BUTTERFLIES

Ecology and Evolution Taking Flight

D1388315

BUTTERFLIES

Edited by

Carol L. Boggs,
Ward B. Watt, and
Paul R. Ehrlich

Ecology and Evolution Taking Flight

The University of Chicago Press
Chicago and London

CAROL L. BOGGS is consulting professor and director of the Center for Conservation
Biology at Stanford University and a senior investigator at the Rocky Mountain
Biological Laboratory. WARD B. WATT is professor of biology at Stanford University
and a senior investigator at the Rocky Mountain Biological Laboratory.
PAUL R. EHRLICH is the Bing Professor of Population Studies at Stanford University.

The University of Chicago Press, Chicago 60637
The University of Chicago Press, Ltd., London
© 2003 by The University of Chicago
All rights reserved. Published 2003
Printed in the United States of America

12 11 10 09 08 07 06 05 04 03   1 2 3 4 5

ISBN: 0-226-06317-8 (cloth)
ISBN: 0-226-06318-6 (paper)

Library of Congress Cataloging-in-Publication Data

Butterflies : ecology and evolution taking flight / edited by Carol L. Boggs,
    Ward B. Watt, and Paul R. Ehrlich.
       p.   cm.
    Includes bibliographical references (p.   ) and index.
    ISBN 0-226-06317-8 (cloth : alk. paper)—ISBN 0-226-06318-6 (pbk. : alk. paper)
    1. Butterflies—Ecology.   2. Butterflies—Evolution.   I. Boggs, Carol L.
    II. Watt, Ward B.   III. Ehrlich, Paul R.
    QL542 .B88   2003
    595.78'9—dc21
                                                                    2002015813

This book is printed on acid-free paper.

To our doctoral advisors, Charles D. Michener, Charles L. Remington, and Lawrence E. Gilbert

CONTENTS

Butterflies have been ideal organisms for scientific study for a very long time. They have also been the favorite group for serious study and important publications by many brilliant amateur naturalists. The best resulting works are fully equal to those of professionals with advanced academic degrees. To me, indistinguishable from one another in scientific significance are, for instance, S. H. Scudder, W. H. Edwards, J. H. McDunnough, W. J. Holland, J. A. Comstock, V. Nabokov, L. P. Grey, W. T. M. Forbes, E. B. Ford, H. Eltringham, G. S. Porter, A. B. Klots, E. A. Cockayne, J. H. Gerould, P. S. Remington, E. B. Poulton, H. E. K. Jordan, H. G. Dyar, Z. Lorkovic, E. Suomalainen, S. R. Bowden, H. B. D. Kettlewell, S. A. Hessel, and O. Buchholz, to name but a few. Perhaps half of these authors had advanced academic degrees in biology, the others none; yet, from scrutiny of their publications, it is not obvious which did and which did not. Observational research, often largely in the field, constituted most of their work, resulting in a large corpus of important discoveries.

From the 1930s and 1940s to the 1960s and 1970s, there began to be more explicit synergism between amateurs and professionals, as well as between workers with different specializations. This trend manifested itself in the founding of the Lepidopterists' Society, and later of other groups worldwide. The Stallings family, M. M. Carey, S. A. Hessel, L. P. Grey, and S. R. Bowden entered into diverse collaborations with C. L. Remington, C. F. dos Passos, W. B. Watt, and others, again to identify only a few of such interactions. I suggest that future scientists looking back to the present time will find that up to about 1990 there was a continuum of more or less steady progress in the classic descriptive biology of butterflies and in their use to study questions in ecology, evolution, and systematic theory. This progress included increasingly elegant studies of systematics using adult and larval characters, population genetics, food plant coevolution, mimicry, migration, endangered or threatened species status, and other studies that could be carried out by knowledgeable butterfly enthusiasts with or without years of university-based training, but increasingly in collaboration. The First International Symposium on Butterfly Biology in London in 1981, and the book that resulted (Ackery and Vane-Wright 1984), represented these activities very well.

However, a new trend toward enlarging the scope of our knowledge of butterflies, and toward their use as "model" systems for studying general biological questions, is becoming evident. A new cluster of breakthroughs has been produced by applying new techniques and combinations of techniques, and new attitudes and approaches, to problems previously thought insoluble or dauntingly complex. Research teams whose members use different yet complementary methods to attack different sides of complex problems have begun to achieve success, as in studies carried out at Rocky Mountain Biological Laboratory on the physiological ecology of resource allocation and life history strategies by Boggs and colleagues, on biochemical adaptations to stressful environments in phylogenetic context by the Watt research group, on the complexities of population ecology and their conservation implications by the Ehrlich research group, and on the diversity of species-specific color vision adaptations to ecological settings by G. Bernard and the Remingtons, using contemporary behavioral and biophysical techniques. Some of these studies could have been done only by professionals with advanced training and costly equipment (as was true in earlier times), yet even here new ways of collaboration with enthusiastic amateurs who know their organisms well can and should be sought for.

The present volume expresses this trend in many different contributions. To me, the application of molecular biology to ecological and population phenomena is especially notable, as in the DNA microsatellite-based study of population fragmentation in high-altitude *Parnassius* by Keyghobadi and colleagues, the role of dopa decarboxylase in *Papilio glaucus*'s yellow and black morphs as studied by ffrench-Constant and Koch, or the dazzling clarification of phylogenetic problems using molecular techniques by Sperling, Martin and colleagues, Campbell and Pierce, and others. Especially evocative of the spirit of synthesis of old and new approaches are the elegant studies of mechanisms underlying wing pattern elements in the African satyrid genus *Bicyclus*, summarized by Brakefield and Monteiro. And a welcome sign of the times is the diversity of studies in response to the rise of an urgent conservation crisis, including the work of Hanski, Hill and colleagues, Kremen and colleagues, Parmesan, and others. But certainly each reader will find her or his own favorite foci of new understanding among the many equally excellent studies presented here. Not only the broad intellectual scope, but also the increased international representation of the work and participating workers in this volume is most encouraging for the future.

Charles Lee Remington
Honorary President
Third International Butterfly Ecology and Evolution Symposium

In August 1998, butterfly biologists from around the world met in Mt. Crested Butte, Colorado, for the Third International Butterfly Ecology and Evolution Symposium. That symposium, building on momentum generated by the first "butterfly meeting" in London in 1981 and a much later meeting in Stockholm in 1994, marked a milestone for the maturation of butterflies as model systems for the study of ecology and evolution. This book is one outcome of the symposium, containing invited presentations plus expansions of selected contributed talks and posters from the meeting.

The chapters that follow are a combination of newly reported work and review and synthesis. We have grouped the chapters into five principal parts, with short introductory comments preceding each part. Readers will quickly notice, however, that many chapters are integrated across several areas, illustrating the depth and breadth of the current use of butterflies in research.

A Web site related to this book, at www.press.uchicago.edu/books/boggs/, contains appendixes for several chapters and a complete copy of the abstracts of papers and posters presented at the meeting. Data contained in the appendixes are also available from the chapter authors.

We wish to thank the U.S. National Science Foundation for partial support for graduate student and Third World participants attending the meeting. Thanks also go to Deborah Levoy, Sharon Carey, and Jennifer Manson for patient and expert word processing and organizational help. Ann McMillan helped with the figures and miscellaneous tasks. Sylvia Fallon provided immensely valuable aid in the logistics associated with the meeting. The efforts of our colleagues who contributed to the symposium and this volume are deeply appreciated. We think they have, with this book, greatly advanced the usefulness of butterflies as tools for answering important scientific questions.

As editors of this volume, we dedicate it, with much respect and affection, to our doctoral advisors: Prof. Charles D. Michener of Kansas (P. R. E.), Prof. Charles L. Remington of Yale (W. B. W.), and Prof. Lawrence E. Gilbert of Texas (C. L. B.). An academic advisor's task is always to convert students into colleagues, thence colleagues into friends, and our lives have all been enriched by the success of these, our mentors, at this task. Indeed, the interconnection of academic relationships is nowhere better illustrated than among the six of us: Charles Michener pointed Paul Ehrlich toward initial acquaintance and friendship with Charles Remington; Paul was Larry Gilbert's doctoral advisor; and Ward Watt sat on Larry's thesis committee. Other ties of academic association also weave among the authors of the chapters that follow in this volume.

In the context of butterfly ecology and evolution, one of our three mentors merits special notice. Charles Remington, the Honorary President of this Third International Symposium on Butterfly Ecology and Evolution, has always been forward-looking. Educated initially as an insect systematist, he perceived the need to blend systematics with the study of the processes giving rise to species' characteristic adaptations and to differences among taxa. From the outset, then, he incorporated into his own research and his teaching alike an awareness of population and ecological genetic research, whether in the Wright-Dobzhansky tradition in North America, the Fisher-Ford tradition in Britain, or parallel stirrings elsewhere in the world. In contrast to some of these other schools of thought, however, Charles has always emphasized the importance of *reciprocal* interactions between theory and empiricism, with the latter testing the former and stimulating its modification or further development, rather than merely validating it. Thus his own work and that of his students have contributed mightily to expanding butterfly biology beyond its taxonomic roots while remaining faithful to them—in the study of mimicry, of natural polymorphism within species, and of the nature of population differentiation over space and across the species boundary. Charles has thus played a leading catalytic role in the emergence of butterflies as a premier test system in population ecology, evolutionary biology, conservation biology, and other disciplines with which these now make contact.

Charles's passion for butterflies and their biology is extremely contagious, and not just to his academic offspring. As one of the founders of the Lepidopterists' Society, he played a major role in encouraging amateurs in the United States both to work with scientists to help develop the grounding for butterflies as model systems and to get involved in conservation efforts. His understanding of ecology and his concerns about conservation of butterflies and their habitats led him to an early understanding of the effects of human population size on the environment, such that he was one of the co-founders of Zero Population Growth, along with one of us (P. R. E.). This concern for the development of basic science, both for its own sake and to support conservation efforts, has been a hallmark of Charles's career, and is reflected in this symposium. It is with the deepest respect and affection that we dedicate this volume to Charles, in appreciation of his many accomplishments and in anticipation of more to come.

PART I

Introduction:
Butterflies, Test Systems, and Biodiversity

Paul R. Ehrlich

Humanity is now faced with the greatest crisis in its history, a crisis that in some senses is shared by butterflies and which, as an important test system, they can help to ameliorate. In the past 150 years a combination of population growth and increased per capita consumption has vaulted humanity into the role of a global geophysical force. Combined with the use of environmentally malign technologies (and flawed socioeconomic and institutional arrangements), these factors are causing the human enterprise to threaten the ecosystem services that are critical to the maintenance of society. These services include, among others, maintenance of the gaseous quality of the atmosphere, recycling of nutrients, running of the hydrologic cycle and control of floods, pollination of crops, control of potential pests, and maintenance of a "genetic library" from which humanity has already withdrawn the very basis of civilization in the form of crops and domesticated animals (as well as antibiotics, pharmaceuticals, fibers, structural materials, and so on). Of course, past civilizations, from the Classic Maya to that of Easter Island, also have overstressed their environmental underpinnings and collapsed. But those were local or regional events; now, for the first time, a global civilization has overshot its resource base and is living on its natural capital, rather than on the income streams that capital generates (Daily 1997)—and that is a temporary game (Ehrlich and Ehrlich 1990; Ehrlich et al. 1995).

What does all this have to do with butterfly biology and butterfly biologists? Plenty. Along with most of the rest of the genetic library, the other animals, plants, and microorganisms with which we share Earth, butterflies are disappearing. Losses of important species have not been well documented (although I am concerned about the status of *Styx infernalis*), in part because it is hard to tell when an insect is truly extinct—especially in the tropics. But there is no doubt that there have been major losses of butterfly *populations*. I can well remember watching, just after World War II, butterfly populations disappear from New Jersey under the assault of rampant development and broadcast spraying of DDT. So the human predicament is a predicament for the global butterfly fauna as well—we are destroying our life-support systems, and butterflies are part of those systems.

But aside from the compassion we might feel for some of the most beautiful and interesting of our companions on Spaceship Earth, and the fear of what their decimation might mean to our aesthetic sense or the functioning of natural ecosystems, there is another reason that the loss of butterflies should be a topic of concern. All scientists are involved in finding out how the world works, and fundamental knowledge of how it works is vital to preserving a habitable planet. It has become increasingly apparent that the efficient way of acquiring the needed information is by developing a taxonomically and geographically stratified sample of model systems on which numerous research teams concentrate their efforts, building a picture of how the system functions in many different dimensions. Such systems have played key roles in disciplines as diverse as genetics (think *Drosophila, Escherichia,* and *Neurospora*), development (*Caenorhabditis*), and neurophysiology (squid giant axons).

As this volume demonstrates, butterflies have now become an important model system for expanding basic knowledge in ecology, evolutionary biology, animal behavior, systematics, and conservation biology. These are fields that have suffered greatly from a lack of model systems (Ehrlich 1997). Each issue of journals such as *Ecology* and *Evolution* is a monument to the folly of population biologists in gathering tidbits of information from otherwise little-known organisms—information that is difficult or impossible to use in constructing a coherent view of how populations, communities, and ecosystems function. As a model system, butterflies have, for example, become key organisms for the monitoring of biodiversity, and are one of the first groups of organisms in which shifts in distributions that may be due to global warming have been documented (Parmesan et al. 1999). The main reason they can play these important roles is that the widespread interest their beauty attracts has led to the publication of many books and papers, frequently produced by dedicated amateurs, detailing their taxonomy, life histories, and distributions. This accumulated knowledge provides the basic foundation needed before a group can serve such crucial functions.

From the viewpoint of the delivery of vital ecosystem services, populations are at least as important as species (Hughes et al. 1997, 2000), and their extinction is likely to be a more sensitive measure of the loss of those services than the extinction of species. But beyond that, the loss of populations also limits the possibilities for using butterflies as a model system. Not only are there fewer populations to investigate, but those that persist are likely to be more remote from research centers and often are under some sort of government protection that encumbers research projects. Restrictions on butterfly collecting are generally tightening worldwide, which is certain to discourage amateurs and thus restrict that important source of information for professional biologists working with butterflies. Those professionals must recognize the urgency of enhancing our understanding of one of Earth's few "indicator taxa" that can give us clues about the conservation value of various areas as well as serving to monitor the health of ecosystems in areas chosen for preservation. Such indicator taxa must be ones that are well known taxonomically and for which adequate field guides exist for many regions—criteria fully met by butterflies. Then, of course, it is a major responsibility of professionals to make every effort to utilize that knowledge to help save our life-support systems. And conserving butterflies themselves is one way to work toward that primary goal. Not only do butterflies serve as a model system for research and function as indicators, but they can also serve as "umbrella species"—ones whose preservation is likely, by protecting certain areas, to conserve many less charismatic organisms as well.

In a world in the grip of a great extinction episode, the butterflies not only can play crucial roles in conservation biology (as numerous papers and posters in this symposium indicate), but also have the potential to be one of the few major taxonomic groups that in some sense can be "finished." By that I mean that in the next few decades we should be able to obtain a more or less complete picture of butterfly phenetic and cladistic taxonomy (see the fine review of the current state of affairs by Vane-Wright in this volume), zoogeography, and coevolution with larval host plants. We can never know everything about butterflies, but we can sample widely enough to learn the basic patterns in the group and increase its usefulness as a test system for ideas at all levels of biological organization.

All this should be feasible *if* the taxonomic and ecological communities have the sense, in the face of severe time and resource constraints, to concentrate their efforts on a few key model groups (Ehrlich 1997). Butterflies clearly should be one such model; no other group of insect herbivores of comparable size has the same potential. The phenetics and cladistics of the major groups are already reasonably well known, most species have been described, and the larval host plants of a good sample of the species have been identified. Work proceeds on improving our understanding of butterfly systematics (I was especially pleased to see several papers at this symposium tackling the confused taxonomic structure within the Nymphalidae.) But more coordinated effort needs to be put into such things as the phenetics of preadult stages and the evaluation of larval host plant and nectar source usage of the populations of a larger sample of species.

Butterflies already have been used to test a wide range of ideas about how the world works, from the interplay of adaptation and constraint in mechanisms of energy processing (e.g., Watt 1992, 1994; Watt, chap. 15 in this volume) to how organisms orient to their environments, especially mates (e.g., Bernard and Remington 1991; Oliveira et al. 1998; Rutowski 1991; and Deinert, chap. 5, Rutowski, chap. 1, Wiklund, chap. 4, and Van Dyck, chap. 16, all in this volume). They have been the subject of some of the most important research on the dynamics of natural populations (Ehrlich 1984), with key long-term studies on checkerspot butterflies (Ehrlich et al. 1975; Hanski 1999; Ehrlich and Hanski 2003) that have illuminated, among other things, the crucial need to identify demographic units before drawing conclusions about mechanisms of population regulation (Brown and Ehrlich 1980). Butterflies have played a major role in illuminating metapopulation dynamics (e.g., Ehrlich and Murphy 1987; Hanski et al. 1994; Hanski and Gilpin 1997; Harrison et al. 1988; and Crone and Schultz, chap. 25, Hanski, chap. 26, and Keyghobadi et al., chap. 8, all in this volume), as recently brilliantly summarized by Ilkka Hanski (Hanski 1999).

Similarly, butterflies have added greatly to our understanding of the significance of hybridization in animal speciation (e.g., Jiggins et al. 1996; Mallet 1993; Mallet and Barton 1989; Remington 1968b; Scriber et al. 1989; Scriber et al. 1995b; and Scriber et al., chap. 17, and Gilbert, chap. 14, in this volume). Butterflies have also been prominent as a test system in the study of coevolution (e.g., Ehrlich and Raven 1964; Gilbert 1983; Pierce 1989; Campbell and Pierce, chap. 18 in this volume), as exemplified by Michael Singer's splendid work on the host plant relationships of *Euphydryas* (Singer 1971a, 1982a, 1986, 1994; Singer et al. 1988, 1991; Singer, chap. 10 in this volume); phenology (Clench 1967; Morisita 1967; Shapiro 1975b; Shapiro et al., chap. 6 in this volume) and biogeography (e.g., Parmesan et al. 1999; and Hill et al., chap. 7, and Parmesan, chap. 24, in this volume). They are increasingly being used as tools for looking at developmental problems (Brakefield 1998; Nijhout 1994a, 1994b; Brakefield and Monteiro, chap. 12, and ffrench-Constant and Koch, chap. 13, in this volume) and issues related to resource allocation (Boggs 1990, 1992, 1997a, 1997c; Boggs and Ross 1993; Karlsson 1995; Leimar et al. 1994; Wiklund et al. 1998; Boggs, chap. 9 in this volume).

The past half-century has seen amazing progress in some of these areas, especially coevolution (Berenbaum 1983, 1995a, 1995b; Farrell et al. 1992; Janz et al. 1994), and the chapters by Janz (chap. 11), Raguso and Willis (chap. 3), and Singer (chap. 10) in this volume show that the pace is not slowing—that the potential of butterflies as a model system has barely been scratched. A major lacuna in the use of butterflies as a test system, one I had hoped to fill myself, is to see how the phenetics and genetics of larval and adult butterflies map onto one another, a biologically important question of great generality that has been lost in the craze for cladistics (which is a fine approach to questions of butterfly-plant coevolution, but is misleading as a basis for general classification and useless for answering the larva versus adult question). I leave that one to some intellectual great-great-great grandchild of Charles Remington—someone with both the steady hands to dissect caterpillars and the skills to discover which genes are "turned on" at what stage of development.

Because time is so short, it is critical that butterflies be further developed into a tool for understanding the best ways of preserving biological diversity. Work on metapopulation dynamics, response to climatic and topoclimatic change, conservation genetics, conservation behavior, and the like is already well advanced in both Europe and North America, as this volume clearly demonstrates. Butterflies were even important factors in the design of Masoala National Park in Madagascar (e.g., Kremen 1994; Kremen, Lees, and Fay, chap. 23 in this volume). Work in the field that Gretchen Daily calls "countryside biogeography" has been started by her group (Ricketts et al. 2001) and others. Although it was too early to report results in this symposium, in my view this work is potentially the most important of all—especially in the tropics. There is no longer a cubic centimeter of the biosphere that has not been altered by human activities, and it is crystal clear that even most *relatively* undisturbed areas will soon be taken over by intensive farming and other activities. As my old friend Bill Klots recognized in his classic field guide to the butterflies (Klots 1951), "Primeval conditions are gone beyond recall" (p. 51). We all must put much more effort into understanding how to make disturbed areas more hospitable to the working parts of humanity's life support systems, which is the main mission of countryside biogeography. In practical terms, butterflies are one of the few tools available to do that job, but much more work is needed to discover exactly how the diversity of butterflies relates to biodiversity in general.

Of course, if all we professionals do is research on our beloved butterflies, we're going to lose most of them *and* the battle to save enough biodiversity to support anything resembling today's scale of the human enterprise—let alone the vast increase in the scale of that enterprise projected for the near future. All of us need, in our own ways, to tithe to our species, and spend at least one-tenth of our time trying to promote a declining human population size, restrict wasteful consumption, educate young people about evolution and ecology, encourage a move from environmentally malign to environmentally benign technologies, or work for the changes in economic, social, and political arrangements that are necessary to achieve such a revolution. Here again we can follow Charles Remington's lead. Almost 30 years ago he and I were co-founders of Zero Population Growth, and he is still educating Yale students on the dimensions of the environmental crisis, evolution, and ecology. We butterfly biologists have a special educational responsibility. Because of the great appeal butterflies have for the public at large, we are in a better position than most biologists to disseminate broad conservation messages. I wonder, for example, how many members of the Lepidopterists' Society or others fascinated by the beauty and diversity of butterflies understand that growing human populations and increasing wasteful consumption gravely threaten the objects of their interest.

Biologists doing research on butterflies are developing these insects into one of the most important model systems for basic biological research. The chapters in this volume show that first-rate researchers are pursuing that goal with vigor. They are in the enviable position of both working with lovely and intriguing creatures and helping to save the world. What more could any scientist ask?

PART II

Behavior

The study of behavior initially focused on descriptive analysis of actions of animals or groups of animals, but has diversified significantly over the past three decades to include causal mechanisms of behavior. These mechanisms include anatomic, physiological, and biochemical determinants of behavior. Such phenotypic characters also may provide the constraints within which the evolution of behavior operates. As evidenced by the chapters presented here, butterflies continue to be instrumental in such studies, particularly those focusing on reproductive and foraging behavior.

The first two chapters explore the diversity of phenotypic structures making up the visual systems of butterflies and its implications for behavior. Ron Rutowski (chap. 1) leads off with an overview of butterfly vision at the organismal level and an analysis of the implications of visual abilities for adult flight and reproductive behaviors. Adriana Briscoe (chap. 2) then explores the physiology and molecular biology of visual pigments. Her chapter includes a case study from *Papilio* examining the implications of color vision and color preferences for behavior. The differentiation of multiple opsin isozymes in this genus allows examination of the coevolution of molecular sensors and behavioral specialization. In combination, these two chapters trace the integration of factors from the molecular through the organismal levels into resultant behaviors.

For some behaviors, such as foraging, multiple sensory input is important. For nectar-feeding adults, both visual and olfactory stimuli are obvious candidates for cues determining behavior, given the diversity of colors and odors associated with flowers. Robert Raguso and Mark Willis (chap. 3) outline a case study of the dual role of vision and olfaction in nectar-feeding hawkmoths, evaluating factors that may be common across Lepidoptera.

The cues associated with nectar feeding provide a classic example of the coevolutionary interaction between lepidopteran foraging behavior and host characters, and in the case described here, work on moths provides a comparative basis for understanding butterfly behavior.

Both the evolution of behavior and the role that behaviors play in sexual and natural selection have been of deep interest to students of reproductive biology, including mating systems. The extensive work of Christer Wiklund and co-workers in Stockholm, which has played a seminal role in developing our understanding of the interaction between mating systems and sexual selection, is synthesized here (chap. 4). The section ends with a chapter by Erika Deinert (chap. 5), detailing a case study of one unusual mating system, pupal mating, and describing the selection pressures and morphologies associated with particular male behavioral choices. Her work combines mating systems and foraging behavior (by males for pupae).

In combination, these studies illustrate the current synthetic understanding of butterfly behavior and raise intriguing questions about the coevolution of behavior and ecology in the context of morphological constraints. This theme is continued in the next section, on ecology, in the contexts of host plant choice and use and of population dispersion and dynamics.

CHAPTER 1

Visual Ecology of Adult Butterflies

Ronald L. Rutowski

Biologists have long been interested in how adult butterflies use vision to solve many of the problems of survival and reproduction they face during the course of their adult lives. This is evident in the record of review articles on the nature of butterfly vision, from one of the first by Eltringham in 1919 to one of the most recent by the late Robert Silberglied in 1984, a contribution to the first symposium in this series. These reviews summarize the literature and new observations on how the visual system of butterflies is structured and how butterflies behave, and conclude in a broad way that while butterflies do not see as well as, for example, humans, they are capable of making biologically relevant color and pattern discriminations.

Since Silberglied's review, however, a variety of new and more detailed questions about interactions between the visual system, behavior, and ecology of butterflies have emerged for several reasons. First, we know more now about the complexities and diversity of visually guided behavior and assessments in butterflies. Second, new information on the structure of butterfly eyes has appeared in the literature. Third, the general understanding of arthropod vision has grown (Land 1989, 1990, 1997; Warrant and McIntyre 1992, 1993). Finally, there is a growing recognition of the importance of ecological context in examining the adaptive features of vision and visually guided behavior (e.g., Endler 1993; Endler and Théry 1996). Some issues of special contemporary interest stimulated by the new ideas and information are (1) the potential constraints visual system performance may place on behavior in butterflies and in arthropods generally; (2) the proximate visual mechanisms underlying specific behavioral tasks performed by butterflies, such as mate recognition; (3) how behavior and vision are affected by their ecological setting; and (4) how interactions between behavior and vision have shaped the evolution of visual system structure and behavior.

The approach taken here in addressing these issues will roughly follow what Dusenbery, in his book *Sensory Ecology* (1992), refers to as the analytic approach, in which three questions are asked: (1) What problems must butterflies solve? (2) What visual strategies do they use to solve these problems? (3) What morphological and behavioral mechanisms are used by butterflies to implement these strategies? These questions are pursued within two limits. First, in dealing with visual system performance, I focus on what can be inferred about performance from the structure of the peripheral components of the visual system; namely, the eyes and their morphology. The nature of compound eyes is such that we can learn a great deal about how butterflies see the world by studying the details of their morphology and their peripheral processing of visual signals and cues (e.g., Land 1997). Second, I deal with a limited set of problems in survival and reproduction; namely, control of flight, location and recognition of nectar sources and oviposition sites, and location and recognition of mates. The major issue omitted in the body of the review is visual detection of predators. While this issue will be taken up in the discussion, there is too little information on this problem and how it is solved to warrant detailed consideration at this point.

Before launching into this analysis, I first provide updated background information on the structure of the butterfly visual system and its performance. I do not cover in full detail the structure of the butterfly eye and the underlying neural networks, but deal primarily with those features that might affect visual system performance in a way that would be expected to be reflected in the behavior and ecology of butterflies.

BUTTERFLY VISION

Butterflies, like other insects, have two compound eyes, each of which is composed of a more or less hemispherical array of several thousand individual photoreceptive elements called ommatidia (Chapman 1971; Horridge 1977; Kolb 1977; Yagi and Koyama 1963). Each ommatidium is a long cylindrical structure that gathers light from a small part of the visual field. At the distal end, an ommatidium is capped with a facet lens that gathers light and sends it through another lens, called the crystalline cone, down the long ommatidium to an array of photosensitive cells. Up to nine of these photosensitive cells, called retinula cells, are radially arrayed around the optical axis of the ommatidium (fig. 1.1; also see Briscoe, chap. 2 in this volume). Each of the retinula cells has a photosensitive part and sends an axon to processing centers just below the eye (the lamina or the medulla) and in the central nervous system. Together, the photosensitive parts of all the retinula

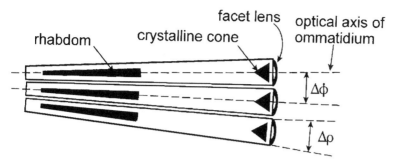

rhabdom   crystalline cone   facet lens   optical axis of ommatidium

$\Delta\phi$

$\Delta\rho$

Figure 1.1 A schematic diagram showing the major features of three adjacent ommatidia, including the facet lens, through which light enters; the crystalline cone, and the rhabdom, where the light is transduced into a neuronal signal encoding information about its intensity and spectral composition. This figure also illustrates the interommatidial angle ($\Delta\phi$) and the acceptance angle ($\Delta\rho$), both of which are important peripheral determinants of visual acuity.

cells form the rhabdom. In what follows I discuss aspects of the structure of the eye and how they affect various aspects of butterfly vision, including the sensitivity of the eye, the dimensions of the visual field, the spatial resolution of the eye, and the perception of color and movement.

SENSITIVITY

The butterfly compound eye is a type of apposition eye (Nilsson et al. 1984, 1988; van Hateren and Nilsson 1987), which means that the rhabdom in each ommatidium processes only light that enters the ommatidium from the facet above it and not from adjacent facets. Screening pigments prevent light from bleeding from the light path of one ommatidium into the next (Ribi 1979). Compared with superposition eyes, apposition eyes make the least efficient use of light entering the eye and so are found most often in arthropods, such as most species of butterflies, that are active during the day in well-lit environments (Warrant and McIntyre 1992).

For apposition eyes, sensitivity is a function of the size of the aperture allowing light into each ommatidium. The maximum size of this aperture is set by the facet size (Warrant and McIntyre 1992). Because butterflies are generally active in high-illuminance environments, it is not surprising that their facet diameters are relatively small compared with those of other insects, typically about 15 to 30 μm (Yagi and Koyama 1963) and trade off ommatidial sensitivity for tighter packing and the higher acuity it brings. The aperture of each ommatidium can be adjusted by a pupillary mechanism so as to optimize photoreceptor performance at a variety of illuminance levels. Interestingly, the position of the curve describing the pupillary response as a function of illuminance level is shifted toward low light levels in species such as members of the genus *Caligo*, which are active when ambient light is typically dim (Järemo Jonson et al. 1998). This finding suggests that the evolution of the mechanisms underlying pupillary response patterns has been shaped by the light environment. As an added complexity, Horridge et al. (1984) suggest that sensitivity is wavelength-dependent.

A paradoxical feature of the eyes of butterflies other than papilionids is the occurrence of a tapetum, or reflecting layer, at the basal end of the ommatidium, which with proper illumination generates an eyeshine or luminous pseudopupil (plate 1.1A; Stavenga 1979). The tapetal reflectance is created by a tracheolar structure and directs any light not absorbed on the first pass back through the rhabdom (Miller and Bernard 1968). In general, such structures are associated with nocturnal animals that are active in low-illuminance environments (Bradbury and Vehrencamp 1998). Why butterflies have such a structure is not clear. However, as will be seen, the tapetal reflectance is a useful tool for students of insect vision.

DIMENSIONS OF THE VISUAL FIELD

When one looks through the facet lens down an ommatidium, the ommatidium appears dark relative to other parts of the eye's surface because light that has entered has been absorbed by the pigments in the light path of the ommatidium. An ommatidium appears dark when its optical axis is aligned with, or even close to, the axis of viewing, and so we typically see a dark spot that includes several ommatidia in the eye (plate 1.1B). This spot, known as the principal pseudopupil, can be used to identify the part of the eye directed at the region of space from which the eye is being examined (Stavenga 1979). This means that the pseudopupil can be used to determine how characteristics of the ommatidial array change from one part of the eye to the next. For example, if a pseudopupil is evident from a certain region in space around the butterfly eye, that means there are ommatidia pointed at that region in space, and thus that the butterfly is gathering visual information from that region in space. Thus, the dimensions of the visual field can be mapped as those regions in space from which a pseudopupil is apparent. The luminous pseudopupil (plate 1.1A) permits precise identification of ommatidia pointed at the viewer because for the eye glow to be seen, the axis of viewing must be even closer to the optical axis of the ommatidium than is necessary to visualize the principal pseudopupil.

Using the luminous pseudopupil, we have measured the visual field of the Empress Leilia, *Asterocampa leilia* (Rutowski and Warrant 2002), and several other species of nymphalids (Rutowski, Warrant, and Gislén, unpub.). In general, each eye has a visual field that approximates one hemisphere. There is little binocular overlap in the fields of the two eyes, about 15° frontally and none posteriorly. Figure 1.2 plots the dimensions of the visual field in the horizontal plane surrounding the head for *A. leilia*. In this plane males have a slightly larger visual field than females by about 10°, with more binocular

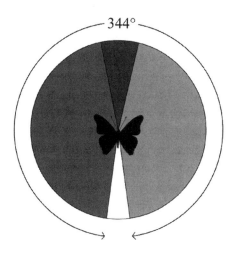

Figure 1.2 The span of the visual field in the horizontal plane at the equator of the head for the Empress Leilia butterfly, *Asterocampa leilia*. The visual fields of both the right and left eyes are shown, as well as the extent to which they overlap (darkest shading) and the extent of the area not seen by either eye (no shading).

overlap and a smaller blind spot. Sexual differences in the dimensions of the visual field are known for other insects (e.g., Beersma et al. 1977) and are likely to be a general feature in butterflies, because males consistently have larger eyes than females when body size is controlled (Yagi and Koyama 1963; Rutowski 2000). What interspecific differences in visual field dimensions exist is not well known, and we also have much to learn about differences between the sexes and species in how the degree of binocular overlap and the size of the blind spot vary as one moves away from the eye equator. Binocular vision can be used in distance perception, especially when animals are moving slowly or not at all and motion-induced parallax is at a minimum.

SPATIAL RESOLUTION

Silberglied (1984) reviewed the spatial resolution of butterfly eyes in general terms and reiterated the point made by others that spatial resolution is a function of how densely the visual field is sampled. Land (1997) lists three structural and two environmental features that affect visual field sampling and, thereby, acuity. The three structural features are (1) the angle between the optical axes of adjacent ommatidia, or interommatidial angle ($\Delta\phi$, see fig. 1.1; a smaller angle produces higher acuity), (2) the diameter of the photoreceptors (a larger diameter produces higher acuity), and (3) the quality of the optics (better quality produces higher acuity). The two environmental features are (1) ambient light levels (higher levels permit higher acuity) and (2) the motion of viewers or targets (higher speeds produce lower acuity). Land and others have provided excellent reviews of how these variables interact (Land 1989, 1990, 1997; Warrant and McIntrye 1992, 1993; Wehner 1981). Here I discuss the major lessons from these reviews about the acuity of butterfly vision.

A key question about acuity from the ecological perspective of this review is at what distance a butterfly should be able to resolve biologically important information, such as the presence of a potential mate, the shape of a leaf, or the shape of a flower. There are two measures of acuity that can help us begin to answer this question: single object threshold and maximum spatial frequency. Single object threshold is the crudest measure and indicates the maximum distance at which an object's presence will be detectable. First detection of an approaching object may in theory occur when the object causes a perceptible change in light intensity in a single ommatidium. The conditions under which this occurs will be a function of two eye features: how much of the visual field is sampled by an ommatidium, and the sensitivity of the photoreceptors in the ommatidium to changes in light intensity. Under conditions of high ambient light levels and reasonable photoreceptor performance, we would expect the single object threshold to be no more than the acceptance angle of the photoreceptors ($\Delta\rho$, see fig. 1.1) and probably less than this value, because even if an object does not fully fill the field of a photoreceptor, it may produce a detectable change in the intensity of light. In fact, in some cases, measured single object thresholds have been less than half of the measured $\Delta\rho$ (Land 1997). $\Delta\rho$'s have been measured for only two butterflies and are in the range of 1.5°–2° (Land 1997; Rutowski and Warrant 2002). Figure 1.3 gives a sense of how the size of an object is related to the maximum distance at which it is likely to be detected when $\Delta\rho = 2°$. Later in this review, the limits on acuity implied by these measurements are discussed relative to the effective distances at which butterflies can perform the various visually guided tasks they face.

Another measure of acuity is maximum spatial frequency. The spatial frequency of a pattern of alternating black and white lines is the reciprocal of the angle between the center of one black line and the next black line (one cycle). Maximum spatial frequency (cycles per degree) is the frequency above which the black lines cannot be resolved, and so gives a sense of a butterfly's ability to resolve patterns. However, it has not been measured in the classic way using optomotor responses for any butterfly. Nonetheless, it can be estimated using the interommatidial angle (Warrant and McIntyre 1993). $\Delta\phi$ has been reported for only three butterflies and is in the range of 1°–3° (Land 1997; Rutowski and Warrant 2002; Stavenga et al. 2001). Hence, the maximum spatial frequency for butterflies ranges from about 0.2 to 0.6 cycles per degree. Figure 1.4 gives a sense of how the size of one cycle of a pattern affects the maximum distance at which it will be seen as a pattern.

Beyond these two measures of acuity, there is the question of how the shapes of objects are encoded by the visual system. Presumably this requires the simultaneous stimulation of multiple ommatidia, which means that the minimum angle an object must subtend for its shape to be encoded by the

Ronald L. Rutowski

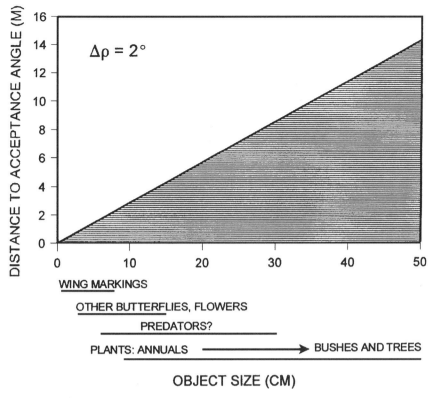

Figure 1.3 The distance at which an object will subtend the typical acceptance angle of a butterfly ommatidium ($\Delta\rho = 2°$) as a function of object size. The line provides a rough estimate of the single object threshold; in other words, the maximum distance at which the presence of objects of various sizes would be detected. The shaded area under the line is that set of distances and object sizes at which the object would be detectable. The approximate size ranges of various classes of objects of potential interest to butterflies are shown below the graph.

visual system will be several degrees (Wehner 1981). Hence the distance at which an object's shape can be recognized should be much smaller than the distance at which its presence can be detected.

Because of trade-offs between morphological characteristics that produce high acuity and eye size, the visual systems of many insects have regions of the eye specialized for high acuity, called acute zones, which have at the least small $\Delta\phi$'s and large facets with small $\Delta\rho$'s (high signal-to-noise ratios) (Land 1989, 1990, 1997). Based on measurements of $\Delta\phi$ in butterflies reported by Rutowski and Warrant (2002) and Stavenga et al. (2001), butterflies are no exception, showing two patterns of variation in $\Delta\phi$'s that have been found in many insects. First, $\Delta\phi$'s tend to be smallest along the equator of the eye. As one moves above and below this band, $\Delta\phi$'s increase. Second, within the equatorial band, $\Delta\phi$'s tend to decrease from front to back. The overall result of these two patterns is that butterfly vision is most acute in the frontal direction and in the equator of the visual field around the head. In other insect species, special regions of high acuity with small $\Delta\phi$'s and

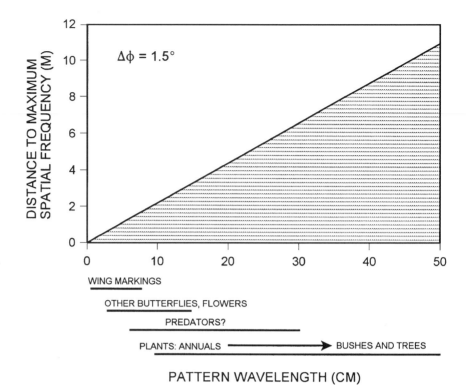

Figure 1.4 The distance at which the linear wavelength of a visual pattern will match the maximum spatial frequency of the typical butterfly eye ($\Delta\phi = 1.5°$). The line provides a very rough estimate of the maximum distance at which patterns of various dimensions would be detected. The shaded area under the line is that set of distances and object sizes at which the object's shape would be detectable. The approximate ranges of cycle widths or wavelengths for various visual patterns of potential interest to butterflies are shown below the graph.

large facets are known to occur outside the equatorial band. These regions can be related to specific visual demands, such as prey or mate detection (Land 1997).

Perception of Color

Many insects, including butterflies, are known or inferred to have color vision (see Ilse 1929; Silberglied 1984; Horridge et al. 1984 for review). True color vision (not just wavelength-specific behavior) has recently been rigorously demonstrated experimentally using learning paradigms in papilionid butterflies (Kelber and Pfaff 1999; Kinoshita 1999). The individual photoreceptors within an ommatidium typically vary in their spectral sensitivity, so that the spectral composition of light entering a rhabdom may be encoded in the response patterns of the photoreceptors (see Briscoe, chap. 2 in this volume). Peripheral processing of the wavelengths reaching the photoreceptors can also occur as a result of filtering of light before it reaches the rhabdom, variation within and between species in the spectral sensitivities of the retinula cells, and selective reflection of wavelengths by the tapetum.

Studies of the spectral absorbances of photoreceptors in ommatidia have led to two major conclusions about color vision in butterflies. First, the spectral sensitivities of the photoreceptors and the visual pigments within them range from the red well into the ultraviolet (Arikawa et al. 1987, 1999a; Briscoe 1998a; Eguchi et al. 1982; Kinoshita et al. 1997; Post and Goldsmith 1969; Shimohigashi and Tominaga 1991; Struwe 1972a, 1972b). Second, there can be as many as five different types of photoreceptors within a single ommatidium (Arikawa et al. 1987). Third, the specific types of photoreceptors found in an ommatidium may be different from the types found in other ommatidia in the same eye region (Arikawa and Stavenga 1997; Kinoshita et al. 1997; Stavenga et al. 2001). Fourth, there may be consistent differences in the spectral sensitivities of ommatidia between eye regions (Arikawa et al. 1987; Bernard and Remington 1991; Stavenga et al. 2001). For example, in *Papilio xuthus,* the ventral region of the eye contains many more receptors that are violet- and ultraviolet-sensitive than the dorsal part of the eye (Arikawa et al. 1987). In summary, the color sensitivity of the eye appears to vary in several ways that could show adaptive modifications for specific tasks.

PERCEPTION OF MOVEMENT

The detection of a moving object depends on the acuity of the eye, the rate of motion of the object, the background against which the object is viewed, and ambient levels of illumination. When moving through the visual field at high angular velocities, the image of an object tends to blur, depending on the response and recovery rates of the photoreceptors and the acceptance angle of the photoreceptors. The recovery rate of the photoreceptors is relatively high, as indicated by the observation that light flashes are not encoded by changes in electroretinogram potentials at flash rates above about 150 Hz (Magnus 1956) and by the speed of the electrical responses of photoreceptors to light flashes (Rutowski and Warrant 2002).

Studies of other insects have revealed that the eye may have specialized underlying neural networks and spectral sensitivities that can be interpreted as adaptations for the detection of moving objects (e.g., Labhart and Nilsson 1995; Buschbeck and Strausfeld 1997). Butterflies also have motion-sensitive neurons in the optic lobes (Ibbotson et al. 1991; Maddess et al. 1991), some of which respond best to temporal frequencies of 10–25 Hz, which would give them an ability to resolve objects moving at higher speeds than could be resolved by humans (O'Carroll et al. 1996). Whether there are interspecific or intersexual differences in the structure or characteristics of these motion-detecting networks in butterflies is not known.

PERCEPTION OF POLARIZATION

A highly ordered arrangement of the internal components of a retinula cell (i.e., the photosensitive microvilli) makes it possible for the cell to be maximally sensitive to light with a certain nonrandom polarization. In particular, the cell must not be twisted so that its microvilli are all oriented in the same way. If there are at least two such retinula cells in a rhabdom that have their microvilli at 90° relative to one another, it then becomes possible for the eye to encode the specific plane of polarization of the stimulating light.

There are nymphalid butterflies whose eyes have been reported to have rhabdoms with the arrangement necessary for polarization detection (Hämmerle and Kolb 1996; Kolb 1986). However, these structures have been reported only in the dorsal rim of the eye, which suggests some regional specialization for detection of the plane of polarization in butterfly eyes. Moreover, Bandai et al. (1992) have found polarization-sensitive photoreceptors in the eye of a swallowtail butterfly.

VISUAL TASKS INVOLVED IN SURVIVAL AND REPRODUCTION

In this section I discuss five problems in survival and reproduction that are faced by adult butterflies, focusing on those whose solutions are either known to or are likely to involve the use of the visual system. In general, insect visual systems cannot be evolutionarily optimized for performance in the context of all visual problems an animal faces, so trade-offs between, for example, sensitivity and acuity will be necessary (Warrant and McIntyre 1992). Thus, by comparing visual system structure to the demands of the various visual tasks butterflies must perform, we can get a sense of the primary determinants of eye structure.

VISUAL CONTROL OF FORWARD FLIGHT

The flight of butterflies is well controlled in that they modulate speed and direction in ways that permit them to avoid impacts with objects, land on uneven surfaces such as branch tips and rocks, compensate for wind drift, and reach overwintering grounds sometimes thousands of miles away. Even in open field situations they maintain fairly constant tracks and velocities (Srygley et al. 1996). The strategies they use can involve either visual cues (Wehner 1981) or cues derived from Earth's magnetic field. I focus here on visual cues.

There are four kinds of visual cues that have been proposed as references at different levels for control of forward flight. The first is the location of the sky and horizon. Information from these sources can be important in keeping the dorsal surface up. The second is the position of the sun. Recent evidence, first from the monarch (*Danaus plexippus;* Perez et al. 1997) and then from a number of Neotropical species (Oliveira et al. 1998), suggests that butterflies use a time-compensated sun compass to guide their migratory flights. Dorsal parts of the eye are probably involved in gathering information about the sun's position. The third reference for guiding forward flight is the pattern of polarization of light coming from the sky. Hyatt (1993) has shown that *D. plexippus* use the pattern of polarization in the sky to set the bearings of their migratory flights. If this mechanism is widespread, we might expect dorsal ommatidia (such as those in the dorsal rim areas) to be especially sensitive to the polarization of light in many butterflies.

A fourth visual cue is the optical flow field (Wehner 1981; Land 1997). As butterflies move on the wing, objects and landmarks in the environment move by at a rate proportional to their distance from the butterfly's body. This flow field and nearby objects in it can be used as a reference to assess speed and constancy of direction. Equatorial acute zones in the eyes of butterflies and other insects have been interpreted as adaptations for monitoring the optical flow field during forward flight (Land 1997). The interpretation of the flow field depends on knowing the relative distances to objects in the field. Given that in butterflies binocular overlap (30°–40°) is small compared with the overall size of the visual field (more than 300°), most distance assessments must be made using movement-induced parallax rather than binocular vision. However, given the relatively poor acuity of the butterfly eye, even large objects such as trees several meters high may not be resolvable at distances of more than 20 to 30 meters.

Detection and Recognition of Oviposition Sites by Females

Female butterflies lay their eggs either singly or in batches, usually on the larval food plant (Stamp 1980). A problem faced by most species is locating and identifying the appropriate plants. Because of the important role plant chemistry plays in the success of the larvae, chemical signals, at both long and close range, are expected to play an important role in finding oviposition substrates. However, vision also plays a role (Prokopy and Owens 1983).

At distances of more than a meter, the role vision plays will depend whether the plants themselves are large, have a distinctive shape, have a unique color, or occur consistently in visually distinctive microhabitats. Bernard and Remington (1991) argue that visual pigments sensitive to long wavelengths in the eyes of some lycaenids may be important for long-range detection of their red-leaved host plants by ovipositing females. At this time there have been no studies in butterflies of the role that vision plays in locating oviposition plants at these distances, although food plant apparency has been considered in general terms (Parmesan 1991).

At the range of a few centimeters, the shapes and colors of leaves or other plant parts may be important cues in food plant recognition. Rausher (1978) has shown that females of *Battus philenor* use leaf shape to select oviposition sites. In *Pieris,* the color of oviposition substrates affects their attractiveness to females (Ilse 1937; Kolb and Scherer 1982), but these color preferences can be modified by experience (Traynier 1984). In some species, in addition to chemical cues (Dempster 1992; Schoonhoven et al. 1990), females use visual cues to detect eggs previously laid on the larval food plants and avoid these plants (Rothschild and Schoonhoven 1977; Rausher 1979a; Shapiro 1981; Williams and Gilbert 1981). However, the specific parts of the eye used in detection of these cues are not known, so we do not know whether there are visual adaptations to aid in these tasks. During inspection of potential oviposition sites, females view plants from in front of or above them, so the frontal and ventrofrontal parts of the eyes of females are expected to be most likely to have features that enhance the detection and recognition of food plants. These features could include adaptive modifications of spectral sensitivity as well as visual acuity superior to that of males. Regional specialization of this sort has not been demonstrated, however.

Almut Kelber has made two interesting suggestions concerning the use of vision in selection of oviposition substrates. First, the receptor interactions that underlie color preferences in the selection of oviposition substrates may permit females to select substrates that are optimal for growth of the newly hatched larvae (Kelber 1999b). Second, by having color receptors that are sensitive to the plane of polarization of light, butterflies may be able to make adaptive discriminations among oviposition substrates on the basis of surface texture (Kelber 1999a). Both of these ideas warrant further testing to better understand the link between vision and oviposition, and thus larval survival, in butterflies and other insects.

Detection and Recognition of Nectar Sources

The problems faced by butterflies in locating and recognizing nectar sources are similar to those faced by females in finding oviposition sites, and both chemical and visual cues, at both long and close range, may be used to solve them (Prokopy and Owens 1983). However, these problems are eased to some extent by the brilliant colors and distinctive shapes of flowers. Nonetheless, whether butterflies use visual cues in locating nectar sources at distances of greater than a few meters is not known. If they do, the cues would have to involve the visual characteristics of appropriate microhabitats or the color of large groups of flowers.

At close range, color is important in locating and recognizing flowers, as has been demonstrated in a variety of studies (see Ilse 1937; Silberglied 1984; Scherer and Kolb 1987b for review). Moreover, color preferences can be altered by learning, so that butterflies visit flowers that are most likely to produce the greatest nectar reward (C. A. Swihart 1970, 1971; Weiss 1995, 1997). Changes in color preference result in correlated changes in the spectral sensitivities of neurons in the visual pathway (S. L. Swihart 1970). Both innate and learned color preferences for nectar sources have been used to demonstrate true color vision in butterflies (Kelber and Pfaff 1999; Kinoshita et al. 1999).

Flower shape and morphology are also important to butterflies in learning which flowers to visit for nectar rewards, as well as how best to approach a flower to minimize handling time (Lewis 1986, 1993). Although these conclusions implicate the use of vision, this has not been confirmed. Again, which specific parts of the eyes are involved in these various discriminations, and whether they show adaptive modification for the task, are not known. I predict that the frontal and ventrofrontal parts of the eyes should be most likely to be used in the detection and recognition of nectar sources, and that if specializations for this task, such as acute zones, finely tuned spectral sensitivities, and areas of large binocular overlap, are found in these parts of the eyes, they should be found in both sexes.

DETECTION OF POTENTIAL MATES BY MALES

No chemical signals produced by females are known that attract or affect the behavior of males at a distance of more than a few centimeters (Rutowski 1991). Instead, male butterflies typically locate females by looking for them, either as they fly about or as they sit and wait at places where females are likely to appear (Rutowski 1991). The visual acuity of males is such that they should be able to discriminate or detect a perched or flying female only from a distance of less than a few meters. However, using visual cues, males may identify or locate places, such as landmarks or hilltops, where females are likely to appear (Dennis and Shreeve 1988). For example, males of a ringlet, *Coenonympha pamphilus*, wait for females near trees that are large and conspicuous. Experiments with artificial trees indicate that the males are using visual cues, but the distance at which they see the trees is not known (Wickman et al. 1995).

The maximum distance at which a male, whether perched or flying, can detect a conspecific female is expected to vary with interspecific variation in body size, for two reasons. First, because of interspecific variation in wing area, some species present much larger visual targets than others. A butterfly with a 15 cm wing span has about fifty times the wing area of a species with a 2 cm wing span. All else being equal, males of larger species should be able to detect conspecific females at greater distances than males of smaller species. But all else is not equal. A number of eye features relevant to visual system performance are correlated with body size in butterflies, including overall eye size, facet number, and facet diameter (Yagi and Koyama 1963; Ziemba and Rutowski 2000; Rutowski 2000). This finding suggests that larger males should have higher overall acuity, a larger visual field, or both. These observations lead to the expectation that males of many small species may be limited to mate location tactics, such as sit-and-wait tactics, that involve detection of females at relatively close range.

The background against which an object is viewed can have an effect on the minimum distance at which that object is detected. Bright uniform backgrounds are generally recognized as permitting detection of small moving objects at the greatest distance (Hailman 1977; Labhart and Nilsson 1995). Therefore, males that use a sit-and-wait tactic to detect females are expected to select perches and body orientations that, given the typical flight paths of females, maximize the chance that the females will be seen against the sky.

Visual stimuli that elicit the approach of males from a distance are generally only broadly similar to conspecifics in shape and size (e.g., Tinbergen et al. 1942; Yamashita 1995), although stimuli with a color matching that of conspecifics may be especially attractive to males at a distance (e.g., Douwes 1975, 1976). For patrollers, females are most likely to fly at about the same height above the ground as males and so will appear in the male visual field near the equator of the eye; a well-developed equatorial acute zone with large facets and small $\Delta\phi$'s is expected. For perchers, a dorsofrontal acute zone is expected in addition to an equatorial acute zone, but this will depend on exactly how the male's visual system is positioned relative to the likely flight paths of passing females.

Given the importance of color in mate detection, spectral sensitivities may also be adaptively modified to enhance the detection of mates. Bernhard et al. (1970) found that the spectral composition of the tapetal reflectance in a heliconiid matched that of markings on the wings of conspecifics that elicit courtship. Swihart (1963, 1967) found in a group of six nymphalids that species differences in the colors eliciting the greatest evoked potential in the male retina were correlated with differences in the species' color patterns.

ASSESSMENT OF POTENTIAL MATES BY MALES AND FEMALES

The problem of mate assessment for males and females involves discriminating conspecifics of the opposite sex from other butterflies encountered while searching for mates. These other butterflies include both conspecifics of the same sex and members of other, often very similar, species. In addition to recognizing individuals of the appropriate sex and species, both males and females may make finer discriminations among potential mates, preferentially interacting with those whose characteristics might yield the highest possible return on investments in sperm, eggs, and nutrients made during mating. The cues used by males for making these discriminations include both chemical and visual signals (Silberglied 1984; Yamashita 1995; Rutowski 1997).

The visual cues that might be used in mate assessment include size, shape, the spatial and temporal structure of displays, and especially the pattern and color of the markings on the wings. In general, these assessments are made in sequential, not simultaneous, evaluations of potential mates. Hence, assessments should be made by comparison either with some internalized absolute standard or with a learned criterion based on previous interactions with individuals in the population. The butterfly eye is such that such discriminations should be made at a few centimeters (see fig. 1.4), but the actual distance is not known. To some extent it will be a function of the size of the relevant pattern variables used to recognize appropriate mates.

At one extreme, males of various pierids are attracted to overall wing colors in both the visible and ultraviolet wavelengths that are typical of conspecific females (Obara 1970; Rutowski 1977b, 1981, 1982; Silberglied and Taylor 1978). At the other extreme, males of *Yoma sabina* (the lurcher) are most attracted to individuals with orange lines only a few millimeters wide on a dark brown or black background (Warzecha and Egelhauf 1995). As another example at this extreme, the yellow bands on the wings of the males of *Papilio polyxenes*, the black swallowtail, are apparently important in intra-sexual competition (Lederhouse and Scriber 1996). In species that use large pattern elements or whole-wing color, discriminations should be made at potentially greater distances, and perhaps more quickly, than in species that use smaller pattern elements. Other visual cues that have been suggested to play a role in mate assessment by males include wingbeat frequency and body size (Magnus 1956). Because other butterflies are approached head first, a male frontal acute zone is expected to maximize the ability to resolve pattern details. Similarly, the frontal ommatidia might be expected to have spectral sensitivities that are tuned to the relevant wavelengths used in mate assessment.

Receptive females may discriminate among potential mates to maximize the genetic or material benefits of mating. In doing so, they may use chemical, visual, and tactile cues. As in males, both whole-wing color and features of specific pattern elements have been implicated in mate assessment by females. Silberglied (1984) discusses the literature on whole-wing color, but since that review Wiernasz (1989, 1995) has shown that females of *Pontia occidentalis* (the western white) discriminate among conspecific males on the basis of dorsal forewing markings that are only a few square millimeters in size. How they make such discriminations while a male courts them with almost constant movement, and what parts of their eyes are used, is not known.

Unreceptive females also respond visually to males by performing behavior patterns that inhibit coupling. In *Pieris rapae* (the cabbage white), for example, unreceptive perched females respond to males by spreading the wings and raising the abdomen. Itoh and Obara (1994) have shown that among the visual cues presented by a courting male fluttering around a perched female, wing motion at a rate typical of flying butterflies and a general white color are among the more important cues.

FUTURE DIRECTIONS

There are a number of promising areas for research on the visual ecology of butterflies that will not only contribute to our understanding of these beautiful animals but also address broad questions in the field of visual ecology. First, we need information on the patterns of intra- and interspecific variation in eye structure in butterflies. Eye size is correlated with body size, and so for reasons discussed earlier, visual system performance should vary with body size. How this variation constrains the behavioral solutions to visual tasks open to butterflies of various sizes remains to be investigated. With such information in hand, we will be able to do comparative studies (like those done for some other insects; e.g., Bauer 1981, 1985) that help us understand the evolutionary relationships among eye structure, behavior, and ecology (Chittka and Briscoe 2001).

Second, to date, studies of visual system performance have for the most part not taken into consideration background and ambient illuminance, including brightness and spectral composition. Because of the preeminent role vision plays in the lives of butterflies, they should prove to be good subjects for testing ideas about the relationship between coloration, visual system structure, and the photic environment (e.g., Endler 1993; Endler and Théry 1996). If nothing else, we must be careful not to assume that what is conspicuous to humans is conspicuous to butterflies.

Third, data on the mechanisms of form detection are needed. Such data will certainly inform our understanding of the solutions open to butterflies facing problems such as recognition of food plants, oviposition sites, and mates. In the context of mate choice, for example, knowing the size limits on pattern elements that can be readily recognized will give us a better idea of the size, shape, and color of the markings that might evolve in the context of mate choice. At this point, it seems that because of the mediocre acuity of the butterfly eye, many of the fine pattern details on the wings of butterflies are unlikely to be important as intraspecific signals.

Finally, behavior determines how the visual system is positioned in space with respect to objects of interest such as flowers, oviposition sites, and potential mates. Detailed studies of body and visual system orientation during visual tasks are required for a complete analysis of the adaptive relationships between behavior, vision, and ecology in butterflies.

SUMMARY

There are two major points to be drawn from this review. First, the effective distance at which various visual tasks can be performed depends on the size of the object of interest and the information that must be gathered about it. The maximum distance at which objects of various sorts can be detected (roughly estimated by the ommatidial acceptance angle) and the maximum distance at which a pattern can be detected (roughly estimated by the interommatidial angle) are both functions of object size. What is striking is that butterflies typically detect resources and mates visually at distances up to only a meter or two. Visual recognition of resources and mates most often occurs at distances of only a few centimeters.

A second theme is that the butterfly eye is regionally specialized with respect to at least acuity and color sensitivity. In some cases these specializations, such as equatorial and frontal acute zones, may be important in several contexts. For the most part these specializations are not as dramatic as those found in the eyes of some other insects, which leaves the impression that the butterfly eye is a general-purpose visual organ. Perhaps predator detection, which more than any of the contexts discussed here would favor a large and uniformly acute visual field, is a critical task that has shaped the evolution of butterfly eyes. Although regional specializations in spectral sensitivity have been demonstrated, their adaptive functions have yet to be experimentally examined.

ACKNOWLEDGMENTS

I thank Carol Boggs, Ward Watt, and Paul Ehrlich for their invitation to contribute to this volume and conference; Eric Warrant and Almut Kelber for discussion concerning the visual capabilities of the compound eye in butterflies; Eric Warrant and Dan-Eric Nilsson for providing the equipment used to make the image of the luminous pseudopupil in plate 1.1A; Almut Kelber and Adriana Briscoe for critiquing early drafts of this chapter; and the U.S. National Science Foundation for financial support (NSF grant IBN 9723160).

CHAPTER 2

Molecular and Physiological Diversity of Visual Mechanisms in *Papilio*

Adriana D. Briscoe

Butterflies are among the most colorful of all living organisms, with wings bearing witness to the work of both natural and sexual selection. In both natural and sexual selection, the faculty of color vision plays a direct role. In the case of natural selection, predators of butterflies, such as birds and lizards, have highly developed color vision systems, which facilitate their detection of these colorful prey (Burkhardt 1996). Butterflies as agents (or victims) of sexual selection in turn have behaviors that reflect complex color vision. Much of what is known about color vision in butterflies has emerged from extensive studies of the swallowtail *Papilio xuthus* (Papilionidae). Anatomic, physiological, and behavioral understanding of the *P. xuthus* visual system is approaching what is known in *Drosophila melanogaster, Apis mellifera,* and humans.

In this chapter I present an overview of the *Papilio xuthus* visual system, as well as selected findings from studies of several other butterfly species. I begin with a discussion of the spatial location and organization of the photoreceptor cells in which the visual pigments are found, then move to photoreceptor cell physiology, visual pigment photochemistry, and the phylogenetic relationships among the opsin proteins giving rise to the visual pigments. These topics provide a structural backdrop for the color vision studies in butterflies that end this chapter.

ANATOMY OF BUTTERFLY VISION

The adult butterfly compound eye presumably has been selected to register and encode spatial, temporal, and chromatic information in response to predation pressure and the need to find food and oviposition sites. The eye accomplishes the processing of visual stimuli by the way in which its photoreceptor cells are patterned and organized, the way in which they encode color, and the way in which they form neuronal connections in the optic lobe of the brain. Besides the photoreceptor cells in the retina, butterflies have other photosensitive cells in the brain, in simple eyes, and even in the genitalia. With the exception of the genitalic photoreceptor cells, the function of these extraretinal photoreceptors is presently unknown.

ADULT COMPOUND EYE

In compound eyes, the retina is the assembly of photoreceptor cells, the eye is the assembly of ommatidia, and the cornea is the assembly of facet lenses (fig. 2.1A). In adults, the eyes may be sexually dimorphic, with males having larger eyes and more facets than females. Facet number varies considerably within butterfly genera. Within *Papilio* species, the number of ommatidia is estimated to range from an average of 12,800 in *P. maackii* females to an average of 15,300 in *P. xuthus* females and 18,200 in *P. xuthus* males (Yagi and Koyama 1963). (For a review of how the structure of the butterfly eye affects its sensitivity, dimensions of the visual field, and spatial resolution, as well as aspects of visual performance such as the perception of motion, see Rutowski, chap. 1 in this volume.)

Ommatidia are themselves composed of many kinds of cells. The various classes of cells include crystalline cone cells, iris pigment cells (i.e., corneagen or corneagenous cells), accessory or secondary pigment cells (also called retinular pigment cells), and photoreceptor cells (also called retinular sense cells). There are, in addition, other structures in the ommatidium formed from the extracellular extrusions of specific subsets of these cells. The cornea, for example, is a product of the iris pigment cells (also called the primary pigment cells).

Starting from the surface of the eye, there is the cornea, which is composed of three layers of cuticle. Beneath the cornea is the corneal process, which is also produced by the iris pigment cell. Directly beneath the corneal process is the crystalline cone, which is composed of four Semper cells and is enveloped in a membrane called the cone sheath. Surrounding the crystalline cone in a nearly cuplike fashion is a pair of iris pigment cells. Below or proximal to the crystalline cone are the light-sensitive photoreceptor cells (fig. 2.1B). The position, arrangement, and patterning of the different classes of photoreceptor cells are highly organized, both within an individual ommatidium and across the entire retinal field. This spatial organization is thought to be the first level of processing of light received from the environment (see Bernard and Remington 1991).

Adriana D. Briscoe

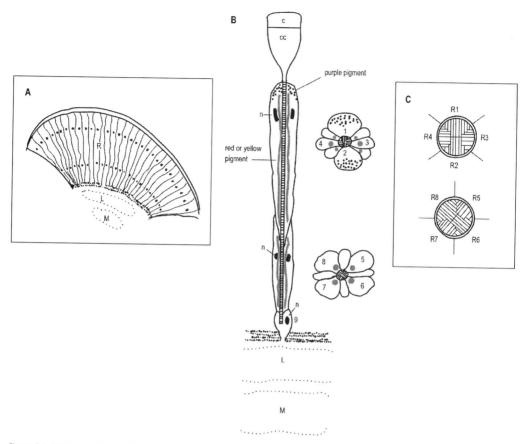

Figure 2.1 Diagram of the *Papilio xuthus* retina, ommatidium, and fused rhabdom. (A) Longitudinal section of the retina, R, and optic lobe, which is composed of the lamina, L, and medulla, M. Three tiers of photoreceptor cell nuclei are present in the retina and are indicated by black dots. (B) Longitudinal section of an ommatidium, showing its organization along the proximal-distal axis. Purple pigment is found at the very distal tip of the R1 and R2 cells and is indicated by small black dots. Yellow or red pigment, which acts as a long-pass filter, is found in the photoreceptor cells close to the rhabdom and is indicated by gray stripes. The rhabdom itself is indicated by black stripes. c, cornea; cc, crystalline cone; n, photoreceptor cell nuclei. Cross sections of an ommatidium at two levels, showing the R1–R8 cell bodies arranged around the central rhabdom, are also shown. Physiologically, the R1 and R2 cells are UV-, violet-, or blue-sensitive; the R3 and R4 cells are green-sensitive, and the R5–R9 cells are either green- or red-sensitive (Bandai et al. 1992). (C) Cross section of the fused rhabdom at two levels in the ommatidium. The rhabdom is composed of parallel microvilli whose orientation varies according to the specific photoreceptor cell contributing microvilli to the rhabdom at that level of the ommatidium (Bandai et al. 1992). (B after Arikawa and Stavenga 1997.)

Papilio ommatidia have nine photoreceptor (R) cells, eight of which are elongate and run the length of the ommatidium to the basement membrane (fig. 2.1B). The ninth photoreceptor cell is much smaller and sits beneath the others just above the basement membrane (Ribi 1987). Each photoreceptor has a specialized structure, the rhabdomere, consisting of microvilli, where the visual pigment molecules (as well as the components of the phototransduction cascade) are located. The rhabdomeres of all the photoreceptor cells within one butterfly ommatidium are juxtaposed and thus form a fused rhabdom. In flies the rhabdomeres are separate and thus compose an open rhabdom. Although the rhabdom is referred to as a fused structure, the parallel microvilli contributed by individual R cells can be uniquely identified (fig. 2.1B, C). The microvilli of opposing pairs of photoreceptor cells contributing to the fused rhabdom have the same angle of orientation (Bandai et al. 1992; Arikawa and Uchiyama 1996) (fig. 2.1C). (More precisely, the microvilli of the R1 and R2 cells are oriented dorsoventrally [0°], those of R3 and R4 are parallel to the anterior-posterior axis [90°], and the remaining R5–R8 cells have microvilli that are oriented diagonally [45°, 135°].) The parallel orientation of the microvilli contributed by each photoreceptor cell remains fixed throughout the length of the cell, and is the basis of *Papilio* butterflies' sensitivity to polarized light (Toh and Sagara 1982; Kelber 1999a).

Surrounding the photoreceptor cells is a group of six accessory or secondary pigment cells (not shown in fig. 2.1), which are densely packed with strongly light-absorbing dark pigment granules. The pigments in the accessory pigment cells are very blackish and always absorb a large proportion of the obliquely incident light. Accessory pigments are also found within the photoreceptor cells. The pigments in the granules surrounding the rhabdom—that is, those within the cell bodies of the photoreceptor cells—act as selective filters. When exposed to bright light, these accessory pigments act as long-pass filters by selectively absorbing short wavelengths and modifying the stray wavelengths of light to which the visual pigments are exposed (described in greater detail below) (Arikawa and Stavenga 1997). At the very bottom of the ommatidium is the basement membrane, which is perforated by the photoreceptor cell axons.

Larval Stemmata and Adult Brain Photoreceptors

The larvae of *Papilio xuthus* have six stemmata, or simple eyes, that are composed of seven photoreceptor cells arranged in a regular semi-tiered fashion (Toh and Sagara 1982; Ichikawa 1991). Each stemma is comparable in size to one adult ommatidium (Toh and Iwasaki 1982). The three classes of photoreceptors found in the stemmata, UV (370 nm), blue (450 nm), and green (530 nm) (Ichikawa and Hideki 1982), have peak sensitivities similar to the photoreceptors found in the adult butterfly and in many other kinds of adult insects (Chittka 1996; Briscoe and Chittka 2001). The larvae, however, lack violet (400 nm) and red (600 nm) photoreceptors, which are present in adults (Arikawa et al. 1987). The distal tier of stemmatal photoreceptor cells is homogeneous in sensitivity (green), while the proximal tier of cells is heterogeneous (either blue and green or UV, blue, and green) (Ichikawa and Tateda 1980, 1982; Ichikawa 1990).

Adriana D. Briscoe

Like the adult ommatidium, the larval stemma has a fused rhabdom. Larval stemmata have a "pupillary response" that functions to increase contrast sensitivity (Gilbert 1994). Dark ommochrome-containing pigment granules migrate radially away from the rhabdom to control the light flux propagating through the rhabdom. Larval stemmata also modulate contrast sensitivity by increasing the surface area of the rhabdom facing the sky, or the acceptance angle of light reaching the rhabdom. The distal tier of cells has a wider acceptance angle than the proximal tier and different neuronal wiring (distal photoreceptors are wired into the lamina, while proximal photoreceptors are wired into the medulla), as well as a different spectral receptor composition. On the basis of these anatomic and physiological differences, Ichikawa and Hideki (1982) and Ichikawa (1990) propose that the distal photoreceptor cells are used in the detection of objects while the proximal photoreceptor cells are involved in the detection of color and shape. (For a summary of how the larval stemmatal neurons are color-coded, see Ichikawa 1990.)

During the prepupal stage of development, the photoreceptor cells of the stemmata migrate into the brain and persist into the pupal and adult stages as brain photoreceptors, retaining their photosensitivity. A small amount of light (<5%) passes through the head and reaches the brain photoreceptors (Ichikawa 1991).

OCELLI AND GENITALIC PHOTORECEPTORS

Besides the retina and brain, adult *Papilio* have other classes of photoreceptor cells. These include a pair of tiny dorsal ocelli, or simple eyes, on top of the head (Dickens and Eaton 1973) and two pairs of genitalic photoreceptors (Arikawa et al. 1980; Miyako et al. 1993). (It should be noted, however, that the developmental and anatomic relationship of the brain photoreceptors described above to the ocelli remains ambiguous and should be further investigated.) The genitalic photoreceptors in males affect male mating performance; ablation of these photoreceptors impairs the successful completion of copulation (Arikawa et al. 1996, 1997). Females use the genitalic photoreceptors in oviposition. They optically confirm whether the ovipositor is sufficiently pushed out, then deposit an egg in response to mechanical stimulation they receive when the ovipositor touches the leaf (Arikawa and Takagi 2001). Genitalic photoreceptors have been found in twenty-two other lepidopteran species from five butterfly families, but not in moths (Arikawa and Aoki 1982). The presence of photoreceptor cells in the adult ocelli, genitalia, and brain suggests that opsins, the protein component of visual pigments, are expressed in these nonretinal structures.

PHYSIOLOGICAL VARIATION OF COLOR RECEPTORS
IN BUTTERFLIES

The sensitivity spectrum describes the physiological response of a photoreceptor to different wavelengths of light. Spectral sensitivities are often measured by recording the mass response of the retina to light (producing an electroretinogram, or ERG) or by measuring the intracellular response of an individually penetrated cell. Electroretinograms can be made from the eye of an intact animal or by removing the eye from the head and bathing the cut end and a "grounding" electrode in saline (Eguchi et al. 1982). A recording electrode is implanted through the cornea into the retina. The eye is left to adapt to dark for a short time before being exposed to light wavelengths starting at one end of the spectrum and ending at the other. The wavelengths the eye is exposed to are modified by changing a set of filters through which the light source is passed.

Spectral sensitivity curves are determined by the reciprocal of the number of light quanta needed to elicit a constant electrophysiological response (Menzel et al. 1986). Usually, curves drawn from ERGs are multipeaked, reflecting the contributions of all receptor types, while those drawn from intracellular recordings comprise one major peak and a minor shoulder, presumably resembling the absorption spectrum of the visual pigments contained within that cell. Spectra estimated from ERGs are arguably roughly the superposition of those estimated from intracellular recordings (Eguchi et al. 1982).

Eguchi et al. (1982) conducted an ERG survey of thirty-five butterfly and moth species. They found considerable variation among the sampled species in the number of spectral classes of photoreceptors present (three to five). Slightly more moths (six species) had three major receptors than had four or more (five species). No major differences were found between nocturnal and diurnal moths in spectral receptor number or type. Among the butterflies tested, nymphalids had three to four spectral classes of photoreceptors, while hesperiids had only three. The UV class was common to all 35 lepidopterans tested. In addition, some butterfly families showed the highest responses in the short-wavelength range (380–400 nm) (Papilionidae, Pieridae, Lycaenidae), while other families of butterflies and moths showed their highest sensitivity to the longer wavelengths (520–580 nm). It is not presently known what is responsible for this difference in relative peak response. It is possible that there are regional differences in the number of photoreceptor types in the retina (see Bernard and Remington 1991), or differences in the distribution of screening pigments that selectively modify the light absorbed by the visual pigments (see below).

The retina of *Papilio xuthus* is among the most spectrally complex of the butterfly retinas that have been studied. Five spectral classes of photoreceptors are present: UV (360 nm), violet (400 nm), blue (460 nm), green (520 nm), and red (600 nm) (Arikawa et al. 1987). In addition, regional differences in spectral sensitivity appear to exist; the ventral part of the *P. xuthus* retina appears to be more sensitive to UV wavelengths than the dorsal part (Arikawa et al. 1987; Kitamoto et al. 2000). The photoreceptor cells in *P. xuthus* also display sensitivity to polarized light (Bandai et al. 1992), which may be utilized by butterflies to recognize open spaces or suitable oviposition sites. Open spaces such as the sky have a high polarized light content, especially in the UV. Differences in degree of polarization also exist between smooth and rough plant foliage (Horváth and Varjú 1997). Behaviorally, *P. aegeus* has been shown to strongly prefer horizontally polarized light over vertically polarized light when choosing oviposition sites (Kelber 1999a).

The sensitivity spectrum of an individually measured photoreceptor cell can, in the absence of filtering by other pigments or cells, conform closely to the absorption spectrum of the visual pigment expressed within that cell (Stavenga 1992). In *Papilio xuthus,* the UV, blue, and one class of green receptors have spectral sensitivity curves that match the expected absorption spectrum of the visual pigments expressed within those cells. However, several spectral classes of photoreceptor cells in *Papilio* species do not have the expected spectral sensitivity curves. The violet receptor (400 nm) and the red receptor (600 nm) have curves that are unusually sharp (Arikawa et al. 1987). In addition, the two classes of green (520 nm) receptors differ in the presence or absence of a secondary UV peak (Bandai et al. 1992). Modifying the spectral properties of the visual pigments expressed within these photoreceptor classes are at least three different kinds of accessory pigments (see Arikawa and Stavenga 1997; Arikawa et al. 1999a, 1999b), the effects of which are discussed below.

PHOTOCHEMISTRY OF VISUAL PIGMENTS

Visual transduction begins with the detection of light by the visual pigments embedded in the rhabdom. Visual pigments are composed of a chromophore molecule, which in butterflies is either 11-*cis*-retinal or 3-hydroxy-11-*cis*-retinal (Seki et al. 1987), and a protein known as an opsin, which forms a binding pocket around the chromophore. When a photon of light hits the visual pigment, the chromophore undergoes a conformational change, whereby the 11-*cis* bond converts to all-*trans* (Wald 1968). The opsin protein also undergoes conformational changes that lead to a cascade of biochemical events, resulting in a signal being sent to the nervous system that light has been detected (reviewed by Stavenga 1995).

Because most butterflies synthesize a single type of chromophore molecule, the spectral diversity of the photoreceptor cells that are found in the eye appears to be due primarily to amino acid differences in the opsin protein itself. Indeed, six opsins have been reported in the butterfly *Papilio glaucus* (Briscoe 1998a, 2000) and five in *Papilio xuthus* (Kitamoto et al. 1998, 2000). However, the full sensitivity spectrum of all the classes of photoreceptor cells is not likely to be due solely to amino acid variation in opsins because of the effects of accessory pigments that modify the spectral content of the illumination of the visual pigments themselves (Arikawa et al. 1999a, 1999b).

Rhodopsin, a term routinely used to identify vertebrate rod cell–specific opsins (Hargrave et al. 1983), is also used as a general term for invertebrate visual pigments. Rhodopsin is the native state of a visual pigment—that is, its state before it has undergone conformational changes induced by light. Each kind of rhodopsin molecule has a characteristic absorption spectrum. After absorption of a photon, the rhodopsin molecule converts to a photoproduct with a different conformation, known as metarhodopsin, which has a different characteristic peak of absorbance. When the rhodopsin peak absorbance is less than 500 nm, the metarhodopsin peak absorbance tends to be greater than 500 nm (a bathochromic shift). Conversely, when the rhodopsin peak absorbance is greater than 500 nm, the metarhodopsin peak absorbance is typically less than 500 nm (a hypsochromic shift) (Stavenga 1992). In insect visual pigments, metarhodopsin can be photoconverted back into rhodopsin by the appropriate wavelengths of light (Stavenga 1992). (In fact, photoreconversion of metarhodopsin also occurs in vertebrate rhodopsin, but it requires photon absorption within the short lifetime of the unstable metarhodopsin.) The thermostability of insect metarhodopsin provides the unique opportunity for photoreconversion to rhodopsin, which can be exploited to maintain sensitivity without the need for a complete renewal of the pigment molecules.

SPECTRAL TUNING BY ACCESSORY PIGMENTS

The sensitivity spectrum of a photoreceptor cell can substantially differ from the absorption spectrum of its visual pigment due to the action of a sensitizing pigment (*Drosophila*) or a spectrally selective light-absorbing filtering pigment (housefly, *Papilio*). Arikawa et al. (1999a), using light microscopy, have documented an UV-fluorescing pigment in approximately 28% of ommatidia in the ventral half of the *Papilio xuthus* retina. The emission spectrum of this UV-fluorescing pigment matches that of 3-hydroxyretinol, the alcohol form of the *P. xuthus* chromophore, 3-hydroxyretinal. The UV-fluorescing pigment co-localizes with the unusually narrow violet photoreceptor and the single-peaked green photoreceptor found in a certain subclass of ommatidia. UV and double-peaked green photoreceptors, which have spectral sensitivity curves more characteristic of photoreceptor cells expressing single visual pigments, were found in nonfluorescing ommatidia.

In addition, Arikawa et al. (1999b) found two other types of screening pigments, which selectively absorb short wavelengths, in the R3–R8 photoreceptor cells in the retina of *Papilio xuthus*. These red and yellow pigments, which are arranged in granules around the rhabdom, function to filter the light reaching the proximal photoreceptor cells. The red pigment is found in about three times as many ommatidia as the yellow pigment, and the occurrence of each is correlated with a distinct spectral class of photoreceptor. The red pigment is found in ommatidia with red-absorbing visual pigments, while the yellow pigment is found in ommatidia with green-absorbing visual pigments. Using a model that takes into account the light transmitted by the red and yellow pigments, Arikawa et al. (1999b) estimate that the 600 nm red photoreceptor is the result of a visual pigment with a peak absorbance at 575 nm filtered by the red pigment. Similarly, the 520 nm green photoreceptor is the result of a visual pigment with a peak absorbance at 515 nm that is filtered by the yellow pigment.

Eye regionalization of screening pigments is commonly found in other insects, such as the male honeybee, or drone (Stavenga 1992). Red pigments of the kind found in *Papilio xuthus*, which predominantly absorb short-wavelength light, may also function to increase the sensitivity of photoreceptor cells by passing on more long-wavelength light, which can then be absorbed by the green rhodopsins that are the most abundant in all ommatidia (Stavenga, pers. comm.).

MOLECULAR BASIS OF VISION IN *Papilio:* PHYLOGENY AND SPATIAL EXPRESSION PATTERNS

Opsins are members of the large multigene G protein–coupled receptor family, which includes such proteins as odorant and neurotransmitter receptors (Fryxell and Meyerowitz 1991). The global spectral properties of an opsin appear to be roughly predictable by analyzing its relationship to other known opsins using phylogenetic analysis (e.g., Crandall and Cronin 1997; Briscoe 1999). Using RT-PCR, Briscoe (1998a, 2000) isolated six distinct opsin-encoding cDNAs (*PglRh1–6*) from the tiger swallowtail, *Papilio glaucus,* and Kitamoto et al. (1998) identified three homologues (*PxRh1–3*) from *Papilio xuthus*. Phylogenetically, the opsins from *P. glaucus* and *P. xuthus* fall into three distinct clades: UV-, blue-, and long-wavelength-absorbing (Briscoe 1998b) (fig. 2.2). The four long-wavelength opsins in *Papilio* are three more than are presently known in any other insect, including *Drosophila,*

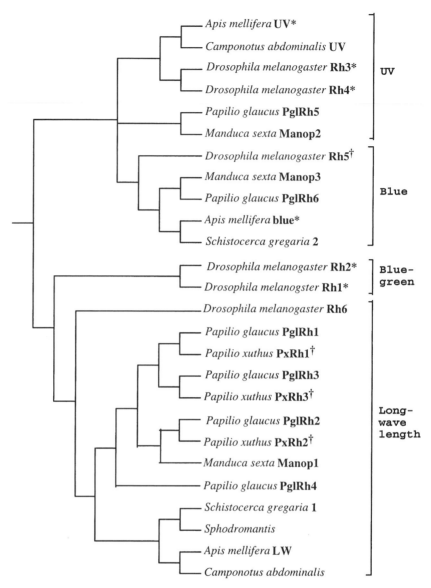

Figure 2.2 Cladistic analysis of insect opsin amino acid sequences. The tree shown is simplified from the analysis of a larger dataset of fifty-four opsin sequences (Briscoe 2000). Only representative insect species from available orders or suborders are shown. Brackets indicate measured (asterisks) or inferred (daggers) spectral properties of the visual pigments in each clade. Inferred spectral properties are based on in situ hybridization or immunohistochemistry in combination with electrophysiological studies. Measured peak sensitivities are 345–375 nm in the UV clade, 439 nm in the blue clade, 420–480 nm in the blue-green clade, and 515–575 nm in the long-wavelength clade. References for measured spectra are from *Apis mellifera* (Townson et al. 2000) and *Drosophila* (see Briscoe 1999). For inferred *Papilio xuthus* spectra, see Kitamoto et al. (1998) and Arikawa et al. (1999b).

in which all classes of photoreceptor cells in the retina are accounted for (Chou et al. 1996; Papatsenko et al. 1997; Salcedo et al. 1999).

Somewhat surprisingly, the *P. glaucus* molecular data suggest a larger diversity of opsins (six) in *Papilio* than might be expected from the number of spectral classes of photoreceptors (five) found in the retina of *P. xuthus* (Arikawa et al. 1987; Briscoe 1998a, 2000). There are a number of possible explanations to account for this discrepancy. First, as suggested earlier, it is conceivable that at least one of these opsins is expressed in the ocelli or in extraretinal brain receptors and is not used in vision. *Drosophila*, for instance, have an ocellar-specific opsin (Rh2) that is not expressed in the retina (Pollock and Benzer 1988). Second, there may be some functional redundancy between some of the long-wavelength opsins (i.e., nearly identical spectral properties or overlapping spatial expression patterns; see below). Kitamoto et al. (1998), in fact, showed that two long-wavelength opsins, Rh1 and Rh2, coexist in R3 and R4 photoreceptor cells in the ventral eye region of *P. xuthus,* a clear example of such redundancy. Phylogenetic analysis alone cannot distinguish which of the long-wavelength visual pigments are likely to be more red-shifted relative to the others, nor can a good prediction be made based on the amino acid differences between the sequences, because we currently lack a model of spectral tuning in insect visual pigments.

The identification of spectrally distinct classes of photoreceptor cells by physiological methods does not require that each class of photoreceptor cell have a unique kind of opsin. The *P. xuthus* violet receptor is a good example of this in which the shape of the spectral sensitivity curve can be adequately explained by an UV-filtering pigment that is modifying the light experienced by an UV-absorbing visual pigment. Kitamoto et al. (2000), in fact, have shown through in situ hybridization studies that the *P. xuthus* UV-absorbing rhodopsin mRNA is expressed in both UV-sensitive and violet-sensitive photoreceptor cells. Kitamoto et al. (1998) have also reported the cloning and in situ hybridization of three long-wavelength-sensitive rhodopsin mRNAs from *P. xuthus,* whose expression patterns display some surprising differences relative to those known from *Drosophila.*

Double- and triple-labeling experiments using antibodies derived from the six *Drosophila* opsins have confirmed the "one opsin per photoreceptor cell" rule in *Drosophila* (Chou et al. 1996) developed from earlier electrophysiological and gene expression studies (Cowman et al. 1986; Fryxell and Meyerowitz 1987; Huber et al. 1997; Papatsenko et al. 1997). However, evidence for the expression of *two* opsins within a photoreceptor cell is accumulating from studies of the crab *Hemigrapsus sanguineus* (Sakamoto et al. 1996) and *Papilio xuthus* (Kitamoto et al. 1998). Significantly, a function for such opsin coexpression has been reported: artificial coexpression of two different visual pigments within a single *Drosophila* photoreceptor cell results in a summed sensitivity spectrum (Feiler et al. 1992), and could be a mechanism for broadening sensitivity to light. In fact, Kitamoto et al. (1998) have reported two different cases of opsin mRNA co-localization within the *Papilio xuthus* eye. They found that in some ommatidia, either the *PxRh1* or the *PxRh2* transcript is expressed in the green-sensitive R3–R4 cells, and in a third ommatidial class the two transcripts are expressed simultaneously. They also found in some ommatidia that either *PxRh2* or *PxRh3* mRNA is expressed in the green- or red-sensitive R5–R8 photoreceptor cells; in others these two transcripts are expressed simultaneously. Whether these opsin transcripts are translated into proteins awaits verification using opsin-specific antibodies. Nevertheless, on the basis of the expression pattern of *PxRh1–3* in the retina, Kitamoto et al. (1998) postulate that PxRh1 and PxRh2 are green-absorbing opsins, while PxRh3 is red-absorbing, a hypothesis that can be rigorously tested by transgenic expression and photochemical or physiological characterization (e.g., Townson et al. 1998).

BEHAVIORAL CORRELATES OF VISION IN BUTTERFLIES

The vast array of colors on the wings of butterflies implies an obvious conclusion about their sensory systems; namely, that butterflies have color vision. The demonstration of color vision, however, requires more than anatomic and physiological analyses or simple behavioral tests such as matching different-colored papers of unknown spectral content. Advocates of a rigorous experimental approach have long upheld von Frisch's famous demonstration of the color vision capacity of honeybees as the method of choice. This approach requires an animal flexible enough in its behavior that it can be trained to tell the difference between visual stimuli of different chromatic content without regard to brightness. In practice, this method may involve training the animal to distinguish "colored" objects from each other and from objects of varying shades of gray, or in a modern advance, using a light-emitting diode array, in which light intensity can be carefully controlled (Kelber and Pfaff 1999). The gradations of color that can be distinguished depend critically on the kind of photoreceptor system the animal has. Likewise, there exist thresholds of brightness beyond which an animal may not be able to distinguish one color from another (e.g., Kinoshita et al. 1999). Although initial attempts at studying the visual systems of butterflies have been somewhat challenging (e.g., Ilse 1928), there have been notable successes in documenting innate color preferences (Weiss 1997) and color vision in butterflies (Kinoshita et al. 1999).

True color vision in butterflies, as opposed to inflexible wavelength-dependent behavior, has been demonstrated in *Papilio xuthus* (Kinoshita et al. 1999) and in *P. aegeus* (Kelber and Pfaff 1999). Wavelength-dependent behaviors are behaviors mediated by different spectral classes of photoreceptors, or by different combinations of such spectral classes, and are thought to be the result of "neuronal filtering," either by the CNS itself or by specialized regions of the eye, in such a way that particular spectral cues are interpreted in specific ways (Goldsmith 1994). Such behaviors have been argued to be adaptive for organisms with a small nervous system and a short life span whose behaviors have immediate consequences for survival and reproduction (Wehner 1981). Behavioral studies that measure innate color preferences, but which do not incorporate training experiments, or do not vary the intensity of the "preferred color" (Kelber and Pfaff 1999), may not be interpretable as demonstrating color vision. In the absence of training, it is impossible to rule out the chance that a particular behavior is "hardwired." For instance, a study by Scherer and Kolb (1987a) found that in *Pieris brassicae,* the escape reaction is stimulated by UV light, egg laying by green (540 nm), feeding by blue (450 nm) or secondarily by red (600 nm), and drumming by green (560 nm). In this instance, because the butterflies could not be trained to associate arbitrary colors with objects in the experiments, and because the intensity of the stimulus was not varied, the contributions of particular spectral photoreceptor types to the response, and their positive or negative interactions, are unknown. In a related set of experiments on *P. aegeus,* Kelber (1999b) demonstrated that the oviposition response is mediated by linear interactions between blue, green, and red photoreceptors, in which the effect of the green photoreceptors is positive and that of the blue and the red is negative. Modeling the chromatic stimulus most likely to elicit a response given the spectral sensitivities of the photoreceptor cells in the retina, their positive or negative interactions, and the background light level (Kelber 1999b) seems a particularly fruitful direction for future research on the evolution of color vision in butterflies.

In its idealized sense, color vision is the capacity to use chromatic cues uncoupled from other features of visual stimuli, such as shape and motion, as well as any obligatory significance for behavior (Goldsmith 1994). Because of the need to demonstrate the ability of the animal to sense color in a general way, the work of Kinoshita et al. (1999) on the swallowtail *Papilio xuthus* contains a key ingredient not found in previous studies: experiments that involve extensive training and which demonstrate the capacity for learning on the part of the animal. Kinoshita and colleagues tested the butterflies' ability to distinguish colors without regard to brightness in two ways: first, by presenting the training color along with disks of varying shades of gray, and second, by using neutral density filters over the training color until the butterfly was not able to distinguish the training color from other colors. As a control against residual scents left by other butterflies, they periodically wiped down the test area, and to guard against the possibility of testing for butterflies' spatial learning ability, they rotated the colored disks during each experiment. Under the light conditions used (400–700 nm), they found the observed color vision ability of *P. xuthus* to depend mostly on the blue, green, and red receptors. They suggest, however, that under different light conditions, the UV (360 nm) and violet (400 nm) receptors of *P. xuthus* (Arikawa et al. 1987) may also be used in color vision. Kelber and Pfaff's (1999) study of the color vision system of *P. aegeus* more rigorously explored the requirement of color recognition independent of light intensity by deployment of an LED array that could vary light over two log units. Together, the results of these studies demonstrate that color vision in *Papilio* is at least tetrachromatic, and it may be found to be pentachromatic when further tests are made.

Although they cannot demonstrate true color vision, studies that record the innate color preferences of butterflies are nevertheless of interest because they may document biases in the rate at which butterflies are able to learn new color associations. For instance, Weiss (1997) found that pipevine swallowtail butterflies (*Battus philenor*) more easily switched to foraging on yellow flowers (a preferred color) after being trained on magenta flowers than vice versa. Likewise, Kinoshita et al. (1999) found that yellow and red were more easily learned by *Papilio xuthus* than blue and green. The fact that there is considerable variation in innate color preferences among butterfly species may provide a partial behavioral basis for niche separation in feeding strategies between closely related butterfly species (see Weiss and Lamont 1997). For example, C. A. Swihart (1970) found that *Papilio troilus* showed a feeding preference for blue, with a lesser preference for orange; Ilse and Vaidya (1956) found that *P. demoleus* preferred blue and purple. Other hypotheses on the reason for color preferences include the trade-offs incurred in having to learn the handling of novel flower species (Goulson et al. 1997) and the dependence of the preference on the intensity of the stimuli (Kelber and Pfaff 1997). How these preferences come about, and under what circumstances they might evolve, remain mysteries. Anatomic and photochemical studies, such as the work of Bernard and Remington (1991) on species of sympatric *Lycaena* (Lycaenidae), suggest that the photoreceptor arrays themselves may harbor a great deal of interspecific and intersexual variation. Changes in the expression pattern of opsins and their spectral tuning by amino acid substitutions and accessory pigments in the peripheral nervous system (the retina) may play a role in mediating the responses of butterflies to their light environment.

SUMMARY

Studies of *Papilio* have revealed a remarkable degree of visual system complexity at the level of molecules, morphology, physiology, and behavior.

Adriana D. Briscoe

Papilio have three more long-wavelength opsins than are presently known in other insects. Studies of the expression patterns of these and other invertebrate opsin transcripts are revealing surprising exceptions to the "one receptor per photoreceptor cell" rule found in *Drosophila*. Accessory pigments play a prominent role in modifying the sensitivity functions of photoreceptors in *Papilio*. True color vision, defined as the ability to discriminate colors based on their spectral composition regardless of brightness, has been demonstrated in *Papilio xuthus* and *Papilio aegeus*. Finally, photoreceptors not only play a role in the long-range detection of host plants, conspecifics, and mates in butterflies, probably mediated by color processing, but they also play a direct role in the success of male mating behavior itself.

ACKNOWLEDGMENTS

I am grateful to K. Arikawa for preprints and for sharing unpublished data. A. Fraser, I. Jones, D. Lambert, L. Nagy, C. Nulsen, R. Reed, R. Rutowski, and an anonymous reviewer provided useful comments on the manuscript. D. G. Stavenga deserves special mention for an excellent and exceptional editing of the manuscript. Finally, I am grateful to my dissertation co-advisors, R. C. Lewontin and N. E. Pierce, for their generous support of my work.

CHAPTER 3

Hawkmoth Pollination in Arizona's Sonoran Desert: Behavioral Responses to Floral Traits

Robert A. Raguso and Mark A. Willis

Adult butterflies forage for a broad spectrum of resources, including floral nectar, pollen, fruit, sap, fungal fluids, mineral salts, and animal tissues, secretions and waste products (Owen 1971; Gilbert and Singer 1975; Ray and Andrews 1980; Boggs 1987b; DeVries 1988a; Boppré 1990). Flower-visiting butterflies have long been recognized as important pollinators (Delpino 1874; Knuth 1898; van der Pijl 1961), as their patterns of movement affect plant outcrossing distances and population structure (Levin 1978; Murawski and Gilbert 1986; Johnson and Bond 1994). Recent studies have explored the role of butterflies as pollen vectors (Cruden and Hermann-Parker 1979; Wiklund et al. 1979; Murphy 1984; Venables and Barrows 1985; Stanton et al. 1986), their effectiveness as pollinators of specific plants (Levin and Berube 1972; Opler et al. 1975; Spears 1983; Jennersten 1984; Schemske and Horvitz 1984; Erhardt 1990), their learning abilities in the context of floral feeding (Lewis 1986; Goulson and Cory 1993; Weiss 1995, 1997), and their allocation of nectar resources to flight energetics and reproductive output (Watt et al. 1974; Boggs 1981a; Murphy et al. 1983; May 1992).

In parallel with butterflies, adult nectar feeding has evolved in a number of moth families and is especially prominent among hawkmoths (Sphingidae: Rothschild and Jordan 1903; Newman 1965; Hodges 1971; Schreiber 1978; Miller 1997). Nectar-feeding hawkmoths constitute an important class of pollinators in warm temperate and tropical habitats worldwide (Baker 1961; Gregory 1964; Silberbauer-Gottsberger and Gottsberger 1975; Grant 1983; Bawa et al. 1985; Nilsson et al. 1985; Haber and Frankie 1989; Singer and Cocucci 1997; Johnson et al. 1998). By virtue of their hovering flight, large body size, and high vagility, hawkmoths visit more flowers per foraging bout (Cruden et al. 1976; Heinrich 1983; Herrera 1989), carry larger pollen loads (Kislev et al. 1972; Haber 1984; Nilsson et al. 1987), and move pollen greater distances (Stockhouse 1976; Linhart and Mendenhall 1977; Nilsson and Rabakonandrianina 1988) than do most other flower-visiting Lepidoptera. These characteristics, combined with hawkmoths' ability to travel long distances in search of mates, host plants, and appropriate habitat (Janzen 1971; Cross and Owen 1970; Powell and Brown 1990; Nilsson et al. 1992), underscore the importance of hawkmoth pollination to plant population dynamics. These insects effect pollen transfer and gene exchange between widely dispersed individual plants and plant populations (Schemske 1980; Haber 1984). Thus, fluctuations in hawkmoth abundance, whether natural or anthropogenic (Grant 1931; Kislev et al. 1972; Buchmann and Nabhan 1996), may have dire consequences for rare plants that depend exclusively on hawkmoths as pollinators, especially in fragmented habitats (Suzán et al. 1994; Buchmann and Nabhan 1996), dune remnants (Pavlic et al. 1993), and on islands (Lammers 1989; Boucher 1996).

During the past four years, we have studied the interactions between nectar-feeding, crepuscular hawkmoths and a guild of night-blooming, hawkmoth-pollinated plants in Arizona's Sonoran Desert. Specifically, we have characterized the chemical and physical properties of floral attractants produced by night-blooming plants, and we have performed behavioral assays testing the relative importance of visual and olfactory cues in attracting hawkmoths to flowers. Our investigations were motivated by the surprising paucity of studies on hawkmoth foraging behavior, despite decades of research on hawkmoth thermal biology, pollination ecology, and sensory neurophysiology. This chapter presents an overview of hawkmoth pollination and introduces our studies of the sensory ecology of hawkmoth-flower interactions. It is important to note that much of the previously published literature, at least for nocturnal hawkmoths, is anecdotal or based on observations from uncontrolled or unbalanced experiments. We begin with an overview of the ultimate and proximate reasons why hawkmoths visit flowers, then ask whether *both* visual and olfactory cues are *necessary* for hawkmoth attraction and feeding. We then summarize the behavioral experiments with which we addressed this question using naive and experienced hawkmoths, and conclude by discussing our results in the context of other studies of hawkmoth behavior.

Why include a chapter on hawkmoth nectar foraging in a book on butterfly ecology and evolution? From a phylogenetic perspective, butterflies are a monophyletic lineage of specialized, largely diurnal moths (Weller and Pashley 1995) whose neurosensory capabilities, physiological demands, and reproductive imperatives are comparable to those of most large moth families (Chapman 1998). Therefore, the questions that drive our experimental system—how hawkmoths integrate visual and olfactory cues during foraging and how larval diet, adult experience, and the physical environment modify such behaviors—are broadly relevant to the evolutionary, ecological, and physiological concept structure by which butterflies and, indeed, all nectar-feeding insects are studied (Gilbert and Singer 1975; Heinrich 1983; Watt 1985b). In this way, the study of pyrrolizidine alkaloid use by arctiid moths (Pliske 1975; Boppré 1990; Conner et al. 1990), mud puddling (Smedley and Eisner 1995), and Müllerian mimicry (Miller 1996) in notodontid moths has provided important insights and context for considerations of butterfly chemical ecology and mating system evolution. Studies such as ours will contribute to an eventual comparative assessment of the effects of sensory physiology and life history parameters on the evolution of adult feeding strategies throughout the Lepidoptera (see Boggs and Ross 1993; Boggs 1997a; D. M. O'Brien 1998).

BRIGHT AND SWEET: FLORAL ADVERTISEMENTS AND REWARDS OF HAWKMOTH-POLLINATED PLANTS

Why do hawkmoths visit flowers? Floral nectar is an important energetic resource for hawkmoths, supporting their metabolically expensive poikilothermic flight physiology (Heinrich and Casey 1973; Casey 1976; O'Brien 1999) and long-distance dispersal (Cross and Owen 1970; Janzen 1986). Adult nectar feeding also may contribute directly to reproductive fitness via egg maturation in some hawkmoths (Ziegler 1991; D. M. O'Brien 1998). In Arizona's Sonoran Desert, at least seventeen species of hawkmoth-pollinated, night-blooming plants (representing twelve angiosperm families) produce large volumes of sucrose-dominated nectars (R. Raguso, unpub.). The nectar in hawkmoth-pollinated flowers is typically less concentrated (18–37% w/w) than the 40–50% syrups that characterize bumblebee-pollinated flowers (Pyke and Waser 1981; Baker and Baker 1983), but mean standing crop nectar volumes are often quite a bit larger, ranging in our sample from 3 to 80 μL per flower (R. Raguso, unpub.). Following the calculations of Bartholomew and Casey (1978) and Cruden et al. (1983), the caloric content of one of these flowers would support 25 seconds to 15 minutes of hovering flight by a hawkmoth weighing 2 g. Thus, Arizona's night-blooming flowers offer a nectar resource that is 10- to 360-fold richer in energy content per flower than that available from most day-blooming, bee-pollinated flowers (see Heinrich 1983).

The chemical composition and viscosity of nectars produced by hawkmoth-pollinated plants presumably represent a balance between the moths' high energetic demands and the biomechanical limitations of fluid extraction through a tubular proboscis (Watt et al. 1974; Kingsolver and Daniel 1979; Pyke and Waser 1981; Heyneman 1983). For example, in preference experiments, day-flying *Macroglossum stellatarum* L. hawkmoths choose to visit artificial flowers offering 20–50% (w/w) sucrose solutions over those with 10% and 60% solutions (Josens and Farina 1997). The degree to which the moths' choices were based on sugar concentration versus viscosity remains an open question.

Hawkmoth-pollinated flowers secrete nectar within deep corolla tubes or spurs, whose length frequently approaches or exceeds that of an extended hawkmoth proboscis (Gregory 1964; Miller 1981; Grant 1983; Nilsson et al. 1985). Nilsson's (1988) elegant manipulative experiments suggest that this geometric relationship is a result of directional selection, in which longer tubes or spurs enhance plant reproductive fitness through pollen removal (male function) and receipt (female function) via contact with the moth's body (Darwin 1865; plate 3.1). In some cases, hawkmoth-mediated runaway directional selection has resulted in nectar spurs exceeding 20 cm in length (Nilsson et al. 1987; Haber and Franckie 1989; Wasserthal 1997).

Hawkmoth-pollinated plants typically advertise the presence of nectar through both olfactory and visual displays. Their tubular or trumpet-shaped flowers often open at dusk and produce powerful, usually pleasant aromas, which are thought to attract hawkmoths from distances ranging from tens to hundreds of meters (Kerner von Marilaum 1895; Tinbergen 1958; Haber 1984). Although oxygenated terpenoids, aromatic esters, and nitrogenous volatiles are frequently present, chemical composition, blend complexity, and relative emission rates of floral scent have been found to vary greatly among hawkmoth-pollinated plants in Ecuador (Knudsen and Tollsten 1993), Japan (Miyake et al. 1998), and Arizona (R. Raguso, unpub.). This lack of tight chemical convergence reflects the diverse biosynthetic pathways available for volatile production in plants (Croteau and Karp 1991; Knudsen et al. 1993; Raguso 2001) and suggests that hawkmoths may respond to a broad spectrum of floral volatiles or learn to associate species specificity in fragrance chemistry with differences in nectar quality or quantity during foraging (see Roy and Raguso 1997).

In contrast to their fragrance, the coloration of hawkmoth-pollinated flowers worldwide and in Arizona is highly convergent: pale or white and strongly reflective at twilight, with deeply dissected or grooved petals, suggesting visual and mechanosensory guidance to the nectaries (Knoll 1925; Baker 1961; Kugler 1971; Brantjes and Bos 1980; White et al. 1994; plate 3.2A). Most flowers in our survey were bright white, reflecting light in all human-visible wavelengths but lacking UV reflectance, which is known to suppress feeding responses in *Manduca sexta* hawkmoths (White et al. 1994; Cutler et al. 1995). The combination of large, reflective individual flowers, densely clustered inflorescensces, and patchy populations can produce extraordinary visual displays, probably visible to foraging moths over tens of meters (plate 3.2B), but also visible to florivores and nectar thieves. Similar visual displays, along with the tubular floral morphology, sucrose-rich

Robert A. Raguso and Mark A. Willis

nectar, and strong fragrances described above, typify hawkmoth-pollinated plants worldwide, have evolved repeatedly in most angiosperm families, and strike the observer as exaggerated or "supernormal" cues (*sensu* Baerends 1950).

Given the opportunistic foraging patterns of most hawkmoths (Kislev et al. 1972; Haber 1984; Wasserthal 1993) and the well-documented temporal fluctuations in their abundance (Miller 1978, 1981; Willmott and Búrquez 1996), many hawkmoth-pollinated plants employ alternative reproductive strategies, such as self-compatibility (Motten and Antonovics 1992), recruitment of secondary pollinators (Barthell and Knops 1997), or a long-lived perennial growth form (Suzán et al. 1994). Moreover, Haber and Frankie (1989) have suggested that obligately hawkmoth-pollinated plants may need to overproduce floral rewards and advertisements in order to compete with more predictable or abundant floral resources. Such elevated investment in pollinator attraction bears a heavy cost in photosynthetic currency (Vogel 1963, 1983) and in increased apparency to natural enemies (Baldwin et al. 1997), underscoring the importance of hawkmoth visitation to the plants' reproductive fitness.

HAWKMOTH ATTRACTION AND FEEDING: HYPOTHESES AND PREDICTIONS

What are the relative contributions of olfactory and visual information to the foraging decisions made by nocturnal hawkmoths? Several lines of evidence suggest that hawkmoths can use olfaction or vision to find flowers. Hawkmoths have keen vision in dim light, many times more sensitive than that of humans (Schlecht 1979; Bennett and White 1989), and they often probe at bright nonfloral objects while foraging at flowers (Clements and Long 1923; Kugler 1971). In addition, both wild and laboratory-reared hawkmoths show acute olfactory sensitivity to individual floral volatiles and complex blends in electroantennogram (EAG) assays (Brantjes 1973; Raguso et al. 1996; Raguso and Light 1998), and they track floral odors to their sources in the absence of visual targets (Kerner von Marilaum 1895; Tinbergen 1958; Brantjes 1973, 1978). Many species of hawkmoths have been trapped with floral odor lures (Morgan and Lyon 1928; Hodges 1971) and fermenting fruit (Knoll 1925; Newman 1965; Brou and Brou 1997), implying olfactory attraction.

Thus, hawkmoths respond physiologically and behaviorally to the visual and olfactory characteristics of the night-blooming flowers that specialize on them as pollinators. To what extent do inputs from these two sensory modalities interact? How does the scale at which visual or olfactory cues attract hawkmoths affect pollen movement within and between plant populations?

Are hawkmoths' responses to floral cues modulated by their physiological state or prior experience?

Based on published studies of other flower-feeding Lepidoptera, we established six working hypotheses to consider the potential roles played by floral scent and visual display in hawkmoth attraction and feeding:

H_0: *Null.* Floral scent has no attractive function; hawkmoth attraction and feeding are accomplished purely through visual stimuli. Rather, floral scent compounds might function as antimicrobial agents in nectar (Lawton et al. 1993), or could represent pleiotropic by-products of null mutations within pigment biosynthetic pathways (e.g., the aromatic precursors of anthocyanin pigments resulting in white flowers; see Dooner et al. 1991).

H_1: *Scent releases visually guided feeding.* The presence of floral scent elicits visual searching or feeding behavior. This hypothesis implies synergistic interactions between visual and olfactory inputs within visual range (Ilse 1928; Baerends 1950; Tinbergen 1958; Brantjes 1973, 1978).

H_2: *Visual attraction to flower, with scent-elicited landing or probing.* After visual guidance to a flower, scent triggers proboscis extension, landing, and feeding, as observed in some nymphalid butterflies (Pellmyr 1986) and noctuid moths (Brantjes 1978; Nilsson 1978).

H_3: *Scent as the complete attractant/feeding cue.* Scent guides hawkmoths from a distance, orients them at close range, and modulates landing and feeding in the absence of visual cues, as observed for some geometrid and noctuid moths (Nilsson et al. 1990).

H_4: *Olfactory distance attraction, with visually guided feeding (at least in part).* Hawkmoths enter an odor plume and fly upwind toward the odor source from a distance, but may transition to visual guidance at close range (Kerner von Marilaum 1895; Morgan and Lyon 1928; Haber 1984).

H_5: *Scent as a positive or negative associative learning cue.* Scent may not be required for initial floral visits, but hawkmoths learn to associate nectar quality at different flowers with scent chemistry, perhaps in combination with visual cues. This possibility was suggested by the learned avoidance of deceptive nectarless flowers by hawkmoths (Haber 1984) and confirmed by recent experiments in which *Manduca sexta* were trained to floral odors as Pavlovian conditioned stimuli (Daly and Smith 2000).

Not all of these hypotheses are mutually exclusive, and floral cues could have different functions depending on distance from the flower or on the physiological state or experience of an individual moth (see reviews by Williams 1983; Dobson 1994). Note that each of these hypotheses has some precedent among groups of flower-visiting Lepidoptera (table 3.1).

Our laboratory and field experiments directly test the hypotheses (H_0–H_3) that are relevant to close-range (0–10 m) hawkmoth attraction and

Robert A. Raguso and Mark A. Willis

Table 3.1 Functions of floral scent for diverse nectar-feeding Lepidoptera

Function	Taxa Studied	Family	Reference
A. Butterflies			
Distance attraction and landing	Ithomiines (8 genera) *Lycorea cleobaea* *Danaus plexippus*	Nymphalidae	Pliske et al. 1976 DeVries and Stiles 1990 Wagner 1973
Landing/probing	*Danaus gilippus* *Argynnis paphia* *Argyronome ruslana*	Nymphalidae	Myers and Walter 1970 Pellmyr 1986
	Pieris napi *Pieris rapae*	Pieridae	Goulson and Cory 1993 Honda et al. 1998
No function?	*Battus philenor* *Papilio demoleus*	Papilionidae	Weiss 1997 Ilse and Vaidya 1956
Releasing cue	*Aglais urticae* *Nymphalis polychloros* *Hipparchia semele* *Pararge aegeria*	Nymphalidae	Ilse 1928 Tinbergen et al. 1942 Scherer and Kolb 1987b
B. Moths			
Distance attraction and landing	*Cisseps fulvicollis* *Prochocrodes transversata* *Evergestis pallidata* Plusiines and Heliothines *Trichoplusia ni* *Autographa gamma* *Cucullia umbratica* *Hadena bicruris*	Ctenuchidae Geometridae Pyralidae Noctuidae	Cantelo and Jacobsen 1978 Haynes et al. 1991 Brantjes 1978
Landing/probing	Hadenine, cuculliine, and plusiine noctuids *Zygaena trifolii*	Noctuidae Zygaenidae	Nilsson 1978 Naumann et al. 1991
Complete attractant	*Gigantoceras perineti* *Melimoessa catenata*	Noctuidae Geometridae	Nilsson et al. 1990
Associative learning	*Spodoptera littoralis*	Noctuidae	Fan et al. 1997
No function?	*Macroglossa stelletarum*	Sphingidae	Kelber and Pfaff 1997

feeding. Three critical predictions allow us to distinguish among these hypotheses (see Alcock 1993a): (1) scent is required to initiate a feeding bout, (2) visual cues are required for feeding, and (3) scent is required for feeding at each flower (table 3.2). If hawkmoths do not feed at scentless flowers, then H_0 and H_1 would be rejected, and the two remaining alternative hypotheses could be evaluated after testing whether visual cues are necessary. In addition, we assessed the ability of naive hawkmoths to orient to floral fragrance in flight by challenging them to track floral scent plumes in a laboratory wind tunnel. While this experiment simulated potential hawkmoth responses to floral scent on a scale of meters to tens of meters, we did not directly test long-distance attraction (H_4) in the field. Potential roles for scent-based associative learning in the context of foraging behavior (H_5)

Table 3.2 Hypothesis tree for hawkmoth attraction to flowers

		Alternative Hypotheses for the Function of Scent in Hawkmoth Attraction and Feeding			Experimental Results	
Critical Predictions	H_0 No Role	H_1 Releasing Cue	H_2 Land or Probe	H_3 Complete Attractant	Greenhouse Bioassays	Field Tests
Scent is required to initiate feeding	−	+	+	+	+	+
Visual cues are required for feeding	+	+	+	−	+	+
Scent is required to feed at each flower	−	−	+	+	−	−

have not yet been addressed directly with hawkmoths, although classical conditioning of *Manduca sexta* and noctuid moths to floral scent has been demonstrated recently in laboratory settings (Hartlieb 1996; Fan et al. 1997; Daly and Smith 2000).

INNATE RESPONSES OF NAIVE HAWKMOTHS TO FLORAL CUES

UPWIND ORIENTATION TO FLORAL SCENT PLUMES

Laminar flow flight tunnels are the arena of choice for demonstrating olfactory attraction and investigating odor-modulated insect behavior (Baker and Linn 1984). Odor-guided upwind flight orientation has been demonstrated previously for *M. sexta* males and females (Willis and Arbas 1991). In these experiments, the odor-modulated flight of male moths to female sex pheromone and of female moths to fresh leaves of *Nicotiana tabacum* L. (Solanaceae), a larval host plant, were found to be broadly similar. In both cases, the moths generated a temporally regular zigzagging flight pattern as they flew upwind to the appropriate odor source. Upon reaching the source, male moths initiated copulatory behavior and females attempted oviposition. Given that both sexes of *M. sexta* use similar strategies to locate distant unseen odor sources in flight, we predicted that they would use the same strategies to locate sources of floral volatiles when tested in our laboratory's flight tunnel.

The results of our flight tunnel experiments are summarized in table 3.3. As predicted, naive, unfed, and unmated male *M. sexta* hawkmoths were attracted to floral targets in the flight tunnel, executing zigzag upwind flight

Robert A. Raguso and Mark A. Willis

Table 3.3 Naive *Manduca sexta* responses to floral scent in wind tunnel assays

Trial, Sex	Fraction of Hawkmoths Responding to:		
	Single Compound	Complete Floral Blend	Control Odors
1. Male	0/9[a]	2/10[b]	3/4[c]
2. Male	—	5/13[d]	—
3. Male	0/4[a]	2/11[d]	7/7[c]
4. Male	0/6[e]	3/10[d]	—
Female	—	2/8[d]	6/8[f]
5. Male	—	2/14[g]	—
Female	—	1/8[g]	—
6. Male	—	2/8[h,i]	0/8[j]

[a] Linalool (most abundant component of floral scent in c, d, e below)
[b] *Peniocereus greggii* (Cactaceae)
[c] One female-equivalent *M. sexta* sex pheromone extract
[d] *Telosiphonia nacapulensis* (Apocynaceae)
[e] Nerolidol (second most abundant component of floral scent in d below)
[f] Leaves of tomato, *Lycopersicon esculentum* (Solanaceae), oviposition host plant for *M. sexta*
[g] *Oenothera caespitosa* (Onagraceae)
[h] *Calylophus toumeyi* (Onagraceae): scent introduced into wind tunnel via Teflon tube
[i] 2/8 moths flew upwind to odor source, but did not extend proboscis
[j] Filtered air, introduced into wind tunnel via Teflon tube

tracks similar to those observed in males tracking pheromone plumes and females tracking plumes of host plant odors (fig. 3.1B, D). Our observations revealed several important features of the moths' innate responses to floral odors. First, no naive *M. sexta* were attracted to odor plumes of single compounds. None of the test moths showed any responses to linalool or nerolidol, two of the most abundant and widespread fragrance compounds found in hawkmoth-pollinated flowers (Kaiser 1993; Knudsen and Tollsten 1993; Miyake et al. 1998; Levin et al. 2001). Second, when offered living, open flowers, approximately 30% of naive test moths tracked the odor plume along the 3 m length of the flight tunnel, showing the slow, zigzag path characteristic of odor-guided flight, then actively fed at the flowers (fig. 3.1C, E). Moths that did not respond to the odor stimulus flew around the flight tunnel showing no preferred orientation (fig. 3.1A). Finally, when fragrance from living flowers was trapped and introduced as a plume into the flight tunnel, again approximately 30% of the naive moths tracked the plume to its source. In this case, however, the moths never extended their proboscides or attempted to feed. Thus, naive *M. sexta* can track plumes of floral scent to their source, but once there, feeding behavior is not elicited in the absence of a visual cue. These results are supported by the behavior of moths in the trials with living flowers, which displayed a typical odor-modulated flight track until they approached the flower, then extended their proboscides and flew a more direct line to the flower to feed (fig. 3.1C, E). This adjustment during approach to the flower suggests a switch from odor-guided to visually guided flight.

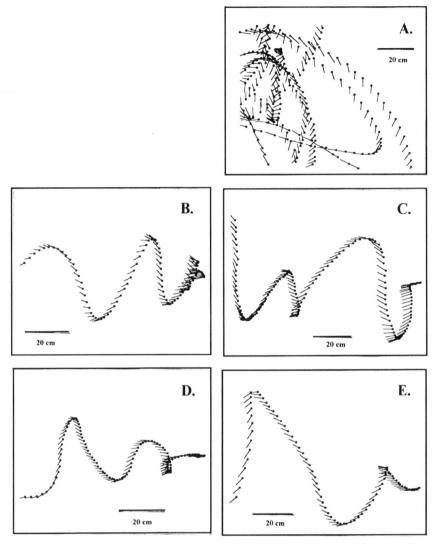

Figure 3.1 Flight tracks of *Manduca sexta* recorded in flight tunnel experiments. Direction of wind flow is R to L, velocity = 60 cm/s. (A) Nondirected flight of male moth that did not respond to odor stimulus. (B) Male moth flying upwind to female sex pheromone. (C) Same individual flying upwind to *Peniocereus greggii* (night-blooming cactus) flower. (D) Female moth flying upwind to tomato leaves. (E) Same individual flying upwind to *Telosiphonia nacapulensis* (rock trumpet) flower. Note linear approach flights to the target in C, D, E. Scale bars = 20 cm.

Although investigations of the chemical ecology of moth attraction to flowers have been ongoing for some time (e.g., Grant 1971), only recently has the technology to fully characterize floral scent chemistry become generally available (Dobson 1994; Raguso and Pellmyr 1998). In experiments investigating the interaction between the noctuid moth *Trichoplusia ni* (Hübner) and flowers of *Abelia grandiflora* (André) (Caprifoliaceae), no significant differences were found between the number of naive moths that flew upwind to a synthetic blend matching the floral scent and the number that flew

Robert A. Raguso and Mark A. Willis

to phenylacetaldehyde, the single most abundant compound in the blend (Haynes et al. 1991). Heath et al. (1992) observed the same pattern in *T. ni* moths' responses to the nearly identical floral scent of *Cestrum nocturnum* L. (Solanaceae). Our results suggest that *M. sexta*'s behavior does not fit this model, as naive moths of this species appear to require a complex blend of compounds to elicit upwind orientation to a flower. An earlier report of *M. sexta* being attracted to single compounds was based on field trapping of wild hawkmoths with amyl salicylate, a compound found in many night-blooming flowers (Morgan and Lyon 1928). In this case it must be assumed that the trapped moths were not naive and had already experienced this compound in the context of a blend emitted by flowers they had visited. It is possible that once a moth has formed an association between a nectar reward and a complex floral scent blend, it is able to "generalize" that association and respond to a simpler scent (i.e., to one or a few of the compounds in the blend). Generalization in olfactory learning has been clearly demonstrated in honeybees (Smith 1993; Smith and Getz 1994; Menzel and Müller 1996), and also appears to occur in *M. sexta* (Daly et al. 2001). Alternatively, the odor lure may have been *perceived* as a complex blend, as the traps were located along the borders of large tobacco fields, which produced formidable vegetative and floral emissions detectable by the moths.

Our flight tunnel work clearly demonstrates that naive *M. sexta* moths can track floral scent plumes to their source from at least 3 meters away, supporting the idea that wild moths may use strong fragrances to locate floral resources at greater distances in nature (Haber 1984). The responses of naive *M. sexta* to diverse floral scent blends from three different plant families are comparable, suggesting a flexible, chemically unspecialized response to floral volatiles. Additionally, these data suggest that once moths reach the odor source, proboscis extension does not occur in the absence of a visual target.

CLOSE-RANGE ORIENTATION AND FEEDING WITHIN PATCHES OF FLOWERS

We observed the behavioral responses of naive *M. sexta* moths to arrays of artificial flowers with and without floral scent in small greenhouse arenas (Raguso and Willis 2002). In these experiments, the artificial flowers were modeled after those of *Oenothera* sp., using paper that matched the reflectance spectrum of the real flowers and artificial nectaries filled with 25% sucrose. Floral scent was provided by living *Oenothera neomexicana* (Small) Munz plants concealed within a cheesecloth cage below the artificial flower array. A similar array with an empty cheesecloth cage served as a control.

Three important aspects of naive hawkmoths' foraging behavior were revealed in this study. First, artificial flowers that were arranged in a clump or bouquet were far less attractive than 3 × 3 arrays of evenly spaced individual

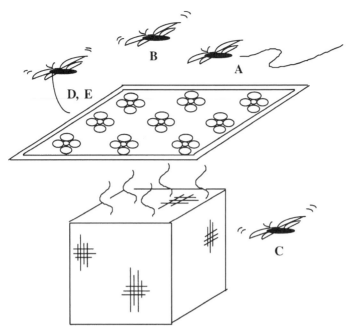

Figure 3.2 Schematic of *Manduca sexta* behavioral responses to visual and olfactory stimuli in greenhouse experiments. Lateral spacing between paper flowers is 25 cm; diagonal spacing is 33 cm. Curling traces above the cheesecloth-covered box denote odor. In the scented greenhouse, blooming *Oenothera neomexicana* plants were hidden within the box beneath the floral array; the box was empty in the control greenhouse. Paper flowers contained 1 mL of 25% sucrose solution in plastic nectary. Hawkmoth behaviors were as follows: A, close pass: a rapid directed flight 1 m or less over the array; B, hover: stationary flight 1 m or less above the array; C, approach to cheesecloth-covered box beneath array (source of odor in scented greenhouse); D, approach to paper flowers (within 10 cm, proboscis not extended); E, feeding behavior, with proboscis extended.

flowers. Second, naive moths were attracted to artificial flowers without floral scent present, but did not approach or feed from them. Third, the introduction of floral scent to an array of artificial flowers elicited feeding behavior from naive moths (see fig. 3.2 and plate 3.3), as well as approaches to the hidden odor source (without probing). All measured parameters of the moths' behavioral responses (i.e., duration of visit, number of hovering events, etc.) increased significantly when floral odors were presented with the artificial flowers (Raguso and Willis 2002).

When we repeated the experiments using a modified floral array of five paper flowers and four natural *Oenothera* flowers, the total number of feeding events increased from 10 to 61, and the proportion of experimental animals that fed increased from 16 to 52%. Other behavioral states were less dramatically affected. Interestingly, no consistent preference (positive or negative assortative visitation) for natural or paper flowers was observed: hawkmoth flower visits simply reflected the relative abundance of each flower type in the array. Similarly, the moths showed no visitation constancy, as the number of transitions within and between natural and paper flowers was essentially

Robert A. Raguso and Mark A. Willis

random (Raguso and Willis 2002). Thus, despite measurable differences in odor, nectar volume, relative brightness, and texture between the natural and paper flowers, the hawkmoths did not distinguish between them. In light of this result, it is more likely that increased feeding from the mixed arrays was a response not to the presence of scented individual flowers, but to the enhanced odor plume emanating from the entire array. In sum, either visual cues or floral scent alone were sufficient to attract the attention of naive *M. sexta* moths, but both cues were necessary to elicit feeding.

FORAGING DECISIONS OF EXPERIENCED WILD HAWKMOTHS

How do wild, presumably experienced moths respond to visual and olfactory floral stimuli? We performed three experiments on the grounds of the Arizona-Sonora Desert Museum, in thornscrub habitat within the Tucson Mountains, Pima County, AZ. We observed a guild of nocturnal hawkmoths (*Agrius cingulatus* [Fabricius], *Manduca quinquemaculata* [Haworth], *M. rustica* [Fabricius], and *M. sexta*) feeding at the flowers of a native night-blooming plant, *Datura wrightii* Regel (Solanaceae). We physically decoupled floral scent and visual display by covering *Datura* flowers with clear acetate bags (visual display, no odor, no nectar) or cheesecloth bags dyed green-brown (odor, no visual display, no nectar) and creating paper model flowers (visual display, nectar, no odor). We designed a series of experiments, in each case observing hawkmoth approaches and visits to evenly spaced flowers modified with respect to olfactory or visual traits (fig. 3.3A).

In the first experiment (fig. 3.3A), hawkmoths approached all floral treatments in two mixed plots, but significantly more visits occurred at open control and paper flowers, where nectar was available, than at either class of bagged flowers. Interestingly, a few hawkmoths poked at the plastic-bagged flowers with extended proboscides, but essentially ignored the cloth-bagged flowers. However, due to the large plume of floral and vegetative volatiles emanating from the plants, no treatment in this experiment was truly scentless.

In the second experiment (fig. 3.3B), hawkmoths were attracted to each of three treatments in homogeneous plots, but attempted to feed only when visible flowers were present. Although the moths approached the cloth-bagged flowers, none extended their proboscides to probe or feed. The combination of paper flowers and floral scent attracted more visits than did paper flowers alone, but surprisingly, the differences were not statistically significant (R. Raguso and M. Willis, unpub.). One interpretation of these results is that the strong *vegetative* odor of *Datura* foliage, when present with visual stimuli, was sufficient to elicit hawkmoth attraction and feeding in the

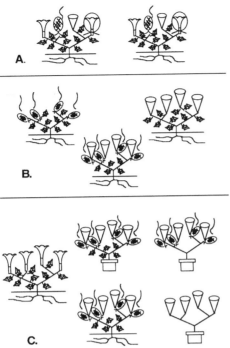

Figure 3.3 Manipulation of *Datura wrightii* plants for field experiments at Arizona-Sonora Desert Museum. (A) Experiment 1, with two mixed-treatment plants, 10 m apart, each with six evenly spaced flowers per treatment. Treatments (L to R in each plant) are open control flowers, cloth-bagged flowers, paper model flowers containing 50 μL of 25% sucrose solution, and plastic-bagged flowers. Curling traces above cloth bags denote floral scent. Note that all treatments were associated with floral and vegetative odors from each plant. (B) Experiment 2, with three homogeneous-treatment plants, 10 m apart, each with eight evenly spaced flowers. Treatments (clockwise from top left) are cloth-bagged flowers, paper model flowers, and a combination thereof. (C) Experiment 3, with five homogeneous-treatment plants, 15 m apart, each with twelve evenly spaced flowers. Treatments (clockwise from far left) are open control flowers (rooted, fixed position); cloth-bagged flowers, paper models, and vegetation (mobile); cloth-bagged flowers and paper models (mobile); paper models (mobile); and cloth-bagged flowers, paper models, and vegetation (rooted).

absence of *floral* scent. An alternative explanation is that wild hawkmoths learn landmarks, return to the same location, and orient to visual cues alone. Another alternative is that the moths may have made an association between floral shape and display and *Datura wrightii*'s impressive nectar rewards. A truly hungry, experienced hawkmoth might relax its normal requirements for the presence of both visual and odor cues in order to feed.

To distinguish between these possibilities, we performed a third experiment controlling for the presence of vegetative odors and proximity to landmarks, using two large *Datura* plants growing 15 m apart in soil and three potted plant treatments rotated between different positions nearby (fig. 3.3C). Since hawkmoths fed from open control *Datura* flowers during all observational periods, the small number of approaches and the absence of feeding at the scentless treatment throughout the experiment indicated that visual cues alone were insufficient to promote hawkmoth attraction

Robert A. Raguso and Mark A. Willis

and feeding. Thus, the functional distance of a *Datura* odor plume as a cue eliciting visually guided approach and feeding behavior must have been less than 15 m in this experiment. The remaining treatments did not differ significantly in their attractiveness to hawkmoths, suggesting that (1) relative position did not affect attraction, and (2) the presence of vegetation neither enhanced nor diminished the attractiveness of floral scent in combination with visual cues.

The results of our field experiments clearly suggest that either bright visual displays or plant odors, whether vegetative or floral, can attract foraging nocturnal hawkmoths, but a combination thereof is required to elicit naturally observed levels of feeding. These results do not differ substantially from those observed for naive *M. sexta* moths in the greenhouse experiments. In the presence of plant odors, hawkmoths attempted to feed from any bright object, while in the absence of floral scent, strong vegetative volatiles appeared to function as a reasonable surrogate cue. Given our results, it appears unlikely that the wild nocturnal hawkmoths in our study are able to find flowers and feed without some plant odor.

SYNTHESIS AND DISCUSSION OF FUTURE DIRECTIONS

A COMBINATION OF FLORAL CUES IS NECESSARY TO ELICIT HAWKMOTH FEEDING

Visual and olfactory stimuli clearly interact at close range (0–10 m) to mediate the nectar-feeding behavior of both naive and wild hawkmoths in Arizona's Sonoran Desert. In flight tunnel assays, greenhouse experiments, and field tests, a combination of visual cues and plant odors was necessary for *M. sexta* and related hawkmoths to extend the proboscis and feed from flowers. These findings allow us to reject the null hypothesis (H_0) that scent has no behavioral function in hawkmoth attraction and feeding and an alternative hypothesis (H_3) that scent functions as the complete floral attractant/feeding stimulant (see table 3.2). Furthermore, while scent cues were required for feeding, scent was not required on an individual flower level, as both naive and experienced hawkmoths foraged avidly from both natural (scented) and paper (unscented) flowers in the presence of a larger cloud of plant volatiles. Thus, scent does not function strictly as a landing or feeding cue (H_2). The model (H_1) propounded by Baerends (1950) and Brantjes (1978), in which scent releases visually guided foraging, is the most likely explanation for how nocturnal hawkmoths respond to floral scent and visual cues within 10 m of their source. For *M. sexta* and other nocturnal hawkmoths, the presence of a "scent cloud" above a patch of flowering plants, as described by Baker (1961), Cruden (1970), Nilsson (1978), and Eisikowitch and Rotem (1987), provides the contextual cue that elicits visually guided close-range orientation, proboscis extension, and feeding.

However, scent may play additional roles in hawkmoth-flower interactions. First, there appears to be an incremental effect of scent concentration, as the inclusion of natural scented flowers within our greenhouse arrays increased the frequency of *M. sexta* feeding above that observed when scent was emanating from beneath paper model flowers. Additional work will be needed in order to identify the minimum threshold of odor concentration required to initiate upwind orientation flight as well as the functional subset of scent components and their potential synergism with other plant cues (e.g., plumes of carbon dioxide or water vapor). Second, our flight tunnel data indicate that scent can induce upwind flight in the absence of visual cues and suggest that strong fragrances could attract moths from distances greater than 3 m (H_4). Field trapping and release-recapture studies will be needed to quantify the distances from which hawkmoths can be attracted by fragrance alone.

Our experimental findings, if broadly applicable to other nocturnal hawkmoths, suggest the following predictions for hawkmoth-pollinated plants:

1. Floral scent attracts hawkmoths at a patch or population level and should not affect fine-scale movement of hawkmoths between individual flowers or neighboring plants. In fact, odor need not emanate from floral tissues, as we found to be the case in *Calylophus hartweggii* (Onagraceae), *Ipomopsis longifolia* (Polemoniaceae) (R. Raguso, unpub.), and our experiments with *Datura wrightii* foliage.

2. If fragrance production has fitness-related costs, there should be balancing selection for optimum emission levels, frequency-dependent selection for scentless mutants within a population, or scentless "parasitic" species that co-bloom with and exploit fragrant plants.

3. The attraction of hawkmoths to bright, reflective flowers with fragrance can be exploited by Batesian mimics whose flowers lack nectar, such as *Plumeria rubra* (Apocynaceae: Haber 1984), or by fraudulent female flowers in dioecious, automimetic plants, such as *Carica papaya* (Caricaceae: Knudsen and Tollsten 1993).

THE EFFECT OF LARVAL DIET AND ADULT PHYSIOLOGICAL STATE ON NECTAR FEEDING

The hawkmoths used in our laboratory and field experiments differed in at least two important details: adult feeding experience and larval diet. Disparity in larval diet may explain what appeared to be gross differences in the

Robert A. Raguso and Mark A. Willis

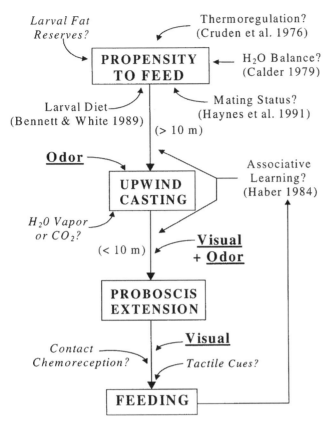

Figure 3.4 Summary flow diagram of nectar-feeding behavior in *Manduca sexta* and similar hawkmoths. The central axis consists of behavioral states (in capitals, boxed) and transitions between them (arrows). Factors affecting specific state changes are denoted with smaller arrows. Factors identified through our study are boldfaced and underlined. Factors demonstrated or suggested in the relevant literature are given in regular print, with appropriate references. Potential factors identified from our own observations are given in italics.

feeding rates of wild versus laboratory-reared hawkmoths. The hawkmoths used in our flight tunnel and greenhouse assays were reared as larvae on an artificial diet, did not wander extensively before pupation, and eclosed as adults with substantial abdominal fat bodies (R. Raguso and M. Willis, unpub.). This large "onboard" energy store may affect the propensity of the moths to feed (fig. 3.4), which could explain the low numbers of moths responding to whole-flower emissions (see table 3.3), even after being starved for 3 days (see Simpson and Raubenheimer 1996). However, similar results have been observed in feeding behavioral assays of other laboratory-reared moths (Fan et al. 1997), and *M. sexta* needed to be starved for a week before being conditioned to odor cues by Daly and Smith (2000). In contrast, the lean, wild hawkmoths studied in our field experiments carried negligible fat bodies (R. Raguso and R. Chapman, unpub.) and often were so eager to feed that they would pry apart unopened *Datura* and *Calylophus* buds with their proboscides and legs (plate 3.4, see Gregory 1964). We are currently studying ways to rear adult hawkmoths with reduced fat bodies in an effort to increase the efficacy of our laboratory assays.

There are other ways that larval diet or adult physiological state could potentially influence a hawkmoth's propensity to feed, including (1) the effects of ambient temperature and thermoregulatory requirements (Cruden et al. 1976; Heinrich 1983; Martinez del Río and Búrquez 1986), (2) the effect of exposure to plant compounds in the larval diet on neurosensory development (Bernays and Chapman 1998), (3) the effect of a larval diet deficient in carotene precursors of visual pigments (Bennett and White 1989), (4) adult physiological water balance and its relation to nectar use (Calder 1979; Pyke and Waser 1981), (5) starvation or frequency of adult feeding and exercise (Brantjes 1978), and (6) the effect of mating status and a potential refractory period toward feeding (see Haynes et al. 1991). Few of these avenues have been explored in the context of any nectar-feeding insect's response to floral attractants. It will be important to address the contributions of these factors directly in our continuing investigations of hawkmoth flower-feeding behavior.

OBSERVATIONS OF DIVERSE HAWKMOTHS AND HABITATS

Our experiments are the first to examine hawkmoth responses to both visual and olfactory floral attractants using balanced experimental designs and controlling for previous foraging experience. However, our results are consistent with anecdotal observations and circumstantial evidence from other studies using naive *M. sexta* moths in laboratory feeding experiments (table 3.4). Earlier experiments on the feeding response of *M. sexta* to artificial flowers or other visual stimuli (Bell and Joaquim 1976; White et al. 1994; Cutler et al. 1995) were confounded by the presence of a live tobacco plant in the same room, included to encourage female oviposition for unrelated purposes. Again, tobacco vegetative volatiles probably were sufficient to provide the necessary contextual odor cues eliciting feeding behavior in these moths. Brantjes (1973, 1978) performed flight cage bioassays in which naive *M. sexta* responded to the introduction of floral odor into a small flight chamber by wing shivering, initiating flight, and active searching behaviors. Interestingly, Brantjes (1973) observed proboscis extension and probing by *Deilephila elpenor* L. hawkmoths at flowers hidden within a perforated box in the flight cage, a behavior not observed by himself or us in similar experiments with *M. sexta*. However, the unexplored potential for visual contrast in Brantjes' experiments, combined with the unknown physiological status of his experimental animals (e.g., starved vs. fed, wild-collected vs. laboratory-reared) precludes further interpretation.

Table 3.4 Comparison with other published studies of hawkmoth feeding behavior

Critical Predictions	Releasing Cue Model	Naive Hawkmoths (Lab)			Experienced Hawkmoths (Field)			
		Knoll 1925 H. lineata livornica	Brantjes 1973, 1978 M. sexta, D. elpenor	White et al. 1994 M. sexta	Clements and Long 1923 M. quinquemaculata	Baker 1961 H. lineata	Kugler 1971 A. convolvuli	Haber 1984 Many Spp.
Scent is required to initiate feeding	+	+/?[a]	+	+/?	?[b]	+/?	?	+/?
Visual cues are required for feeding	+	+	+/−[c]	+	+	+	+	+
Scent is required to feed at each flower	−	−	−	−	−	−	−	−

[a] +/? = circumstantial evidence
[b] ? = not directly tested
[c] + for M. sexta, − for D. elpenor

Although comparable data are limited, our observations of hawkmoth feeding behavior in the field appear to be applicable to other nocturnal nectar-feeding hawkmoth species in temperate and tropical habitats worldwide (see table 3.4). Many species of wild hawkmoths collected at light traps will feed from artificial paper or plastic flowers in outdoor flight cages when natural fragrant flowers are present (Haber 1984, in Costa Rica) or when scented corollas are attached to plastic model flowers (Wasserthal 1993, 1997, in Madagascar). Our observation that visual cues govern approaches to individual flowers at close range is in agreement with published reports of various hawkmoth species flying directly between flowers once they arrive at a patch (*Hyles lineata* [Fabricius] in California: Baker 1961; *Eumorpha achemon* [Drury] and *Sphinx chersis* [Hübner] in Utah: Cruden 1970) or probing at white or highly reflective objects while feeding from flowers in natural settings (*Manduca quinquemaculata* in Colorado: Clements and Long 1923; *Agrius convolvuli* [L.] in Yugoslavia: Kugler 1971). It also is consistent with Knoll's (1925) laboratory experiments with naive *Hyles lineata livornica* (Esp.), in which the moths repeatedly probed at scentless natural and paper flowers pressed between sheets of glass while in the presence of the scented flowers and foliage of *Lonicera implexa* Aiton (Caprifoliaceae), *Nicotiana affinis* (= *alata*) Moore (Solanaceae), and *Salvia officinalis* L. (Labiatae). Knoll correctly concluded that *H. l. livornica* was guided to flowers by visual signals at close range, but did not consider that the plant odors permeating the air of his experimental chamber were eliciting visually guided feeding in his assays, as was suggested later by Ilse (1928), Tinbergen et al. (1942), and Baerends (1950).

Diverse adult feeding strategies abound within the Sphingidae, which range from large guilds of nocturnal nectar-feeding hawkmoths (Nilsson et al. 1985; Haber and Frankie 1989) to diurnal species that ignore odor during foraging (e.g., *Macroglossum stellatarum*: Kelber 1996; Kelber and Pfaff 1997; Josens and Farina 1997), specialists that feed on unusual foods (*Acherontia atropos* L. on beehive honey: Knoll 1925; Newman 1965), and species whose adults do not feed at all (e.g., *Pachysphinx modesta* Harris: Hodges 1971). Given the diverse functions of scent documented for flower-feeding nymphalid butterflies and noctuid moths (see table 3.1), it is reasonable to expect some sphingid species to respond differently to olfactory and visual stimuli in the context of feeding. Electroantennogram studies suggest that butterflies and moths can detect most floral volatiles, such that sensory discrimination is more likely to result from central nervous system processing than peripheral olfactory screening (Topazzini et al. 1990; Naumann et al. 1991; Gabel et al. 1992; van Loon et al. 1992; Raguso et al. 1996; Raguso and Light 1998; Omura et al. 1999a, 1999b). Field studies in Central America (Haber 1984; Haber and Frankie 1989), Israel (Eisikowitz and Galil 1971; Kislev et al. 1972), Africa and Madagascar (Harris and Baker 1958; Nilsson et al. 1985, 1987; Baum 1995; Wasserthal 1997), and Japan (Miyake et al. 1998) suggest that there is little evidence for extreme specialization in flower choice among nectar-feeding hawkmoths worldwide. The combination of multivoltinism and high vagility in many hawkmoth species underscores the adaptive nature of generalized floral foraging. *Acherontia atropos,* the death's head hawk, has a short, stiff proboscis that is ideal for piercing honeycombs, a major source of adult nutriment, and may limit its extraapiary foraging to flowers with short nectar tubes (e.g., citrus and privet: Newman 1965) or, perhaps, to nectar robbery. The potential to use fragrance alone as the complete attractant/feeding cue is greatest for this species and those that include fermenting fruit and sap in their adult diets, such as *Amphion floridensis* B. P. Clark (D. M. O'Brien 1998) and *Darapsa pholus* Cramer (Hodges 1971).

Finally, the effects of daily foraging periodicity on the feeding strategies of different hawkmoth species have been largely ignored. For example, the diurnally active *Macroglossum stellatarum* uses exclusively visual cues to feed from flowers in well-lit laboratory and field settings, but is also known to forage from fragrant plants in the evening along the Mediterranean coast of Europe (Newman 1965; Herrera 1992). Similarly, *Hyles lineata,* the most abundant and widespread hawkmoth in North America, forages under daylight, crepuscular, or purely nocturnal conditions, depending on altitude, temperature, and perhaps other factors (Holland 1903; Grant 1937; Chase and Raven 1975; Miller 1978, 1981; Willmott and Búrquez 1996). The possibility that these species' behavioral responses to floral stimuli vary with relative light intensity deserves closer scrutiny, and could explain such paradoxical observations as *Hyles*'s apparent preference for white over red *Ipomopsis* flowers in northern Arizona (Paige and Whitham 1985) but for red and pink over white *Ipomopsis* flowers in montane Colorado (Elam and Linhart 1988; Campbell et al. 1997). Assays testing the behavioral responses of *Hyles lineata* to visual and olfactory floral cues, performed under light regimes appropriate to diurnal, crepuscular, and nocturnal foraging, would provide insights into the complex contributions of these moths to floral evolution in western North America.

SUMMARY AND CONCLUSIONS

We have discussed the available evidence from our own and others' investigations of the use of floral fragrance and visual cues by nectar-feeding nocturnal hawkmoths. Naive *Manduca sexta* track floral scent plumes to their sources in laboratory assays, indicating their innate ability to orient to plant odors from a distance. The small proportion of naive individuals performing this behavior under our experimental conditions strongly suggests modulation of feeding responses by nutritional state, available energy reserves, and other adult physiological conditions that beg further study. At close range, both naive and experienced *M. sexta* are attracted to bright visual arrays or hidden odor sources, but require the combination of visual and olfactory signals in order to approach a flower, extend the tubular mouthparts, and feed. We were surprised to observe that wild, experienced *M. sexta* do not visit scentless artificial flowers, given that a wide array of bats (Voigt and Winter 1999), butterflies (Weiss 1997), bees (Real 1981), and diurnal hawkmoths (Farina and Josens 1994) can learn to feed from odorless plastic feeders. However, there is ample variation among flower-feeding insects in their ability to generalize among sensory modalities and signals (see Roy and Raguso 1997). The associative learning capabilities of hawkmoths have only recently begun to be studied (Kelber 1996; Kelber and Henrique 1999; Daly and Smith 2000). Relatively little is known about the factors that constrain lepidopteran learning and memory with respect to floral characteristics (Lewis 1986; Murawski and Gilbert 1986; reviewed by Weiss 2001).

Our observations suggest at least two discrete roles for floral scent in this system: long-distance attractant and close-range contextual cue, synergizing with visual stimuli to elicit nectar feeding. Depending on the density of the visual display, large floral aggregations may also attract moths visually from a distance, and visual cues *within* flowers clearly play important roles in proboscis placement and feeding, as they do for bees, long-tongued flies, and many butterflies (reviewed by Dafni and Kevan 1996). These findings are consistent with what little is known of other nocturnal hawkmoth species worldwide. Rather than considering these patterns static rules for foraging behavior, we see them as a framework of hypotheses from which to explore the limits of plasticity and adaptability in nectar foraging within and among hawkmoths and other flower-feeding lepidopterans.

ACKNOWLEDGMENTS

R. A. R. would like to express his gratitude to Ward Watt, Carol Boggs, and Charles Remington for many formative years of friendship, mentorship, and encouragement, and to the Center for Insect Science, University of Arizona, for providing a most stimulating intellectual environment. Reg Chapman, John Hildebrand, Robb Schneider, and Martina Wicklein made important contributions to experimental design. Maria Clauss and Katja Selchow generously translated and discussed papers by Drs. Ilse, Knoll, and Kugler. We acknowledge A. A. Osman for insect culture and Judith Bronstein, Holly Campbell, Gretchen LeBuhn, Randi Papke, and Thomas Tully for helpful suggestions during pilot experiments. Special thanks to Betsy Arnold, Alexandra Chetochine, Amanda Fox, Laurel Hester, Rachel Levin, Jim Tuttle, and an army of volunteer UA moth watchers, and to Laurel Johnston for preparing the flight tracks. We are grateful to Steve Buchmann for his encouragement and access to the resources of the USDA Carl Hayden Bee Lab, and to the Arizona-Sonora Desert Museum staff, especially Mark Dimmitt and Gary Nabhan, for their support and permission to conduct research on museum grounds. R. A. R was supported by an NIH Training Program in Insect Science grant (T32 AI07475) through the Center for Insect Science, an NSF grant to the Research Training Group in Biological Diversification (BIR-9602246), NSF grant DEB-9806840 to the Department of Ecology and Evolutionary Biology, and by a University of Arizona Foundation small grant. M. A. W. was supported by NSF grant IBN-9511742.

CHAPTER 4

Sexual Selection and the Evolution of Butterfly Mating Systems

Christer Wiklund

In Ron Rutowski's (1984) review on sexual selection and the evolution of butterfly mating behavior, he stated that "sexual selection is the evolutionary process proposed by Darwin (1871) to explain traits whose primary function appears to be that of insuring an individual's success in courtship and mating." He went on to say that sexual selection is the mechanism that Darwin arrived at when he tried to understand a conspicuous class of traits that defied explanation by ordinary natural selection for improved survival. Malte Andersson, in the preface to his book *Sexual Selection* (1994), specifies that the traits in question (quoting from Darwin 1871) are "sexual differences...such as the greater size, strength, and pugnacity of the male, his weapons of offence or means of defence against rivals, his gaudy coloring and various ornaments, his power of song and other such characters." The mere ferocity of most of these traits would seem to leave the butterfly student out in the cold, but then again, Darwin himself would disagree, as he writes, "Although butterflies are such weak and fragile creatures, they are pugnacious, and an Emperor butterfly has been captured with the tips of its wings broken from a conflict with another male." In fact, when Darwin suggested that these traits are favored by sexual selection either because they increase a male's chances of winning contests for females with other males (intrasexual selection) or because they increase a male's chances of successfully seducing a female (intersexual selection), he specifically used butterflies to illustrate both of these processes. Disagreeing with Wallace, who believed that in cases of sexual color dimorphism it was the female sex that had departed from the ancestral gaudy coloration to acquire crypsis through dull coloration, Darwin adamantly argued for the alternative explanation, saying that "it is impossible to admit that the brilliant colors of butterflies...have commonly been acquired for the sake of protection. We have seen that their colors and elegant patterns are arranged and exhibited as for display. Hence, I am led to suppose that the females generally prefer, or are most excited by the more brilliant males."

Ever since Darwin, the importance and relevance of sexual selection have been under debate, and its advocates have sometimes been criticized for adopting a rather too narrow approach. In this review I hope to demonstrate the usefulness of the sexual selection approach, and I also attempt to widen its scope by including life history traits, because in so doing I feel that the patterns that we wish to understand will become clearer. Hence, in this review, I will treat mate location systems, mating patterns, sperm competition, and the trade-offs and life history consequences associated with the different mating systems.

MATE LOCATION

MATE LOCATION AND BUTTERFLY DESIGN

Mate location strategies in butterflies can be divided into two main categories (cf. Scott 1974) relating to the situation in which the sexes meet, which can be described by the terms "perching" and "patrolling." Patrolling males typically spend their whole adult lives on the wing searching for females, resting from their incessant search only to refuel their energy stores, or when weather conditions make continued searching unfeasible. Patrolling males typically discover a female, most often in flight but occasionally alighted on vegetation, and approach her to engage in courtship. Perching males typically sit and wait at some vantage point and fly up to inspect any object remotely similar to a conspecific female that comes within their field of vision.

Because the perching mode of encounter demands greater aerial control and agility, sexual selection theory predicts that males in perching species should exhibit traits associated with high acceleration ability and speed, whereas males in patrolling species should exhibit traits associated with flight endurance. To test this idea, Wickman (1992b) did a comparative study involving forty-four species of temperate butterflies. To control for historical effects due to shared ancestry, twenty-five of the species were assigned to eight contrasts; that is, comparisons were made between species in clades in which a change from patrolling to perching mate location behavior, or vice versa, had occurred. In agreement with the prediction, perching species had larger thorax/body mass ratios, higher wing loadings, and higher aspect ratios (wing span squared divided by wing area) than patrolling species. Hence, mate location behavior has influenced male design. Wickman's analysis also showed that male mate location behavior has affected female design in a similar way. However, this effect could be explained by genetic correlation with males, and when the covariance between the sexes was removed, only male design was explained by mate location behavior.

It is obvious that the high-powered flight behavior of perching species is more energetically demanding than that of patrolling species, and so male design also might influence the spatial aspects of mate location strategies. Under ecological circumstances in which the distribution of receptive females is unpredictable and widely spaced, searching males roam widely in search of mating opportunities. This mating system corresponds to an ecological system in which males cannot economically monopolize females, or resources that females use, and can be characterized as a prolonged searching polygyny (*sensu* Thornhill and Alcock 1983). When the distribution of receptive females is clumped and predictable, males are expected to monopolize females, or resources that females use, and males should be selected more for resource-holding power (*sensu* Parker 1974) than for the ability to roam widely in search of females.

Here there is an interesting connection to butterfly antipredator adaptations. As demonstrated in the early 1990s (Chai and Srygley 1990; Srygley and Chai 1990a, 1990b; Marden and Chai 1991), unpalatable and warningly colored butterflies that have an effective defense against predators typically have a design that is vastly different from that of palatable species. The reason for this difference is that whereas palatable species are dependent on flight speed to evade their potential predators, unprofitable aposematic species are not. Therefore, palatable butterflies typically have shorter and stouter bodies, with more mass allocated to flight muscles, and also have shorter wings and smaller wing areas than unpalatable species. Hence, predation pressure has selected for a body morphology that increases flight speed and maneuverability. In a comparative analysis of eighteen Neotropical heliconiine species, Srygley (1994) demonstrated that this difference in design remains in Batesian mimicry groups; although wing coloration patterns have evolved to be closely similar between model and mimic, the difference in body design remains. Because high flight speed and maneuverability are so energetically demanding, this could mean that there is interdependency between palatability and mate location strategy in butterfly males. Hence, palatable species may be more likely to adopt perching behavior, as this strategy allows them to spend less time in active flight than do patrolling males. Moreover, the patrolling mate location strategy also means that males expose themselves more freely to potential predators— a frivolous kind of behavior that can best be afforded by the unpalatable. Moreover, it might also be that the exquisite maneuverability required of perching species is unattainable by really unpalatable patrolling species— thinking of the slow flapping flight of the European wood white butterfly, *Leptidea sinapis*, it is difficult to envisage a male exhibiting the aerial agility so characteristic of males of perching species. At least among the European pierines, which are considered to belong to a Müllerian mimicry ring, there is an association between unpalatability and patrolling behavior, as might be expected from the reasoning above.

THE ECOLOGY OF MATE LOCATION STRATEGIES

Mate location strategies in butterflies include not only patrolling and perching behaviors, but also hilltopping and lekking. Hilltopping is a system in which males aggregate on hilltops or ridges to wait for or search for receptive females, and has been described for a number of butterflies (Shields 1968; Scott 1970; Thornhill and Alcock 1983; Wickman 1988). Hilltopping is not an alternative to perching and patrolling, but can be seen as a system that reduces the total area where males may engage in patrolling or perching. Lekking is a mating system in which males form aggregations that females visit only to mate. Lekking butterfly males typically perch, and may or may not defend territories, but regardless, the resulting distribution of males is highly clumped.

Although the mode of male mate location behavior can be species-specific, there are many species in which males can shift between perching and patrolling strategies (cf. Scott 1974, 1975; Shreeve 1990, 1992b). This observation raises the question of what factors favor the adoption of perching and patrolling behaviors.

There are several ecological factors that might influence the mate location behavior of butterfly males. One class of explanations relates to demography, with population density being a key factor, such that low population density favors perching and high density favors patrolling (Scott 1974; Willmer 1991). The rationale is that the cost of being territorial increases with the number of intruders and becomes uneconomical above a certain threshold (Alcock 1985). Habitat-related explanations are based on the idea that female distribution, which in turn depends on resource distribution, is decisive for male mate location behavior (Thornhill and Alcock 1983; Dennis and Shreeve 1988). According to this idea, as explained above, a predictable distribution of receptive females is prerequisite to perching behavior. Resources that could make female distribution predictable include host plants, nectar plants, microclimate (warm and sunny spots in cold climates and cooler sites in hot climates), and landmarks (Shreeve 1990, 1992b; Rutowski 1991). The distribution of larval host plants, for example, might function as a good predictor of eclosion sites of virgin females, and in species in which females are receptive immediately upon eclosion, males would benefit from choosing a perching site in immediate proximity to host plants. Two examples exist in which males have gone beyond the use of ecological cues and instead target female pupae themselves. This male capacity for finding female pupae and alighting on them to mate with the female immediately upon eclosion has evolved at least twice, in the lycaenid *Jalmenus evagoras* (Elgar and Pierce 1988) and a clade of nine *Heliconius* species (Gilbert 1991; see also Deinert, chap. 5 in this volume).

For ectotherms such as butterflies, ambient temperature and solar radiation can be regarded as resources as well. When these resources are not homogenously distributed—as, for instance, in forests—basking sites such as sunspots may provide rendezvous sites where territoriality and perching may be favored (Davies 1978; Kemp and Wiklund 2001). Other ecological circumstances in which the distribution of solar radiation determines female movements and male territorial perching include those of temperate butterflies that mate in south-facing forest edges in spring and along warm paths in woodlands (Wickman and Wiklund 1983; Ravenscroft 1994; Bitzer and Shaw 1983; Lederhouse 1993). Willmer (1991) has argued that in ectotherms, alternative mate location strategies may often be thermally related and dependent on body size and temperature. As Dennis (1993) has pointed out, temperature and solar radiation are important to most species, since weather and climate are significant modifiers of activity in small ectotherms. Temperature may influence several aspects of perching or patrolling behavior, including wing positioning and perch height (Rutowski et al. 1994). More importantly, changes in temperature may also cause shifts from patrolling to perching, such that a patrolling individual in a sunny landscape will change abruptly to perching when the sun disappears behind the clouds. Accordingly, in *Coenonympha pamphilus* and *Lasiommata megera,* Wickman (1985a, 1988) concluded that population density is of small, often negligible, importance for determination of mate location behavior. Because flight requires high body temperatures, high ambient temperatures are positively correlated with flight duration, which is relevant for patrolling (Shreeve 1984).

In cases in which there is intraspecific variation in male mate location behaviors, there is an interaction between the factors mentioned above. In species that are territorial, for example, there can be a shortage of suitable territorial sites, so that only a fraction of males can become territorial, which leaves only the patrolling option open to competitively inferior males. Moreover, the importance of owning a territory may vary with the weather and the season, so that in cases in which a major advantage of territory ownership is that it permits the resident to maintain higher activity levels than patrollers (e.g., sunspot territories in the speckled wood butterfly, *Pararge aegeria*), territory ownership is devalued under warm weather conditions. These interacting factors create a dynamic equilibrium between patrolling and territorial males that changes both diurnally and seasonally. Hence, a higher proportion of males should be found perching within territories in the early morning and in the early spring than later in the day or season (Wickman and Wiklund 1983; Wickman 1985a; Dennis and Williams 1987).

With respect to the importance of thermoregulation for male choice of mate location behavior, it is well documented that there is adaptive variation in morphology both with latitude and elevation (Hovanitz 1941; Dennis and Shreeve 1989) and with season (Shapiro 1976; Kingsolver 1985, 1987a, 1987b; Kingsolver and Wiernasz 1991a, 1991b). In the speckled wood, Van Dyck et al. (1997a; see also Van Dyck, chap. 16 in this volume) recently demonstrated an interesting interaction of within-season variation in male coloration with mate location behavior. Pale males spend most of their time perching in sunspots, exhibiting territorial behavior, while darker males adopt a kind of patrolling behavior, flying between sunspots and spending a larger proportion of their time in the shaded part of the forest. The adaptive rationale is that darker individuals seem to warm up faster, which means that they can remain in flight in shady areas for a longer time, while pale males do not suffer from overheating as soon as dark males when perching within a sunspot.

THE FEMALE VIEW

The previous treatment of mate location behavior has focused on male behavior, as if female behavior were of little consequence. However, females are ultimately in control, and male behavior and distribution is completely dependent on female behavior and distribution. The importance of female behavior is apparent with respect to several aspects of mate location systems, and many of the interesting questions that remain to be answered relate directly to female behavior. First, all mate location systems that rely on male perching require a great deal of female "cooperation" because in all of these systems, including hilltopping and lekking systems, it is basically females that move around in search of suitable males. Second, insofar as females do not mate before they leave their point of eclosion, female movement is highly pertinent to mate location systems.

Mate location behavior by females has been looked at by Wickman and Jansson (1997) in their study of female searching costs in the lekking small heath butterfly (*Coenonympha pamphilus*). This species exhibits a lekking system in which the most competitive, and largest, males establish small territories close to one another and close to landmarks such as trees and bushes in open grassland, whereas the rest of the males spend their lives as vagrant patrollers (Wickman 1985a, 1985b, 1986). Release of virgin females has shown that they actively fly toward the landmarks where the leks are located, whereas mated females are indifferent to these landmarks (Wickman et al. 1995). Moreover, receptive virgin females of *C. pamphilus* seem determined to mate with territorial males, and are unwilling to mate with patrolling males that intercept them on their way to the lek. Accordingly, receptive female *C. pamphilus* do not solicit courtship from males that pass over them while they are perched, a behavior that is exhibited by some butterflies (Wiklund 1982), and notably by the congener *Coenonympha tullia* (Wickman 1992a). The coyness of a virgin female *C. pamphilus* is confined to the period when she is making her way to the lek—upon reaching the lek, she changes her behavior completely and encourages detection by males with a lengthy, conspicuous circling flight.

The reason for this difference between the two *Coenonympha* species might be related to the fact that *C. tullia*, with an average life expectancy of 3.3 days (Turner 1963b), is considerably shorter-lived than *C. pamphilus*, with an average life expectancy of 7.0 days (Wickman 1985b) so that *C. pamphilus* females can afford to be more choosy. The difference in female mate location behavior between the two species means that the experimentally measured time between the release of virgin females and mating is 4.4 times shorter in *C. tullia*, with *C. pamphilus* females mating on average 200 minutes after being released. Although it is obvious that *C. pamphilus* can better afford to pay a time cost, it remains obscure why they should want to pay this cost at all. Wickman and Jansson (1997) assessed the cost female *C. pamphilus* pay by releasing virgin females and noting how much sooner the females could have mated if they had mated with the first male that passed through the vicinity instead of withdrawing from soliciting courtship and mating until their arrival at the lek. By integrating the effects of age at mating on fecundity with field measures of fecundity and longevity, Wickman calculated the resulting fecundity loss to be between 2.8 and 1.3%. Wickman concludes that the fitness cost for *C. pamphilus* is large, but probably too small to eliminate the possibility of indirect benefits of mating with males on leks.

The lek polygyny system of *C. pamphilus* amply demonstrates that the spatial aspects of butterfly mate location systems result from male and female behaviors combined. Recently Wickman and Rutowski (1999) adopted a novel approach to this issue by concentrating on non-resource-based mating systems. They considered first the extent to which females actively seek males by moving toward sites where males are likely to occur, with the goal of analyzing how the interaction between male and female movements shapes the evolution of male tactics and mating dispersion in insects. Second, they focused on the non-resource sites where mating actually occurs, rather than just on the dispersion of males, and in so doing emphasized the interaction between male and female behaviors. Third, they argued that lekking and prolonged searching polygyny—that is, patrolling—are two alternative endpoints on a continuum of mating dispersion that ranges from highly clumped to widely dispersed. They arrived at the conclusion that six variables are pertinent to variation in mating dispersion in insects; namely, habitat heterogeneity, travel speed, detection distance, female choice, population density, and mating frequency.

MATING AND COURTSHIP

COURTSHIP AND MATE CHOICE

Once mate location behavior has resulted in a male and a female butterfly establishing contact, courtship ensues, during which it is "decided" whether mating will occur or not. Although the previous section has established that females often play an active part in mate location in perching species, it is virtually always the male that is the active partner in establishing close contact. In patrolling species, contact is preceded by a male discovering a conspecific female either on the wing or alighted on the ground; in perching species, final contact is usually preceded by a perched male having flown up to investigate a butterfly that has come within his field of vision. However, final contact is occasionally made by the female, as described in the satyrines *Aphantopus hyperantus* and *Coenonympha tullia,* in which alighted females fly up and solicit courtship from males passing overhead (Wiklund 1982; Wickman 1992a), and in some polyandrous pierids, in which females with collapsed spermatophores solicit courtship by chasing males in flight (Rutowski 1980a; Rutowski et al. 1981).

As pointed out in the excellent reviews by both Rutowski (1984) and Silberglied (1984), male and female butterfly behavior during courtship agrees well with observations on other organisms, as well as with sexual selection theory (Andersson 1994). Males are aggressive toward rivals and persistent in locating and courting females, while females are coy and effective at rejecting males. Female mate rejection behaviors have been described in several species, and males are usually incapable of forcing females to mate (Scott 1973a; Svärd and Wiklund 1989; Wiklund and Forsberg 1991).

In butterflies, courtship seems to consist of two phases, a "species recognition phase" and a "decision-making" phase, after which mating does, or does not, occur. There is no clear-cut border between these two phases, and the "species recognition phase" has too often been overlooked (Andersson 1994). Yet, as Andersson points out, quoting Fisher (1930), species recognition is essential: "The grossest blunder in sexual preference which we can conceive of an animal making would be to mate with a species different from its own."

In this context, it is relevant to return to Darwin, who believed that females were most excited by the most brilliant, beautiful males, and that by choosing mates on the basis of color, females would select for males that departed from the duller ancestral pattern, resulting in the evolution of brilliant male coloration and striking cases of sexual dimorphism. However, after careful analysis of several experiments involving tests of male and female mate preferences for dummies whose colors had been experimentally changed, Silberglied (1984) concluded that "there has been a widespread assumption of color discrimination by females.... Yet all experiments ... point to the fact that color is used less by females than by males, as a basis for discrimination, that females use color little, if at all, and that when females use visual cues, these are primarily in the UV" (see also Silberglied and Taylor 1978; Rutowski 1981). Realizing that such a statement necessitates the explanation of "the peculiar sexual distribution of color and pattern in butterflies," Silberglied advanced the hypothesis that *"intrasexual communication between males ...,* rather than intersexual or interspecific communication, *is the major selective agent responsible for brilliant male coloration,* low male color variability, lack of male-limited polymorphism, and absence of male sex-limited mimicry" (italics in original).

Although the initial courtship begins in response to the sight of the female, the later stages of courtship generally seem to be governed by olfactory cues. These cues can be released both by males and by females. In those species that have been carefully studied, olfactory signals released by the male are usually required for successful mating (Brower et al. 1965; Magnus 1950; Rutowski 1977a, 1978a, 1980b; Tinbergen et al. 1942). The more elaborate behavior associated with courtship appears at this stage, with the male disseminating his odor(s) in the vicinity of, or directly upon, the female's antennae. In *Danaus gilippus,* for example, the male may disseminate "love dust" on the female's antennae during flight or when she is resting (Brower et al. 1965), and in *Hipparchia semele,* the male catches the female's antennae between his wings and rubs them on the sex patches filled with androconia (Tinbergen et al. 1942).

Because most female butterflies mate soon after eclosion, and because females generally have a lower reproductive rate (*sensu* Parker and Simmons 1996) than males, the operational sex ratio in virtually all butterflies is strongly male-biased (Wiklund et al. 1998). For example, males of the green-veined white butterfly, *Pieris napi,* with ad libitum access to receptive females are capable of mating every sixth hour—in other words, they can mate twice on the same day—whereas the mating interval for females is on average 50–80 hours, translating to 5 to 9 days. This means that most courtships in butterflies involve an eagerly courting male and an already mated female that is unwilling to remate. During such encounters, females exhibit a variety of mate-refusal tactics, which can consist of a posture in which the wings are spread and the abdomen is lifted straight up in the air (which makes coupling virtually impossible) (Obara 1964; Rutowski 1978a, 1978b; Wiklund and Forsberg 1985; Forsberg and Wiklund 1989) or an ascending flight 10–15 m high, during which the pursuing male often loses sight of the female during the descending phase (Rutowski 1978b; Wiklund 1977a).

When performing the mate-refusal posture, it seems that females disseminate some pheromone that makes it possible for males to decide whether they have mated or not. This inference is based on the observations that the female's valves are opened when the behavior is performed, and that virgin females, while exhibiting the wings-spread-abdomen-in-the-air posture, are continually and eagerly courted by males (e.g., in *Pieris napi* and *Anthocharis cardamines*), whereas the same posture adopted by a recently mated female makes the courting male leave within seconds (Wiklund and Forsberg 1985; Forsberg and Wiklund 1989). In the polyandrous butterfly *P. napi,* females are maximally unattractive to males immediately after mating, and thereafter become increasingly attractive with the passing of time—an observation that is consistent with the belief that some sort of pheromone is being disseminated and that the concentration of the pheromone decreases with time (Andersson et al. 2000). By performing genetic crosses between races of *Heliconius erato* that differ in the odor of the female abdominal glands, Gilbert (1976) concluded that the odor originates in the male and is transferred to the female at mating. He also made behavioral observations suggesting that the odor is an antiaphrodisiac that helps to enforce monogamy among females.

Although Darwin strongly believed in female mate choice, the extent to which female butterflies exert active mate choice is presently undetermined. In *Coenonympha pamphilus,* for example, while females actively reject patrolling males on their way to the landmark leks, they will as a rule accept the first lekking male that courts them. Moreover, insofar as females would benefit from mating with fresh virgin males rather than with recently mated males, it seems that females in some species are not skilled in choosing an appropriate mate. In *P. napi,* virgin females having access to one virgin male and one previously mated male did not exhibit any preference for virgin males, or for large males (Kaitala and Wiklund 1995). The same was true in an outdoor experiment in which equal numbers of virgin and previously mated males were released together with sixty-five virgin females, thirty-four of which were found in copula. In *Pieris protodice,* however, males behave like "honest salesmen," with recently mated males courting females less intensely than virgin males (Rutowski 1979). In *Dryas julia* and some species of *Colias,* female choosiness increases with time: young females are unable to distinguish recently mated males from virgin males, whereas older females seemingly acquire this ability (Boggs 1995; Watt 1992). Hence, overall, there is no clear-cut evidence as to whether females exert adaptive mate choice in butterflies.

MATING DURATION

When a female butterfly is willing to mate with a courting male, she signals this either by abandoning the mate-refusing posture and going quiescent, as in the pierids *Pieris napi* and *Anthocharis cardamines* (Obara 1964; Wiklund and Forsberg 1985), or by changing from being quiescent to actively signaling that she is receptive by allowing the tip of her abdomen to protrude from between her wings, as in the pierids *Eurema lisa* and *Leptidea sinapis* (Rutowski 1978a; Wiklund 1977a). Upon noticing that the female is receptive, the male aligns himself alongside her, bends his abdomen, and copulates with her. When butterflies in copula are disturbed, either the male or the female flies away, with the passive partner hanging underneath more or less motionless. The sex of the flying partner is species-specific and appears to be a phylogenetically conservative trait. In the Swedish fauna, it is invariably the female that takes flight in the Satyrinae, whereas it is the male who takes flight in virtually all Pieridae (Wiklund and Forsberg 1991). In species in which the female is the active sex, nothing much happens once coupling is achieved; the male simply adjusts his position so that he faces in the direction opposite to the female. However, in species in which the male carries the couple in flight, a postnuptial flight is common.

During mating the male transfers sperm and products from his accessory glands to the bursa copulatrix of the female, where a spermatophore is formed. This proteinaceous package remains in the female bursa for the rest of her life, and permits the determination of how many times a female has mated (Burns 1968). After mating termination, the spermatophore is ruptured by chitinous teeth on the inner wall of the bursa (the lamina dentata), allowing the release of sperm and other constituents. The sperm travel to the receptaculum seminis, where they are stored. Later they travel to the oviduct, where the eggs are fertilized just before being laid by the female. As a rule, females emerge in the early morning and mate relatively soon after emergence, so the majority of matings involving virgin females occur in the morning. Matings involving previously mated females, however, usually occur in the late afternoon, as has been shown in *P. napi* (Forsberg and Wiklund 1989). This timing allows females to lay eggs in the morning, and therefore reduces reproductive time costs associated with remating.

The duration of copulation in butterflies varies from a low of 10 minutes in *Coenonympha pamphilus* (Wickman 1985b) to up to a week in *Gonepteryx rhamni* (Labitte 1919). Much of this variation is explained by the fact that recently mated males remain in copula for much longer than virgin males mating for the first time (Svärd and Wiklund 1986, 1989; Kaitala and Wiklund 1995; Bissoondath and Wiklund 1996). The longest mating durations involving virgin males occur in those nymphalids in which matings are initiated in the afternoon and do not terminate until sometime at night. Hence, in *Polygonia c-album,* which conforms to this pattern, the duration of copulations involving virgin males is on average 330 minutes, ranging from 160 minutes to 745 minutes (C. Wiklund, unpub.), and in *Danaus plexippus,* in which nightfall acts as a cue for the start of ejaculate transfer, the duration of copulation decreases with the time of day when it is initiated, lasting for up to 800 minutes when starting relatively early in the morning (Svärd and Wiklund 1988a).

The observation that copulation duration is dependent on male mating history provides strong evidence in favor of the consensus that whereas females seem to decide whether or not copulation will occur, once copulation has been initiated, it is the male that decides the timing of its termination. When mating a second time soon after their first mating, males always transfer a much smaller ejaculate (Svärd and Wiklund 1986, 1989; Bissoondath and Wiklund 1996). However, in spite of this poorer performance, recently mated males happily remate at the earliest opportunity. This strategy makes sense, as female butterflies are invariably unreceptive for a couple of days after mating, and so receptive females are a rare resource. Hence, the operational sex ratio in butterflies seems invariably to be male-biased, and the reproductive rate (measured as 1/time out, where time out signifies the length of time an individual is unwilling to mate: cf. Parker and Simmons 1996) of males to be much higher—up to ten times higher—than that of females (Wiklund et al. 1998). Therefore, even if a male needs time to recuperate after finishing a mating, he benefits from mating with a second female as soon as possible (even though he is able to deliver only a small ejaculate, which takes a long time to produce and transfer), rather than waiting until he has recuperated, because the likelihood of his encountering another receptive female is so small.

Sperm Competition

The duration of female unreceptivity is influenced by the size of the male's ejaculate. Females have stretch receptors in the bursa that inform them about the size of the ejaculate they have received (Sugawara 1979). For this reason, male butterflies should maximize their mating effort so as to prolong the duration of female unreceptivity as long as possible, because once a female remates, the second male's sperm will compete with those of the first male. The first male to mate with a female benefits from delaying female remating because the second male to mate with her usually fertilizes the majority of eggs laid after that mating, as shown for Edith's checkerspot butterfly, *Euphydryas editha*, by Labine as early as 1966. Studies on sperm competition in a variety of insects have shown last-male sperm precedence to be a general pattern (cf. R. L. Smith 1984). Various explanations for this pattern have been offered, from the structure of the female reproductive system, which exhibits features making a "last in–first out" system likely, to adaptive explanations, which argue that females can somehow exert post-mating choice and, judging the sizes of the ejaculates received, use sperm from the largest ejaculate to fertilize their eggs (LaMunyon and Eisner 1993a, 1993b). However, on theoretical grounds, Simmons and Parker (1989) have argued that sperm precedence patterns are more likely to be a reflection of male adaptations than of female adaptations, because the selective forces acting on males are likely to be much stronger than the selective forces acting on females (cf. Parker 1984).

In agreement with this prediction, comparative analyses across butterfly species have shown that the level of sperm competition influences ejaculate and sperm morphology and composition. Gage (1994) compared reproductive characteristics across seventy-four butterfly species and found that relative testis size increased with the risk of sperm competition. In butterflies, as in all Lepidoptera, males produce two types of sperm: fertilizing, eupyrene, sperm and nonfertilizing, apyrene, sperm (cf. Silberglied 1984). In the same set of seventy-four species, Gage showed that relative eupyrene sperm lengths are greater in species in which males experience higher risks of sperm competition. These results strongly suggest that sperm competition in butterflies selects for increased investment in spermatogenesis and, specifically, in longer sperm. The larger size of competing eupyrene sperm argues against the scramble mode of sperm competition envisaged in the raffle metaphor (Parker 1982, 1990a, 1990b, 1993), and is more consistent with interference competition. Apyrene sperm lengths are not affected by risk of sperm competition, which is consistent with the hypothesis that the function of apyrene sperm is to delay female sexual receptivity by moving while in storage.

The importance of sperm size within species has also been shown in the moth *Plodia interpunctella,* in which males suffering resource restrictions during larval feeding maintained the size of both eupyrene and apyrene sperm, reducing their numbers rather than their size, and did not alter the relative proportions of apyrene and eupyrene sperm produced from a "normal" 9:1 ratio. In addition, recent studies on *Pieris rapae* have shown that males may adjust the composition of their ejaculates to levels of sperm competition by increasing the absolute numbers of both apyrene and eupyrene sperm when mating for the second time, when the likelihood of mating with an already mated female is greater, and by adjusting the relative proportions of the two sperm types, so that remating males transfer a relatively higher number of fertilizing eupyrene sperm (Cook and Wedell 1996; but see Watanabe et al. 1998).

Even though the function of apyrene sperm has now begun to become discernible, what remains to understand is the high individual variation in sperm precedence within species. The practice of presenting the percentage of offspring sired by the second male, usually referred to as the P_2 value, as a species-specific average (cf. R. L. Smith 1984) tends to obscure the profound variation that seems to prevail within species. In 1992 Simmons and Parker presented data on interindividual variation in sperm precedence in the dung fly *Scatophaga stercoraria.* They demonstrated that P_2 varied between 0 and 1, and that longer copulation duration and larger male size were associated with greater fertilization success. In the arctiid moth *Utetheisa ornatrix*, LaMunyon and Eisner (1993a, 1993b) showed that the offspring of twice-mated females showed a low incidence of mixed paternity, and that most progeny were sired by one male—the larger one—largely irrespective of age, mating order, between-mating interval, or copulation duration. Their results led them to speculate that females exert control over the process by which one set of sperm is utilized at the expense of the other (postcopulatory female choice). In *P. napi*, P_2 values ranged from 0 to 1, with sperm precedence being influenced both by male size and by mating order, with second males having an advantage over first males and larger males having an advantage over smaller males (Bissoondath and Wiklund 1997).

Recently Cook et al. (1997) approached the problem of understanding the pattern of intraspecific variation in P_2 by means of an integrated experimental and theoretical analysis, using the moth *Plodia interpunctella*. They compared the fertilization success of small and large ejaculates containing known numbers of sperm, then observed the distribution of P_2. The observed variance was higher than predicted by the fair raffle model, so they concluded that sperm from *P. interpunctella* do not mix randomly before fertilization, and therefore, that sperm competition in this species might be influenced by sperm displacement or stratification. Cook et al. emphasized that their paper is in essence a starting point for further analysis of P_2 data, and suggested that variance in sperm numbers can be used to predict P_2 distributions, and so increase our understanding of sperm competition mechanisms.

The importance of sperm competition in butterflies is contingent upon the prevalence of multiple matings. Spermatophore counts have been performed in many species of butterflies. The degree of female polyandry, measured as the mean number of spermatophores per mated female, has been found to vary between a low of 1.00 in the satyrine *Erebia ligea* (Svärd and Wiklund 1989) and a high of 4.02 in the danaid *Danaus gilippus*, in which one female contained fifteen spermatophores—a record for butterflies (Pliske 1973; Drummond 1984). These findings suggest that female mating systems range from strict monandry to strong polyandry, and that the degree of female polygamy might be a species characteristic. Although the number of matings is bound to vary with female age (Pliske 1973; Drummond 1984; Rutowski and Gilchrist 1986) and with the size of previous spermatophores in the female bursa (Wiklund 1982; Wickman and Wiklund 1983; Drummond 1984), the evidence strongly indicates that variation in polygamy occurs in butterflies and that species can be regarded as describing a continuum from strict monogamy to strong polygamy. The main reason for this conjecture is that both males and females exhibit a variety of traits that can be understood only as adaptations to their specific mating systems.

LIFE HISTORY ADAPTATIONS

MALE ADAPTATIONS TO POLYGAMY

In species in which females mate more than once, it seems likely that sexual selection more strongly targets the quality and quantity of ejaculate than in species in which females mate only once. We have already seen that sperm competition has led to "ejaculate adaptations" in relation to female polygamy, with regard to both sperm characteristics and the proportion of eupyrene and apyrene sperm. Polyandry also has led to adaptations that are related to both male mating effort and paternal investment.

Males of polygynous species exhibit a range of adaptations to multiple matings that set them apart from males of more monogamous species. Because female butterflies can determine the size of ejaculates they receive, and remate sooner when they have received a small ejaculate, polyandry should select for males that transfer large ejaculates. There are two ways in which males can increase ejaculate size: by growing larger (insofar as ejaculate size scales positively with body size) and by transferring proportionally larger ejaculates (i.e., with the scaling of ejaculate to body size exhibiting a higher elevation). There is evidence that sexual selection has resulted in males of polyandrous species doing both (Nylin and Wedell 1994). As a rule, females are larger than males in butterflies, as they are in most animals (cf. Darwin 1871). However, relative male size increases with the degree of female polygamy in Swedish Pieridae and Satyridae, and in the most strongly polyandrous species males are actually larger than females (Wiklund and Forsberg 1991). Moreover, males in polyandrous species also transfer proportionally larger ejaculates than males in more monandrous species (Svärd and Wiklund 1989), probably as a result of having proportionally larger testes (Gage 1994). The mean relative size of the ejaculate (measured as a percentage of adult male body mass) ranges from a low of 1.4% in the monandrous *Pararge aegeria* to a high of 15.1% in *Pieris napi* (with individual males transferring ejaculates that correspond to 25% of their body mass) (Svärd and Wiklund 1989; Forsberg and Wiklund 1989). In addition, males of polyandrous species recuperate more speedily after copulation, and can transfer a larger second ejaculate when remating, than males of more monandrous species (Svärd and Wiklund 1989). Moreover, whereas most investigated males in strongly polyandrous species do seem to recuperate fully and transfer second ejaculates that are as big as the first ejaculate after some days' rest, there is evidence that males in more monandrous species are never able to transfer a second ejaculate matching the size of the first (Svärd and Wiklund 1989).

The adaptations of males of polyandrous species described above are all compatible with a mating effort explanation; that is, that males transfer large ejaculates so as to maximize the number of eggs they fertilize by delaying female remating. There is also abundant evidence that the nutritional value of the ejaculate increases with the degree of polyandry. In a comparative study of eleven butterfly species, nine pierids and two satyrids, the protein content of first ejaculates increased with the degree of polyandry (Bissoondath and Wiklund 1995). There seem to be at least two reasons why male protein investment increases with the degree of polyandry. First, a comparative study of twenty-one species showed that male allocation of mass to reproduction, measured as the ratio of abdomen to total body mass at eclosion, increased with the degree of polyandry (Karlsson 1995). In addition, another comparative study has recently shown that the amount of nitrogen in the abdomen of males increases with the degree of polyandry (Karlsson 1996), which presumably underlies the capacity of males in more polyandrous species to transfer more protein in their ejaculates.

FEMALE ADAPTATIONS TO POLYGAMY

Why do females mate more than once? Drummond (1984) mentions four possible explanations: (1) to achieve an adequate sperm supply, (2) to enhance female survivorship or reproduction through indirect paternal investment, (3) to increase genetic diversity within a female's progeny, and (4) to minimize the loss of time and energy required to resist insistent males. Although there is evidence that all of these factors may be relevant in some species, the explanation that has the widest general applicability is indirect paternal investment.

In Karlsson's (1995) study in which he demonstrated that male reproductive resources scaled positively with the species' degree of polyandry, females showed the opposite pattern: relative abdomen size decreased with the degree of female polygamy. The only conceivable explanation for this surprising finding is that adult females of polyandrous species have a higher expected nutrient income. This explanation is consistent with the idea that females benefit from male nutrient donations transferred through mating. The idea that females might benefit from these nuptial gifts derives from Boggs and Gilbert's (1979) discovery that nutrients from spermatophores were incorporated into the soma and eggs of female butterflies.

Although attempts to find out whether multiply mated females have an increased reproductive output have yielded negative results in some studies (Jones et al. 1986; Svärd and Wiklund 1989, 1991), there are now several studies that have reported a positive association (Oberhauser 1989; Watanabe 1988; Rutowski et al. 1987; Wiklund et al. 1993, 1998, 2001; see also Boggs 1990). For example, laboratory experiments comparing singly and multiply mated females of the naturally polyandrous butterfly *Pieris napi* have shown that multiply mated females live longer, lay larger eggs, and have much higher lifetime fecundity than singly mated females. When females have had access to high-quality food as larvae, their mean fecundity typically increases 1.6 times, from an average of 380 to an average of 610 eggs. The difference was even higher when larvae were raised on poor-quality food, in which case lifetime fecundity increased 2.5 times, from 150 to 375 eggs (Wiklund et al. 1993; C. Wiklund, unpub).

In a recent study on females of the polyandrous butterfly *Pieris napi*, Karlsson (1998) has shown that male ejaculates are made use of in a female's nutrient budget in quite intricate ways. The amount of nitrogen transferred by a virgin male to a female is equivalent to that in about 70 eggs, and females show a positive relationship between the amount of ejaculate material received and lifetime reproductive output. Moreover, female thorax mass decreases with age, which indicates that old females are able to use more of the resources from the thorax than younger females. Because male-donated materials also increase female longevity, multiply mated females also use more of their resources from the thorax, and so make a relatively higher reproductive investment than singly mated females in the sense that they transform a larger part of their body reserves into egg production.

There is now ample evidence that females of polyandrous species benefit nutritionally from mating multiply, and that females show behaviors to procure this extra source of nutrient income (see also Oberhauser 1992; Boggs 1990, 1992, 1997a, 1997b). Experiments have shown, for example, that female *P. napi* forage for matings. Females that are given access only to recently mated males, which deliver small ejaculates, compensate by accepting a higher lifetime number of matings than do females given access only to virgin males, which consistently deliver large ejaculates (Kaitala and Wiklund 1994). Females receiving small ejaculates mated on average 5.1 times (range 2–10), compared with an average of 2.8 times (range 1–4) for females receiving large ejaculates, and in so doing they achieved a lifetime fecundity that was not significantly different from that of the latter females.

Although female butterflies can receive extra nutrients by mating multiply, the average lifetime number of matings observed in wild populations (determined by spermatophore counts) exceeds three matings in only two of seventy-six investigated species (Drummond 1984; Wiklund and Forsberg 1991). The reason why females do not mate more often may be that there is limited space for ejaculates in the female bursa, and that spermatophores are time-consuming to break down (cf. Oberhauser 1992). There appears to be room for a conflict between the sexes with respect to the rate of spermatophore breakdown. It seems likely that males would benefit from a slow rate of degradation, insofar as female remating is delayed, whereas females should benefit from fast degradation to make possible the reception of another nutritious ejaculate (cf. Boggs 1981b). A radiotracer study (in which male-transferred protein was labeled with ^{14}C and ^{3}H) showed that the incorporation of male-derived nutrients into eggs laid by female *P. napi* peaked about 3 to 4 days after mating (Wiklund et al. 1993). In all butterflies examined to date, radioactively labeled male-derived nutrients are found in the next eggs laid by females, although the peak of incorporation is delayed by several days (Boggs and Gilbert 1979; Boggs 1981b, 1990; Boggs and Watt 1981). Hence, the relatively restrained polyandry practiced by most female butterflies may result from a relatively slow rate of nutrient incorporation in combination with a relatively short life expectancy.

The Evolution of Capital and Income Reproductive Investment among Females

When taking into account the fact that adult females can derive nutrients from mating multiply, the question arises, why don't female butterflies in all species practice polyandry? However, this question, in turn, begs another question: why do some males transfer nutrients as well as sperm to females? Hence, the coevolutionary relationship between the sexes comes into focus.

From the male point of view, nutrient transfer could be easily understood if male-donated nutrients were used solely to increase the number and quality of the donating male's own offspring. In butterflies, these benefits necessarily accrue to the last male to mate with a female, and so the problem for a male encountering a somewhat worn receptive female is perhaps not so much whether the nutrients he donates will be exclusively used to benefit his own offspring, but whether the reproductive value of the female is high enough to warrant his investment. However, since the nutrients that an old female receives at mating help boost her egg production, the nutrient donation per se increases the likelihood that mating with an old female will be advantageous.

A male encountering a virgin female faces a different problem, because the reproductive value of the female is beyond doubt. The problem is how much he should optimally invest because of the risk that the nutrients he invests will be used to increase the number and quality of not only his own offspring, but also those sired by other males that subsequently mate with the female. Radiotracer studies have established beyond doubt that nutrients transferred by a female's first mate show up in eggs laid by the female long after she has mated a second time with a new male (Wiklund et al. 1993). In the light of second-male sperm precedence, this makes it virtually certain that nutrients delivered by a male mating with a virgin female are used to benefit offspring sired by other males (cf. Oberhauser 1992; Wiklund and Kaitala 1995). However, this does not necessarily mean that nutrient donation by males mating with virgin females is suboptimally large, not only because the nutrients qualify as paternal investment in the sense that they increase the number and quality of the male's own offspring (up to the time when the female remates), but also because they delay female remating, hence making sense also from the mating effort point of view. There has been some heated debate as to whether male nutrient donation in insects really qualifies as "paternal investment" or "merely" constitutes "mating effort" (cf. Simmons and Parker 1989). From the point of view of butterfly biology, these two functions of male nutrient donation are not mutually exclusive, and so the intense debate attempting to dichotomize the issue seems without merit (Boggs 1981a, 1981b, 1995; Wiklund and Kaitala 1995).

One route that the evolution of nuptial gifts may have taken is selection for male delivery of large ejaculates that contain an abundance of eupyrene sperm, for sperm competition purposes, but also apyrene sperm and accessory substances serving mainly to delay female remating (cf. Gage 1995; Cook and Gage 1995). Sperm competition selects for large ejaculates, which can result in both an increase in male body mass and a proportionate increase in the mass of male gonads and accessory glands. Once a system has evolved in which males transfer a large ejaculate, it is easy to envisage that selection for male nutrient donation could occur, given that it benefits the male's own reproductive output.

The evolution of male nuptial gifts might be related to the unpredictability of larval food supply and sexual size dimorphism (Leimar et al. 1994). The principle of trade in a market is that variation in need to obtain and ability to provide results in more intense transactions, and the same principle should hold when nuptial gifts are traded for offspring. If some males are better able to produce gifts, and some females are in greater need of gifts, those males and females have an incentive to remate. Moreover, a female should remate more quickly after receiving a small gift, because better options are available on the market. Unpredictable food supplies, either for juveniles or for adults, could lead to this kind of variation, and food variation could be an important factor explaining differences among species in nuptial gift giving, and thus in sexual size dimorphism. More generally, any random variation causing males and females to vary in adult size could produce the same effect. Thus, nuptial gifts should be larger in species with greater within-population size variation.

This prediction was borne out by a comparative study involving sixteen butterfly species on relative ejaculate mass, which was taken as proportional to the size of the nuptial gift, and variation in female wing length, which was taken as indicative of the unpredictability of larval food availability or quality. The largest ejaculates were delivered by males in the species in which variation in female wing length was greatest. Moreover, the degree of polyandry was positively correlated with variation in female wing length (Karlsson et al. 1997), which suggests that females are most eager to obtain nuptial gifts in those species in which females have the greatest need to obtain extra nutrients.

In this kind of system, there is a fundamental asymmetry between males and females, because a male's ability to invest in reproduction is constrained by the resources he can accumulate as a larva, whereas a female can obtain resources for reproductive investment both from larval feeding and from nuptial gifts she receives as an adult. Hence, males essentially exhibit capital investment in reproduction, whereas females practice a combined capital and income investment tactic (*sensu* Sibly and Calow 1984, 1986; and explored by Boggs 1992, 1997a, 1997b). This generalization is contingent upon the contention that adult butterflies have limited opportunities to obtain essential nutrients such as protein. Hence, the genus *Heliconius* is not included in this group, as it exhibits many life history adaptations that relate to the ability of adults to acquire protein from pollen feeding (Gilbert 1972; Boggs 1990, 1997a, 1997b). Interestingly both male and female *Heliconius* departed from the pattern described above, in which male reproductive reserves at eclosion increased with the degree of polyandry and female reproductive reserves decreased with polyandry (Karlsson 1996).

In butterflies that do not acquire proteins by feeding as adults, the asymmetry between the sexes should have consequences for larval feeding decisions and individual plasticity in adult size. If females receive substantial resources through nuptial gifts, a female should react to larval food shortage by maturing at a smaller size, since her own lack of reproductive resources will be partly compensated by male contributions. However, a male larva experiencing food shortage must pay the full cost of decreased reproduction if he matures at a very small size, making it more important for him to keep on growing. The resulting adult size dimorphism should vary with growing conditions, with the male-to-female size ratio being greatest for larvae experiencing poor conditions. These predictions were supported by an experiment in which larvae of the polyandrous *P. napi* were subjected to two food regimes, high-quality cruciferous plants (*Alliaria petiolata* or *Berteroa incana*) in fresh condition and ample supply, or low-quality plants of the same two species that were older and smaller (Leimar et al. 1994).

The same theory leads to the opposite prediction in monandrous mating systems. In monandrous species, males deliver small ejaculates relative to their body mass, which suggests that proteinaceous nuptial gifts to females are small under this mating system (cf. Bissoondath and Wiklund 1995). Under these conditions, a female is not expected to benefit from mating repeatedly, and will therefore be dependent on acquiring resources for reproduction on her own through larval feeding. Hence, under monandry, female larvae should continue to grow under poor conditions because they cannot compensate for small reproductive reserves once they have matured. Although male size may be an important factor in male reproductive success (Phelan and Baker 1986; Wickman 1985b; Wiklund and Kaitala 1995; Deinert, chap. 5 in this volume; but see Suzuki and Matsumoto 1992), success may be less strongly associated with size when no nuptial gifts are delivered. Hence, under monandry, male larvae should react to food shortage more strongly than females and mature at a smaller size. Therefore, the shift in sexual size dimorphism with differences in larval food conditions observed in the polyandrous gift-giving butterfly *P. napi* should be absent, or take the opposite direction, in monandrous non-gift-giving butterflies. This prediction was supported by an experiment using the monandrous butterfly *Pararge aegeria*, in which the male ejaculate corresponds to 1.4% of male adult body mass: relative adult male-to-female size decreased with the deterioration of larval food conditions (Karlsson et al. 1997).

PROTANDRY

Although the size, mate location behavior, and courtship behavior of male butterflies may have important consequences for mate acquisition, males also compete for females in the time dimension. Since the operational sex ratio is virtually always strongly male-biased, receptive females are always in short supply, and males should be expected to evolve timing strategies to maximize the number of receptive females they encounter during their lifetime. In systems in which females mate only once, and soon after eclosion, mathematical models have shown that male mating success selects for protandry; that is, the emergence of males before females (Wiklund and Fagerström 1977; Iwasa et al. 1983; Parker and Courtney 1983; Bulmer 1983). Taking the female perspective, it is obvious that females also benefit from males emerging earlier, insofar as this ensures that females can minimize the time spent unmated (Fagerström and Wiklund 1982).

The earlier emergence of males should have consequences for sexual size dimorphism, as Singer (1982b) pointed out: "If males are to emerge before females as a result of selection for protandry, they must have shorter development times than females, and hence they will be smaller, if they grow at the same rate as larvae." However, although sexual size dimorphism was shown to be sensitive to sexual selection, with relative male size increasing with the degree of female polygamy, no evidence was found for the expected negative relationship between relative male size and protandry (Wiklund and Forsberg 1991). This result strongly suggests that males must have the ability to grow at a faster rate than females, a conclusion that has been borne out by experiments.

Growth rates of butterfly larvae are very flexible and can vary adaptively not only with respect to sex and developmental pathway, but also with the season (Nylin et al. 1989, 1993, 1996a; Wiklund et al. 1991; Gotthard et al. 1994, 1999). In areas where *Pieris napi* is bivoltine, the influence of sexual selection on sex-specific growth rate is particularly evident. In this species, in which males are larger than females, the development time of males is indeed longer than that of females in individuals that exhibit a univoltine life cycle—those that diapause in the pupal stage before emerging as adults the following spring. However, when individuals develop without diapausing, male development time is considerably shorter than that of females— nevertheless, the male-to-female size ratio is even more pronounced under direct development (Wiklund et al. 1991). Although the male-biased sexual size dimorphism does not decrease under direct development, protandry does, with males emerging on average 1.4 days before females in the diapausing generation and only 0.3 days before females in the directly developing generation. One possible interpretation of these findings is that sexual selection on male size is stronger than that on early emergence in a polyandrous system.

If this is so, the opposite prediction can be made with respect to the importance of male size versus early emergence in a monandrous system. This prediction is supported by observations on the relationships of these variables to the life cycle in the monandrous butterfly *Leptidea sinapis*, which has a life cycle similar to that of *P. napi*. When larvae are reared under the "critical" photoperiodic condition, in which half of the individuals develop according to a univoltine life cycle and the other half develop without diapausing, protandry is identical in the two generations, with males emerging some 2.5 days before females (Wiklund and Solbreck 1982). However, under direct development, relative male-to-female size is smaller than under diapause development. Hence, early emergence of males may be more important than size in a monandrous system.

The idea that selection for early male emergence should be relaxed under polyandry has been mathematically modeled by Zonneveld (1996a, 1996b). In general, the models showed that polyandry per se did not really relax protandry, mainly because the individual death rate used in the models was so high that repeated matings by females did not have a strong enough effect on male reproductive success. Only when nuptial gift–giving was associated with male size and relatively later emergence was the prediction of relaxed selection for protandry under polyandry upheld.

The timing of male emergence relative to that of females can also influence the size of the ejaculate that a male transfers to the female at mating. It is evident that both the size of the ejaculate and the number of sperm are essential components of the materials transferred to the female at mating. As would be expected, the size of the ejaculate transferred to females increases with male body size, both between and within species (Oberhauser 1988; Svärd and Wiklund 1989; Wiklund and Kaitala 1995). However, the size of the ejaculate that a male can transfer to a female is not fixed at male eclosion, but usually seems to increase with male age, as has been shown, for example, in *Danaus plexippus* (Oberhauser 1988). Hence, early male emergence is not associated only with costs, but also with the benefit of delivering larger ejaculates. This benefit may be contingent on life cycle; it could be particularly important in species that eclose in midsummer and overwinter as adults, but mate only after hibernation. In *Gonepteryx rhamni,* which exhibits this kind of life cycle, males usually emerge up to 3 weeks before females in the spring, and indeed, seem to use this period to increase their ejaculate delivery capacity (Wiklund et al. 1996).

SUMMARY

Sexual selection is the evolutionary process proposed by Darwin to explain traits whose primary function appears to be ensuring an individual's success in courtship and mating; hence, it is believed to have a strong effect on the evolution of animal mating systems. In this review of sexual selection in butterflies, I pay particular attention to its effect on male and female mate location patterns, courtship and mating behavior, sperm competition, and life history traits.

The mate location behaviors of male butterflies have been reasonably well studied. Males typically adopt one of two strategies: patrolling, in which males range widely in search of mates, or perching, in which males remain in one place (and often defend territories) to obtain a mate. Female mate location behaviors have been considerably less well studied, a shortcoming that is beginning to be realized by many workers. I argue that the evolution of butterfly mate location patterns is the combined result of male and female behaviors, and hence, that a full understanding of these patterns requires detailed understanding of both male and female behaviors.

The observation that male butterflies are more brilliantly colored than females in species that exhibit sexual color dimorphism led Darwin to suggest that female preference for gaudy males was the underlying force driving sexual selection. However, the weight of the evidence strongly suggests that Darwin was wrong. Repeated attempts to show that female butterflies are attracted to particularly colorful males have failed, and it seems that olfactory cues are dominant when it comes to stimuli governing female choice.

Some thirty years have now passed since the first demonstration (in *Euphydryas editha*) that second males generally enjoy higher fertilization success than first males with doubly mated females. Second-male sperm precedence is still the prevailing pattern, but recent research has begun to focus on understanding the strong individual variation in sperm precedence. Although the second male, on average, may fertilize some 80% of the doubly mated female's offspring, variation in second-male fertilization success ranges from 0 to 100% in most species. Male size is associated with success in sperm competition because large males transfer more sperm, but recent interest has also been directed toward female postcopulatory choice, holding the issue open whether females can somehow influence which male's sperm will be used for the fertilization of their eggs.

Sexual selection and mating systems have manifold effects on male and female life history traits. Under polygamy, relative male size increases with the degree of female polygamy, and males typically deliver large, nutritious ejaculates that serve as nuptial gifts, whereas males in monandrous systems typically are smaller than females, and they deliver small ejaculates that seem to contain few nutrients. Mating systems also strongly affect female life history traits. Females in monandrous species lean more toward capital investment in reproduction, in which most of the proteins allocated to reproductive effort derive from reserves they have assembled during the larval stage, whereas females in polyandrous species, which receive repeated nuptial gifts during their lifetime, exhibit a kind of income investment in breeding. Capital and income investment can be viewed as integrated parts of different life history syndromes and may interact with other life history traits, such as male and female habitat preference, displacement behavior, and host plant choice.

CHAPTER 5

Mate Location and Competition for Mates in a Pupal Mating Butterfly

Erika I. Deinert

Intermale competition that involves direct combat generally favors morphological features such as large body size (Andersson 1994). Searching for mates can also be considered competitive in species in which females mate only once, experience a refractory period after mating, or become more selective once mated. This form of competition, however, is expected to favor increased spatial and perceptual abilities (Schwagmeyer 1995). At the very least, male search tasks involve correctly identifying and intercepting potential mates. Males whose search strategies and perceptual abilities allow them to encounter relatively more potential mates may realize higher reproductive success.

In some species, searching males can expect to encounter the same females repeatedly. If those females vary in quality, then males should adjust their searching and inspection behavior to target known individuals of higher quality. A corollary of this prediction is that if males can routinely expect to encounter the same females in known locations, and if the quality of each female varies over time, then males should adjust their searching behavior in a way that takes this changing status into account. In other words, males should assign priorities when searching for, selecting, and competing for mates, and those priorities should change as female status changes.

Female physiological and behavioral receptivity is an important aspect of female "quality" for searching males. Males that can distinguish between receptive and unreceptive females rapidly are at an obvious competitive advantage. When males anticipate changes in female receptivity and adjust their behavior accordingly, this too confers an advantage (e.g., Schwagmeyer 1995).

Lepidoptera exhibit a broad range of mate location strategies and mating systems. Reviews characterizing these systems often examine factors that affect the distribution of receptive females. The number and duration of available females during the flight season (Odendaal et al. 1985), the distribution of host plants (Scott 1974), and the behavior of males and females at encounter sites (Bradbury 1985; Rutowski 1991) have all been proposed as determinants of mating system structure (see also Wiklund, chap. 4 in this volume). Receptive females are rarely randomly distributed, so that some locations are expected to be more profitable to searching males than others (see Courtney and Anderson 1986 for review). Such encounter sites may include adult food resources (Suzuki 1976; Rutowski et al. 1991), oviposition sites (Courtney and Parker 1985; Lederhouse et al. 1992b), topographic features such as hilltops (Alcock 1985, 1993b), spots affording high visibility (Rutowski et al. 1991; Rosenberg and Enqvist 1991), or spots containing favorable thermal properties (Ravenscroft 1994). In species in which females mate only once, mating is predicted to occur immediately after female eclosion (Ridley 1989). In such species males may defend emergence sites such as larval host plants or search them for virgin females, especially when such sites are patchily distributed (e.g., Courtney and Parker 1985; Elgar and Pierce 1988; Matsumoto and Suzuki 1992; Deinert et al. 1994; see Rutowski 1991 for review).

Regardless of the mate location strategy employed, most lepidopteran males have limited opportunities to interact repeatedly with known females. Certainly, males can rarely expect to find known females in known locations, so advance information on female status would be of little use in most species. The *Heliconius* pupal mating system provides one exception.

Pupal mating is an extreme encounter site strategy in which males locate clutches of pupae, inspect them for several days, eventually compete for a position on one pupa, and mate with the emerging female. Pupae are immobile, and thus males can reliably relocate these potential mates. Moreover, since pupae are "available" for several days but females can be mated only as they eclose, the receptivity, or value, of the pupae changes as the pupae age. Under these circumstances, males would be expected to adjust their inspection behavior and their competitive interactions to target higher-value females.

The goal of this chapter is to describe several aspects of the mate location behavior of *Heliconius hewitsoni,* to examine how this behavior changes in response to changing pupal maturity, and to consider how this and other behavioral and morphological traits affect male competitive success.

PUPAL MATING AND *Heliconius* AS A MODEL SYSTEM

Pupal mating occurs in 42% of *Heliconius* species (Gilbert 1991), but in only one butterfly outside the genus (Elgar and Pierce 1988), and thus constitutes a rare mate location strategy within Lepidoptera. Outside Lepidoptera, pupal mating occurs in several insect orders, including Diptera (Eberhard 1970; Conner and Itagaki 1984), Hymenoptera, and Coleoptera (see Thornhill and Alcock 1983, table 7.5). Precopulatory guarding of larvae occurs in some species that lack a pupal stage (Anstensrud 1992). In general, pupal mating can be seen as an extreme strategy in a continuum of mate location strategies that range from opportunistic encounters to waiting at emergence sites (e.g., Roubik 1990) to precopulatory mate guarding of adults (e.g., Wen 1993) and immatures (e.g., Anstensrud 1992).

Heliconius butterflies are excellent subjects in which to study male mating behavior. *Heliconius* are long-lived, unpalatable (Chai 1986), aposematic tropical butterflies that are easily caught, marked, and observed. *Heliconius* species breed year round and have broadly overlapping generations. They have home ranges, repeatedly return to the same floral and oviposition sites (Brown 1981; Turner 1981; Murawski and Gilbert 1986), and roost communally (Waller and Gilbert 1982; Mallet 1986a). In addition, males repeatedly and routinely visit the same individual larval host plants searching for pupae. Because pupal mating precludes active female choice, both male inspection behavior and intermale competition can be studied without its confounding effects.

Heliconius hewitsoni is one of several pupal mating (Edwards 1881; Gilbert 1991) species in the genus *Heliconius*. Female *H. hewitsoni* lay clusters of eggs on the terminal growth of the passion vine, *Passiflora pitierii*. The larvae feed gregariously, passing through five instars in 3 weeks, then pupate on or near the host plant. Larvae within a clutch pupate, and later eclose, simultaneously. During the 9-day pupal stage, adult males repeatedly visit the pupae. As early as 48 hours before pupal eclosion, males begin to land and sit on female pupae (Deinert 1997). The operational sex ratio is male-biased, and males actively compete with one another for a position on a pupa and for subsequent access to the female (Deinert et al. 1994). Several males may sit on a single pupa simultaneously while other males circle it, attempting to land and dislodge the sitting males. When not displaced, males remain on the pupa until the female ecloses.

As metamorphosis nears completion, the pupal casing thins, and one or two, but never more than three, sitting males puncture the pupal cuticle and insert several abdominal segments under the pupal skin (plate 5.1). Actual mating takes place as the female begins to eclose. As the female begins to drop down out of the pupal casing, one male is able to clasp the female, and she emerges attached (mated) to this male. Once a male has clasped a female, he is not displaced (E. I. Deinert, unpub.). Mating may last 30 minutes to several hours (E. I. Deinert, unpub.), during which time the male transfers a spermatophore and an antiaphrodisiac pheromone to the female (Gilbert 1976). The spermatophore contains a substantial amount of lipid and protein, which contribute to egg production and maintenance (Boggs and Gilbert 1979). Based on evidence from other *Heliconius* species, males probably have a limited ability to make up the loss of these nutrient reserves (Boggs 1981a) and transfer smaller spermatophores with repeated matings (C. L. Boggs, pers. comm.). In *H. hewitsoni*, males that mate on successive days take substantially longer to transfer the second spermatophore ($n = 6$ males, $\overline{X}_{first} = 94.83$ min ± 9.53 SE, $\overline{X}_{second} = 383.67$ min ± 136.84 SE, Mann-Whitney U test, $U = -10.5$, $p < 0.016$). Males may mate repeatedly during their lifetime, but can compete for access to only one female in a given clutch. Females of other pupal mating species rarely, if ever, mate more than once (Ehrlich and Ehrlich 1978). *Heliconius hewitsoni* females have never been observed to mate multiply in captivity (L. E. Gilbert, pers. comm.), nor have wild-caught females been found to contain more than one spermatophore or spermatophore remnant ($n = 20$ females: M. Cardoso and E. I. Deinert, unpub.). Nevertheless, females continue to lay eggs throughout their lifetime. Both males and females may live up to 6 months under greenhouse conditions (L. E. Gilbert, pers. comm.) and live approximately 4 months under field conditions (E. I. Deinert, unpub.).

Competition for mates is costly in most species. Once a male *H. hewitsoni* chooses to sit on and compete for access to a female pupa, he does not leave the pupa to feed. Field observations suggest that this is a potentially large energetic commitment: males that have sat on a pupa for more than 24 hours will sometimes drop off overnight and be found lying under the pupa, alive but unable to fly, in the morning. In the absence of an analysis of the nutritional status of the male, this observation could alternatively be interpreted as a difference in the thermoregulatory abilities of the males sitting together on a pupa and a lone male on the ground. Either interpretation supports the idea that competition is costly: only males that have sat on pupae for more than 24 hours are found on the ground, and males on the ground are frequently preyed upon by ants. Males sitting on pupae have not been observed to be attacked (E. I. Deinert, pers. obs.).

MALE VISITATION AND INSPECTION PATTERNS

Given that competition for mates is costly, males should be prudent in their allocation of limited resources. Species such as *H. hewitsoni* that engage in prolonged precopulatory mate inspection and mate guarding experience extended periods of intrasexual competition as well as extended periods during which they have an opportunity to evaluate potential mates. When the value of those potential mates changes over time, individuals should respond to those changes by adjusting their inspection behavior. *Heliconius hewitsoni* pupae are available for male inspection over the course of 9 days, but females can be mated only as they emerge. In order to maximize the number of females for which they can compete, males should distinguish between receptive and unreceptive females. In particular, male *H. hewitsoni* should adjust their inspection behavior as a clutch of pupae ages, allocating more resources to pupae close to emergence.

METHODS

The study was conducted in the lowland tropical wet forest (Tosi 1969; Holdridge et al. 1971) of Estación Sirena (8°29′N, 83°36′W) in Corcovado National Park, Costa Rica. To assess male visitation and inspection patterns, nine clutches were observed during the 1996 and 1997 field seasons. Clutches were continuously monitored throughout the fifth-instar larval, prepupal, and pupal stages, and scan samples were taken every half hour to note the number and identity of males investigating the host plant. A marked population was maintained throughout the study. Marks of unique color combinations on the hindwings allowed males to be identified in flight. Since *Heliconius* butterflies are known to respond to capture by leaving the area upon release, and since they may subsequently avoid the site of capture for a limited time (Mallet et al. 1987), capture of males near pupae might alter male visitation patterns. Therefore, for the purposes of the studies presented here, males were not caught near the larval host plant while larvae or pupae were present.

The number of males visiting the site each day was considered to be the number of unique individuals that visited between 0700 and 1700 hours, regardless of the number of times a male visited. Visitation frequency was calculated as the total number of nonconsecutive scans in which a male was present. In other words, visitation frequency is an estimate of the number of times a male left and reappeared at the site per day.

To determine male ability to discriminate between male and female pupae, five clutches were observed. Pupal sex was determined by examining the extent of the genitalic scar found on the terminal abdominal segments (Scoble 1992). Focal males entering the area were allowed to inspect pupae freely. As a focal male moved back and forth between pupae, the amount of time he spent with male and female pupae was measured using two stopwatches. Male inspection time was measured until the male left the area.

Since larvae and pupae of different ages from different clutches are sometimes present on a host plant simultaneously, and since this may confound results, only a single clutch was allowed to remain on the host plant during these observations. Other clutches were removed and the butterflies reared under laboratory conditions for later release.

RESULTS AND DISCUSSION

Males inspected available clutches daily throughout the larval, prepupal, and pupal stages, returning several times a day for visits of varying duration. The number of males inspecting pupae fluctuated throughout the observation period, with a pulse of visitations at the prepupal stage (the day of pupation). The number of visiting males then decreased, increasing again as the pupae neared maturity (fig. 5.1). The duration of visits by individual males showed a similar pattern: a pulse at the prepupal stage, a decrease, and then a gradual increase in visit duration as pupae matured (Deinert 1997). The daily visitation rate for individual males decreased, however, as the pupae matured (fig. 5.2). Taken together, the general pattern is one of frequent short visits early in the pupal stage and less frequent but longer visits later in pupal development. The prepupal stage is an exception to this pattern. Prepupae appear to be relatively more attractive than either fifth-instar larvae or early-stage pupae. It is likely that prepupae emit a strong pheromonal signal that acts to attract males to the site. Many "first-time visitors" appear on this

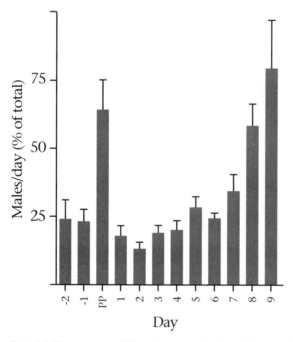

Figure 5.1 The percentage of the total number of males visiting pupae that visited on each of the 12 days of larval and pupal maturity. Days −2 and −1 represent fifth-instar larvae; PP represents the prepupal stage. The percentage of males per day was calculated as the number of unique individuals that inspected a clutch on a given day divided by the total number of unique individuals that inspected that clutch over the course of the 12 days represented. Data represent visitation patterns to nine different clutches. The total number of males ranged from 7 to 22. Error bars represent standard errors.

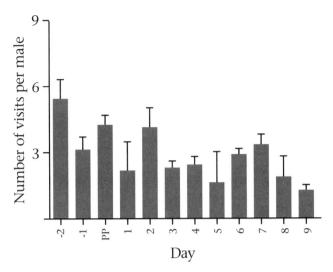

Figure 5.2 The average number of visits per male to pupae on each of the 12 days of larval and pupal maturity. Days −2 and −1 represent fifth-instar larvae; PP represents the prepupal stage. Data represent visitation patterns to nine different clutches. Error bars represent standard errors.

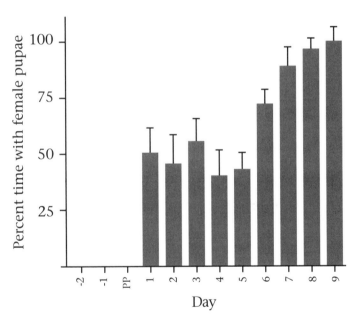

Figure 5.3 The percentage of time males spent inspecting female pupae rather than male pupae on each of the 12 days of larval and pupal maturity. Days −2 and −1 represent fifth-instar larvae; PP represents the prepupal stage. Data are averaged over five clutches. Error bars represent standard errors.

day. Overall, the amount of time individual males spend at the clutch site increases as pupae mature (Deinert 1997).

Males initially did not discriminate between pupae on the basis of pupal sex, but spent significantly more time inspecting female pupae on and after day 6 of pupal maturity (fig. 5.3). Males rarely chose to sit on male

pupae. Males making such mistakes did so only briefly and only while females were eclosing or mating nearby. Perhaps newly emerged virgins emit
strong pheromonal signals that temporarily overwhelm the ability of males
to assess the pheromonal cues of pupae. No males attempted to mate with
male pupae during the course of this study, but anecdotal observations suggest that this can sometimes occur (L. E. Gilbert, pers. comm.). "Mistakes"
in mate choice, or time allocated to pursuing inappropriate matings, is not
a phenomenon restricted to *H. hewitsoni*. Males of another pupal mating
species, *Heliconius charitonius,* have been observed attempting to copulate
with male pupae under high-density conditions, and with *Passiflora* fruits
near an eclosing female (C. L. Boggs, pers. comm.). Pupal mating *Jalmaeus
evagorus,* a lycaenid butterfly in Australia, appear to be unable to discriminate between pupae on the basis of pupal sex at all, and are as likely to
sit on and compete for male pupae as for female pupae (Elgar and Pierce
1988).

It appears, then, that male *H. hewitsoni* are able to assess pupal maturity and adjust their searching behavior according to changes in pupal age,
allocating more time to older pupae. Similar inspection patterns have been
observed in *J. evagorus* (Elgar and Pierce 1988). In the *Jalmaeus* system males
land on pupae more frequently when pupae are about to eclose. However,
Jalmaeus males visit the pupal site as often when pupae are young as when
pupae are close to eclosion. Moreover, *Jalmaeus* males do not distinguish
between male and female pupae (Elgar and Pierce 1988). For *H. hewitsoni,*
whose males sit on pupae long before mating is possible, the costs of allocating resources to unprofitable potential mates is high, and selection for
discrimination may be more stringent.

MATE CHOICE AND RISK TAKING AS A RESPONSE TO PUPAL AGE

If male *H. hewitsoni* are to benefit from assessing the receptive state of potential mates, then they should not only adjust their mate inspection behavior
as pupae mature, but they should also use the resulting information to discriminate among potential mates (Bateson 1983). This information should
allow them to maximize the number of receptive females with which they
interact, and to make decisions about the relative costs and benefits of competing for access to females of various ages.

In binary choice experiments, individual males were allowed to choose
between pupae that were matched for size but that varied in age by 1 day.
Although both pupae were within 48 hours of eclosing, focal males chose to
sit on the older pupae (Deinert 1997). However, as with pupal sex, males discriminated on the basis of pupal age only toward the end of pupal maturity.
Early in the pupal stage males spent as much time inspecting the young as the

old pupae (Deinert 1997). This shift from indiscriminate to discriminating behavior is most likely pheromonally mediated. It also makes sense from an evolutionary perspective. Males are able to gather information about potential mates before choosing one over the other, but they choose in such a way as to maximize the number of pupae with which they can potentially mate. By concentrating competitive efforts on older pupae, males are potentially able to compete for access to both young and old pupae.

When responding to a potential predator males also alter their risk-taking behavior according to pupal maturity. Typically males leave and return to reinspect a clutch of pupae at least once during the course of a day. Males leaving a site return to reinspect pupae more rapidly when the pupae are close to eclosing than when pupae are young (Deinert 1997), an observation that agrees well with the mate inspection patterns described above. Males respond to simulated predation attempts (see Deinert 1997) by increasing the length of time needed to return to the site. The magnitude of this response depends on pupal maturity. When pupae are young, focal males take, on average, 6 times longer to return to the site than males not exposed to predation attempts. When tested on the day males begin to sit on pupae, males increase their time to return by a factor of only 2.5 on average (Deinert 1997).

Mallet et al. (1987) demonstrated that *Heliconius* butterflies respond to capture at adult resources, such as flowers, by avoiding the site of capture for a period of up to several days. Such behavior may reduce the risk of capture if potential predators such as birds are site faithful. If adult resources are available elsewhere, butterflies might incur little cost in avoiding such sites. However, males that avoid sites where pupae are available might decrease their chances of successfully competing for this limited resource. Therefore males should behave in such a way as to minimize their predation risk but maximize reproductive success. Clearly males respond to predation risk at pupal mating sites by leaving the site of capture, but the response is mitigated by changes in mating opportunity and the need to return to the site to compete for late-stage pupae. When pupae are young, males avoid risky sites. As pupae near eclosion and males begin to compete for them, males increase their risk-taking behavior and return to the site quickly (Deinert 1997).

MATE INSPECTION PATTERNS AND MALE COMPETITIVE SUCCESS

Numerous studies of sexual selection have revealed associations between male competitive ability and male morphological or behavioral characters. While large size is perhaps the most commonly reported correlate of male mating success (Andersson 1994), several studies suggest that the amount of time spent searching or competing for mates is also an important predictor of male success (e.g., Dickinson 1992; Simmons 1995).

Methods

To determine whether patterns of male visitation to pupae enhance competitive success in *H. hewitsoni,* male inspection behavior was scored for nineteen clutches between 1993 and 1996. Clutches were monitored as described above throughout the pupal stage until the onset of direct intermale competition—that is, when males began sitting on pupae. Clutches were then continuously monitored. Each male was scored with respect to sitting, inserting, and mating and the time spent in each state was noted. Males were recorded as "sitting" if they sat on a pupa and assumed the head-down position necessary for pupal mating, as "inserting" if they later punctured the pupal cuticle to angle the abdomen upward under the pupal casing, and as "mating" if they achieved copulation with the emerging female. Several potential determinants of male mating success were investigated: the total number of visits to the site prior to the beginning of direct competition, the total number of days on which individual males visited pupae, the total time spent sitting on a pupa, and presence at the site on the first day of direct competition.

Results and Discussion

For the nineteen clutches monitored, 143 males competed for access to pupae; of those, 77 sat on pupae, and of those, 43 mated with eclosing females. Competition for mates occurs as a linear sequence of three stages: (1) competing for a position on a pupa, (2) insertion of abdominal segments under the pupal casing, and (3) clasping the female as she emerges. Males that competed successfully for access to females passed through all three stages. All mated males first successfully competed for a "seat" on a pupa and then later punctured the pupal cuticle with the abdomen ("inserted").

Since direct intermale competition proceeds in stages but is initiated only toward the end of pupal maturity, it seems likely that male inspection behavior might provide important information about pupal quality, other male competitors, and the timing of the onset of competition. However, neither precompetition inspection behavior nor the amount of time males spent with a pupa was a determinant of mating success. Mated males visited pupae on precompetition days as often as unmated males, both in terms of the total number of visits to the site and in terms of the number of days on which they visited (Mann-Whitney U test, $p = 0.18$, 0.23, respectively). Sitting priority, measured as the amount of time on a pupa, also failed to predict mating success. There was a nonsignificant trend, however, for mating success to decrease as sitting time increased: mean time sitting on pupae was slightly less for mated than for unmated males (16.1 hours $\pm$ 1.8 SE, 17.3 hours $\pm$ 3.3 SE, respectively; Mann-Whitney U test, $p = 0.06$).

Being present on the day of onset of direct competition, on the other hand, was a correlate of mating success. Of 43 mated males, only 9 were absent on the day males began sitting on pupae. Of 34 unmated males, 16 were absent that day (Fisher's exact test, two-tailed, $p = 0.026$).

Interestingly, not all males that inspected pupae early in pupal development continued to inspect them. Seventeen males visited pupae, but did not arrive to compete for access to them once direct competition had begun. Since 14 of these males were identified in routine mark-recapture the following day, it is assumed that these males were present in the population but ignored the presence of potential mates. These males are not included in the analyses above.

It appears, then, that while males visit pupae over the entire course of pupal development, this behavior has little direct effect on male mating success. Neither the number of times males visited the site nor the length of time they competed for pupae had an effect on male mating success. Males may have a limited ability to make use of advance information to direct their efforts in competing for access to females when only one clutch is available. Advance information about pupae might be most useful in allowing males to allocate their time to older clutches at the same site or at other sites. However, males do benefit from being present on the day that direct competition begins. It is likely that repeated visits to pupae over the course of pupal development function to keep males informed of pupal maturity and of the timing of onset of competition. This hypothesis makes sense in light of behavioral observations that suggest that once one male begins to sit, others rapidly follow. If the timing of the onset of competition is important, then males should behave in a way that allows them to keep track of one another. Sitting simultaneously may not be necessary, but males arriving after many males have covered the pupa may find it difficult to gain a purchase. And since at most three males per pupa can pass to the "inserted" stage of competition, males arriving after other males have inserted their abdomens will compete in vain for access to the female. Perhaps it is for this reason that males increase their risk-taking behavior with the onset of direct intermale competition.

The trend toward a negative relationship between mating success and length of time on a pupa is consistent with the suggestions, made in an earlier section, that there is an energetic cost to competition and that male nutritional state or energy reserves may play an important role in competitive ability. If this is the case, then individual males may face a trade-off between being present at the onset of competition and leaving to forage for additional resources. Such a trade-off might help to explain why not all males visiting the site on the day of competition onset attempt to sit on pupae immediately: some return later that day, while a very few do not attempt to sit until the following day (E. I. Deinert, pers. obs.). It might also explain why a small percentage of males inspect pupae but do not compete for them.

MORPHOLOGICAL COMPONENTS OF MALE SUCCESS

Overall size and symmetry of bilateral characters have been implicated as determinants of male competitive success in many animal systems. In competition for access to mates, large males may displace smaller males (Elgar and Pierce 1988; Day et al. 1990), more successfully defend mates or territories (Rosenberg and Enqvist 1991), or be more likely to retain a grasp on females that resist them (McLain et al. 1993). Some studies also suggest that smaller males have a competitive advantage in certain situations (Marshall 1988; Zamudio et al. 1995; Hernandez and Benson 1998). Trait asymmetry in normally symmetrical traits has been recognized as an epigenetic measure of an individual's ability to cope with stress. Thus, a high degree of symmetry may be associated with overall fitness (Thornhill 1992). In some systems females display preferences for symmetrical males (e.g., Thornhill 1992). Similarly, symmetrical males may consistently outcompete less symmetrical individuals for access to mates.

In *H. hewitsoni,* body size, measured as wing length and body length, plays a complicated role in determining the outcome of male contests for mates. Larger males have an advantage in competing for a position on a pupa (fig. 5.4A), while smaller males have an advantage in achieving matings once seated (fig. 5.4C). Body size is not a determinant of male success in competition for inserting abdominal segments (fig. 5.4B). Thus the relative body sizes of competing males play a role in two of the three stages of competition for mates. The same male trait is not a determinant of success in both stages of competition, however. Selection gradient analysis (Lande and Arnold 1983; Arnold and Wade 1984a, 1984b) reveals that males with longer wings are favored in competition for access to pupae, while males with shorter abdomens are favored in subsequent competition for matings (Deinert et al. 1994). Interestingly enough, however, mated and unmated males do not differ in wing length or body length, nor has there been a decrease in trait variance (Deinert et al. 1994). This finding suggests that because wing length and body length are highly correlated, and because selection acts on each in opposite directions, the overall effect of these two opposing selective forces is no net detectable selection on either trait (Deinert et al. 1994). That this interaction should result in no net selection, rather than in stabilizing selection, is not intuitive, but figure 5.5 shows how it could occur.

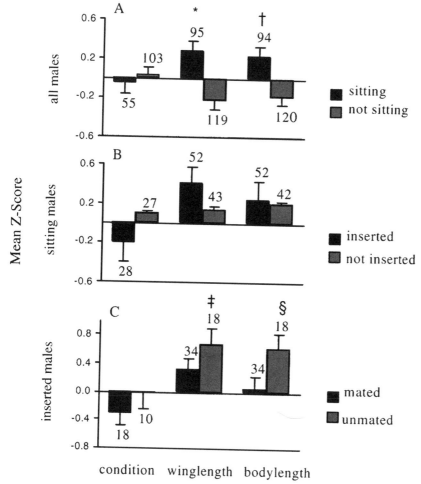

condition   winglength   bodylength

Figure 5.4 A comparison of the mean *Z* scores of male condition, wing length, and body length for (A) males that were successful and unsuccessful in gaining a position on a pupa, (B) sitting males that were successful and unsuccessful in inserting their abdomens under the pupal casing, and (C) sitting, inserted males that were successful and unsuccessful in mating with the eclosing female. Wing condition, or scale loss, is an indicator of male age ($r = 0.7$, $p < 0.001$, $n = 217$) and was scored on a scale of 1–7. Condition is not a predictor of male success at any stage and is included here as a reference. Trait scores are converted to *Z* scores because a given individual will be relatively large within the context of competition for one set of pupae, but relatively small compared with males competing for a different clutch months later. Trait scores were therefore standardized within each group of competing males to a mean of 0 and a variance of 1 (*Z* scores). *$p < .001$; †$p = .002$; ‡$p = .03$; §$p = .02$.

Wing asymmetry, measured as the absolute difference between right and left wing length, did not differ between mated and unmated males (Mann-Whitney *U* test, $p = 0.45$).

Several studies suggest that interspecific differences in wing and body morphology are related to the different requirements of a perching (sit-and-wait) and a patrolling mate location strategy (see Wiklund, chap. 4 in this volume; Van Dyck, chap. 16 in this volume). For example, perching *Pararge aegeria* have larger wing/body ratios than patrolling butterflies, indicating a

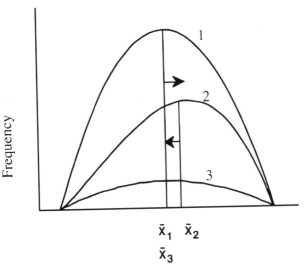

Winglength or Bodylength

Figure 5.5 Schematic diagram illustrating how opposing forces of directional selection could result in no net selection. Curve 1 represents the frequency distribution of the wing length and body length of all males that compete for access to pupae. $\bar{X}_1$ represents the mean wing or body length of competing males. Curve 2 represents the trait distribution of males that have gained access to a pupa. $\bar{X}_2$ represents the mean wing or body length of males sitting on pupae. Curve 3 represents the trait distribution of males that have mated with a female. $\bar{X}_3$ represents the mean wing or body length of mating males. The force of selection acting at each stage is represented by an arrow. Selection favors males with long wings in the first stage of competition. Selection favors males with short bodies in the third stage of competition. Since wing length and body length are correlated characters, both traits are affected by both selective events, and there is no net selection on either trait. (Data from Deinert et al. 1994.)

relatively large allocation of mass to the thorax (Van Dyck, chap. 16 in this volume). In *Heliconius* butterflies, morphological differences across species are similarly related to mate location strategy. The opposing forces of selection generated by competition for pupae appear to have led to a shift in the wing length/body length ratio of pupal mating species relative to non–pupal mating species. While males that were successful in obtaining a copulation did not differ from unsuccessful males in either wing length or body length, as mentioned above, one might suspect that the opposing selective forces would favor males with relatively long wings and short bodies. Because variation in the wing length/body length ratio is extremely low in the study population (coefficient of variation $= 4.13$, $n = 213$), it was not possible to test this hypothesis within the species. However, such selective forces should be acting on all pupal mating species, which suggests that pupal mating and non–pupal mating species should differ morphologically. Pupal mating *Heliconius* do have relatively longer wings and shorter bodies than non–pupal mating species, although absolute wing length and body length do not differ between the two groups (Deinert et al. 1994).

Morphological differences between butterflies using perching and patrolling mate location strategies result from a need for different types of flight. In *Heliconius* butterflies, non–pupal mating species are patrollers, while pupal mating species can be thought of as using a combination of both strategies. Although pupal and non–pupal mating species do not differ in mean wing or body length, males of pupal mating species have larger wing length/body length ratios. This difference may be due in part to differences in optimal flight design. It is probably also due to forces generated by direct competition among males. Males with larger wings are better able to defend pupae against conspecifics, while males with smaller, skinnier abdomens are likely to have an advantage in inserting their abdomens farther under the pupal casing (Deinert et al. 1994). Thus males with relatively longer wings and shorter bodies are favored in competition for pupae. These selective forces generated by direct competition for mates do not act on non–pupal mating species. Direct competition between males is known to be a selective force in territorial perchers, in which males engage in physical battles (see Rosenberg and Enqvist 1991). In the *Heliconius hewitsoni* system direct competition occurs without territoriality.

Hernandez and Benson (1998) report that *Heliconius sara* males may use alternative mate location strategies, and that these strategies are size-based. *H. sara* is a pupal mating butterfly, yet small males hold territories and consistently defeat larger individuals in territorial contests. How this affects the mating success of territory holders and non–territory holders is unknown, yet this finding suggests that in this species small males may be at an overall disadvantage in competition for access to pupae and thus may employ an alternative mate location and mate acquisition strategy. Since the proportion and the relative success of males employing these two strategies is not known, it is impossible to know what effect this alternative strategy might have on the *H. sara* body plan. *Heliconius sara* in Costa Rica conforms to the long wing–short body morphology typical of pupal mating species.

Heliconius hewitsoni males do not appear to be territorial. Nevertheless, some data support the idea of a possible size-based difference in mate location strategies. The mean size of males that arrive at a clutch *for the first time* on the day females eclose is smaller than that of males that have visited the site during the precompetition and competition stages (chi-square test, $G = 12.5$, $p = 0.003$). These males are ones that are either previously unknown from the study population or that have not previously been seen inspecting pupae (E. I. Deinert, unpub.). Males that arrive on the day that females eclose are usually unsuccessful in obtaining mates since all females are mated by sitting males. If clutches occasionally contain more female pupae than there are males in the surrounding population, then late-arriving individuals may be successful in foraging for "leftover" females. Why late arrivals should be smaller males, however, is unknown, since Deinert et al. (1994) indicate that smaller males that compete for access to mates are as likely to achieve matings as larger males. It may be that, in addition to being small, these are males with low energetic reserves that are unable to compete for access to pupae directly.

DIRECTIONS FOR THE FUTURE

What we know about the factors affecting and resulting from the evolution and maintenance of the pupal mating strategy is eclipsed by what we do not know. Unlike most other Lepidoptera, *H. hewitsoni* males can expect to find known females in known locations over a period of several days. Since females are available for mating only toward the end of the pupal stage, males in this system have a unique opportunity to use advance information about female location and status in making decisions about how to allocate time and energy to competition for mates. The results presented here demonstrate that males do respond to changes in pupal age in a way that could maximize the number of receptive females for which they are able to compete. To what extent, however, are males able to adjust their searching and competitive strategies? To what additional factors are they able to respond?

Ideally, males should maximize not the number of females for which they can compete, but the number of females for which they can successfully compete. This implies that males should not only make use of immediate and advance information about females, but should also adjust their competitive strategy based on immediate and advance information about competitors. The relative ages, experience, and physiological state of competing males play a role in determining the outcome of intermale competition in some systems (e.g., Gribbin and Thompson 1991; Fiske et al. 1994; Cook 1995). In *H. hewitsoni,* male size and the timing of arrival are known determinants of male success. In addition, generations are overlapping and male size is determined by larval diet, so males may vary in size within and between clutches. Thus males can expect to compete with other males that differ unpredictably in experience, ability, and morphology. However, males encounter one another at regular intervals, especially while inspecting pupae. Thus males have an opportunity to evaluate not only available pupae, but also competitors, before the onset of competition.

Do males make use of advance information? The existence of such an opportunity leads to several unanswered questions: Do males assess other males when making decisions about which of several pupae to compete for? Do males assess their own condition in making decisions about whether or not to compete for a known clutch of pupae? Are males that disappear after several days of pupal inspection predictably different from males that decide to compete? And is this a decision based on the evaluation of available pupae in other locations or on a male's own chances of competing successfully in the current forum? Does competitive ability or the probability of encountering future clutches change with male age; if so, do older males behave differently?

On a recent trip to Panama (October 2001) I observed *Heliconius sara* and *Heliconius sapho,* both pupal mating species, engaged in apparent territorial behavior in small gaps along the side of Pipeline Road. It may be that alternative mate location strategies are more common in *Heliconius* species than is currently known. Or perhaps the pupal mating system is breaking down in these species. If so, what ecological factors have caused the mating system to break down in these populations? Has a host plant shift to more ephemeral and dispersed plants made searching for pupae less fruitful than adopting a sit-and-wait strategy? Or, if these species possess mixed mating strategies, are these strategies fixed for individuals, or are they plastic? What information about pupal availability or competitors would lead males to adopt one strategy over the other?

Little is known about the decision-making capabilities of insects that have access to advance cues about potential mates and competitors. *Heliconius* butterflies are capable of sophisticated behaviors, such as traplining along adult resources, avoiding sites of capture within the home range, and adjusting to changing mating opportunities. The extent to which males are able to make use of both immediate and advance information may provide us with a greater understanding of the behavioral and morphological traits that affect decision making in the contexts of mate location and mate choice.

SUMMARY

A central theme in behavioral ecology is that there are costs associated with mate acquisition. Whether foraging for food or for mates, fitness gains depend on the relative value of the resource and the costs associated with obtaining it. Animals with flexible behaviors should adjust their activity in response to changes in the associated costs and benefits. In species in which males gain nothing by mating with unreceptive females, female receptivity is an important component of female quality, and one that changes over time. Males of species that engage in precopulatory mate guarding should benefit by anticipating the onset of female receptivity, evaluating the relative value of still immature females, and responding to the behavior of competitors.

In *Heliconius hewitsoni* female pupae are present on the larval host plant during a 9-day pupal stage, but mating takes place only as the female emerges. Males compete for access to female pupae and begin to sit on pupae only 24–48 hours before females eclose. Therefore, while females are available for inspection during an extended period, they are a valuable resource in terms of mating opportunities only toward the end of the pupal stage.

Male *H. hewitsoni* respond to changes in pupal maturity in a variety of ways. Male inspection patterns change as pupae mature: males allocate more total time to visiting clutches when pupae are more mature. Males also assess pupal age when discriminating among potential mates and when responding to risk. Male visitation patterns have little to do with male success in direct competition, however. Rather, male success in competition for mates is determined by an interaction of morphological characters and by being present at the site on the day that direct competition for pupae is initiated. It seems likely, then, that changing male inspection patterns in response to pupal maturity reflect a trade-off between the need to forage and the need to be present when competition begins. Overall, these patterns allow males to concentrate their search activities on higher-value, more mature pupae and thus to maximize the number of pupae for which they can compete.

ACKNOWLEDGMENTS

I thank Carol Boggs for helpful comments on the manuscript and for being unfailingly cheerful and patient as we experienced all manner of electronic and postal communications glitches. Suggestions from two anonymous reviewers greatly improved the clarity of the presentation. Larry Gilbert introduced me to the *Heliconius* system, for which I am eternally grateful. Both he and Mike Ryan helped with comments while the work was in progress. Thanks to the Costa Rican Sistema Nacional de Areas de Conservacion (SiNAC) and the Area de Conservacion Osa (ACOSA) for permission to work in Corcovado Nacional Park. Special thanks to Paulino Valverde, director of Sirena Station, for logistic support while I was in the field.

PART III

Ecology

Population dynamics, species distributions and interactions, and community structure are determined by organisms' physiology and behavior interacting with the environment across diverse temporal and spatial scales. Butterflies have been used in many classic ecological studies because they exhibit so much variation in their ecology, with, for example, population structures ranging from large, continuous open populations to metapopulations and species distributions ranging from worldwide to highly endemic. The need to understand the causes of these ecological patterns is becoming increasingly urgent, particularly as humans continue to modify the environment. Butterfly ecologists are thus using a variety of tools and concepts, from molecular techniques to theoretical models, in order to examine population, community, and landscape structure under various environmental scenarios.

The chapters within this section exemplify this work. Art Shapiro and colleagues (chap. 6) lead off with an exploration of the temporal aspects of butterfly community structure. They use two California datasets on phenologies of whole butterfly faunas to ask what we can learn about issues such as temporal niche partitioning and phenological predictability within and among sites. Equally important, the methods for studying the influences of weather patterns, climate change, and other physical parameters on phenological patterns are relatively poorly understood.

The next two chapters shift the focus from temporal variation to spatial variation. Jane Hill and colleagues (chap. 7) explore temporal changes in the spatial aspects of butterfly community structure. They analyze the influence of climate and habitat fragmentation on the observed range distributions of three European satyrines with contrasting current ranges. They use this analysis to predict future range distributions under current climate change expectations, but at present-day levels of habitat fragmentation. Moving to the population level, Nusha Keyghobadi and colleagues (chap. 8) focus on the effects of habitat fragmentation on population isolation, individual dispersal, and gene flow in *Parnassius* in Alberta, using standard mark-and-recapture techniques as well as molecular markers. They conclude that landscape structure is a strong determinant of population structure for these butterflies.

How are the observed population distributions and dynamics shaped by the interaction between spatial or temporal environmental variation and life history traits? Carol Boggs (chap. 9) outlines studies that use resource allocation as a context to answer general questions concerning the effects of different types of environmental variation on life histories and population dynamics, concluding that there is much more to be learned.

The final two chapters in this section demonstrate effectively that while ecology has been said to be the theater within which the evolutionary play occurs (Hutchinson 1965), as time goes on, the boundaries between theater and play may blur. Michael Singer (chap. 10) synthesizes much of his recent work on the relationships between *Euphydryas editha* and its larval host plants, combining ecological, behavioral, and evolutionary perspectives. The result is an understanding of spatial and temporal patterns of insect-larval host plant association, including the evolution of new host associations. Niklas Janz (chap. 11) addresses the relationship between genetic control of oviposition preference and of larval performance, using *Polygonia c-album* as a study system. He finds that the former is sex-linked, while the latter is not. This finding has strong implications for the ease of host race formation and population differentiation, as well as for patterns of association between insects and their hosts. Both studies provide a link to the next section, which explores genetics and evolution explicitly.

Taken together, the studies in this section illuminate the factors that shape the distribution and abundance of butterfly faunas in space and time, but with take-home messages that translate well to other species and interactions due to the generality of the deduced concept structure and the range of variation exhibited by butterflies.

CHAPTER 6

Phenofaunistics: Seasonality as a Property of Butterfly Faunas

Arthur M. Shapiro, Richard VanBuskirk, Greg Kareofelas,
and William D. Patterson

For growth and nourishment the climate is the most important factor, and in general the character of the season as a whole; for when rain, fair weather, and storms occur opportunely, all crops bear well.... It is the year that bears, not the field.

Theophrastus, *Inquiry into Plants*, ca. 300 B.C.

WHY PHENOLOGY?

Phenology, the study of the timing of biological events, is one of the oldest of the agricultural sciences. Theophrastus and other authors of classical antiquity collected, collated, and commented upon the folk wisdom of agrarians and pastoralists of many cultures. All had developed methods for estimating the timing of events often critical to their survival. The importance of biological seasonality to ancient and modern indigenous peoples is manifest in the centrality of calendrical systems and astronomy in their lives. Modern phenology, like that of the ancients, concerns itself with understanding, modeling, and predicting the effects of seasons and weather on the life cycles of individual species—commonly, crops and pests. Today, however, the study of phenology has taken on new urgency in the context of "global change" and a perceived conservation crisis. Although species remain at issue in this context, larger ecological units are also of concern under the umbrella of "biodiversity." Economic considerations are no longer the only drivers of phenological research.

Phenology was incorporated into both European and American ecological traditions, largely (but not entirely) as an autecological or physiological rather than a synecological specialty. European (essentially Braun-Blanquet) phytosociology is an efficient method for characterizing and mapping plant associations employed in much of the world. Within this tradition, "symphenology" (community-level seasonality) has been used both descriptively and analytically, particularly with reference to community "development" or succession (reviewed by Kruesi 1981). Such uses lay largely outside the consciousness of most recent American ecologists. It was evident to Darwin and other nineteenth-century naturalists that seasonality was an important element in shaping life histories, and what were later called "reproductive strategies," via natural selection. It was thus incorporated, albeit sporadically, at the interface of evolution and ecology where single-species life histories were at issue (and this is where phenology has continued to be of interest to butterfly workers). As a community-level phenomenon, however, phenology remained at the fringes of evolutionary ecology in America, surfacing briefly in Fretwell's *Populations in a Seasonal Environment* (1972) and in McMillan's (1960) attempt to embed the ecotype concept in some kind of community context. Phenology has suffered partly because most Americans are unfamiliar with the European approaches; partly because it is perceived as "a field technique of agricultural meteorology" (Lieth 1974, p. 3); and because the nature of phenological data poses frequently difficult statistical problems. We believe, however, that the foremost problem has been how to move from *phenomenology* to *analysis:* that is, how to use phenology to answer intellectually challenging ecological questions. This chapter is an introductory gesture in that direction, with butterflies the model system. It is not about hypothesis testing in the experimentalist's sense. Rather, it asks about pattern recognition in large datasets and how one can extract testable hypotheses from them. We are being consciously—and, we hope, intelligently—inductivistic here, even if that approach is out of fashion.

There is a vast literature of phenology, but the literature of insect phenology (except for agricultural pests) is surprisingly sparse, and that of butterfly phenology both sparse and very scattered. There is much phenological data embedded in local and regional faunas, but its suitability for analysis varies greatly, and rarely has any attempt been made to analyze it. A rare and fascinating exception, the extremely long "Marsham family dataset" (Sparks and Carey 1995), includes only one insect species—a butterfly, but as a hibernator, a singularly uninformative one! The "Leopold dataset" (Bradley et al. 1999), another long series successfully applied to the problem of recognizing climate change, includes no Lepidoptera. These cases may still be methodologically instructive. The best applications of phenology to insect ecology have consistently been by pollination ecologists, who have not only recognized many of the right questions to ask, but have also developed quantitative methods to deal with some of them. In the next two sections we briefly skim the butterfly literature, then that of pollination ecology.

    Arthur M. Shapiro, Richard VanBuskirk, Greg Kareofelas, and William D. Patterson

The first systematic and detailed study of the phenology of butterfly faunas was carried out in southern Europe by Roger Verity in the early twentieth century, and was brought together in two very wordy and diffuse, but conceptually rich, papers (Verity 1919, 1920). It is unclear how much of a debt Verity owes to the botanical phenologists, particularly the emerging Zurich-Montpellier school; certainly many of his concepts are very similar to theirs. He is particularly concerned with the rate of upslope progression of the season and the correspondence of altitude to latitude (a theme with roots extending at least back to Humboldt at the beginning of the nineteenth century). In the next 40 years phenology appears casually and anecdotally in the butterfly literature, but only rarely as a focus in itself. This silence was punctuated by a series of works on moth phenology by E. P. Wiltshire, culminating in an attempt at a "phenological classification of the Palearctic Lepidoptera" (Wiltshire 1941).

The two Donner Pass papers of Emmel and Emmel (1962; Emmel 1963) explored aspects of the climatic determination of phenology in a montane setting. These two papers were ahead of their time in relating flight seasons to climatic variation and in treating them as adaptive phenomena. They also represented the first phenological study done in a montane setting in North America, raising anew issues Verity had considered in isolation over 40 years before. Very soon thereafter, the "MacArthur school" of ecology allowed phenology to be placed squarely within an evolutionary-ecological context: after the publication of Ricklefs's 1966 paper, time could be seen as a *resource,* potentially the object of competition, and subject to selective influences just as food or territories were.

At exactly this time a butterfly paper incorporating such thinking appeared in *Ecology.* It emanated not from a MacArthurian ecologist, but from Harry K. Clench, a butterfly taxonomist at the Carnegie Museum (Clench 1967). It argued that hesperiid phenology at a locality in western Pennsylvania had been shaped by competition for nectar. There was no attempt at a quantitative demonstration that the alleged phenomenon was real, or reproducible elsewhere. (In fact, A. M. S. wrote Clench that it was not the same in eastern Pennsylvania, and the point was made emphatically for other localities by Shuey [1986] 19 years later.) This paper would never survive the review process today, but the field is much richer for its having done so then, as its appearance placed important issues on the table.

Another study independently embracing faunal-level phenology appeared on the West Coast at about this time (Opler and Langston 1968), and was followed by several tropical papers (Emmel and Leck 1970; Owen and Chanter 1972; Sears 1970) and a cluster of papers from Japan (Morisita 1967; Yamamoto 1973, 1976, 1977). Opler and Langston approached phenology in relation to geography and ecology, including host plant relationships; like that of the Emmels, their work was not only descriptive but at least qualitatively analytical. In 1974 Langston followed up on the themes of Opler and Langston (1968) by examining the prolonged emergence periods of coastal fog-belt butterflies in California.

Shapiro had discussed phenology in previous faunistic works, but in 1975 gave a prospect and overview of a long-term study across northern California, informed by a MacArthurian viewpoint. Austin (1978) presented a butterfly phenology for Pima County, Arizona, and Scott and Epstein (1987) a very informative one for Red Rocks Park, Jefferson County, Colorado. Kulfan (1990) published a related study for Borská nízina, Slovakia. A series of studies emanating from the Museum of Zoology of the National Autonomous University of Mexico (UNAM) has included outstanding phenological data and analysis (Luis and Llorente 1990; Luis et al. 1991; Vargas et al. 1991). All of these papers followed the Emmels and Opler and Langston in viewing phenology as an adaptation, or perhaps the result of a compromise among multiple selective pressures. Their faunas incorporated temperate, tropical lowland, and tropical montane components. Franco-Gaona et al. (1988) explored this aspect of phenology in a guild of crucifer-feeding Mexican Pieridae.

By far the largest pool of butterfly phenological data to have entered the literature is embedded in the British Butterfly Monitoring Scheme (Pollard 1991a; Pollard and Yates 1992). The BBMS and the deep, rich lepidopterological tradition in the United Kingdom have led to a number of well-designed and evolutionarily informed studies there, but the BBMS data have as yet not been "mined" very deeply. A good conceptual overview has been done by Porter et al. (1992); empirical examples of BBMS data are given by Pollard and Yates (1993). The shallow "mining" of these data reflects the difficulties in quantitative analysis.

From the standpoint of conservation, the importance of phenology has been underscored in the long-term studies of *Euphydryas editha* by the Ehrlich group (Ehrlich and Murphy 1987), and it appears with increasing frequency in life table, key factor, and viability analyses of rare and endangered butterflies, as well as in studies of reproductive biology and resource allocation. These studies, however, are at the autecological level, or at most address host plant–herbivore or herbivore-parasitoid trophic interactions, and we will not review them here.

Wolda (1988), in a sweeping review of insect seasonality, lamented the lack of statistical methods available for treating such data. Wolda's review cites various attempts at methodological innovation, nearly all of which have languished as dead ends—and not only in the butterfly literature. Some of these, such as the "seasonal standard deviation" of Greenfield (1982),

Arthur M. Shapiro, Richard VanBuskirk, Greg Kareofelas, and William D. Patterson

deserved better. Wolda missed Crowley and Johnson's (1982) adaptation of Hurlbert's (1978) methods of quantifying temporal niche relationships in odonates. Undoubtedly there are many other similar efforts embedded in the ecological literature, but recovering them in the absence of distinctive keywords is a problem. Kruesi (1981), Lieth (1974), and Schnelle (1955) present methods derived from symphenology that might be adaptable to interesting mechanistic questions, but most are not obviously so—any more than Braun-Blanquet phytosociology has been instructive at the level of mechanisms of community organization. (Just as Raunkiaer's abundance classes led to the negative binomial and ultimately to MacArthurian approaches to resource partitioning, descriptive statistics have an essential foundational role in an analytical phenology.)

THE POLLINATION ECOLOGY PRECEDENT

The best model for butterfly workers is provided by pollination biologists, who almost alone among those concerned with phenology have made use of the MacArthur tradition. Wolda's review largely misses this point. Phenology has interested pollination biologists because of the possibility that the seasonal distribution of flowering in plant communities reflects competition for a resource: pollinators. A working hypothesis has been that this distribution reflects the process of character displacement (Rathcke 1988; Murray et al. 1987). Table 6.1 is an attempt to translate the parameters of flowering phenology used by pollination biologists into lepidopterological terms, with some references to published methods. Most of these methods depend on counts and thus need to be redesigned to apply to qualitative (presence-absence) data. Most use fixed plots in which species-specific phenophases are quantified. For butterfly workers, transect methods are likely to work better.

Another strength of pollination ecology as a model is that it has been strongly influenced by the "Florida State school," which demands rigorous statistical demonstration of the reality of a phenomenon before it can or should be "explained." This "null model approach" appears in a related context in the limnological literature (Richerson et al. 1976). It is precisely this approach, well demonstrated in the work of Poole and Rathcke (1979) and Rathcke (1984), that by its absence vitiates the work of Clench (1967). Butterfly ecology has remained arrested at the stage of Anderson and Hubricht (1940), who, by classifying plant species by eyeball into phenophases, developed habitat-specific phenological summaries for the plants at the Missouri Botanical Garden and related these narratively to climate—precisely what Shapiro (1975b) did for California butterflies 35 years later!

Table 6.1 Some equivalencies between parameters used in pollination ecology and (potentially) by lepidopterists

Parameter in Pollination Ecology	Butterfly Equivalent	References
Flowering commencement (date of first flowering)	First flight or appearance date	
Rate of flowering (cumulative number of flowers vs. time)	Cumulative number of adults counted vs. time	
Course of flowering (number of flowering units vs. time) (date vs. proportion of all flowers observed, that were open that date)	Number of adults counted vs. time (substitute adults counted)	Rathcke 1988
Peak of flowering (date of maximum number of flowers)	(substitute adults counted)	
Dispersion of flowering (uses variance/mean ratio or compares observed variance to expected variance based on randomly dispersed means and a uniform distribution)	(substitute adults counted; measures degree of aggregation in time in the adult population)	Poole and Rathcke 1979
Flowering overlaps (several methods, some based on null models)	Computational methods and required data vary. Some OK with +/− only	Herrera 1986; Murray et al. 1987; Rathcke 1988; Poole and Rathcke 1979; Primack 1980
Consistency of flowering sequence among years	Consistency of adult flight periods (example in this paper, a variant on the method in the reference)	Rathcke 1984
Flowering termination	Last flight or appearance date	
Sexual sequence (commonly protandrous; complicated by monoecious vs. dioecious vs. andromonoecious spp.)	Number or percentage of each sex by date, or sex ratio	

Source: Modified from Dafni 1992, table 3.

Pollination ecology provides methodological guideposts for us, as table 6.1 shows. Whether or not butterflies as pollinators are important selective forces in flowering phenology is beside the point.

THE VACA HILLS: A SPECIMEN FAUNA

The Vaca Hills are part of the Inner North Coast Ranges, located near Vacaville, California. The climate is Mediterranean, with mild, wet winters and hot, dry summers. The prevailing vegetation types are blue oak (*Quercus douglasii*) woodland; "hard chaparral" (dominated by chamise, *Adenostoma fasciculatum*); interior live oak (*Quercus wislizenii*) woodland; and a rich riparian woodland including Fremont cottonwood (*Populus fremontii*),

Arthur M. Shapiro, Richard VanBuskirk, Greg Kareofelas, and William D. Patterson

several willows (*Salix* spp.), big-leaf maple (*Acer macrophyllum*), and white alder (*Alnus rhombifolia*). A butterfly fauna for Thompson Canyon, located in this range, with ecological and geological overviews was published by Shields (1988). One of us (A. M. S.) began monitoring the butterfly fauna of another canyon in this range, Gates Canyon, in 1976. Gates Canyon (elevation 190–600 m) is an east-west oriented, mostly steep-sided canyon traversed by Alamo Creek. The creek flows all year in wet years but dries up at the surface in summer in dry years. The north-facing slope of Gates Canyon is dominated by interior live oak, which forms a nearly continuous canopy, with a rich, diverse, mostly perennial understory. The south-facing slope supports relatively open blue oak woodland, with a grassy understory dominated in most places by Mediterranean annuals. The ridgetops are occupied mostly by chamise. These habitats support distinctive faunas, with some species largely limited to one or another of them (see also Sugden et al. 1985).

G. K. and W. D. P. were authorized by the Quail Ridge Wilderness Conservancy, a local land trust, to conduct a butterfly survey of another site in the Vaca Hills. Quail Ridge is a small peninsula (780 ha) at the southern end of Lake Berryessa some 14.1 km north of Gates Canyon. It has a jumbled topography with elevations of approximately 120–400 m and is covered mostly by mixed oak woodland, with native bunchgrass on north-facing slopes as well as chaparral on south-facing slopes and ridges and some riparian habitat: substantially the same set of communities as at Gates Canyon, but in different proportions. Sampling was conducted from 1993 through 1997.

The sampling protocols were not designed for comparison, and were not identical. A. M. S. samples Gates Canyon by walking the road, which follows Alamo Creek for most of its length. G. K. and W. D. P. walked a convoluted trail through Quail Ridge. A. M. S. attempts to sample at as close to 14-day intervals as possible. Sampling at Quail Ridge has been less regular. All species seen are recorded by all observers. Individuals are not normally counted. At the peak of species richness the numbers of both individuals and species are too great to permit simultaneous counting, even orally by tape recorder or with a battery of hand-held tally counters. A. M. S.'s data are collected only on "good butterfly days," and if the weather changes for the worse during a sample, the data are discarded (this rarely happens). G. K. and W. D. P. recorded all species seen, regardless of weather, but for this study "poor butterfly days" are excluded. The habitats, methodology, and butterfly faunas will be described elsewhere, and are not terribly important here. The purpose of this chapter is to use the resulting data to test quantitative approaches to such datasets, and for this it is necessary only to assume that the data were collected using consistent methods and that the identifications are accurate. A. M. S. has 27 years of data from Gates Canyon; we chose to compare only the 5 years for which simultaneous sampling was in effect. We thus ignore for the purposes of this chapter any additional species recorded in other years.

During 1993–1997, we recorded 66 butterfly species at Quail Ridge and 69 at Gates Canyon. Each site has two resident species at or near the edges of their ranges, not found at the other site. There is a significant fauna of weedy, low-elevation, multivoltine species associated with agriculture in the lower third of Gates Canyon. These species are not resident at Quail Ridge, but colonize it, typically in the second half of the season, when Lake Berryessa is low and agricultural weeds appear on the exposed shoreline; they are then exterminated when the lake level rises. During the latter part of the study period the lake was high, and these species (hereinafter referred to as "weedy") occurred only sporadically at Quail Ridge. During the extended drought of the 1980s they had been a regular component of the fauna.

The actual seasonal, faunistic data are available at www.press.uchicago.edu/books/boggs/ or from the first author. Tables 6.2 and 6.3 break down the faunal overlap between sites.

Given these observations, what can we say quantitatively about phenology as a property of butterfly faunas *as faunas?*

The data can be represented graphically in a variety of ways. The simplest is a plot of the number of species flying versus the date, as in Anderson and Hubricht (1940). Figure 6.1 plots the numbers of species flying at both sites each year. Figure 6.2 combines the five yearly plots by site. The former allows a visual assessment of within-year, between-site consistency, the latter of between-year, within-site consistency. Both figures give an impression of nonrandomness. Each site has a more or less characteristic seasonal curve. There is a strong spring maximum (seemingly divided into an early and a late spring peak, more distinct in some years than in others), often with a late summer–early autumn secondary peak. For both sites, the curve for 1995 looks aberrant, and in the same way. Can we move beyond this vagueness?

ARE THERE PATTERNS HERE? REALLY?

An alternative way to visualize the progress of the flight season is by the accumulation of species with time. Figure 6.3 compares the species accumulation curves within years and between sites; figure 6.4 does the reverse. Again, 1995 seems anomalous. We can test the notion of pattern in these curves by comparing them statistically with an appropriate null model. This is not as straightforward as it sounds. What *is* an appropriate null model?

One could use a Kolmogorov-Smirnov (KS) test against a uniform distribution, assuming that new species would accumulate uniformly over the flight season so that the rate of species accumulation with time would be linear. One cannot make any assumptions about the distribution of the data, so a nonparametric test is called for. The problem, as posed, creates an odd

Arthur M. Shapiro, Richard VanBuskirk, Greg Kareofelas, and William D. Patterson

Table 6.2 Species lists for Gates Canyon and Quail Ridge

Species Name	Gates	Quail	Species Name	Gates	Quail
Adelpha bredowii	X	X	Lycaena xanthoides	X	X
Amblyscirtes vialis		X	Mitoura johnsoni		X
Anthocaris sara	X	X	Nymphalis antiopa	X	X
Atalopedes campestris	X	X	Nymphalis californica	X	X
Atlides halesus	X	X	Nymphalis milberti	X	
Battus philenor	X	X	Ochlodes agricola	X	X
Brephidium exile	X	X	Ochlodes sylvanoides	X	X
Callophrys dumetorum	X	X	Papilio eurymedon	X	X
Celastrina a. echo	X	X	Papilio multicaudatus	X	
Cercyonis p. boopis		X	Papilio rutulus	X	X
Charidryas palla	X	X	Papilio zelicaon	X	X
Coenonympha tullia	X	X	Paratrytone melane	X	X
Colias eurytheme	X	X	Pholisora catullus	X	
Danaus plexippus	X	X	Phyciodes mylitta	X	X
Epargyreus clarus	X		Pieris napi	X	X
Erynnis b. lacustra		X	Pieris rapae	X	X
Erynnis pacuvius	X	X	Polites sabuleti	X	
Erynnis persius	X		Polygonia satyrus	X	X
Erynnis propertius	X	X	Polygonia zephyrus	X	
Erynnis tristis	X	X	Pontia protodice	X	X
Euchloe ausonides	X	X	Pontia sisymbrii	X	X
Euphydryas chalcedona	X	X	Pyrgus communis	X	X
Euphydryas editha		X	Satyrium auretorum	X	X
Everes comyntas	X	X	Satyrium californicum	X	X
Glaucopsyche lygdamus	X	X	Satyrium saepium	X	X
Habrodais grunus		X	Satyrium sylvinus	X	
Heliopetes ericetorum	X	X	Satyrium tetra	X	X
Hesperia columbia	X	X	Speyeria callippe		X
Hesperia lindseyi		X	Speyeria coronis	X	X
Hylephila phyleus	X	X	Strymon melinus	X	X
Icaricia acmon	X	X	Tharsalea arota	X	
Icaricia icarioides	X	X	Thessalia leanira	X	X
Incisalia a. iroides	X	X	Thorybes pylades	X	X
Junonia coenia	X	X	Vanessa annabella	X	X
Leptotes marina	X		Vanessa atalanta	X	X
Lerodea eufala	X		Vanessa cardui	X	X
Limenitis lorquini	X	X	Vanessa virginiensis	X	X
Lycaena gorgon	X	X	Zerene eurydice	X	X
Lycaena helloides	X	X			
			Totals:	69	66
			(77 spp. combined)		

statistical difficulty. If species occurred completely at random (such that one were equally likely to see them on any day of the season), then they would accumulate in a uniform manner only if each species were observed only once during the season. Otherwise, the first date when a species is observed is always the date of interest, which inevitably pushes the distribution toward the early part of the season. Poole and Rathcke (1979) and Wolda (1988) both recognized this problem.

Table 6.3 Missing species by year for Gates Canyon and Quail Ridge

	1993	1994	1995	1996	1997
A. Gates Canyon					
Brephidium exile	(2)	(1)	(5)	Absent	Absent
Epargyreus clarus	Absent	(1)	Absent	Absent	Absent
Erynnis pacuvius	(1)	(2)	Absent	Absent	Absent
Heliopetes ericetorum	(2)	(1)	(1)	Absent	(2)
Hesperia columbia	(1)	Absent	(1)	(2)	(2)
Icaricia icarioides	(3)	(3)	Absent	(3)	(4)
Leptotes marina	Absent	(1)	Absent	Absent	Absent
Lerodea eufala	(2)	Absent	Absent	(4)	(1)
Lycaena helloides	Absent	Absent	(2)	Absent	(1)
Lycaena xanthoides	Absent	Absent	(1)	(1)	(1)
Nymphalis milberti	Absent	Absent	Absent	(1)	Absent
Polites sabuleti	Absent	Absent	Absent	(1)	(3)
Polygonia zephyrus	(1)	(2)	Absent	(2)	(1)
Pontia protodice	(2)	(2)	(1)	Absent	Absent
Tharsalea arota	Absent	Absent	(1)	(1)	(1)
Thessalia leanira	Absent	(1)	Absent	Absent	(1)
Thorybes pylades	(3)	(3)	Absent	(4)	(3)
Vanessa atalanta	Absent	(9)	(8)	(14)	(14)
Vanessa virginiensis	(1)	(3)	(4)	(3)	Absent
Total absences	9	7	10	8	7
B. Quail Ridge					
Amblyscirtes vialis	(5)	(2)	Absent	(2)	(4)
Atalopedes campestris	(4)	(3)	(1)	Absent	(2)
Brephidium exile	(2)	(1)	Absent	Absent	Absent
Cercyonis p. boopis	(4)	(3)	(3)	(3)	Absent
Erynnis b. lacustra	(1)	Absent	Absent	Absent	Absent
Erynnis pacuvius	(1)	Absent	(1)	(1)	(1)
Euchloe ausonides	(5)	Absent	(6)	(3)	Absent
Euphydryas editha	(1)	Absent	Absent	Absent	Absent
Everes comyntas	Absent	(1)	Absent	Absent	(1)
Habrodais grunus	(1)	Absent	Absent	Absent	Absent
Heliopetes ericetorum	Absent	Absent	(1)	Absent	Absent
Hesperia lindseyi	Absent	(1)	Absent	Absent	Absent
Hylephila phyleus	(4)	(1)	Absent	Absent	Absent
Icaricia icarioides	(2)	Absent	(3)	(1)	(1)
Lycaena helloides	(2)	(5)	(1)	Absent	Absent
Lycaena xanthoides	(2)	(2)	Absent	(2)	(1)
Mitoura johnsoni	Absent	Absent	Absent	(1)	Absent
Ochlodes sylvanoides	(6)	(4)	(4)	(2)	Absent
Pieris rapae	(15)	(7)	Absent	(4)	Absent
Polygonia satyrus	(1)	Absent	Absent	(2)	(2)
Pontia protodice	(1)	(3)	Absent	Absent	Absent
Pyrgus communis	(3)	Absent	(2)	Absent	Absent
Speyeria callippe	Absent	Absent	(2)	Absent	Absent
Speyeria coronis	Absent	Absent	Absent	Absent	(1)
Zerene eurydice	(1)	(1)	Absent	(1)	(2)
Total absences	6	12	15	14	16

Note: Parenthetical numbers indicate the total number of weeks a species was present in years when it was present.

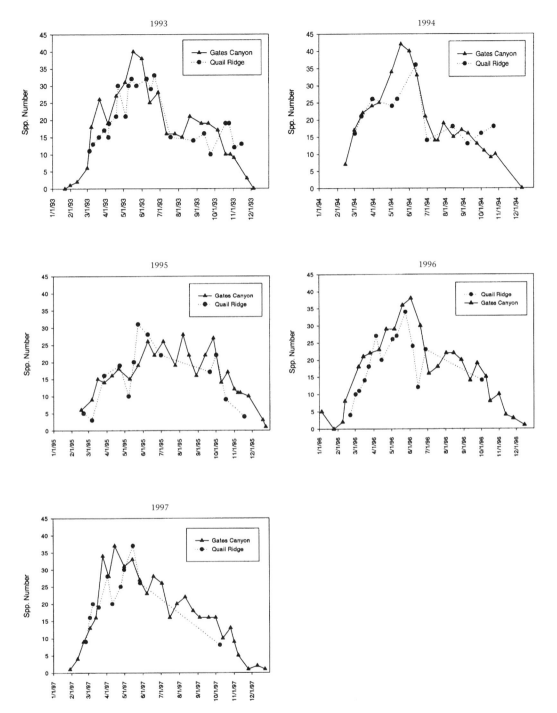

Figure 6.1 Numbers of species flying at different times of the year at Gates Canyon and Quail Ridge in the years 1993–1997.

A

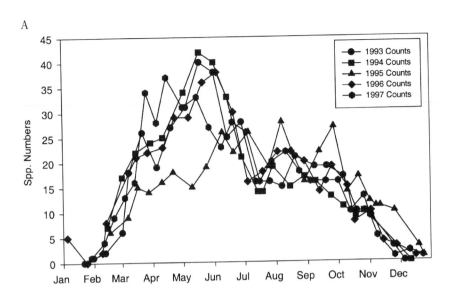

B

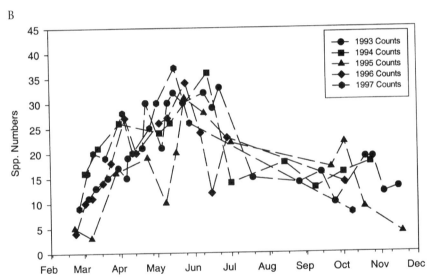

Figure 6.2 Numbers of species observed at different times of the year across all years at (A) Gates Canyon and (B) Quail Ridge.

One solution is to derive a null distribution of first appearance dates by randomly mixing up the observation dates and calculating the empirical distribution of first appearance times for each species under a large number of permutations. For the *n* census dates in a given year at a given site, there are *n*! possible permutations of the presence-absence data. Each permutation can be scored for the earliest census date on which there is a recorded presence. Since *n*! is very large for this dataset, a subset of 500 random permutations was generated for each site/year combination. This collection of random permutations accounts for the apparent bias described above and

Arthur M. Shapiro, Richard VanBuskirk, Greg Kareofelas, and William D. Patterson

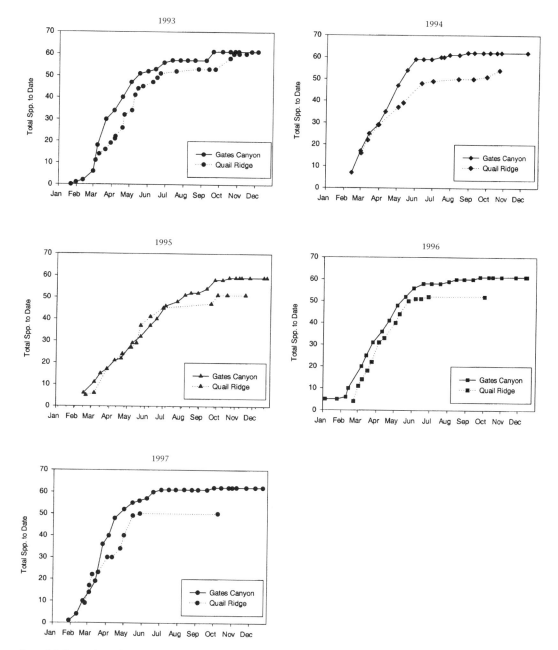

Figure 6.3 Comparison of species accumulation curves for Gates Canyon and Quail Ridge in the years 1993–1997.

generates a hypothetical distribution under the assumption of uniformity. The permutation-derived dates of first appearance are then used to calculate the expected proportion of species first seen on a given census date, which can be plotted for all census dates in a given year. This null distribution of species accumulation can finally be compared with the observed species accumulation curves (figs. 6.5A, 6.5B).

A

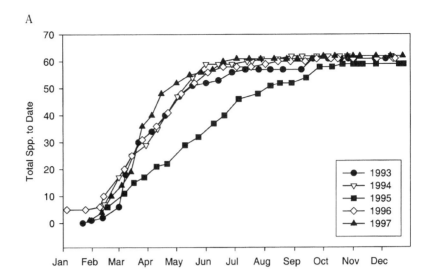

B

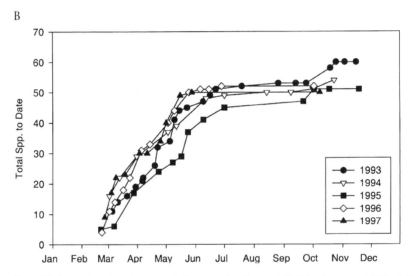

Figure 6.4 Comparison of species accumulation curves for all years at (A) Gates Canyon and (B) Quail Ridge.

In practice, we settled on the Smirnov statistic J rather than the more familiar KS test, which would apply if both distributions were unknown rather than theoretical. The results are given in table 6.4. The only year for which the uniform distribution was a good approximation was 1994, for which the null hypothesis was not rejected at either site, though barely so for Gates Canyon. We conclude, with a reasonable degree of confidence, that there is a nonrandom pattern to seasonal emergence in these butterfly faunas. If it were otherwise, this chapter would be over. (If the 5 years at each site are treated as replicates of the same dataset, the statistics are much more equivocal; then only half the years are significantly different from random.) We would expect this pattern to reflect adaptation to climate and resources, just as Raunkiaer's life form spectra do.

Arthur M. Shapiro, Richard VanBuskirk, Greg Kareofelas, and William D. Patterson

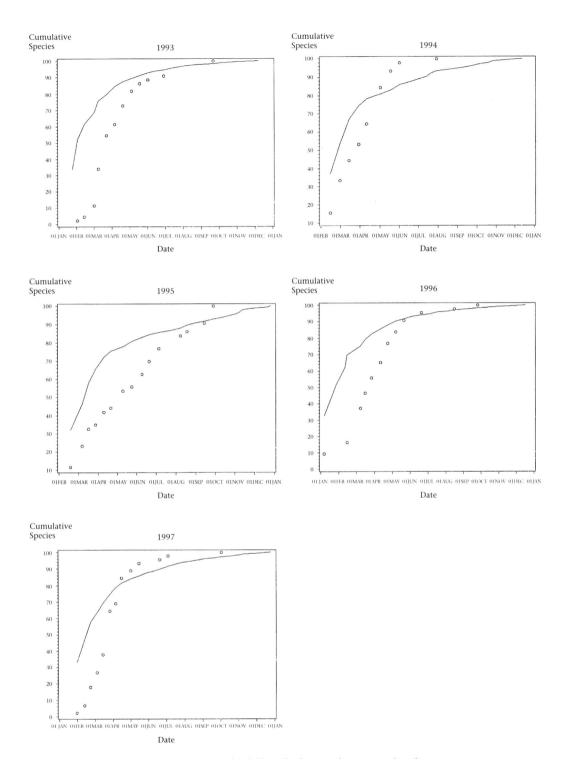

Figure 6.5A Observed (open circles) and theoretical (solid line) distributions of emergence dates for Gates Canyon, 1993–1997.

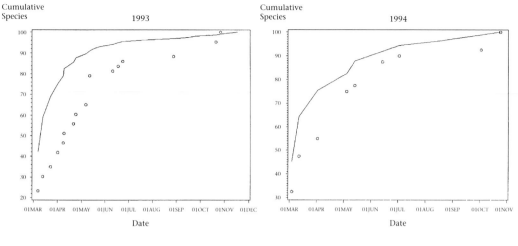

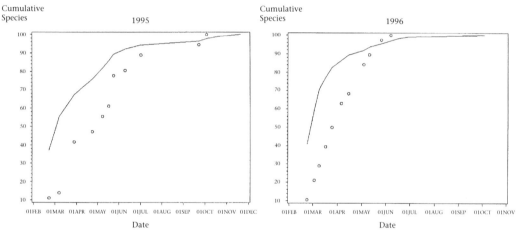

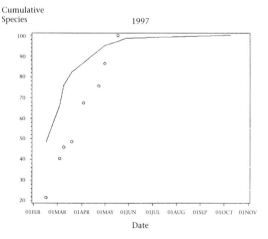

Figure 6.5B Observed (open circles) and theoretical (solid line) distributions of emergence dates for Quail Ridge, 1993–1997.

Table 6.4 Statistical analysis of comparisons between null and observed distributions of emergence times

Site	Year	n	Δ	J	p Value
Gates Canyon	1993	69	0.24	1.98	0.0004
Gates Canyon	1994	69	0.14	1.19	0.0599
Gates Canyon	1995	69	0.18	1.50	0.0110
Gates Canyon	1996	69	0.18	1.47	0.0135
Gates Canyon	1997	69	0.19	1.56	0.0079
Quail Ridge	1993	66	0.20	1.62	0.0052
Quail Ridge	1994	66	0.09	0.72	0.3412
Quail Ridge	1995	66	0.18	1.50	0.0112
Quail Ridge	1996	66	0.22	1.80	0.0015
Quail Ridge	1997	66	0.20	1.61	0.0056

BETWEEN AND WITHIN SITES AND YEARS

The empirical distribution of first appearance dates can be used to compare distributions between sites within years and among years within sites. Since the compared distributions are all unknown and estimated from data, KS tests are appropriate here. If observations were more similar between sites within years than the reverse, the first set of KS pairwise statistics should be smaller as a group than the second set. There is a potential pseudoreplication problem here, since there are 10 pairs of years that can be compared at any one site, but based only on 5 years of data. Let us, however, ignore that problem and look at tables 6.5 and 6.6.

Within each site there are one or two years that are clearly different from the others. At Gates Canyon (as usual) 1995 stands out, while at Quail Ridge 1996 and 1997 are significantly different from the others. However, at Quail Ridge, the years differ among themselves overall more than at Gates Canyon, where 1993, 1994, and 1996 are quite similar among themselves. In addition to the more irregular sampling regime at Quail Ridge, we suspect this reflects the buffering effect of the dominant north- and south-facing slopes at Gates (which tends to prolong overall flight seasons for species shared between the two sites). If we look at variability between sites within years, the differences are less marked, with a more than marginally significant difference only in 1994.

There are several ways of further treating these data to make them easier to assimilate, cluster analysis and multidimensional scaling analysis among them. We opted for the latter (fig. 6.6). This graph emphasizes that 1995 was a very unusual year phenologically, especially at Gates Canyon. (The spring of 1995 was very cold and wet *regionally*, with many species emerging very late and even losing an entire generation at low elevations. This was "obvious" to an observer on the ground, but it is reassuring that it is recoverable from the dataset even in the absence of such first-hand impressions.)

Table 6.5 Statistical analysis of patterns of emergence between years for
Gates Canyon and Quail Ridge

Comparison	Δ	J	p Value
A. Gates Canyon			
93 × 94	0.22	1.290	0.358
93 × 95	0.38	2.210	0.0001
93 × 96	0.12	0.730	0.3309
93 × 97	0.23	1.356	0.0253
94 × 95	0.42	2.465	<0.0001
94 × 96	0.17	1.001	0.1342
94 × 97	0.24	1.436	0.0162
95 × 96	0.40	2.322	<0.0001
95 × 97	0.45	2.626	<0.0001
96 × 97	0.19	1.135	0.0759
B. Quail Ridge			
93 × 94	0.33	1.867	0.0009
93 × 95	0.24	1.351	0.0260
93 × 96	0.24	1.364	0.0242
93 × 97	0.41	2.329	<0.0001
94 × 95	0.34	1.931	0.0006
94 × 96	0.23	1.293	0.0354
94 × 97	0.31	1.809	0.0014
95 × 96	0.37	2.125	0.0001
95 × 97	0.39	2.256	<0.0001
96 × 97	0.22	1.243	0.0456

Table 6.6 Statistical analysis of patterns of emergence between Gates Canyon and
Quail Ridge by year

Year	Δ	J	p Value
1993	0.21	1.240	0.0461
1994	0.33	1.934	0.0006
1995	0.22	1.276	0.0386
1996	0.18	1.020	0.1245
1997	0.19	1.120	0.0814

This graph also tells us that the most similar site/year combinations
are for the same site in different years—Gates Canyon 1994/1996 and
1993/1997, and Quail Ridge 1993/1995 and 1994/1996/1997. Note that good
matches at one site may not be mirrored at the other. Note also that there
is plenty of variability within sites, so that, for example, 1993 and 1996 at
Quail Ridge are no more similar than a number of the intersite comparisons,
even those not involving the same year (compare table 6.6). There is considerable individuality in annual patterns even within the broader site-specific
interannual ones—that is to say, each site has a characteristic pattern, but
the data are quite noisy. The interannual similarities and differences may be

Arthur M. Shapiro, Richard VanBuskirk, Greg Kareofelas, and William D. Patterson

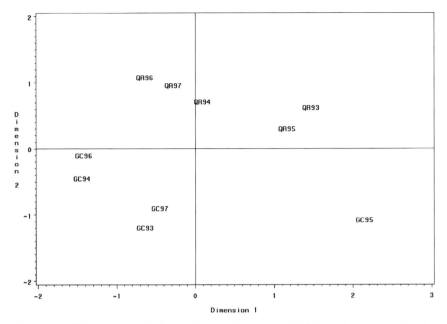

Figure 6.6 Multidimensional scaling for Kendall correlations among distributions of emergence dates at Gates Canyon (GC) and Quail Ridge (QR) by years. Proximity implies similarity.

quite useful in identifying weather events important to butterfly phenology, but that goes beyond the scope of this chapter. It is, however, useful to know that purely local noise can be recognized superimposed on regional pattern.

There is nothing sacred about Kendall correlations here. We could repeat the analysis using Spearman or Pearson correlations to see how sensitive the picture is to the type of correlation used. Intuitively, we would expect little difference. But a multidimensional scaling analysis involves reducing high-dimensionality data down to a lower dimension in a way that loses as little information as possible. If the second and third dimensions were very similar in the amount of information they contained, a change in the type of correlation might reverse their order; thus the plot generated from Spearman correlations might involve essentially the first and third dimensions from the Kendall analysis, and thus might look quite different.

POINTS OF ORDER

Now that we are entitled to say that the butterfly flight season is phenologically nonrandom, we are in a position to examine the properties of the specific sequences of emergences: is the *order* of species emergence patterned within sites between years and between sites within years? We need to do more Kendall correlations.

Kendall's τ_b statistic is based on the proportion of species pairs that are concordant between the two datasets, meaning that they appear in the same

Table 6.7 Kendall concordance coefficients for species sequences by site and year

Comparison	Concordance (W)	p Value
Among years at Quail Ridge	0.3909	<0.0001
Among years at Gates Canyon	0.1941	<0.0001
Among sites in 1993	0.0625	0.1336
Among sites in 1994	0.1512	0.0196
Among sites in 1995	0.0069	0.6171
Among sites in 1996	0.0123	0.5050
Among sites in 1997	0.0193	0.4047

order in the particular comparison. If the two sets are unrelated, the proportion should be about 0.5. However, τ_b is rescaled so it can be interpreted as a correlation coefficient (it ranges between -1 and $+1$; independence generates a 0 value). This approach can be generalized to more than two populations—for example, to a summary statistic based on all 5 years' data at a site—using Kendall's coefficient of concordance, W. Testing for independence based on W is equivalent to a Friedman test for systematic differences in the emergence dates of the butterfly species.

To do this comparison we must reduce the data to the species appearing at both sites during each year, and so on—usually about 35 species. The results are striking (table 6.7). There is a very strong similarity in species sequence within sites among years, but almost none within years between sites. That is, the sequence of species emergences is site-specific; *pace* Theophrastus, it is the field that bears, not the year.

EVENNESS OF TURNOVER

We now know that emergence dates are not uniformly distributed over the flight season. But are they clustered, as Clench (1967) and Shapiro (1975b) both thought their faunas were? Consider Gates Canyon in 1996. There were 26 sampling days. Between any two samples there was usually some change in species composition: things come and go. There may be times of the year when there is little change and spurts of high turnover at other times.

As usual, this question can be approached in a number of ways. We can look at the actual numbers of species gained and lost, or the percentage of change in the fauna between samples, or we can use one or more indices of faunal similarity. Such indices—there are many of them—incorporate information about the number of species in each sample and the number shared between them. The various indices in common use weight these items differently, some emphasizing similarity, some emphasizing difference, and some emphasizing the comparability of the faunal sizes. There is no reason why they cannot be used in the temporal as well as the spatial dimension.

Arthur M. Shapiro, Richard VanBuskirk, Greg Kareofelas, and William D. Patterson

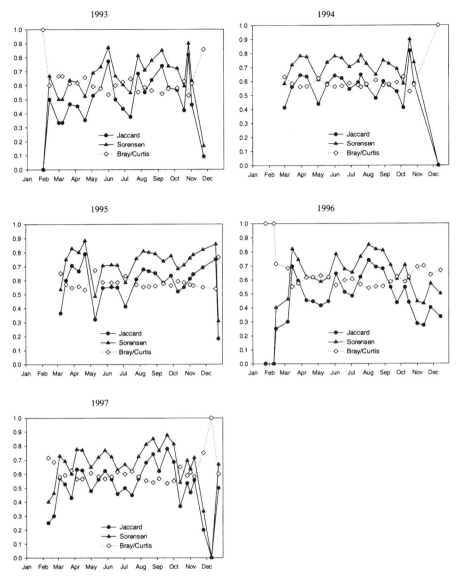

Figure 6.7A Indices of similarity/dissimilarity for Gates Canyon fauna for the years 1993–1997. Similarity/dissimilarity is calculated between the date on which the index is plotted and the previous date.

We calculated two indices of similarity, Jaccard's and Sørensen's (Magurran 1988), for each successive pair of samples for each site and year and plotted these as a curve against Julian date. The results (figs. 6.7A, 6.7B) give some idea of the evenness of faunal turnover and the timing and consistency of periods of high versus negligible turnover during the flight season. We also used an index of dissimilarity (Bray and Curtis 1957), which should be approximately the mirror image of the others. Visual inspection of the results reveals some obvious problems with this approach.

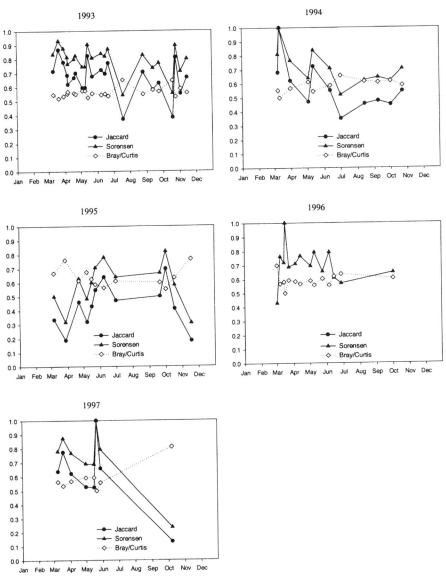

Figure 6.7B Indices of similarity/dissimilarity for Quail Ridge fauna for the years 1993–1997. Similarity/dissimilarity is calculated between the date on which the index is plotted and the previous date.

Faunal similarity at our sites behaves differently early and late in the flight season. This is partly due to the smaller faunas after early summer and partly due to the weedy species that figure in the faunas mainly later in the season, more consistently at Gates Canyon than at Quail Ridge. Strays of weedy species may cause the species composition to oscillate wildly, but in "good" autumns the weedy species may saturate the region and produce faunal uniformity instead. At the very end of the season everything is very scarce, and there is a high contribution of chance to what is actually picked up in a given sample. (One way to get at this problem is to observe the

Arthur M. Shapiro, Richard VanBuskirk, Greg Kareofelas, and William D. Patterson

frequency of reappearances in successive samples. When species wink in and out repeatedly, this normally reflects low density and a high risk of missing them.)

At both sites one thing is clear: there is a major species turnover in late spring-early summer, corresponding to the disappearance of the set of mostly univoltine species that use buckeye (*Aesculus californica*) as a major nectar source: *Euphydryas chalcedona,* several *Satyrium* species, *Ochlodes agricola,* and the second brood of *Celastrina argiolus echo.* The consistency of this association suggests that the timing of adult emergence in these species may have been selected regionally, if not globally, to coincide with the availability of this resource.

We expect to develop this subject further by using overlap indices, as employed by pollination ecologists (Rathcke 1988). The methods of Vargas et al. (1997), which appeared too late for development in this chapter, may be very useful in addressing this and other phenological problems, and we are exploring their applications. Another approach that impinges on both this question and the sequence of emergences involves correlating the faunal compositions for the closest-Julian-date samples in the 5-year period for each site, then plotting the correlations for each over the entire year. This approach should diagnose times of high and low predictability in the fauna. (One complication is Julian "ties," in which two samples in year 2 are equidistant in time from one in year 1. We could do the correlation in both directions, but cumulative errors in successive years would vitiate the method; we need a decision rule.) We will explore these themes in separate publications.

PREDICTABILITY OF FIRST FLIGHT DATES

How predictable are the first flight dates of species within sites? What ecological parameters might influence these dates? Shapiro and Shapiro (1973) claimed that for Staten Island, New York, the first flight dates of univoltine species emerging later in the season varied less in response to weather than did those of univoltines emerging earlier. But they had a sample of only 2 years. Our data are presented in tables 6.8 and 6.9.

We need to have a dimensionless measure, getting rid of calendar dates. We calculated the mean first appearance dates for each species across the 5 years at each site (for species present in at least 3 of the 5 years, thereby excluding the least frequent weedy and stray species). We then computed the departure from the mean for each original observation. Thus, for each species, we derived a table of 3–5 numbers representing the absolute value of the difference between each year's first appearance date and the mean first appearance date for that species. (Note that, since we are interested only in whether early or late emergence influences the predictability of emergence

Table 6.8 Mean date of first sighting and standard deviation for species at Gates Canyon

Species	Mean	SD (Days)	Species	Mean	SD (Days)
Adelpha bredowii	14 Apr	16.97	*Nymphalis californica*	17 Feb	14.81
Anthocaris sara	27 Feb	8.41	*Nymphalis milberti*	15 Mar	—
Atalopedes campestris	18 May	50.11	*Ochlodes agricola*	13 May	16.33
Atlides halesus	26 Apr	78.28	*Ochlodes sylvanoides*	14 Jul	16.65
Battus philenor	3 Mar	13.61	*Papilio eurymedon*	19 Apr	17.80
Brephidium exile	4 Sep	32.81	*Papilio multicaudatus*	2 May	16.33
Callophrys dumetorum	3 Apr	11.86	*Papilio rutulus*	29 Mar	7.28
Celastrina a. echo	10 Feb	21.87	*Papilio zelicaon*	27 Mar	14.54
Charidryas palla	20 Apr	18.80	*Paratrytone melane*	29 Apr	31.28
Coenonympha tullia	21 Mar	11.41	*Pholisora catullus*	26 Apr	44.09
Colias eurytheme	11 Mar	20.12	*Phyciodes mylitta*	5 Mar	2.88
Danaus plexippus	27 Apr	62.77	*Pieris napi*	27 Feb	8.41
Epargyreus clarus	2 May	—	*Pieris rapae*	12 Feb	24.20
Erynnis pacuvius	14 Jun	19.09	*Polites sabuleti*	6 Aug	68.59
Erynnis persius	9 Apr	49.01	*Polygonia satyrus*	21 Apr	91.16
Erynnis propertius	28 Feb	12.48	*Polygonia zephyrus*	13 Mar	36.75
Erynnis tristis	5 Apr	29.35	*Pontia protodice*	23 Jul	73.58
Euchloe ausonides	5 Mar	2.88	*Pontia sisymbrii*	21 Mar	13.09
Euphydryas chalcedona	26 Apr	12.97	*Pyrgus communis*	13 Apr	46.73
Everes comyntas	31 May	77.10	*Satyrium auretorum*	4 May	13.86
Glaucopsyche lygdamus	1 Mar	5.76	*Satyrium californicum*	4 May	13.86
Heliopetes ericetorum	19 May	77.98	*Satyrium saepium*	9 Jun	15.55
Hesperia columbia	13 Jul	84.41	*Satyrium sylvinus*	19 May	13.85
Hylephila phyleus	20 May	38.62	*Satyrium tetra*	25 May	11.22
Icaricia acmon	17 Apr	35.05	*Speyeria coronis*	22 May	14.87
Icaricia icarioides	11 Apr	17.46	*Strymon melinus*	17 Apr	38.20
Incisalia a. iroides	28 Feb	12.82	*Tharsalea arota*	10 Jul	25.24
Junonia coenia	11 Mar	10.26	*Thessalia leanira*	16 May	2.12
Leptotes marina	30 Mar	—	*Thorybes pylades*	5 Apr	12.00
Lerodea eufala	11 Sep	24.58	*Vanessa annabella*	4 Mar	51.25
Limenitis lorquini	12 Apr	16.64	*Vanessa atalanta*	4 Mar	81.29
Lycaena gorgon	16 May	10.64	*Vanessa cardui*	6 May	66.58
Lycaena helloides	14 Aug	95.46	*Vanessa virginiensis*	20 May	44.56
Lycaena xanthoides	19 Jun	16.00	*Zerene eurydice*	15 Apr	41.94
Nymphalis antiopa	5 Feb	18.26			

Note: No deviation is reported for species recorded in only one year.

date, it is the magnitude, and not the direction, of the deviation that is important. Hence, we discarded sign. On the other hand, the signs of the deviations would be important for other uses—such as deriving an index of overall earliness or lateness of the flight season for all species, or for designated subsets of them, such as univoltines, spring species, or tree feeders—all of which could potentially be informative anent certain hypotheses.)

Returning to the matter of predictability: using ANOVA, we can ask not only whether earliness and lateness are correlated with predictability, but a variety of other questions as well. We selected weediness, voltinism, and

Arthur M. Shapiro, Richard VanBuskirk, Greg Kareofelas, and William D. Patterson

Table 6.9 Mean date of first sighting and standard deviation for species at Quail Ridge

Species	Mean	SD (Days)	Species	Mean	SD (Days)
Adelpha bredowii	6 Apr	19.15	Lycaena gorgon	23 May	12.46
Amblyscirtes vialis	28 Apr	5.62	Lycaena helloides	31 Aug	70.09
Anthocaris sara	27 Feb	4.76	Lycaena xanthoides	1 Jun	14.71
Atalopedes campestris	21 Jun	70.84	Mitoura johnsoni	3 May	—
Atlides halesus	20 Jun	108.75	Nymphalis antiopa	27 Feb	4.76
Battus philenor	21 Mar	7.30	Nymphalis californica	26 Feb	5.39
Brephidium exile	21 Oct	2.83	Ochlodes agricola	11 May	8.23
Callophrys dumetorum	20 Mar	12.50	Ochlodes sylvanoides	15 Jul	21.59
Celastrina a. echo	26 Feb	5.39	Papilio eurymedon	5 Apr	17.85
Cercyonis p. boopis	16 Jun	10.66	Papilio rutulus	19 Apr	18.10
Charidryas palla	7 May	21.18	Papilio zelicaon	9 Mar	11.04
Coenonympha tullia	12 Mar	12.36	Paratrytone melane	23 May	27.25
Colias eurytheme	11 Mar	13.88	Phyciodes mylitta	18 Mar	14.45
Danaus plexippus	29 Apr	53.90	Pieris napi	1 Mar	6.04
Erynnis b. lacustra	15 May	—	Pieris rapae	21 Apr	19.63
Erynnis pacuvius	17 May	21.00	Polygonia satyrus	3 Mar	5.69
Erynnis propertius	6 Mar	12.97	Pontia protodice	28 Aug	82.02
Erynnis tristis	23 Mar	26.30	Pontia sisymbrii	2 Apr	27.83
Euchloe ausonides	20 Apr	50.72	Pyrgus communis	5 Oct	19.80
Euphydryas chalcedona	21 Apr	14.22	Satyrium auretorum	8 May	9.47
Euphydryas editha	9 Jun	—	Satyrium californicum	10 May	9.08
Everes comyntas	4 Jul	156.27	Satyrium saepium	4 Jun	14.77
Glaucopsyche lygdamus	8 Mar	7.44	Satyrium tetra	29 May	11.59
Habrodais grunus	26 Aug	—	Speyeria callippe	24 May	—
Heliopetes ericetorum	2 Oct	—	Speyeria coronis	16 May	—
Hesperia columbia	6 Apr	9.80	Strymon melinus	4 Jun	69.38
Hesperia lindseyi	12 Jun	—	Thessalia leanira	14 May	14.96
Hylephila phyleus	21 Oct	2.83	Thorybes pylades	20 Apr	10.43
Icaricia acmon	13 Mar	11.71	Vanessa annabella	2 Apr	42.76
Icaricia icarioides	29 Apr	8.37	Vanessa atalanta	16 Mar	23.80
Incisalia a. iroides	27 Mar	20.63	Vanessa cardui	30 Mar	14.82
Junonia coenia	6 Mar	12.19	Vanessa virginiensis	22 Jun	101.12
Limenitis lorquini	2 May	4.82	Zerene eurydice	3 Apr	16.39

Note: No deviation is reported for species recorded in only one year.

overwintering stage a priori as species attributes likely to affect year-to-year variation in emergence dates, without making predictions as to how they would do so. Each species was characterized as "weedy" or "nonweedy," uni-, bi-, or multivoltine, and by overwintering stage (egg, larva, pupa, adult; where more than one stage can overwinter, only the most common was entered; e.g., *Colias eurytheme,* larva; *Vanessa annabella,* adult). "Weedy" butterfly species were defined roughly as those for which there was a high probability of extinction or colonization in any given year at a site, equivalent to saying that there are no long-term site-bound populations in the region. All our weedy species are multivoltine, but not all multivoltines are weedy (*Pholisora catullus* is weedy; *Erynnis tristis* is not). Weediness of the host plant is relevant, but not decisive (*Lycaena xanthoides* and *Erynnis persius* feed in part on weedy plants but are themselves nonweedy; *Plebeius acmon* and *Junonia coenia* are weedy butterflies, some of whose hosts are nonweedy). All these classifications are available at www.press.uchicago.edu/books/boggs/ or from the first author.

Since we are interested in the predictability of first appearance dates in species grouped by life history attributes, we again turn to our standardized metric, deviation from mean first appearance date, but this time for subsets of the fauna. Overall, the variances in deviation from mean first appearance date are homoscedastic for both sites, but when we test for normality, the raw data are way off. However, a log_{10} transformation (of each number plus 1, to account for the zeros and numbers less than 1) converts the data into beautifully normal (by eyeball) distributions, and we can proceed.

To look at comparisons among overwintering stages, we ran a single-classification ANOVA to see whether the groups were significantly different; to see which differed from which, we ran a multiple-comparisons ANOVA using the Tukey-Kramer criterion for significance, providing an output of pairwise comparisons. We did the same for voltinism and weediness. We then calculated standard errors and generated histograms that sum up the analysis (figs. 6.8, 6.9). Bars that are significantly different are identified by letters; unlabeled bars are not significantly different from the rest.

These results are again encouraging. They tell us that multivoltine species have higher variances in first appearance dates than do univoltines, and weedy higher than nonweedy species. Of course, some of this variation, even with the infrequent colonizers excluded, is still due to year-to-year variance in the arrival times of weedy multivoltines that spill up into the Vaca Hills from the valleys below. The results by overwintering stage are not overwhelming. At Quail Ridge there are no significant differences, while at Gates Canyon the highest variance is found in species that overwinter as adults, and those overwintering as eggs or pupae are significantly more predictable. This finding is mildly surprising, but not very compelling. The difference between the two sites may be a function of the year-to-year variation in the dates of our earliest samples: the first species out are almost always the adult hibernators, and A. M. S. usually visits Gates Canyon earlier than G. K. and W. D. P. visited Quail Ridge for the first time.

Returning to the effect of earliness or lateness of emergence on predictability of first appearance dates, we lumped the species into 2-week intervals based on mean first appearance dates and calculated means and standard deviations over the 5 years for all the departures within these groups over the 5 years, by site. We then calculated coefficients of variation for these data versus mean first Julian dates. To our surprise, mean first appearance date has little effect on predictability (figs. 6.10, 6.11).

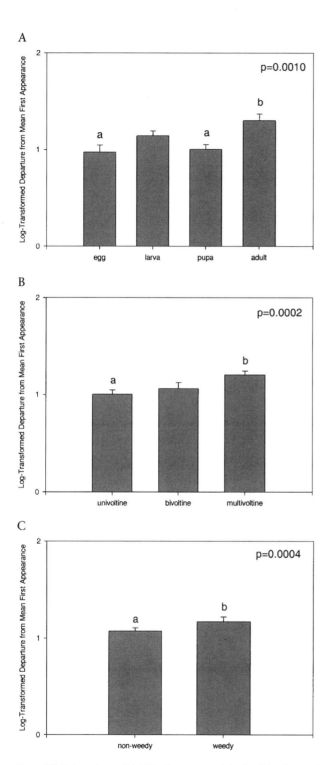

Figure 6.8 Variance in predictability of emergence dates for Gates Canyon fauna, based on departure (in days) from 1993–1997 mean day of first appearance, by (A) overwintering stage, (B) voltinism, and (C) weediness. Different letters above the bars indicate categories that are significantly different.

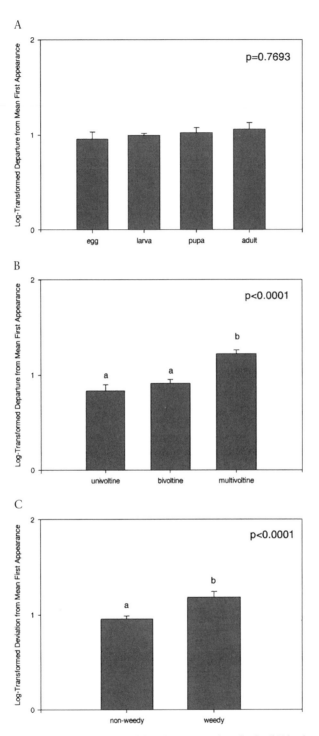

Figure 6.9 Variance in predictability of emergence dates for Quail Ridge fauna, based on departure (in days) from 1993–1997 mean day of first appearance, by (A) overwintering stage, (B) voltinism, (C) weediness. Different letters above the bars indicate categories that are significantly different.

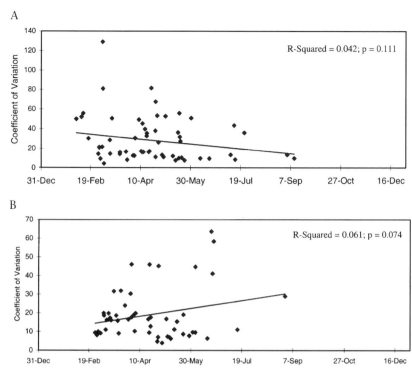

A

B

Figure 6.10 Regression of mean date of first sighting and coefficient of variation for (A) Gates Canyon and (B) Quail Ridge faunas.

NEARING THE END

What about *last* recorded appearance dates? We repeated the same procedures for the last date each species was seen in each year within sites (tables 6.10 and 6.11). Here again, the highest variance is found in species that overwinter as adults—in this case, at both sites. At both sites, voltinism affects the predictability of last dates, with bivoltine species being the most variable at Gates Canyon, but multivoltines the most variable at Quail Ridge. Weediness is highly significant at Quail Ridge, but not at Gates Canyon. Again, this last observation probably reflects the greater rarity and unpredictability of the weedy species overall at Quail Ridge. Table 6.12 compares the variation in first and last dates for these three life history attributes at both sites.

Given the intriguing differences between the two sites, we were curious whether there was a significant correlation between first and last dates as affected by ecology. We therefore calculated Pearson product-moment correlation coefficients for the two sites, based on departure from mean date of first and last appearance for the years 1993–1997. In this case, the signs of the deviations were retained: first dates before the mean first date and last dates before the mean last date were treated as negative, and conversely. When

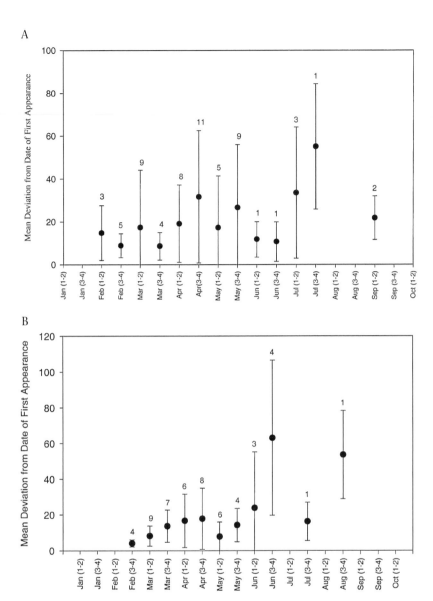

Figure 6.11 Indices of predictability for (A) Gates Canyon and (B) Quail Ridge faunas. Each index is calculated by grouping species falling within a 2-week interval for date of first appearance. Mean departure is plotted with an error term of one standard deviation. The numerals above each point indicate the number of species used to calculate the mean.

interpreting the data (tables 6.13 and 6.14), keep in mind that a positive correlation between first and last appearances reflects a shift forward or backward in time while the absolute length of the flight season varies little (e.g., early first, early last); a negative correlation reflects either a lengthening (i.e., early first, late last) or shortening (late first, early last) of the flight period.

The resulting patterns are complex. Some make obvious sense relative to the weather of the year, while others do not. One would expect multivoltine

Arthur M. Shapiro, Richard VanBuskirk, Greg Kareofelas, and William D. Patterson

Table 6.10 Mean date of last sighting and standard deviation for species at Gates Canyon

Species	Mean	SD (Days)	Species	Mean	SD (Days)
Adelpha bredowii	25 Oct	5.81	*Nymphalis californica*	19 Jun	75.05
Anthocaris sara	1 Jun	12.76	*Nymphalis milberti*	15 Mar	—
Atalopedes campestris	3 Nov	12.40	*Ochlodes agricola*	28 Jun	6.19
Atlides halesus	30 Jul	63.56	*Ochlodes sylvanoides*	1 Oct	7.14
Battus philenor	13 Oct	15.45	*Papilio eurymedon*	13 Jun	10.56
Brephidium exile	8 Oct	63.12	*Papilio multicaudatus*	10 Jul	27.70
Callophrys dumetorum	21 May	20.33	*Papilio rutulus*	27 Aug	11.90
Celastrina a. echo	13 Jul	62.28	*Papilio zelicaon*	28 Aug	35.59
Charidryas palla	5 Jun	15.86	*Paratrytone melane*	25 Sep	10.21
Coenonympha tullia	17 Sep	29.36	*Pholisora catullus*	30 Sep	30.48
Colias eurytheme	15 Nov	21.69	*Phyciodes mylitta*	20 Oct	17.04
Danaus plexippus	8 Oct	17.05	*Pieris napi*	17 Jun	31.46
Epargyreus clarus	2 May	—	*Pieris rapae*	9 Nov	14.31
Erynnis pacuvius	21 Jun	9.90	*Polites sabuleti*	27 Sep	4.95
Erynnis persius	11 Jul	52.00	*Polygonia satyrus*	24 May	83.25
Erynnis propertius	8 Jun	27.30	*Polygonia zephyrus*	3 Apr	28.15
Erynnis tristis	22 Sep	7.26	*Pontia protodice*	26 Sep	36.06
Euchloe ausonides	3 May	32.05	*Pontia sisymbrii*	9 Apr	15.98
Euphydryas chalcedona	19 Jun	11.80	*Pyrgus communis*	4 Nov	13.76
Everes comyntas	2 Sep	42.59	*Satyrium auretorum*	27 May	7.92
Glaucopsyche lygdamus	24 Apr	7.98	*Satyrium californicum*	16 Jun	9.20
Heliopetes ericetorum	8 Jul	78.38	*Satyrium saepium*	10 Jul	21.28
Hesperia columbia	25 Sep	4.65	*Satyrium sylvinus*	28 Jun	6.19
Hylephila phyleus	3 Nov	23.27	*Satyrium tetra*	23 Jun	8.40
Icaricia acmon	4 Nov	11.63	*Speyeria coronis*	19 Jun	54.96
Icaricia icarioides	14 May	15.11	*Strymon melinus*	24 Oct	25.54
Incisalia a. iroides	10 May	38.39	*Tharsalea arota*	10 Jul	25.24
Junonia coenia	13 Nov	12.39	*Thessalia leanira*	16 May	2.12
Leptotes marina	30 Mar	—	*Thorybes pylades*	6 May	15.56
Lerodea eufala	13 Oct	16.64	*Vanessa annabella*	29 Nov	28.89
Limenitis lorquini	9 Sep	22.37	*Vanessa atalanta*	21 Nov	24.85
Lycaena gorgon	17 Jun	16.13	*Vanessa cardui*	7 Oct	44.07
Lycaena helloides	25 Aug	110.31	*Vanessa virginiensis*	11 Sep	57.71
Lycaena xanthoides	19 Jun	16.00	*Zerene eurydice*	3 Jul	71.60
Nymphalis antiopa	9 Jul	60.82			

Note: No deviation is reported for species recorded in only one year.

species to have the most flexibility in life history, and to be capable of adding or skipping entire generations based on weather conditions. Cold, wet springs give them a late start. A very warm summer might enable them to catch up at least partly, while a cool one would maintain the lateness of their breeding cycle through to the end. When a multivoltine species is lagging—say, by half a generation relative to the mean phenology—how does it behave at the end of the season? Specifically, does the last generation of adults emerge, albeit a few weeks late (generating a positive first-last correlation)? Or does the sensitive period for environmental diapause cues occur

Table 6.11 Mean date of last sighting and standard deviation for species at Quail Ridge

Species	Mean	SD (Days)	Species	Mean	SD (Days)
Adelpha bredowii	25 Oct	21.43	*Lycaena gorgon*	6 Jun	13.59
Amblyscirtes vialis	18 May	8.66	*Lycaena helloides*	16 Oct	12.74
Anthocaris sara	27 May	16.46	*Lycaena xanthoides*	13 Jun	19.94
Atalopedes campestris	16 Oct	14.50	*Mitoura johnsoni*	3 May	—
Atlides halesus	15 Aug	86.70	*Nymphalis antiopa*	13 Jun	38.20
Battus philenor	10 Aug	54.50	*Nymphalis californica*	5 Jul	88.98
Brephidium exile	24 Oct	1.41	*Ochlodes agricola*	19 Jun	19.58
Callophrys dumetorum	29 May	13.82	*Ochlodes sylvanoides*	17 Oct	10.42
Celastrina a. echo	18 Jun	13.80	*Papilio eurymedon*	13 Jun	12.01
Cercyonis p. boopis	23 Aug	40.82	*Papilio rutulus*	1 Jul	31.25
Charidryas palla	3 Jun	12.82	*Papilio zelicaon*	22 Jul	47.84
Coenonympha tullia	17 Oct	12.57	*Paratrytone melane*	22 Aug	82.92
Colias eurytheme	19 Oct	16.99	*Phyciodes mylitta*	22 Sep	67.71
Danaus plexippus	13 Sep	67.98	*Pieris napi*	2 Jun	42.40
Erynnis b. lacustra	15 May	—	*Pieris rapae*	23 Oct	22.01
Erynnis pacuvius	17 May	21.00	*Polygonia satyrus*	8 Mar	7.23
Erynnis propertius	23 Jun	19.76	*Pontia protodice*	13 Oct	16.97
Erynnis tristis	24 Sep	13.22	*Pontia sisymbrii*	15 Apr	19.63
Euchloe ausonides	1 Jul	104.31	*Pyrgus communis*	24 Oct	31.11
Euphydryas chalcedona	9 Jun	9.09	*Satyrium auretorum*	6 Jun	11.43
Euphydryas editha	9 Jun	—	*Satyrium californicum*	18 Jun	13.80
Everes comyntas	4 Aug	113.14	*Satyrium saepium*	21 Jun	14.34
Glaucopsyche lygdamus	19 Apr	17.09	*Satyrium tetra*	15 Jun	12.62
Habrodais grunus	26 Aug	—	*Speyeria callippe*	9 Jun	—
Heliopetes ericetorum	2 Oct	—	*Speyeria coronis*	16 May	—
Hesperia columbia	9 Aug	68.82	*Strymon melinus*	13 Sep	67.98
Hesperia lindseyi	12 Jun	—	*Thessalia leanira*	31 May	16.93
Hylephila phyleus	3 Nov	16.26	*Thorybes pylades*	6 Jun	11.64
Icaricia acmon	22 Sep	67.71	*Vanessa annabella*	15 Sep	87.32
Icaricia icarioides	12 May	9.46	*Vanessa atalanta*	14 Sep	95.99
Incisalia a. iroides	18 Jun	13.80	*Vanessa cardui*	2 Aug	98.36
Junonia coenia	25 Oct	21.43	*Vanessa virginiensis*	5 Aug	100.24
Limenitis lorquini	7 Aug	60.84	*Zerene eurydice*	5 Apr	16.87

Note: No deviation is reported for species recorded in only one year.

early enough to program dormancy, so that most or all of the animals lay over to next year rather than eclosing? (In that case, a late first date would be paired with an early, perhaps very early, last date, generating a negative correlation.) In the real world, something intermediate often happens: many animals go into dormancy, but enough develop directly to extend the season to at least its normal length, if not beyond, though the numbers flying may be quite low. (Indeed, under these circumstances, these species may wink in and out repeatedly at the end of the season.) These phenomena also bear on the overwintering stage for species with facultative diapause (thus excluding univoltines). The whole pattern is further complicated by the modulating effect of temperature on photoperiod in at least some species, such that

Arthur M. Shapiro, Richard VanBuskirk, Greg Kareofelas, and William D. Patterson

Table 6.12 Comparison of departure (in days) from mean first sighting and mean last sighting for all species by life history attribute at Gates Canyon and Quail Ridge

	Gates Firsts	Gates Lasts	Quail Firsts	Quail Lasts
A. Overwintering stage				
Egg	16.27[a]	9.36[a]	12.47	16.90[a]
Larva	19.81	16.34[a]	13.11	21.20[ab]
Pupa	17.33[a]	22.18[b]	19.23	28.42[b]
Adult	32.59[b]	36.75[c]	21.69	51.93[c]
Overall significance	$p \ll 0.01$	$p \ll 0.01$	n.s.	$p \ll 0.01$
B. Voltinism				
Univoltine	14.46[a]	14.31[a]	10.03[a]	14.17[a]
Bivoltine	20.12	35.37[b]	8.96[a]	26.54[a]
Multivoltine	26.92[b]	19.38[b]	27.56[b]	44.02[b]
Overall significance	$p \ll 0.01$	$p \ll 0.01$	$p \ll 0.01$	$p \ll 0.01$
C. Weediness				
Weedy	22.94[a]	20.10	23.36[a]	40.25[a]
Nonweedy	20.42[b]	20.62	15.13[b]	25.12[b]
Overall significance	$p \ll 0.01$	$p = 0.1050$	$p = 0.0145$	$p \ll 0.01$

Note: Means are grouped by species' overwintering stage, voltinism, and weediness (see figs. 6.8 and 6.9). Superscripts denote groups that differ significantly (within columns) based on multiple-comparisons ANOVA of log-transformed data using the Tukey-Kramer criterion for significance. Overall *p* values were calculated from single-classification ANOVA of log-transformed data to test for differences among groups. Data are presented here as means of nontransformed values.

warm nights tend to push the critical photoperiod for dormancy later in the season, while cold nights make it earlier.

We would predict that univoltines would be resistant to weather effects on the length of the flight period. In 1995, which had a very cold, wet spring with late emergences, the first-last correlations were strongly positive—that is, the seasonal length was conserved. The same was true of the bivoltines, in which the lateness of the first flight carried over through the second. The multivoltines, however, showed no significant effects; at Quail Ridge the season was insignificantly shortened for them. Some of the significant correlations are related to specific weather events; we will explore them in more detail elsewhere. We note in passing that extreme summer heat, especially after a relatively dry winter, tends to bring the season to an early close. A warm, dry spring and early first appearance dates will generate a positive first-last correlation. Circumstances generating significant negative first-last correlations are rare because of climatic autocorrelations built into the data.

Table 6.13 Pearson correlation analysis of first and last appearance dates grouped by life history attribute for Gates Canyon

| | Weediness | | | Voltinism | | | Overwintering Stage | | | |
	All $n = 62$	Nonweedy $n = 44$	Weedy $n = 18$	Uni $n = 23$	Bi $n = 11$	Multi $n = 28$	Egg $n = 9$	Larva $n = 23$	Pupa $n = 19$	Adult $n = 10$
Year										
1993	-0.0262	0.0131	-0.1585	0.0727	0.1270	-0.2051	-0.1458	0.1798	0.0031	-0.2052
	$p > 0.5$	$p > 0.5$	$p > 0.5$	$p > 0.5$	$p > 0.5$	$0.5 > p > 0.2$	$p > 0.5$	$0.5 > p > 0.2$	$p > 0.5$	$p > 0.5$
1994	0.1251	0.5543	-0.3512	0.4890	0.6452	-0.2099	0.4354	0.4485	0.0674	0.0051
	$0.5 > p > 0.2$	$p < 0.001$	$0.2 > p > 0.1$	$0.02 > p > 0.01$	$0.05 > p > 0.02$	$0.5 > p > 0.2$	$0.5 > p > 0.2$	$0.05 > p > 0.02$	$p > 0.5$	$p > 0.5$
1995	0.3505	0.4579	-0.2624	0.5240	0.5890	0.0129	-0.2815	0.7095	0.2465	0.3076
	$0.01 > p > 0.005$	$0.002 > p > 0.001$	$0.5 > p > 0.2$	$0.02 > p > 0.01$	$0.1 > p > 0.05$	$p > 0.5$	$0.5 > p > 0.2$	$p < 0.001$	$0.5 > p > 0.2$	$0.5 > p > 0.2$
1996	0.2512	0.4250	-0.3045	0.1379	0.8650	-0.0862	-0.0085	-0.0311	0.5266	0.3713
	$0.05 > p > 0.02$	$0.005 > p > 0.002$	$0.5 > p > 0.2$	$p > 0.5$	$p < 0.001$	$p > 0.5$	$p > 0.5$	$p > 0.5$	$0.05 > p > 0.02$	$0.5 > p > 0.2$
1997	0.0251	-0.0889	0.1821	0.2270	-0.2836	0.1035	-0.1430	-0.1054	0.3257	-0.2384
	$p > 0.5$	$p > 0.5$	$0.5 > p > 0.2$	$0.5 > p > 0.2$	$0.5 > p > 0.2$	$p > 0.5$	$p > 0.5$	$p > 0.5$	$0.2 > p > 0.1$	$0.5 > p > 0.2$

Table 6.14 Pearson correlation analysis of first and last appearance dates grouped by life history attribute for Quail Ridge

| | Weediness | | | Voltinism | | | Overwintering Stage | | | |
	All $n = 53$	Nonweedy $n = 41$	Weedy $n = 12$	Uni $n = 22$	Bi $n = 10$	Multi $n = 21$	Egg $n = 8$	Larva $n = 20$	Pupa $n = 15$	Adult $n = 9$
Year										
1993	0.4472	0.5446	0.1513	0.1938	-0.1561	0.4382	-0.3687	0.0300	0.5472	0.5169
	$p < 0.001$	$p < 0.001$	$0.5 > p > 0.2$	$0.5 > p > 0.2$	$p > 0.5$	$0.05 > p > 0.02$	$0.5 > p > 0.2$	$p > 0.5$	$0.05 > p > 0.02$	$0.2 > p > 0.1$
1994	0.0050	0.1174	-0.3516	0.0048	0.1991	0.0033	-0.0336	0.1512	0.1650	-0.1516
	$p > 0.5$	$0.5 > p > 0.2$	$0.02 > p > 0.01$	$p > 0.5$	$p > 0.5$	$p > 0.5$	$p > 0.5$	$p > 0.5$	$p > 0.5$	$p > 0.5$
1995	0.1483	0.3483	-0.2980	0.4503	0.6962	-0.1197	-0.1741	-0.2039	0.1632	0.3232
	$0.2 > p > 0.1$	$0.02 > p > 0.01$	$0.05 > p > 0.02$	$0.05 > p > 0.02$	$0.05 > p > 0.02$	$p > 0.5$	$p > 0.5$	$0.5 > p > 0.2$	$p > 0.5$	$0.5 > p > 0.2$
1996	0.5351	0.5346	0.6605	0.1176	0.7951	0.5107	-0.4948	0.2979	0.7644	0.6413
	$p < 0.001$	$p < 0.001$	$p < 0.001$	$p > 0.5$	$0.01 > p > 0.005$	$0.02 > p > 0.01$	$0.5 > p > 0.2$	$0.5 > p > 0.2$	$p < 0.001$	$0.1 > p > 0.05$
1997	0.3151	0.4748	-0.4400	0.0767	-0.2578	0.2058	-0.4255	0.0791	0.4860	0.4309
	$0.05 > p > 0.02$	$0.002 > p > 0.001$	$0.002 > p > 0.001$	$p > 0.5$	$0.5 > p > 0.2$	$0.5 > p > 0.2$	$0.5 > p > 0.2$	$p > 0.5$	$0.1 > p > 0.05$	$0.5 > p > 0.2$

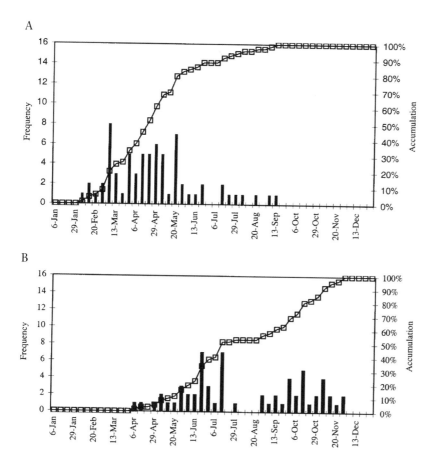

Figure 6.12 Seasonal distribution of (A) mean first and (B) mean last dates of appearance at Gates Canyon with species accumulation curves. Data for Quail Ridge are not presented due to the infrequency of late-season sampling.

Plenty of data for specific species and years at other locations can be found in the literature. A particularly good two-species (British!) case is Brakefield (1987).

Figure 6.12 represents the first and last appearance dates in a different way, as seasonal distributions compared with accumulation curves. This presentation is an alternative to our earlier representations of evenness of turnover. Again, such treatment can be decomposed by life history attribute if useful. This figure also showcases a phenomenon pointed out by Shapiro (1975b): the extreme rarity of autumn univoltines in temperate butterfly faunas, observed in climates as different as central New York and Mediterranean California. This is obviously a nonrandom phenomenon, and it remains unexplained. In many locations, including the Vaca Hills, there are plenty of nectar resources in autumn (in this case, coyotebrush, *Baccharis pilularis*), which are, in fact, crowded with multivoltine butterflies. The problem is not that it is difficult to overwinter as an egg: plenty of species do it (but their adults fly mostly in early summer).

LAST THOUGHTS

Some things we tried worked well; some didn't. Phenological data are complex, noisy, and sloppy. Our goal has been to promote discussion of the questions one can ask of such data and the possible ways to answer them. In this chapter we have not introduced weather data and multivariate comparisons of phenology with them. We will do that elsewhere. The "Leopold dataset" analysis (Bradley et al. 1999) hints at the sorts of problems one faces in doing so. At the level of individual species, phenological modeling has been in place a long time and continues to evolve (Podolsky 1984); the challenge is to extend it to multispecies systems. In addition to the simple statistical methods used here, various techniques exist in the literature that might be useful with data like ours, but which have not been tried yet. Rather than comment on them here, we will continue to experiment with them.

One of us (A. M. S.) teaches a course in the community concept from both an ecological and an evolutionary standpoint. In this course, one of the intellectual "heroes" is the Danish plant ecologist Christen Raunkiaer, who was mentioned in passing earlier in this chapter. At the beginning of the twentieth century Raunkiaer had the insight—comparable to Mendel's quantitative breakthrough in genetics—to approach community structure as a statistical problem. He was particularly interested in the distribution of individuals among species, a phenomenon and an approach that, pursued imaginatively, led to most of the "hot" themes in contemporary community ecology. He was also interested in convergent evolution at the community level and experimented with various indices of "life form," whereby he could characterize species and look for convergent "life form spectra" in the vegetations of widely separated but climatically similar regions. He thus made physiognomy a statistical science as well.

Butterfly phenology—indeed, community-level phenology in general—is now at roughly its Raunkiaer stage of intellectual evolution. Are there broad regional phenological patterns comparable to plant life form spectra, and quantifiable as functions of climate? Shapiro (1975b) speculated as much. What he needed was not only a good enough database, but a set of analytical methods to deal with it. Quantification is better than eyeball judgments. We are gratified, however, as we begin to subject our data to statistical treatment, to find that our eyeballs have been mostly truthful. We can now say with quantitative confidence that 1995 really was a strange year in the Vaca Hills. Perhaps eventually we will be able to say a lot more—such as why.

Arthur M. Shapiro, Richard VanBuskirk, Greg Kareofelas, and William D. Patterson

SUMMARY

Using a 5-year database for two nearby sites in the Inner North Coast Ranges of northern California, we developed and tested some quantitative approaches to phenology as a property of entire butterfly faunas. Using a null model approach, we demonstrated that the seasonal pattern of first appearance dates is probably nonrandom at both of our sites. Each site has a characteristic, but variable within limits, shape of species-versus-Julian-date curve, sequence of appearance of species, and rhythm of seasonal species turnover. When first and last dates are analyzed with respect to voltinism, weediness, and overwintering stage, complex, noisy, and not entirely consistent patterns emerge. Earliness or lateness of flight period is not statistically correlated with variance in first flight dates. More complex datasets and more sophisticated multivariate methods offer the hope that one can mine much more ecologically meaningful information from butterfly phenology. Such datasets exist. Perhaps the methods do too.

ACKNOWLEDGMENTS

We are immensely grateful to Neil Willits for statistical advice—both conceptual and computational—and to Scott L. Gardner for his input on some earlier versions of these ideas. The Quail Ridge data were obtained with the support of the Quail Ridge Wilderness Conservancy, especially Frank Maurer and Lenora Timm. The Gates Canyon data were collected with the support of NSF grant DEB 93–06721 to A. M. S. Computation was supported in part by a grant from the Committee on Research, University of California, Davis, and a grant from the Program on Nature and Culture, University of California, Davis. We dedicate this chapter to the memory of two of A. M. S.'s mentors of 30 years ago, Robert MacArthur and Harry K. Clench, who—had they lived—would probably have solved these problems long ago.

CHAPTER 7

Modeling Present and Potential Future Ranges of European Butterflies Using Climate Response Surfaces

Jane K. Hill, Chris D. Thomas, and Brian Huntley

In 1995, the Intergovernmental Panel on Climate Change concluded that "the balance of evidence suggests that there is a discernible human influence on global climate" (IPCC 1996), and in its most recent report, the IPCC concluded that "there is new and stronger evidence that most of the warming in the past 50 years is attributable to human activities" (IPCC 2001a). These conclusions, coupled to the obligation of signatories to the UN Framework Convention on Climate Change to "achieve . . . stabilization of greenhouse gas concentrations . . . within a time frame sufficient to allow ecosystems to adapt naturally," have generated an increasing need to be able to predict the effects of potential climate change on species' abundances and distributions (Hughes 2000; McCarty 2001). The need for such assessments is particularly acute in the case of insects because they constitute a large fraction of terrestrial biodiversity and include pests and disease vectors as well as numerous rare and endangered species. Their poikilothermic nature, dispersal abilities, high fecundities, and short generation times are likely to render them especially responsive to climate change.

In north temperate latitudes, climate warming is likely to result in insect distributions shifting northward and to higher elevations (Coope 1978; Parmesan 1996; Parmesan et al. 1999). As is common in insects, many butterfly species have distributions that appear to be directly constrained by climate (Pollard 1979; Turner et al. 1987). However, the spatial distributions of host plants and habitats are likely to affect the capacity of insects to respond to climate change, and recent anthropogenic habitat destruction may mean that new climatically suitable habitats are beyond the reach of migrants, thus preventing species from tracking climate changes. Many butterfly species conform to a metapopulation structure (e.g., Thomas and Hanski

1997) such that the spatial and temporal availability of habitat is crucial for the persistence of populations. The presence of apparently suitable habitat that is unoccupied, together with low colonization rates in fragmented landscapes, has highlighted the difficulties butterflies have in reaching isolated habitats (Thomas et al. 1992). Thus, butterfly distributions will be unable to shift in response to climate change if new habitats are fragmented and too distant to be colonized (Warren et al. 2001).

We have investigated the relative importance of climate and habitat in determining distributions of the speckled wood butterfly, *Pararge aegeria* (L.) (Hill et al. 1999b, 2001b). In this chapter we review those data and also extend the study to consider the importance of climate in determining the distributions of two other satyrine butterflies: the ringlet, *Aphantopus hyperantus* (L.) (Hill et al. 2001b), and the large heath, *Coenonympha tullia* (Müll) (Hill et al. 2002). We compare results for *P. aegeria* with results for these two species, which have contrasting distributions in Britain. We then model the potential distributions of all three species under predicted future climate change.

USE OF BUTTERFLIES FOR MODELING EFFECTS OF CLIMATE CHANGE

The relationship between a species' geographic distribution and the present climate can be modeled by a surface representing the probability of encountering that species under a given combination of climatic conditions. This "climate response surface" can then be used to predict potential future distributions of the species in response to forecast climate scenarios (Beerling et al. 1995; Huntley et al. 1995). Climate response surfaces have been effective in demonstrating the importance of climate in determining plant distributions (Beerling et al. 1995; Huntley et al. 1995), and we have shown that they are also valuable in modeling butterfly distributions (Hill et al. 1999b; Hill et al. 2001b). Butterflies are excellent model organisms for this type of investigation for the following reasons:

1. Many species are constrained by climate (Pollard 1979; Turner et al. 1987; Dennis 1993; Roy and Sparks 2000; Roy et al. 2001), occupying only a part of the range of their host plants (Dennis and Shreeve 1991).
2. Distributions of many species have shifted northward during the twentieth century, apparently in response to climate change (Pollard 1979; Parmesan 1996; Parmesan et al. 1999).
3. Many butterflies form metapopulations, in which the spatial distribution of habitat is crucial to their ability to colonize new areas (e.g., Thomas and Hanski 1997).

4. There are extensive records of current and historical distributions (Heath et al. 1984; Emmet and Heath 1990; Tolman 1997; Asher et al. 2001).
5. The British fauna contains a range of species that reach either their southern or their northern range margins within Britain.

In this chapter we compare the performance of climate response surfaces in simulating the distributions of three different European butterflies with contrasting distributions. The combination of chosen species also allows us to investigate potential distributional changes at both northern and southern range margins under predicted future climate change.

ECOLOGY AND DISTRIBUTION OF *Pararge aegeria*

The speckled wood butterfly, *Pararge aegeria,* is one of several British butterflies whose distributions appear to be climatically determined (Pollard 1979) and which have undergone marked changes in their distributions over the past 150 years that may have been related to climate change (Emmet and Heath 1990). *Pararge aegeria* is a western palearctic species, occurring from Madeira east to the Ural Mountains, and from the Atlas Mountains in Morocco north to central Scandinavia (Tolman 1997). Several subspecies have been recognized, although for the purposes of this study, these subspecies have not been differentiated.

During the nineteenth century, *P. aegeria* was widely distributed, probably occurring throughout Britain as far north as central Scotland. However, its distribution began to contract toward the end of the nineteenth century (Burrows 1916; Gibbs 1916), and between 1915 and 1939 it was essentially restricted to Wales and southwestern England (fig. 7.1A). Although there were a number of refuge sites in northern England (e.g., Jackson 1980, 1983) and on the west coast of Scotland (Downes 1948; Thompson 1980), it apparently disappeared from large areas of eastern England (e.g., Chalmers-Hunt and Owen 1952) during this time. However, since 1939, it has reexpanded its distribution, with major periods of expansion during the 1940s (fig. 7.1B) and 1970s (fig. 7.1C; Hill et al. 2001a). In 1976, it was also first recorded on the island of Madeira, approximately 540 km off the coast of North Africa in the northern Atlantic (Owen et al. 1986). It is continuing to expand at its northern margin, but has not yet recolonized all formerly occupied areas (fig. 7.1D).

There are several aspects of its ecology that make *P. aegeria* a particularly good model species for this type of investigation. First, there are good current and historical records of its distribution—it is not easily confused with other species and can be recorded reliably from the ground (as opposed to

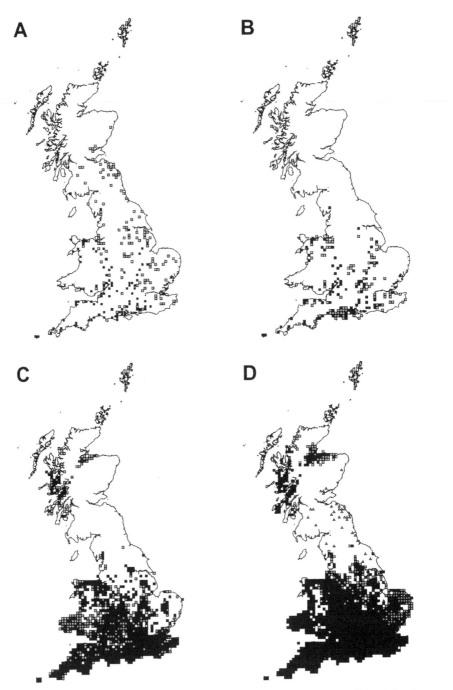

Figure 7.1 Changes in the British distribution of *Pararge aegeria* at a 10 km grid resolution during the past 150 years. (A) Historical (pre-1915, gray squares) and most restricted (1915–1939, black squares) distribution. (B) Expansion during the 1940s; symbols show restricted distribution (1915–1939, black squares) and 1940–1949 records (gray squares). (C) Expansion during the 1970s; symbols show 1940–1969 distribution (black squares) and areas with first recent record 1970–1979 (gray squares). (D) Current expansion; symbols show 1940–1989 distribution (black squares) and areas with first recent record 1990–1997 (gray squares). Triangles show areas with historical (pre-1915) records that have not been recolonized.

those woodland species that spend a large proportion of their time in the canopy, and for which ground-based surveys may underestimate current distributions). Second, it develops through one or more generations per year in Britain, depending on temperature. Populations can thus rapidly increase in size (Pollard et al. 1997), giving them the potential to respond rapidly to changes in the environment. Third, adults are fairly mobile and can probably track changing climates quickly; distributions thus could be at equilibrium with current climatic conditions. Fourth, *P. aegeria*'s host plants (grasses) are ubiquitous and thus unlikely to limit current distributions. Finally, it is restricted to coniferous and deciduous woodlands toward its northern and eastern margins in Britain. This habitat can be mapped reliably from remotely sensed satellite data and readily incorporated into models.

GENERATING THE MODEL

We have generated a climate response surface for the main study species, *P. aegeria* (Hill et al. 1999b). However, *P. aegeria* does not reach its southern

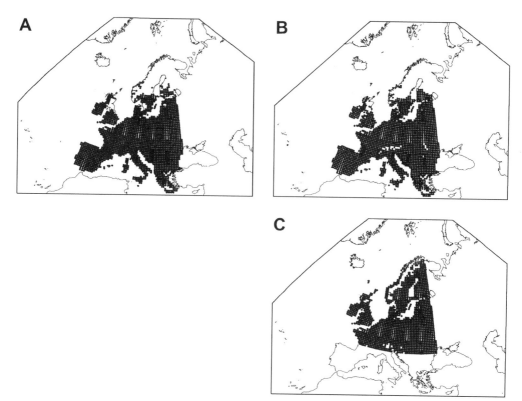

Figure 7.2 European distribution of *Pararge aegeria* mapped on a 50 km UTM grid (including only areas west of 30°E longitude). (A) Current records. (B) Simulated current distribution using the climate response surface. (C) Simulated future distribution for the period 2070–2099 (applies only to areas north of 45°N latitude).

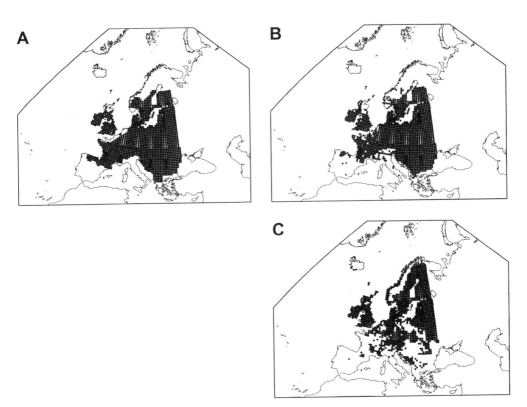

Figure 7.3 European distribution of *Aphantopus hyperantus* mapped on a 50 km UTM grid (including only areas west of 30°E longitude). (A) Current records. (B) Simulated current distribution using the climate response surface. (C) Simulated future distribution for the period 2070–2099.

range margin within the study area (see below). Therefore, in order to investigate the effects of climate change on southern as well as northern range margins, we have also generated climate response surfaces for two other species: *Aphantopus hyperantus*, which reaches its northern range margin in Britain and central Fennoscandia and its southern range margin in northern Spain, and *Coenonympha tullia*, which has a much more northerly distribution than either *P. aegeria* or *A. hyperantus*, reaching its southern range margin in Britain and central Europe. Current European records of *P. aegeria* were collated from a number of sources (e.g., Aagard and Gulbrandsen 1976; Marttila and Saarinen 1996; Tolman 1997; Asher et al. 2001) as well as through direct contact with local butterfly recorders in many European countries (fig. 7.2A). Distributions of *A. hyperantus* (fig. 7.3A) and *C. tullia* (fig. 7.4A) were taken from maps by Tolman (1997), Emmet and Heath (1990), and Asher et al. (2001). Records were converted to presence-absence data on a 50 km UTM grid extending from the Azores east to 30°E longitude (records were not considered to be reliable for areas farther east), and from the Mediterranean Sea (reliable records for *P. aegeria* could not be obtained for North Africa) north to Svalbard (a total of 2,648 grid cells).

Jane K. Hill, Chris D. Thomas, and Brian Huntley

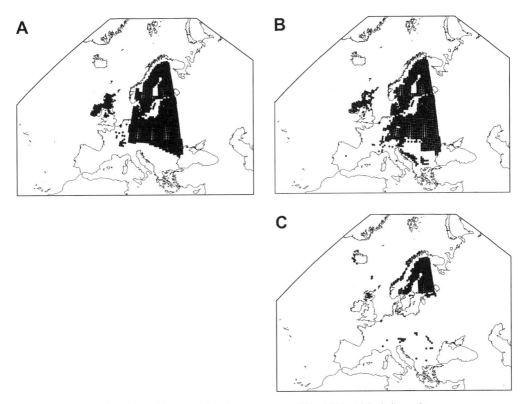

Figure 7.4 European distribution of *Coenonympha tullia* mapped on a 50 km UTM grid (including only areas west of 30°E longitude). (A) Current records. (B) Simulated current distribution using the climate response surface. (C) Simulated future distribution for the period 2070–2099.

We used mean monthly temperature, precipitation, and cloudiness from a meteorological station dataset for the climate normal period of 1931–1960 (Leemans and Cramer 1991) to interpolate values for locations at the midpoint and mean elevation of each 50 km cell (Huntley et al. 1995). We chose three bioclimate variables that reflect principal limitations on butterfly growth and survival: annual temperature sum above 5°C (GDD5, the developmental threshold for larvae: Lees 1962; Blakeley 1997), coldest month mean temperature (MTCO, related to overwintering survival); and moisture availability (AET/PET, related to host plant quality and expressed as an estimate of the ratio of actual to potential evapotranspiration: Huntley et al. 1995). We have also run the models using different combinations of bioclimate variables (e.g., warmest month mean temperature), but the three bioclimate variables described above consistently gave the best fit to current distributions for all three species considered here. It is possible, of course, that other bioclimate variables may be more appropriate for other species (e.g., number of sunshine hours for species with thermoregulating larvae). We computed values for GDD5, MTCO, and AET/PET, and fitted climate response surfaces describing European distributions of the three species in terms of these three variables (Huntley et al. 1995). The response surfaces were fitted using locally weighted regression techniques (Huntley et al. 1995) and, for each species, describe the probability of the species occurring at a given point in climate space.

SIMULATING CURRENT DISTRIBUTIONS

We used the response surfaces to simulate distributions of the three species under current climatic conditions. The goodness of fit between simulated and observed butterfly distributions was used as a test of the response surface and was assessed using the kappa statistic (Monserud and Leemans 1992). For the main study species, *P. aegeria*, as well as for the two other species, there was a good fit between current observed and simulated butterfly distributions (*P. aegeria*, $\kappa = 0.803$ at a threshold probability of butterfly occurrence of 0.45, 2,096 simulated occurrences vs. 2,064 observed occurrences, fig. 7.2B; *A. hyperantus*, $\kappa = 0.788$ at a threshold probability of butterfly occurrence of 0.61, 1,601 simulated occurrences vs. 1,674 observed occurrences, fig. 7.3B [Hill et al. 2001b]; *C. tullia*, $\kappa = 0.810$ at a threshold probability of butterfly occurrence of 0.55, 1,229 simulated occurrences vs. 1,212 observed occurrences, fig. 7.4B).

Given, however, that all three species occupy a high proportion of grid cells (e.g., >77% of cells are currently occupied by *P. aegeria*), a more valuable test of the response surface is its ability to simulate accurately the species' range margins. Visual inspection showed that this simulation was also very good overall, although there were a number of mismatches between observed and simulated distributions.

Pararge aegeria. The model predicted occurrence in several areas beyond *P. aegeria*'s current limits (fig. 7.2B; Hill et al. 2001b). In Britain, these areas included the Isle of Man and the Western Isles, localities that currently are probably too isolated to be occupied (Dennis and Shreeve 1997). However, the model also predicted occurrence in areas along the east and west coasts of England, where the species was historically present before its nineteenth-century range contraction, indicating that distributions are lagging behind current climates. The model also predicted occurrence in an area of southwestern Sweden where *P. aegeria* has never been recorded. The model predicted absence in the core of the Alps in grid cells where *P. aegeria* is restricted to specific habitats (e.g., south-facing slopes and valley bottoms) below the mean elevation of the grid cell; such predicted absences are to be expected, given that the model was fitted to bioclimate values for the mean elevation of the grid cells.

Aphantopus hyperantus. At the northern margin of *A. hyperantus*'s range, in Sweden and Finland, observed and simulated distributions were very similar (fig. 7.3B; Hill et al. 2001b), although the response surface did not simulate quite such extensive distributions as are currently observed in southern Scotland and Norway. At the southern margin, the response surface simulated a few occurrences beyond the observed range in Spain and Italy, and it did not simulate the extensive distributions in northern Spain. As with *P. aegeria*, some areas where the response surface did not perform well were mountainous regions, where *A. hyperantus* occurs only in very specific habitats below the mean elevation of the grid cells.

Coenonympha tullia. The response surface performed well for *C. tullia* in Britain and Fennoscandia, but simulated more southerly distributions in France, Bulgaria, and the former Yugoslavia than are currently observed, as well as two outlying populations in Spain and Italy (fig. 7.4B). However, it did not simulate any populations in Belgium or northern France, where there are currently several isolated populations.

Although there were excellent fits between the observed and simulated distributions, the observed distributions of *C. tullia* and *A. hyperantus* were taken from coarse-grained published maps, and some of the mismatches may be due to inaccuracies in these maps, rather than an inability of the bioclimate variables to match the existing distribution. However, comparison of simulated distributions for *P. aegeria* from response surfaces generated using more accurate collated records (fig. 7.2A) as well as the published map in Tolman (1997) showed that, although there were a few differences at range margins, the differences were not that great (Hill et al. 2001b). Thus we are confident that our conclusions would be valid even if more accurate distribution data were obtained. It is inevitable that distribution-climate lags, as well as detailed patterns of habitat use (e.g., resulting from geology) and microclimate (e.g., resulting from aspect) at range margins, will make it difficult to produce completely accurate distributions based on only three variables. Nevertheless, the simulated distributions appear to be good representations of current distributions.

INCORPORATING EFFECTS OF HABITAT AVAILABILITY

For the main study species, *P. aegeria*, we have also focused on British distributions at a finer resolution to investigate the importance of habitat availability, in combination with climate, in determining distributions (Hill et al. 1999b, 2001b). We obtained 10 km resolution data for the current distribution of *P. aegeria* in Britain. We derived values for the same three bioclimate

Figure 7.5 (A) Distribution of woodland (measured as maximum percentage cover of any 1 km cell within each 10 km cell) in Britain at a 10 km resolution (data from satellite Landcover data combining coniferous and deciduous woodland categories). Small circles, 50–75% cover, large circles >75% cover. Arrows point to locations referred to in the text: southerly arrow indicates the Wash; northerly arrow indicates the Vale of York. (B) Predicted current British distribution of *P. aegeria* at a 10 km resolution incorporating climate suitability and habitat availability. Black circles = simulated occurrence coinciding with recorded presence; open circles = simulated absence coinciding with recorded absence; dark gray circles = simulated occurrence coinciding with recorded absence; pale gray circles = simulated absence coinciding with recorded presence. (C) Simulated future British distribution (black circles) for the period 2070–2099, incorporating current habitat availability.

variables for locations at the midpoint and mean elevation of each 10 km cell (for a total of 2,805 cells) using the same datasets and techniques as before (see "Generating the Model" above). We then applied the climate response surface generated from the 50 km resolution data to these finer-scale climatic data to simulate the probability of occurrence of *P. aegeria* in Britain at a 10 km resolution under the current climatic conditions. The distribution of potential *P. aegeria* woodland habitat was determined using the CEH Landcover dataset, derived from remotely sensed satellite data (Fuller et al. 1994). From these data we calculated the availability of woodland (combining deciduous and coniferous woodlands) in each 10 km cell as the maximum percentage cover of woodland in any 1 km square within each 10 km cell (fig. 7.5A). This measure was chosen to distinguish grid cells within which there are extensive woodlands from others containing numerous small patches classified as woodland (the pixel size of the Landcover dataset is 25 m).

We used logistic regression to model the species' observed British distribution in relation to climate suitability and woodland cover. Both variables were significantly and positively related to butterfly presence, and the model predicted *P. aegeria* presence-absence in 78% of grid cells correctly ($\chi^2 = 1236.1$, 2 d.f., $p < 0.0001$; fig. 7.5B). As at the European scale, the majority of the grid cells where *P. aegeria* occurs but was not simulated are grid cells of high relief (e.g., the Welsh Mountains and the western highlands of Scotland), where the bioclimate variables used reflect the mean elevation, whereas the species occurs in specific habitats at low elevation. Again, as before, *P. aegeria* was predicted to occur in areas currently beyond its northern range margin in England, but which it occupied in the nineteenth century (see fig. 7.1A). Like the results from the European-scale model, and even after incorporating the effects of habitat availability, this model also indicates that *P. aegeria* has failed to keep up with the changing climates of the twentieth century.

SIMULATING POTENTIAL FUTURE DISTRIBUTIONS

We predicted the potential future European distribution of *P. aegeria* for the end of the twenty-first century (Hill et al. 1999b, 2001b) and compared the results with predictions for *C. tullia* and *A. hyperantus* for the same time period. We obtained output from a transient climate change simulation, made using the HADCM2 general circulation model, for the period 2070–2099. The simulation chosen combined the negative forcing of sulfate aerosols with the positive forcing of greenhouse gases (Mitchell et al. 1995) and can be viewed as a conservative simulation of the likely magnitude of climate change over the next century (IPCC 2001a). Mean anomalies

Table 7.1 Mean values for three bioclimate variables used to simulate current and future butterfly distributions

	GDD5 (Degree-Days)	MTCO (°C)	AET/PET
1931–1960	1,915.5 (1,079.0)	−1.36 (6.21)	0.842 (0.288)
2070–2099	2,788.6 (1,354.4)	3.41 (5.17)	0.837 (0.201)
Change	+873.1 (320.5)	+4.77 (1.32)	−0.006 (0.256)

Note: Data for the climate normal period 1931–1960 are from the Leemans and Cramer (1991) dataset; future climate variables for the period 2070–2099 are derived from the HADCM2 scenario. GDD5 = annual temperature sum >5°C; MTCO = mean temperature of the coldest month; AET/PET = actual/potential evapotranspiration. Standard deviations are in parentheses.

between the periods 1931–1960 and 2070–2099 were computed for thirty-six meteorological variables (monthly mean temperature, precipitation, and cloudiness) in the transient simulation. These anomalies were interpolated to the 50 km UTM grid across Europe and added to the previously interpolated observed climate values for the period 1931–1960. The new values were then used as before to compute values for the three bioclimate variables (GDD5, MTCO, and AET/PET) for the climate scenario for 2070–2099. These predicted future values were then used with the climate response surfaces fitted to the 50 km grid data to generate simulated potential distributions for the three butterfly species for the period 2070–2099. Table 7.1 shows mean differences for the three bioclimate variables between the climate normal period of 1931–1960 and future predicted climates. These data indicate that climates within the European study area will on average get warmer and drier by the end of the twenty-first century. Simulated future distributions for the three butterfly species are shown in figures 7.2C, 7.3C, and 7.4C (using the same probability thresholds of occurrence that were used for simulating current distributions; see "Simulating Current Distributions" above).

Pararge aegeria. The model predicts considerable northward extension of the potential distribution of *P. aegeria,* and indicates that *P. aegeria* would have the potential to extend its range throughout Britain, with only the highest mountains in Scotland being excluded (fig. 7.2C; Hill et al. 2001b). In Fennoscandia, the species' potential range extends almost to the Arctic coast, reaching southern Finnmark, and extends along the west coast of Norway as far as the Lofoten Islands. The southern range margin of *P. aegeria* (in North Africa) was not included in the current response surface, making it impossible to predict future changes there, and so areas south of 45°N latitude have been excluded from the simulated future distribution.

Aphantopus hyperantus. The model also predicts considerable northward extension of the potential range of *A. hyperantus* (fig. 7.3C; Hill et al. 2001b), whose potential northern range margin is predicted to be similar to that of *P. aegeria.* In addition, the model predicts northward contraction of the southern range margin, with only isolated populations predicted to persist in

Jane K. Hill, Chris D. Thomas, and Brian Huntley

some mountainous regions at the current southern range margin in southern Europe.

Coenonympha tullia. Because *C. tullia* has a northern distribution, there is little potential for its northern range margin to expand. However, the model predicts considerable northward contraction of its southern range margin, with the butterfly predicted to occur in only a few isolated mountainous sites in continental Europe and Britain (fig. 7.4C). These changes would result in *C. tullia* having a much more restricted distribution than at present (a reduction from simulated occurrence in 1,229 grid squares under current climatic conditions to 331 squares in the future).

PREDICTING POTENTIAL FUTURE BRITISH DISTRIBUTIONS

In order to simulate potential *P. aegeria* distributions in Britain at a 10 km resolution, we applied the anomalies from the HADCM2 simulation to the meteorological data for the 10 km grid (see "Incorporating Effects of Habitat Availability" above), and computed values for the three bioclimate variables for the period 2070–2099 as before (Hill et al. 1999b). We used the climate response surface for *P. aegeria* generated from the 50 km grid to predict the butterfly's probability of occurrence in Britain under the changed climate scenario. We then used the resulting values for probability of occurrence in the logistic regression equation to predict *P. aegeria*'s potential distribution in Britain taking account of habitat availability. The habitat availability values used were those for the present because we have no basis for predicting how they might change over the next century. Predictions from the logistic regression model are for *P. aegeria* to occur throughout Britain during the period 2070–2099, with the exception of the high mountain areas in central Scotland (fig. 7.5C; Hill et al. 2001b). It appears that at a 10 km resolution, a sufficient extent of woodland is present almost everywhere the climate is predicted to be suitable for *P. aegeria,* so that habitat availability at a 10 km resolution does not generally constrain *P. aegeria*'s potential future range.

ESTIMATING DISPERSAL RATES

Direct estimates of dispersal rates are not available for any of the three species studied here. We have estimated the time required for *P. aegeria* to colonize new climatically suitable habitats in Britain by calculating its expansion rate in Britain during the twentieth century using the area method (Van den Bosch et al. 1990; Hill et al. 1999b, 2001a, 2001b). We plotted the area occupied each decade (the square root of area of the number of 10 km grid cells containing butterfly records) against year, then calculated the velocity

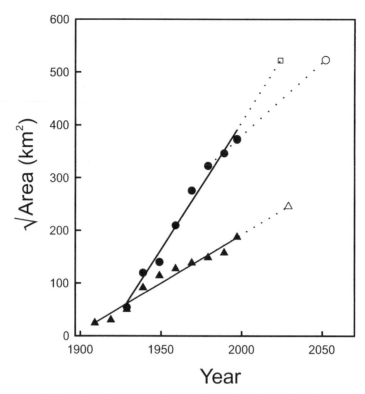

Figure 7.6 Expansion of *P. aegeria* in Britain (solid circles) and Denmark (solid triangles) during the past 100 years. Open symbols indicate time needed to colonize all new climatically suitable habitat in Denmark (triangle) and Britain in the period 2070–2099, assuming expansion rates since 1930 (square) and since 1970 (circle).

of range expansion (*E*) from the slope (*C*) of this line ($E = C/\sqrt{\pi}$; Lensink 1997) (fig. 7.6). This gave an estimated expansion rate of *P. aegeria* in Britain during the twentieth century of 2.7 km/yr (without correcting for geometric distribution of potential new areas for colonization; Lensink 1997). We have also obtained independent estimates of dispersal in Denmark over a similar time period, which gave an estimated expansion rate of 1.03 km/yr during the twentieth century. The lower estimated rate of expansion in Denmark than in Britain may reflect differences in the distribution of potential new areas for colonization and/or differences in the availability of woodlands between the two countries.

Our recent studies showing a twofold increase in expansion rates in regions within Britain with more woodland habitat (Hill et al. 2001a) demonstrate the importance of habitat availability for range expansion. In contrast to Denmark, expansion in Britain was not only a result of expansion at the range margin, but also of expansion from refuge sites beyond the main distribution and of infilling of the main distribution (this pattern contrasts with the pattern of colonization in Denmark, where *P. aegeria* was not recorded in the twentieth century and recent colonization has been into empty habitat).

Jane K. Hill, Chris D. Thomas, and Brian Huntley

These factors may have contributed to expansion rates in Britain approximately twice those in Denmark. Extrapolation of British range expansion rates since 1900 suggests that *P. aegeria* could colonize all currently suitable habitat in the next 3 years. However, this estimate is probably unrealistic because it does not take into account the locations of empty habitats, and expansion into more isolated areas may take much longer.

There is some indication in figure 7.6 that rates of expansion in Britain have declined over the past 30 years, and so we recalculated expansion rates from 1970 onward. This recalculation resulted in a lower estimated expansion rate of 1.6 km/yr. The lower rate may reflect colonization of areas with relatively low woodland cover, or the fact that the colonizing front has now overtaken most refuge sites, which are no longer contributing to the expansion rate. Extrapolation of this lower rate of recent areal expansion predicts that *P. aegeria* will have colonized all currently suitable habitats in the next 7 years, and that it will be able to colonize all areas in Britain that are predicted to be suitable in the future over the next 50 years (Hill et al. 1999b). However these estimates, too, are likely to be unrealistic because, once again, they do not account for the location of suitable empty habitat, much of which is remote from occupied areas at present.

Global mean surface air temperature has increased by 0.3°–0.6°C since the late nineteenth century (IPCC 1996). Although there are regional differences, Europe has warmed by approximately 0.8°C during this period (Watson et al. 1998), shifting the climatic isotherms northward by an average of 120 km (Parmesan et al. 1999). During this period, distributions of *P. aegeria* have shifted northward in Britain by approximately 107 km (England and Wales populations only; Hill et al. 2001b). Future climate change scenarios predict further global warming of up to 6°C by 2100 (IPCC 2001a), and climate within the study area is also predicted to get warmer and drier during this period (see table 7.1). Values of MTCO, for example, are predicted to increase by an average of 4.77°C by the end of the twenty-first century, compared with a mean increase of only 1.19°C between 1901 and 1996 (Hill et al. 1999b). Given that future rates of warming are predicted to be greater than any seen in the last 10,000 years (1996, 2001a), it is likely that any current distribution-climate lags will increase.

DISCUSSION

CLIMATE, HABITAT FRAGMENTATION, AND BUTTERFLY DISTRIBUTIONS

Many butterfly species had more extensive distributions in Britain during the nineteenth century than they do today (Thompson 1980), but underwent marked range contractions toward the end of the nineteenth century. It is likely that these contractions were related to climate change. However, there are no nineteenth-century climate datasets currently available that could be incorporated into the response surfaces to allow us to test whether these range contractions were consistent with climate cooling. There were, however, marked cool periods during the mid- and late nineteenth century (Central England Temperature record; Jones and Hulme 1997), and range expansions since 1900 appear to be consistent with general climate warming during this period (Hill et al. 1999b).

Results from this study show that climate is important in determining distributions of butterfly species at a European scale, and that butterfly distributions can be modeled very successfully using three appropriate bioclimate variables. Our data support the notion that this type of modeling approach will be valuable in investigating potential effects of climate change on other species. In this study, a combination of the same three bioclimate variables gave the best fit for all three species' distributions, but it is possible that other combinations of variables (e.g., sunshine hours, mean temperature of the warmest month, etc.) may be more appropriate for other species with different ecological requirements or physiology.

Our results indicate that at both European and British scales, distributions of *Pararge aegeria* are lagging behind current climates. Incorporation of habitat availability significantly improved the fit of the model at a British scale, but still predicted that *P. aegeria* should be able to occur in several areas beyond its current range margin (fig. 7.5B). Some of these areas were occupied historically (e.g., northern England and lowland Scotland; fig. 7.1B), but have not yet been recolonized; we interpret these findings as a lag between climate change and the species' distributional response. Other areas with simulated occurrence have never been occupied (e.g., the Western Isles of Scotland and the Isle of Man) and are probably too isolated currently to be colonized (Dennis and Shreeve 1997).

Pararge aegeria is essentially a woodland species in Britain, although it is much less restricted to woodland habitats in the south and west of its British distribution. The logistic regression model, however, was generated throughout the British distribution, and may therefore be predicting *P. aegeria* in areas at its range margin with less woodland than it actually requires (e.g., areas around the Wash and the Vale of York where there is very little woodland; fig. 7.5A), and thus overestimating its current range limit. However, given that many areas where the logistic model predicts it to occur do appear to have large areas of woodland (e.g., southern Scotland; fig. 7.5A), it seems that the lag effects are real. The spatial distribution of woodland within grid cells, as well as the area of woodland per se, also affects the species' distribution (Thomas and Jones 1993; Thomas et al. 1992): we interpret the lag effects as consistent with fine-scale habitat fragmentation affecting colonization rates in *P. aegeria* (Hill et al. 2001a). We have recently used the same techniques to

Jane K. Hill, Chris D. Thomas, and Brian Huntley

model climate and habitat availability in Britain for species that differ from *P. aegeria* in their habitat requirements (Hill et al. 2001b; Warren et al. 2001). These analyses indicate that distribution-climate lags are greatest in species with the most restricted habitat requirements. This finding gives further support to the notion that these lag effects are real and related to fine-scale habitat fragmentation. This is clearly an area that requires more study.

Comparison of observed and simulated distributions indicates that both *A. hyperantus* and *C. tullia* appear to be currently occupying most areas of climatically suitable habitat. Like *P. aegeria*, *A. hyperantus* has undergone contraction and expansion of its British distribution over the past 150 years, although distributional changes have not been as great as those observed in *P. aegeria* (Emmet and Heath 1990). *A. hyperantus* occurs in a greater variety of habitats at its range margin than does *P. aegeria*, and thus it is likely that *A. hyperantus* has been able to recolonize empty habitats more quickly: the wider availability of suitable habitats may allow *A. hyperantus* to track climate change more rapidly than *P. aegeria*. Differences in dispersal rates between the two species could also contribute to these differences, but there are currently insufficient data to test this. By contrast, *C. tullia*, which has a more northern distribution than the other two species, has undergone progressive contraction of its British distribution during the twentieth century. This contraction has been blamed primarily on habitat loss (Emmet and Heath 1990), although our model indicates that *C. tullia* currently appears to be occupying nearly all climatically suitable areas (fig. 7.4B). Climate warming over the twentieth century could have contributed to declines in its British distribution.

Predicting Future Distributions

Maps of simulated potential future distributions, such as those shown in this chapter (figs. 7.2C, 7.3C, 7.4C) do not represent forecasts of future distributions, but do provide an indication of the magnitude of the potential effects of climate change on species' distributions. Species are likely to respond individualistically to future climate change (Thomas et al. 2001), and new associations among species are likely to arise as climate changes. Newly suitable habitats may also contain new predators and competitors, making the actual outcomes of any change difficult to predict precisely (Huntley et al. 1995; Davis et al. 1998a, 1998b). However, the results presented here are in agreement with current empirical data showing a general poleward shift of species distributions over the twentieth century (Parmesan 1996; Parmesan et al. 1999).

Our models predict considerable potential northward expansion of *P. aegeria* and *A. hyperantus*. Our estimates of expansion rates of *P. aegeria* over the twentieth century suggest dispersal rates of approximately 1 km per generation (Hill et al. 2001a). Although there are currently no direct estimates of dispersal rates for any of the study species, data for other relatively mobile species (Hill et al. 1996) indicate that these rates, estimated from 10 km resolution data, are likely to be realistic for *P. aegeria,* and are probably also realistic for *A. hyperantus,* which is likely to have broadly similar dispersal rates. Thus these data indicate that distributions have expanded over the twentieth century at rates that are consistent with likely dispersal rates. However, the potential range expansions of more than 500 km that the models predict in Fennoscandia in the twenty-first century are far greater than what these species are likely to achieve in the course of this century. Thus realized ranges are likely to lag well behind potential ranges if climate changes of the rate and magnitude forecast do indeed occur. By contrast, the climate models predict little opportunity for range expansion for *C. tullia,* but predict considerable contraction of its southern range margins, resulting in a much more restricted distribution than at present and increasing the likelihood that *C. tullia* will go extinct in large areas of its current distribution in central and northern Europe and Britain.

Our study shows that even relatively mobile species such as *P. aegeria* appear to be lagging behind current climates. Such lags are likely to be even greater in less mobile species in fragmented landscapes and in species with more restricted habitat requirements. The consequences of lags for these species will be of particular concern because these species are likely to have high conservation value. Our recent research indicates that the majority of British butterflies have failed to track recent climate warming (Warren et al. 2001). Thus, range shifts under future climate warming may be the exception, not the rule. Over the past 30 years, during which the climate has been warming, most British butterflies have declined, particularly those species that are sedentary habitat specialists. These declines are almost certainly due to habitat loss (Warren et al. 2001). Thus, in the future, the loss of natural habitats, together with the inability of many species to track climate warming, will lead to biological communities becoming increasingly dominated by widespread, generalist species as habitat specialists continue to decline.

SUMMARY

We use climate response surfaces to investigate the importance of climate in determining the limits of the distributions of three nonmigratory satyrine butterfly species that have contrasting European distributions: *Pararge aegeria* and *Aphantopus hyperantus* have northern range margins in Britain, whereas *Coenonympha tullia* has its southern range margin in Britain. Climate response surfaces were generated for each species using a combination of three bioclimate variables chosen to reflect principal limitations on butterfly

Jane K. Hill, Chris D. Thomas, and Brian Huntley

growth and survival. The goodness of fit of observed distributions and simulated distributions from the climate models ($\kappa > 0.78$ for all species) indicated that climate is important in determining the distributions of all three species at a European scale. The models predict that butterfly distributions will shift substantially northward under predicted future climate change, and that *P. aegeria* and *A. hyperantus* will have the potential to shift their ranges into northern Fennoscandia. The climate models also predict considerable contraction of southern range margins, and *C. tullia* is predicted to have a much more restricted distribution than at present.

Pararge aegeria has undergone marked fluctuations in its British distribution over the past 150 years, and the model indicates that current distributions are lagging behind current climates. Incorporation of habitat (woodland) availability into the model significantly improves its fit to observed *P. aegeria* distributions, but still predicts distributions of *P. aegeria* farther north in Britain than they currently occur. This lag effect indicates that habitat fragmentation is likely to be affecting colonization even in a relatively mobile species such as *P. aegeria* and highlights the importance of considering habitat availability in predicting species' responses to future climate change.

ACKNOWLEDGMENTS

We thank the Biological Records Centre (CEH Monks Wood), Richard Fox (Butterfly Conservation), Per Stadel Nielsen (Denmark), Nils Ryrholm (Sweden), Øistein Berg (Norway), Kimmo Saarinen (Finland), and many recorders in Britain for providing butterfly records. We also thank Wolfgang Cramer (PIK Potsdam) for providing spline surfaces used to interpolate both the present and HADCM2 anomalies. The output from the HADCM2 transient simulation was supplied by the Climate Impacts LINK Project (Department of the Environment Contract EPG 1/1/16) on behalf of the Hadley Centre and the U.K. Meteorological Office. David Viner (CRU UEA) kindly facilitated access to these data. This study was funded by NERC grant GR9/3016 and GR3/12542.

CHAPTER 8

Ink Marks and Molecular Markers: Examining the Effects of Landscape on Dispersal Using Both Mark-Recapture and Molecular Methods

Nusha Keyghobadi, Jens Roland, Sherri Fownes, and Curtis Strobeck

APPROACHES TO THE STUDY OF SUBDIVIDED BUTTERFLY POPULATIONS

The importance of population patchiness and subdivision in determining both ecological and evolutionary dynamics has long been recognized for many organisms (Nicholson 1933; Andrewartha and Birch 1954; Wright 1931; Ehrlich and Raven 1969), including butterflies (Dowdeswell et al. 1940). Population subdivision may affect single-species dynamics (Hastings 1991), extinction rates (Levins 1970; Hanski and Gilpin 1991), interspecific competitive interactions (Caswell and Cohen 1991; Bengtsson 1991), predator-prey dynamics (Nicholson 1933; Hassell et al. 1991), and other trophic interactions (Polis et al. 1997), as well as effective population size and genetic variation (Wright 1978; Varvio et al. 1986; Gilpin 1991; Hastings and Harrison 1994). Population subdivision and spatial structure are also recurring themes in the field of conservation because fragmentation of natural habitats is a common result of human activities (Forman 1995).

Butterflies have been model systems for the study of subdivided populations because of their habitat specificity (often a result of host plant specificity), well-known natural history, and relatively well understood taxonomy. Empirical approaches to the study of subdivided butterfly populations have been varied and numerous, including, for example, mapping of occupied and unoccupied habitat patches (Thomas et al. 1992; Thomas and Harrison 1992), parametrization of patch occupancy models (Hanski et al. 1994), and examination of among-patch synchronicity in population fluctuations using long-term monitoring data (Sutcliffe et al. 1997b). Some of the approaches commonly used to study subdivided populations fall into two general categories, which have been described as "direct" and "indirect" (Slatkin 1985). For butterflies, the former category often involves the use of mark-release-recapture (MRR) methods (e.g., Dowdeswell et al. 1940; Dowdeswell et al. 1949; Ehrlich 1961b; Brussard and Ehrlich 1970; Ehrlich and Gilbert 1973; Watt et al. 1977; Gall 1984; Harrison et al. 1988; Baguette and Nève 1994; Warrington and Brayford 1995; Hill et al. 1996; Kuussaari et al. 1996; Nève et al. 1996a; Lewis et al. 1997; Sutcliffe et al. 1997a) or point-release methods (e.g., Harrison 1989; Schultz 1998a). MRR allows for description of the distribution and abundance of individuals in a given area, and both types of methods provide details on movements of individuals. The "indirect" approaches involve the description of the distribution of genetic variation among local populations (e.g., McKechnie et al. 1975; Cullenward et al. 1979; Rosenberg 1989; Baughman et al. 1990; Descimon and Napolitano 1993; Debinski 1994; Napolitano and Descimon 1994; Britten et al. 1995; Porter and Geiger 1995; Johannesen et al. 1996; Nève et al. 1996b; Peterson 1996; Lewis et al. 1997; Meglécz et al. 1997). Data on genetic variation can be used to estimate genetic distances and gene flow among subdivided populations (Slatkin 1985) and to determine whether most genetic variation occurs within or among local populations. Movement may be inferred indirectly from the observed patterns.

Several studies of subdivided populations have successfully combined direct and indirect approaches (e.g., Cullenward et al. 1979; Rosenberg 1989; Britten et al. 1995; Nève et al. 1996b; Peterson 1996; Lewis et al. 1997; Meglécz et al. 1997). Many of these have used dispersal data from MRR to aid in the interpretation of geographic patterns of genetic variation and to assess the importance of gene flow in determining population genetic structure. The combination of these approaches improves our understanding of the causes and consequences of population structure.

In many cases, the ecological and genetic approaches cannot be applied at the same spatial scale. The scale at which genetic differences among local populations are detectable is often considerably greater than the scale over which MRR or point-release studies can be feasibly executed. This is particularly true when genetic markers such as allozymes, which have been the most popular markers in such studies, are used. These markers do not have the "resolving power" to detect genetic variation at a small spatial scale. Microsatellite DNA loci, on the other hand, are highly variable genetic markers that are rapidly becoming the markers of choice for many population genetic studies, and have been used to detect genetic structuring among populations in which variation at allozyme loci was insufficient to do so (Hughes and Queller 1993; Paetkau and Strobeck 1994). Thus, microsatellites may allow the description of genetic structure at smaller spatial scales than is possible using allozymes. In particular, they may do so at the same scales at which ecological studies of butterflies are commonly conducted.

Nusha Keyghobadi, Jens Roland, Sherri Fownes, and Curtis Strobeck

EFFECTS OF LANDSCAPE ON DISPERSAL
AND POPULATION STRUCTURE

Unsuitable habitats may act as barriers to movement and genetic exchange in Lepidoptera (Fisher and Ford 1947; Dowdeswell et al. 1949). However, few studies have quantified such effects. Empirical studies of butterfly dispersal using direct methods typically focus on the distribution of high-quality patches of habitat, but have not generally considered the effects of different types of intervening habitat on between-patch movements (Watt et al. 1977; Harrison 1989; Baguette and Nève 1994; Hill et al. 1996; Lewis et al. 1997). Studies of the effects of such landscape variables in highly subdivided populations are almost nonexistent (but see Moilanen and Hanski 1998).

A limited number of population genetic studies of Lepidoptera using indirect methods have considered how the type of habitat separating local populations can contribute to their genetic differentiation. Some populations separated by a physical barrier have been shown to be more genetically dissimilar than populations not separated by such a barrier (Napolitano and Descimon 1994; Johannesen et al. 1996; Nève et al. 1996b; Meglécz et al. 1997). Patterns of genetic variation in regions of highly fragmented versus unfragmented habitat have also been shown to differ (Britten et al. 1995; VanDongen et al. 1998). For example, Britten et al. (1995) found low levels of gene flow and lack of isolation by distance among populations of the butterfly *Euphydryas editha* in the Great Basin, but not in the Rocky Mountains. They ascribe these results to limited dispersal in the Great Basin area, where the species' high-elevation boreal habitat is highly fragmented.

An understanding of the relative effects of different landscape components (e.g., habitat types) on dispersal and gene flow is essential for predicting the impacts of anthropogenic changes to the landscape on the ecology and long-term persistence of species. In some alpine areas, for example, the tree line is rising because of global warming and fire suppression (Kearney 1982; Grabherr et al. 1994; Taylor 1995; Woodward et al. 1995). This results in the meadows that are habitat to subalpine and alpine butterflies, including our study organism, *Parnassius smintheus,* growing smaller and more isolated. Though *P. smintheus* is common in North America, other species in the genus, such as *P. mnemosyne* and *P. apollo,* are endangered in other parts of the world (Heath 1981; Väisänen and Somerma 1985; Bengtsson et al. 1989; Meglécz et al. 1997; Witkowski et al. 1997). To predict how such changes in the distribution of forest and meadow habitats over time will affect butterfly species, it is necessary to understand and estimate how easily individuals can move through each of these habitat types.

In this chapter, we present the results of a MRR study and a population genetic study conducted simultaneously, at the same spatial scale, on the same set of local populations of the alpine butterfly *P. smintheus*

(Papilionidae) in the Kananaskis region of Alberta, Canada (Keyghobadi et al. 1999; Roland et al. 2000). The most distant sites in our study are approximately 12 km apart, which is a relatively large spatial scale for a MRR study, but a small spatial scale for a population genetic study. We use microsatellite DNA loci as genetic markers, which permit us to detect population genetic structure at a small spatial scale. Thus, we are able to integrate MRR data and population genetic data more directly than has been possible previously, and we can measure the decline in genetic similarity of local populations that results from decreased dispersal.

In these studies, we focus on how the type of habitat separating local populations of *P. smintheus* affects rates of dispersal and genetic structure. *P. smintheus* inhabits alpine and subalpine meadows (Sperling and Kondla 1991) that have a patchy distribution within a largely forested landscape. Also, within a given meadow, individuals tend to be localized to "hotspots" of abundance, in contrast with other meadows or portions of meadows where *P. smintheus* is rarely seen. Thus, *P. smintheus* is an ideal subject for a study of the effects of different habitat types on dispersal and gene flow because movements between local populations can occur both through meadow habitat and through forest habitat.

METHODS

MARK-RELEASE-RECAPTURE STUDY

Field Methods

We used mark-recapture methods to estimate the distances moved by *P. smintheus,* and to obtain relative indices of population size, in a series of alpine meadows (fig. 8.1). Meadows were sampled three or four times in both 1995 and 1996. Individuals were captured by hand net and marked with a three-letter identification code, using a fine-tipped permanent marker. We recorded the sex of the butterfly, the meadow in which it was captured, an *x* and *y* coordinate for the capture location, the date, and the time of day. At each subsequent recapture, we recorded the identification code, date, time, meadow of recapture, and the *x* and *y* coordinates of the location. Distances that butterflies moved were estimated as the straight-line distance between initial and subsequent capture locations, but these lines were restricted to follow ridgetops, given that this species is largely restricted to alpine habitats. Craig's method (Craig 1953; Southwood 1978) was used to estimate population size from the mark-recapture data; estimates were averaged for the different sample times over each summer.

Nusha Keyghobadi, Jens Roland, Sherri Fownes, and Curtis Strobeck

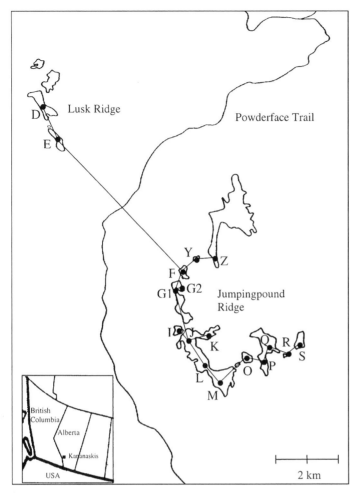

Figure 8.1 The study area, showing locations of sample sites. Outlined patches denote high-altitude (>2000 m elevation) meadow habitat. Distances between sites were measured along lines running along ridgetops. (Adapted from Keyghobadi et al. 1999.)

Statistical Analysis of Landscape and Movement

We wanted to estimate the effects of the type and amount of intervening habitat (meadow and forest) on the number of butterflies moving between pairs of meadows. Between each pair of meadows, three distances were calculated using topographic maps (1:50,000) and 1993 aerial photographs (1:40,000): total distance, distance through forest, and distance through meadow. The total distance was the sum of the forest and meadow components. These distances were taken from the centroids of butterfly capture at each site and were constrained to the ridgetops (see fig. 8.1). We constrained our measurements in this way because in our study area individuals are largely restricted to the ridgetops. Because some meadow pairs had other meadows between them, the distance through meadow and forest between them was the sum of individual segments of each habitat type. For each pair of sites, we also measured the cumulative change in elevation (both up and down) between the centroids at each site.

For each pair of meadows in an individual's recapture event, the "source" meadow is where the butterfly was originally marked, and the "target" meadow is where it was recaptured. Many butterflies were marked and recaptured in the same meadow (i.e., no net movement), and for these "pairs" the distance was zero. Most butterflies that left their source meadow moved only to the immediately adjacent meadow. Because butterflies were marked in all meadows, there was potential for detecting dispersal in both directions between the two meadows of a pair. Movements in the two directions were used as separate estimates of the effect of the intervening landscape, resulting in some lack of independence among estimates (Roland et al. 2000).

Model Fitting

We used generalized linear models with Poisson errors (McCullagh and Nelder 1989), using S-Plus software (Mathsoft, Seattle), to model the number of recaptures moving from each source meadow to each target meadow. The number of *Parnassius* recaptured for each meadow pair was modeled as a function of

1. the number marked in the source meadow, as a controlling variable for marking effort
2. the year (1995, 1996)
3. the summed distance (km) through open meadow between the two meadows
4. the summed distance (km) through any intervening forests between the two meadows
5. the cumulative change in elevation (meters, both down and up) between the two meadows
6. the area (ha) of the source meadow
7. the area (ha) of the target meadow
8. the index of population size in the source meadow
9. the index of population size in the target meadow

All independent variables, except year, were log-transformed for the analysis, so the coefficients in the model were exponential coefficients. The best-fitting model (see Roland et al. 2000 for details on model selection) was subsequently used to predict the number of the butterflies marked in the source meadow that would be captured in the target meadow for all possible pairs of meadows. In this way, estimates of butterfly movement were obtained for all meadow pairs, including those between which no dispersal was actually observed. These estimates of movement were used subsequently for comparison to genetic distance estimates. To control for marking effort, estimates of movement from mark-recapture were expressed as the proportion of butterflies marked in one meadow expected to be recaptured in the second meadow. These predictions were not necessarily symmetrical, and the proportion of marked butterflies from site A recaptured at site B would not usually equal the proportion of marks from B recaptured at A. Since only one genetic distance is calculated for each pair of meadows, the two estimates of butterfly movement were averaged to yield a single estimate of dispersal between each pair of meadows. The resulting estimates of dispersal were then log-transformed to linearize the relationship with genetic distance.

POPULATION GENETIC STUDY

Sample Collection and DNA Isolation

Adult butterfly samples were collected from seventeen sites in the MRR area in 1995 and 1996 (see fig. 8.1). During the mark-recapture study, small (approx. 0.15 cm^2) wing clippings were taken from butterflies the first time they were captured. In 1995, clippings were taken from all butterflies marked, and in 1996 they were taken from 50% of the butterflies marked. We assessed the effect of wing clipping by comparing the distributions of distances moved by clipped and unclipped butterflies, as well as the distributions of minimum number of days alive for the two groups (Kolmogorov-Smirnov two-sample test). Also, in 1995, whole adult butterflies were collected from each site on the last day the site was visited for MRR. Samples were placed in glassine envelopes and stored at −80°C. Genomic DNA was isolated from samples using QIAamp spin columns (QIAGEN). For wing clippings, the entire sample was used; for whole butterflies, a sample of abdominal tissue (for males) or thoracic tissue (for females) was used.

PCR Amplification and Analysis of Microsatellites

From each sample, four microsatellite loci, previously isolated from *P. smintheus* (Keyghobadi et al. 1999), were amplified using the polymerase chain reaction (PCR). Amplification products were electrophoresed and detected using an ABI 373A Automated Sequencer and analyzed using Genescan and Genotyper software (ABI).

Statistical Analysis

Because of the presence of null or nonamplifying alleles (Callen et al. 1993; Paetkau and Strobeck 1995; Pemberton et al. 1995) at all loci, for each locus at each site we had to estimate of the frequency of the null allele, and the frequencies of all other alleles, using the estimation-maximization (EM) algorithm (Ceppellini et al. 1955; Yasuda and Kimura 1968; Long et al. 1995). This algorithm is commonly used to estimate allele frequencies for the ABO blood group system, in which the O allele is recessive to both the A and B alleles and homozygous phenotypes include both true homozygotes and heterozygotes with one O allele. A microsatellite null allele is analogous to the O allele because it is recessive to all other alleles and homozygous phenotypes may be truly homozygous or heterozygous with a null allele. The algorithm provides maximum likelihood estimates of allele frequencies, which we used to calculate Nei's standard genetic distance (Nei 1972) between all pairs of sites.

We investigated the associations between pairwise genetic distances, a subset of the landscape variables (total distance, distance through forest, and distance through meadow), and the predicted proportion of marked butterflies moving between sites using Mantel tests of matrix correspondence (Mantel 1967). The Mantel test determines the significance of the correlation between two variables that are measured pairwise between the same set of n objects. The significance of a particular correlation coefficient is determined by comparing the observed value to a distribution generated by random permutation of one of the $n \times n$ pairwise matrices. We also used partial Mantel tests (Smouse et al. 1986), a method analogous to determining partial correlations, to control for associations between our measures of landscape structure. All Mantel tests were performed using the R Package (Legendre and Vaudor 1991), and 3,000 matrix randomizations were used for each test. The total experimental error for all tests was limited to 0.05 by using a sequential Bonferroni adjustment (Sokal and Rohlf 1995).

RESULTS

MARK-RELEASE-RECAPTURE STUDY

General Results

We recorded a total of 1,171 recaptures of 2,774 individuals over the two years of the study. Movements of up to 1,729 m were observed, but on average, movements were less than 160 m. Over the two years, less than 9% of marked butterflies left the site of marking, and less than 4% emigrated through at least some forest (table 8.1). The sexes did not differ in mean distance moved in either year, but butterflies tended to move farther in 1996. There was no effect of wing clipping on mean distance moved (table 8.2) or on survival (Roland et al. 2000).

Nusha Keyghobadi, Jens Roland, Sherri Fownes, and Curtis Strobeck

Table 8.1 Total captures and recaptures of *Parnassius smintheus* at Jumpingpound Ridge and Lusk Ridge in 1995 and 1996

Year	No. Captures	No. Recaptures, Total	No. Recaptures, Emigrating (%)	No. Recaptures Emigrating through Forest (%)
1995	1,574	726	33 (4.6)	15 (2)
1996	1,200	445	67 (15)	26 (6)
Total	2,774	1,171	100 (8.5)	41 (3.5)

Note: Percentages emigrating are percentages of the total number of recaptures including both recaptures at the site of marking and recaptures at other sites.

Table 8.2 Distances moved by *Parnassius smintheus* butterflies at Jumpingpound Ridge and Lusk Ridge, Alberta

Group	Mean Distance in Meters (SE)	P
Males (1995)	131.9 (6.06)	0.62
Females (1995)	131.6 (21.6)	
Males (1996)	162.4 (9.38)	0.11
Females (1996)	118.0 (36.7)	
Clipped (1996)	159.8 (17.1)	0.75
Unclipped (1996)	153.6 (9.9)	

Note: Distributions of distances moved compared using Kolmogorov-Smirnov two-sample test.

Effect of Landscape on Movement

Not surprisingly, the number of butterflies marked in the source meadows had a large effect on the number subsequently recaptured; this variable was included, therefore, as a factor controlling for marking effort in all subsequent models. There was no effect of year on the rate of recapture after controlling for number marked (deviance = 1.021, $P = 0.31$), and year was not included as a factor in subsequent models.

All three landscape variables (distance through meadow, distance through forest, and elevation change) had significant effects on the number of marked butterflies moving between pairs of meadows (table 8.3). Distance through both meadow and forest had a negative effect on number recaptured, but distance through forest had a much steeper effect (table 8.3; fig. 8.2), implying greater "viscosity" (Wiens et al. 1977) of forest than of open meadow. This greater viscosity was also evident from the fact that no observed movement occurred if there was more than 1 km of forest between meadow pairs, whereas movement of over 1.7 km was observed through meadow (fig. 8.2). There were also fewer recaptures when two meadows were separated by large changes in elevation, suggesting, not surprisingly, that larger valleys are greater barriers even after controlling for the effects of the amount of intervening meadow and forest.

Table 8.3 Model parameters for significant terms in the generalized linear model (S-Plus)

Variable	d.f.	Coefficient	t	P for t Test	P^* for Randomization	Change in Deviance	P for χ^2 Test on Deviance
Null	160					4,113.03	
Intercept		−4.429	−8.25	0.000	0.000		
Number marked	1	1.050	29.66	0.000	0.000	1,176.46	0.000
Distance through meadow	1	−0.588	−4.35	0.001	0.009	1,015.25	0.000
Distance through forest	1	−1.115	−6.44	0.000	0.000	1,686.80	0.000
Elevation change	1	−0.354	−6.50	0.000	0.006	27.38	0.000
Population size in source	1	−0.556	−6.17	0.000	0.005	40.70	0.000
Population size in target	1	0.566	6.87	0.000	0.001	15.14	0.000
Residual deviance	154					150.30	

Note: Coefficients were also tested for significance by randomization methods (see Roland et al. 2000); data were randomized and refit to the GLM, and the number of times that the coefficients were equal to or greater than our observed coefficients (out of 1,000 randomizations) was used to estimate a probability P^*. Dispersion parameter = 0.98.

Neither the size of the source meadow nor the size of the target meadow affected the number of recaptures. The fact that the size of target meadows did not affect the number of butterflies moving to them may be because movement of this species tends to be constrained to ridgetops, so that all meadows are encountered, regardless of their size. Population size in both the source and target meadows had significant effects on the number of recaptures. More butterflies left small source populations ($\beta = -0.556$, $t = -6.17$, $P = 0.000$), and more immigrated into target meadows with large populations ($\beta = 0.566$, $t = 6.87$, $P = 0.000$). It is of interest that the two coefficients for emigration and immigration have almost the same magnitude, although they are opposite in sign (see table 8.3). We believe that the reason for the observed effects of population size may be that population size is a surrogate of meadow quality. Good-quality meadows produce large butterfly populations, and dispersing butterflies may tend to move to and remain in those meadows; poor-quality meadows, on the other hand, may produce small populations from which individuals emigrate at a greater rate in search of better sites.

Our model separating the effects of distance through meadow and distance through forest provides a better predictor of butterfly movement than does an equivalent model using only total distance (change in deviance

Nusha Keyghobadi, Jens Roland, Sherri Fownes, and Curtis Strobeck

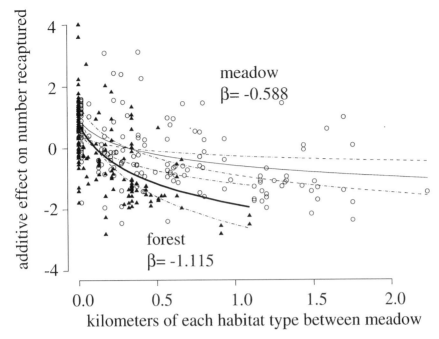

Figure 8.2 Effects of distance between source and target sites through meadow (thin line) and through forest (thick line) on the number of butterflies recaptured at the target site. Plots show the additive effect of each variable on the number of recaptures, within the full generalized linear model with exponential fit. Data for each meadow pair are represented twice, by one point for the distance through meadow (open circles) and one point for distance through forest (solid triangles).

between models $= 21.49$, change in d.f. $= 1$, $F = 15.65$, $P = 0.001$). By taking into account the differential viscosity of the two habitat types, we are better able to estimate landscape connectivity for *P. smintheus*. Having done so, the model permits us to predict movement across other landscapes, or to estimate movement at the same sites in the past when there was less forest (see Roland et al. 2000).

POPULATION GENETIC STUDY

There was a significant negative correlation between Nei's standard genetic distance and the estimated proportion of marked animals moving between sites ($r = -0.443$, $P = 0.002$) (fig. 8.3). Genetic distance was significantly positively correlated with total geographic distance ($r = 0.430$, $P = 0.006$) (fig. 8.4), distance through meadow ($r = 0.344$, $P = 0.007$), and particularly with distance through forest ($r = 0.471$, $P = 0.011$). The coefficient of determination (r^2) between genetic distance and distance through forest ($r^2 = 0.222$) was almost double that between genetic distance and distance through meadow ($r^2 = 0.118$).

Distance through forest and distance through meadow were themselves correlated ($r = 0.732$, $P = 0.000$), so we used partial Mantel tests to

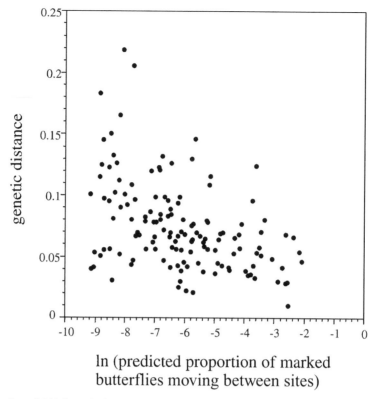

y-axis: genetic distance

x-axis: ln (predicted proportion of marked butterflies moving between sites)

Figure 8.3 Nei's standard genetic distance versus ln of the average predicted proportion of marked butterflies moving between a pair of sites. The negative association between the two variables is significant ($r = -0.443$, $P = 0.002$, Mantel test). (Adapted from Keyghobadi et al. 1999.)

separate the effects of these two landscape features. The partial correlation between genetic distance and distance through forest, controlling for distance through meadow, was not significant using an adjusted α level, even though the correlation coefficient was fairly high ($r = 0.343$) and the probability value was low ($P = 0.04$). In contrast, the partial correlation between genetic distance and distance through meadow, controlling for distance through forest, was also not significant, with a correlation coefficient that was extremely low ($r = -0.001$, $P = 0.49$). The coefficient of multiple determination (R^2), the multivariate analogue of r^2 that describes the proportion of variation in genetic distance accounted for jointly by distance through forest and distance through meadow, was 0.222, which was equal to that for forest alone. Thus, although the effects of distance through meadow and distance through forest are both significant, once the correlation between these two variables is accounted for, it is the effect of distance through forest that accounts for almost all of the variation in genetic distance.

Nusha Keyghobadi, Jens Roland, Sherri Fownes, and Curtis Strobeck

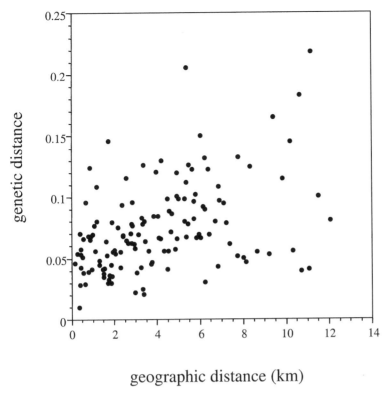

Figure 8.4 Nei's standard genetic distance versus total geographic distance. The positive association between the two variables is significant ($r = 0.430$, $P = 0.006$, Mantel test), indicating a pattern of isolation by distance. (Adapted from Keyghobadi et al. 1999.)

DISCUSSION

Microsatellite DNA markers are powerful tools for the study of population genetic structure, allowing us, in this case, to detect population subdivision at a very small spatial scale (<12 km). The significant correlation that we observed between genetic distance and geographic distance (see fig. 8.4) suggests a pattern of isolation by distance. Our results contrast with those from other butterfly populations that showed very little genetic structure at scales of 30 km to 475 km (Cullenward et al. 1979; Rosenberg 1989; Peterson 1996). Our ability to detect such differences may be due not only to the use of microsatellite markers, but also to the one-dimensional distribution of meadows along ridgetops in our study area. In general, movement constrained to a one-dimensional habitat is more amenable to the detection of isolation by distance than movement through a two-dimensional habitat would be (Slatkin 1993). Our results may also reflect the combined effects of patchy habitat distribution and the low vagility of *P. smintheus* through forested areas (Roland et al. 2000) in reducing rates of gene flow in this species.

The ability to detect genetic differentiation of populations at a small spatial scale allowed us to integrate the genetic data with MRR data obtained at the same scale. We observed a significant negative correlation between pairwise genetic distances and predicted rates of dispersal (see fig. 8.3). Because gene flow depends on successful breeding as well as dispersal (Gilbert and Singer 1973; Slatkin 1985), dispersing individuals in our study area must be contributing to the gene pool of local populations into which they move. If they do not reproduce after dispersal—for example, if they are not afforded matings or suitable oviposition sites—then the relationship between dispersal and genetic structure should be very weak or nonexistent. Such a situation could conceivably arise for butterflies because they have short adult lifetimes, imposing a narrow window of time in which immigrants must mate or oviposit successfully. It should be even more likely to arise in *Parnassius* because females mate only once, very soon after emergence, at which time the male lays down a sphragis to prevent further copulations (Scott 1973b).

In a number of population genetic studies, patterns of genetic variation suggest more gene flow than would be expected given known dispersal distances (e.g., McKechnie et al. 1975; Peterson 1996). It is hypothesized that in such cases gene flow may be a result of infrequent episodes of long-distance dispersal or extinction-colonization dynamics (Slatkin 1985), and not the types of dispersal events that have been observed. The correlation between genetic distance and dispersal that we observed suggests that, within our study area, considerable gene flow does result from the types of "normal" dispersal events we recorded using MRR.

We have demonstrated consistent effects of different matrix types for dispersal and gene flow in *P. smintheus;* in particular, we have shown that forests act as stronger barriers to both of these processes than do open meadows. Thus, population isolation is not just a function of distance; the viscosities of intervening habitat elements may be equally important in defining the degree of "functional" isolation. Meglécz et al. (1997) suggest that forests are also barriers to gene flow for the congener *P. mnemosyne.* Our results stand in contrast to those of Moilanen and Hanski (1998), who found that incorporating landscape variables into a model of the *Melitaea cinxia* metapopulation did little to improve the fit of the model to observed data. This difference may, again, reflect increased ability to detect such effects for a species moving through a one-dimensional series of patches (*P. smintheus*) versus one moving through a two-dimensional series of patches (*M. cinxia*). Our methods may thus be most applicable to species occupying one-dimensional habitats, such as riparian meadows, coastal margins, or ridgetops.

The effect of matrix type on dispersal and gene flow is an important consideration in the conservation of naturally subdivided populations. Where a naturally subdivided population is affected by habitat fragmentation, the distances between the local populations may remain constant while the nature of the matrix separating them changes. Our results suggest that the rising tree line in the alpine landscape, by increasing the amount of forest separating local populations, reduces dispersal and gene flow in *P. smintheus*. This reduction will lower levels of genetic variation within populations because genetic drift will be less strongly countered by gene flow. Concomitant reductions in habitat patch size and population size will probably also act to reduce genetic variation. Reduced genetic variation has negative implications for population survival in the short term (Saccheri et al. 1998) and for adaptation to changing environmental conditions in the long term (Templeton et al. 1990).

SUMMARY

We combined mark-release-recapture (MRR) and molecular techniques to study dispersal and population structure in the alpine butterfly *Parnassius smintheus*. Using highly variable microsatellite DNA markers, we described genetic structure among the same set of local populations we studied using MRR. We were able to measure the decline in genetic similarity of local populations with decreasing dispersal rate; there was a significant negative correlation between genetic distance and dispersal. These data suggest that gene flow in the study area is largely a result of the types of movements that can be observed using MRR. With both methods we detected effects of landscape on population structure; in particular, we found that forests were strong barriers to dispersal and gene flow.

ACKNOWLEDGMENTS

Field work was assisted by Norine Ambrose, Mark Caldwell, Sue Cotterill, Marian Forrester, Fiona Johnson, Chris Schmidt, Lynnette Scott, Kirsty Ward, and Arliss Winship. Advice on laboratory methods was provided by John Coffin, Corey Davis, and David Paetkau. Nancy Heckman, Phil Taylor, and John Brzustowski provided support with statistical analyses. We are thankful to Ilkka Hanski and one anonymous reviewer for very helpful comments on the manuscript. Research was supported by NSERC, Challenge Grants in Biodiversity, Parks Canada, and the Alberta Sports Recreation Parks and Wildlife Foundation.

CHAPTER 9

Environmental Variation, Life Histories, and Allocation

Carol L. Boggs

Environmental variation influences the realized life histories of organisms through changes in their allocation of resources and time to reproduction, survival, growth, storage, and foraging. Yet, because our understanding of allocation is limited, we have little ability to predict changes in life history traits in the face of variable environments. Do constraints on allocation exist, limiting possible combinations of life history traits, and hence limiting the organism's ability to respond to environmental change? Does the form or type of environmental variation make a predictable difference in the allocation response, and hence in realized life histories? The answers to these and related questions determine how effectively individuals can maintain survival and reproduction, buffering their resulting net fitness against the effects of environmental variation.

This relative ability of individuals to buffer fitness against environmental variation in turn affects population dynamics and species persistence. Understanding the physiological or behavioral mechanisms that organisms use to buffer life histories against environmental variation is thus critical to understanding or predicting, for example, range shifts or population dynamics under global change scenarios (e.g., Hellmann 2002; McLaughlin et al. 2002b), effects of introduced predators or hosts, or the abundance and distribution of individuals (e.g., Gatto et al. 1989; Koojiman et al. 1989; Gurney et al. 1990; Hallam et al. 1990; McCauley et al. 1990; Boggs 1992; Boggs 1997a). To achieve these larger-scale goals, we need a general understanding of the circumstances under which individuals can and cannot buffer their life histories against environmental variation.

Consideration of the effects of environmental variation on individuals can profitably be divided into three parts, based on the temporal or spatial frequency of the environmental variation relative to the individual's life span or home range (fig. 9.1). First, if variation occurs at a temporal scale that is longer than an individual's life span, or at a spatial scale that is broader than an individual's range, it will be experienced as a consistent difference from the mean environmental condition previously experienced by members of the population (fig. 9.1A). For example, in the case of food supply, such variation would be experienced as a change in food availability to either consistent resource scarcity or abundance. Functionally, this is coarse-grained or long-term environmental variation. Second, if variation occurs at a scale shorter than an individual's life span or smaller than an individual's range, but longer than the time constant of an organism's behavioral or physiological response, that variation may be experienced as variance around a mean value for the environmental parameter in question (fig. 9.1B). Again, in the case of food supply, such variation would be experienced as fluctuations in food availability. Functionally, this is intermediate-grained or short-term environmental variation. There is a third option that is more complex and will not be dealt with in this chapter: the organism experiences changes in both the mean and variance of an environmental parameter (fig. 9.1C). Functionally, the environmental parameter is varying simultaneously over two scales, coarse- and intermediate-grained or short- and long-term. Such an event could happen in a deteriorating environment—for example, one in which a mean shows a clear trend, yet variance still occurs at an intermediate scale—as could happen under some global climate change scenarios.

Here I synthesize data available from butterflies to begin addressing the effects of both long-term and short-term environmental variation on individual life histories. Such effects occur through changes in the time and resource budgets of individuals and can result in changes in population size and distribution.

The analyses summarized here will be used to begin to answer some of the following key questions concerning the operation of mechanisms used by individuals to buffer life history traits against variation in the environment:

Does the identity of the varying environmental factor affect individuals' ability to buffer life histories through changed allocation patterns? If so, why? In particular, do variation in the availability of time and of physical resources have the same effects on allocation patterns?

Does the frequency or intensity of environmental variation affect individuals' ability to buffer life histories through changed allocation patterns? That is, do organisms use different allocation strategies to respond to slow environmental changes (perceived as changes in the mean) and rapid environmental changes (perceived as changes in the variance)? Does the mean value of an

Carol L. Boggs

A.

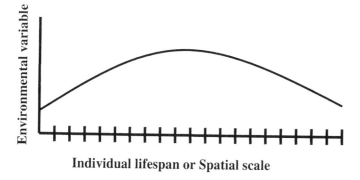

B.

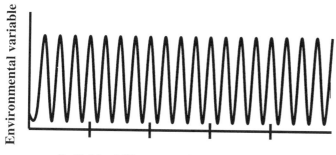

C.

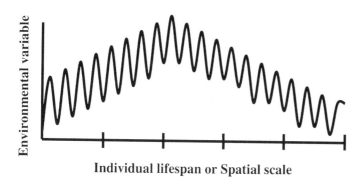

Figure 9.1 Three patterns of environmental change. (A) Change in the mean environment as experienced by individuals when the frequency of environmental variation is coarse-grained in space or time. (B) Variance in the environment as experienced by individuals when the frequency of environmental variation is intermediate-grained in space or time. (C) Changes in both the mean and the variance of the environment, as experienced when environmental variation is complex.

environmental parameter determine how much variation around it can be effectively buffered? Does buffering ability against environmental extremes depend on the frequency with which those extremes are encountered? Is variation at the edge of a species' range generally larger and more difficult for individuals to buffer? Is the mean around which the variation occurs more extreme at range edges?

Are there constraints on resource or time allocation, and hence on ability to buffer life histories? That is, under what circumstances do developmental constraints, or forced trade-offs, circumscribe an individual's allocation patterns and hence life history options? Under what circumstances does the need for resource congruence (the use of nutrient types in a specified ratio: Bazzaz 1996) affect an organism's allocation patterns? Are there some environmental variables for which phylogenetic constraints are more likely to limit allocation responses and hence life history possibilities?

Under what conditions is environmental variation most likely to affect population dynamics? In other words, when is buffering of life history traits most likely to fail? Do variation in the availability of time and of physical resources to individuals have equivalent effects on population dynamics? What temporal and spatial scales of environmental variation are most important in determining the dynamics of populations with different types of population structure? Can apparent density-independent effects of environmental variation on population dynamics be mediated by resource or time allocation mechanisms in a density-dependent manner, blurring the distinction between the two?

To provide a background for addressing these questions, I now turn to two sets of case studies of the effects of environmental variation on resource allocation and life history traits. The first considers allocation responses to variation in a physical resource, food; the second addresses responses to variation in time availability.

CASE STUDIES: EFFECTS OF VARIATION IN FOOD RESOURCES

An obvious variable physical environmental factor is food supply, which may change over space or time. To analyze changes in an individual's resource allocation in response to such variation, we first need to understand the baseline allocation patterns under conditions of plentiful food. Next, we need to pick apart allocation responses to different temporal patterns of adult and larval food restriction or surplus in order to explore their effects on life history parameters and thence on fitness and population dynamics. In the process we will gain insight into the ways in which organisms can or cannot use resource allocation to buffer their life histories against variation in food availability at both long and short time scales. For this analysis, I focus primarily on my own work on *Speyeria mormonia,* but draw on others' studies for comparison.

BACKGROUND

Speyeria mormonia Life History

Speyeria mormonia (Nymphalidae) inhabits montane grasslands of North America. This butterfly has a univoltine life cycle. At my study site at 2,880 m near the Rocky Mountain Biological Laboratory (RMBL), in Gunnison County, Colorado, USA, adults fly from July to September (Boggs 1987a). The species exhibits strong protandry, with the peak of female adult emergence approximately 2 weeks after that of the males. Adults feed on nectar as well as on mud and dung (in a behavior termed "mud puddling"). Young males are most common at mud and dung, followed by older individuals of both sexes. Young females are rarely seen mud puddling (Boggs and Jackson 1991; Sculley and Boggs 1996), but presumably obtain nutrients derived from mud puddling from males at mating (Adler and Pearson 1982; Pivnick and McNeil 1987). Females mate once on average (Boggs 1986), receiving a spermatophore from the male. Male-derived nutrients are used for egg production (Boggs 1997b) and probably for other purposes. Adult butterflies are capable of behavioral thermoregulation via dorsal solar basking as well as occasional shivering. The ability to shiver probably increases the range of ambient environmental conditions over which flight (hence foraging and reproduction) is possible, but at an as yet unmeasured energy cost.

Females lay eggs singly. Newly hatched larvae overwinter as unfed first instars. After spring snowmelt, larvae feed on *Viola* spp. (Violaceae).

This life history indicates that larval host plants, adult nectar sources, mud and dung, and spermatophores are potential foci for the effects of variation in food supply on female resource allocation patterns and resultant life histories. Given that females do not spend much time mud puddling and that spermatophores depend on male allocation responses, I focus here on larval host plants and adult nectar sources.

Sources of Variation in Availability of Larval Host and Adult Nectar Plants

Three broad factors driving variation in food availability for *S. mormonia* are weather, anthropogenic habitat alteration, and, potentially, competition. The first factor, weather, influences the quantity and quality of nectar and larval host plants through soil moisture, relative humidity, and temperature (e.g., Boggs 1987b; de Valpine and Harte 2001). Weather also influences the ability of butterfly larvae to eat and of adults to fly to find food, mates, and oviposition sites, as has been documented for other species. Under cold cloudy, rainy, or snowy conditions, it can be difficult or impossible for butterflies to raise their body temperatures sufficiently high to allow activity (e.g., Watt 1968; Kingsolver 1983a, 1983b; C. L. Boggs and S. Fallon, unpub.). Such weather conditions may result in food stress for individuals over a period of a day to a lifetime.

A second factor influencing variation in food availability is anthropogenic habitat alteration, which can affect food supplies for *S. mormonia* both positively and negatively. For example, grazing can lower flower availability both on a short-term basis, if flowers are eaten, and on a long-term basis, if cattle or sheep stocking patterns select against the Compositae favored by the butterflies. Alternatively, introduction of exotics such as bull thistles can increase flower availability (E. Fleishman, pers. comm.). Fertilizing, either intentionally or unintentionally through dry deposition of air pollutants, seeding with non-native grasses, and controlled burning of habitat have also been shown to alter the density of both larval and adult host plants of related butterfly species in the short and long term (Weiss 1999; Fleishman 2000).

Finally, food availability is influenced not only by the density of resources and the ability of the butterfly to exploit those resources, but also by the relative densities of the butterfly and all other users of the resources. The possible effects of competitors for either violets or nectar have not been studied. However, we know that both plant densities and *S. mormonia* larval and adult abundances fluctuate through time and space, suggesting, at the least, that levels of intraspecific competition for food resources may likewise vary. For example, adult butterflies congregate in areas with flowers that are still in bloom at the end of the flight season (C. L. Boggs, pers. obs.; Lerner 2000). Further, butterfly and plant population numbers also change across years, which may alter the intensity of any competition. This change is sometimes dramatic, as with a late season freeze in 1985 that reduced the butterfly population by two orders of magnitude and caused the abortion of most flowers used by the butterflies for nectar (C. L. Boggs and D. Inouye, unpub.). Changes in butterfly and plant population sizes need not be synchronous, however; in the following year, 1986, the number of flower heads of the primary nectar plant used by the butterflies increased by sixfold, yet the butterfly population only approximately doubled in size (C. L. Boggs and D. Inouye, unpub.).

The effects of weather, anthropogenic habitat alteration, and possible competitors on resource availability for *S. mormonia* are likely to be spatially heterogeneous. For example, for other butterfly species, topography and vegetation structure ameliorate or amplify the effects of weather through provision of microclimates (Weiss et al. 1988; Cherrill and Brown 1990). Likewise, topography and vegetation influence the outcome of habitat alterations such as fire management (Fleishman 2000).

Evidence for Variation in Availability of Larval Host and Adult Nectar Plants in the Wild

The sources of variation in food availability outlined above could result in changes in the mean or variance of food availability as experienced by individual butterflies in the wild. No direct measures of variance in violet or nectar availability yet exist for *S. mormonia* in the field; however, indirect evidence exists for shifts in mean food availability. The body mass and wing length of newly emerged adults decrease in response to larval food stress in many species (e.g., Nylin and Gotthard 1998). Variation in these parameters among years in the field can thus be used to detect possible changes in mean larval food availability. Both mass and wing length were lower in newly emerged field-caught female *Speyeria mormonia* in 1994 than in 1990 or 1995. This decrease in 1994 was not due to some change in genetics in the population. The field-caught 1994 females also had lower body masses and wing lengths than did females from the same generation and site that were fed ad libitum as larvae in a laboratory greenhouse; in other years, greenhouse-reared females have the same body mass and wing length as females from the field (C. L. Boggs, unpub.). Further, violets may have been stressed in 1994 by drought. The summer of 1994 brought the worst drought experienced in central Colorado in decades, with exceedingly small rainfall amounts in June and July, when the larvae were developing (EPA Dry Deposition Station, R. Shaw, pers. comm.).

Evidence further suggests that adult nectar stress may be quite common for *S. mormonia* in my study area, even in years with very different weather regimes and flower availabilities. Age-specific changes in adult body mass can be used to track adult food intake, since these patterns differ between butterflies fed ad libitum and those fed 50% of an ad libitum diet in the laboratory. In 1994 and 1995, age-specific body mass patterns for field-caught females paralleled those seen in females fed 50% of ad libitum (C. L. Boggs, unpub.). This similarity occurred even though weather conditions and flower availability at RMBL were very different in the two years, with 1994 being unusually dry and 1995 being unusually wet. That is, rainfall during July and August 1994 was 26% of the 1991–1996 average, with essentially no rain between late June and early August (EPA Dry Deposition Station, R. Shaw, pers. comm.). Snowfall during the winter preceding 1995 was 148% of normal (W. Barr, pers. comm.), causing plant and animal phenologies to be several weeks late during the summer and maintaining soil water content (C. L. Boggs, pers. obs.). Compounding the effect of weather on differences in nectar availability between the two years, the number of flowers of the

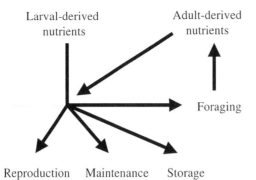

Figure 9.2 Allocation of nutrients to life history traits in holometabolous insects.

primary nectar host, *Erigeron speciosus* (Asteraceae), in 1994 was 5% of the number in 1995 in permanent plots maintained by David Inouye at RMBL (D. Inouye, pers. comm.).

"NORMAL" FOOD AVAILABILITY: ALLOCATION TO REPRODUCTION FROM LARVAL AND ADULT SOURCES

In order to understand changes in allocation to reproduction under conditions of varying food resources, we must first describe the pattern of resource allocation that occurs when food is available ad libitum in *S. mormonia*.

Nutrients that are used for reproduction or other life history traits may come from larval or adult sources (fig. 9.2). From the perspective of the adult, larval food may be used either to manufacture an adult body of a given size or stored for support of adult reproduction, maintenance, or defense. For organisms with determinate growth, incoming adult food is allocated to reproduction, maintenance, or defense or stored for future use. The combination of these allocation patterns determines life history traits, including age-specific fecundity, which is the focus here.

Complicating matters somewhat, adult and larval diets differ in their composition, particularly with respect to nitrogenous compounds and carbohydrates. Nitrogenous compounds such as essential amino acids come primarily from larval feeding in most Lepidoptera, and sugars predominate in adult nectar diets (reviewed in Boggs 1987b; but see Erhardt and Rusterholz 1998). Further, egg production, maintenance, defense, and so forth all require specific ratios of nutrient types, so allocation of each nutrient type must be meshed with allocation of other nutrient types for maximum efficiency.

We thus needed to determine allocation patterns to reproduction both by nutrient type and by the life stage (larval vs. adult) during which the nutrients were taken in. To obtain a baseline picture of the allocation process,

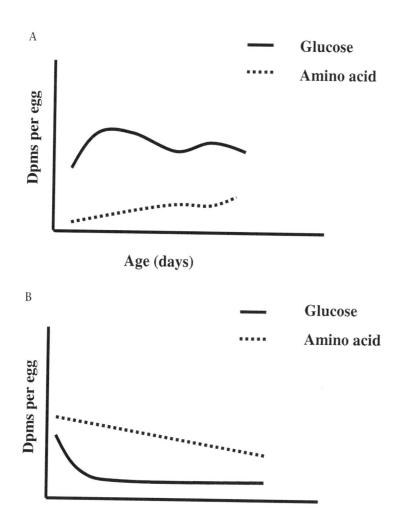

A

Dpms per egg

Age (days)

— Glucose

····· Amino acid

B

Dpms per egg

Age (days)

— Glucose

····· Amino acid

Figure 9.3 Schematic representation of radiotracer data showing the presence in eggs of compounds formed from glucose or amino acids fed to (A) adults and (B) larvae. (Adapted from Boggs 1997b.)

I used both ^{14}C and ^{3}H radiolabeled glucose and amino acids to explore the allocation of larval-derived and adult-derived nutrients to reproduction under ad libitum feeding conditions (Boggs 1997b).

The radiotracer data showed that adult feeding dominated as a source of glucose-derived compounds allocated to egg production in *S. mormonia*, and increased significantly with subsequent egg batches (Boggs 1997b; fig. 9.3A). Label from larval-derived glucose did show up in initial eggs, but dropped off significantly with subsequent eggs, although it never dropped to zero. The consistent minimal presence of larval-derived glucose in eggs probably occurs because oogenesis happens prior to adult emergence (Boggs 1986); thus, compounds from larval-derived glucose will be incorporated into oocytes during their initial development before adult emergence and feeding.

In contrast, the radiotracer data are consistent with the hypothesis that larval feeding is a major, but not the sole, source of nitrogenous compounds used in egg production (Boggs 1997b; fig. 9.3B). Label from larval-derived amino acids was found in consistently high quantities in eggs, yet showed a significant small decrease in later eggs. When available, compounds from adult-derived amino acids were also used in egg production. Label from adult-derived amino acids initially increased in eggs, then leveled off.

These radiotracer data show whether egg constituents derived from glucose or amino acids came from adult or larval feeding, but do not say anything about the source of specific compounds. For example, butterflies can make "nonessential" amino acids from other compounds. The radiotracer data do not indicate whether these amino acids were the result of transamination using carbon skeletons from glucose eaten by adults or derived directly from plants eaten by larvae. More recently, we have used stable carbon isotopes specifically to explore the source of the amino acids in eggs, testing the hypothesis that essential amino acids must be derived from larval feeding (and thus can limit egg production in nectarivorous species, since larval reserves of such amino acids cannot be increased by adults), while nonessential amino acids could be made in part from adult-derived sugars (O'Brien et al. 2002; D. O'Brien et al., unpub.). We analyzed eggs that were laid later in life, when adult and larval contributions could be shown to be in equilibrium. The carbon in essential amino acids was derived from larval feeding as predicted; in contrast, a significant fraction of the carbon in nonessential amino acids derived from adult as well as larval feeding.

These combined data support two generalizations about allocation of resources under ad libitum feeding conditions. First, incoming food is used immediately in preference to stored resources. That is, adult-derived glucose was incorporated into eggs preferentially over larval-derived glucose. Likewise, adult-derived amino acids were used in egg production when available.

Second, resource congruence (the use of nutrient types in a specified ratio) must be considered in any conceptual model of resource allocation. In particular, congruence among compounds that are primarily available from different parts of the life cycle will be important. For *S. mormonia,* compounds derived from carbohydrates and from amino acids showed different patterns of incorporation into eggs. Likewise, the sources of essential and nonessential amino acids used in egg production differed.

LONG-TERM VARIATION IN FOOD AVAILABILITY: EFFECTS ON LIFE HISTORY AND ALLOCATION

Long-term variation in food availability is expressed as changes between generations in mean food availability and hence in mean food intake, assuming that foraging cannot increase enough to maintain intake. Given that larval and adult food resources are generally different (and are definitely so for *S. mormonia*), I examine the allocation and life history effects of food deprivation on each life stage separately.

Long-Term Variation in Larval Food Availability

A decrease in the mean amount of available larval food generally results in a decrease in eventual adult body mass and size in Lepidoptera. The effects of such a decrease on life history will depend on any resulting changes in adult allocation patterns, as well as on the trade-off in the allocation of larval resources during metamorphosis to building an adult body or to reserves for use in reproduction or survival by the adult. As a first possibility, reduction in larval food supply could result in a body size/reserves trade-off function that follows that seen under ad libitum larval feeding. That is, larval-derived reserves could change with body size at a rate that could be predicted based on the relationship between body size and reserves in butterflies fed ad libitum. If adult allocation patterns are also similar between butterflies with reduced and ad libitum larval food availability, then, for *S. mormonia,* the life history traits of individuals stressed and fed ad libitum as larvae should be similar, since neither fecundity nor adult life span depend on wing length in *S. mormonia* fed ad libitum (Boggs 1986; C. L. Boggs, unpub.). As a second possibility, allocation of larval resources during metamorphosis to reserves for adult use could decrease disproportionately to the decrease in body size, resulting in a lower than expected allocation to reproduction and survival relative to body size. In this case, adult reproduction and survival could both decrease, or might exhibit a trade-off not seen under ad libitum larval feeding.

To examine these alternatives, we reared offspring of field-caught female *S. mormonia* on *Viola sororia* (C. L. Boggs and K. Freeman, unpub.). Larvae were fed ad libitum until the middle of the last instar, when half of each brood was shifted to a restricted diet treatment in which about 50% of the leaf area eaten by larvae fed ad libitum was made available. We chose to restrict food during the last instar because the exponential growth pattern of larvae should mean that last-instar larvae accumulate a significant proportion of larval-derived reserves.

As expected from results on many (but not all: see Nylin and Gotthard 1998) other Lepidoptera, *S. mormonia* adult body mass was significantly lower for both male and female butterflies fed a restricted larval diet, and potential female fecundity (eggs laid + eggs remaining in the ovaries at death) was smaller in females fed a restricted larval diet. However, when body mass was included in the analysis, potential female fecundity was not significantly different between females from the ad libitum and restricted larval diet treatments. Females raised on the restricted diet had shorter adult life spans than those fed ad libitum (C. L. Boggs and K. Freeman, unpub.).

These combined results support the hypothesis that proportionately fewer larval-derived reserves are available for adult allocation to reproduction or survival when larval food availability is restricted. Further, larval-derived reserves either are not as important for reproduction as for survival or are allocated preferentially to reproduction under conditions of larval nutrient stress.

Conventional wisdom holds that carbohydrates obtained by adult nectarivores limit survival, while nitrogenous compounds obtained by their larvae limit reproduction. Clearly, however, as found in adult food deprivation experiments, resource congruence between the adult and larval stages is critical: some compound(s) derived from larval feeding must be present in sufficient quantities to match carbohydrates used in adult metabolism in support of survival.

Data on the effects of larval food deprivation on adult life history are scarce in other Lepidoptera. We do, however, have an initial understanding concerning the effects of host plant quality on larval growth rates and fitness (reviewed by Nylin and Gotthard 1998). For example, working with *Pieris napi* (Pieridae), Leimar et al. (1994) showed that larvae grown on low-quality host plants had slower development times, markedly lower female abdomen mass, and in some cases increased mortality, than did larvae grown on high-quality host plants. However, whether the effects of changes in food quality are comparable to the effects of quantitative changes remains to be explored in this species.

Long-Term Variation in Adult Food Availability

What are the effects of reduced adult nectar availability on allocation to reproduction and survival? The simplest case is that of lifelong food restriction, as probably happened to adult *S. mormonia* at my study sites in Colorado during the 1994 drought.

Experimental reduction of adult food (honey-water) availability to 33–75% of ad libitum reduced fecundity, although it did not affect individual egg mass or the life span of individuals of either sex, in *S. mormonia* (Boggs and Ross 1993). Further, the lifetime total fecundity decreased significantly across treatments with decreasing adult food intake. Egg resorption drove this decrease in fecundity under stress. That is, potential fecundity (number of eggs laid + number remaining in the ovaries at death) was lower in stressed females than in control females fed ad libitum. Females fed 50% of ad libitum had 49% of the potential fecundity of control females, and females fed 33% of ad libitum had 32% of the potential fecundity of controls.

This strong effect of adult food availability on fecundity, furthermore, is consistent with observations that daily food intake is correlated with daily fecundity throughout the life span for females fed ad libitum (Boggs and Ross 1993).

This finding, that life span is preserved in the face of adult nutrient stress while fecundity is greatly reduced, was somewhat unexpected for a nectarivore. The accepted wisdom has been that fecundity is limited by larval nitrogen reserves, since nectar is low in nitrogenous compounds (reviewed in Boggs 1987b). Data from *S. mormonia* suggest that these constraints are visible only if adult resources are available ad libitum. This finding is consistent with the radiotracer data, which indicated that glucose from adult feeding is shunted to egg production in preference to use of larval glucose sources. Understanding resource congruence is thus critical to understanding how allocation to life history traits functions.

In general, nectar-feeding species in which not all eggs are mature at adult emergence (and hence in which nectar can play a role in egg production) should be expected to show an effect of nectar restriction on fecundity (see also Boggs 1986, 1997a). Reduction or elimination of sugar in the adult diet of such lepidopteran species does lead to reductions in fecundity like those seen in *S. mormonia*. This was shown to be true in *Jalmenus evagoras* (Lycaenidae: Hill and Pierce 1989), *Euploea core corinna* (Nymphalidae: Hill 1989), *Euphydryas editha bayensis* (Nymphalidae: Murphy et al. 1983), *Panolis flammea* (Noctuidae: Leather 1984), *Colias eurytheme* (Pieridae: Stern and Smith 1960), *Pieris rapae* (Pieridae: Norris 1935), and *P. brassicae* (Pieridae: David and Gardiner 1962). Effects on longevity were less predictable and may have depended on the severity of the particular feeding treatments used, or on food supplies available to larvae.

Since all of these species are nectarivorous, amino acids are probably present in the normal adult diet in relatively small amounts. In contrast, adults of the nymphalid genus *Heliconius* feed on pollen as well as nectar (Gilbert 1972), greatly increasing their adult intake of nitrogenous compounds over that of strictly nectarivorous butterflies. Dunlap-Pianka et al. (1977) showed that *H. charitonius* deprived of pollen have both reduced fecundity and reduced longevity; both can be "rescued" if pollen is restored before a critical period has passed. Further, many Lepidoptera feed on items such as dung, rotting carrion, or sap, which may have relatively high concentrations of nitrogenous compounds. In general, very little is known about the nutritional ecology of such resources, although emerging data suggest that there are phylogenetic patterns at the family level in the use of mud versus dung or carrion by mud-puddling butterflies (Beck et al 1999; C. L. Boggs and B. Dau, unpub.; L. Walling and C. L. Boggs, unpub.). Further, in many species, males predominate at these food sources and probably pass the nutrients on to females at mating (Adler 1982; Adler and Pearson 1982; Pivnick and McNeil 1987; Boggs and Jackson 1991; Sculley and Boggs 1996). This observation suggests that specific compounds from adult male foraging may be of particular importance in the female's resource budget; however, little work has been done exploring this point.

SHORT-TERM VARIATION IN NECTAR AVAILABILITY: EFFECTS ON LIFE HISTORY AND ALLOCATION

Short-term variation in nectar availability results in fluctuations in adult food intake within an individual's lifetime. Such fluctuations can occur in a number of ways; for example, monsoonal moisture may produce rainstorms in an area for several days, causing the butterflies to roost continuously, after which foraging is again possible. Or cattle may enter an area during the flight season and eat the flowers, reducing the nectar supply partway through an individual butterfly's life. Given that fecundity was affected by longer-term variation in nectar supply in *S. mormonia* while survival was unaffected, we would expect that short-term variation in nectar supply could also affect fecundity. However, it could do so in any of several ways. First, the effect on fecundity could be directly related to the duration of the adult nutritional stress. Fecundity could fall off during the stress and rebound later. Second, fecundity could show a threshold effect, being buffered against short-term adult nutrient stress up to a given number of days of stress, after which it would decrease. Alternatively, of course, the butterflies might be able to buffer fecundity against short-term food stress, with the result that fecundity would not decrease.

I used newly emerged adult *S. mormonia* captured in the field to test these alternative hypotheses (C. L. Boggs, unpub.). The experimental treatments consisted of initial food reduction after capture followed by ad libitum feeding, food reduction only later in life, or an alternating cycle of reduction and ad libitum feeding. Each treatment was repeated with different numbers of days of food stress. The entire experiment was replicated with two types of food stress treatment. The first used a 50% reduction from ad libitum feeding, and the second involved placing the butterflies in a glassine envelope in a refrigerator at 5°C to mimic the effects of monsoonal weather patterns. Honey-water was again used as the adult food resource.

Only nutrient stress occurring in early adulthood reduced mean fecundity and potential fecundity, and it did not matter whether the stress was reduced feeding or refrigeration (C. L. Boggs, unpub.). However, the fecundity and potential fecundity of butterflies exposed to early adult stress covered the range from that expected under ad libitum feeding to that expected under constant adult food stress. This result indicates that individuals are able to buffer fecundity against adult food stress occurring later in life, and that short-term stress early in life has a linear effect on fecundity, although the differences occur among individuals within a given treatment, rather than across treatments of differing length.

What caused some individuals to be able to buffer fecundity against early adult nutrient stress, while others could not? The data do not point to compensatory feeding, but rather support the hypothesis that larval reserves are used to buffer reproduction against early adult nutrient stress (C. L. Boggs, unpub.). If reserves (measured as initial adult body mass) are large, the butterfly is able to maintain fecundity; if reserves are small, it cannot. This effect highlights the interaction between larval and adult allocation patterns in response to short-term food stress.

RESOURCE ALLOCATION AND POPULATION DYNAMICS

The above results showing that nectar availability constrains fecundity, and the circumstantial evidence from nectar limitation in the field suggests that nectar availability may be a strong determinant of the population dynamics of *S. mormonia*. Tests of this hypothesis are currently under way.

The importance of nectar resources in the population processes of other lepidopteran species is reflected in studies demonstrating that floral resources affect local egg and adult densities. This effect is presumably due either to habitat choice or the previous effects of nectar availability on population size, combined with spatial autocorrelations in nectar availability. For example, the population density of the lycaenid *Icaricia icarioides fenderi* is positively related to the amount of native nectar in a patch (Schultz and Dlugosch 1999). Likewise, for the nymphalids *Euphydryas gilletti* and *Boloria acrocnema,* population density is higher, or populations are more likely to be present, in areas with a greater floral species diversity (Williams 1988; Britten and Riley 1994). Eggs of both *Euphydryas chalcedona* and the papilionid *Papilio glaucus* tend to be concentrated in areas with extensive floral resources (Murphy et al. 1984; Grossmueller and Lederhouse 1987). These studies point to the general role that floral nectar plays in population distributions, if not also in population regulation.

CASE STUDIES: EFFECTS OF VARIATION IN TIME AVAILABILITY

Time may constrain the ability of organisms to utilize resources even when they are abundant. Like food resources, the amount of time available for various activities (including reproduction) may vary with differing amplitudes or frequencies across the landscape. For behavioral thermoregulators such as butterflies, the time available for activity will depend on weather conditions at the microhabitat scale. Available time, therefore, will vary within a population over the short term as weather conditions change and over the long term as climate changes. Long-term changes, or changes in the mean amount of available time, can also occur over ecological gradients. My co-workers and I have studied the effects of changes in mean time availability across populations along an elevational gradient, using *Colias philodice eriphyle* (Pieridae).

C. *p. eriphyle* populations in the western United States are distributed across an elevational gradient ranging from roughly 1,500 m on the eastern slope of the Sierra Nevada in California, to 1,700 m at the western edge of the Colorado Rocky Mountains, to as high as 2,900 m in the Elk Range of the Rocky Mountains near RMBL. The daily time available for adult flight decreases as elevation increases, even though individuals at higher elevations have more melanin on the areas of the wings covering the thorax and thicker insulating modified scales on the thorax, which allow increased absorption of solar radiation and heat retention. Such adaptations increase the butterflies' ability to raise their body temperatures under the colder and cloudier conditions found at higher elevations (Watt 1968; Kingsolver 1983a, 1983b; Kingsolver and Watt 1984).

Flight is necessary for feeding, mating, and oviposition in *C. p. eriphyle*, so variation among populations in available flight time should be associated with differences in time and resource allocation to these fitness-related activities. To test this hypothesis, Springer and Boggs (1986) examined evidence for a genetically based change in the number of oocytes in the ovaries at emergence (and hence eggs that could be laid) in populations across the elevational gradient in the Colorado Rocky Mountains. In *C. p. eriphyle*, the total number of oocytes in the ovaries is fixed at adult emergence (Stern and Smith 1960). Given decreasing flight time at higher elevations, we predicted that the number of oocytes would decline as elevation increased. We showed that the number of oocytes in newly emerged adult female *C. p. eriphyle* from populations at different elevations raised in a common environment decreased among populations from increasing elevations (Springer and Boggs 1986). Further, we used a model based on flight time available over a mean adult life span under optimal weather conditions at each elevation to predict the number of eggs a female in that population could lay over her lifetime. The mean number of oocytes found in females from each population fit the predictions of the model. Finally, variation in oocyte number was heritable within at least one population.

These data show that time availability can constrain the evolution of life history traits within a population through its effects on resource allocation. In this case, the cause may not be solely a constraint on incoming resources (as seen above for *S. mormonia*), but a constraint on outgoing resources (oviposition) as well. The data also suggest that one factor limiting the species' elevational range may be fecundity, as constrained by flight time.

ALLOCATION RESPONSE TO ENVIRONMENTAL VARIATION: TOWARD TESTABLE GENERALIZATIONS

With this background on the effects of variation in food resources and time availability on allocation patterns and life history traits, I now consider the case for some general conclusions concerning the interaction between environmental variation and allocation responses. We clearly do not have answers yet for many of the questions posed in the introduction to this chapter, but data from butterflies yield some clear insights nonetheless.

DOES THE IDENTITY OF THE VARYING ENVIRONMENTAL FACTOR AFFECT INDIVIDUALS' ABILITY TO BUFFER LIFE HISTORIES THROUGH CHANGED ALLOCATION PATTERNS?

The data from *Colias* and *Speyeria* show that time availability can constrain allocation to reproduction in a manner similar to resource availability. In both cases, adult time or nutrient shortages affected reproduction, but not survival. The life history trait affected may depend on the details of ovarian dynamics, the timing of nutrient intake, and patterns of nutrient congruence for each life history trait (see also Boggs 1986, 1990). The details of these relationships remain unexplored.

These data also suggest a parallel to the debate as to whether time or egg load limits oviposition in parasitoids and other insects (e.g., Rosenheim 1999). In our case, resource availability substitutes for egg load, and life history traits (reproduction and survival) substitute for oviposition. The parallel question, then, is whether (or under what circumstances) the availability of time or resources in the environment limits life history traits, such as fecundity or survival. It would be interesting to explore such parallel models to determine whether the results arising in both lines of work are broadly generalizable.

A permutation of the question asked above is also of interest: Are there some varying environmental factors whose effects on life history traits are more easily buffered by changes in time or in resource allocation? We do not yet have appropriate case studies to construct an answer to this question. However, it seems likely that the phylogenetic history of the organism in question, as well as the antiquity and frequency of the environmental stress, will play a role in the answer.

Does the Frequency or Intensity of Environmental Variation Affect Individuals' Ability to Buffer Life Histories through Changed Allocation Patterns?

Variable and constant adult resource stress in *S. mormonia* yielded contrasting results, with some buffering possible under the variable stress regime, but not under the constant stress regime. The intensity of the stress was reflected in the intensity of the response, as greater reductions in adult food supplies were linearly related to greater reductions in fecundity. These findings suggest that, for environmental variation operating at the scale of an individual's lifetime or less, the frequency and intensity of the variation will be key factors determining the individual's response, and hence the population response over the longer term.

Other related and important questions were outlined in the introduction to this chapter: Does the mean value of an environmental parameter determine how much variation around it can be buffered? What is the effect of the frequency with which extremes are encountered? What are the characteristics of variation at the edge of a species' range and their implications for ability to buffer variation at that edge? These questions remain unanswered. For the most part, researchers have yet to examine the variance and mean in the field for environmental parameters that affect allocation, let alone effectively apply those values to butterflies in an experimental test. Our study of the response of *S. mormonia* adults to recurrent nectar stress versus one-time short-term nectar stress is an example of the type of work that needs to be done, particularly as theoretical studies suggest that the effects of variable and constant environments should be different (Gurney and Middleton 1996).

Are There Constraints on Resource or Time Allocation, and Hence on Ability to Buffer Life Histories?

The butterfly case studies outlined here shed light on the effects of constraints on individual life histories due to resource allocation. In *S. mormonia* and other Lepidoptera, as a general rule, incoming resources are used in preference to stored reserves. When incoming resources are in excess of immediate requirements, they are stored; early storage, including that from larval feeding, is critical to buffering life history traits against later stressful events and maintaining maximal fitness. These results are consistent with empirical studies of plant storage and life history patterns (e.g., Bazzaz et al. 1987; Chapin et al. 1990), as well as work on *Daphnia* (e.g., McCauley et al. 1990; Bradley et al. 1991). They are also consistent with the general theoretical predictions of Gatto and Ghezzi (1996). Making a series of standard assumptions that included a constant intrinsic rate of increase and exponential population growth, these authors found that, in organisms faced with recurrent stress, the optimal strategy is to build up reserves early in life and use them to buffer fitness against each later stress event.

These data and models suggest that the level of stored reserves accumulated by an individual early in life may be matched to an expectation of environmental variation in resource or time availability later in life, during reproduction. We know that this conclusion holds true across species of butterflies, since allocation to reproductive reserves in a series of nymphalid species correlates with an index of expected food availability and reproductive output (Boggs 1981a). In a reverse case, Leimar et al. (1994) showed that variation in female wing length within a species, used as an index of variation in the larval resource environment, is positively correlated with the species' mean spermatophore size. Spermatophores represent stored nutrients for females, but are received after the larval stage. This finding thus suggests that storage in the form of male-derived nutrients increases as the larval nutrient environment becomes more variable, providing insurance against the reproductive costs of variation occurring earlier in the life cycle. Both of these comparative studies are focused at the species level, however. The effects on storage patterns of environmental variation experienced at the population or individual level remain to be explored for the most part.

The role of resource congruence in enhancing or detracting from the buffering ability of organisms is highlighted by the radiotracer and stable isotope studies on *S. mormonia*. There are four major generalizations that can be inferred from the data for later further testing. First, resource congruence can determine the level of stress actually suffered by an organism. Lack of intake of a nutrient that is in short supply in storage should be more detrimental than lack of intake of a nutrient that is abundantly represented in stored reserves. Second, resource congruence could result in selection to mesh or integrate different stages of the life cycle and different nutrient sources, including male nutrient donations. This hypothesis could be tested by further study of the interaction between storage patterns and environmental variation experienced at different life stages. Third, while nectar-feeding Lepidoptera can use amino acids from the adult diet for reproduction, as evidenced by the radiotracer studies on *S. mormonia*, small amounts of additional amino acids available to adults generally had little effect on reproduction or survival. While offspring survival has not been studied in this context, the data suggest that resource congruence may limit the effectiveness of qualitative nutrient supplementation in enhancing fitness. That is, to have significant effects on life history traits, qualitative enhancement of a nutrient at any given stage of the life cycle would have to be accompanied by changes in the intake, storage, or allocation (for example, to oocyte formation) of other nutrients, perhaps even at other life history stages. Finally, which nutrient is limiting can vary depending on the relative availability of all nutrients necessary to support a given life history trait.

UNDER WHAT CONDITIONS IS ENVIRONMENTAL VARIATION MOST LIKELY TO AFFECT POPULATION DYNAMICS?

The expectation is that nectar availability will affect population dynamics in *S. mormonia* either when nectar is scarce throughout adult life or when its availability is restricted early in the butterfly's adult life span and larval food has been relatively scarce. This expectation assumes that fecundity plays a regulatory role in the butterfly's population dynamics. Thus environmental variation is predicted to be important when it affects key life stages controlling population size.

Data from other butterflies presented above also suggest that local population densities are affected by the spatial distribution of adult or larval resources. This is not a particularly novel conclusion; however, it would be interesting to examine the pattern of autocorrelation in environmental parameters for several such cases in order to explore the circumstances under which this pattern results from habitat choice as opposed to reflecting the history of local population dynamics.

The interaction among population structure, the temporal or spatial scale of environmental variation, and resource allocation patterns in driving the dynamics of local populations remains largely unexplored. The concept of source and sink habitats (e.g., Pulliam 1988) is relevant when thinking about the effects of spatial variation on population dynamics, as are studies of the patterns of variation resulting in metapopulation dynamics (e.g., Hanski 1999; Fleishman et al. 2002). Studies or models utilizing these concepts have generally considered only relatively large-scale environmental variation, however. We need comparative work examining the effects of smaller-scale environmental variation on the dynamics of populations with contrasting structures. Butterflies are ideal candidates for such work, as they span a range of population structures (Brussard and Ehrlich 1970; Ehrlich and Gilbert 1973; Watt et al. 1977; Boggs 1987a; Harrison et al. 1988; Hanski et al. 1994; Fleishman et al. 2002).

CONCLUDING COMMENTS

An understanding of the allocation of time and resources in variable environments provides the mechanistic framework for understanding life history and foraging traits at the level of the individual, as well as distribution patterns and dynamics at the level of the population. Most of the studies outlined above are focused on physiology and ecology, giving insight into underlying allocation mechanisms; a stronger focus on the role of genetics in allocation will be critical to understanding the evolution of individual traits and their consequent effects at the population level.

There are a handful of model organisms in which allocation studies are being carried out, including butterflies, plants, lizards, bruchids, orthopterans, parasitic hymenopterans, gerrids, and *Daphnia*. For example, the relative role of resources (eggs) versus time in limiting reproduction in parasitoids has been hotly debated (Rosenheim 1996; Sevenster et al. 1998; Rosenheim 1999). Likewise, our understanding of the costs of reproduction and the evolution of senescence has benefited from resource allocation studies in beetles and *Drosophila* (e.g., Tatar and Carey 1995; Rose and Bradley 1998; Srgo and Partridge 1999). I have argued here, however, that a more thorough understanding both of the structure of variable environments and of time or resource allocation by organisms in those environments is basic to understanding life histories, foraging, and population distributions and dynamics in general. Only by building on our knowledge base in these model organisms can we expect to reach that understanding.

Finally, in a world in which anthropogenic variation is superimposed on natural environmental variation through global climate change, introductions of invasive species, and land management practices, the need to understand organisms' responses to environmental variation is urgent. We have taken on the role of determining the environment for many other species; we had best understand our impacts on that environment and the organisms within it, as well as our likelihood of success in modifying those impacts. The need to understand allocation in variable environments is thus more urgent than ever.

SUMMARY

The environment varies over space and time due to changes in abiotic and biotic factors. Such variation affects an organism's allocation of time and nutrients to reproduction, survival, growth, storage, and foraging. Allocation patterns thus provide the mechanism linking environmental variation to life histories and population dynamics.

In order to understand the role and effect of environmental variation in determining life history and foraging traits, as well as population distributions and dynamics, we need a set of generalizations regarding resource and time allocation in variable environments, including the degree to which life history traits can be buffered against environmental variation. These generalizations touch on both the characteristics of the environment and the physiological, ecological, behavioral, and genetic responses of the individual. Such generalizations can be divided into four sets of questions: the effects of the type of environmental variation on resource and time allocation; the effects of the frequency or intensity of environmental variation on allocation; the effects of constraints acting at the individual level on allocation; and the effects of environmental variation on population dynamics.

I explore these questions using case studies drawn from my work on *Speyeria mormonia* and *Colias philodice eriphyle* and supplemented by information from other Lepidoptera. Many questions remain unanswered, particularly those involving a characterization of environmental variation. Nonetheless, the beginnings of a framework are apparent, and that framework will help us to understand the effects of both natural and anthropogenic sources of environmental variation on the distribution and dynamics of populations.

ACKNOWLEDGMENTS

I thank J. Ellers, E. Fleishman, J. Hellmann, C. Kremen, and W. B. Watt for helpful comments on the manuscript. Parts of the work summarized here were supported by funds from the Undergraduate Research Opportunities office at Stanford University and the U.S. National Science Foundation (IBN 9983044).

CHAPTER 10

Spatial and Temporal Patterns of Checkerspot Butterfly–Host Plant Association: The Diverse Roles of Oviposition Preference

Michael C. Singer

We can view a spatial pattern of plant-insect association entomocentrically and describe it as spatial variation in the diets of particular insect species. Alternatively, we can view exactly the same pattern phytocentrically and describe it as spatial variation in guild structure on particular plant species. An entomocentric description may seem to carry the implication that some trait of the insects is spatially variable, while a phytocentric description may seem to imply variation among plants. These appearances are misleading, however, and we should not be beguiled by our own verbiage into thinking that we understand the sources of variation. When plants and/or insects vary in traits that affect their interaction, we may observe only the variable interaction, not the variable traits, whose identities may be less than obvious. In order to understand these associations mechanistically, it is necessary to pinpoint the sources of variation and to distinguish between traits of the plants, traits of the insects, and emergent traits that are solely traits of their interaction.

Because both plants and insects vary within and among populations in traits that influence patterns of plant-insect association (Singer and Parmesan 1993; Rausher 1984; Abrahamson and Weis 1996; Mopper 1998; Strauss and Karban 1998), there are practical difficulties in identifying these traits and teasing them apart. But such a process is necessary for both evolutionary and ecological understanding of plant-insect systems. This chapter concentrates on the role of one particular insect trait, oviposition preference, as a mechanistic cause of patterns of association between melitaeine butterflies and their hosts. I show how variation in preference can be identified and separated from variation among plants, even in the context of host plants that are themselves also variable.

This chapter begins with spatial variation, first reviewing published work showing how the North American butterfly Edith's checkerspot, *Euphydryas editha*, becomes associated with different host species at different sites as a result of variation among both plants and insects. I then turn to work with Ilkka Hanski's group on spatial patterns of host association in the Finnish Glanville Fritillary, *Melitaea cinxia* (pronounced "keenksia" in Finnish). This work shows that patterns of host-biased habitat patch colonization observed in the field may or may not represent interactions among the patches, depending on whether the mechanism underlying the patterns stems from variation among plants or among insects. Consequently, our view of what is happening in a system may be dramatically different depending on whether particular observed correlations are caused by variable plant traits or by variable insect traits.

In the section on temporal variation I discuss diet shifts, especially the colonization of novel hosts. Finally, I deal with the possibility that constraints on diet evolution may stem from the genetic architecture of preference. While stressing our own work, I've summarized related studies of other butterflies and indicated the manner in which work on these topics in butterflies contributes to our general understanding of plant-insect interactions. (For more general reviews of butterfly-host relationships, readers should consult Gilbert 1978; Chew and Robbins 1984; Jaenike 1989; Thompson and Pellmyr 1991; Renwick and Chew 1994; and Nylin and Janz 1999.)

PATTERNS IN SPACE

SPATIAL VARIATION IN ASSOCIATIONS BETWEEN BUTTERFLIES AND THEIR HOSTS

More than workers with any other insect group, butterfly biologists have been intrigued by spatial variation in insect diets (Singer 1971a; Wiklund 1974; Tabashnik 1983; Scriber 1986a; Mazel 1986; Papaj 1986a; Williams 1990; Bowers et al. 1992; Scriber and Lederhouse 1992; Bossart and Scriber 1995a; Singer and Thomas 1996; Thompson 1993, 1998; Wehling and Thompson 1997; Janz and Nylin 1997; Bossart 1998; Boughton 1999, 2000; Kuussaari et al. 2000; Hanski and Singer 2001). Their studies have used spatial variation for a variety of purposes. Thompson (1994) argued that spatial variation is important because decisive events in insect-plant coevolution occur in "coevolutionary hot spots" where spatial variation of plant and insect traits creates particular combinations of interacting traits. Several authors have used spatial variation in degree of host specialization to test hypotheses about causes of spatial pattern in plant-insect associations. Wiklund (1974) argued that specialization is greater in more predictable habitats.

Nylin (1988) suggested that "if a species has several possible hosts on which larval development time differs, the choice of host would be expected to be more specialized when a short larval development time is of greater relative importance." He used this argument to predict that oviposition preferences should vary geographically and be more specialized on hosts that support rapid larval development where two generations occur, with barely enough time to complete them, than where there is only one generation with ample time for development. He found both interpopulation and intergeneration variation in specialization of *Polygonia c-album*, which he interpreted in this light. Scriber and Lederhouse (1992) independently proposed the same hypothesis, which they named the "voltinism-suitability hypothesis." They examined diet breadth across a wide latitudinal range in *Papilio glaucus*, and they confirmed the prediction that where there was ample time for X generations per year, but not time for $(X + 1)$ generations, the diet was broad. Conversely, where time for the fixed number of generations was short, the butterflies had narrow diets centered on the hosts that supported the most rapid larval development.

Singer (1971) suggested that diet variation in space might be considered a surrogate for diet variation in time. Several authors have done this, deriving generalizations about temporal patterns from the study of spatial patterns. A prominent example, which I discuss in detail below, is the deduction from the observation that host preference is less variable than expected in space that it should be evolutionarily conservative in time (Thompson 1993; Wehling and Thompson 1997). In a similar vein, spatial variation has often been used to study rapid diet evolution by comparing insects from populations that have recently undergone diet shifts with those that have not (Tabashnik 1983; Thomas et al. 1987; Bowers et al. 1992; Singer et al. 1992a; Camara 1997).

TEASING APART PREFERENCE, ACCEPTABILITY, AND ELECTIVITY USING CHECKERSPOTS

Over the last 30 years, checkerspots have proved convenient organisms for studying the ecology and evolution of diet. They possess a combination of traits that both set up natural comparisons and make them amenable to controlled experimentation. Specifically, they are relatively sedentary, so that discrete populations can be identified as study units (Ehrlich 1961b, 1965; Hanski et al. 1994; Kuussaari et al. 1996); they are docile and therefore easily manipulated in the field as well as in the laboratory; and they frequently exhibit large variations in diet over small geographic scales (Singer 1994; Singer and Thomas 1996; Thomas and Singer 1998; Kuussaari et al. 2000).

Part of the spatial variation in checkerspot diet is simply a function of host availability. This can be demonstrated by showing that a plant is both acceptable to ovipositing adults and suitable for larval development although it does not occur locally (Mazel 1986; Thomas et al. 1987). However, both *Euphydryas editha* and *Melitaea cinxia* often conspicuously choose different host species in apparently similar plant communities (Singer and Parmesan 1993; Singer 1994; Singer et al. 1994; Thomas and Singer 1998; Kuussaari et al. 2000). When this happens, some qualitative trait of either plants or insects must be spatially variable.

In *E. editha*, we have been able to trace the mechanistic basis for these more complex instances of diet variation to traits of both the plants and the insects. Below, I describe the most detailed study. I hope that this work is informative as an example of experimental design that allows the possibility that both plants and insects may vary both within and among populations.

The Basis of Variation in Electivity between Two Populations of *E. editha*

First, I should define "electivity," "preference," and "acceptability," since I shall use these terms freely. *Electivity* is the proportional use of a resource as a function of its relative abundance (Ivlev 1961; Singer 2000). So, if we find, as we do, that the proportion of *E. editha* eggs laid on two host species varies between sites in a manner that is not explained by variation in the relative abundance of the hosts, then we can describe this finding as spatially variable *electivity*. Oviposition *preference* is the set of likelihoods of acceptance by an insect of particular, specified plants that it encounters. Pre-alighting preferences are responses to encounters with visual (Rausher 1978; Wiklund 1984; Parmesan et al. 1995) or chemical (Feeny et al. 1989) stimuli detectable at a distance from the plant, and "acceptance" following such an encounter comprises turning toward the plant and receiving further stimuli (Singer 1986). Post-alighting preferences are responses to chemotactile and physical stimuli (Oyeyele and Zalucki 1990; Sachev-Gupta et al. 1992; Renwick and Chew 1994), and acceptance is expressed as an attempt to oviposit. Some butterflies show clear sequential responses to visual, chemical, and physical stimuli. In *Euphydryas,* it seems that the response to acceptance of visual stimuli is to assess plant chemistry, and the response to acceptance of chemical stimuli is to assess the mechanical properties of the plant (Singer 1986, 1994; Parmesan et al. 1995).

Preference as defined here is a trait of an individual female insect, manifested with respect to a specified array of plants. The reciprocal plant trait, *acceptability,* is likewise a trait of an individual plant, manifested with respect to a specified array of insects: acceptability is the set of likelihoods that a plant will be accepted for oviposition by particular insects that encounter it. Using these definitions, preference can be viewed as an insect trait, acceptability as a plant trait, and electivity as a trait of the interaction (Singer 2000).

Singer and Parmesan (1993) devised a series of experiments to measure butterfly preference and host plant acceptability in two natural populations in order to understand their very different patterns of electivity. These two populations of *E. editha* chose different plant species for oviposition out of apparently similar arrays of potential hosts growing at similar densities. *E. editha* at Frenchman Lake fed principally on *Penstemon rydbergii*, while those at Sonora Junction fed principally on *Collinsia parviflora*. Both *P. rydbergii* and *C. parviflora* occurred at both sites in about the same proportions and abundances. The experiments are described below.

1. Reciprocal transplant experiment to determine whether plant acceptability and/or insect preference differs between sites

We captured insects in the field and tested each of them with two plant pairs: one pair comprising a *Collinsia* and a *Penstemon* from Sonora, and one comprising the same two species from Frenchman. During each preference test, we staged repeated encounters between the insect and the two plants (Singer et al. 1992b). The plants were offered to the insect in alternation. If the insect attempted to oviposit, it was not allowed to do so, but acceptance of the plant was recorded, and the insect was tested on the other plant. If plant X was accepted and plant Y was subsequently rejected, we recorded that X was preferred over Y. This technique is designed to control for level of oviposition motivation when estimating preference (Singer et al. 1992b). After each test, we discarded both the insect and the two plant pairs and started afresh.

Both butterflies and plants differed between the two sites. The difference in the butterflies was significant, regardless of the origin of the plants (table 10.1A, B). The plant effect was tested by rearranging the same dataset (table 10.1C, D). Frenchman insects always preferred *Penstemon* over *Collinsia,* regardless of the origin of the plant pair, giving no evidence that plants differed between the sites (table 10.1C). However, the rankings produced by Sonora butterflies differed significantly depending on the site of origin of the plant pair (table 10.1D). Sonora insects were significantly more likely to prefer *Penstemon* over *Collinsia* when the plant pair was from Frenchman, the site where *Penstemon* is used. This finding suggests that, at least from the perspective of Sonora butterflies, Frenchman *Penstemon* is more acceptable than Sonora *Penstemon,* and/or that Sonora *Collinsia* is more acceptable than Frenchman *Collinsia*.

Note that this experimental design asks how insects taken from each site interact with plants from each site, in a general sense. Each insect and each plant are independently sampled from their respective populations. Such an experiment can tell us (as it did) that insects from Sonora tend to rank the two plant species differently depending on their origin. It does *not*

Table 10.1 Rank order of plant species by insects offered local or foreign plant pairs

	Number of Times *Penstemon > Collinsia*	Number of Times *Collinsia > Penstemon*	Significance
A.			
Frenchman insects, Frenchman plants	26	0	
Sonora insects, Frenchman plants	8	10	$p < 0.01$
B.			
Sonora insects, Sonora plants	1	15	
Frenchman insects, Sonora plants	22	0	$p < 0.001$
C.			
Frenchman insects, Frenchman plants	26	0	
Frenchman insects, Sonora plants	22	0	$p = 1.0$
D.			
Sonora insects, Sonora plants	1	15	
Sonora insects, Frenchman plants	8	10	$p = 0.02$

Note: C and D rearrange the data from A and B.

estimate variation within either plant or insect populations. For example, if two Sonora butterflies were offered plant pairs from the same site and produced different ranks, we could not tell whether the butterflies or the plants were different. So, this experimental design has its limitations, but it does take fully into account the fact that both plants and insects vary both within and among populations.

2. Determination of genetic variation of insect preference: Maintenance of home preference by insects tested with experimental plant standards

In the second experiment we offered all insects the same plant pair, comprising one *Collinsia* and one *Penstemon,* both from the same site (Sonora). We did this in order to reveal variation that was clearly among insects, not among plants. When using insects raised in the laboratory, we fed all the larvae *Collinsia* and avoided testing sibs in order to maintain independence of data points. Whether we used field-caught insects (table 10.2A) or lab-raised insects (table 10.2B), we found a significant difference in preference between insects from the two sites in the direction that would contribute to the observed difference in diet. We concluded that genetic variation in oviposition preference among insect populations was at least part of the mechanism producing spatial variation of electivity (but see Singer and Lee 2000 for some additional complexities in interpreting this type of experiment).

3. Determination of genetic variation of plant acceptability: Consistent difference between plant populations in a completely crossed, reciprocal transplant experiment

The third experiment used plant pairs that were conspecific rather than heterospecific. Once again, each insect and plant pair were used only once to generate the dataset. Each plant pair comprised a *Penstemon rydbergii* from Frenchman and one from Sonora. Butterflies from both sites preferred the plants from Frenchman, whether the plant pairs comprised freshly transplanted plants from the field or plants grown from seed in common soil (table 10.3).

Table 10.2 Rank order of plant species by insects all offered the same plant pair

	Number of Times *Penstemon* > *Collinsia*	Number of Times *Collinsia* > *Penstemon*	Significance
A. Field-caught insects			
Frenchman insects	28	0	
Sonora insects	1	6	$p = 1.3 \times 10^{-6}$
B. Lab-raised insects			
Frenchman insects	17	0	
Sonora insects	0	9	$p = 3.2 \times 10^{-7}$

Table 10.3 Rank order of acceptability of *Penstemon* from Frenchman (FM) and Sonora (SJ)

	Number of Plant Pairs in Which			
	FM > SJ	FM = SJ	SJ > FM	Significance
A. Field-grown plants (transplanted)				
Frenchman insects	11	0	0	$p = 0.0005$
Sonora insects	9	3	0	$p = 0.002$
B. Plants grown from seed				
Frenchman insects	9	3	0	$p = 0.002$
Sonora insects	9	2	0	$p = 0.002$

The conclusion from these three experiments is that both plant and insect genetic variation contribute substantially to the spatial pattern of plant-insect association. *Penstemon* was virtually excluded from the diet at Sonora (we found only one egg cluster on it), partly because the local *Penstemon* population was genetically unacceptable and partly because the local butterfly population was genetically *Collinsia*-preferring. Neither of these effects alone would have sufficed, as table 10.1D shows: if Sonora butterflies were transplanted to Frenchman, *Penstemon* would instantly become a major host. In fact, since these experiments were done, *Penstemon has* become a major host at Sonora (B. Wee and M. C. Singer, unpub.). This shift occurred after the butterfly population became extinct and was recolonized; we suspect, but do not yet know, that the identity of the source population of the colonizing insects may be responsible for the diet change.

This set of experiments makes clear that variation among plant populations in acceptability should be important in the evolution of insect-host associations (cf. Thompson 1994). If we knew, for example, how plant acceptability varied with habitat quality or history of insect attack, we might be able to predict the invasibility of particular habitats by particular insects.

Application to *Melitaea cinxia* of the Approach Developed with *E. editha*

Hanski and Singer (2001) have applied a similar approach to understand the role that spatial variation in plants and butterflies may play in generating host-biased colonization of unoccupied habitat patches by *Melitaea cinxia*. In the Åland Islands, this butterfly uses two hosts, *Plantago lanceolata* and *Veronica spicata*. The Hanski group's data show that empty patches containing principally *Veronica* are more likely to be colonized if there is a history of high relative use of *Veronica* in nearby patches. Independently, empty patches containing principally *Plantago* are more likely to be colonized when there is a history of high relative use of *Plantago* in surrounding patches. Just like the spatial pattern described above for *E. editha*, this resource-biased colonization pattern could be caused by variation among plants or by variation among insects, or both.

First, consider an insect-based explanation: We know that the insects evolve local adaptations in the form of oviposition preferences for either *Plantago* or *Veronica* (Kuussaari et al. 2000). In areas where *Plantago* is preferred, electivities are expected to be biased toward that plant; that is, it will be used more than expected from its relative abundance (Kuussaari et al. 2000). Preference may also affect patch colonization, either by influencing insect movement among patches (Thomas and Singer 1987; Singer and Thomas 1996; Boughton 2000) or by affecting the likelihood that immigrants to a patch will oviposit there.

Michael C. Singer

Second, consider a plant-based explanation: An empty patch containing *Plantago* may be empty because the plants are unacceptable to ovipositing butterflies or unsuitable for growing larvae. If there is spatial autocorrelation of plant quality, an empty patch with low-quality *Plantago* will tend to be surrounded by other patches with low-quality *Plantago*, where the insects have been concentrated on *Veronica*.

So, the apparent influence of diet on the colonization of surrounding patches could be a sophisticated interaction among patches mediated by local adaptation of insect preference (an insect-based mechanism). Alternatively, it could be much more passively caused by a relatively simple and general response of insects to the spatial scale of variation in plant quality, with no interaction among patches other than that already known from rules of insect emigration and immigration (Hanski et al. 1994; Kuussaari et al. 1996). A series of experiments, similar in spirit to those described above for the Frenchman-Sonora comparison, showed that the insect-based mechanism is the principal driver in this case (Hanski and Singer 2001).

I hope that these two examples, using *E. editha* and *M. cinxia,* illustrate the value of understanding the relative roles of plant and insect variation in generating patterns of plant-insect association. Only when we have done this can we realistically incorporate these plant-insect systems into either ecological or (co)evolutionary models.

PATTERNS IN TIME

HOST SHIFTS AND COLONIZATION OF NOVEL HOSTS

How difficult are host shifts for insects to achieve, what obstacles must be overcome, and how are host shifts associated with speciation? I begin with an apparent paradox: Ehrlich and Raven (1964) observed a systematic pattern in which related butterfly species utilize related host plants. From this pattern they painted a portrait of a shift to a host unrelated to the current host as a rare event, difficult to achieve, requiring evolutionary novelty on the part of the insect, and leading to adaptive radiation once an effective host defense has been overcome. On the other hand, Strong (1974) showed that the number of insect species feeding on cultivated cacao was correlated with the area occupied by the host, not with the length of time the plant had been in the region or with whether it was native or introduced. Strong's result suggests that introduced cacao had been colonized by local insects so quickly that equilibrium species diversity of insects on cacao had been achieved even in areas where cacao had been cultivated merely for decades.

This result does not apply to all plant species—indeed, it was phrased as a counterpoint to the very first study of this type: Southwood (1961) had implicated history as well as area occupied as a correlate of insect diversity on particular plant species. At least in the case of cacao, we can conclude either that the insects must have rapidly evolved novel adaptations to use the plant or that no such adaptations were required—that is, that the host shift involved no immediate evolutionary change. Thus, the patterns described by Strong and by Ehrlich and Raven tend to generate opposing pictures of the ease with which novel insect-host associations arise.

Do these two classic studies reveal a paradox? Or can they both be understood in terms of common underlying mechanisms? To better understand these large-scale patterns, I focus on the details of a relatively simple but enticingly dynamic circumstance: What occurs when an opportunity for a host shift arises, such as when an insect population is confronted with an introduced plant?

Butterflies are suitable organisms for this type of work because oviposition choice behavior and larval performance can be studied both in captivity and in the field, and because these two traits can be cleanly separated (in contrast to insects that feed on the same host individuals as larvae and as adults). When an herbivorous insect population comes into contact with a novel plant species, the plant may be both acceptable to ovipositing insects and suitable for larval development. This sets the stage for incorporation of the plant into the insect's diet (Tabashnik 1983; Thomas et al. 1987; Bowers et al. 1992; Camara 1997). Alternatively, the plant may be suitable for larvae but unacceptable to adults. Karowe (1990) identified such a case, concluding that the plant had failed to be drawn into the insect's diet solely because of lack of genetic variation for oviposition preference. The reciprocal case, in which the plant is acceptable to adults but unsuitable for larvae, has been more frequently reported (Dethier 1954; Straatman 1962; Chew 1977; Feldman and Haber, 1998). This situation incurs simultaneous selection on adults to reject the plant and on larvae to be able to use it. If oviposition preference is the first trait to respond to selection, the plant is excluded from the diet; if larval performance responds first, then the plant is drawn into the diet (Thomas et al. 1987).

There are many more reported cases of oviposition on toxic plants than of failure to oviposit on suitable ones. But this difference may be misleading, since oviposition on toxic plants is readily observed without experimental intervention: eggs are found in the field on plants that do not support larval growth. Failure to oviposit on usable plants is much less likely to be discovered because it cannot be simply observed, but instead requires experimental demonstration of successful larval development on plants that do not naturally receive eggs.

Geographic and Temporal Comparisons

When a host shift is still in progress or has recently occurred, it is often possible to compare insects that have undergone the shift with those that have not, which represent the putative starting condition. This has been done for *Colias philodice* and *Papilio zelicaon* on native and cultivated hosts (Shapiro and Masuda 1980; Tabashnik 1983), for *Junonia coenia* (Camara 1997), and for two North American *Euphydryas* species, *E. phaeton* (Bowers et al. 1992) and *E. editha* (Thomas et al. 1987; Singer et al. 1992a; Singer and Thomas 1996).

It is possible to make direct observations of changes in butterfly-host associations over time. For example, it would be interesting to revisit the study sites used by Chew (1977), Shapiro and Masuda (1980), and Tabashnik (1983) to see what changes have occurred in insects or plants since those studies were done. Our own work on *E. editha* shows that such changes can be very rapid. At one site (Schneider's Meadow, Carson City), the proportion of butterflies preferring the introduced *Plantago lanceolata* rose from about 5 to about 55% in the course of six generations (Singer et al. 1993). At a second site (Rabbit Meadow, Sequoia National Forest), the proportion of butterflies developing naturally on *Collinsia torreyi* that actually preferred this novel host rose from 5 to 24% over about eight generations (Singer et al. 1993). At Schneider's Meadow, we were able to show that the change stemmed from genetic changes in the insect because the change in the field was mirrored in the laboratory. The family mean preferences of lab-raised offspring of field-caught 1983 butterflies differed significantly from the family mean preferences of lab-raised offspring of 1990 butterflies.

A Host Shift in the Face of a Phenological Barrier and Maladaptation to the Novel Host: Patterns of Maladaptation and Their Proximate Mechanisms

A different way to ask whether host shifts by herbivorous insects are easy or difficult to achieve is to ask what obstacles have been overcome when a host shift actually does occur. To this end, we have performed a series of observations and experimental manipulations to elucidate the (mal)adaptation to a novel host in a natural population of *E. editha* (reviewed in Singer 1994). At the Rabbit Meadow site, we studied host use in two adjacent patches of habitat, which we call a "patch-pair." One member of the pair was a clear-cut, where the principal host was *Collinsia torreyi,* the novel host for the insects in this metapopulation. The second patch comprised undisturbed open coniferous forest, where the insects still used their traditional host, *Pedicularis semibarbata,* even though *Collinsia* was present and abundant (Singer 1983;

Singer and Thomas 1996). There was sufficient dispersal among the patches (Thomas and Singer 1987; Boughton 2000) to ensure that many butterflies spent time in both of them. *Collinsia* had been rendered a usable host in this region following logging that began in 1967, which created clear-cut habitat patches supporting plant individuals that were phenologically highly suitable for larval survival (Singer 1983; Boughton 1999). *E. editha* had begun to colonize these patches sometime between 1967 and 1979, when we started work at this site. By 1985 a large set of clear-cut patches had been colonized. In the undisturbed patches of open forest, *Collinsia* was abundant but unsuitable, undergoing senescence before larvae feeding on it would have reached diapause. Here, the butterflies retained their traditional diet of *Pedicularis* (and occasionally *Castilleja*). The Rabbit Meadow patch-pair was part of a network of habitat patches within a 10 km × 10 km area consisting of the same two patch types—suitable for use of the novel host or suitable for use of the traditional host.

Over several years of working on individual components of host use, from in-flight behavior of females to larval growth, we have been able to compile a detailed assessment of how the insects interacted with their novel and traditional hosts. This composite picture illustrates the various obstacles that have been overcome in the colonization of *Collinsia*. (This description updates the treatment of the same topic in Singer 1994.)

1. The phenological barrier

Phenological barriers may be frequent obstacles to host shifts (Feder et al. 1998). In the present case, *Collinsia* frequently underwent senescence too soon for many larvae to survive, placing a premium on early oviposition (Boughton 1999). Early oviposition was more readily achieved by adults that had developed in clearings, where they emerged on average a week earlier than those in adjacent undisturbed habitats (Singer 1983; Boughton 1999). In consequence, survival in clearings was higher among the offspring of local insects than among the offspring of immigrants from *Pedicularis* patches. Thus, there was a phenological barrier to colonization of *Collinsia* patches in clearings from *Pedicularis* patches in undisturbed forest, but no barrier in the reverse direction (Boughton 1999).

2. Patterns of maladaptation and their proximate mechanisms

Other obstacles to the host shift stemmed principally from maladaptations of the insects to their novel host. I describe these maladaptations in the context of the sequence of events in host choice: first host finding, then selection of a chemically acceptable host individual, then the choice of a physically acceptable oviposition site, and finally the number of eggs laid.

Mackay (1995) observed naturally searching females and discovered that *Pedicularis* was found efficiently, but *Collinsia* was not. He suggested that the insects had not had time to evolve efficient searching for their novel host. Parmesan et al. (1995) repeated and confirmed Mackay's observations several years later. They also performed an experiment, releasing in the Rabbit patch-pair a set of teneral females found in mating pairs in a nearby (500 m distant) *Collinsia*-feeding population in a clearing. Those that were released in the *Pedicularis*-feeding patch found their (traditional) host efficiently, from the very first alighting of the first search of their lives. However, those released in the adjacent (150–300 m distant) *Collinsia*-feeding patch found their (novel) host *less* efficiently than random alighting would have predicted, and they failed to improve their host finding with experience (Parmesan et al. 1995). These differences in ability to find the two hosts in flight were consistently found with naturally searching females in different years of study (Mackay 1985; Parmesan et al. 1995).

After alighting, female *E. editha* taste potential hosts with their atro-phied foretarsi. Acceptance of host chemistry is indicated by curling of the abdomen and sweeping of the extruded ovipositor across the underside of the leaf surface. In the early stages of the host colonization at Rabbit, most butterflies showed post-alighting (chemical) preference for their traditional host, even though fitness was higher on the novel host (Singer 1983; Moore 1989; Singer and Thomas 1996). Some insects that developed in clearings on *Collinsia* would not accept *Collinsia* at all; many others were so averse to it that their oviposition was delayed (Singer et al. 1992b). Additional exper-iments confirmed that preferences expressed at this stage are strongly heri-table both within populations (Singer et al. 1988) and among them (Singer et al. 1991; Singer and Parmesan 1993) and are apparently unaffected by prior experiences of host encounter (Singer 1986; Thomas and Singer 1987).

This aversion of butterflies in clearings to *Collinsia,* and possibly also to that habitat type (Boughton 2000), resulted in a striking pattern of patch occupancy and a strong relationship between clearing size and larval density (Thomas and Singer 1998). Only the larger clear-cut patches were colonized, and among colonized patches, larval density was strongly positively cor-related with patch size (Thomas and Singer 1998). We know that the insects in general tended to leave the clearings (Boughton 2000), and we suspect that *Pedicularis*-preferring insects normally succeeded in doing so be-fore becoming sufficiently motivated that they would oviposit on *Collinsia.* The larger the patch, the more likely that an insect would remain in it long enough to accept a low-ranked host. Evidence that the relationship between patch size and larval density stemmed somehow from lack of adaptation to *Collinsia* comes from the absence of any such pattern among patches of traditional hosts. We found no such relationship between patch size and density either at Rabbit among patches of *Pedicularis* or at Tamarack Ridge among patches of *Collinsia*, where this host is not novel (M. C. Singer and D. A. Boughton, unpub.).

After alighting on a host plant, females exhibited a consistent set of differences in their treatment of the novel and the traditional hosts. The combined works of Rausher et al. (1981), Ng (1988), and Mackay (1985) showed that females using *Pedicularis* could discriminate adaptively among individuals, while those using *Collinsia* tended to pick the individual plants least likely to support larval survival. This maladaptive choice among *Collinsia* individuals repeated itself in studies over several years. Its mechanism appears to lie in responses to host phenology. Since two studies in different years have shown that host senescence is a major cause of larval mortality in this population (Moore 1989; Boughton 1999), females should choose the youngest plants for oviposition. However, they did the reverse: in a series of pairwise tests, with each plant pair and each butterfly used only once, *Collinsia* plants that had finished blooming were significantly preferred over blooming plants—quite the reverse of the expected adaptive direction of preference (M. C. Singer, unpub.).

After a plant had been chosen for oviposition, fixed behavior patterns again caused problems with the novel host. The *Collinsia*-feeding butterflies dropped to the ground and attempted to oviposit at the base of the plant, often failing to do so because the plant did not have a rosette of leaves spread on the ground (as did *Pedicularis*). They were seen walking through the vegetation with their ovipositors probing in front of them, apparently unable to find a physically acceptable oviposition site that would provide resistance when the ovipositor was pressed against it. This search for physical resistance to probing with the ovipositor often led them to oviposit in areas of extremely high plant density, exacerbating their tendency to select plants that would undergo early senescence. For the same reason, many females oviposited on fallen logs, which could result in death of the eggs from desiccation in hot weather. When interacting with their traditional hosts, *E. editha* never laid eggs on logs, always ovipositing on the host itself or occasionally on adjacent plants.

An adaptive strategy should result in females laying smaller clusters of eggs on *Collinsia* than on *Pedicularis*. This expectation stems from experiments that indicated that 20–50 eggs per cluster was an adaptive cluster size on *Pedicularis,* but that in most years 5 eggs per cluster generated higher larval survival than 20 or 50 per cluster on *Collinsia* (M. C. Singer, C. McNeely, R. Moore, and D. Ng, unpub.). In practice, the mean cluster size of freshly laid eggs was 48 on *Pedicularis* and 52 on *Collinsia,* a significant difference in the maladaptive direction (Moore 1989). The likely cause of this maladaptive behavior is that when Rabbit *E. editha* lay eggs, they lay all the eggs that are currently mature (Agnew and Singer 2000). So females searching in a field of *Collinsia* for their beloved but absent *Pedicularis* would accumulate a high egg load and deposit large clusters as a result of an extended search (Singer et al. 1992b).

This suite of experiments and related natural field correlations indicate that the insects' behavioral patterns associated with host finding and oviposition were maladaptive toward the novel host and adaptive toward the traditional host. Insects using the novel host found it inefficiently, selected the individual plants and plant parts least likely to support their offspring, and had physical difficulty in finding oviposition sites, in which they then placed egg clusters of maladaptive size. These maladaptive interactions with the novel host added to the phenological barrier between the habitats to generate a set of obstacles to the host shift itself, making it quite surprising that the shift had occurred and that (in most years) insect fitness was higher on the novel than on the traditional host (Singer and Thomas 1996; Thomas et al. 1996).

3. Origin of constraints on incorporation of the novel host

Our finding that insects were maladapted to their novel host (*Collinsia*) but relatively well adapted to their traditional host suggests the following possibilities:

1. Adaptive finding and handling of *Collinsia* cannot be achieved because of some evolutionary constraint.
2. Adaptive behavior cannot be achieved toward more than one host species at once by a single butterfly population (or by populations with substantial gene exchange, as at Rabbit).
3. Adaptive behavior toward multiple hosts *can* be achieved, but this had not occurred at Rabbit because there had not been sufficient time (fewer than twenty butterfly generations since colonization of *Collinsia*).

The results of several different studies bear on these questions. With respect to host searching, it is possible that inefficient finding of the small, erect annual *Collinsia* relative to the larger perennial rosette *Pedicularis* stems from differences in plant apparency: the visual system of *E. editha* may not be adequate for efficient finding of *Collinsia* (Wiklund 1984). This hypothesis was tested by examining host finding at a different site (Schneider's Meadow), where the roles of the plants were reversed: the novel host was a perennial rosette (*Plantago lanceolata*) and the traditional host was a small, erect annual *Collinsia* (*C. parviflora*). At Schneider, *E. editha* found *both* hosts efficiently (Parmesan 1991), thereby refuting hypotheses (1) and (2) above, and supporting hypothesis (3). Parmesan (1991) argued that the interaction between insect visual acuity and host apparency was not a long-term constraint on the evolutionary diet expansion at Rabbit.

We have gleaned further understanding of the host shift at Rabbit by examining the responses to hosts of a population of *E. editha* at a similar site with a different history, Tamarack Ridge. This site is about 60 km distant from Rabbit, at the same elevation, and contains the same potential host species, *Pedicularis semibarbata* and *Collinsia torreyi*. At Tamarack, *Pedicularis* is used by *Euphydryas chalcedona* and avoided by *E. editha*. Indeed, these two butterfly species show significant diet displacement in the Sierra Nevada range (Thomas et al. 1990). *E. editha* at Tamarack feed principally on *Collinsia torreyi* and secondarily on *Veronica serpyllifolia* and *Mimulus* sp. (Singer et al. 1994).

Unlike Rabbit insects, Tamarack butterflies colonized small *Collinsia* patches, chose *Collinsia* plants that were destined for late rather than early senescence, and laid small egg clusters (mean = eggs) close to the top of the plant. Furthermore, they produced larvae that did not move to the base of the plant (which consisted of only an inedible stem), but remained at the top (M. C. Singer, unpub.). Thus, butterflies at Tamarack, where there is no evidence that *Collinsia* is a novel host, have evolved a completely different suite of behavioral patterns, from adult search to larval movement, all apparently adapted to the use of *Collinsia*.

Collectively, these observations argue against hypothesis (1) above: the insects can evolve adaptive finding of *Collinsia*, as they have done at Schneider. They have not done so at Rabbit because of evolutionary lag (Parmesan 1991) (but see Courtney 1982 and Chew and Courtney 1991 for the opposite conclusion). They can also evolve adaptive discrimination among individual *Collinsia*, adaptive egg placement, and adaptive egg cluster size, as they have done at Tamarack. They have not done this at Rabbit because of some presently unknown combination of evolutionary lag and constraints that prevent adaptive responses to two hosts at once (hypotheses 2 and 3 above). Camara (1997) studied an analogous situation and argued that detailed chemical coevolution between *Junonia coenia* and its two hosts was prevented because "natural selection on diet breadth by natural enemies is stronger than selection from host plants."

Resolving the Paradox (in Part)

How does this information from butterflies bear on the apparent paradox that comes from comparing the results of Strong (1974) and Ehrlich and Raven (1964)? Our repeated observations of rapid diet evolution (Singer et al. 1993) are supported by intraspecific molecular phylogenies of *E. editha*, which also imply that this species' diet has been labile and that each host has been colonized and abandoned several times (Radtkey and Singer 1995). These results suggest that one reason for Strong's result with cacao was that local insects rapidly evolved the ability to use this plant. However, a second mechanism underlying Strong's result is also suggested by the butterfly data: Strong's insects may have colonized cacao without becoming adapted to it at all. This scenario is supported by two findings. First, in our studies of *E. editha*, we found two independent instances in which a novel host was edible by larvae and had been acceptable to at least some adults *before* it was colonized (Thomas et al. 1987; Singer et al. 1992a). This result resembles Tabashnik's (1983) finding with *Colias philodice* colonizing alfalfa. Second, we observed that Rabbit insects successfully colonized a host to which they were ill-adapted in many ways. The host shift came first; the adaptation may (or may not) come later. In the absence of competition, a newly available plant can be colonized by insects that do not perform very well on it and would probably be excluded later by competitors if they did not evolve appropriate adaptations. In general, our observations support Strong's view of insect diets as labile, and they demonstrate both possible causes (of rapid colonization of cacao) implied by Strong's data: colonization without evolutionary change and extremely rapid evolution of adaptations to a novel host.

But what of the patterns shown by Ehrlich and Raven, also using butterflies as examples? The answer may lie in the level at which Ehrlich and Raven were working. All *Heliconius* feed on Passifloraceae. Ehrlich and Raven surmise that some ancestor of *Passiflora* evolved a very successful set of defenses, and that some ancestor of *Heliconius* successfully overcame them. Since then, the insects have been tied to this group of plants. We can be fairly sure that it would be difficult for a heliconiine to colonize a non-passifloraceous plant because this has not happened in a *very* long time. But it may be quite easy for host shifts to occur from one passifloraceous plant to another. As Gilbert (1978), Futuyma (1991), and Berenbaum (1995b) have argued, host associations can be evolutionarily labile at one level but constrained at another.

EVOLUTIONARY DIMENSIONALITY OF PREFERENCE

Wiklund (1981) found that the host preferences of individual *Papilio machaon* varied in intensity or specificity, but not in rank order. These and subsequent similar findings in other species have led some butterfly biologists (Wehling and Thompson 1997; Thompson 1993; Bossart and Scriber 1999) to join *Drosophila* biologists (Courtney et al. 1989) in arguing that preference hierarchies are evolutionarily viscous or constrained, with consequences for diet evolution. If adult insects are constrained to a preference rank of A > B > C, for example, then if A and C are both in the diet, B cannot be excluded, even if it is toxic to larvae. So the insects would have two potentially viable evolutionary options: monophagy on A or oligophagy on all three plants. This hypothesis is clearly related to the idea that neural constraints are important in the evolution of insect diet breadth (Futuyma 1983; Dukas and Real 1991; Bernays 1998).

Thompson's (1993) evidence for evolutionary constraints on preference hierarchies in *P. zelicaon* stems from the observation that these hierarchies are invariant among populations with different diets. Bossart and Scriber (1999) found variation in both preference rank and specificity in *Papilio glaucus,* but could detect heritable variation only in specificity, concluding that the variation in rank order was environmental. In contrast, *E. editha* show genetically variable preference rank both among populations (Singer et al. 1991, 1994; Singer and Parmesan 1993; Singer and Thomas 1996) and within them (Singer 1983; Singer et al. 1988). This pattern of variation suggests that preference hierarchies are evolutionarily labile. However, we have additional evidence for lability that is even stronger: direct observations of population-level changes in preference rank order (Singer et al. 1993). We have also been able to test whether preferences for different plant categories (within a plant species) evolved independently of preferences for different plant species. This work constitutes a test of a special case of the "fixed hierarchy" hypothesis advanced by Courtney and Thompson.

If preference hierarchies are highly constrained, then the relationships between discriminations made by insects within and among host species should tend to be conserved. However, we have evidence from *M. cinxia* that preferences expressed within and among host species can vary among individual insects (Singer and Lee 2000) and evidence from *E. editha* that the relationships between these two types of preferences have evolved over less than twenty generations (Singer et al. 1992a). We studied the same population of *E. editha* described above, at Rabbit Meadow, where *Collinsia torreyi* had recently been incorporated into the diet, but where most insects still prefer their traditional host at that site, *Pedicularis semibarbata.* Early work showed that some insects discriminated among individual *Pedicularis* plants, while others did not (Rausher et al. 1981; Ng 1988). Later, Singer et al. (1992a) found that the trait of discrimination among individual *Pedicularis* plants was highly correlated with acceptance of the novel host, *Collinsia.* Within a population (at Rabbit) that used *Collinsia,* those insects that accepted *Collinsia* most readily were nondiscriminators within *Pedicularis.*

We were excited to think that we had found an important novel constraint on insect diet breadth. Our observation suggested an evolutionary hypothesis: when a novel host is incorporated into the diet, adaptive discrimination among individuals of the traditional host is lost. If this adaptive discrimination were important, then diet expansion would have a fitness cost stemming from this constraint. Diet expansion would be rendered less likely, and when a broader diet did evolve, it would be associated with reduced intraspecific host discrimination. Unfortunately for this hypothesis, at least in this particular case, we were able to test it directly. The diet shift at Rabbit had been caused by logging, and we had access to insects in an unlogged habitat only 12 km away, at Colony Meadow in Sequoia National Park. We considered Colony insects to represent the putative ancestral condition of the Rabbit butterflies before the diet shift occurred. We compared insects from the two sites to assess the nature of the changes associated with the diet shift.

First, we showed that the proportion of insects accepting *Collinsia* had increased dramatically since the diet shift, but that no change at all had occurred in discrimination among *Pedicularis* plants. Second, we showed that the association between discrimination within and among hosts was significantly different at Colony than at Rabbit. At Colony, there was a (nonsignificant) trend in the opposite direction from Rabbit: butterflies that accepted *Collinsia* most readily were *more* likely to discriminate among *Pedicularis* individuals. So, the exciting result for which we had hoped did not materialize, and we produced a manuscript with the less-than-exciting title "Rapid evolution of associations among preferences fails to constrain evolution of insect diet breadth" (Singer et al. 1992b). However, this result does show clearly that host preference has at least two independently evolving dimensions, and thereby invalidates (for this specific case) a simple model in which all plants are arranged in a single evolutionarily viscous hierarchy.

The idea that specialists make more adaptive discriminations within plant species has, however, received recent support. Among butterflies whose diets include nettles, larvae of oligophagous butterfly species suffered from low nettle quality just as much as did the monophagous species. However, ovipositing adults of three monophagous species made clearer discriminations among nettles of differing quality than did two oligophagous species (Janz and Nylin 1997).

In contrast to Wiklund's and Thompson's work with the *Papilio machaon* group of swallowtails, Bossart and Scriber (1995b) show geographic variation in preference rank in *Papilio glaucus,* implying that the preference hierarchy may differ in viscosity even between two groups of swallowtails. Detailed investigation of this type of difference may prove informative about diet evolution.

THE ROLE OF BUTTERFLY BIOLOGY IN PLANT-INSECT INTERACTIONS

I've chosen a few topics from our melitaeine research that illustrate areas in which I believe butterfly biology can make a contribution to the understanding of insect-plant relations in a general sense. Because it is not feasible to raise butterflies in the numbers that can readily be achieved with flies or beetles, it behooves us to tailor our ambitions to the possible and tackle problems for which butterflies are either exceptionally suitable research organisms or for which there is some indication that they may differ systematically from other well-studied groups. An example to show what I mean by such a "systematic difference" is that the general advantage of broad diet that stems from the physiological benefits of diet mixing in Orthoptera seems to be missing in Lepidoptera, so that the action of natural selection on diet breadth must be quite different in the two groups (Bernays and Minkenberg 1997). In fact, butterflies have played a continuing role in research on insect diet breadth. The hypothesis that diet breadth depends on time constraints originated in butterfly work (Nylin 1988; Scriber and Lederhouse 1992). The recent emphasis on predators as agents of selection for a narrow diet, stemming from the work of Bernays and Graham (1988), has received empirical support from work with Neotropical caterpillars (Dyer 1995). Understanding of the role of constraints on preference hierarchies in diet breadth centers on work with both flies (Courtney et al. 1989) and butterflies (Singer et al. 1992a; Janz and Nylin 1997; Thompson 1998), but traces its origins to butterflies (Wiklund 1981). And, of course, butterflies have loomed large in plant-insect coevolution from the start (Ehrlich and Raven 1964; Feeny 1975; Berenbaum 1995b; Janz and Nylin 1998).

Where are we now? Is butterfly biology doomed to a minor role in the future study of plant-insect interactions because our study subjects are harder to raise in numbers than mites, beetles, or flies? The power to investigate the genetic architecture of preference and performance has been best realized in flies (Jaenike 1986) and beetles (Fox 1993) (but see Camara 1997 and Sheck and Gould 1996). Gould's classic (1979) experimental work on diet evolution in mites required large numbers and short generation times. Butterfly biologists are, in general, condemned to lower-than-*Drosophila* sample sizes. Perhaps, if the conceptual questions in which we are interested are really better tackled with beetles, then we should consider doing just that?

But this is a book about the biology of butterflies, not about plant-insect interactions. So must we really all switch to beetles? Before we resort to what to some of us must seem drastic measures, we should take heart: samples in the thousands aren't always necessary for chemical ecology studies (Feeny 1995; Berenbaum 1995b) or phylogenetic studies of diet history (Mitter et al. 1991; Radtkey and Singer 1995; Janz 1998a). More to the point, we should at least try to ask ourselves what unique contributions butterfly biology can continue to make.

Two conceptual problems eminently suited to testing with butterflies come to mind. First, testing evolutionary predictions about relationships between adult preference and larval performance is simpler when larval and adult resources can be cleanly separated. In beetles and flies, these parameters are often intertwined. An adult beetle or fruit fly may feed on a suboptimal resource because it is an excellent oviposition substrate, and may oviposit on a resource suboptimal for offspring because it makes excellent adult food. It's hard enough to make and test evolutionary predictions in butterflies, in which adult nutrition is not an issue, but the oviposition host that confers the highest fitness must still meet a daunting plethora of criteria (Rausher 1979b). It should be easy to find and handle, appropriate in microclimate for adult activity, harbor few enemies of either ovipositing adults or larvae, support high offspring survival, and generate larval growth rates that lead to adaptive phenology in the next adult generation.

A second way in which butterflies excel is that they can be readily marked as individuals, recognized upon resighting without being disturbed by recapture, and followed as they search for hosts. Efficiency of host finding can be readily estimated and compared among butterflies (Rausher 1978; Stanton and Cook 1983) or host types (Parmesan et al. 1995). Encounters with hosts can be clearly observed and their results, in terms of host acceptance or rejection, unequivocally recorded (Oyeyele and Zalucki 1990). Although workers with tephritids have performed equivalent observations (Feder et al. 1998 and references therein), butterflies are clearly ideal for studies of host search behavior and its correlations with prior experience or diet breadth. The classic work in this field by Jones (1977), Rausher and Papaj (e.g., Rausher 1978; Papaj 1986a, 1986b; Papaj and Rausher 1987; reviewed by Rausher 1993), and Stanton and Cook (1983) seems peripheral in recent reviews of plant-insect interactions. We should dig it out again, and consider expanding on it in our work.

SUMMARY

Ten years ago, studies of insect-host plant associations centered largely on the insects' relative performance on different hosts, rather than on their relative chances of selecting those hosts for feeding or oviposition. Now preference and performance are recognized as equally important, and we see a proliferation of papers on relationships between them. In this chapter, I discuss how butterfly oviposition preference interacts not with performance, but with the reciprocal trait of the host plants, acceptability. This interaction generates spatial and temporal patterns of insect-host association. I then discuss the evidence that preference constrains diet evolution, and I describe examples in which it has failed to do so during the colonization of novel host species. In conclusion, I suggest how butterfly biologists might make the best use of their study organisms in contributing to advances in the understanding of plant-insect interactions in general.

ACKNOWLEDGMENTS

Paul Ehrlich introduced me to *E. editha,* cheerfully paid for my projects whether or not he thought them wise, and tolerated my various insurrections. I hope I have been equally tolerant of my own collaborators less aged than myself, particularly Duncan Mackay, David Ng, Camille Parmesan, Chris Thomas, and David Boughton. Recently, I'm especially grateful to Ilkka Hanski for wholeheartedly welcoming me as part of his group. I've also been helped by Bernard Barascud, David Bauer, Henri Descimon, John Emmel, Wille Fortelius, Niklas Janz, Mathieu Joron, Sterling and Eileen Mattoon, Robert Mazel, Emese Meglecz, Dennis Murphy, Gabriel Neve, Saskya van Nouyhuys, Gordon Pratt, Nils Ryrholm, Michel Savourey, Constanti Stefanescu, Niklas Wahlberg, Brian Wee, Ray White, Christer Wiklund, and Marie Zimmerman.

CHAPTER 11

Sex Linkage of Host Plant Use in Butterflies

Niklas Janz

Herbivorous insects account for much of the diversity of life, and this great diversity appears to some extent to have been caused by radiation onto an equally manifold food resource, the seed plants (Ehrlich and Raven 1964; Jermy 1984; Mitter et al. 1988, 1991; Janz and Nylin 1998). Recent hybridization studies on butterflies have offered new insight into the genetic mechanisms behind this relatively rapid diversification, suggesting an intriguing role for the X chromosome in speciation in the Lepidoptera (Thompson 1988b; Jaenike 1989; Thompson et al. 1990; Sperling 1993; Scriber 1994; Sperling and Harrison 1994; Scriber et al. 1995a, 1996; see also Sperling, chap. 20 in this volume). Even taking into account the possibility of a sampling bias in the available data, it appears clear that species differences are disproportionately affected by genes on the X chromosome (e.g., Charlesworth et al. 1987; Sperling 1994). The traits involved include diapause control, mimetic coloration, host plant ranking, pheromone composition, mate selection, and female fecundity (Sperling 1994, and references therein). These are all also important life history traits. What is the reason for this bias toward the X chromosome?

Charlesworth et al. (1987) have shown theoretically that major genes on the X chromosome will evolve faster than those on the autosomes if mutations are fully or partially recessive. The reason for this is that recessive genes on the X chromosome will be more exposed to selection in the heterogametic sex. In contrast, there will be no comparable difference in rate of evolution between the chromosomes for traits controlled by a number of loci with additive effects (Charlesworth et al. 1987). The increased rate of evolution will allow faster spread and fixation of favorable mutations in the population, especially for traits that are expressed only by the heterogametic sex.

Because females are heterogametic in the Lepidoptera, this phenomenon is especially suggestive as an explanation for X-linkage of traits expressed only by females, such as host plant selection. On the other hand, X-linked characters in the Lepidoptera that are restricted to males, such as male-limited wing coloration, cannot be explained by this mechanism, as males have two X chromosomes. However, as dosage compensation does not appear to occur in butterflies, males will have twice the dose of an X-linked enzyme that females have, making it possible for a male-limited trait to be turned on or off by a large or small dose of a certain enzyme (Johnson and Turner 1979).

The accumulation of genes on the X chromosome will be further facilitated by the reduced rate of recombination for genes on the X chromosome. Eventually this process could result in the buildup of "coadapted gene complexes" that would simplify fast and major changes in whole suites of traits coadapted to, for example, local climatic conditions (Scriber 1994). With time, these changes could then lead to population differentiation and speciation. Furthermore, the empirical finding that heterogametic hybrids often suffer from reduced viability or fertility, known as Haldane's rule (Haldane 1922; Coyne 1992), would further reinforce this differentiation and help keep these gene complexes intact (e.g., Charlesworth et al. 1987; Sperling 1993; Scriber 1994).

Among the traits that make up these proposed coadapted complexes of traits with X-linked inheritance is host plant preference. Several studies comparing interspecific hybrids between pairs of closely related *Papilio* butterflies have demonstrated a strong effect of the X chromosome on host plant ranking (Thompson 1988b; Scriber et al. 1991a; Scriber 1994), a suggestive finding in light of the ongoing discussion of sympatric speciation via host plant races (e.g., Bush 1975; Futuyma and Peterson 1985; Butlin 1987; Bush 1994). However, any host plant–mediated diversification also requires understanding of the evolution and maintenance of local adaptations on an ecological scale (e.g., Singer and Thomas 1996; see also Singer, chap. 10 in this volume). We need to know more about the genetic control of *intraspecific* differences in host plant preference (Jaenike 1989).

A NEW PIECE IN THE PUZZLE

Evidence on X-linkage of important life history traits in butterflies is accumulating, but some important questions remain. I have conducted an intraspecific hybridization experiment on the comma butterfly, *Polygonia c-album,* in an attempt to answer two of those questions (Janz 1998b). The first is the more general: if interspecific differences tend to be X-linked, is *within*-species variation similarly X-linked? The second concerns the difference between host plant ranking and specialization. In all the studies on host plant preference mentioned above, the investigators performed hybridizations of closely related species that differed in ranking; that is, they preferred different plants. The question is, will the degree of specialization on one preferred plant be inherited in a similar way (i.e., be X-linked), or will it show autosomal inheritance, as could be expected from the more quantitative nature of this trait?

The comma butterfly is unusually well suited to address these questions, and I will briefly outline some important characteristics of this species. It is the only representative in northern Europe of the Holarctic genus *Polygonia* (tribe Nymphalini, family Nymphalidae). It has a wide distribution, ranging from western Europe to Japan, and in Europe from Scandinavia to the Mediterranean. Its host plant range is unusually wide for a butterfly, including plants from seven families in four orders (Urticaceae, Ulmaceae, and Cannabidaceae in Urticales, Salicaceae in Salicales, Grossulariaceae in Rosales, and Betulaceae and Corylaceae in Fagales). Of these plants, females usually prefer, and larvae perform best on, the plants in Urticales (Nylin 1988; Janz et al. 1994). There is a relatively high correspondence at the population level between female preference and larval performance in this species (Nylin 1988; Nylin and Janz 1993; Janz et al. 1994; Nylin et al. 1996b), indicating that females base their choices largely on intrinsic qualities of the plants, and that external factors such as predators play a limited role in the establishment of the preference hierarchy.

Like most of its relatives in Nymphalini, the comma hibernates in the adult stage. Under favorable conditions it can produce a brighter-colored, direct-developing form that cannot normally survive the winter, but must mate and give rise to a second summer generation (Nylin 1989). Because the length of the favorable season changes with latitude, southern populations regularly produce the direct-developing form, while populations closer to the northern limit of the species' distribution are strictly univoltine. At the latitude where there is barely enough time for a second summer generation, there is increased selection for oviposition on plants that can support the shortest development times, leading to increased specialization on these plants (Nylin 1988; see also Scriber and Lederhouse 1992). On the other hand, a bit farther north, there is never enough time for a second generation, but still plenty of time for one, and consequently there is lower selection pressure for specialization on plants that can support the fastest growth.

This phenomenon has provided us with the opportunity to find and compare populations of *P. c-album* that differ in degree of oviposition specialization while retaining the same host ranking (Nylin 1988; Janz and

Nylin 1997). The populations used in these experiments came from southern England (a partially bivoltine population) and Stockholm, Sweden (a univoltine population). These populations were also used in a hybridization experiment to investigate the inheritance of oviposition specificity in *P. c-album* (Janz 1998b). Butterflies from the two populations were cross-mated in all possible combinations, and females were tested in simultaneous choice trials with *Urtica dioica* as the preferred plant and *Salix caprea* as the less preferred plant. Offspring were all reared on *U. dioica* under a photoperiod and temperature regime known to cause direct development in both populations (Nylin 1989). Female F_1 offspring of all the crosses were then given the same oviposition choice trial. (See Janz 1998b for a more comprehensive method description.)

COMPONENTS OF HOST PLANT USE

Host plant use in butterflies can conveniently be divided into two complex traits, female oviposition preference and larval performance (Thompson 1988a). Oviposition preference refers to the sequence of behavioral traits involved in locating and evaluating a potential host plant that ultimately leads to the decision to oviposit or not. Most butterfly species are relatively specialized, restricting oviposition to a few related plant species or genera. Even so, the host plant species in a butterfly's repertoire usually vary in quality, and preference is generally expressed as a hierarchical ranking of those plants. Singer (1971a) and Wiklund (1975, 1981) provided some of the first empirical evidence for the hierarchical nature of host plant range in butterflies and other herbivorous insects. Females are more likely to oviposit on a high-ranked plant, but will accept lower-ranked plants to a lesser degree, especially if the higher-ranked plants are not available.

There is a good deal of confusion surrounding the terms used to describe different types of oviposition behavior and strategies. To avoid adding to this confusion, I briefly define my use of these terms, while trying to follow and combine existing definitions as much as possible (cf. Thompson 1988b; Singer et al. 1992b; Singer, chap. 10 in this volume). All terms refer to oviposition behavior under controlled conditions; actual host use may differ depending on the abundance and availability of potential host plants in nature.

Host plant ranking is the order of host plants as ranked by number of eggs oviposited on them (in simultaneous choice trials), or the order of plants as they become acceptable (in sequential choice trials).

Host plant range is the number of plant species actually oviposited on in any type of choice trial.

Specificity is a relative measure of how many eggs a female lays on a preferred plant in relation to other plants in the trial (in simultaneous choice trials) or of the length of the discrimination time on a preferred plant in relation to other plants (in sequential choice trials).

Oviposition preference is perhaps the most vague of these terms, often simply referring to the fact that a female shows a higher willingness to oviposit on certain plants than on others (see Singer, chap. 10 in this volume, for a more thorough definition).

Larval performance refers to a measurable trait or set of traits that adequately approximate, or correlate well with, offspring fitness on a given host plant (Thompson 1988a; Nylin et al. 1996b). Popular traits to investigate are development time, survival, pupal or adult weight, and growth rate. In some circumstances it may also be necessary to include female fecundity as well as the quantity and quality of the male contribution to fitness (i.e., spermatophore size and protein content) (Wiklund and Kaitala 1995; Nylin et al. 1996b; Wedell 1996).

HOST PLANT RANKING VERSUS SPECIALIZATION

Two hybridization studies on *Papilio* butterflies have demonstrated that host plant preferences in these butterflies are strongly influenced by genes on the X chromosome (Thompson 1988b; Scriber et al. 1991a). In both of these studies, the species that were hybridized preferred different host plant species—that is, they showed differences in ranking; no comparable studies have been made on differences in oviposition specificity. The relationship between ranking and specificity is not at all clear, but traditionally they have been treated as two rather different phenomena, caused by different mechanisms. This view dates back to the 1970s and was formally described by Courtney et al. as "the hierarchy-threshold model" (1989). According to this model, host plant ranking is largely determined by external, plant-specific factors, such as plant chemistry, while specificity is determined by a threshold value that is dependent on the insect's internal motivational state (fig. 11.1). Thus, specificity is not directly determined by plant characteristics, but is a property of the ovipositing female. Several interesting predictions can be made from this distinction. First, the genetic basis of a threshold trait is most likely to have polygenic determination, and thus to be best understood in terms of quantitative genetics (Courtney et al. 1989). Because the X-linked genes discussed above are selected for essentially as major genes (Charlesworth et al. 1987), there is no reason to expect a disproportionate effect of the X chromosome under the hierarchy-threshold model. Second, motivation to oviposit can vary, even over a single female's life span, and thus specialization should be a relatively labile trait. Ranking,

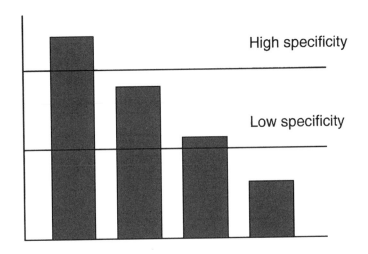

Rank order of host plants

Figure 11.1 Schematic description of host plant ranking and specialization, according to the hierarchy-threshold model (Courtney et al. 1989). While host ranking is determined by external factors, such as host plant chemistry, oviposition specificity is a result of the current motivational state of the ovipositing female. Changes in motivational state will cause the motivational threshold to move up or down, making the female accept or reject plants further down in the hierarchy.

on the other hand, should not change as readily, and should be much more evolutionarily stable (Courtney et al. 1989; Scriber 1994).

The results from my hybridization experiment on *P. c-album* demonstrated very clearly that oviposition specificity is strongly influenced by genes on the X chromosome (fig. 11.2, see also Janz 1998b), showing a mode of inheritance very similar to that of host plant ranking in *Papilio* butterflies. The exact genetic mechanisms remain unknown, but at the very least, this finding suggests that factors other than a threshold mechanism have a significant influence on what is expressed as specificity in *P. c-album*. One possibility is that one or more modifier genes on the X chromosome influence the threshold value, but the simplest explanation would perhaps be that ranking and specificity are different expressions of the same genes. This explanation requires that the acceptability of the different host plant species vary independently.

There is some evidence in support of the prediction that specialization should be more evolutionarily labile than ranking: while several studies have demonstrated individual variation in specificity, few have been able to demonstrate such variation in ranking (e.g., Jaenike 1990). However, this evidence is compatible with the view that both ranking and specificity are determined by the same genes. Typically, small changes in ranking would be expressed as changes in specificity, while only larger changes would result in

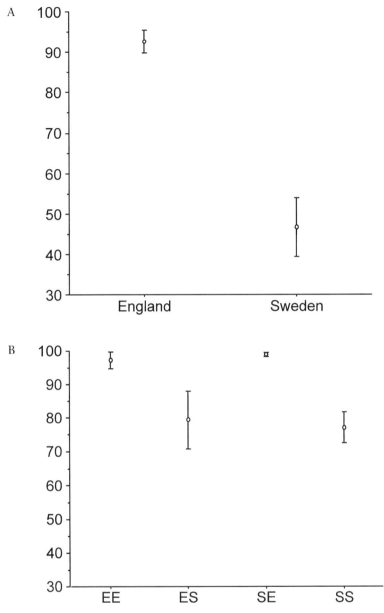

Figure 11.2 Degree of preference (means ± SE) for the higher-ranked *Urtica dioica* over the lower-ranked *Salix caprea* by ovipositing females of *Polygonia c-album*. (A) Parental generation (hibernated), English and Swedish populations. (B) F₁ crosses (summer generation). E = English; S = Swedish; mother's origin is given first. If preference is sex-linked, then it should vary with the father's origin. (Data from Janz 1998b.)

reversals in ranking, and small changes would undoubtedly be more common that large ones. Furthermore, there have been indications of reversals in ranking within the Swedish population of *P. c-album* (Janz et al. 1994). While that particular experiment did not clearly distinguish between genetic and environmental effects, recent experiments on the same population indicate a strong genetic component in the variation in host plant preference (S. Nylin, J. Windig, and G. Nygren, unpub.).

OVIPOSITION PREFERENCE VERSUS LARVAL PERFORMANCE

Because most butterfly larvae are relatively immobile and lack the specific adaptations for dispersal and host plant selection found in some other Lepidoptera (e.g., Tammaru et al. 1995), most host plant selection is exerted by the ovipositing female. For this reason, one should expect a relatively high correspondence between the plants that are selected by females for oviposition and the plants on which offspring fitness is highest. It has been hypothesized that oviposition preference and larval performance should be genetically linked, or even be pleiotropic effects of the same genes (Bush 1975; Rausher 1984; Futuyma and Peterson 1985; Via 1986). Many studies have investigated the correlation between female oviposition preference and larval performance, and the results are mixed (reviewed by Thompson 1988a). There could be several reasons why the correspondence between these traits is not always perfect (Thompson 1988a; Thompson and Pellmyr 1991). There could, for example, have been insufficient time to adapt to a novel host plant, or the preferred host might be so rare that it does not pay to search for it. Other factors that could influence the preference hierarchy are not easily quantified in a controlled choice trial in the laboratory: a favorable plant might grow in unfavorable habitats or be exposed to enemies. Moreover, oviposition preference should really be expected to correlate with total offspring fitness, not with any single measure of performance (Thompson 1988a; Reavey and Lawton 1991; Janz et al. 1994; Nylin et al. 1996b). Choosing an adequate performance measure is as important as it may be difficult and requires good knowledge of the system under study.

Still, on average, we should expect, and often find, a good correlation between oviposition preference and traits that contribute to offspring performance, and some form of physical linkage between the traits would seem to make sense. Curiously, several studies, on organisms as diverse as papilionid butterflies (Thompson 1988b; Thompson et al. 1990), chrysomelid beetles (Keese 1996), and aphids (Guldemond 1990), have demonstrated that oviposition preference shows a different type of inheritance than larval performance. Similarly, in my intraspecific cross of *P. c-album,* there was no evidence of X-linked inheritance of growth rate on the preferred host plant *Urtica dioica.* This trait appeared to be largely determined by genes on the autosomes (fig. 11.3). Consequently, there was no indication of X-linkage of larval performance. Hence, in none of these species was there any evidence for either pleiotropy or physical linkage between the genes that influenced preference and performance.

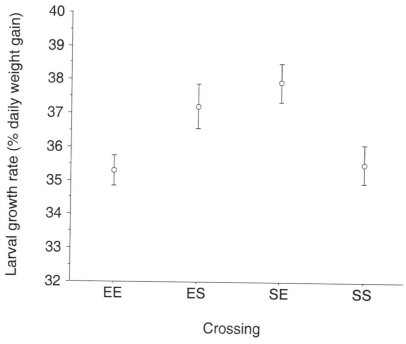

Figure 11.3 Larval growth rate (means ± SE) on *U. dioica* for F_1 crosses of Swedish and English *Polygonia c-album,* measured as the percentage of daily weight gain. E = English; S = Swedish; mother's origin is given first.

As it must be very important for the female to oviposit on plants that the larvae can feed most efficiently on, why is a good correlation not assured by linkage or pleiotropy? To put it differently, why are the genes that influence larval performance not included in the "coadapted gene complexes" described in the introduction to this chapter? Part of the answer may lie in the asymmetrical relationship between the two traits. While ovipositions on plants that the larvae cannot survive on are very costly for the female, there is not necessarily a high cost associated with the capacity to feed on a wider range of plants than the female normally oviposits on. On the contrary, this capacity would probably be adaptive, because females sometimes make oviposition mistakes (Chew 1977; Larsson and Ekbom 1995), and because the original food plant could be depleted. Several authors have also shown empirically that larvae are able to grow and survive on a wider range of plants than females actually oviposit on (Wiklund 1975; Smiley 1978; Roininen and Tahvanainen 1989). Furthermore, the often proposed physiological trade-off between larval feeding efficiency on different host plant species has received relatively weak support (see Janz and Nylin 1997), making it less costly to retain presently unused plants in the larval host plant range. Thus, opportunistic oviposition strategies and conservative larval performance can both be seen as adaptations to a constantly changing environment, making a close linkage between the two traits nonadaptive.

In his review of the genetic basis of species differences in the Lepidoptera, Sperling (1994) found that more than half of all reported differences between species were controlled by X-linked genes, a striking result considering that Lepidoptera have about thirty pairs of chromosomes. This finding indicates a strong bias for X-linkage of genes that account for species differences. Many species of Lepidoptera vary geographically in host plant use, in terms of both ranking and specificity (Nylin 1988; Singer et al. 1989; Scriber 1992; Thompson 1993; Singer and Thomas 1996; Janz and Nylin 1997; Thompson 1997). Are the genetic determinants of intraspecific variation in host plant preference of the same sort as the interspecific variation studied by Thompson (1988b) and Scriber et al. (1991a)?

Based on the theories of Charlesworth et al. (1987) and Jaenike (1989), Scriber (1994) hypothesized that while interspecific differences should be controlled by X-linked, recessive genes, intraspecific differences should be controlled by autosomal, dominant, or quantitative factors. However, my study of *P. c-album* showed a very strong influence of the X chromosome on intraspecific differences in host plant specificity (Janz 1998b). The two populations used in my study are widely separated geographically, and gene flow between them is probably minimal. If X-linkage is to play a role in diversification, genes on the X chromosome should also account for much of the variation among populations on a geographic scale. An interesting and unexplored question concerns the role of the X chromosome in maintaining local adaptations in conspecific populations. Many of the traits that have been suggested to be involved in the coadapted gene complexes on the X chromosome (see Scriber 1994) are also traits that can be expected to vary locally—for example, with latitude in temperate regions. It is also extremely important that local covariation of traits such as photoperiod sensitivity, host plant specialization, diapause control, and so forth not be broken by gene flow from other populations.

Variation *within* populations deserves more attention, too. A few studies have demonstrated a significant heritability of oviposition preference, indicating that variation at this level is significantly influenced by genes with additive effects (Tabashnik et al. 1981; Singer et al. 1988; Carriere and Roitberg 1995). Preliminary results from a recent experiment on the Swedish population of *P. c-album* show that at least some of the within-population variation is determined by autosomal genes, although X-linked genes could also contribute to that variation (S. Nylin, J. Windig, and G. Nygren, unpub.). The relationship of the genetic determination of variation between individuals in the same population, between conspecific populations, and between closely related species remains a puzzle that needs attention.

SUMMARY

X-linkage of coadapted suites of life history traits has been hypothesized to play an important role in speciation in the Lepidoptera. Among the traits that have been shown to be strongly influenced by the X chromosome are species differences in host plant ranking. I have shown that even intraspecific differences in the degree of oviposition specialization can be X-linked, suggesting a common genetic background for host plant ranking and oviposition specialization. In contrast, larval performance seems to be inherited differently from oviposition preference, which should make speciation via host plant races more difficult. The studies done thus far raise several suggestive hypotheses about population differentiation and maintenance of local adaptations. To answer these questions, more attention must be directed toward understanding the relationship between genetic variation within and between populations and species.

PART IV

Genetics and Evolutionary Dynamics

Because no evolution is possible without heritable variation, genetics has been at the heart of evolutionary study since the rediscovery of Mendel's work in 1900. But as powerful as the formal theory of population genetics is, there is growing awareness that when standing alone, it is incomplete (Feder and Watt 1992). The interactions (often reciprocal, rather than unidirectional) between heritable phenotypes and the environments in which they occur are the driving forces of evolutionary dynamics and must be studied alongside their population genetic effects. The depth of our knowledge of butterflies' breeding biology and natural history makes them superb model systems for this sort of work. It allows us to see clearly how genotype-phenotype-environment interactions first determine differences in variants' performances of immediate biological tasks in the wild, and thence through demography lead to differences in evolutionary fitness among the variants—the essential grist of the evolutionary mill. Such work will be needed if we are to gain any general picture of how such fitness differences, which population genetic theory takes among its starting conditions, are actually distributed in nature.

The chapters in this part of the book use diverse strategies for assembling such a general picture. Several chapters focus on wing patterns, the displays of butterflies' identities to one another, to their potential predators, and to biologists. The work ranges from the formal properties of pattern determination to underlying mechanistic developmental genetics. Larry Gilbert (chap. 14) uses the interfertility of seemingly disparate *Heliconius* to dissect the genetic control of their striking Müllerian-mimetic wing patterns, showing how very different pattern geometries may result from small, often hierarchical, genetic changes. Paul Brakefield and Antónia Monteiro (chap. 12) offer an initial synthesis of the workings of such developmental genetics in phenotypic evolution. Studying the variability of eyespots in *Bicyclus anynana*, they explore the contrasts between genes with large and small effects on genotypes. At an even more mechanistic level, Richard ffrench-Constant and Bernhard Koch (chap. 13) describe the biochemical genetics of melanin formation during development, which produces dramatic differences in wing color among different *Papilio glaucus* morphs.

The theme of adaptive responses, at diverse levels of organization, to variable habitats continues in other taxa and phenotypic systems. Ward Watt (chap. 15) synthesizes work on the thermal biology and metabolic evolution of *Colias*, tracing the effects of genetic variants from molecular to organismal performance and thence to fitness itself, but emphasizing the role of constraints, no less than natural selection, in shaping phenotypes and organism-environment interactions. Working with *Pararge*, Hans van Dyck (chap. 16) discusses the interaction between mate location strategies and associated morphological adaptations that allow males to deal effectively with the thermal stresses associated with each strategy.

Adaptive organism-environment interactions may change in the transition from intraspecific to transspecific evolution. Mark Scriber and his colleagues (chap. 17) end part 4 with a study of trait clines in regionally distinct host plant preferences, multigenic determinants of growth rate, and other potentially specifically adaptive characters across hybrid zones between partially reproductively isolated *Papilio glaucus* and *P. canadensis* in North America. They make a strong case for the usefulness of mechanistic study of character state variation in such zones as a means of dissecting the relationship between adaptive specialization and phylogenetic differentiation. This work thus makes a helpful bridge to the consideration of phylogeny and systematics in part 5.

CHAPTER 12

The Evolution of Butterfly Eyespot Patterns

Paul M. Brakefield and Antónia Monteiro

One of the most dramatic, as well as beautiful, examples of morphological diversity is displayed by the color patterns of butterfly wings. The functional aspects of this diversity have fascinated biologists for a long time. Butterflies have provided the material for examining many hypotheses about how natural selection influences phenotypic variation both within and across species (Ford 1964; Brakefield 1984; Endler 1986; Joron and Mallet 1998).

Studies of Müllerian mimicry in species of *Heliconius* with geographic races in South America have detected stabilizing selection on color patterns in the wild (Mallet and Barton 1989). More recently, Kingsolver (1995a, 1995b, 1996) has used another example of phenotypic variation in butterflies to expand our understanding of adaptive evolution. A series of elegant field experiments quantified the change in relative fitness of the seasonal color forms of the western white, *Pontia occidentalis,* across the environments in which they fly (see Brakefield 1996). Such seasonal forms are the result of phenotypic plasticity, in which sensitivity to variation in the environment during development leads to alternative adult phenotypes (Shapiro 1976; Jacobs and Watt 1994; Brakefield and French 1999). Kingsolver's experiments support the hypothesis that differences between the color forms in thermoregulation underlie the seasonal changes in relative fitness. These types of studies have thus enabled both the detection of natural selection and the examination of the biological reasons for differences in fitness (see Endler 1986).

At the same time as butterfly wing patterns have provided the impetus for studies of natural selection, the genetic basis of their variability has been analyzed. The genetics of several examples of polymorphism in mimetic color patterns, both Batesian and Müllerian, have been especially well described. Clarke and Sheppard (1959, 1960, 1963), for example, used detailed series of genetic crosses to describe the genetic differences among the Batesian mimetic forms of the African swallowtail *Papilio dardanus*. Comparable analyses have been made for other mimetic species of *Hypolimnas, Danaus,* and *Papilio* (see Ford 1964; Turner 1984; Nijhout 1991, 1994a). Philip Sheppard was also involved in the study of the color pattern races of the South American *Heliconius* butterflies, especially the Müllerian co-mimics *H. erato* and *H. melpomene* (Sheppard et al. 1985). The work on *Heliconius* has been supplemented by studies of natural hybrid zones between geographic races distinguished by sometimes spectacular divergence in color pattern (e.g., Mallet and Joron 1999). The widest of such differences in color pattern can usually be accounted for by fixation of alternative alleles at a small number of gene loci. On the other hand, many other differences in wing pattern among populations of particular species of butterflies are likely to be due to a larger number of genes, each of which has only a small phenotypic effect (see Ford 1964; Brakefield 1984).

Another approach to accounting for the diversity of wing patterns was initiated in the 1920s by comparative morphologists, especially B. N. Schwanwitsch and F. Suffert (reviewed by Nijhout and Wray 1986; Nijhout 1991). Detailed morphological examination of representative species from within particular families of butterflies led to descriptions of how wing patterns may have become modified during evolution to provide the array of present-day color patterns. Perhaps the most important contribution of this approach was the concept of an ancestral or prototype wing pattern known as the nymphalid groundplan (fig. 12.1). This prototype shows parallel columns of particular pattern elements extending across the proximal-distal axis of each wing. These pattern elements include those making up the central symmetry system of a pair of medial bands, the concentric eyespots of the border ocelli system, and the parafocal chevron elements along the wing margins. Each wing subdivision or wing cell (an area bounded by wing veins) shows the presence of several pattern elements of different types. A particular type of element, such as an eyespot, is thus represented by repeats of the element in adjoining wing cells. Evolutionary change is envisaged as involving the presence or absence, or modifications of the color, size, and shape, of the repeats of each type of element. The fusion of repeats of a particular element across wing veins and wing cells can lead to a continuous pattern, such as a stripe or band, that extends across the whole wing. The combination of changes within individual wing cells and divergence across the cells provides the basis of the spectacular diversity within groups of butterflies.

Finally, early studies on the development of wing patterns in the flour-moth, *Ephestia kuhniella* (Kuhn and von Engelhardt 1933), were followed up with great success by Nijhout (1980b, 1991) using eyespots of the buckeye

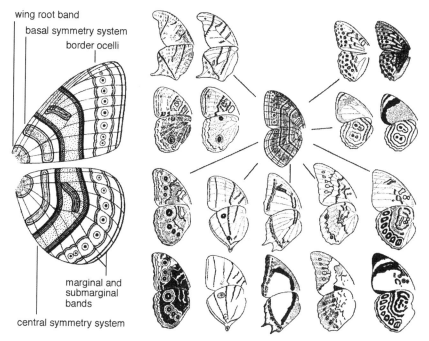

Figure 12.1 The nymphalid groundplan (left), modified to produce representative wing patterns of extant species (right). (After Nijhout 1991, figs. 2.1 and 2.4.)

Labels on figure:
wing root band
basal symmetry system
border ocelli
marginal and submarginal bands
central symmetry system

butterfly, *Precis coenia*. These studies, together with further work on the eyespots of the African satyrid butterfly, *Bicyclus anynana*, have provided the potential for directly linking developmental insights with the genetic basis of the phenotypic variation (Brakefield and French 1993, 1999; Brakefield 1998). Thus it is now possible to fill the gap between genes and phenotypes for examples of functional traits involved in adaptive morphological evolution. We concentrate here on our attempts to fill this gap for the eyespot patterns of *Bicyclus* butterflies.

EYESPOT PATTERNS AND DEVELOPMENTAL MODULES

The color pattern of a butterfly wing is made up of a mosaic of scale cells arranged like the tiles on a roof. The wild type of *B. anynana* has a series of eyespots on each wing surface except the dorsal hindwing, where eyespots only occasionally occur (plate 12.1). While the ventral hindwing shows a full row of seven or eight eyespots, the forewing surfaces usually have only a large posterior and a small anterior eyespot. The eyespots have a central white pupil, an inner black disc, and an outer gold ring (with additional rings in ventral eyespots). Each concentric ring of color within an eyespot is made up of many scale cells, all of which have synthesized the same color pigment. The row of eyespots represent serial developmental homologues, with each eyespot based on a common developmental mechanism.

In the terminology elaborated by Wagner (1996), the eyespot pattern as a whole constitutes a single developmental module. The different parallel columns of pattern elements identified in the nymphalid groundplan, then, reflect a series of different modules. Certain directions of change within a single module involving developmentally integrated traits may be relatively difficult to achieve in evolution, while different modules can change freely and independently of one another. Nijhout's writings have emphasized the great flexibility or freedom in the evolution of wing pattern diversity that arises from the independence of the different modules or series of pattern elements (Nijhout 1991, 1994b, 2001; Paulsen and Nijhout 1993; Paulsen 1994, 1995; see fig. 12.1). Our studies of eyespots concentrate on changes within one of these modules.

The following section of this chapter reviews our laboratory studies on the eyespots of a single species, *B. anynana*. This work has focused on the developmental processes underlying eyespot formation, on the genetic variation underlying different traits or features of the eyespot pattern, and on the developmental mechanisms that link the genes to the phenotypic variation. The next phase of these laboratory studies on a single species will not only probe the genes and developmental mechanisms more effectively, but will also explore more empirically whether some changes in the eyespot pattern can be attained more readily than others. If so, then factors depending on the genetic and developmental bases of this pattern could act as constraints tending to bias the directions taken by evolution. Under such a scenario, the observed diversity in eyespot patterns across species would reflect not only the history of natural selection in relation to the functional requirements of environments, but also bias introduced by the genetic and developmental architectures of the traits (Brakefield and French 1993; Brakefield 1998).

The final sections of this chapter will show how combining phylogenetic studies of the species-rich genus *Bicyclus* with comparative descriptions of divergence in wing patterns is beginning to reveal the evolutionary trajectories that have been followed in the clade. Linking the top-down and bottom-up approaches allows us to begin to make predictions about which paths are most likely to be taken by evolution, both from mechanistic and from functional perspectives.

THE FORMATION OF EYESPOTS: THE DEVELOPMENTAL REPERTOIRE

The forewings and hindwings of butterflies develop in the larva as two sets of imaginal discs. Each disc is an internal pouch of epidermal cells that

Paul M. Brakefield and Antónia Monteiro

evaginates at metamorphosis to form the pupal wings. The color pattern of each wing surface (dorsal and ventral) is formed by a single cell layer, the epidermis. Certain epidermal cells, the scale mother cells, secrete a cuticular projection, the scale, which in the late pupa incorporates a particular color pigment. It is cell interactions at earlier stages that determine the particular pigments synthesized by these cells and hence define the adult wing pattern. The cell layers of the pupal wings are stacked one above the other under the pupal wing case. In the first few hours following pupation, the dorsal cell layer of the forewing is attached to the pupal cuticle. This arrangement is important because it enables surgical transplantation experiments as first done by Nijhout (1980b) in his work with eyespots.

The results of surgical experiments demonstrate that in both *P. coenia* and *B. anynana,* each eyespot is specified from a central signaling region known as the focus (Nijhout 1980b, 1985a, 1991; French and Brakefield 1992, 1995; Brakefield and French 1995; Brakefield et al. 1996). First, damage experiments in which fine needles are used to ablate the focus in early pupae (with or without heat) remove or shrink the entire eyespot. Second, and more critically, transplanting the focus to another wing position in the very early pupa induces an ectopic eyespot pattern in the epidermis surrounding the graft. Interestingly, focal grafts to proximal positions in *B. anynana* fail to yield ectopic patterns, while in *P. coenia* they induce rings of color using pigments of the proximal banding pattern, rather than those characteristic of the marginal eyespots; apparently the particular pigments produced in response to the focal signal depend on the competence of the epidermal cells surrounding the focus. Also, on some wing surfaces at certain times after pupation, local damage to the epidermis can induce the formation of an ectopic eyespot (although without the central white pupil). Nijhout (1980b) suggested that the eyespot focus may act as a local source that generates a conical morphogen gradient, with different concentrations specifying the concentric rings of the eyespot. The overall results of the surgical experiments favor a long-range signal from the focus, such as a gradient, but a relay of short-range signals propagated outward from the focus cannot be excluded (Monteiro et al. 2001). Mathematically, both models are interchangeable (Hammer 1998) and thus predict similar phenotypes. Similarly, a contrasting scenario to one in which the focus acts as a local source—namely, a sink model—cannot be ruled out (see French and Brakefield 1992). Evidence to support one or the other model will have to come from sophisticated molecular genetic experiments similar to the ones preformed in *Drosophila* imaginal discs with the morphogen Decapentaplegic and two of its target genes, *Spalt* and *optormotor-blind* (Nellen et al. 1996).

The surgical experiments have been supplemented by the monitoring of focal activity using a molecular marker: expression of the protein product of the homeobox gene *Distal-less* (a regulatory gene controlling limb or appendage development in arthropods: Panganiban et al. 1995). Carroll et al. (1994) first demonstrated that *Distal-less* was expressed in the foci of the eyespots in *P. coenia*. Brakefield et al. (1996) used this marker to track both the early and later periods of eyespot pattern determination in *P. coenia* and *B. anynana*. In discs dissected from final-instar larvae, *Distal-less* is first expressed in rays between the disc's lacunae (later the wing veins) and then becomes enhanced in small spots at the centers of future eyespots (plate 12.2). Finally, after pupation, *Distal-less* expression is observed in epidermal cells surrounding the foci. This gene has recently been shown to harbor genetic variance that can contribute to a gradual response to artificial selection on eyespot size in *Bicyclus anynana* (Beldade et al. 2002a). *Distal-less* and other transcription factors have also now been found to be expressed both in the focal organizer and later on in pattern determination in association with the color rings of the adult eyespot (Brunetti et al. 2001). This pattern of gene expression is shown by all eyespots of both species, while there is no comparable expression within the wing blade in species that express no adult eyespots (nor is there any expression associated with other pattern elements). These observations are consistent with a common developmental process underlying the formation of all butterfly eyespots. Nijhout (1985a, 1991) has further suggested that modifications of a focal signaling mechanism may also specify the symmetry systems of bands and perhaps other elements of the wing pattern. However, empirical evidence for signals from discrete foci underlying other pattern elements is lacking (see Brakefield and French 1999; Beldade and Brakefield 2002; McMillan et al. 2002), and in *P. coenia* (Carroll et al. 1994) there is some indication that the proximal bands of the central symmetry system may be associated with an early stripe of expression of the Wingless signaling protein.

Tying these observations on *Distal-less* expression together with the results of the surgical experiments has enabled a preliminary description of the developmental pathway for eyespot formation (plate 12.3). With this background, we can enquire about how different patterns of phenotypic change correlate with genetic variation regulating the different steps of this pathway.

THE GENETICS OF EYESPOT TRAITS: OPTIONS FOR CHANGE

B. anynana is readily raised in large numbers in the laboratory. Furthermore, it is tolerant of pathogens and has a short life cycle of 5 weeks at 27°C. These features have made the species valuable for genetic research. We have established a large outcrossed laboratory stock from many founders collected at a locality in Malawi. Our work has focused on several mutant alleles with abrupt effects on the eyespot pattern, as well as on smooth, continuous responses to artificial selection on eyespot traits that are probably accounted for by many alleles of small phenotypic effect.

Spontaneous single-gene mutants (plate 12.4) have been isolated from our laboratory stocks and their modes of inheritance determined. We have also begun to analyze how these genes may perturb the different developmental stages of eyespot formation (Brakefield and French 1993; Brakefield et al. 1996; Brakefield 1998). *Spotty* is a semidominant mutant allele that produces extra forewing eyespots. Both grafting experiments and examination of *Distal-less* expression patterns have demonstrated that the *Spotty* allele specifies the determination of additional signaling foci in two cells of the forewing where foci do not usually occur. The *Cyclops* mutant is homozygous lethal. In heterozygotes, it produces a highly perturbed wing venation and eyespot pattern. The most extreme phenotype has a single large ellipsoidal eyespot with a central white pupil highly elongated along the anterior-posterior axis. The recessive mutant *comet* produces dramatically pear-shaped eyespots, with each color ring elongated toward the wing margins. These three mutant phenotypes all appear to result from genetic effects in the early stages of eyespot formation that lead to the determination of active signaling foci. A fourth mutant, *Bigeye,* shows dramatically enlarged eyespots. The *Distal-less* expression pattern indicates that the *Bigeye* allele probably influences aspects of the response to the focal signal rather than the signal itself (Brakefield et al. 1996).

The artificial selection experiments have concentrated on the posterior eyespot of the dorsal forewing (see plate 12.1). They have examined responses to truncation selection over numerous generations for different features or traits of this eyespot. Selection has usually produced lines that were completely divergent for the eyespot trait within five to ten generations. A first pair of upward and downward lines selected for eyespot size diverged rapidly, demonstrating a high level of additive genetic variance (plate 12.5). A regression analysis of the rate of response and intensity of selection yielded an estimate of realized heritability for eyespot size of about 50% (Monteiro et al. 1994). More prolonged selection led to the complete elimination of both dorsal eyespots in butterflies of the downward (low) line (Brakefield 1998). Surgical experiments on pupae from the selected lines showed that the genetic variation underlying eyespot size exists for both the response and, in particular, the signaling components of the developmental pathway (Monteiro et al. 1994). Thus, grafts of foci from the upward (high) line consistently yielded larger ectopic eyespots than those from low-line donors, but the same foci transplanted into high-line hosts tended to produce slightly larger ectopic eyespots than in low-line hosts.

An interesting aspect of the response to selection on eyespot size is the similarity of the phenotype of the selected high line to that of the *Bigeye* mutant. Such examples beg the question of whether predictions can be made about the type of genetic and developmental change likely to be involved in a given evolutionary change in nature (Brakefield 1998). Does how and when in development a given change is produced affect the likelihood of its involvement in evolutionary change either within or across species? It will be a challenge for the future to compare the actual genetic and developmental bases of specific examples of eyespot divergence (including divergence in size) observed across species and assess how these phenomena relate to predictions developed from the intensive work on a single species.

Artificial selection on the color composition of the posterior eyespot produced a response similar to selection on eyespot size: divergent "black" and "gold" lines were rapidly established with narrow and broad outer gold rings, respectively (plate 12.5). Thus, there is a similar amount of additive genetic variance in our stock for size traits and color traits (Monteiro et al. 1994, 1997a). However, surgical experiments comparable to those used in analyzing the size lines failed to trace any genetic effect on color composition to focal signaling activity. Rather, the phenotypic difference between the color lines was fully accounted for by genetic effects on the epidermal response to the focal signals. Therefore, while eyespot size and color behave similarly with respect to additive genetic variances, they are different from a developmental perspective. The apparently wider range of developmental options for changing eyespot size may have consequences for the breadth of evolutionary change likely to be observed for this trait in the pattern as a whole relative to the color composition of the eyespots (Brakefield 1998).

Eyespots in *B. anynana* are usually close to being circular in shape. The rate of response to selection on the shape of the posterior eyespot (elongated either along the anterior-posterior or proximal-distal axis) was substantially slower and less marked than that for either size or color composition (Monteiro et al. 1997b). The estimate for realized heritability was low at about 15%. Surgical experiments indicated that there was no genetic variation traceable to the signaling foci (Monteiro et al. 1997b). Furthermore, measurements of the spacing of the rows of scale cells around the forewing eyespots suggested the involvement of changes at this level in the limited divergence of eyespot shape between the "fat" and "thin" lines (Monteiro et al. 1997c). Thus, the standing genetic variance in our laboratory stock provides only a rather limited ability to respond to selection for a bilaterally symmetrical change in eyespot shape. There are, however, single-gene mutants available that can produce specific, dramatic changes in eyespot shape (i.e., *Cyclops* and *comet*). These observations suggest that from a developmental perspective, certain specific shifts in the shape of an eyespot may be more readily obtained than others, and that quantitative changes in shape are less likely to occur than those in other eyespot traits.

Artificial selection on the position of the eyespots has been applied in only a single direction (Brakefield 1998). A line has been produced in which all the eyespots are aligned along the extreme margins of the wings. As with eyespot size and color, the eyespots on the targeted wing surface have responded in a concerted manner, although in this case selection was applied to the whole pattern.

The genetic covariances for a given trait among a set of individual eyespots, especially when on the same wing surface, are positive. Thus, the alleles of genes with small phenotypic effect that influence one particular eyespot tend to produce similar effects on the other eyespots on the same wing surface. Although such genetic correlations may be high, they do not reach unity. There may thus be some genes within the standing variation of populations that can provide the potential for evolutionary independence among the elements of a set or module of eyespots, even over comparatively small numbers of generations. The extent of this potential has been examined by a new series of selection experiments designed to compare the responses to different combinations of selection on both of the forewing eyespots of *B. anynana* (see Beldade et al. 2002b). In these experiments, selection is applied to the anterior and posterior eyespots in either a concordant or antagonistic manner. Despite the genetic correlations and the developmental coupling between the two eyespots, there is much flexibility for independent evolution of eyespot size. Response to selection in the laboratory produced all forewing patterns found within the genus and even a candidate "forbidden morphology" not represented in the eighty or so *Bicyclus* species described (Condamin 1973). This type of study will quantify the relative freedom of components of the eyespot module to change along different axes within potential morphological space.

Two of the spontaneous mutants we have isolated to date, *Spotty* and *Cyclops,* have divergent effects on eyespots within a single wing surface; for example, *Spotty* adds two eyespots between the existing forewing eyespots without influencing the most anterior or posterior wing cells. Such uncoupling genes may play an important facilitating role in evolution both within and among species by providing the opportunity for novel and independent change. Thus, through the involvement of these genes, subsets of eyespots may be able to respond in a different direction from others, even those on the same wing surface (Brakefield and French 1993; Brakefield 1998). The following sections cover studies in which evolutionary divergence in eyespot patterns is beginning to be examined across species of *Bicyclus* for which the phylogenetic relationships are known.

EYESPOT VARIATION ACROSS THE GENUS *Bicyclus*

The nearly eighty species in the genus *Bicyclus* live throughout Africa in lowland tropical rainforests, in mountain forests, and in arboreal savanna regions (Condamin 1973). These species have a wide variety of wing patterns that include morphological variation in the number, size, color composition, and position of the marginal eyespots.

The number of eyespots present on the ventral surface of the forewing is very stable across the genus and is always two. The number of ventral hindwing eyespots varies from five to eight. The dorsal forewing pattern is highly variable, consisting of zero, one, or two eyespots and/or a broad transversal band.

In *Bicyclus* butterflies, eyespots vary in size as well as in color composition and in position relative to the wing margin—all traits that have been successfully modified through artificial selection in *B. anynana* (see plate 12.5). In contrast, there is little variation in eyespot shape across the genus, which is in accordance with the low levels of additive genetic variance found for this trait in *B. anynana*.

Changes in eyespot morphology, however, are not restricted to correlated increases or decreases in size, changes in the proportions of the color rings, or coordinated shifts in eyespot position relative to the wing margin. There are many *Bicyclus* species in which the relative size of the eyespots is very different from that in *B. anynana*. In species in which both dorsal forewing eyespots are present, the relative sizes of those eyespots can vary from the anterior being the largest of the two to being the smallest. Furthermore, there are species in which only one of the two eyespots is present (fig. 12.2A). On the hindwing, individual eyespots have been reduced or increased in size independently of the others in the row (fig. 12.2B). Also, in some species, individual eyespots or subsets of eyespots have shifted along the proximal-distal axis of the hindwing independently of others, breaking the curvilinear arrangement characteristic of many species (fig. 12.2C). Species with eyespots with marked differences in color ring proportions on the same wing surface are also found in the genus (fig. 12.2D). Clearly, the diversity of wing patterns seen across the genus still exceeds the limits of what we, so far, have achieved with artificial selection in *B. anynana*.

On the other hand, mutations of large phenotypic effect, such as *Bigeye*, may have been involved in overall increases in eyespot size across the genus. Unfortunately, there is no evidence that mutants such as *Spotty*, *Cyclops*, or *comet* have been fixed in any of the *Bicyclus* species (although *Spotty*-like phenotypes are found in *B. safitza:* Brakefield et al. 1996). Some satyrid species of the South American genus *Euptychia*, however, do appear to be fixed for a *Spotty*-like gene, as well as expressing a combination of *comet* and *Spotty* eyespot phenotypes in two wing cells on the hindwing (in positions homologous to those of the two forewing wing cells where *Spotty* introduces extra eyespots in *B. anynana*).

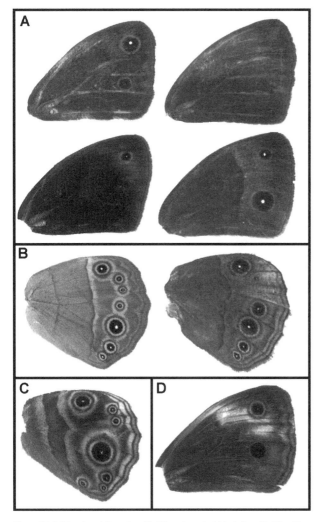

Figure 12.2 The dorsal forewing (A, D) and ventral hindwing (B, C) patterns of *Bicyclus* species.
(A) Clockwise from top left: *B. procorus, B. golo, B. mollitia, B. vansoni.* (B) Left to right: *B. analis* and
B. angulosus. (C) *B. ignobilis.* (D) *B. alboplagus.*

In summary, variation in overall eyespot size, color composition, and
position across the genus *Bicyclus* is at least partly consistent with the
variation resulting from genes of small phenotypic effect of the type involved in the gradual responses to artificial selection in *B. anynana.* Single
genes of large effect are also likely to underlie some of the differences among
species, perhaps especially those between groups of closely related species
with highly divergent eyespot patterns.

In order to understand the evolutionary history of changes in eyespot
morphology, as well as to gain insight into the evolution of other wing
pattern elements, a molecular phylogeny of the genus *Bicyclus* has been

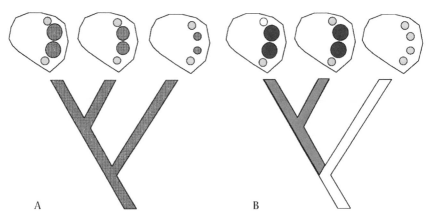

Figure 12.3 Possible ways for a subset of eyespots to achieve a size uncoupling from the other eyespots in the row: (A) gradually, through the accumulation of alleles with a small and independent effect on the subset of eyespots; or (B) saltationally, through the deployment of genes of large phenotypic effect. (The same idea could be applied to variation in eyespot position or color composition.)

constructed (Monteiro and Pierce 2001). One of the aims of this work is to identify possible instances of rapid evolution due to the deployment of genes with large discontinuous effects on the phenotype, as well as instances in which wing pattern evolution follows a gradual transformation process. A question of particular interest is, how does the evolution of genes of large effect compare with the evolution of genes of small effect? Two hypotheses can be tested (fig. 12.3):

1. Given the high additive genetic variances for eyespot size, color composition, and position in *B. anynana,* and assuming similar levels across species, we expect these traits for the eyespot pattern *as a whole* to be relatively unconstrained across the phylogeny of the genus. In this case, it will not be unusual to find closely related species with very different phenotypes or distantly related species with similar phenotypes.
2. Abrupt evolution within the genus, resulting in changes such as the introduction or removal of particular eyespots, will be found in more restricted lineages within the phylogeny. The resulting phenotypes will also tend to be shared by more closely related species.

AN EXAMPLE OF MORPHOLOGICAL EVOLUTION IN A *Bicyclus* CLADE

A small clade of seven related species of *Bicyclus* from within the wider phylogeny under construction illustrates the evolution of relative eyespot size on the ventral hindwing (plate 12.6). The row of ventral hindwing eyespots

Paul M. Brakefield and Antónia Monteiro

was mapped onto the tips of the phylogeny. There is overall variation in eyespot size between the different species (compare, for instance, *campus* with *angulosus* or *auricrudus*), but most interestingly, there are marked variations in relative eyespot size across the clade. Note the gradual shift in the size of eyespot 1, relative to eyespot 2, as one progresses from the base of the *anynana-campus-angulosus* clade to the tips. The size relationship between eyespots 3 and 4 changes more dramatically. In *mollitia* these two eyespots have approximately the same size. In the *anynana-campus-angulosus* lineage, the size relationship shifts gradually, until there is a very small third eyespot and a large fourth eyespot in *angulosus*. The lineage that gives rise to the *auricrudus-mandanes* clade completely eliminates these two eyespots. In this case it is not clear whether the change results from fixation of a gene(s) of large uncoupling effect or from a gradual reduction in eyespot size. The other eyespots in both species tend to be small, and eyespots 3 and 4 in their closest relative, *mollitia*, are the smallest in the hindwing row. However, we have recently isolated a phenotype of *B. anynana* from our laboratory stock that lacks eyespots 3 and 4 (the other eyespots are of normal size) (Brakefield 2001). Early breeding results suggest that this phenotype breeds true and may, therefore, have a simple genetic basis. Future studies with this mutant may elucidate its developmental basis and eventually determine whether it is actually involved in instances of phenotypically similar change across species.

TOWARD A NEW SYNTHESIS

It is clear that a fuller understanding of how the developmental mechanisms specifying eyespot patterns evolve will come from an examination of the relevant genetic variability present within and across species. To study more fully how the eyespot pattern evolves, from genes to development to phenotypic diversity, the following complementary approaches will prove useful:

1. Combining artificial selection experiments on eyespot features with QTL gene-mapping techniques and candidate gene approaches. The transcription factors, including Distal-less, Spalt, and Engrailed, and the ligands Hedgehog, Decapentaplegic, and Wingless provide the obvious choice for the latter approach (McMillan et al. 2002; Beldade and Brakefield 2002).
2. Developing a transgenic system in which the regulatory function and epistatic relationships of the candidate genes mentioned above can be tested by ectopically expressing these genes in the wing.
3. A mutagenesis screen to probe for more single genes of large phenotypic effect on the eyespot pattern in a single species

(*B. anynana*). Such screens may reveal genes that can account for observed patterns of divergence across species, and further developmental studies may then be able to tie certain mutations to the regulation of known signaling pathways.

4. Using the phylogenetic approach to identify clades with comparatively wide changes in wing pattern morphologies. In such cases, it may prove valuable to attempt to hybridize representative species from different clades to study the segregation patterns in any viable F_1 hybrids.

5. Applying the comparative method to the patterns of gene expression in early wing development. Shifts in domains of gene expression can be traced through the phylogeny. A phylogenetic framework could eventually enable identification of those developmental pathways that change frequently (and thus appear more labile) and those that are more invariant (and thus appear more constrained). Also, this approach could determine whether there are patterns of correlated changes among smaller subsets of eyespots or whether each eyespot has an equal opportunity to evolve independently from the others.

Studying the patterns of expression of early developmental genes across selection lines, mutants, and closely related species will provide valuable insights into the evolution of eyespot individuality as well as into the mechanisms that are shared by all developing eyespots. Understanding the way in which eyespot individuality has evolved, and the options that are available at this level of character organization, will be the key to describing evolutionary constraints. A possible explanation for the genetic and developmental architecture observed in the anterior-posterior row of serially homologous eyespots may have parallels in the process of establishing segmental identity in the serially homologous body segments of insects and other arthropods (Akam et al. 1994; Carroll 1995). The identity of a segment is achieved by the combinatorial expression of certain regulatory genes (Hox genes) laid out very early in embryogenesis. The establishment of these early expression patterns leads to very different developmental cascades being followed in each segment, resulting in distinct adult segmental morphologies. Different body patterns may evolve through changes in Hox gene number, regulation, or function (Carroll 1995; Carroll et al. 1995; Akam 1998; Weatherbee and Carroll 1999).

In butterfly wings, one can envisage a similar chain of events that starts in early wing disc development with the establishment of several gene expression domains. So far, Carroll and co-workers (Carroll et al. 1994; Brakefield et al. 1996; Keys et al. 1999) have found a few regulatory genes that are expressed in broad wing domains (e.g., *vestigial, engrailed, Distal-less, Cubitus Interruptus*), but there may be many more that criss-cross the wing and give cells in separate wing cells, or groups of wing cells, or parts of a wing cell, a separate identity or positional information (see McMillan et al. 2002). From this perspective, an allele such as *Spotty* could be a *cis*-regulatory mutation of a gene involved in focal differentiation. The mutation could involve, for instance, the elimination of the binding sites for a regional regulator gene, expressed in wing cells 3 and 4 and involved in repressing *Spotty* in these wing cells. If the regional regulator were prevented from repressing *Spotty*, the latter would become active and turn on a cascade of downstream genes leading to the differentiation of two additional eyespots. Moreover, *Spotty* may be a very early developmental gene because it influences eyespots in both ventral and dorsal wing surfaces. Its pattern of expression crosses that early developmental boundary and must, therefore, presumably be established when the imaginal disc is still small (J. A. Williams et al. 1994).

Examining eyespot size variation across the genus *Bicyclus*, one can imagine that the interplay of focal signal and response that controls eyespot size across the wing could be modified in particular wing cells, or subsets of wing cells, by the regional regulator genes. How does the evolution of wing cell or focal individuality (size of focus) occur? Possibly in one of two ways, or a combination of the two:

1. There is genetic variance for the total gene product of the genes expressed in a particular compartment, also affecting the final identity of focal cells differentiating in that compartment.
2. There is genetic variance for the regulatory regions of the genes involved in focal differentiation, focal signaling, or focal response, which are under the control of the regional regulator genes. Variation, for instance, in the number or type of binding sites in the *cis*-regulatory region of their target genes could determine differential expression of these genes in different areas of the wing.

Also, in the evolution of the genus *Bicyclus*, one can envisage gradual, quantitative modulation of these regional regulator genes or of their target binding sites, or abrupt "larger-scale" changes derived from loss of function of the regional regulator gene itself or of some downstream receptor. Further multidisciplinary research on butterfly eyespots should provide the necessary data to test such ideas.

SUMMARY

The spectacular diversity of color patterns on butterfly wings has provided material for many influential studies on natural selection, genetics, and comparative morphology. Much recent research has concentrated on the evolution of the eyespot patterns of African *Bicyclus* butterflies. Multidisciplinary studies linking genes with phenotypes via development and studies of differentiation within the *Bicyclus* phylogeny are beginning to provide new insights into the developmental and evolutionary processes that are the basis of morphological diversity. Field studies will be necessary to uncover the details of how different processes of natural selection can influence pattern change.

Each of the eyespots of the border ocelli system within a species of *Bicyclus* has evolved a characteristic size, color composition, and position relative to the wing margin. The differences found across the row of eyespots are rather stable and identify particular species. Artificial selection experiments performed on a single species have shown that there is substantial additive genetic variance within a species, which can produce rapid changes in eyespot morphology. These changes can either be achieved simultaneously in the whole row of eyespots or can target individual eyespots, and reflect the way in which eyespot individuality is established within and across species. The involvement of genes of large "uncoupling" effect, as exemplified by several spontaneous mutants in a laboratory stock, may also have enabled the evolution of the distinctive morphological features within a row of eyespots. A phylogeny of the group will be used to describe the patterns of morphological change, such as the frequency and distribution of particular types of change, and indicate which eyespot features may be more labile or more constrained. It will also provide insights into patterns of eyespot covariation across the genus. Future work will highlight the genetic variability within developmental pathways that underlies the evolution of eyespot morphology both within and across species.

ACKNOWLEDGMENTS

We would like to thank all our colleagues at Leiden for their help and enthusiasm, as well as Vernon French (Edinburgh), Sean Carroll (Madison), and Fred Nijhout (Duke). Thanks to Naomi Pierce for inspiration and for providing the DNA sequencing facilities; to André Mignault, Maya Michino, Jennifer Fines, Cara Forster, and Laela Sturdy for help with DNA sequencing; and to William Piel, Christoph Haag, José Pedro Tavares, Fausto Brito e Abreu, and Patrícia Salgueiro for help with collecting *Bicyclus* specimens. The Human Frontier Science Program Organization provided generous funding to P. M. B. and A. M., and the Junta Nacional de Investigação Científica e Tecnológica provided extra funds to A. M.

CHAPTER 13

Mimicry and Melanism in Swallowtail Butterflies: Toward a Molecular Understanding

Richard ffrench-Constant and P. Bernhard Koch

The development and evolutionary genetics of butterfly wing patterns have been reviewed elsewhere in this book (see Brakefield and Monteiro, chap. 12 in this volume). In this chapter, we use the specific example of melanism in swallowtail butterflies to dissect the genetics and developmental biology underlying wing color pattern formation. Moreover, we attempt to bring together the different mechanisms of color pattern change under a unifying developmental model, which suggests that the genes controlling melanism in fact drive rates of scale development, in turn dictating the final color of a given wing area.

In many cases of mimicry, melanism is used to make the mimics resemble their models. This is particularly apparent in the striking examples of mimicry found among the swallowtail butterflies. This topic has been extensively reviewed elsewhere (Nijhout 1991), but is summarized again here to give context to the developmental hypotheses extended in this chapter. In examining the different color patterns associated with melanism, Nijhout called for efforts to identify the homologies between different parts of these patterns. Without this, he suggests, there is "no basis for critically judging how color patterns and mimicry systems evolve." He further postulates that the complicated and qualitative phenotypic effects of many genes can be seen as relatively simple variations on existing forms. Since this variation must arise during the ontogeny of the wing pattern, we have investigated differences in the late stages of wing development between melanic and wild-type butterflies. We propose that changes in rates of scale development, potentially driven by a single major gene, can ultimately control complex color patterns.

In this chapter, we attempt to dissect the biochemical basis of melanism in the eastern tiger swallowtail of North America, *Papilio glaucus*. Before doing so, however, we need to step back and examine the developmental basis of wing color pattern formation, first in butterflies as a whole, and then specifically as it underlies the wild-type pattern of *P. glaucus*. We then go on to derive a general model for the regulation of patterning, scale maturation, and pigment formation. This developmental model forms the basis for our discussion of the control of the biochemical changes underlying melanism.

THE DEVELOPMENTAL BASIS OF BUTTERFLY WING COLOR PATTERN FORMATION

PATTERN DETERMINATION AND EXPRESSION OF PATTERN-CORRELATED GENES

For those lepidopteran wing pattern elements that have been experimentally investigated, pattern determination occurs during a developmental window extending from the middle of the last larval instar to a point approximately 48 hours after pupation. This timing has been inferred from cautery and transplantation assays (Nijhout 1980b; French and Brakefield 1992) on eyespot-forming tissue (not found in papilionids). These experiments, as well as more direct assays of gene expression (Carroll et al. 1994; Brakefield et al. 1996), indicate that during this period a developmental spatial coordinate system is set up and maintained relative to the wing margin and veins.

On this basis, we can divide the black pattern in papilionids into two kinds of elements: vein-dependent and vein-independent. The vein-dependent pattern elements correspond to the black stripes that match the positions of the wing veins. The vein-independent pattern elements are those that are either independent of the veins and lie in central wing areas or match the position of the wing boundary (the black bands along the edges of the forewings and hindwings). We can speculate that the vein-dependent stripes are driven either by the same developmental system that produces the veins or by the presence of the veins themselves. The importance of the veins in this type of pattern element is reinforced by a *veins reduced* mutant of the Japanese swallowtail *P. xuthus* collected from the field. In this mutant, the absence of the black vein-dependent stripes corresponds to a lack of the veins themselves (plate 13.1). Interestingly, the black bands along the edge of the wing remain, but they are not dissected as they are in the wild-type, suggesting that the veins also have a role as spatial compartment borders in shifting patterns along the veins (P. B. Koch and H. F. Nijhout, unpub.). Unfortunately, no direct experimental data on pattern determination in

Richard ffrench-Constant and P. Bernhard Koch

papilionids exists, but the above observations suggest that it occurs in the early pupal or late larval stage, is closely associated with wing venation (which develops in the middle of the last larval instar), and can be directly affected by sex-linked control genes and their sex-specific modifiers.

Hormones and the Development of the Adult Butterfly Wing

Wing development in butterflies is a part of larval-pupal-adult metamorphosis and is regulated by ecdysteroid hormones distributed in the hemolymph. During the pupal stage there is a long peak of ecdysteroid concentrations, and the rising phase of this peak appears to be associated with pattern formation. The falling phase of the same peak appears to be responsible for scale pigmentation and maturation (see plate 13.7).

After the pupal molt, the increasing hormone titer induces cuticular apolysis, scale cell differentiation, and outgrowth of the scale cells. It is not known whether typical color pattern determination occurs independently of ecdysteroid action or whether a hormonal signal induces pattern determination. However, in the case of seasonal polyphenisms in butterflies (in which the same species adopts different patterns in different seasons), ecdysteroids are clearly involved in color pattern determination (Rountree and Nijhout 1995; Koch et al. 1996). After a broad pupal peak of hormone titer, ecdysteroids in the hemolymph decrease, and wing maturation continues with the final pigmentation and sclerotization of the scales. Thus, steroid hormones coordinate multiple aspects of tissue development, including activation of all the genes leading to the complex fine structure of the scales.

The precise mechanism whereby the ecdysteroids exert their complex coordinate control over wing development is poorly understood. However, we do know that the ecdysteroid titer is important in controlling the differentiation of scales within the wing epidermis, and several observations begin to suggest the underlying mechanisms. The total ecdysteroid titer in the hemolymph is in fact made up of successive peaks of different ecdysteroid molecules, most importantly ecdysone and 20-hydroxyecdysone (Gilbert 1989). On a molecular level, ecdysteroids are known to govern a hierarchy of differential gene expression in their target cells via nuclear receptors (Thummel 1995). Expression studies on early and late genes in larval epidermis have revealed that 20-hydroxyecdysone, alone or in combination with ecdysone, acts differentially on the expression of different ecdysteroid receptor isoforms, suggesting a potential role for the different ecdysteroids present in the total hemolymph titer. Further, the expression of different ecdysone receptor isoforms, and of subsequent regulatory genes, during lepidopteran scale development also appears to be involved in the complex process of final scale maturation (L. Riddiford, pers. comm.). Interestingly, a decrease in the total ecdysteroid titer is needed to allow the final steps of pigmentation and wing maturation, as was first shown in *Manduca sexta* (Schwartz and Truman 1983). This decrease in ecdysteroids is central to the regulation of the enzyme dopa decarboxylase, or DDC, which has a regulatory role in melanization of the larval epidermis and in melanin synthesis in butterfly wings (Koch 1994, 1995). Clearly, a further understanding of color pattern development, and of how it is changed in melanism and mimicry, must therefore include an understanding of how ecdysteroids interact with pattern-determining genes.

Color Development Is Highly Conserved

The color pattern in butterfly wings is formed by the color and arrangement of the individual scales on the wing surface (Nijhout 1991). Wings develop within the larva from embryonic cells that form wing buds or anlagen, and by the time the pupal case hardens following the larval-pupal molt, the fully everted wing disc has adopted its final shape, tracheal pattern, and total preinflation area. During the pupal stage, scale cells differentiate from the wing disc epidermis, and it is these cells that synthesize the pigments underlying the color pattern shortly before adult emergence. These pigments belong to a range of different chemical classes: pteridines forming white, yellow, or red; ommatins forming red or red-brown; and melanins forming gray or black (Nijhout 1980a; Koch 1991; Koch and Kaufmann 1995). Interestingly, some additional pigments are found only in certain groups of Lepidoptera; for example, the yellow papiliochromes discussed here are exclusive to the papilionids (Umebachi 1985).

Production of the final wing color pattern proceeds through a clear succession of stages in all butterfly species that have been examined (Koch et al. 1998). In other words, scales with different color fates meet their fates at different times in development. The final color of a scale is therefore determined by its rate of development. Specifically, these stages correspond to periods of synthesis and deposition of different pigments, in which initially white coloration appears, then red, and then black. Given that papilionids have evolved unique biochemical pigments, we were interested in documenting whether a similar sequence of pigment synthesis occurs in this butterfly family. Such a pattern is indeed observed in the swallowtail *P. glaucus*, with white appearing first (later becoming blue iridescent scales), then red and yellow, then black. This ordered succession of color deposition is conserved despite the fact that the different butterfly families are using different pigments to make the different colors. In the nymphalids, following the appearance of the white pteridines, the tryptophan-derived red ommatins (Koch 1991, 1993) are synthesized before the start of melanization. In the papilionid *P. glaucus*, the yellow and red papiliochromes, which are tightly linked to the tryptophan pathway, are again synthesized before melanization. Thus, despite the fact that the final pigments have different chemical compositions in the different butterfly families, the tryptophan-derived pigments are always deposited *before* those derived from tyrosine (the melanins). Different butterfly species therefore appear to display an evolutionarily conserved sequence of pigment synthesis, despite divergence in the details of the synthetic pathways involved in depositing the final colored pigments.

COLOR DEVELOPMENT AND SCALE MATURATION

In the context of spatially regulated color development, it is important to recognize that scale maturation—or, more specifically, the final sclerotization of the scales—occurs in a timed succession that is synchronous with color development. This sequence was first reported in a nymphalid butterfly (Nijhout 1980a). If wings are air-dried at different stages during pigment formation, unpigmented scales collapse, while those that are fully pigmented remain erect and show their final architecture. Scales derive from epidermal cells, and their complex surface structure is therefore a specialization of the epidermal cuticle. Consequently, scales must be sclerotized to give them their final stiffness and structure.

Sclerotization is achieved by the cross-linking of cuticular proteins, predominantly by N-acyl-catecholamines such as N-acetyl-dopamine (NADA) and N-β-alanyl-dopamine (NBAD) (Hiruma and Kramer 1992). We speculate that the principal sclerotization of the insect cuticle, and the formation of sclerotized hairs or bristles (Galant et al. 1998), predate the appearance of colored scales in butterflies and therefore may represent an older evolutionary pathway. The sclerotizing agents NADA and NBAD derive from tyrosine via dihydroxy-phenylalanine, which is decarboxylated by DDC to form dopamine and subsequently N-acetylated with acetic acid (to form NADA) or β-alanine (to form NBAD) (fig. 13.1). Hence DDC has a role in wing development, not only in melanin synthesis, but also in delivering agents for sclerotization. The final synthesis of NADA and NBAD involves the enzymes N-acetyl-transferase and N-β-alanyl-transferase, respectively. Therefore, in evolutionary terms, the latter enzyme and its product NBAD may have been secondarily co-opted from its role in sclerotization into synthesis of papiliochrome, a pigment unique to the swallowtails (Umebachi 1993).

TYPES OF MELANISM

As a prelude to a mechanistic dissection of swallowtail melanism, we first briefly review the visual classification of melanism proposed by Nijhout

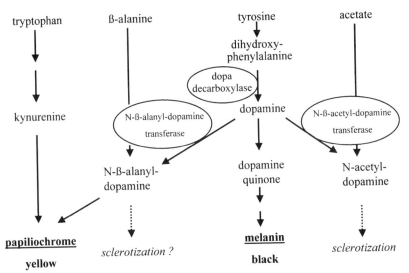

Figure 13.1 Synthesis pathway for the *P. glaucus* pigments (underlined) papiliochrome and melanin and for sclerotizing agents (in italics). The enzymes assayed in this study are circled. These pathways were predicted from previous studies (Umebachi 1985; Hiruma and Kramer 1992; Koch 1995).

(Nijhout 1991), then examine the evidence for the number of genes that control these types of melanism.

THREE TYPES OF MELANISM

Nijhout recognized three morphologically distinct types of melanism: (1) general darkening of the background color of the wing, (2) broadening of existing dark pattern elements, and (3) darkening of pattern elements. Interestingly, in those species in which they have been studied, each of these mechanisms appears to be controlled by a single dominant genetic locus. The primary challenge is therefore to understand how developmentally complex mechanisms can be controlled by a single major gene. Further, we need to determine whether the occurrence of similar forms of melanism in different species is determined by the same major locus or by numerous different single loci. Here we briefly review each of the types of melanism and the potential mechanisms proposed for them based on visual examinations.

General darkening of the background color. A good example of this first type of melanism is seen in the melanization of the yellow background color in the dark female form of *P. glaucus* (plate 13.2A, B) (believed to mimic *Battus philenor*). Here the wild-type black pattern is unaltered and can be seen below the darkened (melanized) background pattern. Such a darkening could stem from either a switch in the pigments synthesized—in the case of *P. glaucus*, a switch from the background yellow papiliochrome to dark

Richard ffrench-Constant and P. Bernhard Koch

melanin—or an increase in the frequency of dark versus light scales—in the case of *P. glaucus,* an increase in the frequency of dark melanin-containing scales among the yellow scales of the background. We suggest that these two alternatives are in fact differing levels of penetrance of the *same* phenotype. Thus, in fully melanic individuals, every scale in the background domain switches pigment synthesis, and all the originally yellow scales make dark melanic pigment, whereas in partially penetrant individuals, some of the yellow scales fail to produce the melanic pigment and remain as yellow scales in a melanic background (see the discussion of penetrance below). Melanism itself therefore arises from originally yellow scales making dark melanic pigment, and not from a change in the ratio of yellow to black scales (except in the case of partial penetrance). We note that the dark melanic pigment is not black, like the melanized area of the wild-type pattern, but is in fact a very dark brown. Although we have little idea of what the underlying differences in chemical composition between this "brown" melanic pigment and the normal black pigment are, we can speculate that they correspond to different chemical forms of melanin.

In relation to the potential biochemical switches underlying these two alternative mechanisms, Nijhout suggested that a switch in pigment synthesis could depend on a simple switch within a biochemical pathway, such as activation or inactivation of a specific enzyme, whereas a change in the frequency of differently colored scales would be more difficult to understand, as it would involve discrete switching between biochemical pathways at the single-cell (single-scale) level (Nijhout 1991).

Broadening of existing dark pattern elements. In the second type of melanism, existing dark pattern elements (constituting the "foreground") are enlarged to cover lighter areas (representing the "background"). This type of melanism is seen in females of *Papilio polyxenes,* which are darker than males because the black area of the pattern is broadened to exclude the yellow background (plate 13.2C, D). Nijhout suggests that this type of melanism could arise from a change in the position of the boundary between pattern elements and ground color (Nijhout 1991). This could occur through a change in the timing, or in the rate of propagation, of the signal that establishes this boundary.

Darkening of the pattern elements. In the final type of melanism, pattern elements change their color, but not their shape, as seen, for example, in the dark and light forms of the nymphalid *Hypolimnas bolina.* In this species, the light *pallescens* form is light tan and the dark *naresi* form is black, but the pattern elements themselves do not change shape (Nijhout 1991). We stress that this type of melanism does not seem to occur in *P. glaucus* and is therefore mentioned here only for the sake of completeness; it is therefore not discussed further in this chapter.

These descriptions of the three types of melanism stress the developmental differences among them. Two of the modes of melanism do not affect the positions of the boundaries between different domains of the wing. In one of these modes, the background changes; in the other, the pattern elements change. The remaining type of melanism involves movement of the borders of the pattern elements themselves. Having described these developmental differences, we must explain any differences in their underlying biochemistry. In the case of *H. bolina,* for example, Nijhout suggests a switch between "phaeomelanin" (brown) and "eumelanin" (black) synthesis (Nijhout 1991). This change might involve a switch in the use of melanin substrates, rather than a switch in the enzymes involved in melanin synthesis (Kayser 1985; Nijhout 1985b).

THE NUMBER OF GENES CONTROLLING MELANISM AND MIMICRY

Although the remainder of this chapter is focused on a discussion of melanism in *P. glaucus* as a model system, it is interesting to compare the relatively simple changes observed in *P. glaucus* and *P. polyxenes* with the apparently more complicated examples of mimicry in other papilionids such as *P. dardanus, P. memnon,* and *P. polytes* (Nijhout 1991). In these species, while the males typically remain recognizable as swallowtails, the females mimic a number of different unpalatable species in different parts of their geographic range. *P. dardanus* is perhaps the classic example, in which the males are black and yellow and the females mimic a number of different unpalatable danaids of the genera *Amauris, Bematistes,* and *Danaus* with a range of different colors and wing patterns. Despite the larger number of color changes that appear to be involved in this type of mimicry, the same basic processes seem to be at work. Thus, the difference in *P. dardanus* patterns can be explained in terms of a combination of variation in the width of existing black bands and changes in the background color from yellow to colors ranging from white to brown (Nijhout 1991).

Extensive genetic crossing work by Clarke and Sheppard and others (reviewed by Nijhout 1991) has led to the suggestion that such complex mimicry is controlled either by single major genes or by "supergenes" (in which two or more loci controlling color pattern are closely linked). Nijhout (1991), however, suggests that the evidence for supergenes in the control of complex mimicries in *Papilio* is actually weak or circumstantial. The single major genes involved are thought to be under the influence of sex-specific modifiers as well as modifiers that refine the pattern of the mimic in a given geographic region in relation to the specific model in that area. In the context of this review, this conclusion therefore raises the interesting possibility that switches between visually complex phenotypes could be under the control of a very few, or even a single, gene(s). This observation therefore drives

Richard ffrench-Constant and P. Bernhard Koch

our investigation of developmental control in trying to explain how single changes in wing pattern development can be expressed as multiple color and pattern changes.

SEX-LINKED MELANISM IN *P. glaucus* AND OTHER SWALLOWTAILS

Melanic sexual polymorphisms are common in many papilionids. Melanism in *P. glaucus* provides a particularly striking example. In this species, males are always yellow, whereas females can either be yellow (nonmimetic) or black (mimicking the unpalatable pipevine swallowtail, *B. philenor*) (see plate 13.2A, B). The genetics of melanism in *P. glaucus* have been studied extensively (Clarke and Sheppard 1959, 1962; Clarke et al. 1976; Scriber et al. 1996), and the trait is known to be sex-linked. Typically, yellow females give rise only to yellow female offspring and black females to black female offspring. Males are always yellow regardless of their parentage. In a rare case, paternal transmission of the dark female form was reported (Scriber and Evans 1986). In Lepidoptera, females are the heterogametic sex (XY, also referred to as WZ), and males are homogametic (XX or ZZ) (Lauge 1985). These observations are therefore consistent with melanism being controlled by a single locus on the Y (female) chromosome that is either absent from the X or is present, but suppressed (Nijhout 1991). Scriber and others (Scriber et al. 1996; see Scriber et al., chap. 17 in this volume) proposed a single sex-linked gene (the Y-linked *black* or *b* gene), which causes the melanic phenotype, and a modifying gene (the X-linked *suppressor* or *s* gene), which suppresses it, based on hybrid crosses to the closely related *P. canadensis*.

The conclusion that a similar single sex-linked gene controls melanism in other swallowtails is reinforced by a comparison of *P. glaucus* with species from the *Papilio machaon* complex. The genetics of melanism were studied in interspecific crosses between four species in the complex: *P. machaon, P. polyxenes, P. zelicaon,* and *P. brevicauda* (Clarke and Sheppard 1955b). The same single major gene appears to control the melanic form in at least two of these species (*P. polyxenes* and *P. brevicauda*), and sexually dimorphic expression of melanism is controlled by modifier genes that are present in some species, but not others. Thus, *P. machaon,* which is normally nonmelanic and monomorphic, becomes dimorphic in the presence of the introgressed dominant melanic gene from a different species. In conclusion, melanism in swallowtails, whether due to darkening of the background color or extension of the black pattern elements, is usually under the control of a single sex-linked gene of major effect that affects the process of color pattern formation. Sex-specific suppressors, which control the differences between males and females, can therefore be documented by interspecific crosses.

THE DEVELOPMENT OF COLOR PATTERN AND SCLEROTIZATION IN *P. glaucus*

CONCLUSIONS FROM RADIOLABELED PRECURSORS

Before examining melanism, we needed to define the normal biochemical processes underlying the formation of the wild-type yellow and black pattern in *P. glaucus*. We therefore followed the formation of yellow and black pigments using radiolabeled compounds predicted to be incorporated into specific chemical classes of pigments (see fig. 13.1). We examined the temporal and spatial incorporation patterns of the three main pigment precursors, tyrosine, β-alanine, and tryptophan, both in vivo (by injecting them into developing pupae) and in vitro (by using them as supplements to wings isolated in tissue culture medium).

Based on the current state of knowledge of papiliochrome synthesis in *Papilio xuthus* (Ishizaki and Umebachi 1990; Umebachi 1993) and of melanin formation in *Precis coenia* (Koch 1994; Koch and Kaufmann 1995), we predicted that both tryptophan and β-alanine would be incorporated into the yellow papiliochrome. We further expected that tyrosine would be the major precursor for the melanin synthesis pathway and would also be incorporated into papiliochrome; that is, that it would be incorporated into both black and yellow pigments (see fig. 13.1). This latter expectation arises from the fact that in the wing, dopamine is complexed with β-alanine (by N-β-alanyl-transferase) to give NBAD, a necessary component for papiliochrome synthesis (Umebachi 1985).

In order to test the hypothesis that both tryptophan and β-alanine are incorporated into yellow papiliochrome, we examined autoradiographs of adult wings following the injection of pupae with radiolabeled precursors (plate 13.3A–E), and traced the temporal pattern of precursor incorporation into wings at different stages of development in vitro (plate 13.3F). As predicted, β-alanine was incorporated only in the yellow areas of wild-type females, both in vivo (plate 13.3A) and in vitro (plate 13.3F). Tryptophan also showed incorporation into yellow areas in vivo (plate 13.3E). Unexpectedly, tryptophan was not incorporated into yellow areas in vitro (Koch et al. 1998). The lack of in vitro incorporation can be explained by the fact that a tryptophan metabolite, kynurenine, the ultimate precursor of papiliochrome, occurs at high concentrations in the hemolymph and must be taken up directly by the scale cells (Umebachi 1985). It is therefore kynurenine that is taken up as a papiliochrome precursor, rather than tryptophan itself.

Tyrosine was indeed incorporated, in vivo and in vitro, into both yellow and black areas, as expected. However, there was a distinct temporal difference: tyrosine was first incorporated into yellow areas early in development

Richard ffrench-Constant and P. Bernhard Koch

(plate 13.3B), and only later was it incorporated into the black pattern (plate 13.3C). Thus, the temporal pattern of pigment precursor uptake reflects the observed sequence of pigment deposition seen in *P. glaucus* wing patterning. This finding suggests that the switch between the black and yellow synthesis pathways is under tightly regulated developmental control.

SCLEROTIZATION PATTERNS IN *P. glaucus*

As well as studying the developmental succession of pigment deposition in *P. glaucus* scales, we also investigated the relative rates at which these differently colored scales were sclerotized. This was achieved by air-drying wing sections at different developmental stages (proceeding from VI to I) and then examining scale morphology via scanning electron microscopy or SEM (fig. 13.2). At stage VI, when no pigments are visible, the scales collapse after air-drying (fig. 13.2A). In contrast, at stage V, when yellow pigmentation starts, papiliochrome-containing scales start to become sclerotized and remain erect after air-drying (fig. 13.2B). Later, at stage IV (fig. 13.2C), fully sclerotized yellow scales can be seen. At stage III (fig. 13.2D), when melanization of the prospective black scales begins, sclerotization also starts in these areas. Full sclerotization is then reached at stage I (fig. 13.2E), shortly before adult emergence. These results demonstrate that the relative rates at which the differently colored scales become sclerotized match the developmental succession of pigment deposition, suggesting that the two processes are regulated in a coordinated manner.

THE ROLE OF DDC AND OTHER ENZYMES IN THE YELLOW-BLACK PATTERN

We have shown, via a combination of precursor incorporation studies (see fig. 13.1 and plate 13.3), enzyme activity assays (see the discussion below), and in situ hybridization analysis of *Ddc* mRNA abundance (plate 13.4), that the differential spatial and temporal expression of the enzymes underlying pigment synthesis is involved in the yellow-black color decision taken by each individual wing scale cell (Koch et al. 1998). There is a clear inversion of the spatial pattern of *Ddc* mRNA accumulation over time, which shows that *Ddc* gene expression is dynamically regulated. Thus DDC supplies dopamine early in wing development for papiliochrome synthesis in presumptive yellow areas and later for melanization of the black stripes and the marginal bands of the swallowtail wing. However, the correlation of DDC activity with the differential timing of yellow-black patterning, as well as with the differential timing of sclerotization, implies that other elements of the dopamine pathway must also be regulated to dictate the production of one pigment or another.

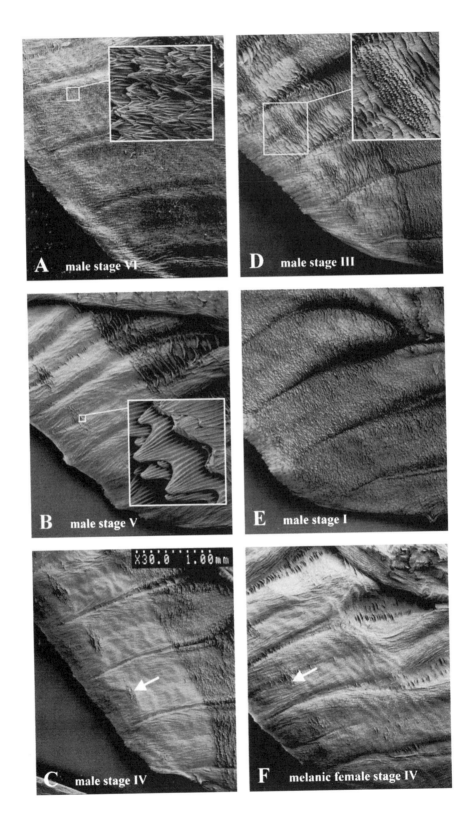

A male stage VI

D male stage III

B male stage V

E male stage I

C male stage IV

X30.0 1.00mm

F melanic female stage IV

These other elements are the enzymes N-β-alanyl-transferase and N-acetyl-transferase. Thus dopamine can either be processed into NADA by N-acetyl-transferase, to take part in sclerotization, or into dopamine quinone to form melanin (see fig. 13.1). Alternatively, dopamine can be processed into NBAD, which can also be used in sclerotization (as well as in papiliochrome), by N-β-alanyl-transferase. Recently we have developed radiochemical assays to measure the activities of both of these enzymes in the same wing homogenates. Our results show that in whole forewings of male *P. glaucus* (in which large areas of yellow papiliochrome are displayed), both enzymes show an increase and then a subsequent decrease in activity over time. N-β-alanyl-transferase activity peaks sharply at stage IV, when papiliochrome synthesis is maximal (see plate 13.7). In contrast, N-acetyl-transferase activity in the same tissue increases at stage VI and peaks at stage V, which is shortly before the period of maximum papiliochrome synthesis and sclerotization of most of the wing area at stage IV. Enzyme activity then slowly decreases toward stage II, when most pigmentation and sclerotization has already occurred (see plate 13.7). Additionally, in the yellow central forewing of the male, the enzyme activities are even higher than in the wing as a whole because this tissue contains exclusively yellow and sclerotizing scales. These results suggest that NADA is probably involved in sclerotizing yellow scales.

A DUAL ROLE FOR DDC IN SCALE DEVELOPMENT

Our results demonstrating the incorporation of dopamine into both the yellow and black pigments as well as into sclerotizing agents (as inferred from N-acetyl-transferase activities) suggest a dual role for the enzyme DDC and its product dopamine. Transcription of the *Ddc* gene and expression of the active enzyme is therefore clearly a part of the scale maturation program, enabling dopamine to be used both in pigments (papiliochrome or melanin) and as a component of scale cuticle maturation (NBAD and/or NADA). Hence, the spatial and temporal expression of DDC controls both the start of pigment formation and sclerotization, but does not regulate the decision of a given scale to be yellow or black. We speculated that this role may be performed by N-β-alanyl-transferase, which shunts dopamine out of melanin synthesis and into the papiliochrome synthesis pathway (as discussed below).

Figure 13.2 Morphology of scale color development under scanning electron microscopy after air-drying of wing tissues. The plates compare scale development in male *P. glaucus* at stages VI (A), V (B), IV (C), III (D), and I (E) with that in a melanic female at stage IV (F). Note that the yellow scales in the wild-type male pattern are sclerotized first, and then subsequently those in the black stripes. In contrast, in the melanic female, the sclerotization of the (normally yellow) central forewing is delayed (F), and this area is finally sclerotized at the same time as the black stripes. Arrows indicate sclerotized yellow scales of the marginal spots in wild-type (C) and melanic (F) wings. The scale for all plates is given in C (magnification ×30). Magnification of the inserts ranges from ×150 to ×2000.

MELANISM: CHANGES IN BOUNDARIES OR BACKGROUND COLOR

Following this dissection of the developmental and biochemical processes underlying color pattern formation, we can now attempt to explain the alterations in these processes underlying the three types of melanism described above: first, simple changes in the position of a color boundary, and second, true changes in background color.

CHANGES IN THE POSITION OF A COLOR BOUNDARY

In the type of melanism exemplified by the *P. machaon* complex, we need to explain the movement of a yellow-black boundary that increasingly diminishes the area of the background yellow color left visible. To explain this change, we need to understand what originally drives the black pattern of the central wing area. A recent examination of mutant color patterns may help to explain these changes. From the *veins reduced* mutant of *P. xuthus,* it is evident that the black vein-dependent stripes depend directly on vein formation, as the loss of the veins in the mutant also removed those stripes (see plate 13.1). In contrast, the marginal bands may be defined by signals from the wing margin. The factors driving the yellow-black border of the central wing area and the tigerlike stripes in the forewing remain unclear.

In this type of melanism, therefore, the yellow-black border must be shifted or extended toward the wing margin, as exemplified by a comparison of male versus female *P. polyxenes* (plate 13.2C, D). Clearly sex-linked genes must be involved in the process that shifts this border, but the molecular mechanisms or signaling molecules involved remain unknown. However, we can speculate that these changes in the placement of a pattern boundary might be most easily affected by changes in the timing of the underlying patterning signals. Therefore, as suggested above, it seems likely that either the timing of ecdysone secretion itself or the expression of the associated receptors is altered.

P. glaucus MELANISM IS A CHANGE IN BACKGROUND COLOR

Two very different mechanisms could account for *P. glaucus* melanism. First, a mixture of yellow and melanic scales could cause an overall change in color. Second, melanic pigment could be substituted for the yellow pigment in normally yellow scales. We propose that both mechanisms are in fact present, but that their relative apparency depends on the penetrance of the melanic gene.

In fully penetrant individuals, our visual observations of color development show that yellow pigment (papiliochrome) is not deposited in the

Richard ffrench-Constant and P. Bernhard Koch

central forewing, and that this area is then later melanized (plate 13.5). Perhaps more importantly, the final melanic scales themselves are not as black as those in the normal black pattern elements, but are a dark *brown*. These observations suggest, first, that papiliochrome synthesis may be absent from the central forewing, and second, that the pigment in the melanic scales may be different from the melanin in normally black scales, as discussed above.

In contrast, Nijhout, in reviewing the different types of melanism, proposed that the dark female form of *P. glaucus* corresponds to an increase in the frequency of dark scales in the yellow background (Nijhout 1991). Although yellow scales can be found co-occurring with melanic scales in individual melanic females (plate 13.6A), we propose that these specimens are poorly penetrant for the melanic phenotype. Thus, in fully penetrant individuals, yellow scales are totally absent from the melanic areas; that is, all the formerly yellow scales produce brown melanin (plate 13.6B). In partially penetrant individuals, not all of the yellow scales undergo this switch, and some remain yellow, producing a pattern of yellow scales in a melanized background. We therefore propose that the darkening of the central area of the wings results not from a simple change in the ratio of yellow to black scales, but rather from a change in the actual amount or composition of the pigment the scales contain.

Several lines of biochemical evidence support these two suggestions. First, the patterns of precursor incorporation into the various color pattern elements differ between wild-type females and melanic females. In the central presumptive black areas of the melanic females, there is no β-alanine or tyrosine incorporation during papiliochrome synthesis (which occurs only in the row of marginal yellow spots) (plate 13.3D, F). Tyrosine is incorporated only into melanin at a later time (plate 13.3F). This failure to incorporate β-alanine suggests that papiliochrome synthesis is absent from this area of the wing, which is consistent with the observation that the yellow pattern element is missing from the central wing of the melanic female. Thus, the formation of the yellow and black elements of the wild-type pattern involves differential timing of pigment synthesis, while the dark area of the fully penetrant melanic female appears to be regulated by the absence of, or suppression of, yellow pigment synthesis in the central part of the wing.

Second, early in wing color development, the high levels of DDC activity normally present in the central wing area of wild-type females are much reduced in the same region in melanic females (Koch et al. 1998). The presence or absence of DDC activity is therefore correlated with the decision of tissues to be either yellow or black and, respectively, to sclerotize early or late. This correlation is demonstrated by the lack of scale sclerotization observed in the central wing area of melanic females at the time when the scales in the yellow marginal spots are in the process of sclerotization (fig. 13.2F). Thus, in melanics, the early abnormal absence of DDC activity in the central wing area is correlated with the subsequent atypical melanization of the same area, suggesting that these two processes may be under the same coordinated genetic regulation.

Obviously a decrease in early DDC activity is probably not sufficient to suppress papiliochrome synthesis in melanic individuals. We are therefore currently investigating the role of N-β-alanyl-transferase, the enzyme that shunts dopamine out of the melanin pathway and into the papiliochrome pathway to complex it with β-alanine, forming NBAD, an ultimate precursor of papiliochrome. Our recent measurements of N-β-alanyl-transferase activity show a sharp peak at stage IV, corresponding to maximal papiliochrome synthesis, and little or no apparent activity in the central forewing of melanic females, supporting this interpretation.

Despite the involvement of very different color pigments, the sharp cutoff of β-alanine incorporation into black (or very dark) scales observed in the nymphalid *Precis coenia* (Koch and Kaufmann 1995) also suggests that β-alanine uptake and the formation of NBAD (as a sclerotizing agent) may be the key regulative step in separating non-melanin synthesis (always early) from melanin synthesis (always late). Interestingly, N-β-alanyl-transferase is encoded by the homologue of the *Drosophila* gene *ebony* (Hovemann et al. 1998), null mutants of which are melanized black (Wright 1987). Melanization in *P. glaucus* may therefore correspond to coordinated regulation of *both* DDC and N-β-alanyl-transferase activity, whereby early DDC activity is decreased and N-β-alanyl-transferase activity is completely shut down. This suppression of both enzyme activities correlates with a delay in the development (sclerotization) of the presumptive yellow scales, which are then melanized later in development.

A DEVELOPMENTAL MODEL OF MELANISM

Two basic processes appear to underlie swallowtail melanism, and perhaps mimicry as a whole: first, changes in the position of color boundaries, and second, actual changes in the background colors themselves. This conclusion raises the fascinating question of how such apparently different changes, one spatial and one chemical, could be regulated by the same sex-linked melanic gene. Our recent examinations of scale development suggest a developmental model for color pattern formation that essentially combines these two processes (plate 13.7) and proposes that coordinated control of color development is exerted through control of the timing of scale maturation.

Our initial visual observations showed that in all the species that we examined, there was a clear developmentally ordered succession of pigment deposition, with the deposition of colored pigments preceding the later melanization of uncolored areas. Further, the corresponding areas of the

Richard ffrench-Constant and P. Bernhard Koch

P. glaucus wing showed a direct correlation between the rate of scale maturation and the resulting color (see fig. 13.2). Thus, scales that mature early synthesize papiliochrome and are yellow, whereas scales that mature late are melanized black. Simple changes in color boundaries can therefore be executed by changing the relative rates of scale development in a given area, perhaps in reference to a gradient of signaling molecules that defines different pattern elements (e.g., vein-dependent stripes, as suggested by the *veins reduced* mutant of *P. xuthus*). Such boundary changes would involve no change in the biochemistry of pigment synthesis in the scales, merely a redistribution of the cells developing at different rates, resulting in a redistribution of the corresponding boundary (fig. 13.3A).

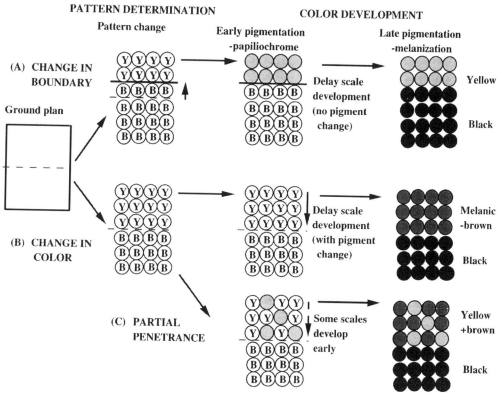

Figure 13.3 A model differentiating the putative mechanisms underlying the two types of melanism in *P. glaucus*, a change in boundary or a change in background color. (A) During pattern determination, the position of the yellow-black boundary is shifted from that in the original groundplan. Subsequently, during color development, the presumptive yellow and black scales are colored early and late in development, respectively. In this type of melanism there is a delay in development between yellow and black scales, but no changes in cell color fate are apparent. (B) In a change of background color, there is no change in the prepattern boundary, but the development of cells originally destined to be yellow is delayed so that they are abnormally melanized (to brown) at the same time as normal black scales are melanized. (C) In partially penetrant melanic individuals, the signal to delay scale development is not interpreted equally by all the scales. Therefore some develop early and become yellow, and others delay their development and become melanized (brown). This process leads to a mixture of yellow and brown scales.

As a hypothesis, we suggest that pattern-determining genes may set the threshold of decreasing ecdysteroid concentration in the different wing areas, which in turn *both* induces final scale maturation *and* co-regulates DDC and N-β-alanyl-transferase expression. Such a threshold-sensing mechanism could involve the differential expression of ecdysteroid receptors or their isoforms. However, such a model can *also* be used to explain changes in background color if a resulting change in biochemistry is inferred. SEM analysis of melanic *P. glaucus* scales shows that these scales, originally destined to be yellow, show delayed development similar to that of wild-type black scales. Given that their papiliochrome synthesis pathway is apparently deficient, and that they were not originally destined to synthesize black melanin, these cells then undergo an atypical melanization corresponding to their late development. This process produces the atypical melanin colored dark brown. Although we have not biochemically analyzed this "dark brown" melanin, it will be interesting to document how it differs biochemically from the normal black melanin of the black pattern elements and how it relates to the eumelanin (black) and phaeomelanin (brown) discussed by Nijhout (1991). In this second type of melanism, scales originally programmed to be one color (yellow) have their rates of development delayed so that they are colored in the wrong time window (that of the later black melanization phase) (fig. 13.3B). In this way, regulation of a single process, the rate of scale development, can cause both spatial changes in color boundaries (in which cell color fates remain unaltered) and changes in background color (in which cell color fates are changed).

MELANIC ABERRATIONS: WHAT ARE THEY TELLING US?

During the course of examining a large number of melanic *P. glaucus,* several authors have noted two abnormal forms or aberrations: the first apparently relating to the penetrance of the melanic phenotype (Ritland 1986), and the second in which putative mosaics of wing tissue of different sexes, traditionally termed "gynandromorphs," are formed, (Clarke and Clarke 1983). Following our presentation of a model describing the developmental basis of melanism, we therefore need to reexamine how each of these aberrations can be explained within the context of that model.

VARIABLE PENETRANCE OF THE MELANIC PHENOTYPE

In explaining melanism in *P. glaucus,* Nijhout originally drew attention to the frequent presence of yellow scales within the darkened central areas of the wing (Nijhout 1991). Further, he proposed that the melanic

Richard ffrench-Constant and P. Bernhard Koch

phenotype itself could be explained by a change in the proportions of yellow and black scales within the melanic area. Although yellow scales can certainly be found in the central wing area of many melanic females, we suggest that this phenomenon represents an example of variable penetrance. Thus, normally penetrant melanic females show no yellow scales in the central wing area, whereas partially penetrant individuals show a large proportion of yellow scales in the same area (see plate 13.6A). Thus the two processes of melanism (a change in the rate of scale development and a shift in the underlying biochemistry) and the penetrance of the phenotype (the proportion of scales that adopt the melanic developmental pathway) exist in parallel to one another.

This gradient of penetrance therefore appears to correspond to the ability of individual scales to respond to the melanizing signal. Cells therefore appear to behave autonomously and respond individually to a threshold of signal, above which they develop early, and are colored yellow, and below which they develop late, and are melanized (see fig. 13.3C). Presumably, if the signal is present at or around this threshold level, then a mixture of responses by individual scales is observed, as in the partially penetrant individuals. Interestingly, this threshold appears to be temperature sensitive, as raising melanic butterflies at higher temperatures has been reported to reduce penetrance—that is, to increase the proportion of yellow scales present (Ritland 1986).

Finally, it is important to note that in rare specimens (see plate 13.6C), even the marginal yellow spots can be occluded by the melanic wing area. It is hard to relate these specimens to the concept of penetrance, and thus we must conclude that they actually represent rare examples of boundary shifts, in which the melanic background area is actually shifted to extend to the margin of the wing. Although we cannot determine whether this change in pattern is under the same genetic control as normal melanization of the background color, if it is, it would provide another example of how a single gene can exert changes in both color and boundary effects.

Sexual Mosaics or Gynandromorphs

In a second type of aberration involving melanism, gynandromorphs—individual butterflies that appear to be a mosaic of wild-type male and melanic female tissues—are produced (plate 13.6D). Specimens similar to the one shown here have been reported elsewhere (Clarke and Clarke 1983), and this type of mosaic is thought to be possible, given that sex determination in insects is cell-autonomous (Lauge 1985) (that is, individual cells are genetically predetermined to be either male or female). Different scale cells could therefore respond differently to the same patterning signals in the same individual insect, depending on whether they are male or female. Thus, in the specimen shown in plate 13.6D, female cells in the central area of the wing are melanized, whereas male cells have responded to the same signals with the normal wild-type pattern. From this example, we can see that the sex-linked control genes, and their sex-linked modifiers, that underlie the genetic basis of melanism must exert their effects by differential interpretation of the patterning signal. For example, interpretation of the signal imposing a delay in the development of melanic scales in melanic females is female-specific, and male scale cells exposed to this signal develop normally.

These two examples of aberrations in the melanic phenotype emphasize the autonomy of the developing scale cells. Individual cells respond differently to the same patterning signals, based on both their predetermined sex (as to whether their development is wild-type or is predisposed to melanism) and the intensity of the signal they receive (as to whether a threshold triggering normal development is achieved or not).

SUMMARY AND CONCLUSIONS

Swallowtail butterflies show a range of forms of sex-specific melanism and mimicry, apparently driven by single major genes and sex-specific modifiers. Although a wide variety of final effects are derived, ranging from a simple darkening of the overall butterfly to close mimicry of an unrelated species involving numerous color changes, two basic kinds of changes are observed: changes in color boundaries (such as the extension of a black area over a light background color) and changes in the background color itself. Through a comparative examination of the biochemistry of pigment formation, melanic and veinless mutants, and relative rates of scale development, we have derived a developmental model to explain how these apparently divergent processes may be controlled by the same genes. Given the strictly developmentally ordered pattern of pigment synthesis and its correlation with the rate of scale development in differently colored areas, we propose that the genes controlling mimicry are developmental genes driven by hormonal signals that alter rates of scale development and, correspondingly, the final color of the scales. In the absence of associated changes in the underlying biochemistry, the activities of these genes result merely in changes in color borders, but concomitant with changes in pigment biochemistry, they can drive changes in background color as well. This model helps to explain how genes spatially controlling rates of scale development, and thus pigment boundaries, can also cause changes in pigment colors.

Richard ffrench-Constant and P. Bernhard Koch

ACKNOWLEDGMENTS

We dedicate this chapter to Professor Yoshishige Umebachi, whose pioneering work on the biochemistry of papiliochrome synthesis enabled us to define an effective experimental plan for examining melanism in *P. glaucus*. We thank Ute Lorenz (Ulm) for help with the figures, Bettina Behnecke and Marga Lenz (Ulm) for recent enzyme assays, Thomas Rocheleau for technical assistance and provision of specimens, and David Keys (Madison) for DDC in situ hybridization and extensive comments on the manuscript. We also thank Katsuhiko Endo (Yamaguchi) for mutant *P. xuthus* and Fred Nijhout (Durham, NC) for helpful discussions.

CHAPTER 14

Adaptive Novelty through Introgression in *Heliconius* Wing Patterns: Evidence for a Shared Genetic "Toolbox" from Synthetic Hybrid Zones and a Theory of Diversification

Lawrence E. Gilbert

TAXONOMIC, GEOGRAPHIC, AND ECOLOGICAL PATTERNS OF *Heliconius* WING PHENOTYPES

WING PATTERN DIVERSITY IN *Heliconius*

The Neotropical genus *Heliconius* has long fascinated evolutionary biologists because of the puzzles presented by the variation in wing pattern within and among species. The strikingly diverse wing patterns that characterize different races of a species apparently evolve rapidly (Brower 1994a) and at rates different from overall genomic divergence (Turner et al. 1979). Studies of gene flow in hybrid zones between races show that genes controlling conspicuous pattern elements exhibit much steeper clines of frequency than genes with little or no effect on pattern (Mallet 1986b; Mallet et al. 1990; Jiggins et al. 1996; Linares 1989). Manipulative experiments (Benson 1972; Mallet and Barton 1989) support the idea that visual selection by predators exerts a strong conservative effect to preserve the predominant phenotypes within the boundaries of a race. Perhaps the biggest puzzle, then, is how such qualitatively distinct patterns arise, persist, and come to characterize an area of a species' range in the first place. Many aspects of this general problem have been thoroughly explored and convincingly explained by Turner and Mallet (1996), but the source of the novelty that fuels this adaptive radiation remains an unexplored question.

A second puzzle concerns coexisting species of *Heliconius* within a local community: why are the patterns among such species so diverse? Although eight of nine local *Heliconius* species in Corcovado Park, Costa Rica, are unpalatable to a common butterfly predator (e.g., Chai 1990), at least three

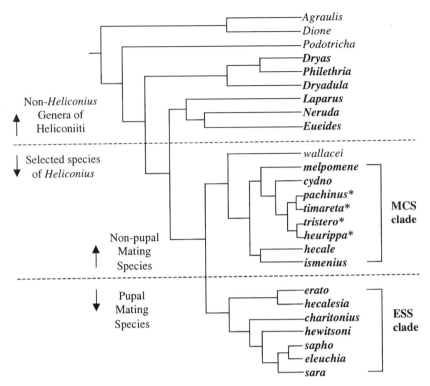

Non-*Heliconius*
Genera of
Heliconiiti

↑

Selected species
of *Heliconius*
↓

Non-pupal
Mating
Species
↑

Pupal
Mating
Species
↓

Agraulis
Dione
Podotricha
Dryas
Philethria
Dryadula
Laparus
Neruda
Eueides

wallacei
melpomene
cydno
*pachinus**
*timareta**
*tristero**
*heurippa**
hecale
ismenius

MCS
clade

erato
hecalesia
charitonius
hewitsoni
sapho
eleuchia
sara

ESS
clade

Figure 14.1 Annotated phylogeny of the subtribe Heliconiiti (Nymphalidae, Heliconiinae), showing the *Heliconius* species and species groups discussed in the text. Higher-level relationships are based on Penz (1999), and species-level relationships for *Heliconius* follow Brower and Egan (1997), modified to include *H. hecalesia* within the ESS clade as proposed by Brown (1981). Taxa in boldfaced type are discussed in the text. An asterisk indicates a described species from the *cydno* group suggested to arise from *cydno* × *melpomene* hybridization.

distinctive pattern themes (called mimicry rings) coexist there (plate 14.1a–f), as is the case in any Neotropical rainforest community of eight to ten *Heliconius* species. Why do so many color pattern mimicry rings coexist at once when, in theory, Müllerian mimicry should favor community-wide convergence (see Joron and Mallet 1998)? A hint to the answer comes from the way in which the distinct pattern themes within a habitat are related phylogenetically (fig. 14.1). For example, in Corcovado Park, the *erato/sapho/sara* (ESS) clade (see Brower 1994b; Penz 1999), a group that contains five pupal mating species (all of which share the lack of a signa in the female bursa copulatrix: Brown 1981), exhibits four distinct pattern themes. Similarly, each of four sympatric species in the *melpomene/cydno*/silvaniform (MCS) clade possesses a different pattern theme, and three of these participate in intimate Müllerian partnerships with a pupal mating ESS comodel. In addition to sharing wing patterns, mimetic comodels from different clades also exhibit similar patterns of overall habitat use, including heights of nocturnal roosts (Mallet and Gilbert 1995).

Lawrence E. Gilbert

Within the MCS clade, interspecific mating leads both to nonmimetic F$_1$ phenotypes, vulnerable to differential sampling by bird predators (e.g., Benson 1972), and sterile F$_1$ females (in keeping with Haldane's rule). Within the ESS clade, interspecific matings often result in complete inviability of F$_1$ zygotes (L. E. Gilbert, pers. obs.). ESS (pupal mating) males are known to compete intensively for mates (Deinert et al. 1994; Deinert, chap. 5 in this volume), and will attempt mating with heterospecific pupae or emerging adults discovered near conspecific pupae in greenhouses or in the field (L. E. Gilbert, pers. obs.). This phenomenon has been suggested as one selective force driving host plant and microhabitat separation within the *Heliconius* community (Gilbert 1984, 1991) because ESS males not only sterilize female pupae of other ESS species, but may also disable and kill both sexes of MCS teneral individuals found on or near hosts they are searching for pupae (L. E. Gilbert, pers. obs.).

Realistic scenarios for the assembly of species-rich local communities of *Heliconius* (e.g., plate 14.1) must take account of the potential for such reproductive interference along with other aspects of interspecific interaction (Gilbert 1991). Thus, the probability that sibling species will be able to establish breeding populations and coexist after arrival in a suitable patch of habitat should depend on the degree to which each has evolved distinct microhabitat or host plant preferences while geographically isolated (Jiggins et al. 1997b; Mallet 1993; Mallet et al. 1998b). Incipient niche divergence would reduce competitive and reproductive interference between a newly arrived species and a resident sibling species, or any other *Heliconius* species that already inhabited the area.

WING PATTERNS AND SPECIES PACKING

Does possessing a highly distinct wing pattern assist a new arrival's establishment in a local community? If it does, then the local species diversity of *Heliconius* could be at least partly due to its capacity to generate different wing patterns. Wing pattern diversity seems most causally connected to local species diversity in groups such as the MCS clade, which appears to rely heavily on visual signals in courtship. The probability that an additional species could be packed into a local community would depend on its wing pattern being sufficiently distinct from those of close relatives to minimize confusion in courtship that might lead to hybridization. By the same token, the new arrival's degree of mimicry of a well-established non-MCS aposematic wing pattern (not necessarily that of other *Heliconius*) should promote its chances of establishment.

Such mimetic convergence of wing patterns in a local community of *Heliconius* (see plate 14.1) tends to be found between species from different clades that are able to share microhabitat (e.g., Mallet and Gilbert 1995) by virtue of having distinctly different mating and oviposition habits. Such cross-clade combinations may coevolve (in the microevolutionary sense) toward identical wing patterns as Müllerian mutualists (Gilbert 1983) in spite of also being competitors for resources (Templeton and Gilbert 1985). Excluding the highly polymorphic *H. numata,* whose various forms mimic different ithomiine butterflies (Brown and Benson 1975), the intrageneric mimicry we find in *Heliconius* ensures that the number of different wing pattern themes coexisting locally will be always be somewhat less than the total number of *Heliconius* species present.

WING PATTERNS IN SPACE AND TIME

From region to region, quantum jumps with respect to wing pattern are taken in concert by each species of a Müllerian partnership. Müllerian pairs such as *H. erato* and *H. melpomene* exhibit concordant racial changes and parallel hybrid zones (Turner 1981), providing comparative systems for the study of the ecological and evolutionary genetics of mimetic adaptation (e.g., Mallet et al. 1990; Jiggins and McMillan 1997), behavioral mimicry (Srygley 1999), coevolution and phylogeny of mimetic races (Brower 1996b), and speciation (e.g., Mallet 1993).

It is also striking that novel, superficially unrelated wing patterns "punctuate" racial variation within species such as *H. erato* and comodel *H. melpomene* (see Turner 1983) no less than they characterize interspecific variation across the entire genus *Heliconius.* This generality is most interesting in terms of pattern evolution *within clades* of *Heliconius* for two reasons: first, the underlying mechanisms of pattern development are likely to be shared by all members of a clade, and second, genes that determine pattern are known to pass across species boundaries in some clades, such as MCS.

How do pattern novelties arise within a lineage? To date, the approach to this question has been at the level of evolutionary mechanisms (e.g., Turner and Mallet 1996), such as "biotic drift" (Brown et al. 1974), or "shifting balance" (Mallet 1993; but see Coyne et al. 1997); that is, processes that would filter, concentrate, and preserve pattern novelty within species. Implicit in this literature is the assumption that mutation is sufficient to provide the variation necessary for these novelty-selecting mechanisms to work. But if that is all there is to it, one has to ask why *Heliconius* should be so extraordinary in its display of intraspecific and intrageneric wing pattern novelty. Linares (1989, 1997b) has implicated hybridization as a process generating pattern novelty, but introgression, while of major importance in this system, is not sufficient to explain why *Heliconius,* but not related genera, displays such a variety of patterns, so rapidly evolved.

In this chapter I attempt to account for the origin of novel wing patterns in *Heliconius* by proposing developmental-genetic mechanisms that enhance the capacity of introgression to generate qualitative genetic variation. I then attempt to explain the diversification of the genus in light of these mechanisms and our knowledge of its natural history and ecology. This chapter will address the following questions:

1. Why are so many wing patterns available to *Heliconius?*
2. Why are so few wing patterns successful in nature?
3. What are the likely circumstances for cross-species recombination in nature?
4. What are the relative contributions of mutation and introgression to pattern evolution?
5. How might evolving *Heliconius* jump from one adaptive peak to another without crossing fitness valleys below?
6. Does one clade typically drive the evolution of novel patterns?
7. Does *Heliconius,* and particularly its MCS clade, possess unique developmental-genetic mechanisms for generating wing patterns?
8. How did these developmental mechanisms—i.e., "the toolbox"—originate?

METHODS, MODELS, METAPHORICAL AIDS

BACKGROUND

The ideas on the genetic control of wing pattern described in this chapter have emerged from 25 years of maintaining *Heliconius* populations in insectaries and observing the products of seminatural or "synthetic" hybrid zones during the era when the molecular genetic mechanisms of pattern formation were first being revealed. The ideas presented later in the chapter about the ecology and evolution of diversity were shaped by my own three decades of studying *Heliconius* populations in their community context and by my exposure over those years to the ideas and findings of other *Heliconius* workers, who have been integrating behavioral and physiological ecology, ecological and evolutionary genetics, and phylogenetics to a degree unprecedented for any genus of animals. I have focused on one group of *Heliconius,* the MCS clade, because this group hybridizes most frequently in culture and nature (see Mallet et al. 1998b).

During population studies of Costa Rican *Heliconius* communities in the early 1980s, I observed that the *Heliconius* communities on the two sides of the Meseta Central, the montane barrier that divides that country, share nearly identical color pattern themes, with one striking exception (plate 14.1g–h): the wing coloration of Müllerian partners that fly in the forest understory varies from iridescent blue-black with broad white forewing patches (*H. sapho, H. cydno galanthus*) on the Atlantic side to flat black with bold yellow forewing and hindwing bars (*H. hewitsoni, H. pachinus*) on the Pacific side. The two pupal mating species *H. sapho* and *H. hewitsoni* are specialists on *Passiflora pittieri* and possess virtually identical life histories and larval and pupal morphology. Nevertheless, they prove to be distinct species: they have different chromosome numbers (56 vs. 21: Brown et al. 1992), and matings between them in greenhouse cultures fail to produce offspring (L. E. Gilbert, pers. obs.).

In contrast, crosses between *H. cydno galanthus* and *H. pachinus* are readily obtained. These two species are host plant or oviposition generalists using species in the genus *Passiflora* and have similar larval and pupal morphology. Nevertheless, it is not difficult to understand why taxonomists traditionally separated these populations into different species: no hybrid zones have been previously recognized in the (ca. 50 km wide) zone of potential contact centered on the Meseta Central. However, it is now clear that a hybrid zone has been present, but not perceived, since many hybrid individuals, due to the nature of wing pattern genetics in this group, display rather novel phenotypes, as accounts to follow will illustrate. Moreover, *H. pachinus* is identical to both *H. cydno galanthus* and Colombian *H. c. weymeri* in terms of rDNA restriction sites (Lee et al. 1992), it groups within a clade of *cydno* races in terms of mtDNA (Brower 1996b), and it is fully interfertile with *H. cydno galanthus* and with other *H. cydno* (L. E. Gilbert, pers. obs.). Based on these observations, *H. pachinus* is assumed for the present to represent a well-differentiated race of *H. cydno,* approaching but not broaching the race/species boundary described for *Heliconius* by Mallet et al. (1999).

While conducting genetic crosses and maintaining *cydno* × *pachinus* offspring in insectaries with other *Heliconius* species, I obtained unexpected matings between *H. melpomene* males and *H. cydno* group females. F_1 females of this cross are sterile, in keeping with Haldane's rule, but males are fertile and can be backcrossed to pure females of both species. By repeatedly ("iteratively") backcrossing successive generations of hybrid males showing a particular trait of one species (e.g., the red band on the forewing of *melpomene*) to pure females of the other species, it was possible eventually to obtain fertile hybrid males and females showing the heterospecific trait. I term broods from the crossing of such individuals "pseudo F_2" broods, since they provide a look at some of the phenotypes one might find in a true F_2 cross between two species.

By this method, I discovered the expression of the *melpomene* gene for forewing red to be useful for testing hypotheses developed to explain certain results of *cydno* × *pachinus* crosses. To account for the observed interaction of pattern genes in these three phenotypically distinct taxa (plate 14.4, top left panel, a–c), it was necessary to develop the concept of a shared wing pattern "toolbox." This toolbox includes those pattern genes that behave essentially the same in both *cydno* and *melpomene* genomes.

Little of the genetic data underlying the toolbox model of pattern control to be outlined in the pages to follow has been published (but see Nijhout et al. 1990). However, broods from experimental crosses have been, and continue to be, made accessible to interested researchers working on *Heliconius* genetics and butterfly wing pattern development (see Nijhout 1991). For the present purposes, I refer only to robust conclusions secured by the most definitive results, which I illustrate with photos of representative critical broods. Because of logistic and time constraints, I could not rear every potentially interesting brood arising from all the unique and potentially informative hybridizations that have occurred in my insectaries. Rather, I used greenhouse "hybrid zones" created with known founders to prospect for any phenotypes whose mere appearance would force a rethinking of a current paradigm, or conversely, for rare recombinants predicted by the model. Subsequent test crosses were focused on the most interesting phenotypes and presumptive genotypes. Finally, because obtaining large families from *Heliconius* females requires that they be kept several months and fed pollen or appropriate amino acid diets (Gilbert 1972), I often worked with the combined broods of several sisters mated to a single male or to several males of the same genotype, sacrificing details of minor individual variation for the ability to observe the behavior of major loci in larger communal families.

For several reasons, including space constraints, I have not attempted to relate my genetic hypotheses to gene classifications from prior *Heliconius* studies or to utilize their terminology (although ultimately that will be an informative and important exercise). A glance at the terminology of Sheppard et al.'s (1985) epic work on *Heliconius* demonstrates why only hardcore specialists can process and utilize the results or conclusions of the largest analysis of *Heliconius* genetics ever undertaken. Likewise, although subsequent works more specifically focused on races of the *H. cydno* group (e.g., Nijhout et al. 1990; Linares 1996; Kapan 1998) developed terminology in the context of knowledge of some of my own work on the MCS toolbox elements and would be more compatible with the scheme I use in this chapter, I do not attempt to show the correspondence between these works and the hypotheses I present here. Nijhout (1991), in his synthesis, provides the most valuable summary of *Heliconius* wing color and pattern genes to date. I focus here on describing a few important wing pattern groundplan elements along with those few genes whose effects and interactions are recognizable across races and species of the MCS clade as (1) homologous and (2) significant in determining major aspects of wing pattern phenotype.

Early in this work I attempted to understand the mechanisms underlying the origin of novel patterns in *Heliconius* in terms of general models of insect developmental genetics based on *Drosophila*. Although some of the early ideas from that literature are outmoded, they helped me to organize hypotheses and suggested intuitive metaphors to explain the correspondence between genes and wing patterns that seemed to account for pattern variation in synthetic hybrid zones. Beyond the fact that *Drosophila* wing bristles and butterfly wing scales are now known to be homologous (Galant et al. 1998), I see heuristic value in retaining the *Drosophila*-inspired conceptual structure in thinking about how *Heliconius* may be different from other well-studied models of butterfly development.

SCALE-LEVEL VERSUS PATTERN-LEVEL CONTROL IN DEVELOPMENT

The biochemical events involved in the maturation and pigmentation of butterfly scales during development are relatively well known for *Papilio*, a genus famous for dramatic intraspecific pattern variation, and for *Precis*, a model for the study of eyespot development (Koch et al. 1998; ffrench-Constant and Koch, chap. 13 in this volume). With respect to the chemistry of different scale types, Gilbert et al. (1988) and Koch (1993) have shown that brown and red pigments in *Heliconius* are ommatins, probably derived from kynurenine. These pigments, along with melanin, account for black scales, as well as many of the brown, red, and yellow scales of other butterfly groups (see ffrench-Constant and Koch, chap. 13 in this volume). However, Gilbert et al. (1988) went further to document the correlation of scale ultrastructure and pigmentation in *Heliconius*, revealing that white scales in this genus are structural white, lacking any pigment. A recessive allele adds 3-hydroxy-L-kynurenine to convert these scales to yellow.

The fact that the white/yellow scale morphotype constitutes an important element of the *Heliconius* wing pattern groundplan for mimetic evolution is critical to the discussions of genetics to follow. The model of scale differentiation developed for *Heliconius* by Gilbert et al. (1988, fig. 7) reflects an order of appearance of pigment types corresponding to that documented by Koch et al. (1998) for other taxa. However, in contrast to their findings for *Papilio*, our observations of *Heliconius* indicate that the class of pigment within a scale morphotype does not vary progressively over time.

In general, however, there may be few features that distinguish *Heliconius* from butterflies such as *Precis* with respect to late events in the maturation of scales. The more difficult and overarching issue is the question of how genes create patterns of differentiated scales across the wing. Even with the same or similar basic biochemical mechanisms for pigmenting scales at the terminus of adult development, there may be great variety in how genes determine the dominant patterns that attract us to different butterfly taxa.

Thus, knowing that eyespot patterns in nymphaline butterflies are somehow determined by the positions of morphogen sources and sinks begs the question of how earlier-acting genes determine the spatial arrangements of those critical foci. ffrench-Constant and Koch (chap. 13 in this volume) provide an integrated and compelling model for how pattern fields and boundaries might be determined in *Papilio*. The question of whether the genetic control of wing pattern in *Heliconius* is qualitatively distinct from that proposed for other taxa will be discussed further at the conclusion of this chapter.

The *Heliconius* Wing as a Computer Screen

To explain my working hypothesis for the genetic control of wing pattern in the MCS clade of *Heliconius*, I find it convenient to envision the wing as a computer screen. The following scheme of how genes determine scale phenotypes is based on Gilbert et al. (1988). If each scale is analogous to a pixel, then in the case of *Heliconius*, there are three basic pixel types: (I) white (= pigmentless)/yellow (3-hydroxy-L-kynurenine), (II) black (melanin), and (III) brown/red (xanthommatin and di-hydro-xanthommatin). The placement of these three pixel types on the *Heliconius* "wing monitor screen" can be approximated most simply if we imagine turning off the color on the monitor and simply viewing the image formed by white (type I), black (type II), and gray (type III) pixels. These three scale types are the essential subunits at the disposal of the pattern-forming mechanism in *Heliconius*—that is, those genes that determine the two-dimensional array of the three pixel types on the *Heliconius* screen. Whether pixel type I is white or yellow, pixel type II dull black or reflective, or pixel type III brown or red is genetically trivial as far as the mechanism that forms the spatial pattern is concerned, just as turning a monitor's color control to the black-and-white mode does not affect the essential pattern viewed on the screen. In the case of *Heliconius*, the three major scale types are morphologically distinct at the ultrastructural level (Gilbert et al. 1988) and resemble photoreceptor subunits of *Drosophila* ommatidia in that structure correlates with associated pigments (Tomlinson and Ready 1986).

Unlike pixels on a computer screen, the scales of a *Heliconius* wing develop from undifferentiated trichogen cells (scale precursors). If one selects a coordinate point on the wing that bears type I, II, or III scales and observes the fate of scale phenotypes at that point over a series of crosses, it appears that "realizator genes" (*sensu* Garcia-Bellido 1977) for scale type generally interact in the following order of dominance or epistasis at the scale level: III > II > I. (Gilbert et al. [1988] used the term "selector genes," which is here changed to "realizator" for compatibility with Garcia-Bellido's model.) Type I scales do not require pigments to mature and stiffen, and are thus considered a default condition. If realizator gene *M* switches on, then the scale may develop into type II (melanic) or type III (xanthommatin). Type III scales occur if realizator gene X switches on in a trichogen cell with M also in the "on" position.

These binary rules account for most of what we observe in crosses within and between species in the MCS clade. There are exceptions, however, with some cases of melanic (type II) regions being dominant or epistatic to xanthommatin (type III) regions (e.g., see the discussion of the "forceps" shutter below). Furthermore, on the ventral hindwing only, regions in which scales should be I/II heterozygotes exhibit a strange structural modification that increases reflectance and allows the position of the recessive white/yellow pattern to be seen as a reflectance shift in otherwise melanic scales, a useful diagnostic for heterozygous genotypes.

If one assumes, first, that the realizator genes specifying the three scale types in the *Heliconius* model act by altering the rate of scale development relative to the timing of pigment deposition, and second, that pigment type determines scale morphology, then the epistatic relationships mentioned above are consistent with developmental data on similarly pigmented scales in other butterflies (e.g., Koch et al. 1998). Nevertheless, realizator genes are relatively uninteresting unless a class of regulatory genes, which Garcia-Bellido (1977) termed "selector genes," specifies the regions of realizator gene activities across the wing in order to create a pattern. Metaphorically, I think of selector genes as the computer program that chooses among folders containing bitmap files of pre-scanned images to be viewed in a particular window on the screen as an array of pixels (= scales on the wings of *Heliconius*).

Initially, I thought that these metaphorical windows on *Heliconius* wings might correspond to developmental "compartments" as described or hypothesized in *Drosophila* (e.g., Lawrence and Morata 1976; Kaufmann et al. 1978; Kaufmann 1981). Compartment theory suggested that cell surface properties, determined by the "on" or "off" states of a hierarchy of selector genes, help to organize polyclones of cells that come to occupy discrete, sharply bounded zones, or compartments. Although aspects of compartment theory are now understood (e.g., Blair and Ralston 1997), work over the last 15 years has demonstrated other mechanisms that may establish regions of the *Drosophila* wing differing in regulatory gene expression (e.g., O'Brochta and Bryant 1985), For simplicity, I occasionally refer to such regions of the *Heliconius* wing as "compartments," with the reader's understanding that the term is not used in its strict drosophilan sense, even though the strict definition may actually apply to some parts of *Heliconius* wings. Obviously, extending the simplistic computer screen metaphor to spatial patterns of scales becomes more complex if a variety of lineage restriction mechanisms are at work and if zones of the wing surface are reserved for more ancestral nymphaline developmental schemes. However, simplistic models can be useful for guiding research, even when we suspect that they are largely wrong.

Regulatory Genes and Computer Screens

In order to illustrate what happens on a *Heliconius* wing while maintaining the computer analogy, it is necessary to mimic the way developmental compartments (windows) might organize the expression of pattern genes on real wings. For simplicity, imagine proximal and distal, dorsal and ventral compartments on the forewing and hindwing. This requires eight windows, one to represent a "compartment" in each of eight wing sectors. Each window is uniquely associated with a different set of applications, representing the regulatory genes that are constrained by compartments in the developing wing. To open any image file and display a pattern in the appropriate window, the appropriate application must first be opened.

An intuitive case to which this model probably applies is the forewing of *H. melpomene*. A quick examination of the wing surfaces of some *H. melpomene* races leaves no doubt that the dorsal and ventral (D/V) surfaces of *Heliconius* wings represent strikingly different realms of regulatory gene activity, if not compartments. The Central American race, *rosina*, possesses red (type III) scales in a narrow band distal to the median on the forewing dorsal surface (best seen in plate 14.1f). However, differentiation in the same pattern region on the ventral surface is separately controlled and results in white (type I) scales, a juxtaposition that accounts for the bright rose-pink color of the wing (L. E. Gilbert, pers. obs.). Therefore, the realizator gene that creates red scales in the distal part of the *Heliconius melpomene/cydno* dorsal forewing ("window 1") does so after interpreting information provided by appropriate regulatory (homeotic?) genes (i.e., the selector genes in Garcia-Bellido's model, or the "application" in the computer metaphor), which in turn are constrained by compartment boundaries (the window's frame). Thus, only inside the compartment on the dorsal forewing is the realizator for "all red" expressed. Meanwhile, on the ventral forewing ("window 2"), red scales do not appear in the homologous area because the appropriate selector genes are not active in that particular compartment. Thus, in terms of the computer screen metaphor, window 2, representing a ventral compartment of the distal forewing, contains the image file that would specify an all-red (type III) pixel image in the application's window, but it cannot be opened (leaving default, type I pixels in that area). That image file, however, can be opened and displayed within the bounds of window 1, representing a compartment on the distal part of the dorsal forewing (see also plate 14.2a,b and the genetic discussion below).

If, during development, a somatic mutation in the appropriate homeotic gene occurs, realizator genes normally expressed on another wing surface can be expressed in any scales derived clonally from the original mutant cell. Such "exotic" clones are cell-autonomous in that their differentiation proceeds independently of that of adjacent "native" cells. Such homeotic mutations, or their phenocopies, can result in patterns from one wing surface appearing as a mosaic patch within a novel region. This phenomenon, known as homeosis, has been reviewed and analyzed for the Lepidoptera by Sibatani (1980). Although D/V homeosis is not known in *Drosophila* (making the hypothesis of D/V compartments suspect), it has been diagnosed in butterflies such as lycaenids, in which scale types can differ strikingly between dorsal and ventral forewing surfaces (Sibatani 1980).

The size of such a mosaic patch is a function of how early the causal somatic mutation occurred. Likewise, certain developmental boundaries, established prior to the origin of the homeotic mutant clone, may constrain its distribution on the wing, an observation that originally led to the compartment concept in other insects. My observations of spontaneous homeosis in *Heliconius* (L. E. Gilbert, unpub.) demonstrate cell-autonomous differentiation of scales with respect to scale type and color (e.g., plate 14.3a). Likewise, experimental induction of somatic mutations in *Heliconius* embryos, which generally reflect phenomena known from clonal analysis of *Drosophila* imaginal discs (Nöthiger 1981), also indicates cell-autonomous differentiation of scale types and suggests that determination of some major pattern boundaries on the wing may occur very early in development (e.g., plate 14.3b). No other similar work from butterflies is available for comparison.

WINDOWS, SHUTTERS, AND WALLS: THE WING PATTERNS OF THE MCS CLADE

Dorsal Hindwing

The foregoing metaphorical connections to *Drosophila*-based concepts of how regulatory genes might organize the development of pattern evolved from attempts to make sense of the phenotypes emerging from synthetic hybrid zones of *cydno, pachinus,* and *melpomene* (e.g., plate 14.4, upper left panel). The first major surprise (and the event that triggered further investigation) was the appearance of a striking and novel hindwing pattern, a large white or yellow oval, in hybrid populations derived from crosses of *cydno* and *pachinus* (see plate 14.5a,b). Recall that *cydno*'s dorsal hindwing pattern is solid black (plate 14.1h), while that of *pachinus* consists of a well-defined rectangular yellow bar that sweeps horizontally across the wing (plate 14.1d). To account for this phenotype in F_2 and particular backcross test broods, it was necessary to question two long-standing assumptions.

First, the usual assumption that black scales represent a ground color had to be rejected. To account for the observed hindwing pattern, an alternative assumption was needed: that these two species share a common scheme of windows of type I (white or yellow) scales, defined by compartment boundaries against a surrounding "wall" of black type II scales (from here on, "window-wall boundary" will be equivalent in the analogy to the window-monitor screen boundary). In Costa Rican *melpomene*, this window can be seen as the hindwing yellow bar. In the *pachinus* hindwing, only its lower part is visible because a realizator gene has placed a "shutter" of black scales over the upper part of the window, completely obscuring the window-wall boundary. In *cydno galanthus,* no evidence of the window can be seen on the dorsal hindwing surface because a realizator gene has placed black scales over the entire window, a complete shuttering of the hindwing window (see plate 14.1h).

Second, the usual attribution of most alternative phenotypes at a particular site on the wing to the action of alternative alleles at the "site locus" had to be questioned. How would a complete white oval have been revealed in the hybrid broods if the alternative shutters in question were the expression of alternative alleles at a locus? It must be concluded from the segregation of novel, shutter-free phenotypes in the F_2 of *cydno* × *pachinus* that different and unlinked realizator genes compete for expression in the same compartment of the wing, just as different images compete to be placed "in front" in a particular window on a computer monitor. In principle, several unlinked realizators capable of modifying the groundplan in an area of the wing could be organized in an epistatic pecking order, just as many alternative images can be called up one at a time within a window on a computer screen.

It is easy to see how a system of differently shaped or differently positioned black shutters placed over a window in a dark room could create an almost endless variety of patterns of light in the unshuttered parts of the window. Apparently an analogous scheme accounts for some of the diversity of the white or yellow bands and bars observed in *Heliconius* wings, as illustrated by hindwing patterns in broods derived from genetic crosses of *cydno galanthus* and *pachinus* (see plate 14.4, upper right panel). Furthermore, in crosses of Costa Rican *H. cydno* and *melpomene*, the gene for the dorsal hindwing shutter of *cydno* is epistatic to the hindwing yellow window of *melpomene* (see plate 14.4, lower right panel), with the exception that a scattering of yellow scales sometimes occurs in the window region of heterozygous males, a phenotype seen in presumptive natural zones of introgression between these species, as illustrated in Brower (1996a, fig. 5A).

The dorsal melanic scales of most *H. melpomene* races are flat black, while those of *cydno* are typically a reflective blue-black. On the Pacific slopes of Colombia and Ecuador, *melpomene* hindwing windows are totally shuttered dorsally (but expressed ventrally), and they display the *cydno* traits of reflective dorsal scales and white borders, traits critical for mimetic tracking of co-occurring *H. erato.* Meanwhile, *cydno* races in this region show a number of reciprocal influences of introgression from *melpomene,* manifested on the dorsal hindwing by variation in the width of the white marginal band (plate 14.7, top panel: i, j, k). This is a reflection of underlying segregation of *melpomene* genes and *cydno* genes for small versus large window size, respectively, and can be obtained in laboratory crosses of the Costa Rican races of these species (plate 14.7, top panel: h). Even though the hindwing window may not be visible if covered by a shutter, its size limits the area of the wing available for other "program windows," such as remnants of the ancestral nymphaline groundplan (Nijhout et al. 1990) around the margin. Thus, when *melpomene*'s small hindwing window is placed in a *cydno* background, marginal white lines or bands are unveiled. Ecuadorian *H. cydno* also show occasional segregation of *melpomene* hindwing yellow windows, most often seen in heterozygous expression (D. D. Kapan and L. E. Gilbert, unpub.; L. E. Gilbert and D. D. Kapan, unpub.).

Dorsal Forewing

Uncovering the concept of windows and shutters in the hindwing led me to reevaluate my interpretation of genetic variation in the dorsal forewing white band of *H. cydno.* All the patterns of that area seen in the F$_2$ of *cydno* × *pachinus* can be attributed to approximately two shutter gene loci, with different alleles at each characterizing the revealed parts of the underlying forewing windows of *cydno* and *pachinus,* as discussed in Nijhout et al. (1990). Why do such close relatives look so different? The answer is that several trivial differences in scale color and shutter position create a major shift in pattern phenotype: first, *pachinus* forewing type I scales are recessive yellow, not white as in *cydno* (Gilbert et al. 1988). Second, the *pachinus* shutter sits centrally in the wing's forewing window, allowing yellow (type I) scales to be expressed both distally and proximally to the shutter, just as a shutter in the middle of a real window allows light to enter above and below, while that of *cydno* is like a shutter pulled up against the wall above the window. A sample of one brood (plate 14.4, upper right panel) provides a dorsal view of segregation of most of the major forewing and hindwing shutter phenotypes.

In a darkened room it is not possible to perceive the boundary between wall and window where a shutter is attached. Analogously, in *cydno galanthus,* it is not possible to perceive this boundary directly because both shutter and wall consist of melanic (type II) scales. The presence of this shutter was initially deduced from the pattern of shutter positions in *cydno* × *pachinus* hybrids. For example, in the F$_1$ of *cydno* × *pachinus,* the hybrid shutter shifts proximally (roughly averaging the position of the parental shutters), revealing the distal edge of the white window (plate 14.6e). This phenotype, produced by introgression of shutter alleles from *pachinus* into *cydno galanthus,* is not uncommonly seen in the Atlantic forests east of Costa Rica's Meseta Central (across which gene flow occurs), but is not found in *cydno* populations away from that zone (L. E. Gilbert, pers. obs.).

Serendipitously, the hybridization of Costa Rican *melpomene* with pure *cydno,* pure *pachinus,* and their various hybrid offspring verified the homology of the *cydno* group forewing shutter system. Central American *melpomene* is fixed for a realizator gene that replaces type II (melanic) scales with type III (xanthommatin) scales exclusively in the forewing shutter region. Crossing a male heterozygous for this red gene (a *cydno* × *melpomene* F_1) with a *cydno* × *pachinus* F_2 hybrid heterozygous for different settings of the forewing black shutters showed a 1:1 segregation of fully expressed red shutters in the forewing (plate 14.4, lower center panel), indicating epistasis in a single dose or complete dominance. Of greater interest is that the *melpomene* red gene is in essence a forewing shutter "marker," highlighting the shutter's boundaries, and hence the window-wall boundary, in cases, such as *H. cydno galanthus,* in which the melanic forewing shutter precisely abuts the window's distal boundary with surrounding melanic pattern elements. Based on its apparent early determination (see plate 14.3b), I hypothesize that this boundary represents a true compartment boundary in the strict sense.

The expression of the *melpomene* forewing red gene, which I isolated in the *cydno* genome through a process of reiterative backcrossing of fertile male hybrids displaying red forewings to pure-race females of *cydno* or *pachinus,* confirms for *cydno* (compare plate 14.1h vs. i) and for *pachinus* (compare plate 14.1d vs. j), first, that the red gene of Central American *melpomene* acts to precisely "mark" the forewing shutter system (i.e., that clone in which shutter realizators are switched on) in these species, and second, that the forewing shutter system of *melpomene* is homologous to that of the *cydno* group. Because in pure *melpomene rosina* no white or yellow scales show either distally or proximally to the (red) shutter, it, by definition, must completely obscure *melpomene's* forewing window. This observation predicts that in crosses involving *melpomene* (e.g., Amazonian races) lacking red on the distal forewing (or *cydno,* for that matter) and those of Central America displaying solid red bands, solid black distal forewing phenotypes should segregate in F_2 broods (i.e., individuals simultaneously homozygous for red null alleles and pure *melpomene rosina* window and shutter genotypes). Such phenotypes occur both in interracial crosses within *melpomene* (see Sheppard et al. 1985) and, more interestingly, in interspecific crosses of Costa Rican populations of *melpomene* and *cydno/pachinus* (see plate 14.4, upper left panel, d). I have also obtained individuals virtually identical in both hindwing and forewing to the Colombian *H. c. weymeri* form *gustavi* (see plate 14.7, lower left panel, b) from synthetic hybrid zones restricted to *melpomene rosina* and *cydno galanthus* (not shown). These experiments indicate that to achieve the all-black state in the distal half of the forewing, as seen in the

Colombian *H. c. weymeri* f. *gustavi,* one need only infuse both the *melpomene* window and shutter system into an otherwise pure *cydno* genome in which the gene for red does not exist.

An important complication for interpreting hybrid phenotypes must be mentioned at this point: wing shape and size, along with the relative shape, size, and position of the yellow/white window, vary between species and races. If the window-wall boundary does represent a compartment boundary as hypothesized, then *melpomene* × *cydno* broods have an interesting developmental conflict in heterozygotes across the zone of the distal forewing window between their respective small versus large window "settings" of that boundary. This conflict is apparently manifested by the feathering of this otherwise sharp boundary, as seen, for example, in *cydno* × *melpomene* F$_1$ (big × small window) and many of the offspring of the backcross to *melpomene* (plate 14.4, lower right panel). I believe that the genetics of variation in developmental boundaries has not been considered by *Drosophila* workers because without patterns of diverse scale types, as one has in *Heliconius,* it is much more difficult to detect boundaries on wings. Moreover, at levels more central to organismal function than peripheral, physiologically neutral wing patterns, identity of genetically determined boundaries on the action of homeotic genes might be required for hybrid viability in the first place. So even if compartments are real, their interspecific variation is not likely to be an interesting issue for understanding *Drosophila.*

To compare properly the genes that add shutters to the yellow or white windows of MCS clade hybrids, it is necessary to view their expression in the same window. This can be done, for example, by isolating *melpomene* shutter genes in a *pachinus* background and highlighting them with *melpomene* red to assure homology. The proximal boundary of the forewing distal window appears to be perpendicular to the wing's long axis at the top of the discal cell in all the MCS clade members (see the sharp line at this location in *cydno* × *melpomene* F$_1$ individuals and in broods that they parent: plate 14.4, lower right, lower center, and upper left panels). However, the position of the window's distal boundary varies. The lower left panel of plate 14.4 shows pure *melpomene* (a) and pure *pachinus* (d). The two middle specimens resulted from selecting for *melpomene* shutters and red color on a *pachinus* window (b) and *pachinus* shutters converted to *melpomene* red on a *pachinus* window (c). Along a transect from the top of the discal cell to the top of the *cydno* window, *melpomene* and *pachinus* distal forewing shutter boundaries occur at approximately 1/2 and 3/4 the distance to *cydno*'s position on the boundary, respectively (compare plate 14.4, lower left panel, b and c, with plate 14.1i). As the forewing shutter position is set by approximately two loci (Nijhout et al. 1990), it would appear that *cydno* is fixed for "distal" shutter alleles (*dd, dd*) at each locus, while *melpomene* is fixed for proximal alleles (*pp, pp*) at the same loci. According to this hypothesis, the *pachinus* shutter genotype is predicted to be (*pp, dd*). Thus, when we can visualize MCS forewing shutters displayed on the same window, it appears that the *pachinus* forewing shutter phenotype represents a *cydno* × *melpomene* hybrid for that trait! This hypothesis is supported by *H. cydno gadquae* from the Tachira, San Juan de Colon, area of Venezuela. This race shows a *pachinus*-like position of the forewing shutter in combination with strong evidence of *melpomene* influence on the ventral hindwing forceps motif (see below). A survey of Venezuelan *Heliconius* clearly places the race *gadquae* in an active zone of *cydno-melpomene* introgression (Brown and Fernandez-Yepez 1984, figs. 165–177). Moreover, I have created virtually the same phenotype (not shown) from synthetic hybrid zones of Costa Rican races of these species (L. E. Gilbert, unpub.).

From these and other initial analyses of dorsal forewing pattern genetics, carried out independently with various races of *H. cydno* and *H. melpomene* by M. Linares and myself, we must conclude that many of the more distinctive forms, races, or species of the *H. cydno* complex arise from introgression with *H. melpomene* (and vice versa). In addition to the distinctive shutter position that creates two forewing bands in *pachinus*, two other traits of the *pachinus* forewing may reflect the influence of *melpomene*. The first is the recessive yellow scales of the window (although not expressed because of epistatic realizator/shutter genes, the type I scale genotype for the *melpomene* forewing window is in fact yellow, and this phenotype segregates 1:1 in the [*cydno* × *melpomene* F$_1$] × *melpomene* backcross shown in plate 14.4, lower right panel). Second, the melanic (type II) scales of *pachinus* are more dull black, like those of *melpomene* and its Müllerian partner *H. hewitsoni,* than reflective, like those of conspecific *cydno galanthus.*

In addition to the previously mentioned Colombian *cydno weymeri* form *gustavi*, which tracks Müllerian partner *H. erato chestertonii* (Linares 1997a), I attribute another important example of *cydno* variation to introgression from *melpomene*. The polymorphic variation seen in the forewing of *H. cydno* from the Pacific slope forests of Ecuador (Kapan 1998) exactly matches the types of variation that can be produced in synthetic hybrid zones of *melpomene* and *cydno* from Costa Rica (L. E. Gilbert and D. D. Kapan, unpub.). This intrapopulation variation, which includes yellow versus white forewing windows and various settings of window sizes and shutter positions, allows for the polymorphic mimicry of *H. sapho* (white) and *H. eleuchia* (yellow) by the same *cydno* population (plate 14.7, top panel, i, j). This population has also evolved recessive forewing yellow scales, which, because they would not be expressed as rare mutants in heterozygous form, are more likely to have been derived from introgression than by mutation. Moreover, the absence of linkages of collaborating mimetic loci and their appropriate alleles into *Papilio dardanus*-like supergenes (Kapan 1998) is consistent with a recent introgressive origin of this variation. Other polymorphic *cydno* races in

South America, such as *H. c. hermogenes,* show similar evidence of multiple influences by *melpomene.*

Ventral Forewing

The interesting case of the forewing red gene of *melpomene* was mentioned above in explaining my computer window metaphor. The oft-described "pale" red of the ventral forewing surface of some *melpomene* races results from viewing dorsal red scales through the translucent wing membrane and (type I) white (pigmentless) scales in the ventral homologue of the forewing distal window. To my knowledge, this D/V switch in scale type is an exclusively *melpomene* trait. Note that even *cydno* races with white forewing windows displayed both dorsally and ventrally possess an epistatic gene for expression of type III scales (red/brown) on the ventral forewing, such that all crosses of the *cydno* group with red-banded *melpomene* races convert the ventral forewing window from white to brown or red scales (e.g., see plate 14.2c). This case and the ventral hindwing patterns discussed below provide ample evidence of the independent regulation of realizator genes between dorsal and ventral surfaces. However, whether the switch is the type of selector gene envisioned in Garcia-Bellido's compartment model is not known.

The semi-independence of the ventral and dorsal forewing patterns means that the precise overlay of homologous pattern elements is itself under (canalizing) selection. One frequent trait of interracial and interspecific hybrids (or even strongly inbred lines) is the disruption of this D/V coordination such that boundaries do not line up (e.g., plate 14.5e), or a patch on one surface that appears smaller than on the opposing surface (e.g., Brower 1996a, figs. 8A vs. 8B). This phenomenon can occur on either forewing or hindwing, but I notice it most frequently on the forewing. It should be useful in the detection of natural cases of interspecific introgression.

Ventral Hindwing

This final wing surface has been the most complex to interpret in *H. cydno,* and was ignored in previous attempts to reconcile *Heliconius* genetics with the nymphaline groundplan (Nijhout et al. 1990), but has been studied in Colombian *cydno* by Linares (1989, 1996, 1997a). In Costa Rica, the ventral hindwings of *pachinus* and *cydno* share large windows, which although polygenically different in size and shape, are sufficiently similar to allow the realizator genes for shutter traits of the two races to be visualized in essentially the same window framework. Fortunately for unraveling the details, several other major ventral hindwing differences between these taxa appear to consist of presence vs. null alleles or +/− states of unlinked shutter loci, some of which are also expressed on the dorsal hindwing (e.g., the *cydno* shutter) and some of which simultaneously act on the forewing with respect to homologous wing-vein landmarks (e.g., the *pachinus* shutter).

The *pachinus* shutter

The *pachinus* hindwing is basically that of *melpomene rosina*, except that the yellow window is much larger, and the top half of that window is replaced by a shutter just beyond (proximal to) the discal cell. Simultaneously, this gene (or one tightly linked to it) shutters the proximal half of the forewing from the end of the forewing discal cell. (Compare the *pachinus* × *cydno* F_1, plate 14.6, to a mating pair of parents, plate 14.5c and d.)

The *galanthus* shutter

The shutter that totally obscures the dorsal hindwing window characterizes *cydno galanthus* and is also present ventrally, although the interaction of two other realizators in the same area obscures its presence. Fortunately, because these other loci are unlinked and are represented only by null alleles (at least with respect to major effects) in *pachinus*, it is possible to recover homozygotes and heterozygotes for the *galanthus* shutter and view its effects on the ventral hindwing. A shutter-free individual showing a *pachinus* window and the "brown line" of *cydno* (plate 14.5a) is shown mating with a heterozygote for *galanthus* (plate 14.5b). Note that the reflectance shift of melanic scales heterozygous for this gene allow one to detect the window boundary.

The red/brown realizator for shutter type (II vs. III)

Just as in the case of the forewing shutter system in *melpomene,* the "shutter color gene" for type III scales (red/brown) converts the *cydno galanthus* shutter region of the hindwing window from melanic to brown scales. This phenotype is easily obtained in laboratory crosses, and plate 14.5e shows a natural version of the same phenotype collected in central Costa Rica early this century and described by William Schaus (1913).

The "forceps" shutter of *cydno*

In pure *cydno galanthus,* a realizator gene converts most of the brown (*galanthus*) shutter back to black scales, but leaves an arching line of these brown scales visible parallel to the upper ventral hindwing margin. A heterozygote phenotype for this pattern gene is seen in plate 14.5g and in homozygous form in wild-type *cydno galanthus* ventral hindwing (plate 14.5c). I call this the "forceps shutter" because in combination with the nonhomologous brown line that arches parallel to the lower ventral hind-wing margin, it creates the forceps-like brown pattern on this wing surface. It is the homozygous "null" at this locus, due to gene flow from *pachinus,* that produces the phenotype shown in plate 14.5e.

Note that one influence of introgression from yellow hindwing win-dow races of *melpomene* into *cydno* is the replacement of the large window with much smaller versions depending on the degree of *melpomene* influence. As the hindwing window's size decreases, the brown line moves to keep its relationship to the edge of the window, and the sides of the forceps motif straighten and close to near touching. Such *cydno* phenotypes (e.g., plate 14.7, top panel, e and f) are common in areas of Venezuela, Colombia, and Ecuador where other evidences of introgression from yellow hindwing window *melpomene* are abundant. As the brown line pulls away from the lower margin to follow the smaller *melpomene* window, broad streaks of white scales move in behind, creating, for example, the marginal white bands seen on the Pacific side of Ecuador (see the discussion above). Remarkably, this phenomenon can be replicated in synthetic hybrid zones involving these species using only the wing pattern toolbox options available in Costa Rica (e.g., plate 14.7, top panel, f, h).

While it is *melpomene*'s influence that widens a hindwing marginal win-dow (as seen in plate 14.7, top panel, e, f, and h), it is *cydno galanthus* that provides the previously mentioned white pattern elements in an area that is solid melanic in *melpomene rosina* and, incidentally, in *pachinus.* In the latter population, submarginal white dots on the ventral hindwing are best viewed as evidence of gene flow from *H. c. galanthus.* In northwestern South America, introgression from *cydno* supplies the dorsal hindwing shutter, the reflective blue sheen on the melanic scales, and the white borders that allow *H. melpomene vulcanus* and *H. m. cythera* to track their respective Müllerian partner races of *H. erato, venus,* and *cyrbia* (both of which display their yellow bands on the ventral, but not the dorsal, hindwing).

It is appropriate to mention here that under the MCS toolbox hypothe-sis, Amazonian races of *melpomene* showing a yellow forewing, a narrow or-ange hindwing window, and "rays" on both surfaces of the hindwing would be more closely related to *cydno galanthus* than to *melpomene rosina* with respect to the essential pattern elements employed. Indeed, crosses of those *melpomene* races with Costa Rican *cydno* show that a principal element of *melpomene* that is not immediately recognizable as homologous—the system of hindwing rays—may be a "streaked out" version of the brown line, according to the mechanism just detailed above (plate 14.7, top panel: compare a, d, m). And, of course, in *melpomene,* the brown-shuttered hind-wing window and the accompanying system of rays (= *cydno* brown line) appear dorsally as well as ventrally. In synthetic hybrid zones of Amazonian *melpomene* crossed with Costa Rican *cydno, melpomene* contributes the null (−) allele for the realizator that keeps the dorsal hindwing surface black in *cydno galanthus*. This allele, when homozygous in a *cydno* background, permits the display of *cydno* ventral hindwing brown forceps phenotypes dorsally as well (L. E. Gilbert, pers. obs., not shown).

Basal red

H. pachinus is alone among races of *cydno* in lacking ventral hindwing brown and in possessing red basally like its Müllerian partner, *H. hewitsoni.* The Müllerian partner of *H. cydno galanthus, H. sapho,* also sports basal red, yet *cydno* has not followed suit. I believe this is a consequence of the ease of mimicking the white forewing of *sapho* on the one hand and the difficulty of tracking the red pattern, given fact that neither *melpomene* × *cydno* F_1 nor backcrosses to *cydno* produce the homozygous recessive *melpomene* basal red pattern. While it is possible to synthesize better *sapho* mimicry in the laboratory via reiterative backcrosses and production of "pseudo F_2" broods, the crosses required to produce recessive basal red would be highly unlikely in nature without isolation from backcrosses to standard *cydno* and/or much stronger mimetic selection on the ventral hindwing. In contrast, the hypothesized *cydno* × *melpomene* hybrid forerunners of *H. pachinus* faced jumping to an adaptive peak of black, yellow, and red (*H. hewitsoni* colors). It is worth noting that the latter two scale colors are recessive to their respective white and brown counterparts. Therefore, in any small and isolated hybrid populations that would have allowed the occurrence and fixation of forewing yellow homozygotes by genetic drift, the co-occurrence of the red basal pattern on the ventral hindwing could be expected. Moreover, mimicking the hindwing yellow band of *H. hewitsoni* required the removal of all those nasty *galanthus* shutters (as just reviewed), and with them the genes epistatic or dominant to the basal red.

Shutter interaction and novelty

Without going into much further detail, it is worth repeating that peeling away these layers of interacting realizator genes, particularly on the ventral hindwing, would not have been possible without the serendipity of their independent assortment between *pachinus* and *cydno* and the communal sharing of the same toolbox for pattern generation across the MCS clade. By the same token, it is the independence of these unlinked realizator loci and the cell-autonomous nature of their effects across bold patches of wing surface that provide the creative power of the MCS toolbox. Virtually all departures from the common pattern themes within the *cydno* clade (e.g., *H. heurippa*, *H. timareta*, *H. pachinus*, *H. cydno weymeri* f. *gustavi*) can be explained by introgression of toolbox elements from *melpomene*. Reciprocally, several *melpomene* races show the clear influence of *cydno* in its adaptive tracking of *H. erato*. In addition to *vulcanus* and *cythera*, already mentioned, I regard the white forewing patches and black hindwing shutters of *m. plessini* and the all-black hindwing of *m. flagrans* as possible examples of *cydno* influence on *melpomene* pattern evolution.

WHAT ABOUT THE SILVANIFORMS?

Although species in the silvaniform group—the "S" in the MCS clade—are equal in unpalatability to other *Heliconius* (Chai 1990), their wing pattern evolution is asymmetrically influenced, much as Batesian mimics would be, by pattern themes of the more unpalatable ithomiine butterflies (see Mallet and Gilbert 1995, plate 1b). As a consequence, some silvaniforms superficially appear to be using quite different wing pattern rules from other members of the MCS clade. While genetic contact between this group and *melpomene/cydno* is probably very rare, F_1 crosses of *H. ismenius* and both *pachinus* and *cydno* suggest that they are using the same wing pattern toolbox (Gilbert 1984, plate 1A). A recent cross of Costa Rican *ismenius* and Ecuadorian *cydno* produced credible mimics of an Ecuadorian race of the pupal mating species *H. hecalesia* in the F_1 generation (plate 14.7, middle right panel). Needless to say, such quantum events, even though extremely rare, could move mimetic evolution along much more rapidly than gradual substitutions of new mutant alleles. Backcrosses of the F_1 males of this cross to pure *cydno* indicate the possibility of introgression between silvaniforms and *cydno/melpomene* (L. E. Gilbert, pers. obs.).

Although F_1 products of *melpomene* crosses with silvaniforms such as *H. hecale* (plate 14.1b) and *H. ethilla* (not shown) are known, successful backcrosses are not known to me. Yet the link between *cydno* and the silvaniforms could provide a route for *melpomene* genes to move into the silvaniforms. Expression of the red gene of *melpomene* in Costa Rican *H. hecale* (not shown) indicates that on the forewing, the homologue of the *cydno/melpomene* window/shutter system is restricted to a thin band just distal to the end of the discal cell (these hybrids were received from R. Boender, Butterfly World). Based on what one observes in *cydno* × *melpomene* pseudo F_2 broods (plate 14.7, top panel, f and h; note both forewing and hindwing), reducing the forewing window in ancestors of Costa Rican *hecale* would account for the expanded marginal zone expressing the standard nymphaline groundplan; that is, the white/yellow spots needed to mimic toxic ithomiines. Several *H. cydno* races in South America, including *weymeri* and *hermogenes*, may track the Apocynaceae-feeding ithomiine *Elzunia* (see Linares 1997a) by this mechanism. The variety of wing patterns in *H. ethilla, H. hecale, H. ismenius,* and especially the highly polymorphic *H. numata* (Brown and Benson 1975), suggests that the same wing pattern toolbox, along with introgression, may be functioning to create novelty, mimicry, and rapid diversification across the entire MCS clade.

Occurrence of Natural Introgression in *Heliconius*

Without doubt, the types of hybridization events herein described for synthetic hybrid zones do occur in nature (Ackery and Smites 1976, and, more recently, Mallet et al. 1999; M. Linares et al., unpub.). It is straightforward to map obvious *melpomene-cydno* hybrids occasionally captured by collectors. It is a more difficult challenge to locate, gain access to, and document currently active areas of introgression, given the extent of ongoing political turmoil in key Neotropical regions. Even then, the outcomes of introgression may be difficult to interpret without detailed study of both wing patterns and molecular traits.

From our observations of greenhouse hybridizations, it would appear that the forewing red gene and certain window/shutter schemes cross the *melpomene-cydno* boundary almost exclusively via initial mating of male *melpomene* with female *cydno*. In natural hybrid populations, recombinants from backcrosses to *cydno* that accidentally hit an adaptive peak for Müllerian protection and eventually come to characterize a race or species should (1) possess *cydno* mitochondrial DNA, (2) possess the larger size of *cydno*, typically 5–7% larger in terms of wing span than *melpomene,* and (3) show pattern elements of *melpomene* such as red forewing bands (e.g., the half-red forewing [plate 14.4, lower center panel] of *H. heurippa*), all-black forewing (e.g., the forewing of *H. cydno weymeri* f. *gustavi* [plate 14.7, lower left, b]) or the ventral hindwing closed forceps pattern described above (plate 14.7, top panel, d, e, f, and h). *H. cydno* races or populations that have taken adaptive steps in color pattern by this introgressive process may prove problematic for phylogenies based on mitochondrial DNA. Naturally occurring hybrid individuals originating in this manner often appear sufficiently distinct to be described as new species. This scenario, along with the systematist's null assumption that novel molecular and morphological trait combinations arise by new mutation, not by interspecific introgression, is the likely explanation for a recently described MCS species, *H. tristero* (Brower 1996a), which I refer to below as *H. (cydno) tristero* to reflect my opinion of its likely status.

If the *cydno* × *melpomene* F_1 males in the same hybrid zone backcross to pure *melpomene* females (e.g., plate 14.4, lower right panel), the segregates will have red forewings (the red gene being epistatic) and possess *melpomene* mtDNA. A phylogeny based on mtDNA would place such hybrids with *melpomene* and, if sufficiently distinct, they might be described as a new race, as was *H. melpomene mocoa,* an assumed mimic of *H. (c.) tristero* (Brower 1996a). Because it is straightforward to produce wing pattern/mtDNA combinations closely resembling Brower's new taxa, even using Costa Rican *cydno* and *melpomene* stocks, in synthetic hybrid zones, it is likely that the type specimens were generated in an area that favors occasional *melpomene* × *cydno* hybridization followed by occasional backcrosses by F_1 males to pure females of both *melpomene* and *cydno*. Thus, in the case of *(cydno) tristero* and *melpomene mocoa,* we probably have a case of *melpomene* forewing red patterns shared by common descent from F_1 fathers in an area of natural hybridization, rather than mimicry between *cydno* and *melpomene* (which is not known to exist).

A diagnostic clue to introgression is provided by Brower's (1996a) figures of the ventral forewing of these newly described taxa. First, *H. (c.) tristero,* in addition to the red band on the dorsal forewing, shows white scales ventral to the dorsal red, as seen in Brower's figure 7B. As mentioned previously, this is an exclusively *melpomene* trait. I obtain *cydno* similar to *H. (c.) tristero* only after repeated backcrossing to pure *cydno* females by successive generations of hybrid males that display *melpomene* forewing red. Eventually the forewing red is isolated in hybrids that are sufficiently "*cydno*" genomically to overcome Haldane's rule. At that point it is possible to cross male and female hybrids (a pseudo F_2 produced by crossing hybrid males and females once genomic compatibility is achieved with respect to the filtered traits) and observe the segregation of the recessive "white below red" forewing trait of *melpomene* in nearly pure *cydno* broods (e.g., plate 14.2a and b). Certainly, based on these considerations, the type specimen of *tristero* as described is not a simple first-generation backcross and would indicate prolonged contact between pure *cydno* females and hybrid males, as outlined above.

Other *cydno* group species and races discussed above that are good candidates to have been produced by hybridization have definable geographic ranges based on a century of collections. The lack of older collections of these new forms described by Brower suggests that he is describing the products of a relatively recent hybrid zone, possibly promoted by habitat change, as in the case of Colombian *H. cydno* (Linares 1989, 1997a). In the end, I doubt that both of these new taxa will coexist long as Müllerian partners of *erato* because of the problems of reproductive interference explained in the beginning of this chapter. This is another reason to suspect that *cydno tristero, melpomene mocoa,* and *H. erato dingus* represent a transient mimetic triangle maintained by introgression. If and when *cydno* mitochondria go extinct in the *H. c. tristero* system, *H. m. mocoa* may live up to its new status as a race tracking *H. erato.* Perhaps *H.c.w.* f. *gustavi* (plate 14.7, lower left panel, b) flew briefly with a parallel *melpomene* "race" (which shared a

Lawrence E. Gilbert

common hybrid male ancestor) before the latter became extinct in the Cali region of Colombia, where Mauricio Linares studies a *cydno* hybrid zone.

We have seen that striking and novel phenotypes can be generated in hybrid zones between such genomically close taxa as *cydno galanthus* and *(cydno) pachinus*. The tracks of introgression between species can be subtle, yet unmistakable once recognized. Thus, further understanding of the developmental genetic toolbox for MCS pattern along the lines described in this chapter is required to search properly for and detect the possible mimetic steps that have been enabled by this process in natural populations. That interspecific gene exchange can account for rather subtle mimetic differences between nearby races of a *Heliconius* species was first shown by measuring elements of wing pattern in greenhouse populations of *H. cydno* introgressed with *H. melpomene* and then by discriminant function analysis to compare experimental hybrids with wild *H. cydno weymeri* and *cydnides* (Linares 1989).

So far, all comparisons of experimentally produced hybrids, natural hybrids, and naturally occurring mimetic patterns of various MCS races suggest that major evolutionary advances in wing pattern during the history of the *Heliconius* MCS clade have been based on variation arising from introgression rather than de novo from mutation.

DISCUSSION: EVOLUTIONARY QUESTIONS

In this chapter I have described a hypothesis of wing pattern genetics and mimetic evolution in *Heliconius* based on empirical observations of hybridization within the *melpomene/cydno*/silvaniform clade of *Heliconius*. These species apparently share a "toolbox" for generating wing pattern, which I intentionally described with minimal reference to other schemes for describing the genetics and wing pattern development of *Heliconius*. To harmonize this hypothesis with prior hypotheses and systems of gene nomenclature, while important, would require a much longer and potentially more confusing text than the present chapter. I described my concept of pattern determination in *Heliconius* in terms of developmental genetic hypotheses based on *Drosophila*, with two metaphorical aids. First, I compared major pattern-determining zones of *Heliconius* wings to computer program windows to explain a possible way in which regulatory gene hierarchies might operate independently in different wing compartments or lineage restriction zones. Second, I described these zones in terms of actual windows on walls and shutters on windows as an aid in visualizing their simplicity and elegance. Both of these analogies highlight the ease with which extensive qualitative pattern variety can arise through introgression. Specific ways in which the toolbox/introgression hypothesis assists in interpreting the wing patterns of known species, races, and forms of the MCS clade were discussed in reference to particular wing surfaces. Therefore, it is finally possible to return to the more general evolutionary questions, posed earlier, about *Heliconius* wing patterns.

1. WHY ARE SO MANY WING PATTERNS AVAILABLE TO *Heliconius?*

As I pointed out in the introduction to this chapter, the focal question has been, "Given a given amount of available genetic variation, why does so much variety evolve?" While this is still a central problem that could occupy us for many more decades, in this chapter I shifted focus to the question, "Why does *Heliconius* seem to have such a great supply of variation in the first place?" My own perspective began to shift in the early 1980s. Working with synthetic hybrid zones, I found that the sum total of the patterns that exist over the entire geographic range of the MCS clade are but a fraction of the myriad patterns potentially available to that clade even within parts of its range (e.g., plates 14.4, 14.7, and 14.8). In the MCS clade, novel patterns are generated through introgression at rates unimaginable by mutation. Thus, this chapter has been focused on how regulatory genes that establish the identity of autonomous scale cell lineages early in development could account for the remarkable capacity of a few genes to generate so much qualitative variety in pattern. It is the relative allocation to this particular mode of gene governance over scale pattern that may set *Heliconius*, and species such as *Papilio dardanus,* apart from other butterflies.

However, just as genotype variation in a population depends on allelic variation at genetic loci, the mechanisms of developmental genetics and introgression that I describe depend on hybridization between already present, distinctly patterned, species or races. Furthermore, just as standard genetic recombination can produce greater variety if frequency-dependent selection or heterosis maintains genetic polymorphism in a population, the creative potential of introgression in this case depends at some level on the diversity of wing patterns maintained in local *Heliconius* communities. But, as discussed earlier, wing pattern diversity in a community depends on habitat heterogeneity and external sources of pattern variation, which brings us full circle.

Novel developmental genetic mechanisms, on the one hand, and rules for the diversification and storage of novel pattern programs in local communities, on the other, are adequate to explain why *Heliconius* has available a greater source of pattern variation to recombine through introgression than do many other nymphaline taxa, such as *Precis* (e.g., Hafernik 1982). However, since novel wing pattern genotypes arise through introgression between already diverse races or species, as we have seen, how does a new variant emerge from the dizzying milieu of patterns in a hybrid zone to achieve recognition as a wing pattern race? Ultimately it does appear, as Mallet, Turner, and others have suggested, that processes such as the shifting balance are needed at some stage to preserve novel genotypes in nature by increasing their frequencies to the level of recognized taxa. These taxa may later hybridize to fuel further diversification through introgressive recombination.

Once again, such lines of logic bring us full circle in terms of answering the question of why *Heliconius* seems to have more wing pattern variation available. This is because the mechanisms and processes discussed promote one another, and positive feedback systems or cycles tend to be circular. While many other butterfly genera, including other members of the heliconiine tribe, use the same pigments to color their wing scales, share some common mechanisms for genetic control of some aspects of scale pattern, have diverse, mimetic species and hybrid zones (e.g., *Limenitis:* Platt 1983), and are exposed to the evolutionary forces of drift and selection, they certainly cannot match the punctuated nature of pattern evolution seen on *Heliconius* wings (Turner 1983), nor match the rate of diversification of that genus.

What traits of *Heliconius* might account for its exceptional capacity to generate biodiversity (as illustrated in plate 14.8)? I argued in the introduction to this chapter that the unique trait of pupal mating might promote local diversity, one of the key ingredients of the feedback system envisioned. Another unique trait of *Heliconius,* adult pollen feeding, by promoting individual longevity and residence time, allows local populations to persist at extremely low densities (Gilbert 1972, 1991). Such resilience of local demes, in the context of metapopulations in a hybrid zone, should improve the opportunity for shifting balance to work effectively. However, while features of adult life history probably play a role, they represent quantitative rather than qualitative departures from what we know about related butterflies. I must conclude, therefore, that the catalyst for setting off the complex feedback cycles that sequentially depend on, then generate, the pattern diversity found in *Heliconius* is to be found in the toolbox of developmental genetics as revealed by studying the MCS clade.

2. Why Are So Few Wing Patterns Actually Successful in Nature?

There are several possible answers to this question, such as "few of the extant racial varieties are able to form zones of contact in nature." While that is true, synthetic introgression among just a few adjacent races of *cydno* and *melpomene,* which can and do hybridize, generates much more variety of pattern than occurs in nature in races and species of that clade. For example, plate 14.4 (upper left panel) shows a small sample of possible varieties that quite likely have occurred at one time or another in central Costa Rica. The fact that the realized pattern diversity of described taxa is well below what we know is possible, given the potential of known hybrid zones, presents an interesting question. It is abundantly clear that even in relatively short evolutionary time frames, any lack of pattern variety is *not* due to developmental genetic constraints on pattern evolution!

There are a few more possible reasons why so few of the possible *Heliconius* wing patterns are found to exist in nature. The first is a sensory bias in predators: those patterns that survive are the best signals to predators in terms of recognition and learning. This hypothesis is certainly testable, since both the relevant predators and the extent of heritable pattern variation are known. Mimicry rings may be constrained to a few modal color patterns because of the way light environments in different habitats interact with the ability of predators to perceive, discriminate, and learn visual signals.

Second, adaptive peaks may be limited. In most areas at any given time, common aposematic species are few, and those few would create a large selection gradient in favor of a small fraction of possible hybrid patterns. This hypothesis could be tested, for example, by introducing identical interracial F_1 *cydno* into several isolated sites, each harboring abundant *Passiflora* hosts, naive birds, and no other *Heliconius*. Each site would receive prior releases of model phenotypes (different for each site) to experimentally create different adaptive peaks. The variable F_2 population emerging at each site should evolve a different monomorphic pattern predicted by the experimental model for that area. Such an experiment could be conducted in conjunction with the use of *Heliconius cydno* in biocontrol of the pest liana of Hawaiian forests, *Passiflora mollissima* (Waage et al. 1981).

Third, the rules of meiosis, epistasis, and dominance may ensure that in a hybrid zone some phenotypes will outnumber others, all other things being equal. One possibility is that isolated hybrid populations may be initiated in disturbed patches temporarily free of predator pressure. Later, when predators colonized the patch, they would quickly learn the most common phenotype, which would thus form its own adaptive peak (e.g., Kapan 1998). This possibility is testable by reviewing the genetic rules that govern pattern in interracial and interspecific crosses and checking whether the successful patterns tend to be those that would be the most abundant in the absence of selection. Note that in a typical hybrid zone between mimetic races with predators constantly present, novel alleles flowing into an area are more likely to persist if they are recessive (e.g., Mallet et al. 1990), just the reverse of the scenario suggested.

Finally, areas ideal for the operation of evolutionary processes such as biotic drift or shifting balance may be limited. Geomorphology and climatic history determine where patterns can be stable and where conditions will promote revolution.

3. What Are the Likely Circumstances for Cross-Species Recombination in Nature?

While I have never witnessed the process of interspecific hybridization in nature, I have seen areas where hybrids have been collected or observed, I have collected wild hybrids, and I know what is required to establish synthetic hybrid zones in a greenhouse. As long as both species populations are relatively equal in density, it is actually possible to keep *cydno* and *melpomene* in the same 13 ft × 21 ft greenhouse for years without the occurrence of interspecific courtship or mating (L. E. Gilbert, pers. obs.). My method of obtaining interspecific matings involves releasing a virgin female into an insectary containing males of a second species. The question, then, becomes, when or where does such a numerical and sex ratio imbalance occur in natural communities of *Heliconius?*

In lowland rainforests, *Heliconius* exist in habitat patches formed by disturbance gaps. These gaps are colonized first by host plants, then by the butterflies. Populations thrive, then disappear as succession converts the gaps back to shaded forest. A large gap might allow a second-growth species such as *melpomene* to thrive, but differential dispersal by females (Gilbert 1991) could produce local male bias. Meanwhile, in a *cydno* population that typically has densities on the order of 1–2 adults per hectare (Gilbert 1991), it is not difficult to imagine that a virgin female *cydno* might wander onto the edge of a forest gap and be surrounded by male *melpomene* seeking to mate.

Differential colonization and extinction in remote unoccupied habitat patches constitutes a more likely crucible for interspecies crosses. If *melpomene* arrived in a small mountain valley a month before the first dispersing *cydno* female parent, then no mature *cydno* males would greet first-generation virgin *cydno* females in that patch, even if they emerged with cohort brothers (it typically takes 72 hours before males are competent to mate). Such females very likely would be mated by mature *melpomene* males. It seems likely that forest fragmentation, either natural or anthropogenic, could provide the conditions for MCS clade species to exchange the contents of their genetic toolboxes. Indeed, the areas that show the most active production of novel patterns in *Heliconius* consist of steep, dissected montane landscapes where isolation, natural disturbance, and funnel points for insects dispersing between valleys provide the ingredients for bringing this patchy hybrid zone scenario to life (e.g., Linares 1997b).

4. What Are the Relative Contributions of Mutation and Introgression to Pattern Evolution?

My answer to this question is obvious from the topic and content of this chapter. With respect to mutations, I have cultivated *Heliconius* populations for 29 years and conducted long-term mark-release-recapture studies in the field. I estimate that I have personally examined several tens of thousands of *Heliconius* in that time. Although I have found several interesting (but non-transmissible) homeotic alterations of the wing pattern, I have spotted only three apparent mutants, a white-eyed *H. cydno;* a white-banded *H. charitonius,* which appears to be an alteration of color, but not pattern; and one *H. cydno* with a heritable modification of the forewing shutter. D. D. Kapan (pers. comm.) has noted two dominant color mutants (yellow to white in *H. eleuchia*) at the same location in Western Ecuador. Interpreting this finding as one event with two offspring captured in Kapan's total sampling effort indicates an approximate 1:4,000 probability for the occurrence of this mutation.

Virtually all novel and heritable alterations of wing scale pattern seen in my cultures over three decades have proved to be the results of introgression, as discussed in this chapter. In the field or in museum collections, and with the exception of nonheritable developmental anomalies, I have yet to see a phenotype of the MCS clade that is not clearly interpretable as a product of introgression between adjacent races or between sympatric species. Mallet et al. (1999) have documented the fact that hybridization is common in *Heliconius.* Yet mutations of genes affecting wing pattern do occur. Why don't mutations constitute a significant source of adaptive variation in this genus?

To answer this question, it is useful to consider the probable fate of pattern mutants in natural populations. Because of their long adult life span and sedentary behavior, *Heliconius* are capable of persisting as small, local demes at densities of less than one adult per hectare (Gilbert 1991). Benson's (1972) experimental studies of selection suggest that if dominant or epistatic mutants for pattern novelty arose in such small populations, they would be removed rapidly by birds. During episodes of environmental change, predator pressure may be relaxed (see Turner 1984). But even in this context, pattern mutants that are recessive are likely to be lost by genetic drift before they can support an episode of rapid pattern evolution. If a novel recessive pattern allele were fixed by drift in a small local population during an episode with no predator pressure, it is possible that the entire population would quickly be eliminated by birds, which, having learned other aposematic patterns elsewhere, would recolonize the patch and begin to sample unrecognized patterns.

Thus, one compelling feature of introgression in the system described here is that the variation it generates is renewable and continues generating macromutation-like variants in spite of genetic drift, strong selection by local predators, or sequential combinations of both. Moreover, these "macromutants" are likely to be compatible with any MCS "operating system." Clearly, introgressive recombination would be orders of magnitude more likely than basic mutational processes to generate the type of genetic variation necessary for rapid adaptive responses to shifts in adaptive peaks for predator protection. Hybridization as a source of novelty has been reviewed by Maynard Smith (1983), and hybridization as a source of adaptive variation in insects has been suggested for *Drosophila* (Lewontin and Birch 1966) and for *Heliconius* (Linares 1989, 1997b).

5. How Might Evolving *Heliconius* Jump from One Adaptive Peak to Another without Crossing Fitness Valleys Below?

Single-allele changes in regulatory genes (such as those controlling shutters and shutter color in the MCS clade) can create strikingly novel patterns. Because major pattern themes are varied qualitatively by so few genes in this clade, hybridization of pattern genotypes having strikingly different phenotypes can produce offspring resembling macromutation-like variants. Only a few such changes can instantly "beam" hybrids onto or near new peaks of mimetic protection without necessitating gradual evolution that puts between-peak variants at risk. Sheppard (1962) developed such ideas in reference to "major gene" mutation.

Examples of the potential of the MCS toolbox to promote colonization of new peaks of protection can be found in synthetic hybrid zones. In one example, only two steps were required for hybridization of distinct *cydno* races to produce a near-perfect mimic of a toxic moth (plate 14.7, lower left panel) and in another, the F_1 of a *cydno* × *ismenius* cross show close mimicry of *H. hecalesia,* an ESS clade species with a pattern distinctly different from the parents of the cross (plate 14.7, middle right panel). These are but two of many examples that have I have noticed in the course of watching hybrid populations.

I previously mentioned examples from nature in which mimetic adaptation by both *cydno* and *melpomene* may have been enabled by genes crossing the species boundary. Specifically, I hypothesize that the steps that allowed *cydno* to rapidly colonize the black forewing *erato* peak of protection in Colombia (Linares 1989, 1997a) and to obtain the variation that allows some populations of *Heliconius* to simultaneously track two distinct Müllerian co-models as polymorphic populations under frequency-dependent selection in Ecuador (Kapan 1998) arose from introgression with *melpomene.*

6. Does One Clade Typically Drive the Evolution of Novel Patterns?

Müllerian pairs from the pupal mating ESS clade and the MCS clade are known to coevolve locally with respect to polygenic adjustments in pattern elements, such as the width of the hindwing window in *melpomene* and *erato* (Gilbert 1983). However, the pattern variety among races of *erato* (ESS) and *melpomene* (MCS) and the precise mimetic tracking of one by the other clearly shows that novel steps occur and that mimetic tracking ensues. The question is whether novel steps are taken by an ESS species in some places while comparable steps are taken by its counterpart MCS species in others.

At least two ESS species do not appear to be comodels driving pattern evolution among other *Heliconius*. First, *H. charitonius,* the most palatable *Heliconius* species tested by Chai (1990), is remarkably uniform over its range, from Texas and Florida to Panama, and does not participate with other *Heliconius* in mimicry. (In Peru, a sibling species of *H. charitonius* converges on the ithomiine *Elzunia*.) Likewise, the pupal mating species *H. hecalesia,* along with *H. hecale,* converges on the pattern of the much more unpalatable ithomiines (Chai 1990).

These species aside, there are several reasons to implicate the ESS clade as the principal generator of novelty. First, to the degree that females of pupal mating species lack the ability to choose mates, sexual selection is minimized as a conservative force maintaining wing pattern. (In contrast to MCS females, which mate multiply, ESS females are typically monogamous, usually mating only once at eclosion.) Second, pupal mating species, in comparison to the MCS clade, form larger and more gregarious nocturnal roosting groups (L. E. Gilbert, pers. obs.). Dense pre-roosting congregations might increase the apparent local density of a novel trait to local predators and promote its establishment (Mallet 1986b; Mallet and Gilbert 1995). Third, pupal mating species often occur in marginal habitats on the edge of *Heliconius* distributions, where they can evolve novelty by mutation without the swamping effects of gene flow.

Fourth, the group of ESS species that includes *sapho, hewitsoni,* and *eleuchia* utilizes the woody Astrophea group *Passiflora,* and all deposit large clusters of eggs on new shoots, which appear in pulses and grow very rapidly. Consequently, in these species, large cohorts of new adults often pulse into local concentrations of their older kin, which themselves have previously emerged in a particular host patch (Kapan 1998; Deinert, chap. 5 in this volume; L. E. Gilbert, pers. obs.). This population structure provides an unusual opportunity for local inbreeding, which in turn would promote the rapid karyotype evolution in this group (see Brown et al. 1992) as well as fixation of rare combinations of mutant alleles. The result might be rapid production of genetically isolated species with novel karyotypes and wing patterns (e.g., *H. eleuchia*). Moreover, species of this group are unique among *Heliconius* in their "hyperactive" sequestration of host cyanogens (Engler 1998) and may be less dependent on adult pollen feeding for unpalatability than is assumed for most *Heliconius* (Gilbert 1991). Occasional large local congregations, unpalatability, and a high potential for inbreeding are possible ingredients for the evolution of pattern novelty without invoking introgression.

The working hypothesis emerging from these considerations is that populations of the ESS clade are more likely to establish new adaptive peaks for warning pattern autonomously than are those of the MCS group. Species of the pupal mating group tend to be well isolated from one another, often by chromosome differences, and thus form, as *sapho* and *hewitsoni* illustrate in Costa Rica, stable templates for their Müllerian partners.

Whether MCS *Heliconius* have unique tools in their wing pattern toolbox is a question deserving of intensive study. Because of the frequent failure of interspecific crosses within the ESS clade, it is more difficult to make progress in defining the nature of shared pattern genes in this group. It is worth noting that Turner (1981, 1983), in applying Haldane's sieve to polarize pattern genes as traits for constructing parallel phylogenies of *erato* and *melpomene,* predicted that both species descended from ancestors possessing yellow bands (= windows) on both forewing and hindwing. This prediction, along with the fact that it is possible to obtain this predicted phenotype at the bottom of an epistatic pecking order of pattern genes in crosses of *cydno* and *pachinus* (e.g., plate 14.4, upper right panel, g), suggests that similar underlying mechanisms are at work in the ESS and MCS clades. Yet, from the crosses I have conducted (not shown here) or reviewed in the literature involving *erato* races, as well as those involving different species at the species/race boundary (e.g., *erato* and *himera,* Jiggins and McMillan 1997), it is apparent that some of the shutter tools in the wing pattern toolbox of the MCS clade represent developmental innovations unique to the *cydno/melpomene* part of that clade. I suggest that these innovations may have allowed the MCS group to diversify rapidly against the template of ESS-generated adaptive peaks typically characterized by warning patterns unique to *Heliconius*. To understand the level at which coevolution might operate in these parallel radiations, it will be helpful to know to what degree the ESS side has taken the evolutionary initiative and what aspects of the parallel wing pattern evolution of these clades have been based on similar developmental genetic systems throughout their joint histories.

7. Does *Heliconius* Possess Unique Developmental Genetic Mechanisms for Generating Wing Pattern?

It has long been assumed that the diversity of lepidopteran wing patterns must have arisen from very different developmental mechanisms, which in some cases can be seen competing for space on the same wing (e.g., see plate 14.7, lower right panel). The most elegant summary of the early literature in this regard is that of Munroe (1983), beautifully expanded for butterfly patterns by Nijhout (1991). Viewed in the broader context of lepidopteran wing patterns, *Heliconius* seems exceptional only in the degree to which important aspects of wing pattern, such as key pattern boundaries, appear to be determined early in development by putting scale type specification under the control of regulatory genes, which, in turn, respond to compartments or other lineage restriction boundaries.

Koch et al. (1998) and ffrench-Constant and Koch (chap. 13 in this volume), working on sexually dimorphic *Papilio*, suggest one alternative way in which genes might control qualitative changes in wing pattern. A single gene, by controlling the production of hormones that regulate the rate of scale maturation relative to circulating pigment precursors, can change scale pigmentation from yellow to melanic over most of the wing in females. However, sexual mosaics and gynandromorphs in *Papilio* indicate that if scale precursor cells are genetically male, threshold responses to the same signals are below that required for melanization. I have proposed in this chapter that in *Heliconius,* such scale cell lineage autonomy can also arise more generally through somatically or germ-line heritable changes in the settings of regulatory genes (realizators) in early development, providing another way in which a few genes can govern entire pattern fields of the wing. This possibility is supported by recent molecular studies of the expression of *Drosophila* regulatory genes during butterfly wing development, as reviewed by Brakefield and Monteiro (chap. 12 in this volume). They point out that mutations in such a gene might alter, for example, whether the eyespots they study are expressed dorsally and ventrally. In spite of the elegance of this scenario and its recognition of regulatory switches that govern major pattern fields, as described for *Heliconius,* it cannot fully contend with the novelty and quantum variety one must consider in this genus.

Window boundaries in *Heliconius* (plate 14.6) are apparently determined by a primary, nonplastic pattern program similar to that which determines the positions of eyespot foci that are sources of morphogens. Second-order patterns are created as scale cells mature differently according to local concentrations of such morphogens on the pupal wings of *Precis* (Nijhout 1980a, 1980b; Bard and French 1984). Primary patterns of elements such as eyespot foci are established by early-acting regulatory genes (see review in Brakefield and Monteiro, chap. 12 in this volume). The possibility of homology between *Heliconius* window boundaries and certain eyespot foci in *Precis* is supported by the expression pattern of Hedgehog signaling protein on the hindwing of *Precis* (Keys et al. 1999). In addition to helping to define a major eyespot center in a standard nymphaline groundplan species, Hedgehog defines a boundary across the pupal wing that, in relation to wing venation, corresponds closely to the anterior boundary of the hindwing window of *H. cydno.* It should now be possible to establish whether window boundaries in *Heliconius* are essentially eyespot foci stretched into lines, rather than lineage restriction boundaries established in earlier development, as I have proposed.

In *Precis,* and in other nymphaline groundplan species, scales developing in zones around eyespot foci on the pupal wing are developmentally plastic with respect to thresholds of response to morphogen concentrations, and thus plastic with respect to abiotic factors such as cold shock as well (Nijhout 1984). The idea that a gene that changed the sensitivity of scale precursor cells to some diffusing morphogen (ffrench-Constant and Koch, chap. 13 in this volume) could change a pattern boundary agrees with my hypothesis for how the proximal boundary of the forewing shutter (plate 14.6b) is determined in the MCS clade of *Heliconius.* In contrast to the forewing window-wall boundary nearby (plate 14.6e), which apparently is determined in early embryogenesis, the forewing shutter's distal boundary shows plasticity with respect to its precise position and sharpness (L. E. Gilbert, pers. obs.). This and other elements, such as the white marginal spots (previously mentioned), suggest that in many aspects of pattern, *Heliconius* differs in degree, but not in kind, from other nymphaline butterflies. Indeed, expression patterns of the *Drosophila distal-less* gene in *Heliconius* wing discs are virtually identical to those seen in *Precis* (S. Carroll and J. Gates, pers. comm., and see review in French and Monteiro 1994).

8. How Did the Toolbox Originate?

Almost certainly, what I have been metaphorically calling "the wing pattern toolbox" involved an innovation with respect to how and when in development scale cell fates are determined such that changes in few regulatory genes might have large qualitative effects on wing pattern. The question of what precisely these innovations might have been may be revealed by investigations of wing pattern development in *Philaethria,* a heliconiine that displays open windows of green wing membrane characterized by highly reduced scales. However, within these "windows" on both forewing and hindwing, these paddle-like structures are basically type I (yellow/white) scales (L. E. Gilbert, pers. obs.). Thus, *Philaethria* wings show important traits one might expect of a proto-*Heliconius* wing pattern. With its closest relatives, *Dryas* and *Dryadula, Philaethria* constitutes an outgroup to *Heliconius* (Penz 1999). *Dryas* and *Dryadula* show type III scales over all window regions and would therefore provide useful comparisons for any developmental studies of *Philaethria.* The evolution of the genes that switched the groundplan of the windows from type III to type I scales in *Philaethria* may represent the first steps in creating the toolbox shared by *Eueides, Neruda, Laparus,* and *Heliconius,* all genera that separate from other Heliconiiti with respect to their potential for evolving wing pattern variety under mimetic selection.

Does the genus *Heliconius* represent an additional adaptive radiation based on some further improvement in the contents of the wing pattern toolbox? I think not. I have argued elsewhere that pollen feeding represents the crucial adaptive zone for this genus (Gilbert 1991), and that this innovation led to unpalatability and selected for adult behavioral traits that in turn led to population structures that promoted niche diversification.

Early in the history of *Heliconius,* the wing pattern toolbox might have gradually diversified through mutation. However, if we are indeed dealing with a simple set of on/off switches that govern a cascade of regulatory genes in a few sectors of the wing, and those at the bottom are in charge of only three scale types, the major ways in which species and races now differ may have been quickly accumulated among early-evolving species of the genus. At that point, we can imagine that hybridization and introgression would have begun to accelerate in importance and quickly would have replaced mutation as the proximate generator of novel pattern genotypes in *Heliconius.*

The recent history of diversification of the genus *Heliconius* does, I think, reflect two intertwined adaptive zones. The first of these is based on the habit of pupal mating and its indirect but positive effects on wing pattern diversification (as detailed for the ESS clade above). The second, and to me the most amazing, adaptive zone, reflected in the adaptive radiation of intrageneric mimicry by the *melpomene/cydno* group and of ithomiine mimicry by *cydno*/silvaniforms of the MCS clade, is based on an upgrade of the window/shutter system (it is now more flexible, and there is a shutter color option). This upgrade further accelerated the rate at which hybridization and introgression could facilitate rapid evolution of wing pattern in the tracking of comodels. For lack of access, I have ignored the so-called "primitive species" of *Heliconius* (e.g., Brower 1994b), all from South America. This clade may be important in testing the hypotheses developed in this chapter.

SUMMARY AND CONCLUSION

Genes that regulate the differentiation of scales and patterns of scale types within developmental compartments or lineage restriction zones of *Heliconius* wings account for major adaptive changes in aposematic pattern between races and species in at least one clade of these Neotropical mimetic insects. The addition of early-acting regulatory genes, possibly even homeotics, to the toolbox of pattern genetics may be one way in which bold, qualitative steps in morphology and behavior evolve in this genus. There is no evidence that mutation has played a role recently in providing the variation needed for mimetic evolution in the MCS clade. Given the known rules of the wing pattern toolbox described above and assuming interracial and

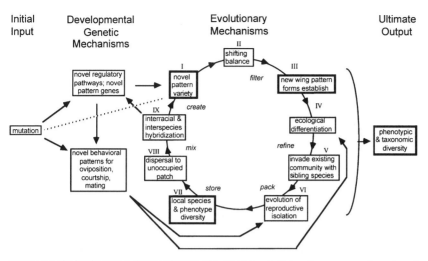

Figure 14.2 The biodiversity cycle for *Heliconius*. This diagram summarizes the sequence of events and processes that constitute a positive feedback loop generating both wing pattern diversity and species diversity in *Heliconius*. The unique thing about the *Heliconius* system, as proposed in this chapter, is the *creation* of novel wing pattern variants when genes of the MCS "toolbox" recombine by introgression in hybrid zones (step I). Co-occurring evolutionary processes of migration, drift, and selection, summarized here as "shifting balance" (step II), which *filter* the available variants; geographic differentiation in allopatry or parapatry (step III), which *refines* the genomic correlates of a newly established pattern (step IV), and later the evolution of reproductive isolation (step VI) complete the prerequisites for *packing* into an existing community (steps V–VII). These mechanisms have been previously proposed with the assumption that mutation alone (indicated by the dotted line) produces step I. Major innovations in courtship and mating (e.g., pupal mating), or in behaviors, such as larval host preference, or in habitat preferences promote the evolution of niche differences (step IV) as well as reproductive isolation (step VI) and lead to local saturation in coexisting species and mimicry rings. This local genetic diversity is *stored* in local communities (step VII), from which individuals occasionally disperse into hybrid zones to mate with and *mix* genes with those of individuals whose source populations experienced a different history (steps VIII and IX). Not shown are factors that constrain local diversity (relevant to steps II–IV and VI–VII), such as microhabitat and host plant diversity and predator-imposed selection for Müllerian convergence. While the packing of species and wing patterns is limited locally, diversity builds among areas so that the cycle described continues to increase the overall biodiversity of the genus with respect to taxonomic as well as phenotypic diversification. Bold squares enclose the major products of the processes described, from novel patterns in hybrid zones to their ultimate output: genus-wide biodiversity.

interspecific introgression, it is possible to account for all the wing patterns so far seen in this group, including many that have not been seen in nature.

In *Heliconius*, cycles of population differentiation, diversification, hybridization, and introgressive recombination constitute positive feedback systems in which diversity of genotypes promotes diversity of races and species, and vice versa (fig. 14.2). Yet, at any instant, only so many patterns are displayed by a given species or clade, in spite of the fact that the feedback system described has been at work through the much of the history of the genus. Where are all the past patterns generated by this process? They may have been lost, like alleles that have been lost through drift or by selection. Another possibility is that these patterns are present but suppressed, and are recovered only as recombinants in hybrid zones. Thus we expect to, and do, recover patterns that may have been part of past mimicry systems, as suggested by Linares (1997a). But it is also possible that the wing pattern toolbox, at least as described for the MCS clade, has the potential to generate virtually any known pattern from the few basic components described: three scale types, displayed as components of alternative patterns that compete to varying degrees with ancestral nymphaline pattern elements on compartments of the wing. All that is required to generate many basic patterns of this clade is the presence of several distinct species capable of occasionally exchanging genes, and that's what we usually have.

Finally, it seems likely that developmental genetic innovations similar to those that promote novelty in *Heliconius* wings, but which instead affect more cryptic attributes of behavior or morphology, may underlie intrageneric adaptive radiation in many groups of organisms. Increasing the number of coexisting species per genus is a major way in which species diversity increases toward tropical latitudes. Therefore, the genus *Heliconius* is an ideal model system for helping us to understand how such global patterns come about, and, as figure 14.2 suggests, provides an opportunity to develop an integrative theory of biodiversity.

ACKNOWLEDGMENTS

I thank M. Linares for many useful discussions and for the opportunity to see and work with the Colombian races of *H. cydno* early in the gestation of these ideas (1984–1986). K. Brown has been a much-appreciated long-term source of general encouragement for my work with *Heliconius*. The work of, and personal contacts with, W. Benson, P. Sheppard, and J. Turner stimulated my initial interest in some of the problems discussed here. Thanks to J. Mallet, O. McMillan, and C. Jiggins for sharing unpublished manuscripts and for their comments on this manuscript. I thank the many colleagues in developmental biology who provided useful feedback, education, and encouragement; especially S. B. Carroll, F. Nijhout, K. Kalthoff, S. M. Cohen, and S. Dyby. Reviewers R. ffrench-Constant and A. Monteiro made very useful suggestions and criticisms. I am especially grateful to D. Kapan, C. Penz, P. Schappert, and M. Cardoso for extensive help in improving the manuscript and for useful discussions, and to S. Bramblett and P. Schappert for help with computer graphics. I thank the dozens of hapless visitors to my lab, colleagues, students, and seminar audiences who listened patiently while I tried to explain these ideas. Questions and stimulating feedback from these folks helped me form the approach taken in this chapter. Research and collecting permits from the Costa Rican Park Service and Vida Silvestre and importation permits from USDA APHIS made these studies possible. Greenhouse facilities were developed under NSF grants DEB-79060332 and BSR-8315399 and with the support of the University of Texas, Austin.

CHAPTER 15

Mechanistic Studies of Butterfly Adaptations

Ward B. Watt

Adaptation is the central, causal concept in Darwin's (1859) argument for evolution by natural selection, encompassing diverse aspects of organisms' suitedness to their environments (Feder and Watt 1992; Watt 2000). Butterflies are excellent systems in which to analyze how adaptation works. Two centuries of study have produced a wealth of background knowledge of butterflies' ecology, distributions, and behavior. Their abundance, manageable physical sizes, and relative ease of laboratory rearing support the use of diverse techniques, from molecular to ecological, for the rigorous study of their adaptations. Further, they have many adaptive challenges in common with other creatures; for example, their need for energy-intensive locomotion is shared with other animals, and their need for water-economizing gas exchange through surface apertures is shared with plant leaves. Thus, if butterfly study yields specific answers to questions about adaptation, these answers may generalize readily to other creatures.

Genetic variation is prerequisite for adaptive evolution, but the study of adaptation only begins there. Adaptive differences among genetic variants are differences in how those variants' phenotypes perform biological tasks in their habitats. Fitness differences are the effects of performance differences on reproductive success. Natural selection, thus summarized, is a recursion of four stages (Feder and Watt 1992):

1. genotype → phenotype, in which adaptive variation may alter metabolism or development
2. phenotype → performance, in which variation may be adaptive at many phenotypic levels

3. performance → fitness, in which survivorship and fecundity, the demographic results of adaptive performance, sum or integrate into fitness over the life cycle
4. fitness → genotype, in which genotypic fitness interacts with random genetic drift, inbreeding, and so forth to yield genotype frequencies for the next generation

Distinguishing adaptation, as performance in stages 1 and 2, from the resulting fitness that arises in stage 3 dispels confusion about the logic of evolution (Watt 1994, 2000). Adaptation is not ubiquitous: variants may be neutral, or constraints on adaptive precision may arise from factors such as geometry or history (Gould and Lewontin 1979; Watt 1995a). But, with these caveats in mind, biologists are paying renewed attention to the nature of adaptation (Rose and Lauder 1996; Watt 2000).

The method of identified genes makes use of genetic variation for the rigorous study of adaptation (Watt 2000). It works with genes of known molecular and physiological function: variants of such genes are used to assess how genetic changes in phenotype do or do not change organismal performances, and thus do or do not lead to fitness differences. This method often uses variants of genes encoding metabolic enzymes—allozymes—but genes encoding other functions can now also be studied in this way (e.g., Brakefield and Monteiro, chap. 12 in this volume).

Evolutionary study of allozymes was at first embroiled in the "neutralist-selectionist" controversy. This fruitless debate was based on the statistical study of allozyme frequencies in population samples, often without relation to biogeography or population structure, let alone comparative ecological or functional study. At this level of abstraction, opposed population genetic processes (e.g., the infinite alleles neutral model and fluctuating environment selection models) predict similar patterns of variant frequencies (e.g., Gillespie 1978, 1991; Rothman and Templeton 1980; Watt 1985a, 1995a). Careful study of allozyme patterns in nymphaline and satyrine butterflies has shown that much genetic complexity can arise from the interactions of factors such as genetic drift, migration, natural selection, and vicariant range changes (Mueller et al. 1985; Brussard et al. 1989; Baughman et al. 1990; Britten and Brussard 1992; Goulson 1993). To see which of these causes are operating in actual cases, the method of identified genes is essential.

My colleagues and I use identified gene variants to probe adaptations from molecular to ecological levels, using as test systems the sulfur butterflies, *Colias* (Pieridae). This chapter aims to show both the analytical power of this approach and its support for new syntheses and generalizations. We will have to consider and integrate diverse biological specialties, but the resulting understanding will be worth the effort.

ADAPTIVE PERFORMANCES ARE UNIFIED
BY METABOLIC BIOENERGETICS

BIOENERGETICS AS AN ADAPTIVE CONTEXT

If we are to study adaptive processes in a generalizable way, we need common contexts in which to test phenotypes' adaptiveness against alternatives—or else we will only assemble lists of specific results, with no chance for general principles to emerge. In Endler's review of studies of natural selection (1986, table 5.1), 80% of studies in which a cause of selection was identified used bioenergetics—that is, the flow of energy through organisms—as the context for evaluating the adaptiveness of variation.

Bioenergetics is implemented by temperature-dependent mechanisms of metabolism or physiology, which underlie organismal performances (Watt 1985b, 1986). Flight is energy-intensive, and all adult butterflies' fitness components depend on it. We have focused much of our study of *Colias*'s adaptation at the bioenergetic intersection of metabolic organization, its thermal dependence, thermoregulation itself, and the interaction of natural variation in these phenotypic subsystems with ecological thermal niche variables to alter flight performance. Here, I first review *Colias*'s adaptations to thermally variable habitats, then explore the causes of the thermal dependence of their energy processing mechanisms. This review addresses general questions about thermal adaptation, positioning us to see later how functional differences among genetic variants can result in large adaptive changes in flight performance and thence in components of fitness.

FLIGHT, TEMPERATURE, AND THERMOREGULATORY ADAPTATIONS

Most smaller butterflies, and certainly *Colias*, are behavioral thermoregulators, dependent on energy from sunlight to raise their body temperature (T_b) above air temperature (T_a). *Colias*'s T_b limits their flight: voluntary flight occurs at $29° \leq T_b \leq 41°C$, and its occurrence, as well as wingbeat frequency, is maximized at $35° \leq T_b \leq 39°C$ (Watt 1968, 1997; Tsuji et al. 1986). Yet habitat T_a may routinely be as low as $10°–12°C$ during flight periods. Flight-permissive T_bs are achieved in the face of such conditions by a group of phenotypic traits called a "thermal filter," which receives habitat thermal variables—solar energy flux (S), T_a, ground temperature (T_{grd}), and wind velocity (v)—as inputs and yields T_b as output (Kingsolver and Watt 1983; Tsuji et al. 1986). "Active" filtering comes from orientation to sunlight: the insects sit with wings folded dorsally, orienting perpendicular to the solar beam to maximize absorption of S when $T_b < 35°C$, or parallel to minimize absorption when $T_b > 39°C$ (Watt 1968). This behavior is the same for *Colias* in all habitats. "Passive" filtering comes from characters such as absorptivity (light vs. dark color) and insulation against heat loss (thick or thin "fur," modified thoracic scales): cold-habitat *Colias* are dark and furry, while those in warmer habitats are less so (Watt 1968; Kingsolver 1983a, 1983b).

Flight patterns of whole populations are constrained by the quantitative balance of individuals' heat gains and losses at rest (Watt 1968; Kingsolver 1983a, 1983b; Tsuji et al. 1986). This is clear in the results of Kingsolver (1983a, especially figs. 1–3): daily flight activity in a wild population begins only when the T_b of *Colias* in basking posture in that habitat (measured by an implanted thermocouple) rises above 29°–30°C, and maximum population flight occurs only when basking insects' T_bs reach 35°–39°C.

The study of thermal balance once insects are in the air is equally important for understanding the duration of flight and the resulting ability to feed, find mates, and carry out other activities once flight has begun (Watt 1997). Using a wind tunnel (Tsuji et al. 1986), we have begun to explore *Colias*'s thermal balance in flight. For example, the dynamics of rapid cooling in flight may be especially important in arctic or alpine habitats, in which T_a may decrease, and v increase, very sharply only a few centimeters above protected basking sites (Watt 1997). Microscale variation of climate parameters is an important cause of flight heterogeneity within or among habitats (Kingsolver 1983b; Kingsolver and Watt 1983, 1984).

Such a clear picture of a species' thermal niche depends on the investigator's measuring *all* thermal aspects of the organism's phenotype-environment interactions. First, one must monitor insect T_b over a full range of behavioral and ecological conditions by chronic implantation of suitably small sensors (Watt 1968; Stone and Willmer 1989). Second, one must measure all thermal niche variables—S, T_a, T_{grd}, and v—and insect thermal parameters—such as absorptivity and degree of insulation against convective cooling—to allow the construction of an explicit "climate space" expressing the dependence of insect T_b, and hence activity, on the values of the niche variables (Kingsolver 1983a; Tsuji et al. 1986). Finally, one must perform proper control experiments and independent cross-checks of all conclusions (Watt 1968, 1997; Kingsolver 1983a, 1983b).

Complex as such work may seem, microelectronics puts it within the reach even of amateur biologists. Despite this, some workers still rely on "grab-and-stab," one-time sampling of butterfly T_b, neglecting the three points above. "Grab-and-stab" data can be useful if interpreted carefully, but often they have not been, and major confusion can result from misinterpretations (Stone and Willmer 1989; Watt 1997). This method is also costly in insect lives, as each datum requires the serious injury or death of an individual. When feasible, it is better to implant thermocouples chronically into a smaller but representative sample of butterflies from a study population to maximize experimental insight into thermal ecology and minimize the impact on populations.

WHY THERMOREGULATE? METABOLISM AS A LIKELY SOURCE OF FLIGHT'S THERMAL DEPENDENCE

The contraction of animal muscles, specifically insects' flight muscles, is fueled by splitting the high-energy phosphate compound adenosine triphosphate, or ATP (e.g., Sacktor 1975). The metabolic supply of this ATP "fuel" to flight muscles is a major potential source of the thermal constraints on insect, and notably *Colias,* flight. But why? And why, therefore, must *Colias,* like so many other animals, thermoregulate?

It's almost too obvious to reply that all chemical reaction rates covary with temperature. Classic explanations of the evolution of thermoregulation proceed from this observation to make three claims:

1. Metabolic power sufficient for intense activity is possible only at high T_b, so to maximize metabolic output, animals should thermoregulate to as high a T_b as possible, short of values denaturing their proteins (the common "maxithermy" hypothesis).
2. Small animals can't have a T_b far from the ambient (surrounding) temperature, as dictated by their high surface/volume ratio and the heat capacity of the ambient medium.
3. Large, active animals can't avoid having a T_b well above the ambient temperature, due to their intense metabolisms and low surface/volume ratios; they must evolve active cooling mechanisms to hold T_b below damage limits, and they then evolve to keep T_b high routinely, for reasons of metabolic efficiency, resulting in complete thermoregulation (Bartholomew 1981; Heinrich 1977).

Claim 1 is wrong: metabolic reactions *can* have high power (rate of throughput) at low to moderate T_b, by means such as high enzyme concentrations or changed thermal dependence of enzyme-substrate binding kinetics—albeit at costs of greater enzyme synthesis, possible lower enzyme stability at high T_b, or other opposing effects (Crawford and Powers 1989; Watt 1986, 1994).

Claim 2 is demonstrably true for very small insects (e.g., *Drosophila* or micropterygid moths) in air, and for most aquatic insects in water, as dictated by the heat capacity of these media.

Claim 3 may explain the evolution of active cooling mechanisms in large vertebrates and the largest insects (Heinrich 1974). But the more general view, that all thermoregulation evolves from a mass- and activity-driven need to lose excess heat, is wrong. While facultatively endothermic insects (e.g., saturniid or sphingid moths, large bees or beetles) are all large, insects of diverse sizes thermoregulate in other ways. A small insect's flight metabolism alone cannot overheat it (Tsuji et al. 1986; Watt 1991). Small insects reach high T_b only via evolved physical and behavioral traits (as in *Colias*); for example, only heavy insulation allows small nocturnal moths' T_b to rise above 30°C in flight through the cool night air (Casey 1981). In such cases, overheating risk comes only from thermoregulation itself. Why do *Colias* or other such insects not fly at lower, broader T_b, as very small insects must? What favored their evolution of high, narrow T_b in flight?

Small insects might have had large ancestors, whose size and activity forced early evolution of thermoregulation, but the evidence suggests otherwise. The most basal, generalized lepidopterans are small and are weak fliers; their early ancestry shows no evidence of large, possibly endothermic insects (Common 1975; Kristensen 1981; Scoble 1992).

Moreover, even when insects don't maintain high T_b, they usually show thermal *narrowness*. *Colias* larvae, for example, show T_b maxima for feeding and growth; these maxima differ among taxa, and are much lower than the adult flight maximum, but are just as narrow: 25°–29°C for *C. eurytheme*, 21°–26°C for *C. p. eriphyle* (Sherman and Watt 1973).

We have not one but two problems here: the narrowness of thermoregulatory T_b ranges and their frequent high values. Running metabolism at high T_b may be more cost-effective than making more enzyme to run it at low T_b, but that idea needs further testing. As for narrowness, the coevolution of metabolic steps may constrain maximum throughput to a narrow T_b range (Watt 1991). To see why, we must inspect the molecular basis of metabolic T_b dependence.

THERMAL DEPENDENCE OF BIOCHEMICAL REACTION KINETICS

A chemical rate constant (k) is intrinsically temperature-dependent, and is defined by the equation

$$k = Ae^{-(E_a/RT)},$$

where A is an "Arrhenius constant" unique to each reaction, e is the base of natural logarithms, E_a is energy of activation, R is the gas constant, and T is temperature in kelvins. But this equation only begins to describe the metabolic effect of T. The simplest reversible one-substrate (S), one-product (P), enzyme (E)-catalyzed reaction has six such constants:

$$\begin{array}{ccc} k_1 & k_2 & k_3 \\ E + S \rightleftarrows ES \rightleftarrows EP \rightleftarrows E + P, \\ k_{-1} & k_{-2} & k_{-3} \end{array}$$

where ES and EP are enzyme-substrate and enzyme-product complexes. The rate constants k_i give rise to summary enzyme parameters (see fig. 15.1). k_{cat} is the catalytic rate constant, k_2 or k_{-2}, depending on the reaction direction, and K_m is the Michaelis constant, a measure of substrate affinity (low

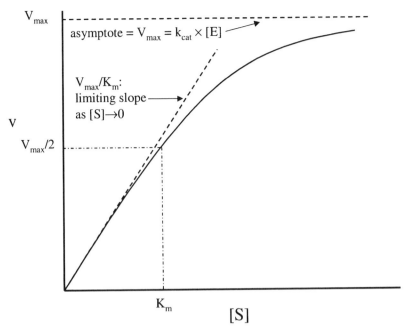

Figure 15.1 Relationships of enzyme parameters to a plot of initial velocity (*v*) against substrate concentration [S] for an enzyme-catalyzed reaction. Because "initial velocity" conditions mean that product is not initially present, these relationships are true for either direction of reversible reactions, in which case all kinetic parameters would display direction-specific values. V_{max} = maximum specific activity, approached in the limit of infinite [S]; k_{cat} = catalytic rate constant; [E] = enzyme concentration; K_m = Michaelis constant, numerically equal to the substrate concentration giving half-maximal velocity as shown; V_{max}/K_m = "pseudo-first-order" rate constant in the limit as [S] tends toward 0. In most cases in vivo, [S] is near K_m to well below it (e.g., Hochachka and Somero 1973).

K_m = tight binding), the ratio of the sum of rate constants dissociating the ES complex (or EP complex for the reverse reaction) to the sum of those forming it. [E], enzyme concentration, varies with enzyme stability and synthesis rate, and is part of V_{max}, maximum specific activity ($\equiv k_{cat} \times$ [E]). All of these parameters make up the Briggs-Haldane equation (the reversible reaction generalization of the Michaelis-Menten equation) for the velocity (*v*) of an enzyme-catalyzed reaction:

$$(15.1) \quad v = \frac{(V_{max}/K_m)_f \times [S] - (V_{max}/K_m)_b \times [P]}{1 + ([S]/K_{m_f}) + ([P]/K_{m_b})},$$

where the subscripts f and b refer to forward and back reaction directions. Since the thermal dependences of the underlying k_i are semi-independent, adaptive adjustment of one enzyme's thermal responses to maximize enzyme function in an environmentally appropriate temperature range is no simple task for natural selection. But as we will see next, *all* enzymes in a metabolic pathway must be thermally coadjusted by selection if the pathway is to process resources effectively.

Mechanistic Studies of Adaptations   325

Fuel—that is, ATP—is supplied to insect flight muscles by metabolic pathways made up of many single reaction steps, each of whose products (P_i) are substrates (S_{i+1}) for the next steps. The organization of such pathways demands kinetic coadjustment of their enzyme-catalyzed steps, each with its own suite of rate constants, as described above. Further, despite "population biologists'" common but mistaken assumption that any phenotypic task can be done in several ways, metabolism is not redundant: limitations at one point in the pathway can seldom be well compensated elsewhere. To see how metabolic adaptations to varying T_b evolve under the constraint of the multiplicity of pathway steps, we must summarize metabolic organization theory, which expresses that constraint.

Metabolite concentrations or pool sizes, $[S]_i$, and fluxes are *dependent* metabolic variables, varying with *in*dependent ones—state variables (such as temperature) and biological supply or demand—and with parameters of metabolism. The latter include enzyme parameters, as described above, as well as V_{max}/K_m ratios, for each step. V_{max}/K_m is a "pseudo-first-order rate constant" at the low $[S]_i$ values seen in vivo: as [S] and [P] shrink relative to K_{m_f} and K_{m_b}, equation (15.1) reduces to a difference of first-order terms involving V_{max}/K_m. V_{max}/K_m is thus the best measure of enzyme function in vivo (e.g., Watt 1983; Powers 1987; see fig. 15.1). Adaptive change in fluxes or pools occurs through genetic change in these parameters (or in state variable regulation). Amino acid sequence variants alter K_m, k_{cat}, or, via stability, [E], and hence V_{max}/K_m; "control gene" variants alter V_{max}/K_m by changing enzyme expression, and hence [E] (e.g., Crawford and Powers 1989).

In a metabolic pathway, all steps may, in principle, influence flux or the duration of flux changes. But often a few enzymes are "rate-limiting" or "control" steps, while the rest intervene among them; this arrangement must result from coadaptive adjustment of all the steps under natural selection (Watt and Dean 2000). The control steps' kinetics must yield enough flux to meet biological demand, while at the intervening steps, V_{max}/K_m must appear "in excess" of system flux so as not to constrain the control steps' action (Watt 1983; Watt and Dean 2000; see below). Different metabolic states impose these coadaptive demands on pathways with different degrees of stringency.

In a steady state—for example, during the steady growth or slow movement of insect larvae—all steps show the same flux, and no metabolite pools change. Steady-state metabolic theory is perforce a theory of small change, because large change, by definition, disrupts the steady state (Kacser and Burns 1973). Control coefficients (C_i; formerly Z_i) express the effect of change in the kinetics of the ith step (i.e., change in k_{cat}, K_m, or $[E]_i$) on pathway flux. C_i are assigned to steps as

$$C_1 : C_2 : C_3 \ldots :: \frac{K_{m_1}}{V_{max_1}} : \frac{K_{m_2}}{V_{max_2} \times K_{eq_1}} : \frac{K_{m_3}}{V_{max_3} \times K_{eq_1} \times K_{eq_2}} \ldots,$$

so a higher V_{max}/K_m at a step gives it a lower C_i. In unbranched steady-state pathways, $C_i > 0$ and $\Sigma C_i = 1$ (the "summation theorem"; Kacser and Burns 1973, 1979), so the focusing of control in a large C_i at one step, such as phosphofructokinase (PFK) in glycolysis (cf. fig. 15.2 below), means that enzymes at the intervening steps must be selected for low C_i (i.e., high V_{max}/K_m) (Watt 1983; Watt and Dean 2000). This selection may reach a zone of diminishing returns (Hartl et al. 1985), in which kinetic variants at a step whose C_i is small will tend to be phenotypically recessive or, indeed, neutral. But, despite an exaggerated claim (Kacser and Burns 1981), this phenomenon is not universal, and heterozygous variants often affect steady states (e.g., Savageau and Sorribas 1989; Watt and Dean 2000).

Transient metabolism shows large changes in pool sizes and step fluxes; there is no one pathway-wide flow rate. Transients are especially common in insect flight. Easterby (1973, 1990) found that (1) a step's response to transient metabolic change varies inversely with its V_{max}/K_m ratio; (2) a step's transition time (τ) varies with K_m/V_{max} ($\tau \equiv$ time needed for $[1 - (1/e)]$ of the change to occur; 5τ spans 99% of the change); and (3) the system transition time is the sum of the steps' times, $\tau_{sys} = \Sigma \tau_i$ (the transient summation theorem).

Watt and Boggs (1987) proved a useful corollary: for the τ of a control step c to approach that of the system (i.e., $\tau_c \rightarrow \tau_{sys}$), $\tau_{i \neq c}$ must approach zero (i.e., $(K_m/V_{max})_{i \neq c} \rightarrow 0$ as $(V_{max}/K_m)_{i \neq c} \rightarrow \infty$). That is, for a step c to control system transience, $(V_{max}/K_m)_{i \neq c}$ must be very large for all other steps. Diminishing returns of increasing $(V_{max}/K_m)_i$ are reached much more slowly in transient than in steady state because the transient summation theorem does not limit the sizes of τ_i (e.g., Easterby 1990), as the steady-state case limits C_i.

We can now see why high-throughput metabolic performance should be so constrained to a narrow temperature range. *Colias*'s (and other insects') flight fuel is supplied by metabolic pathways in series—glycolysis, the Krebs cycle, oxidative phosphorylation (cf. Sacktor 1975; Watt and Boggs 1987)—each made up of many reactions, as figure 15.2 summarizes. This metabolic complexity must be coadapted for function according to the constraining principles just summarized above, and this must be done in the face of varying T_b. Over a broad T_b range, the differing Arrhenius constants and activation energies of the k_i at each step mean that coadaptation of those steps' V_{max}/K_m ratios, mandated by the above principles, is possible only within a

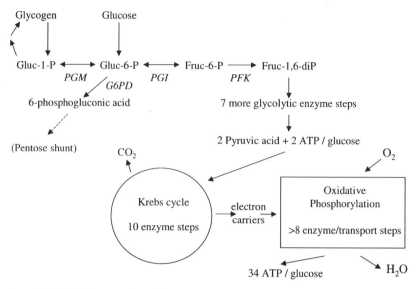

Figure 15.2 Overall diagram of central energy processing reactions in *Colias*. Enzyme steps mentioned in the text are italicized. PGI = phosphoglucose isomerase; PGM = phosphoglucomutase; G6PD = glucose-6-phosphate dehydrogenase; PFK = phosphofructokinase. Metabolite abbreviations: Gluc = glucose; P = phosphate; ATP = adenosine triphosphate. (For further details of these pathways or for structures of metabolites, consult any contemporary biochemistry text.)

few degrees. Thus, thermoregulation to *narrow* T_b is an evolved adaptive response to the constraints of metabolic organization (Watt 1991). Regulation to *high* T_b, if possible, may be adaptive in achieving high metabolic flux with less enzyme synthesis cost than is needed for the same flux in a lower, but equally narrow, T_b range (Watt 1991), but that is a separate issue from the basic constraint of thermal narrowness imposed by metabolic organization.

Ultimately, of course, metabolic performances are measured in terms of delivery of metabolic products—such as fuel or "building blocks"—to organismal performances: do the performing phenotypic subsystems—locomotion, gametogenesis, and so forth—receive enough resources that their carriers can survive and reproduce effectively (Watt 1986)? A butterfly's metabolic performance connects to its flight as an organismal performance, whose effectiveness then translates over the life cycle into fitness. Thus, metabolic organization and temperature jointly constrain the evolution of insect flight, shaping adaptive refinements from specific enzymes to thermoregulation itself, according to the principles we have just discussed.

CHANGING STATE VARIABLES TO TEST METABOLIC HYPOTHESES ABOUT THE NEED FOR THERMOREGULATION

Gould and Lewontin (1979) complained justifiably about the prevalence of armchair biology—mere plausible reasoning without testing—in studies of adaptation. The cure for this disease is not to ignore adaptation, as some have wrongly advised, but to test alternative hypotheses about the adaptiveness, constraint, or neutrality of the phenotypes in question (Feder and Watt 1992; Watt 2000). One way to test alternative explanations for the thermal dependence of metabolism is to manipulate the key state variable, T_b, to see whether metabolism's responses resolve different explanations for thermoregulation. We have done so (Kohane and Watt 1999), studying (by high-pressure liquid chromatography, HPLC) high-energy adenylate levels in the flight muscles of individual *Colias eurytheme*. Adenosine triphosphate (ATP) is the high-energy reactant that drives muscle actomyosin contraction, breaking down to its diphosphate (ADP) and a phosphate ion in the process. We measured the [ATP]/[ADP] ratio, a close correlate of the mass action ratio for actomyosin-ATPase, in *Colias* flying for standard times at suboptimal T_b (31°C) and at the base (35°C) and the top (39°C) of the T_b optimum. We tested three hypotheses:

1. Neutrality: T_b has no effect on [ATP]/[ADP] (unlikely, but imaginable).
2. Maxithermal adaptation: [ATP]/[ADP] rises monotonically with T_b throughout this temperature range, as even 39°C is not high enough for protein denaturation or other thermal damage to occur in *Colias* (Kingsolver and Watt 1983; Kohane and Watt 1999).
3. Constrained metabolic system performance: [ATP]/[ADP] passes through a maximum within the T_b flight optimum, declining on both sides of it.

Figure 15.3 shows these alternatives as idealized curves, then plots the results of our initial test. Setting aside the details of experimental control and accounting for other variables (found in Kohane and Watt 1999), the "bottom line" relationship of [ATP]/[ADP] to T_b in flight was a peak at the thermal optimum, followed by a decline above it: at 31°C, 2.30 ± 0.23 ($n = 20$); at 35°C, 3.04 ± 0.19 ($n = 45$); and at 39°C, 2.03 ± 0.10 ($n = 54$). This result is significant by analysis of variance at $P = 2.6 \times 10^{-5}$! It falsifies hypotheses 1 and 2, but supports hypothesis 3, that of metabolic thermal constraint.

There are other ways to test the metabolic constraint hypothesis for the thermal dependence of flight, or of other performances, and hence the need for thermoregulation, in *Colias* or other animals. Specifically, one can manipulate glycolytic performance with functional genetic variants to see how those variants alter flight muscle [ATP]/[ADP] responses to changing T_b. Conversely, the bioenergetics of flight is an essential context for interpreting functional differences among genetic variants. Such studies can clarify metabolic reasons for thermoregulation as well as other aspects of metabolic adaptation. I now turn to a review of such a study.

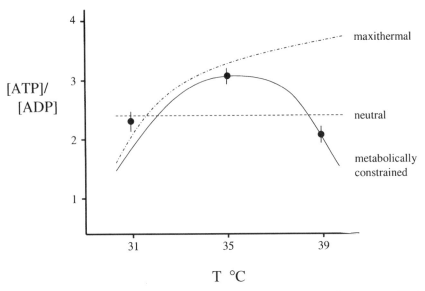

Figure 15.3 Test of alternative hypotheses for effects of body temperature on metabolic support of flight muscle ([ATP]/[ADP] ratios). Values of [ATP]/[ADP] (solid circles: means ± standard errors of means from table 3 of Kohane and Watt 1999) are plotted against lines predicted by the three alternative hypotheses elaborated in the text: (1) neutrality (no effect of T_b on [ATP]/[ADP]); (2) maxithermal performance ([ATP]/[ADP] increases monotonically with T_b; curve details arbitrary); (3) constrained metabolic performance ([ATP]/[ADP] passes through a narrow maximum and declines with T_b beyond it; curve details arbitrary).

IDENTIFIED GENE VARIATION IN THE CONTEXT OF FLIGHT METABOLISM AND THERMAL CONSTRAINT

ADAPTIVE VARIATION OF AN ENERGY-PROCESSING ENZYME IN LOWLAND *Colias*

Natural genetic variants of *Colias*'s energy-processing metabolism, which are useful as probes of bioenergetic adaptation, occur in the lowland North American species complex (*C. eurytheme, C. philodice,* and relatives) in several enzymes that share glucose-6-phosphate (G6P) as substrate (Watt 1977; Carter and Watt 1988). This branch point in the energy-processing pathway (see fig. 15.2) allocates carbohydrate among biosynthesis, via the pentose shunt, whose first enzyme is G6P dehydrogenase (G6PD); storage as glycogen, whose first enzyme is phosphoglucomutase (PGM); and glycolysis, whose first enzyme is phosphoglucose isomerase (PGI). Initial evidence of survival differences among PGI genotypes led us to study their effects from metabolism all the way to fitness in the wild.

PGI's variation is ideal for probing adaptive interactions among flight, thermoregulation, and metabolic constraints. PGI interconverts G6P and fructose-6-phosphate (F6P) (see fig. 15.2). As an intervening step in flight-muscle glycolysis next to the control-step enzyme phosphofructok-inase, PGI undergoes some of the most demanding transient metabolic changes known to biology (Sacktor 1975; Watt 1977). Major functional differences occur among the common polymorphs of PGI in lowland *Colias* (Watt 1977, 1983). We tested predictions of genotypic performance and fitness differences, based on these functional differences interpreted in the context of transient metabolic theory, against the neutral null hypotheses in the wild. Our results are summarized under the stages of the evolutionary recursion discussed above.

1. Genotype → Phenotype

Four PGI alleles ($\equiv 2, 3, 4,$ and 5) are common in the wild. Their ten genotypes differ by up to fourfold in V_{max}/K_m and/or thermal stability, falsifying the neutral hypothesis of functional equivalence of variants. Most heterozygotes (3/4, 2/3, 2/4, etc.) have higher V_{max}/K_m than most homozygotes (3/3, 4/4, etc.) due to large K_m differences (Watt 1983). There is also a strong trade-off of thermal stability versus V_{max}/K_m (as predicted for many proteins by Hochachka and Somero 1973), especially in homozygotes. PGI in its native state is a dimer of protein subunits; in heterozygotes, each allele codes for half the subunits, and half the enzyme in an individual is heterodimers containing one subunit from each allele. Subunit interaction in these heterodimers appears to promote both high V_{max}/K_m and some relief from structural constraints on stability.

2. Phenotype → Performance

Steady-state larval metabolism is less demanding than adult transient metabolism, so *Colias* PGI variants have little effect on preadult performance, and adults emerge from pupae at close to Hardy-Weinberg frequencies (Watt 1977). But genotypes of high V_{max}/K_m are predicted by metabolic theory to minimize PGI's transition time under the demands of flight muscle glycolysis. In other words, such genotypes are predicted to have a faster glycolytic response to flight than other genotypes. Using ^{14}C tracers with primitive paper chromatography separation techniques, we tested this prediction with 3/4 (high V_{max}/K_m) and 4/4 (low V_{max}/K_m) genotypes, and confirmed it (Watt and Boggs 1987). We are developing HPLC methods for analyzing ^{14}C-labeled glycolytic metabolites to pursue this question in more detail. Genotypes with high V_{max}/K_m are also predicted to fly over a broader span of the daily thermal flight cycle (Watt 1977, 1983), because such genotypes should maintain enough kinetic capacity for metabolic support of flight over a broader T_b range than do those with low values (the genotypes are *not* kinetically specialized to high or low T_b ranges). In field studies, this prediction was tested against the neutral null hypothesis of "no organismal effect." The three most common genotypes rank as $3/4 > 3/3 \gg 4/4$ in terms of V_{max}/K_m values, so this order of flight activity through the day was predicted, and was found in six replicates, with strong statistical support (Watt et al. 1983).

3. Performance → Fitness

Adult fitness components depend on flight, so *Colias*'s PGI genotypes should differ congruently in survival, male mating success, and female fecundity, in accordance with predictions from their metabolic and flight performances. New methods were needed to study these fitness components in the wild. Here, especially, the accessibility of butterfly biology was of crucial utility. For example, direct behavioral observations of *Colias* courtship in the field would need to be impractically extensive to test PGI genotype–specific male mating success by this means. However, we had previously found that while *Colias* females do mate several times in their lives, there is "absolute sperm precedence": the last male to mate with a female fathers all of her eggs until her next mating, and earlier males' sperm never reappear (Boggs and Watt 1981). Thus, we could examine male mating success by the following method (Watt et al. 1985): First, we took a large sample of both sexes from a population during peak flight at midday. We genotyped the males in this sample as representative of the males available to the females in that population as mates. We then obtained eggs (which all, because of sperm precedence, were fathered by the most recently mating male) from each female, then genotyped all the females. We raised and genotyped enough larvae from each female's eggs to infer their father's genotype with $\geq 99\%$ likelihood, according to binomial distribution statistics appropriate to Mendelian genetic segregation. Finally, we compared the distribution of PGI genotypes among males actually mating females with that of the available mates to test for differences and thence to estimate male mating success. This experimental design also allows simultaneous testing for both assortative mating and segregation distortion (= "meiotic drive"), neither of which has been found at PGI (or other allozyme genes) in *Colias*. It has been successfully applied to several other populations, genes, and taxa within the genus (Watt et al. 1985, 1986, 1996; Carter and Watt 1988).

Other features of *Colias* biology have been exploited in turn to allow measurement of other fitness components in the wild. Such testing in the wild, replicated widely for the most part among years, sites, and semispecies, has confirmed the biochemically predicted fitness effects of lowland *Colias*'s PGI variants, without exception (Watt 1983, 1992; Watt et al. 1985, 1986).

4. Fitness → Genotype

Adaptively predictable fitness differences interact with nonadaptive aspects of population structure. Studies of the latter are crucial in testing alternative interpretations of field data: for example, a study of dispersal and allelic covariance rejected the hypothesis that multi-allele Wahlund effects cause the heterozygote excess at the *Colias* PGI, leaving better survival of high-V_{max}/K_m genotypes as the only viable hypothesis (Watt 1983).

Despite experimental rejection of the null hypothesis at each stage of these analyses, one last, subtle null hypothesis must be addressed: that of association with linked variants of other genes, or "hitchhiking." For example, variants at the gene studied might be neutral, but closely linked to other variants at an unknown gene that is actually being selected (Maynard Smith and Haigh 1974; Thomson 1977). For *Colias* PGI, this hypothesis can be rejected. Associative hypotheses generally predict that any performance or fitness differences seen among neutrally hitchhiking variants should not be related to differences in those variants' own molecular function (Watt 1983, 1992). When variants' functional differences do accurately predict genotype-specific performance and fitness differences, as they do here, the associative hypothesis is rejected.

By tracking *Colias*'s PGI variation through the whole evolutionary recursion, we've seen that strong natural selection acts on it. Molecular differences in kinetic function and thermal stability among PGI genotypes interact with *Colias*'s thermal niche to adapt fuel supply to flight demands and, through resulting differences in flight performance, affect each fitness component examined: survival, male mating success, and female fecundity. Table 15.1 illustrates these genotypic effects for the three most common genotypes and for heterozygotes and homozygotes overall.

The resulting selection regime is not simple. First, there is heterozygote advantage, notably for genotype 3/4, whose PGI has a very high V_{max}/K_m ratio and near-maximal thermal stability, and hence superior glycolytic performance, flight performance, and fitness. Other heterozygotes show better (harmonic or geometric) mean functional performances, compared to those of related homozygotes, among locally patchy (in space or time) habitats (Watt 1977, 1983, 1992; Haldane and Jayakar 1963; Levene 1953; Gillespie 1991). Other complex phenotype-environment interactions arise from the kinetics versus stability trade-off seen in homozygotes. For example, the kinetically favored homozygote 2/2 never survives to old age (indexed by wing wear; Watt 1977) in the wild, apparently because of its PGI's poor thermal stability, while thermally stable 4/4 is poor in kinetics and thus suffers in fitness except under heat stress (Watt 1983, 1992).

Lowland populations vary temporally in PGI frequencies within sites as a result of these differences in performance and resulting fitness, but their

Table 15.1 Illustrative biochemical properties and resulting relative fitness component differences for subsets of lowland *Colias* PGI genotypes

Genotype	V_{max}/K_m[a]	Stability (1 hr at 50°C)[a]	Survival[b]	Male Mating Success[c] G 8/8/83	T 9/24/83	T 11/3/83	Female Fecundity[d]	Relative Fitness[e] Male (G)	Female
3/3	2.32	72%	1.00	1.00	1.00	1.00	1.00	1.00	1.00
3/4	2.49	83%	1.38	1.21	2.08	2.23	1.34	1.67	1.85
4/4	1.58	90%	0.35	0.49	0.20	0.27	0.53	0.17	0.19
All homozygotes			0.90	0.82	0.91	0.83	0.89	0.77	0.69
All heterozygotes			1.36	1.70	2.37	2.24	1.18	2.31	1.61

Note: 3/3, 3/4, and 4/4 are the most common genotypes in both lowland "semi-species" considered here: *C. p. eriphyle* and *C. eurytheme*. The 3/3 genotype, as the most common homozygote and as having moderate values of kinetic parameters and stability, was chosen as the standard for relative fitness component and fitness calculations. Statistical validation of differences among genotypes was conducted in the original references, and is not repeated here.

[a] V_{max}/K_m and stability data from Watt (1983); V_{max}/K_m units are rate units/μM × min/mg.

[b] Survival was calculated from data underlying fig. 2 of Watt (1977), taken at Crested Butte Mountain, CO, on *C. p. eriphyle*.

[c] Male mating success was calculated from data on *C. p. eriphyle* at Gunnison, CO (G) and on *C. eurytheme* at Tracy, CA (T), underlying table 2 of Watt et al. (1985).

[d] Female fecundity data on *C. p. eriphyle* from Gunnison, Co, is from Watt (1992).

[e] Male relative fitness is the product of survival with G values for male mating success; female relative fitness is the product of survival with fecundity.

mean allele and genotype frequencies are very similar among sites many hundreds of kilometers apart (table 15.2; Watt et al. 2002). This finding is expected, because observed PGI genotypic performance and fitness differences are closely similar among these sites (Watt 1983, 1992; Watt et al. 1983, 1985, 1986). As noted above, the major selection on PGI stems from the insects' thermal experiences. These are apparently kept similar by local thermoregulatory adaptations to shallow gradients of elevation, and hence of thermal niche variables, across North America (Kingsolver 1983a, 1983b, Kingsolver and Watt 1984; Watt et al. 2002), leading to the striking uniformity of polymorph frequencies seen across this region.

These variants will be useful as tools for further study in both laboratory and field. We can use them to manipulate the organization of flight fuel metabolism and observe the effects on fuel output performance, testing new hypotheses about molecular mechanisms of adaptation and constraint in metabolic processes. We can also probe metabolic responses to T_b variation, further testing alternative hypotheses about the metabolic causes of the evolution of animal thermoregulation and the fitness consequences of variation in such systems.

SOME GENERAL IMPLICATIONS OF THIS SPECIFIC STUDY

The fact that some allozyme genes are subject to extremely strong natural selection, whose nature is predictable from the allozymes' molecular

Table 15.2 Representative samples of PGI allele frequencies from lowland and alpine species complexes

Taxon	Site and Elevation[a]	Date	n (Genotypes)	p_1	p_2	p_3	p_4	p_5	p_6
Lowland									
C. eurytheme	Tracy, CA, 30 m	9/85	178	0.006	0.062	0.626	0.270	0.037	0.000
C. p. eriphyle	CB Mtn, CO, 2,700 m	8/76	53	0.000	0.047	0.623	0.245	0.009	0.000
C. p. eriphyle	Olathe, CO, 1,650 m	8/77	40	0.000	0.063	0.663	0.238	0.038	0.000
C. p. eriphyle	Gunnison, CO, 2,350 m	8/94	80	0.006	0.063	0.650	0.244	0.031	0.006
Alpine[c]									
C. meadii	Blue Park (S), CO, 3,300 m	7/97	51	0.039	0.529	0.422	0.010		
C. meadii	Brooklyn Lake (S), WY, 3,200 m	7/97	63	0.024	0.484	0.492	0.000		
C. meadii	Brooklyn Lake (S), WY, 3,200 m	8/98	47	0.021	0.489	0.457	0.032		
C. meadii	Mesa Seco (S), CO, 3,400 m	7/78	45	0.022	0.511	0.444	0.022		
C. meadii	Mesa Seco (T), CO, 3,750 m	7/78	44	0.011	0.625	0.330	0.034		
C. meadii	Mesa Seco (S), CO, 3,400 m	8/88	156	0.013	0.554	0.407	0.026		
C. meadii	Mesa Seco (T), CO, 3,750 m	8/97	47	0.032	0.628	0.287	0.053		
C. meadii	Cottonwood Pass (T), CO, 3,750 m	8/91	155	0.032	0.670	0.287	0.010		
C. meadii	Jones Pass (T), CO, 3,690 m	8/96	53	0.019	0.623	0.311	0.047		

Note: Note that, as emphasized in the text and by Watt et al. (1996), electromorphs in the two species complexes that have similar mobilities in ordinary-resolution gels are *not* the same in charge, shape, or functional properties—they represent distinct alleles. G tests for heterogeneity of allele frequencies: all lowland populations, $G_{12} = 6.315$, $0.8 < P < 0.9$; all steppe populations of *C. meadii*, $G_{12} = 12.125$, $0.3 < P < 0.5$; all tundra populations of *C. meadii*, $G_9 = 10.579$, $0.3 < P < 0.5$; steppe vs. tundra populations of *C. meadii*, $G_3 = 28.542$, $P \ll 0.001$.

[a] The lowland populations span roughly 2,000 km of map distance. Mesa Seco populations below and above tree line are separated by only by ~0.5–0.75 km, and exchange a percentage of their adults per generation (Watt et al. 1977). Blue Park, Mesa Seco, and Brooklyn Lake span 300+ km, while Mesa Seco, Cottonwood Pass, and Jones Pass span roughly 200 km.

[b] p_i = frequency of electromorph allele i.

[c] (S) denotes a montane steppe population below tree line; (T) denotes a tundra population above tree line.

Source: Data from Watt et al. 2002.

properties when placed in the context of organismal physiology and ecology, is a finding of general importance. It marks one end of a spectrum of strengths of selection on individual genes at a very high value. How often do allozymes occupy different ranges of this spectrum? For example, *Colias* PGI genotypes 4/4 and 4/5 are equal in their high heat stability and low values of V_{max}/K_m, and as a result are equal in fitness components; they are neutral with respect to one another even while differing by severalfold in function and fitness from other PGI genotypes (Watt 1983, 1992). Thus, even for a single gene and its variants, let alone among multiple genes, "selection" and "neutrality" are ends of a spectrum of performance and consequent fitness differences among variants, from large to zero.

Next, uniformity of genetic frequencies over wide areas need not arise only from homogenization of neutral variation by dispersal ("gene flow").

Costa and Ross (1994), finding uniformity of allozyme frequencies across the range of the moth *Malacosoma,* noted that geographic similarity of positive selection would explain this just as well as neutrality plus dispersal. The fact that the same large fitness differences occur among *Colias* PGI genotypes at many sites reinforces Costa and Ross's suggestion and a similar one for *Maniola jurtina* (Goulson 1993). It supports Ehrlich and Raven's (1969) view that uniformity of a species over long distances may owe more to similarity of local selection than to "genetic cohesion" via dispersal, and may have implications for choice of species concepts (cf. Martin et al., chap. 21 in this volume).

Further, population genetic sampling of other taxa should, in the future, take explicit account of temporally as well as spatially varying habitat or population conditions. Demographic stage in a generation or a season of activity, habitat temperature, and time of day, via the daily thermal cycle, all affect *Colias*'s PGI genotype frequencies (Watt 1983; Watt et al. 1983). If sampling is random with respect to such variables, important evolutionary dynamics may go undetected.

In even broader terms, this case shows that one can understand the evolutionary meaning of natural variants only if one knows how they affect their carrier organisms' phenotypes and their ecological niche interactions, *in mechanistic terms.* The hope of many population biologists that population genetic statistics alone, without functional study of the variants' actions, could tell us all we needed to know about evolutionary processes is clearly a vain one.

DIFFERENTIATION OF AN ADAPTIVE MECHANISM AMONG SPECIES

One obvious route to testing the generality of studies of adaptation within one species is to extend them to progressively more distant taxa. *Colias meadii,* an alpine North American species, shows PGI polymorphism, maintained by strong fitness differences predictable from genotypic differences in function and flight, just as do lowland taxa (Watt et al. 1996). Further, alpine tundra populations show great similarity of PGI frequencies even when located far apart, as do lowland taxa (see table 15.2, also Watt et al. 2002). But similarity to the lowland taxa stops there, and comparisons among PGI alleles of these taxa, from molecular to biogeographic levels, are provocative.

Absence of Allelic and Genotypic Identity among Taxa

C. meadii's common PGI genotypes differ functionally, showing heterozygote advantage in kinetics and a trade-off of kinetics versus thermal stability in homozygotes, as do those of the lowland taxa. However, this functional parallelism does *not* reflect identity of alleles between the two groups. Allozymes of *C. meadii* and of the lowland taxa, which have similar mobilities in ordinary-resolution electrophoresis, are in fact different on more careful inspection (Watt et al. 1996). First, in high-resolution gels, enzymes appearing to represent "the same" alleles and genotypes between these taxa turn out to have subtly different shapes and charges. Second, PGI genotypes of like mobility among taxa are quite dissimilar in function— e.g., *C. meadii*'s allozymes are generally less thermally stable than those of lowland taxa, and genotype for genotype, there is no resemblance in thermal stability or in kinetic constants. However, the functional differences nonetheless lead to parallel genotypic differences in flight performance and fitness components, apparently by the same organismal mechanisms.

These observations underscore a warning, first given by Coyne (1976) but ignored by "allozyme systematists": it is *very unsafe* to assume allelic identity among taxa from similar mobility of allozymes in ordinary electrophoresis gels. This assumption may lead to the underestimation of differences among relatives otherwise thought to share "the same" alleles and to differ only in their frequencies. Worse, this underestimation may not be uniform, as differences of identity and function, obscured by similar mobility, may occur to different extents among lineages of many creatures. But this warning is only one of several important implications of our results.

Adaptive Differentiation on Ecological, Biogeographic, and Systematic Scales

As noted earlier, populations of *C. meadii* located above tree line show geographic uniformity of PGI frequencies among sites separated by 500 km or more. Remarkably, though, *C. meadii* PGI variants can show large frequency shifts over distances of little more than 500 *meters* where populations cross tree line in an ecotone (Endler 1977) from tundra to montane steppe (Watt et al. 2002). These shifts are reproducible among years and among sites. Some populations occur entirely isolated below tree line, and these, too, are similar among themselves in PGI frequencies despite wide geographic separation. Further, their frequencies are closely similar to those of populations at the lower ends of the tree line–crossing gradients (see table 15.2). Thus, a major shift in selection pressure on this polymorphism, strong enough to overcome counterdispersal of reproducing adults each generation, occurs reproducibly *between* steppe and tundra ecosystems, even while selection *within* each ecosystem appears uniform over hundreds of kilometers (Watt et al. 2002). This feature of alpine *Colias* PGI variation offers new and important research opportunities.

First, we can compare the scaling of ecological change with the scaling of evolutionary response. That is, we can study how changes in niche variables produce changes in organism-environment interactions (the PGI variants themselves are the same across tree line; only their frequencies change) and thus changes in the balance of fitness components yielding the frequency changes. In so doing, we will be studying an actual mechanism for adaptive specialization in the face of migration. Conversely, by extending this study to sites above, below, and crossing tree line in different parts of *C. meadii's* range, we can see what keeps genotypic fitnesses similar within microhabitat types over long distances. The coexistence of within-habitat fitness stasis over long distances with sharp between-habitat fitness differentiation over short distances and in spite of migration is truly striking.

Further, we can compare the intraspecific shift in polymorphism among habitats with genetic change in PGI polymorphism across a taxonomic boundary. The subspecies *C. m. elis* occurs north of *C. m. meadii,* but only below tree line (e.g., Layberry et al. 1998). It shows allele frequencies that parallel or extend those of *C. m. meadii* below tree line, if the alleles in question are the same (but we do not know that yet: C. Wheat et al., unpub.). This observation raises an evolutionary question: Which of the allele frequency states in *C. m. meadii* is actually the derived condition? Could *C. m. meadii's* tundra presence be secondary, so that the direction of the frequency shift has been, for example, from an ancestral, lower p_2 below tree line to a derived, higher p_2 above it?

More distant relatives of *C. meadii* (e.g., *C. canadensis, C. hecla*) are also very polymorphic at the PGI gene, which will allow us eventually to explore the adaptive evolution of this gene over an even broader range of phyletic divergences (C. Wheat et al., unpub.). Indeed, surveys of about 25% of the 70+ *Colias* species and two of the three species of the sister genus *Zerene* (Geiger 1980; Pollock et al. 1998; H. Geiger et al., unpub.) reveal no *population,* let alone taxon, in which PGI is not highly variable. PGI polymorphism may be older than entire clades in this insect group!

INTERWEAVING OF ADAPTATION, CONSTRAINT, AND PHYLOGENY: IMPORTANT UNANSWERED QUESTIONS

These comparisons of PGI polymorphism among taxa raise a host of new questions about the interaction of adaptation and constraint in the evolution of both protein structure and metabolic organization, and about the ways in which adaptation at specific loci changes as the genes' carriers themselves differentiate in the phylogenetic sense.

A trade-off of enzyme thermal stability versus kinetics may arise, at the level of protein structure, from conflict between the structural rigidity needed to resist thermal agitation and the flexibility needed for substrate binding and catalytic speed (Hochachka and Somero 1973). Such a constraining trade-off is seen among *Colias* PGI homozygotes in each species complex, but some heterozygotes may be nearly exempt from it (Watt 1983; Watt et al. 1996). Testing the structural basis of this constraint requires us to discover how the varying alleles differ in amino acid sequence (by DNA sequencing: C. Wheat et al., unpub.) and then to use physical methods such as X-ray crystallography to reveal PGI's molecular structure and see where those amino acid changes fall within it. Three-dimensional structures for pig (Achari et al. 1981) and rabbit (Jeffery et al. 2000) PGI suggest a reason for heterozygotes' kinetic advantage: each subunit has its own active site, but each of the two subunits making up the native dimeric protein contributes one side, and a key amino acid residue, to the other subunit's active site. (Insect and vertebrate PGIs do differ in many respects, so this needs molecular-structural checking in *Colias* itself.)

Such information may also address, in terms of protein structure, a question arising at a more abstract evolutionary level. These *Colias* taxa are abundant and widespread, so their genomes, including the PGI gene, should have been broadly scanned by recurrent mutation; in other words, there has been much opportunity for the rise of a wide range of new mutants. Why, then, has no PGI allele arisen that maximizes all aspects of function when homozygous? The answer, when found, may have general implications for the evolution of protein structure.

On another but related point, have *Colias*'s and *Zerene*'s PGI variants diverged from a common ancestral polymorphism, or have there been multiple origins? The latter alternative seems less plausible, but a rigorous answer requires a comparison of PGI allelic sequence phylogeny with the *taxon* phylogeny of these clades, as estimated independently (e.g., from mitochondrial DNA sequences, as in Pollock et al. 1998). Multiple origins would pose the problem of why monomorphic ancestors were so susceptible to polymorphic "invasion." A deep common origin for the variants would suggest that the gene diverged by successive allele replacements while remaining polymorphic, since no monomorphic populations are known in (*Colias* + *Zerene*).

Insight into these issues must come from an interplay of empirical work with questions that move broadly among levels of biological organization, and from the evolutionary generality and implications of the answers to those questions. Another way in which specific studies may lead to generality is by extension of those studies to other genes, as the following sections explain.

COMPLEXITY IN PROXIMITY: DIVERGENT ADAPTATIONS OF ADJACENT ENZYME GENES

Glucose phosphate dehydrogenase (G6PD) and phosphoglucomutase (PGM) share a common substrate, G6P, with PGI. These genes' allozymes do not directly affect *Colias*'s flight, as PGI's do, but they also have large fitness effects, apparently by changing other metabolic phenotypes (Carter and Watt 1988). PGM interconverts G6P and G1P en route to or from glycogen storage; G6PD converts G6P + NADP to 6-phosphogluconate + NADPH as the first step of the pentose shunt (see fig. 15.2). The pentose shunt does not run in flight muscle, and PGM plays only a minor role there, as most flight muscle G6P comes from hemolymph sugar, not muscle glycogen (Watt and Boggs 1987). Thus PGM and G6PD variants should not impact flight. However, they could interact with one another, and potentially with PGI variants, at the G6P branch point in the fat body, a major site of insect biosynthesis and one in which glycolysis, the pentose shunt, and glycogen storage all run at once (e.g., Sacktor 1975). Moreover, the genes that code for PGM and G6PD are loosely linked, showing slightly more than 40% recombination, though they assort independently of the PGI gene. (This is the first well-defined autosomal linkage group in *Colias*, though several genes have been identified as sex-linked by Grula and Taylor [1980b].)

There are five alleles at PGM, and four at G6PD, in *C. eurytheme* and *C. eriphyle* (Carter and Watt 1988). While testing fitness predictions about PGI, we scored PGM and G6PD in the same samples. As expected, flight was unchanged by G6PD genotypes and little affected by PGM, and there were no survival differences at either gene. Heterozygotes at both genes were advantaged in male mating success (25–40% for PGM; nearly twofold for G6PD), as much as for PGI variants but independent of them—showing the distinctness of effects resulting from the enzymes' metabolic roles. We also saw epistasis between PGM and G6PD: some genotype combinations were favored, and others disfavored, in male mating success (Carter and Watt 1988).

We are beginning a functional study of variation at these genes, asking several key questions. First, does the kinetics versus stability trade-off, seen in PGI, extend to these enzyme genes? Second, how do these enzymes' roles in their separate, though interconnected, pathways shape their variants' performance effects, compared with PGI? Clearly qualitative differences in metabolic tasking are important, as, for example, the predictable absence of flight alteration by G6PD variants makes clear, but possible quantitative performance and fitness differences based on the nature or magnitude of functional differences will need careful evaluation, as with PGI. Finally, how does epistasis, or nonadditive interaction among the genotypes of multiple genes, among enzymes vary with their places in metabolism? Is it true, as may be theoretically expected, that epistasis mainly occurs among genes acting within single pathway branches, dividing metabolism into "modules" (cf. Savageau and Sorribas 1989; Wagner 1996)?

Whatever the answers to these questions prove to be, one lesson is already clear: even sharing a common substrate in the metabolic map does not force gene products into similar organism-environment interactions, commonality of adaptive nature, or resulting selective regimes. Only approaches founded on recognition of biological specificity—most notably, the method of identified genes—can hope to analyze effectively the evolutionary meaning of such variation.

REGULATORY AND STRUCTURAL GENE VARIATION: COADAPTATION AND COEVOLUTION

Some genes do not code for proteins, but regulate the expression of other genes. The variability of regulatory and of protein coding genes could interact in important ways. Evolutionary studies of yet another *Colias* enzyme gene have looked at just such interactions—once again, in a broadly bioenergetic context.

Early in the study of allozyme variation in the wild, Burns discovered extraordinary variation in a dimeric esterase (Es-D) of *Colias* (Burns and Johnson 1967). First found in the North American lowland species complex, in which some populations have 20–25 or more alleles, this polymorphism is universal among North American *Colias* (Burns 1975) and also occurs in two species of *Colias*'s sister genus, *Zerene* (H. Geiger et al., unpub.). Numbers of *Es-D* alleles, and some other features of Es-D phenotypes, covary with *Colias*'s larval host plant specializations (Burns 1975).

Superimposed regulatory variation appeared during Burns and Johnson's study of the transmission genetics of this extensive allelic variation (1967). They found several progenies of single-pair matings that included more than four phenotypes—which is not possible for a single gene in diploid organisms! Rather than shrug off their findings as "unexplained mistakes," as many might have done, Burns and Johnson had the insight to report the data in detail and hypothesize the action of one or more "modifier genes," of unknown nature, in their anomalous Es-D progenies.

There are two keys to understanding these progenies. First, each progeny involves four or fewer electromorph alleles, a number consistent with single-gene inheritance; and second, the additional phenotypes reflect increases or decreases in the intensity of Es-D band staining, segregating in Mendelian ratios within electromorph allele classes. Thus the "modifiers" must be variants of regulatory genes that affect the Es-D gene's transcription or translation into protein. Figure 15.4 displays two possible models for such regulation. Figure 15.5 shows how the model in figure 15.4A, isomorphic to the bacterial lactose operon system (Jacob and Monod 1961), can explain one of Burns and Johnson's anomalous crosses. However, Adriana Briscoe, while in our laboratory, found that such an operon analogue must be augmented: in *C. eurytheme,* there are three or more genes affecting Es-D expression (Briscoe 1993); a final count awaits further study.

A. "operon" model

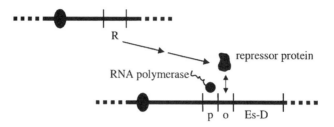

B. one multi-site regulation model

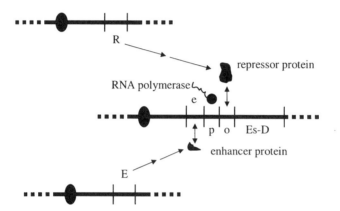

Figure 15.4 Two possible models of regulation of the expression of esterase-D (Es-D). (A) A model analogous to the lactose "operon" in bacteria. The Es-D structural gene is found on an autosome, with a "promoter" site, p, which binds RNA polymerase, upstream from the gene and separated from it by an "operator" site, o, which binds a repressor protein. If o is obstructed, RNA polymerase cannot reach the Es-D gene to transcribe messenger RNA from it, and thus Es-D is not expressed from that gene copy. A gene, R, on another autosome codes for the "repressor" protein that can bind o, obstructing it. At the o site, genetic variants o^+, allowing the repressor to bind, and o^c, not allowing it to do so, are possible. At the R site, genetic variants R^+, producing a functional repressor, and R^-, producing a dysfunctional repressor, or none at all, are possible. (For further details of the lactose operon system, consult any recent genetics text.) (B) One possible multigene regulation system, in which an "enhancer" gene, E, on yet another autosomal chromosome is added to the system. E produces an "enhancer" protein that binds at site e on Es-D's chromosome, facilitating the initial binding of RNA polymerase to site p. Genetic variants of E that affect the level of Es-D expression by enhancing this binding to lesser or greater extents would be possible. Note that repression of Es-D expression would override such variation and thus would be epistatic to it.

Burns's finding of phylogenetic correlations between Es-D variation and larval host plant use suggested that Es-D might detoxify the defensive chemicals of *Colias*'s larval host plants. This hypothesis gains further support from the observation that Es-D is very active against esters of dual-ring naphthol derivatives, similar in structure to indolizidine alkaloids and other multi-ring defensive compounds found in some legume host plants of *Colias* (e.g., Molyneux and James 1982). Further study of Es-D will let us examine three general issues: the adaptive importance of the cosegregation of structural protein variation and variation in multiple regulatory loci controlling

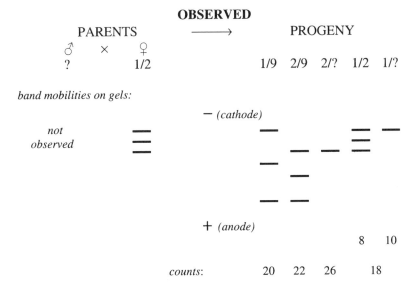

OBSERVED

PARENTS $\longrightarrow$ PROGENY

♂ × ♀
?   1/2   1/9   2/9   2/?   1/2   1/?

band mobilities on gels:

− *(cathode)*

not observed

+ *(anode)*

                     8   10

counts: 20   22   26   18

HYPOTHETICAL GENETIC MODEL

♂ × ♀

Es-D: $2^r/9^c$ × $1^c/2^c$ $\longrightarrow$ $1^c/9^c$ $2^c/9^c$ $2^c/2^r$ $1^c/2^r +1^c/2^r$
                                          1   :   1   :   1   :   1

R
gene: R^-/R^- R^-/R^+
         or R^-/R^- : R^-/R^+
     R^-/R^+ R^-/R^- 1   :   1

Figure 15.5 Explanation of Burns and Johnson's (1967) cross 66–3 by model A of figure 15.4. The cross of a female heterozygous for Es-D alleles 1 and 2 with an unknown male produced five progeny classes; female and progeny Es-D electrophoretic phenotypes are diagrammed, and progeny counts are given. The "operon-like" genetic model can explain this pattern if several assumptions are made: first, that one parent was homozygous for a repressor-negative (R⁻) allele while the other was heterozygous for repressor-positive and repressor-negative alleles (R⁺/R⁻), making all Es-D progeny classes segregate 1:1 for presence/absence of repression; and second, that the father was heterozygous for Es-D allele 2 linked to a repressible promoter-operator site and allele 9 linked to a constitutive, not repressible, promoter-operator site ($2^r/9^c$), while the mother's Es-D alleles were both linked to constitutive promoter-operators ($1^c/2^c$). The progeny classes 1/9 and 2/9 are straightforward. The single-banded progeny class 2/? contains two classes of expression that are not distinguishable on starch gels; and the "fourth and fifth" classes 1/2 and 1/? actually represent the segregation of R⁺ and R⁻ within the Es-D genotype $1^c/2^r$, and sum to give the fourth part of a 1:1:1:1 segregation at Es-D itself.

protein expression in the wild; the genetic basis of the insect side of co-evolution between *Colias* and its host plants, testing some predictions of the Ehrlich and Raven (1964) coevolutionary model; and the integration of variation at genes affecting food acquisition into the overall scheme of the organismal energy budget. In short, Es-D's evolution should be understandable as that of a molecular foraging tool, falling into place within the bioenergetic adaptive context in a quite different way than the enzymes of intermediary metabolism considered up to this point.

FROM BUTTERFLIES TO THE REST OF BIODIVERSITY: EXTENDING AND RESYNTHESIZING FROM SPECIFIC RESULTS

The method of identified genes has proved its analytical worth in diverse cases, such as our *Colias* studies. But analyses of such cases only accumulate detailed facts unless resynthesis from the analyses is possible. How should we proceed from diverse results on *Colias,* or on other butterflies, to candidate generalities that might apply broadly across the living world?

The difficulties of evolutionary generalization, arising from biological complexity, have been of concern to many distinguished workers. Levins (1968) suggested that evolutionists might not achieve reality, generality, and precision of understanding all at the same time. Clegg (2000) asked, given genetic variation in a population, how (if at all) can we address its evolutionary meaning rigorously and quickly, given the intricacy of the functional context inside an organism and the ecological context around it? Does the complexity of phenotype-environment interaction mean that only rarely can we understand adaptation in causal terms? Must our knowledge be limited because adaptive biology, while causal in its basis, is too multivariate for us to unravel the interwoven threads of that basis, or too complex to allow us to perceive common features?

Our experience argues that pessimistic answers to these questions are *not* warranted, and that mechanistic evolutionary studies may be able to address these problems effectively where older, amechanistic approaches cannot (cf. Watt 2000). We focus here on two related challenges: extending specific empirical understanding to additional cases or systems, and generalizing results on diverse genes or taxa into meaningful heuristic principles.

THE FEASIBILITY OF EXTENDING SPECIFIC KNOWLEDGE OF ADAPTATION

As with any new area of science, the first few rigorous studies of adaptive mechanisms have been the slowest and most difficult to articulate. Some insights into how to facilitate such work are in hand, though doubtless many others remain to be realized. The following list is surely not comprehensive, but it is well supported by experience so far.

Knowledge of natural history is prerequisite (though not, alone, sufficient) to the usefulness of any model system. Knowledge of natural history may be fostered by any careful observer of individual behavior patterns, life cycle strategy and details, seasonal phenology and microhabitat distribution, and so forth. Our extensive knowledge of their natural history is one reason why butterflies are such fine model systems for observation or experiment in the study of ecology and evolution.

In dealing with complex systems, one may first achieve local understanding, then expand from that beginning. The method of identified genes exemplifies this principle, since focusing on variation at one gene in a metabolic or developmental pathway, then expanding to study the genes with which it interacts, may be very productive. But if this approach is to succeed, overeager criticism of early-stage studies as "incomplete" must be resisted. Science often advances by cycles of successive refinement, and in dealing with living complexity, intermediate stages of knowledge are necessary way stations on the path to greater clarity.

Idiosyncrasies of study systems can often form elements of experimental design. For example, sperm precedence in the remating of *Colias* (Boggs and Watt 1981) is central to a design for studying male mating success in the wild (Watt et al. 1985). Our ability to assay how often a female butterfly has mated by counting spermatophores (Burns 1968) allows the testing of a female choice mechanism favoring kinetically effective male PGI genotypes in *Colias*'s courtship, with general implications for mating system evolution (Watt et al. 1986; Brown 1997). In a different but analogous case, the planar nature of butterfly wing patterns has fostered their use as models for the evolution of development (Nijhout 1991; Brakefield and Monteiro, chap. 12 in this volume).

Scientists must broaden their approaches to gain new understanding of evolution. They must acquire new technical tools and skills, and cross subdisciplinary boundaries, to analyze adaptive phenomena that cut across traditional specializations on taxa, conceptual subareas, or "layers" of biological organization. This is not a matter of unusual talent, but of willingness to think in new ways. An early example was Klots's (1951) focus on the relation of butterfly ecology to host plant distributions; this is now "conventional wisdom" for butterfly biology, especially following Ehrlich and Raven's recognition of coevolution among plants and herbivorous insects (1964). As another example, understanding the functional roles of genes in phenotypic organization is crucial for understanding natural selection on them; one must learn what is known about phenotypic organization to understand the adaptive variation of genes within it.

This insight applies equally to amateur biologists. Many "technical" evolutionary areas, such as the study of butterflies' thermal adaptations, are accessible to self-educated workers. Background knowledge can be gained from the literature (and/or by collaboration with professionals), and the cost of needed instruments may be *much* less than that of the field vehicles often owned by collectors. There is every reason why amateur biologists should contribute to mechanistic evolutionary study, just as serious amateurs contribute to "technical" areas of astronomy.

Functional subdivisions of the phenotype are real and must be recognized. In other words, if specific traits are to function, the connections among them must have sharp limits—"pleiotropy" cannot be unconstrained. Different genes or phenotypic subsystems interact with the same niche variables differently according to their functions. For example, photoperiodically cued shifts of absorptivity and of insulating hair thickness between a cool-season spring-fall morph and a warm-season summer morph in *Colias* display similar but independent response curves (Jacobs and Watt 1994). Further, while PGI variants and thermoregulatory phenotypes are both subject to strong thermally based selection in *Colias*, their interactions with those selection pressures are not correlated (Watt 1992). Since the interconnection of phenotypic subsystems is constrained by their functions, their experimental analysis must in fact be feasible, contrary to assertions of "irreducible holism" by earlier workers (critiqued also by Depew and Weber 1995).

INEFFECTIVE AND EFFECTIVE WAYS OF SEARCHING FOR EVOLUTIONARY GENERALITY

To generalize successfully about evolution, one cannot merely average or summarize over cases to erase functional differences among genes or phenotypic subsystems and isolate some purely formal principle. Fisher (1958) asserted in his "fundamental theorem of natural selection" that assessing "genetic variance in fitness" would suffice to explain the dynamics of natural selection, and Levins (1965) praised this view as supposedly avoiding the problems posed by biological complexity. But by so doing, the study of evolution is limited to post hoc summary. There is no hope of *predictive* generality without studying the mechanistic interplay of adaptation and constraint that gives rise to fitness differences in the first place.

In this regard, results from the method of identified genes oppose the assumption, often made by population biologists, that allozymes behave as a uniform class of variants. This idea may have arisen because allozymes are all detected with one technique (electrophoresis), but it is nonetheless a delusion. Gillespie and Kojima (1968) first saw that enzymes' distinct metabolic functions lead to their variants having differently specific effects on organismal performance, and thence on fitness. It follows that electrophoretic screening of multigene allozyme variation is mainly useful for initial surveys, and should be followed by more functionally focused study.

Thus, studies that correlate holistic measures of organismal performance (e.g., growth rate or oxygen consumption: cf. Mitton 1997, chap. 7) with multigene allozyme heterozygosity serve mainly to suggest targets for gene-by-gene study—as done by Powers et al. (e.g., 1991) for fish LDH following a survey by Mitton and Koehn (1975), by Pogson (1991) for oyster PGM, and many others. Multigene heterozygosity is a useful summary statistic, but we must not overestimate its biological reality. Some of the variants underlying this statistic may be functionally neutral, while others differ sharply in function and thence in their effects on diverse fitness-related performances—foraging, growth, maintenance, and reproduction (Watt 1985a, 1985b, 1986).

Further, some genes may affect a given part of the phenotype while other genes, because they serve other functions, do not. *Colias*'s PGM and G6PD variants, which affect male mating success, but not through flight, do not change survival, while PGI variants, which affect flight, change both fitness components. Or, a given selection pressure may engage only a few genes; e.g., in sea bass exposed to osmotic stress, some allozymes showed large frequency shifts (without functional studies, the causes aren't known yet), while others' frequencies stayed constant, and randomly assayed neutral nuclear DNA "markers" drifted randomly (Allegrucci et al. 1994, 1995). Whether variation is adaptive, occurs within constraints, or is neutral—and *why?*—are questions *necessarily* first asked variant by variant, gene by gene, habitat by habitat.

Thus, "meta-analysis" of multigene correlative studies of allozymes, as attempted by Britten (1996), may only compound confusion. Meta-analysis assumes that the entities varying in the studies analyzed are truly comparable, as if allozymes were randomly sampled from a single distribution of genes affecting performance and fitness in the same ways, important or not. Demonstrably, they are not. We (Watt et al. 1986) agree with Britten's doubts that heterozygosity per se "must" be of adaptive value, but his claim that "selection . . . has at most a weak effect at allozyme loci" is just as undermined by the diversity of the varying genes' phenotypic functions in the studies he considered as are some of those studies' conclusions themselves.

However, recognizing functional diversity among genes and their variants need not lead to despair of generality, and model systems need not limit the scope of the generalizations whose formulation they provoke. The bioenergetic context for our studies of adaptation, developed from metabolic theory in response to specific findings about *Colias* variants, already unifies studies of butterflies, flies, fish, mice, crustaceans, plants, and bacteria under its simple initial principles (Watt 1985a, 1986, 1991; Feder and Watt 1992; Watt and Dean 2000):

The effect of genetic variants on fitness varies with the nature and size of their functional differences. Thus *Colias* PGI genotypes vary dramatically in fitness according to their functional differences (e.g., Watt 1992 and table 15.1 above), while PGI allozymes of *E. coli* all behave neutrally—that is, have equivalent fitness—because their functional differences are negligible in the conditions in which fitness was tested (Dykhuizen and Hartl 1983; Watt 1985a).

Variants' effects depend on their gene's role in its metabolic (or developmental) pathway as governed by theory applying to that pathway. Thus *Colias* PGI variants, which have large effects on the transient metabolism of adult flight, seem functionally neutral in the larval steady state, as is consistent with theoretical expectations of the demands of transient versus steady-state metabolism. Further, in *E. coli*'s steady-state lactose use pathway, kinetic variants of galactoside permease, the pathway's first enzyme, have a much greater fitness effect than kinetic variants of similar size at the second enzyme, following steady-state theory (e.g., Watt and Dean 2000).

Variants' effects depend on the role of their gene's pathway in the organism's processing, allocation, or biosynthetic/growth machinery. Thus variants of PGI, at the start of glycolysis, have large effects on flight performance and thence on all adult fitness components, while variants of PGM and G6PD, affecting two other pathways, have little or no effect on flight or survivorship, and apparently exert their large effects on male mating success by quite different functional routes (Carter and Watt 1988), even though all three pathways share the branch-point metabolite G6P.

The fraction of the organism's energy budget that a pathway affects gives a scale for the effect of genetic variants in that pathway. Variants of large difference, in pathways with major effects on organismal energy budgets, have similarly large performance and fitness effects in *Colias* PGI (e.g., Watt 1992), killifish LDH (Powers et al. 1991), and *Drosophila* G6PD (Labate and Eanes 1992). In *E. coli*, 6PGD variants differing by 35–40% in K_m had undetectable fitness effects when that step of the pentose shunt was peripheral to overall carbon flow, but strong fitness effects when genetic rearrangement of metabolism made 6PGD central to major carbon flow into cells (Dykhuizen and Hartl 1980; Hartl and Dykhuizen 1981; Watt 1985a).

Further tests of these simple principles will be feasible as other specific gene studies, in butterflies and other model systems alike, are developed—but no failure to support them has yet been found in any case tested. They may extend readily to other situations, such as the cost-benefit trade-off between variants that change V_{max}/K_m by affecting the rate of enzyme production and hence [E], and situations in which an enzyme's kinetics or stability are altered by amino acid substitution (Watt 1986). As in other areas of biology, the path to truly productive generality leads through the understanding and resynthesis of diversely specific empirical results (e.g., Judson 1996).

SUMMARY

Beyond the specific adaptive mechanisms revealed by the study of butterflies with the method of identified genes, and the methodological lessons that experience of such study teaches, what general conclusions about evolutionary facts and processes have come from this work? And, even acknowledging that much of the future of this approach may be unanticipatable, where *might* it take us?

Conclusions

Bioenergetics is a powerful context for unifying specific case studies of adaptations in, and constraints on, evolutionary variation. Specific model system results have been extended to a general view of thermal limitation of metabolic performance, forcing the evolution of thermoregulation to narrow, and separately to high, body temperature ranges by diverse means in diverse groups of animals. The integration of thermodynamic boundary conditions and constraint by principles of pathway kinetics supports generalizable cost-benefit analyses of the adaptive effects of natural variation on metabolic organization.

The method of identified genes allows prediction of the performance and fitness effects of genetic variants in the wild. If not yet routine, the method of identified genes at least now provides a clear strategy for studying variants' molecular and physiological differences (especially in the bioenergetic context), assessing their interactions with ecological niche variables, and thus predicting their evolutionary dynamics in empirically testable ways.

Variants of single major genes may often have large, positive fitness effects. This conclusion overturns earlier views that such cases ought to be exceptional. The first three enzymes studied in our test system each show at least one fitness component differing among genotypes by more than 10%. A related point is that major gene variants may have large fitness effects *through* their alteration of "complex" traits such as locomotion. This conclusion falsifies the view of many population biologists that complex traits must be polygenic, with little scope for the action of major genes.

Natural genetic variants of metabolic enzymes are not a unitary functional class. Because metabolic enzymes have diversely specific roles in metabolism, their performance effects and fitness consequences may be very divergent. Even when enzymes share common substrates, their polymorphisms may have independent evolutionary experiences, though such functional proximity can also lead to important epistatic interactions. Empirical study designs and methods of data analysis must acknowledge the importance of this functional heterogeneity, but it does not preclude productive generalization from specific cases, as our first three conclusions emphasize.

Similarity of allozyme (or other protein) mobility in ordinary electrophoresis is not a sound criterion of allelic or genotypic identity. Indeed, genotypes of similar mobility may have entirely distinct functional properties in different taxa. "Allozyme systematics" may often misestimate—usually *underest*imate—differences among related taxa, as those taxa are assumed to share alleles, albeit with different frequencies, on the basis of ordinary electrophoresis.

Either clinal differentiation or uniformity of polymorphic genotype frequencies over space may be driven by strong local selection pressures. Such effects may coexist when reproducible shifts in local selection pressure recur over broad geographic ranges. Thus, when comparing local differences in genetic variation with uniformity of other variant frequencies over geography, one should not assume a priori that any of the variation is either selected or neutral, but should test all alternatives empirically.

Constraints on protein structure and metabolism frustrate the "optimization" of metabolic traits, so that adaptation occurs only within those constraints. Such constraints begin, in ways that remain to be determined, by preventing co-maximization of different functional properties, such as kinetics and thermal stability, in homozygotes, despite ample mutational opportunity for such optimizing alleles to arise. These constraints, in turn, interact with the metabolic constraints imposed by principles of pathway organization.

Selection within mechanistic constraints may maintain functional polymorphism for long periods of time. There is evidence from PGI and other genes that polymorphisms may persist continuously for longer than the time spans of individual species' existence. At the same time, those polymorphisms can diverge evolutionarily among taxa in functional respects. In short, genetic polymorphism need not be "a transient phase of molecular evolution," but may in some cases be an alternative stable state of molecular evolution, perhaps lasting millions of years.

PROSPECTS FOR THE FUTURE

Many of these conclusions point to future advances. We can look forward to the extension of bioenergetic theories of adaptation, and of the empirical bases for testing these theories, in several ways.

We can explore metabolic adaptation using natural genetic variants. We can examine the effects of variants' functional differences on a pathway's performance, and especially on its thermal sensitivity, to test quantitative aspects of metabolic adaptation within system constraints and to make further tests of alternative theories on the need for animal thermoregulation.

The study of natural variants' sequences will shed light on the evolution of protein structure. The placement of adaptive (or neutral) amino acid changes in protein structures will clarify how functional, and thence performance and fitness, differences among variants arise from molecular structure. How such changes interact with protein structure to constrain functional optimization in homozygotes, perpetuating polymorphic variation, will be an especially interesting question.

The study of adaptation at diverse specific genes will extend the testing, and thus the generality, of bioenergetic adaptive principles. Understanding functional differences among genotypes of PGM, G6PD, Es-D, and other variable genes in *Colias* (and relatives) will clarify the evolutionary interaction of phenotypic subsystems with diverse areas of Hutchinsonian "niche space." In the case of Es-D especially, the role of specific major gene adaptations in *co*evolutionary processes may be clarified. Moreover, the complementary, rather than "either/or," roles of regulatory and structural gene variants may be clarified as the study of Es-D unfolds.

The connections of intraspecific adaptive processes with processes of species differentiation will become accessible to study. A number of important questions arise here: How do specific adaptive mechanisms evolve across taxonomic boundaries? How do major parts or "subspaces" of the Hutchinsonian organism-environment niche interaction evolve across taxonomic boundaries or among differently divergent relatives? How, if at all, are adaptive innovations associated with particular stages of speciation? How much similarity and difference among taxa is based on "phylogenetic constraints," and how much on differential adaptation (Harvey and Pagel 1991)? Finally, what is the repeatability of evolution? Are unique combinations of epistatic variants at different genes, or of variants with diverse genetic backgrounds, often important? Will similar genetic solutions evolve repeatedly under the same pressures, given realistic constraints?

In final conclusion: While the study of evolutionary mechanisms will require new intellectual approaches in many respects, these approaches will be different from, but not intrinsically more difficult than, previous paths to understanding. Our background knowledge of butterflies, our ability to study them in both laboratory and field settings, our ability to compare details of their adaptive machinery among different habitats and taxa, and our ability to assimilate new techniques and thought processes from the study of other organisms will all be extremely helpful to our success in meeting this intellectual challenge. We may look forward confidently to further uses of butterflies as model systems for the mechanistic study of evolution.

ACKNOWLEDGMENTS

I owe gratitude of long standing, as noted elsewhere (Watt 1995b), to Charles Remington for collegiality, friendship, and intellectual stimulus. Too many other colleagues to thank individually have contributed ideas and assistance to the work summarized here; they have, however, been acknowledged elsewhere. I thank Carol Boggs, Paul Ehrlich, Erica Fleishman, Jessica

Hellmann, Everett Meyer, Chris Wheat, and Paul Wright for helpful commentary on drafts of this chapter. Our research has been supported over several decades by Lois and Ralph Watt, the Joseph Fels Foundation, the National Geographic Society, the U.S. Department of Energy, the U.S. National Institutes of Health, the U.S. National Science Foundation, and the Ford Motor Company through the Center for Evolutionary Studies at Stanford University.

CHAPTER 16

Mate Location: A Matter of Design? Adaptive Morphological Variation in the Speckled Wood Butterfly

Hans Van Dyck

MATE LOCATION IN MALE BUTTERFLIES: WAIT OR SEEK

Species, and individuals within a species, differ in several aspects of their phenotype, including morphology, physiology, and behavior. At the behavioral level, an animal may have two different options for finding a resource, such as food or a mate: "wait" or "seek." This dichotomy appears widely applicable to different kinds of behavior and has universally been used to classify the variation in visually cued mate location behavior in butterflies and in some other groups of insects (e.g., Odonata: Heinrich and Casey 1978; Thysanoptera: Crespi 1988; Hymenoptera: Alcock and Houston 1996). A male butterfly can sit and wait at a particular site in order to meet females, or he can move around, searching for females. Scott (1974) classified these strategies as "perching" and "patrolling," respectively. For a broader review of mate location, mating systems, and sexual selection in butterflies, I refer the reader to Rutowski (1997) and Wiklund (chap. 4 in this volume), and for other groups of insects, including information on their alternative mate location strategies, to Choe and Crespi (1997).

In the life of an adult male butterfly, mate location is an important activity, since most of his active time is spent trying to find mates (Shreeve 1992a). Some butterfly species are exclusive patrollers, others predominant perchers, whereas in some others there is clear evidence that both strategies occur, even within a single population. In most animals, mate location strategies are described in relation to demography (e.g., population density, operational sex ratio, or individual age), but in many ectotherms (including butterflies), mate location strategies may be related to body size and temperature (Willmer 1991). Mate location is clearly related to flight behavior, and perching and patrolling imply different types of flight. A percher requires a short, powerful flight in order to approach a passer-by very quickly, while a patroller needs a searching flight at a more or less constant and lower speed. Different types of flight, which vary in their biomechanics and aerodynamics, may require different designs, including differences in distribution of body mass, wing loading, and wing shape (Betts and Wootton 1988; Dudley 1990; Chai and Srygley 1990; Srygley and Chai 1990a). Therefore, we might expect mate location behavior to be related to body and wing morphology. Indeed, at the interspecific level, perching and patrolling species differ morphologically (Wickman 1992b): perching species have, among other differences, larger relative thorax masses (i.e., thorax mass/total body mass) and higher wing loadings (i.e., body mass/wing area). Scott (1983) concluded in a similar vein that perching butterflies have a more powerful thorax relative to the size of the wings than patrolling species.

The goal of the work reviewed in this chapter is an understanding of intraspecific variation in mate location behavior when both perching and patrolling co-occur within a population. The speckled wood butterfly, *Pararge aegeria* (L.), is such a species. The underlying working hypothesis is that the observed links between morphology and mate location behavior reflect variation in morphological adaptedness to the different strategies. First, I discuss the relationships between morphological traits and mate location behavior and the functional mechanisms underlying them. Second, I shift the focus to implications for other flight behaviors, to female behavior and design, and to possible implications when habitat conditions change, particularly within a context of habitat fragmentation.

THE SPECKLED WOOD BUTTERFLY

The speckled wood is a temperate satyrine butterfly of the western Palearctic that occurs mainly within and at the edges of different types of woodland where sunlight can penetrate to the forest floor. Adult males and females rely on sunlit patches to thermoregulate behaviorally by dorsal basking (*sensu* Clench 1966). They feed mainly on honeydew, but also to a lesser extent on fluids of trees, rotten berries, and nectar. In Belgium, where our fieldwork was conducted, the speckled wood is a bivoltine butterfly of common status. Compared with other temperate butterflies, the speckled wood has an exceptionally variable life cycle, with different possible pathways depending on overwintering stage (larval or pupal) and the occurrence of summer or winter diapause. Studies by the Stockholm Evolutionary Ecology group (Wiklund et al. 1983; Nylin et al. 1989, 1993, 1995) show complex reaction norms of development with strong plasticity in relation to environmental factors (photoperiod and secondarily temperature).

The dorsal wing surface of the speckled wood butterfly is light to dark brown with small yellow patches. In the submarginal zone of the dorsal hindwings, a variable number of black eyespots is present (rarely two, usually three or four). The eyespots vary in size and in the presence or absence of a white center. The intensity of the brown background wing color can be scored visually and with high repeatability in the field (Van Dyck et al. 1997a). When specimens are collected, this variation in color can be measured as gray values by means of an image analyzing system (cf. Windig 1991). Females are on average larger than males. The phenotypic composition of a population changes seasonally, but there are no discrete seasonal forms (Packer 1984; Shreeve 1987; Van Dyck et al. 1997c). In the first generation, successively emerging butterflies are darker and larger, while in the second generation they remain rather dark and of intermediate size. In several other insects, including butterflies, spring individuals are more melanized than summer individuals for thermoregulatory reasons (e.g., Shapiro 1976; Holloway 1993), which is contrary to the pattern found here. However, this temporal pattern agrees with the seasonal changes in the light levels within a temperate woodland (Van Dyck et al. 1997c). In temperate regions, ambient temperatures, and particularly light levels, are highest in summer (June to August), but climatic conditions vary differently at the floor of a deciduous forest, since there is interference by foliage: light levels at the forest floor peak in April or May (Larcher 1995).

Starting with the classic paper of Davies (1978), the mate location behavior of speckled wood males has been the focus of much attention (Austad et al. 1979; Davies 1979; Wickman and Wiklund 1983; Shreeve 1984, 1987; Van Dyck et al. 1997a, 1997b, 1997c; Van Dyck and Matthysen 1998; Stutt and Willmer 1998; Hardy 1998). Males can either perch in a territorial manner in a sunlit patch where females come to bask (not containing food or oviposition sites) or patrol by flying through the forest and searching for females at and between sunlit patches. The contest behavior of territorial males has been interpreted as an example of the Bourgeois strategy following from game theory, with the conventional rule "the resident always wins" (Davies 1978). However, observations and manipulative experiments by Stutt and Willmer (1998) have recently shown that asymmetries in thoracic temperature between contestants determine the outcome: warmer males were more likely to win. Hence, the winning of contests reflects temperature-related fighting ability, and not a convention based on prior residence. The issue of speckled wood battles and the importance of hot property has recently been reviewed by Hardy (1998).

Here I focus mainly on relationships between the alternative perching and patrolling strategies and the butterfly's morphological design. Davies (1978) considered perching to be the optimal strategy, since territorial perching males gained the most matings. In his study, some "patrolling" males resided in the canopy and frequently came down into the sunlit patches and tried to take over any vacancies. However, in our study areas (small oak-dominated forest patches near Antwerp in Belgium; cf. Van Dyck et al. 1997a), patrolling males flew in the 1–2 m space above the ground, like those observed by Wickman and Wiklund (1983) and Shreeve (1984, 1987). Shreeve (1984) showed that these patrollers located females at a faster rate than did the perching males, but emphasized that their flights are restricted by the necessity of maintaining a high body temperature. We also observed some individuals in the canopy, which were probably closer in behavior to the "patrollers" in Davies' study, being excluded from territorial sites and following a suboptimal strategy of waiting for vacancies. So, the issue of the relative payoffs of perching and patrolling has not yet been clarified yet, but the situation appears in every respect not to be as simple as assumed by Davies (1978).

RELATIONSHIPS BETWEEN ADULT DESIGN AND BEHAVIORAL STRATEGIES

Although there is evidence that the frequencies of perchers and patrollers change during the season (Wickman and Wiklund 1983), individual males were found to be more consistent in adopting one strategy than expected by chance (Van Dyck et al. 1997b). From different types of behavioral observations (including short "snapshot" observations of activity before the butterfly was captured and measured, as well as long observations on a random selection of individuals with the purpose of collecting time budget data), we found consistent relationships between a male's phenotype and his behavior (Van Dyck et al. 1997a, 1997b). When studying the relationships of behavior to wing color, submarginal eyespots, and forewing length (controlling for seasonal variation), we found wing color to be of overriding importance. Pale males spent most of their time resting within a sunlit patch and engaged more often in short flights and intra- and interspecific interactions; that is, they followed a perching strategy. Darker males flew more frequently between sunlit patches through the shaded forest (cf. fig. 16.1) and initiated interactions less frequently; that is, they followed a patrolling strategy. This difference was not an effect of age, since wing wear did not affect wing color.

Interestingly, Shreeve (1987) has shown a different relationship between phenotype and mate location strategy in speckled woods: males with four eyespots were mainly perchers, while three-spot males were patrollers. In our study, the relationships of behavioral parameters with spot type were much weaker than those with wing color, and in fact the trends were the opposite:

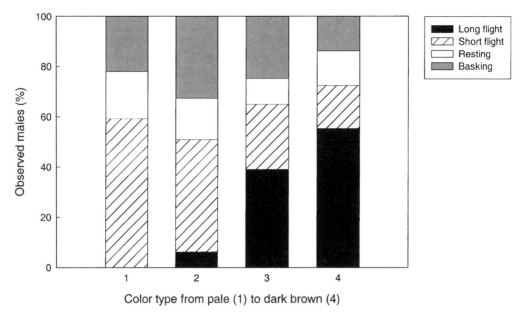

Figure 16.1 Percentages of speckled wood males with different wing colors ($N = 187$) engaging in four different activities. Sample sizes for the four color categories were 32, 49, 77, and 29 individuals respectively. (From Van Dyck et al. 1997a; with permission of Academic Press.)

three-spot males engaged in long flights (an indication of patrolling) less often, and tended to initiate more intraspecific conflicts (an indication of territorial perching), than four-spot males (Van Dyck et al. 1997a). This relationship makes sense in terms of the predator deflectance model of Brakefield (1984), which predicts a positive correlation between spotting and level of activity. The fact that a relationship between behavioral strategy and spot type can be the reverse is a further indication of the importance of some factor other than spot type. However, it is not clear to what extent the difference between our results and Shreeve's may be attributable to variation in selection pressures between habitats.

Independently of these relationships with wing color and spot type, we found that perchers had relatively large thorax sizes compared with patrollers. To measure relative thorax size, we used forewing length/body length as an index for thorax mass/total body mass (for justification see Van Dyck et al. 1997b). Lengths are easier to measure accurately in the field than the small mass of butterflies; additionally, this method does not require killing the animal. Perchers and patrollers did not differ in wing length, but the former had shorter bodies. The relatively larger thoraxes of perchers fit with the interspecific pattern shown by Wickman (1992b). This finding also agrees with the interspecific comparisons between palatable and unpalatable Neotropical butterflies (Chai and Srygley 1990; Srygley and Chai 1990a): unpalatable species that engage in evasive flights and need a high maneuverability to escape from bird predators also had larger thoraxes and shorter bodies. A lack of correlation between absolute size (wing length) and mate location strategy was also found in perching and patrolling tiger blue butterflies, *Tarucus theophrastus* (Courtney and Parker 1985).

CAUSES BEHIND THE PATTERNS: THERMOREGULATION AND BIOMECHANICS

The observation that perching males have paler wings and larger thoraxes than patrolling males points to functional relationships between these traits and aspects of flight ability, including thermoregulation. We hypothesized that relatively small differences in wing color imply considerable variation in thermoregulation (Van Dyck et al. 1997a). This idea arose from well-established observations in butterflies of increased melanization with elevation or latitude (e.g., Watt 1968; Roland 1982; Guppy 1986; Kingsolver and Wiernasz 1987). In the alpine butterfly *Parnassius phoebus,* increased basal wing melanism has been associated with increased movement of males within a population, whereas size (wing length) had no effect (Guppy 1986). Wing color influences thermoregulation, but what really matters for dorsal basking butterflies such as the speckled wood is the basal part of the wing; heat energy can be transferred from this basal part to the thorax by conduction and convection of trapped warm air (Wasserthal 1975). The thermal characteristics, particularly the absorptivity, of butterfly wings vary among species by type of basking behavior, color, and surface structure (Schmitz 1994). Thermocouples (e.g., copper-constantan thermocouple in a hypodermic needle microprobe: cf. Van Dyck and Matthysen 1998) can provide accurate measurements of thoracic temperature in living butterflies under field conditions or in experimental setups in the laboratory.

In the speckled wood, patrollers fly from one sunlit patch to another through shady, cooler conditions, while perchers remain in a sunlit patch. The optimal body temperature for flight varies between 32° and 34.5°C, well above normal ambient levels (Shreeve 1984), and flight reduces body temperature (Shreeve 1984), as is also the case in three other satyrine butterflies (Heinrich 1986; Shelley and Ludwig 1985; Wickman 1988). For these reasons, we hypothesized that darker males are better designed for patrolling (Van Dyck et al. 1997a). Darker males may be better able to recover from heat loss in flight and quickly regain the necessary body temperature for flight by a higher absorption of energy while basking, and thereby spend more time flying and searching for females (Wickman 1988). Hence, patrollers are probably true shuttling ectotherms (Pivnick and McNeil 1986; Dennis 1993; Rutowski et al. 1994; Dreisig 1995). Perching males, particularly if they are too dark, may suffer from overheating in permanent sunlight on a perch.

Table 16.1 Mean thoracic temperature ($\pm$ SE) of speckled wood males engaged in different activities under field conditions

Activity	N	Thoracic temperature (°C)
Long flight	33	31.20 ± 0.26
Basking	70	31.22 ± 0.31
Short flight	36	32.24 ± 0.19
Fighting	14	33.36 ± 0.36
Resting	59	34.03 ± 0.16

Source: Van Dyck and Matthysen 1998; with permission of Springer-Verlag.

From this hypothesis we made three predictions. First, body temperature should vary with behavior, since more flight activity (especially flying between sunlit patches) implies convective cooling and hence more frequent lower temperatures. Second, body temperature should vary with color, since darker males are more often found patrolling (flying) and hence are faced with more convective cooling. Finally, the color types should differ in heating rate: darker males should heat up faster. All three predictions were confirmed by observational data in the field and a heating experiment in the laboratory (Van Dyck and Matthysen 1998). In the field, darker males had lower body temperatures on average than paler males. Different activities (e.g., resting, flying: table 16.1) and behavioral strategies (perching or patrolling) were associated with differences in thoracic temperature: patrolling males that primarily engaged in long flights and periods of basking had lower thoracic temperatures than did perching males. The thoracic temperatures of resting males did not differ between males practicing perching or patrolling. Under laboratory conditions (i.e., an experimental setup of mercury vapor lamps similar in spectrum and intensity to solar radiation), cooled males heated up significantly faster if they were darker (fig. 16.2), but there was no difference in the threshold thoracic temperature for flight. Further experiments using dummies with darkened wings (by means of dark brown paint marker) failed to find an overall effect on thermal properties, but this finding could be an artifact of the manipulation, as supported by results of absorption measurements (Berwaerts et al. 2001).

With respect to the relationship between mate location behavior and thorax mass, the reasoning is identical to that at the interspecific level (Wickman 1992b). Territorial perching speckled woods may need the power from a large thorax (and hence a larger muscle investment) not only to approach a passer-by very quickly, but also to increase the probability of winning a contest. Long male-male conflicts have been shown to be real fights taking the form of spinning-wheels, in which males bounce into each other (Wickman and Wiklund 1983). Consequently, a percher should benefit from a powerful thorax conferring a high capacity to maneuver. Fighting ability varies among males: interactions between some individually

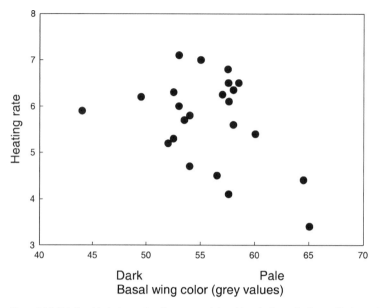

Figure 16.2 Relationship between heating rate and dorsal basal wing color in speckled wood males (*N* = 23). Heating rate is expressed as the slope of thoracic temperature-log time regression in the interval 26°–32°C. (From Van Dyck and Matthysen 1998; with permission of Springer-Verlag.)

marked speckled woods were both more frequent and considerably longer than contests between others (Wickman and Wiklund 1983). Forewing length had no effect on the outcome of interactions between males (Shreeve 1987). However, relationships between flight performance and morphology have often been assumed, but seldom tested. Using an experimental setup with tethered flight, we recently found that acceleration capacity indeed increased with relative thorax size (among other morphological traits) in speckled woods (Berwaerts et al. 2002).

So far, we have ignored the origin or causation of these morphological traits. Basal wing color and thorax size differed highly significantly among families in a "common garden" breeding experiment, and hence those traits appear to have a heritable component (Van Dyck et al. 1998), a prerequisite for selection on flight ability. More detailed work on the production of phenotypic variation in these traits in relation to genetics and environmental influences is in progress (e.g., Van Dyck and Wiklund 2002).

The results of Shreeve and Smith (1992) strongly suggest that relationships among morphology, thermoregulation, and mate location similar to the ones from our intraspecific work exist at the *Pararge* species level as well. They compared the endemic Madeiran speckled wood *Pararge xiphia* and the European speckled wood *P. aegeria*, which was introduced into Madeira in 1976 (Higgins 1977). They found that (1) *P. xiphia* is larger and much darker than *P. aegeria*; (2) *P. xiphia* flies for longer periods and is active at lower temperatures and in cooler microclimates than *P. aegeria;* and (3) both species engage in perching and patrolling, but *P. xiphia* patrols more often than *P. aegeria.* Similar results were independently shown by Jones and Lace (1992).

FROM MATE LOCATION TO LARGER-SCALE MOBILITY AND FEMALE DESIGN

Since mate location behavior is strongly related to flight ability, its relationships with morphological variation may have relevance to other flight behaviors as well. For instance, in a limited mark-recapture study, we found that larger and darker males had a higher probability of moving out of the forest (Van Dyck et al. 1997a). Thus, whereas wing length did not differ between perchers and patrollers (i.e., mobility at the local scale), it appears to be important in the context of dispersal (i.e., mobility at the landscape scale). For the Glanville fritillary, *Melitaea cinxia,* Kuussaari et al. (1996) have similarly shown that emigrating females were larger than resident females. With respect to wing color, the results are comparable for mate location and dispersal: higher mobility is associated with darker wing color.

Our observation was based on samples of males only, but when dealing with mobility at the population level (dispersal and colonization), females should—obviously—also be taken into account. Far away from woodlands, Baker (1984) found only females of the speckled wood. Unfortunately, the present knowledge of morphological and behavioral variation in speckled wood females is very scanty. Since speckled wood females deposit their eggs singly on grasses in shaded, relatively wet parts of the forest, and since searching time for suitable habitat and host plants is thought to be a limiting factor for their fitness (Wiklund and Persson 1983), a female might benefit from being larger and thermally more stable (e.g., more fur on thorax) in order to maintain an optimal body temperature over longer time periods for oviposition and dispersal flights (Van Dyck et al. 1998). Scott (1983) suggested that females of several butterfly species have a patrolling design, but it seems not entirely justified to typify a female's behavior (and design) from the point of view of mate location by males. However, selection on male design could affect female design if there is a high genetic correlation between the sexes (Wickman 1992b). Much more work remains to be done on functional relationships between female design and behavior and how they parallel (or not) those relationships in males. In this context, the observation by Nylin et al. (1993) that speckled wood females are larger than males regardless of whether they are from populations with or without protandry may point to flight-related and thermoregulation-related sexual dimorphism.

A CHANGING DESIGN IN A CHANGING LANDSCAPE?

Knowing that there are consistent relationships between design and be-havior (particularly in males), and that there is evidence to consider them functional, adaptive associations relating to biomechanics and thermoregulation, the next question is whether speckled woods from different types of habitat differ morphologically or behaviorally. Different types of woodland may have different habitat structures and hence different microclimates (or general conditions). Shreeve (1985) found that significantly more males adopted a territorial perching strategy in dense coniferous woodland (where sunlit patches were relatively scarce) than in more open deciduous woodland. Similarly, in a limited census (with data only from a 3-week period in the summer generation), I found a significantly higher proportion of patrollers in a deciduous forest (52%) than in a dense coniferous woodland (23%) and a dense swamp woodland (25%) (Van Dyck, unpub.). An in-depth comparison of morphological traits and behavior among habitat types has not yet been done. However, selection on flight and thermoregulatory abilities may also change when habitat is fragmented. The effects of habitat fragmentation are more commonly studied with respect to population dynamics (e.g., Hanski and Gilpin 1997), but it may have consequences for selection on flight-related design as well. This idea was first put forward by Dempster et al. (1976) in their morphometric study of a time series of cabinet specimens of British *Papilio machaon*. Recent studies provide further evidence for the potential of such evolutionary changes (cf. Van Dyck and Matthysen 1999).

In a preliminary analysis, we compared morphological variation (particularly basal wing color and relative thorax mass) in speckled wood males from four sites differing in the degree of habitat fragmentation: a large woodland, a set of moderately isolated woodland fragments, a set of more strongly isolated woodlots, and a highly fragmented area with very small woodlots and hedgerows scattered in an intensively used agricultural landscape (Berwaerts et al. 1998). Although there were no replicates in this limited study, the results suggest that relative thorax size increases significantly with degree of habitat fragmentation (fig. 16.3). Individuals from the large woodland were significantly paler than the butterflies from the fragmented areas (fig. 16.4). These patterns can be explained by the microclimatic conditions experienced by males in these different habitats.

The microclimatic conditions a speckled wood faces will be very different depending on whether it is active in a large woodland, in tiny woodlots, or along a hedgerow. From a thermoregulatory point of view, the cost of flying in more open conditions may be higher, since the flying time that is "bought" after a period of basking will be smaller. This also applies to very dense woodlands with only a few scattered sunlit patches. Since darker

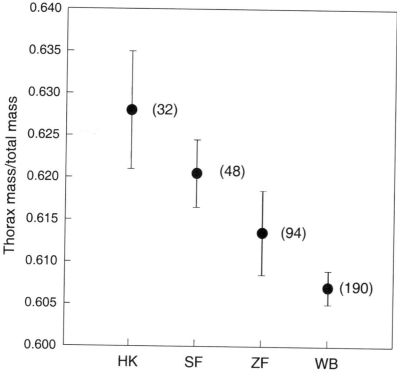

Figure 16.3 Relative thorax size (±SE) in relation to degree of woodland fragmentation for speckled wood males. WB, a relatively large woodland; ZF, a set of moderately isolated woodland fragments; SF, a set of more strongly isolated woodlots; HK, an area with very small woodlots and hedgerows in an intensively used agricultural landscape. Samples sizes are given in parentheses. (Data from Berwaerts et al. 1998.)

speckled woods heat up faster, the presence of darker speckled woods in more open conditions (with more severe convective cooling) seems to make sense. Furthermore, flying in more open conditions may require more power, and hence a larger thorax would be beneficial. So far, there are no data to test whether mate location behavior also varies with fragmentation. In this context, there are several possibilities, including parallel shifts in behavior and related design traits, or a change in the relationship between behavior and design.

Thomas et al. (1998) provided evidence of complex evolutionary changes in flight-related morphology in the lycaenid *Plebejus argus* in response to changes in landscape structure. They found that, within metapopulations of this butterfly, relative thorax size increased with declining habitat area. One of the possible explanations is an effect of mate location strategy on emigration rates. If males with relatively large thoraxes are more likely to perch, they may then be more likely to remain within a small habitat fragment; those that patrol may disperse more widely and be lost from small and isolated patches (Thomas et al. 1998). Hill et al. (1999c)

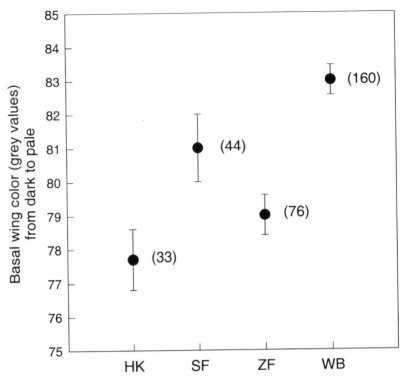

Figure 16.4 Color of the basal part of the dorsal wing surface (expressed as mean gray values ±SE) in relation to degree of woodland fragmentation for speckled wood males. WB, a relatively large woodland; ZF, a set of moderately isolated woodland fragments; SF, a set of more strongly isolated woodlots; HK, an area with very small woodlots and hedgerows in an intensively used agricultural landscape. Samples sizes are given in parentheses. (Data from Berwaerts et al. 1998.)

found heritable responses in the skipper, *Hesperia comma,* when morphological traits among individuals from different patches and metapopulations were compared. When reared in a common environment, colonizing individuals of the northern European speckled wood were larger and also had relatively larger thoraxes than individuals from sites that had been continuously occupied (Hill et al. 1999a). Different butterfly species probably show a wide range of evolutionary responses to changes in the landscape because flight has so many functions, including adult foraging, mate location, finding oviposition sites, predator avoidance, and dispersal (Thomas et al. 1998; Van Dyck and Matthysen 1999).

Apparently such responses to habitat fragmentation are not restricted to very localized, threatened species only, but can also be found in more common species such as the speckled wood. Responses to fragmentation (or changes in land use generally) may interfere with, or even confound, geographic patterns of morphological variation. This observation may shed new light on the complex pattern of morphological variation in this satyrine at a larger geographic scale in Europe. As Brakefield and Shreeve (1992) remarked, this variation follows neither geographic boundaries nor easily explainable clinal patterns.

FUTURE RESEARCH: TOWARD A MULTIDISCIPLINARY UNDERSTANDING

Given the amount of basic knowledge of behavior and morphology in the speckled wood (which is also an easy butterfly to breed, and hence to use for experiments), it is an interesting model for developing new research programs aimed at a more complete understanding of the relationships of morphological design to aspects of flight behavior (including mate location and dispersal) and how these relationships may change and evolve. To reach this goal, future research needs to emphasize experimental approaches (e.g., flight tunnel experiments) as well as correlative studies. Further insights are needed on the causation of the phenotypic variation, the selective forces acting on this variation, and how morphology-behavior links relate to variation in fitness components (cf. Nielsen and Watt 1998). In other words, we need answers to questions such as, What is the quantitative variation in flight-related performance (e.g., acceleration, maneuverability, endurance) among different phenotypes? How is this variation influenced by environmental conditions, such as ambient temperature? To what extent is the variation in performance and morphological design a reflection of genetic variation, and what is the influence of breeding conditions? Are there genetic correlations that may stimulate or break down the simultaneous evolution of different traits of a design? How (and for which aspects of butterfly flight) is variation in performance translated into variation in reproductive output or survival? In addition to a more complete understanding of morphology-behavior links within an evolutionary, adaptive framework, data on fitness components of perching versus patrolling males will be necessary to tackle the behavioral ecological issue of the relative payoffs of the two alternatives (and hence better understand the variation in their frequencies), which are still unclear.

With respect to the causation and development of adult designs, a new observation has recently emerged suggesting a novel trade-off between juvenile and adult investment. Speckled woods can have either green or brown pupae. We found that green pupae produced larger adults with a larger relative thorax mass than brown pupae, and that green pupae also produced adults with a paler basal wing color in females, but not in males (Van Dyck et al. 1998). Further research is definitely required into the mechanism of this possible trade-off between pupal color and adult design.

Understanding the mechanisms underlying the relationships between morphological variation and behavioral or ecological patterns (e.g., habitat use, mate location) can be a powerful explanatory tool in ecological and evolutionary research, since morphological variation among individuals (or species) can be causally linked to variation in resource use and fitness (Wainwright 1994). A further understanding of aspects of butterfly flight (including mate location) will benefit from a multidisciplinary approach integrating functional morphology with biomechanics, thermal ecophysiology, behavioral ecology, and quantitative genetics.

SUMMARY

To locate females, male butterflies either perch or patrol. These two strategies co-occur in some species, such as the speckled wood butterfly (*Pararge aegeria*), a temperate satyrine of woodlands. Perching males have paler wings and larger thoraxes than patrolling males. This observation points to functional relationships with flight ability and thermoregulation. Small differences in basal wing color were shown to result in considerable variation in thermoregulatory properties. The relationships of thorax size to mate location strategy are similar to the known relationships at the interspecific level. A percher will benefit from a large, powerful thorax (muscle mass) to approach a passer-by quickly and to fight with other males. A detailed comparison of flight performance between phenotypes remains to be done. These relationships also have relevance to other behaviors, particularly dispersal. However, little is known about females (the more important sex for dispersal) and how their design relates to behavioral variation. A preliminary analysis of morphological variation in relation to habitat fragmentation suggests that selection may act on this variation: relative thorax size increased with degree of habitat fragmentation, and individuals from a large woodland were paler than individuals from fragmented areas. The species appears to be an interesting model for developing new research programs investigating how design relates to aspects of flight behavior (including mate location and dispersal) and how this relationship may evolve. This research will require the integration of functional morphology, thermal ecophysiology, behavior ecology, and quantitative genetics.

ACKNOWLEDGMENTS

I thank Erik Matthysen, Christer Wiklund, and an anonymous referee for valuable comments on the manuscript. This research is supported by a grant of the University of Antwerp (GOA 15R/3942). H. V. D. is supported by the Fund for Scientific Research Flanders-Belgium (F.W.O.).

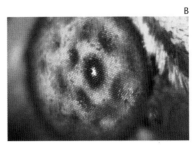

Plate 1.1 *(above & right)* The left eye of a male *Asterocampa leilia*. (A) The principal pseudopupil can be clearly seen as the dark spot above and a little to the left of the center of the eye. (B) A close-up of the pseudopupil as seen with orthodromic illumination. With this type of illumination, the luminous pseudopupil or eyeshine is visible.

Plate 3.1 *(left & below)* The geometry of hawkmoth pollination. (A) *Hyles lineata* visiting flowers of *Aquilegia chrysantha* (Ranunculaceae) in the Catalina Mountains, Pima County, AZ. The length of the moth's proboscis is comparable to that of the nectar spurs (white arrow), and pollen is deposited and removed from the moth's ventral thorax (black arrow). (B) *Manduca quinquemaculata* foraging in a mixed garden of *Calylophus hartweggii* (not shown) and *Oenothera caespitosa* (Onagraceae), in the Tucson Mountains, Pima County, AZ. Pollen from the short-tubed *Calylophus* is deposited on the proboscis (black arrow), while that of *Oenothera* is on the legs (white arrow). The moth's 12 cm proboscis enables it to rob nectar from most Sonoran Desert flowers.

A

Plate 3.2 *(above & left)* (A) Members of the night-blooming, hawkmoth-pollinated guild from south-western North America (a U.S. quarter is included for scale). From left to right, *Ipomoea longifolia* (Convolvulaceae), *Mirabilis longiflora* (Nyctaginaceae), *Telosiphonia brachysiphon* (Apocynaceae), *Hymenocallis sonorensis* (Amaryllidaceae), and *Datura discolor* and *D. wrightii* (Solanaceae).
(B) A population of *Oenothera deltoides* (Onagraceae), Algodones Dunes, California, pollinated by *Hyles lineata*. Note the density of flowers per plant, the relative scarcity of other dune plants, and the visual guides indicating the center of each flower.

B

Plate 3.3 *(left)* Naive male *Manduca sexta* moth approaching a paper flower in a greenhouse experiment; note partially extended proboscis (white arrow). A flowering *Oenothera neomexicana* plant is hidden beneath an array of paper flowers.

Plate 3.4 *(above)* *Hyles lineata* moth probing at unopened flower of *Calylophus hartweggii* (Onagraceae), Tucson Mountains, Pima County, AZ. Note proboscis slipping beneath sepal (white arrow). Photograph by Charles Hedgecock, RBP, with permission.

Plate 5.1 *(left)* Pupal mating in *Heliconius hewitsoni*.

Plate 12.1 *(top) Bicyclus anynana* wild type: dorsal (left) and ventral (right) wing surfaces.

Plate 12.2 *(middle)* The protein product of the *Distal-less* gene (in white) is produced during early development of the ventral hindwing of *Bicyclus anynana*. (A) An early wing imaginal disc from an early fifth-instar larva, showing *Distal-less* expression along the wing margin and midway between the veins in small incipient rays. (B) The rays extend proximally and become more defined in the mid-fifth-instar imaginal disc. (C) By the late fifth instar, the protein accumulates at high levels at the end of each ray. (D) The foci of high expression correspond to the centers of the future eyespots on the ventral hindwing (same developmental stage as C). (Photos courtesy of Steve Paddock and Sean Carroll.)

Plate 12.3 *(bottom)* Eyespot formation and diversity. The contrast between the top and bottom rows reflects the differences between species that arise in the developmental pathway. There are four steps in eyespot regulation. (A) In the larva, a prepattern of gene activity creates the potential focal pattern reflected by early *Distal-less* expression (see plate 12.2). (B) Foci are determined and *Distal-less* expression is stabilized only in specific wing cells; the number of foci differs between wing surfaces and butterfly species. (C) In the pupa, a signal from the focus induces surrounding cells; the size of the eyespot is controlled by the size of the focus. (D) Induced cells later differentiate into scales of different colors depending on their distance from the focus and their position in the wing. (From Brakefield et al. 1996.)

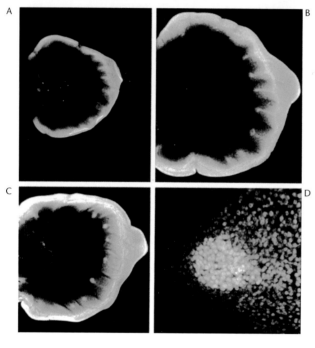

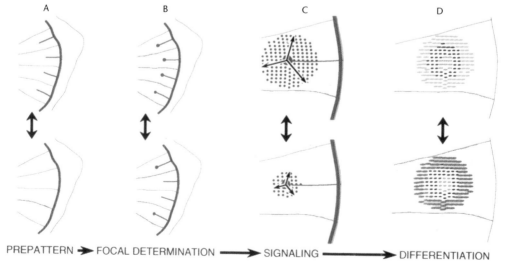

PREPATTERN ➡ FOCAL DETERMINATION ⟶ SIGNALING ⟶ DIFFERENTIATION

Plate 12.4 Mutant ventral phenotypes of *Bicyclus anynana* that appeared spontaneously in the stock population. Clockwise from top left: *Spotty*, *Cyclops*, *comet*, and *Bigeye* (all specimens are homozygous for *Spotty*).

A

B

C

D

Plate 12.5 *(left)* Representative specimens of *Bicyclus anynana* from four lines selected for different morphologies of the dorsal posterior eyespot on the forewing: (A) LOW and (B) HIGH (selected for a small and large eyespot, respectively); (C) GOLD and (D) BLACK (selected for a large and small width of the gold ring, respectively).

Plate 12.6 *(below)* A clade of close relatives from the larger tree of *Bicyclus* butterflies. This phylogeny was constructed with DNA sequence data from two mitochondrial genes (*COI* and *COII*) and a nuclear gene (*EF1α*), using maximum parsimony. Eyespots are numbered from 1 (most anterior at the top of the figure) to 7 (most posterior).

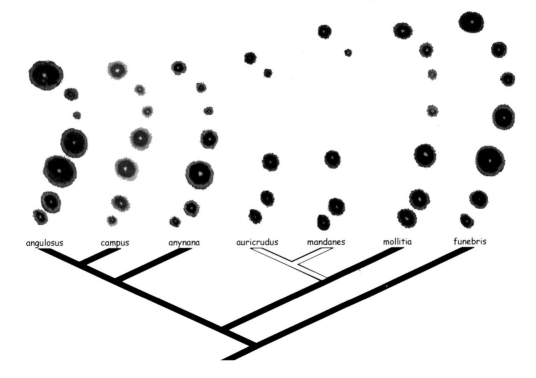

angulosus   campus   anynana   auricrudus   mandanes   mollitia   funebris

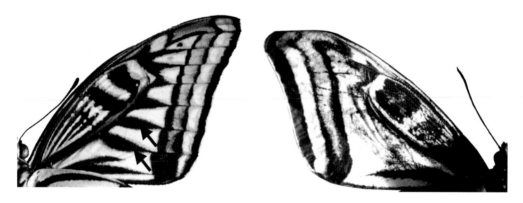

Plate 13.1 Male forewing from a wild-type specimen (left) and a *veins reduced* field-collected mutant (right) of *Papilio xuthus*. Note that the vein-dependent stripes (arrows) are absent in the mutant, in which the corresponding veins are also missing.

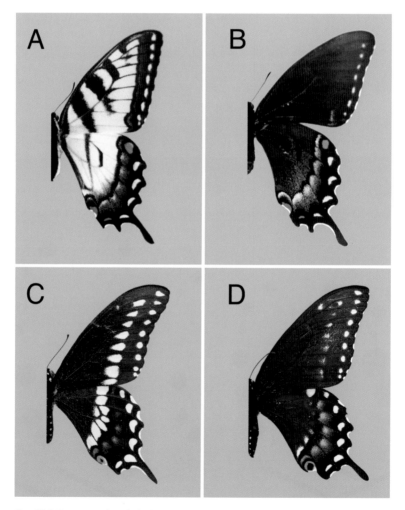

Plate 13.2 Two types of sex-linked melanism in swallowtails. (A, B) A change in the background color. Compare a wild-type yellow female *P. glaucus* (A) with a melanic female (B), in which the yellow background is replaced with melanic brown in the central area of the wing. Note that the yellow in the marginal row of yellow spots is still present. (C, D) A change in the yellow-black boundary. Compare a male *P. polyxenes* (C) with a female (D). Note that the melanism of the female derives from a movement of the black boundary, which displaces the yellow background.

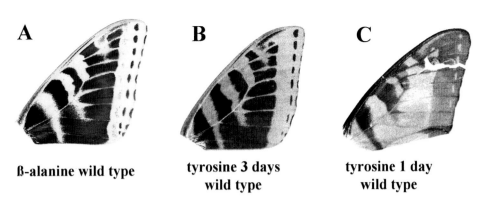

A **B** **C**

ß-alanine wild type

tyrosine 3 days
wild type

tyrosine 1 day
wild type

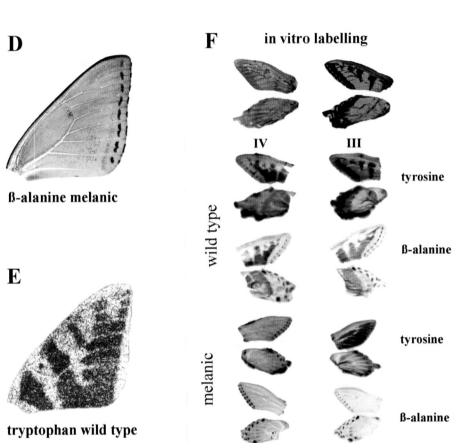

D

ß-alanine melanic

E

tryptophan wild type

F   **in vitro labelling**

IV   III

tyrosine

ß-alanine

wild type

tyrosine

ß-alanine

melanic

Plate 13.3 Autoradiographic patterns of incorporation of different radiolabeled precursors into *P. glaucus* wing scales in vivo (A–E) and in vitro (F). (A) Radiolabeled β-alanine injected into a wild-type pupa labels yellow areas. Tyrosine injected 3 days before adult emergence labels yellow scales (B), but when injected 1 day before emergence, labels black scales (C). (D) β-alanine injected into a melanic female pupa labels only the yellow marginal spots, but not the central wing area (which is yellow in the wild-type). (E) Tryptophan is incorporated only into yellow scales. (F) Wings were dissected from developing pupae at stage IV and at stage III (top wing pairs) and then incubated in Grace's medium. The autoradiographs below show the incorporation patterns of radiolabeled precursors that were added to the medium for 5 hours. In a wild-type individual, tyrosine is incorporated early (stage IV) into yellow and later (stage III) into black. In the corresponding wing pairs of the same butterfly, β-alanine is incorporated only into yellow. In a melanic female, the same temporal pattern of incorporation occurs. Note that here only the yellow marginal spots incorporate β-alanine. Tyrosine is incorporated into the marginal spots only during early papiliochrome formation, but the central wing is labeled during melanin synthesis.

wild type pattern color developement

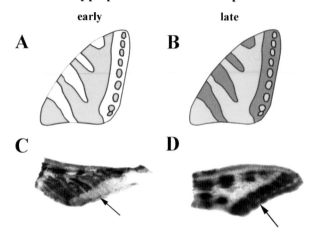

early

A

late

B

C

D

Plate 13.4 DDC gene expression is temporally and spatially regulated in *P. glaucus* wing development. The diagram shows the early stages of papiliochrome formation (A) and the corresponding stage IV in situ hybridization of ^{33}P-labeled antisense DDC RNA probe (C). Note that DDC mRNA is expressed only in presumptive yellow areas. Later (at stage II), during melanin synthesis, DDC mRNA is expressed in presumptive black areas (B). Note that there is *no* label in the marginal yellow spots. DDC therefore shows a complete inversion of pattern from early expression in presumptive yellow to late expression in presumptive black areas.

wild type   **melanic**

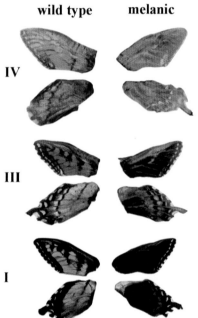

IV

III

I

Plate 13.5 The sequence of color development in wild-type and melanic wings of *P. glaucus* (dorsal views of female wings). Stage IV of color development represents the intense yellow coloration present before the start of melanization. During stage III, melanization occurs on the dorsal, but not on the ventral surface (not shown). Stage I wings are fully pigmented. Note that in stage IV melanic females, the central wing area is not yellow, and that this same area is later melanized brown in stage III.

Plate 13.6 Aberrant examples of melanism in *P. glaucus*. (A) Right forewing of a partially penetrant melanic female, showing the abnormal presence of a mixture of yellow and melanic scales in the central area of the wing. Note the normal row of yellow spots on the wing margin (large arrow). Note also the abnormal presence of a high density of yellow scales in one cell of the central forewing (large arrow) and the lower density of yellow scales throughout the rest of the central wing area (small arrows). (B) Right forewing of a fully penetrant melanic female, showing the normal absence of yellow scales from the central area of the melanic wing. Note the normal row of yellow spots on the wing margin (large arrow). (C) Rare individual in which the marginal yellow spots themselves are occluded by the melanic wing area (no arrow), suggesting a change in the boundary of the melanic background pattern element. (D) Putative gynandromorph, which is a mosaic of yellow male tissue and melanic female tissue. Note the presence of blue scales on the hind part of the right hindwing, which is diagnostic of females, and their absence from the forward part, showing that this section of the wing is male. Note also that where the melanic female tissue abuts the black pattern of the male, it is clearly dark brown and not true black.

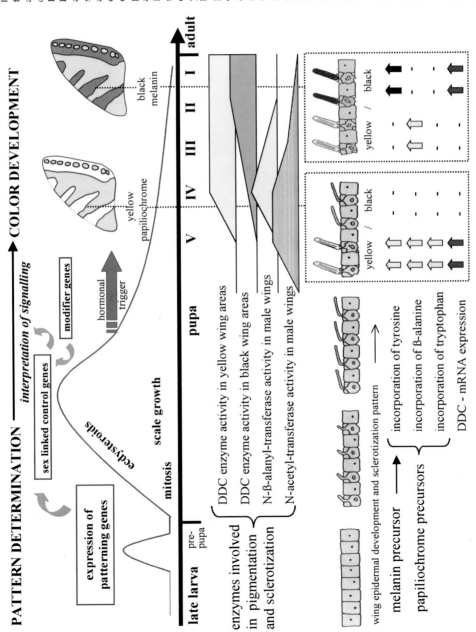

Plate 13.7 A general developmental model for color pattern formation in butterflies, adapted to the swallowtail pattern of *P. glaucus*. Development is regulated by ecdysteroid hormones. A sharp peak at the end of the last larval instar induces prepupal development and pupal molt. The broad peak in the pupal stage controls pupal-adult metamorphosis, and its decline triggers the onset of scale color development and sclerotization. Pattern determination, guided by the expression of patterning genes, occurs during late larval and early pupal development. These patterning signals are interpreted by the developing scales and result in pattern-specific color development (indicated schematically by the yellow and black pattern). These signals can be modified by sex-linked control genes and putative modifier genes, resulting in sexual dimorphism. The wing epidermis develops as the scales grow and then sclerotize in two stages, at first parallel to the lamina and then upright. The stages of pigment deposition (proceeding from V to I) correspond to those shown in figure 13.2 and discussed in the text. Note the differences in the timing of scale development between yellow and black areas, with black scales developing later. Arrows within the boxes indicate the incorporation of pigment precursors and in situ expression of *Ddc* mRNA in the different color patterns at different stages in development. The graphs above the boxes show the changes in enzyme activities in the male wild-type pattern and refer to stages V to I of color development during the last 2 days before adult emergence. The hormone titer and developmental events are idealized and do not reflect events in real time. This model includes data described elsewhere (Carroll et al. 1994; Brakefield et al. 1996; Koch et al. 1998) and our own unpublished data on sclerotization and enzyme activities.

Plate 14.1 *(left)* Top panel: Three pattern themes exhibited by six *Heliconius* species in Corcovado Park, in the Pacific lowlands of Costa Rica. Left column, ESS (pupal mating) clade: (a) *hecalesia,* (c) *hewitsoni,* (e) *erato;* right column, MCS clade: (b) *hecale,* (d) *pachinus,* (f) *melpomene.* Middle panel: Rainforest understory Müllerian partners in the Atlantic forests of Costa Rica: (g) *H. sapho* and (h) *H. cydno.* Bottom panel: Red (di-hydro-xanthommatin) gene from *H. melpomene* (f) expressed as shutter marker in (i) *H. cydno galanthus* and (j) *H. pachinus.*

Plate 14.2 *(below)* A hybrid derived from *cydno galanthus* × *melpomene rosina* is completely shuttered, and the red dorsal forewing *cydno* window (a) is opposed on the ventral forewing by white (type I) scales (b). This D/V "shutter off" switch is derived from *melpomene.* (c) The shutter of the ventral forewing distal window is converted to brown (type III scales) in this F1 *pachinus* × *melpomene.* The ventral "shutter on" of the *cydno* group is epistatic to the "shutter off" of *melpomene* (compare with b).

Plate 14.3 (a) A spontaneously produced ventral forewing to ventral hindwing homeosis transfers several forewing scale patches to homologous areas of the hindwing, demonstrating the cell-autonomous nature of pattern control. (From L. E. Gilbert, unpub.) (b) X-irradiation of an egg 72 hours after oviposition produced this clone of white scales, which originates at the base of the dorsal forewing and terminates precisely at the window-wall boundary, as highlighted the by red shutter in this individual from a *cydno × melpomene* hybrid population. It is not precisely known how long after fertilization treatment was given (terminal eggs in the oviduct can be held several days post-fertilization before being laid), and genetic damage might slow the development of a mutant clone. Nevertheless, one can con-clude that the forewing window-wall boundary had to have been established before this clone, which occupies approximately 6% of the forewing, could spread the full length of the wing. (From L. E. Gilbert, unpub.) (c–f) Examples of clones of contrasting scale pigmentation and morphotype resulting from somatic crossing-over induced by X-rays. In these cases, recessive alleles or repressed loci were expressed as ho-mozygous scale phenotypes on the wings of het-erozygous individuals in pattern fields otherwise expressing dominant or epistatic phenotypes. Note that such clones become progressively larger according to how early in development the embryos were irradiated, demonstrating lineage autonomy in cells that give rise to wing scales. Clones comparable to that of c in size occur only if early-stage larvae are irradiated. Irradiation of pupae results in single-scale changes. (c) Scales homozygous for lack of shutter (patch of yellow, type I scales) on dorsal hindwing window region otherwise expressing type II scales (melanic). (d) Patch of homozygous red scales interrupts ventral hindwing brown line in an individual heterozygous for brown/red ommatin in type III scales. (e) Patch of homozygous black scales (type II) within dorsal forewing shutter composed of red (type III) scales on individual heterozygous for shutter color locus. (f) Clone of homozygous yellow scales (type I) expressed against field of white (type I) within a forewing window heterozygous for 3-hydroxy-L-kynurenine gene.

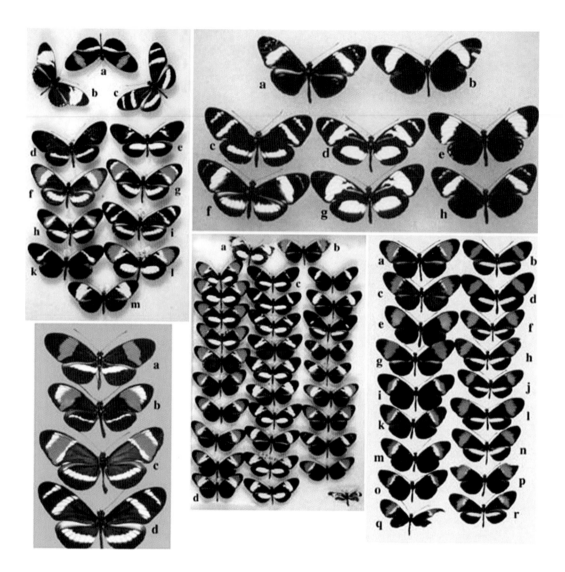

Plate 14.4 Upper left panel: Sample of novel patterns arising in synthetic hybrid zones involving Costa Rican *melpomene rosina* (a), *cydno galanthus* (b), and *pachinus* (c). Individuals (d) and (e) share *melpomene* window and shutter settings in the forewing distal window, but lack red. Individuals (f) and (h) share hybrid shutters (red), but differ in window size. The *pachinus* proximal forewing/ hindwing shutter affects (d), (f), (g), (i), and (l). Upper right panel: Segregation of forewing and hindwing shutters in hybrids of *H. pachinus* and *H. cydno galanthus*. Parents (a and b) were offspring of pure *pachinus* backcrossed to *cydno × pachinus* F_1. These patterns are among the many that also appear in F_2 broods in nature in central Costa Rica. Lower left panel: Independence of shutters and windows in pseudo F_2 of *H. melpomene* (a) × *H. pachinus* (d). (b) is interpreted as homozygous for the *melpomene* forewing shutter position and *pachinus* window. (c) is interpreted as near homozygous at two or three loci (?) for the *pachinus* shutter position on the *pachinus* window. The shutters are red in (b) and

(c). Lower center panel: One brood from a three-way "hybrid zone" of *cydno galanthus*, *pachinus*, and *melpomene rosina* (all Costa Rican). Parents are a female F_2 of *cydno × pachinus* showing shutter-free hindwing windows (a) and a male F_1 of *melpomene × cydno* (b). This 1983 brood demonstrated that the *melpomene* red marked the forewing shutter, and suggested a clade-wide "toolbox," as well as hybrid origins for *H. heurippa* (which resembles d) and *H. cydno weymeri* (with a distal forewing like c). A specimen resembling (d) was taken in 1993 on the Rio Sarapiqui in Costa Rica and is deposited in the Museo Nacional of Costa Rica. Lower right panel: Backcross of *melpomene × cydno* to pure *melpomene*. Forewing window type I scale color segregates yellow/white approximately 1:1, as does hindwing shutter (of *cydno* origin). Note pattern of shuttering of proximal half of forewing revealed by removal of red in that region (e.g., a, c, i, k, etc.). This trait distinguishes the form *alithea* from *haenshii* in polymorphic *cydno* in western Ecuador (see plate 14.7).

Plate 14.5 (a–b) Two ventral hindwing phenotypes that appeared in a synthetic hybrid zone of *cydno × pachinus:* (a) unshuttered hindwing window bordered by brown line; (b) heterozygote for *cydno* hindwing shutter, lacking brown line. (c–d) Ventral pattern of wild-type (c) *cydno galanthus* (compare with e below) and (d) *pachinus.* (e) This Costa Rican specimen of *H. cydno* was described as a new species by Schaus (1913). It represents a phenotype that appears in the F$_2$ of *cydno × pachinus.* The hindwing window area, completely "shuttered," is highlighted by brown scales. Note lack of D/V match on proximal boundary of forewing shutter, a common feature of hybrids. (f) This synthetic hybrid zone specimen is homozygous for the brown shutter phenotype and is probably the same genotype as e. (g) Heterozygote for "forceps" shutter, which in *cydno* converts brown shuttered oval window into an arch matching the opposite brown line, thus creating a forceps motif. The schematic diagram indicates the sequence of layers revealed by hybridization and illustrated by the specimens in this figure. Proceeding from (a) to (c): unshuttered window (a); heterozygous for *cydno* hindwing shutter (b); homozygous for same shutter (no photo); heterozygous for brown shutter color (no photo); homozygous for same locus (e/f); heterozygous for "forceps" shutter (g); homozygous for "forceps" shutter (c).

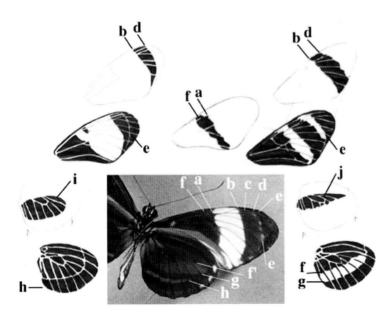

Plate 14.6 Diagrams of the windows and shutters of *cydno* (left) and *pachinus* (right) related to the ventral pattern of the *cydno × pachinus* F$_1$ wing, showing many of the pattern elements discussed in the text: the proximal boundary of the forewing distal window (a), the proximal boundary of the forewing hybrid shutter (b), the forewing distal shutter (c), the distal boundary of that shutter (d), the window-wall boundary (e), the *pachinus* proximal shutter on the forewing (f), the homologous shutter on the hindwing (f′), the position of the *pachinus* yellow bar, shuttered, which is seen as a zone of higher reflectance, and the brown line (h). Note that the "forceps" shutter of *cydno* is not perceptible, as it is overlapped by both *cydno* hindwing (i) and *pachinus* hindwing (j) shutters. The hindwing window-wall distal boundary is (g).

Plate 14.7 Top panel: Expression of some *H. melpomene* pattern genes in *H. cydno* background. (a) *H. melpomene*-typical "dennis-ray" race from western Amazonia. (b) *H. cydno galanthus*, Costa Rica; (m) shows ventral of this race. (c) *H. melpomene rosina*, Costa Rica; (l) shows ventral of this race. (d) Ventral view of backcross [(a × b) F₁ × b]; compare to ventral of pure *galanthus* (m). (g) "Pseudo F₂" derived from (b × c) shows *melpomene* yellow forewing distal window with hybrid shutter on its distal half. Note that shuttering of cell region of proximal forewing identical to that seen in this laboratory hybrid occurs in nature as a trait of *cydno* form *haenshii* (j). (e), (f), and (h) are also "pseudo F₂" phenotypes derived from (b × c). Compare these with

naturally occurring forms (i) and (k), *H. cydno alithea*, and (j), *H. c. haenshii*, from western Ecuador. Lower left panel: Mimicry of novel pattern in two steps. *H. cydno* races *galanthus* (a) and *weymeri* f. *gustavi* (b) produced intermediate F₁ (c, d). F₂ brood produced several novel patterns (e–k), including (g), which is a close mimic of an unpalatable pericopid moth common on the Osa Peninsula of Costa Rica (lower right panel). Middle right panel: One-step mimicry. Crossing species *H. cydno alithea* (a) and *H. ismenius* (b) yields F₁ phenotypes (c, d, e) that mimic Ecuadorian *H. hecalesia* (f, g). Males of F₁ are fertile. Lower right panel: *Colobura dirce*, called the "mosaic," appears to illustrate two modes of pattern-determining mechanisms.

Plate 14.8 A sample of novel patterns generated in synthetic hybrid zones involving several races each of *H. cydno* and *H. melpomene*.

Plate 23.1 Map of Madagascar, showing rainforest cover and sampling sites for recent (1996–1998) butterfly inventory.

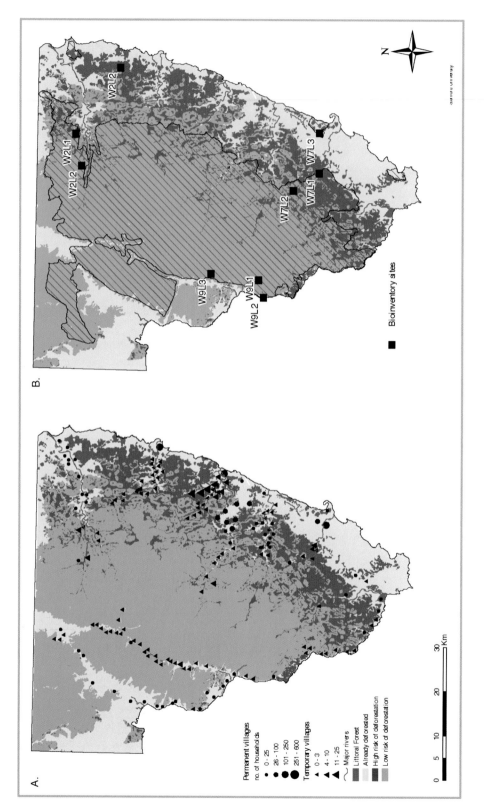

Plate 23.2 (A) The Masoala Peninsula, showing the remaining forests and the area predicted to be deforested within the next quarter century. The distribution of villages is
also indicated. (B) The Masoala National Park. An area of 230,000 ha (cross-hatched area)
was gazetted in 1997 following the recommendations of the Masoala Project (Kremen et
al. 1999b). Sites where biodiversity surveys were conducted are noted. The forests outside
of the park (note that most are highly threatened) will serve as an economic support zone
for the populace and a buffer to the reserve. Sustainable enterprises (harvest of rainforest
products, tourism) are being encouraged in this zone.

CHAPTER 17

Hybrid Zone Ecology and Tiger Swallowtail Trait Clines in North America

J. Mark Scriber, Mark Deering, and Aram Stump

The 475–575 species of swallowtail butterflies in the Papilionidae are distributed among six tribes (Triodini, Graphiini, Papilioniini, Zerynthiini, Parnassiini, and Baronini), with relatively few new species added since Munroe's (1961) taxonomic study (Tyler et al. 1994; Scriber 1995). Most of the species are found in the lower (tropical) latitudes and are reported to feed on only a few host species within only one or two plant families (Scriber 1973, 1984b). This latitudinal pattern of species richness in the Papilionidae has been repeatedly noted for its general ecological and evolutionary significance for biodiversity and conservation (Collins and Morris 1985; New and Collins 1991; Sutton and Collins 1991; Scriber 1995; Speight et al. 1999).

The occurrence of natural hybridization in the Papilionidae (Descimon and Geiger 1988; Luebke et al. 1988; Sperling 1990) and the surprising degree of genetic compatibility of some hand-paired hybrids (Clarke and Sheppard 1955a, 1957; Ae 1979; Scriber and Lederhouse 1989; Scriber et al. 1990a, 1991b, 1995a) raise important questions about reproductive isolation, speciation, and the variable numbers of species in the Papilionidae recognized by different authors (Scriber 1995).

HYBRID ZONES AND INTROGRESSION

Hybrid zones have recently been described as "places where two or more populations of individuals that are distinguishable on the basis of one or more heritable characters overlap spatially and temporally, and cross to form viable and at least partially fertile offspring" (Arnold 1997). Introgression is "the movement of genes or alleles from one population or species into another" where hybrids are the result of natural hybridization and are associated with behavioral, biochemical, ecological, and genetic changes in the hybridizing populations (Arnold 1997; see also Harrison 1993; Endler 1998). As these authors point out, these definitions are advantageous for several reasons: first, they do not depend on any particular "species concept" (e.g., "biological," "recognition," "cohesion," or "phylogenetic"); second, the participating populations do not need to be classified into any particular taxa; third, it is not essential to know the relative fitnesses or adaptive trait responses of the hybrids relative to those of their parents; and finally, the definitions are easy to use.

Most species concepts are founded upon the perspective that hybridization and hybrids are "bad," or unlikely to be of much evolutionary significance. This perspective involves several assumptions (see Harrison 1993; Whitham et al. 1994; Levin et al. 1996; Rhymer and Simberloff 1996; Arnold 1997; Endler 1998): that hybrid offspring "always" show lower or no fertility and viability; that exceptionally fit hybrids will "tarnish" the purity, integrity, distinctiveness, or wholesomeness of the parental species; that hybridization reverses the process of divergent evolution (furthermore, most species concepts do not acknowledge the existence of hybrids, since "good" species do not hybridize); and that hybridization violates the assumptions of cladistic analyses. Taxonomists, conservationists, and their administrative lawyers tend to view hybridization as confusing, sloppy, or "illegitimate."

This chapter will examine some of these concepts and assumptions about hybrids by examining the extensive geographic and phylogenetic differentiation seen among the North American tiger swallowtail butterflies (Scriber 1996a). Results of recent studies examining prezygotic, postmating, and postzygotic reproductive isolation, as well as environmental factors and ecological adaptations, will be described for the Great Lakes hybrid zone between the two most closely related species, the Canadian (*Papilio canadensis*) and eastern (*Papilio glaucus*) tiger swallowtails.

THE *Papilio canadensis/P. glaucus* HYBRID ZONE

One of the earliest recognized hybrid zones involving the tiger swallowtail butterflies is a rather narrow band of overlap that extends from Wisconsin and Michigan to New England (at about 41°–44° N latitude), including much of New York State and Pennsylvania (fig. 17.1; Edwards 1884; Rothschild and Jordan 1906; Scriber 1990). Although the taxonomic status of the butterflies in this zone has been debated since it was first described (Tyler et al. 1994), the *P. glaucus* to the south and the *P. canadensis* to the north have long been recognized as separate parapatric species (Hagen et al. 1991; Sperling 1993). These two species were originally distinguished by differences in adult size

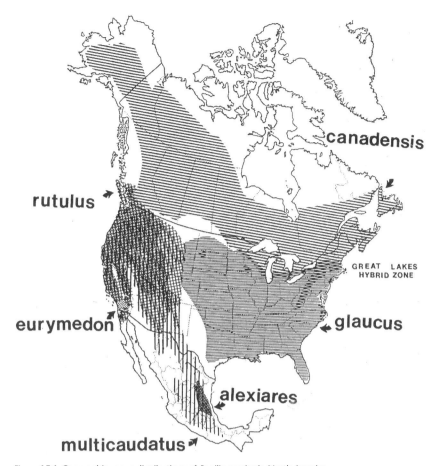

Figure 17.1 Geographic range distributions of *Papilio* species in North America.

and details of wing color patterns (Rothschild and Jordan 1906; Scriber 1990). Our studies have found clear heritable differences between the two species for a variety of characteristics (table 17.1: Scriber 1982, 1996a; Rockey et al. 1987a; Luebke et al. 1988; Hagen and Scriber 1989; Hagen 1990;). Allozyme frequencies have highlighted the geographic center of the hybrid zone, with mixed frequencies of diagnostic loci within the zone and essentially fixed differences on either side of the zone (fig. 17.2; Scriber 1996a). The two species appear distinct, with nearly complete concordance in the trait clines, where the zone is narrow (50–100 km wide), whereas more individuals with a mixture of *canadensis/glaucus* traits occur in central New York State and Pennsylvania, where the zone may be several hundred kilometers wide, with extensive elevational variation created by the mountains of the Appalachian chain that run north and south throughout these regions. The Great Lakes (Lakes Michigan, Huron, and Erie) disrupt this continuous latitudinal band of hybrid interaction from Wisconsin to Massachusetts.

Table 17.1 Summary of physiological, biochemical, and behavioral differences between *P. glaucus* and *P. canadensis* and their modes of inheritance, if known

Character	*P. glaucus*	*P. canadensis*	Inheritance	Reference[a]
Environmental determination of pupal diapause	Yes	No	X-linked	1, 2
Oviposition preference	Tulip tree	Aspen	X-linked	3
Larval survival (aspen)	Very low	High	Polygenic	4, 5, 6
Larval survival (Tulip tree)	High	Very low	Polygenic	4, 5
Polymorphism (dark females)	Present	Absent	Y-linked	8, 9
Suppression of melanic color	Absent	Present	X-linked	1, 9, 10
Hexokinase (*Hk*) alleles	"100"	"110"	"Autosomal"	11
Lactate dehydrogenase (*Ldh*) alleles	"100"	"80," "40"	X-linked	1, 7, 11
6-Phosphogluconate dehydrogenase (*Pgd*) alleles	"100," "50"	"125, 80, and 150"	X-linked	1, 7, 11
Neonate white bands	One only	Three	Autosomal	13
Adult hindwing width black on anal cell	30–40%	50–90%	Autosomal	14, 15
Mitochondrial DNA	3 RFLPs	4 RFLPs	Maternal	17
Haldane effect	In hybrids between species		X-linked	This study, 12
X-effects	In hybrids between species		X-linked	This study, 12

[a] References: 1, Hagen and Scriber 1989; 2, Rockey et al. 1987a; 3, Scriber 1994; 4 Scriber 1986b; 5, Scriber 1988; 6, Scriber et al. 1989; 7, Hagen 1990; 8, Clarke and Sheppard 1962; 9, Scriber et al. 1996; 10, Scriber et al. 1987; 11, Hagen et al. 1991; 12, Hagen and Scriber 1995; 13, Scriber 1998; 14, Scriber 2002; 15, Scriber 1982; 16, Luebke et al. 1988; 17, Sperling 1993.

Regardless of how the *P. canadensis/P. glaucus* hybrid zone was established (i.e., by primary parapatric divergence or by secondary contact: Scriber 1988), the interaction of the taxa in the zone of overlap could result in several potential scenarios. First, if the hybrids are inferior as judged by natural selection, the taxa could evolve reproductive isolation by the process of "reinforcement" (Blair 1955; Howard 1993; Butlin 1995). Second, the hybrid zone could be stabilized on an ecological time scale by a combination of selection and dispersal (Barton and Hewitt 1985; Mallet 1993; McMillan et al. 1997; Mallet et al. 1998a). Third, the two taxa could diffuse into each other, with their unique characters eventually fading away as their trait clines "decay" and become broader or less steep (Rhymer and Simberloff 1996; Porter et al. 1997); Fourth, one taxon could completely replace the other (Remington 1968b; Rhymer and Simberloff 1996). Finally, a combination of the above scenarios could result in a geographic "mosaic" in which local populations differ in composition and in the fitness of the genotypes (Moore 1977; Rand and Harrison 1989), including hybrids that are in some cases more fit than parental types (Arnold and Emms 1998).

J. Mark Scriber, Mark Deering, and Aram Stump

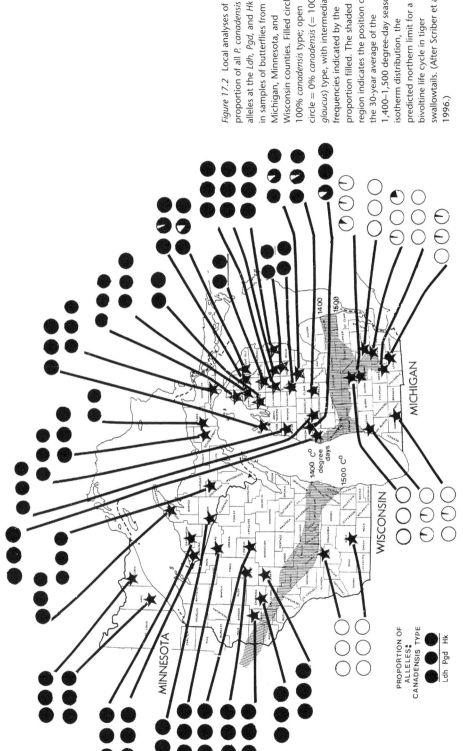

Figure 17.2 Local analyses of proportion of all P. canadensis alleles at the Ldh, Pgd, and Hk loci in samples of butterflies from Michigan, Minnesota, and Wisconsin counties. Filled circle = 100% canadensis type; open circle = 0% canadensis (= 100% glaucus) type, with intermediate frequencies indicated by the proportion filled. The shaded region indicates the position of the 30-year average of the 1,400–1,500 degree-day seasonal isotherm distribution, the predicted northern limit for a bivoltine life cycle in tiger swallowtails. (After Scriber et al. 1996.)

GENETIC DIVERGENCE IN SWALLOWTAILS

Phylogenetic Context and Ecological Distances

The genus *Papilio* alone has had more than 220 species attributed to it (more than 40% of the entire Papilionidae: Scriber 1995). Within the New World *Papilio,* the subgenus *Pterourus* (Hancock 1983) includes the North American *glaucus* group (*canadensis, glaucus, rutulus, eurymedon, multicaudatus,* and *alexiares*), whose members are among the most polyphagous swallowtail species in the world (Scriber 1984b). The South/ Central American *Papilio* subgenus *Pyrrhosticta* contains the next most polyphagous species (those in the *scamander, homerus,* and *garamas* groups: Scriber et al. 1991c; Tyler et al. 1994). Both of these subgenera have members that feed on the ancient and probably ancestral angiosperm host plant families of Magnoliaceae and Lauraceae (Scriber et al. 1991c).

The presumed sister group to the North American *P. glaucus* group has been the *P. troilus* group of Lauraceae specialists (*troilus, palamedes,* and *pilumnus:* Scriber 1996a) (fig. 17.3); however, we have learned through inter-specific hand pairings (Scriber et al. 1991b) and molecular genetics (Sperling 1991; Caterino and Sperling 1999; Reed and Sperling 1999) that the *scamander, garamas,* and *homerus* groups from South/Central America appear to be more closely related to the North American *glaucus* group than is the *troilus* group from eastern North America. This finding suggests that the detoxification adaptations required for processing phytochemicals in the Magnoliaceae may in fact have been derived long ago in the common stock of these North and South American *glaucus/scamander* prototypes (Scriber 1996a).

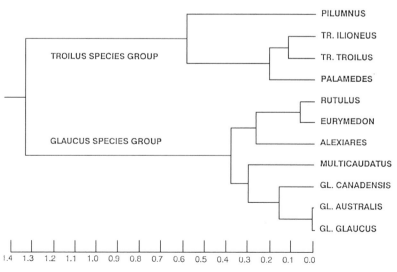

Figure 17.2 Phylogenetic relationships between the *P. troilus* and *P. glaucus* species groups.

In contrast, some members of the *glaucus* group (*P. canadensis* and *P. rutulus*) have apparently recently evolved the ability to detoxify the phenolic glycosides of the Salicaceae, which allows them to feed and grow successfully on aspens, willows, cottonwoods, and related poplars (Scriber 1988). Thorough literature searches indicate that these are the only two species of Papilionidae in the world that can survive well and grow to pupation on the Salicaceae (Scriber 1982; Lindroth et al. 1988; Scriber et al. 1989, 1991c). These species may have had a relatively recent genetic divergence in their character states during the recent Pleistocene glaciations (Scriber 1988; Scriber et al. 1991c). Near the Great Lakes ecotone, where boreal forests meet temperate deciduous forests (Curtis 1959), *P. canadensis* populations contain females that still prefer the putative ancestral magnoliaceous hosts, such as tulip tree (*Liriodendron tulipifera*), in laboratory three-choice oviposition studies (including black cherry, *Prunus serotina,* and quaking aspen, *Populus tremuloides*), even though this tree is toxic to all of their larvae (Scriber et al. 1991c; Bossart and Scriber 1995a). Other morphological and biochemical traits suggest that *canadensis* has only relatively recently diverged from *glaucus* (Hagen and Scriber 1991; Hagen et al. 1991; Sperling 1993). In this chapter we add behavioral (mate preference) data supporting this concept.

These North and South American Papilionidae provide a valuable framework within which we can examine a suite of adaptive traits in both space and time (ecological as well as evolutionary). Intergeneric hybrids (Scriber et al. 1991b) and interspecific hybrids of almost all pairwise combinations of the North American *glaucus* and *troilus* species groups have produced some viable offspring when hand-pairing techniques were used (e.g., Scriber and Lederhouse 1989; Scriber et al. 1990a, 1990b, 1995a). In fact, intergroup copulation between a free-flying *P. palamedes* male and our experimentally tethered *P. canadensis* female was observed recently (Deering and Scriber 1998). Natural hybrids have also been reported between *P. rutulus* and *P. eurymedon* and between *P. multicaudatus* and *P. glaucus* (Brower 1959; Wagner 1978; Garth and Tilden 1986), and there is more extensive natural hybridization evidence for *P. glaucus* and *P. canadensis* (Luebke et al. 1988; Scriber 1990).

PARTIAL HALDANE EFFECT AND REPRODUCTIVE ISOLATION IN SWALLOWTAIL BUTTERFLIES

Two rules that have emerged from hybridization studies on a variety of animals are "Haldane's rule" (in hybridization, the heterogametic sex, which is the female in Lepidoptera, is most often negatively affected: Haldane 1922) and the "X-rule" (genes affecting hybrid fitness are often on the sex chromosome: Coyne 1985; Orr 1987, 1989). The Haldane effect arises due to deleterious interactions between two loci: any of X-linked and autosomal alleles, X-linked and Y-linked alleles, Y-linked and autosomal alleles, or in Lepidoptera (with heterogametic females), X-linked alleles and cytoplasmic factors. Males may escape these effects because they lack Y-linked genes and recessiveness of the X factor, or because expression is limited to females (see Orr 1993; Hagen and Scriber 1995; Prowell 1998; see also Sperling, chap. 20 in this volume). The causal mechanisms of the Haldane effect have not been resolved (Coyne et al. 1991; Frank 1991; Read and Nee 1991; Wu 1992; Coyne and Orr 1993; Orr 1993, 1995; Hurst 1993; Davies and Pomiankowski 1995; Hagen and Scriber 1995; Turelli and Orr 1995).

Sex-linked alleles are more exposed to selection in the hemizygous state, and could accumulate differences more rapidly than autosomal alleles (Charlesworth et al. 1987; Rice 1988; Coyne and Orr 1989). Whether or not evolution toward hybrid sterility proceeds faster than hybrid inviability (Orr 1993; Wu and Davis 1993), the Haldane and X effects suggest that genes important in speciation need not be additive genes of small effect (Virdee 1993; but see Nijhout 1994a).

Our studies of interspecific hybridization using *P. glaucus* females mated to members of the *glaucus* group (Hagen and Scriber 1995) showed increased female pupal mortality (permanent diapause? see Oliver 1979a, 1979b) with increasing genetic distance. Pupal mortality reduced the sex ratio below the expected 50%, as predicted by theory (Coyne and Orr 1989) (*glaucus-glaucus*: 48.8% female, $n = 7,101$ pupae; *glaucus-alexiares*: 46.7%, $n = 555$; *glaucus-canadensis*: 39.4%, $n = 1,426$; *glaucus-multicaudatus*: 16.7%, $n = 67$; *glaucus-rutulus*: 3.4%, $n = 781$; *glaucus-eurymedon*: 0.4%, $n = 474$). The corresponding reciprocal interspecific crosses (with *P. glaucus* fathers) showed no such Haldane effect in female pupal mortality, and the sex ratios were not significantly different from 50% (*glaucus-glaucus*: 48.8%, $n = 7101$; *alexiares-glaucus*: 42.4%, $n = 130$; *canadensis-glaucus*: 51.3%, $n = 780$; *multicaudatus-glaucus*: more than 40 unsuccessful pairings; *rutulus-glaucus*: 46.5%, $n = 30$; *eurymedon-glaucus*: 40.0%, $n = 40$) (Hagen and Scriber 1995).

Hand-paired interspecific hybrids were produced using virgin females of the *glaucus* group each mated to a male from a different species. With *P. glaucus* mothers, the percentage of interspecific hybrid eggs that were viable ranged from 72% with *canadensis* males to only 26% with *multicaudatus* males and only 4% with South American *P. scamander* males (table 17.2). These results are supportive of the genetic incompatibility predicted with increasing phylogenetic distance. The interspecific crosses using *P. glaucus* males show significantly higher egg mortality in every case than the corresponding reciprocal pairings using *glaucus* females (table 17.2). Again, this inviability is more intense with greater phylogenetic distance. Among the highlights of the few interspecific pairings not including *P. glaucus* is the exceptionally high compatibility between *P. rutulus* and *P. eurymedon*, with

J. Mark Scriber, Mark Deering, and Aram Stump

Table 17.2 Egg viability in reciprocal crosses of *Papilio glaucus* and some *canadensis* with other members of the *glaucus, scamander,* and *troilus* groups (1983–1989)

Cross (Female × Male)	Egg Hatch (%)	Total Eggs	No. Mothers
glaucus × canadensis	71.1	3,249	17
canadensis × glaucus	45.1	260	28
glaucus × alexiares	58.9	2,269	16
alexiares × glaucus	24.3	37	3
glaucus × rutulus	41.4	3,386	37
canadensis × rutulus	30.2	2,730	36
rutulus × glaucus	0.0	68	2
rutulus × canadensis	0.0	156	5
glaucus × eurymedon	29.1	3,139	43
canadensis × eurymedon	47.1	1,824	29
eurymedon × glaucus	(No eggs obtained)	0	2
eurymedon × canadensis	33.6	134	5
glaucus × multicaudatus	25.5	149	5
canadensis × multicaudatus	6.3	112	2
multicaudatus × glaucus	(No pairings were successful)		
multicaudatus × canadensis	(No pairings were successful)		
glaucus × scamander	2.7	393	7
scamander × glaucus	0.0	10	2
glaucus × troilus	0.0	144	1
troilus × glaucus	8.0	155	2

86% egg viability and 56% with the reciprocal cross (Scriber et al. 1995a). This finding supports the suggestion of Sperling (1993, 1994) that species sharing the same mtDNA, as these two do, should have little incompatibility.

It should be noted that an index of interspecific genetic compatibilities using hybrid egg viability has been developed for use in assessing phylogenetic relationships among many different species of the Papilionidae (Ae 1979, 1995). We are aware of some limitations on the conclusions to be drawn from data such as these and our own (table 17.2). For example, the total number of eggs laid by our hand-paired females was used in the viability index denominator, but only a single mating was conducted for each pairing. Since multiple matings are necessary to restore fertility in *glaucus* and *canadensis* females (Lederhouse and Scriber 1987), laboratory egg production and viability may not reflect their actual lifetime reproductive potential. In addition, the ability of any male to transfer a large and usable spermatophore depends on male age and time since last mating (Lederhouse et al. 1989), and the use of field-captured males makes this factor an unknown. (Laboratory-reared males usually have considerably lower fertility unless a strong supplementary feeding regime is used: Lederhouse et al. 1990.) For example, a sample of field-captured *glaucus* group females that were allowed to oviposit until death generally averaged only 51–68% egg viability (table 17.3). Also, a single gene with a large effect could influence

Table 17.3 Fecundity and egg viability of wild (field-captured) female *Papilio* butterflies

Species	Mean (SE) Total Eggs	No. Females	Mean (SE) % Viable	Total Larvae per Female
P. australis	136.9 (17.5)	31	58.7 (5.7)	80.4
P. glaucus	94.3 (7.8)	50	59.3 (4.0)	55.9
P. canadensis	88.5 (6.8)	63	55.9 (4.0)	49.5
P. alexiares	76.8 (12.4)	11	51.3 (8.4)	39.4
P. rutulus	56.8 (16.8)	13	56.8 (10.2)	32.3
P. eurymedon	49.0 (23.2)	4	68.0 (15.0)	39.4

hybrid incompatibility, obscuring any simple relationship between phylogenetic relationship and hybrid index.

SEX CHROMOSOMES AND THE *glaucus/canadensis* HYBRID ZONE

This section focuses on the hybrid zone dynamics of the Canadian tiger swallowtail, *P. canadensis* (elevated from subspecies status: Hagen et al. 1991), and its closely related and parapatric congener, *Papilio glaucus*. Both species of tiger swallowtails are polyphagous, each feeding on plants from at least five different families (Scriber 1984a; Scriber et al. 1995a). The hybrid zone is located across the central Great Lakes region of North America (Luebke et al. 1988; Scriber 1996a), near the ecotone or suture/transition zone (Merriam 1894; Remington 1968b) of hybrid interaction described for several other butterflies and insect species (Platt and Brower 1968; Ebner 1970; Showers 1981; Wagner et al. 1981; Scriber 1983; Giebink et al. 1984; Scriber and Hainze 1987; Waldbauer et al. 1988; Feder et al. 1990; Howard and Waring 1991).

The mechanisms responsible for speciation and differential ecological adaptations across this zone have been the primary focus of our group's recent research. We have previously looked at host plant distributions and differential host use abilities as potential primary explanations of the hybrid zone location (Scriber 1983, 1986b, 1996a, 1996b; Lindroth et al. 1986; Nitao et al. 1991; Scriber et al. 1991c; Lederhouse et al. 1992a; Scriber and Lederhouse 1992; Ayres and Scriber 1994; Scriber and Gage 1995). We have more recently investigated premating, prezygotic, and postzygotic processes to determine how reproductive isolation and parapatric range distributions are maintained between these two tiger swallowtail species.

That so many loci determining traits that differ between *P. glaucus* and *P. canadensis* are sex-linked is especially intriguing and may provide a unique perspective on the origins of host shifts in *Papilio* as compared with other insect herbivores (Sperling 1994; Thompson 1995). It is unlikely that this association is due solely to chance, since the haploid number of chromosomes is 30 or 31 (Emmel et al. 1995). A preliminary map of the X chromosome of *glaucus* and *canadensis* has been constructed (Hagen and Scriber 1989; Scriber 1994; Hagen and Scriber 1995). Two diagnostic loci, *Ldh* (lactate dehydrogenase) and *Pgd* (6-phosphogluconate dehydrogenase), are X-linked, as are *Tpi* (triose phosphate isomerase), *Acp* (acid phosphatase), and *P3gdh* (phosphoglycerate dehydrogenase). The sex linkage of these allozyme loci appears to be conserved throughout the *glaucus* group, and with the potential exception of *Ldh*, these loci are also sex-linked in a noctuid moth (Heckel 1993). It is not known whether these alleles are selectively neutral, although allozyme variation at *Pgd* can affect fitness through metabolic flux and partitioning differences (Hughes and Lucchesi 1977; Powers 1987; see also Watt 1985b). There is evidence from vertebrates for a selective basis for allozyme differentiation at *Ldh* loci related to thermal adaptation (Merritt 1972; Powers et al. 1986).

GEOGRAPHIC DISTANCE FROM HYBRID ZONE DOES NOT INCREASE INCOMPATIBILITY IN HYBRID CROSSES

A series of *P. canadensis* males, all from northern Wisconsin populations, were paired with *P. glaucus* females from three locations at varying distances from the center of the hybrid zone (southern Wisconsin, southeastern Pennsylvania, and central Florida). No significant differences between these three pairings in hybrid egg viability (percentage eclosion) were observed (Wisconsin: 75.1%, SE = 8.1; Pennsylvania: 70.3%, SE = 5.2; Florida: 73.8%, SE = 2.4).

It was interesting that *canadensis* × *canadensis* pairs from northern Wisconsin had lower egg viability (64.2%, SE = 5.3; $n = 27$ females) than the hybrid pairs described above, as did *glaucus* × *glaucus* pairs from southeastern Pennsylvania (69.8%, SE = 5.2; $n = 16$ females). This finding raised the possibility that hybrids are not always disadvantaged relative to their parental genotypes (Collins 1984; Arnold and Hodges 1995) and may actually have higher fitness in some environments (see review by Arnold 1997).

HYBRID VIGOR/HETEROSIS?

A series of laboratory hand pairings of *P. glaucus* and *P. canadensis* from different families (table 17.4) showed variation in fecundity, hybrid egg viability, and the survival of neonates on their common host plant, black cherry. The

Table 17.4 Fecundity, egg viability, and neonate larval survival on black cherry leaves of two tiger swallowtail species and their hybrids

Genotype	Mean (SE) Total Eggs per Female	Mean (SE) % Viable Eggs	% Neonate Survival	No. Mothers	Total Eggs
P. glaucus	94.3 (7.8)[a]	59.3 (4.0)[b]	78	50	6,411
P. canadensis × P. glaucus	75.8 (9.3)[b]	45.1 (5.4)[c]	68	28	260
P. glaucus × P. canadensis	84.8 (17.1)[ab]	71.1 (5.3)[a]	80	17	3,249
P. canadensis	88.5 (6.8)[ab]	55.9 (4.0)[b]	73	63	3,290

Note: Significant differences between means ($p = 0.05$) are indicated by different superscript letters (Tukey's test for unequal sample sizes).

Table 17.5 Growth rates (first instar neonate to pupa) and pupal weights of two tiger swallowtail species and their hybrids

Genotype	Pupae	Duration (Days)	Mean Pupal Wt (SE), Mg Live	Growth Rate (Wt/Days)
P. glaucus	1,005	32.5 (0.2)[bc]	927 (8)[b]	28.5
P. canadensis × P. glaucus	21	26.2 (0.6)[a]	1,009 (43)[a]	38.5
P. glaucus × P. canadensis	92	30.6 (0.5)[b]	1,089 (21)[a]	35.6
P. canadensis	17	34.1 (0.7)[c]	752 (23)[c]	22.0

Note: Significant differences ($p = 0.05$) are indicated by different letters (Tukey's test for unequal sample sizes).

canadensis (female) × *glaucus* (male) crosses had fewer eggs, lower egg viability, and lower neonate larval survival than the parental types. However, the reciprocal crosses, *glaucus* (female) × *canadensis* (male), produced about as many eggs as the parental types, but had the highest egg viability, and the largest percentage of neonate larval survival, of all types, including the parentals (table 17.4).

An analysis of *P. glaucus* from southeastern Pennsylvania and *P. canadensis* from northern Wisconsin and their reciprocal hybrids also suggests "hybrid vigor"(table 17.5). Both (reciprocal) hybrid types (*canadensis* × *glaucus* and *glaucus* × *canadensis*) showed a shorter duration of the developmental period from neonate larva to pupa, a higher average pupal weight, and a more rapid lifetime growth rate than the parental types. In addition, a series of interspecific pairings of *glaucus* with the closely related *alexiares* (table 17.6) from Mexico produced 200–300% more eggs, with higher viability, than pairings of either parental type, resulting in a significantly larger number of larvae.

In summary, we saw earlier that increased genetic distance resulted in a partial Haldane effect in female pupae in one direction of interspecific crossing of *P. glaucus*. Egg viability also declined with increased genetic distance

Table 17.6 Heterosis in crosses of Mexican and eastern tiger swallowtails

Species	Mean (SE) Total Eggs	Mean (SE) % Viable Eggs	No. Females (n)	Larvae per Female
P. glaucus	94.3 (7.8)	59.3 (4.0)	501	55.9
P. glaucus × *P. alexiares*	173.9 (29.7)	66.1 (6.1)	16	115.0
P. alexiares	76.8 (12.4)	51.3 (8.4)	11	39.4

in both directions of reciprocal interspecific crosses, but the crosses with *glaucus* males (rather than females) produced hybrid eggs that were more severely affected (see table 17.2). However, variable results in egg viability and neonate larval survival were evident in reciprocal crosses between *glaucus* and *canadensis,* suggesting that both heterosis and hybrid dysgenesis (negative heterosis; Ritchie and Hewitt 1995) are likely.

HETEROTIC GROWTH: A SOLUTION TO SEASONAL THERMAL CONSTRAINTS?

The observation that the growth rates and final pupal sizes of *glaucus* × *canadensis* hybrids are superior to their parental types (see table 17.5) suggests a potential solution to the seasonal thermal constraints faced by these species at latitudinally critical zones (Scriber and Lederhouse 1992) or in locally cold "pockets" (Scriber 1994, 1996a; Tesar and Scriber 2002). Faster growth of hybrid genotypes at any given temperature could circumvent these ecological challenges and select for hybridization. Metabolic capabilities for molting, feeding, and growth at very low temperatures have been selected for naturally in Alaskan populations of *canadensis* (Ayres and Scriber 1994). While we have not yet investigated molting duration for hybrids at different temperatures, it is likely to be of fundamental ecological importance as a parameter of a particularly vulnerable life stage, as well as part of the overall duration of larval life, and may be enhanced in hybrids at low temperatures (as were hybrid growth thresholds). Alaskan caterpillars have elevated metabolic rates (36% higher) at low temperatures (e.g., 12°C) compared with Michigan caterpillars (Ayres and Scriber 1994), which allows considerably faster molting and growth, and may be a favorable trait in our interspecific hybrids as well.

An examination of the thermally controlled developmental thresholds of pure *glaucus,* pure *canadensis,* and their hybrids shows that the hybrids begin to develop at 8°–9°C, whereas most *canadensis* and *glaucus* require a temperature of 10°–11°C or even higher (table 17.7) (Scriber and Lederhouse 1983; Ritland and Scriber 1985). This physiologically extrapolated developmental threshold could potentially allow 2–3 extra degree-days each day throughout the otherwise thermally constrained growing season all across

Table 17.7 Developmental threshold temperatures and lifetime growth rates (neonate larva to pupa) for two tiger swallowtail species and their hybrids

Genotype	Pupae (n)	Developmental Threshold (°C)	Mean Lifetime Growth Rates (SE), mg/days		
			16°–18°C	21°–22°C	28°C
P. canadensis (cWI)	105	10.1	13.0 (0.2)	21.7 (1.0)	28.0 (1.6)
Pg (WI) × Pc (nWI)	14	10.2	14.1 (1.0)	43.2 (1.9)	57.5 (3.2)
Pg (PA) × Pc (nWI)	62	8.7	16.6 (0.4)	33.9 (0.9)	42.1 (2.1)
Pg (PA) × Pc (cWI)	69	9.0	16.5 (1.0)	34.9 (1.3)	45.6 (1.3)
P. glaucus (WI)	59	10.3	21.8 (1.0)	33.2 (1.7)	46.4 (3.9)
(WI, 2nd)	58	12.8			
P. glaucus (PA)	26	9.4	25.6 (2.2)	39.5 (0.7)	55.4 (2.1)
(PA, 2nd)	48	13.2			

Note: After Ritland and Scriber 1985.

the hybrid zone area and in cold pockets. In addition, growth would be possible even on days below the normal thermal threshold for the parental types (i.e., not just extra growth on the warm days above 10°–11°C). All of these changes could result in very significant additional thermal accumulations (150–250 degree-days), which could increase the northern range of *P. glaucus* for bivoltinism (see Scriber and Gage 1995) and enhance the chances for northern populations of *canadensis* to successfully complete their single generation (Ayres and Scriber 1994). These changes could also reduce or eliminate the selection pressure on females in the cold pockets to select only the most nutritional host plant species (e.g., *Fraxinus:* Scriber 1996b; see also Giroux 1998).

However, we have observed very little electrophoretically detectable introgression into these areas, although some introgression of *Pgd* into the cold pockets of northern Michigan is noticeable (Hagen et al. 1991; Scriber 1996a). The advantages of hybrid genotypes for rapid development and growth have not been rigorously compared at different temperatures or under different photoperiods, yet may prove to be of considerable ecological significance. Spring pupal eclosion is closely regulated by ambient temperatures, but hybrid pupae do not eclose before *canadensis* and are intermediate between the two parental types in eclosion time (Scriber et al. 2002). At temperatures above 30°C, diapausing pupae of *P. canadensis* experience higher mortality than do hybrid pupae (Scriber et al. 2002).

The hybrids between *glaucus* and *canadensis* are more efficient and capable of faster growth at 23°C than are the parental types on aspen, cherry, and tulip tree (fig. 17.4; Scriber 1986b). A concurrent study of parental types and reciprocal hybrids across a range of temperatures and host plants for a complete suite of life history traits would help to clarify which environmental conditions might favor hybrids over parental types (Arnold and Hodges 1995).

J. Mark Scriber, Mark Deering, and Aram Stump

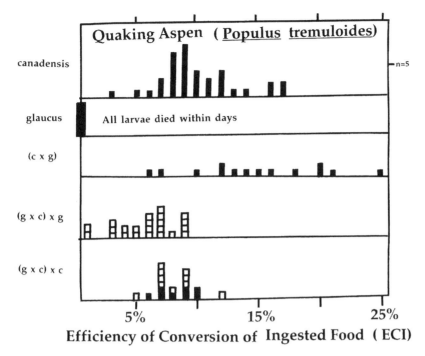

Figure 17.3 Variation in the overall efficiency (ECI) of conversion of quaking aspen leaves into larval growth by penultimate instar larvae of two *Papilio* species, their hybrids, and backcrosses. Note that all *P. glaucus* died, and that the hybrids appear to have a higher mean efficiency than even the parental *P. canadensis*. (After Scriber 1986b.)

DO DIFFERENTIAL HOST PREFERENCES AND DETOXIFICATION ABILITIES MAINTAIN THE SHARPLY DEFINED PARAPATRIC HYBRID ZONE BETWEEN *glaucus* AND *canadensis*?

Relatively strong concordance is observed in clines for several traits transecting the hybrid zone between *P. canadensis* and *P. glaucus,* including X-linked diapause regulation (obligate vs. facultative: Rockey et al. 1987a, 1987b), the distribution limits of a Y-linked dark (i.e., mimetic) female morph, and the X-linked suppressor/enabler allowing the expression of that trait (Scriber et al. 1996), as well as alleles at the *Ldh, Pgd,* and *Hk* loci (Hagen et al. 1991), neonate larval banding patterns (Scriber 1998), and adult wing color and morphology (Luebke et al. 1988; Scriber 1990, 2002). However, the differential ability to detoxify aspens (e.g., *Populus tremuloides*) and magnolias (e.g., *Liriodendron tulipifera*) and the X-linked control of oviposition behavior toward these host plant species do not have sharp geographic delineations. In other words, these clines for host plant use abilities and oviposition preference are significantly broader than those observed for diagnostic alleles, morphological differences, northern limits to bivoltinism capability (and southern limits to obligate diapause), and northern limits to the dark (mimetic) morph (and southern limits of the dark form color suppressor gene). However, analyses of allele frequencies across Michigan based on numerical likelihood methods (Szymura and Barton 1991; Porter et al. 1997) show that *Ldh, Pgd,* and *Hk* clines are highly significantly different in shape than the cline of *Hk* introgression from *P. canadensis* southward into *P. glaucus,* and that the *Ldh* cline is displaced southward of the other clines ($P < 0.001$; A. Porter and J. M. Scriber, unpub.).

P. glaucus's ability to detoxify tulip tree (*Liriodendron tulipifera*) has a sharp northern truncation at the hybrid zone, and not simply at the range limits of tulip tree distribution (Scriber 1986a). For *Callosamia* silkmoths, there are similarly broad geographic clines of host use ability that transcend the range limits of sweet bay magnolia, *Magnolia virginiana* (Johnson et al. 1996). The oviposition preferences of *Papilio* are often less distinct than larval survival abilities on particular host plant species in relation to the plant's geographic range (Scriber et al. 1991c), and some females collected as far north as Fairbanks, Alaska, actually preferred tulip tree in a three-choice study (with black cherry and quaking aspen: see also Bossart and Scriber 1995a). There is an intriguing decline in the proportion of these toxic "mistakes" by *P. canadensis* females with proximity to the central Michigan region, as the chances of encountering such a tree become increasingly likely. Alaskan populations are thousands of kilometers away from the nearest tulip tree.

The extension of aspen (*Populus tremuloides*) detoxification abilities southward beyond the hybrid zone center is more extensive and shows a gradual decay with distance (except in some "relict" *Papilio* populations of the Appalachian Mountains, which possess detoxification abilities in an increased proportion of the individuals: Scriber 1986b, 1988). The inheritance of esterase detoxification abilities in hybrids and backcrosses appears to be multilocus and quantitative in nature (Scriber et al. 1989) and has been used to detect induced levels of phytochemical resistance in hybrid poplars that could not be detected by either pure parent (Scriber et al. 1999). The selection of quaking aspen as an oviposition substrate in three-choice arenas is always very low in *P. glaucus* populations, but does persist all the way south to central Florida (Scriber et al. 1991a; Bossart and Scriber 1995a, 1995b). In fact, females of this most polyphagous swallowtail in the world (Scriber 1984b, 1995) consistently place 2–10% of their eggs on toxic or "non-" host plant leaves in multichoice oviposition arenas with normal hosts as the alternate choices (Scriber 1993), unlike other species such as the Lauraceae-specialized *P. troilus* and *P. palamedes* (Frankfater 1996; table 17.8). However, if in an arena with no normal host plants, most *P. glaucus* females refuse to lay any eggs (Scriber et al. 1999). Many other hosts for the polyphagous *canadensis* and *glaucus* species exist both north and south of the hybrid zone (Scriber 1986a), and it is unlikely that host plants alone select for the sharp borders between these species' ranges (Scriber 1988, 1996a; Hoffman and Blows

J. Mark Scriber, Mark Deering, and Aram Stump

Table 17.8 Oviposition preferences of *Papilio* females in revolving multichoice arenas[a] using host plant species from six major families (Lauraceae, Magnoliaceae, Rutaceae, Rosaceae, Salicaceae, Rhamnaceae)

Species	Females (n)	Mean Percentage of Total Eggs[b]					
		SP	TT	HT	BC	QA	RH
P. troilus	1	97.6	0.0	0.0	0.0	1.2	7.2
P. glaucus (Law. Co., OH)	13	3.4	31.9	49.1	11.7	3.5	0.8
P. glaucus (Gallia Co., OH)	25	13.7	46.7	30.5	4.6	2.6	1.6
P. glaucus (Clark Co., GA)	6	3.6	48.9	29.3	12.9	1.7	3.6
P. canadensis (Fairbanks, AK)	5	11.1	9.4	22.7	15.0	39.6	2.2

[a] See Scriber 1993.

[b] *SP* = spicebush, *Lindera benzoin;* TT = tulip tree, *Liriodendron tulipifera;* HT = hop tree, *Ptelea trifoliata;* BC = black cherry, *Prunus serotina;* QA = quaking aspen, *Populus tremuloides;* RH = *Rhamnus* spp.

1994). Genetically based adult oviposition preferences and differential larval detoxification and growth on sweet bay magnolia (*M. virginiana* L.) varied geographically (Scriber 1986a; Bossart and Scriber 1995a), although no electrophoretically detectable differentiation was observed from populations in central Florida through Georgia and into Ohio (Bossart and Scriber 1995b).

Individual tiger swallowtails from central New York State (near the center of the wide section of the hybrid zone) exhibit a composite of *glaucus* and *canadensis* traits (Scriber 1982). Some individuals have *P. glaucus Pgd* alleles and *P. canadensis Ldh* alleles (Hagen 1990). While many males from this area suppress the expression of the dark mimetic female morph in their hybrid daughters in pairings with dark mothers, some do not (Scriber et al. 1996). In the area of Tompkins County, individuals naturally oviposit on both tulip tree and quaking aspen, and their larvae develop well on both (Scriber 1975; Scriber and Feeny 1979; Scriber and Lederhouse 1992). In the central New York area, emergence of overwintering pupae is bimodal, but not likely bivoltine (Scriber 1975; Scriber and Lederhouse 1983; Hagen and Lederhouse 1985). This apparent mixture of *P. glaucus* and *P. canadensis* traits contrasts strongly with observations from the more western parts of the extensive Great Lakes hybrid zone (e.g., Michigan and Wisconsin; fig. 17.5). In the western areas of the zone, the concordance between traits is high; the exceptional "recombinant" individual is mostly *P. glaucus* with the occasional *canadensis* allele and is found toward the southern edge of the hybrid zone (Scriber 1996a; cf. Hagen 1990).

The possibility exists that linkage at the selected loci for diapause, color polymorphism, and oviposition preferences could intensify barriers to gene flow across the hybrid zone (Barton 1983; Barton and Hewitt 1985), which could be sufficient to prevent the free exchange of neutral alleles at other linked loci (Weir and Cockerhan 1978; Weir 1979). Thus the *Pgd* allozymes

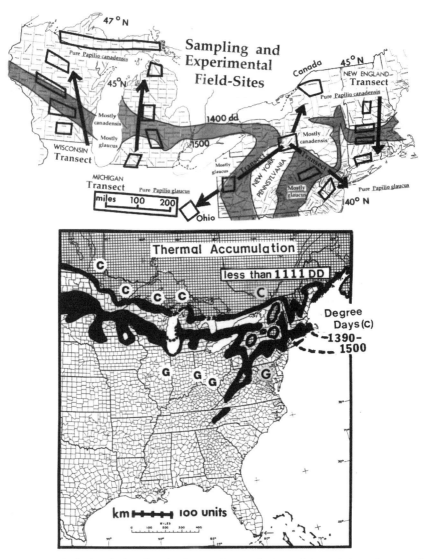

Figure 17.4 Distribution of selected *Papilio glaucus* and *P. canadensis* populations relative to the seasonal (20-year) average of thermal unit accumulation above a base threshold of 10°C across the Great Lakes and Appalachian Mountain regions of the eastern United States. The "C" and "G" designate the geographic sources of the *P. canadensis* and *P. glaucus* reference populations used in the multivariate morphometric discriminate analyses by Luebke et al. (1988).

of *glaucus* and *canadensis* need not be under selection to account for their clinal distribution. However, *Ldh* may be too far away from the diapause-*Pgd*-female color complex for hitchhiking to account for this X chromosome allele frequency cline (Hagen and Scriber 1989, 1995). Other factors in addition to linkage disequilibrium could also affect the ability of neutral alleles to cross the hybrid zone, such as low population densities and interruptions to gene flow (Endler 1977; Thorpe 1984; Rand and Harrison 1989; Mallet 1993; Hilton et al. 1994; Bert and Arnold 1995; Harrison and Bogdanowicz 1997).

The extent of average individual dispersal and subsequent gene flow across this hybrid zone has not been systematically examined. Mark-release-recapture studies of *P. glaucus* (Lederhouse 1995; Scriber et al. 1998a, 1999) have consistently found some very local individuals along with some that quickly disperse (but probably not more than 15 kilometers). In fact, the northern distribution of dark morph females has been closely watched by lepidopterists for many decades, even back into the mid-nineteenth century (Edwards 1884), and has changed amazingly little throughout that period, even with some variation due to several warm or cold seasons (Scriber and Gage 1995). Stray dark morph female individuals are rarely, if ever, observed at distances more than 50–100 kilometers from the center of the hybrid zone (Ebner 1970; Shapiro 1974; Scriber et al. 1996). However, a single specimen was recently collected in the Michigan Upper Peninsula (250–350 kilometers from the nearest *glaucus*); biochemical and other evidence led to the conclusion that this was a very atypical blow-in on a strong weather front that had passed through from the southwest the previous day (Scriber et al. 1998b).

IS THERE PREZYGOTIC ISOLATION BETWEEN *canadensis* AND *glaucus?*

Interspecific hybrids between members of the *P. glaucus* group sometimes exhibit hybrid dysgenesis (or "negative heterosis," in the form of Haldane effects, X effects, egg mortality, and pupal deaths), but also exhibit hybrid vigor or heterosis (in egg production, viability, growth rates, and efficiencies of growth), relative to the parental types. Reduced fitness in hybrids could select for prezygotic reproductive isolation and an increase in "assortative mating" (Mayr 1963), especially in zones of overlap or hybridization, possibly by the process of "reinforcement" (see discussions in Howard 1993; Butlin 1995; Futuyma and Shapiro 1995; Veech et al. 1996). In a review of the literature involving heterogametic males, Reinhold (1998) showed that X-linked genes had a pronounced effect on sexually selected traits in three groups: *Drosophila,* other insects, and mammals. We would predict that sexual selection in butterflies (with heterogametic females) would also be controlled by traits on the X chromosome. Tethering of reciprocal hybrid female virgins would help to determine whether this occurs for mate selection traits used by males.

While sex chromosome effects have few significant roles in premating reproductive isolation (Wu and Johnson 1996), some Lepidoptera do exhibit sex-linked genes affecting premating isolation (*Ostrinia,* the European corn borer: Roelofs et al. 1987; *Colias:* Silberglied and Taylor 1978; Grula and Taylor 1980a, 1980b; budworms: Sanders et al. 1977). These sex-linked traits have enhanced isolation and are significant in speciation (Sperling 1994;

Sperling, chap. 20 in this volume; Prowell 1998). However, the breakdown of hybrid zones may result due to neutral introgression or the selection of alleles that reduce the degree of "hybrid unfitness" (whether dependent or independent of the environment: Riesenberg and Wendell 1993; Arnold and Hodges 1995; Ritchie and Hewitt 1995).

FIELD STUDIES SHOW ASYMMETRY IN MATING PREFERENCES

Few studies of mating biology among hybridizing species have ever been conducted in the field (Brower 1959; Hewitt et al. 1987; Saetre et al. 1997; Deering 1998; Mallet et al. 1998a), despite the importance of habitat-specific mating preferences that cannot be simulated in the laboratory (Feder et al. 1994; Rhymer and Simberloff 1996). Our goal recently was to compare the mating preferences of males in their natural habitats for different species of females in two-choice tests.

We used tethered, size-matched virgin yellow females of *Papilio canadensis* and *P. glaucus* at locations with high concentrations of free-flying males of one or the other species (northern Michigan for *canadensis* and central Florida for *glaucus:* Deering 1998) as part of a larger study of geographic variation in hybrid zone mating dynamics (Deering and Scriber 2002). In Florida, the conspecific *P. glaucus* females dominated the preferences and activities of the local males in both 1997 (93% of copulations) and 1998 (100%). With regard to contacts (attempted matings), the same basic pattern of results was obtained in the Florida populations (Deering 1998). In northern Michigan (near the Charlevoix/Emmet/Cheboygan county intersect location, 250 kilometers or more from the hybrid zone), however, the local *P. canadensis* males did not prefer their own species, and the matings were not random; there was a strong preference for the heterospecific yellow *glaucus* females! More than 82% of all matings ($n = 493$) and more than 80% of the attempted matings ($n = 119$) of free-flying *canadensis* males were with the tethered female *glaucus* (Deering and Scriber 2002).

Not only do these observations fail to support the concept of species recognition and reinforcement, but the observed behavior could reflect phylogenetically old traits. It is clear that *canadensis* males are still attracted to the ancestral female form (*P. glaucus*) even more than to females of their own species. Such heterospecific mating preferences have been seen in swordtails (Ryan and Wagner 1987), frogs (Ryan et al. 1990), and least auklets (Jones and Hunter 1998), suggesting that ancestral traits may be preferred due to previously possessed sensory biases (Basolo 1990) or viability indicators (or the "good genes" or "handicap" process: see Andersson 1994).

However, preliminary evidence (J. M. Scriber, M. Deering, and H. Hereau, unpub.) suggests that this strong preference of *canadensis* males for the ancestral *glaucus* female type does not extend to the dark (mimetic) form of

J. Mark Scriber, Mark Deering, and Aram Stump

P. glaucus. They fly over, and basically ignore, the dark females and mate with *canadensis* or yellow hybrid females tethered out as the other member of the pair. Tethered dark females of *glaucus* were also ignored by western members of the *glaucus* group, especially *multicaudatus* males (Brower 1959). Males of *P. glaucus* do not seem to have difficulty recognizing and mating with conspecific dark morph females, preferring the locally more abundant color morph. We have observed a preference for yellow among males in central Florida, where the proportion of dark females in the population is only 20–40% (Scriber et al. 1998a), in contrast to Ohio, where the dark form represents 80–85% of the females and is preferred by males there (R. Lederhouse and J. M. Scriber, unpub.). It has been suggested that male *glaucus* use ultraviolet hindwing cues (Rutowski 1998), which may be found on both morphs of *glaucus* females (Platt et al. 1984). Perhaps *canadensis* and the western species (*rutulus, multicaudatus,* and *eurymedon*) that do not have conspecific dark morph females may "cue in" more on the yellow wing pattern, or other factors, rather than the ultraviolet of the hindwings, which *glaucus* males use. Alternatively, it may be that *canadensis* females have little ultraviolet pattern showing on their wing scales.

We need to continue our mating preference studies with special emphasis on the geographic variation in this heterospecific preference to see whether it is extensive or occurs only near the northern Michigan "cold pocket" where *canadensis* males exhibited these unexpected and intensive heterospecific mating preferences. It will also be essential to increase replicates of tethering studies inside the "hybrid zone" itself. Very preliminary studies (J. M. Scriber, unpub.; $n = 3$ pairings) do show 100% preference for *canadensis* females (when paired with *glaucus* or hybrids as the other choice) by local males (probably all *canadensis,* judged by wing patterns) near our Isabella/Clare County population at the north side of the hybrid zone.

DO MULTIPLY MATING *canadensis, glaucus,* AND OTHER SWALLOWTAILS SELECT CONSPECIFIC SPERM, OR DOES SPERM PRECEDENCE PREVAIL?

The Canadian and Eastern tiger swallowtail butterflies usually mate three to five times in the field (Lederhouse and Scriber 1987; Lederhouse et al. 1989; Lederhouse 1995). The fact that hybrids are rare (Luebke et al. 1988; Scriber 1990, 1996a), while interspecific matings may not be (Deering 1998), leads us to consider the possibility that females may be selecting conspecific sperm when they have mated with males of two or more different species. This would reflect "postmating, prezygotic" or "cryptic sexual selection" (Thornhill 1983; LaMunyon and Eisner 1993a; Eberhard and Cordero 1995; Eberhard 1996). Post-insemination barriers to gene flow in crickets have been reported recently (Howard and Gregory 1993; Gregory and Howard 1994, 1996), in which multiply mated females select conspecific rather than heterospecific sperm, whereas, if mated by two conspecifics, their offspring would be sired by both males. A direct role for such prezygotic, postmating barriers to hybridization in the evolution of reproductive isolation has been suggested for lacewings (Albuquerque et al. 1996) and for numerous other species (Eberhard 1996; Holland and Rice 1997). It has even been suggested that female dung flies can store sperm of different males in different places and subsequently select different sperm (to lay eggs of different genotypes) depending on environmental conditions (Ward 1998). Dung flies that were heterozygous at the *Pgm* (phosphoglucomutase) locus grew better under variable conditions (Ward 1998), and *Pgm* variation is known to have fitness effects for butterflies as well (Watt et al. 1985).

Our ability to hand-pair *Papilio* species and obtain viable hybrids of many interspecific combinations (Scriber et al. 1995a), combined with adult diagnostic allozymes (Hagen and Scriber 1991) that work for larvae as well (Stump 2000) and diagnostic morphological traits for larvae (Scriber et al. 1995a; Scriber 1998) and adults (Luebke et al. 1988), provide valuable tools for determining whether cryptic sexual selection can or does occur, or whether sperm precedence prevails in all cases, as previously assumed (Parker 1984). We hand-paired females twice, each to a conspecific and a heterospecific male. Some of the females were mated first to a conspecific male, followed by a heterospecific male, and the others were sequentially mated in the reverse order. Eggs were collected, and hatching larvae were frozen at −80°C. We found that the *Pgd* locus, for which *P. glaucus* and *P. canadensis* have different allozymes (Hagen and Scriber 1991), showed the same allozymes in third-instar larvae as in adults. This allowed allozyme electrophoresis of *Pgd* to be used to determine the paternity of larvae produced after a second mating.

Twenty-three twice-mated females produced larvae before and after a second mating. Of these, sixteen continued to produce offspring sired exclusively by the first male, three produced a mixture of offspring sired by both males, and four switched entirely to producing offspring sired only by the second male. This finding shows that there is no absolute first-male or last-male sperm precedence. Of the eleven females that were mated to a conspecific male first, eight showed no switching, and three showed some or total switching. Of the twelve females that were mated to a heterospecific male first, eight showed no switching, and four showed some or total switching. This finding suggests that there is no block to interspecific fertilizations even when there is conspecific sperm available. However, the possibility of local adaptation in and near the hybrid zone means that it is important to continue studying sperm precedence in these areas. In addition to assessing these behaviors in relation to geographic distance from the center of the *canadensis/glaucus* hybrid zone, we plan to assess the effects of increased phylogenetic distance in these interspecific crosses.

J. Mark Scriber, Mark Deering, and Aram Stump

A number of variables need to be taken into account when interpreting the offspring identities of multiply mated females. For example, the size of the first (and second) spermatophore transferred and the nutrients provided by apyrene sperm or other material in the spermatophore could affect the results (Watanabe 1988; Lederhouse et al. 1989, 1990; Wedell and Cook 1998). The propensity for the female to remate or refuse our attempts could also bias the interpretation of our hand-paired experimental results (Rutowski 1984; R. L. Smith 1984; Lederhouse and Scriber 1987; Ringo 1996).

CONCLUSION: THE IMPORTANCE OF A GEOGRAPHIC PERSPECTIVE IN EVOLUTIONARY ECOLOGY

It has become clear that multiple transect studies of hybrid zones may yield more than just geographic "pattern"; they will provide a means by which to evaluate the "processes" of genetic differentiation and speciation as well (Oliver 1979b; Collins 1984; Rand and Harrison 1989; Howard et al. 1993; Futuyma and Shapiro 1995; Scriber et al. 1996). These "geographic mosaics of hybrid interaction" are a mixture of local environmental selection pressures, such as those seen in northern Michigan cold pockets (Scriber 1996b), that are dynamic, changing with climate (Giroux 1998). Whether or why some traits critical to differentiation and speciation in the Canadian and eastern tiger swallowtail butterflies have become almost universally (as opposed to locally) established and "diagnostic" of the species is still not clear, but the reason seems to be a combination of selection and gene flow.

We have observed an asymmetry in assortative interspecific mating in field populations using tethered females such that *canadensis* females seem nowhere preferred (Deering 1998; Deering and Scriber 2002), but multiply mated *canadensis* females do not always show conspecific sperm precedence (Stump 2000). Results of such asymmetrical mating behavior should be detectable using mitochondrial DNA, which, being maternally inherited, should indicate the parentage of each hybrid individual.

Some asymmetry in key host plant detoxification abilities also seems to exist across the hybrid zone with regard to tulip tree and quaking aspen. The ability to use tulip tree stops rather abruptly going northward at the center of the hybrid zone, while aspen detoxification and larval survival is observed at various low levels well south of the hybrid zone center into the midwestern states of Illinois, Indiana, and Ohio, as well as in the southern Appalachian Mountains (Scriber 1994). Similarly, univoltinism should not by itself be a barrier to southward movement of *canadensis,* and many excellent host plant species exist southward all the way to central Florida (Scriber 1986a). However, recent studies (Scriber et al. 2002) suggest that several days at temperatures in the range of 30°–36° are more lethal for diapausing pupae of *P. canadensis* than for hybrids or *P. glaucus*. While temperatures in excess of 35°C are common for more than 10 consecutive days throughout most of the United States, this is rare north of the hybrid zone (NOAA 1999). It is very likely that gene flow northward in *P. glaucus* is severely limited by thermal constraints (combined with host plant quality variation within and among plant species), such that a genetic sink or "ecological trench" exists across the hybrid zone for any attempts at a second generation too far north in this facultatively diapausing species. Thus, it seems that a combination of selective forces (Haldane's rule, X-linkage, behavioral, physiological, ecological), as well as gene flow, are important in the historical maintenance of this hybrid zone.

While it is unlikely that the insect-plant interactions involved in the *glaucus/scamander/troilus* species groups are "coevolutionary" in nature (Scriber 1988; Scriber et al. 1991b; Thompson 1993), the concept of a "geographic mosaic" used by Thompson (1994) in this regard directly applies to "interactions and adaptations" of *Papilio* with their biotic and abiotic environment. Certainly a geographic perspective is essential with regard to host plant "quality/suitability" (Scriber 1984b; Mattson and Scriber 1987), especially at the edges of host plant ranges, in hybrid zones (Arnold et al. 1999), and in cold pockets (Johnson and Scriber 1994; Hoffman and Blows 1994; Bell 1997), and with regard to differential levels of previous herbivory (Dankert et al. 1997; Scriber et al. 1999). These biotic and abiotic factors are interactive and dynamic, involving climate, habitat disturbances, pollution, and associated interactions at the tri-trophic and general community level (Scriber 1994; Scriber and Gage 1995).

There is no better laboratory than a natural hybrid zone. We will focus our immediate attention on determining the overall strength of the selection pressures, number of genes involved, rate of individual dispersal, and ease with which different alleles cross from one gene pool to another using frequencies of various genotypes found across the hybrid zone (Charlesworth et al. 1998).

SUMMARY

Many of the North American species of swallowtail butterflies of the Papilionidae family are known to hybridize naturally, and interspecific laboratory hand pairings of species from different continents have produced viable hybrid offspring. The focus of this chapter has been on the natural hybrid zone between *Papilio glaucus* and *P. canadensis* and the potential reproductive isolating mechanism and ecological factors maintaining it for the past two decades (1980–1998).

J. Mark Scriber, Mark Deering, and Aram Stump

Different "species diagnostic" traits (including morphological, physiological, and behavioral features as well as biochemical allozymes) have generally appeared to be geographically stable and basically concordant in their frequency cline changes across the narrow Great Lakes hybrid zone in Wisconsin and Michigan, with less step cline concordance of traits observed in the mountainous eastern United States (New York, Vermont, Pennsylvania, and southern New England). Continuing geographic analyses will be needed to assess the influence of recent regional climate warming on the location and stability of these multiple trait clines in transects across the hybrid zone. A geographically/temporally extensive and ecologically comprehensive foundation, such as that described in this chapter, will better enable us to determine the role of ecological factors in natural selection and genetic divergence between these hybridizing taxa, improving our understanding of the processes leading to speciation.

ACKNOWLEDGMENTS

This research was supported in part by several NSF grants, Doctoral Dissertation Improvement awards, and Research Experience for Undergraduate awards (BSR-87–18448, BSR 88–01184, BSR 90–37153–5263, BSR 91–071390, DEB 91–20122, DEB [LTER]: 9221022, DEB 9510044 and DEB 9981608), the Michigan Agricultural Experiment Station (Projects 1640, 1644, 1722, 8051, and 8072), and the Michigan State University Foundation. Several students received Hutson Research Grants (Department of Entomology). The Michigan Biological Field Station at Douglas Lake, the Archbold Biological Field Station, and the Highlands Hammock State Park generously provided laboratory and field facilities. Special thanks are extended to Professor Martine Rahier and the plant/animal ecology group at the University of Neuchatel for their generous hospitality during this, J. M. S.'s first, sabbatical leave, and for their patience during my preparation of this chapter.

PART V

Systematics and Species Diversification

Systematic biology infers, displays, and constructs systems of communication about the present relatedness among organisms and groups of organisms, and, so far as possible, infers the history leading from common ancestors through time to those present patterns of relatedness. It can thus provide, from these inferred historical patterns, an organizing framework for diverse kinds of comparative study in biology. When systematic inferences are sufficiently strong, and robust, they can interact synergistically with the study of present-day processes to illuminate ecological and evolutionary mechanisms, and they can supplement mechanistic understanding in addressing important problems in applied biology, particularly problems in conservation and environmental science at large.

The initial chapters in part 5 illustrate very different choices of character sources and yield different kinds of results. Dana Campbell and Naomi Pierce (chap. 18) summarize their molecular approach to the long-vexing questions of the relationships between lycaenid (blues, coppers, and hairstreaks) and riodinid (metalmarks) butterflies, and of these groups to other butterfly families. Their evidence from one nuclear gene argues strongly for sister status of Lycaenidae and Riodinidae as monophyletic subclades within a common clade, helping the study of adaptive coevolution with ants within this clade, but in contrast, shedding little light on relations to other butterfly groups. Paulo Motta (chap. 19), working with the Ithomiinae, explores the utility of morphological characters from larvae as compared with adults for clarifying relationships both within and outside the group. Considering these two studies together shows the importance of diverse views on character choice, on the biological usefulness of the rank concept, and other such questions on which extreme positions are often taken in systematic debate.

How are species best defined *in practice?* What is the role in phyletic differentiation of the frequent sex linkage of mate recognition and other taxon-diagnostic traits? What different character sources are useful for what different kinds of analyses in Lepidoptera? Why might single-gene and multigene phylogenetic hypotheses clash? Felix Sperling (chap. 20) raises these questions in the context of using molecular methods to address the systematics of papilionid butterflies. In the course of providing exemplary answers to his questions, he calls for consistency in molecular systematists' choice of DNA sequence sources across the Lepidoptera to allow more rapid accumulation of directly comparable evidence. Jean-François Martin and colleagues (chap. 21) take a complementary approach, extending the consideration of species definitions to a case study, using both morphological and molecular evidence, of a classic "cryptic" or "sibling" species pair in the biogeographically isolated dismorphiine pierid genus *Leptidea*. They find that morphological and molecular characters resolve the taxa in question to quite different extents. Their findings raise ecological studies of the species' organism-environment interactions, to understand what may have driven their differentiation, to a high priority.

Knowledge of the identity of an organism or group is fundamental to considering any of its more specific features. What *is* identity, in systematic principle or in the practical context of the need for conservation decisions? Richard Vane-Wright (chap. 22) concludes part 5 by using work on butterflies to pose fundamental, philosophically driven questions about what systematics is and what it does, even as he summarizes current progress in understanding the history of butterfly origins and diversification and in applying this understanding to conservation issues.

CHAPTER 18

Phylogenetic Relationships of the Riodinidae: Implications for the Evolution of Ant Association

Dana L. Campbell and Naomi E. Pierce

PHYLOGENETIC HYPOTHESES OF THE PAPILIONOIDEA

Although not for lack of study, the evolutionary history of the major lineages of "true" butterflies (Papilionoidea, including Hesperiidae) is still unknown, and multiple conflicting phylogenetic hypotheses exist in the literature. Assessing the systematic position of the metalmark butterflies (family Riodinidae) has been a particular challenge for this field. Furthermore, there is disagreement about the monophyly of this large group, which contains over 1,200 species. Most morphological studies place the riodinid butterflies as most closely related to the lycaenid butterflies, and identify the nymphalids as the closest relatives to this riodinid + lycaenid clade (Ehrlich and Ehrlich 1967; Kristensen 1976; Scott and Wright 1990; de Jong et al. 1996a) (fig. 18.1A, B). These relationships have been inferred with a variety of phylogenetic methods and are supported by a number of adult, larval, and pupal synapomorphies, although few are universal or uniquely derived. An alternative hypothesis of the placement of the riodinids was proposed by Robbins (1988a). Based on a cladistic analysis of nine character states among four characters of the foreleg coxa, trochanter, and basal femur, Robbins suggested that the Riodinidae are more closely related to the Nymphalidae than to the Lycaenidae (fig. 18.1C), and split the lycaenids into two groups, which may not compose a monophyletic lineage: Lycaeninae-Theclinae-Polyommatinae and Lipteninae-Poritinae-Miletinae-Curetinae.

Two molecular studies have explored papilionid relationships, but their results conflict with each other and with the morphological hypotheses (fig. 18.1D, E). In comparing nucleotide characters from the 28s subunit of nuclear ribosomal RNA, Martin and Pashley (1992) found no close

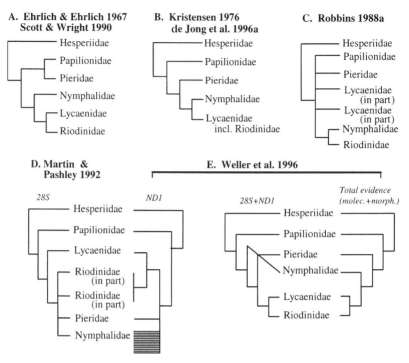

Figure 18.1 Results of previous studies addressing the relationship of the Riodinidae to the other butterfly families.

phylogenetic relationship between the Riodinidae and the Lycaenidae, and instead found the monophyly of the Riodinidae uncertain. Analysis of a portion of a second gene, the mitochondrial NADH dehydrogenase subunit 1 (ND1) (Weller et al. 1996), resulted in a monophyletic interpretation of the Lycaenidae + Riodinidae, but did not resolve the sister to the Lycaenidae + Riodinidae clade, nor did it recover a monophyletic Nymphalidae. When characters from both genes were analyzed in combination, the riodinid + lycaenid relationship was recovered, and the Pieridae came out as the sister to the riodinid + lycaenid clade. A total evidence analysis combining the molecular data from both genes with morphological characters taken from all five of the morphological studies mentioned above once more supported a riodinid + lycaenid clade with a sister relationship to the Nymphalidae (Weller et al. 1996).

TAXONOMIC RANKING

Previous studies of butterfly relationships vary in their interpretation of the taxonomic rank of the riodinids, with some conferring familial (Eliot 1973; Harvey 1987; Robbins 1988a; Martin and Pashley 1992; Weller et al. 1996) and some subfamilial (Ehrlich 1958; Kristensen 1976; Scott and Wright 1990;

Dana L. Campbell and Naomi E. Pierce

de Jong et al. 1996a) status. In this chapter we refer to the Riodinidae as a family due to the precedence of this terminology in studies examining within-riodinid relationships (Stichel 1928; Clench 1955; Harvey 1987; Robbins 1988a). Hence, we use the term Lycaenidae to refer to the non-riodinid lycaenids *sensu* Eliot (Eliot 1973; but not Eliot in Corbet et al. 1992).

ANT ASSOCIATION IN THE PAPILIONOIDEA

The Riodinidae and the Lycaenidae are distinct among the Papilionoidea in that they have evolved the ability to form complex larval associations with ants (myrmecophily: Hinton 1951; Pierce 1987; DeVries 1991; Fiedler 1991; Pierce et al. 2002). In many cases, these are mutualistic associations whereby the larvae secrete nutritious solutions from specialized glands (ant organs) to multiple species of ants in exchange for protection from predators and parasites (Malicky 1970; Pierce and Easteal 1986; DeVries 1991; Axen and Pierce 1997). Some myrmecophilous larvae have evolved separate organs that are thought to secrete chemicals to appease the ants and further mediate larval-ant interactions (Clark and Dickson 1956; Malicky 1970; Claassens and Dickson 1977; DeVries 1988b, 1991). While many consider ant association to have evolved once in a riodinid + lycaenid ancestor and been subsequently lost in multiple lineages (Hinton 1951; Vane-Wright 1978; Scott 1984; Scott and Wright 1990), it has also been argued that riodinid and lycaenid ant organs may not be homologous, since they are found on different larval segments in these two families. Thus, instead of having a single origin in the Papilionoidea, ant association may have evolved independently in the riodinids and in the lycaenids (DeVries 1991, 1997; see also Fiedler 1991).

In order to settle the placement of the riodinid butterflies and to examine the evolution of myrmecophily from a phylogenetic perspective, molecular sequence characters from the 3' exon of *wingless* were generated (Campbell et al. 2000). This developmentally active nuclear gene evolves rapidly in nymphalid butterflies (at rates exceeding those of the mitochondrial genes *Cytochrome Oxidase I* and *Cytochrome Oxidase II*) and has been informative for reconstructing relationships in a large dataset of nymphalid butterflies (Brower and DeSalle 1998). Applications of sequence characters derived from *wingless* to problems involving relationships within riodinids and among butterfly families have confirmed the utility of *wingless* for problems at this phylogenetic level (Campbell 1998; Campbell et al. 2000). In this chapter we review the phylogenetic relationships among riodinid, lycaenid, and nymphalid butterflies as recovered by *wingless,* and we examine the implications of the phylogenetic placement of the Riodinidae with respect to the other butterfly families for our understanding of ant association in the Papilionoidea.

METHODS

SAMPLING SCHEME, OUTGROUPS, AND AVAILABLE VOUCHER SPECIMENS

Taxa were selected to represent each of the main lycaenid, riodinid, and nymphalid lineages (table 18.1). Two representatives of the Pieridae and one species of the Papilionidae were also included. A hesperiid representative was included as an outgroup based on previous studies of butterfly systematics, which agree on the Hesperiidae as the basal lineage of the Papilionoidea. Adult butterflies were collected as fresh specimens and the bodies stored in 100% ethanol at −80°C. Wings were retained as voucher specimens in the Harvard Museum of Comparative Zoology (riodinids, lycaenids, *Papilio glaucus,* and *Ancyloxypha numita*) and the American Museum of Natural History (nymphalids and *Pieris rapae*). PCR and sequencing were carried out as described by Campbell et al. (2000). All sequences have been submitted to Genbank (for accession numbers, see Campbell et al. 2000).

PHYLOGENETIC ANALYSIS

Our extensive exploration of the signal in *wingless* characters, and our phylogenetic analysis of *wingless* characters using various character weighting strategies as well as model-based analytical methods for these taxa, are discussed in detail elsewhere (Campbell 1998; Campbell et al. 2000). Here we present a conservative parsimony analysis in which third codon position transitions are excluded on the basis that these characters were found to be saturated in some taxa (however, they do contain signal for other taxa, particularly taxa in the family Riodinidae; see Campbell et al. 2000). Heuristic parsimony searches were performed with TBR branch swapping and fifty random addition replicates using the computer program PAUP*4 test versions d49 and d56, kindly provided by D. Swofford (Swofford 1998b). One hundred bootstrapping replicates were done to assess nodal support.

PHYLOGENETIC PATTERNS

Parsimony analysis of *wingless* characters excluding third position transitions recovered four most parsimonious trees. A strict consensus of these trees is shown in figure 18.2. The results of this analysis are summarized by family below.

Table 18.1 Taxa used in this study and their classification

Family	Subfamily	Tribe	Species	Locality
Riodinidae	Euselasiinae		*Euselasia* sp.	Ecuador: Sucumbios Province
	Hamearinae		*Taxila haquinus*	Malaysia: FRIM Kepong
			Abisara saturata	Malaysia: Kuala Woh, Papah
	Riodininae	incertae sedis	*Cremna actoris*	Ecuador: Sucumbios Province
		Eurybiini	*Eurybia* sp.	Ecuador: Sucumbios Province
		Mesosemiini	*Mesosemia* sp.	Ecuador: Sucumbios Province
		Riodinini	*Riodina lysippus*	Ecuador: Sucumbios Province
		Charitini	*Sarota* sp.	Ecuador: Sucumbios Province
		Emesini	*Emesis* sp.	Ecuador: Sucumbios Province
		Nymphidiini	*Nymphidium cachrus*	Ecuador: Sucumbios Province
		Helicopini	*Helicopis cupido*	Ecuador: Sucumbios Province
		Lemoniini	*Thisbe irena*	Ecuador: Sucumbios Province
Lycaenidae	Poritiinae	Poritiini	*Poritia phama*	Malaysia: Genting Tea Estate
			Simiskina pheretia	Malaysia: Awana FR, Pahang
		Liptenini	*Baliochila minima*	Kenya: Arabuko-Sokoke
	Curetinae		*Curetis bulis*	Malaysia: FRIM Kepong
	Miletinae	Miletini	*Miletis ancon*	Malaysia: FRIM Kepong
		Liphyrini	*Liphyra brassolis*	Australia: Queensland
			Spalgis epius	Malaysia: Genting Tea Estate
	Theclinae		*Habrodais ganus*	USA: Nevada, Lang Crossing
			Jalmenus daemeli	Australia: Queensland, Townsville
	Polyommatinae		*Candalides geminus*	Australia: Queensland, Burra Range
			Jamides alecto	Malaysia: FRIM Kepong
	Lycaeninae		*Heliophorus kiana*	Malaysia: Kinabolu Park
Nymphalidae	Heliconiinae		*Heliconius erato*	French Guiana: Pointe Macouria
	Libytheinae		*Libytheana carineta*	Brazil: Rondonia, Ariquemes
	Satyrinae		*Cercyonis pegala*	USA: New York, Ithaca
	Morphinae		*Morpho helenor*	Brazil: Rondonia, Ariquemes
	Limenitidinae		*Limenitis arthemis*	USA: New York, Caroline
			Diaethria clymena	Brazil: Rondonia, Ariquemes
	Nymphalinae		*Hypolimnas misippus*	Reared in captivity, ex. C. Clarke
			Siproeta steneles	Brazil: Rondonia, Ariquemes
	Danainae		*Danaus plexippus*	Colombia: Meta, Villavisencia
	Ithomiinae		*Melinaea maenius*	Brazil: Rondonia, Ariquemes
Pieridae	Pierinae		*Pieris rapae*	USA: New York, Ithaca
			Delias sp.	Australia: NSW, Lismore
Papilionidae	Papilioninae		*Papilio glaucus*	USA: Colorado, Gunnison
Hesperiidae			*Ancyloxypha numita*	USA: Massachusetts, Boston

Note: Classifications are according to Harvey 1987 (riodinids), Eliot 1973 (lycaenids), and Harvey 1991 (nymphalids).

Strong bootstrap values support riodinid monophyly, lycaenid monophyly, and a sister relationship between the riodinids and the lycaenids (see fig. 18.2). The power of *wingless* is considerably lower, however, at the next deeper level of comparison. It is unable to establish unambiguously the sister taxon to the riodinid + lycaenid lineage. This analysis recovers the Nymphalidae + Pieridae + Papilionidae as the sister clade to the Riodinidae + Lycaenidae; however, this arrangement is not supported by bootstrapping, and should be interpreted very cautiously.

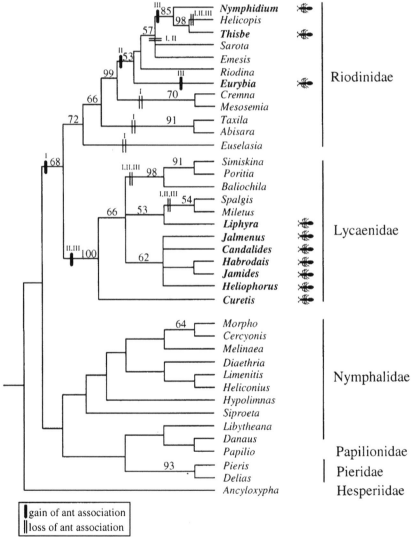

Figure 18.2 Strict consensus of the four most parsimonious trees resulting from an analysis in which third position transitions were excluded. Bootstrap values are shown for nodes with 50% or greater support. Taxa that have ant organs are shown in boldfaced type and identified with an ant icon.

Dana L. Campbell and Naomi E. Pierce

Riodinidae

The *wingless* data establish strong evidence for the monophyly of the Riodinidae, countering the possibility of a polyphyletic Riodinidae raised by Martin and Pashley (1992). Molecular studies have yet to test the phylogenetic affiliation of the rare monotypic riodinid subfamilies Styginae and Corrachiinae, although recent morphological analyses place these within the Riodinidae (Harvey 1987; Robbins 1988a, 1988b; Scott and Wright 1990). Most relationships within the Riodinidae are well resolved and well supported by bootstrapping (see fig. 18.2) and are largely concordant with the most recent hypothesis of riodinid subfamilial and tribal relationships (Harvey 1987).

Except for the position of *Euselasia, wingless* recovers the same riodinid topology under different analytical conditions, indicating that these are robust conclusions (maximum likelihood, distance methods, and parsimony under different weighting strategies were examined; see Campbell et al. 2000). In some analyses, *Euselasia* was found to be the sister group to the Hamearinae, represented by *Abisara + Taxila.* The ant-associated tribes Lemoniini, Nymphidiini, and Eurybiini form two clades, with the Eurybiini evolving earlier and the Lemoniini and Nymphidiini derived from a common ancestor. A larger study using more taxa (Campbell 1998) and a morphological analysis (Penz and DeVries 1999) indicate that although the Lemoniini and Nymphidiini make up a monophyletic group, they are not, as Harvey suggested, distinct lineages. Relationships within the riodinids, in an analysis involving more extensive taxon sampling, are discussed further in Campbell (1998).

Lycaenidae

Very few morphological characters supporting the monophyly of the Lycaenidae exist in the systematic literature, although only two studies have suggested that the lycaenids are paraphyletic (Scott 1984; Robbins 1988a, 1988b). Both of these studies consider the lycaenid subfamily Curetinae to be more closely related to the riodinids than to the lycaenids, although Scott later changed this view to a monophyletic Lycaenidae (Scott and Wright 1990). The *wingless* gene contributes multiple characters that strongly support a monophyletic Lycaenidae including the Curetinae.

Our *wingless* analysis places *Curetis* as the most basal lycaenid group; this interpretation is supported by Eliot (in Corbet et al. 1992). The curetines share many morphological characters with the Riodinidae, especially characters that are not found in other lycaenids, such as a large anepisternum, uncus, and transtilla and tibial spurs (Scott and Wright 1990). The basal position of the curetines is consistent with the parsimonious interpretation that these are symplesiomorphic traits that were lost once, in the ancestor of the non-curetine lycaenids. Noise or conflicting signal generated by third position transitions in *wingless* reduces support for this basal relationship, however, and analyses employing alternative weighting schemes (for example, when all third positions are included in the parsimony analysis: Campbell et al. 2000) place the Curetinae as a highly derived lycaenid lineage (as do Scott and Wright 1990), albeit with no bootstrap support. The position of the curetines requires further examination. Reconstruction of lycaenid relationships is currently in progress using *wingless* and other molecular characters as well as more extensive taxon sampling.

Nymphalidae

In the analysis presented here, the Nymphalidae are found to be paraphyletic with respect to the pierid representatives and *Papilio*. However, none of the recovered relationships among the Nymphalidae have bootstrap support greater than 50%, and when different weighting schemes or analytical methods are used, the topology of the nymphalids is very different (Campbell et al. 2000). For example, unweighted parsimony finds the Nymphalidae to be polyphyletic with respect to the riodinid + lycaenid clade (again, with little or no bootstrap support: Campbell et al. 2000).

Monophyly of the Nymphalidae is not supported by *wingless*, yet at the same time *wingless* does not strongly refute the possibility of nymphalid monophyly (i.e., nodes contradicting nymphalid monophyly are not supported by bootstrapping; furthermore, forcing the constraint of monophyly of all nymphalids or forcing monophyly of all nymphalids except *Libytheana* in heuristic searches does not significantly increase tree length). Short internal branch lengths render almost all within-nymphalid relationships unstable and highly dependent on the weighting method used for analysis. Furthermore, the informative changes among nymphalids appear to consist of mostly third position changes, and only a few first and second position changes. In riodinids and lycaenids, on the other hand, first and second position informative sites are much more common (Campbell 1998). This may explain the difference in the utility of the *wingless* gene in recovering relationships within and between these families. The monophyly of the Nymphalidae and its relationship to the Lycaenidae + Riodinidae is still in need of rigorous investigation using other genes and more extensive taxonomic sampling.

It is notable that, using characters from a portion of the ND1 gene, Weller et al. (1996) also did not recover the monophyly of, or any resolution within the nymphalids. On the other hand, characters from the 28s gene recovered the Nymphalidae, but not riodinid + lycaenid monophyly (Martin and Pashley 1992). These findings suggest that the inability to resolve all families at once may not be due to the shortcomings of a particular gene itself, but might instead be due to biological differences in the radiations of these lineages, or a different rate of molecular evolution in the Nymphalidae. Alternatively, there is some evidence that *wingless* may be evolving at a different rate in the riodinids and lycaenids than in the nymphalids (Campbell 1998). Differing rates of evolution among taxonomic groups may reflect interesting evolutionary histories of the organisms or of the genes; this difference among the riodinids, lycaenids, and nymphalids is being examined further (D. Campbell, P. J. DeVries, and N. Pierce, unpub.). For these reasons, substitution rates (and thus phylogenetic signal) for a particular gene in one taxonomic group may not translate to other groups, even closely related ones, of the same taxonomic ranking. This complicates the process of choosing a gene for phylogenetic reconstruction based on the results of studies performed on other similarly aged radiations of taxa.

IMPLICATIONS FOR THE EVOLUTION OF ANT ASSOCIATION

As reviewed in the previous section of this chapter, phylogenetic analysis of *wingless* indicates that the Lycaenidae and Riodinidae, both of which have evolved specialized larval adaptations for mediating associations with ants, belong to a single clade. Although other Lepidoptera are known to engage in interactions of various kinds with ants (Hinton 1951), no cases of myrmecophily of a similar nature are known in other butterflies. It is also clear from this work that the evolutionary pattern of ant association is not a simple one. For instance, when species possessing ant organs are mapped onto the phylogeny in figure 18.2, we find that the most basal riodinid lineages do not have any ant-associated members. This finding implies that myrmecophily has been lost and/or gained multiple times.

The phylogenetic approach is powerful in that it allows us to access this interesting pattern, and it becomes the basis for framing the question of how ant association evolved. Knowing the relationship between the riodinids and lycaenids enables us to form three hypotheses: (1) ant association is a shared, derived character that evolved at the base of the riodinid + lycaenid lineage and was apomorphically lost in non-myrmecophilous branches in both families; (2) the ancestor to the riodinids and lycaenids was not associated with ants, and ant relationships evolved independently in the riodinid and lycaenid lineages; (3) ant association evolved independently in the lycaenids and in the two myrmecophilous riodinid lineages: Eurybiini and Lemoniini+ Nymphidiini (DeVries 1991, 1997). Yet even a thorough phylogenetic knowledge of these groups will not, by itself, distinguish among these hypotheses.

Table 18.2 Inferred numbers of evolutionary events for three hypotheses for the evolution of ant association when myrmecophily is mapped onto the phylogeny in figure 18.2

	Gains	Losses	Total
Hypothesis I	1	7–9[a]	8–10[a]
Hypothesis II	2	4–6[a]	6–8[a]
Hypothesis III	3	3	6

[a] Number of losses is dependent on the resolution of *Sarota*, *Emesis*, and *Riodina* (Riodinidae).

Although we can theoretically estimate the minimal number of evolutionary changes required by each hypothesis (table 18.2), interpreting the most parsimonious pattern of gains and losses of myrmecophily is an arbitrary distinction when the mechanism underlying these gains and losses is not understood. That is, we do not know, for example, whether one gain and two losses is more or less likely than two gains and six losses. Thus, examining the origin of myrmecophily in the butterflies requires more than a phylogenetic analysis.

The homology of the structures that riodinid and lycaenid caterpillars use in their myrmecophilous lifestyles (ant organs) provides perspective on ant association. If, for instance, lycaenid and riodinid ant organs are not homologous, then it is likely that ant association has also evolved independently. DeVries (1991, 1997) has begun to explore this question. He notes that the riodinid larvae secrete food for ants through a paired set of "tentacle nectary organs" (TNOs), located on the eighth abdominal segment (A8). The lycaenids, on the other hand, use a nontentacular organ (the dorsal nectary organ, or DNO) on the seventh abdominal segment (A7) for this purpose (fig. 18.3). Likewise, the riodinids secrete chemical stimuli to ants through paired anterior tentacle organs (ATOs) on the third thoracic segment (T3), whereas the lycaenid organs with equivalent function (tentacle organs, or TOs) are located on the eighth abdominal segment (A8). Thus the organs for feeding ants and the organs for controlling ants chemically are located on different body segments in lycaenids and riodinids, and since they do not derive from the same body part, DeVries interprets them as having independent origins. Under this interpretation, a myrmecophilous ancestor of the riodinids and lycaenids would be very unlikely.

However, despite their different placements, histological studies of riodinid and lycaenid ant organs show unmistakable parallels, especially the three kinds of tentacular organs (ATOs, TNOs, and TOs). In both lycaenids and riodinids, these organs are glandular and secretory (Ross 1964, 1966; Kitching 1983; Kitching and Luke 1985; DeVries 1988b), have glandular tissue that is connected via ducts to terminal setae (Ross 1964; Malicky 1970; Cottrell 1984; DeVries 1988b), and are retracted into the body when

Dana L. Campbell and Naomi E. Pierce

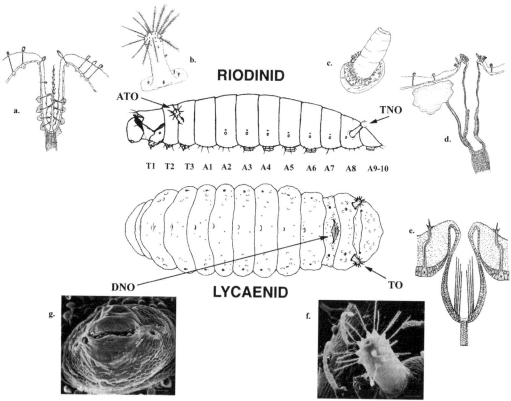

Figure 18.3 Placement of riodinid and lycaenid ant organs. Electron micrographs and histological diagrams demonstrate the similarity of structure among these organs. Body segments are labeled T1–T3 (thoracic segments 1–3) and A1–A10 (abdominal segments 1–10). (A) Histological section of a riodinid anterior tentacle organ (ATO; *Anatole rossi*). (B) Line drawing of a riodinid ATO (*Anatole rossi*). (C) Line drawing of a riodinid tentacle nectary organ (TNO; *Anatole rossi*). (D) Histological cross section of a riodinid TNO (*Anatole rossi*). (E) Histological cross section of a lycaenid tentacle organ (TO; *Phaedrotes piasus*). (F) Electron micrograph of a lycaenid TO (*Lysandra coridon*). (G) Electron micrograph of a lycaenid dorsal nectary organ (DNO; *Lysandra coridon*). (Riodinid line drawing from De Vries 1988b; A–D from Ross 1964; E from Hinton 1951; lycaenid line drawing and F–G from Kitching and Luke 1985.)

not in use. Clark and Dickson's (1956), Claassens and Dickson's (1977), and Hinton's (1951) illustrations of the histology of lycaenid tentacular organs show a structure similar to that in Ross's (1964) illustration of the riodinid counterpart (fig. 18.3).

The tentacular organs might be more parsimoniously explained as homologous structures, with shifts in function and position over time. The required changes in function (between secreting food and secreting chemical substances) may be trivial if food secretions also contain chemicals that are important in mediating interactions with ants, as Pierce (1983, 1989) and DeVries (1997) have suggested. Thus the nectar-supplying TNOs on the eighth abdominal segment of riodinids would be homologous to the chemical-secreting organs on the lycaenid eighth abdominal segment (Cottrell 1984; Kitching and Luke 1985). Furthermore, the riodinid

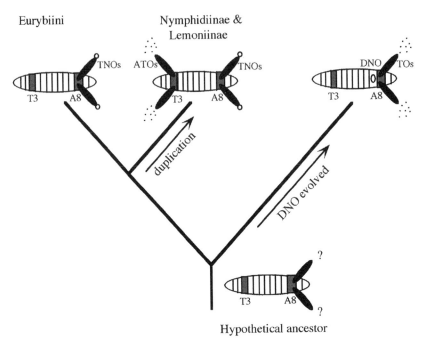

RIODINIDAE   LYCAENIDAE

Eurybiini   Nymphidiinae &
                             Lemoniinae

Figure 18.4 Simplified tree of riodinid and lycaenid relationships, showing only lineages with ant organs. The diagrams show, for lycaenid and riodinid caterpillars, the full complement of ant organs discussed in this chapter, although species (especially lycaenids) vary in their endowment of ant organs and may have a subset of this complement. DNO = dorsal nectary organ. Tentacle organs (TNO, ATO, TO) are shown in black, and their function is indicated next to the diagram by a series of dots (volatile chemical secretions) or a droplet (liquid food secretion). ? represents the unknown secretion of the ancestor.

chemical-secreting ATOs on the third thoracic segment might be explained as an iterative homologue to the tentacular organs on the eighth abdominal segment under a broader definition of homology; that is, as structures derived from the same ancestral developmental cascade (Wagner 1994; Lauder 1994; Abouheif 1997). This kind of evolutionary change is especially possible in metameric organisms in which much positional identity is under the control of homeobox genes, allowing regulatory changes to cause duplications or shifts among segments (Roth 1991; Abouheif 1997).

A possible model of the evolution of ant organs, based on phylogenetic relationships and this concept of serial homology, is illustrated in figure 18.4. In this model, the riodinid + lycaenid ancestor is postulated as having one set of tentacular organs on the eighth abdominal segment. These organs diversified in function, becoming food producers in riodinids and chemical secretors in lycaenids. At some point in lycaenid evolution, the DNO developed on segment A7 (perhaps as an independent organ, or perhaps as a serially repeated pair of tentacular organs, subsequently modified into a single structure) to provide food rewards for ants. In the riodinids, one

Dana L. Campbell and Naomi E. Pierce

lineage (the Eurybiini) retained ancestor-like organs, while in the more derived Nymphidiini + Lemoniini lineage the tentacular organs were serially duplicated on the third thoracic segment and their function changed to chemical secretion. While speculative, this hypothesis provides a mechanism for the existence of genetically homologous ant organs on different segments, and relieves the requirement for entirely separate evolutionary events to independently create ant organs de novo. This level of homology allows the possibility that ancestral riodinids and lycaenids had ant organs (and were myrmecophilous) even if the ant organs on extant riodinids are not homologous on the basis of their position (*sensu* DeVries 1991, 1997) to those on extant lycaenids.

It is too early to determine whether ant association, tentacular organs, or the genetic pathways specifying tentacular organs in the lycaenid + riodinid lineage are ancestral or have evolved independently. Phylogenetic reconstruction will eventually resolve the relationships within the lycaenid and riodinid families, and will be crucial in reconstructing the evolution of variation within ant-associated lineages. However, interpreting the origins of myrmecophily also requires testing the theories based on phylogenetic understanding through an exploration of the developmental genetics, physiology, and structure of the ant organs themselves.

One possible starting point for future research in this direction is to compare expression patterns in riodinid and lycaenid larvae for genes involved in the development of ant organs. Homologous structures have been examined in this way in other systems; for example, in studies of the genes involved in the establishment of eyespots on butterfly wings in different taxa (see Brakefield and Monteiro, chap. 12 in this volume). While comparable expression patterns in these ant organs would not in themselves guarantee functional homology of a gene in different taxa, they would suggest that the development of the organs may be parallel, and that a regulatory shift producing iterative structures is a possible evolutionary scenario. The genetics of ant organ development is unknown, but investigations of related systems have furnished potentially involved genes. For example, a promising starting candidate is the gene *distal-less* (*dll*), which shows expression at the tip of most protruding structures, such as limbs, antennae, and setae, in a variety of Lepidoptera, as well as in other insects and invertebrates (Carroll et al. 1994; Panganiban et al. 1995). Different expression patterns of *dll* certainly would indicate different origins of the riodinid and lycaenid organs. Similar *dll* expression patterns might be a result of homology among ant organs, or could represent convergence, and would require testing of other gene products, working down the developmental cascade if possible. Research in insect developmental genetics is now quickly making the job of finding candidate genes more and more feasible. A more immediate challenge is finding representative ant organ–bearing riodinid species whose biology and larval host plants are well enough known that larvae can be reared in numbers in the laboratory. This needs to be accomplished soon, before habitat destruction reduces the number of species from which to choose.

SUMMARY

Phylogenetic characters derived from the *wingless* gene provide the first strong molecular evidence for two important phylogenetic conclusions: (1) that the riodinids and lycaenids each form monophyletic groupings, and (2) that the riodinids and lycaenids are sister lineages. Interestingly, while *wingless* provides robust support for relationships within and between the riodinids and lycaenids, it is less informative about nymphalid relationships. Nymphalids appear to cluster as part of an unsupported group along with pierid and papilionid representatives; *wingless* does not consistently recover a monophyletic Nymphalidae, nor does it resolve relationships within the Nymphalidae with confidence. Elucidating riodinid origins enhances our understanding of how ant association may have evolved in the Papilionoidea. We present a model of the evolution of ant association based on the phylogenetic relationships recovered here coupled with a genetic interpretation of ant organ homology and development, which suggests that ant association may have been an ancestral feature of riodinid and lycaenid butterflies. Comparing expression patterns of genes involved in ant organ development is suggested as a possible direction for testing this hypothesis.

ACKNOWLEDGMENTS

We thank Kelvin Dunn, André Mignault, Karen Nutt, Art Shapiro, Man-Wah Tan, Diane Wagner, and especially Phil DeVries for assistance in collecting and/or sequencing butterflies. Andy Brower, Belinda Chang, Phil DeVries, Brian Farrell, Toby Kellogg, Roger Kitching, Kerry Shaw, Chris Simon, Ward Watt, and an anonymous reviewer contributed greatly to improving the ideas presented here. David Swofford allowed us to publish results from his test versions of PAUP* (d49 and 56). This research was supported by grants from the Harvard Putnam Expedition Fund, a Doctoral Dissertation Improvement Grant to D. C. from the National Science Foundation, and NSF DEB-9615760 to N. P.

Dana L. Campbell and Naomi E. Pierce

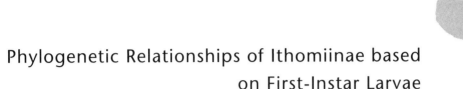

CHAPTER 19

Phylogenetic Relationships of Ithomiinae based on First-Instar Larvae

Paulo César Motta

Ithomiinae is a group (containing about 301 species) confined exclusively to the American tropics, and is related to *Tellervo* (of the Australian region) and the holotropic Danainae. The ithomiines are considered aposematic, resemble unpalatable models by both Batesian and Müllerian mimicry, and are examples of coevolution between insects and plants. Their host plants are mostly Solanaceae; of fifty-two genera, only *Elzunia, Tithorea,* and *Aeria* feed on Apocynaceae, while *Hyposcada* uses Gesneriaceae along with Solanaceae (Gilbert and Ehrlich 1970; Drummond 1976, 1986; Muyshondt et al. 1976; Haber 1978; Young 1978; Brown 1985, 1987; Drummond and Brown 1987; Brown et al. 1991).

The Ithomiinae have played an important role in biogeographic and phylogenetic studies. Despite the previously suggested proximity of Ithomiinae to Satyrinae (Fox 1949; Gilbert and Ehrlich 1970), the current thought is that Danainae, Ithomiinae, and *Tellervo* form a monophyletic group. This conclusion is supported by a wide range of morphological, behavioral, and ecological characteristics (Ehrlich 1958; Gilbert and Ehrlich 1970; Kristensen 1976; Ackery and Vane-Wright 1984; Scott 1984; Ackery 1987; Robbins 1988a). However, the phylogenetic relationships among these three groups are not clear. *Tellervo* may be considered to be closest to Ithomiinae (Fox 1949, 1956; Ehrlich 1958; D'Abrera 1971; Emmel et al. 1974; Sbordoni and Forestiero 1984; Brown 1985, 1987; Drummond and Brown 1987; Trigo and Motta 1990), to Danainae (Ackery 1987), or to both subfamilies as an outgroup (Freitas 1999). Thus, these three groups are usually treated as having equal status, as an unresolved trichotomy (Reuter 1896, cited in Ackery 1987; Ackery and Vane-Wright 1984; Ackery 1984, 1987, 1988; Kitching 1985; Harvey 1991; de Jong et al. 1996a; Janz and Nylin 1998).

Different researchers have included different numbers of tribes in the Ithomiinae. The number of tribes has ranged from three to fourteen (Fox 1940, 1961; D'Almeida 1978; Mielke and Brown 1979; Brown 1985, 1987; Motta 1989). Currently there are eleven accepted tribes (Brown and Freitas 1994).

Fox reviewed the tribes Tithoreini, Melinaeini, Mechanitini, and Napeogenini (Fox 1940, 1949, 1956, 1960, 1961, 1965, 1967; Fox and Real 1971), and Brown (1977) studied the systematics and biology of Ithomiini, Oleriini, Dircennini, and Godyridini. The phylogenetic relationships among the genera of Ithomiinae were first studied by Brown (1985, 1987), using ninety morphological and chemical characteristics, as well as eggs, fifth-instar larvae, pupae, and adults. Motta (1989), using 28 species, reconstructed a phylogeny based on 32 chorionic structures of the eggs. Brown and Freitas (1994) used 9 characters from the egg, 3 from first-instar larvae, 26 from last-instar larvae, and 21 from the pupae of 47 genera.

This study focuses on evaluating the utility of characters (especially chaetotaxic ones) from first-instar larvae. Larval characters, such as the setae of the body and head, the mouthparts, and the legs, have been used in systematic studies of several butterfly groups (Fleming 1960; Downey and Allyn 1984; Igarashi 1984; Kitching 1984, 1985; DeVries et al. 1985; García-Barros 1987; Nakanishi 1988; García-Barros and Martín 1991). Chaetotaxy, the study of the arrangement of setae on the larval body, is very common in morphological descriptions because this approach is simple and informative and the patterns obtained are easily comparable across taxa. Chaetotaxic characters have never been used for ithomiine systematics, and the importance of these characters for understanding relationships in the Ithomiinae is unknown.

All of the setae and tubercles of many (if not all) first-instar butterfly larvae occur in even numbers, symmetrically across the body, and are primary setae. After the first ecdysis, many ontogenetic differences appear (Fleming 1960; Downey and Allyn 1984; Igarashi 1984). The pattern of setae in first-instar larvae appears to be nonadaptive and thus evolved in a neutral manner, so that systematic studies are not confounded by adaptive, convergent character change.

In this study I use two approaches: first, I address the phylogenetic relationships of Ithomiinae based on first-instar larvae; second, I discuss the cladistic position of *Tellervo* in relation to Danainae and Ithomiinae.

MATERIALS AND METHODS

Twenty-nine species (of 24 genera) of Ithomiinae were examined. *Tellervo zoilus* was used as the outgroup. Species of Danainae (*Lycorea cleobaea, Danaus plexippus,* and *Anetia briarea*) were used in some comparisons and in exploring the relationships among these groups. Eggs or first-instar larvae were obtained from host plants in the field. Observation of oviposition or rearing of individuals in the laboratory makes the identification reliable. The number of individuals of each species examined is given in table 19.1.

The larvae were preserved in Kahle's solution (Peterson 1962), clarified in 10% KOH, and then stored in phenol. The head capsule was first separated from the body, followed by the labrum and mandible. All the material was microscopically examined, with magnification ranges from 100× to 400×. The terms and homologies used here are from Hinton (1946), Peterson (1962), Kitching (1984), and Stehr (1987). The segments of the thorax were coded as T1–T3 and those of the abdomen as A1–A10. The characters were obtained mainly by comparing seta position, length, and distance in relation to other setae or structures.

The cladistic analysis of Ithomiinae was executed using PAUP 2.4 (Swofford 1985), with the following options: swap = global, mulpars, maxtree = 100. The number of trees stored in computer memory (hold command) and the taxon addition sequence (addseq command) were as recommended (Platnick 1987). All characters were treated as ordered and weighted equally. The cladistic analysis of relationships among Danainae, Ithomiinae, and *Tellervo* was done by the exact branch-and-bound algorithm, which is guaranteed to find all optimal trees. The strict consensus tree was generated from the multiple equally parsimonious trees.

RESULTS AND DISCUSSION

FIRST-INSTAR LARVAL CHAETOTAXY

The majority of lepidopteran larvae possess a distinct head, with a distinct epicranial suture in the form of an inverted Y, and six stemmata situated in a lateroventral semicircle, near the antennae. The mouthparts consist of a labrum, mandibles, maxillae, and a labium. The body consists of three thoracic segments, with legs and spiracles along the prothorax, and ten abdominal segments, with prolegs with crotchets at the base of the third to sixth and tenth segments, and spiracles on segments 1–8. The setae of the larvae are sensory organs, although they may also have other functions, such as defense.

Live, feeding first-instar larvae of Ithomiinae measure 2–5 mm in length, with a cephalic capsule width of 0.3–0.5 mm. The head color may be black, brown, or light beige; in the last case it is sometimes granulated in coloration. The stemmata are black, and the labrum is brown. Some species possess colored rings, but most first-instar ithomiine larvae are light green,

Table 19.1 Species examined in this study

Species	Location[a]	Number of Individuals	Collector[b]
Tithorea harmonia (Cramer, 1777)	Mogi-Guaçu (SP)	4	1
Aeria olena (Weymer, 1875)	Campinas/Jundiaí (SP)	11	1
Aeria elara (Hewitson, 1855)	Uberlândia (MG)	4	1
Methona themisto (Hübner, 1818)	Campinas (SP)/Uberlândia (MG)	8	1
Placidula euryanassa (C. & R. Felder, 1860)	Rio (RJ)/Santos (SP)	20	2, 3
Melinaea ludovica (Cramer, 1780)	Rio (RJ)/Santos (SP)	3	2, 3
Melinaea menophilus (Hewitson, 1855)	Alto Juruá (AC)	1	2, 3
Athesis clearista Doubleday, 1847	Caraballeda, Venezuela	2	2
Thyridia psidii Hübner, 1816	Campinas (SP)	3	1, 3
Scada karschina (Herbst, 1792)	Santa Tereza (ES)	1	3
Mechanitis lysimnia (Fabricius, 1793)	Campinas (SP)	4	1
Mechanitis polymnia (Linnaeus, 1758)	Campinas/Santos (SP)	14	1
Paititia neglecta Lamas, 1979	Alto Juruá (AC)	1	2
Oleria aquata (Weymer, 1875)	Santos (SP)	3	1, 3
Epityches eupompe (Geyer, 1832)	Sete Barras (SP)	1	3
Hypothyris ninonia (Hübner, 1806)	Juiz de Fora/Uberlândia (MG)	8	1
Hypothyris euclea (Godart, 1819)	Campinas (SP)	10	1
Miraleria cymothoe (Hewitson, 1854)	Mérida, Venezuela	3	2, 3
Ithomia lichyi D'Almeida, 1939	Jundiaí (SP)	1	1
Callithomia lenea (Cramer, 1780)	Mogi-Guaçu (SP)	3	1
Talamancana lonera (Butler & H. Druce, 1872)	Costa Rica	2	4
Hyalenna pascua (Schaus, 1902)	Jundiaí (SP)	1	1
Dircenna dero (Hübner, 1823)	Jundiaí (SP)/Uberlândia (MG)	4	1
Ceratinia tutia (Hewitson, 1852)	Alto Juruá (AC)	1	3
Prittwitzia hymenaea (Prittwitz, 1865)	Campinas (SP)/Florianópolis (SC)	2	1, 3
Episcada clausina (Hewitson, 1876)	Jundiaí (SP)	2	1
Episcada philoclea (Hewitson, 1854)	Extrema (MG)	1	1
Pteronymia carlia Schaus, 1902	Santos (SP)	1	1, 3
Pteronymia euritea (Cramer, 1780)	Linhares (ES)	1	3
Pseudoscada genetyllis (D'Almeida, 1922)	Santa Tereza (ES)	1	3
Pseudoscada quadrifasciata Talbot, 1928	São Vicente (SP)	1	3
Greta andromica (Hewitson, 1854)	Venezuela	1	2
Hypoleria adasa (Hewitson, 1854)	São Vicente (SP)	1	1
Heterosais edessa (Hewitson, 1854)	São Vicente (SP)	3	1, 3
		127	

Outgroups

Tellervo zoilus (Fabricius, 1775)	Queensland, Australia	4	5
Lycorea cleobaea (Godart, 1819)	São Vicente (SP)	2	3
Danaus plexippus (Linnaeus, 1758)	Jundiaí (SP)/Uberlândia (MG)	5	1
Anetia briarea (Godart, 1819)	Constanza, Dominican Republic	5	2
		16	
Total number of individuals examined		143	

[a] Most species are from Brazil (city and state are given).
[b] Collector code: 1, P. C. Motta; 2, K. Brown; 3, A. V. L. Freitas; 4, W. Haber; 5, A. G. Orr.

without rings or lateral or dorsal stripes. In most species the setae are usually imperceptible to the naked eye; in some species, however, they may be relatively large and conspicuous.

Ninety-nine taxonomic characters were delineated (see table 19.2 for the character list and table 19.3 for the data matrix). The cephalic capsule (see example in fig. 19.1) showed 17 pairs of long setae, 5 pairs of microscopic setae, and 16 pairs of punctures, as is the case for most Lepidoptera. The cephalic setae are designated as anterior (A1–A3), posterior (P1–P2), frontal (F1), and so on. The position of the A3 setae relative to an imaginary line between stemma iv and the P1 setae represents character 17 and is one of the 52 characters delineated in the head (see other examples of head characters in fig. 19.2). The absence of setae, considered apomorphic, occurs only in the adfrontal region. The AF1 setae are absent in the following ithomiines: *Athesis clearista, Talamancana lonera, Episcada clausina, Ceratinia tutia, Pteronymia euritea,* and *Prittwitzia hymenaea,* and the AF2 are absent in *Hyalenna pascua, Dircenna dero, Episcada philoclea, Greta andromica,* and *Pseudoscada quadrifasciata.* The puncture AFa was not observed in *Episcada philoclea.*

The labrum (19 characters) has a distal notch, is laminal, bilobed, and gives rise to 6 pairs of primary setae, 3 being lateral (L1, L2, and L3) and 3 medial (M1, M2 and M3), and a pair of campaniform sensilla (puncture S). The mandibles (3 characters) are solid, compact, and heavily sclerotized. They have five large incisor teeth and a variable number of small protuberances, which are the molar teeth.

The most conspicuous macroscopic body traits (6 characters) are the tubercles, the length of the setae, and the crotchets. Historically, the tubercles have been important in considering some ithomiine species as "primitive," since they are present in *Tellervo* and Danainae. In relation to position, the tubercles can be on T2, A2, and A8 (*Danaus gilippus*), T2 and A8 (*D. plexippus, D. genutia*), T2 only (*Tithorea, Aeria, Melinaea, Anetia, Lycorea,* and probably *Tirumala*), or T3 only (*Tellervo*).

The most common ithomiine body pattern is the occurrence of 97 or 98 pairs of setae (fig. 19.3). Generally there are 10 setae on the prothorax, from which 4 characters were defined. XD1 and XD2 are equivalent in length; D1, positioned between them, is more posterior and smaller; SD1 and SD2 are aligned with them, SD2 being dorsal and smaller than SD1; L2 is ventral, caudal, and longer than L1; and SV1 is bigger than SV2. The cervical sclerite (fig. 19.4) under XD1, XD2, and D1 is present in Danainae, *Tellervo,* and *Tithorea.* The meso- and metathorax bear 8 setae, which generated 6 characters. Sometimes the L2 setae are absent, as in Danainae, *Tellervo,* and *Tithorea* (plesiomorphic condition). The abdominal setal pattern is very homogeneous in Ithomiinae, with 8 setae on A1, 9 on A2, 6 on the segments with prolegs (A3–6), 8 on A7, 8 on A8, 6 or 7 on A9, and 8 on A10 (9 characters on the abdomen). In general, D1 and D2 are aligned and of similar

Table 19.2 List of ninety-nine characters defined in this study

1. Relative position of C1 to the frontal and anteclypeal suture: (0) equidistant; (1) nearer to one of them.
2. C1–C2 distance: (0) equal distance between C1 and median imaginary line; (1) C2 nearer to C1.
3. C2 length in relation to C1: (0) both the same size; (1) C2 as long as double the length of C1.
4. Relative position of F1 to C2: (0) F1 subtly more dorsal than C2; (1) F1 undoubtedly more dorsal.
5. Relative position of F1 to C2 and the coronal suture bifurcation: (0) equidistant; (1) F1 nearer to C2.
6. Relative position of F1 to the frontal suture and the median imaginary line between the coronal suture bifurcation and the clypeus median point: (0) equidistant or subtly nearer to the frontal suture; (1) nearer to the frontal suture.
7. Relative position of Fa to F1: (0) aligned or subtly above; (1) clearly overhead (more posterior).
8. Distances between Fa's and between Fa and F1: (0) longer distance between Fa's; (1) same distance; (2) shorter distance between Fa's.
9. Presence of AF1, AF2, and AFa: (0) all present; (1) at least one is absent.
10. Relative position of AFa to AF1 and AF2: (0) much more dorsal, forming a triangle; (1) aligned or subtly more dorsal.
11. Relative distance of AFa to AF1 and AF2: (0) nearer to AF2; (1) equidistant (or subtly nearer to AF2).
12. Length of AF1 and AF2: (0) similar; (1) AF2 longer.
13. AF2 position: (0) aligned to the coronal suture bifurcation, subtly lower (anterior/distal) or subtly above; (1) above (toward the posterior).
14. AF2 distance to the coronal suture: (0) similar to the distance between AF1 and the frontal suture; (1) more distant.
15. Relative position of Aa relative to the A2–AF1 line, frontal view (when AF1 absent, its probable position was considered): (0) above the line (posterior); (1) aligned or subtly above or below; (2) below the line.
16. Relative distance of Aa to A2 and AF1: (0) equidistant; (1) nearer to A2.
17. Relative position of A3 to an imaginary line between stemma iv and P1: (0) nearly aligned to iv–P1 or more frontal; (1) posterior.
18. Relative position of A1 to stemmata i and ii: (0) A1 aligned to i; (1) A1 between i and ii, forming a triangle; (2) anterior to i.
19. Relative position of A2 to an imaginary line between stemma ii and AF1: (0) aligned; (1) anterior.
20. A3 length compared with the lengths of A2 and L1: (0) same or A3 subtly different; (1) A3 much longer than A2.
21. Relative position of Pa to the line A2–A3: (0) nearly aligned or subtly more ventral; (1) ventral.
22. Relative distance of Pa to the line A2–A3: (0) nearer to A3; (1) equidistant or subtly nearer to A2; (2) nearer to A2.
23. Relative position of Pb to the line P1–P2: (0) aligned or subtly ventral or distal; (1) dorsal.
24. Relative distance of Pb to P1 and P2: (0) equidistant or nearer to P1; (1) nearer to P2.
25. Distance between P1 and the coronal suture compared with P2: (0) equidistant or subtly dorsal or ventral; (1) longer than P2 (more ventral); (2) much more dorsal.
26. Lengths of P1 and P2: (0) same or P1 longer; (1) P1 double the length; (2) P1 much more than twice the length of P2.
27. Relative distance of La to L1 and A3: (0) 1/3 of the distance between L1 and A3; (1) half the distance between L1 and A3; (2) much closer to L1 (less than 1/3).
28. Relative position of La to L1 and A3: (0) aligned; (1) form a triangle (L1 posterior or anterior).
29. Relative position of O1 relative to stemmata i, ii, iii, iv and the line between i and iv: (0) aligned to i and iv, equidistant to ii and iii; (1) aligned to i and iv, equidistant to iii and iv.
30. Relative position of O2 to stemmata iv and v (triangle): (0) form an angle less than 90°; (1) form an angle more than 90°.
31. Relative distance of O2 to stemmata iv and v (triangle): (1) nearer to v; (1) nearer to iv; (2) equidistant.
32. Relative length of O2 to O1 and O3: (0) similar lengths; (1) O2 longer.
33. Relative length of O3 to O1 and O2: (0) similar lengths; (1) O3 shorter.
34. Relative position of O3 to stemma v and the "groove": (0) aligned or subtly more ventral; (1) posterior.
35. Relative position of Oa to stemma i and A1: (0) aligned to i with A1, very near i; (1) more anterior than the i–A1 line.
36. Relative position of Ob to stemma v, O2, and O3: (0) aligned to v and O2 or subtly ventral; (1) forming an angle; (2) aligned to v and O3 or subtly anterior to this line.

Table 19.2 *continued*

37. Relative distance of Ob to stemma v, O2 and O3: (0) equidistant to v and O2 or nearer to O2; (1) nearer to v; (2) equidistant to v and O3.
38. Relative position of SO1 to SO3 and the antennal socket: (0) in the ventral end of the socket (distance to its end is shorter than 1/2 the distance between SO1 and SO3); (1) same distance between SO3 and the end of the socket.
39. Relative position of SO2 to v and vi: (0) subtly ventral; (1) aligned or subtly dorsal; (2) ventral.
40. Relative distance of SO2 to stemmata v and vi: (0) equidistant or nearer to v; (1) nearer to vi.
41. Distance between SO3 and the antennal socket or the relative position of SO3 to the imaginary line between stemma vi and SO1: (0) aligned; (1) posterior to the line.
42. Relative position of SOa to the line between SO3–G1 and the ventral suture: (0) aligned; (1) nearer to the suture than G1; (2) more distant to the suture than G1.
43. Relative distance of SOa to the SO2 line and the suture: (0) SOa aligned to SO2; (1) SOa nearer to SO3.
44. Relative position of SOb to the antennal socket: (0) very near; (1) distant.
45. Relative position of SOb to vi and SO3: (0) nearer to vi; (1) equidistant to vi and SO3; (2) nearer to SO3.
46. Relative position of G1 to the "groove" and the "fold": (0) nearer to the fold; (1) equidistant; (2) nearer to the groove.
47. Relative position of Ga to the line G1 and O3: (0) aligned; (1) subtly dorsal.
48. Relative distance of Ga to G1 and O3: (0) near O3; (1) equidistant.
49. Relative distance of V1 to P2 and to group V (V2, V3, Va): (0) equidistant; (1) nearer to V2; (2) nearer to P2.
50. Relative diameter of the stemmata: (0) similar sizes; (1) iv and v longer or ii is the longer.
51. Distance between the stemmata: (0) Similar distance between i, ii, iii, and iv; (1) distance between iii and iv is shorter than the distance between i and ii, ii and iii.
52. Position of stemma v: (0) near vi; (1) equidistant to iv and vi; (1) nearer to iv.
53. Relative position of M2 to L1 and L2: (0) between L1 and L2 or aligned to L1 or subtly basal to L1; (1) aligned to L2 or basal to L1.
54. Relative position of M2 to the line drawn between M1 and L2: (0) level or subtly dorsal; (1) distal; (2) basal.
55. Relative position of M1 to M2: (0) aligned or subtly posterior; (1) posterior; (2) anterior.
56. Comparative distance between M1 and M2 in relation to the distance between the M1 setae: (0) shorter between M1 and M2 than between M1's; (1) much shorter; (2) equivalent.
57. Lengths of M1 and M2: (0) M2 longer; (1) M2 much longer.
58. Anterior-posterior position of puncture S (relative to M1 and M2): (0) posterior (basal); (1) anterior, nearly aligned.
59. Dorsal-ventral position of puncture S (relative to M1 and M2): (0) equidistant to M1 and M2 or a little closer to M2; (1) dorsal (nearer to M1); (2) ventral (nearer to M2).
60. Mean angle between the lines that connect M1 and M2, and M1 and the puncture S: (0) 40°–70°; (1) 70°–90°; (2) less than 40°. (It is more than 90° only in *Danaus* and *Anetia*.)
61. Relative position of puncture S to M1 and M2 and the posterior border: (0) nearer to M1/M2; (1) equidistant or subtly nearer to M1/M2; (2) nearer to the border.
62. Relative position of puncture S to the widest point of labrum: (0) basal; (1) level or distal.
63. M3 position: (0) on the distal border of the labrum; (1) behind the margin, more than one diameter of the socket; (2) before the margin, more than one diameter of the socket.
64. L2 position: (0) equidistant to L1 and L3 or nearer to L1; (1) much nearer to L1.
65. Relative position of L1 to the widest point of the labrum: (0) distal; (1) level; (2) basal.
66. Less sclerotized region: (0) near the labrum notch and to M1 and M2; (1) spreading/near M3; (2) along the distal, and sometimes lateral, margin; (3) absent.
67. Less sclerotized basal patches: (0) absent; (1) present.
68. Internal border of the labral lobe: (0) angled; (1) smoothly curved.
69. Basal angle of labral notch: (0) acute or about 90°; (1) very obtuse.
70. Length relation of labral notch to the labral length: (0) between 1.2 and 1.3; (1) longer than 1.3; (2) shorter or equal to 1.1.
71. Relation between the widest point (L1) and the longest point (labral lobe and base): (0) longer or equal to 1.8; (1) shorter or equal to 1.7.
72. Number of molar teeth (small ones): (0) larger than or equal to 3; (1) fewer than 3.

(*continued*)

Table 19.2 *continued*

73. Length of the incisors 2 and 3: (0) similar or tooth 2 subtly shorter; (1) tooth 2 much shorter than 3.
74. Lateral grooves on the incisor 4: (0) one on the internal side; (1) two, one on both sides.
75. Tubercles on the thorax: (0) filament or protuberance in the segments T2 or T3; (1) absent.
76. Tubercles on the body from the second to fifth instar: (0) present; (1) absent.
77. Seta length (in relation to segment width): (0) short; (1) medium; (2) long.
78. Disposition of the crotchets on the prolegs: (0) circle; (1) semicircle.
79. Crotchet length of the prolegs: (0) equivalent lengths; (1) external crotchets shorter than internal ones.
80. Mean number of crotchets on the prolegs: (0) 14 or more; (1) between 11 and 13.5; (2) 10 or fewer.
81. Cervical sclerite on XD1, XD2, and D1: (0) present; (1) absent.
82. Relative lengths of XD1, D1, and XD2: (0) D1 is shorter, XD1 and XD2 are equivalent; (1) XD1, XD2, and D1 are equivalent or one of the setae is longer than the other two.
83. Position of SD1 and SD2: (0) aligned or SD2 subtly posterior; (1) SD2 posterior.
84. Relative position of L1 and L2 to the spiracle: (0) dorsal; (1) level (L2 median to the spiracle).
85. D1 and D2 sizes: (0) equivalent; (1) D1 longer.
86. Relative distance of SD2 to SD1 and D2: (0) nearer to SD1; (1) equidistant; (2) nearer to D2.
87. Relative position of SD1 and SD2: (0) aligned; (1) SD2 posterior or anterior.
88. Relative position of SD2 to D1 and D2: (0) ventral (aligned); (1) ventral, aligned to D1 with D2 anterior; (2) ventral and posterior to D1 and D2.
89. SD1 and L1 sizes: (0) equivalent; (1) SD1 a bit shorter; (2) SD1 much shorter.
90. L2 setae: (0) absent (7 setae); (1) present (8 setae).
91. D1 and D2 lengths: (0) equivalent; (1) SD2 longer.
92. SD2 and D1/D2 lengths: (0) equivalent; (1) SD2 longer.
93. SD1 length relative to D1, D2, and SD2: (0) SD1 longer; (1) equivalent; (2) SD1 shorter than SD2.
94. Relative lengths of SD1 to L1 and L2: (0) equivalent or SD1 longer; (1) SD1 equivalent to the shortest setae (L1 or L2); (2) SD1 much shorter.
95. L1 and L2 lengths: (0) equivalent or L2 subtly longer; (1) L2 longer; (2) L1 longer.
96. Additional SV seta in A1–7: (0) absent; (1) present.
97. A9 compared with A7 and A8: (0) without one seta (L1); (1) without two setae (SD2 and L1).
98. Epiproct setae (A10): (0) D1 longer, SD1 and L1 similar, D2 shortest of all; (1) similar lengths, D2 subtly shorter; (2) similar sizes.
99. P1 and SP1 setae: (0) normal, both present; (1) presence of one extra seta (SP2).

Note: All characters except character 76 are from the first larval instar. Characters 1–52 derive from the cephalic capsule, 53–71 from the labrum, 72–74 from the mandible and 75–99 from the body. Most characters are original; however, 18 is from Kitching 1984; 1–7, 10, 11, 12, 15, and 17 are modifications from Kitching 1984; 54, 60, 62, 63, 65, 68, 69, and 70 are from DeVries et al. 1985. Characters from cephalic capsule are divided by regions: clypeus (1–3), front (4–8), adfront (9–14), anterior (15–20), posterior (21–26), lateral (27–28), stemmata (29–37 and 50–52), substemmata (38–45), genal (46–48), and vertical (49).

lengths; SD2 is posterior, ventral, and larger, and more proximal to them than to SD1; and L1 and L2 are of similar lengths.

PHYLOGENETIC ANALYSIS

The PAUP analysis produced 70 equally most parsimonious trees (length = 562, CI = 0.24). Four different tree topologies were found; the most common of them is depicted in figure 19.5. The relationships found among the main clades in each of these four topologies are summarized in figure 19.6.

Six distinct clades in the Ithomiinae were revealed in nearly all analyses (see the components of each clade in fig. 19.5), but the relationships among

Table 19.3 Data matrix used in the analyses, with 99 characters and 36 taxa

```
         1111111111222222222233333333334444444444555555555566666666667777777777888888888899999999999
1234567890123456789012345678901234567890123456789012345678901234567890123456789012345678901234567890123456789

Tit.har  00?0100101000010000?0000011011001000100?02122100000000
Aer.ole  1010110101000?100?0?010000000???112?0000001?110000000000
Aer.ela  1010110101010101010000000000020101200000010210200000000
Met.the  0011100100011100001010101101010101022110010101221012010010
Pla.eur  0111011010000010100110-000000101010101010101120111011212110
Mel.men  0111100010001000000011011100000021000002010102001001000120
Mel.lud  ?011100100010??????00???????00100??????10022?1000?000120
Ath.cle  0001110011001--0-0100001010000200101001001111000002012000120
Thy.psi  0001100110101101010020001110200101001001001010021012000120
Sca.kar  0101011200010--010012111?2001200010010000110101011201001010120
Mec.lys  0111101010010010101101011012000101101001000111001010001000101
Mec.pol  0011112000010--001000210110100120001100101101000001001000100
Pai.neg  0111001010011010100011200001102001101001001010011110001000101
Ole.aqu  0101010101010101111000201000000000201010101001010101122100200010
Epi.eup  0100001000010012011210002010010000012100010101001?0200?00?10100
Hyp.nin  0100001000101010?11001?011210021001021001000?0100100?01100110
Hyp.euc  0100000100001-1100001-10000010201001010101010011110000200001110000
Mir.cym  11000101000001-1100010-1000010101010101010101121110010001000100
Ith.lic  1010100100001000112101012010101010101?00?10110012121010001000100
Callen   0111001100011111020000111100000111000020010200?0?10?0?0?01100011100110
Tal.lon  00000111-0-0-0?00001?10211101011010002001010021?11200010011201100
Hya.pas  010010110-----1101011-11221011110000010101021010210102121??00100?0
Dir.der  010110110-----1101101121101110000010000002221020002013010101010000100
Cer.tut  011011011-----0100001110220010120001002011010202001010202001010100
Pri.hym  011001001--0-01000010011012010000000001021101110010010221100000100
Epi.cla  101000011---0-010000012110110002?0001100101010100101010010100100
Epi.phi  101010011---?-?000?-?000?0?00?00100???10?01120001?????????0??0??
Pte.eur  0100010110-----0-11001101210100101100010001110001?0002020010020100
Pse.gen  010011011------1110-0110011000021000010110202011000112000120100
Pse.qua  000011011-----011001100002?000010110010010010?011002020010020100
Gre.and  0000000011------11000???????010000?????1100??00110?0??0011?????????
Het.ede  1100010000021100010111000021010100010000??????00?1000110112110120100

Tel.zoi  00000000000000000000000000?0000000000000000000000000000000??0
Dan.ple  01111010000210000100001000001010001001000011000-100000010010
Lyc.cle  0011100001000110100000001000010011011200100000001101?0
Ane.bri  1001100001000010000001000000000011111001-100010010001000110
         1111111111222222222233333333334444444444555555555566666666667777777777888888888899999999999
1234567890123456789012345678901234567890123456789012345678901234567890123456789012345678901234567890123456789
```

Note: The species codes are derived from the species names in table 19.1. The symbols "?" and "—" represent unknown and inapplicable states, respectively.

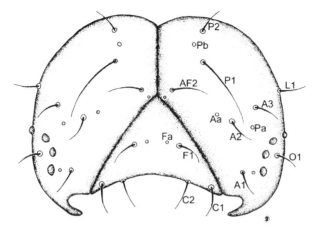

Figure 19.1 Chaetotaxy of the cephalic capsule: overview of *Athesis clearista* head, with names of the setae and punctures.

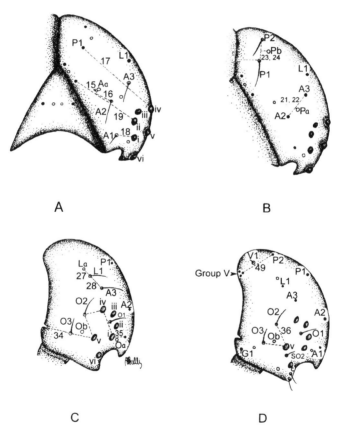

Figure 19.2 Chaetotaxy of the cephalic capsule: examples of characters in different regions. (A) Anterior region (characters 15–19). (B) Posterior region (characters 21–25). (C) Lateral (L) region (characters 27, 28, 34, 35). (D) Stemmatal (O), genal (G), or vertical (V) regions (characters 36 and 49). Codes: P1, A1, L1, and so on are setae, except V1 and G1, which are microsetae; Aa, Pa, and so on are punctures; i–vi are stemmata. Black and white points are nonrepresented setae and punctures respectively. See table 19.2 for character descriptions.

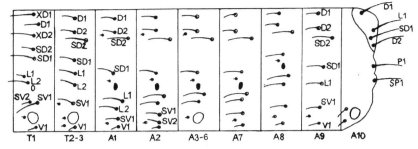

Figure 19.3 Example of ithomiine setal map (*Methona themisto*). The large open circles are legs or prolegs; the small solid circles are spiracles. The microsetae are not named.

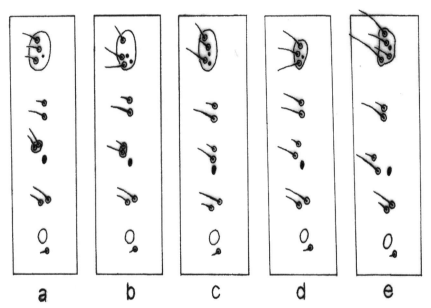

Figure 19.4 Chaetotaxy of the prothorax, showing the cervical sclerite. The names of the setae are as in figure 19.3. (A) *Danaus plexippus*, (B) *Anetia briarea*, (C) *Lycorea cleobaea*, (D) *Tellervo zoilus*, (E) *Tithorea harmonia*.

them are not exactly the same in every topology. The internal relationships within each clade are identical in all 70 trees. The character states supporting the labeled clades are listed in table 19.4. There is only one basal lineage (clade A, consisting of *Aeria elara*, *A. olena*, and *Tithorea harmonia*). Clade B may be a sister group of the remaining parts of tree (figs. 19.5 and 19.6A), forming a monophyletic group together with clade D (fig. 19.6B, C), or may be a subgroup of clade D (fig. 19.6D). In the last case, there are five distinct clades. Similarly, clade C may be a sister group of the remaining clades (fig. 19.6A, B, D), or of clades B and D (fig. 19.6C). The sister group of *Athesis clearista* (clade E) is a large clade F. These two sister clades were the most advanced in all analyses.

The fact that the species analyzed here are not exactly identical to those used in other studies (24 of the 52 genera) makes comparison difficult.

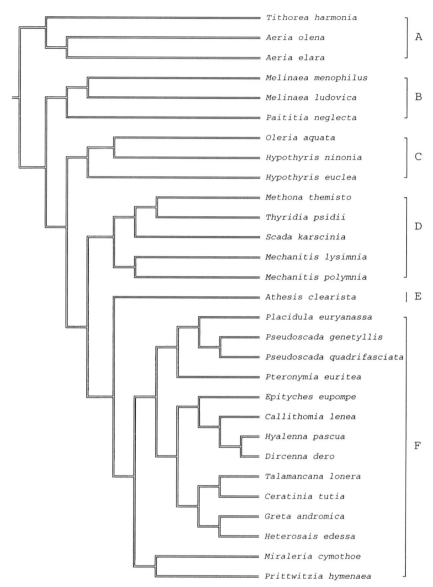

Figure 19.5 The most common of the equally parsimonious trees (length = 562, CI = 0.24); the same tree was found 28 times. The outgroup used was *Tellervo zoilus.*

However, some observations may be made. The relationship between *Tithorea* and *Aeria* as members of the most primitive Neotropical group of ithomiines originated in the works of Brown (1985, 1987). *Melinaea* and *Paititia* were always considered to be in some way members of primitive or intermediate groups (Fox 1940, 1961; D'Almeida 1978; Mielke and Brown 1979; Brown 1985, 1987), and Brown and Freitas (1994) put them in the tribe Melinaeini, together with *Athesis, Olyras,* and *Eutresis.*

Fox (1940, 1961), D'Almeida (1978), and Mielke and Brown (1979) placed the monotypic genus *Athesis* in the tribe Tithoreini. Brown (1985,

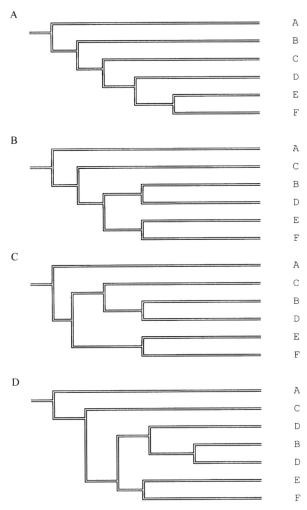

Figure 19.6 Phylogenetic relationships among clades (see fig. 19.5 for the members of each clade) in the four most common equally parsimonious tree topologies. Number of equally parsimonious trees: (A) 28, (B) 14, (C) 14, (D) 14.

Table 19.4 Synapomorphies supporting the clades in figure 19.5

Clade	Characters and States
A	5(1), 10(1), 35(1), 36(2), 68(1), 84(1), 87(1), 88(2)
B	13(1), 33(0), 37(1), 49(1), 53(1), 56(1), 60(2), 62(1), 64(1), 69(1), 70(1), 73(1)
C	4(0), 17(1), 28(1), 30(0), 45(2), 59(2), 79(1), 80(1), 89(2)
D	7(1), 13(1), 14(0), 18(1), 23(1), 25(1), 33(0), 35(1), 53(0), 61(2), 74(1), 89(0)
E+F	9(1), 22(1), 40(1), 55(0), 73(1), 85(1), 86(2), 94(1)
E	2(0), 5(0), 8(0), 36(0), 56(1), 59(0), 63(1), 76(1), 95(1)
F	4(0), 26(1), 48(1), 49(1), 88(2)

Note: See table 19.2 for character descriptions.

Table 19.5 Ithomiinae tribes resulting from this study

ITHOMIINAE Godman & Salvin, 1879
  TITHOREINI Fox, 1940
    Aeria Hübner, 1816 [3]
    Elzunia Bryk, 1937 [2]
    Tithorea Doubleday, 1847 [2]
  MELINAEINI Clark, 1948
    Athesis Doubleday, 1847 [1]
    Athyrtis C. Felder & R. Felder, 1862 [1]
    Eutresis Doubleday, 1847 [2]
    Melinaea Hübner, 1816 [7]
    Olyras Doubleday, 1847 [2]
    Paititia Lamas, 1979 [1]
    Patricia Fox, 1940 [2]
    Roswellia Fox, 1948 [1]
  MECHANITINI Fox, 1949
    Forbestra Fox, 1967 [3]
    Mechanitis Fabricius, 1807 [4]
    Methona Doubleday, 1847 [7]
    Sais Hübner, 1816 [2]
    Scada Kirby, 1871 [5]
    Thyridia Hübner, 1816 [1]
  ITHOMIINI Godman & Salvin, 1879
    Aremfoxia Real, 1971 [1]
    Garsauritis D'Almeida, 1938 [1]
    (New genus 1) *orestilla* [1]
    Hyalyris Boisduval, 1870 [10]
    Hyposcada Godman & Salvin, 1879 [8]
    Hypothyris Hübner, 1821 [16]
    Ithomia Hübner, 1816 [29]
    Napeogenes Bates, 1862 [17]
    Oleria Hübner, 1816 [33]
    Ollantaya Brown & Freitas, 1994 [1]
    Pagyris Boisduval, 1870 [1]
    Rhodussa D'Almeida, 1939 [1]
  DIRCENNINI D'Almeida, 1941
    Callithomia Bates, 1862 [3]
    Ceratinia Hübner, 1816 [5]
    Ceratiscada Brown & D'Almeida, 1970 [3]
    Dircenna Doubleday, 1847 [8]
    Dygoris Fox, 1945 [1]
    Episcada Godman & Salvin, 1879 [11]
    Epityches D'Almeida, 1938 [1]
    (New genus 2) *derama* [1]
    Godyris Boisduval, 1870 [10]
    Greta Hemming, 1934 [16?]
    Heterosais Godman & Salvin, 1879 [1]
    Hyalenna Forbes, 1942 [4]
    Hypoleria Godman & Salvin, 1879 [20]
    Hypomenitis Fox, 1945 [1]
    Mcclungia Fox, 1940 [1]
    Miraleria Haensch, 1903 [1]
    Placidula D'Almeida, 1922 [1]
    Prittwitzia Brown & Ebert, 1970 [1]

Table 19.5 *continued*

Pseudoscada Godman & Salvin, 1879 [8]
Pteronymia Butler & Druce, 1872 [32]
Talamancana Haber, Brown & Freitas, 1994 [1]
Veladyris Fox, 1945 [1]
Velamysta Haensch, 1909 [5]

Note: The genera within each tribe are listed in alphabetical order; the number of species in each genus is given in square brackets. (Data from D'Almeida 1978; Mielke and Brown 1979; Brown and Freitas 1994.)

1987) later considered it to be a member of a new tribe together with *Patricia* and *Roswellia,* and later still it was placed in Melinaeini, together with *Melinaea* and *Paititia* (Brown and Freitas 1994). According to first-instar larval analyses, *Athesis clearista* is a sister group of clade F.

The tribe Mechanitini, which corresponds to the group in this study composed of *Mechanitis, Scada, Thyridia,* and *Methona,* was established by Fox (1961). Later, D'Almeida (1978), Lamas (1979), and Mielke and Brown (1979) included *Forbestra* and *Paititia,* and Motta (1989) and Brown and Freitas (1994) also included *Methona* and *Placidula.*

The relationship of the genus *Placidula* to all other Ithomiinae is one of the most intriguing, as this genus has so far been placed in Ithomiini by Fox (1940, 1961) and D'Almeida (1978), in Napeogenini by Mielke and Brown (1979; following Fox and Real 1971), in a new tribe with a primitive position by Brown (1985, 1987), and in Mechanitini by Motta (1989) and Brown and Freitas (1994). The first-instar larval results indicate a proximity to *Pseudoscada* and *Pteronymia* in a more advanced group. Since the work of Fox (1940, 1961), the members of the most recent group have been considered to be relatively united, divided into only two tribes, Dircennini and Godyridini. The divergent genera, with the notable exception of *Placidula* discussed above, are *Callithomia* and *Talamancana,* already pertaining to Dircennini. However, Brown and Freitas (1994) isolated them into a new tribe (without name) near Mechanitini and Oleriini. *Epityches,* considered by D'Almeida (1978), Mielke and Brown (1979), and Brown (1985,1987) as a typical intermediary member (tribe Napeogenini), demonstrates a greater affinity to the more advanced group, as had already been suggested by Fox (1961).

The group consisting of *Oleria* (Oleriini tribe) and *Hypothyris* (Napeogenini) is curious, since the genus *Hypothyris* may be polyphyletic, as has already been suggested by egg analyses (Motta 1989). Perhaps the inclusion of other genera (such as *Ithomia* and *Napeogenes*) in this analysis would suggest certain links with the intermediate or advanced groups.

Brown (1985, 1987). Brown and Freitas (1994), and Motta (1989) suggest the allocation of the 52 genera (except *Tellervo*) to five tribes (see table 19.5).

The main differences are the grouping together of the Oleriini, Ithomiini, and Napeogenini as Ithomiini, and of the Dircennini and Godyridini under Dircennini.

ABOUT THE CHARACTERS

In order to evaluate the phylogenetic importance of various suites of characters in resolving ithomiine species relationships, the dataset was also analyzed by character subsets (cephalic capsule, labrum, mandibles, and body) and by combinations of these subsets. Considering each subset separately, the labrum (19 characters) contributes the least, and the mandibles (only tree characters) contribute nothing. The 25 body characters (thorax and abdomen) contain a degree of information similar to those of the head (52 characters), even though there are only half as many body characters. Analyzing pairs of character subsets, the head characters coupled with those of the body were the most informative, reflecting the global phylogeny relatively well. The most informative combination of three characters subsets was the head, body, and labrum, as would be expected.

While the mandible may provide only a very small amount of information, that is not to say that it should be disregarded, as it makes a contribution when combined with head characters. However, the goal here is to prioritize character subsets based on the amount of information furnished in relation to the energy spent in obtaining character measurements for studies within subfamilies, tribes, and genera. Thus, in future studies, I would discard the mandible and refine the labrum and head characters.

This is the first study of Neotropical butterflies to make extensive use of first-instar larval chaetotaxy (except for character 76) for phylogenetic purposes. Little is known about the quality of chaetotaxic characters as evaluators of phylogenetic relationships, nor is it known how many of the variations in these characters correspond to the individual, population, or specific levels. Despite the considerable homoplasy in the ithomiine data (CI = 0.24), I now present some considerations of the adaptability, correlations, confidence, variations, and anomalies of these characters.

Some characters, such as 1, 2, 42, 43, 63, and 84, are of questionable consistency due to the difficulty of observation and possible populational variation. Some characters appear to be more sensitive to populational variation than others, or to have anomalous states in individuals. Among these, the most important are related to the punctures Fa, Aa, Pa, Pb, La, and Ob and to seta position and number. Asymmetry commonly occurred; for example, on one side of the cephalic capsule, Pb was in line with and equidistant from P1 and P2, and on the other side it was ventral and anterior to P1. Extra punctures may also occur. La was sometimes transformed into a seta on one side, or, more rarely, two setae in the same socket. Of the 37 occurrences of anomalies, 30 (81%) were on the cephalic capsule, and the most anomalous characters were 23 and 24 (position and distance of Pb in relation to P1 and P2), with anomalies found in seven species, followed by 15 (position of Aa in relation to A2 and AF1) and 18 (position of A1 in relation to stemmata i and ii), with anomalies found in three species each.

There is apparently no correlation between seta length (character 77) and the gregarious or solitary habits of the larvae. Of the six species that have gregarious larvae, two have medium setae (*Hypothyris euclea* and *Miraleria cymothoe*) and four have long setae (*Placidula euryanassa, Mechanitis polymnia, M. lysimnia,* and *Episcada clausina*); of the twelve species with long setae, four have gregarious habits and eight are solitary. Many species of clade F have long setae and solitary larvae.

In general, setae do not vary in size among different segments. Setae D1 and D2 may have different sizes on different segments; in most cases, however (69%), their sizes on the meso-metathorax and abdomen coincide (characters 85 and 91, states 0–0, $n = 21$, and 1–1, $n = 3$).

Apparently there is no relationship between the mandible morphology of first-instar larvae and leaf toughness or pilosity. For example, the mandibles of *Aeria* spp., which feed on soft, hairless leaves of *Prestonia* sp. (Apocynaceae), are identical to those of *Mechanitis* spp., which feed on the highly pilose leaves of *Solanum* (Solanaceae, subgenera *Leptostemonum* and *Minon*). Another example is the species of *Pteronymia,* which feed on tender, smooth leaves (*Cestrum* spp.) as well as pilose leaves (*Solanum* subgenus *Minon*).

The Position of *Tellervo*

The phylogenetic position of *Tellervo,* a genus of the Australian region, in relation to Danainae and Ithomiinae has been debated for a long time. Larval characters may help to clarify the phylogenetic relationships among these groups.

The secondary setae on the labrum of the mature larva (second to fifth instar) are present in *Danaus plexippus* and *Lycorea cleobaea,* but are absent in *Tellervo zoilus* and in the ithomiines examined (*Tithorea harmonia, Aeria olena, Melinaea ludovica, Methona themisto, Mechanitis lysimnia, Mechanitis polymnia, Ithomia lichyi, Dircenna dero, Epityches eupompe, Episcada clausina, Prittwitzia hymenaea, Hypoleria adasa,* and *Heterosais edessa*).

The tubercles on the thorax of the first-instar larva (character 75; table 19.2) are present in Danainae, *Tellervo, Tithorea, Aeria,* and *Melinaea* (P. C. Motta, unpub.). Another important character is the sclerotized cervical plate of the prothorax (character 81, see fig. 19.4). This cervical sclerite

Table 19.6 List of characters used to assess position of *Tellervo*

1. Labrum, secondary setae in second to fifth instar: (0) present; (1) absent.
2. Tubercles on thorax: (0) present; (1) absent.
3. Cervical sclerite on prothorax: (0) present; (1) absent.
4. Prothorax, L1 and L2 setae on common pinaculum: (0) present; (1) absent.
5. L2 setae on meso- and metathorax: (0) absent; (1) present.

Note: All characters are from first-instar larvae, except character 1.

is common in the first-instar larvae of several Nymphalidae, including Nymphalinae (Nakanishi 1988), Danainae (Kitching 1984), Libytheinae (Scott 1986), Heliconiinae (Fleming 1960; P. C. Motta, pers. obs.), and some moths, including *Catocala* (Noctuidae: Johnson 1984). As *Tithorea harmonia* is the unique ithomiine with this plate, its absence is considered an apomorphic state in Ithomiinae. When the cervical sclerite is present, the prothoracic L1 and L2 setae may be on a common pinaculum (*Danaus plexippus* and *Anetia briarea*). The L2 setae on the meso- and metathorax (character 90) are absent in Danainae, *Tellervo,* and *Tithorea* and a few other ithomiine genera (such as *Mechanitis, Ithomia, Callithomia,* and *Ceratinia*).

These five characters, summarized in table 19.6, were used to evaluate the phylogenetic relationships among Danainae, *Tellervo,* and some primitive (*Tithorea harmonia* and *Aeria olena*), intermediary (*Melinaea ludovica*), and advanced (*Dircenna dero*) ithomiine lineages.

Nine equally most parsimonious trees (length = 5, CI = 1.0) were found using these characters. Figure 19.7 shows the consensus tree and the summarized tree topologies. *Tellervo* and *Tithorea* are genera that show basic danainoid plesiomorphic characters (characters 2, 3, and 5, table 19.6) and share the same host plant family (Apocynaceae). This finding probably indicates that both genera diverged quite early from the danainoid stock. In accordance with this hypothesis, the eggs of these genera are extremely similar, and are more similar to those of *Aeria* than to those of *Danaus, Anetia,* and *Lycorea* (Motta 1989). If *Tellervo* and *Tithorea* are sister groups (fig. 19.7C), would Ithomiinae then be paraphyletic?

One additional character, obtained from adult morphology, sheds light on these relationships and was necessary to choose the one preferred cladogram: In the adult male, hairpencils are found on the abdomen (Danainae), wings (Ithomiinae) or absent (*Tellervo*).

Based on biogeographic grounds and the adult male hairpencil, the hypothesis shown in figure 19.7B can be discarded, unless one supposes that this character appeared twice in the course of evolution. In figure 19.7C, *Tellervo* and *Tithorea* are monophyletic, and the *Tellervo* lineage has lost the hairpencil. In this case, *Tithorea* would be reallocated and considered the Neotropical member of Tellervinae.

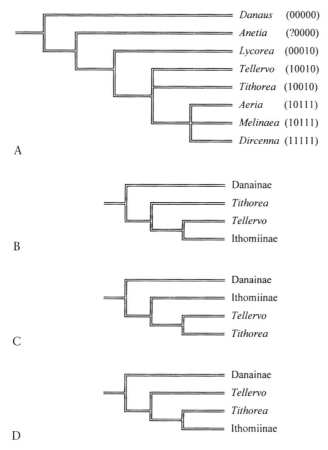

Danaus (00000)
Anetia (?0000)
Lycorea (00010)
Tellervo (10010)
Tithorea (10010)
Aeria (10111)
Melinaea (10111)
Dircenna (11111)

A

Danainae
Tithorea
Tellervo
Ithomiinae

B

Danainae
Ithomiinae
Tellervo
Tithorea

C

Danainae
Tellervo
Tithorea
Ithomiinae

D

Figure 19.7 Relationships among Danainae, *Tellervo,* and Ithomiinae. An exhaustive search of all possible topologies was performed. (A) Consensus from nine trees (the numbers after the genera are character states; see table 19.6); (B–D) The three topologies found. ($n = 3$ trees for each topology).

In the last topology (fig. 19.7D), the ithomiines are monophyletic, and the hairpencil appears once. I consider this hypothesis the most plausible. As such, *Tellervo* is more closely related to the Ithomiinae, mainly *Tithorea,* than to the Danainae. The adult characters and geographic isolation may give subfamily status to *Tellervo* (Tellervinae), but still place it nearer to Ithomiinae than to Danainae.

CONCLUSIONS

At what taxonomic level are first-instar larval characters, principally chaetotaxic ones, most informative in evaluating phylogenetic relationships: species, genus, subfamily, or family? If immature characters in fact evolve more slowly than those of the adult, then they may be less informative when applied to studies of recent radiations (Miller 1996). Therefore, the study of such characters would be more useful for evaluating relationships among subfamilies than within subfamilies, given the intraspecific variation of head characters and the relative homogeneity of the ithomiine body.

The taxonomic characters obtained from first-instar larval chaetotaxy provide new hypotheses concerning the phylogenetic relationships among the studied genera, questioning some classic views. Five large monophyletic groups were suggested for the 52 Ithomiinae genera: Tithoreini, Melinaeini, Mechanitini, Ithomiini, and Dircennini. This last tribe includes the more advanced genera formerly placed in the tribe Godyridini.

The characters obtained through larval body chaetotaxy were fewer in number compared with those of the cephalic capsule, but of greater confidence due to lower intrapopulational variation. The first-instar larval characters, principally the cervical sclerite of the prothorax, were also useful in evaluating phylogenetic relationships among *Tellervo*, Ithomiinae, and Danainae. They indicated that *Tellervo* is more closely related to Ithomiinae than to Danainae and may represent an independent monophyletic group, deserving subfamilial status. This analysis of the characters of first-instar larvae provides the first phylogenetic evidence to support the traditional viewpoint that Tellervinae is closely related to Ithomiinae.

Hypotheses concerning the phylogenetic relationships among the Ithomiinae (from this and other studies) continue to become more consistent and stable. An analysis of the maximum possible number of species of all 52 genera, the refinement and redimensioning of the characters outlined here, and a survey of additional character systems, using characters from all stages of the life cycle and from behavior, ecology, chemistry, and molecular data, would be useful in understanding the phylogenetic affinities among the taxa studied here.

SUMMARY

The subfamily Ithomiinae was investigated from a macroevolutionary point of view in a search for cladogenetic events, using first-instar larval morphology to generate hypotheses on the phylogenetic relationships among genera and tribes. The chaetotaxy of the head capsule, labrum, mandible, and body for 35 ithomiine and 3 danaine species (143 individuals) was used to delineate 99 taxonomic characters. Phylogenetic relationships in the Ithomiinae were evaluated. The monophyletic groups did not correspond to generally accepted tribes, and new tribal groups were suggested. Some characters were important in the discussion of the phylogenetic position of *Tellervo* (a genus restricted to the Australian region) in relation to Danainae (a nearly cosmopolitan group) and Ithomiinae (a Neotropical group).

ACKNOWLEDGMENTS

I would like to express my gratitude to Keith S. Brown Jr. for his valuable advice and helpful comments during this study. For loans of material I thank K. S. Brown Jr., A. V. L. Freitas, W. Haber, and A. G. Orr. I also thank A. V. L. Freitas and R. B. Francini for assistance in the field and comments, and O. H. H. Mielke. I am also deeply indebted to Cláudia V. A. Dansa for constant encouragement. The universities of Campinas, Uberlândia, and Brasília provided support at various times during this study. The chaetotaxy figures were drawn by Núbia S. L. de Souza. Two anonymous referees offered incisive remarks and suggestions that contributed to a much improved final version. Funding was provided by the Brazilian National Council for the Development of Science and Technology (CNPq).

CHAPTER 20

Butterfly Molecular Systematics: From Species Definitions to Higher-Level Phylogenies

Felix Sperling

Butterfly systematics is experiencing a renaissance. Its renewed vigor is due to the widespread realization that robust phylogenies and objective species delimitations are crucial for comparative investigations in biology and conservation, as well as to the recent development of easily applied techniques for assaying DNA sequences and other molecular variation (Hillis et al. 1996). Molecular techniques have allowed a surge in systematic investigations ranging in scope from surveys of gene flow among intraspecific populations to examinations of deep phylogenetic divergences (e.g., Brower 1994a; Sperling and Harrison 1994; Weller and Pashley 1995).

However, the advantages of molecular investigations may also be a source of fundamental problems. A student can usually produce reliable molecular datasets in a matter of months, whereas it often takes years to train a researcher who is proficient at morphological character analysis. On the other hand, the ease of producing sequence data has produced an ever-growing patchwork that is difficult to compare meaningfully among studies. Furthermore, proper sampling and analysis of molecular data is not straightforward, and neglect of these issues can seriously limit the value of studies.

The purpose of this chapter is to evaluate the use of genetic markers in butterfly systematics with respect to both species-level problems and higher-level relationships. Specifically, I ask two questions: (1) Are some kinds of genetic markers particularly effective in delineating butterfly species boundaries? (2) What DNA sequence regions are most useful for resolving higher-level phylogenies in butterflies? First, I argue that species should be recognized as populations that maintain their genomic integrity when they contact each other. Then I make the case that X-linked genes and mitochondrial DNA (mtDNA) are particularly good markers of species boundaries, and

I use species problems in two groups of *Papilio* to illustrate my points. Finally, I review the kinds of gene sequences that have been used to reconstruct butterfly phylogenies. I recommend that gene sequences used for species-level problems be accumulated with an eye to building community-wide databases that are informative for resolving deeper divergences.

SPECIES DEFINITIONS

Before anyone can hope to determine whether some kinds of markers are better than others for delimiting species boundaries, it is necessary to define what is meant by species. As is well known, species concepts have had a long and contentious history, and the controversy has not abated to this day (e.g., Claridge et al. 1997; Howard and Berlocher 1998). The current debate appears to be polarized between the battered, but still strong, proponents of the biological species concept (Mayr 1963) and those who support the advantages, particularly for conservation purposes, of the phylogenetic species concept (Cracraft 1983, 1997).

This debate may not be as intractable as it seems. I believe that a pragmatic resolution can be obtained by applying a conceptually mixed, two-part species definition. According to this definition, species are (1) populations that maintain their genomic integrity when they contact each other, even if they occasionally exchange genes, *or* (2) allopatric populations that have overall genetic divergences equivalent to the average for taxonomically relevant sister species that are in contact with each other. To simplify communication, I refer to this concept as the genomic integrity species definition. It shares conceptual elements with several other species definitions, differing from them in the way that these elements are combined and emphasized. The second part of the definition addresses an issue that is ambiguous or less explicit in other definitions.

Reference to genomic integrity begs two questions: what is it, and how can it be demonstrated? Genomic integrity is the extent to which the genome, or at least a central core of it, holds together (remains stable and cohesive) in the face of gene flow from related species or natural selection across different environments. A conceptually similar but more ambiguous phrasing for genomic integrity is implied in Templeton's cohesion species concept (1989).

The clearest way to establish or quantify genomic integrity is to provide evidence of reproductive discontinuity among populations. Preliminary evidence of such discontinuity can rely on a single locus in sympatric populations. A more general demonstration of genomic integrity involves comparing the extent of gaps between clusters of individuals plotted in multivariate character space (Mallet 1995). The interpretation of such clusters should be tempered by extensive experience with the organisms. Any particular set of markers or formulae used for measuring gene flow is likely to have exceptions and violations of its assumptions (Porter and Geiger 1995; Bossart and Prowell 1998). Therefore, genomic integrity should ideally be assessed using a variety of kinds of characters and lines of evidence.

For most butterflies, the criterion of reproductive continuity, as emphasized in the biological species concept (Mayr 1963), remains operationally useful and conceptually meaningful for ranking populations. In practice, however, reproductive continuity can be assessed only in sympatric or parapatric populations. The ranking of extended populations as species may rely on determining whether those populations form distinct gene clusters over most of their area of contact. Populations with distinct gene clusters also have diagnostic character combinations, even if they do not have complete allele substitutions at any one locus. Diagnosable populations thus qualify as species in the sense of the phylogenetic species concept (Cracraft 1997).

The first part of the genomic integrity species definition, which refers to the maintenance of integrity in areas of contact, leaves allopatric populations and parthenogenetic lineages without an objective criterion for ranking them. The "potential for interbreeding" that Mayr (1942) included in his early definitions of the biological species concept is largely untestable due to the difficulties involved in duplicating natural conditions in a hybridization experiment, especially over a few generations. Artificial hybridization is certainly useful for assaying species status in cases in which there is significant postzygotic incompatibility, but such hybridization bypasses most meaningful prezygotic incompatibility. A more internally consistent ranking criterion for allopatric or parthenogenetic populations is a comparison with overall genetic divergences between naturally interacting sister species.

Although it may take only a single fixed difference in a heritable trait to demonstrate that two interacting populations maintain a statistically significant degree of genetic integrity in sympatry, ranking allopatric populations on the basis of such a minimum divergence could lead to species recognition for innumerable small populations with only single diagnostic differences. This is the key drawback of the phylogenetic species concept, since the number of species recognized will be an arbitrary function of the extent to which new molecular markers and techniques have been employed (Avise 1994; Mallet 1995).

Uncritical use of particular measures of genomic divergence, even if corrected for different rates of evolution in different lineages, can potentially lead to the slippery slope of operationalism. As convenient as it may be to rely on one or a few genes as the final arbiter of species status, allopatric populations must instead be ranked using a variety of heritable characters.

These should, wherever possible, include characters that are morphological, ecological, behavioral, and molecular in order to obtain a reasonable estimate of the degree of overall genomic divergence. Only when this overall divergence is similar to average, rather than minimum, divergences between interacting sister species pairs should an allopatric population be ranked as a species. The species pairs used to set up divergence baselines should normally be closely related to the allopatric populations under consideration (perhaps at the genus or tribe level for butterflies) in order to minimize the effect of significant variation in rates of evolution in different phylogenetic lineages.

The genomic integrity species concept outlined above is obviously related to the main elements of the biological, cohesion, and recognition (Paterson 1985) concepts by its reference to assessments of genetic continuity within and between populations. However, it clarifies the role of natural hybridization by explicitly including the potential for gene exchange as long as the genomic integrity of species is maintained over most of the geographic area over which they overlap and potentially interbreed. Like the "genotypic clusters" concept of Mallet (1995), this definition focuses on the detection of character combinations that are not broken up upon contact or under disruptive selection, rather than on inferences regarding the process of interbreeding. However, it provides more explicit guidance regarding the recognition of allopatric populations than Mallet offered. It also provides wording that is a bridge to other species concepts. It is similar in emphasis to the evolutionary species concept (Wiley 1978), by reference to the maintenance of genomic integrity as a more explicit phrasing of "identity," but goes further by specifying how allopatric versus sympatric populations are to be treated. Unlike the genealogical species concept (Baum and Shaw 1995), it has no requirement that sister species be reciprocally monophyletic at any gene loci. Finally, this definition is likely to be more consistent in its application to isolated allopatric populations than the phylogenetic species concept, since it specifies a more general, biologically meaningful level at which gene clusters should be recognized as species.

Hull (1997) suggests that no single species concept can serve all masters effectively. No two concepts emphasize generality, applicability, or theoretical significance equally, and concepts differ primarily in the extent to which they focus on one or two of these three attributes at the expense of the others. In Harrison's (1998) view, different species concepts may simply focus on different stages of the divergence, or "life history," of species. The genomic integrity definition is intended to emphasize theoretical significance and conceptual interrelationships more than the gene cluster or phylogenetic species concepts do, but like them, its application is likely to result in species recognition being given to populations at a relatively early stage of divergence.

SPECIES BOUNDARIES AND MARKERS

HALDANE'S RULE

Regardless of how species are defined, it is often a challenge to find reliable markers to distinguish sister species. There are few rules for finding such markers. Haldane's rule is the only general rule about the process of speciation that has so far been shown to apply to all known groups of animals (Haldane 1922; Orr 1997). Haldane's rule observes that any differential sterility or inviability between males and females in interspecific hybrids will be greater in the heterogametic sex (see appendix 20.1 below: in Lepidoptera, females are the heterogametic sex). The fact that hybrid female Lepidoptera are overwhelmingly more likely to show inviability than hybrid males was used by Haldane (1922) as strong empirical support for his generalization.

The causes of Haldane's rule have been at the center of a great deal of research over the last 15 years, particularly by *Drosophila* geneticists. Recent developments have solidified support for two mechanisms, both of which may act simultaneously (Civetta and Singh 1998; Presgraves and Orr 1998; Turelli 1998), and a third explanation remains a possibility. The first explanation is the dominance theory, which states that Haldane's rule is a result of recessive X-linked loci that have incompatibilities with autosomal loci and that, owing to their recessiveness, are exposed to selection only in the heterogametic sex. The second explanation is the faster-male theory, which combines the empirical observation that males tend to diverge faster than females, particularly in traits affected by sexual selection leading to sterility, with the fact that males are the XY sex in *Drosophila* and most animals. The third explanation for Haldane's rule has not received much support in *Drosophila* (Orr 1997). This explanation states that there is faster evolution of X-linked loci due to the generally greater exposure of recessive X-linked traits to natural selection, especially if those traits are expressed in only one sex.

The dominance theory is a less satisfactory fit for Lepidoptera than for *Drosophila*, although it remains a plausible explanation (Turelli 1998). Incompatibilities with autosomal loci are expected to be less important due to the larger number of chromosomes in Lepidoptera (typically $n = 30$) than in *Drosophila* ($n = 4$) and the consequently fewer opportunities for incompatibilities between X chromosomes and autosomes. The second explanation, the faster-male theory, is expected to oppose Haldane's rule in Lepidoptera, since males are the XX sex but are still expected to be the sex that is more responsive to sexual selection. The faster-X theory remains a reasonable explanation for Lepidoptera, however weakly supported it may be in Diptera (Orr 1997). It is clear that investigations in Lepidoptera are likely to provide important tests of the generality of any explanations of Haldane's rule (Ritchie and Phillips 1998).

A finding that is related to Haldane's rule is that genes on X chromosomes appear to contribute disproportionately to hybrid inviability and sterility. This phenomenon has been called the "large X effect" by Coyne and Orr (1989). *Drosophila* geneticists have concentrated on postzygotic aspects of the large X effect, which include inviability and sterility. However, the tendency of genes that control species differences to be located on the X chromosome appears to apply just as much to genes that control prezygotic isolation in Lepidoptera, such as those affecting seasonal phenology and mate recognition (Sperling 1994). Compared with *Drosophila*, this phenomenon is even more striking in Lepidoptera because of their greater number of chromosomes. Since the 30 pairs of chromosomes in most species of Lepidoptera are of approximately similar size (Robinson 1971), only 1/30, or 3%, of genes should be on the X chromosomes if the genes are located randomly.

Prowell (1998), building on a survey by Sperling (1994), reviewed eleven well-studied pairs of species or well-differentiated races in the Lepidoptera, including three pairs of butterflies. Prowell's review listed a total of 77 traits that distinguished the eleven pairs of species or races. Fully 39% of these traits were on X chromosomes, while 10% were maternal or Y-linked, and 51% were autosomally inherited. Furthermore, X chromosome bias was greater for traits recognized to be directly important for speciation, such as mating behavior (76%) and host performance (60%), than for morphological traits (38%) and allozymes (24%). X-linked allozyme loci that showed differences between species had an average allele frequency difference of 83%, compared with only 50% for autosomal loci. Of traits whose expression was limited to one sex, 63% were on the X chromosomes. There was considerable taxonomic variation in the extent to which traits were X-linked, ranging from complete X-linkage of species differences in *Colias* butterflies to no X-linkage in *Yponomeuta* ermine moths. Prowell concluded that traits that distinguish closely related species in Lepidoptera exhibit a clear X-linkage bias. The distribution of these traits was consistent with an explanation for Haldane's rule that is based on generally faster evolution of X-linked genes, particularly if they are limited to expression in only one sex.

The observation that a disproportionate number of genes for species differences are X-linked in Lepidoptera is in need of further investigation. This finding could be a consequence of the ease with which X-linkage can be demonstrated, as well as the possibility that X-linkage is considered interesting enough to be published more often than is autosomal linkage. Furthermore, many of the traits listed by Prowell were not completely controlled by X-linked genes, and therefore 39% may be an overestimate of the proportion of species differences that are exclusively X-linked. Nonetheless, it is difficult to explain the difference between 3% (random association for the 1/30 of the genome that X chromosomes constitute) and 39% (the observed frequency) as being due only to observational bias or incomplete X-linked control. Neither of these two factors explains why allozyme allele frequency differences at diagnostic loci tend to be larger for X-linked than autosomal loci (Prowell 1998).

In fact, rather than being overestimated, the proportion of X-linked traits that distinguish species may even be underestimated. This is because comparisons between species pairs are made at varying time intervals after speciation, rather than right at speciation. The number of species-specific genes that are X-linked appears to be most disproportionate in *Drosophila* and *Caenorhabditis* at the point of speciation, and these genes show rapid saturation of X-linked nucleotide substitutions between more distantly related species (Civetta and Singh 1998). This is particularly true of sex-related genes, such as those involved in mating behavior, fertilization, spermatogenesis, or sex determination. If this pattern also applies to Lepidoptera, then X-linkage bias will be partially obscured in comparisons between species that are some distance past the point of speciation.

There are two particularly interesting consequences of the finding that a large proportion and variety of recently evolved species differences appear to be X-linked in Lepidoptera. First, such a bias could be of practical use to molecular systematists searching for diagnostic markers to distinguish ecologically distinct but morphologically similar species. It may be possible to find diagnostic markers more quickly, either by concentrating on loci known to be X-linked in related species or by looking for differences between the two types of F_1 hybrid females (see appendix 20.1). A second consequence of disproportionate X-linkage in species or race differences is that such a phenomenon could function to keep combinations of traits together in spite of gene exchange at autosomal loci (Charlesworth et al. 1987; Scriber 1994; Janz 1998b). Several species pairs in Prowell's review (1998) had X-linked genes for species differences that controlled ecological traits (e.g., diapause termination, oviposition preference) as well as ones that controlled mating traits (e.g., pheromone production, sex-specific wing coloration). With both ecological and mating traits linked in this fashion, it would be relatively easy for ecological or sexual selection to drive speciation, as has been suggested on the basis of models of sympatric speciation (e.g., van Doorn et al. 1998) as well as empirical studies (e.g., Sperling 1990; Orr and Smith 1998; Rice 1998).

Although not universally accepted, the hypothesis that sympatric speciation is a common phenomenon is gaining support (Bush 1994; Howard and Berlocher 1998). In fact, sympatric speciation may be a more general mode of speciation than the widely accepted allopatric mode. If close association between ecological traits and mating traits is the key to divergence in spite of continued opportunity for genetic interchange, then allopatric isolation may simply force a particular form of association between such traits. In the allopatric case, attenuated gene flow would be genome-wide and due to geographic distance.

In contrast, a recombination-decreasing phenomenon such as X-linkage bias could allow the formation of a divergent core of the genome, which could grow by accretion of epistatically linked traits in the rest of the genome until eventually no gene exchange with sister species is possible. If faster evolution of X-linked genes is the underlying process driving disproportionate X-linkage, then that process could be a key genetic mechanism leading to speciation. The phenomenon of divergence of a limited core of the genome, in spite of greater gene exchange in the rest of the genome, will be particularly exciting to study in greater detail (Sperling 1994). The most extreme example so far may be *Colias eurytheme* versus *C. philodice,* in which all species differences seem to be X-linked (Grula and Taylor 1980a). In this case, it is at least theoretically possible that the species differences are controlled by one or a few tightly linked genes on the X chromosomes and act much like an intraspecific polymorphism.

MATERNALLY INHERITED MARKERS

The ease with which mtDNA variation can be assayed, together with its relatively rapid nucleotide divergence rates, has made mtDNA a commonly surveyed genetic marker in insects at both the species level and above (Simon et al. 1994; Caterino et al. 2000). The pattern of accumulation of nucleotide mutations in mtDNA is not disrupted by recombination, and its analysis is relatively simple even at the population level (Avise 1994). The almost exclusively maternal inheritance of mtDNA also means that it has one-fourth the effective population size of an autosomal gene and therefore is more susceptible to genetic bottlenecks. This feature has been considered advantageous in conservation studies, since mtDNA should be a sensitive indicator of evolutionarily significant units (Moritz 1994a, 1994b). The key disadvantage of mtDNA as a genetic marker is that it represents only a single linked marker of maternal gene flow and hence may not be informative about patterns of male gene flow or nuclear gene relationships.

In Lepidoptera and other taxa with heterogametic females, mitochondrial DNA, like Y-linked markers, has another advantage as a genetic marker (Sperling 1993). In these taxa, the effects of Haldane's rule mean that females are the sex that is preferentially eliminated in interspecific hybrid interactions. Thus both mtDNA and Y-linked markers should also be disproportionately eliminated in such interactions. In fact, if Haldane's rule holds and if all else remains equal, mtDNA and Y-linked genes should generally be better markers of species boundaries than any other genes. The fact that mtDNA proved to be a good diagnostic marker in all five of the species pairs for which this marker was reviewed by Prowell (1998) supports this hypothesis. The same was true of the one putatively Y-linked marker. It will be difficult to distinguish selective elimination of maternal markers due to the Haldane effect from the effect of their greater susceptibility to genetic bottlenecks. Nonetheless, it is clear that analysis of mtDNA alone is as effective as a survey of a whole battery of allozyme loci for determining lepidopteran species boundaries and phylogenies (Sperling et al. 1995, 1996; Prowell 1998).

EXAMPLES FROM *Papilio* SPECIES COMPLEXES

Discussion of species concepts and species markers is helpful only if it brings clarity to real problems in taxonomically difficult species complexes. In butterflies, most species are relatively unambiguous units that would probably be delimited in the same way under most species concepts. However, a substantial number of butterfly species complexes cannot be dealt with so easily. These complexes provide a rich substrate for studies of speciation.

The genus *Papilio* contains numerous examples of such difficult species complexes. Comprising over two hundred well-studied species that range across all major biotic regions of the world, this genus is divided into approximately forty species groups (Munroe 1961; Hancock 1983). A huge amount of background information is available for these charismatic insects and has contributed to many influential studies with broad relevance to biology (e.g., Wallace 1865; Jordan 1896; Clarke and Sheppard 1960; Ehrlich and Raven 1964).

Among the best-known species groups in *Papilio* are the *P. machaon* (Old World swallowtail) and *P. glaucus* (tiger swallowtail) groups. These two groups are relatively distantly related to each other within *Papilio* (Caterino and Sperling 1999). The problems that the *P. machaon* and *P. glaucus* species groups pose for studies of species and speciation range from geographic variation and cryptic species, which prompted the development of the biological species concept, to hybrid swarms and host races, which are a problem for any of the major species concepts. The *P. machaon* group has long been considered a challenge, and, as Clarke and Sheppard (1955b) commented, "it is clear that the Machaon-group provides some of the most suitable material ever investigated in animals for studying the process of speciation in detail, taking into account genetic, ecological and behavior differences as well as time."

Mitochondrial DNA in *Papilio*

Mitochondrial DNA can provide an enormous range of information about species boundaries and phylogenetic history. Its usefulness is illustrated by a survey of mtDNA restriction site variation in the *Papilio machaon* group (Sperling and Harrison 1994). Four major mtDNA lineages are evident in the North American members of the group, and these lineages correspond to *P. machaon, P. zelicaon, P. polyxenes,* and *P. indra* (fig. 20.1). In North America, *P. indra* is the only species in the group with divergent genitalic morphology, and this species also has the most divergent mtDNA. A fifth lineage, corresponding to *P. hospiton,* occurs in Europe. On the basis of larval color pattern and host plant, the Mediterranean species *P. alexanor* had previously been placed in the *P. machaon* group (Munroe 1961), but phylogenetic analyses of mtDNA and nuclear gene sequences across *Papilio* have

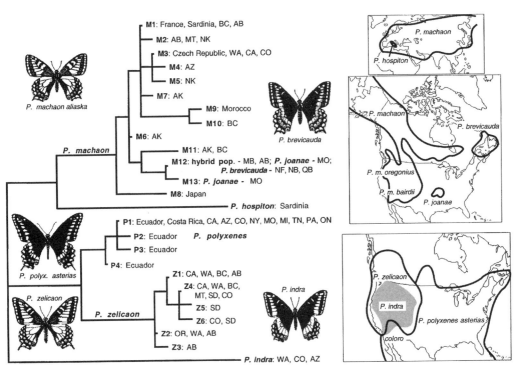

Figure 20.1 Mitochondrial DNA phylogeny for the *Papilio machaon* species group, based on restriction site data of Sperling and Harrison (1994). The tree shown arbitrarily represents one phylogram out of six most-parsimonious trees obtained using an unweighted heuristic search with PAUP 3.0Q (Swofford 1991), with trees not shown here having the position of the H lineage at the base of the M + (P + Z) lineage, or the M9 + M10 lineage with the M3 or M1 lineage. The geographic sources of specimens are given beside the haplotype names. For the United States and Canada, AB = Alberta; AK = Alaska; AZ = Arizona; BC = British Columbia; CA = California; CO = Colorado; MB = Manitoba; MI = Michigan; MO = Missouri; MT = Montana; NB = New Brunswick; NF = Newfoundland; NK = Nebraska; NY = New York; ON = Ontario; PA = Pennsylvania; QB = Quebec; SD = South Dakota; TN = Tennessee; WA = Washington.

now placed *P. alexanor* far outside this group (Caterino and Sperling 1999; Reed and Sperling 1999).

Mitochondrial DNA strongly supports a sister species relationship for *P. polyxenes* and *P. zelicaon,* and this has now been confirmed independently with sequences from a nuclear gene, *elongation factor-1α* (*EF-1α*) (Reed and Sperling 1999). In *P. polyxenes,* mtDNA shows no variation across a large geographic range extending from southern Canada to Central America, but has a pocket of variation in the southernmost part of the range in Ecuador (Sperling and Harrison 1994). The fact that mtDNA variation is limited to South America can be interpreted as the result of either a recent range expansion northward, with attendant bottlenecks, or a sweep of selectively advantageous mtDNA variants across the northern part of the range.

The uniformity of mtDNA across most of the range of *P. polyxenes* also contrasts with the substantial amount of ecological and wing pattern variation evident in populations that occur in California and Arizona. Here *P. polyxenes coloro* has such a different wing pattern, larval host plant, and habitat affinity that many early authors considered it a separate species. More recent work showed a clinal frequency shift in these characters through New Mexico into more typical *P. polyxenes asterias* in Texas (Ferris and Emmel 1982). MtDNA provided the first unambiguous confirmation of that assessment (Sperling and Harrison 1994).

Papilio zelicaon contains noticeably more mtDNA variation across its range than *P. polyxenes* (see fig. 20.1). While only a single mtDNA haplotype is evident across virtually all of the range of *P. polyxenes, P. zelicaon* in most localities where mtDNA was sampled had multiple haplotypes. *P. zelicaon* also shows a shift in the proportions of mtDNA variants from the eastern (CO, SD, MT) to the western (CA, OR, WA, BC) parts of its range. This shift provides some weak evidence of differentiation for Remington's (1968a) "*P. gothica,*" which he described from the Colorado Rocky Mountains and considered to be reproductively differentiated from Californian *P. zelicaon.* However, the relatively tight clustering of *P. zelicaon* mtDNA across its range supports Shapiro's (1975a) contention that most differentiation is due to recent, ecologically induced plasticity.

The major mtDNA lineage that occurs in *P. machaon* shows considerably more variation and differentiation than in related species (see fig. 20.1). Nonetheless, mtDNA analysis supports the genetic continuity of *P. machaon* populations from Europe and North Africa across Asia to North America. In western North America, *P. m. oregonius* and *P. m. bairdii* (AZ, AB, CA, CO, MT, NK, and WA) had previously been treated as one or more species separate from *P. machaon* from Eurasia and northern North America (BC and AK). This taxonomic assessment was largely founded on their unusual larval host plants in the Asteraceae, rather than the Apiaceae or Rutaceae as in all related *Papilio* species. However, Asteraceae-feeding populations have some of the same mtDNA variants (M1, M3) as Apiaceae-feeding European populations. Although allozymes and multivariate analyses of color pattern characters had recently indicated that these Asteraceae-feeding populations should be placed in *P. machaon* (Sperling 1987), mtDNA provided a simple, clear confirmation of this relationship.

In contrast to the preceding situations in which mtDNA confirmed conspecificity, mtDNA indicated that two species, *P. joanae* and *P. brevicauda,* are substantially different from *P. polyxenes* in at least one marker, even though they are morphologically very similar to that species (see fig. 20.1). In fact, the mtDNA of *P. joanae* and *P. brevicauda* is clearly part of the mtDNA lineage of *P. machaon*, a species that neither of them resembles in color pattern. Populations of *P. machaon* are now located at least 1,000 km distant from these two species. The distribution of mtDNA among *P. joanae, P. brevicauda,* and some populations of *P. machaon* suggests relatively recent genetic continuity, perhaps during glacial periods when forested regions were compressed south of the continental ice sheet. On the other hand, it is likely that the black wing and body color pattern that *P. joanae* and *P. brevicauda* share with *P. polyxenes* was first derived in *P. polyxenes* (see discussion of the black morph below). This possibility suggests that *P. joanae* and *P. brevicauda* evolved as a result of interspecific hybridization between *P. machaon* females and *P. polyxenes* males thousands of years ago, when the ranges of some *P. machaon* populations shifted southward in front of continental ice sheets.

Unfortunately, no other comparative genetic surveys have been done on *P. joanae* and *P. brevicauda.* It will be particularly instructive to determine what proportions of their genomes resemble *P. polyxenes* versus *P. machaon.* In contrast to hybrid populations in western Canada (see below), in which allozyme studies as well as multivariate analyses of color pattern characters have been done (Sperling 1987), I currently prefer to treat *P. joanae* and *P. brevicauda* as taxonomically distinct species. I do this primarily to retain nomenclatural stability, a principle that I believe should take precedence when biological information is incomplete or inconclusive.

Although many intriguing questions remain, it is clear that a survey of mtDNA variation has been of as much utility in determining species boundaries and relationships in the *P. machaon* group as any other suite of markers, including morphology, allozymes, and life history characters.

X-LINKAGE AND HALDANE'S RULE IN *Papilio*

The *P. glaucus* group provides an illustration of the potential interrelationships between X-linkage, maternal markers, and Haldane's rule. This group has three broadly sympatric species across western North America (*P. rutulus, P. eurymedon,* and *P. multicaudatus*) and three parapatric species with ranges extending from northern North America across the eastern

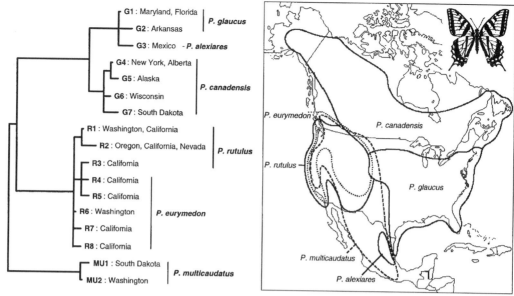

Figure 20.2 Mitochondrial DNA phylogeny for the *Papilio glaucus* species group, based on restriction site data of Sperling (1993). The tree shown arbitrarily represents one phylogram out of four most-parsimonious trees obtained using an unweighted heuristic search with PAUP 3.0Q (Swofford 1991), with trees not shown here differing within the topology of *P. canadensis* (G4–7) and *P. eurymedon* (R6–8). The geographic sources of specimens are given beside the haplotype names.

United States and into Mexico (*P. canadensis, P. glaucus,* and *P. alexiares*) (fig. 20.2).

Of the three parapatric species, *P. glaucus* and *P. canadensis* have only recently been considered distinct at the species level (Hagen et al. 1991). They hybridize across a relatively narrow zone extending through Wisconsin, Michigan, and New York State (Hagen 1990), but differ genetically in larval host plant use, pupal diapause termination, oviposition preference, three allozyme loci, mtDNA sequences (see fig. 20.2), and a dark female color morph that allows mimicry of an unpalatable species and may also influence male mating preference (Hagen and Scriber 1989; Hagen et al. 1991; see also Scriber et al., chap. 17 in this volume). Most of these traits are X-linked or determined maternally. The mimetic morph is controlled by one X-linked and one Y-linked gene, and the only autosomally controlled traits are larval feeding and one of the three allozyme loci.

Hybrids between *P. glaucus* and *P. canadensis* conform to Haldane's rule, since females are significantly more inviable than males (Hagen and Scriber 1995). Thus it is easy to explain why maternally inherited traits, which include mtDNA and one of the mimetic morph genes, show steep allele frequency shifts along the hybrid zone. The potential causal relationship between Haldane's rule and the disproportionate X-linkage of diagnostic traits is not as obvious. Nonetheless, disproportionate X-linkage, mtDNA differences, and conformance to Haldane's rule are all found in the *P. glaucus-P. canadensis* pair (Sperling 1993; Hagen and Scriber 1995).

In contrast, the western species of the *P. glaucus* group include a pair, *P. rutulus* and *P. eurymedon,* that are undoubtedly distinct species, since they regularly contact each other in nature but maintain distinct adult color patterns, larval host plants, and ecological zone associations. Yet they have only minor allozyme allele frequency differences (Hagen and Scriber 1991), and their mtDNA is not autapomorphic (see fig. 20.2). None of the species differences appear to be X-linked, nor do they show a Haldane effect (Sperling 1993). This case shows that mtDNA and X-linked genes are not universal markers of species boundaries. It also demonstrates a correlation among mtDNA differences, X-linked allele frequency differences, and the Haldane effect that is consistent with the possibility of a causative relationship and encourages further investigation of these phenomena in other species complexes.

There are fewer reports of X-linkage between species in populations that interact naturally in the *P. machaon* group than in the *P. glaucus* group. None of the allozyme loci that have been sampled are X-linked (Sperling 1987; Aubert et al. 1997). However, *P. joanae,* which is surrounded by populations of *P. polyxenes,* shows mtDNA differences as well as a strong Haldane effect in hybrids with *P. polyxenes* (Heitzman 1973; J. R. Heitzman, pers. comm.). For *P. machaon* versus *P. zelicaon,* mtDNA is diagnostic, and one crucial behavioral difference, oviposition preference, is significantly X-linked (Thompson 1988b). In Sardinia and Corsica, where *P. hospiton* and *P. machaon* are sympatric, mtDNA is diagnostic, and the control of pupal diapause termination may be X-linked (Aubert et al. 1997). Since oviposition preference and diapause termination may indirectly influence mating location and phenology in *P. zelicaon* or *P. hospiton* versus *P. machaon,* these findings raise the possibility that associations between mating behavior and ecological traits contribute to these two species pairs maintaining their genetic integrity in sympatry (Sperling 1990; see the discussion of consequences of X-linkage above).

Maintenance of Genetic Integrity in *Papilio*

The central theme of the species definition outlined at the beginning of this chapter is that species maintain their genomic integrity when they contact each other, though they may still exchange some genes. *Papilio hospiton* illustrates the utility of this way of viewing species (Aubert et al. 1997). This species is endemic to the Mediterranean islands of Sardinia and Corsica, which have also been invaded by *P. machaon.* The two species have distinct genitalia, wing color patterns, wing shapes, and ecological associations. However, they hybridize commonly when they contact each other in nature.

Papilio hospiton and *P. machaon* have some genetic incompatibilities, since inappropriate pupal diapause termination causes high inviability of female hybrids. Mitochondrial DNA is diagnostic, whereas the nine variable allozyme loci that have been surveyed show only allele frequency differences rather than complete allele substitutions (Aubert et al. 1997). In fact, *P. machaon* populations on Corsica share some allozyme alleles with *P. hospiton*, even though these alleles are not found in *P. machaon* populations on the mainland, where *P. hospiton* is not present. This finding suggests there has been some gene introgression between the species, and that they maintain their genetic integrity in spite of the potential for gene flow.

An even more complex genetic situation is found in the *P. machaon* group in western Canada (Sperling 1987). Here, some regions have hybrid swarms that appear to be the result of genetic mixture, in various proportions, among *P. machaon, P. zelicaon,* and *P. polyxenes* (fig. 20.3; for larger ranges, see fig. 20.1). This hybridization predates significant habitat disturbance by European settlers. In central Manitoba, the dark morph and the yellow morph found in hybrid populations had been given separate taxonomic names, but allozymes and mtDNA indicate that these are part of a dimorphic, self-sustaining hybrid population derived from both *P. polyxenes* and *P. machaon.*

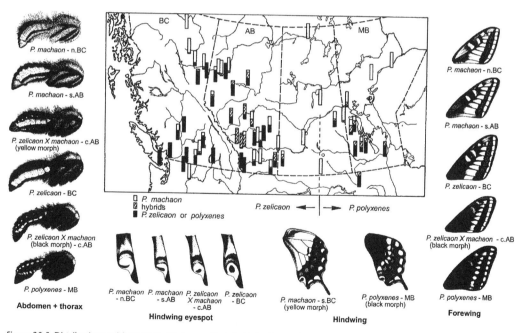

Figure 20.3 Distribution and frequency of interspecific hybrids in the *Papilio machaon* species group in western Canada. The drawings around the periphery of the map illustrate the kinds of color pattern characters studied and their ranges of variation. c. = central; n. = northern; s. = southern; AB = Alberta; BC = British Columbia; MB = Manitoba. (Map from Sperling 1990; drawings from Sperling 1987.)

In Alberta, hybrid swarms between *P. zelicaon* and *P. machaon* have been studied in greater detail (Sperling 1987). A multivariate analysis of color pattern traits and allozyme alleles indicates that specimens with intermediate character combinations predominate in central Alberta (see fig. 20.3). Populations outside of this region have a more bimodal distribution of character combinations. Thus, in spite of the fact that *P. zelicaon* and *P. machaon* maintain their genetic integrity over most of their very large region of range overlap in western North America, they show the ability to merge into hybrid swarms under some circumstances.

The interaction between *P. zelicaon* and *P. polyxenes* also shows some evidence of gene exchange (Sperling 1987). The black adult color pattern that characterizes *P. polyxenes* is probably inherited as a simple autosomal dominant (Fisher 1977). These two species are parapatric along the front range of the Rocky Mountains in Colorado. The black adult color morph that characterizes *P. polyxenes* occurs as a genetic polymorphism in populations of *P. zelicaon* along the front edge of its range from Colorado to Alberta (see fig. 20.3 for illustrations of black versus yellow wing pattern and body coloration). However, no apparent hybrid swarms of just *P. zelicaon* and *P. polyxenes* have been found. In central Alberta, the low-frequency presence of the black morph of *P. polyxenes* in hybrid swarms indicates that these populations are actually a three-way combination, even if they are predominantly composed of genes from *P. zelicaon* and *P. machaon* (Sperling 1987). In Arizona and California, the black morph has introgressed at high frequency into the southernmost Asteraceae-feeding populations of *P. machaon*.

It is likely that these kinds of hybrid situations are common. A minimum of 6% of *Papilio* species hybridize in nature, and many of these hybrid combinations are between pairs that are not each other's closest relatives (Sperling 1990). Similar examples are known from a wide variety of animals and especially plants (Avise 1994; Mallet 1995). Since these hybridizing populations represent character combinations that maintain their integrity in spite of hybridization, most biologists who have field experience have considered them to be species. However, they represent a real challenge to both the biological species concept, through its focus on reproductive isolation, and the phylogenetic species concept, through its focus on diagnosability.

CALIBRATING DIVERGENCES IN ALLOPATRIC POPULATIONS

One of the first things that a molecular systematist is asked by other biologists is what percentage of mtDNA sequence divergence or allozyme distance is the cutoff above which populations should be recognized as separate species. Even the few *Papilio* examples described above demonstrate that it is unreasonable to expect any kind of simple relationship between percentage of sequence divergence and the maintenance of genetic integrity.

For example, *Papilio rutulus* and *P. eurymedon* are distinct species by almost any species definition, but have no evident mtDNA differences and only small allozyme allele frequency differences (see fig. 20.2; Hagen and Scriber 1991; Sperling 1993). On the other hand, samples of *P. machaon* from some localities contain a substantial amount of mtDNA variation, while other variants are found across the entire Holarctic region (see fig. 20.1; Sperling and Harrison 1994).

It is equally unreasonable to expect that an allopatric population that happens to be fixed for a single mutation should be recognized at the species level. Instead, an experienced systematist or field biologist should take into account the combination of morphological, genetic, behavioral, and life history divergences between allopatric populations and ask whether these are quantitatively and qualitatively equivalent to the average difference between sister species that are in contact with each other. For example, most Asteraceae-feeding populations of *P. machaon* in western North America are disjunct from the Holarctic Apiaceae-feeding populations and have some wing pattern characters that, in combination, allow an experienced person to have a high probability of determining the origin of a specimen. However, these distinctions are clearly less than those that are found in the contiguous part of the range of *P. machaon* and cluster nicely within them. Thus there is little reason to recognize these populations as separate species, even if there is no current gene flow between the northern and southern populations in North America.

Eventually, enough butterfly species will have their mtDNA surveyed so that statistically supported statements can be made about the probability that a particular percentage of sequence divergence—say, 2%—is associated with species that are recognized on other grounds as taxonomically distinct. To a large extent, this has already been done for allozymes (Thorpe 1982; Brussard et al. 1985). By themselves, however, these numbers will provide useful guidance only for cases with unusually high or low divergences, and therefore should be used in concert with other, more classic characters such as wing pattern, genitalic morphology, and life history. Separations between species should be assessed as directly as possible by sampling populations in areas where they may contact each other.

DNA MARKERS FOR PHYLOGENIES

RELIABILITY OF MOLECULAR PHYLOGENIES

Phylogenies are useful constructs. They serve as a record of nature's experiments and provide a historical framework for understanding the evolution of traits through comparative analysis. The proliferation of molecular data has been a boon to the building of phylogenies, but it is important to keep in mind that any phylogeny is a reconstruction that carries with it some element of uncertainty. Prior to the availability of DNA sequence data, it was difficult to determine whether such uncertainty was due to inadequacy of the data or real conflict between genes, since so little information was available for any one gene. In one sense, there was a bright side to this problem, since it forced systematists to obtain information from many different genes. Now, however, it is possible to determine the phylogeny of a single gene with a high degree of certainty, and it is clear that any one gene's phylogeny may not trace the phylogeny of the species in which it is found. Since this calls into question the meaning of a species phylogeny, a species phylogeny may be defined as the modal phylogeny of the genes it contains (i.e., the most frequently occurring gene phylogeny).

Legitimate conflicts between separate gene phylogenies can arise because of interspecific hybridization or retained ancestral polymorphism. Some kinds of genes are more likely to reflect the modal gene phylogeny than others, and these genes are the ones that we should concentrate on in our attempts to reconstruct species phylogenies. Such genes can be expected to conform to species boundaries, which should mean that they are less likely than other genes to be exchanged between recently diverged species. Genes ideal for determining species phylogenies should also have a fast enough rate of evolution that their phylogeny can be reconstructed, but should not have so much intraspecific polymorphism that separate allele lineages are likely to sort independently of the modal gene phylogeny.

In butterflies, mtDNA qualifies as a good marker on both accounts. The biased inviability of females due to the Haldane effect should generally make mtDNA a good marker of species boundaries. The maternal inheritance of mtDNA also implies lower effective population sizes than for most nuclear genes, as well as reduced opportunities for recombination, which should mean less polymorphism and reticulation. It remains to be seen, however, to what extent these arguments from first principles hold true, and there continues to be a need to use multiple genes in addition to mtDNA to reconstruct phylogenies. For example, there is real conflict between mtDNA and *EF-1α* with respect to the placement of *Papilio multicaudatus* (Reed and Sperling 1999), and several more gene phylogenies will be needed to determine what the modal phylogeny is.

Phylogenies can also be uncertain because there are simply not enough data. In this case, the ability to generate copious character data from DNA sequences has been one of the major advantages of molecular systematics. This ability, however, has encouraged an exemplar approach to reconstructing phylogenies, in which a few species are surveyed and effort is focused on maximizing the amount of sequence available for each species. The drawback of DNA sequence data is that they may not provide useful information about closely spaced divergences at the bases of long branches deep within a phylogeny, since the few character changes that occur at this level are likely to be obscured by subsequent substitutions.

One solution to the problems caused by sequences saturated with multiple substitutions is to maximize the number of taxa surveyed in a study (Hillis 1998; Goldman 1998). The addition of taxa within an ingroup helps to resolve internal nodes by cutting long branches (Graybeal 1998) and by making more informed reconstructions of ancestral nodes (Yang 1998). Thus, the most accurate phylogeny for a group of butterflies is likely to be the one that samples the most species, particularly those that break up long, deep branches. For logistic and budgetary reasons, however, comprehensive resolution of butterfly phylogenies as part of a single research project will generally be possible only for small groups of species from regions that are easily sampled.

Fortunately, a solution is near at hand, just as it has been for large genome sequencing projects. By using a divide-and-conquer strategy of working through the butterflies in a fashion coordinated among multiple researchers, and by focusing on a few genes that are likely to be informative across a broad range of taxonomic levels, it should be possible to provide a much firmer phylogenetic foundation for butterfly ecology and evolutionary biology in the near future (Caterino et al. 2000). This strategy has already allowed excellent progress in resolving the notoriously difficult basal relationships of angiosperms (Chase and Albert 1998).

Work in my laboratory on the phylogeny of the Papilionidae provides an example of the potential of DNA sequences to be informative from the species level to the subfamily level (fig. 20.4; Caterino et al. 2001). In combination, the COI + COII mtDNA gene region and the nuclear gene *EF-1α* remain informative to the level of subfamilies in the Papilionidae, although this approach may require judicious weighting of codon positions and use of maximum likelihood approaches. The minimum evolution tree in figure 20.4 includes most of the tribes of the family and is based on simultaneous analysis of 2.3 kb of COI + COII and 1 kb of *EF-1α*. Virtually all the clades that were supported on the basis of prior morphological investigations were retained in the tree derived from DNA sequence data. This result encourages taxonomically comprehensive surveys in which different researchers working at shallower levels in a phylogeny can then pool their sequences to reconstruct relationships at deeper levels.

COMPILATION OF DNA SEQUENCE STUDIES

Unfortunately, different research groups working on the same butterfly taxa are now commonly sequencing nonhomologous gene regions. In addition, a few otherwise reputable journals have published DNA sequence

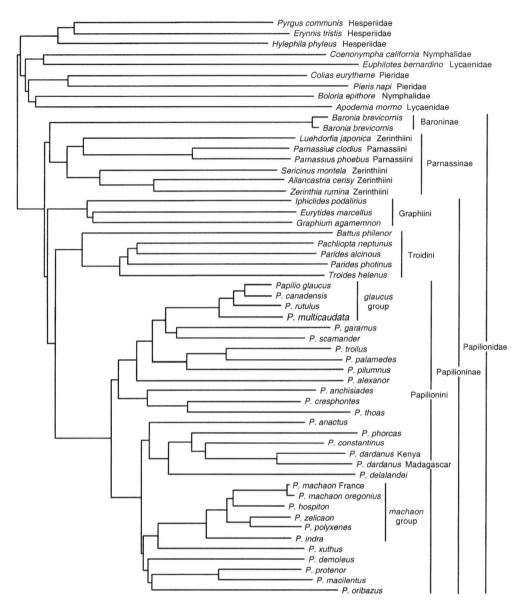

Figure 20.4 Phylogeny for Papilionidae, based on a combined analysis of DNA sequence for 2.3 kb of mitochondrial COI + COII and 1 kb of *EF-1α*. The tree was obtained with the minimum evolution method implemented in PAUP 4.0b1 (Swofford 1998a), using equal weighting for all characters. (Data from Caterino et al. 2001 and F. Sperling, unpub.).

surveys of butterflies without requiring the authors to deposit the sequences in DNA databanks or present the sequences in the publication. If data cannot be combined meaningfully, then there is little chance that the whole assemblage of sequences will ever be more than the sum of its parts.

The compilation of DNA sequence studies in this section is intended to provide an overview of the kinds of genes and gene regions that have been

sequenced in butterflies. It is also intended to encourage researchers to maximize the relevance of their work by choosing gene regions that will allow
them to contribute to preexisting pools of sequences. A larger compilation
of sequencing studies published up to May 1999 across all insects was
prepared by Caterino et al. (2000). In that review, we concluded that the best
DNA sequence regions for use in the insects as a whole were the COI and
16s genes in mtDNA and the 18s and *EF-1α* genes in nuclear DNA. However,
there was a great deal of variation in the extent to which these regions were
used in different insect orders.

Numerous sources of molecular data other than DNA sequences have
been used in butterfly systematics. These are not reviewed here because they
are not nearly as easily combined across studies to produce global phylogenetic analyses. For example, characters from allozymes, restriction fragment
length polymorphisms (RFLPs), and random amplified polymorphic DNA
(RAPDs) are difficult to compare across different taxa. Other markers, such
as microsatellites (e.g., Keyghobadi et al. 1999), single-stranded conformational polymorphisms (SSCPs), and restriction sites in polymerase chain
reaction (PCR) fragments, can more easily be reduced to sequence data, but
are only briefly listed here because they generally use loci that evolve too
quickly to be informative at the species level and above.

For DNA sequences, more than 22,000 separate lepidopteran submis-
sions were deposited on GenBank/EMBL/DDBJ by January 2002. Of these,
1,817 were for butterflies (1,799) or skippers (18), and the sequences were
widely dispersed across many taxa. In contrast, the remaining moth sequences were concentrated on a few model organisms, including *Bombyx
mori* and *B. mandarina* (15,951), *Manduca sexta* (1,793), and *Antheraea
yamamai* (637). The gene-prospecting and characterization studies of these
model-organism moths have provided a helpful foundation for developing phylogenetically useful nuclear markers for butterflies and other insects
(Friedlander et al. 1992, 1994).

Mitochondrial DNA

Phylogenetically oriented mtDNA sequence surveys of butterflies and
skippers are summarized in figure 20.5. This compilation includes studies
that have been published in some form or have had their sequences
deposited in databanks up to January 2002.

Although sequence studies of mtDNA are far more common than studies of any nuclear gene, it is evident from figure 20.5 that mtDNA studies have surveyed a wide variety of nonhomologous gene regions. For
butterfly mtDNA, the COI + COII gene region has been sequenced the
most frequently, mainly by North American researchers. However, different

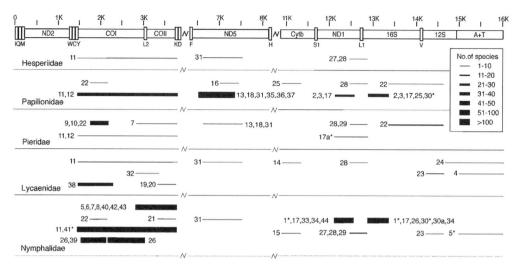

Figure 20.5 Compilation of mitochondrial DNA sequencing studies for butterflies, by family and gene region. The scale at the top gives gene arrangement and numbering as in *Drosophila yakuba* (Clary and Wolstenholme 1985). Bars show regions sequenced for most specimens in each study, with the width of each bar indicating number of species. Intraspecific variation is not shown, and duplicate species are counted only if based on independent sequence obtained by different research groups. Numbers by bars denote references as follows: 1, Aubert et al. 1996; 2, Aubert et al. 1997; 3, Aubert et al. 1999; 4, Brookes et al. 1997; 5, Brower 1994b; 6, Brower 1994a; 7, Brower and DeSalle 1998; 8, Brower and Egan 1997; 9, Brunton 1998; 10, Brunton and Hurst 1998; 11, Caterino et al. 2001; 12, Caterino and Sperling 1999; 13, Morinaka et al. 2000; 14, Aagard et al. 2001; 15, Joyce and Pullin 2000; 16, Makita et al. 1999; 17, Martin et al. 2000; 17a, Martin et al., chap. 21 in this volume; 18, Morinaka et al. 1999; 19, Nice and Shapiro 1999a; 20, Nice and Shapiro 1999b; 21, Nice and Shapiro 2001; 22, Pollock et al. 1998; 23, Sutherland and Axton 2000; 24, Taylor et al. 1993; 25, Vane-Wright et al. 1999; 26, Wahlberg and Zimmermann 2000; 27, Weller and Pashley 1995; 28, Weller et al. 1996; 29, Weller et al. 1994; 30, Wink and von Nickisch-Rosenegk 1997; 30a, Wink et al. 1998; 31, Yagi et al. 1999; 32, Yokoyama et al. 1998; 33, Zimmermann et al. 1999; 34, Zimmermann et al. 2000; 35, Yagi et al. 2001; 36, Makita et al. 2000; 37, Makita et al. 2001; 38, Rand et al. 2000; 39, Lushai et al. 2001; 40, Blum et al. 2001; 41, Monteiro and Pierce 2001; 42, Beltran et al. 2001; 43, Williams 2000; 44, Nylin et al. 2001. Asterisks indicate publications for which sequence was not included in the publication or made available in major databanks (e.g., GenBank) as of 20 January 2002.

laboratories have focused on different ends of this region. The sequence of the full COI + COII gene region has nonetheless been published for some representatives of all families of butterflies and skippers (Caterino et al. 2001), as well as for eight other families of Ditrysia (Sperling et al. 1995, 1996, 1999; Landry et al. 1999; Caterino et al. 2001).

The ND1 + 16s mtDNA gene region has also received a substantial amount of attention in butterflies (see fig. 20.5) and other Lepidoptera (Caterino et al. 2000), although the total length of sequences has usually been less than for COI + COII. This region has most frequently been used by European researchers in recent years. Fewer studies have sequenced parts of ND5, 12s, or cytb. The most notable exception is the ND5 region in papilionids, which has received attention in several Japanese studies (summarized in fig. 20.5). In general, the 12s and 16s rDNA genes are more conserved than protein coding genes in mtDNA, but all studies of mtDNA protein coding or RNA gene variation in Lepidoptera found usable phylogenetic signal at the level of genera and in some cases up to the level of subfamilies.

In contrast, the AT-rich region of mtDNA seems to be informative only within species or between closely related species. Taylor et al. (1993) sequenced the AT-rich region in several related lycaenid species. They found that the region was substantially shorter than in *Drosophila yakuba* and was bracketed by tRNA methionine, suggesting a gene rearrangement relative to Diptera. PCR amplification, followed by restriction site digestion of a fragment from the AT-rich region, was used by Brookes et al. (1997) to generate markers that were distinguished by fragment length differences in a lycaenid species. Brower (1994b, 1996b) also sequenced this region in intraspecific surveys of two nymphalid species and reported extensive indels and short AT repeats.

Unfortunately, few studies have explicitly compared the phylogenetic utility of different mtDNA gene regions, so few clear statements can be made about their relative value. In the absence of rigorous comparisons among gene regions, Caterino et al. (2000) recommend reliance on those regions that have received the most sequencing studies and therefore provide the largest pool of sequences for phylogenetic studies using combined datasets. The mitochondrial COI + COII and 16s gene regions have been the most commonly employed across insects, including Lepidoptera.

Nuclear rRNA

The 18s and 28s ribosomal RNA genes, as well as associated genes and spacers, have received extensive characterization in many organisms. In Lepidoptera, a series of dispersed regions from both the 18s and 28s rRNA genes were sequenced by Martin and Pashley (1992) and by Weller et al. (1994). They found that no section of the 18s gene and only the 28B section of the 28s gene provided enough variation to be worth surveying in butterflies. Even for the 28B section, there were problems with aligning some portions of the sequences, and the butterfly phylogeny that was derived from these sequences had several unreasonable clades (Martin and Pashley 1992). The same taxa were reexamined using additional sequences from the ND1 mitochondrial gene (Weller and Pashley 1995; Weller et al. 1996). Combined analysis of the ND1 and 28B sequences gave a much more reasonable phylogeny for butterfly families, with the shallower nodes being resolved primarily by the ND1 sequences and the 28s sequences contributing to the resolution of the deeper nodes.

More recent sequencing of the 18s and 28s genes has been done using *Papilio troilus* as an exemplar of Lepidoptera, as part of an examination of the phylogenetic relationships of the holometabolous insect orders by Whiting et al. (1997), as well as by Lushai et al. (2001) and Makita et al. (2001).

Sequences have also been obtained for the 18s gene of a number of species of basal lepidopteran clades, and their analysis gave trees that were highly congruent with phylogenies based on morphological data (Wiegmann et al. 2000).

Nuclear Protein Coding Genes

Two nuclear protein coding genes, *EF-1α* and *wingless* (*wg*), have given excellent phylogenetic information at divergence levels beyond the point at which mitochondrial protein coding genes start to suffer from loss of information due to sequence saturation (Cho et al. 1995; Brower and DeSalle 1998). Both genes appear to have only a single locus per genome in Lepidoptera and have either no introns (*EF-1α*) or a long exon region of 450 bp between introns (*wg*).

Originally used to reconstruct relationships within a subfamily of Noctuoidea (Cho et al. 1995; Mitchell et al. 1997), the *EF-1α* gene has now been used to complement mitochondrial COI + II sequences in swallowtails (Reed and Sperling 1999; Caterino et al. 2001). Sequences for the *wg* gene were used by Brower and Egan (1997), Brower (2000b), and Nylin et al. (2001) to complement COI + COII sequences in nymphalids. The nuclear genes were slower-evolving and gave better resolution of relationships among species groups and genera than the COI + COII sequences. However, at the shallowest levels within species groups, these two nuclear genes provided too few nucleotide differences among species to be as useful as mtDNA. At deeper levels, among subfamilies and families, the *EF-1α* sequences were not as informative as at the tribal level, due primarily to exceedingly conservative amino acid sequences (Mitchell et al. 1997; Caterino et al. 2001). Sequences for *wg* were used alone to reconstruct well-supported family- and subfamily-level phylogenies in the Lycaenidae (including riodinids) (Campbell et al. 2000).

Several other single-copy nuclear protein coding genes have been developed. These appear to be very informative at the level of genera and families in Lepidoptera, though none have been applied extensively to butterflies. They include *dopa decarboxylase* (*DDC*) (Fang et al. 1997; Friedlander et al. 1998), *period* (Regier et al. 1998), *glucose-6-phosphate dehydrogenase* (*G6pdh*) (Soto-Adames et al. 1994), and *arylphorin* (Shimada et al. 1995). A somewhat slower-evolving gene that is informative about early subordinal divergences of the Lepidoptera is *phosphoenolpyruvate carboxykinase* (*PEPCK*) (Friedlander et al. 1996). Unfortunately, all of these genes contain several introns, and it is difficult to obtain sequence without using RNA template and reverse transcriptase PCR. Thus there is little potential to obtain these sequences from relatively degraded material such as papered butterflies, as is possible for mtDNA and to some extent also for *EF-1α* and *wg*.

Mitochondrial DNA protein coding genes have numerous advantages that should make them the first priority for any phylogenetic study using DNA sequences in butterflies, at least for shallow divergences and up to the level of subfamilies. The maternal mode of inheritance of mtDNA makes it likely to be a good marker of species boundaries. The mtDNA molecule is also robust enough that it can be amplified from dried material and long enough that kilobases of sequence can easily be obtained. Divergence rates for third-position nucleotides make mtDNA protein coding genes an excellent source of information within species and species groups.

Numerous previously obtained sequences for several mtDNA gene regions also provide a jumping-off point for further systematic study. In particular, COI + COII, ND1 + 16s, and ND5 have a sufficient critical mass of previous work that development of alternative mitochondrial gene regions would be a suboptimal use of resources. Except for COI versus COII (Caterino and Sperling 1999; Reed and Sperling 1999), no detailed comparisons of divergence rates have been published for any combination of mitochondrial genes in butterflies. Nor have comparisons of relative divergences among the full set of COI, COII, ND1, and ND5 been done in any Lepidoptera. However, such comparisons are available for *Drosophila melanogaster* versus *D. yakuba* (Wolstenholme and Clary 1985; Garesse 1998) and for *Anopheles gambiae* versus *A. quadrimaculatus* (Beard et al. 1993). These two intrageneric comparisons show no consistent pattern in the relative magnitude or ranking of nucleotide divergences, nor in the magnitude of amino acid divergences. Thus there is little reason to prefer any one of these protein coding genes for reconstructing divergences among closely related species. For more distant comparisons, amino acid divergence rates vary greatly, with COI being the most conservative, followed by COII, then ND1, and finally ND5 (Simon et al. 1994). However, it remains to be seen at what divergences the faster protein evolution rates of ND1 and ND5 cause saturation relative to COI and COII.

Among nuclear genes, *EF-1α* and *wg* are preferred because of the relative ease of obtaining sequences from suboptimally preserved material, while their information content is similar to that of other nuclear genes. *Wingless* is more difficult to consistently obtain sequences from than *EF-1α*, since only a single pair of "universal" primers is currently available and the usable sequence length is less than 400 bp. In contrast, over 1 kb can consistently be obtained for *EF-1α*, and multiple "universal" primers have been designed for the gene, giving overlapping PCR fragments that will allow design of new internal primers (Cho et al. 1995; Reed and Sperling 1999; Caterino et al. 2001). *EF-1α* and *wg* complement COI and COII well because their slower divergence rates allow them to be informative at deeper, but still overlapping, taxonomic levels relative to the mitochondrial genes. Thus sequencing of these two genes is recommended for phylogenetic surveys of butterflies, in combination with the COI + COII mitochondrial protein coding genes.

SUMMARY

This chapter reviews the kinds of genetic markers that are effective in delineating butterfly species boundaries, as well as the DNA sequence regions that are useful for reconstructing higher-level phylogenies.

Butterfly species are defined as populations that maintain their genomic integrity when they contact each other, even though they may occasionally exchange genes. For geographically isolated populations, species recognition should be given only if genetic divergences between those populations and their closest relatives are equivalent to the average divergences of taxonomically relevant sister species pairs that are in contact with each other.

Information about the kinds of genes that have been exchanged recently between species, as well as genes that are consistently not exchanged when others are, provides valuable insight into the mechanisms that allow populations to maintain their genomic integrity in spite of incomplete reproductive isolation. In butterflies and in Lepidoptera in general, X-linked genes and mtDNA appear to be particularly good indicators of species limits. This phenomenon is related to the Haldane effect, which in Lepidoptera results in selective inviability or sterility of females of hybrid origin. It also suggests that genetic associations between mating traits and ecological traits may play a role in allowing divergence of a limited core of the genome of species in spite of greater gene introgression into the rest of the genome. The *Papilio machaon* and *P. glaucus* species groups provide a variety of illustrations of the utility of mtDNA and X-linked traits as markers of species boundaries.

For reconstructing butterfly species phylogenies using DNA sequence data, it is clear that some sequences are more useful than others. A species phylogeny is defined as the modal, or most frequently represented, gene phylogeny. MtDNA protein coding gene sequences are useful in this context because of their likely informativeness, particularly within species groups but also across a wide range of taxonomic levels. Work on these mtDNA gene regions is also relatively technically tractable. The COI + II gene region is the best candidate for phylogenetic studies since this mtDNA region has been the most widely sequenced within the Lepidoptera. Two nuclear protein coding genes, *EF-1α* and *wingless,* also provide highly informative sequence that is reasonably easy to obtain. These two nuclear genes give sequences that complement mtDNA in higher-level phylogenies. Although many different butterfly gene regions are currently being sequenced by different research groups, it is becoming apparent that one of the best ways to optimize the informativeness of a study is to sequence regions for which there already exists a critical mass of prior sequences.

APPENDIX 20.1: DETERMINING LINKAGE RELATIONSHIPS IN LEPIDOPTERA

In Lepidoptera, unlike most other animals, females are the heterogametic (XY) sex. Lepidopteran sex chromosomes are frequently referred to as W and Z chromosomes to emphasize their lack of homology with X and Y chromosomes (Robinson 1971). However, chromosomes designated as X and Y are clearly not homologous across all lineages either, so for the sake of simplicity the more general XY system of naming is used here.

X-linkage can be relatively easy to demonstrate in Lepidoptera without sophisticated equipment. It is only necessary to rear a single generation of reciprocal hybrid crosses. I have outlined the basic methods for determining sex linkage relationships below, in the hope that this will encourage genetic examination of a wider range of species pairs.

The diploid genome of a butterfly can be symbolized as AAXXmt for males and AAXYmt for females, where A indicates autosomes, X indicates X chromosomes, Y indicates Y chromosomes, and mt indicates mitochondrial DNA. All 30 or so pairs of autosomes are treated here as a single pair. A subscript is used to indicate whether the genes are from parental species 1 or 2. One hybrid cross can then be represented as an $A_1A_1X_1Y_1mt_1$ female mated with an $A_2A_2X_2X_2mt_2$ male. This cross will give hybrid offspring in which females are $A_1A_2X_2Y_1mt_1$ and males are $A_1A_2X_1X_2mt_1$. The reciprocal cross is an $A_2A_2X_2Y_2mt_2$ female mated with an $A_1A_1X_1X_1mt_1$ male. This cross will give hybrid offspring in which females are $A_1A_2X_1Y_2mt_2$ and males are $A_1A_2X_1X_2mt_2$.

Note that in these crosses the hybrid female gets her Y chromosome from her mother and her X chromosome from her father. The hybrid male gets one X from his mother and one X from his father. Hybrids of both sexes get one autosomal chromosome of each diploid pair from their mother and one from their father. Males and females both get their mitochondrial DNA from their mother. The two types of hybrid females have the same combination of autosomes (A_1A_2), but they are different in that one is $X_1Y_2mt_2$ and one is $X_2Y_1mt_1$. The two types of hybrid males have the same combination of both autosomes and X chromosomes ($A_1A_2X_1X_2$) and differ only in their mitochondrial DNA.

From these inheritance patterns, it follows that a trait is X-linked if the two types of hybrid females differ from each other with respect to that trait and resemble their respective fathers, or at least inherit their fathers' genes. In contrast to hybrid females, the two types of hybrid males will resemble each other. An example might be a wing coloration trait that is found in both males and females, for which reciprocal hybrid females have the same wing coloration as their respective fathers (e.g., *Colias eurytheme* wing color: Grula and Taylor 1980a).

It is more difficult to demonstrate X-linkage for traits that are expressed only in females. For example, oviposition preference might be different between reciprocal hybrid females, but it is not possible to assay oviposition preference directly in their fathers (e.g., *Papilio machaon:* Thompson 1988b). In this case, X-linkage can be determined by knowing the oviposition preference of the paternal grandmothers of the hybrid females.

Autosomal inheritance is the most logical explanation for a trait if the two types of hybrid females resemble each other. In this case, hybrid females may have a phenotype intermediate between the parental traits, indicating codominant genes, or they may resemble one of the two parental species, indicating a dominant gene (e.g., *Papilio machaon:* Clarke and Sheppard 1955b).

There are two general kinds of maternally inherited traits. For cytoplasmically inherited traits, both female and male hybrids resemble their respective mothers, or at least have their genes. Mitochondrial DNA is usually a good example of this type of inheritance (Avise 1994). A second kind of maternal inheritance in Lepidoptera is Y-linkage. For such traits, female hybrids resemble their respective mothers, and males do not have the gene (e.g., *Papilio glaucus:* Hagen and Scriber 1989). At a practical level, a specific Y-linked or cytoplasmic DNA probe must be available for Y-linkage to be distinguished from a cytoplasmically inherited trait that is expressed only in females.

ACKNOWLEDGMENTS

I thank J. Burns, M. Caterino, M. Collins, J. Herbeck, D. Rubinoff, W. Watt, and an anonymous reviewer for critical readings of various drafts of this chapter, and E. Zakharov for helping to update the sequence compilation. My work was supported by grants from NSERC Canada and NSF-PEET.

CHAPTER 21

Species Concepts and Sibling Species: The Case of *Leptidea sinapis* and *Leptidea reali*

Jean-François Martin, André Gilles, and Henri Descimon

Species concepts have been the subject of many debates (Ehrlich and Raven 1969; Avise 1994; Mallet 1995). One of the reasons is that species definitions are often linked to, or determined by, a speciation theory and the assumptions of taxonomic approaches. Sibling species (Cuénot 1936) can provide case studies to test species concepts at work. Many studies have established the occurrence of sibling species complexes (Duvernell and Aspinwall 1995; Questiau et al. 1998; Jiggins et al. 1997a), but the implications of such case studies for species concepts have rarely been examined.

In the case of the pierid *Leptidea sinapis* L. (the "wood white"), the discovery of a sibling species came as a surprise and was subject to controversy (Mazel and Leestmans 1996). The ecology and wing morphology of this well-known European species had been studied in many classic works (e.g., Frohawk 1914) and, more recently, by Warren et al. (1986). Under these conditions, the discovery by Réal (1988) that such an apparently homogenous, very common and widespread entity was in fact composed of two largely sympatric specific units elicited some skepticism. After resolving nomenclature constraints, the recently discovered taxon was definitively named *Leptidea reali* Reissinger 1989 (Reissinger 1989; Lorkovic 1994).

L. reali and *L. sinapis* present several characteristics that make their taxonomic resolution difficult. They occur in sympatry in the field, and their wing pattern elements are not sharply diagnostic (Lorkovic 1994). Furthermore, they have overlapping adult phenologies. It was only the observation that there were two slightly distinguishable forms (in the clearness of the wing patterns) emerging with a small lag in time that introduced doubts about the homogeneity of *L. sinapis* and led to the discovery of the second taxon. The two forms were first explained by the coexistence of two kinds of habitat with different ecological characteristics, each holding its own ecotype (Réal 1962). However, a morphological analysis of the genitalic structures revealed two classes of individuals, with *L. reali* showing a long form of the penis and *L. sinapis* with a shorter one (Lorkovic 1994; Mazel and Leestmans 1996). But, since these studies did not address the variability of these genitalic structures, it could not be yet decided whether the observed difference represented intraspecific variability or, conversely, a reliable distinction between two closely related species that are almost identical in more obvious morphological characters.

An approach using a combination of morphological and molecular techniques should allow discrimination of even the best-concealed sibling species (Ayala and Powell 1972; Jermiin et al. 1991; Silberman and Walsh 1992). To determine whether or not there are two different clades in this case, a portion of mitochondrial DNA was sequenced. The presence of gene flow in several population samples was studied using the variability of the male genitalic structures, allozyme markers, and restriction fragment length polymorphism (RFLP) on a portion of amplified mitochondrial DNA (mtDNA). Localities where both forms occur and presumptive allopatric populations were sampled to assess the level of reproductive isolation in a zone of sympatry and to calibrate the different markers. The phylogenetic position of the two taxa within the genus *Leptidea* was assessed independently based on mtDNA sequences.

MATERIALS AND METHODS

BIOLOGY OF *Leptidea sinapis* AND *L. reali*

The two putative taxa *Leptidea sinapis* and *L. reali* are found in similar habitats. Larvae of both taxa feed on species of the family Fabaceae, particularly *Lathyrus pratensis* (L.) (Lorkovic 1994), but *L. sinapis* is also known to feed on *Vicia cracca* (L.) and *Lotus* species (Warren et al. 1986). *L. sinapis* has a very large distribution in the Palearctic region, whereas *L. reali* seems to be more locally present in western Europe. For this study, samples were collected from three localities in the eastern Pyrenees (France), where both taxa occur in sympatry, and from three other localities in the south of France, chosen as being allopatric, based on the preliminary morphological results of Mazel and Leestmans (1996) (table 21.1).

The specimens of the two putative taxonomic entities (PTE) were analyzed using the genitalic structures as sources of morphological characters, the allozymes as nuclear gene characters, RFLPs as mtDNA characters, and mtDNA sequences as a source of quantitative phylogenetic evidence, as detailed below.

Jean-François Martin, André Gilles, and Henri Descimon

Table 21.1 Localities and sizes of the population samples used in the study of genetic relationships between the two putative taxonomic entities

Abbreviation	Sample Size	Locality[a]
Sainte Baume	21	Sainte Baume (SF)
Orgnac	25	Orgnac (SF)
Niave	26	Forêt de Niave (SF)
Nyer	28	Nyer (EP)
Nohèdes	31	Nohèdes (EP)
Coustouges	32	Coustouges (EP)

[a] EP, eastern Pyrenees; SF, south of France.

Table 21.2 Collecting localities of *Leptidea* used in the molecular phylogenetic analysis

Taxon	Genbank Accession Code	Locality
Leptidea amurensis	AF485919	Manchuria
Leptidea lactea	AF485918	China
Leptidea duponcheli	AF485920	Provence (France)
Leptidea sinapis	AF485916	Spain
Leptidea sinapis	AF485917	Provence (France)
Leptidea reali	AF485914	Spain
Leptidea reali	AF485915	Eastern Pyrenees (France)
Leptidea morsei	AF485921	Austria
Dismorphia cubana	AF485913	Cuba

Note: Each taxon is represented by one sample except for *L. sinapis* and *L. reali,* which are represented twice.

Molecular Phylogenetic Analysis of the Genus *Leptidea*

One individual each from six of the seven species of the genus *Leptidea* (table 21.2) was studied (*L. gigantea* occurs in China and we could not obtain usable samples of it). For *L. sinapis* and *L. reali,* we chose individuals from what were considered allopatric sites following the morphological work of Mazel and Leestmans (1996). To root the phylogenetic relationships, we used a butterfly representing another genus of the subfamily Dismorphiinae, *Dismorphia cubana.*

We amplified a mtDNA fragment of 728 bp corresponding to the final portion of the 16s rRNA (*Drosophila yakuba* positions 12756–12885), the entire tRNA-Leu (positions 12691–12755), and the beginning of subunit 1 of NADH dehydrogenase (ND1) (positions 12151–12680). These three genes are contiguous on the mtDNA molecule and are separated by a few nucleotides with uncertain function (Pashley and Ke 1992). They display different levels of variability in mtDNA sequences, since rRNA and tRNA genes evolve at a slower rate than protein coding genes (see Sperling, chap. 20 in this volume). Extraction of total DNA was done by the method of Sambrook et al. (1989) for fresh and dry samples. Polymerase chain reaction (PCR) amplification used Biotaq polymerase (Quantum biotechnologies) with the primers 5′ CTGTTCGATCATTAAAATCTTAC 3′ (forward) (Aubert et al. 1997) and 5′ ATCAAAAGGAGCTCGATTAGTTTC 3′ (reverse) (Aubert et al. 1996).

Cycle parameters were as follows: 1 min at 92°C (1 cycle); 15 s at 92°C, 45 s at 48°C, 2 min 30 s at 62°C (5 cycles); 15 s at 92°C, 45 s at 52°C, 2 min 30 s at 62°C (30 cycles); 7 min at 62°C (1 cycle). Fragment sequencing was then done with an automated sequencer (Genome Express S.A.). Sequences were aligned by eye using the MUST package (Philippe 1993). In the protein coding gene, no gaps were found in the alignment, and the open reading frame was checked with ORF-Finder (1997) using the invertebrate mitochondrial genetic code. The sequences are available on Genbank (see table 21.2) through the Butterfly Net International Web site (www.ent.orst.edu/bnet/).

Molecular systematic analyses were performed using the neighbor-joining algorithm (Saitou and Nei 1987) based on a matrix of pairwise nucleotide differences (percentage of divergence) as implemented in PAUP* 4.0d64 (provided by D. Swofford) and a cladistic approach following the maximum parsimony criterion (branch-and-bound algorithm of PAUP*). Robustness of nodes was assessed by the bootstrap method (Felsenstein 1985) (resampling of 1,000 datasets) in both cases and by the decay index (Bremer 1994) for parsimony analysis.

RELATIONSHIPS BETWEEN *L. sinapis* AND *L. reali*

RFLP Analysis

As a preliminary step, five individuals of each PTE were sequenced for the same mtDNA block used in the phylogenetic work to search for a reliable diagnostic site between the two PTE and to avoid randomly variable sites that could introduce a homoplasic signal. A restriction map was drawn using DNA-Strider (Marck 1990). Visualization of the patterns obtained by digestion with the restriction enzyme chosen was done on a vertical polyacrylamide gel (6%) after electrophoresis under 60 V for about 2 hours to test the repeatability of the two haplotypes found. The use of such genetic markers allows us to assess whether the mitochondrial haplotypes are correlated with allozyme and morphological marker variation within the dataset.

Morphology

Only the male genitalia were studied, since too few females were available. Four traits were measured: saccus, penis, and uncus lengths and valvae

Jean-François Martin, André Gilles, and Henri Descimon

width. The genitalia were isolated after softening of the tissues in 0.1 M NaOH, then stored in a solution composed of water, alcohol, and glycerol [20:75:5]. The statistical analysis was performed using the computer package Statistica 5.0 (Statsoft 1997).

Allozymes

Our aim was, first, to discover whether diagnostic loci for the two PTE exist. Further, these markers were used to estimate the genetic relationships between and within the PTE. A total of sixteen enzyme loci were studied. Proteins were extracted from the thorax and the anterior part of the abdomen of each individual by the method of Wynne et al. (1992), then stored at $-80°$C. Enzyme electrophoresis was conducted according to Richardson et al. (1986) on "Helena" cellulose acetate plates. Genetic relationships and population structures were assessed using Genepop 3.1 (Raymond and Rousset 1995), Biosys 1.0 (Swofford and Selander 1981), and Phylip 3.57c (Felsenstein 1993) computer packages.

RESULTS

MOLECULAR PHYLOGENY OF THE GENUS *Leptidea*

The mtDNA of butterflies displays a major base composition bias in favor of A–T pairs (Pashley and Ke 1992). The present study corroborates this finding, with about 80% A–T in the ND1, 16s rDNA, and tRNA sequences. In the ND1 gene, the bias differs according to codon position. The variation is proportional to the constraints applied to each of the three positions, the third position being the least constrained and showing an A–T composition of more than 90%. Although this A–T-rich composition favors A–T transversions, a comparison of distance matrices based on transitions and transversions respectively yields no major sign of saturation within the genus. Therefore, all substitutions were used to assess the phylogenetic relationships within the genus. The aligned sequences display 174 variable sites, 56 of which are parsimony-informative.

Parsimony analysis using the total evidence approach (Kluge 1989) (simultaneous analysis of RNA and coding genes) yields two equally parsimonious trees 256 steps long with a consistency index (CI) (Farris 1969) of 0.867 and a retention index (RI) (Farris 1989) of 0.605. The skewness of tree lengths (Hillis 1991; Huelsenbeck 1991) $g_1 = -0.967$ indicates a strong phylogenetic signal in the dataset.

The strict consensus of the two trees leads to a topology similar to the one obtained by bootstrap analysis. The cladistic (fig. 21.1A) and the phenetic

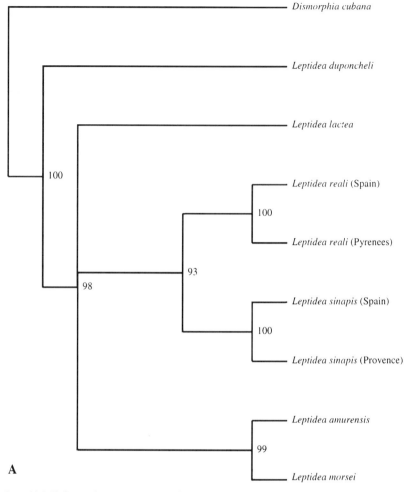

A

Figure 21.1 Phylogenetic reconstruction of the genus *Leptidea* using both (A) neighbor-joining and (B) maximum parsimony approaches yields identical tree topologies. In the parsimony analysis, values above the branches correspond to average step numbers in the bootstrap method; values below the branches are decay indices. In both trees, values on the nodes are bootstrap proportions (1,000 replicates).

(fig. 21.1B) approaches yield identical tree topologies. *L. lactea* takes an unresolved position as sister species to the (*L. amurensis, L. morsei*) cluster or the (*L. sinapis, L. reali*) one. The sequences of the two putative *L. sinapis* and *L. reali* representatives display 3% divergence, corresponding to 18 steps in the most parsimonious tree. These last results demonstrate that *L. sinapis* and *L. reali* are two distinct clades, represented, respectively, by haplotypes "A" and "B." They are two distinct genetic entities with differences not ascribable to homoplasy.

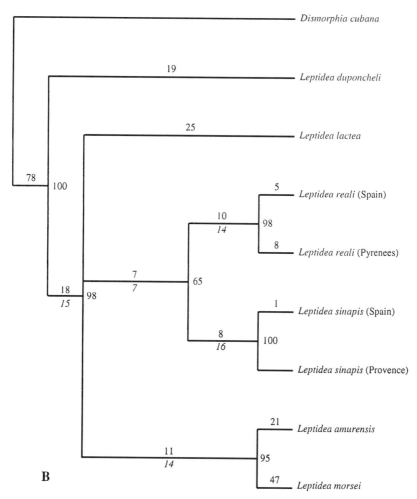

The following tree contains the labels and values:

- Dismorphia cubana
- 19 — Leptidea duponcheli
- 25 — Leptidea lactea
- 78 / 100
- 5 — Leptidea reali (Spain)
- 10 / 14 — 98
- 8 — Leptidea reali (Pyrenees)
- 7 / 7 — 65
- 18 / 15 — 98
- 1 — Leptidea sinapis (Spain)
- 8 / 16 — 100
- Leptidea sinapis (Provence)
- 21 — Leptidea amurensis
- 11 / 14 — 95
- 47 — Leptidea morsei

B

Figure 21.1 (continued)

RELATIONSHIPS BETWEEN *L. sinapis* AND *L. reali*

RFLP Study

The two haplotypes, A (*L. sinapis*) and B (*L. reali*), found in the systematic analysis of the genus *Leptidea* differ by a restriction site for the ssp1 endonuclease, which cuts DNA stretches with a pattern of AATATT, allowing a quick RFLP-based test for the distribution of these haplotypes among the sampled populations.

The results of this experiment show that haplotype B (*L. reali*) is absent from the Orgnac and Sainte Baume population samples, but is present in the other ones: Niave, Nyer, Nohèdes, and Coustouges (only two individuals at the Niave locality). Haplotype A (*L. sinapis*) is present in all six sampled populations, indicating a widespread distribution. The two haplotypes are found together in the eastern Pyrenees and determine two taxa (PTE A and PTE B).

Morphological Analysis

Is there a correlation between the assignment of each individual to a PTE and the morphological variables? To answer this question, we looked for statistically significant differences in the recorded morphological variables between individuals of each PTE.

Although this problem is one of the most classic of morphometry and systematics, the use of continuously variable traits still remains difficult. Unlike the molecular data, which provide Boolean answers, overlapping distributions in quantitative characters often give ambiguous replies. This point is especially important in the present case, since the first clue to the existence of two entities was genitalic morphology.

The variables measured did not conform to a normal distribution (chi-square test, $p < 0.05$); therefore, nonparametric testing was adopted. The gamma test of independence (preferable to the classic "r of Pearson" in case of equal ranks) between the variables reveals a correlation of 0.69 between the variables "saccus" and "penis," which is not surprising in such a morphological complex. Consequently, the results inferred from these variables are redundant and must not be independently interpreted.

The distribution of each variable within the dataset was first studied, with each individual assigned by the previous molecular data to one of the PTE. Molecular and morphological criteria indeed appeared to be in good coincidence for the variables "saccus" and "penis" (fig. 21.2) (bimodal distribution), but the variables "valvae" and "uncus" yielded no significant results. Consequently, only the former two variables were retained in subsequent analyses.

What is needed at this step of the analysis is to know whether the observed morphological differences between the individuals of PTE A and PTE B are significant or not. The two genitalic markers were measured in two geographically distant populations where only PTE A occurs (Orgnac and Sainte Baume) in order to calibrate the inferred variation within PTE A for variables "saccus" and "penis" and to assess the position of each individual inside or outside this range of variation. For this purpose, we adapted the allele discriminant value (ADV) method of Bert and Arnold (1995) to the quantitative traits under study. An index value was assigned to each individual, combining measurements of the variables "saccus" and "penis." The index was calculated as follows:

$$\sum_{i=1}^{n} (f_i A - f_i B)/n,$$

where n is the number of characters (two in this case), $f_i A$ is the mean frequency of the ith character in the calibration dataset of PTE A; and $f_i B$,

Jean-François Martin, André Gilles, and Henri Descimon

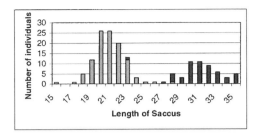
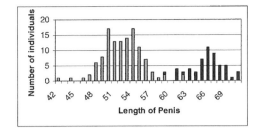
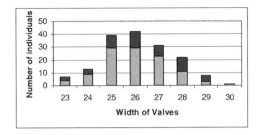
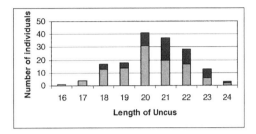

P.T.E. A   P.T.E. B

Figure 21.2 Distributions of the four genitalic variables used in the morphological study. PTE A individuals have the smallest values for the variables "saccus" and "penis," whereas the graphs show a shuffled distribution for the variables "valves" and "uncus," indicating that the latter variables are not discriminant between the two PTE.

in our case, is equal to zero if the value is in the PTE A range and equal to 1 in other cases, due to our inability to find isolated PTE B populations.

This procedure allows us to define three categories of individuals:

1. Individuals for which both values are compatible with the PTE A defined range. These individuals were all assigned to PTE A using molecular analysis.
2. Individuals with both values excluded from the PTE A range. These individuals were all assigned to PTE B by molecular analysis.
3. Six "intermediate" individuals, with only one of the two variables compatible with the PTE A range. Among these six individuals, four had been assigned to PTE A and two to PTE B (by RFLP criterion).

According to this analysis, the two morphological groups display some over-lap, with six individuals of ambiguous assignment.

In conclusion, the variation of the "saccus" and "penis" variables is strongly coincident with the molecular marker assignments, with fewer than 5% of the individuals (six) difficult to sort using genitalic morphology. The joint use of molecular and morphological approaches provides strong evidence that the two PTE are distinct genetic entities.

It was tempting to try to develop discriminant wing pattern features using the same approach. But, as Lorkovic (1994) had already noted, intraspecific variation overwhelms interspecific differences to such an extent that even the sharpest "systematist eye" is powerless when facing this problem. Such a situation is rare in butterfly systematics.

Allozyme Data

The question we wanted to address with the allozyme study is whether a concordance between nuclear markers (allozymes) and the two mitochondrial haplotypes exists. We found that the MDHb locus has two alleles, A and B, that are completely correlated with the mtDNA haplotypes: all the individuals with the mitochondrial haplotype A show an A allele for MDHb, whereas all the haplotype B individuals have a B allele for MDHb. Furthermore, no heterozygote was found. Such an allozyme system has all the features of a diagnostic marker for two distinct lineages.

The allozyme study thus shows the concordance of mitochondrial (RFLP) and nuclear (MDHb) markers for assignment of individuals to a particular lineage. These results confirm the identification of two distinct genetic entities using both mitochondrial and nuclear criteria.

The conjunction of mtDNA, morphology, and allozyme results allows us to conclude that the specific rank of each genetic entity is no longer in doubt. In this context, PTE A may be associated with *L. sinapis*, usually considered a widespread taxon with the smallest "saccus" and "penis" lengths (Lorkovic 1994; Mazel and Leestmans 1996), whereas PTE B is associated with *L. reali.*

ALLOZYME COMPARISON OF THE TWO SPECIES

Since the existence of two species is no longer in doubt, we have to separate the populations from sympatric localities (Nohèdes, Nyer, and Coustouges) into distinct populations for each species. For the Niave locality, only the *L. sinapis* population was studied, since only two *L. reali* individuals were present in the sample.

On the sixteen loci scored, eleven were polymorphic in samples of each of the two species (table 21.3). The percentage of polymorphic loci is greater in the *L. sinapis* allopatric populations (in the south of France) than in sympatric ones (Pyrenees), except for the Nyer locality, where polymorphism is high (37.5%). Polymorphism is low in the *L. reali* samples from all three eastern Pyrenees localities.

A pairwise test of genotypic differentiation (as implemented in Genepop v3.1) clearly discriminates the *L. sinapis* populations from the *L. reali* ones for the MDHb locus, as expected. This locus is diagnostic for the

Table 21.3 Measures of genetic variability calculated for the nine populations

Population	Mean Sample Size per Locus	Mean No. of Alleles per Locus	Percentage of Loci Polymorphic[a]	Mean Heterozygosity	
				Direct Count	Hardy-Weinberg Expected[b]
Orgnac (*L. sinapis*)	29.0 (0.0)	1.6 (0.3)	25.0	0.075 (0.05)	0.126 (0.06)
Sainte Baume (*L. sinapis*)	30.0 (0.0)	1.9 (0.4)	25.0	0.075 (0.04)	0.138 (0.06)
Niave (*L. sinapis*)	27.0 (0.0)	1.6 (0.3)	25.0	0.088 (0.05)	0.143 (0.06)
Nohèdes (*L. sinapis*)	17.0 (0.0)	1.4 (0.2)	18.8	0.070 (0.03)	0.097 (0.05)
Nyer (*L. sinapis*)	10.0 (0.0)	1.8 (0.3)	37.5	0.075 (0.04)	0.166 (0.06)
Coustouges (*L. sinapis*)	16.0 (0.0)	1.5 (0.3)	18.8	0.059 (0.03)	0.113 (0.06)
Nohèdes (*L. reali*)	14.0 (0.0)	1.3 (0.2)	12.5	0.036 (0.03)	0.052 (0.04)
Nyer (*L. reali*)	21.0 (0.0)	1.5 (0.3)	12.5	0.045 (0.04)	0.074 (0.04)
Coustouges (*L. reali*)	28.0 (0.0)	1.6 (0.3)	18.8	0.045 (0.04)	0.066 (0.04)

Note: Each of the three sympatric localities is separated into two distinct populations according to the ADV and RFLP-MDHb results. Standard errors are in parentheses.

[a] A locus is considered polymorphic if more than one allele was detected.

[b] Unbiased estimate (Nei 1978).

two species. Moreover, the AK locus allows us to differentiate the two species: it is fixed on the allele B in the *L. reali* populations and polymorphic (alleles A and B) in the *L. sinapis* populations (see data at www.press.uchicago.edu/books/boggs/). The PGI locus is highly polymorphic (see data at www.press.uchicago.edu/books/boggs/). Two alleles, B and D, were present only in the *L. sinapis* populations of Sainte Baume and Orgnac. The allele C was more frequent in *L. reali* samples, being fixed in the population of Nohèdes and prevalent in the populations of Nyer and Coustouges, with frequencies of 0.952 and 0.929, respectively.

Finally, populations' genetic relationships based on allozyme frequencies were assessed using a maximum likelihood method as implemented in the Phylip package (Felsenstein 1993). The bootstrap technique was used to test the robustness of nodes. The resulting tree (fig. 21.3) displayed robust separation of the two PTE (bootstrap proportion = 93) with an estimated variance (represented by the branch length) linking the two species equal to 0.081.

Multiple comparisons of F_{st} values for all samples showed low differentiation within both species in the eastern Pyrenees (all F_{st} values < 0.10),

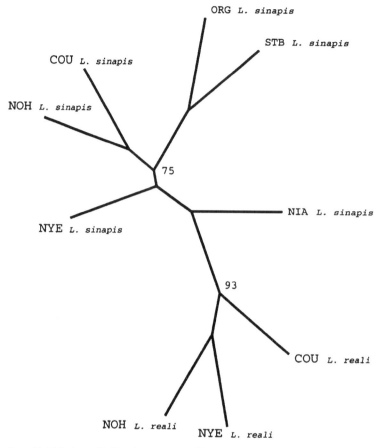

ORG *L. sinapis*

STB *L. sinapis*

COU *L. sinapis*

NOH *L. sinapis*

75

NYE *L. sinapis*

NIA *L. sinapis*

93

COU *L. reali*

NOH *L. reali*

NYE *L. reali*

Figure 21.3 Maximum likelihood tree computed from allele frequencies for the nine population samples (sympatric localities are separated into two populations according to the ADV and RFLP-MDHb results). Bootstrap values are given at each node (100 replicates).

but significant differentiation (with $\alpha = 0.05$) between Pyrenean and Orgnac or Sainte Baume populations of *L. sinapis*. A genotypic disequilibrium test (implemented in Genepop v3.1) showed no significant linkage (with $\alpha = 0.05$) in the genotypic compositions of any the population samples, except for the pair AK-PGI, which was linked with $P = 0.016$ in *L. sinapis* at Coustouges.

DISCUSSION

The results of the present study are surprisingly clear: a pair of "almost perfect" sibling species, which escaped systematists' notice until the advent of molecular genetics, is composed of two "good" species, fully distinct by multiple genetic criteria. This discovery offers a good opportunity to test the value of some concepts as practical tools. Here we successively consider the species concepts and definitions set forth by various schools of biological

Jean-François Martin, André Gilles, and Henri Descimon

thought and their usefulness in practical work, the significance of "barriers" to gene flow, especially under the form of the lock-and-key hypothesis, and finally the usefulness of biogeographic and speciation scenarios in understanding the genetic and systematic relations between extant taxa.

How applicable Are Alternative Species Concepts to *Leptidea?*

The role of species concepts is double: on the one hand, they are cornerstones in the general theory of evolution; on the other hand, they are supposed to provide tools to study particular cases under scrutiny and to locate them relative to this general theory. The implications of a conceptual definition of species may be strong, because one will recognize speciation events or relationships between a pair of taxa differently according to the species definition accepted as a basic hypothesis. Further, Mallet (1995, 1996a) has argued that, for better resolution of the problems of practical systematics, operational procedures are needed, rather than concepts laden with essentialist connotations.

In the last few decades, the most often adopted species definition has been the biological species concept (BSC) (Dobzhansky 1937; Mayr 1942), associated with the "modern synthesis" view of evolution. This concept defines a species as "a reproductive community, separated from other such communities by isolating mechanisms." The BSC definition is well suited for sibling species to which the morphological species concept (in which a species is defined by its phenotype rather than by its genetic complement and potential for interbreeding) is not applicable. Considerable debate has taken place about the importance of the two notions of "reproductive community" and "isolating mechanisms" (Masters and Spencer 1989). Two distinct schools focus on the "recognition" concept (RC) and the "isolation" concept (IC), respectively. According to the former, a species is primarily defined as a community of organisms that share a specific mate recognition system (Paterson 1985). For the latter, a species is above all a group of organisms isolated from other analogous groups (Dobzhansky 1970). Pheneticists and cladists (Ehrlich 1961a; Sokal 1973; Donoghue 1985; Cracraft 1989) have criticized the theoretical validity and practical utility of the BSC. Further, the application of the BSC to some groups is problematic because hybridization occurs and results in some amount of gene exchange (McCourt and Hoshaw 1990). Furthermore, breeding experiments, on which the BSC depends, may be inconclusive, interbreeding in nature being heavily influenced by variable environmental factors.

Many current studies using molecular data for phylogenetic reconstruction support the phylogenetic species concept (PSC), which defines a species as a basal group of organisms all of whose genes show more recent coalescence with one another than with those of any organisms outside that group (Baum and Donoghue 1995). This definition avoids the problem of assessing reproductive isolation, but raises an important question about the distinction between trait history (the gene tree) and organism history (the species tree), since the two can differ in various ways due to lineage sorting or reticulate evolution. This concept is of no help as a guide to discriminating ranks of taxa, and indeed, its adherents often deny the value of the rank concept in systematics. By analogy with already studied and related groups, a threshold value for genetic distances could be contrived. In recent times, however, some workers have offered a synthetic view of species concepts, reconciling cladist and classic views on species through a "general lineage concept" (de Queiroz 1998). The merit of this approach is that it defines a zone of uncertainty during the process of speciation in which various criteria can give conflicting indications.

Much of the initial recognition of "operational taxonomic units" or "putative taxa" is still done by relatively typological, or other pre-BSC, taxonomic practices, using, for instance, a combination of morphological and eco-ethological criteria (Cuénot 1936). In practice, this approach is often used as a precursor to use of either the BSC or the PSC, particularly in the Lepidoptera (Guillaumin and Descimon 1976). However, the reference to ecological criteria based on Gause's principle (1934)—which states that different species occupy different ecological niches—is often neglected at present in favor of genetic criteria (but see Schluter 2000). The genealogical concordance principle of Avise and Ball (1990) proceeds from a logic similar to that of Cuénot: the recognition of differences in each of several independent genetic traits is necessary to establish the separation of two species; this idea is also developed by Futuyma (1986, p. 112). The concepts of "genotype clusters" (Mallet 1995) and cytonuclear disequilibrium (Asmussen et al. 1989) follow the same path. Carson's (1975) more theoretical definition of a species as "a field for gene recombination" implicitly involves reticulate inheritance and obviously proceeds from the same logic.

The two *Leptidea* species studied here give a clear illustration of the efficiency of some of the previous principles and of the joint use of molecular and morphological criteria. Molecular analysis of the genus *Leptidea* led to the discovery of two distinct mitochondrial haplotypes corresponding to the two suspected taxa. This mtDNA evidence was sufficient to assign individuals to two distinct genetic entities of species rank, according to the PSC definition for a pair of closely related species. Since female butterflies are heterogametic, and mtDNA is inherited maternally, Haldane's rule (cf. Sperling 1993) means that mtDNA phylogeny is maximally likely to correspond to actual species phylogeny. As we pointed out, this species concept avoids the question of gene flow between two sister taxa.

Moreover, a full coincidence of species-diagnostic molecular markers, both RFLPs and allozymes, was observed for all the individuals studied.

Among 163 individuals, from both sympatric populations (eastern Pyrenees) and those of *sinapis* alone, no heterozygote at the MDHb locus was found. It is unlikely that intraspecific selective pressure against heterozygotes could explain this structure, as both entities would have shown the same geographic structure of haplotypes, which they did not. Cytonuclear disequilibrium (Asmussen et al. 1989) equal to 1 indicates a total absence of nuclear or mitochondrial genetic shuffling between the two species. Furthermore, one of the alleles of AK is specific to *L. sinapis*. This allele was present in samples from all *L. sinapis* populations, whether they are found alone or are sympatric with *L. reali*. This case study is "perfect" in the BSC context because no sign of interspecific gene flow is found in any of the data. Other studies of sibling species in insects have found some evidence of hybridization (e.g., Battisti et al. 1998), but even then, the level of gene flow was very low. The recognition of *L. reali* as a fully valid species is therefore confirmed. Although genitalic dissection is generally sufficient for identification, the existence of a few individuals whose genitalic morphology contradicts molecular genetic criteria means that it should not be used as the sole diagnostic marker.

The genetic distance (Nei's $D = 0.08$) recorded between the two taxa is compatible with sibling species pairs (Battisti et al. 1998). The divergence between mtDNA sequences is also within the range observed for fully distinct species in various families of butterflies (Aubert et al. 1997; Martin et al. 2000).

The Lock-and-Key Hypothesis and "Barriers" to Gene Flow

The morphological variation study is consistent with the molecular analyses, recognizing two separate, if slightly overlapping, distributions of values for two potentially coadaptive genitalic characters ("saccus" in females and "penis" in males). Often, differences in genitalia between two PTE are considered evidence of reproductive isolation between them because they could imply an impossibility of cross-fertilization through mechanical incompatibility. This "lock and key hypothesis" has been vigorously debated recently (Porter and Shapiro 1990; Sota and Kubota 1998). In the present case, the differences between the two PTE could lead to mechanical incompatibility and thus constitute a prezygotic barrier, but the small morphological overlap between the two taxa could allow for hybridization. However, even if the morphological differences play an active role as prezygotic barriers, it is more likely that they do not act alone. Differences in pheromones or behavior probably constitute other such barriers; the latter are known to be extremely differentiated and precise in *Leptidea* (Wiklund 1977b).

The few morphologically ambiguous individuals could be an indication of a recent speciation event that led to the two distinct genetic entities with undiscernible wing pattern morphology. It could also be interpreted as a failure to diverge, or as an adaptive convergence of the wing pattern features due to common ecological conditions. However, the great congruence among the genetic markers is unlikely to be due to common selection pressures in all cases.

BIOGEOGRAPHY AND THE POSSIBLE HISTORY OF SPECIATION

The lower level of heterozygosity in the *L. reali* populations than in *L. sinapis* leads to thoughts about a later emergence of this taxon, a foundation zone, or a bottleneck effect. In the last case, the biogeographic hypothesis of geographic isolation between two gene pools in a common ancestor of the two taxa may be explored. This scenario implies an allopatric speciation process associated with glacial events.

In recent times, the history of the Palearctic region has been dominated by periods of glaciation, which caused the majority of temperate biota to be crowded into "refuges" located at the southernmost tips of Europe and the Middle East (De Lattin 1967). These events may have led to genetic differentiation and possibly allopatric speciation in numerous groups. The distribution patterns of *L. sinapis* and *L. reali* suggest such a scenario. This hypothesis supposes a recolonization of *L. sinapis* from the eastern Mediterranean region (the Ponto-Mediterranean refuge: de Lattin 1967), as for many other Euro-Siberian butterfly species. *L. reali* probably recolonized from southern Spain (the Atlanto-Mediterranean refuge: de Lattin 1967) and may have been subjected to a more restricted ecological niche. However, only more information about the genetic differentiation within and between the populations of both *Leptidea* across Europe and their precise distribution patterns will allow us to determine their historical biogeography.

Orr and Orr (1996) showed that speciation occurs just as quickly in a species that splits into a few large populations as in one that splits into many small populations. Indeed, when divergence is driven by natural selection, speciation occurs most rapidly when a species is split into two large populations. So, even if both species did not pass through a bottleneck, divergence time is still sufficient for them to have acquired sufficient genetic incompatibilities.

This case study is problematic when we consider Gause's principle: when two closely related species are sympatric, they should be associated with two different ecological niches (with at least quantitative differences). No such niche separation is yet known for these species, which appear to share the same food plants, flight places, behavior, overlapping flight periods, and so forth, but the apparent problem may be simply due to the difficulty of conducting precise field studies in the absence of reliable wing pattern identification criteria (Mazel 1996).

Jean-François Martin, André Gilles, and Henri Descimon

CONCLUSIONS

Sibling species represent particularly interesting case studies for situations in which little or no external morphological difference does not imply little or no genetic differentiation. The *L. sinapis–L. reali* pair displays no less divergence than other butterfly species pairs. This finding indicates that morphological and molecular evolution can be uncoupled in nature, leading to a reassessment of species concepts based on phenotypic relationships in the absence of morphological and/or ecological differentiation, which have led a number of authors to find only one species. The present case study clearly shows that the BSC still works, and even that molecular criteria assist its use, providing both robust identification criteria and information about the level of genetic isolation between taxonomic units.

Practical systematists must navigate between the Charybdis of confusing two or more actually separate species in a single one and the Scylla of spuriously splitting a cohesive gene pool. The first error is relieved by criteria from the "isolation" concept, while the second may be avoided mainly by using arguments derived from the "recognition" concept. There is some parallelism between the genesis of species in nature and, in the systematist's mind, the recognition of two separate species within a previously single unit. At first, the two "recognized" PTE may be considered subspecies, ecotypes, or pleiotropic single-gene variants (for instance). Their status as distinct species may be confirmed if the isolation of their gene pools is established by marker studies. Actually, problems arise not when "recognition" by systematists is difficult, as in the case of sibling species such as the two *Leptidea* under study, but when the isolation of gene pools is dubious. This is especially the case in "hybrid zones" (Barton and Hewitt 1989); while evolutionary biologists enjoy the opportunity to study speciation in progress, systematists deal with the impossible task of defining as specific or intraspecific genetic entities that are neither. For a while, the definition of intermediate categories such as semispecies (Mayr 1940) appeared to provide a solution for those cases in which speciation processes are at work and species criteria are conflicting. In the present case, the two *Leptidea* studied are not semispecies, but rather tricky "good" species that deceived European butterfly systematists for almost a century.

Clearly, Mallet (1995, 1996a) is right in arguing that what is needed by working systematists and evolutionists is not an abstract definition of species, but a practical tool for defining and recognizing species. Species concepts, in this view, are most useful as bridges between theory and practice in understanding the genesis and maintenance of distinct species. In this context, insistence on a conflict between recognition and isolation concepts seems pointless. It seems best to come back to the original views of

Dobzhansky (1937) and Mayr (1942): species are both cohesive inside and separated outside.

SUMMARY

The very common and widespread Palearctic pierid *Leptidea sinapis* L. has been recently recognized as encompassing two entities, *L. sinapis s. str.* and *L. reali* Reiss. They are characterized by some details of male and female genitalic morphology; *"reali"* is less widespread than *"sinapis."* *L. reali* has always been found sympatrically with *L. sinapis*. The absence of clear differences between these entities in wing patterns, adult behavior, larval food plants, and habitat choices raised doubts about their specific status. A study using molecular markers (a 728 bp fragment of mitochondrial DNA and sixteen enzyme loci) was conducted on six populations from southern France. Two entities are discriminated by consistent differences in the mtDNA sequences, by the existence of diagnostic alleles at a MDH locus, and by a perfect concordance between the two types of markers. Morphometry of genitalic features yielded data coinciding fairly closely with the molecular data, although there is a slight overlap in some of the lengths. Both taxa can thus be assigned a species rank, in spite of the absence of qualitative detectable ecological differences between them, challenging Gause's principle of the uniqueness of ecological niche. A phylogenetic analysis of members of the genus *Leptidea* and the Pieridae using sequences of a mtDNA fragment showed that these two *Leptidea* taxa correspond to a pair of sister species. Enzyme loci displayed significant genetic differentiation between the two species. Both species also are geographically differentiated, but *L. reali* is less variable within and among populations.

This pair of sibling species is an interesting case study for testing the usefulness of species concepts. For the pair *L. sinapis–L. reali,* species concepts do clarify the biological evidence, with Avise's concordance principle and Mallet's genotypic clusters serving as the most practical explanatory definitions. Finally, the significance of the "lock-and-key" hypothesis is doubtful, since a small proportion of individuals, clearly assigned to one species by molecular criteria, present genitalic features compatible with the other one.

ACKNOWLEDGMENTS

We are grateful to W. B. Watt, J. Mallet, and R. Mazel for major improvements in earlier versions of this manuscript, and to E. Meyer, E. Carson, S. Bertram, and S. Walsh for careful reading and helpful discussions. We also thank D. Swofford, who provided test versions of PAUP*.

CHAPTER 22

Evidence and Identity in Butterfly Systematics

Richard I. Vane-Wright

Butterfly systematics entered the modern era just over four decades ago, with publication of Paul Ehrlich's (1958) work on comparative morphology and higher classification. Ehrlich was, in those far-off days, an emergent and unabashed pheneticist. Based on Ehrlich and Ehrlich (1967) and his comments at Crested Butte in 1998, it is evident that he is now an abashed but unrepentant pheneticist. As I am an abashed but unrepentant cladist, it may be asked why I consider Ehrlich's 1958 contribution to be the benchmark. I have two major reasons: for its introduction of so many new or little-known character systems, and for its strictly and fully comparative organization. The "cladistic revolution," involving the widespread adoption and development of Willi Hennig's earlier ideas (e.g., Hennig 1950), occurred during the following two decades (e.g., Hennig 1965; Brundin 1966; Nelson 1971, 1979; Patterson and Rosen 1977; Platnick 1979; Wiley 1981), and progressed, methodologically, through the adoption of two operational principles: use of character matrices, and use of algorithms for computing special resemblance (homologies in the sense of Patterson, e.g., 1980). The latter principle was necessarily introduced by a cladist (Farris 1970), but the former was already well in place, thanks to the numerical taxonomists (e.g., Sokal and Sneath 1963).

Another reason to celebrate Ehrlich's 1958 paper is the fact that, even though he was about to help create the ideas of phenetics, his section on "phylogeny" (Ehrlich 1958, p. 326–330) revolved around a discussion of the necessity "to determine the primitive state of butterfly characters by inference from their states in various groups considered to be related to the butterflies." The influence of lepidopterist and proto-cladist W. T. M. Forbes at the Museum of Comparative Zoology at Harvard may have been responsible for this; Ehrlich thanks Forbes warmly for "a lengthy and constructive correspondence over many aspects of the work." Thus, using a more or less explicit outgroup method, Ehrlich recognized 64 "primitive and specialized characters in the Papilionoidea" (Ehrlich 1958, table 1). Moreover, it is quite clear that the young Ehrlich was in no doubt about the fundamental importance of homology for phylogenetic analysis (Ehrlich 1958, p. 307–308). One is left to wonder what might have happened had he worked in Stuttgart rather than Kansas! What is clear is that, without the wealth of empirical data and methodical presentation that epitomizes Ehrlich's 1958 work, the first definitive application of cladistic principles to butterfly higher classification (Kristensen 1976) would scarcely have been possible.

The present overview is based on two recent reviews with which I have been involved as a co-author (de Jong et al. 1996a; Ackery et al. 1999). These, in turn, rest on a huge body of butterfly literature, some documented therein, but little of which is referred to directly here. In addition, I have taken into account some more recent work, including certain advances reported at Crested Butte in 1998, and since.

BUTTERFLY HIGHER CLASSIFICATION: THE CURRENT STATE

DOUBT AND CERTAINTY

The first thing that must be acknowledged about the present state of butterfly higher classification, in cladistic terms at least, is the incredible variation in the quality of our understanding of different taxa and taxonomic levels. This understanding ranges from near certainty to almost complete uncertainty. According to de Jong et al. (1996a), Ackery et al. (1999), and Kristensen and Skalski (1999), major doubts include the following:

* Relationship of butterflies to other higher Lepidoptera (Obtectomera and Macrolepidoptera)
* Inclusion of Hedyloidea with butterflies (see Weller and Pashley 1995)
* Monophyly of true butterflies (Papilionoidea) + skippers (Hesperioidea)
* Naturalness of many current subfamily divisions
* Monophyly of the (Pieridae + Papilionidae), versus monophyly of the (Pieridae + Lycaenidae + Nymphalidae) to the exclusion of the Papilionidae

To give an idea of the type of problem involved, just consider the last of these examples. Among the features suggesting that the Pieridae form a group with the (Lycaenidae *s.l.* + Nymphalidae) are the following: absence of a foretibial epiphysis, absence of a prospinasterno-procoxal muscle, and a secondary sclerite behind the metascutellum (Brock 1971). In contrast, three characters suggest that the Pieridae form a group with the Papilionidae: a unique type of proboscis extensor muscle system (Schmitt 1938), an upright pupa with a girdle passing over a thickened abdominal groove, and an unusual quadrifid forewing cubitus. Among the first set of three characters, two are absences, two are not widely confirmed, and at least one is uncertain in other ways. In the second set, all appear to be positive features, and only one is not widely confirmed. Thus we might be tempted to conclude in favor of the second, more traditional view (e.g., Kirby [1871] placed whites, sulfurs, swallowtails, and parnassians all in one family, the Papilionidae). However, the proboscis extensors have been looked at in few species, it is not certain that the pupal girdle and abdominal thickening are homologous in the two groups (and even if they are, this may be symplesiomorphy), and the quadrifid forewing cubitus is found in only one subfamily of pierids, and could be homoplasious. In Kristensen's (1976) phylogenetic analysis, in the cladistic analysis of morphological characters by de Jong et al. (1996a), and in the combined morphological plus molecular analysis of Weller et al. (1996), total evidence was more in favor of the pierids as sister group to the "four-footed" butterflies (Lycaenidae *s.l.* + Nymphalidae) than to the Papilionidae. Ackery et al. (1999) could only conclude, lamely but reasonably, that "the position of the Pieridae needs more attention."

Near-certainties include the monophyly of the two superfamilies (Papilionoidea and Hesperioidea), and of each of the five major families accepted by Ehrlich: Hesperiidae, Papilionidae, Pieridae, Lycaenidae *s.l.* (including Riodinidae) and Nymphalidae *s.l.* (including libytheines). Recent work by Campbell (Campbell and Pierce, chap. 18 in this volume; Campbell et al. 2000) and others (e.g., Weller et al. 1996) suggests that the vexed question of the riodinids and lycaenids will resolve with the two groups recognized as monophyletic sister taxa (see below). In the following sections I discuss the major family groups in turn, together with various problems affecting their subdivision and current understanding of their mutual relationships.

HESPERIIDAE

As a group, the skippers (about 3,500 species) are abundantly distinct from all other Lepidoptera. Striking synapomorphies include wide basal separation of the antennae (twice width of scape or more), conspicuous marginal eye ring of reduced ommatidial facets, wide and roughly Y-shaped third axillary sclerite of the forewing base, main hindwing discal cell with short additional cell just anterior to base formed by the radial and subcostal veins, mesoscutellum extended over metanotum (a somewhat similar condition occurs in libytheids), and a distinctive patch of specialized scales, found in both sexes, located near or over the base of vein R on hindwing upper side. All of these are adult characters, and it seems likely that careful systematic examination of the early stages, especially larvae, would reveal further synapomorphies for the whole group, or, more usefully, for subgroups. One well-known larval peculiarity of hesperiids is the "neck" (a narrowing of the prothoracic region immediately behind the head), but it is not universal, not being shown by *Megathymus* and related genera. Some specialists have placed these so-called giant skippers in a separate subfamily (or even family, the Megathymidae: e.g., Freeman 1969; Kuznetzov and Stekol'nikov 2001), but others consider them to be no more than a subordinate group of the Hesperiinae (Ackery et al. 1999), a view followed here.

Apart from the megathymids, skippers have in general been divided into about six subfamilies. However, few if any of these groupings are well characterized, and their interrelationships are uncertain. The Coeliadinae (Old World tropics) comprise about 75 species brought together by their unique, awl-like third segment of the labial palp. Pyrrhopyginae (about 150 New World, mainly Neotropical species) have two synapomorphies (greatly compressed abdominal tergum I; stout "golf-club" antennal club). The Pyrginae (about 1,000 species, worldwide) lack recognized universal synapomorphies, while the characters of the Heteropterinae (about 150 species from the Americas, Palearctic, and Afrotropics) are little better. Trapezitinae (a small group of about 60 Australasian species) are characterized by a particular formation of the hindwing discocellular veins. Finally, many of the Hesperiinae show a peculiarity in the forewing venation, with M_2 curving to M_3, but this is not distinct in all the many species located in this group (over 2,000 species, with worldwide distribution except New Zealand, and including the American megathymines). Ackery et al. (1999) discuss the possible relationships of these six more or less weakly defined subfamilies, and find some evidence in favor of the Coeliadinae as sister group to the rest, with the latter divisible into two plausibly monophyletic groups, to give (Coeliadinae [{Pyrrhopyginae + Pyrginae} {Heteropterinae + Trapezitinae + Hesperiinae}]).

Papilionidae

Measured by effort per species, more work has gone into trying to understand the interrelationships of the 600 or so species of Papilionidae than any other family of Lepidoptera. Schemes abound, but we remain far from any consensus.

The group as a whole does at least appear monophyletic. Evidence in its favor includes free vein 2A of forewing (Miller 1987; diagnostic, even though it might seem plesiomorphic), extended third axillary sclerite of forewing base (de Jong et al. 1996a), joined cervical sclerites (Kristensen 1976; Miller 1987), quadrifid cubitus (Clench 1955; also occurs in dismorphiine pierids), and, perhaps most convincingly, the unique eversible osmeterium of the larval prothorax (confirmed by Vasquez and Perez 1966, for *Baronia*). (For discussion of these and other characters, see Ackery et al. 1999.)

Division of Papilionidae into three subfamilies (based on Ehrlich 1958) is now conventional. The Baroniinae (1 extant species) form a very distinct clade, the characters of which include unique patagia (Ehrlich 1958), curiously thickened forewing radial vein, unusual membranous lateral lobe to male valve (Miller 1987), and a special female scent organ (Häuser 1992). Although *Baronia* is widely accepted as the stem lineage of the family (e.g., Munroe and Ehrlich 1960; Hancock 1983; Tyler et al. 1994), in the exploratory cladistic analyses of de Jong et al. (1996a) it did not emerge as sister to the remaining Papilionidae; instead, this position was most often occupied by *Parnassius*. The Parnassiinae, which include up to 80 species in 8 genera, can be linked by their asymmetrical tarsal claws and highly sclerotized aedeagus and ostium. However, these features are absent in *Hypermnestra*, which should perhaps be excluded as a result, as suggested by Hiura (1980) and urged by Häuser (1993a). Thus the Parnassiinae might represent a paraphyletic stem group to the rest of the Papilionidae (Baroniinae and Papilioninae). Such a departure from the accepted position for *Baronia* would be surprising, and should be entertained only as a possibility worth investigating (Tyler et al. [1994] offer apparently strong support for the conventional view). Caterino et al. (2001) have found evidence from mitochondrial and nuclear DNA data that the Parnassiinae are indeed most probably paraphyletic, but in most of their analyses *Baronia* remained in stem position; unfortunately they did not obtain data for *Hypermnestra*. Yagi et al. (1999), using mitochondrial DNA evidence, also suggest that the Parnassiinae may not be monophyletic.

The bulk of papilionids (about 550 species in 17 or so genera) are placed in the Papilioninae, but the group has only one really convincing synapomorphy, and this has yet to be checked in the majority of species (metathorax with distinct meral suture, including internal lamella: Ehrlich 1958; Miller 1987). The pseuduncus and the basal spur of forewing cubital vein may be other good characters (Miller 1987). Munroe (1961) divided the Papilioninae into three tribes, Troidini, Leptocircini (= Graphiini, including *Teinopalpus*), and Papilionini. The composition of the second of these tribal groups, and the mutual and internal relationships of all three, remain uncertain. For example, both Hancock (1983) and Miller (1987) concluded that the Troidini and Papilionini have a sister group relationship, with the Leptocircini in stem position. Miller recognized an additional tribe for *Teinopalpus* (as did Ehrlich 1958), placing the Teinopalpini as sister to (Papilionini + Troidini). In some contrast, in a series of analyses, Tyler et al. (1994) often found Leptocircini to be sister to Papilionini (in agreement with the earlier suggestion of Munroe and Ehrlich [1960]), with Troidini basal, although they finally concluded that there was "ambiguity still remaining as to which tribe (Troidini or Graphiini

[= Leptocircini]) stands alone." In their analyses, *Teinopalpus* always maintained high rank, most often as sister to (Leptocircini + Papilionini). More recently, to complete the set of possibilities, Yagi et al. (1999) found molecular evidence in favor of a sister group relationship for (Troidini + Leptocircini), but this relationship is not supported by the independent work of Caterino et al. (2001).

Within the three major tribes, regardless of their interrelationships, no stable classification exists. For Papilionini, the major instability relates to subdivision of the otherwise very large genus *Papilio* (>200 species). For example, Tyler et al. (1994) recognized several generic divisions made by Hancock (1983), while Parsons (1999), following Miller, recognized none; Collins and Morris (1985), by ranking Hancock's genera as subgenera of *Papilio,* sought a compromise—also favored by the present author as a practical interim. The two main rival classifications for Leptocircini (Hancock 1983; Miller 1987) differ substantially. However, the greatest uncertainty relates to the Troidini (discussed in detail below).

Pieridae

As discussed by Ackery et al. (1999), a number of features can be cited in support of the Pieridae as a natural group, comprising over 1,000 species. These characters include unfused lateral plates of the pronotum, fully bifid (equal) claws of the foretarsus, outer edge of forewing third axillary sclerite with tooth, median plate of forewing basal sclerites fused with third axillary sclerite, and pterins in wing scales (including pterin, leucopterin, isoxanthopterin, and xanthopterin; perhaps coupled with absence of β-alanine). Most of these, together with some other potentially informative characters (such as the uni- or trisulcate antennae described by Jordan [1898]), need further study, and the Pieridae did not always emerge as a monophyletic group in the analyses of de Jong et al. (1996a). Despite this slight uncertainty, and despite the lack of strong support for Pieridae in the molecular work of Pollock et al. (1998), it seems unlikely that the integrity of the Pieridae as a group will be challenged.

At the level of subfamilies and their interrelations, however, we are faced with considerable uncertainty. Four subfamilies are currently recognized. Of these, the Pseudopontiinae include a single, highly autapomorphic African species. The Dismorphiinae, a group of about 100 species, are distinguished among the Pieridae by their "quadrifid" cubitus and, possibly among all butterflies, by their trisulcate antennae (Jordan 1898). Other peculiarities of this group, including the forewing radial venation, need to be clarified, even if only to confirm that the Palearctic wood whites (*Leptidea*) really do belong with this otherwise entirely Neotropical group (a view that Yoshimoto [2000] appears to question). The two remaining conventionally recognized subfamilies, the Coliadinae (sulfurs) and Pierinae (whites), include about 250 and 700 species respectively; neither group has very convincing synapomorphies. Venables (1993) considered the sulfurs to be paraphyletic, and it is conceivable that the Pierinae are polyphyletic (de Jong et al. 1996a). However, the widespread occurrence of structurally produced UV "colors" in male Coliadinae and of UV-absorbing pterins in male Pierinae, coupled with differences in host plant use, suggest that it is premature to abandon either of these groups at present. In a recent molecular analysis of a limited sample of 21 coliadinine and pierine taxa, with a nymphalid and a papilionid as outgroups, Pollock et al. (1998) recovered both groups as monophyletic (and further unpublished work by Francie Chew and Ward Watt finds support for Pierinae as a natural group: W. B. Watt, pers. comm.). Osamu Yata and Takeo Yamauchi have carried out recent work based in part on Venables' dataset, and find evidence in favor of monophyly of the Coliadinae, but with the sclerotised patagia (originally noted by Ehrlich) as the only clear, apparently secondarily derived, potential synapomorphy (O. Yata, pers. comm.).

With respect to the interrelations of the four subfamily groups, various schemes have been proposed, of which two seem most favored on current evidence: either (Pseudopontiinae + Dismorphiinae) form a group (as Klots [1933] proposed), together with (Pierinae + Coliadinae) as a second coordinate pairing (Scott and Wright 1990; Ehrlich 1958), or the Dismorphiinae are the stem group, with *Pseudopontia* being the first branch of the crown group, to give (Dismorphiinae [Pseudopontiinae {Coliadinae + Pierinae}]), as more or less proposed by Clench (1955), Venables (1993) and F. S. Chew and W. B. Watt (unpub.). Some support for the latter view was found by de Jong et al. (1996a), although *Pseudopontia* seemed more internal to the representatives of the Pierinae than expected (*Pseudopontia* could be related to *Leptosia:* W. B. Watt, pers. comm.). Yoshimoto (2000) has recently questioned the conventional wisdom that the Dismorphiinae, and *Leptidea* in particular, can be regarded as "primitive." Kuznetzov and Stekol'nikov (2001, fig. 127) evidently agree, as they propose the novel classification (Pierinae [Coliadinae {Dismorphiinae + Pseudopontiinae}]). Evidently, much more work is required if a rich and stable higher classification of the Pieridae is to be established.

Lycaenidae *sensu lato*

Formal classification of the Lycaenidae *s.l.* (over 6,000 species) has been beset with problems regarding family limits and the status and rank of subgroups. Ehrlich (1958) included the metalmarks (Riodininae, together with the monobasic Styginae) within the Lycaenidae *s.l.,* which thus included just three subfamilies. The cladistic analyses of Kristensen (1976) and de Jong et al. (1996a) suggested that, on available evidence, exclusion of the metalmarks would render the residual Lycaenidae paraphyletic. While many lepidopterists have adopted the concept of Lycaenidae *s.l.* (e.g., Scott 1986; Eliot 1990; Nielsen and Common 1991; Parsons 1999), others have continued to give both groups family-level status (e.g., Harvey 1987; Fiedler 1991; DeVries 1997). Robbins (1988a, 1990) has even suggested that the Lycaenidae *s.l.* do not form a natural group, the metalmarks possibly having a closer relationship with the Nymphalidae than the Lycaenidae *s.s.* Some recent research on genitalic morphology by Kuznetzov and Stekol'nikov (1998) could support this view, but this does not seem to be their current interpretation (Kuznetzov and Stekol'nikov 2001).

The molecular work of Dana Campbell (Campbell et al. 2000; Campbell and Pierce, chap. 18 in this volume; see also Weller et al. 1996) suggests, however, that this problem is most likely to be resolved by recognition of the two groups as a pair of monophyletic sister taxa. If so, this solution rejects the Kristensen/de Jong et al. view and upholds the Ehrlich system (other than downgrading *Styx*), leaving only the question of absolute rank. Having arrived at Crested Butte not prepared to defend a paraphyletic Lycaenidae *s.s.* simply to promote the more clearly monophyletic Riodinidae, seen the work of Campbell, and listened subsequently to arguments by Robbins and others, I now accept Lycaenidae *s.s.* and Riodinidae (including *Styx*: Harvey 1987; Robbins 1988b) as full families in a sister group relationship (Lycaenidae *s.l.* = Lycaenoidea *auctt.*) as the best current classification (Campbell et al. 2000; Kuznetzov and Stekol'nikov 2001). However, Pierce et al. (2002), in a current review of ant associations in these butterflies, revert to the metalmarks as a subfamily within the Lycaenidae. As Rienk de Jong (pers. comm., Jan. 2002) points out, recalling Kristensen's (1976) position, "What is at stake here is not the monophyly of the Riodinidae (nobody disagrees), but of the Lycaenidae without Riodinidae." On the other hand, Bob Robbins (1988a; pers. comm., Jan. 2002) cites characters of the male foretarsus in support of monophyly of the Lycaenidae *s.s.*, and is of the firm opinion that there is "no evidence suggesting that Lycaenidae [are] paraphyletic in terms of Riodinidae." I suspect there is quite a lot of life left in this particular piece of systematic doubt!

Morphological characters of the Lycaenidae *s.l.* include "indentation" of the compound eye adjacent to base of the antenna, reduced metathoracic wing case in pupa, mesoseries of crotchets on larval prolegs interrupted by a lobe, and larva lacking eversible prothoracic gland. These characters are not universal (some Nymphalidae have indented eyes), or are absences, or have not been corroborated for more than a fraction of species. In practice, any butterfly with the combination (modified male foreleg + non-tricarinate antenna + indented eye) will be a member of the Lycaenidae *sensu lato*. The male genitalia almost certainly offer additional characters. However, the single most striking peculiarity of the Lycaenidae *s.l.* is their widespread association with ants ("myrmecophily") and their associated adaptations, most notably the various glandular structures of the larvae used to appease or deceive ants ("ant organs").

Detailed knowledge of the ant organs of Lycaenidae *s.s.* has grown over a long period (Cottrell 1984 provides an excellent overview). However, it was not until DeVries took a serious interest in the riodinids, most of which are restricted to the Neotropics, that sufficient knowledge became available to make a systematic comparison of the two major groups. DeVries (1991, 1997) demonstrates, in terms of classical morphology, that the ant organs of the two are not homologous. Previous workers (including Vane-Wright 1978) often assumed that at least one class of ant organs in the two groups would prove to be homologous morphological expressions of a single ancestral shift to a myrmecophilous relationship. Given that both riodinids and lycaenids *s.s.* include a number of subgroups that do not exhibit myrmecophily, and that some of these lack even vestigial ant organs, DeVries (1991; also Fiedler 1991) very reasonably argued that the evolution of ant association occurred independently at least twice—at least once in the Riodinidae, and at least once in the Lycaenidae *s.s.*—citing the nonhomologous nature of the ant organs of the two groups as evidence.

To argue against DeVries and Fiedler on this issue would seem nonparsimonious and, in my case at least, even disingenuous. However(!), recent advances in molecular biology are pointing to regulatory gene systems thought to control, for example, the development of structures as different (and seemingly nonhomologous) as vertebrate and arthropod eyes (e.g., Xu et al. 1999). Comparable puzzles may occur elsewhere in butterflies, such as the pouched versus pocketed hindwing cubital organs of the very closely related danaine genera *Danaus* and *Tirumala*. Scored grossly, as the only invaginated cubital wing organs found in butterflies (and given that both receive the abdominal hairpencils in pre-courtship behavior), these structures seem to shout "homologous!" But, scored in terms of how the organs develop and their precise function, they are radically different (Boppré and Vane-Wright 1989). Even so, at some other level they may prove to be homologous, their noncomparable developmental paths and functions perhaps being different expressions of a shared regulatory gene system. The apparently sharp differences noted by Parsons (1996a, 1996b) between the hindwing androconia of *Ornithoptera* and *Troides* could prove to be another such case (discussed further below).

Riodinidae

Characters of the Riodinidae (about 1,300 known species: Hall and Harvey 2002) include reduction (relative to Lycaenidae *s.s.*) of the male prothoracic legs (less than one-half length of pterothoracic, as in many nymphalids), trichoid sensilla of female foretarsus in single cluster, and absence of posterior apophyses of female genitalia. DeVries (1997) reanalyzed Harvey's (1987) original work, and confirmed that, on present evidence, division into five major subfamilies is supportable: Styginae (1 species), Corrachiinae (1 species), Euselasiinae (>140 species), Nemeobiinae (= Hamearinae; <100 species), and Riodininae (about 800 species), although Hall and Harvey (2002) now suggest that the first two taxa should be included within Euselasiinae. The largest subfamily, the Riodininae, is divided into about nine tribes (Harvey 1987; DeVries 1997; Hall and Willmott 2000). Although great progress has been made, it is evident that much remains to be done on the characterization and interrelationships of the members of this fascinating group (e.g., see Penz and DeVries 1999; Hall and Harvey 2002). Current excellent work by Phil DeVries, Carla Penz, Jason Hall, Donald Harvey, and others is very encouraging.

Lycaenidae *s.s.*

With removal of the riodinids, as noted by Kristensen (1976) and de Jong et al. (1996a) and discussed above, unequivocal morphological characterization of the entire 5,000 species constituting the Lycaenidae *s.s.* is problematic. This difficulty is reflected in DeVries (1997, table 2), in which the distinct features listed refer to the Riodinidae rather than the Lycaenidae. This approach recalls Clench's (1955) division of the Lycaenoidea into four separate families, Riodinidae, Lycaenidae, Liptenidae, and Liphyridae, to which Shirôzu and Yamamoto (1957) added Curetidae. However, as already noted, Campbell's molecular work (e.g., Campbell et al. 2000), as well as certain features of the foreleg, does support monophyly, although only a single sequence is apparently involved. Eliot (1973) divided the Lycaenidae *s.s.* into eight subfamilies, but his later, very conservative summary classification (Eliot 1990) recognizes just four: Poritiinae (to include Lipteninae; about 600 species), Miletinae (to include Liphyrinae; about 150 species), Curetinae (18 species), and Lycaeninae (to include the familiar Theclinae, Polyommatinae, and also the apparently rather distinct Aphnaeini; a total of about 4,000 species). G. Lamas et al. (unpub.), in an attempt to develop a global "baseline" classification for all butterflies, adopt Eliot's most recent published scheme, with the exception that they continue to give the theclines and polyommatines subfamily rank (table 22.1). Exactly the same arrangement has been proposed independently by Kuznetzov and Stekol'nikov (2001, fig. 127). However, the characters used to support these groups, other than the monobasic Curetinae, are not very convincing (Ackery et al. 1999), and very much remains to be done on the higher classification of these butterflies.

Table 22.1 Summary classification of butterflies (Hesperioidea + Papilionoidea), to subfamily

HESPERIOIDEA Latreille (skippers)
  Hesperiidae Latreille
    Coeliadinae Evans
    Pyrrhopyginae Mabille
    Pyrginae Burmeister
    Heteropterinae Aurivillius
    Trapezitinae Waterhouse & Lyell
    Hesperiinae Latreille

PAPILIONOIDEA Latreille (true butterflies)
  Papilionidae Latreille
    Baroniinae Bryk
    Parnassiinae Duponchel
    Papilioninae Latreille
  Pieridae Swainson
    Dismorphiinae Schatz
    Pseudopontiinae Reuter
    Coliadinae Swainson
    Pierinae Swainson
  Lycaenidae Leach
    Poritiinae Doherty
    Miletinae Reuter
    Curetinae Distant
    Theclinae Swainson
    Lycaeninae Leach
    Polyommatinae Swainson
  Riodinidae Grote
    Euselasiinae Kirby
      (incl. Stygini Ehrlich)
      (incl. Corrachiini Stichel)
    Nemeobiinae Bates
    Riodininae Grote
  Nymphalidae Swainson
    Libytheinae Boisduval
    Calinaginae Moore
    Morphinae Newman
    Satyrinae Boisduval
    Charaxinae Guenée
    incertae sedis Cyrestini Guenée
    incertae sedis Biblidini Boisduval
    incertae sedis Pseudergolini Jordan
    Apaturinae Boisduval
    Nymphalinae Swainson
    Danainae Boisduval
    incertae sedis Limenitidini Behr
    Heliconiinae Swainson
      (= Argynninae Swainson)

Note: This table reflects the initial consensus (both classification and nomenclature) most likely to be accepted by GloBIS (Global Butterfly Information System). The classification to be adopted by GloBIS will be reviewed regularly, and changes can be anticipated whenever significant progress is made in resolving any of the many areas of uncertainty. (Data from G. Lamas et al., unpub.)

The approximately 6,000 species of butterflies included by Ehrlich (1958) in the Nymphalidae have often been divided into a number of separate families, notably Danaidae, Acraeidae, Satyridae, and Morphidae, usually complemented by a variable number of other families, and an omnibus "Nymphalidae" soaking up misfits as well as the typical. All these butterflies are ambulatory tetrapods in both sexes, with the forelegs unused for walking. However, because the male forelegs of Riodinidae are also unused for walking, the most reliable and widely confirmed synapomorphy for the entire assemblage is the three-ridged, "tricarinate" antenna (Jordan 1898; Brower 2000b; see the excellent illustration in Bascombe et al. 1999, fig. 9.1).

This antennal character is, however, also present in libytheids (which can use the female forelegs for walking). This, plus the occurrence of a von Siebold organ in female *Libythea* (Häuser 1993b) and the robust position of this group as sister to the Nymphalidae *sensu* Ehrlich, persuaded de Jong et al. (1996a) to include the libytheids within the Nymphalidae *s.l.*, as the stem subfamily. With division of the Lycaenidae *s.l.* into two coordinate families (Riodinidae and Lycaenidae), it might seem logical to restore the Libytheidae to family rank as well. However, given that there now seems to be little doubt about their relationship to other nymphalids, and that libytheines form such a small group of species, in this case, unlike the situation with Riodinidae, no practical issues attach to "low rank." Therefore I do not propose to depart from the arrangement adopted in Ackery et al. (1999). Indeed, Brower's (2000b) most recent molecular investigation of the Nymphalidae *s.l.* has a "biblidine" (*Chersonesia*) in stem position, with *Libytheana* following as sister to the rest. This seems a rather bizarre placement in an otherwise very interesting and intuitively "good" cladogram, but nonetheless it seems to confirm the Libytheinae as a very high-ranking or stem group *within* the Nymphalidae *s.l.*

Including the Libytheinae, Ackery et al. (1999) recognized 10 major subfamilies. Half seem to be good monophyletic groups: Libytheinae (12 species), Calinaginae (about 8 species), Charaxinae (about 400 species), Apaturinae (about 430 species), and Danainae *s.l.* (including Tellervinae and Ithomiinae; over 450 species). The other five, which between them include the majority of nymphalid species, were poorly characterized: Heliconiinae *s.l.* (including Acraeinae, Argynninae, and Pardopsidini; over 400 species), Nymphalinae (about 350 species), "Limenitinae" (correctly Limenitidinae, but junior to the name Biblidinae; >1,000 species), Morphinae (including Amathusiinae and Brassolinae, about 230 species), and Satyrinae (about 2,400 species).

This classification of the Nymphalidae *s.l.* differs from that of Harvey (1991) only by placing Brassolinae within Morphinae *s.l.* (cf. Ehrlich 1958, except for inclusion of *Bia, Caerois,* and *Antirrhea,* which Ehrlich placed in the satyrines), and Tellervinae and Ithomiinae within Danainae *s.l.* This last change, introduced by Ackery et al. (1999), practically reverts to the danoid Heliconiidae of Bates (1862), and differs from the Danainae *sensu* Kirby (1871) only by inclusion of *Anetia.* Brower's (2000b) results, based on partial sequences of the *wingless* gene from 103 nymphalid species, do not conflict with this last arrangement of Danainae *s.l.,* or with any of the other four well-supported subfamilies listed above (although the Apaturinae appear to be of low rank), and do give additional support to the Heliconiinae *s.l.* and the Nymphalinae (to include Coeini). However, the Biblidinae ("Limenitinae") appear polyphyletic, and G. Lamas et al. (unpub.), following a suggestion by Don Harvey, propose to divide them into at least four tribes, not grouped within a formal subfamily, placed provisionally instead as *incertae sedis* within the Nymphalidae as a whole. In some contrast, the (Morphinae + Satyrinae) taken together may form a natural group (as now proposed in Kuznetzov and Stekol'nikov 2001, fig. 127, with family status), but not the Morphinae *sensu* Ehrlich. Very interestingly, in Brower's most favored cladogram, *Amathusia* groups with two Old World satyrines (*Mycalesis* and *Melanitis*) to the exclusion of a large group of Neotropical Satyrinae, while the (Morphini + Brassolini), to include *Bia, Caerois,* and *Antirrhea,* seem to form a distinct clade. If Brower's results are confirmed, in the future we may be able to recognize the Satyrinae *s.l.,* with two subgroups, the Morphini (to include Brassolini, *Bia, Caerois,* and *Antirrhea*), and the Satyrini (to include *Haetera, Melanitis,* and Amathusiina). The current scheme of G. Lamas et al. (unpub.), with nine subfamilies and four tribes *incertae sedis,* is reflected in table 22.1.

The morphological characters used to establish these various subgroups are summarized in a series of recent papers (Ackery 1988; Harvey 1991; de Jong et al. 1996a; Ackery et al. 1999). This is an active area of research, with rapid developments to be expected from molecular systematics (e.g., Brower and DeSalle 1998; Brower 2000b; Wahlberg and Zimmerman 2001), detailed study of early stages (e.g., Brown and Freitas 1994; see also Motta, chap. 19 in this volume), and even reinvestigation of adult characters (e.g., Angel Viloria's as yet unpublished 1998 thesis on Satyrinae, compared with Miller 1968). As with the Lycaenidae, the internal classification of the Nymphalidae, arguably the most familiar of all butterflies, remains uncertain.

HEDYLIDAE

The Hedylidae comprise a distinct monobasic superfamily of about 40 species (Scoble 1990a, 1990b; Ackery et al. 1999), of which the adults, but not the larvae, are rather mothlike in appearance. Their status as "butterflies," and their possible relationships to the Geometroidea (from which they differ fundamentally in certain respects), Hesperioidea, and Papilionoidea remain uncertain. However, what does seem clear is that the Hedyloidea are closely related to the butterflies (e.g., Weller and Pashley 1995; de Jong et al. 1996a; Weller et al. 1996), and they should be included in any future assessments of butterfly higher classification and comparative evaluations of butterfly biology.

COMPARATIVE BIOLOGY, ECOLOGY, AND CLADOGRAMS

A recent, and at times acrimonious, debate over the nature of comparative biology (e.g., *sensu* Rieppel 1988) versus the comparative method (e.g., *sensu* Harvey and Pagel 1991) has revealed that two different agendas are involved. According to Coddington (1994), these can be encapsulated as the "homology approach" and the "convergence approach." The first is concerned with specific history: typically, with the sequential changes that have occurred within a particular lineage, in the hope of understanding that lineage's unique properties. The second is concerned with general trends: typically, with the comparison of multiple, independent historical events, in the hope of identifying ecological and evolutionary processes.

Either way, it has become apparent that modern comparative biology is dependent on phylogenetic systematics or cladistics to provide the essential framework. As Coddington (1994) notes, "the convergence approach uses the same data and cladistic model as the homology approach." According to Miller and Wenzel (1995), "just as ecologists have learned to use chemistry and geography to study abiotic processes, so should they learn to use cladograms in their search for evolutionary patterns." Thus, further advances in the comparative study of butterfly ecology, and in understanding the biogeographic and biological peculiarities of individual butterfly taxa, will continue to be dependent on (and limited by) advances in butterfly systematics (e.g., Hall and Willmott 2000).

The search for the origin of mimetic patterns of *Papilio dardanus* offers an example of the "homology" approach that, due to an inadequate phylogenetic framework, was long misconstrued. Trimen (1869) proposed three hypotheses about the evolutionary problems posed by this remarkable African species: a genetic hypothesis (the various males and female forms all constituted a single, polymorphic species); an ecological hypothesis (the various tailless female forms were Batesian mimics); and a phylogenetic hypothesis (the mimetic forms evolved from a condition like that seen on Madagascar, where all females of *P. dardanus meriones* are male-like). Over the next hundred years, a vast amount of evidence supporting the first of these hypotheses accumulated. Little critical evidence concerning the mimetic status of any of the female morphs has been forthcoming, but the ecological explanation has not been seriously contested. The phylogenetic hypothesis has been questioned from time to time, but Turner's (1963a) complex scenario, whereby the mimetic patterns could be derived from the pattern of the male-like female morph found on Madagascar, was entirely in keeping with Trimen's original and untested supposition. Trimen's idea (and Turner's elaboration) was finally challenged by an explicit phylogenetic hypothesis linking *P. dardanus* to two other African swallowtail species, *P. phorcas* and *P. constantinus,* with the clear implication that the male-like pattern of female *dardanus* is not the ancestral phenotype, and that the mimetic morphs were more likely evolved from a form similar to that of the narrow-banded *constantinus* phenotype than from the highly specialized, largely yellow *dardanus* andromorph.

The morphological analysis of Vane-Wright and Smith (1991) and the recent molecular investigation reported by Vane-Wright et al. (1999) appear at first sight conclusive regarding the sister species relationship of (*P. dardanus* + *P. phorcas*), and their sister group relationship to *P. constantinus*. However, closer inspection makes it clear that both the cladistic and interpretative debates must continue. The independent morphological work of Hancock (1993) suggested that *constantinus* links with two Madagascan swallowtails, *P. delalandei* and *P. mangoura,* before collectively forming the sister group of (*phorcas* + *dardanus*). In contrast, the molecular investigations of Caterino and Sperling (1999) and Reed and Sperling (1999) place *constantinus* as sister to *phorcas,* before linking with *dardanus,* or in a trichotomy with *dardanus* and *phorcas* (Reed and Sperling 1999). More recently still, *P. delalandei* has been sequenced and found to be closely related to the *phorcas* group, but not internal to it (Felix Sperling, pers. comm.). Regarding interpretation, Clarke et al. (1996) raise a number of important questions. Whatever the final outcome, the need for a dependable cladogram (i.e., a cladogram based on far more extensive data, or one that survives testing by considerable additional data) for all Afrotropical swallowtails is now essential for finding worthwhile answers to Trimen's phylogenetic and ontogenetic questions.

Given the famous single diagram in Darwin's *Origin,* it seems strange that more than a century elapsed before the need for such diagrams was seen as part of "normal" evolutionary biology. Even so, we must acknowledge that cladograms are constructs that are open to revision (they "cannot be claimed to match some supposedly 'extra-subjective' reality of nature": Rieppel 1988, p. 170), that our findings based on phylogenetic trees should not be overstated (Eggleton and Vane-Wright 1994, p. 362), and that evolutionary theory is not needed as an assumption for cladistic analysis to be undertaken (Brower 2000a)—although I would contend that a general theory of evolution is still needed to justify the hierarchical pattern-seeking procedures adopted in all cladistic methods normally employed (Vane-Wright 2001).

An already "classic" example of the convergence approach is that of Sillén-Tullberg (1988), who explored the possible relationship between unpalatability and gregarious behavior in butterfly larvae. Her study began with the assumption that warningly colored caterpillars are generally unpalatable, and made use of "existing phylogenies" for the Rhopalocera (in reality, a series of "paste-ups" of quasi-cladistic classifications to give convenient branching diagrams or supertrees, which the author was unable to evaluate critically). Sillén-Tullberg mapped the known occurrences of larval aposematism and gregariousness onto these "phylogenies" (to use the ghastly misnomer that has spread throughout the entire comparative literature!) and analyzed this set of discrete data by the directional method (Nylin and Weddell 1994). The results suggested that unpalatability was of great significance for the evolution of gregarious behavior, whereas, by the same token, kin selection was of little importance for the evolution of warning coloration. Maddison (1990) was critical of Sillén-Tullberg's methodology and, by use of a new statistical test, endeavored to show that her results were not significant. Others (e.g., Wenzel and Carpenter 1994; Miller and Wenzel 1995) have fiercely debated the relevance of such tests that aggregate disparate events—probably because they are essentially members of the "homology school" and tend to see the general picture as the sum of not only independent, but also unique episodes ("it seems likely that warning coloration is associated with gregariousness in some taxa, while in others it is not": Miller and Wenzel 1995, p. 401).

My point here is not to take sides in these particular issues, but to emphasize again the primacy of the cladistics on which such analyses rest and the uncertainties that still attach to many of our phylogenetic constructions. In her analysis of the Heliconiini, Sillén-Tullberg (1988, fig. 11) used the evolutionary classification of Brown (1981). Brown's classification differs significantly from subsequent efforts, and these efforts also differ among themselves. Thus Brower's (1994b) consensus tree based on mtDNA data differs from his later preferred cladogram based on a combined analysis of mtDNA and *wingless* data (Brower and Egan 1997), and both differ from Penz's (1999) consensus tree based on adult and larval morphology. Mapping the traits of interest to Sillén-Tullberg onto these various trees results in differing estimates of the number of independent evolutionary gains and losses. Mitter and Brooks (1983) had earlier used a "phylogeny" of the Heliconiini based on Brown's (1981) classification to explore potential coevolutionary patterns between the butterflies and the Passifloraceae. While substitution of the later cladograms makes little difference to Mitter and Brooks's conclusions in this case, it is clear that their "test" (assuming Brown's classification to be wrong) lacked empirical validity. Thus, until some stability is reached, those who wish to use "phylogenies" to explore such matters as coevolution, or the quasi-lawlike generalities that are the object of the convergence approach, are at the mercy of cladistic reassessments—whether they use statistical procedures or not. The same is also true, of course, for those concerned with the homology approach, but, as their aim is normally specific, they are not offering grand theories, and thus mistakes based on inadequate systematics will not be so conspicuous or contentious. To give a final example, the interpretation of gregariousness in the Nymphalidae (Sillén-Tullberg 1988, fig. 7) is quite a different proposition when based on the cladogram of Brower (2000b) instead of the "phylogeny" of Scott (1984).

Many ecologists and evolutionary biologists thus give the impression that they wish to use phylogenetic trees to draw conclusions about processes, but without care for the data or the critical methodology of cladistics. Although such apparent lack of concern for evidence is most unfortunate, the current impatience of evolutionary biologists (in contrast to their former indifference) for the delivery of the required cladograms is as much a thing to be wondered at as to be concerned about. In my view, it is imperative that the small band of classical taxonomists and the growing throng of molecular systematists combine their efforts to deliver what is really needed. Such well-intended but as yet largely unfunded initiatives as Butterfly Net International (BNI: www.ent.orst.edu/bnet/) and the Global Butterfly Information System (GloBIS: www.ento.csiro.au/globis/) need to become fully operational, rather than just dreams.

In this context, the recent paper of Janz and Nylin (1998) may represent a way forward on the comparative side, embracing as it does both the homology and convergence approaches, with numerous well-formulated historical and evolutionary questions to be answered from a common biological and cladistic information base. What is most needed now, therefore, is more and better cladograms, tested and improved as studies progress. Until then, a greater degree of appreciation by ecologists of the current limitations of cladograms would be wise (Eggleton and Vane-Wright 1994). Although Janz and Nylin use a "paste-up" tree in their 1998 paper (with all the uncertainty that this entails: a comprehensive character matrix for the entire assemblage analyzed using parsimony would probably not give an identical result), it is encouraging to see that members of the same group are also engaged in empirical cladistic work on the Nymphalini (Nylin et al. 2001). However, the following example offers a particular warning regarding incautious use of existing cladograms and the surprising differences that arise between different specialists.

A CASE IN POINT: TROUBLESOME TROIDINES

The Papilionidae are the smallest and evidently the oldest family of Papilionoidea (in terms of the current noncoordinate classification). Even if the Papilionidae, and notably the Parnassiinae and Papilioninae, were ultimately to prove to be paraphyletic groups (as some of the difficulties revealed by Häuser [1993a] might suggest; see also Caterino et al. 2001), their low species richness and great age would lead us to expect their higher classification to be well resolved, with large gaps giving a strong and unequivocal phylogenetic "signal." But this seems not to be the case. Despite intensive effort, there is no agreement on swallowtail higher classification (cf. Munroe and Ehrlich 1960 versus Hancock 1983 versus Miller 1987 versus Tyler et al. 1994). Nowhere is this lack of agreement more apparent than in the Troidini—according to some, the most charismatic of all butterflies—for which three radically different phylogenetic classifications have been proposed within the last two decades (Hancock 1983; Miller 1987; Parsons 1996a, 1996b).

According to Hancock (1983), the first division of the troidines (fig. 22.1A) leads to *Battus* (Battina) and the rest (Troidina). The Troidina are divisible into *Euryades* + *Cressida* in one daughter lineage, and another with *Parides* as sister to a crown group of three genera, in which *Atrophaneura* (including *Pharmacophagus*) is sister to *Trogonoptera* + *Troides*. This last genus, according to Hancock (1983), comprises three subgenera (sg. *Troides*, sg. *Ripponia*, and sg. *Ornithoptera*). Hancock subsequently treated *Ornithoptera* as a full genus again, but apparently only for the sake of convention ("taxonomically, it is best regarded as a subgenus . . . or synonym . . . of *Troides*": Hancock 1991).

Miller's (1987) system corresponds to Hancock's at the most basal level, with *Battus* sister to the rest (fig. 22.1B). *Pharmacophagus* (widely separated from *Atrophaneura*) then appears as the basal lineage of the Troidina. *Euryades* and *Cressida* retain their sister group relationship, but are here sister to *Pachliopta*, another group removed from Hancock's concept of *Atrophaneura*. This group of three genera is sister to a final group of two sister genera, *Troides* (including *Ornithoptera* as a synonym, and *Trogonoptera* as a subgenus) and a differently constituted *Parides*, which, in Miller's scheme, includes not only *Parides s.s.* and *Panosmia* as subgenera, but also *Atrophaneura s.s.* as a third subgenus. Thus Miller's arrangement differs radically from Hancock's in a number of ways, although several of these relate to the splitting of Hancock's *Atrophaneura* into three widely separate groups, together with lumping *Atrophaneura s.s.* with *Parides* to form a terminal genus (as opposed to two lineages, one of them basal, in Hancock's treatment).

Parsons' (1996a, 1996b) system (fig. 22.1C) differs even more radically from Hancock's. The first division separates *Euryades* from the rest, and at the next division, *Cressida* is separated likewise. Then comes (*Pharmacophagus* + *Ornithoptera*) as sister to a crown group of six genera with the following relationships: (*Battus* [*Parides* {(*Trogonoptera* + *Troides*) (*Atrophaneura* + *Pachliopta*)}]). Parsons thus rejects Miller's association of the South American *Parides* with the Asian *Atrophaneura*, differs from Hancock and Miller alike

Richard I. Vane-Wright

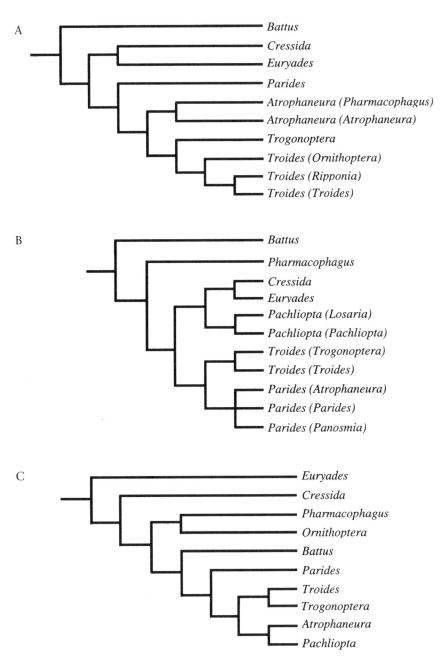

Figure 22.1 The included genera of Troidini (Papilionidae) and their cladistic relationships, according to (A) Hancock (1983); (B) Miller (1987); and (C) Parsons (1996a, 1996b).

in withdrawing *Battus* from stem lineage position, and, perhaps most surprisingly of all, not only separates *Ornithoptera* from (*Trogonoptera* + *Troides*), but also places them far apart in his divisions of the tribe. In this he departs from a tradition going back more than a century. The interest of Parsons' arrangement largely relates to this separation, as it is fundamental to his claim that the biogeography of the troidines, so reclassified, can be explained by the breakup of Pangaea. Thus, according to Parsons, the true birdwings, restricted to lands east of Weber's line, owe their largely parapatric distribution to *Troides s.s.* to their Gondwanic origin.

To justify the generic distinction of *Troides* (including *Trogonoptera*) and *Ornithoptera,* Parsons (1991, 1996a, 1996b, 1999) points to a number of consistent differences between them, notably venation, androconia, shape and stridulation of the pupae, and various larval characters, including pupation site. Miller (1987), following Hancock and Rothschild before him, regarded the two as congeneric (with *Ornithoptera* not even worthy of subgeneric rank). Miller based his conclusion on five characters of the male and female genitalia, four of which he considered almost universal in birdwings but otherwise unique within Troidini. He also noted the androconia as a potential synapomorphy (but it is clear that his studies of this feature were not complete).

With regard to his wide separation of *Troides* and *Ornithoptera,* Parsons was aware that the natural hybrids (Sands and Sawyer 1977) found where the two groups overlap (in New Guinea) could be used as a counterargument. So he pointed out that "only males result, confirming that the parent species are genetically distinct from each other" (Parsons 1999). As the parent species are *O. priamus* (common green birdwing) and *T. oblongomaculatus* (eastern yellow birdwing), genetic distinction is not the issue. The extensive studies of Ae (1979) on species hybrids in Papilionini indicate that artificial hybrids between many species conventionally placed in *Papilio* do not develop as far as adulthood. Thus, among African *Papilio* of the subgenus *Princeps,* artificial hybridization between *P. dardanus* and *P. demodocus* results only in infertile males, while sequence studies confirm that these two species are distinct but nonetheless quite closely related (Vane-Wright et al. 1999). Thus the fact that *O. priamus* and *T. oblongomaculatus* hybridize naturally to produce fully winged males is good prima facie evidence of *relatively* close relationship (further evidence of this compatibility is the production of fully winged artificial male hybrids of *O. priamus* × *T. helena* and *O. priamus* × *T. hypolitus,* illustrated by Matsuka 2001, p. 235). This situation is rather like that of the Danaini, in which we now accept that species such as *plexippus* (monarch: *Danaus*) and *hamata* (blue tiger: *Tirumala*) should no longer be placed in the same genus, being abundantly distinct in various characters (notably remarkable differences in their androconia), but nonetheless are indeed very closely related, as their former inclusion within the "old" paraphyletic *Danaus s.l.* always suggested (Boppré and Vane-Wright 1989). Thus, while I find myself quite prepared to accept full generic separation for *Ornithoptera* and *Troides,* I am skeptical, because of the ready production of hybrid males, about the two genera being separate for over 100 million years, as Parsons' biogeographic scenario seems to imply. Even though some recent unpublished work by

Angel Viloria (1998) on the classification of Neotropical Satyrinae suggests that we might need to think about even advanced groups of butterflies having histories that go back to the breakup of Gondwana, fossil evidence for the age of the Lepidoptera, even though very fragmentary and uncertain, seems to suggest that Gondwanic origins for any groups of higher Ditrysia are unlikely (David Grimaldi, pers. comm.).

Tyler et al. (1994) gave a series of cladograms for a selection of 43 swallowtail species, exemplars chosen to represent a wide range of papilionid genera. In their analyses, cladograms derived from partitioned adult and larval datasets were not congruent. On combining the datasets to give a total evidence analysis, they found the supposedly "optimal" solution to be very sensitive to the addition of even a second species of one particular genus (*Chilasa:* Papilionini) already represented. This instability resulted in great changes among the troidines (unfortunately, Tyler et al. included only one species of *Troides s.s.* in their datasets, with no representative of *Ornithoptera*). Although elements of the Hancock, Miller, and Parsons schemes can be recognized in the various results of Tyler et al., it is clear that no consensus is even beginning to emerge. Anyone wishing to base elaborate evolutionary or ecological hypotheses on existing "phylogenies" of the Troidini should beware!

As a short postscript to this section, some recent work by Morinaka et al. (1999), using data from the mitochondrial gene ND5, has even questioned the monophyly of the Troidini. However, the analyses of Caterino et al. (2001), based on data from two genes, give little support for this controversial view. Perhaps more significantly, in all analyses reported by Morinaka et al., *Ornithoptera* and *Troides* emerged as sister groups; unfortunately, they were not able to obtain data for the critical *Trogonoptera*.

A NOVEL DEVELOPMENT: COMPARING DIET BREADTHS

Finally, considering this ecological context, the emergence of biological measures that themselves depend on the availability of cladistic reconstructions is notable. Symons and Beccaloni (1999) have developed and applied a novel comparative method for measuring larval diet breadths for species, genera, or other higher taxa—although, for empirical work, Beccaloni and Symons (2000) are forced to resort to a "paste-up" supertree for the hosts, with all of its potential limitations. For butterflies, this approach involves evaluating the degree to which the host plants of particular taxa are scattered or clumped over a cladogram for all land plants. This family of measures has emerged from recent ideas about adding a phylogenetic component to the measurement of biological diversity (see, e.g., P. H. Williams et al. 1994; Faith 1994), as described next.

PHYLOGENETICS AND THE EVALUATION OF BIOLOGICAL DIVERSITY

Whittaker (1972) was one of the first to appreciate that a complete measure of biological diversity would need to take into account the evolutionary divergence between species and the genetic diversity within them (see also Hendrickson and Ehrlich [1971], who were similarly concerned with measuring individual and specific ecological differences). Such an approach is crucial to appreciating the different potential values of biodiversity and the implications of making different choices in the light of such understanding (Humphries et al. 1995; Vane-Wright 1996). However, despite amazing advances in molecular genetics, we still have little empirical data directly relevant to the first of these problems—not least because most living species have not even been catalogued, let alone investigated at deeper levels. Instead, over the last decade, a series of papers has debated various possible ways of modeling character, genetic, or phylogenetic diversity based on phylogenetic trees (see Crozier 1997 for an excellent review). As most phylogenetic trees lack convincing branch lengths, many of these papers have focused simply on cladograms, or even classifications (e.g., P. H. Williams et al. 1994; Faith 1994; Williams and Humphries 1996). To the extent that (according to some views of evolution, at least; e.g., punctuated equilibrium theory) major changes are primarily associated with nodes, this focus may not be unrealistic.

However, with respect to conservation applications such as area selection, in which large numbers of species can be taken into account, species richness may prove to be an adequate surrogate for overall genetic diversity (Williams and Humphries 1996; but see also Crozier 1997, p. 255, and Butlin and Tregenza 1998), and the additional computational burden of modeling genetic diversity, especially given all the assumptions, is probably unnecessary. The same probably applies to another promising but imperfect measure, higher taxon richness (Williams and Gaston 1994; Crozier 1997). At present, there are no significant applications to conservation evaluation and area selection at faunal, regional, or even national levels that rely on a knowledge of lepidopteran diversity, distribution, and phylogenetic relationships. However, this could change through the use of available data for better-known areas (e.g., the United States, Europe), the influence of worldwide bioinformatics projects such as GloBIS, and wider appreciation of the issues at stake (e.g., Solis and Pogue 1999).

Spurred on by the advances in molecular biology and molecular systematics, related developments have also been occurring at the population level, and these developments could have a more direct effect on practical decisions about butterfly ecology and conservation. In particular, application of the MU (management unit) and ESU (evolutionarily significant unit) concepts discussed by Moritz (1994b) could affect decisions regarding which populations of endangered species are most worthy of attention (and which populations might be used for reintroductions). Readers are referred to Vogler and DeSalle (1994), Moritz (1994b, 1995), Moritz et al. (1995), Crozier (1997), Butlin and Tregenza (1998), and, notably, evolutionary geneticist and butterfly specialist Jim Mallet (1996b) for an introduction to this rapidly expanding field, some implications of which are explored below.

BUTTERFLY HIGHER TAXA AND CONSERVATION PRIORITIES

In a first attempt to incorporate interspecific evolutionary divergence into conservation evaluation, Vane-Wright et al. (1991) proposed a measure of diversity that took into account information on the interrelationships of taxa, in addition to simply counting the number of branch terminals (as in species richness or other measures of "ecological diversity"). Although the particular measure employed (root-weight) has been superseded by the measures already discussed above (e.g., Faith 1994; Humphries et al. 1995), Vane-Wright et al. (1991) had two goals in mind that remain valid: mitigation against conservation priority being increased by false inflation of taxonomic rank (as when a local population or race is advanced to full species status to improve claims for the area in which it is found), and, conversely, promotion of taxonomically isolated, high-ranking species or species groups, on the expectation that such taxa represent significant genetic diversity not found elsewhere. In a sense, the idea was to promote greater concern for "living fossils" at the relative expense of other, less genetically distinct species (cf. May 1990).

Such a procedure makes sense only if the selected taxa really *are* distinct. Indeed, if the absolute or phylogenetic rank of a taxon is inflated by poor systematics (for whatever reason), then paying special attention to it will, at best, confer no advantage over selecting species at random. Thus, current uncertainties, such as those related above regarding the Troidini, could affect conservation priorities. Notwithstanding these limitations, the conservation status of "living fossil" butterflies, based on the current classification, is now assessed.

Among the Hesperiidae, the Coeliadinae seem good candidates for the stem group. However, as the 70+ species are (collectively) widespread throughout the Old World tropics, no special conservation action seems necessary. The Papilionidae offer a very obvious candidate in *Baronia* (one Mexican species: Baroniinae); other high-ranking, species-poor swallowtail lineages are *Hypermnestra* (one species, in desert regions from Iran to Kyrgyzstan; a possible stem lineage) and *Teinopalpus* (two or three montane Sino-Himalayan species: Teinopalpini). Based on conventional classifications, *Pseudopontia* (one species from western and central Africa: Pseudopontiinae) stands out among the Pieridae. Of the Riodinidae, *Styx* (one Peruvian species) and *Corrachia* (one montane Costa Rican species) have recently been placed as stem group subfamilies, although Hall and Harvey (2002) now propose demoting them as subordinate taxa of the Euselasiinae. Within Lycaenidae, the Curetinae (Oriental Region) have eighteen species; among Nymphalidae, the curious Sino-Himalayan Calinaginae (about eight species), and most certainly the globally widespread Libytheinae (twelve species), have high rank.

Of these groups, only four seem of any immediate conservation concern. *Teinopalpus* butterflies are avidly sought by collectors, but their mountain habitats surely provide good protection. Likewise, although known only from a single small country, the rarely encountered *Corrachia leucoplaga* is probably safe in its mountain habitats. *Styx infernalis* is perhaps even more rarely met with, and a serious effort to relocate this curious species and discover its life history would surely be justified, even if only from an academic perspective (since writing this, this has apparently been done: D. Harvey, pers. comm.). *Baronia* is perhaps of greatest concern, and has Red Data Book status. *B. brevicornis* is restricted to southwestern Mexico, where it is very local. However, as described by Tyler et al. (1994), some of its populations can be extraordinarily dense, and it would appear to be secure at present. Collins and Morris (1985) noted that at least one colony occurs in a national park, and New and Collins (1991) suggest that little action is currently required "other than monitoring to increase ecological and biological knowledge of the species as an aid in any future conservation need."

Recently there has been a further exploration of these ideas with respect to nonrandom patterns of speciation and extinction rates across the phylogenetic tree (e.g., Nee and May 1997; Heard and Mooers 2000). This approach could be applied, perhaps, to temperate butterfly species, first endeavoring to estimate probabilities of extinction by following up ideas such as those of Fritz Bink (1992). However, what has emerged most clearly from work on phylogenetic measures, paradoxically, is the realization that the pattern of turnover of identified terminal taxa, notably species, is crucial for area selection. This "complementarity" (Kirkpatrick 1983; Vane-Wright et al. 1991; Williams 2001) can be thought of as "labeled" beta- or gamma-diversity, whereby the identities of the terminal taxa provide the essential area attributes for all area comparisons (and are not lost sight of, as in ecological diversity measures, by reducing each area comparison to a single numerical value). Complementarity is not only fundamental for effective and efficient area selection (e.g., Williams et al. 1996; Williams 2001), but it can also have a major role to play in the recognition of biogeographic regions, another procedure of potential significance for conservation evaluation (e.g., Williams et al. 1999). This recent appreciation of the importance of complementarity places a new emphasis on generic and species-level classification, and on the very nature of taxonomic "identity"—a question returned to below.

BUTTERFLY SPECIES AND THEIR CONSERVATION FROM A SYSTEMATIC VIEWPOINT

The previous section, which set out to look at priorities for conserving higher taxa, was soon reduced to the discussion of single species. Despite the often-stated (and indeed very real) need to consider conservation at the ecosystem level on the one hand and genetic diversity on the other, the species retains a key role in ecology and conservation biology. For all sexually reproducing species (leaving aside transduction, introgression, genetic engineering, and any other form of lateral gene transfer: Doolittle 1999), the gene pool of the extended species is the universe within which genetic novelties usually arise and are initially contained. Subsequently, such novelties may survive speciation, but they can do so over the long term only insofar as one or more of those daughter species survive, typically through their own fragmentation into yet further successful lineages. Thus, we presume, for example (but it is a presumption), that some genetic novelties of the original libytheine survive in all twelve living species of "snouts" and in some way are responsible for the various synapomorphies by which we recognize these butterflies as a natural group.

Through our struggles with the needs and concepts of biodiversity, it has become apparent that conservation should focus on entire ecosystems or assemblages, which must be preserved through the application of our knowledge of landscape and community ecology. However, success or failure will almost inevitably be judged by whether a variety of keystone, indicator, or charismatic species continue to exist in the chosen area networks. Even though the focus may be on management of the whole system, the measure of success is the persistence of species—perhaps idealistically, of all the "native" species considered, collectively, to characterize the particular ecosystem in question. Despite our growing awareness of biodiversity as a whole, conservation action for a group such as the butterflies is largely driven by the desire to avoid global, or even national, extinction of species. When extinction occurs, there may be a public demand for restoration through reintroduction. In the United Kingdom reintroduction has been attempted for two spectacular lycaenids, *Maculinea arion* and *Lycaena dispar*—only the former with success so far.

In considering such action, the question naturally arises, "which available population would be most appropriate to use as a source of breeding stock?" This question presupposes that we have an agreed value system for judging different options. In terms of historical fidelity, one might argue in favor of using the most closely related population by descent. Such a choice would be limited by our ability to make effective phylogenetic classification schemes below the species level (Vogler and DeSalle 1994; Vogler 1998; Goldstein et al. 2000). This problem brings us to a dilemma regarding

Ryder's (1986) concept of evolutionarily significant units, which are likely to be genetically homogeneous populations (Moritz 1994b; Vogler 1998), and thus inherently likely to be endangered (Vogler 1998; Butlin and Tregenza 1998). Genetically variable populations may not only represent greater biodiversity, and thus arguably be more valuable, but may also have greater evolutionary potential (Butlin and Tregenza 1998) and thus a better chance of persistence. Given a free choice for reintroduction, however, a third possibility arises: current adaptation may be of more importance than either a concern for history or taking a gamble on unproven evolutionary potential.

Local adaptation in butterflies, at least in temperate species, could be indicated by a suite of biological characteristics such as fecundity, migration potential, growth rate, voltinism, host synchronization, and so forth, as discussed by Bink (1992), coupled with size, coloration, and other phenotypic traits known from various studies to be affected by or reflect local conditions. Depending, then, on the biodiversity value assumed or identified at the time of making a decision to reintroduce a species, within-species taxonomic judgment could be exercised on the basis of cladistics (history), heterozygosity (evolutionary potential), or phenetics (ecological adaptation). The different choices, if matched by using appropriate methods, would be likely to produce different results. In the case of attempts to reintroduce *Maculinea arion* to England, the founding populations from Sweden were selected on the basis of being "physiologically and phenotypically suited to conditions in the UK" (Thomas and Elmes 1992, p. 121). Thus, in this successful example of reintroduction, those involved had little hesitation to opt for a phenetic approach based on some combination of presumptively adaptive characters. Unfortunately, in this case, there was no control available to see whether a choice based on identifying the population most closely related by descent (or the nearest ESU), or on maximizing heterozygosity, would have worked better—or not. Assuming, however, that the existing methods of measurement are capable of classifying populations effectively with respect to the different value systems, then, at this level, historical pattern, contemporary process, or future process may each be legitimate goals—but they are unlikely to be mutually compatible.

These problems, relating to "the dilemma of subspecies" (Ryder 1986), raise other difficulties for the relationship between systematics and conservation. Butlin and Tregenza (1998) comment that in practice, ecologists have to "make pragmatic use of the species defined by systematists," but conclude that "species are not equivalent units of biodiversity" (cf. Hendrickson and Ehrlich 1971). As noted above, when aggregated in large numbers for the comparison of areas, the species of systematists do seem to provide an acceptable surrogate for genetic (or character) diversity (Williams and Humphries 1996), precluding the need for sophisticated indices taking genetic distinctness into account. However, with the demonstration that complementarity (Williams 2001) is the key to efficient area selection, the species problem has shifted to another familiar difficulty: the question of the status of allopatric populations. Because complementarity depends on recognizing parapatric and allopatric populations as either belonging to the same taxon or not, and because most species are manifestly not geographically uniform in terms of genetic polymorphism, effective population size, or local adaptation (e.g., García-Barros 2000), the nature of taxonomic "identity" becomes a conservation issue.

A QUESTION OF IDENTITY

Putting a name to specimens, either directly or through the provision of keys and identification guides for use by others, is a major activity of taxonomists. The matching of individuals to the established system of classification is called "identification." Despite its crucial importance in almost all areas of biology, the concept of identification appears to have little or no theory. Certainly, scant attention is paid to the nature of taxonomic identity in books on systematics and classification, other than to the problems of constructing keys and other practical systems for "naming." As pointed out by Simpson (1961), even the distinction between classification and identification is not always clearly drawn.

In the 1970s a keen amateur lepidopterist used to ask me, with great earnestness, "What characters make a genus, and what characters define a species?" After a while he tired of my evasions, which ran along the lines, "It all depends on the particular group you are studying; what might signify generic rank in one case might be no more than individual variation in another." Although empirical genetic observations seem to bear this out (e.g., Avise and Aquadro 1982), the notion of an absolute criterion can reappear in seemingly more sophisticated guise as the question of genetic distance and rank: how great a difference is typical (defining?) for a subspecies, and how much greater is it (or should it be?) for a full species? Thus, when it was first discovered just how similar humans, gorillas, and chimpanzees are in terms of genetic distance, surprise was sometimes expressed along the lines, "If these were values for *Drosophila* samples, they would probably be regarded as subspecies." Even so, human, gorilla, and chimpanzee continue to be placed in separate genera. Somebody in primatology could presumably have given the answer my amateur colleague was looking for. Perhaps they could also help Felix Sperling decide on the status of such taxa as *Papilio dardanus meriones* from Madagascar and *P. dardanus humbloti* from Grande Comore, long treated by classical geneticists as subspecies, but revealed by molecular work to be more distinct from each other and from mainland *P. dardanus* than a number of sympatric swallowtail species (Caterino and Sperling 1999).

According to the psychologist Flavell (1963), "One cannot really grasp the concept of a class without understanding what a classification system entails, because the single class is only an abstraction from the total system . . . the isolated operation can never be the proper unit of analysis, because it gains all its meaning from the system to which it is a part." This quotation reflects a general view of current observational science, and systematics has also moved on from notions of absolute significance or rank, consistent with a view of the universe in which God created genera or species (which ideally he would *reveal* to us), to ideas of relative relationship. This change in perspective is consistent with an evolutionary model of life in which descent with modification and phyletic divergence are the dominant modes of change through time. The ideal for most systematists now, I would suggest, is to *discover* and recognize natural groups that reflect this history of diversification (rather than *define* them).

But how does relativism affect our notions of identification, of identity? In sexually reproducing organisms, due to genetic polymorphism and recombination, no two individuals are ever likely to be genetically identical. A person is only Paul Ehrlich or not Paul Ehrlich. Even another person given the same name is not thereby made identical. There is no relativity here (cf. Wilson 1999). However, if I consider an individual bonobo, is it or is it not identifiable as a chimpanzee? Yes, if we accept bonobo as a subspecies of chimpanzee and we are discussing species; no, if we regard bonobo and chimpanzee as separate species, or yes and no, if we regard them as subspecies but are concerned with a question about subspecific rank. Thus the concept of identification in taxonomy transcends individual "sameness" or continuity (Paul Ehrlich tomorrow is "the same" as Paul Ehrlich today, even though thousands of cells in his body have changed) to embrace classification (cf. Wiggins 1980, on Locke's notion of "sortals"). Understanding how two or more individual organisms can be identified as the same, or not the same, makes sense only in relation to the whole system. So identity, in the sense of classification, is also a relative concept.

Taxonomic methods are generally either agglomerative (e.g., phenetics) or divisive (cladistics, *sensu* Løvtrup 1987). These categories correspond to two different ways of making actual decisions about taxonomic identity: *synthetic recognition* versus *sequential analysis*. Synthetic recognition is akin to Gestalt perception, "jizz," or classification by overall similarity. For most of us, recognizing an elephant or a *Trogonoptera* does not appear to involve going through, in our minds, step by step, the characteristics of Metazoa: Chordata: Tetrapoda: Mammalia: Proboscidea; or Arthropoda:

Insecta: Holometabola: Lepidoptera: Papilionidae: Troidini, and so forth. On the other hand, identifying an unfamiliar mouselike marsupial, or a danaid-like zygaenid, may require even specialists, starting with Mammalia or Lepidoptera, to adopt the method of sequential analysis, and thereby arrive at an "intellectual" answer (cf. Minelli 1993, p. 210). This is possible because of the hierarchical nature of biological classification and the existence of diagnostic features specified (at least in theory) for each and every named level within the system.

For the comparison of entire biotas, the use of the analytical method is quite appropriate, as the hierarchical placement of numerous individuals within a taxonomic framework provides a basis for assessing the genetic (or phylogenetic) diversity of the particular assemblage. At the population level, however, we are faced with a different problem. Because of tokogenetic relationships, a simple hierarchical approach is no longer really possible (even though certain subpopulations may be recognized as ESUs). Despite insistence to the contrary, and despite promotion of the phylogenetic species concept even below the conventional species level by certain molecular systematists (e.g., Goldstein et al. 2000), at the population level we may often be forced adopt a recognition approach based on overall phenetic or genetic similarity. In this relatively uncharted territory for biological classification, the fields of automated pattern recognition (as in scanning machines able to read handwriting) and artificial intelligence (e.g., Weeks et al. 1997) are likely to hold some clues. In this context, however, genetic similarity may be of greater importance than phenetic similarity.

In response to the need to explore "naturalness" in classification, Mayr proposed that the fundamental basis of this concept is the proportion or number of genes held in common by any two taxa: "if we knew the entire genotype of each organism, it would be possible to undertake a grouping of species that would accurately reflect their 'natural affinity'" (Mayr 1969, p. 81). The empirical approach closest to this idea is the use of pairwise distance data representing the entire genome (e.g., immunological data and, notably, DNA-DNA hybridization data), and complete nucleotide sequences for the entire genomes of various organisms are now becoming available for direct comparison. Interestingly, in this context, Caccone et al. (1996) reported that the simultaneous analysis of sequence data for thirteen genes from seven *Drosophila* species produced similar results to DNA-DNA hybridization. Even though the latter approach may founder on some of the fundamental problems of numerical taxonomy (Panchen 1992; cf. Ehrlich 1964), Mayr's proposal that "genes-in-common" provides the ultimate arbiter of natural classification is an important concept, as it encapsulates the only well-articulated rival to the phylogenetic nexus, first suggested by Darwin, as the basis of natural classification.

The relative number of genes-held-in-common as a basis for identifying individuals, demes, or taxa is fundamentally a synthetic recognition criterion. Like all methods based on overall similarity, it conflates similarities due to loss or absence with those due to homology and descent with modification. Moreover, there is no reason to expect, for example, that the biological effects of chromosomal rearrangement or gene duplication can be anticipated through simple comparisons based on sequence data. They may be underestimated or overestimated. Even so, at the demic level, it seems plausible that comparison of the total number of genes-in-common would be the best arbiter currently available if questions of identity at infraspecific level are involved. Alternatively, we may need to consider special classifications at this level: if different populations of a species are locally adapted to different host plants, for example, then a reintroduction plan may need to focus of this single criterion, perhaps above all others.

Two Notions of Identity: Discontinuous and Continuous Relationships

The notion of identity is probably neglected because it lies at the interface of pattern and process (part of the two "world views" discussed by Olivier Rieppel). This is especially true at the species level, where evolutionary biologists seek to establish a series of singularities based on knowledge of reproductive and ecological processes, while taxonomists try to derive whole systems from general hierarchical patterns (compare Templeton [1989] on species with Cracraft [1989] on species). (In this context, note that it might be possible to entertain both world views at once by the "trick" of getting sexually reproducing organisms to reveal their own identities through knowledge of their mate recognition systems: Vane-Wright and Boppré 1993.) If Hennig's notion of the three-taxon statement (Hennig 1965) can be extended to the question of identity, then species separation and recognition becomes a relative, not an absolute, criterion. This approach could be appropriate for the construction of classifications for use in conservation evaluation, as it enables us to apply complementarity without being held hostage to special pleading based on quirks of reproductive biology (some lineages divide into many small, reproductively separate, but otherwise not very divergent species, while others encompass numerous locally differentiated populations despite gene flow). For the purposes of conservation management, however, such a taxonomy may or may not be the most appropriate. Here we may see the practical consequences of the fundamental divisions that have affected major branches of biology throughout this century. It may be necessary to admit a plurality of approaches without losing sight of the need to set clear values, goals, and objectives that will determine the type of taxonomy to which we need to attend.

PROSPECTS

Is "Total Evidence" an Answer?

Over the past 40 years, a consensus has emerged on the relationship of *Heliconius* and *Eueides* as sister genera, but until recently no rigorous cladistic analysis had been carried out. So it was that Andrew Brower (1994b) caused consternation when, based on an explicit analysis of mtDNA data, he claimed that *Heliconius* was paraphyletic and that *Eueides* was sister not to the whole group, but only to the *H. charithonia* species group. His view was challenged on morphological evidence. Brower then rejected his own view, not out of "respect" for the morphological data, but because when the mtDNA data were combined with sequences for a second gene fragment (*wingless*), an explicit cladogram based on molecular evidence confirmed the traditional expectation (Brower and Egan 1997). Interestingly, the recent cladistic analysis by Penz (1999) of *Heliconius* and its allies, based on detailed morphology, produced results from the partitioned immature and adult datasets that were different from each other, and both were different from Brower and Egan's (1997) best result. Penz preferred the cladogram arising from the combined immature and adult dataset, which was well resolved, and in which both *Heliconius* (six species included) and *Eueides* (three species included) emerged as monophyletic groups. Although it became fashionable for a while to adopt a hard-line total evidence approach, the logical imperative to do so, as urged so forcefully by Kluge (1998) and some others, has now been challenged, with a strong trend toward conditional combination based on levels of congruence (Cunningham 1997; Caterino et al. 2000).

Whatever the philosophical or practical arguments over data combination, a clear trend in systematics is the exploration of ever larger datasets. Datasets can become larger in at least three "dimensions": taxon sampling density, individual sampling intensity, and number of characters.

Taxon Sampling Density

In making a classical taxonomic revision, it is normal practice to assess, ideally by personal examination, all of the terminal taxa involved (e.g., all species within a genus). Since the arrival of numerical techniques, dependent on character matrices in which "unknowns" are kept at a minimum while the number of characters is maximized, higher classifications have generally been explored using exemplars. Thus Paul Ehrlich's classic work focused on "300 [listed] species of [the known 15,000 papilionoid] butterflies . . . dissected . . . as well as 41 representatives of 24 families of moths and skippers" (Ehrlich 1958, p. 309). With the introduction of molecular techniques requiring fresh or frozen materials, at first the density of taxon sampling inevitably dropped. Thus Martin and Pashley (1992) tried to address the question of butterfly phylogenetic relationships by examining a short segment of ribosomal RNA sequenced from 28 species of Papilionoidea.

There is now a growing appreciation that, due to the effects of homoplasy and unique character combinations, cladistic analyses based on global parsimony can be radically altered by individual or "rogue" taxa (e.g., the effect of adding a second *Chilasa* species to the analysis of 43 Papilionidae carried out by Tyler et al., as noted above). Thus, restricting our analyses to a limited number of exemplars can give rise to false confidence in the results: one additional taxon can change those results more or less dramatically. Given the rapid increase in the power of automated sequencers, there is now a trend toward greater and greater taxon sampling density in molecular work (see Caterino et al. 2000 for succinct discussion of a number of related issues). Brower's (2000b) recent molecular investigation addresses as many nymphalid exemplars as the morphological study of de Jong et al. (1996a) on the Rhopalocera as a whole.

Individual Sampling Intensity

In their revision of the genus *Phulia*, Field and Herrera (1977) recorded the number of specimens they examined for every species or subspecies of this obscure group of montane pierids. This number varied from 4 for *P. paranympha ernesta,* collected at one locality high in the Bolivian Andes, to 389 for *P. nymphula nymphula,* the specimens having been obtained by different collectors from numerous places in Chile, Argentina, and Bolivia, at altitudes varying from 2600 to 4875 m. Morphotaxonomists frequently go to considerable lengths to examine long series of specimens until they are satisfied they have the best samples they can reasonably get. With the introduction of molecular methods, taxonomic pronouncements were initially made on the basis of relatively few specimens, sometimes only a singleton, or a single sample of "pooled" specimens, per species (e.g., Martin and Pashley 1992). However, given that polymorphism can affect the results of cladistic analysis (Wiens 1999), ideally at least 100 specimens of each taxon should be examined. But with geographic variation so apparent in many butterflies, perhaps an even tenfold greater sampling intensity than this could be justified. To sample, let us imagine, just 50 *P. nymphula nymphula* from Caracoles in Chile and 50 from Las Cuevas in Argentina might simply not be enough to assess the full extent of its variation. Thus, to evaluate the status of the nominal subspecies *Phulia nymphula nympha,* considered by Field and Herrera probably to be no more than a localized, nonpolymorphic ("homogeneous") population of *nymphula* found within the mountains of Bolivia, might still not be possible without much more intensive sampling of the "rest" of *P. nymphula*.

NUMBER OF CHARACTERS

Ehrlich (1958) reported on 43 characters for 300 species of Papilionoidea—in theory, a minimum total of 12,900 data points. De Jong et al. (1996a) struggled to deliver a matrix of 103 characters for 49 Papilionoidea, a minimum total of 5,047 data points for these butterflies. Ackery and Vane-Wright (1984) considered 226 characters for 157 species of Danainae, but did not present this as a single matrix with the 35,482 cells required. Gathering morphological data for large groups is labor-intensive, as is obtaining systematic chemotaxonomic information (it took Stefan Schulz and Michael Boppré an enormous effort to produce a systematic matrix for the 214 scent organ compounds for just 10 African danaid species, as reported in Schulz et al. 1993). In contrast, DNA sequencing can now generate vast amounts of discrete data relatively quickly. However, certain attempts to produce classifications based on just mtDNA data, or just a small number of gene fragments, have been found wanting (e.g., Brower 1994b, as discussed above). The trend now is to sequence multiple genes or gene fragments, and attempts to subsample the entire genome cannot be far off. One can imagine attempts to get sequence data for 50 gene fragments at a taxon density of, say, 2,000 butterfly species (about 10% of known taxa), spread evenly over an initial "paste-up" butterfly supertree, sampling an average of 200 specimens per species.

Whatever the foreseeable technical developments, handling up to 20 million individual sequences as required in this scenario would involve massive efforts, not the least being the logistical task of obtaining up to 400,000 butterfly specimens in suitable condition at the outset: this is more specimens than most national museums have of these insects, and one-seventh the size of the Natural History Museum butterfly collection in London, accumulated over more than 200 years. Moreover, this scenario assumes that all molecular data are valuable and that other data are of little consequence.

IS "PARTITIONING" AN ANSWER?

An alternative approach to overdosing on molecular sequences alone is to reconsider congruence methods (partitioned data analysis). Multiple datasets (e.g., eggs, larvae, pupae, adults, pheromones, separate gene sequences, etc.) could be analyzed and compared for common patterns. Partitioning allows each data type to be analyzed by the most appropriate means (de Queiroz et al. 1995). Claims that certain datasets are inherently superior (e.g., the suggestion by Parsons [1999, p. 126] that early-stage data are more informative than data from adults) are misguided, and this probably applies to claims for molecular versus morphological data as well (Patterson et al. 1993).

Even working just with molecular data, Reed and Sperling (1999) reported a case in which combining three different gene sequences studied in 25 Papilionidae obscured the phylogenetic signal rather than enhancing it, supposedly due to very different substitution rates affecting the individual genes (see also Caterino et al. 2001). However, it is also true that if a total evidence approach is adopted, cladistic analysis of a single, combined dataset is always likely to converge, through successive weighting or a similar procedure, on a single preferred tree. With simultaneous analysis, such a result can be tested only by adding more data to the total pot, which is only likely to produce yet another, more or less different, singular outcome. Comparing different trees produced from different datasets according to a variety of different procedures (perhaps several for each dataset, not only the supposedly "best" method) could lead, through such procedures as combinable components analysis, to trees in which certain nodes are identified with a high degree of confidence (less resolved groups subtended by such nodes could then be subjected to further, intensive study: de Jong et al. 1996a, p. 98).

Such a picture corresponds to the current reality for butterfly higher classification reviewed at the outset of this chapter, a "taxon-scape" of doubt and certainty that departs from the grail of the one-true-tree apparently pursued by DNA-DNA hybridization and total evidence approaches. A similar dichotomy almost certainly recurs at the population level, between those who anticipate the evolution of reciprocal monophyly among sister lineages as the norm, opposed to those who (like myself) believe that, at all levels in the hierarchy, the evolution of a recognizable autapomorphy in one lineage is independent of events affecting the stem group populations, leading directly to the mosaic of doubt (paraphyly) and certainty (monophyly) that we observe in nature. This pattern, it seems to me, is exactly what we would expect from an evolving and largely divergent biological system.

CONCLUSIONS

WHAT CONSERVATION GOALS CAN CLASSIFICATION AFFECT? THE NEED FOR PLURALITY

The long-standing division between those concerned with the general patterns of evolution and those engaged with the directly observable processes of genetics and ecology by which it is thought such patterns must

Richard I. Vane-Wright

originate has been characterized by Rieppel (1988) as "two ways of seeing." As in the famous ambiguous figures of cognitive psychology, both views of life cannot be entertained by one mind simultaneously. Rieppel argues, however, that a complete view of nature necessarily involves an appreciation of both. The two ways of seeing also extend to the matter of time. Thus the "pattern" approach can be linked to macroevolutionary time scales of eons, while the direct investigation of processes (microevolution) is largely limited to time scales measured in hours, months and, in some sense at the limit, to the working life spans of individual human beings. These differences have consequences for the application of systematic studies on butterflies to the purposes of conservation (and also for our understanding of ecology).

The late Graham Caughley (1994) pointed to two major strands of work in conservation biology: planning and management. For successful management, either of individual species, as in recovery programs, or of entire ecosystems or landscapes, an understanding of environmental processes and the dynamics of population biology is clearly fundamental. For planning the use of limited resources, however, wider perspectives on commonness and rarity, global distributions, and interrelationships are desirable. The "pattern perspective" is necessary to inform us about priorities, whereas the "process perspective" is essential to taking effective action on those priorities, once they have been established. Thus, for planning, it is necessary that we continue with the business of describing new butterfly taxa, establishing subjective synonymies (identity again!), improving higher classification and means of identification, and sampling and monitoring to improve our general knowledge of distribution. For management, it is necessary that we continue discovering life histories, endeavoring to understand community ecology, and assessing the minutiae of population biology as they affect individual species. Perhaps most challenging of all, as I have tried to suggest above, where these two activities converge, it is necessary to be very precise about what goals are being pursued. Many aspects of empirical research and conservation applications depend on classification at the level of species and subspecies (Goldstein et al. 2000). To avoid misunderstandings and poor science at this level, we need to acknowledge a plurality of approach that is unavoidable at the crossover point between pattern and process.

This volume is ample demonstration that these two strands of investigation are being pursued vigorously by those interested in butterflies. However, the two strands need to be continually pulled together. We must neither underestimate nor overestimate what has been achieved so far. Systematists and ecologists alike need to appreciate the strengths and weaknesses of both the present system of classification and our understanding of ecology, at all levels, and strive to support each other. This will involve a greater concern for evidence and its interpretation, especially at the level of higher classification and the use of cladograms in comparative biology and macroecology.

Equally, the nature of taxonomic identity at the species level is a matter for interpretation and careful debate, rather than hostile confrontation, due to the unique position of species-level phenomena in our understanding of ecology and evolution and the applications of systematics in conservation planning and management.

FUTURE TRENDS

The future of butterfly classification lies largely, but I very much hope not entirely, with molecular systematics. At all levels, we can expect to see increasing density of taxon sampling and a move toward genome-level characterization. These shifts will be important, as they will allow direct comparison of the number or proportion of genes (alleles) in common, thus providing a suitable (and healthy) challenge to cladistics as the sole arbiter of distinctness and rank. In practice, I suspect that genome-level comparisons will be of most importance at the population level, where they are likely to be significant with respect to such matters as choosing source populations for reintroductions—or in relatively benign GMO sci-fi mode, even to the engineering of extinct ESUs from genetic components extant in other populations. All of this presupposes a will to sample extensively from wild populations and carry out the necessary molecular investigations. Quite apart from the growing ethical concerns over the use of wildlife (although sampling even from endangered butterfly populations need not be more than minimally invasive with advanced techniques: Mallet 1996b), it seems unlikely that in the near future more than a handful of north-temperate butterfly taxa could benefit from such a labor- and cost-intensive approach, let alone the myriad of other organisms that would have at least equal claims on our attention.

Methodologically, it seems likely that simultaneous analysis will simply become a special case of partitioned analysis: one further investigation to make, along with various partitions, when it is possible to do so. In terms of applications, there seems to be no dearth of ecologists looking for good cladograms to be handed down as tablets of stone—in which case, as Paul Ehrlich (1964) hinted at long ago, systematists have a duty to point to the complex mosaic of doubt and certainty that continues to affect classifications, a fractal and unfolding pattern that may be inherent to the subject, and to the inevitably provisional nature of all scientific discovery.

SUMMARY

This chapter reviews the current state of butterfly systematics, with particular emphasis on higher classification. The use of higher classification in both comparative and conservation biology is then briefly explored, and its relationship to species-level systematics considered with reference to conservation issues. The concept of "identity," basic to many aspects of taxonomic theory and application, is poorly developed. This problem relates to the dual nature of species in the pattern-process debate, and the consequences of this duality are briefly discussed in relation to different conservation values and goals.

ACKNOWLEDGMENTS

To Ward Watt and Carol Boggs (for extraordinary patience). To Paul Ehrlich (for inspiration). To Bob Robbins, Gerardo Lamas, Niels P. Kristensen, the late Ebbe Nielsen, and Phil DeVries (for further inspiration). To my collaborators Phillip Ackery, Michael Boppré, Harish Gaonkar, Christoph Häuser, Chris Humphries, Rienk de Jong, Campbell Smith, Alfried Vogler, and Paul Williams (for things diverse). To Andy Brower (for access to unpublished data) and Don Harvey (for invaluable discussion). To Rory Post (for good lunches), Paul Henderson (for forbearance), Hazel (even greater forbearance), and my parents (for identity). To all of these friends and to other colleagues who have helped me, I am very grateful.

PART VI

Conservation and Biodiversity

Given the scope of human impacts on the environment, it is urgent that we understand the forces contributing both to population extinction or persistence and to species richness patterns (see Ehrlich, introduction to this volume). Without this understanding, we are operating blind as we design land management schemes, and we run the risk both of inefficient allocation of the scarce resources available for conservation and of unnecessarily diminishing the living legacy that we leave to future generations.

The rich history of amateur work on butterflies, their habitat and host plant specificity, and their amenability to field and laboratory experiments made butterflies one of the early model taxa used in conservation and biodiversity studies. The chapters in part 6 reflect the evolution of this tradition. The first, by Claire Kremen and colleagues (chap. 23), explores the use of evolutionary radiations, widely distributed species groups, and endemic species as biodiversity indicators for broader taxonomic groups. It then applies this knowledge to a case study, the establishment of a new national park in Madagascar. Kremen et al. illustrate how selected biodiversity indicators can be combined effectively with social indicators in land use planning.

Camille Parmesan (chap. 24) continues with the consideration of butterflies as bioindicators, but now of climate change. She summarizes evidence for the effects of climate change during the past 100 years on the range boundaries of many butterfly species in Europe and of *Euphydryas editha* in the western United States, and she explores possible mechanisms responsible for the range shift in *E. editha*.

As Parmesan indicates, what happens to whole faunas depends on the mechanisms operating at the population level on single species. Elizabeth Crone and Cheryl Schultz (chap. 25) report on a case study of Fender's blue butterfly (*Icaricia icarioides fenderi*), which lives in patchy populations of varying sizes. The movement of individual females within and between patches influences the number of eggs laid in each patch, and hence local population persistence within a patch. Crone and Schultz are thus able to calculate the "critical minimum patch size" necessary for population persistence, given specific patch quality constraints. This interplay between patch size, quality, and location is of general importance for population persistence in fragmented habitats.

Ilkka Hanski (chap. 26) concludes part 6 by summarizing his work on *Melitaea cinxia* and other species, which highlights the causes of extinction of local populations and whole metapopulations. He argues that spatial scale is important, and that factors operating at multiple scales must be included in analyses of extinction dynamics.

As is evident from the chapters in this part of the book, the conceptual understanding needed to guide our actions in response to practical problems builds on themes raised throughout the book: behavior, ecology, genetics and evolution, and systematics. It is important that these themes be unified, in a model system such as butterflies, and then further integrated with other disciplines, such as economics, psychology, and public policy, to give us a sound basis for understanding and consciously shaping the changes we are making in the world.

CHAPTER 23

Butterflies and Conservation Planning in Madagascar: From Pattern to Practice

Claire Kremen, David C. Lees, and John P. Fay

Conservation biologists generally agree that the next one to two decades are all that remain for selecting additional lands to place in protected area networks (Noss and Cooperrider 1994). However, the enormous gaps in our knowledge of the distributions, and even the identities, of most organisms tremendously limit our ability to prioritize areas for conservation in a timely, yet educated, fashion (di Castri et al. 1992; Kremen et al. 1993). Much interest has therefore been generated in the idea of using indicator or surrogate taxonomic groups as proxies in conservation planning (Noss 1990; Ryti 1992; Faith and Walker 1996a; Dufrene and Legendre 1997). If indicator taxa that mirror patterns of species richness, endemism, or turnover in other taxonomic groups could be selected, these indicators could then be used for planning an efficient reserve network (Margules et al. 1988; Dobson et al. 1997; Howard et al. 1998) that represents the maximum biodiversity in a minimal area (Margules and Usher 1981).

Recently, however, numerous studies using a variety of taxa, scales, and geographic areas have demonstrated low concordance in cross-taxonomic patterns of species richness, shaking confidence in the indicator or surrogacy approach (Prendergast et al. 1993; Dobson et al. 1997; Flather et al. 1997; Kerr 1997; Howard et al. 1998; Lawton et al. 1998; Oliver et al. 1998; Vanjaarsveld et al. 1998). In addition, within taxa, hotspots of species richness often do not coincide with concentrations of geographically rare species, dashing hopes that analysis of richness patterns will identify areas of vulnerable taxa (Prendergast et al. 1993; Simmons et al. 1998; but see Kerr 1997; Vanjaarsveld et al. 1998). Nonetheless, the key parameter of a useful biodiversity indicator taxon is representativeness (Reid 1998). An indicator taxon demonstrates high representativeness when its richness hotspots or complementary set (the minimal set of areas required to include each of its species at least once) include a high proportion of the other taxa studied. Some of the same studies that have demonstrated low concordance in other biodiversity parameters have shown high representativeness for specific indicator taxa (Prendergast et al. 1993; see also Csuti 1997; Dobson et al. 1997; Howard et al. 1998), leading to continued hope for the utility of indicators in conservation planning (Balmford 1998).

We have investigated patterns of species richness, endemism, and complementarity in Madagascan butterflies and nine other higher taxa to assess levels of cross-taxonomic concordance. In this chapter, we examine species distributional patterns in the entire rainforest biome of Madagascar and suggest the implications of these patterns for reserve selection there. Next, we show how we applied biodiversity data in conjunction with other information layers in the design of a new national park in Madagascar.

We also revisit a general hypothesis about the efficient selection of biodiversity indicators. This hypothesis proposes that within a defined biogeographic zone, evolutionary radiations should be superior indicators of biodiversity patterns compared with their higher taxa (Kremen 1994). Evolutionary radiations could display cross-taxonomic distributional correlations due to vicariance (Nelson 1984; Cracraft 1991); that is, simultaneous speciation caused by the same geographic event affecting unrelated lineages (for examples, see Griswold 1991, 2000; Crisp et al. 1995). Alternatively, evolutionary radiations could display correlations with patterns of environmental heterogeneity due to parallel niche partitioning; that is, the segregation of species in unrelated lineages along the same fine-scale spatial or temporal gradients. Fine-scaled niche partitioning of species from evolutionary radiations is known in a variety of taxa (for examples, see Adams 1986; Fisher 1996, 1998, 1999; Samson et al. 1997; Warheit et al. 1999), and parallelisms between unrelated lineages due to similar physiological or evolutionary constraints are plausible. In support of this hypothesis, preliminary studies showed that the distribution of species in the mycalesine subtribe of satyrine butterflies of Madagascar (a large evolutionary radiation of sixty-seven species in five genera: Lees 1997) reflected a variety of ecological gradients more faithfully than the entire butterfly assemblage or equally sized subsets of butterflies constructed across families (Kremen 1994). These earlier studies, however, did not make cross-taxonomic comparisons.

Claire Kremen, David C. Lees, and John P. Fay

CROSS-TAXONOMIC PATTERNS OF SPECIES RICHNESS, ENDEMISM, AND TURNOVER

METHODS

Madagascar is a large island or mini-continent (ca. 580,000 km^2) containing desert, tropical dry forest, savanna, and humid evergreen forest. The current distribution of humid evergreen forest (plate 23.1) spans almost the length of the island, from 12.25° to 25.25°S latitude, and occupies a relatively narrow band on the eastern side of the island, except in the extreme north, where it also occurs across a mountainous zone that extends to the western Sambirano region (Green and Sussman 1990; Nelson and Horning 1993). Previously, humid evergreen forest occupied a broader area, extending eastward down to the coast along the length of the island. The central portion of the island (high plateau) may once have contained humid evergreen forest (Gade 1996) or a forest-savanna mosaic (Burney 1988), and small pockets of humid evergreen forest still remain there (Du Puy and Moat 1996). However, the vast majority of the eastern coastal lowlands and the central high plateau has been completely denuded by slash-and-burn farming and cattle ranching (Green and Sussman 1990; Nelson and Horning 1993). The humid evergreen forest region, in both its past and its present condition, forms a distinct biogeographic region in Madagascar, geographically bounded to the north, south, and east by the ocean and to the west by the increasing aridity that results from a rain shadow effect.

We examined the distributions of ten taxonomic groups (butterflies, primates, birds, frogs, chameleons, tiger (cicindelid) beetles, enariine scarab beetles, syntomine arctiid moths, tenrecs, and rodents) representing 637 species endemic to the humid evergreen forest zone of Madagascar. All of these groups contained at least one significant evolutionary radiation (table 23.1). For butterflies, we used distributional data from our field studies conducted over the period 1988–1996 (plate 23.1; see also Lees et al. 1999 and C. Kremen, D. Lees, and H. Raharitsimba, unpub.). Historical data on butterflies (Lees 1997) and cicindelids (Andriamampianiana 1996, Andriamampianiana et al. 2000) were obtained from an exhaustive survey of museum specimen records (Natural History Museum, London, and the Muséum National d'Histoire Naturelle, Paris) and the literature. Distributional records for all other taxonomic groups were obtained from the recent literature (as referenced in Lees et al. 1999).

Many species in Madagascar are poorly sampled, leading to gaps in records of species occurrence across the landscape (Ganzhorn et al. 1997). We therefore interpolated the available distributional records to produce range maps for each species. Range maps were constructed so as to represent likely *current* species distributions, based on the availability of appropriate

Table 23.1 Large taxonomic groups and evolutionary radiations included in the study

Taxonomic Groups	N (Rainforest Occurrence)	N (Strict Rainforest Endemics)	Evolutionary Radiations within the Rainforest Biome	N (Rainforest Endemics : Whole Radiation)
Butterflies	277	145	Satyrinae: Mycalesina[a]	54:67
			Satyrinae: *Strabena*	36:42
Syntomine arctiid moths	80	95	*Maculonaclia*	31:31
			Thyrosticta	15:23
Cicindelid tiger beetles	134	85	*Pogonostoma*	46:81
			Physodeutera	33:48
Enariine scarab beetles	103	87	*Cherbatazina*	19:30
Birds	104	36	Brachypteraciidae	4:5
Chameleons	47	35	*Brookesia*	17:23
			Calumma	15:18
Frogs	157	126	*Mantidactylus*	49:61
			Boophis	29:37
Tenrecs	23	19	Tenrecidae	19:27
Rodents	21	15	Nesomyinae	15:21
Primates	22	9	Strepsirrhini[b]	9:30
Total	983	637		391:544

[a] *Heteropsis, Henotesia, Masoura, Houlbertia,* and *Admiratio*
[b] All extant lemur families: Cheirogaleidae, Megaladapidae, Lemuridae, Indriidae, Daubentoniidae

habitat within elevational, latitudinal, and longitudinal range extremes for each species. We used forest cover from 1985 (the most recent data available to us: Green and Sussman 1990) updated with more recent (1991) satellite imagery from Masoala (Kremen et al. 1999b) and Mantadia. Only current distributions or predicted current distributions are useful in a conservation planning context. We used a quarter degree grid square (727 ± 29 km^2) of Madagascar in Worldmap IV, a software mapping tool that provides access to a number of reserve selection algorithms (Williams 1998), to map the occurrence of appropriate habitat for each species (all cells containing areas within the elevational range of the species and with appropriate forest type covering $\geq 1\%$ of the cell, i.e., ≥ 727 ha). Many recent studies have used a somewhat finer grid size (e.g., 100 km^2: Prendergast et al. 1993; Vanjaarsveld et al. 1998), while others have used a coarser grid (Dobson et al. 1997; Kerr 1997; Pearson and Carroll 1998). We then mapped the historical and recent occurrences of each species, drew a minimum convex polygon around these occurrences (Rapoport 1982), and accepted the appropriate habitat within the polygon as that species' range (see also Lees et al. 1999). The effect of this interpolation is to smooth over sampling gaps by providing many more species records; for example, from 5,057 actual grid square occurrences of butterfly species, 56,615 interpolated occurrences (i.e., predicted occupied grid cells) were produced. However, in contrast to other range mapping procedures, this procedure is both faithful to the empirically recorded range

Claire Kremen, David C. Lees, and John P. Fay

extremes and allows gaps within a species' range that reflect unsuitable habitat, and is thus more realistic than simple range filling.

Because of the north-south orientation of the humid evergreen forest zone, it was also possible to describe a species' range one-dimensionally, simply by latitudinal spread. Thus, we used latitudinal spread to define widespread versus "narrow-spread" species. We defined any species with a latitudinal spread of less than half the entire span (12.25°–25.25°S) as being narrow-spread. While arbitrary, this method of differentiating species by range size is entirely objective, generalizable, and relates to a null model used to describe range size and species richness distributions in Madagascan rainforest (Lees 1997; Lees et al. 1999; Colwell and Lees 2000), against which we could test empirical range size distributions and their relationship to gradients in species richness.

This uniform null model generates expected patterns of species richness based on geometric considerations (see also Colwell and Hurtt 1994; Willig and Lyons 1998; Colwell and Lees 2000 for alternative models). In its simplest form, it assumes (1) that all range sizes up to the latitudinal limit imposed by the maximum rainforest span are equally probable (i.e., following a random uniform distribution), (2) that range midpoints are distributed randomly within the constraints determined by the range size, and (3) that ranges are unfragmented. In other words, midpoints for range sizes approaching the length of the latitudinal span would be constrained to the midpoint of the span, while midpoints for vanishingly small ranges would be effectively unconstrained within the span. To increase the reality of the model, the assumption of uniformity of range was relaxed by incorporating increasing proportional approximations to the empirically observed range size frequency distribution (Lees et al. 1999; Colwell and Lees 2000).

Widespread species, as defined above, will by definition have ranges that overlap the middle of the span, while the distributions of narrow-spread species may or may not do so. When species ranges are distributed in this fashion, this model predicts that species richness will be low at latitudinal extremes and will increase symmetrically in a quasi-parabolic fashion toward middle latitudes. This null model was tested against observed species richness using the Mann-Whitney U test, which emphasizes differences in central tendency, and the Kolmogorov-Smirnov two-sample test, which emphasizes goodness of fit (Sokal and Rohlf 1995).

To look at patterns of endemism, we considered all species whose one-dimensional latitudinal range spans were less than 3.25° (one-fourth of the available span). Ranges of locally endemic species were mapped in Arcview 3.1 (Environmental Systems Research Institute), using an Arcview script and following the same interpolation procedure outlined above. Here, however, species ranges were mapped exactly to the forest cover layer within each species' elevational range, rather than to grid squares containing 1% or more of forest cover. Thus the range maps developed using Arcview have better spatial resolution than those used in Worldmap at that grid size. Despite the better resolution, the ranges of rare species generally tend to be underestimated (Colwell and Hurtt 1994; Gaston 1994), and this is certainly the case for many Madagascan species due to the many gaps in sampling (Ganzhorn et al. 1997).

Clusters of locally endemic taxa were then defined for various taxonomic groups in Arcview by identifying species with overlapping ranges. For example, if species A's predicted range overlapped with that of species B, and species B overlapped with species C, then species A, B, and C were designated as belonging to the same cluster (see also Griswold 1991 for a related method of defining areas of endemism). Clusters therefore also define distinct species assemblages; they are delineated so that there is complete species turnover between clusters.

We used the near minimum set selection algorithm in Worldmap (rarity-based algorithm: see Csuti et al. 1997) to select the set of complementary grid squares necessary to protect all 637 taxa, and then compared the selected areas against those already overlapped by protected area polygons (Direction des Eaux et Forets et al. 1993; L. Andriamampianiana, pers. comm.) in order to generate a predicted list of unprotected rainforest species. Using the same algorithm, we also generated the complementary set of areas required for protecting each higher taxon, and then compared the overlap in complementary sets between taxa using the Jaccard similarity index (number of shared complementary areas/total number of complementary areas: see also Magurran 1988; Vanjaarsveld et al. 1998).

Patterns of Species Richness

A striking pattern was observed in the distribution of species richness across the humid evergreen forest zone of Madagascar for many groups. Species richness peaked around the middle of the latitudinal gradient for all species taken together, with a fairly symmetrical and convex decline to both north and south (see fig. 23.3A below). The overall species richness pattern was broadly similar for many groups and subgroups (table 23.2, and see fig. 23.1A, C, D, E, F, G, H). However, three groups displayed different patterns. Tiger beetles and syntomine moths, the two groups with the lowest proportion of widespread species, had a northern skew in species richness, while lemurs had a bimodal distribution (see fig. 23.1B, I, J, and table 23.2). The distributions of subgroups were often similar to those of higher taxon groups (for example, mycalesines within butterflies, fig. 23.1E, F, and *Pogonostoma* within tiger beetles, fig. 23.1I, J; see also Gaston and Blackburn 1995; Balmford 1998).

Claire Kremen, David C. Lees, and John P. Fay

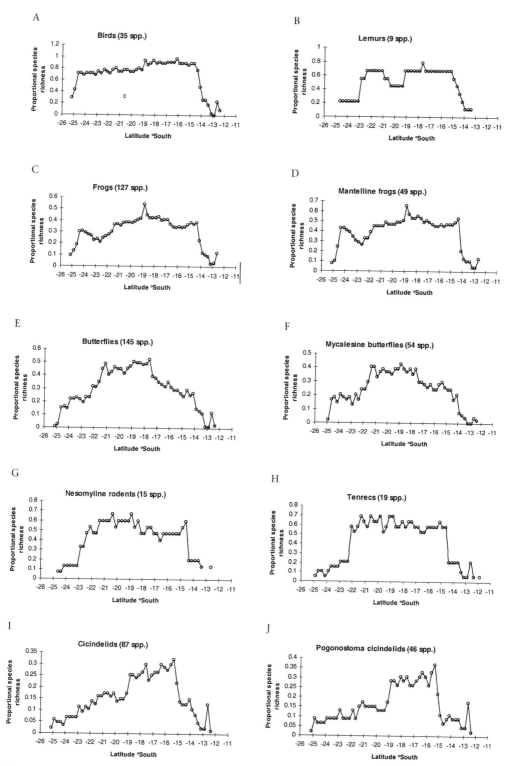

Figure 23.1 The distribution of species richness (as a proportion of richness of the taxon) as a function of latitude in Madagascar for (A) birds, (B) lemurs, (C) frogs, (D) mantelline frogs, (E) butterflies, (F) mycalesine satyrine butterflies, (G) nesomyiine rodents, (H) tenrecs, (I) tiger beetles, and (J) tiger beetles in the genus *Pogonostoma*.

Table 23.2 Latitudinal peak ("hotspot") and tendency of the species richness distribution for rainforest-restricted species in each taxonomic group

Tendency of the Species Richness Distribution	Taxonomic Group	Latitude of Hotspot (°S)	Percentage of Widespread Species
Central peak; more or less symmetrical convex curve	All taxa; butterflies, frogs, enariine beetles, birds, chameleons, rodents, tenrecs	18.1–18.8	17.2–83.3
Skewed distribution with northern peak	Tiger beetles, syntomine moths	14.4–15.6	7.1–11.3
Bimodal distribution	Lemurs	17.6 and 22.1	44.4

Concern that the mid-latitudinal peaks of richness in many taxa might have resulted from a high concentration of sampling in the accessible Andasibe and Mantadia complex of reserves (18.75°S) led us to repeat the interpolations and replot species richness after omitting all recent or historical records from this grid square. However, the removal of these records did not change either the shape of the curve for one-dimensional species richness plotted against latitude or its central tendency, effectively shifting the hotspot latitudinally by only two grid squares to the north (Lees et al. 1999). Thus oversampling of these areas clearly did not cause the symmetrical mid-latitudinal gradients in species richness observed for many of the taxonomic groups in this study.

From a conservation perspective, one might therefore conclude, first, there is high concordance between the distribution patterns of different animal groups in Madagascar, and second, that much of the rainforest fauna could be protected simply by establishing significant reserves in the mid-latitudinal region of the humid evergreen forest zone. However, such conclusions would be spurious.

Looking more closely at the distribution of the mycalesine satyrines, which is now one of the best-known insect groups in Madagascar in terms of its ecology and taxonomy (Kremen 1992, 1994; Lees 1997; Lees et al. 1999; Kremen et al. 2001; C. Kremen and D. Lees, unpub.), a much different picture emerges. In the mycalesine satyrines, the overall convex distribution of species richness and its mid-latitudinal peak results from overlap in the ranges of widespread species (fig. 23.2). Narrow-spread species contribute little to the convex pattern and, in fact, create deviations from it. In all taxonomic groups studied, there are narrow-spread species whose ranges do not overlap the mid-latitudinal area, and thus would not be protected by a mid-latitudinal rainforest reserve. Two of the three groups not displaying a mid-latitudinal richness peak (tiger beetles and syntomine moths) were largely composed of narrow-spread species (see table 23.2). Since narrow-spread species are at greatest risk of global extinction from the destruction of their

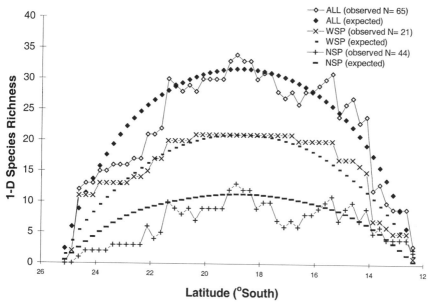

Figure 23.2 Observed and expected distributions of species richness as a function of latitude for the mycalesine satyrine butterflies, partitioned into separate curves for widespread (WSP, >50% of the latitudinal span) and narrow-spread species (NSP). Overlap of the distributions of widespread species produces the upper convex curve for the entire taxon (ALL), which is not significantly different from the uniform null model. Narrow-spread distributions (the lower curve), however, deviate significantly from the convex pattern produced by the null model. (Adapted from Lees et al. 1999, fig. 7.)

habitats (Noss and Cooperrider 1994), disproportionate attention should be paid to such sensitive species. In contrast, while habitat destruction may cause local extinction of widespread species, such species are more likely to persist elsewhere across their range.

In the mycalesine satyrines, we found that the overall convex pattern of species richness was statistically indistinguishable from the uniform null model of species richness (Lees et al. 1999). Partitioning the taxon into widespread and narrow-spread species, however, demonstrated that while the distribution of the widespread species is similar to that of the uniform null model (Mann-Whitney, $U = 0.165$, $p > 0.8$), the narrow-spread species have a significantly different distribution (Mann-Whitney, $U = 3.263$, $p < 0.01$; see fig. 23.2). Similarly, when looking at all taxonomic groups combined, the curve for widespread species was indistinguishable from that of the uniform null model (Mann-Whitney, $U = 0.1643$, $p > 0.8$, Kolmogorov-Smirnov, 0.1731, $p = 0.42$, fig. 23.3A), but narrow-spread species displayed a significantly different, skewed pattern with a northern peak (Mann-Whitney, $U = 1.25$, $p > 0.2$, Kolmogorov-Smirnov, 0.31, $p = 0.014$, fig. 23.3B).

No other environmental gradients in Madagascar, with the exception of area, displayed a convex pattern when plotted against latitude. The gradients investigated included mean annual temperature, mean monthly rainfall,

A

1-D widespread species (N = 293); oooo: obs.; - - - -: pred.

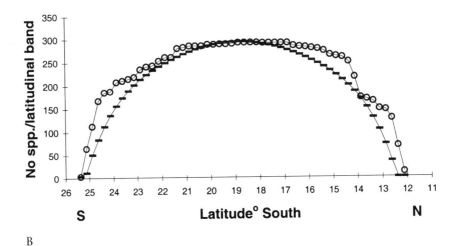

B

1-D narrow-spread species (N= 479); oooo: obs. - - - -: pred.

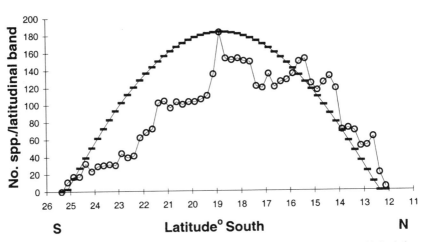

Figure 23.3 (A) The distribution of observed and expected species richness as a function of latitude for widespread species, all taxa. (B) The distribution of observed and expected species richness as a function of latitude for narrow-spread species, all taxa.

hydric credit, potential evapotranspiration, daily solar radiation, elevational range, mean elevation, land cover, humid evergreen forest cover, habitat diversity, and area of the quarter degree grid cell occupied (Lees 1997; Lees et al. 1999). Many of these gradients have been used to explain patterns of species diversity, and in general, there are two principal hypotheses: (1) species diversity increases along energy or productivity gradients (Wright 1983; Currie 1991; O'Brien 1993; E. M. O'Brien 1998) and (2) species diversity increases with increasing area or habitat diversity (Williams 1943; Connor and McCoy 1979). In Madagascar, species richness gradients related to

Claire Kremen, David C. Lees, and John P. Fay

energy/productivity had a slight tendency to increase from south to north, although in general these correlations (uncorrected for spatial autocorrelation) were much lower ($0.04 < r^2 < 0.45$: Lees et al. 1999) than that of the null model ($r^2 = 0.85$: Colwell and Lees 2000).

Although land area per latitudinal band did have a roughly convex pattern, humid evergreen forest cover did not. Thus, range overlap of widespread species within the geometrically constrained humid evergreen forest biome appears to be the most parsimonious explanation for the convex distribution of species richness in Madagascar.

PATTERNS OF ENDEMISM

To look at patterns of endemism, we mapped the distributions of locally endemic taxa ($<3.25°$ latitudinal span) for six of the largest evolutionary radiations (butterflies: Mycalesina and *Strabena;* syntomine moths: *Maculonaclia;* cicindelid beetles: *Pogonostoma* and *Physodeutera;* frogs: *Mantidactylus;* see table 23.1), identified discrete clusters of endemic species whose ranges overlap, and looked for concordant spatial patterns of clustering between taxa (fig. 23.4). All six radiations showed an important concentration of locally endemic taxa in the northern region (although details differ between taxa; this region encompasses the Sambirano zone, the mountainous Tsaratanana and Marojejy region, and the Masoala Peninsula/Baie d'Antongil region). Northern clusters contained between 36% (*Strabena*) and 82% (*Physodeutera*) of the locally endemic rainforest species in each taxon, although in some taxa the northern cluster included species whose ranges extended toward middle latitudes (e.g., *Maculonaclia, Physodeutera*). Separate mid-latitudinal cluster(s) were found in all taxa except *Physodeutera,* which, as previously mentioned, does not have complete turnover between locally endemic species inhabiting northern and central areas. The lowest level of similarity was found among the southern cluster(s), which rarely showed congruence between evolutionary radiations. Diversity of locally endemic taxa declined from north to south for all taxa except *Strabena,* which had the greatest richness at central latitudes.

At a coarse scale, reasonable concordance therefore appears to exist between large evolutionary radiations in richness trends, spatial distributions of clusters, and patterns of species turnover among these locally endemic species. However, determining whether these radiations show concordant patterns at a finer scale would require either comparison via appropriate spatial statistics (Cressie 1991; Carroll and Pearson 1998a, 1998b) or phylogenetic analysis of areas of endemism (*sensu* Cracraft 1991), which is beyond the scope of this chapter. A phylogenetic approach might additionally allow us to distinguish between two models that might explain the high diversity of locally endemic species in the north: (1) a vicariance model or (2) gradient

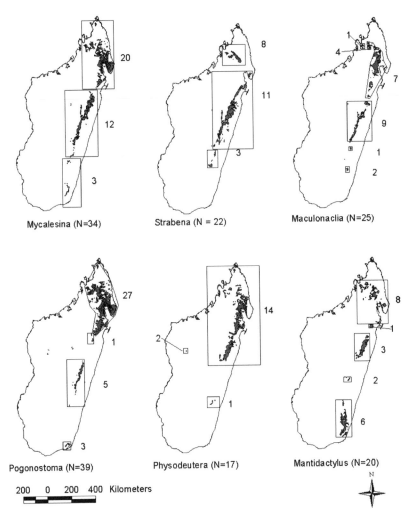

Figure 23.4 Map of Madagascar showing clusters of locally endemic taxa (<3.25° latitudinal span) for six major rainforest radiations (mycalesine butterflies, *Strabena* butterflies, *Maculonaclia* moths, *Pogonostoma* tiger beetles, *Physodeutera* tiger beetles, and *Mantidactylus* frogs). Ranges of species within boxes overlap. In contrast, there is complete turnover between boxes (except for one mycalesine species that occupies both the southern portion of the middle box and the most northerly portion of the southern box). Numbers refer to the species richness of each box.

models based on habitat diversity (potentially higher in the north due to the complex topography) or energy (higher in the north).

PATTERNS OF SPECIES TURNOVER (COMPLEMENTARITY)

Species turnover within a taxon can be measured by assessing the complementarity exhibited by assemblages in different areas (Colwell and Coddington 1994). A complementary set of areas is the minimum number

Claire Kremen, David C. Lees, and John P. Fay

of areas required to include each species at least once (Vane-Wright et al. 1991). The similarity in species turnover patterns across taxa, then, can be evaluated by comparing the overlap exhibited by the complementary sets of areas (Vanjaarsveld et al. 1998).

Comparison of complementary sets of areas between higher taxa revealed low levels of concordance. Complementary sets overlapped 0–21% (Jaccard similarity index) between taxa (table 23.3). Sixty grid squares were required to include the entire fauna, and the number of areas (i.e., sets of contiguous grid squares) needed to include each higher taxon varied from two (birds) to twenty-seven (enariine scarab beetles). As expected, as the number of grid cells in a taxon's complementary set increased, so did its similarity to the complementary set required to include the entire fauna and its representativeness of the entire fauna. Thus the complementary areas for birds ($N = 2$) represented only 30% of the remaining fauna, but those for butterflies ($N = 16$) represented 76%.

EVOLUTIONARY RADIATIONS AS BIODIVERSITY INDICATORS

Can we say, then, that the mycalesine radiation (or any other radiation, for that matter) is a good surrogate, or indicator, for other taxonomic groups? The striking concordance in species richness patterns observed among many of the large taxonomic groups (see table 23.2), as well as among subgroups (see fig. 23.1; see also Lees et al. 1999), appears to be an emergent property of range overlap of widespread species within the constraints of this biome. Thus groups of widespread species could form good surrogates for one another, but evolutionary radiations, being composed of both widespread and narrow-spread taxa, may not.

Locally endemic species, which are species of special concern for conservation, showed a broad level of concordance in patterns of richness and distribution between six large evolutionary radiations, including mycalesines. Concordance between evolutionary radiations and evaluation of their utility as biodiversity indicators deserves further study at a finer scale using additional analytical methods. Nonetheless, based on the extremely low concordance between complementary sets of areas found for higher taxa (see table 23.3), it seems unlikely that fine-scale analyses will reveal concordant patterns in narrow-spread endemics (unless further inventories reveal larger ranges and greater concordance), since nonoverlap among these species contributes greatly to the low concordance values observed. Despite the low similarity between complementary sets, the complementary sets of single indicator taxa can nonetheless represent a large proportion of the remaining biota (e.g., the complementary set of butterflies includes 76% of the remaining fauna; see also Prendergast et al. 1993; Dobson et al. 1997; Reid 1998), and thus there is hope for the indicator concept (Howard et al. 1998).

Table 23.3 Similarity between rainforest-restricted taxa in complementary sets of areas required to include all species within a taxon at least once

	All Taxa	Enariine Beetles	Tiger Beetles	Syntomine Moths	Frogs	Butterflies	Chameleons	Small Mammals	Primates	Birds	Species (N)	Areas (N)
All taxa	1.00	0.40	0.31	0.31	0.30	0.23	0.13	0.05	0.03	0.02	637	60
Enariine beetles		1.00	0.15	0.21	0.21	0.19	0.12	0.07	0.03	0.04	87	27
Tiger beetles			1.00	0.08	0.11	0.16	0.11	0.00	0.00	0.00	85	20
Syntomine moths				1.00	0.22	0.20	0.15	0.14	0.05	0.05	95	20
Frogs					1.00	0.17	0.15	0.15	0.05	0.00	126	19
Butterflies						1.00	0.13	0.11	0.12	0.00	145	16
Chameleons							1.00	0.00	0.00	0.00	35	11
Small mammals								1.00	0.00	0.00	34	4
Primates									1.00	0.00	9	3
Birds										1.00	36	2

Note: Jaccard index = shared complementary areas/total areas.

However, it remains impossible to predict a priori which taxon will be representative of others; in the United States, Uganda, and the United Kingdom, for example, the complementary set and species richness hotspots, respectively, of birds were most representative of all other fauna (Prendergast et al. 1993; Dobson et al. 1997; Howard et al. 1998); while in our study, they were the least representative (see also Saetersdal et al. 1993). Thus a precautionary strategy would be to use as many taxonomic groups as possible when collecting information for the selection and design of nature reserves (Kremen et al. 1993; Reid 1998).

RESERVE SELECTION

This study reinforces the importance of looking at species endemism and turnover patterns, rather than richness patterns alone, as indices for prioritizing areas for protection. Our results clearly show that representation cannot be guaranteed simply by selecting the richest areas for protection, since this strategy may fail to protect local endemics while widespread species are represented repeatedly. In addition, data on species distributions should be used to characterize the level of threat to individual species. Generally, one can assume that locally endemic species bear a greater risk of random walk to extinction the smaller their range (Hanski 1982).

For Madagascar, selecting the minimum set of areas required to represent each of the 637 rainforest taxa of this study at least once led to the choice of 60 grid squares. Madagascar's entire existing reserve network of forty-five protected areas falls over 122 grid cells (including non-rainforest reserves), but this network still leaves out an estimated 66 rainforest species (all narrow-spread species), which would require an additional minimum set of 33 grid cells to be represented at least once. These figures are likely to underestimate the number of unprotected species, and the areas required to protect them, due to the coarseness of the Worldmap grid, which may assign a species and a reserve to the same grid even though the species does not actually occur within the protected area boundaries. While the existing reserve network could hardly be called efficient in species representation relative to the theoretical minimum of 60 grid squares, our database predicts that it includes an estimated 89% of rainforest endemics. This "inefficiency," which results in multiple representation of some species within the protected area network, may be a good insurance policy against catastrophes.

Regardless of the exact number of new reserves required for full protection of local endemics, a strategy of establishing a large number of new reserves is not realistic, nor is it likely to be effective in the long run. Madagascar already has forty-five protected areas, but few of these actually have the infrastructure that they would need to ensure their long-term protection. Perhaps it is not realistic to assume that every species can be included within a reserve network (see also Saetersdal et al. 1993; Howard et al. 1998).

In addition, reserve selection algorithms should incorporate data layers other than species distributions, so as to take into account important ecological and socioeconomic considerations and to provide flexibility in a changing world (Pickett et al. 1992; Vane-Wright 1996; Margules and Pressey 2000). To assess the degree of risk borne by key individual species (e.g., flagship, keystone, or umbrella species: Caro and O'Doherty 1999), one can bring in estimates of the habitat and area requirements for maintaining viable populations (Shaffer 1981) and levels of threat to individual species from overharvesting or other specific actions (Robinson and Redford 1991). Site-specific attributes should also be considered in order to select the reserves most likely to remain viable over time, and thus to contribute maximally to conservation on a regional scale. These attributes include size, naturalness, edge to area ratio (Usher 1986; Noss and Cooperrider 1994), minimum patch dynamic area (Pickett and Thompson 1978), source-sink dynamics (Pulliam 1988), contribution to intra- and inter-reserve connectivity (Noss and Cooperrider 1994), and ecoregional representation (Olson and Dinerstein 1998). Socioeconomic considerations include current and future threats of anthropogenic degradation (Faith and Walker 1996b, 1996c), risks associated with different conservation strategies and with changing trends of population, resources, and environment, and the opportunity costs of setting the area aside for conservation (Kremen et al. 2000). All of these considerations have bearing on either the importance of protecting the area in question or the likelihood of success in attempting to conserve it.

DESIGNING THE MASOALA NATIONAL PARK: A CASE STUDY

METHODS

The Masoala Peninsula is located in northeastern Madagascar. It contains one of the largest remaining tracts of humid evergreen forest, including significant areas of lowland forest (<800 m elevation as defined in Du Puy and Moat 1996). It was identified as a priority for conservation in Madagascar's Environmental Action Plan (World Bank et al. 1988) and subsequent conservation planning exercises (Ganzhorn et al. 1997), particularly since little lowland forest had been included in Madagascar's protected area network. A set of biological and socioeconomic studies was conducted from 1993 to 1996, leading to the design and eventual establishment of a 230,000 ha park (Kremen et al. 1995, 1999b). To evaluate the likely influence of environmental gradients on biodiversity, surveys were conducted at nine localities

Claire Kremen, David C. Lees, and John P. Fay

Table 23.4 Zonal comparisons across environmental gradients

Elevational Gradient	Localities[a]	Number of Sites[b]	Restrictions to the Comparison
Elevation			
Low: <400 m	W9L2	10	1. High rainfall
Medium: 400–700 m	W9L1	10	2. Granitic soils
High: >700 m	W9L3	5	
Rainfall			
Low: eastern	W2L1, W2L2, W7L1, W7L2	26	1. Low elevation
High: western	W9L2	20	2. Granitic soils
Peninsular effect			
Tip: northern	W2L1, W2L2	14	1. Low rainfall
Base: southern	W7L1, W7L2	12	2. Low elevation
			3. Granitic soils
Parent rock type			
Granite	W2L1, W2L2, W7L1,W7L2	15	1. Low rainfall
Basalt	W2L3	8	2. <250 m elevation
Sand	W7L3	5	
Edge effect			
Interior	W2L2, W7L2	14	1. Low rainfall
Periphery	W2L1, W7L1	12	2. Low elevation
			3. Granitic soils

[a] See plate 23.2B for locations.

[b] Not all sites at each locality were included in a zonal comparison, depending on the restriction applied.

representing different zones along gradients of rainfall, elevation, parent rock type, peninsular effect, and edge effects (for details see table 23.4 and Kremen et al. 2001). Taxa studied included butterflies (Kremen et al. 2001), birds (Thorstrom and Watson 1997), small mammals (Razafindrakoto 1995), primates (Sterling and Rakotoarison 1998), and tiger and scarab beetles (Razafimahatratra and Andriamampianiana 1995). To determine the habitat and area requirements of potentially area-demanding species, autecological and population studies were conducted on key species, including the Madagascar serpent eagle (*Eutriorchis astur:* Thorstrom et al. 1995), the Madagascar red owl (*Tyto soumagnei:* Thorstrom et al. 1997), and the red-ruffed (*Varecia variegata rubra:* Rigamonti 1993; Vasey 1997; Merenlender et al. 1998) and white-fronted (*Eulemur fulvus albifrons*) lemurs (Vasey 1996; Merenlender et al. 1998). Economic analyses of the feasibility of alternatives to slash-and-burn farming were conducted (Guillery and Andrianisa 1995; Kremen et al. 1999b), along with socioeconomic studies to determine human use of forest products, land settlement and use, and deforestation rates and patterns (Lance et al. 1995; Raymond 1995; Kremen et al. 1995, 1998, 1999a, 1999b). The biological data were used to establish the locations and sizes of areas to be included in the park to meet the following goals:

(1) protect species of special concern (rare, threatened, or endangered species) (2) include representative species, habitats, and ecosystems found on the Peninsula, including the full length of environmental gradients, (3) ensure the viability of area-demanding species, and (4) promote ecological viability by maintaining connectivity within and between habitat types. Socioeconomic data were used to establish the locations and areas of forest that should be excluded from the park as a support and buffer zone, in order to garner the support of the local population and assure the sustainability of the park project (Hough and Sherpa 1989; Kremen et al. 1999b). A Geographic Information System of the Masoala region was developed in Arcview 3.0 and was used to overlay biological and socioeconomic data layers.

OVERLAYING BIOLOGICAL AND SOCIOECONOMIC DATA

The design of the Masoala National Park exemplifies the concurrent use of biological and socioeconomic data for the goal of establishing an ecologically viable and socially sustainable protected area (Kremen et al. 1999b).

Biodiversity surveys demonstrated high species turnover across rainfall, elevation, and peninsular gradients for the insect groups and small mammals, although birds and primates showed relatively low turnover. Eastern, western, northern, southern, low, middle, and high elevation zones each had a complement of restricted species (Kremen et al. 1999b). In addition, some of the species restricted to particular zones on Masoala are known only from the Peninsula or from a slightly larger region, including five new butterfly species discovered during the inventory (fig. 23.5; Kremen et al. 2001). The presence of species unique to each zone, and especially of range-restricted species within these zones, required the inclusion of representative areas from across the rainfall, peninsular, and elevational gradients within the park.

To define the critical areas for species of special concern, we maximized the accumulation of rare butterfly species (defined for this purpose to include widespread species found at low abundance across their range as well as range-restricted and habitat-limited species: Rabinowitz et al. 1986) across sites, and then compared accumulation curves among different species groups (Kremen et al. 1999b, 2001). Rare butterflies could be protected by selecting the three inventory sites that included the extremes of the elevation, rainfall, and peninsular gradients (fig. 23.6). Forest-restricted butterflies required the addition of only one more site. These same sites also protected all of the rare, threatened, and endangered birds and primates (table 23.5). Additional sites, while also comprising primary forest habitat, primarily added species that tolerated some level of disturbance, and included areas close to the advancing front of deforestation on the eastern side of the Peninsula

Claire Kremen, David C. Lees, and John P. Fay

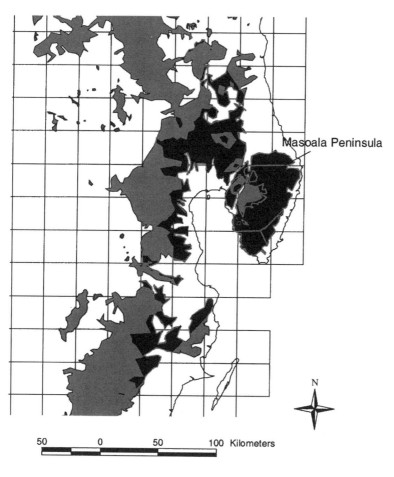

Masoala Peninsula

50   0   50   100 Kilometers

■ Ranges of new species discovered at Masoala
▦ Rainforest cover

Figure 23.5 The spatial distribution of five new butterfly species discovered at Masoala. The squares shown represent the quarter degree grid used in the survey.

(plate 23.2A). However, two species of tiger beetles sampled only in this threatened zone were range-restricted, and eight species of scarab beetles found only there had unknown habitat requirements and ranges. These results clearly demonstrate that it is necessary to protect the full range of the rainfall, peninsular, and elevational environmental gradients on the peninsula within the core area of undisturbed habitat in order to represent fully the majority of species of special concern. At this local scale, then, we found a high level of concordance in the complementary habitat types required for representation of the rare, threatened, and endangered species (see also Reid 1998).

Using Geographic Information Systems, we delineated the area predicted to be deforested by slash-and-burn farming within the next quarter century

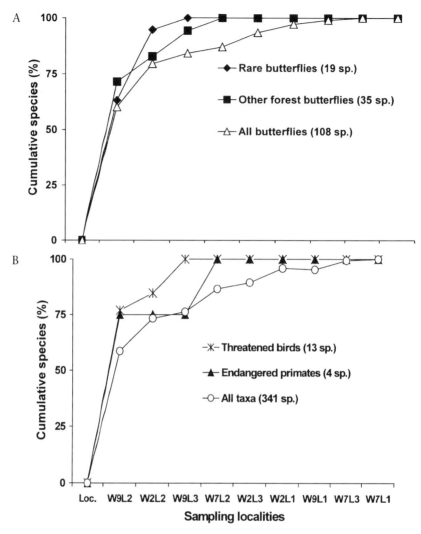

Figure 23.6 (A) Cumulative butterfly species protected by adding inventory sites along the rainfall, peninsular, and elevational gradients. Note that species known to be rare or forest-restricted are all protected within the first four sites; sites in the peripheral, highly threatened zone add widespread species and/or species tolerant of disturbance. (B) A similar pattern was found for other taxa (see table 23.5). (Adapted from Kremen et al. 1999b, fig. 4.)

(plate 23.2A). While this large area of forest (approximately 100,000 ha) consisted largely of primary lowland evergreen humid forest, and would provide additional habitat for many of the species of special concern, none of the sites inventoried within this highly threatened area had added species known to be of special concern, although two of the eleven tiger beetle species inventoried only in the threatened zone were narrow-ranged species.

Additional studies identified this same area as the region most feasible for conducting highly selective, sustainable harvesting of timber and non-timber forest products (Kremen et al. 1999b). The harvesting plan included

Table 23.5 The distribution of species from biological inventory data collected in four core area sites representing the rainfall, peninsular, and elevational gradients, and in five peripheral area sites

Taxonomic Group	Core Areas (N = 4)	Peripheral Areas (N = 5)	Species Characteristics in Peripheral Areas
Butterflies[a]	94	14	Widespread and/or tolerant of disturbance
Primates	10	0	—
Small mammals	19	0	—
Threatened birds[b]	13	0	—
Other birds	85	10	Widespread and/or tolerant of disturbance
Tiger beetles	10	11	9 out of 11 are widespread
Scarab beetles	83	8	Unknown habitat requirements and distributions

Note: Most species found only in the peripheral sites were widespread and/or tolerant of disturbance, although several beetle species have unknown habitat affinities and/or range characteristics.
[a] This analysis includes only the 108 species observed during the inventory, and not the 27 additional species observed incidentally at other sites on the Peninsula (Kremen et al. 2001).
[b] Thorstrom and Watson 1997.

several aspects that would promote sustainability: (1) community-based endeavors, (2) use of major waterways for transporting products, so as to avoid introducing roads into this area, and (3) principles of sustainable harvesting and best management practices. Economic analyses demonstrated that communities could greatly enhance local earnings by engaging in sustainable harvesting of timber species for the export market. Forest certification was identified as a mechanism for developing the appropriate market links. Similar studies and pilot projects are currently under way for ranching of butterflies (enhancement planting of host plants and rearing of larvae in areas protected from predators and parasitoids) for the live and dead markets (H. Raharitsimba, pers. comm.).

Taken together, these various studies led to a clear strategy for park design and regional natural resource management (plate 23.2B). A large core area of about 190,000 ha that included the entire span of the rainfall, elevational, and peninsular gradients was recommended for inclusion within the park. This area included all of the known species of special concern on the Peninsula. An additional 20,000 ha within the highly threatened peripheral zone was also included; while only two range-restricted species had been found uniquely there (the two tiger beetles), it is not known what additional species might be found there as inventories continue to be conducted. The park proposal included corridors that link the Masoala Peninsula to a large unprotected forest on Madagascar's "mainland." With respect to area-demanding species, the park included a large population of the locally endemic lemur subspecies *Varecia variegata rubra* (>14,000 adults: Vasey 1997; Merenlender et al. 1998). In contrast, populations of the extremely rare Madagascar serpent eagle and red owl are still likely to be small (on the order of 250 and 1,500 individuals, respectively) within the park (Thorstrom et al. 1995, 1997). However, these two species are unlikely to be protected in sufficient numbers except by protecting the wide forest corridor to the north of the Masoala Peninsula that connects to the Anjanaharibe Reserve, where these species are also found (Kremen et al. 1999b). Increasing the size of the park on the Peninsula would be of marginal value for these two species, although potentially greatly diminishing the chances of success of the larger conservation endeavor.

This larger conservation endeavor included the consideration of local human needs as an essential component of the conservation strategy for the entire Peninsula. Thus, the majority of the highly threatened peripheral zone was not included within the park. However, the goal was not to sacrifice this area, but rather to protect it with an alternative conservation strategy. This zone contains a large human population (about 9,000), and has a high edge to area ratio, making it extremely difficult to protect. Evicting people from this area would have established a negative relationship with the local population, and ultimately would detract from the ability of park rangers to protect the park. Instead, the conservation strategy adopted was to establish community-based enterprises (including sustainable harvesting of rainforest products and tourism) that depend on the presence of intact forest, and so provide incentives for forest conservation (Kremen et al. 1995, 1999b, 2000). While the forest in this threatened area will not remain pristine, it will continue to provide habitat for species tolerating a low level of forest disturbance (including the red-ruffed lemur and the Madagascar serpent eagle and red owl, all of which have been found in this zone as well as in core areas [Merenlender et al. 1998; Sterling and Rakotoarison 1998; Thorstrom 1995, 1997]). Most important, it will buffer the core park area from encroachment by slash-and-burn farming. By considering biological and socioeconomic factors, this plan included a larger conservation landscape than the protected area itself.

Finally, the park, which was gazetted following these recommendations in 1997, is Madagascar's largest protected area, and the only one to protect a significant tract of lowland humid evergreen forest, a major ecoregion that was formerly virtually absent from Madagascar's protected area system.

SUMMARY: CONCLUSIONS AND LESSONS LEARNED

This work began with the goal of testing the hypothesis that evolutionary radiations might be good choices as indicators for conservation planning, using the mycalesine butterfly radiation of Madagascar as a test system. While patterns of species richness demonstrated remarkable similarity between mycalesines and the majority of taxonomic groups studied, we found that the best explanation for these concordant patterns was the random placement of range midpoints as constrained by the geometry of the biome. We concluded that any species-rich taxonomic group with a substantial proportion of widespread species (ca. 25%; for theoretical explanation, see Lees et al. 1999) could have been chosen as a good surrogate for the richness distributions and mid-latitudinal hotspots of other groups. Notably, the three groups showing different patterns from the rest (lemurs, tiger beetles, and syntomine moths) were either less diverse than the other taxa (lemurs) or had a high proportion of narrow-spread species (see table 23.2).

Widespread species contributed greatly to the range overlap that generated mid-latitudinal richness peaks in many taxa and large radiations. In contrast, narrow-spread species tended to create deviations from the mid-latitudinal pattern. On a broad scale, richness and spatial distributions of locally endemic species (<3.25° latitudinal spread) were fairly concordant between the six large evolutionary radiations examined. However, much more work remains to be done, both in documenting distributions and conducting appropriate spatial analyses at a finer scale. On a scale relevant to conservation planning, however, cross-taxonomic distributional patterns do not match up well, as evidenced by the low levels of similarity in complementary area sets across taxa. In conclusion, our results concur with those of other recent studies in suggesting that multiple taxa should be used in selecting and designing nature reserves.

Butterflies have here served as a model system for investigating patterns of diversity and endemism along environmental gradients in Madagascar and then using this information to evaluate the existing protected area network and to design a new park. At the local scale, rare and forest-restricted butterflies served as good predictors of the complementary *habitat types* required to obtain representation of the species of special concern in other taxonomic groups. At the regional scale, the complementary set of areas for butterflies was predicted to include 76% of the other taxa. However, other groups (those with larger complementary areas) would undoubtedly represent a larger proportion of the other taxa. Can we say that butterflies are "good indicators" for conservation? Again, it seems dangerous to rely on a single taxon for information used to select and design nature reserves, for two reasons. First, we know that different taxonomic groups respond to different spatial scales and environmental parameters, as emphasized by the lack of concordance between cross-taxonomic distributional patterns across scales spanning five orders of magnitude (e.g., hectares to thousands of square kilometers: see Prendergast et al. 1993; Dobson et al. 1997; Lawton et al. 1998; and this study). Second, we cannot single out in advance the taxonomic group or groups whose complementary set will be most representative of other taxa. In conclusion, we do not recommend that butterflies be used as sole indicators for conservation studies, but certainly, given that they are one of the best-known groups of insects, they should be included among the set of indicator taxa whenever possible (Kremen et al. 1993).

Reserve selection algorithms are a good initial step for evaluating existing reserve networks and highlighting a set of conservation priority areas. They can provide an objective and efficient mechanism for selecting priority areas based on species representation. In the case of Madagascar, our analysis demonstrated that the majority of rainforest endemics in the ten taxa we studied are probably protected in the existing reserve network; however, about 10% of species, all narrow endemics, are not. To be realistic, however, reserve selection algorithms need to incorporate other data layers, so as to account for ecological factors (size, connectivity, naturalness, edge to area ratio, source-sink dynamics, representation of ecoregions) as well as social considerations (risks and threats, opportunity costs, and the local population, resources, and culture). Similarly, these factors need to be considered in reserve design, and conservation strategies for reserve design need to be defined within the context of large landscapes to include both managed and protected areas.

In the design of the Masoala National Park, biological and socioeconomic data came together to provide a solution for wildlife and for people. Here, studies of butterflies and other taxa demonstrated that core areas of forest straddling the major environmental gradients were required to protect the biodiversity of the area, as well as to provide representation of a key missing ecoregion (lowland humid evergreen forest) in Madagascar's protected area network. Peripheral areas of forest needed to be excluded from the park and managed for sustainable use to buffer the park and provide economic support for local people.

ACKNOWLEDGMENTS

We would like to thank the conference organizers, Carol Boggs, Paul Ehrlich, and Ward Watt, for providing us the opportunity to produce this review. We thank Carol Boggs and two anonymous reviewers for helpful editorial comments, and the Center for Conservation Biology and Wildlife Conservation Society for their support.

Claire Kremen, David C. Lees, and John P. Fay

CHAPTER 24

Butterflies as Bioindicators for Climate Change Effects

Camille Parmesan

Earth's climate is changing. Weather patterns over the last century have shown trends toward warmer temperatures, increased cloudiness (especially at night), and increased precipitation occurring in fewer, more extreme events (Karl et al. 1996; Easterling et al. 1997, 2000; Groisman et al. 1999). Evidence is mounting that these trends bear a human fingerprint: the products of industrialization are altering atmospheric processes at the molecular level (IPCC 2001a). If this assessment is correct, these trends will continue. In particular, what are now extreme events in terms of temperature and precipitation may become the norm. Extreme weather events affect many aspects of natural populations, communities, and ecosystems, from behavior to reproductive physiology to dynamics (Parmesan et al. 2000).

It is important for both scientific understanding and future policy to assess the effects of current climatic trends. Analyses of current impacts are essential for prediction of future impacts on natural populations under global warming scenarios. Further, studies can cross-validate observations stemming directly from climatic data, providing independent support for the conclusion that systematic climate change is occurring. Further, the magnitude of biotic response indicates the importance of the relatively small level of climate change that has already occurred. While biologists have studied biotic responses to past major climatic shifts on a time scale of several centuries (i.e., after equilibrium), responses on a decadal time scale during a transition period are not well understood. Thus, close analyses of biotic changes over the last century are essential to future predictive models.

A first approach to these questions is best taken with a model system in which the effects of climate are understood at a mechanistic level. Much wild plant and animal life has a shared form of population structure characterized by small, discrete populations with low dispersal. Though there are some true migrants, most butterfly species fit this pattern.

In the face of a local environmental change, such as a systematic change in the climate, wild species have three possible responses:

1. Move to a new place to track the environmental changes—either through whole-range shifts or through changes in the timing or destination of migrations
2. Remain in the same place, but change to match the new environment—through either a plastic or a genetic response
3. Suffer local extinction

Studies of responses to past large-scale climate changes during the Pleistocene glaciations provide a good basis for predicting biotic responses to current climate change. Overwhelmingly, the most common response was for a species to track the climate change such that it maintained, more or less, a species-specific climatic envelope in which it lived. Typically, a species' range shifted several hundred kilometers with each 1°C change in mean annual temperature, moving poleward and upward in elevation during warming trends (Woodward 1987; Davis and Zabinski 1992; Coope 1995).

For very mobile or migratory animals, such as many birds, large mammals, or pelagic fishes, range movement occurs via the process of individuals moving or migration destinations changing. Thus, these movements actually track yearly climatic fluctuations, causing range changes on an annual basis. These mobile species are very sensitive indicators of climate change because they show an immediate response, but, as with climatic data itself, one then needs very long time series in order to distinguish year-to-year variation from the long-term trends. Even then, it may prove difficult to discern a consistent pattern.

Bretherton (1983), for instance, presented some explorations of the arrival dates and subsequent abundances of migrant macro-Lepidoptera in Britain, with some records going back to the 1850s. He noted that while these metrics varied widely over the years, extreme values appeared sporadically without seeming linked to decadal trends. Further, species were not particularly synchronized in their behavior. There is some climatic signal in fluctuations of migrant abundances among years; for example, high abundances of many migrants in 1858 and 1859 followed a decade of favorable weather. However, following a distinct warming period that began in the 1920s, there was only a slight trend toward more subsequent peak years, and migrant numbers were not consistently high every year during this 20-year warm phase. This mismatch between decadal climatic trends and yearly migrant fluctuations is nearly impossible to interpret without considerable detailed analysis: it could be due either to high sensitivity of the butterflies to subtle climatic variations or to relative insensitivity to those variations coupled with nonclimatic factors. Arrival dates appeared even more chaotic, leading Bretherton to lament that "forecasting the arrivals of immigrant species is likely to prove a disappointing pastime."

In contrast, for the bulk of wild species that are sedentary, range changes stem not from changes in the pattern of individual movements, but from the much slower process of population extinctions and colonizations. Because species' responses have an inherent lag time stemming from limited dispersal abilities, ranges may take from decades to centuries to shift noticeably, but are more likely to follow long-term climatic trends than are yearly fluctuations. Detection of such changes occurring in natural populations in recent times is increasing (Grabherr et al. 1994; Parmesan 1996; Parmesan et al. 1999; Pounds et al. 1999; Sagarin et al. 1999; Thomas and Lennon 1999; Hughes 2000, Walther et al. 2002; IPCC 2001b).

Other responses that have been documented are phenological shifts, such that germination, breeding, and so forth are beginning earlier in response to advancement of spring weather conditions (Beebee 1995; Crick et al. 1997; Woiwod 1997; Bradley 1999; Menzel and Fabian 1999; Roy and Sparks 2000; Walther et al. 2002; IPCC 2001b). With these sorts of broad patterns emerging, the challenge is to understand not only the general impacts of climate change, but their mechanistic basis as well.

BUTTERFLIES AS BIOINDICATORS

APPROPRIATE ATTRIBUTES

Ideal target species, communities, or systems in which to look for biotic responses to climate change are those that meet the following criteria:

1. They are known from basic research to be climatically sensitive with respect to the hypothesized change. It is best if the actual mechanism is known, though correlational studies are also indicative.
2. They are robust to some level of anthropogenic influence (i.e., relatively insensitive to possible confounding factors stemming from direct effects of human activities).
3. A short (decadal) or no lag time is expected between climate change and response.
4. There are good historical records for the system, either from being a model system for basic research or from a history of amateur collecting.

5. Current data are available (from monitoring schemes, long-term research) or easy to gather.

6. Data are available over a large area—preferably over the whole species' range.

Though different taxonomic groups might satisfy some of these requirements, butterflies and birds are perhaps the only taxa that meet all of these criteria (even then, not all species within each group fit the list). For example, tree rings provide long time series of growth rates, but it is difficult to determine whether changes in growth were due to changes in temperature or precipitation or to other forms of stress, such as insect attack or disease (Innes 1991; Kullman 1995; Arseneault and Payette 1997; Lloyd and Graumlich 1997).

EARLY STUDIES

Since the early part of the twentieth century, butterfly aficionados and researchers have remarked on their sensitivity to spring and summer temperatures (reviewed by Dennis 1993). Ford, in his masterpiece on British butterflies (1945), noted the northward range shifts of several species in England, including *Limenitis camilla*. Ford attributed these shifts to a warming trend in Britain—particularly noting that attempted introductions of *L. camilla* prior to this warming had failed:

> In 1907 or 1908 Canon Godwin liberated large numbers of the white admiral in Wateringbury Woods, from which the species was then apparently absent, but none survived. Long afterwards, that locality became included within the range of the butterfly, which had extended naturally, and in 1934, Canon Godwin saw at least 200 specimens in the area where he had unsuccessfully attempted to establish the species in the past. (Ford 1945, p. 140)

Kaisila (1962, p. 447) independently documented northward shifts in the ranges of many Lepidoptera (primarily moths) in Finland over the same period:

> A strong tendency to become commoner and to extend the range has appeared during recent decades in the southern element of the Lepidopterous fauna of southern Finland . . . Most of the species concerned, expanding species [*Expansionsarten*], show two periods of extension of their area of occurrence: one in the 1910s, and another which started about 1930 and still continues, to some extent at least. . . . These phases of extension and abundance correspond accurately to the periods of warm summers during

the recent . . . change of climate. . . . Although a considerable proportion of these expanding species favour a cultivated environment, an increase in the intensity of cultivation has but little effect on the extension of the range; the changes in this have taken place very gradually and over a very long period.

ABILITY TO INTERPRET PATTERNS OF CHANGE

The beauty of butterflies as bioindicators lies in the breadth and depth of our basic ecological, evolutionary, and behavioral knowledge. Their macro- and microhabitat requirements are often understood in such detail that the cause of a distributional change can be inferred from known processes operating at the population level. This understanding has become extremely important as the anthropogenic onslaughts of the twentieth century have subjected wild species to a suite of factors that can alter their distributions: competition with invaders, acid rain, nitrogen rain, habitat destruction and general habitat fragmentation, and land management changes. Starting with an observed distributional change and then teasing apart these nonclimatic human impacts from those stemming from climate change requires detailed knowledge of each species' idiosyncratic ecological specificities and sensitivities.

For an example of this process, I again turn to the large literature on British butterflies. Many species ranges that extend over most of Europe have their northern edges situated in Britain. Various analyses of distribution limits and climatic variables show that most British butterflies' northern range limits correspond to species-specific climatic isotherms (Dennis 1993; Thomas 1993). These studies, along with others on correlations between population dynamics and climate (e.g., Pollard 1988; Pollard and Yates 1993), have led to a consensus view that climate largely determines the distributions of British butterflies and that, barring future habitat destruction, most species should respond to climatic warming trends by expanding northward.

But a close look at three of these species paints a more complex picture. The white admiral (*L. camilla*) has a northerly limit corresponding to the 15.9°C mean July isotherm. Two fritillaries, the pearl-bordered and small pearl-bordered (*Boloria euphrosyne* and *B. selene*) follow the 8.9°C mean July isotherm (Dennis 1993). All three species share open woodland habitat, and their host plants extend beyond their ranges, so expansion should be possible. Further, their population structures are similar, being described as "rare and localized" (Pollard and Eversham 1995). From the turn of the twentieth century to the present day, mean annual temperature in Britain has risen by 0.8°C (Beniston et al. 1998). As predicted, *L. camilla* has responded by expanding its distribution: its northern limit now lies about 200 km north of where it was in the early 1900s (Pollard 1979; Burton 1998a). Both

Boloria species, however, have contracted considerably from the eastern half of England (Robertson et al. 1995; Warren 1995).

With only this information, we would conclude that simple correlations between temperature isotherms and range limits provide a false causation. So, while *L. camilla* appears to be limited by summer isotherms and to be responding to an increase in temperature with an expansion of its distribution, *Boloria* species appear to be reacting in an opposite fashion. It would seem, then, that we must consider nonclimatic factors to understand *Boloria*'s distributional changes. In fact, we would still be wrong.

Focusing on micro- rather than macrohabitat requirements indicates that *B. selene* and *B. euphrosyne* are, in fact, extremely temperature-sensitive, laying their eggs only where the air temperature at the host plant surface is 17°–19°C (Thomas 1993). In the southern parts of their ranges (southern France), these temperature requirements are met even when the host plants (violets) are shaded by overgrowing shrubs, but in Britain the violets must be in open clearings to be suitably warm (Thomas 1993). The contraction of *Boloria* species can be explained by changes in coppicing practices in the United Kingdom, which have allowed understory shrubs and saplings to shade ground-level herbs: the hosts are present but are no longer in a suitable microclimate (Thomas and Lewington 1991; Robertson et al. 1995; Warren 1995).

Thus, from the perspective of *Boloria,* the climate of much of Britain has become cooler. In contrast, the honeysuckle host of *L. camilla* is a vine, and females oviposit at a height where the temperature has been much less affected by land management changes. Therefore, in all probability, both of these distributional changes are related to climate: to macroclimatic shifts in the case of *L. camilla* and to microclimatic shifts in the case of *Boloria*. If Britain were to warm by as much as 3°C, then *Boloria* might be able to recolonize those more shaded woodlands and once again be distributed throughout England.

CHANGES IN EUROPE OVER THE TWENTIETH CENTURY

EMERGING PATTERNS

Distributional Changes

Interest among European lepidopterists in distributional changes has only increased since the days of Ford and Kaisila. Most atlases now divide the records by one or two date cutoffs so that one can get a sense of broad changes through time. Burton (1998a, 1998b) calculated a few summaries from published records, which showed some dramatic, systematic trends in movement of the northern range boundaries of many butterflies and moths. Burton (1998a) reported that out of 260 species that had altered their northern limits since 1850, 190 of those showed extensions of their range, primarily to the northwest. No analyses or detailed data were presented, but if one simply counts the number of species reported as moving "north, northwest or west" ($n = 190$) versus other directions ($n = 70$), the change is highly nonrandom ($P < 0.001$). This finding is indicative of a common response to a regional environmental change and is entirely consistent with documented temperature increases over Europe.

Many studies, however, are motivated primarily by concern over species' declines and the need for detailed distributional data to develop sound management and recovery plans. This emphasis can create difficulties in making "global warming" interpretations. In Great Britain, for instance, while about 12 species have fluctuated in density and distribution over the twentieth century, 4 species have gone extinct, and 18 have suffered "major range contractions" (Heath et al. 1984; Warren 1992; Pollard and Eversham 1995). A similar conclusion comes from The Netherlands, where 72% of 71 native species have declined in density since 1901 and 15 species are probably now extinct (van Swaay 1995).

Results from other countries are not quite so dire, and some indicate noticeable expansions of species' ranges. In fact, it has been the good fortune of several northern European countries to have gained a few continental species in recent years. These gains are often attributed to several warm years over the past decade (Henriksen and Kreutzer 1982; Mikkola 1997; Burton 1998a; L. Kaila, J. Kullberg, and N. Ryrholm, pers. comm.). In Finland, Mikkola (1997) showed that 26 new species have been recorded since 1961. Many of these new records are of moths and may be confounded by improved collecting methods, but that cannot be said of the several butterflies on this list, including the scarce heath (*Coenonympha hero*—first seen in Finland in 1968) and the map butterfly (*Araschnia levana*—first seen in Finland in 1973, established by 1983). Both species have continued to expand since their first colonization of the country. *A. levana* likewise arrived in Sweden in the 1970s, implying simultaneous, independent expansions into Sweden and Finland.

To the delight of local lepidopterists, the purple emperor (*Apatura iris*) spread throughout Denmark beginning in the 1940s, hopped across the islands, entered Sweden in 1983, and in the past few years has established several thriving populations along the southern coast (Henriksen and Kreutzer 1982; Parmesan et al. 1999). Independent expansion of *A. iris* in the Baltics led to its entry into Finland in 1991, after a half-century of absence (Mikkola 1997; Parmesan et al. 1999).

Phenological Changes

First spring emergences and arrivals of butterflies in Britain show a trend toward earlier timing similar to that seen in other taxa (birds, frogs, and flowers). Roy and Sparks (2000) analyzed a 22-year series of records for the first spring sightings of 35 butterfly species in Britain and found 26 species appearing earlier, 13 significantly so. Adults in 1998 were being sighted, on average, 8.2 days earlier than in 1976. Burton (1998a) calculated the simple difference between first appearance in the 1990s and in the 1970s for 7 additional species of moths and found it to be 11 days earlier. These phenological shifts closely match the temperature trends over the same time period, during which summer has become 1°C warmer and spring 1.5°C warmer in central England.

In the Roy and Sparks (2000) study, the red admiral (*Vanessa atalanta*) showed the strongest response, appearing more than a month earlier than in the past. Total length of the flight period increased significantly for 11 of the 35 species, becoming up to 39.8 days longer (for *V. atalanta*). Only the grayling (*Hipparchia semele*) is experiencing a shorter season. These observations suggest that facultative multivoltine species may be able to add another generation in their northerly habitats. Interestingly, for at least one butterfly-host plant pair, the synchrony between butterfly and host remained the same in spite of concurrent changes. Earlier emergence of the orange tip (*Anthocaris cardamines*) matched the earlier spring growth of its host plant, the garlic mustard (*Alliaria petiolata*) (Sparks and Yates 1997).

HISTORICAL VERSUS MODERN PERSPECTIVES

In spite of some range extensions, butterfly population densities have tended to decrease across Europe as habitat is lost to urban developments and the plow, "modernization" of forestry and hay meadow practices, and draining of marshes and peat bogs. Even in Finland, which has gained new species in recent decades, a cold look at all butterflies showed that nearly half of the species are declining or threatened (Marttila et al. 1990). Thus, land use changes have not only swamped many of the positive effects that climate change would have had on local butterfly abundances in northern countries, but have also made it much more difficult for species to move around the landscape and track a changing climate: their success in finding suitable new sites to colonize is declining (Thomas et al. 1992; Thomas 1995; Woiwod 1997; Warren et al. 2001).

Let us first consider conditions under the major global climate shifts of the past. Prior to human domination of Earth, we can assume that the following conditions prevailed for most butterfly species (as compared with the current conditions):

1. Single populations were typically larger and lived in larger patches of unbroken habitat.
2. Suitable habitat patches were relatively close to one another, perhaps even within the dispersal abilities of individuals.
3. This network of relatively well "connected" habitat patches allowed for the existence of true metapopulations at the local level and freedom of expansion and contraction at the regional level.

Thus, when historical climate changes occurred, such as the 4°–6°C shifts in mean temperature between each glacial and interglacial period of the Pleistocene, butterfly species had options available that could ensure their continued existence. Populations could shift locally to different microclimates to adjust to small changes in temperature (e.g., from south- to north-facing slopes), or species could shift their whole ranges through extinction of populations at one range edge and colonization of new habitat at the other. Migratory species could, of course, respond even faster.

Clearly, recent anthropogenic alterations of the landscape have created profound limitations on these options. Reduction of habitat patch sizes makes it difficult for populations to seek more suitable microhabitats. Reduced population sizes are likely to lower genetic diversity, which may make extinction more likely (Saccheri et al. 1998), and adaptation less likely, in the face of environmental change. Finally, as noted earlier, habitat fragmentation has made it much more difficult for individuals that wander out of their populations to actually find new, suitable habitat for colonization. Thus, very small changes in climate imposed on a modern landscape are likely to have larger effects than they did in the past. Understanding the interplay between landscape-level habitat changes and climate change will become increasingly important for the creation of robust management and conservation plans.

A DIRECTED SEARCH FOR CLIMATIC IMPACTS

In an attempt to tease apart these many influences on distributional change, I and twelve colleagues set about addressing the specific question of whether there has been a response to the twentieth-century warming trend in European butterflies (Parmesan et al. 1999). Because we were focused on distinguishing whole-range shifts, we made efforts to restrict our species list to those species for which we could obtain data from both the northern and the southern range boundaries. Having whole-range data is essential to distinguish range shifts occurring at the continental scale from local fluctuations at a single range boundary. Further, because we were interested in isolating effects of climate from effects of habitat change, we instituted criteria designed to restrict our study species to those that had not shown major impacts of land use change on the position of either the northern or the southern boundary.

Thus, a species was excluded if (1) it is extremely habitat restricted (e.g., it requires such a narrow combination of microclimate, plant phenology, and other characteristics that it is highly localized even within habitats containing its host) or (2) it cannot tolerate even a modest level of human-mediated habitat modification. A particular country's data for a species were excluded if within that country (1) the species' range is limited by host plant distribution; (2) the range boundary lies in an area with so little potential habitat that it could have changed due to habitat alteration; or (3) the species has suffered severe habitat loss.

In some northern regions, specialists on dry meadows, calcareous grasslands, and marshes were excluded due to severe declines in those habitats in recent decades. In northern Africa, data from sites that no longer provided good butterfly habitat during the period of later censuses were excluded; if good habitat was still available—irrespective of the presence or absence of the target species—the data were included. These were the only criteria used to exclude species; prior knowledge of boundary changes was not considered.

Our European study concluded that among the 57 nonmigratory species evaluated, systematic northward shifts in distributions have indeed occurred over the twentieth century. Of the 35 species for which we had whole-range data (i.e., from both the northern and southern range limits), 63% have shifted their ranges to the north by 35–240 km, and only 6% have shifted their ranges to the south (Parmesan et al. 1999). This trend is highly significantly different from random movement ($P < 0.001$).

In the most extreme cases, the southern edge of the range contracted concurrently with the northern edge expanding. For example, the sooty copper (*Heodes tityrus*) was common in the Montseny region of central Catalonia in the 1920s—the extensive collections of Sagarra harbor long series of individuals from several populations. But modern records are only from the Pyrenees, 50 km to the north. Symmetrically, *H. tityrus* entered Estonia for the first time in 1998, and by 1999 had established several successful breeding populations (Parmesan et al. 1999) (fig. 24.1).

By studying distributional changes at both latitudinal range boundaries, we were able to distinguish general range expansions or contractions from actual range shifts. As an example, I return to *A. levana,* which, as I mentioned earlier, has shown large population booms and rapid northerly colonization in the northern parts of its range—specifically, in northern France,

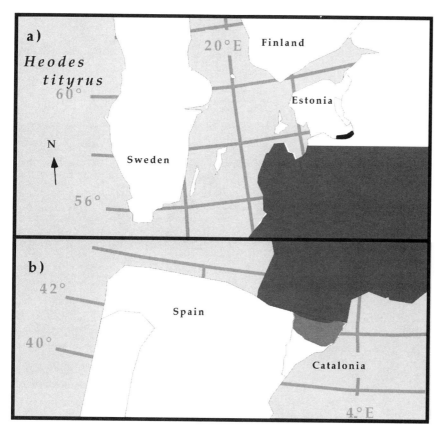

Figure 24.1 Changes in the distribution of *Heodes tityrus* over the twentieth century. Black = areas of extension; medium gray = stable areas; light gray = areas of retraction. (A) The northern range boundary: the species was first seen in Estonia in 1998. (B) The southern range boundary: the range retracted from central Catalonia between 1930s and 1970s, and the species is currently restricted to the Pyrenees.

The Netherlands, and Fennoscandia (Henriksen and Kreutzer 1982; Radigue 1994; van Swaay 1995; Mikkola 1997; Parmesan et al. 1999). Since these dramatic expansions have accompanied a period of warm springs or spring-times, superficially this pattern might appear to be a climate-mediated north-ward shift, as per global warming predictions. But a closer look at what has been transpiring at the southern boundary leads to a quite different conclu-sion. The first sighting of *A. levana* in Spain was in 1962 in the Pyrenees. Since then, *A. levana* has steadily expanded into Catalonia, and is now com-mon nearly to Barcelona (Viader 1993; Parmesan et al. 1999). The cause of this southward expansion is unknown, but the least we can conclude is that it is unlikely to have been climate-mediated (fig. 24.2).

To date, this study provides the only multispecies evidence of poleward shifts in entire species' ranges. This level of replication at a large geographic scale provides the statistical power to interpret broad correlational patterns rigorously. That is, replication allows the idiosyncratic problems of any single

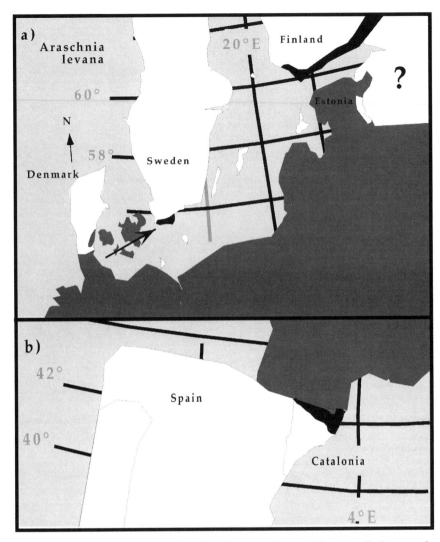

Figure 24.2 Changes in the distribution of *Araschnia levana* over the twentieth century. Black = areas of extension since 1970; medium gray = distribution from 1900 to 1969. (A) The northern range boundary: the species was first seen in Sweden in the 1970s, disappeared in the cold summer of 1987, and returned in 1992, with steady expansion ever since; it was first seen in Finland in 1973 and established breeding there by 1983. The arrow indicates the route of expansion from southeastern Denmark across the islands and into Sweden. (B) The southern range boundary: the species was first seen in the Pyrenees in 1962, with steady expansion into Spain ever since.

species' data to become statistical "noise" when added into a much larger dataset including a multitude of species. By this means, correlational studies can provide a robust means to distinguish the effects of climate from those of other known factors when analyzing observed changes in natural systems.

DETECTION AT MULTIPLE LEVELS: *Euphydryas editha* AND CLIMATE CHANGE

PATTERNS OF CHANGE

Having established that many broad patterns are emerging that are consistent with global warming predictions, what can we say concerning the mechanistic basis of these trends? Edith's checkerspot butterfly (*Euphydryas editha*), which has been studied for 40 years by dozens of researchers, provides an example of how knowledge at many different levels can be integrated to answer complex questions concerning response to climate change.

Using historical records combined with current field censuses, I found an asymmetrical pattern of population extinctions on a continental scale (from Baja California, Mexico, to lower Canada: fig. 24.3). This process had shifted the range of *E. editha* both northward and upward in elevation since the beginning of the twentieth century (Parmesan 1996). The magnitude of the shift (in mean location of populations) was 92 km toward the north and 124 m upward in elevation. This shift closely matched the observed warming trend over the same region, in which the mean yearly temperature isotherms had shifted 105 km northward and 105 m upward (Karl et al. 1996). Further, the altitudinal cline in frequency of population extinction had a breakpoint at 2,400 m (fewer extinctions occurred at elevations higher than 2,400 m). This breakpoint was correlated with that for changes in snowpack depth and in the timing of snowmelt (table 24.1; Johnson 1998).

In this study, direct habitat degradation was controlled for by eliminating those habitats that were no longer suitable for *E. editha*. In other words, if a historical record was at a site that was no longer suitable habitat for this species, it was eliminated from the study. Patterns of surrounding habitat destruction (i.e., proximity to large urban areas) did not correlate with the natural extinction patterns (C. Parmesan, unpub.). The observed correlations make climatic warming the most likely candidate for the cause of the distributional shift.

Fortunately, the story does not end there. Previous studies had pinpointed specific cause-and-effect links between various aspects of climate and weather events and *E. editha* behavior, physiology, fitness, and population dynamics. Thus, the many years of basic research on this butterfly provided inferential power for interpreting the distributional correlations. Synthesizing across all these levels of study, the fingerprint of climate as the principal driver of the observed range shift is revealed.

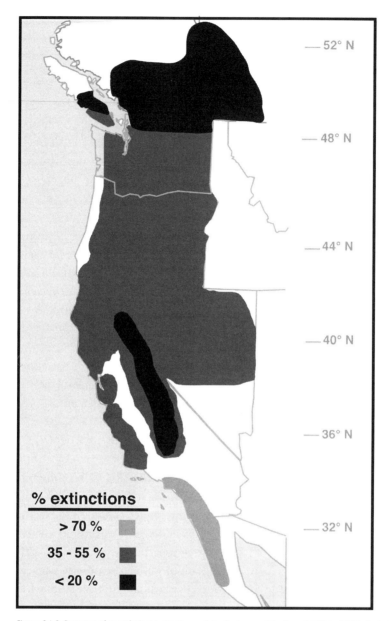

Figure 24.3 Patterns of population extinctions of *Euphydryas editha* from 1860 to 1996. Each shaded area represents multiple populations. The different shades of gray represent the proportion of populations extinct in a given area during the period 1994–1996 that were previously recorded as present during the period 1860–1983.

MECHANISMS AT THE INDIVIDUAL LEVEL: CONSEQUENCES OF BEING IN THE WRONG PLACE AT THE WRONG TIME

Empirical studies of *E. editha* within a population have elucidated many subtle and complex interactions between climatic variability and individuals. A recurring theme from observational and manipulative experiments is

Table 24.1 Relationships between distributional changes of *Euphydryas editha* and climatic trends over the twentieth century

A. Shifts in temperature and in *E. editha* range northward and upward in elevation[a]

	Northward Shift	Upward Shift
Temperature isotherm shift[b]	105 km	105 m
Shift in mean location of *E. editha* range[c]	92 km	124 m

B. Concordant shifts in snowpack and in *E. editha* population extinctions at 2,400 m elevation[d]

	Change in Snowpack/50 Years	Change in Melt Date	Extinct Populations (%)
Below 2,400 m	14% less	7 days earlier	46%
Above 2,400 m	8% more	No change	14%

[a] This shift represents a 0.7° warming over the western United States.
[b] Karl et al. 1996.
[c] Parmesan 1996.
[d] Johnson 1998.

that the relationship between weather and survival of *E. editha* is typically mediated not by the direct effects of climate on the insect, but by their effects on the timing of the butterfly's life cycle relative to that of its host and nectar plants.

The phase relationship between growth of the early juvenile stages and maturation of the host plants has been particularly well studied. Singer (1972) found that host plant senescence was a serious problem for young *E. editha* larvae at Stanford's Jasper Ridge reserve. He showed that more than 98% of pre-diapause larvae died from host senescence, either because the host died before the eggs hatched (80% of egg clusters) or because host senescence occurred before larvae had reached mid–third instar (the earliest stage at which they could respond to lack of food by entering diapause).

The pattern of these spring starvation deaths could be detected the following year in the late winter distribution of post-diapause larvae across the landscape. Singer (1971b, 1972) and Singer and Ehrlich (1979) showed that post-diapause larvae were absent from a south-facing slope in the winter following a very dry spring, although eggs had been laid there. In contrast, post-diapause larvae were well distributed across the same south-facing slope in the winter following a more moderate spring season. These authors suggested that warmer southern exposures caused butterfly and plant to be out of phase in drought years, but not in years of normal rainfall.

Singer and Ehrlich (1979) pointed out that the habitat of one of the few populations that did well following the 1977–1978 drought contained a diversity of slope aspects. They suggested that this diversity had enabled the insects to survive a single adverse year because of the phenological advantage gained by females that emerged early on a south-facing slope and laid eggs on a north-facing slope, where hosts were available later. This compensation mechanism would be successful only in the event of a single bad year. That is, there would be no early-emerging butterflies on the south-facing slopes in the following year, with adverse consequences for the synchrony of plants and insects on the remaining north-facing slopes.

Weiss et al. (1987, 1988) quantified some of these relationships and showed that post-diapause larvae grew up to 31% faster, and that pupal development was up to 56% faster, on south-facing slopes than on north-facing ones. Individual larvae on south-facing slopes attained body temperatures an average of 3.2°C higher, while pupae were an average of 12°C warmer, than individuals on north-facing slopes. Weiss et al. further documented that post-diapause larvae moved about the local landscape—across small mounds—which gave a single individual the opportunity to develop on slopes of different aspect. Thus, they showed that local microtopographic diversity can provide a population with almost as much choice of temperature (= development time), and hence buffering against weather variability, as the larger-scale presence of hills.

Because weather, emergence patterns, and population densities all varied yearly, there was no single "best" strategy that would maximize a butterfly's fitness at the Jasper Ridge site. Whether average fitness was higher on south- or north-facing slopes depended both on the overall weather pattern during the relevant growing season (from about January to April) and on the extent of dispersal of females between slopes of different aspect (Singer 1972; Singer and Ehrlich 1979; Weiss et al. 1988).

Many studies have since shown that the relative phenology of larval development and host plant senescence is a principal driver of *E. editha* population dynamics at many sites, not just at Jasper Ridge. In general, weather conditions that speed the plant life cycle relative to that of the insect (such as warm, cloudy weather) cause increased larval mortality (Singer 1983; Boughton 1999). The reverse is also true: conditions that slow the plants relative to the insects increase insect fitness. In the General's Highway metapopulation (described in detail in a later section), for example, *Collinsia*-feeding populations appeared in clear-cuts after logging, tilling, and burning of wood debris had caused delayed senescence of this host. In unlogged habitat patches, *Collinsia* was more abundant than in clear-cuts, but underwent senescence too quickly to support *E. editha* larvae to diapause (Singer 1983; Singer and Thomas 1996; Singer, chap. 10 in this volume).

Thus, the ultimate population response to systematic climatic trends depends on the interplay between host plant distribution across the micro- and macrotopographic landscape, larval and adult dispersal, and female choice of oviposition sites.

Mechanisms at the Population Level: Extinction and Colonization

Many extinctions of *E. editha* populations have been associated with particular climatic events (Singer and Ehrlich 1979; Ehrlich et al. 1980; Singer and Thomas 1996). The severe drought over California in 1975–1977 caused the extinction of five out of twenty-one surveyed populations (Singer and Ehrlich 1979; Ehrlich et al. 1980). At the other extreme, two consecutive wet winters also caused a population crash for *E. editha bayensis* at Jasper Ridge (San Francisco Bay area) in spring 1983: 1982 and 1983 had 50–150% more precipitation than the average of all other years between 1976 and 1985 (Dobkin et al. 1987). Surprisingly, a similar weather pattern resulted in the opposite response by *E. editha quino* in the far south of the species' range in Baja. Here, two consecutive years with about twice the dry-year rainfall resulted in population booms and active dispersal of adults across the landscape—an extremely rare event for *E. editha* in any part of its range (Murphy and White 1984).

Within a single metapopulation in the Sierra Nevada mountains of California (General's Highway), complete extinction of all *E. editha* populations utilizing a particular host species occurred in response to three distinct extreme climatic events (Singer and Thomas 1996; Thomas et al. 1996). In this metapopulation, there are two possible resource patch types: clear-cut habitat and open forest habitat. The butterflies used *Collinsia torreyi* as their host plant in clear-cut habitat patches and *Pedicularis semibarbata* in surrounding open forest. During the 1980s, butterfly densities were higher in the clearings, which were net exporters of insects. Then a series of climate-caused catastrophes struck the clearing populations, each one reducing population densities in clearings by at least an order of magnitude while leaving the forest populations untouched (Singer and Thomas 1996; Thomas et al. 1996).

The first catastrophe occurred in 1989, when very low winter snowpack led to an early and unusually synchronous adult emergence (large variation in snowpack depth over the mountainous landscape normally extends emergence over 2–3 weeks). The butterfly population was advanced far more than the plants, with the result that adults emerged so early that no nectar sources had matured to flowering. Most adults died from starvation, and the ground was littered with freshly emerged, dead butterflies. The second event took place just one year later. Again, a relatively light snowpack caused adults to emerge early—this time causing a problem for adults in coping with a "normal" (for the date) snowstorm. The finale came just two years later: "The coup de grace came in 1992, when temperatures of −5°C on June 16, without insulating snowfall, killed an estimated 97% of the *Collinsia* [host] plants in the clearing. The butterflies had already finished flying and left behind young larvae that were not killed directly but starved in the absence of hosts" (Singer and Thomas 1996, pp. 524–525).

The cumulative result of these three independent weather events was the total extinction of all local populations in these *Collinsia* patches over a 10 km × 10 km area. The metapopulation as a whole persisted because local populations within the second patch type, where *Pedicularis* was the sole host, were insensitive to these same events. In *Pedicularis* habitats, adult emergence was typically 1–2 weeks later, and this host was robust to freezing temperatures.

Boughton (1999) extended the previous work on the phase relationship of butterfly flight and plant development. He showed that the extent of phase matching not only affects individual survival, but also drives the success or failure of colonization of empty habitat patches. Boughton documented that in the two years following the catastrophic extinction of the early-flying clear-cut populations, later-flying forest populations were unable to colonize the empty (and very suitable) clear-cut habitat patches because the *Collinsia* was already undergoing senescence by the time the adjacent forest populations were ovipositing.

A similar asymmetry of colonization success may occur with elevation. Lower-elevation populations should have a relatively easy time colonizing higher-elevation habitats where plants are at an early stage of development at the time when insects from lower sites are flying. The reverse should not be as successful, for by the time the high-elevation populations are flying, potential host plants are already withering lower down the mountain. Thus, distributional changes may be fundamentally asymmetrical processes, with or without environmental shifts driving them.

THE DETECTIVE IN THE PARLOR

As noted earlier, local *E. editha* population booms were associated with two sequential wet years in southern California and northern Baja (1976 and 1977) (White and Levin 1980; Murphy and White 1984). But over the twentieth century, this region has suffered decreased precipitation, as well as a gradual warming trend (Karl et al. 1996; C. Parmesan, unpub.). When censusing this region in 1996, I observed a phenological mismatch between the host plants and that season's offspring. At one site outside of San Diego, the only larval groups found were all recently hatched, and all were on host plants that were already half-senescent. It was highly unlikely that these plants would support these tiny first-instar larvae up to the fourth- or fifth-instar diapause stage before completely drying out. Surrounding plants were in no better condition, and the probability of survival of these larvae was clearly very poor.

Though difficult to prove, a reasonable working hypothesis is that climatic trends over the twentieth century have been causing increased prediapause larval deaths due to host plant senescence at the southern range edge, and that this process is driving the observed very high extinction rate there. For Mexico and southern California, the first records of E. editha started in the 1930s. By the 1994–1996 census, 80% of these historical populations had gone extinct—the highest proportion of population extinctions in the entire range (Parmesan 1996).

Putting these many studies together points to a probable chain of events that might have led to the continental-scale distributional shift. In the mountains, trends toward lighter winter snowpack at lower elevations have probably caused an increase in detrimental "false spring" events. Conversely, the trend toward heavier snowpack at the highest elevations delays the flight season until the most climatically stable, warm months of July and August, ensuring rapid, unimpeded growth of offspring to diapause (C. Parmesan, unpub.). In the southernmost populations, a gradual warming/drying trend has probably led to a steady shortening of the window of time in which the host is edible. Thus, systematic climatic shifts are highly plausible drivers of the northward and upward range shift of E. editha.

SUMMARY

Butterflies are ideal models for understanding the intersecting effects of modern environmental changes, particularly the hardships imposed by climate change across an increasingly hostile landscape. Range shifts are perhaps the least controversial, as well as the most easily observed, responses expected under global warming scenarios. While changes at single study sites and along single species' range boundaries have been studied in a diversity of taxa, only in butterflies have changes across entire species ranges been documented. In studies that have focused on detection of climatic effects while incorporating controls for other factors known to affect species' distributions, poleward shifts of species' ranges have been found in proportions far higher than one would expect by chance. The magnitudes of the observed range shifts (boundary movements from 35 to 200 km) are on the same order as the magnitudes of regional warming (from $0.7°$ to $0.8°C$). The sensitivity of butterflies to climate, the temporal and spatial breadth of distributional data (especially for European species), and the wealth of basic biological knowledge place butterflies among the very few wild organisms that can provide this quality of information on the current impacts of climate change. Thus, butterflies are, and are likely to remain, model bioindicators for present and future impacts of global warming.

ACKNOWLEDGMENTS

Many thanks to the thousands of amateur lepidopterists whose records are essential for tracking change, and to all of the researchers whose field studies of butterflies provide the details for linking observed trends to climate change. Field assistance for the *E. editha* study came from K. Agnew, D. Boughton, D. Kingsinger, T. Martinez, M. C. Singer, C. D. Thomas, and B. Wee. The bulk of *E. editha* records and historical notes were provided by G. Austin, D. Bauer, J. Brown, P. R. Ehrlich, J. Emmel, L. E. Gilbert, C. Guppy, J. Hinchliff (who compiled all the Washington and Oregon records), S. Matoon, J. Rawlins, O. Shields, and R. R. White; the American Museum of Natural History, California Academy of Sciences, Carnegie Natural History Museum, Center for Conservation Biology (Stanford), Cornell entomology collection, Los Angeles Natural History Museum, the Natural History Museum (London), Nevada State Museum, San Diego Natural History Museum, Smithsonian Natural History Museum, and U. C. Davis entomology collection. The European/North Africa synthesis was made possible with the help of P. Ackery, H. Descimon, I. Hanski, L. Kaila, J. Kullberg, J. K. Hill, B. Huntley, M. Nieminen, N. Ryrholm, M. C. Singer, C. Stefanescu, C. D. Thomas, J. A. Thomas, W. J. Tennent, T. Tammaru, R. I. Vane-Wright, and M. Warren; lepidopterists' societies and butterfly conservation organizations in Estonia, Finland, Great Britain, the Netherlands, and Sweden; Université de Provence and University of Madrid; and natural history museums in London, Paris, Barcelona, and Helsinki. Special thanks to Michael Singer for introducing me to the joys of butterfly research and for being an extremely patient, overqualified field assistant throughout the years.

CHAPTER 25

Movement Behavior and Minimum Patch Size for Butterfly Population Persistence

Elizabeth E. Crone and Cheryl B. Schultz

The vast majority of butterflies have specific habitat requirements, and for these species, the world can be divided into habitat and non-habitat. Many butterfly species exist naturally in small habitat fragments (Warren 1991). Others are threatened by loss of habitat, or persist in a fraction of their historical range. Of 59 species of British butterflies surveyed by Thomas (1984), 46 exist in discrete, "closed" populations; of these, 15 have been recorded with persistent populations on 0.5–1 ha of land. Although these statistics suggest that butterfly populations can survive on remarkably small pieces of land, this conclusion might be very misleading. For example, many butterfly species are thought to behave as metapopulations. Although it appears that individual habitat patches are small, butterfly persistence may depend on immigration from other patches (Thomas 1991; Hanski 1998a). Historically, habitat patches may have been common and between-patch migration rather frequent. Today, however, much habitat has been lost. In these cases, once a local butterfly population goes extinct, the patch is often too isolated to be recolonized (Thomas 1991). Furthermore, butterflies that leave a habitat patch are likely to be lost to the system entirely, rather than finding and reproducing in new patches, as would have happened in more connected systems. As a result, for many butterfly species today, populations in previously well-connected patches must now survive independently of other patches, if they are to persist at all.

We expect smaller patches to be less able to support persistent butterfly populations for several reasons. For example, smaller butterfly populations are generally more susceptible to extinction through demographic, environmental, and genetic stochasticity (Gilpin and Soulé 1986; Hanski, chap. 26 in this volume). In addition, edge effects are proportionally greater in smaller patches. Invasion of small patches by non-native species, for example, could lead to competitive exclusion of necessary butterfly host plants. Finally, for many butterfly species, individuals in small habitat patches are more likely to fly out of suitable habitat by random chance and get lost in the surrounding non-habitat. In this chapter, our primary focus is on this last phenomenon: interactions between movement behavior, patch size, and population persistence.

Butterflies spend less time in smaller habitat patches because of the stochastic nature of butterfly movement behavior. For many butterfly species, flight is described well by a random walk (Jones 1977; Root and Kareiva 1984; Turchin et al. 1991; Turchin 1998). This means that there is a substantial stochastic component to the speed and direction of butterfly movement, even if butterflies also have some affinity for particular landscape features (e.g., patches of suitable host plants). As host plant patches get smaller, butterflies abandon them more quickly, simply because the probability of a butterfly encountering the habitat perimeter is greater in smaller patches (see descriptions of minimum patch size theory for randomly moving organisms in Skellam 1951; Okubo 1984; Holmes et al. 1994). To corroborate these general theories, higher per capita emigration rates in smaller patches have been documented for several butterfly populations (Hill et al. 1996; Sutcliffe and Thomas 1997a). Based on these ideas, we define the critical minimum patch size for butterfly persistence as the smallest patch in which butterflies stay long enough to lay enough eggs to replace themselves before leaving the patch.

In this chapter, we calculate the minimum patch size that could support persistent populations of an endangered butterfly, *Icaricia icarioides fenderi*, based on its movement behavior and population dynamics. We then discuss how similar calculations could be made from other kinds of data that are available for many other butterfly species. After reviewing the effects of movement behavior on patch size and population persistence, we briefly explore the interrelationships between movement behavior and other ecological processes that affect the viability of butterfly populations in small habitat patches.

MINIMUM PATCH SIZE FOR THE FENDER'S BLUE BUTTERFLY

To estimate minimum patch size, we need three kinds of information about a species: movement behavior, demography, and how at least one of these varies with patch size. To explore the effects of movement and patch size on population persistence, we begin with an extensive study of the dispersal behavior of Fender's blue butterfly (*Icaricia icarioides fenderi*) (Schultz 1998a; Schultz and Crone 2001). We combine quantification of individual behavior with limited monitoring data from six *I. i. fenderi* populations and a general knowledge of the butterfly's biology. We build an empirically based, mechanistic model (derived from basic principles of population viability analysis) that predicts how population growth rates of butterfly populations should vary with patch size when a patch is isolated from other butterfly populations.

BIOLOGY OF THE FENDER'S BLUE

I. i. fenderi is an endangered butterfly endemic to upland prairies in the Willamette Valley in Oregon (fig. 25.1). It depends on native perennial lupines, either *Lupinus sulphureus kincaidii* (Kincaid's lupine) or *L. laxiflorus* (spur lupine), as larval host plants. Because the Fender's blue is a habitat specialist, the landscape can be divided into habitat and non-habitat based on the presence of host lupines. Fender's blue habitat has declined dramatically over the last 150 years due to agriculture, urbanization, and the cessation of annual autumn fires set by Native Americans (Ingersoll and Wilson 1991; Noss et al. 1995). Less than 1% of the Willamette Valley's original upland prairie survives, and the remaining fragments are small, isolated, and widely scattered across the valley (Alverson 1993). Forests and weedy shrubs now threaten to overrun these remnants (Hammond and Wilson 1993). Fewer than 4,000 Fender's blues remain (Schultz 1998b; Hammond 1995; Hammond and Wilson 1993), and Kincaid's lupine survives in only a handful of areas greater than a hectare in size (Kuykendall and Kaye 1993). Both the butterfly and Kincaid's lupine were added to the U.S. endangered species list in January 2000 (Federal Register 2000).

The remaining *I. i. fenderi* populations are not connected by dispersal. Baskette Slough National Wildlife Refuge, in the northern part of the Willamette Valley, is owned and managed by the U.S. Fish and Wildlife Service and supports the largest remaining population, about 1,000–1,400 butterflies. From Baskette Slough, it is about 8 km to the nearest neighboring *I. i. fenderi* population. The Nature Conservancy's Willow Creek Natural Area supports the second largest remaining population, about 500–1,000 butterflies. The closest *I. i. fenderi* population to Willow Creek is about 7 km away. Both of these populations are too isolated to facilitate exchange with other nearby populations. At best, an *I. i. fenderi* may fly 1 or 2 kilometers in its lifetime (Schultz 1998a). Therefore, knowing how small a population can persist without immigration is relevant to conservation decision making for extant populations.

In addition, numerous agencies in the Willamette Valley are interested in the conservation of the Fender's blue butterfly and its habitat. The Bureau of Land Management and The Nature Conservancy have recently purchased land that they are interested in restoring as Willamette Valley upland prairie

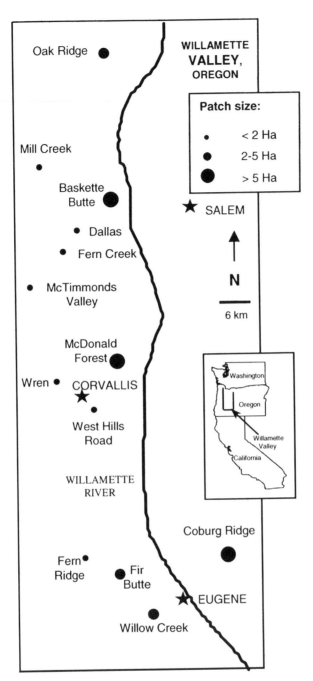

Figure 25.1 Locations and habitat areas for extant Fender's blue butterfly populations.

with the goal of re-creating *I. i. fenderi* habitat. Given limited conservation dollars, we need to direct such efforts at habitat conservation and restoration efficiently. By defining a minimum patch size for *I. i. fenderi*, we can decide which potential restoration and acquisition sites are large enough to support viable *I. i. fenderi* populations.

Elizabeth E. Crone and Cheryl B. Schultz

We began our analysis of minimum patch size by using movement behavior to ask how long butterflies can be expected to stay in habitat patches of different sizes. In other words, if a Fender's blue butterfly emerges in a lupine patch of a given size, how many days will she spend in that patch before randomly dispersing into non-habitat? To make this calculation, we observed movement behavior in the field and estimated parameters for a model of individual dispersal behavior (Schultz and Crone 2001). The model assumed that movement behavior was a function of a butterfly's position relative to lupine habitat. To parameterize the model, we observed 122 *I. i. fenderi* flight paths in lupine, outside lupine, and at the boundary between habitat and non-habitat. Our approach was based on random walk methods for discretizing continuous flight paths into individual moves, characterized by their speed and direction (fig. 25.2). We used parameters estimated from these moves to predict long-term displacement. General methods for this kind of analysis are reviewed by Turchin (1998), and the details of our analyses of *I. i. fenderi* movement behavior are presented elsewhere (Schultz and Crone 2001). Here, we summarize this analysis as a necessary first step in estimating minimum patch size.

I. i. fenderi flight behavior is a combination of random and directed factors (Schultz and Crone 2001). We described these behaviors using the conceptual framework of a biased, correlated random walk. We tested for

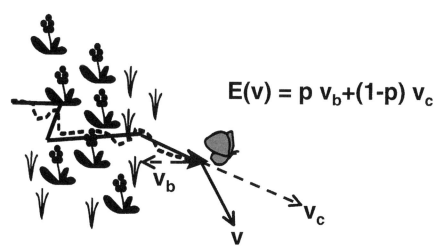

$$E(v) = p\, v_b + (1-p)\, v_c$$

Figure 25.2 Movement path of a butterfly (heavy dashed line) transformed into discrete steps for data analysis (heavy solid lines). Each step is characterized by its speed and direction. Because this butterfly is at a habitat edge (near a lupine patch, but currently in non-habitat), its expected direction of movement (v) is a weighted average of the direction expected due to bias (the direction straight toward the nearest lupine patch, v_b) and the direction expected due to correlation (the direction of the previous movement, v_c). In addition to estimating bias, we compared movement speeds and the tendency for butterflies to deviate from the expected direction between lupine habitat, habitat edges, and non-habitat.

two kinds of directed movement by *I. i. fenderi*: correlation, or the tendency to fly in straight lines (i.e., the direction of each move is correlated with the direction of the previous move); and bias, or the tendency to fly toward lupine patches. We assumed that butterfly dispersal behavior depended on both correlation and bias, such that each move's expected direction was a weighted average of the direction of the previous move (correlation) and the direction of the straightest line to the nearest lupine (bias) (fig. 25.2). Not surprisingly, butterflies demonstrated considerable deviation from the expected movement direction (the random part of a biased, correlated random walk). These parameters formed the basis for stochastic simulations of lifetime butterfly movement. We predicted patch residence times from the averages of 2,000 simulated butterflies in each of ten patch sizes, chosen to span the size distribution of existing and potentially restorable habitat patches for the Fender's blue.

POPULATION VIABILITY ANALYSIS

Next, we combined patch residence times with census data from ongoing monitoring to estimate how population growth rates vary with patch size. The rationale for this procedure comes from assuming that a butterfly's lifetime fecundity (e_t) is primarily limited by the amount of time she spends in lupine habitat (T_L), rather than in non-habitat. The average number of eggs laid in the entire population is therefore the product of the number of female butterflies, their oviposition rate (w), and the average amount of time each spends inside lupine habitat:

$$e_t = T_L {}^* w {}^* 0.5 {}^* N_t,$$

where N_t is the total number of adult butterflies in the population, assuming an approximately even sex ratio. The number of adult butterflies in the next generation (N_{t+1}) is the number of eggs laid by the previous generation, multiplied by their survivorship (s):

$$(25.1) \quad N_{t+1} = T_L {}^* w {}^* 0.5 {}^* N_t {}^* s.$$

This means that the population growth rate (N_{t+1}/N_t) increases linearly with increasing residence time in lupine habitat. From the perspective of movement behavior, the primary negative effect of small patch size on population viability is therefore a decrease in the maximum possible population growth rate, rather then the potential negative effects of small population size per se (see Caughley 1994).

To estimate a minimum size for persistent populations, we employed a simple, density-independent model of population dynamics. As explained by Lande and Orzack (1988) and Dennis et al. (1991), the relationship between population growth rate and population viability depends on the

Elizabeth E. Crone and Cheryl B. Schultz

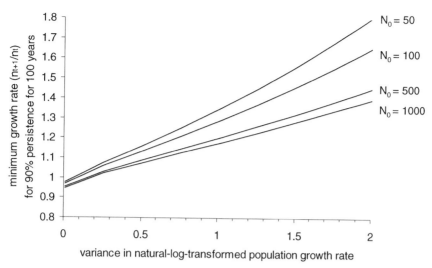

Figure 25.3 Minimum combinations of population growth rate and variance in log-transformed growth rate that predict 90% persistence of populations for 100 years, based on a range of initial population sizes (N_0). Points to the upper left would be less likely to persist, and points to the lower right more likely to persist. Curves were calculated following Dennis et al. (1991), and are directly analogous to the analytical results of Lande and Orzack (1988).

initial population size and the amount of temporal environmental variation (fig. 25.3). All else being equal, larger populations, populations with higher average growth rates, and populations with lower variance in growth rates are more likely to persist. In the context of habitat restoration and butterfly reintroduction, it may be possible to control initial starting population sizes, but it is seldom feasible to directly control long-term population growth rates or the environmental variation that affects them. We are therefore particularly concerned with the effects of patch size (which we directly control in land acquisition and restoration projects) on population growth rates. By using this method, we ignore mechanisms of population regulation, such as density dependence, except to assume that Fender's blue fecundity is primarily limited by time spent inside lupine patches. However, density dependence, at least in the sense of overcrowding, is unlikely to matter at the point where population growth shifts from declining to increasing.

Six Fender's blue populations have been monitored since the early 1990s (C. Schultz and P. Hammond, unpub.; fig. 25.4). Using data from these populations and methods outlined by Dennis et al. (1991; see also Morris et al. 1999), we estimated population growth rate, year-to-year variance in population growth rate, and the minimum growth rate that would be necessary to predict 90% persistence for 100 years based on various population starting sizes (see fig. 25.3). Using this information, we calculated the expected changes in population growth rate with changes in patch size (recruitment/day, multiplied by the number of days spent in patches

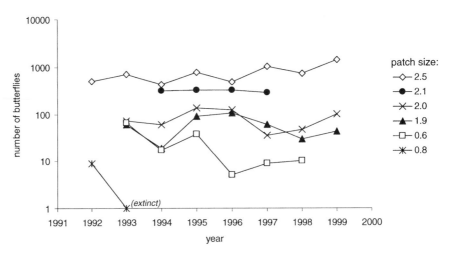

Figure 25.4 Abundance data from six Fender's blue populations with ongoing monitoring programs. These populations are located in habitat patches with sizes from 0.6 to 2.5 ha. Note the log-transformed scale on the *y*-axis.

of different sizes). We fitted a single curve to average trends across sites, weighted by variance in trend parameter estimates.

MINIMUM PATCH SIZE

Within a lupine patch, Fender's blue butterflies moved short distances and turned frequently from the direction of the previous move. Outside lupine patches, butterflies flew longer distances and were more likely to fly in straight lines. At the edges of lupine patches (outside lupine, but within 10–20 m of patch perimeters), butterfly movement behavior was intermediate between behavior inside and outside patches, and butterflies were more likely to fly toward lupine patches than would be expected by chance (table 25.1). Based on these parameters, we found that expected residence time varied dramatically over the size range of existing and potential habitat. For example, in 0.5 ha patches, simulated butterflies stayed 2.9 days, on average, in their natal patch, while in 3.0 ha patches, simulated butterflies stayed in their natal patches an average of 8.7 days. This finding implies that population growth rates of butterflies should also vary widely with patch size across this range of patch sizes.

In the six populations monitored, the average growth rate was higher in larger patches. However, average trends at most sites were poorly estimated because variance in population growth rates was high. Nonetheless, if we assume that population growth rate increases linearly with time spent in lupine habitat, we can be confident about the shape of the residence time curve, based on the movement model. Given the assumptions of the model, Fender's blue butterflies require a minimum population growth rate of 1.04,

Table 25.1 Movement behavior of female Fender's blue butterflies in lupine habitat, in non-habitat, and at habitat/non-habitat edges

Behavior	Parameter Estimates (90% Confidence Intervals)			
	Lupine Habitat	Habitat Edge	Non-Habitat	Edge Width[a]
Movement speed (m/s)	0.035	0.10	0.15	14
Bias (%, relative	(0.03–0.04)	(0.09–0.12)	(0.11–0.21)	(0–50+)
to correlation)		0.38		10
		(0.09–0.61)		(6–18)
Average deviance from	49	47	23	22
expected direction (°)	(46–52)	(43–50)	(18–31)	(16–26)

Source: Summarized from Schultz and Crone 2001.

[a] Edge width is the spatial area (in meters from patch edge) over which butterflies display edge behavior (see further explanation and discussion in Schultz and Crone 2001).

if we assume low year-to-year variance (as observed in the least variable population), and a minimum growth rate of 1.55, if we assume high variance. This finding demonstrates the importance of taking variation into account when estimating population viability. Both estimates of minimum growth rate are considerably higher than the minimum growth rate for replacement in a constant environment. Exact replacement occurs when births equal deaths, or when the multiplicative population growth rate is 1. By scaling population growth rates to residence time, we estimated that Fender's blue butterflies gain a growth rate increment of 0.15 for every day they spend inside lupine. Thus, it seems highly unlikely that a Fender's blue population would persist in an isolated habitat patch of less than 2 ha (fig. 25.5). A conservative estimate of minimum patch size, assuming high stochastic variance in growth rates, is 6 ha.

MINIMUM PATCH SIZE FOR OTHER BUTTERFLIES

How can we estimate minimum patch size for other at-risk butterfly populations? For *I. i. fenderi,* we estimated minimum patch size using detailed behavioral data, which are not available for many species. For endangered species in particular, it is important to be able to base calculations on readily available data. For at-risk butterflies, three kinds of relevant information are often available: life table data (Pollard 1979; Brakefield 1982; Courtney and Duggan 1983; Warren et al. 1986), and repeated censuses of abundance over time (such as the British Butterfly Monitoring Scheme: Pollard 1982, 1991b; Thomas 1983a, 1983b; Warren et al. 1984, 1986; Warren 1991), both of which can be used to estimate population viability; and residence time data from mark-release-recapture (MRR) studies (Warren et al. 1986; Hill et al. 1996), which can be used to estimate the relationship between residence time and patch size.

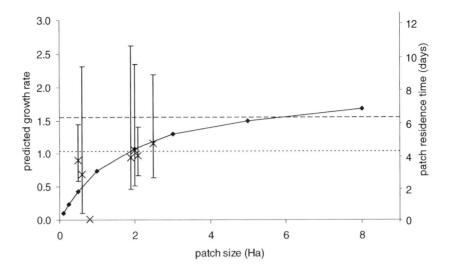

Figure 25.5 Relationship between patch size, butterfly residence time, and population growth rate in six natural Fender's blue populations. For sites that encompass several distinct habitat patches, the size of the largest discrete lupine patch was used in the analysis. For comparison, the horizontal lines indicate minimum growth rates that would predict 90% persistence of populations over 100 years with an initial starting size of 500 butterflies, based on variance in population growth rates typical of these populations (dashed line = minimum growth rate necessary for the most variable population, dotted line = minimum growth rate necessary for the least variable population). For a given level of variance, the critical minimum patch size for population persistence occurs where the residence time curve intersects the horizontal line.

The process of estimating minimum patch size from typically available data would closely resemble our calculation of minimum patch size for *I. i. fenderi*. Instead of using a mechanistic movement model to estimate the relationship between residence time and patch size, MRR studies across a range of patch sizes could be used to estimate this relationship directly. A limitation of MRR data is that, without a mechanistic model (or at least a priori knowledge about the shape of the relationship between residence time and patch size), it is reasonable to infer only within the range of data points. In other words, MRR data from both persistent and too-small populations would be necessary to estimate minimum patch size. Next, it would be necessary to scale residence time to recruitment rates. Monitoring data from clearly isolated populations could be used exactly as we used monitoring data from the six *I. i. fenderi* sites. If populations were not isolated, it would be necessary to quantify and subtract out the contribution of immigrants (see the discussion of immigration below). Alternatively, life table data could be used to measure rates of survivorship and fecundity directly (see equation [25.1]), and these rates could be scaled to account for changes in residence time.

Elizabeth E. Crone and Cheryl B. Schultz

PATCH SIZE AND BUTTERFLY ECOLOGY

Many aspects of butterfly ecology, in addition to residence time, could influence the minimum amount of habitat needed for population viability. Populations of the Fender's blue were probably connected by dispersal before human settlement and habitat fragmentation (Schultz 1998a). The remaining Fender's blue habitat patches have been invaded by weeds. A possible way to reverse this problem is by repeated controlled burning (Schultz and Crone 1998), but this strategy would itself affect population growth rates. In addition, inbreeding depression resulting from isolation could affect the persistence of small populations (Saccheri et al. 1998). Finally, for many butterflies, there are well-documented, discrete shifts in habitat quality with measurable environmental variables (Thomas 1991; Schultz and Dlugosch 1999). Qualitatively, how would these factors change the critical minimum patch size?

IMMIGRATION

Obviously, immigration reduces the minimum patch size required for population persistence because immigration from other patches counterbalances emigration. However, any between-patch movement means that some time (out of a relatively short lifetime) is lost to migration, and butterflies that leave one patch may not find another. Thus, the important demographic variable to track is the number of days spent by butterflies in natal and subsequent habitat patches, rather than the number of immigrants and emigrants. Based on our simulations of Fender's blue behavior, butterflies that leave 2 ha patches spend, on average, 4.2 days in their natal patch. (This differs from the average residence time of 7.2 days because 28% of the butterflies that emerge in 2 ha patches do not leave the natal patch at all during their lifetimes.) Butterflies also spend a substantial amount of time moving from one patch to the next. From simulations based on movement behavior, we predicted that butterflies that successfully migrate to a new patch 1 kilometer away take, on average, 10.8 days to reach it. Given that we estimate the average life span of a Fender's blue at about 15 days, migrating butterflies would thus spend less than a third of their lives, on average, in their second patch, even if they left their natal patch immediately after emergence. This finding highlights a significant difference between butterfly biology and the assumptions of general theories used to predict the dynamics of spatially structured populations (e.g., Hanski and Gilpin 1997; Tilman and Kareiva 1997). Because butterfly movement is often relatively slow and undirected, relative to butterflies' short individual life spans, movement takes a significant amount of time away from other activities, such as feeding and oviposition.

Numerous invasive plant species currently affect butterfly habitats. *I. i. fenderi* habitat is being invaded by several non-native grasses, Scot's broom (*Cytisus scoparius*), blackberry (*Rubus* spp., particularly *R. discolor*), and poison oak (*Toxicodendron diversiloba*). Woody invaders in particular are likely to be best managed by controlled burns. Unfortunately, although fire may be necessary to maintain habitat, many species of butterflies are killed by fire (Reed 1997), including the Fender's blue (Schultz and Crone 1998). If burning became necessary to *maintain* conditions like those at extant Fender's blue sites, its primary effect would be to increase variance in population growth rates, because a substantial fraction of individuals are killed in each burn, but the fecundity of survivors increases after fire. Population persistence, as we have noted, becomes less likely with increasing variance in growth rate. Controlled burning would therefore increase the critical minimum patch size, relative to a scenario in which habitat quality could be maintained without controlled burns. Of course, if fire were the only feasible way to maintain habitat quality, then *not* burning could potentially reduce oviposition rates by increasing female search times, reduce larval survivorship by reducing the availability of host plants, and directly reduce patch size, if weeds invaded from outside locations. Overall, these conclusions imply that our initial estimate of minimum patch size, in the absence of fire, is optimistically small.

INBREEDING DEPRESSION

Although there are many studies of genetic structure in butterfly populations, few studies have measured inbreeding depression (reduction in survivorship or fecundity with increasingly related mates) in butterflies (but see Saccheri et al. 1996). We know absolutely nothing about *I. i. fenderi* genetics. In principle, inbreeding would modify population dynamics as follows (after Ralls et al. 1988):

$$N_{t+1} = T_L {}^* w {}^* 0.5 {}^* N_t {}^* s {}^* \exp\{-B[F_0 + t/(2 {}^* Ne_t)]\},$$

where Ne_t is the effective population size in year t, B is the rate at which survivorship and/or fecundity decline with relatedness (the inbreeding depression parameter), and F_0 is the standard inbreeding coefficient (see Hartl and Clark 1989). As in any model of inbreeding depression without purging of deleterious alleles, recruitment rates decline over time, and no isolated population can be considered secure. (Note, however, that small amounts of immigration can significantly slow rates of inbreeding depression.) This decline in recruitment is much faster in small than in large populations, but here "small" and "large" are relative to the effective population size, which is a derived number, not necessarily directly related to patch size or actual numbers of butterflies (Hartl and Clark 1989). This perspective is fundamentally different from that of a minimum patch size set by movement behavior, in which we are concerned with population growth rates, meaning that population size is changing over time. Larger habitat patches might be likely to have higher environmentally determined carrying capacities, but these would be relevant only for populations in patches large enough that populations are able to grow to carrying capacity (as opposed to declining due to random movement). Thus, the effects of patch size on population size, and on subsequent inbreeding, are relevant only in populations above the minimum patch size set by dispersal behavior. Nevertheless, if anything, inbreeding would increase the minimum patch size, depending on the magnitude of inbreeding depression, the relationship between patch size and effective population size, and how frequently butterflies move among populations.

PATCH QUALITY

Our calculations are based on the assumption that habitat conditions are similar across sites. Larger patch sizes would be required if habitat were of lower quality, because lower-quality patches, by definition, would have lower recruitment rates, relative to patch size, increasing the critical minimum patch size. Mathematically, if habitat patches were of discrete quality (e.g., patches of two different host plant species), one could fit different minimum patch sizes to sets of patches in each habitat quality class (or perhaps to the highest-quality and lowest-quality patches to bound estimates). If quality varied continuously, some index of quality (e.g., grass height for British heathland butterflies: Thomas 1991; nectar sources for the Fender's blue: Schultz and Dlugosch 1999) could be used as a covariate of recruitment rates to estimate the relationship between patch quality and minimum patch size.

Alternatively, habitat quality might vary systematically with patch size. For example, edge effects, in which habitat quality deteriorates markedly near habitat edges, have been documented for many species. Edge effects can be biotic (e.g., increased presence of invasive species) or abiotic (e.g., altered light, temperature, or humidity). Edge effects would probably be greater in smaller patches simply because smaller patches have a higher perimeter/area ratio. This increase could lead to depressed fecundity or survivorship in smaller patches. The relationship between patch size and population viability would therefore differ systematically from the relationship between patch size and residence time: populations in smaller patches would be less likely to persist than expected based on residence time. If anything, the Fender's blue populations for which we have monitoring data show the opposite pattern: higher population growth rates than expected in smaller habitat patches.

FUTURE DIRECTIONS

The minimum patch size for *I. i. fenderi* is about 2–3 ha, larger than the habitat patches available for more than half of the extant populations (see fig. 25.1). Small patch size, combined with isolation, is a likely cause of population declines in this endangered species. With the exception of immigration, all the additions we discuss to make the minimum patch size model more "realistic" increase the minimum patch size. For most species (including *I. i. fenderi*), we will seldom have enough data to parameterize more realistic models of minimum patch size. However, it seems likely that the critical minimum patch size estimated only from dispersal behavior, residence time, and population viability analysis would set an absolute minimum patch size to consider for restoration or protection.

Based on these analyses, we see several profitable areas for future research. First, although butterflies are widely known to have both spatially structured populations and random walk movement behavior, almost no experimental research has been done to compare residence times based on random walk models with those estimated from MRR data, or to link residence times to population viability. These kinds of experiments, done with common butterfly species, would be a valuable companion to predictive studies with endangered species. They would provide a necessary check on the general approach of combining movement behavior and within-patch demography to predict minimum patch size, allowing us to quantify how confident we should be about making decisions based on this approach.

Second, it would be interesting to compare the relative strength of movement-based effects of small patch size with other, more commonly cited effects, such as edge effects or demographic and genetic stochasticity (see, e.g., Hanski, chap. 26 in this volume), in either real or model populations. Extinctions due to movement stochasticity differ fundamentally from extinctions due to demographic, genetic, or environmental stochasticity. The latter three mechanisms result in extinctions because the butterflies in a particular population die. Random movement results in extinctions because butterflies have left a particular habitat patch and are searching the environment for other suitable habitat. When patches are sufficiently isolated, these two mechanisms become equivalent. When patches are somewhat connected, however, their implications could differ markedly (Crone et al. 2001).

Finally, our simulations show that, for butterfly species similar to the Fender's blue, movement occurs slowly relative to the organism's life span.

Elizabeth E. Crone and Cheryl B. Schultz

We cannot necessarily think of movement as an instantaneous process, as assumed by many spatial models of population dynamics. Before applying the results of general spatial theory to butterfly populations, we need to investigate how the assumptions of mechanistic movement models and random walk behavior intergrade with the assumptions of metapopulation theory.

As is emphasized throughout this volume, we know a lot about the biology of both rare and common butterflies. This gives us two strong advantages in managing at-risk butterflies. First, the natural history of many butterfly species, even rare ones, is well known, and quantitative data on historical abundance and recent trends are often available. Second, we understand the fundamental underpinnings of butterfly population dynamics—mechanisms of dispersal, habitat needs and ranges of specialization, broad patterns of variation in ecological needs with phylogeny. Endangered species management requires effective use of very limited resources to make the best decisions possible. For butterflies, we can do this by integrating our general knowledge of butterfly biology with the natural history and limited data available for at-risk species.

SUMMARY

Many butterfly species exist naturally in small habitat fragments, and many others are threatened by habitat loss or fragmentation. In this chapter, we explore the relationship between butterfly movement behavior, demography, and the minimum patch size needed to support persistent butterfly populations. For many butterfly species, movement can be described by a correlated, biased, random walk. These butterflies abandon smaller host plant patches more quickly, simply because the probability that a butterfly will encounter habitat perimeters is larger in smaller habitat patches. If butterflies lay eggs at a constant rate over time, they will have lower rates of population growth in smaller patches. As a case study, we estimate the critical minimum patch size for the Fender's blue (*Icaricia icarioides fenderi*), an endangered prairie butterfly found only in a few isolated habitat remnants. We combine stochastic simulations of movement behavior with population viability models. We find that *I. i. fenderi* requires patches of at least 2 to 6 ha to persist, in the absence of immigration from other patches. We also explore the ways in which predicted minimum patch size is changed by ecological factors, such as weed invasion, inbreeding depression, and spatial variation in patch quality. Not surprisingly, most of these factors increase the area required to maintain butterfly populations. Thus, estimates based on movement and demography alone set an absolute lower limit to habitat requirements for butterfly population persistence.

ACKNOWLEDGMENTS

We thank the Nature Conservancy, the City of Eugene, and the U.S. Army Corps of Engineers for permission to monitor populations and observe butterfly behavior on their land. Support for C. Schultz was provided by the National Center for Ecological Analysis and Synthesis. The Center is funded by an NSF grant (DEB 9421535), the University of California–Santa Barbara, the California Resources Agency, and the California Environmental Protection Agency. Support for E. Crone was provided by the University of Calgary and an NSERC operating grant. Funds for field research and monitoring were provided by an NSF dissertation improvement grant (614558) to C. Schultz and by the U.S. Fish and Wildlife Service.

CHAPTER 26

Biology of Extinctions in Butterfly Metapopulations

Ilkka Hanski

Population ecologists have traditionally studied the processes that contribute to population regulation and long-term persistence (for reviews, see Sinclair 1989; Hanski 1990; Murdoch 1994; Harrison and Cappuccino 1995; Turchin 1995). Persistence is relative, however, as any population has a finite lifetime, and one may as well turn the matter the other way round and ask about the processes that influence population extinction. This is the perspective from which conservation biologists have always viewed population dynamics (Soulé 1986), and the accelerating rate of population and even species extinctions is shifting the attention of ecologists at large to the study of extinction (Lawton and May 1995). The population processes promoting persistence have not suddenly stopped working, of course; rather, the elevated extinction rate is due to environmental changes and especially to habitat loss and fragmentation. Butterfly populations in northern and western Europe and elsewhere in the densely populated regions of Earth are going extinct at an especially high rate (Thomas 1984; Warren 1992; Pollard and Yates 1993; Pullin 1995).

Apart from conservation concerns, there is another reason for the shift of focus from persistence to extinction in population ecology. Traditionally, insect ecologists have studied large populations, with the aim of describing, analyzing, and modeling the mechanisms that contribute to population regulation. Techniques such as key factor (Varley and Gradwell 1960; Morris 1963) and life table analyses (Watt 1961; Morris 1963) were developed for this purpose, to elucidate the forces that cause populations to oscillate, but also to identify and measure the strength of the density-dependent processes that would nonetheless ensure population regulation. But as we well know, not all populations are large, or even relatively large. Hundreds of community studies have demonstrated that most species in local communities are rare (Gaston 1994), on which basis one might conjecture that most local populations are small and therefore prone to local extinction (Hanski 1998b). Many small local populations represent sink populations or are otherwise unimportant for the large-scale persistence of the species, which hinges on the presence of large populations with an insignificant risk of extinction (for a butterfly example, see Harrison et al. 1988). But in other cases, there simply are no large populations within the usual movement range of individuals (for a butterfly example, see Hanski et al. 1994). The latter species are not expected to persist locally for a long time, but they may well persist as metapopulations, defined as assemblages of local populations (Hanski and Gilpin 1997; Hanski 1999). In classic metapopulations (Levins 1969), which have no large "mainland" populations, local extinctions are often rampant, even in the absence of any environmental changes. This is another good reason to be interested in the biology of extinctions and in the ecological, genetic, and evolutionary implications of high extinction rates.

This chapter has a dual aim. First, I review the various causes and mechanisms that are instrumental in the extinction of butterfly populations. Second, I present an overview of population extinction in the Glanville fritillary butterfly (*Melitaea cinxia*), on which much information has been accumulated over the past seven years (Hanski et al. 1995a, 1995b, 1996a; Lei and Hanski 1997; Saccheri et al. 1998; Kuussaari et al. 1998; Hanski 1999). The extinction processes that are important in butterflies are also important in many other taxa; hence the conclusions of this chapter are not restricted to butterflies. My particular aim is to go beyond the traditional viewpoint about extinction in isolated populations and to illustrate, using the Glanville fritillary as a case study, the breadth and the depth of the biology of extinctions in the metapopulation context. Many specific issues are further discussed from the perspective of checkerspot butterflies in the forthcoming volume edited by Ehrlich and Hanski (2003).

LOCAL EXTINCTION: THE TRADITIONAL VIEWPOINT

Population extinctions have been attributed to many processes, which are often classified into two main categories. Some causes of extinction are external to the population, and they are deterministic in the sense that a particular agent can be identified and, at least in principle, be manipulated to change the risk of population extinction. These causes of extinction, which belong to what Caughley (1994) termed the declining-population paradigm, include factors such as habitat destruction, climate change, persecution by humans, and the effects of introduced species. The second class of extinction processes belongs to Caughley's small-population paradigm; these processes are stochastic and intrinsic to the dynamics of populations. Shaffer (1981) identified four kinds of stochasticity affecting populations; namely, demographic, environmental, genetic, and catastrophic stochasticity. Gilpin and Soulé (1986), among others, have elaborated on the various forms of stochasticity and on their interactions. On the other hand, a neat distinction between external causes and internal mechanisms is not always possible, as we will see below, and in any case, the two kinds of processes do not operate in isolation (Hedrick et al. 1996).

Regardless of the actual causes and mechanisms of population extinction, it is generally true that the risk of extinction during some fixed period of time declines with increasing initial population size. This assertion is abundantly supported by theoretical models focusing on particular mechanisms of extinction (MacArthur and Wilson 1967; Leigh 1981; Goodman 1987; Wissel and Stöcker 1991; Lande 1993; Mangel and Tier 1993, 1994; Foley 1994, 1997), as well as by an extensive body of empirical research (Diamond 1984; Williamson 1981; Hanski 1994; Lawton and May 1995). Figure 26.1 illustrates the influence of population size on extinction risk in *Melitaea cinxia* (the Glanville fritillary) in the Åland Islands in southwestern Finland, where a large metapopulation has been studied for several years (Hanski et al. 1995a, 1996a; Hanski 1999). The caterpillars are gregarious, and it is hence both convenient and sensible to measure the sizes of local populations in terms of the number of larval groups. Local populations often consist of just one or a few larval groups, and not surprisingly, the turnover rate is very high—so high that we typically record 150–200 local extinction events per year out of a possible 400–500 events (Hanski 1999).

I have described the spatial population structure of the large *M. cinxia* metapopulation in detail elsewhere (Hanski 1998a, 1998b, 1999). Though the local populations are often very small, they represent discrete breeding units, with typically 60–80% of individuals remaining in the natal meadow during their entire lifetime (Hanski et al. 1994, Hanski 1999; Kuussaari et al. 1996). The majority of the local populations are so small that one might expect demographic stochasticity to essentially explain local extinctions. One purpose of this chapter is to demonstrate that this is not so; instead, many different processes play a significant role in local extinctions in this large metapopulation.

EXTRINSIC CAUSES

Habitat Loss

The most obvious cause of population extinction is habitat loss: species do not survive in places where their ecological requirements are not met. In the case of butterflies, habitat loss occurs both because of natural processes,

A

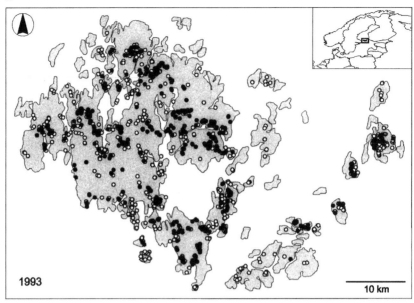

1993

10 km

B

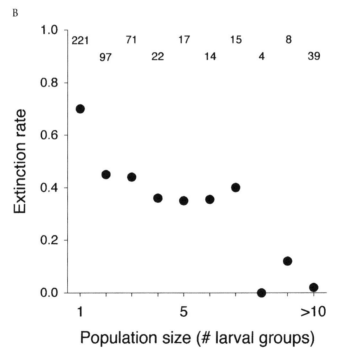

Extinction rate

Population size (# larval groups)

Figure 26.1 (A) A map of the Åland Islands in southwestern Finland, with the locations of about 1,600 habitat patches that are suitable for the Glanville fritillary (dry meadows with *Plantago lanceolata* or *Veronica spicata* or both). Patches that were occupied in 1993 are shown by solid circles, empty patches by open circles. (B) Probability of population extinction during 1 year as a function of the number of larval groups recorded in the population. The small numbers on top of the graph indicate sample size. (From Hanski et al. 1995b.)

such as successional overgrowth (Warren 1987; Thomas and Hanski 1997), and because of habitat destruction caused by humans (Murphy and Weiss 1988; Warren 1992). Habitat loss is the most pervasive cause of population extinction, and ultimately species extinction, worldwide (Morris 1995), so important that, from the conservation viewpoint, one would not lose much by focusing on this single cause alone. Thomas (1984) concluded that the very high rates of local extinction of butterflies on small nature reserves in the United Kingdom have practically always been due to the scarcity or complete lack of suitable habitat.

Habitat loss is not always overt. Ovipositing butterflies often have specific preferences for particular microhabitats (Chew and Robbins 1984); hence amazingly subtle environmental changes may be sufficient to cause population decline and ultimately lead to extinction. The silver-spotted skipper (*Hesperia comma*) went extinct from many sites in the southern United Kingdom when rabbit grazing was reduced and the vegetation became somewhat taller; when rabbit populations recovered, the butterfly metapopulation started to spread back to its previous habitat patch networks (Thomas and Jones 1993; Hanski and Thomas 1994). Subtle changes in the habitat may also influence other species that interact with the focal butterfly. Jeremy Thomas's (1980, 1984) work on the large blue butterfly (*Maculinea arion*) provides a classic example. When grazing at the butterfly sites was reduced, the regular ant host (*Myrmica sabuleti*) of the parasitic caterpillars was largely replaced by another ant species (*M. scabrinodis*), which is a poor host for large blue caterpillars, and butterfly populations went extinct.

Climate Change

Climate change is expected to influence population dynamics and thereby affect the risk of extinction in many taxa, including butterflies. Camille Parmesan's results on the northward range shift of the Edith's checkerspot (*Euphydryas editha*) in California (Parmesan 1996) and of similar shifts in several butterfly species in Europe (Parmesan et al. 1999; Parmesan, chap. 24 in this volume) involve increased rates of population extinction at the southern range limit. The illustrious Jasper Ridge populations of *E. editha* went gradually extinct over a period of 30 years (McGarrahan 1997; Hellmann et al., unpub.; McLaughlin et al. 2002a), possibly due to climate change (McLaughlin et al. 2002b).

At the level of actual mechanisms, climate change–caused extinctions are likely to involve something that we would normally call environmental stochasticity (see below); for instance, an increased frequency of drought years and other unfavorable weather conditions. Climate change in general, and the effects of weather conditions in particular, interact with local environmental conditions; hence, a generalization that, for example, climate change always causes a northward shift of geographic ranges is unwarranted. The Glanville fritillary in Finland provides a counterexample. The Finnish metapopulation occurs right at the northern range limit of the species in Europe, on which basis one might expect that warmer summers would be beneficial for the populations. In reality, just the opposite appears to be the case. In the 1990s, many summers have been exceptionally warm and dry, which has caused widespread starvation of caterpillars in late summer when their host plants have withered in the intrinsically dry meadows on rocky outcrops (I. Hanski, pers. obs.).

Generalist Natural Enemies

It is unlikely that a specialist natural enemy would drive an isolated local population to extinction, but generalist enemies with several prey species may do so. Examples for butterflies are not abundant, but this does not necessarily mean that such extinctions are uncommon. Diego Jordano (pers. comm.) is presently studying a possible example, in which two migratory and multivoltine blue butterflies (*Lampides boeticus* and *Sintarucus pirithous*) are increasing in an area in southern Spain. These butterflies are attacked by an ichneumonid parasitoid (*Anisobas cingulatorius*), which also attacks the silver-studded blue (*Plebejus argus*), and may even cause a local extinction of the latter species, due to the large numbers of the parasitoid produced by the common multivoltine host species.

Van Nouhuys and Hanski (2000) have studied apparent competition involving the braconid parasitoid *Cotesia melitaearum,* which specializes on the Glanville fritillary in the Åland Islands. We added large numbers of cocoons of a related primary parasitoid, *Cotesia glomerata,* to three meadows occupied by the Glanville fritillary and *C. melitaearum,* close to larval groups of the host butterfly. Three other butterfly populations functioned as controls. We knew from the previous study by Lei and Camara (1999) that the generalist hyperparasitoid *Gelis agilis* is strongly attracted to groups of *Cotesia* cocoons, and by adding *C. glomerata* cocoons to the populations, we aimed at increasing the numbers of *G. agilis,* which subsequently would attack *C. melitaearum,* which in turn would reduce parasitism on the Glanville fritillary. The predicted decline in *C. melitaearum* was indeed observed: two of the three treatment populations actually went extinct, and the difference between the treatment and control populations was significant (van Nouhuys and Hanski 2000). On the other hand, there was no systematic effect on the butterfly populations due to the extinction or reduction in the density of *C. melitaearum,* apparently because many other factors apart from parasitism influence the dynamics of the host butterfly (Hanski 1999).

Other Extrinsic Causes

Persecution by humans, which amounts to collecting in the case of butterflies, may cause the extinction of local butterfly populations, though generally collecting is not considered to be an important cause of butterfly extinctions (Thomas 1984). Even when the intention is good, the impact may be substantial. Harrison et al.'s (1991) analysis suggested that intensive long-term mark-release-recapture study and sampling of *Euphydryas editha* populations may have increased their probability of extinction, although Hellmann et al. (2003) conclude that the effect was probably minor.

STOCHASTIC PROCESSES

Three distinct types of stochasticity affecting local populations are demographic, environmental, and genetic stochasticity. Demographic stochasticity refers to the intrinsic uncertainty in birth and death events, which, by definition, is uncorrelated among individuals. Environmental stochasticity, in contrast, refers to temporal variation in birth and death rates that is correlated among individuals, owing to all or most individuals being affected by shared environmental conditions. Environmental stochasticity amplifies variance in demographic rates beyond what could be expected from demographic stochasticity alone. Catastrophes simply represent an extreme form of environmental stochasticity, with correlation among individuals being very high or complete, such as happens when an aberrant freeze (Ehrlich et al. 1972; Thomas et al. 1996) or a drought (Ehrlich et al. 1980; Thomas 1984) causes the deaths of all larvae in a butterfly population. Finally, genetic stochasticity refers to processes, such as genetic drift and inbreeding, that lead to changes in the demographic rates in a population. I will discuss genetic stochasticity below.

Demographic Stochasticity

Demographic stochasticity necessarily has a significant effect in very small populations. The extinction of the last population of the large blue (*Maculinea arion*) in the United Kingdom involved a series of "accidents," such as a biased sex ratio when the population was already exceedingly small and the failure of most females to become fertilized due to lack of potential mates at the right time (Thomas 1980). Two other examples of demographic stochasticity being the final mechanism of extinction are described by Duffey (1977: *Lycaena dispar*) and Dempster and Hall (1980: *Papilio machaon*).

Many local populations of *Melitaea cinxia* in the Åland Islands consist of just one sib-group of larvae in a particular year (see fig. 26.1B). Survival of the larvae in a group is to a large extent correlated, especially because the larvae have no chance of overwintering unless they occur in a relatively large group (Kuussaari 1998). The larval group is therefore an important demographic unit, and the gregarious larval behavior amplifies demographic stochasticity. It is probably not a coincidence that insect species with gregarious larvae tend to have a large amplitude of population oscillations (Hanski 1987; Hunter 1991). This phenomenon is often discussed in the context of outbreak species (Nothnagle and Schultz 1987), but the same argument applies to uncommon species: other things being equal, species with gregarious larvae are especially prone to turn into threatened species.

Environmental Stochasticity

A prime example of environmental stochasticity is the effect of weather conditions on butterfly behavior and larval survival, for which there is abundant evidence. Scores of studies on checkerspots in California have analyzed the effects of drought on population dynamics and extinction (Ehrlich et al. 1975; Singer and Ehrlich 1979). The effects of climate change, which itself is best considered a deterministic environmental change, are manifested in insect populations through environmental stochasticity—for instance, an increased frequency of drought years.

The effects of variable weather conditions on butterfly populations depend critically on habitat quality. In a heterogeneous habitat patch, the same weather conditions have different consequences for larvae that happen to reside in different microhabitats, such as south-facing and north-facing slopes (Weiss et al. 1988). Habitat heterogeneity buffers the population against environmental stochasticity by reducing the among-individual correlation in demographic rates. Kindvall (1995) reports an actual example in a bush cricket species, demonstrating how increased habitat heterogeneity reduces the amplitude of population oscillations. Undoubtedly, the same relationship applies to butterflies (Sutcliffe et al. 1997b). At the regional scale, different populations of *Euphydryas editha* have adapted to different host plants, which have different responses to drought years and thereby influence the extinction risk of the different butterfly populations (Singer and Ehrlich 1979; Ehrlich et al. 1980).

It is clear that weather effects are environmental, but it is less clear to what extent, from the butterflies' viewpoint, weather-caused "environmental stochasticity" is just stochasticity. For instance, host plants for herbivores may wither during a drought, causing elevated mortality and possibly leading to extinction. Is this an instance of "stochastic" extinction, or is it "deterministic" extinction due to the habitat having turned unsuitable? Caughley (1994), Harrison (1994), Simberloff (1994), and Thomas (1994), among others, have suggested that most local extinctions are in fact due to temporary or more permanent environmental changes, not to populations fluctuating to extinction in stationary environments. No doubt examples of all kinds of environmentally caused extinctions can be found, but there is so much empirical evidence to demonstrate the extinction proneness of small populations in apparently suitable habitat that it would be unreasonable to attribute the bulk of extinctions, especially of small populations, to all of the habitat having turned temporarily or permanently unsuitable. Local extinctions in the *Melitaea cinxia* metapopulation can often be attributed to elevated larval mortality during dry spells of weather, though generally not all larvae in a population die at the same time. Local populations in meadows on rocky outcrops are especially sensitive to weather conditions because the host plants (*Plantago lanceolata* and *Veronica spicata*) on such meadows may wither in a matter of weeks. Nonetheless, hundreds of local populations in the *Melitaea cinxia* metapopulation have gone extinct without any apparent change in host plant quality (Hanski 1999).

EXTINCTIONS IN METAPOPULATIONS: AN EXTENDED PERSPECTIVE

Turning to the dynamics of metapopulations consisting of small local populations raises a number of new issues. Though all the extinction processes discussed in the previous section necessarily operate here as well, local extinction in metapopulations may additionally be influenced by processes that are not significant, or are inconvenient to address, in the context of isolated populations. One such process is migration, and there are others that will be discussed below. Completely new questions may be asked about the extrinsic causes and stochastic processes that influence the risk of extinction of entire metapopulations (table 26.1).

THE INFLUENCE OF METAPOPULATION PROCESSES ON LOCAL EXTINCTION

The Influence of Migration

The size of a local population, and ultimately its risk of extinction, is influenced by anything affecting birth and death rates, but also by processes affecting the rates of immigration to and emigration from the population. There are good reasons to expect that migration influences the risk of local extinction in small populations within metapopulations.

Many empirical studies on butterflies (Hill et al. 1996; Kuussaari et al. 1996; Sutcliffe et al. 1997a; see also Crone and Schultz, chap. 25 in this volume) and other insects (Back 1988; Kareiva 1985; Turchin 1986; Kindvall 1995) have demonstrated that per capita emigration rate increases with

Table 26.1 Processes influencing extinction in metapopulations

Scale of Extinction	Type of Stochasticity (Intrinsic Causes)	Extrinsic Causes
Local extinction	**Demographic**[a] **Environmental Genetic**[a]	**Habitat loss** Generalist enemies and competitors **Persecution by humans,** etc.
Metapopulation extinction	**Migration (in small populations) Extinction-colonization Regional**	**Specialist enemies** and competitors **Habitat loss and fragmentation (extinction typically delayed)**

Source: Modified from Hanski 1998a.

Note: The processes that have been observed to operate in the Glanville fritillary metapopulation are printed in boldfaced type.

[a] Demographic and genetic stochasticity assume an increased significance in metapopulations with many small local populations.

decreasing habitat patch size, evidently because of the increasing ratio of patch boundary to patch area with decreasing patch size. A recent modeling study using mark-release-recapture data on *Melitaea diamina* suggested that per capita emigration rate scales as the patch area raised to a power of 0.2 (Hanski et al. 2000). Assuming that the intrinsic rate of population increase is not affected by patch area, which is a reasonable assumption, such scaling of emigration rate with patch area imposes a lower limit on the area of occupied patches and substantially increases the risk of population extinction in patches just above this limit. Additionally, emigration rates may be inversely density-dependent in small populations (Gilbert and Singer 1973; Brown and Ehrlich 1980; Kuussaari et al. 1996), which further increases the extinction risk of the smallest populations. Though it will be difficult to tease apart empirically the influence of emigration and of other factors increasing the risk of extinction in small populations, it is probably true that the contribution of emigration has been generally underestimated (Thomas and Hanski 1997).

The other side of the coin is the reduction in extinction risk caused by immigration, especially in small populations that are located close to large populations. As with the comparable but opposite effect of emigration, there is little doubt that, in principle, immigration could increase the sizes of local populations, which is the core idea in source-sink dynamics (Pulliam 1988, 1996; Stacey et al. 1997). Thomas et al. (1996), studying *Euphydryas editha* in California, have shown that immigration from a source population increases the density of nearby pseudo-sink populations. Because extinction risk generally decreases, for many reasons, with increasing population size, immigration should logically reduce extinction risk. This phenomenon is called the rescue effect (Brown and Kodric-Brown 1977). Demonstrating the rescue effect in practice is not easy, however, and merely showing that there is substantial migration among populations is not quite enough (Stacey et al. 1997).

Table 26.2 gives an example of the rescue effect in *Melitaea cinxia*. This table summarizes the annual extinction rates of populations that had 1, 2, 3–5, and >5 larval groups. Extinctions were modeled with logistic regression, including the following explanatory variables (Hanski et al. 1995b): patch area, the regional trend in population sizes, and a measure of the pooled size of the neighboring populations, denoted by S. A significant rescue effect is manifested as a significant effect of S on extinctions, because when there are many populations close to the focal one (a large S), there is, on average, much immigration to that population. The results demonstrate a significant rescue effect in the case of populations that had 1 or 2 larval groups, but not in the case of larger populations. This finding makes sense, because a given number of immigrants has a greater effect on the dynamics of small than large populations (see also Kuussaari et al. 1998). One complication that should be mentioned here is the possibility that a part of the rescue effect demonstrated in table 26.2 is a "genetic rescue effect," the fitness advantage that immigrants are likely to experience in small populations affected by inbreeding depression (see below).

Table 26.2 The rescue effect in small populations of the Glanville fritillary

Population Size[a]	Extinct	n	Average S[b]	Significance of Rescue Effect t	P
1	Yes	150	2.55		
	No	76	2.84	−2.97	0.003
2	Yes	46	2.78		
	No	58	3.12	−2.24	0.025
3–5	Yes	46	2.88		
	No	202	2.75	−0.63	0.527
>5	Yes	14	3.31		
	No	204	2.83	1.42	0.155

Note: The table gives the numbers of populations that went extinct versus the numbers that survived one year; a measure (S) that is proportional to the expected numbers of immigrants arriving at the population; and results of t test for the rescue effect, which was measured by the effect of S on extinction (in logistic regression models, which also included the effects of patch area and the regional trend in population sizes on extinction).
[a] Number of larval groups in autumn 1993.
[b] S is defined as

$$S_i = \sum_{j \neq i} \exp(-\alpha d_{ij}) N_j$$

and it represents the sum of the contributions from all other populations (indexed by j) to the pooled numbers of immigrants to population i; these contributions increase with the size of population j but decrease with the distance of population j from population i (Hanski 1998a).

It is appropriate to comment here on Harrison's (1991, 1994) distinction between metapopulations and patchy populations. In Harrison's classification scheme, only metapopulations in which the migration rate is very low qualify as "real" metapopulations. She concludes that many population structures considered metapopulations would be better classified as "patchy populations," with much migration among ephemeral aggregates of individuals, not to be considered local populations. While it is true that population structures with more or less complete mixing of individuals in each generation are better studied using some approach other than the metapopulation approach, it is not necessary to restrict the metapopulation concept to cases with insignificantly low migration rates. If the physical structure of the environment forces the species to oviposit in relatively isolated and discrete habitat patches, as is the case with *Melitaea cinxia* in the Åland Islands, it is both appropriate and helpful to employ the metapopulation concept, even if the emigration rate from small habitat patches is very high, and even if the patch network includes some patches so small and so little isolated that migration plays a major role in their dynamics. It should also be noted that there is a substantial theoretical literature addressing metapopulation dynamics in situations in which the migration rate is high enough to influence local dynamics (reviewed in Gyllenberg et al. 1997).

Extinctions Caused by Specialist Natural Enemies

Only generalist natural enemies with alternative host species are likely to pose a threat to the survival of isolated prey populations. In contrast, in metapopulations, specialist natural enemies may increase the risk of local prey extinction and yet persist at a larger spatial scale, like their prey, in a balance between local extinctions and colonizations. Nicholson's (1933; Nicholson and Bailey 1935) pioneering work on host-parasitoid models led him to consider such metapopulation persistence as a "solution" to locally unstable dynamics in simple host-parasitoid models. In Nicholson's own words (1933, p. 177), "the population is broken into widely separated small groups of individuals." Such "groups of host increase geometrically for a few generations, but are sooner or later found by parasites and ultimately exterminated"; "in the meantime there has been a migration of hosts, some of which have established new groups" (p. 163). Here is a clear vision of host-parasitoid metapopulation dynamics. Classic predator-prey metapopulations of the type envisioned by Nicholson do not appear to be common (Taylor 1988; Harrison and Taylor 1997), though one should add here the customary caveat that lack of evidence may reflect lack of appropriate fieldwork.

Studies on *Melitaea cinxia* in Finland have produced evidence for local host extinctions caused by a specialist natural enemy. *Melitaea cinxia* has two specialist larval parasitoids in the Åland Islands, the braconid *Cotesia melitaearum* and the ichneumonid *Hyposoter horticola* (Lei et al. 1997). The two parasitoid species have different biologies and foraging behaviors, and these differences are reflected in their spatial dynamics (Lei and Hanski 1998). *Hyposoter horticola* is a solitary parasitoid with one generation per host generation, and the female wasps move frequently among larval groups, apparently parasitizing only a small number of larvae per visit (see Stamp 1982 for similar behavior in another ichneumonid, *Benjamina euphydryadis,* attacking the American *Euphydryas phaeton*). In contrast, *C. melitaearum* is a gregarious parasitoid with three generations per host generation, and the female wasps often spend several days attending and parasitizing a single larval group (Lei and Camara 1999). *Cotesia melitaearum* is a superior competitor to *H. horticola* in the early host instars, whereas the latter species appears to persist as a fugitive, as it is able to locate larval groups (and small populations) not used by *C. melitaearum* (Lei and Hanski 1998). *Hyposoter horticola* inflicts a relatively constant level of mortality (about 30%) both temporally and spatially, whereas the level of parasitism due to *C. melitaearum* varies from 0 to 100% in local host populations (Lei et al. 1997). Parasitism by *C. melitaearum* has been found to increase the risk of host extinction (Lei and Hanski 1997), though *C. melitaearum* does well only in dense networks of habitat patches and host populations, where establishment of new parasitoid populations is relatively easy. In such circumstances, parasitism may drive much of the turnover in the host populations, just as Nicholson (1933) originally envisioned. On the other hand, in other areas in Åland, the density of host populations is so low that the parasitoid is either absent or plays no significant role in host dynamics (Lei and Hanski 1997).

Demographic and Genetic Stochasticity in Local Populations within Metapopulations

Demographic and genetic stochasticity may play a role in the extinction of isolated populations when the populations have become small, but arguably other causes—the ones that brought about the small population sizes in the first place—are the primary causes of extinction. In contrast, in metapopulations, many local populations are typically small, either because they occur in small habitat patches or because they have become established only recently, and there is accordingly more scope for demographic and genetic stochasticity to operate. I illustrate this phenomenon with recent results showing that inbreeding depression increases the risk of local extinction in the *Melitaea cinxia* metapopulation (Saccheri et al. 1998).

In summer 1996 we collected a small number of female butterflies from 42 local populations across Åland. The butterflies were genotyped using seven polymorphic enzyme loci and one polymorphic microsatellite. The

42 populations differed greatly in size and isolation, as measured in late summer 1995. Given the dynamics of the metapopulation, it is reasonable to assume that the average heterozygosity in the populations, as measured with the above-mentioned markers, reflects the degree of inbreeding in the local populations (Saccheri et al. 1998). We used a previously published logistic regression model of local extinctions (Hanski et al. 1995b) to predict the influence of the following ecological factors on extinction risk among the 42 populations: population size in 1995, the regional trend in population sizes, and habitat patch size. This model was parameterized using data on the 336 populations found in 1995, but excluding the 42 populations involved in the genetic study (this was done so as to parameterize the influence of ecological factors on extinction with independent data). We then applied this model to the sample of 42 populations and added average heterozygosity to the model as a measure of inbreeding. By late summer 1996, 7 of the 42 populations had gone extinct, and these extinctions were predicted well by the model (fig. 26.2). Average heterozygosity had a highly significant effect on extinction risk, on top of the effects of the ecological factors. Laboratory and field results have shown that just one generation of full-sib mating, which must occur frequently in the very small populations that are so common in *Melitaea cinxia* in Åland (see fig. 26.1B), significantly reduces fitness (Saccheri et al. 1998; Haikola et al. 2001). As far as we know, this is the first convincing field study demonstrating a relationship between inbreeding and extinction. It is probably significant, as will be discussed below, that the result came from a metapopulation consisting of numerous small local populations.

METAPOPULATION EXTINCTION

Local extinctions are recurrent events in classic metapopulations, such as the *Melitaea cinxia* metapopulation in Finland. If there are no large and relatively permanent "mainland" populations, and if all local populations therefore face a substantial risk of extinction, the entire metapopulation may go extinct when all local populations happen to go extinct in the same year. It is therefore important to consider processes that influence the risk of extinction of the entire metapopulation as well as the risk of extinction of local populations (see table 26.1).

Habitat Loss and Fragmentation

Two general effects of landscape structure on population processes largely determine the dynamics of metapopulations in highly fragmented landscapes. First, the risk of local extinction typically increases with decreasing habitat patch size because small patches tend to have small populations

Ilkka Hanski

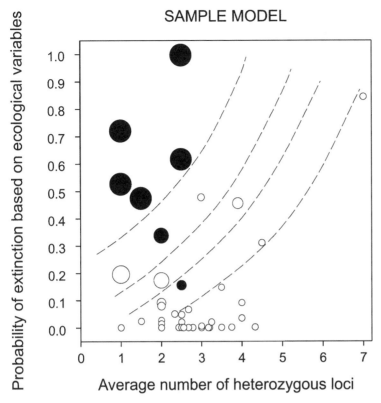

Figure 26.2 The predicted probability of local extinction due to ecological factors (*y*-axis, from a logistic regression model) and the average number of heterozygous loci (*x*-axis) in 42 populations of the Glanville fritillary butterfly. The ecological factors include population size, regional trend in population size, and habitat patch size. The size of the symbol gives the probability of extinction predicted by a logistic regression model incorporating both the ecological factors and the average number of heterozygous loci. The model predicts well the observed 7 extinctions (solid circles), and heterozygosity makes a highly significant contribution to this model. The isoclines of equal extinction risk were drawn by eye. (From Saccheri et al. 1998.)

with a high risk of extinction. Second, the probability of colonization of a currently empty patch decreases with increasing isolation because the movement range of individuals is limited. These two effects generate a continuum of increasing patch occupancy from small and isolated patches to large and well-connected patches (Hanski 1994, 1998a). Considering the consequences of habitat loss and fragmentation for metapopulation persistence, it is easy to see, and can be rigorously demonstrated (Hanski 1994; Hanski and Ovaskainen 2000), that a decreasing average size and increasing average isolation of habitat patches in a patch network leads to a reduction in the fraction of habitat patches occupied and eventually leads to metapopulation extinction.

These predictions can be tested with data on *Melitaea cinxia*. Having surveyed the entire range of the species in the Åland Islands (see fig. 26.1), we divided the study area into 2 × 2 km squares and treated the patch networks

Table 26.3 Effects of average patch area and patch number in 4 km^2 squares on the fraction of occupied patches (P) in replicate metapopulations of the Glanville fritillary

Patch Area			Patch Number/4 km^2		
Average Area	Occupancy		Number of	Occupancy	
(ha)	n	P	Patches	n	P
<0.01	23	0.24	1	61	0.21
0.01–0.1	138	0.24	2–3	70	0.32
0.10–1.0	88	0.40	4–7	58	0.25
>1.0	6	0.56	>7	66	0.41

Note: The replicate patch networks in the 4 km^2 squares have been divided into four classes based on average patch area or patch number (from Hanski et al. 1995a). The effects of average patch area and density on occupancy (P) were tested with ANOVA on ranks, using the four patch area and density classes shown in the table. Both effects were highly significant (area: $F_{3,251} = 5.69$, $p = 0.001$; density: $F_{3,251} = 4.21$, $p = 0.006$; no significant interaction).

in these squares as replicates (Hanski et al. 1995a). The average patch area within a square ranged from less than 0.01 ha to more than 1 ha, and the number of patches per square ranged from 1 to more than 20. The predicted effects of landscape structure were observed (table 26.3): the fraction of occupied patches increased from 0.21 in squares with an average patch size of less than 0.01 ha to 0.56 in squares with an average patch size of more than 1 ha, and the fraction of occupied patches increased with the number of patches per square. It is easy to see that extrapolating these trends to ever sparser networks of ever smaller patches would lead to metapopulation extinction; theory additionally tells us that, as the threshold for persistence is approached, the fraction of occupied patches plummets to zero rather abruptly (Hanski 1999; Hanski and Ovaskainen 2000). *Melitaea cinxia* went extinct from mainland Finland in the 1970s (Kuussaari et al. 1995), as it has done in many other areas in northern and western Europe (Hanski and Kuussaari 1995), most likely because the density of suitable patches has dropped below the threshold density necessary for metapopulation persistence.

Extinction-Colonization Stochasticity and Regional Stochasticity

The two forms of stochasticity affecting local populations, demographic stochasticity and environmental stochasticity, have exact counterparts at the metapopulation level. Consider a classic metapopulation with extinction-prone local populations. Even if the local populations have independent dynamics, as is assumed by most metapopulation models (Hanski 1999), all existing populations may happen to go extinct in the same year without giving rise to new populations, just as all individuals in a particular population may happen to die without producing any surviving progeny. Such stochasticity due to the intrinsically stochastic nature of local extinctions and colonizations is called extinction-colonization stochasticity, and it is analogous to demographic stochasticity in local populations (Hanski 1991).

Theory suggests that extinction-colonization stochasticity is an important mechanism of metapopulation extinction when the number of extinction-prone local populations is less than 15–20 (Gurney and Nisbet 1978; Hanski et al. 1996b). I turn again to our results on *Melitaea cinxia* to test this prediction. Here it is not sensible to use patch networks in 2 × 2 km squares as replicates, as was done in table 26.3, because these networks are not dynamically independent units. For the present purpose, I use as replicates the 127 semi-independent patch networks (SINs) into which Hanski et al. (1996a) have divided the roughly 1,600 habitat patches in the Åland Islands (see fig. 26.1). The SINs are separated from one another by a sufficient distance, usually more than 1.5 km, to make interactions between the respective metapopulations weak, though not so weak as to completely exclude the possibility of recolonization from a nearby SIN. Figure 26.3 shows that, during the 1993 census, roughly one-third of the SINs with fewer than 10 patches were occupied, whereas occupancy reached practically 100% in

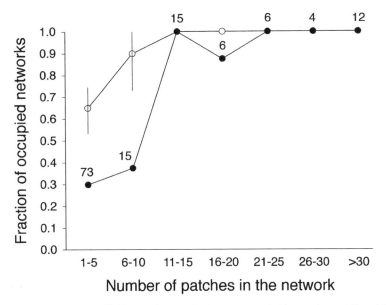

Figure 26.3 Fraction of habitat patch networks that were occupied by a metapopulation of the Glanville fritillary in 1993 as a function of the number of patches in the network. The networks have been arranged in groups with 1–5 patches, 6–10 patches, and so on. The number of networks in each class is given by the numbers above the solid circles. The open circles give the null hypothesis obtained by randomizing the positions of the existing local populations amongst the habitat patches (average, minimum, and maximum values in ten randomizations; based on material described in Hanski et al. 1995a, 1996a).

networks that had 15 or more patches, in good agreement with the above-mentioned theoretical prediction (Hanski et al. 1996b). The observed level of patch occupancy in the networks with fewer than 15 patches is significantly and substantially lower than that predicted by random placement of local populations among the habitat patches, which is an appropriate null hypothesis here.

Other butterfly examples discussed by Thomas and Hanski (1997) support the conclusion that a viable network of small habitat patches should have more than 15–20 patches. On the other hand, results on the specialist parasitoids of checkerspot butterflies suggest that more than 20–40 host populations may be needed for the persistence of the parasitoid metapopulation (Hanski 1999). This figure is higher than the corresponding figure for the host butterflies, possibly because temporal fluctuations in the number of host populations reduce the long-term effective patch number for the parasitoid.

Another reason for the apparently greater threshold patch number for the persistence of parasitoids than of hosts relates to the nonstochastic component of dynamics in fragmented landscapes. For a metapopulation to persist for a long time in a patch network, the following replacement condition must be satisfied: the expected number of new populations generated by one existing local population during its lifetime in an otherwise empty patch network must be greater than one. As only a fraction of the habitat patches suitable for the host are occupied, the average isolation of suitable patches for the parasitoid (= host-occupied patches) is necessarily greater than the average isolation of patches for the host. If the parasitoid does not have a greater migration range and colonization ability than the host, the replacement condition is less likely to be satisfied, in a given habitat patch network, for the parasitoid than for the host. The replacement condition is also a relevant consideration for the proper interpretation of figure 26.3. Some of the potential metapopulations in the smallest patch networks may not satisfy the replacement condition, and are hence expected to go extinct regardless of extinction-colonization stochasticity (see Hanski and Ovaskainen 2000). An important conclusion from figure 26.3 nonetheless is that, whether the replacement condition is met or not, a metapopulation of extinction-prone local populations in a small patch network is necessarily more threatened than are metapopulations in large patch networks.

The counterpart of environmental stochasticity at the metapopulation level is regional stochasticity, which refers, by definition, to spatially correlated environmental stochasticity (Hanski 1991). The most likely cause of regional stochasticity in butterfly metapopulations is spatially correlated weather conditions. We have a strong hunch, though not yet any definite proof, that the distinctly spatially correlated changes observed in the sizes of local populations of *Melitaea cinxia* (fig. 26.4) reflect spatially correlated weather conditions. There are several possible mechanisms by which this could occur. One possibility is localized heavy showers during early larval development, which might wash young larvae off the host plant and cause high mortality. The opposite is also possible: during drought years, local showers in late summer might save larvae from starvation by preventing complete withering of the host plants. Another possible cause of spatially correlated changes in population sizes is related to the spatial distribution of the two host plants, *Plantago lanceolata* and *Veronica spicata*. The latter species occurs primarily in the northwestern part of Åland (Kuussaari et al. 2000), roughly where the population decline was most marked in 1993–1994 and where the recovery was most obvious in 1995–1996 (fig. 26.4). It is possible that in some years *Plantago*-feeding caterpillars do better than *Veronica*-feeding caterpillars, and vice versa, which might contribute to the observed spatial patterns (the two host plants have somewhat different microhabitats and phenologies). This would be another example of interactions between weather conditions and habitat quality, which are well documented for American checkerspot butterflies (Ehrlich and Murphy 1987; Weiss et al. 1993).

Delayed Extinctions

Apart from true catastrophes, such as frost killing all host plants and leading to the starvation of all larvae in a population (Thomas et al. 1996), population extinction typically involves a time delay. The habitat may change from source to sink, reducing the finite rate of population increase below unity, but it takes time before the population actually goes extinct. It typically takes even longer for an entire metapopulation to go extinct following, for example, habitat loss and fragmentation that has caused the finite rate of increase in the metapopulation to drop below unity (Hanski 1998a).

It is hard to demonstrate delayed metapopulation extinctions with actual data, though anecdotal examples of "living dead" metapopulations are plentiful (e.g., Thomas 1984; Hanski and Kuussaari 1995). I resort here to a modeling approach that we have used to study the dynamics of *Melitaea cinxia* (Hanski et al. 1996b) and other butterfly species (Hanski 1994; Wahlberg et al. 1996). Working within an area of 25 km² in northern Åland, Hering (1995) mapped the extent of the suitable habitat for *M. cinxia*. He then reconstructed the extent of suitable habitat some 20 years before, using the results of his fieldwork, old aerial photographs, and interviews with local people. During the 20-year period, the total area of suitable habitat had been reduced to one-third of its original extent, and the number of distinct habitat patches had declined from 55 to 42, largely due to decreased grazing by cattle and sheep. To assess the metapopulation dynamic consequences of this change in the landscape structure, we did the following (Hanski et al. 1996b). For each patch that had lost some area, we assumed that the loss

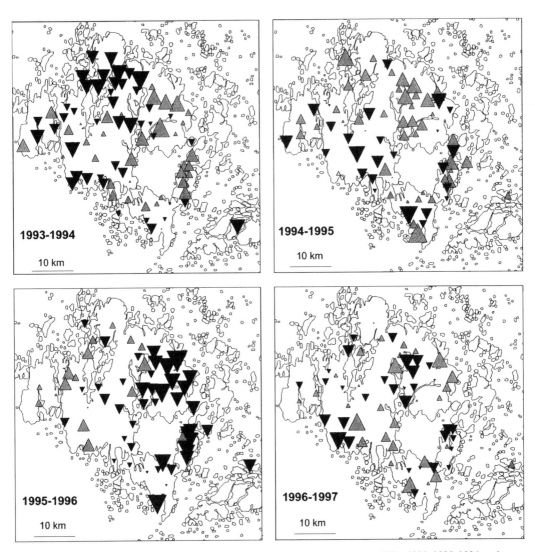

Figure 26.4 Relative changes in metapopulation sizes in 1993–1994, 1994–1995, 1995–1996, and 1996–1997 in the Glanville fritillary in the Åland Islands, Finland. The symbols represent metapopulations in semi-independent patch networks (Hanski et al. 1996a). Solid symbols indicate metapopulation decline; shaded symbols indicate metapopulation increase. The size of the symbol is proportional to the relative change in metapopulation size.

had occurred linearly over a period of T years, where T is a random variable uniformly distributed between 1 and 20 years. We then used the previously parameterized incidence function model (Hanski et al. 1996a) to predict the fraction of occupied patches, P, during and following the 20-year period of habitat loss. Using the model, we also calculated the equilibrium value of P, P^*, at each point in time. The difference between P and P^* reflects the magnitude of the delay in metapopulation dynamics following habitat loss and fragmentation.

The results in figure 26.5A suggest that *M. cinxia* has tracked the amount of suitable habitat with only a small delay. The delay is small because the metapopulation occupied most of the habitat at the beginning of the 20-year period, and because the turnover rate is high in comparison with the rate of environmental change. But what would happen if the same trend in habitat loss continued for another 20 years? For instance, let us assume that each of the present patches will lose yet another 50% of its area in another 20 years. Figure 26.5B shows that this additional habitat loss would lead to a patch network that is not adequate for long-term metapopulation persistence; that is, the equilibrium P^* would drop to zero in less than 20 years. However, the actual metapopulation extinction is predicted to take

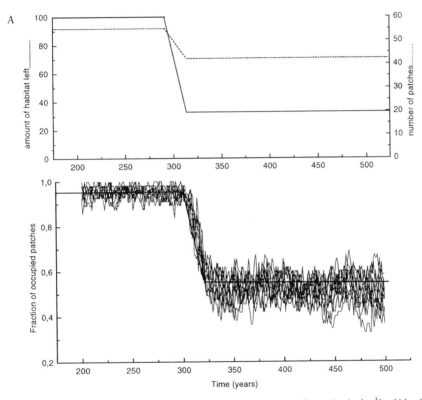

Figure 26.5 Metapopulation dynamics of the Glanville fritillary in a 5 × 5 km region in the Åland Islands, southwestern Finland, in a habitat patch network that lost two-thirds of the area of suitable habitat, as well as entire habitat patches, during a 20-year period. The size of the metapopulation is measured by the fraction of occupied patches (P). The results were obtained with the incidence function model (Hanski 1994) using parameter values estimated by Hanski et al. (1996a). (A) The lower graph gives the predicted equilibrium metapopulation size (thick line) with ten replicate predicted trajectories before, during, and following the observed reduction in habitat area and number of patches over the 20-year period (shown in the upper graph). (B, overleaf) Similar results for a hypothetical scenario of further loss of 50% of the area of each of the remaining patches (upper graph). In this case, the equilibrium moves to metapopulation extinction even though a substantial amount of habitat remains. The simulated trajectories (lower graph), however, show a long delay in the response of the metapopulation to habitat loss. (Reprinted from *Metapopulation Ecology*, by Ilkka Hanski [1999] by permission of Oxford University Press.)

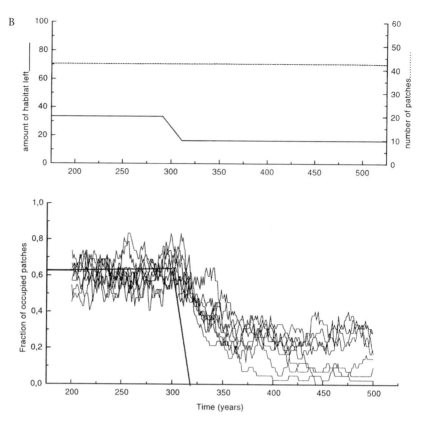

Figure 26.5 (continued)

tens or even hundreds of years, with the largest remaining local populations dwindling to extinction slowly. The inevitable decline to extinction may be temporarily halted for long periods, with the number of occupied patches fluctuating without any obvious trend. This example reflects a general result, which shows that the delay is especially long in situations in which the new equilibrium is close to the extinction threshold (Hanski 1998a). The message is clear: many small metapopulations (rare species) may be around only because they have not yet had time to go extinct.

IMPLICATIONS AND CONCLUSIONS

A wide range of processes influences extinctions in butterflies. Habitat loss and environmental stochasticity, especially variation in larval survival caused by varying weather conditions, are widely considered to be the main cause and the main mechanism of population extinction, respectively. This view is probably correct for newly isolated populations that used to occur in relatively large expanses of suitable habitat that originally supported large local populations. The message of this chapter is that a much richer scenario of population extinction emerges from metapopulation studies. Because metapopulations are common, and are becoming increasingly common due to habitat fragmentation, an extended view of extinctions is warranted.

The reader may raise a fundamental objection here. True, populations go extinct for many reasons when the habitat is very fragmented, but does all this fine-scale fast turnover of small local populations really matter? What benefit do we obtain by considering the details of these often minimally small populations—would it not be sufficient to define populations at a larger spatial scale and to consider the risks of extinction that they face? My answer is that it does matter, and that we should pay attention to the actual spatial structure of populations, regardless of the spatial scale at which it occurs. Chesson (1998) summarizes the argument for considering spatial structure within local populations; here, I give reasons for not being satisfied with spatially averaged data for metapopulations.

Consider first the threats that habitat loss and fragmentation pose to populations. If the real spatial structure of a population or metapopulation is ignored, one can address only the consequences of the reduction in the overall amount of habitat for the total population size. Though the total amount of habitat is often the primary determinant of the expected lifetime of a metapopulation (Hanski 1998a), it is easy to see that in extreme cases, pooling leads to meaningless conclusions: an infinitely large but sparse network of small patches would have an infinite amount of habitat, but species would nonetheless go extinct there due to high extinction and low colonization rates. In other words, a mechanistic understanding of the consequences of habitat destruction can be obtained only by considering the actual spatial population structure and processes. The local populations in small patches are ephemeral, but for exactly this reason, they have a profound effect on the average per capita growth rate in metapopulations lacking large populations by allowing processes that lower growth rates only in small populations to operate. Demographic stochasticity is one such process, and the increase in the extinction rate due to inbreeding observed in *Melitaea cinxia* (see fig. 26.2) is another.

Given the generally very small local population sizes in the large *M. cinxia* metapopulation, one might expect that demographic stochasticity is indeed the key process that largely "explains" local extinctions. Though demographic stochasticity must play a significant role in this kind of population structure, it is sobering to note that our studies have produced strong evidence for practically all the commonly considered processes of local extinction in this single metapopulation, and that these studies have also demonstrated the ways in which entire metapopulations may go extinct (the extinction processes for which there is empirical evidence for *M. cinxia* are printed in boldfaced type in table 26.1). To some extent these findings are due to the great statistical power that one has while analyzing hundreds of extinction events, but that is not the full story, because many of the extinction processes operate strongly in at least some populations in some years. The role of the specialist parasitoid *Cotesia melitaearum* is a case in point. In a study conducted in a dense network of habitat patches during a period when host populations were common, parasitism by *C. melitaearum* was observed to increase the risk of host population extinction (Lei and Hanski 1997). In contrast, in the areas of the Åland Islands where habitat patch networks are sparse, the parasitoid has no role to play, as it does not even persist in these regions, apparently because the dynamic network of host populations is too sparse or too variable in time to support a viable parasitoid metapopulation.

There is an extensive theoretical literature on the population biology of species with spatially structured populations and extinction-colonization dynamics (Hanski and Gilpin 1997), but the corresponding empirical literature is still limited. Butterflies are often structured as classic metapopulations and could thus function as a prominent model taxon for metapopulation studies (Thomas and Hanski 1997). Below, I briefly sketch some research questions and preliminary results on the ecology, genetics, and evolution of butterfly metapopulations with extinction-colonization dynamics, using *Melitaea cinxia* as my showcase.

Caughley (1994) drew attention to the contrast between the bulk of theory in conservation biology, which is largely concerned with the mechanisms of extinction in small populations, and the reality of conservation biology, which is primarily burdened by very practical questions about the causes of population decline. The two inquiries are poorly integrated, but metapopulation ecology builds one bridge between them in having the capacity to address questions about population dynamics in dynamic fragmented landscapes (Hanski et al. 1996a). In other words, it allows us to combine questions about the causes of extinction (habitat loss and fragmentation) with questions about its mechanisms (extinction in small populations). An intimate understanding of the factors influencing local extinction is a prerequisite for mechanistic models of the consequences of habitat loss and fragmentation.

The finding that inbreeding depression increases the risk of local extinction in *M. cinxia* (Saccheri et al. 1998) is at first hard to reconcile with expectations based on the theory developed for single populations (Soulé and Wilcox 1980). *Melitaea cinxia* populations are continuously going through bottlenecks, on which basis one would expect that deleterious alleles have been purged from the metapopulation, that there is no substantial genetic load, and that hence there is no significant inbreeding depression. In contrast, the empirical results indicate a large genetic load and an ample increase in extinction risk with just one generation of mating between full sibs. Apparently, intuition developed for isolated populations is inadequate for highly structured metapopulations such as that of *M. cinxia* (for a review of existing genetic theory of metapopulations, see Barton and Whitlock 1997). There is a real need to develop a more comprehensive theory of population genetics for spatially realistic metapopulation structures, and there is a great opportunity to develop empirical research projects on butterflies to test model predictions—once we have them!

Finally, one more reason to be interested in population turnover at a small spatial scale is that extinction-colonization dynamics may lead to group selection and thereby influence adaptive evolution. This is more likely the faster the turnover rate, and the turnover rate is especially fast when the metapopulation is fragmented into very small local populations, as is that of *M. cinxia* in the Åland Islands. An example relates to the evolution of female host plant preference. *Melitaea cinxia* has two host plants in the Åland Islands, where there is large-scale genetic specialization in female host plant preference, seemingly reflecting geographic variation in host plant abundances (Kuussaari et al. 2000). Recent results indicate that female host plant preference influences the probability of colonization of habitat patches with different mixtures of the two host plants (Hanski and Singer 2001). Even more surprisingly, the results of a combination of modeling and analysis of extensive field data suggest that, because of these host plant–biased colonizations, extinction-colonization dynamics influence the regional evolution of female host plant preference. We could not even start considering such questions if we did not pay attention to the fragmented spatial population structures and extinction-colonization dynamics that characterize many butterflies.

SUMMARY

Population ecologists have traditionally studied the processes that contribute to population regulation and long-term persistence. Persistence is relative, however, as any population has a finite lifetime, and one may as well turn the matter the other way round and ask about the processes that influence population extinction. This chapter reviews the local and metapopulation-level processes that influence the risk of extinction of local populations and entire metapopulations of butterflies. A large-scale study on the dynamics of the Glanville fritillary butterfly (*Melitaea cinxia*) provides many instructive examples. Metapopulation-level processes influencing local extinction include coupled interactions with specialist natural enemies, the influence of migration on extinction risk, and the magnification of demographic and genetic stochasticity in small local populations within metapopulations. Entire metapopulations may go extinct because of habitat loss and fragmentation, but the risk of metapopulation extinction is also increased by two forms of stochasticity, extinction-colonization and regional stochasticity, analogous to demographic and environmental stochasticity in local dynamics. An extended view of population extinction is needed, especially for species, such as many butterflies, that have a highly fragmented population structure. There is a great opportunity for butterfly population biologists to contribute fundamental results on the ecological, genetic, and evolutionary consequences of extinction-colonization dynamics in metapopulations.

Ilkka Hanski

Synthesis: Butterflies as Model Systems in Ecology and Evolution—Present and Future

Ward B. Watt and Carol L. Boggs

WHAT CONSTITUTES A MODEL SYSTEM FOR ECOLOGY AND EVOLUTION?

Model systems for biological study have traditionally been single taxa—"the" mouse, "the" worm, and so forth. These organisms have usually been chosen for aspects of their life cycles that make them convenient to some specific laboratory purpose. This does not, however, render them equally useful for all areas of biology. *Drosophila melanogaster,* for example, became a model system for structural genetics because of its small size, short generation time, tolerance of inbreeding, chromosome structure, and high fecundity, which suited it well to the production of large numbers of segregating offspring from experimental crosses in a short time. Our resulting knowledge of its genetics and our subsequent study of its systematic relationships to its near relatives (*D. simulans,* etc.) have led many evolutionists to study its natural variation. But *D. melanogaster*'s usefulness for this purpose is limited, much more so than often realized (but see Eanes 1999), even compared with that of other *Drosophila,* by lack of knowledge about its ecology in the wild. Recent studies by M. Feder and colleagues (e.g., Feder et al. 1997) have begun to remedy this problem, but even so, cactophilic and forest-floor *Drosophila* provide better ecologically known models for evolutionary study in the wild.

Within the fields of ecology and evolution, diverse candidate model species from different taxa can be identified. A variety of butterfly species have some claim to model species status due to the large body of work on specific aspects of their biology: lowland North American *Colias,* certain *Euphydryas, Melitaea,* and *Pieris* species in North America and Europe, *Papilio dardanus,* various *Heliconius, Pararge aegeria, Bicyclus* spp., and *Maniola jurtina,* to name but a few. *Taricha* newts, *Peromyscus* or other mice, stickleback fish, and a few large game species such as European red deer are exemplary candidates among vertebrate animals, while *Clarkia, Ipomopsis,* morning glories (*Ipomoea*), and various crucifers (including *Arabidopsis, Arabis,* and relatives) are examples among plants. Among fungi, *Neurospora* and yeasts are promising candidates, but are still limited by biomedically based typology and ignorance of environmental reality. Some bacteria are becoming important ecological and evolutionary models (e.g., Hall 1982; Rainey and Travisano 1998; Bohannan and Lenski 2000).

But seldom until recently, except perhaps for Hawaiian *Drosophila,* has it been considered that an entire clade of creatures, or even a sampling of diverse clades whose relationships are explicit, might be an appropriate biodiverse model system for conceptual study in ecology and evolution. Such clade-related systems can support the rigorous pursuit of questions that arise from considering diversity itself, including comparative ecological and evolutionary studies and the study of biodiversity. Such questions cannot be addressed at all by monospecific models: for example, how and why do thermoregulatory strategies vary among animals with respect to their sizes and ecological niche structures (Watt, chap. 15 in this volume) when phylogenetically based similarities are accounted for? Alternatively, what are the sets of foraging and life history traits that are selected for under particular environmental regimes, and why are some sets disfavored, again, once historical phylogenetic constraints are taken into consideration (Boggs, chap. 9 in this volume)? What are the patterns and mechanisms of insect-plant coevolution (Ehrlich and Raven 1964; Berenbaum 1983; Farrell et al. 1992; Singer, chap. 10 in this volume)? What are the factors controlling the distribution of clades in time (Shapiro et al., chap. 6 in this volume) and space (Kremen et al., chap. 23, and Parmesan, chap. 24, in this volume), and do these factors represent general phenomena applicable across broader groups? These kinds of questions contrast with the narrower, taxon-specific, description-oriented foci of the traditional "ologies"—botany, mammalogy, entomology, or even narrower specializations on particular families. As emphasized by Paul Ehrlich in the introduction to this volume, biodiverse model systems are crucial if we are to apply ecological and evolutionary principles to the preservation of planetary viability. They are equally important for the rational development of fundamental understanding in the concept structures of both ecology and evolution. They may even stimulate philosophers of science to come to grips more effectively with intrinsically biodiverse aspects of the life sciences.

As with single-taxon model systems, the successful use of any major clade, such as butterflies, as a biodiverse model system requires appropriate interplay between the characteristics of the clade and the approaches of those studying it. First, tractability for the purposes at hand is obviously important. This means that the system must exhibit characteristics that allow particular questions to be addressed. For example, the wide range of variation in numbers of species between sister butterfly clades (e.g., *Colias,* with seventy or more, and *Zerene,* with three) suits them well to asking, and perhaps answering, questions about what drives species richness to high or low values. Further, as with individual taxa used as model systems, the life histories, sizes, and laboratory compatibility of these systems must not be constraining for the desired studies. One would not choose large, long-lived mammals such as rhinoceroses for pioneering studies of ecological genetics, though results from the study of more genetically tractable model systems might find practical applicability to rhinoceros conservation.

Equally important, any of a series of intellectual pitfalls can preclude investigators' effective use of a potential model system to gain ecological and evolutionary understanding. "Organismal tunnel vision," or a focus solely on the features of one group and not at all on the others with which it interacts, or to which it is related, may cut off workers from crucial insights about processes of diversification, coevolution, or other important features of evolution. Unwillingness to learn and deploy novel technical approaches can leave ecologists and evolutionists alike struggling to answer important questions with inadequate tools. Just as problematic is a misdirected confounding of generality with the mere avoidance of biologically realistic specificity, which can result in generalizations that appear admirably simple, but which may be uninformative or mistaken. In contrast, a productive approach may first ask how a diverse array of related taxa solve some ecological problem, and then seek to determine the general features of the solutions from their specifically understood natures.

Clearly, the contributors to this volume have successfully chosen tractable systems and avoided these intellectual pitfalls in their study. How can we, and those who might join us in this work, build most effectively on these initial successes? What opportunities and needs for empirical system development are apparent? How can we think most effectively about the broader and deeper development of research approaches to the use of butterflies as ecological and evolutionary model systems? Here we consider the opportunities that the features of butterflies already present, many of which are exemplified in this volume. We then consider a nonexhaustive list of needed studies that would notably increase the utility of butterflies as a comprehensive, biodiverse model system. Finally, we suggest some goals for the attention of several overlapping scientific communities concerned with the possibilities of butterflies as model systems, and evaluate the prospects for achieving them.

OPPORTUNITIES OFFERED BY BUTTERFLIES AS
A MODEL SYSTEM

Many common characteristics facilitate both laboratory and field study of the three related but unequally diverse "butterfly" superfamilies: Papilionoidea, Hesperioidea, and Hedyloidea (e.g., Scoble 1992). These characteristics include diurnality and conspicuousness, a phytophagous life cycle strategy, demography that is analyzable in both functional and ecological contexts (e.g., Keyghobadi et al., chap. 8 in this volume), and, in general, a wealth of baseline natural history knowledge.

The phylogenetic characteristics of the butterfly clade also make it a useful model system. Because there are a number of sister clades to this one within the ditrysian Lepidoptera (e.g., Scoble 1992), comparative study using various moth clades as comparison groups is possible (e.g., Raguso and Willis, chap. 3 in this volume). Often, the relative closeness of these relationships means that methods developed for one butterfly group can be readily extended to many others within the butterfly clade, or even to butterflies from moths and vice versa. Indeed, many approaches can be imported to butterflies, and to other Lepidoptera, from the commonly used dipteran *Drosophila* model, since among insect orders the consensus grouping ([Lepidoptera, Trichoptera], Diptera) is a relatively clear and close one, reflecting many biological commonalities.

Superimposed on these fundamental unities among butterflies as a whole is a diversity of solutions to ecological problems, which, as noted above, is critical to generating general understanding. For example, the clade displays conspicuous phenotypic diversity for morphological, physiological, and life history traits within and among taxa and habitat types. This diversity has already begun to facilitate the rigorous comparative study of organism-environment interactions on diverse ecological scales, which is of profound importance for both ecological and evolutionary investigations. Wiklund (chap. 4 in this volume) summarizes one example of such work, focused on mating systems. Yet another example at a different spatial scale, summarized by Scriber et al. (chap. 17 in this volume), incorporates organism-environment interactions in a comparative context into an evaluation of genetic divergence among species.

The clear relationships of butterflies with other community members (e.g., plants, predators, parasitoids) have also allowed rigorous study of species interactions and coevolutionary processes. An early formulation of coevolution between interacting species involved butterflies and their larval host plants (Ehrlich and Raven 1964). Similarly, initial work on the chemical defenses of insects against predators focused on butterfly mimicry systems (Van Zandt Brower 1958a, 1958b; Turner 1977; Brower 1984). Such work on species interactions has continued, as exemplified by the chapters in this volume by Singer (chap. 10) and by Janz (chap. 11).

At yet a larger scale, butterflies have achieved indicator group status in work on conservation biology and biodiversity (e.g., Kremen 1992, 1994; Beccaloni and Gaston 1995; Ehrlich, introduction to this volume; Hill et al., chap. 7, Kremen et al., chap. 23, and Parmesan, chap. 24, all in this volume). This status is due to their susceptibility to alterations of their physical (e.g., thermal or wind circulation variables, which are affected by plant architecture) and biotic niches (e.g., larval and adult dependence on different aspects of the plant community; various sensitivities to predators, parasitoids, and pathogens). Their indicator group status has meant that butterflies have been used both in practical land management decisions (e.g., Kremen et al., chap. 23 in this volume) and to understand general factors controlling patterns of species richness and endemism (e.g., Fleishman et al. 1998; Devine et al. 2002).

These are only some examples of the ways in which butterflies are already serving as model systems to generate conceptual advances in ecology and evolution. Many other examples could be listed, including those from evolutionary developmental biology and its interface with ecology (Brakefield and Monteiro, chap. 12, Gilbert, chap. 14, ffrench-Constant and Koch, chap. 13, all in this volume).

RESEARCH NEEDS FOR THE ENHANCEMENT OF BUTTERFLIES AS A BROAD-SCALE MODEL SYSTEM

We suggest here four areas of research whose energetic development would pay dividends in making butterflies as a group an even more useful model system. Others may well occur to thoughtful readers—the more the merrier.

1. PALEONTOLOGY

The fossil record for butterflies is already informative (e.g., Emmel et al. 1992). But it is nonetheless very fragmentary, and up to now it has been augmented only rarely and fortuitously. How might butterfly paleontology be put on a more solid foundation?

The challenge, as with human paleontology, is developing more organized approaches to looking for fossils—added, in this case, to the difficulty of recognizing butterfly remains when they are present. One might try to develop methods for finding and using taxonomically diagnostic, physically persistent hard chitinous cuticular parts, as has been done so successfully with beetle elytra (Elias 1994). Larval head capsules are possible candidates, especially as they are already known to display numbers of diagnostic characters (Motta, chap. 19 in this volume). Collaboration between those interested in butterflies and in other groups may be critical: for example, the recognition of a fossil moth egg on a Cretaceous fossil plant leaf (Gall and Tiffney 1983) resulted from just such an interaction. More consistent surveying of leaf fossils for insect, lepidopteran, or specifically butterfly eggs, as recognizable by surficial chorion characters (of which there are many), might yield important results. Indeed, screening of finely preserved Cretaceous or Tertiary deposits of many other small-animal groups or of angiosperm taxa, as the appropriate paleoecology would suggest, for the presence in any form of butterflies and closely related moth groups might pay large dividends.

2. Systematics

We need a more comprehensive analysis of butterfly systematics (see Ehrlich, introduction to this volume, and Vane-Wright, chap. 22 in this volume) in order to clarify the inferred history of the entire three-superfamily clade and its relations to sister moth clades. Taxa important to clarifying this history include presently "difficult" groups, uncommon basal taxa, and "key enigmas."

Groups may be "difficult" because their distinguishing characters are esoteric or finely differentiated, because radiation of the group is recent, because parallelism is rampant for obvious character sets, or because speciation has been cryptic to obvious character sets. *Leptidea* (see Martin et al., chap. 21 in this volume) exemplifies both the last problem and a solution. Here, the addition of molecular characters helped to clarify the relations between two previously unrecognized sibling species. Molecular characters are not "superior" in any intrinsic sense, but do offer the advantages of rapid unequivocal acquisition and (usually) a very different potential envelope of present selection pressures and gene-specific histories than classic morphological character sources.

Uncommon basal taxa (e.g., *Baronia*) are critical to a comprehensive analysis of the systematics of butterflies. They may preserve key evidence of branching order, lineage sorting of key characters, and other kinds of information necessary for phylogenetic reconstructions, particularly at deeper nodes. Further, their rarity makes them vulnerable to extinction, increasing the urgency of systematic study and increasing their value as prime candidates for conservation action.

"Key enigmas" are those taxa whose characteristics, while confusing, suggest that they *could* be of primary importance to our understanding of evolution within the clade. One exemplary "enigma" is the monospecific pierid genus *Pseudopontia*, whose adult wing venation and antennal morphology appear severely modified, suggesting major developmental-genetic alteration from any candidate common ancestor. However, *Pseudopontia*'s size and overall wing shape, albeit with scaleless wings, are similar to those of Afro-Asian *Leptosia*. Is this resemblance a convergence or a reliable "hint"? The taxon could be a uniquely derived superficial "twig" of its clade, and thus of only passing interest except for its developmental anomaly, or it could reveal something more profound about pierid history. Here is an obvious case for the speedy deployment of molecular techniques to attempt the resolution of this taxon's place in the systematic context.

3. SUBDISCIPLINES

The utility of butterflies as a biodiverse model system in ecology and evolution will be enhanced by the further development of supporting conceptual or technical subdisciplines using Lepidoptera as study organisms. These subdisciplines include structural genetics and cytogenetics, the study of early development and pupal reorganization, and neurophysiology. Further development of these areas would enhance our ability to understand, for example, the neural mechanisms underlying different flight behaviors associated with foraging and mating, or constraints on combinations of life history traits due to the allocation of resources during metamorphosis. Similarly, butterflies' holometabolous life cycle includes radically different egg, larval, pupal, and adult morphologies, feeding habits, and mobilities. A comparative analysis of these traits across life stages (as called for by Ehrlich in the introduction to this volume) would allow the use of traits with different evolutionary histories and subject to different selective pressures for exploring both systematic and ecological questions. Also, an exploration of the biomechanics of various life cycle stages could prove fruitful; for example, what are all those egg-ribs and diverse egg shapes about? Many such traits are used as systematic characters without an understanding of their functional and, potentially, adaptive roles. An understanding of those roles is necessary to understand the systematic and functional evolutionary biology of the group.

Some of this information may already exist, scattered in the increasingly vast empirical and descriptive literature. If so, it would merely need collection and integration. Other subdisciplinary work, however, will need encouragement, often including collaboration with other kinds of biologists who already have adaptable new techniques, or who can bring needed innovative conceptual approaches to bear on relevant questions using butterflies.

4. NICHE STRUCTURE

The ease of working with butterflies in the field presents an unprecedented opportunity to document their niche structure (*sensu* Hutchinson 1965; Pulliam 2000) in a comprehensive, quantitative, and comparative manner. This documentation would include not only trophic aspects of the niche, for which much information already exists in initial qualitative form, but also physical climate spaces (e.g., Kingsolver 1983a, 1983b; Kingsolver and Watt 1983, 1984) and interactions with biotic components such as predators, pathogens, and competitors. When collected for members of such a biodiverse group, this information will address many important general questions in ecology and evolution. For example, what is the relationship of clade diversification to patterns of ecological innovation? Does local adaptation tend to occur in the context of some niche components but not others? How does niche similarity facilitate species' invasions into new geographic areas?

These identified research needs, combined with progress already made, set the stage for a consideration of future goals and prospects for the study of butterfly ecology and evolution, which we undertake in conclusion.

GOALS AND PROSPECTS

The enormous potential for the study of butterfly biology to make future contributions to ecology and evolution is partially due to the characteristics of the system, the knowledge gained to date, and the diverse ways of tackling biological problems using butterflies, as briefly outlined above. Beyond that, these contributions will be enhanced by the diversity of the people whose expertise can be brought to bear on ecological and evolutionary problems using butterflies, and to whom we hope this book will be useful. These people include ecologists and evolutionary biologists interested in butterflies, both professionals and serious amateurs, as well as other biologists working on different systems but concerned with the progress of knowledge in ecology and evolution. Finally, we hope that this book will stimulate the interest of some more general readers, who might be intrigued by what they have found here and be interested in where it might lead.

To understand fully the prospective importance and utility of butterflies as model systems, we must first realize that all of biology takes its status as a part of natural science from the Darwinian process of evolution by natural selection (e.g., Dobzhansky 1973). This is true of topics ranging from the study of intricate molecular, physiological, and behavioral mechanisms, which may display the results of long ages of adaptive refinement, to the inference of phyletic descent and diversification over those same ages that is central to an evolutionary understanding of systematics. But equally, all organismal complexity and diversity must be understood in terms of organisms' interactions with their environments, and thus in terms of the playing out of both adaptation and diversification within the changing structures of habitats (Hutchinson 1965), which organisms themselves may alter in turn (Lewontin 1983; Laland et al. 1999). Various students of the biology of butterflies (or indeed of other creatures) may be primarily interested in questions falling in very different stages of the evolutionary recursion (Feder and Watt 1992; Watt, chap. 15 in this volume), from genotypes to phenotypes to performances to fitnesses and back to genotypes again. But if such workers maintain awareness of the implications of their findings for neighboring subdisciplines as well, then in the end, their results will find importance and relevance in the context of general ecological and evolutionary understandings, as well as application to urgent problems of conservation and environmental science.

What, then, are some of the ways in which we may look to see the present uses of butterflies as model systems becoming even more diverse, productive, and comprehensive?

The first two stages of the evolutionary recursion, genotype → phenotype and phenotype → performance, overlap substantially as each organism both builds itself in interaction with its environment and performs biological tasks while doing so. The study of these stages includes (but is not limited to) work on both metabolic and developmental organization in an evolutionary context. While "phenotypic evolution" may be studied productively with formal Mendelian genetics (e.g., Gilbert, chap. 14 in this volume) or with the widely used methods of quantitative genetics (e.g., Monteiro et al. 1994; Brakefield 1998), the method of identified genes can make ever more diverse contributions. Its use in identifying specific gene foci for metabolic (Watt, chap. 15, ffrench-Constant and Koch, chap. 13, in this volume), molecular-sensory (Briscoe, chap. 2 in this volume), and developmental (Brakefield and Monteiro, chap. 12 in this volume) studies on butterflies shows its power to open phenotypic "black boxes" and reveal the hierarchical phenotypic organizations, at multiple levels, within which natural genetic variation acts in specific ways to alter phenotypes (see also Stern 2000). Probing complex phenotypes, whether behavioral, morphological, or physiological, "from below" in this specific and experimentally controllable manner will, among other things, show how the integration of phenotypic parts can support the emergence of quite new properties at higher levels of phenotypic organization, but in such a way that changes in the parts can still predict changes in the performance of the whole.

Of course, no evolution occurs independently of specific environments, although some evolutionists seriously neglect the ecological aspects of their discipline, as Endler (1986), Feder and Watt (1992), and Mitton (1997) have warned. Rigorous studies of the organism-environment interactions of naturally variant phenotypes are as central to studies of the first two stages of the evolutionary recursion as are studies of phenotypic mechanisms—indeed, these areas of study form a continuum. A more thorough study of butterfly ecological niche structures, as called for above, if carried out with explicit awareness of evolutionary connections, will tremendously facilitate subsequent evolutionary work as well as a variety of specifically ecological pursuits. It may finally be possible, for example, to bring some rigor and clarity to the long debate over whether apparently unoccupied niche space constitutes identifiably "empty niches," and if so, how and why. But addressing this question will involve comparisons among taxa of alternative classes of phenotypes and their interactions with their environments, as well as taking advantage of the rigorous experimental control afforded by study of natural variants in those phenotypes within taxa and their effects on organism-environment interactions—in short, a practical amalgamation of mechanistic approaches to both ecology and evolution.

A special application of these ideas to systematics will be the illumination of the genotype-phenotype-environment interactions driving "character evolution" as clades diversify. The phenotypic diversity present in the butterfly clade will prove useful for exploring the underlying causes of patterns of "character evolution" within taxa and across subclade and clade divisions—especially, for example, in clarifying the occurrence and causes of parallel or convergent evolution, which has such potential to confound phylogenetic inference if not detected and understood.

The study of the next segment of the evolutionary recursion, performance → fitness, will include analyses of life history trait evolution, fitness components and net fitnesses of organisms in the wild, and resultant population dynamics. Here, too, comparative study within and among taxa will facilitate answers to long-standing questions. For example, what combinations of age-specific survival and reproduction are favored under particular environmental conditions? Are some combinations essentially "forbidden" by evolution? If so, why? The answer to this latter question will require reaching back to earlier components of the recursion to include, for example, the study of bioenergetics, behavior, and interspecific interactions as mechanisms either constraining evolution or generating particular life history traits. Future work in this area of the recursion can also be expected to lead to the further development of methods for assessing fitness components and net fitnesses in the wild. Butterflies, given their tractability for fieldwork and our knowledge of their natural history, should prove ideal test systems for such development.

The fourth stage of the evolutionary recursion, leading from fitness to a new array of genotypes in the next generation via the dynamics of population genetics, is highly accessible to exploration and testing in butterflies. Such studies will build on extensive and continuing studies of mating systems (e.g., Wiklund, chap. 4 in this volume), population censuses and dispersal patterns (e.g., Crone and Schultz, chap. 25 in this volume, and many earlier studies), and hence the ability to assess effective population size, inbreeding, and the role of genetic drift alongside differential fitnesses of genotypes.

Population dynamics over longer time frames, including the dynamics of extinction and colonization, have been studied fairly extensively using butterflies (Hanski, chap. 26 in this volume), yet our ability to predict the circumstances (including intensity of human disturbance) that lead to extinction is still rudimentary. Given that population persistence is critical to species and clade persistence (Hughes et al. 1997), that human disturbance is not likely to abate in the near future, and that butterflies can serve as indicator species, the various components of conservation biology will be important foci for research. These components include causal mechanisms determining patterns of population dynamics, species distributions, and landscape-level diversity. The last component specifically includes countryside biogeography, or the study of the diversity remaining in human-altered landscapes (Daily et al. 2001; Ehrlich, introduction to this volume), whose roots go back to early conservationist thinkers (e.g., Leopold 1949; Hutchinson 1953). In the case of butterflies, its early roots lie in the masterful analysis of the problems of developing "a new . . . balance, consonant with man's presence in and use of each area" (p. 35), articulated by Bill Klots in his magnificent 1951 *Field Guide to the Butterflies*. While present thinking has moved away from concepts of balance to those of natural nonequilibrium states of populations and communities, the message remains: we must learn how to preserve as much diversity as possible around ourselves, not only in remote and isolated refuge areas.

Finally, we believe that the combination of interdisciplinary breadth and specific, thorough in-depth study that our authors have exhibited throughout this volume is the best possible indicator of the future scientific productiveness of butterflies as model systems. If much has already been learned, and we have begun to understand how to apply that learning to the solution of practical problems, nonetheless the way is open for much more, and more comprehensive, understanding, both fundamental and applied. The study of ecology and evolution is indeed taking flight, as it must if we are to preserve our planet and ourselves. Butterflies will be our beautiful companions, as well as critical test systems for our work, as we navigate through that flight to what we all hope will be its successful conclusion.

Aagaard, K., and J. Gulbrandsen. 1976. *Prikkart over Norske dagsommerfugler.* Universitetet I Trondheim, Trondheim.

Aagaard, K., K. Hindar, A. S. Pullin, C. H. James, O. Hammarstedt, T. Balstad, and O. Hanssen. 2002. Phylogenetic relationships in brown argus butterflies (Lepidoptera: Lycaenidae: Aricia) from north-western Europe. Biological Journal of the Linnean Society 75: 27–37.

Abouheif, E. 1997. Developmental genetics and homology: A hierarchical approach. Trends in Ecology and Evolution 12: 405–408.

Abouheif, E., M. Akam, W. J. Dickinson, P. W. H. Holland, A. Meyer, N. H. Patel, R. A. Raff, V. L. Roth, and G. A. Wray. 1997. Homology and developmental genes. Trends in Genetics 13: 432–433.

Abrahamson, W. G., and A. E. Weis. 1996. *The evolutionary ecology of a tritrophic interaction: Goldenrod, the stemgaller and its natural enemies.* Princeton University Press, Princeton, NJ.

Achari, A., S. E. Marshall, H. Muirhead, R. H. Palmieri, and E. A. Noltmann. 1981. Glucose-6-phosphate isomerase. Philosophical Transactions of the Royal Society of London B 293: 145–157.

Ackery, P. R. 1984. Systematic and faunistic studies on butterflies. Pp. 9–21 in R. I. Vane-Wright and P. R. Ackery, eds., *The biology of butterflies.* Academic Press, London.

————. 1987. The Danaid genus *Tellervo* (Lepidoptera, Nymphalidae): A cladistic approach. Zoological Journal of the Linnean Society 89: 203–274.

————. 1988. Host plants and classification: A review of nymphalid butterflies. Biological Journal of the Linnean Society 33: 95–203.

Ackery, P. R., R. de Jong, and R. I. Vane-Wright. 1999. The butterflies: Hedyloidea, Hesperioidea and Papilionoidea. Pp. 263–300 in N. P. Kristensen, ed., *Handbook of Zoology* 4. Walter de Gruyter, Berlin.

Ackery, P. R., and R. L. Smites. 1976. An illustrated list of the type specimens of the Heliconiinae (Lepidoptera: Nymphalidae) in the British Museum (Natural History). Bulletin of the British Museum (Natural History) Entomology 32 (5). London.

Ackery, P. R., and R. I. Vane-Wright. 1984. *Milkweed butterflies.* Cornell University Press, Ithaca, NY.

Adams, M. J. 1986. Pronophiline butterflies (Satyridae) of the three Andean Cordilleras of Colombia. Zoological Journal of the Linnean Society 87: 235–320.

Adler, P. H. 1982. Soil- and puddle-visiting habits of moths. Journal of the Lepidopterists' Society 36: 161–173.

Adler, P. H., and D. L. Pearson. 1982. Why do male butterflies visit mud puddles? Canadian Journal of Zoology 60: 322–325.

Ae, S. 1979. The phylogeny of some *Papilio* species based on interspecific hybridization data. Systematic Entomology 4: 1–16.

———. 1995. Ecological and evolutionary aspects of hybridization in some *Papilio* butterflies. Pp. 229–235 in J. M. Scriber, Y. Tsubaki, and R. C. Lederhouse, eds., *Swallowtail butterflies: Their ecology and evolutionary biology.* Scientific Publishers, Gainesville, FL.

Agnew, K., and M. C. Singer. 2000. Does fecundity constrain the evolution of insect diet? Oikos 88: 533–538.

Akam, M. 1998. Hox genes, homeosis, and the evolution of segment identity: No need for hopeless monsters. International Journal of Developmental Biology 42: 445–451.

Akam, M., M. Averof, J. Castelli-Gair, R. Dawes, and F. Falciani. 1994. The evolving role of Hox genes in arthropods. Development Suppl. 209–215.

Albuquerque, G. S., C. A. Tauber, and M. J. Tauber. 1996. Post mating reproductive isolation between *Chrysopa quadripunctata* and *Chrysopa slossonae:* Mechanisms and geographic variation. Evolution 50: 1598–1606.

Alcock, J. 1985. Hilltopping in the nymphalid butterfly *Chlosyne californica* (Lepidoptera). American Midland Naturalist 113: 69–75.

———. 1993a. *Animal behavior: An evolutionary approach.* 5th ed. Sinauer Associates, Sunderland, MA.

———. 1993b. The effects of male body size on territorial and mating success in the landmark-defending fly *Hermetia comstocki* (Stratiomyidae). Ecological Entomology 18: 1–6.

Alcock, J., and T. F. Houston. 1996. Mating systems and male size in Australian Hylaeine bees (Hymenoptera: Colletidae). Ethology 102: 591–610.

Allegrucci, G., A. Caccone, S. Cataudella, J. R. Powell, and V. Sbordoni. 1995. Acclimation of the European sea bass to freshwater: Monitoring genetic changes by RAPD polymerase chain reaction to detect DNA polymorphisms. Marine Biology 121: 591–599.

Allegrucci, G., C. Fortunato, S. Cataudella, and V. Sbordoni. 1994. Acclimation to fresh water of the sea bass: Evidence of selective mortality of allozyme genotypes. Pp. 486–502 in A. R. Beaumont, ed., *Genetics and evolution of aquatic organisms.* Chapman and Hall, London.

Alverson, E. R. 1993. Assessment of proposed wetland mitigation in West Eugene. Report to the Environmental Protection Agency, Region X.

Anderson, E., and L. Hubricht. 1940. A method for describing and comparing blooming-seasons. Bulletin of the Torrey Botanical Club 67: 639–648.

Anderson, R. A., T. R. Hamilton-Kemp, P. D. Fleming, and D. F. Hildebrand. 1986. Volatile compounds from vegetative tobacco and wheat obtained by steam distillation and headspace trapping. Pp. 99–111 in T. H. Parliment and R. Croteau, eds., *Biogeneration of aromas.* American Chemical Society, Washington, DC.

Andersson, J., A.-K. Borg-Karlson, and C. Wiklund. 2000. Sexual cooperation and conflict in butterflies: A male-transferred anti-aphrodisiac reduces harassment of recently mated females. Proceedings of the Royal Society of London B 267: 1271–1275.

Andersson, M. 1994. *Sexual selection*. Princeton University Press, Princeton, NJ.

Andrewartha, H. G., and L. C. Birch. 1954. *The distribution and abundance of animals*. University of Chicago Press, Chicago.

Andriamampianiana, L. 1996. *Biogeography of enariine (Melolonthidae) and cicindelid beetles in Madagascar*. Durrell Institute of Conservation and Ecology, University of Kent, Canterbury, U.K.

Andriamampianiana, L., C. Kremen, R. Vane-Wright, D. Lees, and V. Razafimahatratra. 2000. Taxic richness patterns and conservation evaluation of Madagascan tiger beetles (Coleoptera: Cicindelidae). Journal of Insect Conservation 4: 109–128.

Anstensrud, M. 1992. Mate guarding and mate choice in two copepods, *Lernaeocera branchialis* (Pennellidae) and *Lepeophtheirus pectoralis* (Caligidae), parasitic on flounder. Journal of Crustacean Biology 12: 31–40.

Arikawa, K., and K. Aoki. 1982. Response characteristics and occurrence of extraocular photoreceptors on lepidopteran genitalia. Journal of Comparative Physiology A 148: 483–489.

Arikawa, K., E. Eguchi, A. Yoshida, and K. Aoki. 1980. Multiple extraocular photoreceptive areas on genitalia of butterfly *Papilio xuthus*. Nature 288: 700–702.

Arikawa, K., K. Inokuma, and E. Eguchi. 1987. Pentachromatic visual system in a butterfly. Naturwissenschaften 74: 297–298.

Arikawa, K., S. Mizuno, D. G. W. Scholten, M. Kinoshita, T. Seki, J. Kitamoto, and D. G. Stavenga. 1999a. An ultraviolet absorbing pigment causes a narrow-band ultraviolet receptor and a single-peaked green receptor in the eye of the butterfly *Papilio*. Vision Research 39: 1–8.

Arikawa, K., D. G. W. Scholten, M. Kinoshita, and D. G. Stavenga. 1999b. Tuning of photoreceptor spectral sensitivities by red and yellow pigments in the butterfly *Papilio xuthus*. Zoological Science 16: 17–24.

Arikawa, K., and D. Stavenga. 1997. Random array of colour filters in the eyes of butterflies. Journal of Experimental Biology 200: 2501–2506.

Arikawa, K., D. Suyama, and T. Fujii. 1996. Light on butterfly mating. Nature 382: 119.

———. 1997. Hindsight by genitalia: Photo-guided copulation in butterflies. Journal of Comparative Physiology A 180: 295–299.

Arikawa, K., and N. Takagi. 2001. Genital photoreceptors have crucial role in oviposition in Japanese yellow swallowtail butterfly, *Papilio xuthus*. Zoological Science 18: 175–179.

Arikawa, K., and H. Uchiyama. 1996. Red receptors dominate the proximal tier of the retina in the butterfly *Papilio xuthus*. Journal of Comparative Physiology A 178: 55–61.

Arnold, M. L. 1997. *Natural hybridization and evolution*. Oxford University Press, Oxford.

Arnold, M. L., M. R. Bulger, J. M. Burke, A. L. Hempel, and J. H. Williams. 1999. Natural hybridization: How long can you go and still be important? Ecology 80: 371–381.

Arnold, M. L., and S. K. Emms. 1998. Paradigm lost: Natural hybridization and evolutionary innovations. Pp. 379–389 in D. J. Howard and S. H. Berlocher, eds., *Endless forms: Species and speciation*. Oxford University Press, New York.

Arnold, M. L., and S. A. Hodges. 1995. Are natural hybrids fit or unfit relative to their parents? Trends in Ecology and Evolution 10: 67–71.

Arnold, S. J., and M. J. Wade. 1984a. On the measurement of natural and sexual selection: Theory. Evolution 38: 709–719.

———. 1984b. On the measurement of natural and sexual selection: Applications. Evolution 38: 720–734.

Arseneault, D., and S. Payette. 1997. Reconstruction of millennial forest dynamics from tree remains in a subarctic tree line peatland. Ecology 78: 1873–1883.

Asher, J., M. Warren, R. Fox, P. Harding, G. Jeffcoate, and S. Jeffcoate. 2001. *The millennium atlas of butterflies in Britain and Ireland.* Oxford University Press, Oxford.

Asmussen, M. A., J. Arnold, and J. C. Avise. 1989. The effects of assortative mating and migration on cytonuclear associations in hybrid zones. Genetics 122: 923–934.

Aubert, J., B. Barascud, H. Descimon, and F. Michel. 1996. Systematique moleculaire des Argynnes (Lepidoptera: Nymphalidae). Comptes Rendus de l'Academie des Sciences. Serie III. Sciences de la Vie 319: 647–651.

———. 1997. Ecology and genetics of interspecific hybridization in the swallowtails, *Papilio hospiton* Gene and *P. machaon* L., in Corsica (Lepidoptera: Papilionidae). Biological Journal of the Linnean Society 60: 467–492.

Aubert, J., L. Legal, H. Descimon, and F. Michel. 1999. Molecular phylogeny of swallowtail butterflies of the tribe Papilionini (Papilionidae, Lepidoptera). Molecular Phylogenetics and Evolution 12: 156–167.

Austad, S. N., W. T. Jones, and P. M. Waser. 1979. Territorial defence in speckled wood butterflies: Why does the resident always win? Animal Behaviour 27: 960–961.

Austin, G. T. 1978. Phenology and diversity of a butterfly population in southern Arizona. Journal of the Lepidopterists' Society 32: 207–220.

Avise, J. C. 1994. *Molecular markers, natural history, and evolution.* Chapman and Hall, New York.

Avise, J. C., and C. F. Aquadro. 1982. A comparative summary of genetic distances in the vertebrates. Evolutionary Biology 15: 151–185.

Avise, J. C., and M. R. Ball Jr. 1990. Principles of genealogical concordance in species concepts and biological taxonomy. Oxford Surveys in Evolutionary Biology 7: 45–67.

Axen, A. H., and N. E. Pierce. 1997. Aggregation as a cost-reducing strategy for lycaenid larvae. Behavoral Ecology 9: 109–115.

Ayala, F. J., and J. R. Powell. 1972. Allozymes as diagnostic characters of sibling species of *Drosophila.* Proceedings of the National Academy of Sciences USA 69: 1094–1096.

Ayres, M. P., and J. M. Scriber. 1994. Local adaptations to regional climates in *Papilio canadensis* (Lepidoptera: Papilionidae). Ecological Monographs 64: 465–482.

Back, C. E. 1988. Effects of host plant size on herbivore density: Patterns. Ecology 69: 1090–1102.

Baerends, G. P. 1950. Specializations in organs and movements with a releasing function. Pp. 337–360. *Symposia of the Society for Experimental Biology, Number IV: Physiological mechanisms in animal behaviour.* Academic Press, New York.

Baguette, M., and G. Nève. 1994. Adult movements between populations in the specialist butterfly *Proclossiana eunomia.* Ecological Entomology 19: 1–5.

Baker, H. G. 1961. The adaptation of flowering plants to nocturnal and crepuscular pollinators. Quarterly Review of Biology 36: 64–73.

Baker, H. G., and I. Baker. 1983. A brief historical review of the chemistry of floral nectar. Pp. 126–152 in B. Bentley and T. Elias, eds., *The biology of nectaries.* Columbia University Press, New York.

Baker, R. R. 1984. The dilemma: When and how to go or stay. Pp. 279–296 in R. I. Vane-Wright and P. R. Ackery, eds., *The biology of butterflies.* Academic Press, London.

Baker, T. C., and C. E. Linn Jr. 1984. Wind tunnels in pheromone research. Pp. 75–110 in H. E. Hummel and T. A. Miller, eds., *Techniques in pheromone research.* Springer-Verlag, New York.

Baldwin, I. T., C. Preston, M. Euler, and D. Gorham. 1997. Patterns and consequences of benzyl acetone floral emissions from *Nicotiana attenuata* plants. Journal of Chemical Ecology 23: 2327–2343.

Balmford, A. 1998. On hotspots and the use of indicators for reserve selection. Trends in Ecology and Evolution 13: 409.

Balmford, A., M. J. B. Green, and M. G. Murray. 1996. Using higher-taxon richness as a surrogate for species richness: I. Regional tests. Proceedings of the Royal Society of London B 263: 1267–1274.

Bandai, K., K. Arikawa, and E. Eguchi. 1992. Localization of spectral receptors in the ommatidium of butterfly compound eye determined by polarization sensitivity. Journal of Comparative Physiology A 171: 289–297.

Bard, J. B. L., and V. French. 1984. Butterfly wing patterns: How good a determining mechanism is the simple diffusion of a single morphogen? Journal of Embryology and Experimental Morphology 84: 255–274.

Barthell, J. F., and J. M. H. Knops. 1997. Visitation of evening primrose by carpenter bees: Evidence of a "mixed" pollination syndrome. Southwestern Naturalist 42: 86–93.

Bartholomew, G. 1981. A matter of size: An examination of endothermy in insects and terrestial vertebrates. Pp. 45–78 in B. Heinrich, ed., *Insect thermoregulation.* J. Wiley and Sons, New York.

Bartholomew, G., and T. M. Casey. 1978. Oxygen consumption of moths during rest, pre-flight warm-up, and flight in relation to body size and wing morphology. Journal of Experimental Biology 76: 11–25.

Barton, N. H. 1983. Multilocus clines. Evolution 37: 454–471.

Barton, N. H., and G. M. Hewitt. 1985. Analysis of hybrid zones. Annual Review of Ecology and Systematics 16: 113–148.

———. 1989. Adaptation, speciation and hybrid zones. Nature 341: 497–503.

Barton, N. H., and M. C. Whitlock. 1997. The evolution of metapopulations. Pp. 183–210 in I. Hanski and M. Gilpin, eds., *Metapopulation biology.* Academic Press, San Diego.

Bascombe, M. J., G. Johnston, and F. S. Bascombe. 1999. *The butterflies of Hong Kong.* Academic Press, London.

Basolo, A. L. 1990. Female preference predates the evolution of the sword in swordtail fish. Science 250: 808–810.

Bates, H. W. 1862. Contributions to an insect fauna of the Amazon valley. Lepidoptera: Heliconidae. Transactions of the Linnean Society 23: 495–566.

Bateson, P. 1983. *Mate choice.* Cambridge University Press, Cambridge.

Battisti, A., A. Boato, and D. Zanocco. 1998. Two sibling species of the spurce web-spinning sawfly *Cephalcia fallenii* (Hymenoptera: Pamphiliidae) in Europe. Systematic Entomology 23: 99–108.

Bauer, T. 1981. Prey capture and structure of the visual space of an insect that hunts by sight on the litter layer (*Notiophilus biguttatus* F., Carabidae, Coleoptera). Behavioral Ecology and Sociobiology 8: 91–97.

———. 1985. Different adaptations to visual hunting in three ground beetle species of the same genus. Journal of Insect Physiology 31: 593–601.

Baughman, J. F., P. F. Brussard, P. R. Ehrlich, and D. D. Murphy. 1990. History, selection, drift, and gene flow: Complex differentiation in checkerspot butterflies. Canadian Journal of Zoology 68: 1967–1975.

Baum, D. A. 1995. The comparative pollination and floral biology of baobabs (*Adansonia bombacaceae*). Annals of the Missouri Botanical Garden 82: 322–348.

Baum, D. A., and M. J. Donoghue. 1995. Choosing among alternative phylogenetic species concepts. Systematic Botany 20: 560–573.

Baum, D. A., and K. L. Shaw. 1995. Genealogical perspectives on the species problem. Pp. 289–303 in P. C. Hoch and A. G. Stevenson, eds., *Experimental and molecular approaches to plant biosystematics*. Missouri Botanical Garden, St. Louis.

Bawa, K. S., S. H. Bullock, D. R. Perry, R. E. Coville, and M. H. Grayum. 1985. Reproductive biology of tropical rain forest trees. II. Pollination systems. American Journal of Botany 72: 346–356.

Bazzaz, F. A. 1996. *Plants in changing environments: Linking physiological, population and community ecology.* Cambridge University Press, Cambridge.

Bazzaz, F. A., N. R. Chiariello, P. D. Coley, and L. F. Pitelka. 1987. Allocating resources to reproduction and defense. BioScience 37: 58–67.

Beard, C. D., D. M. Hamm, and F. H. Collins. 1993. The mitochondrial genome of the mosquito *Anopheles gambiae:* DNA sequence, genome organization, and comparisons with mitochondrial sequences of other insects. Insect Molecular Biology 2: 103–124.

Beccaloni, G. W., and K. J. Gaston. 1995. Predicting the species richness of Neotropical forest butterflies: Ithomiinae (Lepidoptera: Nymphalidae) as indicators. Biological Conservation 71: 77–86.

Beccaloni, G. W., and F. B. Symons. 2000. Variation of butterfly diet breadth in relation to host-plant predictability: Results from two faunas. Oikos: 90: 50–66.

Beck, J., E. Muhlenberg, and K. Fiedler. 1999. Mud-puddling behavior in tropical butterflies: In search of proteins or minerals. Oecologia 119: 140–148.

Beebee, T. J. C. 1995. Amphibian breeding and climate. Nature 374: 219.

Beerling, D. J., B. Huntley, and J. P. Bailey. 1995. Climate and the distribution of *Fallopia japonica:* Use of an introduced species to test the predictive capacity of response surfaces. Journal of Vegetation Science 6: 269–282.

Beersma, D. G. M., D. G. Stavenga, and J. W. Kuiper. 1977. Retinal lattice, visual field, and binocularity in flies: Dependence on species and sex. Journal of Comparative Physiology 119: 207–220.

Beldade, P., and P. M. Brakefield. 2002. The genetics and evo-devo of butterfly wing patterns. Nature Reviews Genetics 3: 442–452.

Beldade, P., P. M. Brakefield, and A. D. Long. 2002a. Contribution of *Distal-less* to quantitative variation in butterfly eyespots. Nature 415: 315–318.

Beldade, P., K. Koops, and P. M. Brakefield. 2002b. Developmental constraints versus flexibility in morphological evolution. Nature 416: 844–847.

Bell, G. 1997. *Selection: The mechanism of evolution.* Chapman and Hall, New York.

Bell, R. A., and F. G. Joaquim. 1976. Techniques for rearing laboratory colonies of tobacco hornworms and pink bollworms. Annals of the Entomological Society of America 69: 365–373.

Beltran, M. S., C. D. Jiggins, V. Bull, O. McMillan, E. Bermingham, J. Mallet, and M. Linares. 2001. Phylogenetic discordance at the species boundary: Comparative gene genealogies in *Heliconius* butterflies. GenBank (http://www.ncbi.nlm.nih.gov).

Bengtsson, B. E., H. Elmquist, and E. Nyholm. 1989. On the Swedish apollo butterfly with an attempt to explain its decline. Entomologisk Tidskrift 110: 31–37.

Bengtsson, J. 1991. Interspecific competition in metapopulations. Biological Journal of the Linnean Society 42: 219–238.

Beniston, M., R. S. J. Tol, R. Delécolle, G. Hoermann, A. Iglesias, J. Innes, A. J. McMichael, W. J. M. Martens, I. Nemesova, R. Nicholls, and F. L. Toth. 1998. Europe. Pp. 149–185 in R. T. Watson, M. C. Zinyowera, and R. H. Moss, eds., *The regional impacts of climate change.* Intergovernmental Panel on Climate Change Working Group II. Cambridge University Press, Cambridge.

Bennett, R. R., and R. H. White. 1989. Influence of carotenoid deficiency on visual sensitivity, visual pigment and P-face particles of photoreceptor membrane in the moth *Manduca sexta.* Journal of Comparative Physiology A 164: 321–331.

Benson, W. W. 1972. Natural selection for Müllerian mimicry in *Heliconius erato* in Costa Rica. Science 176: 936–939.

Benson, W. W., C. F. B. Haddad, and M. Zakon. 1989. Territorial behavior and dominance in some heliconiine butterflies (Nymphalidae). Journal of the Lepidopterists' Society 43: 33–39.

Berenbaum, M. R. 1983. Coumarins and caterpillars: A case for coevolution. Evolution 37: 163–169.

———. 1995a. The chemistry of defense: Theory and practice. Proceedings of the National Academy of Sciences USA 92: 2–8.

———. 1995b. Chemistry and oligophagy in the Papilionidae. Pp. 27–38 in J. M. Scriber, Y. Tsubaki, and R. C. Lederhouse, eds., *Swallowtail butterflies: Their ecology and evolutionary biology.* Scientific Publishers, Gainesville, FL.

Berger, L. A., and M. Fontaine. 1947–1948. Une espèce malconnue du genre *Colias.* Lambilionea 47: 91–98; 48: 12–15, 21–24, 90–114.

Bernard, G. D., and C. L. Remington. 1991. Color vision in *Lycaena* butterflies: Spectral tuning of receptor arrays in relation to behavioral ecology. Proceedings of the National Academy of Sciences USA 88: 2783–2787.

Bernays, E. A. 1998. The value of being a resource specialist: Behavioral support for a neural hypothesis. American Naturalist 151: 451–464.

Bernays, E. A., and R. F. Chapman. 1998. Phenotypic plasticity in numbers of antennal receptors in a grasshopper: Effects of food. Journal of Comparative Physiology 183: 69–76.

Bernays, E. A., and M. Graham. 1988. On the evolution of host specificity in phytophagous arthropods. Ecology 69: 886–892.

Bernays, E. A., and O. Minkenberg. 1997. Insect herbivores: Different reasons for being a generalist. Ecology 78: 1157–1169.

Bernhard, C. G., J. Boëthius, G. Gemne, and G. Struwe. 1970. Eye ultrastructure, color reception, and behaviour. Nature 226: 865–866.

Bert, T. M., and W. S. Arnold. 1995. An empirical test of predictions of two competing models for the maintenance and fate of hybrid zones: Both models are supported in a hard-clam hybrid zone. Evolution 49: 276–289.

Berwaerts, K., H. Van Dyck, and P. Aerts. 2002. Does flight morphology relate to flight performance? An experimental test with the butterfly *Pararge aegeria.* Functional Ecology 16: 484–491.

Berwaerts, K., H. Van Dyck, S. Van Dongen, and E. Matthysen. 1998. Morphological and genetic variation in the speckled wood butterfly (*Pararge aegeria* L.) among differently fragmented landscapes. Netherlands Journal of Zoology 48: 241–253.

Berwaerts, K., H. Van Dyck, E. Vints, and E. Matthysen. 2001. Effect of manipulated wing characteristics and basking posture on thermal properties of the butterfly *Pararge aegeria* (L.). Journal of Zoology 255: 261–267.

Betts, C. R., and R. J. Wootton. 1988. Wing shape and flight behaviour in butterflies (Lepidoptera: Papilionidea and Hesperioidea): A preliminary analysis. Journal of Experimental Biology 138: 271–288.

Bink, F. A. 1992. The butterflies of the future, their strategy. Pp. 134–138 in T. Pavlicek-van Beek, A. H. Ovaa, and J. G. van der Made, eds., *Future of butterflies in Europe*. Department of Nature Conservation, Agricultural University, Wageningen.

Bird, C. D., G. L. Hitchie, N. G. Kondla, E. M. Pike, and F. A. H. Sperling. 1995. *Alberta butterflies*. Provincial Museum of Alberta, Edmonton.

Bissoondath, C. J., and C. Wiklund. 1995. Protein content of spermatophores in relation to monandry/polyandry in butterflies. Behavioral Ecology and Sociobiology 37: 365–371.

——— . 1996. Effect of male mating history and body size on ejaculate size and quality in two polyandrous butterflies *Pieris napi* and *P. rapae* (Lepidoptera: Pieridae). Functional Ecology 10: 457–464.

——— . 1997. Effect of male body size on sperm precedence in the polyandrous butterfly *Pieris napi* L. (Lepidoptera: Pieridae). Behavioral Ecology 8: 518–523.

Bitzer, R. J., and K. C. Shaw. 1983. Territorial behavior of *Nymphalis antiopa* and *Polygonia comma* (Nymphalidae). Journal of the Lepidopterists' Society 37: 1–13.

Blair, S. S., and A. Ralston. 1997. Smoothened-mediated Hedgehog signalling is required for the maintenance of the anterior-posterior lineage restriction in the developing wing of *Drosophila*. Development 124: 4053–4063.

Blair, W. F. 1955. Mating call and stage of speciation in the *Microhyla olivaceae-M. carolinensis* complex. Evolution 9: 469–480.

Blakeley, D. S. 1997. Overwintering biology of *Pararge aegeria*. M. Phil. thesis, University of Leeds.

Blum, M. J., E. Bermingham, and K. Dasmahapatra. 2001. A molecular phylogeny of the Neotropical butterfly genus *Anartia* (Lepidoptera: Nymphalidae). GenBank (http://www.ncbi.nlm.nih.gov).

Boggs, C. L. 1981a. Nutritional and life history determinants of resource allocation in holometabolous insects. American Naturalist 117: 692–709.

——— . 1981b. Selection pressures affecting male nutrient investment at mating in heliconiine butterflies. Evolution 35: 931–940.

——— . 1986. Reproductive strategies of female butterflies: Variation in and constraints on fecundity. Ecological Entomology 11: 7–15.

——— . 1987a. Within population variation in the demography of *Speyeria mormonia* (Lepidoptera: Nymphalidae). Holarctic Ecology 10: 175–184.

——— . 1987b. Ecology of nectar and pollen feeding in Lepidoptera. Pp. 369–391 in F. Slansky and J. G. Rodriguez, eds., *Nutritional ecology of insects, mites and spiders*. John Wiley and Sons, New York.

——— . 1990. A general model of the role of male-donated nutrients in female insects' reproduction. American Naturalist 136: 598–617.

——— . 1992. Resource allocation: Exploring connections between foraging and life history. Functional Ecology 6: 508–518.

—————. 1995. Male nuptial gifts: Phenotypic consequences and evolutionary implications. Pp. 215–242 in S. R. Leather and J. Hardie, eds., *Insect reproduction.* CRC Press, New York.

—————. 1997a. Reproductive allocation from reserves and income in butterfly species with differing adult diets. Ecology 78: 181–191.

—————. 1997b. Dynamics of reproductive allocation from juvenile and adult feeding: Radiotracer studies. Ecology 78: 192–202.

—————. 1997c. Resource allocation in variable environments: Comparing insects and plants. Pp. 73–92 in F. A. Bazzaz and J. Grace, eds., *Plant resource allocation.* Academic Press, New York.

Boggs, C. L., and L. E. Gilbert. 1979. Male contribution to egg production in butterflies: Evidence for transfer of nutrients at mating. Science 206: 83–84.

Boggs, C. L., and L. A. Jackson. 1991. Mud puddling by butterflies is not a simple matter. Ecological Entomology 16: 123–127.

Boggs, C. L., and C. L. Ross. 1993. The effect of adult food limitation on life-history traits in *Speyeria mormonia* (Lepidoptera, Nymphalidae). Ecology 74: 433–441.

Boggs, C. L., and W. B. Watt. 1981. Population structure of pierid butterflies. IV. Genetic and physiological investment in offspring by male *Colias.* Oecologia 50: 320–324.

Bohannan, B. J. M., and R. E. Lenski. 2000. Linking genetic change to community evolution: Insights from studies of bacteria and bacteriophage. Ecology Letters 3: 362–377.

Boppré, M. 1990. Lepidoptera and pyrrolizidine alkaloids: Exemplification of complexity in chemical ecology. Journal of Chemical Ecology 16: 165–185.

Boppré, M., and R. I. Vane-Wright. 1989. Androconial systems in Danainae (Lepidoptera): Functional morphology of *Amauris, Tirumala, Danaus* and *Euploea.* Zoological Journal of the Linnean Society 97: 101–133.

Bossart, J. L. 1998. Genetic architecture of host use in a widely distributed, polyphagous butterfly (Lepidoptera: Papilionidae): Adaptive inferences based on comparison of spatio-temporal populations. Biological Journal of the Linnean Society 165: 279–300.

Bossart, J. L., and D. P. Prowell. 1998. Genetic estimates of population structure and gene flow: Limitations, lessons and new directions. Trends in Ecology and Evolution 13: 202–206.

Bossart, J. L., and J. M. Scriber. 1995a. Genetic variation in oviposition preferences in the tiger swallowtail butterfly: Interspecific, interpopulation, and interindividual comparisons. Pp. 183–194 in J. M. Scriber, Y. Tsubaki, and R. C. Lederhouse, eds., *Swallowtail butterflies: Their ecology and evolutionary biology.* Scientific Publishers, Gainesville, FL.

—————. 1995b. Maintenance of ecologically significant genetic variation in the tiger swallowtail butterfly through differential selection and gene flow. Evolution 49: 1163–1171.

—————. 1999. Preference variation in the polyphagous tiger swallowtail butterfly (Lepidoptera: Papilionidae). Environmental Entomology 28: 628–637.

Boucher, D. 1996. Hawaiian sphinx: *Tinostoma smaragdina.* News of the Lepidopterists' Society 38: 24.

Boughton, D. A. 1999. Empirical evidence for source-sink dynamics in a butterfly: Temporal barriers and alternative states. Ecology 80: 2727–2739.

—————. 2000. The dispersal system of a butterfly: A test of source-sink theory suggests the intermediate-scale hypothesis. American Naturalist 156: 131–144.

Bowers, M. D., N. E. Stamp, and S. Collinge. 1992. Early stage of host-range expansion by a specialist herbivore, *Euphydryas phaeton* (Nymphalidae). Ecology 73: 526–536.

Bradbury, J. W. 1985. Contrasts between insects and vertebrates in the evolution of male display, female choice and lek mating. In B. Hölldobler and M. Lindauer, eds., *Experimental behavioral ecology and sociobiology.* Fisher, New York.

Bradbury, J. W., and S. L. Vehrencamp. 1998. *Principles of animal communication.* Sinauer Associates, Sunderland, MA.

Bradley, M. C., N. Perrin, and P. Calow. 1991. Energy allocation in the cladoceran *Daphnia magna* Straus, under starvation and re-feeding. Oecologia 86: 414–418.

Bradley, N. L., A. C. Leopold, J. Ross, and W. Huffaker. 1999. Phenological changes reflect climate change in Wisconsin. Proceedings of the National Academy of Sciences USA 96: 9701–9704.

Brakefield, P. M. 1982. Ecological studies on the butterfly *Maniola jurtina* in Britain. II. Population dynamics: The present position. Journal of Animal Ecology 51: 727–738.

———. 1984. The ecological genetics of quantitative characters of *Maniola jurtina* and other butterflies. Pp. 167–190 in R. I. Vane-Wright and P. R. Ackery, eds., *The biology of butterflies.* Academic Press, London.

———. 1987. Geographical variability in, and temperature effects on, the phenology of *Maniola jurtina* and *Pyronia tithonus* in England and Wales. Ecological Entomology 12: 139–148.

———. 1996. Seasonal polyphenism in butterflies and natural selection. Trends in Ecology and Evolution 11: 275–277.

———. 1998. The evolution-development interface and advances with the eyespot patterns of *Bicyclus* butterflies. Heredity 80: 265–272.

———. 2001. Structure of a character and the evolution of butterfly eyespot patterns. Journal of Experimental Zoology 291: 93–104.

Brakefield, P. M., and V. French. 1993. Butterfly wing patterns: Developmental mechanisms and evolutionary change. Acta Biotheoretica 41: 447–468.

———. 1995. Eyespot development on butterfly wings: The epidermal response to damage. Developmental Biology 168: 98–111.

———. 1999. Butterfly wings: The evolution of development of colour patterns. Bioessays 21: 391–401.

Brakefield, P. M., J. Gates, D. Keys, F. Kesbeke, P. J. Wijngaarden, A. Monteiro, V. French, and S. B. Carroll. 1996. Development, plasticity and evolution of butterfly eyespot patterns. Nature 384: 236–242.

Brakefield, P. M., and T. G. Shreeve. 1992. Case studies in evolution. Pp. 197–216 in R. L. H. Dennis, ed., *The ecology of butterflies in Britain.* Oxford University Press, Oxford.

Brantjes, N. B. M. 1973. Sphingophilous flowers, function of their scent. Pp. 27–46. in N. Brantjes, ed., *Pollination and dispersal.* Dept. of Botany, Nijmegen, The Netherlands.

———. 1976. Senses involved in the visiting of flowers by *Cucullia umbratica* (Noctuidae: Lepidoptera). Entomologica Experimentalis et Applicata 20: 1–7.

———. 1978. Sensory responses to flowers in night-flying moths. Pp. 13–19 in A. J. Richards, ed., *The pollination of flowers by insects.* Academic Press, London.

Brantjes, N. B. M., and J. J. Bos. 1980. Hawkmoth behaviour and flower adaptation reducing self pollination in two Liliiflorae. New Phytologist 84: 139–143.

Bray, J. R., and J. T. Curtis. 1957. An ordination of the upland forest communities of southern Wisconsin. Ecological Monographs 27: 325–349.

Bremer, K. 1994. Branch support and tree stability. Cladistics 10: 295–304.

Bretherton, R. F. 1983. The incidence of migrant Lepidoptera in the British Isles. Pp. 9–34 in J. Heath and A. M. Emmet, eds., *Moths and butterflies of Great Britain and Ireland,* vol. 10. Harley Books, Colchester.

Briscoe, A. D. 1993. Populational, structural, and regulatory properties of EST-D in *Colias* butterflies. Undergraduate honors thesis, Stanford University.

_____ . 1998a. Molecular diversity of visual pigments in the butterfly *Papilio glaucus.* Naturwissenschaften 85: 33–35.

_____ . 1998b. Evolution of the visual pigments in the butterfly *Papilio glaucus.* Ph.D. dissertation, Harvard University, Cambridge, MA.

_____ . 1999. Intron splice sites of *Papilio glaucus PglRh3* corroborate insect opsin phylogeny. Gene 230: 101–109.

_____ . 2000. Six opsins from the butterfly *Papilio glaucus:* Molecular phylogenetic evidence for paralogous origins of red-sensitive visual pigments in insects. Journal of Molecular Evolution 51: 110–121.

Briscoe, A. D., and L. Chittka. 2001. The evolution of color vision in insects. Annual Review of Entomology 46: 471–510.

Britten, H. B. 1996. Meta-analyses of the association between multilocus heterozygosity and fitness. Evolution 50: 2158–2164.

Britten, H. B., and P. F. Brussard. 1992. Genetic divergence and the Pleistocene history of the alpine butterflies *Boloria improba* (Nymphalidae) and the endangered *Boloria acrocnema* (Nymphalidae) in western North America. Canadian Jounral of Zoology 70: 539–548.

Britten, H. B., P. F. Brussard, D. D. Murphy, and P. R. Ehrlich. 1995. A test for isolation-by-distance in Central Rocky Mountain and Great Basin populations of Edith's Checkerspot butterfly (*Euphydryas editha*). Journal of Heredity 86: 204–210.

Britten, H. B., and L. Riley. 1994. Nectar source diversity as an indicator of habitat suitability for the endangered Uncampaghre fritillary, *Boloria acrocnema* (Nymphalidae). Journal of the Lepidopterists' Society 48: 173–179.

Brock, J. P. 1971. A contribution towards an understanding of the morphology and phylogeny of the Ditrysian Lepidoptera. Journal of Natural History 5: 29–102.

Brookes, M. I., Y. A. Graneau, P. King, O. C. Rose, C. D. Thomas, and J. L. B. Mallet. 1997. Genetic analysis of founder bottlenecks in the rare British butterfly *Plebejus argus.* Conservation Biology 11: 648–661.

Brou, V. A. Jr., and C. D. Brou. 1997. Distribution and phenologies of Louisiana Sphingidae. Journal of the Lepidopterists' Society 51: 156–175.

Brower, A. V. Z. 1994a. Rapid morphological radiation and convergence among races of the butterfly *Heliconius erato* inferred from patterns of mitochondrial DNA evolution. Proceedings of the National Academy of Sciences USA 91: 6491–6495.

_____ . 1994b. Phylogeny of *Heliconius* butterflies inferred from mitochondrial DNA sequences (Lepidoptera: Nymphalidae). Molecular Phylogenetics and Evolution 3: 159–174.

_____ . 1996a. A new mimetic species of *Heliconius* (Lepidoptera: Nymphalidae), from southeastern Colombia, revealed by cladistic analysis of mitochondrial DNA sequences. Zoological Journal of the Linnean Society 116: 317–332.

———— . 1996b. Parallel race formation and the evolution of mimicry in *Heliconius* butterflies: A phylogenetic hypothesis from mitochondrial DNA sequences. Evolution 50: 195–221.

———— . 2000a. Evolution is not a necessary assumption of cladistics. Cladistics 16: 143–154.

———— . 2000b. Phylogenetic relationships among the Nymphalidae (Lepidoptera), inferred from partial sequences of the *wingless* gene. Proceedings of the Royal Society of London B 267: 1201–1211.

Brower, A. V. Z., and R. DeSalle. 1998. Patterns of mitochondrial versus nuclear DNA sequence divergence among nymphalid butterflies: The utility of *wingless* as a source of characters for phylogenetic inference. Insect Molecular Biology 7: 1–10.

Brower, A. V. Z., and M. G. Egan. 1997. Cladistic analysis of *Heliconius* butterflies and relatives (Nymphalidae: Heliconiiti): A revised phylogenetic position for *Eueides* based on sequences from mtDNA and a nuclear gene. Proceedings of the Royal Society of London 264: 969–977.

Brower, L. P. 1959. Speciation in butterflies of the *Papilio glaucus* group. II. Ecological relationships and interspecific sexual behavior. Evolution 13: 212–228.

———— . 1984. Chemical defense in butterflies. Pp. 109–134 in P. Ackery and R. Vane-Wright, eds., *The biology of butterflies*. Academic Press, London.

Brower, L. P., J. Van Zandt Brower, and F. P. Cranston. 1965. Courtship behaviour of the queen butterfly, *Danaus gilippus berenice*. Zoologica, 50: 1–39.

Brown, I. L., and P. R. Ehrlich. 1980. Population biology of the checkerspot butterfly, *Euphydryas chalcedona:* Structure of the Jasper Ridge colony. Oecologia 47: 239–251.

Brown, J. H., and A. Kodric-Brown. 1977. Turnover rates in insular biogeography: Effect of immigration on extinction. Ecology 58: 445–449.

Brown, J. L. 1997. A theory of mate choice based on heterozygosity. Behavioral Ecology 8: 60–65.

Brown, K. S. Jr. 1977. Centros de evolução, refúgios quaternários e conservação de patrimônios genéticos na região neotropical: Padrões de diferenciação em Ithomiinae (Lepidoptera: Nymphalidae). Acta Amazonica 7: 75–137.

———— . 1981. The biology of *Heliconius* and related genera. Annual Review of Entomology 26: 427–456.

———— . 1985. Chemical ecology of dehydropyrrolizidine alkaloids in adult Ithomiinae (Lepidoptera: Nymphalidae). Revista Brasiliera de Biologia (Rio de Janiero) 44: 435–460.

———— . 1987. Chemistry at the Solanaceae/Ithomiinae interface. Annals of the Missouri Botanical Garden 74: 359–397.

Brown, K. S. Jr., and W. W. Benson. 1975. Adaptive polymorphism associated with multiple Müllerian mimicry in *Heliconius numata* (Lepid.: Nymph.). Biotropica 6: 205–228.

Brown, K. S. Jr., T. C. Emmel, P. J. Eliazar, and E. Suomalainen. 1992. Evolutionary patterns in chromosome numbers in Neotropical Lepidoptera. Hereditas 117: 109–125.

Brown, K. S. Jr., and F. Fernandes-Yepez. 1984. Los Heliconiini (Lepidoptera, Nymphalidae) de Venezuela. Boletín de Entomogía Venezolana N.S. 3: 29–76.

Brown, K. S. Jr., and A. V. Freitas. 1994. Juvenile stages of Ithomiinae: Overview and systematics (Lepidoptera: Nymphalidae). Tropical Lepidoptera 5: 9–20.

Brown, K. S. Jr., P. M. Sheppard, and J. R. G. Turner. 1974. Quaternary refugia in South America: Evidence from race formation in *Heliconius* butterflies. Proceedings of the Royal Society of London B 187: 369–378.

Brown, K. S. Jr., J. R. Trigo, R. B. Francini, A. B. B. Morais, and P. C. Motta. 1991. Aposematic insects on toxic host plants: Coevolution, colonization and chemical emancipation. Pp. 375–402 in P. W. Price, T. M. Lewinsohn, G. W. Fernandes, and W. W. Benson, eds., *Plant-animal interactions: Evolutionary ecology in tropical and temperate regions.* Wiley, New York.

Brundin, L. 1966. Transantarctic relationships and their significance as evidenced by midges. Kungliga Svenska Vetenskapsakademiens Handlingar 4: 1–472.

Brunetti, C., J. E. Selegue, A. Monteiro, V. French, P. M. Brakefield, and S. B. Carroll. 2001. The generation and diversification of butterfly eyespot color patterns. Current Biology 11: 1578–1585.

Brunton, C. F. A. 1998. The evolution of ultraviolet patterns in European *Colias* butterflies (Lepidoptera, Pieridae): A phylogeny using mitochondrial DNA. Heredity 80: 611–616.

Brunton, C. F. A., and G. D. D. Hurst. 1998. Mitochondrial DNA phylogeny of brimstone butterflies (genus *Gonepteryx*) from the Canary Islands and Madeira. Biological Journal of the Linnean Society 63: 69–79.

Brunton, C. F. A., and M. E. N. Majerus. 1995. Ultraviolet colours in butterflies: Intra- or inter-specific communication? Proceedings of the Royal Society of London B 260: 199–204.

Brussard, P. F., J. F. Baughman, D. D. Murphy, P. R. Ehrlich, and J. Wright. 1989. Complex population differentiation in checkerspot butterflies (*Euphydryas* spp.). Canadian Journal Zoology 67: 330–335.

Brussard, P. F., and P. R. Ehrlich. 1970. The population structure of *Erebia epipsodea* (Lepidoptera: Satyrinae) Ecology 51: 119–129.

Brussard, P. F., P. R. Ehrlich, D. D. Murphy, B. A. Wilcox, and J. Wright. 1985. Genetic distances and the taxonomy of checkerspot butterflies (Nymphalidae: Nymphalinae). Journal of the Kansas Entomological Society 58: 403–412.

Buchmann, S. L., and G. P. Nabhan. 1996. *The forgotten pollinators.* Island Press, Washington, D.C.

Bulmer, M. G. 1983. Models for the evolution of protandry in insects. Theoretical Population Biology 23: 314–322.

Burkhardt, D. 1996. Ultraviolet perception by bird eyes and some implications. Naturwissenschaften 83: 492–497.

Burney, D. A. 1988. Modern pollen spectra from Madagascar. Palaeogeography, Palaeoclimatology, Palaeoecology 66: 63–76.

Burns, J. M. 1968. Mating frequency in natural populations of skippers and butterflies as determined by spermatophore counts. Proceedings of the National Academy of Sciences USA 61: 852–859.

——. 1975. Isozymes in evolutionary systematics. Pp. 49–62 in C. L. Markert, ed., *Isozymes IV: Genetics and evolution.* Academic Press, New York.

Burns, J. M., and F. M. Johnson. 1967. Esterase polymorphism in natural populations of a sulfur butterfly, *Colias eurytheme.* Science 156: 93–96.

Burrows, C. R. N. 1916. The disappearing *Pararge aegeria.* Entomologists' Record 28: 112–114.

Burton, J. F. 1998a. The apparent effects of climatic changes since 1850 on European Lepidoptera. Societe Royale Belge d'Entomologie 38: 125–144.

———. 1998b. The apparent responses of European Lepidoptera to the climate changes of the past hundred years. Atropos 5: 24–30.

Buschbeck, E. K., and N. J. Strausfeld. 1997. The relevance of neural architecture to visual performance: Phylogenetic conservation and variation in Dipteran visual systems. Journal of Comparative Neurology 383: 282–304.

Bush, G. L. 1975. Sympatric speciation in phytophagous parasitic insects. Pp. 187–206 in P. W. Price, ed., *Evolutionary strategies of parasitic insects and mites*. Plenum, London.

———. 1994. Sympatric speciation in animals: New wine in old bottles. Trends in Ecology and Evolution 9: 285–288.

Butlin, R. 1987. A new approach to sympatric speciation. Trends in Ecology and Evolution 2: 310–311.

———. 1995. Reinforcement: An idea evolving. Trends in Ecology and Evolution 10: 432–434.

Butlin, R., and T. Tregenza. 1998. Levels of genetic polymorphism: Marker loci versus quantitative traits. Philosophical Transactions of the Royal Society of London B 353: 187–198.

Caccone, A., E. N. Moriyama, J. M. Gleason, L. Nigro, and J. R. Powell. 1996. A molecular phylogeny for the *Drosophila melanogaster* subgroup and the problem of polymorphism data. Molecular Biology and Evolution 13: 1224–1232.

Calder, W. A. 1979. On the temperature-dependency of optimal nectar concentrations in birds. Journal of Theoretical Biology 78: 185–196.

———. 1984. *Size, function and life history*. Harvard University Press, Cambridge, MA.

Callen, D. F., A. D. Thompson, Y. Shen, H. Phillips, R. I. Richards, J. C. Mulley, and G. R. Sutherland. 1993. Incidence and origin of null alleles in the (AC)n microsatellite markers. American Journal Human Genetics 52: 922–927.

Camara, M. D. 1997. A recent host range expansion in *Junonia coenia* (Nymphalidae). Oviposition preference, survival, growth and chemical defense. Evolution 51: 873–884.

Campbell, D. L. 1998. Higher level phylogeny and evolution of the Riodinidae (Lepidoptera). Ph.D. dissertation, Harvard University, Cambridge, MA.

Campbell, D. L., A. V. Z. Brower, and N. E. Pierce. 2000. Molecular evolution of the *wingless* gene and its implications for the phylogenetic placement of the butterfly family Riodinidae (Lepidoptera: Papilionoidea). Molecular Biology and Evolution 17: 78–90.

Campbell, D. R., N. M. Waser, and E. J. Meléndez-Ackerman. 1997. Analyzing pollinator-mediated selection in a plant hybrid zone: Hummingbird visitation patterns on three spatial scales. American Naturalist 149: 295–315.

Cantelo, W. W., and M. Jacobsen. 1978. Phenylacetaldehyde attracts moths to bladder flower and to blacklight traps. Environmental Entomology 8: 444–447.

Caro, T. M., and G. O'Doherty. 1999. On the use of surrogate species in conservation biology. Conservation Biology 13: 805–814.

Carriere, Y., and B. D. Roitberg. 1995. Evolution of host-selection behaviour in insect herbivores: Genetic variation and covariation in host acceptance within and between populations of *Choristoneura rosaceana* (Family: Tortricidae), the obliquebanded leafroller. Heredity 74: 357–368.

Carroll, S. B. 1995. Homeotic genes and the evolution of arthropods and chordates. Nature 376: 479–485.

Carroll, S. B., S. D. Weatherbee, and J. A. Langeland. 1995. Homeotic genes and the regulation and evolution of insect wing number. Nature 375: 58–61.

Carroll, S. B., J. Gates, D. N. Keys, S. W. Paddock, G. E. F. Panganiban, J. E. Selegue, and J. A. Williams. 1994. Pattern formation and eyespot determination in butterfly wings. Science 265: 109–114.

Carroll, S. S., and D. L. Pearson. 1998a. The effects of scale and sample size on the accuracy of spatial predictions of tiger beetle (Cicindelidae) species richness. Ecography 21: 401–414.

———. 1998b. Spatial modeling of butterfly species richness using tiger beetles (Cicindelidae) as a bioindicator taxon. Ecological Applications 8: 531–543.

Carson, H. L. 1975. The genetics of speciation at the diploid level. American Naturalist 109: 83–92.

Carter, P. A., and W. B. Watt. 1988. Adaptation at specific loci. V. Metabolically adjacent enzyme loci may have very distinct experiences of selective pressures. Genetics 119: 913–924.

Casey, T. M. 1976. Flight energetics of sphinx moths: Power input during hovering flight. Journal of Experimental Biology 64: 529–543.

———. 1981. Insect flight energetics. Pp. 419–452 in C. F. Herreid and C. R. Fourtner, eds., *Locomotion and energetics in arthropods*. Plenum Press, New York.

Caswell, H., and J. E. Cohen. 1991. Disturbance, interspecific interaction, and diversity in metapopulations. Biological Journal of the Linnean Society 42: 193–218.

Caterino, M. S., S. Cho, and F. A. H. Sperling. 2000. The current state of insect molecular systematics: A thriving Tower of Babel. Annual Review of Entomology 45: 1–54.

Caterino, M. S., R. D. Reed, M. M. Kuo, and F. A. H. Sperling. 2001. A partitioned likelihood analysis of swallowtail butterfly phylogeny (Lepidoptera: Papilionidae). Systematic Biology 50: 106–127.

Caterino, M. S., and F. A. H. Sperling. 1999. *Papilio* phylogeny based on mitochondrial cytochrome oxidase I and II genes. Molecular Phylogenetics and Evolution 11: 122–137.

Caughley, G. 1994. Directions in conservation biology. Journal of Animal Ecology 63: 215–244.

Ceppellini, R., M. Siniscalco, and C. A. B. Smith. 1955. The estimation of gene frequencies in a random-mating population. Annals of Human Genetics 20: 97–115.

Chai, P. 1986. Field observations and feeding experiments on the response of rufous-tailed jacamars (*Galbula ruficauda*) to free-flying butterflies in a tropical rain forest. Biological Journal of the Linnean Society 29: 166–189.

———. 1990. Relationships between visual characteristics of rainforest butterflies and responses of a specialized insectivorous bird. Pp. 31–60 in M. Wicksten, ed., *Adaptive coloration in invertebrates*. Symposium of the American Society of Zoologists. Texas A&M University Sea Grant College Program, TAMU-SG-90-106, College Station, Texas.

Chai, P., and R. B. Srygley. 1990. Predation and the flight, morphology, and temperature of Neotropical rain-forest butterflies. American Naturalist 135: 748–765.

Chalmers-Hunt, J. M., and D. F. Owen. 1952. The history and status of *Pararge aegeria* (Lep. Satyridae) in Kent. The Entomologist 85: 145–154.

Chapin, F. A. III, E.-D. Schulze, and H. A. Mooney. 1990. The ecology and economics of storage in plants. Annual Review of Ecology and Systematics 21: 423–447.

Chapman, R. F. 1971. *The insects: Structure and function.* American Elsevier, New York.

_____ . 1998. *The insects: Structure and function.* 4th ed. Cambridge University Press, Cambridge.

Charlesworth, B., J. A. Coyne, and N. H. Barton. 1987. The relative rates of evolution of sex chromosomes and autosomes. American Naturalist 130: 113–146.

Charlesworth, B., M. Nordborg, and D. Charlesworth. 1998. The effects of local selection, balanced polymorphism, and background selection on equilibrium patterns of genetic diversity in subdivided populations. Genetics Research 70: 155–174.

Chase, M. W., and V. A. Albert. 1998. A perspective on the contribution of plastid rbcL DNA sequences to angiosperm phylogenetics. Pp. 488–507 in D. E. Soltis, P. S. Soltis, and J. J. Doyle, eds., *Molecular systematics of plants II: DNA sequencing.* Kluwer Academic Publishers, Dordrecht, Netherlands.

Chase, V. C., and P. H. Raven. 1975. Evolutionary and ecological relationships between *Aquilegia formosa* and *A. pubescens* (Ranunculaceae), two perennial plants. Evolution 29: 474–486.

Cherrill, A. J., and V. K. Brown. 1990. The life cycle and distribution of the wart-biter *Decticus verrucivorus* (L.) (Orthoptera: Tettigoniidae) in a chalk grassland in southern England [UK]. Biological Conservation 53: 125–144.

Chesson, P. 1998. Making sense of spatial models in ecology. Pp. 151–166 in J. Bascompte and R. V. Sol, eds., *Modeling spatiotemporal dynamics in ecology.* Springer, Berlin.

Chew, F. S. 1977. Coevolution of pierid butterflies and their cruciferous food plants. II. The distribution of eggs on potential food plants. Evolution 31: 568–579.

Chew, F. S., and S. P. Courtney. 1991. Plant apparency and evolutionary escape from insect herbivory. American Naturalist 138: 729–750.

Chew, F. S., and R. K. Robbins. 1984. Egg-laying in butterflies. Pp. 65–79 in R. I. Vane-Wright and P. R. Ackery, eds., *The biology of butterflies.* Academic Press, London.

Chittka, L. 1996. Does bee color vision predate the evolution of flower color? Naturwissenschaften 83: 136–138.

Chittka, L., and A. Briscoe. 2001. Why sensory ecology needs to become more evolutionary: Insect color vision as a case in point. Pp. 19–37 in F. G. Barth and A. Schmid, eds., *Ecology of sensing.* Springer, Berlin.

Cho, S., A. Mitchell, J. C. Regier, C. Mitter, R. W. Poole, T. P. Friedlander, and S. Zhao. 1995. A highly conserved nuclear gene for low-level phylogenetics: Elongation factor-1α recovers morphology-based tree for heliothine moths. Molecular Biology and Evolution 12: 650–656.

Choe, J. C., and B. J. Crespi, eds. 1997. *The evolution of mating systems in insects and arachnids.* Cambridge University Press, Cambridge.

Chou, W.-H., K. Hall, D. Wilson, C. Wideman, S. Townson, L. Chadwell, and S. Britt. 1996. Identification of a novel *Drosophila* opsin reveals specific patterning of the R7 and R8 photoreceptor cells. Neuron 11: 1101–1115.

Civetta, A., and R. S. Singh. 1998. Sex-related genes, directional sexual selection, and speciation. Molecular Biology and Evolution 15: 901–909.

Claassens, A. J. M., and C. G. C. Dickson. 1977. A study of the myrmecophilous behavior of the immature stages of *Aloeides thyra* (L.) (Lep.: Lycaenidae) with special reference to the function of the retractile tubercles and with additional notes on the general biology of the species. Entomologists' Record 89: 225–231.

Claridge, M. F., H. A. Dawah, and M. R. Wilson, eds. 1997. *Species, the units of biodiversity.* Chapman and Hall, London.

Clark, G. C., and C. G. C. Dickson. 1956. The honey gland and tubercles of larvae of the Lycaenidae. Lepidopterists News 10: 37–43.

Clarke, C. A., and F. M. M. Clarke. 1983. Abnormalities of wing pattern in the eastern tiger swallowtail butterfly, *Papilio glaucus*. Systematic Entomology 8: 25–28.

Clarke, C. A., F. M. M. Clarke, and I. J. Gordon. 1996. Mimicry and other controversial topics in East African Lepidoptera. Journal of East African Natural History 84: 3–18.

Clarke, C. A., and P. M. Sheppard. 1955a. The breeding in captivity of the hybrid *Papilio rutulus* female × *P. glaucus* male. Lepidopterists News 9: 46–48.

———. 1955b. A preliminary report on the genetics of the *machaon* group of swallowtail butterflies. Evolution 10: 182–201.

———. 1957. The breeding of the *Papilio glaucus* female and *P. eurymedon* male. Lepidopterists News 11: 201–205.

———. 1959. The genetics of some mimetic forms of *Papilio dardenus,* Brown, and *Papilio glaucus*. Linnean Journal Genetics 56: 237–259.

———. 1960. Supergenes and mimicry. Heredity 14: 175–185.

———. 1962. The genetics of the mimetic butterfly, *Papilio glaucus*. Ecology 43: 159–161.

———. 1963. Interactions between major genes and polygenes in the determination of the mimetic pattern of *Papilio dardanus*. Evolution 17: 404–413.

Clarke, C. A., P. M. Sheppard, and U. Mittwoch. 1976. Heterochromatin polymorphism and colour pattern in the tiger swallowtail butterfly *Papilio glaucus* L. Nature 263: 585–587.

Clary, D. O., and D. R. Wolstenholme. 1985. The mitochondrial DNA molecule of *Drosophila yakuba:* Nucleotide sequence, gene organization, and genetic code. Journal of Molecular Evolution 22: 252–271.

Clegg, M. T. 2000. Limits to knowledge in evolutionary genetics. Evolutionary Biology 32: 35–51.

Clements, F., and F. Long. 1923. *Experimental pollination: An outline of the ecology of flowers and insects*. Carnegie Institute of Washington, Washington, D.C.

Clench, H. K. 1955. Revised classification of the butterfly family Lycaenidae and its allies. Annals of the Carnegie Museum 33: 261–274.

———. 1966. Behavioral thermoregulation in butterflies. Ecology 47: 1021–1034.

———. 1967. Temporal association and population regulation in eastern Hesperiine butterflies. Ecology 48: 1000–1006.

Coddington, J. A. 1994. The roles of homology and convergence in studies of adaptation. Pp. 53–78 in P. Eggleton and R. I. Vane-Wright, eds., *Phylogenetics and ecology*. Academic Press, London.

Collins, M. M. 1984. Genetics and ecology of a hybrid zone in *Hyalophora* (Lepidoptera: Saturniidae). University of California Publications in Entomology, vol. 104. University of California Press, Berkeley.

Collins, N. M., and M. G. Morris. 1985. *Threatened swallowtail butterflies of the world: The IUCN Red Data Book*. IUCN, Gland, Switzerland.

Colwell, R. K., and J. A. Coddington. 1994. Estimating terrestrial biodiversity through extrapolation. Philosophical Transactions of the Royal Society of London B 345: 101–118.

Colwell, R. K., and G. C. Hurtt. 1994. Nonbiological gradients in species richness and a spurious Rapoport effect. American Naturalist 144: 570–595.

Colwell, R. K., and D. Lees. 2000. The mid-domain effect: Geometric constraints on the geography of species richness. Trends in Ecology and Evolution 15: 72–76.

Common, I. F. B. 1975. Evolution and classification of the Lepidoptera. Pp. 765–866 in *The insects of Australia*. CSIRO, Melbourne University Press, Melbourne.

Condamin, M. 1973. Monographie du genre *Bicyclus* (Lepidoptera, Satyridae). IFAN, Dakar.

Conner, W. E., and H. Itagaki. 1984. Pupal attendance in the crabhole mosquito *Deinocerites cancer:* The effects of pupal sex and age. Physiological Entomology 9: 263–267.

Connor, E. F., and E. D. McCoy. 1979. The statistics and biology of the species-area relationship. American Naturalist 113: 791–833.

Connor, W. E., B. Roach, E. Benedict, J. Meinwald, and T. Eisner. 1990. Courtship pheromone production and body size as correlates of larval diet in males of the arctiid moth *Utetheisa ornatrix*. Journal of Chemical Ecology 16: 543–552.

Cook, D. F. 1995. Influence of previous mating experience on future mating success in male *Lucilia cuprina* (Diptera: Calliphoridae). Journal of Insect Behavior 8: 207–217.

Cook, P. A., and M. J. G. Gage. 1995. Effects of different risks of sperm competition upon eupyrene and apyrene sperm numbers in the moth *Plodia interpunctella*. Behavioral Ecology and Sociobiology 36: 261–268.

Cook, P. A., I. F. Harvey, and G. A. Parker. 1997. Predicting variation in sperm precedence. Philosophical Transactions of the Royal Society of London B 352: 771–780.

Cook, P. A., and N. Wedell. 1996. Ejaculate dynamics in butterflies: A strategy for maximizing fertilization success? Proceedings of the Royal Society of London B 263: 1047–1051.

Coope, G. R. 1978. Constancy of insect species versus inconstancy of Quaternary environments. Pp. 176–187 in L. A. Mound and N. Waloff, eds., *Diversity of insect faunas*. Blackwell, Oxford.

———. 1995. Insect faunas in ice age environments: Why so little extinction? Pp. 55–74 in J. H. Lawton and R. M. May, eds., *Extinction rates*. Oxford University Press, Oxford.

Corbet, A. S., H. M. Pendlebury, and J. N. Eliot. 1992. *The butterflies of the Malay peninsula*. Malayan Nature Society, Kuala Lumpur.

Costa, J. T., and K. G. Ross. 1994. Hierarchical genetic structure and gene flow in macrogeographic populations of the eastern tent caterpillar (*Malacosoma americanum*). Evolution 48: 1158–1167.

Cottrell, C. B. 1984. Aphytophagy in butterflies: Its relationship to myrmecophily. Zoological Journal of the Linnean Society 79: 1–57.

Courtney, S. P. 1982. Coevolution of pierid butterflies and their cruciferous hostplants. IV. Crucifer apparency and *Anthocharis cardamines* oviposition. Oecologia 52: 258–265.

Courtney, S. P., and K. Anderson. 1986. Behaviour around encounter sites. Behavioral Ecology and Sociobiology 19: 241–248.

Courtney, S. P., G. K. Chen, and A. Gardner. 1989. A general model for individual host selection. Oikos 55: 55–65.

Courtney, S. P., and A. E. Duggan. 1983. The population biology of the orange tip butterfly, *Anthocharis cardamines,* in Britain. Ecological Entomology 8: 271–281.

Courtney, S. P., and G. A. Parker. 1985. Mating behavior of the tiger blue butterfly (*Tarucus theophrastus*): Competitive mate searching when not all females are captured. Behavioral Ecology and Sociobiology 17: 213–221.

Cowman, A. F., C. S. Zuker, and G. M. Rubin. 1986. An opsin gene expressed in only one photoreceptor cell type of the *Drosophila* eye. Cell 44: 705–710.

Coyne, J. A. 1976. Lack of genetic similarity between two sibling species of *Drosophila* as revealed by varied techniques. Genetics 84: 593–607.

——— . 1985. The genetic basis of Haldane's rule. Nature 314: 736–738.

——— . 1992. Genetics and speciation. Nature 355: 511–515.

——— . 1994. Rules for Haldane's rule. Nature 369: 189–190.

Coyne, J. A., N. H. Barton, and M. Turelli. 1997. Perspective: A critique of Sewall Wright's shifting balance theory of evolution. Evolution 51: 643–671.

Coyne, J. A., B. Charlesworth, and H. A. Orr. 1991. Haldane's rule revisited. Evolution 45: 1710–1714.

Coyne, J. A., and H. A. Orr. 1989. Two rules of speciation. Pp. 180–207 in D. Otte and J. A. Endler, eds., *Speciation and its consequences*. Sinauer Associates, Sunderland, MA.

——— . 1993. Further evidence against meiotic-drive models of hybrid sterility. Evolution 47: 685–687.

Cracraft, J. 1983. Species concepts and speciation analysis. Current Ornithology 1: 159–187.

——— . 1989. Speciation and its ontology: The empirical consequences of alternative species concepts for understanding patterns and processes of differentiation. Pp. 28–59 in D. Otte and J. A. Endler, eds., *Speciation and its consequenes*. Sinauer Associates, Sunderland, MA.

——— . 1991. Patterns of diversification within continental biotas: Hierarchical congruence among the areas of endemism of Australian vertebrates. Australian Systematic Botany 4: 211–227.

——— . 1997. Species concepts in systematics and conservation biology—an ornithological viewpoint. Pp. 325–339 in M. F. Claridge, H. A. Dawah, and M. R. Wilson, eds., *Species, the units of biodiversity*. Chapman and Hall, London.

Craig, C. C. 1953. On the utilization of marked specimens in estimating populations of flying insects. Biometrika 40: 170–176.

Crandall, K., and T. Cronin. 1997. The molecular evolution of visual pigments of freshwater crayfishes (Decapoda: Cambaridae). Journal of Molecular Evolution 45: 524–534.

Crawford, D. L., and D. A. Powers. 1989. Molecular basis of evolutionary adaptation at the lactate dehydrogenase-B locus in the fish *Fundulus heteroclitus*. Proceedings of the National Academy of Sciences USA 86: 9365–9369.

Crespi, B. J. 1988. Adaptation, compromise, and constraint: The development, morphometrics, and behavioral basis of a fighter-flier polymorphism in male *Hoplothrips karnyi* (Insecta: Thysanoptera). Behavioral Ecology and Sociobiology 23: 93–104.

Cressie, N. 1991. *Statistics for spatial data*. John Wiley, New York.

Crick, H. Q. P., C. Dudley, D. E. Glue, and D. L. Thomson. 1997. UK birds are laying eggs earlier. Nature 388: 526.

Crisp, M. D., H. P. Linder, and P. H. Weston. 1995. Cladistic biogeography of plants in Australia and New Guinea: Congruent pattern reveals two endemic tropical tracks. Systematic Biology 44: 457–473.

Croizat, A. 1958. *Panbiogeography*. Published by the author, Caracas.

Crone, E. E., D. Doak, and J. Pokki. 2001. Ecological influences on the dynamics of a field vole metapopulation. Ecology 82: 831–843.

Cross, R. M., and D. F. Owen. 1970. Seasonal changes in energy content in tropical hawkmoths (Sphingidae). Revue de Zoologie et de Botanique Africaines 81: 109–116.

Croteau, R., and F. Karp. 1991. Origin of natural odorants. Pp. 101–126 in P. M. Müller and D. Lamparsky, eds., *Perfumes: Art, science, and technology.* New York: Elsevier Applied Sciences.

Crowley, P. H., and D. M. Johnson. 1982. Habitat and seasonality as niche axes in an odonate community. Ecology 63: 1064–1077.

Crozier, R. H. 1997. Preserving the information content of species: Genetic diversity, phylogeny, and conservation worth. Annual Review of Ecology and Systematics 28: 343–368.

Cruden, R. W. 1970. Hawkmoth pollination of *Mirabilis* (Nyctaginaceae). Bulletin of the Torrey Botanical Club 97: 89–91.

Cruden, R. W., and S. M. Hermann-Parker. 1979. Butterfly pollination of *Caesalpinia pulcherrima,* with observations on a psychophilous syndrome. Journal of Ecology 67: 155–168.

Cruden, R. W., S. M. Hermann, and S. Peterson. 1983. Patterns of nectar production and plant-pollinator coevolution. Pp. 80–125 in B. Bentley and T. Elias, eds., *The biology of nectaries.* Columbia University Press, New York.

Cruden, R. W., S. Kinsman, R. E. Stockhouse II, and Y. B. Linhart. 1976. Pollination, fecundity and the distribution of moth-flowered plants. Biotropica 8: 204–210.

Csuti, B., S. Polasky, P. H. Williams, R. L. Pressey, J. D. Camm, M. Kershaw, A. R. Kiester, B. Downs, R. Hamilton, M. Huso, and K. Sahr. 1997. A comparison of reserve selection algorithms using data on terrestrial vertebrates in Oregon. Biological Conservation 80: 83–97.

Cuénot, L. 1936. *L'espèce.* Doin, Paris.

Cullenward, M. J., P. R. Ehrlich, R. R. White, and C. E. Holdren. 1979. The ecology and population genetics of an alpine checkerspot butterfly, *Euphydryas anicia.* Oecologia 38: 1–12.

Cunningham, C. W. 1997. Is congruence between data partitions a reliable predictor of phylogenetic accuracy? Empirically testing an iterative procedure for choosing among phylogenetic methods. Systematic Biology 46: 464–478.

Currie, D. J. 1991. Energy and large-scale patterns of animal and plant species richness. American Naturalist 137: 27–49.

Curtis, J. T. 1959. *The vegetation of Wisconsin.* University of Wisconsin Press, Madison.

Cutler, D. E., R. R. Bennett, R. D. Stevenson, and R. H. White. 1995. Feeding behavior in the nocturnal moth *Manduca sexta* is mediated mainly by blue receptors, but where are they located in the retina? Journal of Experimental Biology 198: 1909–1917.

D'Abrera, B. 1971. *Butterflies of the Australian region.* Lansdowne, Melbourne.

Dafni, A. 1992. *Pollination ecology: A practical approach.* IRL Press, Oxford.

Dafni, A., and P. G. Kevan. 1996. Floral symmetry and nectar guides: Ontogenetic constraints from floral development, colour pattern rules and functional significance. Botanical Journal of the Linnean Society 120: 371–377.

Daily, G. C., ed. 1997. *Nature's services: Societal dependence on natural ecosystems.* Island Press, Washington, DC.

Daily, G. C., P. R. Ehrlich, and G. A. Sánchez-Azofeifa. 2001. Countryside biogeography: Utilization of human-dominated habitats by the avifauna of southern Costa Rica. Ecological Applications 11: 1–13.

D'Almeida, R. F. 1978. *Catálogo dos Ithomiidae Americanos (Lepidoptera)*. Universidade Federal do Paraná/CNPq, Curitiba.

Daly, K. C., C. Sathees, M. L. Durtschi, and B. H. Smith. 2001. The generalization of an olfactory-based conditioned response reveals unique but overlapping odour representation in the moth *Manduca sexta*. Journal of Experimental Biology 204: 3085–3095.

Daly, K. C., and B. H. Smith. 2000. Associative olfactory learning in the moth *Manduca sexta*. Journal of Experimental Biology 203: 2225–2038.

Dankert, B. A., D. A. Herms, D. Parry, J. M. Scriber, and L. A. Haas. 1997. Mediation of competition between folivores through defoliated-induced changes in host quality. Pp. 71–88 in A. Raman, ed., *Ecology and evolution of plant-feeding insects in natural and man-made environments*. Backhuys, Leiden, Netherlands.

Darwin, C. 1859. *The origin of species*. 6th rev. ed. 1872. New American Library, New York.

———. 1865. *On various contrivances by which British and foreign orchids are fertilized by insects*. John Murray, London.

———. 1871. *The descent of man and selection in relation to sex*. John Murray, London.

David, W. A. L., and B. O. C. Gardiner. 1962. Oviposition and the hatching of eggs of *Pieris brassicae* in a laboratory culture. Bulletin of Entomological Research 53: 91–109.

Davies, N. B. 1978. Territorial defence in the speckled wood butterfly (*Pararge aegeria*): The resident always wins. Animal Behaviour 26: 138–147.

———. 1979. Game theory and territorial behaviour in speckled wood butterflies. Animal Behaviour 27: 961–962.

Davies, N. B., and A. Pomiankowski. 1995. Haldane's rule: Old theories are the best. Trends in Ecology and Evolution 10: 350–351.

Davis, A. J., L. S. Jenkinson, J. H. Lawton, B. Shorrocks, and S. Wood. 1998a. Making mistakes when predicting shifts in species range in response to global warming. Nature 391: 783–786.

Davis, A. J., J. H. Lawton, B. Shorrocks, and L. S. Jenkinson. 1998b. Individualistic species responses invalidate simple physiological models of community dynamics under global environmental change. Journal of Animal Ecology 67: 600–612.

Davis, M. B., and C. Zabinski. 1992. Changes in geographical range resulting from greenhouse warming: Effects on biodiversity in forests. Chap. 22 in R. L. Peters and T. E. Lovejoy, eds., *Global warming and biological diversity*. Yale University Press, New Haven, CT.

Day, T. H., S. P. Foster, and G. Engelhard. 1990. Mating behavior in seaweed flies (*Coelopa frigida*). Journal of Insect Behaviour 3: 105–120.

Debinski, D. M. 1994. Genetic diversity assessment in a metapopulation of the butterfly *Euphydryas gilletti*. Biological Conservation 70: 25–31.

Deering, M. D. 1998. Preferential mate selection by males as a reproductive isolating mechanism between swallowtail species *Papilio glaucus* and *P. canadensis* (Lepidoptera: Papilionidae) M.S. thesis, Michigan State University, East Lansing.

Deering, M. D., and J. M. Scriber. 1998. Heterospecific mating behavior of *Papilio palamedes* in Florida (Lepidoptera: Papilionidae). Holarctic Lepidoptera 2: 49–51.

———. 2002. Field bioassays show heterospecific mating preference asymmetry between hybridizing North American *Papilio* butterfly species (Lepidoptera: Papilionidae). Journal of Ethology 20: 25–33.

Deinert, E. I. 1997. Sexual selection in a pupal mating butterfly, *Heliconius hewitsoni*. Ph.D. dissertation, University of Texas, Austin.

Deinert, E. I., J. T. Longino, and L. E. Gilbert. 1994. Mate competition in butterflies. Nature 370: 23–24.

de Jong, R., R. I. Vane-Wright, and P. R. Ackery. 1996a. The higher classification of butterflies (Lepidoptera): Problems and prospects. Entomologica Scandinavica 27: 65–101.

———. 1996b. *Butterfly net international newsletter,* no. 1 (www.ent.orst.edu/bnet/).

de Lattin, G. 1967. *Grundrisse der zoogeographie.* Iena, Stuttgart.

Delpino, F. 1874. Ulteriori osservazioni e considerazioni sulla dicogamia nel regno vegetale. 2 (IV). Delle piante zoidifile. Atti Societa Italiana di Scienze Naturale. Museo Civile di Storia Naturale 16: 151–349.

Dempster, J. P. 1991. Fragmentation, isolation and mobility of insect populations. Pp. 143–154 in N. M. Collins and J. A. Thomas, eds., *Conservation of insects and their habitats.* Academic Press, London.

———. 1992. Evidence of an oviposition-deterring pheromone in the orange-tip butterfly, *Anthocharis cardamines* (L). Ecological Entomology 17: 83–85.

Dempster, J. P., and M. L. Hall. 1980. An attempt at re-establishing the swallowtail butterfly at Wicken Fen. Ecological Entomology 5: 327–334.

Dempster, J. P., M. L. King, and K. H. Lakhani. 1976. The status of the swallowtail butterfly in Britain. Ecological Entomology 1: 71–84.

Dennis, B., P. L. Munholland, and J. M. Scott. 1991. Estimation of growth and extinction parameters for endangered species. Ecological Monographs 61: 115–143.

Dennis, R. L. H. 1992. *The ecology of butterflies in Britain.* Oxford University Press, Oxford.

———. 1993. *Butterflies and climate change.* Manchester University Press, Manchester.

Dennis, R. L. H., and T. G. Shreeve. 1988. Hostplant-habitat structure and the evolution of butterfly mate-locating behaviour. Zoological Journal of the Linnean Society 94: 301–318.

———. 1989. Butterfly wing morphology variation in the British Isles: The influence of climate, behavioural posture and the hostplant-habitat. Biological Journal of the Linnean Society 38: 323–348.

———. 1991. Climatic change and the British butterfly fauna: Opportunities and constraints. Biological Conservation 55: 1–16.

———. 1997. Diversity of butterflies on British islands: Ecological influences underlying the roles of area, isolation and the size of the faunal source. Biological Journal of the Linnean Society 60: 257–275.

Dennis, R. L. H., and W. R. Williams. 1987. Mate locating behaviour of the large skipper butterfly *Ochlodes venata:* Flexible strategies and spatial components. Journal of the Lepidopterists' Society 41: 45–64.

Depew, D. J., and B. H. Weber. 1995. *Darwinism evolving.* MIT Press, Cambridge, MA.

de Queiroz, A., M. J. Donoghue, and J. Kim. 1995. Separate versus combined analysis of phylogenetic evidence. Annual Review of Ecology and Systematics 26: 657–681.

de Queiroz, K. 1998. The general lineage concept of species, species criteria, and the process of speciation. Pp. 57–75 in D. J. Howard and S. H. Berlocher, eds., *Endless forms: Species and speciation.* Oxford University Press, New York and Oxford.

Descimon, H., and H. Geiger. 1988. Electrophoretic detection of interspecific hybrids in *Parnassius* (Lepidoptera: Papilionidae). Génétique, Sélection, Evolution 20: 435–440.

Descimon, H., and M. Napolitano. 1993. Enzyme polymorphism, wing pattern variability, and geographical isolation in an endangered butterfly species. Biological Conservation 66: 117–123.

Dethier, V. G. 1954. Evolution of feeding preferences in phytophagous insects. Evolution 8: 33–54.

Devine, M. C., G. C. Daily, P. R. Ehrlich, and C. L. Boggs. 2002. Countryside biogeography of tropical butterflies. Conservation Biology. In press.

DeVries, P. J. 1988a. Stratification of fruit-feeding nymphalid butterflies in a Costa Rican rainforest. Journal of Research on Lepidoptera 26: 98–108.

———. 1988b. The larval ant-organs of *Thisbe irenea* (Lepidoptera: Riodinidae) and their effects upon attending ants. Zoological Journal of the Linnean Society 94: 379–393.

———. 1991. Evolutionary and ecological patterns in myrmecophilous riodinid butterflies. Pp. 143–156 in C. R. Huxley and D. F. Cutler, eds., *Ant-Plant interactions*. Oxford University Press, Oxford.

———. 1997. *The butterflies of Costa Rica and their natural history*. Vol. 2, *Riodinidae*. Princeton University Press, Princeton, NJ.

DeVries, P. J., I. J. Kitching, and R. I. Vane-Wright. 1985. The systematic position of *Antirrhea* and *Caerois* with comments on the classification of the Nymphalidae (Lepidoptera). Systematic Entomology 10: 11–32.

DeVries, P. J., and F. G. Stiles. 1990. Attraction of pyrrholizidine alkaloid seeking Lepidoptera to *Epidendrum* orchids. Biotropica 22: 290–297.

Diamond, J. A. 1984. "Normal" extinction of isolated populations. Pp. 191–246 in M. H. Nitecki, ed., *Extinctions*. University of Chicago Press, Chicago.

di Castri, F., J. R. Vernhes, and T. Younes. 1992. A proposal for an international network on inventorying and monitoring of biodiversity. Biology International 27: 1–27.

Dickens, J., and J. Eaton. 1973. External ocelli in Lepidoptera previously considered to be anocellate. Nature 242: 205–206.

Dickinson, J. L. 1992. Scramble competition in the milkweed leaf beetle: Combat, mobility, and the importance of being there. Behavioral Ecology 3: 32–41.

Direction des Eaux et Forets, Projet COEFOR and Conservation International. 1993. *Repertoire et carte de distribution: Domaine forestier national de Madagascar.* Conservation International, Antananarivo, Madagascar.

Dobkin, D. S., I. Olivieri, and P. R. Ehrlich. 1987. Rainfall and the interaction of microclimate with larval resources in the population dynamics of checkerspot butterflies (*Euphydryas editha*) inhabiting serpentine grassland. Oecologia 71: 161–166.

Dobson, A. P., J. P. Rodriguez, W. M. Roberts, and D. S. Wilcove. 1997. Geographic distribution of endangered species in the United States. Science 275: 550–553.

Dobson, H. E. M. 1994. Floral volatiles in insect biology. Pp. 47–81 in E. Bernays, ed., *Insect-plant interactions*, vol. 5. CRC Press, Boca Raton, FL.

Dobzhansky, T. 1937. *Genetics and the origin of species*. Columbia University Press, New York.

———. 1970. *Genetics of the evolutionary process*. Columbia University Press, New York.

———. 1973. Nothing in biology makes sense except in the light of evolution. American Biology Teacher 35: 125–129.

Donoghue, M. J. 1985. A critique of the biological species concept and recommendations for a phylogenetic alternative. Bryologist 88: 172–181.

Doolittle, W. F. 1999. Phylogenetic classification and the universal tree. Science 284: 2124–2128.

Dooner, H. K., T. P. Robbins, and R. A. Jorgensen. 1991. Genetic and developmental control of anthocyanin biosynthesis. Annual Reviews of Genetics 25: 173–199.

Douwes, P. 1975. Territorial behaviour in *Heodes virgaureae* L. (Lep., Lycaenidae) with particular reference to visual stimuli. Norwegian Journal of Entomology 22: 143–154.

———. 1976. Mating behaviour in *Heodes virgaureae* with particular reference to the stimuli from the females (Lepidoptera: Lycaenidae). Entomologica Germanica 2: 232–241.

Dowdeswell, W. H., R. A. Fisher, and E. B. Ford. 1940. The quantitative study of populations in the Lepidoptera I. *Polyommatus icarus* Rott. Annals of Eugenics 10: 9–136.

———. 1949. The quantitative study of populations in the Lepidoptera. II. *Maniola jurtina* L. Heredity 3: 67–84.

Downes, J. A. 1948. The history of the speckled wood butterfly (*Pararge aegeria*) in Scotland, with a discussion of the recent changes of range of other British butterflies. Journal of Animal Ecology 17: 131–138.

Downey, J. C., and A. C. Allyn. 1984. Chaetotaxy of the first instar larva of *Hemiargus ceraunus antibubastus* (Hbn.) (Lycaenidae). Bulletin of the Allyn Museum 90: 1–4.

Dreisig, H. 1995. Thermoregulation and flight activity in territorial male graylings, *Hipparchia semele* (Satyridae), and large skippers, *Ochlodes venata* (Hesperiidae). Oecologia 101: 169–176.

Drummond, B. A. 1976. Comparative ecology and mimetic relationships of ithomiine butterflies in eastern Ecuador. Ph.D. dissertation, University of Florida.

———. 1984. Multiple mating and sperm competition in the Lepidoptera. Pp. 291–370 in R. L. Smith, ed., *Sperm competition and the evolution of animal mating systems*. Academic Press, New York.

———. 1986. Coevolution of ithomiinae butterflies and solanaceous plants. Pp. 307–327 in W. G. D'Arcy, ed., *Solanaceae, biology and systematics*. Columbia University Press, New York.

Drummond, B. A., and K. S. Brown Jr. 1987. Ithomiinae (Lepidoptera: Nymphalidae): Summary of known larval food plants. Annals of the Missouri Botanical Garden 74: 341–358.

Dudley, R. 1990. Biomechanics of flight in Neotropical butterflies: Morphometrics and kinematics. Journal of Experimental Biology 150: 37–53.

Duffey, E. 1977. The reestablishment of the large copper butterfly *Lycaena dispar batavus* Obth. on Woodwalton Fen National Reserve, Cambridgeshire, England, 1969–73. Biological Conservation 12: 143–158.

Dufrene, M., and P. Legendre. 1997. Species assemblages and indicator species: The need for a flexible asymmetrical approach. Ecological Monographs 67: 345–366.

Dukas, R., and L. Real. 1991. Learning foraging tasks by bees: A comparison between social and solitary species. Animal Behaviour 42: 269–276.

Dunlap-Pianka, H. L., C. L. Boggs, and L. E. Gilbert. 1977. Ovarian dynamics in heliconiine butterflies: Programmed senescence versus eternal youth. Science 197: 487–490.

Du Puy, D. J., and J. Moat. 1996. A refined classification of the primary vegetation of Madagascar based on the underlying geology: Using GIS to map its distribution and to assess its conservation status. Pp. 205–218 in W. R. Lourenco, ed., *Biogeographie de Madagascar.* ORSTOM, Paris.

Dusenbery, D. B. 1992. *Sensory ecology: How organisms acquire and respond to information.* W. H. Freeman, New York.

Duvernell, D. D., and N. Aspinwall. 1995. Introgression of *Luxilus cornutus* mtDNA into allopatric populations of *Luxilus chrysocephalus* (Teleostei: Cyprinidae) in Missouri and Arkansas. Molecular Ecology 4: 173–181.

Dyer, L. A. 1995. Tasty generalists and nasty specialists? Antipredator mechanisms in tropical lepidopteran larvae. Ecology 76: 1483–1496.

Dykhuizen, D. E., and D. L. Hartl. 1980. Selective neutrality of 6PGD allozymes in *E. coli* and the effects of genetic background. Genetics 96: 801–817.

———. 1983. Functional effects of PGI allozymes in *E. coli.* Genetics 105: 1–18.

Eanes, W. F. 1999. Analysis of selection on enzyme polymorphisms. Annual Review of Ecology and Systematics 30: 301–326.

Easterby, J. S. 1973. Coupled enzyme assays: A general expression for the transient. Biochimica Biophysica Acta 293: 552–558.

———. 1990. Integration of temporal analysis and control analysis of metabolic systems. Biochemical Journal 269: 255–259.

Easterling, D. R., J. L. Evans, P. Y. Groisman, T. R. Karl, K. E. Kunkel, and P. Ambenje. 2000. Observed variability and trends in extreme climate events: A brief review. Bulletin of the American Meteorological Society 81: 417–425.

Easterling, D. R., B. Horton, P. D. Jones, T. C. Peterson, T. R. Karl, D. E. Parker, M. J. Salinger, V. Razuvayev, N. Plummer, P. Jamason, and C. K. Folland. 1997. Maximum and minimum temperature trends for the globe. Science 277: 364–367.

Eberhard, W. G. 1970. The natural history of the fungus gnats *Leptomorphus bifasciatus* (Say) and *L. subcaeruleus* (Coquillett) (Diptera: Mychetophilidae). Psyche 77: 361–383.

———. 1996. *Female control: Sexual selection by cryptic female choice.* Princeton University Press, Princeton, NJ.

Eberhard, W. G., and C. Cordero. 1995. Sexual selection by cryptic female choice on male seminal products—a new bridge between sexual selection and reproductive physiology. Trends in Ecology and Evolution 10: 493–496.

Ebner, J. A. 1970. *Butterflies of Wisconsin.* Milwaukee Public Museum Press, Milwaukee, WI.

Edwards, W. H. 1881. On certain habits of *Heliconia charitonia* Linn., a species of butterfly found in Florida. Papilio 1: 209–215.

———. 1884. *The butterflies of North America.* Vol. 2. Houghton Mifflin, Boston.

Eggleton, P., and R. I. Vane-Wright. 1994. Some principles of phylogenetics and their implications for comparative biology. Pp. 345–366 in P. Eggleton and R. I. Vane-Wright, eds., *Phylogenetics and ecology.* Academic Press, London.

Eguchi, E., K. Watanabe, T. Hariyama, and K. Yamamoto. 1982. A comparison of electrophysiologically determined spectral responses in 35 species of Lepidoptera. Journal of Insect Physiology 28: 675–682.

Ehrlich, A. H., and P. R. Ehrlich. 1978. Reproductive strategies in the butterflies. I. Mating frequency, plugging, and egg number. Journal of the Kansas Entomological Society 51: 666–697.

Ehrlich, P. R. 1958. The comparative morphology, phylogeny and higher classification of the butterflies (Lepidoptera: Papilionoidea). University of Kansas Science Bulletin 8: 305–370.

_____ . 1961a. Has the biological species concept outlived its usefulness? Systematic Zoology 10: 167–176.

_____ . 1961b. Intrinsic barriers to dispersal in a checkerspot butterfly. Science 134: 108–109.

_____ . 1964. Some axioms of taxonomy. Systematic Zoology 13: 109–123.

_____ . 1965. The population biology of the butterfly *Euphydryas editha*. II. The structure of the Jasper Ridge colony. Evolution 19: 327–336.

_____ . 1984. The structure and dynamics of butterfly populations. Pp. 25–40 in R. I. Vane-Wright and P. R. Ackery, eds., *The biology of butterflies*. Academic Press, London.

_____ . 1997. *A world of wounds: Ecologists and the human dilemma*. Ecology Institute, Oldendorf/Luhe.

Ehrlich, P. R, D. E. Breedlove, P. F. Brussard, and M. A. Sharp. 1972. Weather and the "regulation" of subalpine butterfly populations. Ecology 53: 243–247.

Ehrlich, P. R., and A. H. Ehrlich. 1967. The phenetic relationships of the butterflies. I. Adult taxonomy and the nonspecificity hypothesis. Systematic Zoology 16: 301–317.

_____ . 1990. *The population explosion*. Simon and Schuster, New York.

Ehrlich, P. R., A. H. Ehrlich, and G. C. Daily. 1995. *The stork and the plow: The equity answer to the human dilemma*. Putnam, New York.

Ehrlich, P. R., and L. E. Gilbert. 1973. Population structure and dynamics of the tropical butterfly *Heliconius ethilla*. Biotropica 5: 69–82.

Ehrlich, P. R., and I. Hanski, eds. 2003. *On the wings of checkerspots*. Oxford University Press, Oxford. In press.

Ehrlich, P. R., and D. D. Murphy. 1987. Conservation lessons from long-term studies of checkerspot butterflies. Conservation Biology 1: 122–131.

Ehrlich, P. R., D. D. Murphy, M. C. Singer, C. B. Sherwood, R. R. White, and I. L. Brown. 1980. Extinction, reduction, stability and increase: The responses of checkerspot butterfly (*Euphydryas*) populations to the California drought. Oecologia 46: 101–105.

Ehrlich, P. R., and P. H. Raven. 1964. Butterflies and plants: A study in coevolution. Evolution 18: 586–608.

_____ . 1969. Differentiation of populations. Science 165: 1228–1232.

Ehrlich, P. R., R. R. White, M. C. Singer, S. W. McKechnie, and L. E. Gilbert. 1975. Checkerspot butterflies: A historical perspective. Science 188: 221–228.

Eisikowitch, D., and J. Galil. 1971. Effect of wind on the pollination of *Pancratium maritimum* L. (Amaryllidaceae) by hawkmoths (Lepid.: Sphingidae). Journal of Animal Ecology 40: 673–678.

Eisikowitch, D., and R. Rotem. 1987. Flower orientation and color change in *Quisqualis indica* and their possible role in pollinator partitioning. Botanical Gazette 148: 175–179.

Elam, D. R., and Y. B. Linhart. 1988. Pollination and seed production in *Ipomopsis aggregata*: Differences among and within flower color morphs. American Journal of Botany 75: 1262–1274.

Elgar, M. A., and N. E. Pierce. 1988. Mating success and fecundity in an ant-tended lycaenid butterfly. Pp. 59–75 in T. H. Clutton-Brock, ed., *Reproductive success: Studies of individual variation in contrasting breeding systems*. University of Chicago Press, Chicago and London.

Elias, S. A. 1994. *Quaternary insects and their environments*. Smithsonian Institution Press, Washington. D.C.

Eliot, J. N. 1973. The higher classification of the Lycaenidae (Lepidoptera): A tentative arrangement. Bulletin of the British Museum (Natural History) Entomology 28: 371–505.

———. 1990. Notes on the genus *Curetis* Hübner (Lepidoptera, Lycaenidae). Transactions of the Lepidopterological Society of Japan 41: 201–225.

Eltringham, H. 1919. Butterfly vision. Transactions of the Royal Entomological Society of London 1919 (Part I): 1–49.

Emmel, T. C. 1963. Ecological studies of Rhopalocera at Donner Pass, California. II. Meteorological influences on flight activity. Journal of the Lepidopterists' Society 17: 7–20.

Emmel, T. C., K. S. Brown Jr., P. J. Eliazer, and E. Suomalainen. 1995. Chromosome evolution in the Papilionidae. Pp. 283–298 in J. M. Scriber, Y. Tsubaki, and R. C. Lederhouse, eds., *Swallowtail butterflies: Their ecology and evolutionary biology.* Scientific Publishers, Gainesville FL.

Emmel, T. C., and J. F. Emmel. 1962. Ecological studies of Rhopalocera at Donner Pass, California. I. Butterfly associations and distributional factors. Journal of the Lepidopterists' Society 16: 23–44.

Emmel, T. C., T. S. Kilduff, and N. McFarland. 1974. The chromosomes of a long-isolated monotypic butterfly genus: *Tellervo zoilus* (Nymphalidae: Ithomiinae) in Australia. Journal of Entomology 49: 43–46.

Emmel, T. C., and C. F. Leck. 1970. Seasonal changes in organization of tropical rain forest butterfly populations in Panama. Journal of Research on Lepidoptera 8: 133–152.

Emmel, T. C., M. C. Minno, and B. A. Drummond. 1992. *Florissant butterflies: A guide to the fossil and present-day species of central Colorado.* Stanford University Press, Stanford, CA.

Emmet, A. M., and J. Heath. 1990. *The butterflies of Great Britain and Ireland.* Harley Books, Colchester, UK.

Endler, J. A. 1977. *Geographic variation, speciation, and clines.* Princeton University Press, Princeton, NJ.

———. 1986. *Natural selection in the wild.* Princeton University Press, Princeton, NJ.

———. 1993. The color of light in forests and its implications. Ecological Monographs 63: 1–27.

———. 1998. The place of hybridization in evolution. Evolution 52: 640–644.

Endler, J. A., and M. Théry. 1996. Interacting effects of lek placement, display behavior, ambient light, and color patterns in three Neotropical forest-dwelling birds. American Naturalist 148: 421–452.

Engler, H. 1998. Chemical ecology of passionvine butterflies: Sequestration of cyanogens and patterns of host-plant specialization. Ph.D. dissertation, University of Texas, Austin.

Erhardt, A. 1990. Pollination of *Dianthus gratianopolitanus* (Caryophyllaceae). Plant Systematics and Evolution 170: 125–132.

Erhardt, A., and H. P. Rusterholz. 1998. Do peacock butterflies (*Inachis io* L.) detect and prefer nectar amino acids and other nitrogenous compounds? Oecologia 117: 536–542.

Fagerström T., and C. Wiklund. 1982. Why do males emerge before females? Protandry as a mating strategy in male and female butterflies. Oecologia 52: 164–166.

Faith, D. 1994. Phylogenetic pattern and the quantification of organismal biodiversity. Philosophical Transactions of the Royal Society of London B 345: 45–58.

Faith, D., and P. A. Walker. 1996a. How do indicator groups provide information about the relative biodiversity of different sets of areas? On hotspots, complementarity and pattern-based approaches. Biodiversity Letters 3: 18–25.

————. 1996b. Integrating conservation and development: Incorporating vulnerability into biodiversity-assessment of areas. Biodiversity Conservation 5: 417–429.

————. 1996c. Integrating conservation and development: Effective trade-offs between biodiversity and cost in the selection of protected areas. Biodiversity Conservation 5: 431–446.

Fan, R., P. Anderson, and B. S. Hansson. 1997. Behavioural analysis of olfactory conditioning in the moth *Spodoptera littoralis* (Boisd.) (Lepidoptera: Noctuidae). Journal of Experimental Biology 200: 2969–2976.

Fang, Q. Q., S. Cho, J. C. Regier, C. Mitter, M. Matthews, R. W. Poole, T. P. Friedlander, and S. Zhao. 1997. A new nuclear gene for insect phylogenetics: Dopa decarboxylase is informative of relationships within Heliothinae (Lepidoptera: Noctuidae). Systematic Biology 46: 269–283.

Farina, W. M., and R. B. Josens. 1994. Food source profitability modulates compensatory responses to a visual stimulus in the hawk moth *Macroglossum stellatarum*. Naturwisssenschaften 81: 131–133.

Farrell, B. D., and C. Mitter. 1993. Phylogenetic determinants of insect/plant community diversity. Pp. 253–266 in R. E. Ricklefs and D. Schluter, eds., *Ecological communities: Historical and geographical perspectives*. University of Chicago Press, Chicago.

Farrell, B. D., C. Mitter, and D. J. Futuyma. 1992. Diversification at the insect-plant interface. BioScience 42: 34–42.

Farris, J. S. 1969. A successive approximations approach to character weighting. Systematic Zoology 18: 374–385.

————. 1970. Methods for computing Wagner trees. Systematic Zoology 19: 83–92.

————. 1989. The retention index and homoplasy excess. Systematic Zoology 38: 406–407.

Feder, J. L., S. H. Berlocher, and S. B. Opp. 1998. Sympatric host-race formation and speciation in *Rhagoletis* (Diptera: Tephritidae): A tale of two species for Charles D. Pp. 408–442 in S. Mopper and S. Strauss, eds., *Genetic structure and local adaptation in natural insect populations*. Chapman and Hall, New York.

Feder, J. L., C. A. Chilcote, and G. L. Bush. 1990. Regional, local and microgeographic allele frequency variation between apple and hawthorne populations of *Rhagoletis pomenella* in western Michigan. Evolution 44: 595–608.

Feder, J. L., S. B. Opp, B. Wazlo, K. Reynolds, and S. Spisak. 1994. Host fidelity is an effective pre-mating barrier between sympatric races of the apple maggot fly. Proceedings of the National Academy of Sciences USA 91: 7990–7994.

Feder, M. E., N. Blair, and H. Figueras. 1997. Natural thermal stress and heat-shock protein expression in *Drosophila* larvae and pupae. Functional Ecology 11: 90–100.

Feder, M. E., and W. B. Watt. 1992. Functional biology of adaptation. Pp. 365–392 in R. J. Berry, T. J. Crawford, and G. M. Hewitt, eds., *Genes in ecology*. British Ecological Society, Cambridge Press, UK.

Federal Register. 2000. Endangered and threatened wildlife and plants: Endangered status for *Erigeron decumbens* var. *decumbens* (Willamette Daisy) and Fender's blue butterfly (*Icaricia icarioides fenderi*) and threatened status for *Lupinus sulphureus* ssp. *kincaidii* (Kincaid's lupine). Federal Register 65: 3875–3890.

Feeny, P. P. 1975. Biochemical coevolution between plants and their insect herbivores. Pp. 3–19 in L. E. Gilbert and P. H. Raven, eds., *Coevolution of animals and plants*. University of Texas Press, Austin.

———. 1995. Ecological opportunism and chemical constraints on host associations of swallowtail butterflies. Pp. 9–15 in J. M. Scriber, Y. Tsubaki, and R. C. Lederhouse, eds., *Swallowtail butterflies: Their ecology and evolutionary biology*. Scientific Publishers, Gainesville, FL.

Feeny, P. P., E. Stadler, I. Ahman, and M. Carter. 1989. Effects of plant odor on oviposition by the Black Swallowtail butterfly, *Papilio polyxenes* (Lepidoptera: Papilionidae). Journal of Insect Behavior 2: 803–827.

Feiler, R., R. Bjornson, K. Kirschfeld, D. Mismer, G. M. Rubin, D. P. Smith, M. Socolich, and C. S. Zuker. 1992. Ectopic expression of ultraviolet-rhodopsins in the blue photoreceptor cells of *Drosophila*: Visual physiology and photochemistry of transgenic animals. Journal of Neuroscience 12: 3862–3868.

Feldman, T. S., and W. A. Haber. 1998. Oviposition behavior, host plant use and diet breadth of *Anathassa* butterflies (Lepidoptera: Nymphalidae) using plants in the Acanthaceae in a Costa Rican community. Florida Entomologist 81: 396–406.

Felsenstein, J. 1985. Confidence limits on phylogenies: An approach using the bootstrap. Evolution 39: 783–791.

———. 1993. PHYLIP (Phylogeny Inference Package) version 3.57c. Distributed by the author, Department of Genetics, University of Washington, Seattle.

Ferge, L. 1983. Distribution and hybridization of *Hyalophora columbia* (Lepidoptera: Saturniidae) in Wisconsin. Great Lakes Entomologist 16: 67–71.

Ferris, C. D., and J. F. Emmel. 1982. Discussion of *Papilio coloro* W. G. Wright (= *Papilio rudkini* F., and R. Chermock) and *Papilio polyxenes* Fabricius (Papilionidae). Bulletin of the Allyn Museum 76: 1–13.

Fiedler, K. 1991. Systematic, evolutionary and ecological implications of myrmecophily within the Lycaenidae (Insecta: Lepidoptera: Papilionoidea). Bonn Zoological Monographs 31: 1–210.

Field, W. D., and J. Herrera. 1977. The pierid butterflies of the genera *Hypsochila* Ureta, *Phulia* Herrich-Schäffer, *Infraphulia* Field, *Pierphulia* Field, and *Piercolias* Staudinger. Smithsonian Contributions Zoology 232: iii + 64.

Fisher, B. L. 1996. Ant diversity patterns along an elevational gradient in the Réserve Naturelle Intégrale d'Andringitra, Madagascar. Fieldiana 85: 93–108.

———. 1998. Ant diversity patterns along an elevational gradient in the Réserve Naturelle Intégrale d'Andohahela, Madagascar. Fieldiana 90: 39–67.

———. 1999. Ant diversity patterns along an elevational gradient in the Réserve Spéciale d'Anjanaharibe-Sud and on the western Masoala Peninsula, Madagascar. Fieldiana 94: 129–148.

Fisher, M. S. 1977. The taxonomy and identity of *Papilio nitra* W. H. Edwards in Colorado (Papilionidae). Bulletin of the Allyn Museum 47: 1–7.

Fisher, R. A. 1930. *The genetical theory of natural selection*. Oxford University Press, Oxford.

———. 1958. *The genetical theory of natural selection*. 2d ed., rev., Dover, New York.

Fisher, R. A., and E. B. Ford. 1947. The spread of a gene in natural conditions in a colony of moth *Panaxia dominula* L. Heredity 1: 143–174.

Fiske, P., J. A. Kalas, and S. A. Saether. 1994. Correlates of male mating success in the lekking great snipe (*Gallinago media*): Results from a four-year study. Behavioral Ecology 5: 210–218.

Flather, C. H., K. R. Wilson, D. J. Dean, and W. C. McComb. 1997. Identifying gaps in conservation networks: Of indicators and uncertainty in geographic-based analyses. Ecological Applications 7: 531–542.

Flavell, J. H. 1963. *The developmental psychology of Jean Piaget.* Van Nostrand, New York.

Fleishman, E. 2000. Monitoring the response of butterfly communities to prescribed fire. Environmental Management 26: 685–695.

Fleishman, E., G. T. Austin, and A. D. Weiss. 1998. An empirical test of Rapoport's rule: Elevational gradients in montane butterfly communities. Ecology 79: 2482–2493.

Fleishman, E., C. Ray, P. Sjögren-Gulve, C. L. Boggs, and D. D. Murphy. 2002. Assessing the roles of patch quality, area, and isolation in predicting metapopulation dynamics. Conservation Biology 16: 706–716.

Fleming, H. 1960. The first instar larvae of the Heliconiinae (butterflies) of Trinidad, W. I. Zoologica 45: 91–110.

Foley, P. 1994. Predicting extinction times from environmental stochasticity and carrying capacity. Conservation Biology 8: 124–137.

———. 1997. Extinction models for local populations. Pp. 215–246 in I. Hanski and M. E. Gilpin, eds., *Metapopulation biology.* Academic Press, San Diego.

Ford, E. B. 1945. *Butterflies.* Reprint, 1962. Collins, London.

———. 1964. *Ecological genetics.* Methuen, London.

Forman, R. T. T. 1995. *Land mosaics: The ecology of landscapes and regions.* Cambridge University Press, Cambridge.

Forsberg, J., and C. Wiklund. 1989. Mating in the afternoon: Time-saving in courtship and remating by females of a polyandrous butterfly *Pieris napi.* Behavioral Ecology and Sociobiology 25: 349–356.

Fox, C. W. 1993. A quantitative genetic analysis of oviposition preference and larval performance in two hosts in the bruchid beetle *Callosobruchus maculatus.* Evolution 47: 166–175.

Fox, L. R., and P. A. Morrow. 1981. Specialization: Species property or local phenomenon? Science 211: 1466–1470.

Fox, R. M. 1940. A generic review of the Ithomiinae (Lepidoptera: Nymphalidae). Transactions of the American Entomological Society 66: 161–207.

———. 1949. The evolution and systematics of the Ithomiidae (Lepidoptera). University of Pittsburgh Bulletin 45: 1–12.

———. 1956. A monograph of the Ithomiidae (Lepidoptera). Part I. Bulletin of the American Museum of Natural History 3: 1–76.

———. 1960. A monograph of the Ithomiidae (Lepidoptera). Part II. The tribe Melinaeini Clark. Transactions of the American Entomological Society 86: 109–171.

———. 1961. A check-list of the Ithomiidae. I. Tribes Tithoreini and Melinaeini. Journal of the Lepidopterists' Society 15: 25–33.

———. 1965. Additional notes on *Melinaea* Hubner (Lepidoptera: Ithomiidae). Proceedings of the Royal Entomological Society of London B 34: 77–82.

———. 1967. A monograph of Ithomiidae (Lepidoptera). Part III. The tribe Mechanitini Fox. Memoirs of the American Entomological Society no. 22. American Entomological Society, Philadelphia.

Fox, R. M., and H. G. Real. 1971. A monograph of the Ithomiidae (Lepidoptera). Part IV. The tribe Napeoginini Fox. Memoirs of the American Entomological Institute no. 15. American Entomological Institute, Ann Arbor, MI.

Franco-Gaona, A., J. Llorente B., and A. M. Shapiro. 1988. Abundancia relativa de tres especies de pierinos, evaluada mediante el método de Moore y Pollard en Xochimilco, D.F., México. Folia Entomologica Mexicana 76: 107–128.

Frank, S. A. 1991. Haldane's rule: A defense of the meiotic drive theory. Evolution 45: 1710–1714.

Frankfater, C. 1996. Phytochemical basis for host plant selection by generalist and specialist swallowtail butterflies. M.S. thesis, Michigan State University, East Lansing.

Freeman, H. A. 1969. Systematic review of the Megathymidae. Journal of the Lepidopterist's Society 23 (supplement): 1–59.

Freitas, A. V. L. 1999. Nymphalidae (Lepidoptera): Filogenia incluindo caracteres de imaturos, com testes de troca de planta hospedeira. Ph.D. dissertation, Universidade Estadual de Campinas, São Paulo.

French, V., and P. M. Brakefield. 1992. The development of eyespot patterns on butterfly wings: Morphogen sources or sinks? Development 116: 103–109.

French, V., and P. M. Brakefield. 1995. Eyespot development on butterfly wings: The focal signal. Developmental Biology 168: 112–123.

French, V., and A. Monteiro. 1994. Butterfly wings: Colour patterns and new gene expression patterns. BioEssays 16: 789–792.

Fretwell, S. D. 1972. *Populations in a seasonal environment.* Princeton University Press, Princeton, NJ.

Friedlander, T. P., K. R. Horst, J. C. Regier, C. Mitter, R. S. Peigler, and Q. Q. Fang. 1998. Two nuclear genes yield concordant relationships within Attacini (Lepidoptera: Saturniidae). Molecular Phylogenetics and Evolution 9: 131–140.

Friedlander, T. P., J. C. Regier, and C. Mitter. 1992. Nuclear gene sequences for higher level phylogenetic analysis: 14 promising candidates. Systematic Biology 41: 483–490.

———. 1994. Phylogenetic information content of five nuclear gene sequences in animals: Initial assessment of character sets from concordance and divergence studies. Systematic Biology 43: 511–525.

Friedlander, T. P., J. C. Regier, C. Mitter, and D. L. Wagner. 1996. A nuclear gene for higher level phylogenetics: Phosphoenolpyruvate carboxykinase tracks Mesozoic-age divergences within Lepidoptera (Insecta). Molecular Biology and Evolution 13: 594–604.

Frohawk, F. W. 1914. *Natural history of British butterflies.* Vol. 1. Hutchinson & Co., London.

Fryxell, K. J., and E. M. Meyerowitz. 1987. An opsin gene that is expressed only in the R7 photoreceptor cell of *Drosophila.* EMBO Journal 6: 443–451.

———. 1991. The evolution of rhodopsins and neurotransmitter receptors. Journal of Molecular Evolution 33: 367–378.

Fuller, R. M., G. B. Groom, and A. R. Jones. 1994. The land cover map of Great Britain: An automated classification of Landsat thematic mapper data. Photogrammatic Engineering and Remote Sensing 60: 553–562.

Futuyma, D. J. 1983. Evolutionary interactions among herbivorous insects and plants. Pp. 207–231 in D. J. Futuyma and M. Slatkin, eds., *Coevolution.* Sinauer Associates, Sunderland, MA.

———. 1986. *Evolutionary biology.* 2d ed. Sinauer Associates, Sunderland, MA.

———. 1991. Evolution of host-specificity in herbivorous insects: Genetic, ecological and phylogenetic aspects. Pp. 431–454 in P. W. Price, T. M. Lewinshon, G. W. Fernandes, and W. W. Benson, eds., *Plant-animal interactions: Evolutionary ecology in tropical and temperate regions.* Wiley, New York.

Futuyma, D. J., and S. C. Peterson. 1985. Genetic variation in the use of resources by insects. Annual Review of Entomology 30: 217–238.

Futuyma, D. J., and L. H. Shapiro. 1995. Hybrid zones. Evolution 49: 222–226.

Gabel, B., D. Thièry, V. Suchy, F. Marion-Poll, P. Hradsky, and P. Farkas. 1992. Floral volatiles of *Tanacetum vulgare* L. attractive to *Lobesia botrana* Den. et. Schiff. females. Journal of Chemical Ecology 19: 693–701.

Gade, D. 1996. Deforestation and its effects in Highland Madagascar. Mountain Research and Development 16: 101–116.

Gage, M. J. G. 1994. Associations between body size, mating pattern, testis size and sperm lengths across butterflies. Proceedings of the Royal Society of London B 258: 247–254.

_____ . 1995. Continuous variation in reproductive strategy as an adaptive response to population density in the moth *Plodia interpunctella*. Proceedings of the Royal Society of London B 258: 247–254.

Galant, R., J. B. Skeath, S. Paddock, D. L. Lewis, and S. B. Carroll. 1998. Expression pattern of a butterfly achaete-scute homologue reveals the homology of butterfly wing scales and insect sensory bristles. Current Biology 8: 807–813.

Gall, L. F. 1984. Population structure and recommendations for conservation of the narrowly endemic alpine butterfly, *Boloria acrocnema* (Lepidoptera, Nymphalidae). Biological Conservation 28: 111–138.

Gall, L. F., and B. H. Tiffney. 1983. A fossil noctuid moth egg from the late Cretaceous of eastern North America. Science 219: 507–509.

Ganzhorn, J. U., B. Rakotosamimananana, L. Hannah, J. Hough, L. Iyer, S. Olivieri, S. Rajaobelina, C. Rodstrom, and G. Tilkin. 1997. Priorities for biodiversity conservation in Madagascar. Primate Report Special Issue 48–1.

García-Barros, E. 1987. Morphology and chaetotaxy of the first instar larvae of six species of the *Satyrus* (s.l.) series (Lepidoptera: Nymphalidae). Systematic Entomology 12: 335–344.

_____ . 2000. Comparative data on the adult biology, ecology and behaviour of species belonging to the genera *Hipparchia, Chazara* and *Kanetsia* in central Spain (Nymphalidae: Satyrinae). Nota Lepidoptera 23: 119–140.

García-Barros, E., and J. Martín. 1991. Immature stages of *Hipparchia* Fabricius and the systematics of the "*Satyrus* series" (Lepidoptera: Nymphalidae: Satyrinae). Systematic Entomology 16: 407–426.

Garcia-Bellido, A. 1977. Homeotic and atavic mutations in insects. American Zoologist 17: 613–629.

Garesse, R. 1988. *Drosophila melanogaster* mitochondrial DNA: Gene organization and evolutionary considerations. Genetics 118: 649–663.

Garth, J. S., and J. W. Tilden. 1986. *California butterflies*. University of California Press, Berkeley.

Gaston, K. J. 1994. *Rarity*. Chapman and Hall, London.

Gaston, K. J., and T. M. Blackburn. 1995. Mapping biodiversity using surrogates for species richness: Macro-scales and New World birds. Proceedings of the Royal Society of London B 262: 335–341.

Gatto, M., and L. L. Ghezzi. 1996. Optimal life strategies in organisms exposed to recurrent critical events. Journal of Optimization Theory and Applications 90: 79–94.

Gatto, M., C. Matessi, and L. B. Slobodkin. 1989. Physiological profiles and demographic rates in relation to food quantity and predictability: An optimization approach. Evolutionary Ecology 3: 1–30.

Gause, G. F. 1934. *The struggle for existence.* Williams and Wilkins, Baltimore.

Geiger, H. J. 1980. Enzyme electrophoretic studies on the genetic relationships of pierid butterflies (Lepidoptera, Pieridae). I. European taxa. Journal of Research on Lepidoptera 19: 181–195.

Gibbs, A. E. 1916. The disappearing *Pararge aegeria.* Entomologists' Record 28: 122–126.

Giebink, B., J. M. Scriber, and J. L. Wedberg. 1984. Biology and phenology of the hop vine borer, *Hydraecia immanis* Guenee and detection of the potato stem borer, *H. micacea* (Esper) (Lepidoptera: Noctuidae) in Wisconsin. Environmental Entomology 13: 1216–1224.

Gilbert, C. 1994. Form and function of stemmata in larvae of holometabolous insects. Annual Review of Entomology 39: 323–349.

Gilbert, L. E. 1972. Pollen feeding and reproductive biology of *Heliconius* butterflies. Proceedings of the National Academy of Sciences USA 69: 1403–1407.

————. 1976. Postmating female odor in *Heliconius* butterflies: A male-contributed anti-aphrodisiac? Science 193: 419–420.

————. 1978. Development of theory in the analysis of insect-plant interactions. Pp. 117–154 in D. J. Horn, G. R. Stairs, and R. D. Mitchell, eds., *Analysis of ecological systems.* Ohio State University Press, Columbus.

————. 1983. Coevolution and mimicry Pp. 263–281 in D. J. Futuyma and M. Slatkin, eds., *Coevolution.* Sinauer Associates, Sunderland, MA.

————. 1984. The biology of butterfly communities. Pp. 41–54 in R. I. Vane-Wright and P. R. Ackery, eds., *The biology of butterflies.* Academic Press, London.

————. 1991. Biodiversity of a Central American *Heliconius* community: Pattern, process and problems. Pp. 403–427 in P. W. Price, T. M. Lewinsohn, G. W. Fernandes, and W. W. Benson, eds., *Plant-animal interactions: Evolutionary ecology in tropical and temperate regions.* John Wiley and Sons, London.

Gilbert, L. E., and P. R. Ehrlich. 1970. The affinities of the Ithomiinae and Satyrinae (Nymphalidae). Journal of the Lepidopterists' Society 4: 297–300.

Gilbert, L. E., H. S. Forrest, T. D. Schultz, and D. J. Harvey. 1988. Correlations of ultrastructure and pigmentation suggest how genes control development of wing scales in *Heliconius* butterflies. Journal of Research on Lepidoptera 26: 141–160.

Gilbert, L. E., and M. C. Singer. 1973. Dispersal and gene flow in a butterfly species. American Naturalist 107: 58–72.

————. 1975. Butterfly ecology. Annual Reviews of Ecology and Systematics 6: 365–398.

Gilbert, L. I. 1989. The endocrine control of molting: The Tobacco hornworm, *Manduca Sexta,* as a model system. Pp. 448–471 in J. Koolman, ed., *Ecdysone: From chemistry to mode of action.* Thieme, New York.

Gillespie, J. H. 1978. A general model to account for enzyme variation in natural populations. V. The SAS-CFF model. Theoretical Population Biology 14: 1–45.

————. 1991. *The causes of molecular evolution.* Oxford University Press, Oxford.

Gillespie, J. H., and K.-I. Kojima. 1968. The degree of polymorphism in enzymes of energy production compared to that in nonspecific enzymes in two *Drosophila ananassae* populations. Proceedings of the National Academy of Sciences USA 61: 582–585.

Gilpin, M. 1991. The genetic effective size of a metapopulation. Biological Journal of the Linnean Society 42: 165–175.

Gilpin, M., and M. E. Soulé. 1986. Minimum viable populations: Processes of species extinctions. Pp. 19–34 in M. E. Soulé, ed., *Conservation biology: The science of scarcity and diversity.* Sinauer Associates, Sunderland, MA.

Giroux, P. Y. 1998. Testing the "cold pocket" hypothesis: Oviposition preference in the Canadian tiger swallowtail, *Papilio canadensis.* M.S. thesis, Michigan State University, East Lansing.

Goldman, N. 1998. Phylogenetic information and experimental design in molecular systematics. Proceedings of the Royal Society of London B 265: 1779–1786.

Goldsmith, T. 1994. Ultraviolet receptors and color vision: Evolutionary implications and a dissonance of paradigms. Vision Research 34: 1479–1487.

Goldstein, P. Z., R. DeSalle, G. Amato, and A. P. Vogler. 2000. Conservation genetics at the species boundary. Conservation Biology 14: 120–131.

Goodman, D. 1987. The demography of chance extinction. Pp. 311–334 in M. E. Soulé, ed., *Conservation biology: The science of scarcity and diversity.* Sinauer Associates, Sunderland, MA.

Gotthard, K., S. Nylin, and C. Wiklund. 1994. Adaptive variation in growth rate: Life history costs and consequences in the speckled wood butterfly *Pararge aegeria.* Oecologia 99: 281–289.

——— . 1999. Seasonal plasticity in two satyrine butterflies: State-dependent decision making in relation to daylength. Oikos 84: 453–462.

Gould, F. 1979. Rapid host range evolution in a population of the phytophagous mite *Tetranychus urticae.* Evolution 33: 791–802.

Gould, S. J., and R. C. Lewontin. 1979. The spandrels of San Marco and the Panglossian paradigm. Proceedings of the Royal Society of London B 205: 581–598.

Goulson, D. 1993. Allozyme variation in the butterfly, *Maniola jurtina* (Lepidoptera: Satyrinae) (L.): Evidence for selection. Heredity 71: 386–393.

Goulson, D., and J. S. Cory. 1993. Flower constancy and learning in foraging preferences of the green-veined white butterfly, *Pieris napi.* Ecological Entomology 18: 315–320.

Goulson, D., J. C. Stout, and S. A. Hawson. 1997. Can flower constancy in nectaring butterflies be explained by Darwin's interference hypothesis? Oecologia 112: 225–231.

Grabherr, G., M. Gottfried, and H. Pauli. 1994. Climate effects on mountain plants. Nature 369: 448.

Grant, G. G. 1971. Feeding activity of adult cabbage loopers on flowers with strong olfactory stimulants. Journal of Economic Entomology 64: 315–316.

Grant, K. J. 1937. An historical study of the migrations of *Celerio lineata lineata* Fab., and *Celerio lineata livornica* Esp. (Lepidoptera). Transactions of the Royal Entomological Society of London 86: 345–357.

Grant, V. 1983. The systematic and geographical distribution of hawkmoth flowers in the temperate North American flora. Botanical Gazette 144: 439–449.

Graybeal, A. 1998. Is it better to add taxa or characters to a difficult phylogenetic problem? Systematic Biology 47: 9–17.

Green, G. M., and R. W. Sussman. 1990. Deforestation history of the eastern rain forests of Madagascar from satellite images. Science 248: 212–215.

Greenfield, M. D. 1982. Reproductive isolation in clearwing moths (Lepidoptera: Sesiidae): A tropical-temperate comparison. Ecology 64: 362–375.

Gregory, D. P. 1963. Hawkmoth pollination in the genus *Oenothera.* Aliso 5: 357–384.

——— . 1964. Hawkmoth pollination in the genus *Oenothera.* Aliso 5: 385–419.

Gregory, P. G., and D. J. Howard. 1994. A post-insemination barrier to fertilization isolates two closely related ground crickets. Evolution 48: 705–710.

———. 1996. Multiple mating in natural populations of ground crickets. Entomologica Experimentalis et Applicata 78: 353–356.

Gribbin, S. D., and D. J. Thompson. 1991. The effects of size and residency on territorial disputes and short-term mating success in the damselfly *Pyrrhosoma nymphula* (Zygoptera: Coenagrionidae). Animal Behaviour 41: 689–695.

Griswold, C. E. 1991. Cladistic biogeography of afromontane spiders. Australian Systematic Botany 4: 73–89.

———. 2000. "Afromontane" spiders in Madagascar (Araneae, Araneomorphae, Cyatholipidae, Phyxelididae, Zorocratidae). Pp. 345–354 in W. Lourenco and S. Goodman, eds., *Diversity and endemism in Madagascar*. Mémoires de la Sociéte de Biogéographie, Paris.

Groisman, P. Y., T. R. Karl, D. R. Easterling, R. W. Knight, P. F. Jamason, K. J. Hennessy, R. Suppiah, C. M. Page, J. Wibig, K. Fortuniak, V. N. Razuvaev, A. Douglas, E. Forland, and P. Zhai. 1999. Changes in the probability of heavy precipitation: Important indicators of climatic change. Climatic Change 42: 243–283.

Grossmueller, D. W., and R. C. Lederhouse. 1987. The role of nectar source distribution in habitat use and oviposition by the tiger swallowtail butterfly. Journal of the Lepidopterists' Society 41: 159–165.

Grula, J. W., and O. R. Taylor. 1980a. Some characteristics of hybrids derived from the sulfur butterflies, *Colias eurytheme* and *C. philodice*: Phenotype effects of the X-chromosome. Evolution 34: 673–687.

———. 1980b. The effect of X-chromosome inheritance on mate selection behavior in the sulfur butterflies, *Colias eurytheme* and *C. philodice*. Evolution 34: 688–695.

Guillaumin, M., and H. Descimon. 1976. La notion d'espèce chez les Lèpidoptères in Les problèmes de l'espèce dans le règne animal. Memoires, Societe Zoologique de France 38: 129–202.

Guillery, P., and J. Andrianisa. 1995. Annexe XIV. Inventaire forestier préliminaire de la peninsule Masoala: Faisabilité d'une gestion forestière durable dans la zone périphérique du parc. In C. Kremen, ed., *Proposition des limites du Parc National Masoala*. Care International Madagascar, Wildlife Conservation Society, and The Peregrine Fund, Antananarivo.

Guldemond, J. A. 1990. Evolutionary genetics of the aphid *Cryptomyzus*, with a preliminary analysis of the inheritance of host plant preference, reproductive performance and host-alteration. Entomologica Experimentalis et Applicata 57: 65–76.

Guppy, C. S. 1986. The adaptive significance of alpine melanism in the butterfly *Parnassius phoebus* F. (Lepidoptera: Papilionidae). Oecologia 70: 205–213.

Gurney, W. S. C., E. McCauley, R. M. Nisbet, and W. W. Murdoch. 1990. The physiological ecology of *Daphnia*: A dynamic model of growth and reproduction. Ecology 71: 716–732.

Gurney, W. S. C., and D. A. J. Middleton. 1996. Optimal resource allocation in a randomly varying environment. Functional Ecology 10: 602–612.

Gurney, W. S. C., and R. M. Nisbet. 1978. Single species population fluctuations in patchy environments. American Naturalist 112: 1075–1090.

Gyllenberg, M., I. Hanski, and A. Hastings. 1997. Structured metapopulation models. Pp. 93–122 in I. Hanski and M. E. Gilpin, eds., *Metapopulation biology*. Academic Press, San Diego.

Haber, W. A. 1978. Evolutionary ecology of tropical mimetic butterflies (Lepidoptera: Ithomiinae). Ph.D. dissertation, University of Minnesota.

———. 1984. Pollination by deceit in a mass-flowering tropical tree *Plumeria rubra* L. (Apocynaceae). Biotropica 16: 269–275.

Haber, W. A., and G. W. Frankie. 1989. A tropical hawkmoth community: Costa Rican dry forest Sphingidae. Biotropica 21: 155–172.

Hafernik, J. E. 1982. Phenetics and ecology of hybridization in buckeye butterflies. University of California Publications in Entomology 96: 109.

Hagen, R. H. 1990. Population structure and host use in hybridizing subspecies of *Papilio glaucus* (Lepidoptera: Papilionidae). Evolution 44: 1914–1930.

Hagen, R. H., and R. C. Lederhouse. 1985. Polymodal emergence of the tiger swallowtail, *Papilio glaucus* (Lepidoptera: Papilionidae): Source of a false second generation in central New York State. Ecological Entomology 10: 19–28.

Hagen, R. H., R. C. Lederhouse, J. L. Bossart, and J. M. Scriber. 1991. *Papilio canadensis* and *P. glaucus* (Papilionidae) are distinct species. Journal of the Lepidopterists' Society 45: 245–258.

Hagen, R. H., and J. M. Scriber. 1989. Sex-linked diapause, color, and allozyme loci in *Papilio glaucus:* Linkage analysis and significance in a hybrid zone. Journal of Heredity 80: 179–185.

———. 1991. Systematics of the *Papilio glaucus* and *P. troilus* species groups (Lepidoptera: Papilionidae): Inferences from allozymes. Annals of the Entomological Society of America 84: 380–395.

———. 1995. Sex chromosomes and speciation in the *Papilio glaucus* group. Pp. 211–228 in J. M. Scriber, Y. Tsubaki, and R. C. Lederhouse, eds., *Swallowtail butterflies: Their ecology and evolutionary biology.* Scientific Publishers, Gainesville, FL.

Haikola, S., W. Fortelius, R. B. O'Hara, M. Kuussaari, N. Wahlberg, I. J. Saccheri, M. C. Singer, and I. Hanski. 2001. Inbreeding depression and the maintenance of genetic load in *Melitaea cinxia* metapopulations. Conservation Genetics 2: 325–335.

Hailman, J. 1977. *Optical signals.* Indiana University Press, Bloomington.

Haldane, J. B. S. 1922. Sex ratio and unisexual sterility in hybrid animals. Journal of Genetics 12: 101–109.

Haldane, J. B. S., and S. D. Jayakar. 1963. Polymorphism due to selection of varying direction. Journal of Genetics 58: 237–242.

Hall, B. 1982. Evolution on a petri dish. Evolutionary Biology 15: 85–150.

Hall, J. P. W., and D. J. Harvey. 2002. A survey of the androconial organs in the Riodinidae (Lepidoptera). Zoological Journal of the Linnean Society 136: 171–197.

Hall, J. P. W., and K. R. Willmott. 2000. Patterns of feeding behaviour in adult male riodinid butterflies and their relationship to morphology and ecology. Biological Journal of the Linnean Society 69: 1–23.

Hallam, T. G., R. R. Lassiter, J. Li, and L. A. Suarez. 1990. Modelling individuals employing an integrated energy response: Application to *Daphnia.* Ecology 71: 938–954.

Hammer, O. 1998. Diffuson and direct signaling models are numerically equivalent. Journal of Theoretical Biology 192: 129–130.

Hämmerle, B., and G. Kolb. 1996. Retinal structure of the dorsal region of *Pararge aegeria* (Linn.) (Lepidoptera: Satyridae). International Journal of Morphology and Embryology 25: 305–315.

Hammond, P. C. 1995. 1994 study of the Fender's blue butterfly (*Icaricia icarioides fenderi*) in Benton, Polk and Yamhill Counties. Report to the U.S. Fish and Wildlife Service and the Oregon Natural Heritage Program, Portland, Oregon.

Hammond, P. C., and M. V. Wilson. 1993. Status of the Fender's blue butterfly (*Icaricia icarioides fenderi*). Report to the U.S. Fish and Wildlife Service, Portland, Oregon.

Hancock, D. L. 1983. Classification of the Papilionidae (Lepidoptera): A phylogenetic approach. Smithersia 2: 1–48.

————. 1991. Notes on the phylogeny and biogeography of *Ornithoptera* Boisduval (Lepidoptera: Papilionidae). Tyô to Ga 42: 17–36.

————. 1993. Origins and evolution of the Afrotropical Papilionidae (Lepidoptera). Arnoldia Zimbabwe 9: 557–583.

Hanski, I. 1982. Dynamics of regional distribution: The core and satellite hypothesis. Oikos 38: 210–221.

————. 1987. Pine sawfly population dynamics: Patterns, processes, problems. Oikos 50: 327–335.

————. 1990. Density dependence, regulation and variability on animal populations. Philosophical Transactions of the Royal Society of London B 330: 141–150.

————. 1991. Single-species metapopulation dynamics: Concepts, models and observations. Pp. 17–38 in M. E. Gilpin and I. Hanski, eds., *Metapopulation dynamics*. Academic Press, London.

————. 1994. A practical model of metapopulation dynamics. Journal of Animal Ecology 63: 151–162.

————. 1998a. Metapopulation dynamics. Nature 396: 41–49.

————. 1998b. Spatial structure and dynamics of insect populations. Pp. 3–28 in J. Dempster and I. McLean, eds., *Insect populations*. Kluwer Academic, London.

————. 1999. *Metapopulation ecology*. Oxford University Press, Oxford.

Hanski, I., J. Alho, and A. Moilanen. 2000. Estimating the parameters of survival and migration of individuals in metapopulations. Ecology 81: 239–251.

Hanski, I., and M. Gilpin. 1991. Metapopulation dynamics: Brief history and conceptual domain. Biological Journal of the Linnean Society 42: 3–16.

————. eds. 1997. *Metapopulation biology: Ecology, genetics, and evolution*. Academic Press, San Diego.

Hanski, I., and M. Kuussaari. 1995. Butterfly metapopulation dynamics. Pp. 149–171 in P. Cappuccino and P. Price, eds., *Population dynamics: New approaches and synthesis*. Academic Press, London.

Hanski, I., M. Kuussaari, and M. Nieminen. 1994. Metapopulation structure and migration in the butterfly *Melitaea cinxia*. Ecology 75: 747–762.

Hanski, I., A. Moilanen, and M. Gyllenberg. 1996a. Minimum viable metapopulation size. American Naturalist 147: 527–541.

Hanski, I., T. Moilanen, T. Pakkala, and M. Kuussaari. 1996b. The quantitative incidence function model and persistence of an endangered butterfly metapopulation. Conservation Biology 10: 578–590.

Hanski, I., and O. Ovaskainen. 2000. The metapopulation capacity of a fragmented landscape. Nature 404: 755–758.

Hanski, I., T. Pakkala, M. Kuussaari, and G. Lei. 1995a. Metapopulation persistence of an endangered butterfly in a fragmented landscape. Oikos 72: 21–28.

Hanski, I., J. Pöyry, M. Kuussaari, and T. Pakkala. 1995b. Multiple equilibria in metapopulation dynamics. Nature 377: 618–621.

Hanski, I., and M. C. Singer. 2001. Extinction-colonization dynamics and host-plant choice in butterfly metapopulations. American Naturalist 158: 341–353.

Hanski, I., and C. D. Thomas. 1994. Metapopulation dynamics and conservation: A spatially explicit model applied to butterflies. Biological Conservation 68: 167–180.

Hardy, I. C. W. 1998. Butterfly battles: On conventional contests and hot property. Trends in Ecology and Evolution 13: 385–386.

Hargrave, P. A., J. H. McDowell, D. R. Curtis, J. K. Wang, E. Juszczak, S.-L. Fong, J. K. Mohana Rao, and P. Argos. 1983. The structure of bovine rhodopsin. Biophysical Structural Mechanics 9: 235–244.

Harris, B. J., and H. G. Baker. 1958. Pollination of *Kigelia africana.* Journal of the West African Scientific Association 4: 25–30.

Harrison, R. G. 1993. *Hybrid zones and the evolutionary process.* Oxford University Press, Oxford.

————. 1998. Linking evolutionary pattern and process: The relevance of species concepts for the study of speciation. Pp. 19–31 in D. J. Howard and S. H. Berlocher, eds., *Endless forms: Species and speciation.* Oxford University Press, New York and Oxford.

Harrison, R. G., and S. M. Bogdanowicz. 1997. Patterns of variation and linkage disequilibrium in a field cricket hybrid zone. Evolution 51: 493–505.

Harrison, S. 1989. Long-distance dispersal and colonization in the Bay Checkerspot butterfly, *Euphydryas editha bayensis.* Ecology 70: 1236–1243.

————. 1991. Local extinction in a metapopulation context: An empirical evaluation. Biological Journal of the Linnean Society 42: 73–88.

————. 1994. Metapopulations and conservation. Pp. 111–128 in P. J. Edwards, R. M. May, and N. R. Webb, eds., *Large-scale ecology and conservation biology.* Blackwell Scientific Press, Oxford.

Harrison, S., and N. Cappuccino. 1995. Using density-manipulation experiments to study population regulation. Pp. 131–148 in N. Cappuccino and P. Price, eds., *Population dynamics: New approaches and synthesis.* Academic Press, San Diego.

Harrison, S., D. D. Murphy, and P. R. Ehrlich. 1988. Distribution of the Bay Checkerspot butterfly, *Euphydryas editha bayensis:* Evidence for a metapopulation model. American Naturalist 132: 360–382.

Harrison, S., J. F. Quinn, J. F. Baughman, D. D. Murphy, and P. R. Ehrlich. 1991. Estimating the effects of scientific study on two butterfly populations. American Naturalist 137: 227–243.

Harrison, S., and A. D. Taylor. 1997. Empirical evidence for metapopulation dynamics. Pp. 27–42. in I. Hanski and M. E. Gilpin, eds., *Metapopulation biology.* Academic Press, San Diego.

Hartl, D. L., and A. G. Clark. 1989. *Principles of population genetics.* Sinauer Associates, Sunderland, MA.

Hartl, D. L., and D. E. Dykhuizen. 1981. Potential for selection among nearly neutral allozymes of 6-phosphogluconate dehydrogenase in *Escherichia coli.* Proceedings of the National Academy of Sciences USA 78: 6344–6348.

Hartl, D. L., D. E. Dykhuizen, and A. M. Dean. 1985. The limits of adaptation: The evolution of selective neutrality. Genetics 111: 655–674.

Hartlieb, E. 1996. Olfactory conditioning in the moth *Heliothis virescens.* Naturwissenschaften 83: 87–88.

Harvey, D. J. 1987. The higher classification of the Riodinidae. Ph.D. dissertation, University of Texas, Austin.

————. 1991. Higher classification of the Nymphalidae, Appendix B. Pp. 255–273 in H. F. Nijhout, ed., *The development and evolution of butterfly wing patterns.* Smithsonian Institution Press, Washington, D.C.

Harvey, P. H., and M. D. Pagel. 1991. *The comparative method in evolutionary biology.* Oxford University Press, Oxford.

Hassell, M. P., R. M. May, S. W. Pacala, and P. L. Chesson. 1991. The persistence of host-parasitoid associations in patchy environments. I. A general criterion. American Naturalist 138: 568–583.

Hastings, A. 1991. Structured models of metapopulation dynamics: Concepts, models, and observations. Biological Journal of the Linnean Society 42: 57–72.

Hastings, A., and S. Harrison. 1994. Metapopulation dynamics and genetics. Annual Review of Ecology and Systematics 25: 167–188.

Häuser, C. L. 1992. A new abdominal scent organ in females of *Baronia brevicornis* (Lepidoptera: Papilionidae). Zoologischer Anzeiger 229: 54–62.

———. 1993a. Critical comments on the phylogenetic relationships within the family Papilionidae (Lepidoptera). Nota Lepidopterologica 16: 34–43.

———. 1993b. The internal genital organs in butterflies (Rhopalocera): Comparative morphology and phylogenetic interpretation. Zoologische Jahrbücher, Abteilung für Systematik Oekologie und Geographie der Tiere 120: 389–439.

Haynes, K. F., J. Z. Zhao, and A. Latif. 1991. Identification of floral compounds from *Abelia grandiflora* that stimulate upwind flight in cabbage looper moths. Journal of Chemical Ecology 17: 637–646.

Heard, S. B., and Ø. Mooers. 2000. Phylogenetically patterned speciation rates and extinction risks change the loss of evolutionary history during extinctions. Proceedings of the Royal Society of London B 267: 613–620.

Heath, J. 1981. Threatened Rhopalocera (butterflies) in Europe. Council of Europe, Nature and Environment Series 23: 1–157. Strasbourg.

Heath, J., E. Pollard, and J. A. Thomas. 1984. *Atlas of butterflies in Britain and Ireland.* Viking, Penguin Books Ltd., Harmondsworth, England.

Heath, R. R., P. J. Landolt, B. Dueben, and B. Senczewski. 1992. Identification of floral compounds of night-blooming jessamine attractive to cabbage looper moths. Environmental Entomology 21: 854–859.

Heckel, D. G. 1993. Comparative genetic linkage mapping in insects. Annual Review of Entomology 38: 381–408.

Hedrick, P. W., R. C. Lacy, F. W. Allendorf, and M. E. Soulé. 1996. Directions in conservation biology: Comments on Caughley. Conservation Biology 10: 1312–1320.

Heinrich, B. 1974. Thermoregulation in endothermic insects. Science 185: 747–756.

———. 1977. Why some animals have evolved to regulate a high body temperature. American Naturalist 111: 623–640.

———. 1983. Insect foraging energetics. Pp. 187–214 in C. E. Jones and R. J. Little, eds., *Handbook of experimental pollination biology.* Van Nostrand-Reinhold, New York.

———. 1986. Thermoregulation and flight activity of a satyrine, *Coenonympha inornata* (Lepidoptera: Satyridae). Ecology 67: 593–597.

Heinrich, B., and T. M. Casey. 1973. Metabolic rate and endothermy in sphinx moths. Journal of Comparative Physiology 82: 195–206.

———. 1978. Heat transfer in dragonflies: "Fliers" and "perchers." Journal of Experimental Biology 74: 17–36.

Henriksen, H. J., and I. B. Kreutzer. 1982. *The butterflies of Scandinavia in nature.* Skandinavisk Bogforlag, Denmark.

Heitzman, J. R. 1973. A new species of *Papilio* from the eastern United States (Papilionidae). Journal of Research on Lepidoptera 12: 1–10.

Hellmann, J. J. 2002. Butterflies as model systems for understanding and predicting the biological effects of climate change. Pp. 93–126 in S. H. Schneider and T. L. Root, eds., *Wildlife responses to climate change*. Island Press, Washington, DC.

Hellmann, J. J., S. B. Weiss, J. F. McLaughlin, P. R. Ehrlich, D. D. Murphy, and A. E. Launer. 2003. Structure and dynamics of *Euphydryas editha* populations. In P. R. Ehrlich and I. Hanski, eds., *On the wings of checkerspots*. Oxford University Press, Oxford. In press.

Hendrickson, J. A., and P. R. Ehrlich. 1971. An expanded concept of "species diversity." Notulae Naturae, Philadelphia (439).

Hennig. W. 1950. *Grundzüge einer theorie der phylogenetischen systematik*. Deutscher Zentralverlag, Berlin.

———. 1965. Phylogenetic systematics. Annual Review of Entomology 10: 97–116.

Hering, F. 1995. Habitat patches of the threatened butterfly species *Melitaea cinxia* (L.) on the Åland islands, Finland: Vegetation characteristics and caterpillar-hostplant interactions. M.Sc. thesis, Münster.

Hernandez, M. I., and W. W. Benson. 1998. Dispersed landmark mating territories defended by the aposematic butterfly *Heliconius sara* (Nymphalidae) in lowland tropical forest. Animal Behaviour 56: 533–540.

Herrera, C. M. 1989. Pollinator abundance, morphology and flower visitation rate: Analysis of the "quantity" component in a plant-pollinator system. Oecologia 80: 241–248.

———. 1992. Activity pattern and thermal biology of a day flying hawkmoth (*Macroglossum stellatarum*) under Mediterranean summer conditions. Ecological Entomology 17: 52–56.

Herrera, J. 1986. Flowering and fruiting phenology in the coastal shrublands of Doñana, south Spain. Vegetatio 68: 91–98.

Hewitt, G. M. 1996. Some genetic consequences of ice ages, and their role in divergence and speciation. Biological Journal of the Linnean Society 58: 247–276.

Hewitt, G. M., R. A. Nichols, and N. H. Barton. 1987. Homogamy in a hybrid zone in the alpine grasshopper, *Podisma pedestrisi*. Heredity 62: 343–354.

Heyneman, A. J. 1983. Optimal sugar concentrations of floral nectars: Dependence on sugar intake efficiency and foraging costs. Oecologia 60: 198–213.

Higgins, L. G. 1977. The speckled wood (*Pararge aegeria* L.) in Madeira. Entomologists' Record and Journal of Variation 890: 22–23.

Hill, C. J. 1989. The effect of adult diet on the biology of butterflies. 2. The common crow butterfly, *Euploe core corinna*. Oecologia 81: 258–266.

Hill, C. J., and N. E. Pierce. 1989. The effect of adult diet on the biology of butterflies. 1. The common imperial blue, *Jalmenus evagoras*. Oecologia 81: 249–257.

Hill, J. K., Y. C. Collingham, C. D. Thomas, D. S. Blakeley, R. Fox, D. Moss, and B. Huntley. 2001a. Impacts of landscape structure on butterfly range expansion. Ecology Letters 4: 313–321.

Hill, J. K., C. D. Thomas, and D. S. Blakeley. 1999a. Evolution of flight morphology in a butterfly that has recently expanded its geographic range. Oecologia 121: 165–170.

Hill, J. K., C. D. Thomas, and B. Huntley. 1999b. Climate and habitat availability determine 20th century changes in a butterfly's range margins. Proceedings of the Royal Society of London B 266: 1197–1206.

———. 2002. Climate and recent range changes in butterflies. In G.-R. Walther, C. A. Burga, and P. J. Edwards, eds., *Fingerprints of climate change: Adapted behaviour and shifting species ranges*. Kluwer Academic and Plenum Publishers, UK.

Hill, J. K., C. D. Thomas, B. Huntley, and R. Fox. 2001b. Analysing and modelling range changes in UK butterflies. Pp. 415–442 in I. Woiwod, D. Reynolds, and C. D. Thomas, eds., *Insect movement: Mechanisms and consequences*. Royal Entomological Society (London) 20th Symposium. CABI Publishing, UK.

Hill, J. K., C. D. Thomas, and O. T. Lewis. 1996. Effects of habitat patch size and isolation on dispersal by *Hesperia comma* butterflies: Implications for metapopulation structure. Journal of Animal Ecology 65: 725–735.

Hill, J. K., C. D. Thomas, and O. T. Lewis. 1999c. Flight morphology in fragmented populations of a rare British butterfly, *Hesperia comma*. Biological Conservation 87: 277–283.

Hillis, D. M. 1991. Discriminating between phylogenetic signal and random noise in DNA sequences. Pp. 278–294 in M. M. Miyamoto and J. Cracraft, eds., *Phylogenetic analysis of DNA sequences*. Oxford University Press, Oxford.

Hillis, D. M. 1998. Taxonomic sampling, phylogenetic accuracy, and investigator bias. Systematic Biology 47: 3–8.

Hillis, D. M., C. Moritz, and B. K. Mable, eds. 1996. *Molecular systematics*. 2d ed. Sinauer Associates, Sunderland, MA.

Hilton, H., R. M. Kliman, and J. Hey. 1994. Using hitchhiking genes to study adaptation and divergence during speciation within the *Drosophila melanogaster* species complex. Evolution 48: 1900–1913.

Hinton, H. E. 1946. On the homology and nomenclature of the setae of lepidopterous larvae, with some notes on the phylogeny of the Lepidoptera. Transactions of the Royal Entomological Society of London 97: 1–37.

———. 1951. Myrmecophilous Lycaenidae and other Lepidoptera: A summary. Transactions of the South London Entomological and Natural History Society 1949–50: 111–175.

Hiruma, T. L., and K. J. Kramer. 1992. Insect cuticle sclerotization. Annual Review of Entomology 37: 273–302.

Hiura, I. 1980. A phylogeny of the genera of Parnassiinae based on analysis of wing pattern, with description of a new genus (Lepidoptera: Papilionidae). Bulletin Osaka Museum Natural History 33: 71–95.

Hochachka, P. W., and G. N. Somero. 1973. *Strategies of biochemical adaptation*. W. B. Saunders, Philadelphia.

Hodges, R. W. 1971. *The moths of America north of Mexico*. Fascicle 21: *Sphingidae*. E. W. Classey and R. B. D. Public, London.

Hoffman, A. A., and M. W. Blows. 1994. Species borders: Ecological and evolutionary perspectives. Trends in Ecology and Evolution 9: 223–227.

Holdridge, L. A., W. C. Grenke, W. H. Hatheway, T. Liang, and J. A. Tosi Jr. 1971. *Forest environments in tropical life zones: A pilot study*. Pergamon Press, Oxford.

Holland, B., and W. R. Rice. 1997. Cryptic sexual selection: More control issues. Evolution 51: 321–324.

Holland, W. J. 1903. *The moth book*. Doubleday, Page and Co., New York.

Holloway, G. J. 1993. Phenotypic variation in colour pattern and seasonal plasticity in *Eristalis* hoverflies (Diptera: Syrphidae). Ecological Entomology 18: 209–217.

Holmes, E. E., M. A. Lewis, J. E. Banks, and R. R. Veit. 1994. Partial differential equations in ecology: Spatial interactions and population dynamics. Ecology 75: 17–29.

Honda, K., H. Omura, and N. Hayashi. 1998. Identification of floral volatiles from *Ligustrum japonicum* that stimulate flower-visiting by cabbage butterfly, *Pieris rapae*. Journal of Chemical Ecology 24: 2167–2180.

Horridge, G. A. 1977. The compound eye of insects. Scientific American 237: 108–120.

Horridge, G. A., L. Marcelja, and R. Jahnke. 1984. Colour vision in butterflies. I. Single color experiments. Journal of Comparative Physiology A 155: 529–542.

Horváth, G., and D. Varjú. 1997. Polarization pattern of freshwater habitats recorded by video polarimetry in red, green and blue spectral ranges and its relevance for water detection by aquatic insects. Journal of Experimental Biology 200: 1155–1163.

Hough, J. L., and M. N. Sherpa. 1989. Bottom up vs. basic needs: Integrating conservation and development in the Annapurna and Michiru Mountain conservation areas of Nepal and Malawi. Ambio 18: 434–441.

Hovanitz, W. 1941. Parallel ecogenotypical color variation in butterflies. Ecology 22: 259–284.

Hovemann, B. T., R.-P. Ryseck, U. Walldorf, K. F. Stortkuhl, I. D. Dietzel, and E. Dessen. 1998. The *Drosophila ebony* gene is closely related to microbial peptideal synthetases and shows specific cuticle and nervous system expression. Gene 221: 1–9.

Howard, D. J. 1993. Reinforcement: Origin, dynamics, and fate of an evolutionary hypothesis. Pp. 46–69 in R. G. Harrison, ed., *Hybrid zones and the evolutionary process*. Oxford University Press, Oxford.

Howard, D. J., and S. H. Berlocher, eds. 1998. *Endless forms, species and speciation*. Oxford University Press, New York and Oxford.

Howard, D. J., and P. G. Gregory. 1993. Post-insemination signalling systems and reinforcement. Philosophical Transactions of the Royal Society of London B 340: 231–236.

Howard, D. J., and G. L. Waring. 1991. Topographic diversity, zone width, and strength of reproductive isolation in a zone of overlap and hybridization. Evolution 45: 1120–1135.

Howard, D. J., G. W. Waring, A. Tibbets, and P. Gregory. 1993. Survival of hybrids in a mosaic hybrid zone. Evolution 47: 789–800.

Howard, P. C., P. Viskanic, T. R. B. Davenport, F. W. Kigenyi, M. Baltzer, C. J. Dickinson, J. S. Lwanga, R. A. Matthews, and A. Balmford. 1998. Complementarity and the use of indicator groups for reserve selection in Uganda. Nature 394: 472–475.

Huber, A., S. Schulz, J. Bentrop, C. Groell, U. Wolfrum, and R. Paulsen. 1997. Molecular cloning of *Drosophila* Rh6 rhodopsin: The visual pigment of a subset of R8 photoreceptor cells. FEBS Letter 406: 6–10.

Huelsenbeck, J. P. 1991. Tree-length distribution skewness: An indicator of phylogenetic information. Systematic Zoology 40: 257–270.

Hughes, C. R., and D. C. Queller. 1993. Detection of highly polymorphic microsatellite loci in a species with little allozyme polymorphism. Molecular Ecology 2: 131–137.

Hughes, J. B., G. C. Daily, and P. R. Ehrlich. 1997. Population diversity: Its extent and extinction. Science 278: 689–692.

———. 2000. The loss of population diversity and why it matters. Pp. 71–83 in P. H. Raven, ed., *Nature and human society*. National Academy Press, Washington, DC.

Hughes, L. 2000. Biological consequences of global warming: Is the signal already apparent? Trends in Ecology and Evolution 15: 56–61.

Hughes, M. B., and J. C. Lucchesi. 1977. Genetic rescue of a lethal "null" activity allele of 6-phosphogluconate dehydrogenase in *Drosophila melanogaster*. Science 196: 1114–1115.

Hull, D. L. 1997. The ideal species concept—and why we can't get it. Pp. 357–380 in M. F. Claridge, H. A. Dawah, and M. R. Wilson, eds., *Species, the units of biodiversity*. Chapman and Hall, London.

Humphries, C. J., P. H. Williams, and R. I. Vane-Wright. 1995. Measuring biodiversity value for conservation. Annual Review of Ecology and Systematics 26: 93–111.

Hunter, A. F. 1991. Traits that distinguish outbreaking and nonoutbreaking Macrolepidoptera feeding on northern hardwood trees. Oikos 60: 275–282.

Huntley, B., P. M. Berry, W. Cramer, and A. McDonald. 1995. Modelling present and potential future ranges of some European higher plants using climate response surfaces. Journal of Biogeography 22: 967–1001.

Hurlbert, S. 1978. The measurement of niche overlap and some relatives. Ecology 59: 67–77.

Hurst, L. D. 1993. The incidences, mechanisms, and evolution of cytoplasmic sex-ratio disorders in animals. Biological Review Cambridge Philosophical Society 68: 121–193.

Hutchinson, G. E. 1953. On living in the biosphere. Reprinted in *The itinerant ivory tower*. Yale University Press, New Haven, CT.

———. 1965. *The ecological theater and the evolutionary play*. Yale University Press, New Haven, CT.

Hyatt, M. B. 1993. The use of sky polarization for migratory orientation by Monarch butterflies. Ph.D. dissertation, University of Pittsburgh.

Ibbotson, M. R., T. Maddess, and R. DuBois. 1991. A system of insect neurons sensitive to horizontal and vertical image motion connects the medulla and midbrain. Journal of Comparative Physiology 169: 355–367.

Ichikawa, T. 1990. Spectral sensitivities of elementary color-coded neurons in butterfly larva. Journal of Neurophysiology 64: 1861–1872.

———. 1991. Brain photoreceptors in the pupal and adult butterfly: Fate of the larval ocelli. Zoological Science 8: 471–476.

Ichikawa, T., and T. Hideki. 1982. Distribution of color receptors in the larval eyes of four species of Lepidoptera. Journal of Comparative Physiology 149: 317–324.

Ichikawa, T., and H. Tateda. 1980. Cellular patterns and spectral sensitivity of larval ocelli in the swallowtail butterfly *Papilio*. Journal of Comparative Physiology 139: 41–47.

———. 1982. Receptive field of the stemmata in the swallowtail butterfly *Papilio*. Journal of Comparative Physiology A 146: 191–199.

Igarashi, S. 1984. The classification of the Papilionidae mainly based on the morphology of their immature stages. Tyô to Ga 34: 41–96.

Ilse, D. 1928. Über den Farbensinn der Tagfalter. Zeitschrift Vergleichende Physiologie 8: 658–692.

———. 1929. Zur formwahrnehmung der tagfalter. 1. Spontane bevorzugung von formmerkmalen durch vanessen. Zeitschrift Vergleichende Physiologie 31: 537–556.

———. 1937. New observations on responses to colours in egg-laying butterflies. Nature 140: 544–546.

Ilse, D., and V. G. Vaidya. 1956. Spontaneous feeding response to colours in *Papilio demoleus* L. Proceedings of the Indian Academy of Sciences B 43: 23–31.

Ingersoll, C. A., and M. V. Wilson. 1991. Restoration plans of a western Oregon remnant prairie. Restoration Management Notes 9: 110–111.

Innes, J. L. 1991. High-altitude and high-latitude tree growth in relation to past, present and future global climate change. The Holocene 1,2: 168–173.

Intergovernmental Panel on Climate Change (IPCC). 1996. *Climate change 1995: The science of climate change.* J. T. Houghton, L. G. Meira Filho, B. A. Callander, N. Harris, A. Kattenberg, and K. Maskell, eds. Cambridge University Press, Cambridge.

Intergovernmental Panel on Climate Change (IPCC). 2001a. *Climate change 2001: The science of climate change.* J. T. Houghton, Y. Ding, D. J. Griggs, M. Noguer, P. J. van der Linden, X. Dai, K. Maskell, and C. A. Johnson, eds. IPCC Third Assessment Report. Cambridge University Press, Cambridge.

Intergovernmental Panel on Climate Change (IPCC). 2001b. *Climate change 2001: Impacts, adaptation, and vulnerability.* J. J. McCarthy, O. F. Canziani, N. A. Leary, D. J. Dokken, and K. S. White, eds. IPCC Third Assessment Report. Cambridge University Press, Cambridge.

Ishizaki, Y., and Y. Umebachi. 1990. Further studies on dopamine and N-acetyl-dopamine during the pupal stage of *Papilio xuthus* (Lepidoptera: Papilionidae). Comparative Biochemistry and Physiology B 97: 563–567.

Itoh, J., and Y. Obara. 1994. Visual stimuli eliciting mate refusal posture in the mated female of the cabbage white butterfly, *Pieris rapae crucivora* (Lepidoptera: Pieridae). Applied Entomology and Zoology 29: 377–388.

Ivlev, V. S. 1961. *Experimental ecology of the feeding of fishes.* Yale University Press, New Haven, CT.

Iwasa, Y., F. J. Odendaal, D. D. Murphy, P. R. Ehrlich., and A. E. Launer. 1983. Emergence patterns in male butterflies: A hypothesis and a test. Theoretical Population Biology 23: 363–379.

Jackson, S. M. 1980. Changes since 1900 in the distribution of butterflies in Yorkshire and elsewhere in the north of England. Entomologists' Record 105: 139–142.

———. 1983. Lepidoptera report 1975–1980. The Naturalist 108: 25–29.

Jacob, F., and J. Monod. 1961. Genetic regulatory mechanisms in the synthesis of proteins. Journal of Molecular Biology 3: 318–356.

Jacobs, M. D., and W. B. Watt. 1994. Seasonal adaptation vs. physiological constraint: Photo period, thermoregulation, and flight in *Colias* butterflies. Functional Ecology 8: 366–376.

Jaenike, J. 1986. Genetic complexity of host-selection behavior in *Drosophila*. Proceedings of the National Academy of Sciences USA 83: 2148–2151.

———. 1989. Genetics of butterfly-hostplant associations. Trends in Ecology and Evolution 4: 34–35.

———. 1990. Host specialization in phytophagous insects. Annual Review of Ecology and Systematics 21: 243–273.

Janz, N. 1998a. Ecology and evolution of butterfly host range. Ph.D. dissertation, Stockholm University.

———. 1998b. Sex-linked inheritance of host-plant specialization in a polyphagous butterfly. Proceedings of the Royal Society of London B 265: 1675–1678.

Janz, N., and S. Nylin. 1997. The role of female search behaviour in determining host plant range in plant feeding insects: A test of the information processing hypothesis. Proceedings of the Royal Society of London B 264: 701–707.

_____. 1998. Butterflies and plants: A phylogenetic study. Evolution 52: 486–502.

Janz, N., S. Nylin, and N. Wedell. 1994. Host plant utilization in the comma butterfly: Sources of variation and evolutionary implications. Oecologia 99: 132–140.

Janzen, D. H. 1971. Euglossine bees as long distance pollinators of tropical plants. Science 171: 203–205.

_____. 1986. Biogeography of an unexceptional place: What determines the saturniid and sphingid moth fauna of Santa Rosa National Park, Costa Rica, and what does it mean to conservation biology? Brenesia 25/26: 51–87.

Järemo Jonson, A. C., M. F. Land, D. C. Osorio, and D.-E. Nilsson. 1998. Relationships between pupil working range and habitat luminance in flies and butterflies. Journal of Comparative Physiology A 182: 1–9.

Jeffery, C. J., B. J. Bahnson, W. Chien, D. Ringe, and A. Petsko. 2000. Crystal structure of rabbit phosphoglucose isomerase, a glycolytic enzyme that moonlights as neuroleukin, autocrine mobility factor, and differentiation mediator. Biochemistry 39: 955–964.

Jennersten, O. 1984. Flower visitation and pollination efficiency of some north European butterflies. Oecologia 63: 80–89.

Jermiin, L. S., V. Loeschcke, V. Simonsen, and V. Malher. 1991. Electrophoretic and morphometric analyses of two sibling species pairs in _Trachyphloeus_ (Coleoptera: Curculionidae). Entomologica Scandinavica 22: 159–170.

Jermy, T. 1984. Evolution of insect/host plant relationships. American Naturalist 124: 609–630.

Jiggins, C. D., and W. O. McMillan. 1997. The genetic basis of an adaptive radiation: Warning colour in two _Heliconius_ species. Proceedings of the Royal Society of London B 264: 1167–1175.

Jiggins, C. D., W. O. McMillan, P. King, and J. Mallet. 1997a. The maintenance of species differences across a _Heliconius_ hybrid zone. Heredity 79: 495–505.

Jiggins, C. D., W. O. McMillan, and J. Mallet. 1997b. Host plant adaptation has not played a role in the recent speciation of _Heliconius himera_ and _Heliconius erato_ (Lepidoptera: Nymphalidae). Ecological Entomology 22: 361–365.

Jiggins, C. D., W. O. McMillan, W. Neukirchen, and J. Mallet. 1996. What can hybrid zones tell us about speciation? The case of _Heliconius himera_ and _Heliconius erato_ (Lepidoptera: Nymphalidae). Biological Journal of the Linnean Society 59: 221–242.

Johannesen, J., M. Veith, and A. Seitz. 1996. Population genetic structure of the butterfly _Melitaea didyma_ (Nymphalidae) along a northern distribution range border. Molecular Ecology 5: 259–267.

Johnson, J. W. 1984. The immature stages of six California _Catocala_ (Lepidoptera: Noctuidae). Journal of Research on Lepidoptera 23: 303–327.

Johnson, K. S., and J. M. Scriber. 1994. Geographic variation in plant allelochemicals of significance to insect herbivores. Pp. 7–31 in Ananthakrishnan, ed., _Functional dynamics of phytophagous insects_. Oxford and IBH, New Delhi.

Johnson, K. S., J. M. Scriber, and M. Nair. 1996. Phenyproanoids phenolics in sweetbay magnolia as chemical determinants of host use in saturniid silkmoths (_Callosamia_ spp.). Journal of Chemical Ecology 22: 1955–1969.

Johnson, M. S., and J. R. G. Turner. 1979. Absence of dosage compensation for a sex-linked enzyme in butterflies (_Heliconius_). Heredity 43: 71–77.

Johnson, S. D., and W. J. Bond. 1994. Red flowers and butterfly pollination in the fynbos of South Africa. Pp. 137–148 in M. Arianoutsou and R. H. Groves, eds.,

Plant-animal interactions in Mediterranean-type ecosystems. Kluwer Academic Publishers, Netherlands.

Johnson, S. D., H. P. Linder, and K. E. Steiner. 1998. Phylogeny and radiation of pollination systems in *Disa* (Orchidaceae). American Journal of Botany 85: 402–411.

Johnson, T. 1998. Snowpack accumulation trends in California. M.S. thesis, Bren School of Environmental Sciences, University of California at Santa Barbara.

Jones, I. L., and F. M. Hunter. 1998. Heterospecific mating preferences for a feather ornament in least auklets. Behavioral Ecology 9: 187–192.

Jones, K. N., F. J. Odendaal, and P. R. Ehrlich. 1986. Evidence against the spermatophore as paternal investment in the checkerspot butterflies (*Euphydryas:* Nymphalidae). American Midland Naturalist 116: 1–6.

Jones, M. J., and L. A. Lace. 1992. The speckled wood butterflies *Pararge xiphia* and *P. aegeria* (Satyridae) on Madeira: Distribution, territorial behaviour and possible competition. Biological Journal of the Linnean Society 46: 77–89.

Jones, P., and M. Hulme. 1997. The changing temperature of "Central England." Pp. 173–196 in M. Hulme and E. Barrow, eds., *Climates of the British Isles, present, past and future.* Routledge, London.

Jones, R. E. 1977. Movement patterns and egg distribution in cabbage butterflies. Journal of Animal Ecology 46: 195–212.

Jordan, K. 1896. On mechanical selection and other problems. Novitates Zoologicae 3: 426–525.

———. 1898. Contributions to the morphology of Lepidoptera. Novitates Zoologicae 5: 374–415.

Joron, M., and J. L. B. Mallet. 1998. Diversity in mimicry: Paradox or paradigm? Trends in Ecology and Evolution 13: 461–466.

Josens, R. B., and W. M. Farina. 1997. Selective choice of sucrose solution concentration by the hovering hawkmoth *Macroglossum stellatarum.* Journal of Insect Behavior 10: 631–637.

Joyce, D. A., and A. S. Pullin. 2000. Phylogeography of the Marsh Fritillary *Euphydryas aurinia* (Lepidoptera: Nymphalidae) in the U.K. GenBank (http://www.ncbi.nlm.nih.gov).

Judson, H. F. 1996. *The eighth day of creation.* 2d ed. Cold Spring Harbor Laboratory Press, Plainview, NY.

Kacser, H., and J. A. Burns. 1973. The control of flux. Symposium Society Experimental Biology 27: 65–104.

———. 1979. Molecular democracy: Who shares the controls? Biochemical Society Transactions 7: 1149–1160.

———. 1981. The molecular basis of dominance. Genetics 97: 639–666.

Kaiser, R. 1993. *The scent of orchids: Olfactory and chemical investigations.* Elsevier, Amsterdam.

Kaisila, J. 1962. Immigration und Expansion der Lepidopteren in Finnland in den Jahren 1869–1960. Acta Entomologica Fennica, Helsinki.

Kaitala, A., and C. Wiklund. 1994. Polyandrous females forage for matings. Behavioral Ecology and Sociobiology 35: 385–388.

———. 1995. Female mate choice and mating costs in the polyandrous butterfly *Pieris napi* (Lepidoptera: Pieridae). Journal of Insect Behavior 8: 355–363.

Kapan, D. D. 1998. Divergent natural selection and Müllerian mimicry in polymorphic *Heliconius cydno* (Lepidoptera: Nymphalidae). Ph.D. dissertation, University of British Columbia.

Kareiva, P. 1985. Finding and losing plants by *Phyllotreta:* Patch size and surrounding habitat. Ecology 66: 1810–1816.

Karl, T. R., R. W. Knight, D. R. Easterling, and R. G. Quayle. 1996. Indices of climate change for the United States. Bulletin of the American Meteorological Society 77: 279–292.

Karlsson, B. 1995. Resource allocation and mating systems in butterflies. Evolution 49: 955–961.

———. 1996. Male reproductive reserves in relation to mating systems in butterflies: A comparative study. Proceedings of the Royal Society of London B 263: 187–192.

———. 1998. Nuptial gifts, resource allocation and reproductive output in a polyandrous butterfly, *Pieris napi.* Ecology 79: 2931–2940.

Karlsson, B., O. Leimar, and C. Wiklund. 1997. Unpredictable environments, nuptial gifts and the evolution of sexual size dimorphism in insects: An experiment. Proceedings of the Royal Society of London B 264: 475–479.

Karowe, D. N. 1990. Predicting host range evolution: Colonization of *Coronilla varia* by *Colias philodice* (Lepidoptera: Pieridae). Evolution 44: 1637–1647.

Kauffman, S. A. 1981. Pattern formation in the *Drosophila* embryo. Philosophical Transactions of the Royal Entomological Society of London B 295: 567–594.

Kauffman, S. A., R. M. Shymko, and K. Trabert. 1978. Control of sequential compartment formation in *Drosophila.* Science 199: 259–270.

Kayser, H. 1985. Pigments. Pp. 367–415 in G. A. Kerkut and L. I. Gilbert, eds., *Comprehensive insect physiology, biochemistry and pharmacology.* Pergamon Press, New York.

Kearney, M. S. 1982. Recent seedling establishment at timberline in Jasper National Park, Alta. Canadian Journal of Botany 60: 2283–2287.

Keese, M. C. 1996. Feeding responses of hybrids and the inheritance of host-use traits in leaf feeding beetles (Coleoptera: Chrysomelidae). Heredity 76: 36–42.

Kelber, A. 1996. Colour learning in the hawkmoth *Macroglossum stellatarum.* Journal of Experimental Biology 199: 1227–1231.

———. 1999a. Why "false" colours are seen by butterflies. Nature 402: 251.

———. 1999b. Ovipositing butterflies use a red receptor to see green. Journal of Experimental Biology 202: 2619–2630.

Kelber, A., and U. Henrique. 1999. Trichromatic colour vision in the hummingbird hawkmoth, *Macroglossum stellatarum* L. Journal of Comparative Physiology A 184: 535–541.

Kelber, A., and M. Pfaff. 1997. Spontaneous and learned preferences for visual flower features in a diurnal hawkmoth. Israel Journal of Plant Sciences 45: 235–245.

———. 1999. True color vision in the orchard butterfly, *Papilio aegeus. Naturwissenschaften* 86: 221–224.

Kemp, D., and C. Wiklund. 2001. Fighting without weaponry: A review of male-male contest competition in butterflies. Behavioral Ecology Sociobiology 49: 429–442.

Kerner von Marilaum, A. 1895. *The natural history of plants: Their forms, growth, reproduction and distribution.* Blackie and Son, London.

Kerr, J. T. 1997. Species richness, endemism, and the choice of areas for conservation. Conservation Biology 11: 1094–1100.

Keyghobadi, N., J. Roland, and C. Strobeck. 1999. Influence of landscape on the population genetic structure of the alpine butterfly *Parnassius smintheus* (Papilionidae). Molecular Ecology 8: 1481–1495.

Keys, D. N., D. L. Lewis, J. E. Selegue, B. J. Pearson, L. V. Goodrich, R. L. Johnson, J. Gates, M. P. Johnson, and S. B. Carroll. 1999. Recruitment of a hedgehog regulatory circuit in butterfly eyespot evolution. Science 283: 532–534.

Kindvall, O. 1995. The impact of extreme weather on habitat preference and survival in a metapopulation of the bush cricket *Metrioptera bicolor* in Sweden. Biological Conservation 73: 51–58.

Kingsolver, J. G. 1983a. Thermoregulation and flight in *Colias* butterflies: Elevational patterns and mechanistic limitations. Ecology 64: 534–545.

_____. 1983b. Ecological significance of flight activity in *Colias* butterflies: Implications for reproductive strategy and population structure. Ecology 64: 546–551.

_____. 1985. Thermoregulatory significance of wing melanization in *Pieris* butterflies (Lepidoptera: Pieridae): Physics, posture, and pattern. Oecologia 66: 546–553.

_____. 1987a. Evolution and coadaptation of thermoregulatory behavior and wing pigmentation pattern in pierid butterflies. Evolution 41: 472–490.

_____. 1987b. Predation, thermoregulation, and wing color in pierid butterflies. Oecologia 73: 301–306.

_____. 1995a. Viability selection on seasonally polyphenic traits: Wing melanin pattern in western white butterflies. Evolution 49: 932–941.

_____. 1995b. Fitness consequences of seasonal polyphenism in western white butterflies. Evolution 49: 942–954.

_____. 1996. Experimental manipulation of wing pigment pattern and survival in western white butterflies. American Naturalist 147: 296–306.

Kingsolver, J. G., and T. L. Daniel. 1979. On the mechanics and energetics of nectar feeding in butterflies. Journal of Theoretical Biology 76: 167–179.

Kingsolver, J. G., and S. G. Smith. 1995. Estimating selection on quantitative traits using capture-recapture data. Evolution 49: 384–388.

Kingsolver, J. G., and W. B. Watt. 1983. Thermoregulatory strategies in *Colias* butterflies: Thermal stress and the limits to adaptation in temporally varying environments. American Naturalist 121: 32–55.

_____. 1984. Mechanistic constraints and optimality models: Thermoregulatory strategies in *Colias* butterflies. Ecology 65: 1835–1839.

Kingsolver, J. G., and D. C. Wiernasz. 1987. Dissecting correlated characters: Adaptive aspects of phenotypic covariation in melanization pattern of *Pieris* butterflies. Evolution 41: 491–503.

_____. 1991a. Development, function, and the quantitative genetics of wing melanin pattern in *Pieris* butterflies. Evolution 45: 1480–1492.

_____. 1991b. Seasonal polyphenism in wing-melanin pattern and thermoregulatory pattern in *Pieris* butterflies. American Naturalist 137: 816–830.

Kinoshita, M., M. Sato, and K. Arikawa. 1997. Spectral receptors of nymphalid butterflies. Naturwissenschaften 84: 199–201.

Kinoshita, M., N. Shimada, and K. Arikawa. 1999. Colour vision of foraging swallowtail butterfly, *Papilio xuthus*. Journal of Experimental Biology 202: 95–102.

Kirby, W. F. 1871. *A synonymic catalogue of diurnal Lepidoptera*. John Van Voorst, London.

Kirkpatrick, J. B. 1983. An iterative method for establishing priorities for the selection of nature reserves: An example from Tasmania. Biological Conservation 25: 127–134.

Kislev, M. E., Z. Kraviz, and J. Lorch. 1972. A study of hawkmoth pollination by a palynological analysis of the proboscis. Israel Journal of Botany 21: 57–75.

Kitamoto, J., K. Ozaki, and K. Arikawa. 2000. Ultraviolet and violet receptors express identical mRNA encoding an ultraviolet-absorbing opsin: Identification and histological localization of two mRNAs encoding short-wavelength-absorbing opsins in the retina of the butterfly *Papilio xuthus*. Journal of Experimental Biology 203: 2887–2894.

Kitamoto, J., K. Sakamoto, K. Ozaki, Y. Mishina, and K. Arikawa. 1998. Two visual pigments in a single photoreceptor cell: Identification and histological localization of three mRNAs encoding visual pigment opsins in the retina of the the butterfly *Papilio xuthus*. Journal of Experimental Biology 201: 1255–1261.

Kitching, I. J. 1984. The use of larval chaetotaxy in butterfly systematics, with special reference to the Danaini (Lepidoptera: Nymphalidae). Systematic Entomology 9: 49–61.

―――. 1985. Early stages and the classification of the milkweed butterflies (Lepidoptera: Danainae). Zoological Journal of the Linnean Society 85: 1–97.

Kitching, R. L. 1983. Myrmecophilous organs of the larvae and pupa of the lycaenid butterfly *Jalmenus evagoras* (Donovan). Journal of Natural History 17: 471–481.

Kitching, R. L., and B. Luke. 1985. The myrmecophilous organs of the larvae of some British Lycaenidae (Lepidoptera): A comparative study. Journal of Natural History 19: 259–276.

Klots, A. B. 1933. A generic revision of the Pieridae (Lepidoptera). Entomologica Americana 12: 139–242.

―――. 1951. *A field guide to the butterflies of North America, east of the Great Plains*. Houghton Mifflin, Boston.

Kluge, A. G. 1989. A concern for evidence and a phylogenetic hypothesis on relationships among *Epicrates* (Boidae, Serpentes). Systematic Zooloogy 38: 7–25.

―――. 1998. Total evidence or taxonomic congruence: Cladistics or consensus classification. Cladistics 14: 151–158.

Knoll, F. von. 1925. Lichtsinn und blütenbesuch des falters von *Deilephila livornica*. Zeitschrift Vergleichende Physiologie 2: 329–380.

Knudsen, J. T., and L. Tollsten. 1993. Trends in floral scent chemistry in pollination syndromes: Floral scent composition in moth-pollinated taxa. Botanical Journal of the Linnean Society 113: 263–284.

Knudsen, J. T., L. Tollsten, and L. G. Bergström. 1993. Floral scents—a check-list of volatile compounds isolated by head-space techniques. Phytochemistry 33: 253–280.

Knuth, P. 1898–1905. *Handbuch der blütenbiologie* 1–3. Berlag von Wilhelm Engelmann, Leipzig.

Koch, P. B. 1991. Precursors of pattern specific ommatin in red wing scales of the polyphenic butterfly *Araschnia levana* L.: Haemolymph tryptophan and 3-hydroxykynurenine. Insect Biochemistry 21: 785–794.

―――. 1993. Production of [14 C]-Labeled 3-Hydroxy-L-Kynurenine in a butterfly, *Heliconius charitonia* L., and precursor studies in butterfly wing ommatins. Pigment Cell Research 6: 85–90.

―――. 1994. Wings of the butterfly *Precis coenia* synthesize dopamine melanin by selective activity of dopadecarboxylase. Naturwissenschaften 81: 36–38.

―――. 1995. Colour pattern specific melanin synthesis is controlled by ecdysteroids via dopa decarboxylase in wings of *Precis coenia* (Lepidoptera: Nymphalidae). European Journal of Entomology 92: 161–167.

Koch, P. B., P. M. Brakefield, and F. Kesbeke. 1996. Ecydsteroids control eyespot size and wing color pattern in the polyphenic butterfly *Bicyclus anynana* (Lepidoptera: Satyridae). Journal of Insect Physiology 42: 223–230.

Koch, P. B., and N. Kaufmann. 1995. Pattern specific melanin synthesis and DOPA decarboxylase activity in a butterfly wing of *Precis coenia* Hubner. Insect Biochemistry and Molecular Biology 25: 73–82.

Koch, P. B., D. N. Keys, T. Rocheleau, K. Aronstein, M. Blackburn, S. B. Carroll, and R. H. ffrench-Constant. 1998. Regulation of Dopa decarboxylase expression during color pattern formation in wild-type and melanic tiger swallowtails. Development 125: 2303–2313.

Kohane, M. J., and W. B. Watt. 1999. Flight-muscle adenylate pool responses to flight demands and thermal constraints in individual *Colias* (Lepidoptera, Pieridae). Journal of Experimental Biology 202: 3145–3154.

Kolb, G. 1977. The structure of the eye of *Pieris brassicae* L. (Lepidoptera). Zoomorphology 87: 123–146.

———. 1986. Retinal structure in the dorsal rim and large dorsal area of the eye of *Aglais urticae* (Lepidoptera). Zoomorphology 106: 244–246.

Kolb, G., and C. Scherer. 1982. Experiments on wavelength specific behavior of *Pieris brassicae* L. during drumming and egg laying. Journal of Comparative Physiology 149: 325–332.

Koojiman, S. A. L. M., N. van der Hoeven, and D. C. van der Werf. 1989. Population consequences of a physiological model for individuals. Functional Ecology 3: 325–336.

Kremen, C. 1992. Assessing the indicator properties of species assemblages for natural areas monitoring. Ecological Applications 2: 203–217.

———. 1994. Biological inventory using target taxa: A case study of the butterflies of Madagascar. Ecological Applications 4: 407–422.

Kremen, C., R. K. Colwell, T. L. Erwin, D. D. Murphy, R. F. Noss, and M. A. Sanjayan. 1993. Terrestrial arthropod assemblages: Their use in conservation planning. Conservation Biology 7: 796–808.

Kremen, C., D. Lees, V. Razafimahatratra, and H. Raharitsimba. 2001. Biodiversity surveys in Madagascar rain forest: Using butterfly indicators to evaluate the design of a new national park. Pp. 400–428 in W. Weber, A. Vedder, H. S. Morland, L. White, and T. Hart, eds., *African rain forest ecology and conservation*. Yale University Press, New Haven, CT.

Kremen, C., J. Niles, M. Dalton, G. Daily, P. Ehrlich, J. Fay, D. Grewal, and R. Guillery. 2000. Economic incentives for rain forest conservation across scales. Science 288: 1828–1832.

Kremen, C., J. Rakotomalala, V. Razafimahatratra, O. Rakotobe, P. Guillery, A. Zakandraina, and Jaomanana. 1995. *Proposition des limites du Parc National Masoala*. CARE International, Wildlife Conservation Society, and Peregrine Fund, Antananarivo, Madagascar.

Kremen, C., I. Raymond, and K. Lance. 1998. An interdisciplinary tool for monitoring conservation impacts in Madagascar. Conservation Biology 12: 549–563.

Kremen, C., I. Raymond, K. Lance, and A. Weiss. 1999a. Monitoring natural resource use on the Masoala Peninsula, Madagascar: A tool for managing integrated conservation and development projects. Pp. 63–84 in K. Saterson, R. Margoulis, and N. Salafsky, eds., *Measuring conservation impacts: An interdisciplinary approach to project monitoring and evaluation*. Biodiversity Support Program, Washington, DC.

Kremen, C., V. Razafimahatratra, R. P. Guillery, J. Rakotomalala, A. Weiss, and J. Ratsisompatrarivo. 1999b. Designing the Masoala National Park in Madagascar using biological and socio-economic data. Conservation Biology 13: 1055–1068.

Kristensen, N. P. 1976. Remarks on the family-level phylogeny of butterflies (Lepidoptera: Rhopalocera). Zeitschrift für Zoologische Systematik und Evolutionforschung 14: 25–33.

——— . 1981. Phylogeny of insect orders. Annual Review of Entomology 26: 135–157.

Kristensen, N. P., and A. W. Skalski. 1999. Phylogeny and palaeontology. Pp. 7–25 in N. P. Kristensen, ed., *Handbook of zoology* 4. De Gruyter, Berlin.

Kruesi, B. 1981. Phenological methods in permanent plot research. Veroeffentlichungen. Geobotanisches Institute Ruebel, Zurich 74: 1–68.

Kugler, H. 1971. Zur bestäubung grossblumiger *Datura* arten. Flora 160: 511–517.

Kuhn, A., and M. V. Engelhardt. 1933. Uber die determination des symmetriesystems auf dem vorderflugel von *Ephestia kuhniella*. Wilhelm Roux' Archiv für Entwicklungs Mechanik der Organismen 130: 660–703.

Kulfan, J. 1990. Sezónna dynamika spoločenstiev heliofilných motýl'ovna troch lokalitách zapadného slovenska (Lepidoptera). Ent. Problémy (Bratislava) 20: 177–210.

Kullman, L. 1995. Holocene tree-limit and climate history from the Scandes mountains, Sweden. Ecology 76: 2490–2502.

Kuussaari, M. 1998. Biology of the Glanville fritillary butterfly (*Melitaea cinxia*). Ph.D. dissertation, University of Helsinki.

Kuussaari, M., M. Nieminen, and I. Hanski. 1996. An experimental study of migration in the butterfly *Melitaea cinxia*. Journal of Animal Ecology 65: 791–801.

Kuussaari, M., M. Nieminen, J. Pöyry and I. Hanski. 1995. Life history and distribution of the Glanville fritillary *Melitaea cinxia* (Nymphalidae) in Finland. Baptria 20: 167–180.

Kuussaari, M., I. Saccheri, M. Camara, and I. Hanski. 1998. Demonstration of the Allee effect in small populations of an endangered butterfly. Oikos 82: 384–392.

Kuussaari, M., M. Singer, and I. Hanski. 2000. Local specialization and landscape-level influence of host use in a herbivorous insect. Ecology 81: 2177–2187.

Kuykendall, K., and T. Kaye. 1993. *Lupinus sulphureus* spp. *kincaidii* and reproductive studies. Report to the Bureau of Land Management and the Oregon Department of Agriculture, Salem, OR.

Kuznetzov, V. I., and A. A. Stekol'nikov. 1998. Evolution of the skeleton and muscles of male genitalia in the families Riodinidae and Lycaenidae (Lepidoptera). Entomol. Obozrenie 77: 443–461. [In Russian.]

——— . 2001. *New approaches to the system of Lepidoptera of world fauna (on the base of the functional morphology of abdomen)*. Proceedings of the Zoological Institute, vol. 282. Russian Academy of Sciences, St. Petersburg.

Labate, J., and W. F. Eanes. 1992. Direct measurement of *in vivo* flux differences between electrophoretic variants of G6PD from *Drosophila melanogaster*. Genetics 132: 783–787.

Labhart, T., and D.-E. Nilsson. 1995. The dorsal eye of the dragonfly *Sympetrum:* Specializations for prey detection against the blue sky. Journal of Comparative Physiology A 176: 437–453.

Labine, P. A. 1966. The population biology of the butterfly *Euphydryas editha*. IV. Sperm precedence—a preliminary report. Evolution 20: 580–586.

Labitte, A. 1919. Observations sur *Rhodocera rhamni*. Bulletin du Museum d'Histoire Naturelle 25: 624–625.

Laland, K. N., F. J. Odling-Smee, and M. W. Feldman. 1999. Evolutionary consequences of niche construction and their implications for ecology. Proceedings of the National Academy of Sciences USA 96: 10242–10247.

Lamas, G. 1979. *Paititia neglecta,* gen. n., sp. n. from Peru (Nymphalidae, Ithomiinae). Journal of the Lepidopterists' Society 33: 1–5.

Lammers, T. 1989. Revision of *Brighamia* (Campanulaceae: Lobelioideae): A caudiciform succulent endemic to the Hawaiian Islands. Systematic Botany 14: 133–138.

LaMunyon, C. W., and T. Eisner. 1993a. Postcopulatory sexual selection in an arctiid moth (*Utetheisa ornatrix*). Proceedings of the National Academy of Sciences USA 90: 4689–4692.

———. 1993b. Spermatophore size as determinant of paternity in an arctiid moth (*Utetheisa ornatrix*). Proceedings of the National Academy of Sciences USA 91: 7081–7084.

Lance, K., C. Kremen, and I. Raymond. 1995. Annexe 1. Reconnaissance préliminaire de la peninsule de Masoala: Utilisation de la terre et des resources. in C. Kremen, ed., *Proposition des limites du Parc National Masoala*. Care International Madagascar, Wildlife Conservation Society, and The Peregrine Fund., Antananarivo.

Land, M. F. 1989. Variations in the structure and design of compound eyes. Pp. 90–111 in D. G. Stavenga and R. C. Hardie, eds., *Facets of vision*. Springer Verlag, Berlin.

———. 1990. The design of compound eyes. Pp. 55–65 in C. Blakemore, ed., *Vision: Coding and efficiency*. Cambridge University Press, Cambridge.

———. 1997. Visual acuity in insects. Annual Review of Entomology 42: 147–177.

Land, M. F., and H. Eckert. 1985. Maps of the acute zones of fly eyes. Journal of Comparative Physiology 156: 525–538.

Lande, R. 1993. Risks of population extinction from demographic and environmental stochasticity and random catastrophes. American Naturalist 142: 911–927.

Lande, R., and S. J. Arnold. 1983. The measurement of selection on correlated characters. Evolution 37: 1210–1216.

Lande, R., and S. H. Orzack. 1988. Extinction dynamics of age-structured populations in a fluctuating environment. Proceedings of the National Academy of Sciences USA 85: 7418–7421.

Landry, B., J. A. Powell, and F. A. H. Sperling. 1999. Systematics of the *Argyrotaenia franciscana* (Lepidoptera: Tortricidae) species group: Evidence from mitochondrial DNA. Annals of the Entomological Society of America 92: 40–46.

Langston, R. L. 1974. Extended flight periods of coastal and dune butterflies in California. Journal of Research on Lepidoptera 13: 83–89.

Larcher, W. 1995. *Physiological plant ecology*. 3d ed. Springer-Verlag, Berlin/Heidelberg.

Larsson, S., and B. Ekbom. 1995. Oviposition mistakes in herbivorous insects: Confusion or a step towards a new host plant? Oikos 72: 155–160.

Lauder, G. V. 1994. Homology and the mechanisms of development. Pp. 151–196 in B. K. Hall, ed., *Homology: The hierarchical basis of comparative biology*. Academic Press, New York.

Lauge, G. 1985. Sex determination: Genetic and epigenetic factors. Pp. 295–318 in G. A. Kerkut and L. I. Gilbert, eds., *Comprehensive insect physiology, biochemistry and pharmacology.* Pergammon Press, Oxford.

Lawrence, P. A., and G. Morata. 1976. Compartments in the wing of *Drosophila*: A study of the engrailed gene. Developmental Biology 50: 321–337.

Lawton, J. H., D. E. Bignell, B. Bolton, G. F. Bloemers, P. Eggleton, P. M. Hammond, M. Hodde, R. D. Holt, T. B. Larsen, N. A. Mawdsley, N. E. Stork. 1998. Biodiversity inventories, indicator taxa and effects of habitat modification in tropical forest. Nature 391: 72–76.

Lawton, J. H., and R. M. May, eds. 1995. *Extinction rates.* Oxford University Press, Oxford.

Lawton, R. O., L. D. Alexander, W. N. Setzer, and K. G. Byler. 1993. Floral essential oil of *Guettarda poasana* inhibits yeast growth. Biotropica 25: 483–486.

Layberry, R. A., P. W. Hall, and J. D. Lafontaine. 1998. *The butterflies of Canada.* University of Toronto Press, Toronto.

Leather, S. R. 1984. The effect of adult feeding on the fecundity, weight loss and survival of the pine beauty moth, *Panolis flammea* (D&S). Oecologia 65: 70–74.

Lederhouse, R. C. 1993. Territoriality along flyways as mate-locating behavior in male *Limenitis arthemis* (Nymphalidae). Journal of the Lepidopterists' Society 47: 22–31.

———. 1995. Comparative mating behavior and sexual selection in North American swallowtail butterflies. Pp. 117–131 in J. M. Scriber, Y. Tsubaki, and R. C. Lederhouse, eds., *Swallowtail butterflies: Their ecology and evolutionary biology.* Scientific Publishers, Gainesville, FL.

Lederhouse, R. C., M. P. Ayres, J. K. Nitao, and J. M. Scriber. 1992a. Differential use of lauraceous hosts by swallowtail butterflies, *Papilio palamedes* and *P. troilus* (Papilionidae). Oikos 63: 244–252.

Lederhouse, R. C., M. P. Ayres, and J. M. Scriber. 1989. Evaluation of spermatophore counts in studying mating systems of Lepidoptera. Journal of the Lepidopterists' Society 43: 93–101.

———. 1990. Adult nutrition affects male virility in *Papilio glaucus.* Functional Ecology 4: 743–751.

———. 1995. Physiological and behavioral adaptations to variable thermal environments in North American swallowtail butterflies. Pp. 71–81 in J. M. Scriber, Y. Tsubaki, and R. C. Lederhouse, eds., *Swallowtail butterflies: Their ecology and evolutionary biology.* Scientific Publishers, Gainesville, FL.

Lederhouse, R. C., S. G. Codella, D. W. Grossmueller, and A. S. Maccarone. 1992b. Host plant-based territitoriality in the white peacock butterfly *Anartia jatrophae* (Lepidoptera: Nymphalidae). Journal of Insect Behavior 5: 721–728.

Lederhouse, R. C., and J. M. Scriber. 1987. Ecological significance of a post-mating decline in egg viability in the tiger swallowtail. Journal of the Lepidopterists' Society 41: 83–93.

———. 1996. Intrasexual selection constrains the evolution of the dorsal color pattern of male black swallowtail butterflies, *Papilio polyxenes.* Evolution 50: 717–722.

Lee, C. S., B. A. McCool, J. L. Moore, D. M. Hillis, and L. E. Gilbert. 1992. Phylogenic study of heliconiine butterflies based on morphology and restriction analysis of ribosomal genes. Zoological Journal of the Linnean Society 106: 17–31.

Leemans, R., and W. Cramer. 1991. Research Report RR-91-18, International Institute for Applied Systems Analysis (IIASA). Laxenburg, Austria.

Lees, D. C. 1997. Systematics and biogeography of Madagascar mycalesine butterflies and applications to conservation evaluation. Ph.D. dissertation, University of London.

Lees, D. C., C. Kremen, and L. Andriamampianiana. 1999. A null model for species richness gradients: Bounded range overlap of butterflies and other rainforest endemics in Madagascar. Biological Journal of the Linnean Society 67: 529–584.

Lees, E. 1962. Factors determining the distribution of the speckled wood butterfly (*Pararge aegeria* [L.]) in Gt. Britain. Entomologists' Gazette 13: 101–113.

Legendre, P., and A. Vaudor. 1991. The R Package: Multidimensional analysis, spatial analysis. Version 3.0, Universitè de Montrèal, Montrèal.

Lei, G., and M. D. Camara. 1999. Behavior of a specialist parasitoid, *Cotesia melitaearum:* From individual behavior to metapopulation processes. Ecological Entomology 24: 59–72.

Lei, G., and I. Hanski. 1997. Metapopulation structure of *Cotesia melitaearum,* a specialist parasitoid of the butterfly *Melitaea cinxia*. Oikos 78: 91–100.

———. 1998. Spatial dynamics of two competing specialist parasitoids in a host metapopulation. Journal of Animal Ecology 67: 422–433.

Lei, G., V. Vikberg, M. Nieminen, and M. Kuussaari. 1997. The parasitoid complex attacking Finnish populations of the Glanville fritillary *Melitaea cinxia* (Lep: Nymphalidae), an endangered butterfly. Journal of Natural History 31: 635–648.

Leigh, E. G. 1981. The average lifetime of a population in a varying environment. Journal of Theoretical Biology 90: 231–239.

Leimar, O., B. Karlsson, and C. Wiklund. 1994. Unpredictable food and sexual size dimorphism in insects. Proceedings of the Royal Society of London B 258: 121–125.

Lensink, R. 1997. Range expansion of raptors in Britain and the Netherlands since the 1960s: Testing an individual-based diffusion model. Journal of Animal Ecology 66: 811–826.

Leopold, A. 1949. *A Sand County almanac and sketches here and there.* Oxford University Press, London.

Lerner, A. 2000. The impact of cattle grazing on pollinators of generalist pollinated plants. Undergraduate honors thesis, Program in Human Biology, Stanford University.

Levene, H. 1953. Genetic equilibrium when more than one niche is available. American Naturalist 87: 331–333.

Levin, D. A. 1978. Pollinator behaviour and the breeding structure of plant populations. Pp. 133–150, in A. J. Richards, ed., *The pollination of flowers by insects.* Academic Press, New York.

Levin, D. A., and D. E. Berube. 1972. *Phlox* and *Colias:* The efficiency of a pollination system. Evolution 26: 242–250.

Levin, D. A., J. Francisco-Ortega, and R. K. Jensen. 1996. Hybridization and the extinction of rare plant species. Conservation Biology 10: 10–16.

Levin, R. A., R. A. Raguso, and L. A. McDade. 2001. Fragrance chemistry and pollinator affinities in Nyctaginaceae. Phytochemistry 58: 429–440.

Levins, R. 1965. Genetic consequences of natural selection. Pp. 371–387 in T. H. Waterman and H. J. Morowitz, eds., *Theoretical and mathematical biology.* Blaisdell, New York.

———. 1968. *Evolution in changing environments.* Princeton University Press, Princeton, NJ.

——— . 1969. Some demographic and genetic consequences of environmental heterogeneity for biological control. Bulletin of the Entomological Society of America 15: 237–240.

——— . 1970. Extinction. Pp. 77–107 in M. Gerstenhaber, ed., *Lectures on mathematics in the life sciences*. Vol. 2. American Mathematical Society, Providence, RI.

Lewis, A. 1986. Memory constraints and flower choice in butterflies. Science 232: 863–865.

——— . 1993. Learning and the evolution of resources: Pollinators and flower morphology. Pp. 219–242 in D. Papaj and A. Lewis, eds., *Insect learning: Ecological and evolutionary perspectives*. Chapman and Hall, New York.

Lewis, O. T., C. D. Thomas, J. K. Hill, M. I. Brookes, T. P. R. Crane, Y. A. Graneau, J. L. B. Mallet, and O. C. Rose. 1997. Three ways of assessing metapopulation structure in the butterfly *Plebejus argus*. Ecological Entomology 22: 283–293.

Lewontin, R. C. 1983. Gene, organism and environment. Pp. 273–285 in D. S. Bendall, ed., *Evolution from molecules to men*. Cambridge University Press, Cambridge.

Lewontin, R. C., and L. C. Birch. 1966. Hybridization as a new source of variation for adaptation to new environments. Evolution 20: 315–336.

Lieth, H. 1974. *Phenology and seasonality modeling*. Springer, New York.

Linares, M. 1989. Adaptive microevolution through hybridization and biotic destruction in the Neotropics. Ph.D. dissertation, University of Texas, Austin.

——— . 1996. The genetics of the mimetic coloration in the butterfly *Heliconius cydno weymeri*. Journal of Heredity 87: 142–149.

——— . 1997a. The ghost of mimicry past: Laboratory reconstitution of an extinct butterfly "race." Heredity 78: 628–635.

——— . 1997b. Origin of Neotropical mimetic biodiversity from a three-way hybrid zone of Heliconius butterflies. Pp. 93–108 in H. Ulrich, ed., *Tropical biodiversity and systematics*. Proceedings of the International Symposium on Biodiversity and Systematics.

Lindroth, R. L., J. M. Scriber, and M. T. S. Hsia. 1986. Differential responses of tiger swallowtail subspecies to secondary metabolites from tulip tree and quaking aspen leaves. Oecologia 70: 13–19.

——— . 1988. Chemical ecology of the tiger swallowtail. Ecology 69: 814–822.

Lingren, P. D., G. L. Greene, D. R. Davis, A. H. Baumhover, and T. J. Henneberry. 1977. Nocturnal behavior of four lepidopteran pests that attack tobacco and other crops. Annals of the Entomological Society of America 70: 161–167.

Linhart, Y. B., and J. A. Mendenhall. 1977. Pollen dispersal by hawkmoths in a *Lindenia rivalis* population in Belize. Biotropica 9: 143.

Lloyd, A. H., and L. J. Graumlich. 1997. Holocene dynamics of treeline forests in the Sierra Nevada. Ecology 78: 1199–1210.

Long, J. C., R. C. Williams, and M. Urbanek. 1995. An E-M algorithm and testing strategy for multiple-locus haplotypes. American Journal Human Genetics 56: 799–810.

Lorkovic, Z. 1994. *Leptidea reali* Reissinger 1989 (= *lorkovicii* Real 1988), a new European species (Lepid., Pieridae). Nat. Croat. 2: 1–26.

Løvtrup, S. 1987. On species and other taxa. Cladistics 3: 157–177.

Luebke, H. J., J. M. Scriber, and B. S. Yandell. 1988. Use of multivariate discriminant analysis of male wing morphometrics to delineate a hybrid zone for *Papilio glaucus glaucus* and *P. g. canadensis* in Wisconsin. American Midland Naturatlist 119: 366–379.

Luis, M. A., and J. Llorente B. 1990. Mariposas en el Valle de México: Introducción e historia. I. Distribución local y estacional de los Papilionoidea de la Cañada de los Dinamos, Magdalena Contreras, D.F., México. Folia Entomologia Mexicana 78: 95–198.

Luis, M. A., I. Vargas F., and J. Llorente B. 1991. Lepidópterofauna de Oaxaca I. Distribución y fenología de los Papilionoidea de la Sierra de Juarez. Publicaciones Especiales del Museo del Zoologia UNAM, 3: 1–119.

Lushai, G., D. A. S. Smith, J. A. Allen, D. Goulson, and N. Maclean. 2001. The origin and evolution of Monarch and Queen butterflies, with special references to the African Queen, *Danaus chrysippus* (L.). GenBank (http://www.ncbi.nlm.nih.gov).

MacArthur, R. H., and E. O. Wilson. 1967. *The theory of island biogeography.* Princeton University Press, Princeton, NJ.

Mackay, D. A. 1985. Conspecific host discrimination by ovipositing *Euphydryas editha* butterflies: Its nature and its consequences for offspring survivorship. Researches in Population Ecology (Kyoto) 27: 87–98.

———. 1995. Prealighting search behavior and host plant selection by ovipositing *Euphydryas editha* butterflies. Ecology 66: 142–151.

Maddess, T., R. A. Dubois, and M. R. Ibbotson. 1991. Response properties and adaptation of neurons sensitive to image motion in the butterfly *Papilio aegeus.* Journal of Experimental Biology 161: 171–199.

Maddison, W. P. 1990. A method for testing correlated evolution of two binary characters: Are gains and losses concentrated on certain branches of a phylogenetic tree? Evolution 44: 539–557.

Magnus, D. B. E. 1950. Beobachtungen zur Balz und Eiablage des Kaisersmantels *Argynnis paphia.* Zeitschrift Tierpsychologie 7: 435–449.

———. 1956. Experimental analysis of some "overoptimal" sign stimuli in the mating behavior of the fritillary butterfly *Argynnis paphia* L. (Lep., Nymph.). Proceedings Xth International Entomology Congress (Montreal) 2: 405–418.

Magurran, A. E. 1988. *Ecological diversity and its measurement.* Princeton University Press, Princeton, NJ.

Makita, H., T. Shinkawa, K. Kondo, and T. Nakazawa. 2001. Tribe Graphiini mitochondrial ND5 genes. GenBank (http://www.ncbi.nlm.nih.gov).

Makita, H., T. Shinkawa, and T. Nakazawa. 1999. GenBank (http://www.ncbi.nlm.nih.gov).

Makita, H., T. Shinkawa, K. Ohta, A. Kondo, and T. Nakazawa. 2000. Phylogeny of Luehdorfia butterflies inferred from mitochondrial ND5 gene sequences. Entomological Science 3: 321–329.

Malicky, H. 1970. New aspects on the association between lycaenid larvae (Lycaenidae) and ants (Formicidae, Hymenoptera). Journal of the Lepidopterists' Society 24: 190–202.

Mallet, J. 1986a. Gregarious roosting and home range in *Heliconius* butterflies. National Geographic Research 2: 198–215.

———. 1986b. Hybrid zones of *Heliconius* butterflies in Panama and the stability and movement of warning colour clines. Heredity 56: 191–202.

———. 1993. Speciation, raciation, and color pattern evolution in *Heliconius* butterflies: Evidence from hybrid zones. Pp. 226–260 in R. Harrison, ed., *Hybrid zones and the evolutionary process.* Oxford University Press, Oxford.

————. 1995. A species definition for the modern synthesis. Trends in Ecology and Evolution 10: 294–300.

————. 1996a. Reply to Gittenberger. Trends in Ecology and Evolution 10: 490–491.

————. 1996b. The genetics of biological diversity: From varieties to species. Pp. 13–53 in K. J. Gaston, ed., *Biodiversity: A biology of numbers and difference.* Blackwell, Oxford.

Mallet, J., and N. H. Barton. 1989. Strong natural selection in a warning color hybrid zone. Evolution 43: 421–431.

Mallet, J., N. H. Barton, G. Lamas, J. Santisteban, M. Muedas, and H. Eeley. 1990. Estimates of selection and gene flow from measures of cline width and linkage disequilibrium in *Heliconius* hybrid zones. Genetics 124: 921–936.

Mallet, J., and L. E. Gilbert. 1995. Why are there so many mimicry rings? Correlations between habitat, behavior and mimicry in *Heliconius* butterflies. Biological Journal of the Linnean Society 55: 159–180.

Mallet, J., and M. Joron. 1999. Evolution of diversity in warning color and mimicry: Polymorphisms, shifting balance, and speciation. Annual Review of Ecology and Systematics 30: 201–233.

Mallet, J., J. T. Longino, D. Murawski, A. Murawski, and A. S. de Gamboa. 1987. Handling effects in *Heliconius:* Where do all the butterflies go? Journal of Animal Ecology 56: 377–386.

Mallet, J., W. O. McMillan, and C. D. Jiggins. 1998a. Estimating the mating behavior of a pair of hybridizing *Heliconius* species in the wild. Evolution 52: 503–510.

————. 1998b. Mimicry and warning color at the boundary between races and species. Pp. 390–403 in S. Berlocher and D. Howard, eds., *Endless forms: Species and speciation.* Oxford University Press, Oxford.

Mallet, J., W. Neukirchen, and M. Linares. 1999. The nature of species: Hybridization in *Heliconius* butterflies. Available by Internet pre-publication. http://abacus.gene.ucl.ac.uk/jim/Hyb/helichyb.html.

Mangel, M., and C. Tier. 1993. Dynamics of metapopulations with demographic stochasticity and environmental catastrophes. Theoretical Population Biology 44: 1–31.

————. 1994. Four facts every conservation biologist should know about persistence. Ecology 75: 607–614.

Mantel, N. 1967. The detection of disease clustering and a generalized regression approach. Cancer Research 27: 209–220.

Marck, C. 1990. DNA-Strider 1.2. Service de biochimie et de génétique moléculaire, Gif sur Yvette, France.

Marden, J. H., and P. Chai. 1991. Aerial predation and butterfly design: How palatability, mimicry and the need for evasive flight constrain mass allocation. American Naturalist 138: 15–36.

Margules, C. R., A. O. Nicholls, and R. L. Pressey. 1988. Selecting networks of reserves to maximize biological diversity. Biological Conservation 43: 63–76.

Margules, C. R., and R. L. Pressey. 2000. Systematic conservation planning. Nature 405: 243–253.

Margules, C. R., and R. R. Usher. 1981. Criteria used in assessing wildlife conservation potential. Biological Conservation 21: 79–109.

Markov, A. 1997. Assortative fertilization in *Drosophila.* Proceedings of the National Academy of Sciences USA 94: 7756–7760.

Marshall, L. D. 1988. Small male advantage in mating *Parapediasia teterrella* and *Ariphila plumbfimbriella*, Lepidoptera, Pyralidae. American Midland Naturalist 119: 412–419.

Martin, J. A., and D. P. Pashley. 1992. A molecular systematic analysis of butterfly family and some subfamily relationships (Lepidoptera: Papilionoidea). Annals of the Entomological Society of America 85: 127–139.

Martin, J.-F., A. Gilles, and H. Descimon. 2000. Molecular phylogeny and evolutionary patterns of the European satyrids (Lepidoptera: Satyridae) as revealed by mitochondrial gene sequences. Molecular Phylogenetics and Evolution 15: 70–82.

Martinez del Río, C., and A. Búrquez. 1986. Nectar production and temperature-dependent pollination in *Mirabilis jalapa*. Biotropica 18: 28–31.

Marttila, O., T. Haahtela, H. Aarnio, and P. Ojalainen. 1990. Suomen Päiväperhoset. Kirjayhtymä, Helsinki.

Marttila, O., and K. Saarinen. 1996. Perhostutkimus Suomessa. Etalä-Karjalan Allergia—Ja Ympäristöinstituutti. Finland.

Masters, J. C., and H. G. Spencer. 1989. Why we need a new genetic species concept. Systematic Zoology 38: 270–279.

Matic, T. 1983. Electrical inhibition in the retina of the butterfly *Papilio*. I. Four spectral types of photoreceptors. Journal of Comparative Physiology A 152: 169–182.

Matsuka, H. 2001. *Natural history of birdwing butterflies*. Matsuka Shuppan, Tokyo.

Matsumoto, K., and N. Suzuki. 1992. Effectiveness of the mating plug in *Atrophaneura alcinous* (Lepidoptera: Papilionidae). Behavioral Ecology and Sociobiology 30: 157–163.

Mattson, W. J., and J. M. Scriber. 1987. Nutritional ecology of folivores of woody plants: Nitrogen, fiber and mineral considerations. Pp. 105–146 in F. Slansky Jr., and J. G. Rodriguez, eds., *Nutritional ecology of insects, mites and spiders*. Wiley, New York.

May, P. G. 1992. Flower selection and the dynamics of lipid reserves in two nectarivorous butterflies. Ecology 73: 2181–2191.

May, R. M. 1990. Taxonomy as destiny. Nature 347: 129–130.

Maynard Smith, J. 1983. The genetics of stasis and punctuation. Annual Review of Genetics 17: 11–25.

Maynard Smith, J., and J. Haigh. 1974. The hitch-hiking effect of a favourable gene. Genetical Research 23: 23–35.

Mayr, E. 1940. Speciation phenomena in birds. American Naturalist 74: 249–278.

———. 1942. *Systematics and the origin of species from the viewpoint of a zoologist*. Columbia University Press, New York.

———. 1963. *Animal species and evolution*. Belknap Press, Cambridge, MA.

———. 1969. *Principles of systematic zoology*. McGraw-Hill, New York.

Mazel, R. 1986. Structure et evolution du peuplement d' *Euphydras aurinia* (Lepidoptera) dans le sud-ouest europeen. Vie Milieu 36: 205–225.

Mazel, R., and R. Leestmans. 1996. Relations biogéographiques, écologiques et taxinomiques entre *Leptidea sinapis* Linn, et *L. reali* Reissinger en France, Belgique et régions limitrophes (Lepidoptera: Pieridae) Linneana Belgica 8: 317–326.

McCarty, J. P. 2001. Ecological consequences of recent climate change. Conservation Biology 15: 320–331.

McCauley, E., W. W. Murdoch, R. M. Nisbet, and W. S. C. Gurney. 1990. The physiological ecology of *Daphnia:* Development of a model of growth and reproduction. Ecology 71: 703–715.

McCourt, R. M., and R. W. Hoshaw. 1990. Noncorrespondence of breeding groups, morphology and monophyletic groups in *Spirogyra* (Zygnemataceae; Chlorophyta) and the application of species concepts. Systematic Botany 15: 69–78.

McCullagh, P., and J. A. Nelder. 1989. *Generalized linear models*. 2d ed. Monographs on Statistics and Applied Probability 37. Chapman and Hall, London.

McGarrahan, E. 1997. Much-studied butterfly winks out on Stanford preserve. Science 275: 479–480.

McKechnie, S. W., P. R. Ehrlich, and R. R. White. 1975. Population genetics of *Euphydryas* butterflies I. Genetic variation and the neutrality hypothesis. Genetics 81: 571–594.

McLain, D. K., L. B. Burnette, and D. A. Deeds. 1993. Within season variation in the intensity of sexual selection on body size in the bug *Margus obscurato* (Hemiptera: Coreidae). Ethology, Ecology, Evolution 5: 75–86.

McLaughlin, J. F., J. J. Hellmann, P. R. Ehrlich, and C. L. Boggs. 2002a. The route to extinction: Population dynamics of a threatened butterfly. Oecologia 132: 538–548.

———. 2002b. Climate change hastens population extinctions. Proceedings of the National Academy of Sciences USA 99: 6070–6074.

McMillan, C. 1960. Ecotypes and community function. American Naturalist 94: 246–255.

McMillan, W. O., C. D. Jiggins, and J. Mallet. 1997. What initiates speciation in passion-vine butterflies? Proceedings of the National Academy of Sciences USA 94: 8628–8633.

McMillan, W. O., A. Monteiro, and D. D. Kapan. 2002. Development and evolution on the wing. Trends in Ecology and Evolution 17: 125–133.

Meglécz, E., K. Pecsenye, L. Peregovits, and Z. Varga. 1997. Effects of population size and habitat fragmentation on the genetic variability of *Parnassius mnemosyne* populations in NE Hungary. A. Zool. Acad. Scien. Hung. 43: 183–190.

Menzel, A., and P. Fabian. 1999. Growing season extended in Europe. Nature 397: 659.

Menzel, R., and U. Müller. 1996. Learning and memory in honeybees: From behavior to neural substrates. Annual Review of Neuroscience 19: 379–404.

Menzel, R., D. F. Ventura, H. Hertel, J. M. de Souza, and U. Greggers. 1986. Spectral sensitivity of photoreceptors in insect compound eyes: Comparison of species and methods. Journal of Comparative Physiology A 158: 165–177.

Merenlender, A., C. Kremen, M. Rakotondratsima, and A. Weiss. 1998. Monitoring impacts of natural resource extraction on lemurs on the Masoala Peninsula, Madagascar. Conservation Ecology 2 (www.consecol.org/J./vol2/iss2/art5/).

Merriam, C. H. 1894. Laws of temperature control of the geographic distributions of terrestrial animals and plants. National Geographic Magazine 6: 229–238.

Merritt, R. B. 1972. Geographic distribution and enzymatic properties of lactate dehydrogenase allozymes in the fat head minnow, *Pimephales promelas*. American Naturalist 196: 173–184.

Mielke, O. H. H., and K. S. Brown Jr. 1979. Suplemento ao "Catálogo dos Ithomiidae Americanos de Romualdo Ferreira D'Almeida (Lepidoptera)" (Nymphalidae: Ithomiinae). Universidade Federal do Paraná/CNPq, Curitiba.

Mikkola, K. 1997. Population trends of Finnish Lepidoptera during 1961–1996. Ent. Fennica 3: 121–143.

Miller, J. S. 1987. Phylogenetic studies in the Papilioninae (Lepidoptera: Papilionidae). Bulletin of the American Museum of Natural History 186: 365–512.

———. 1996. Phylogeny of the Neotropical moth tribe Josiini (Notodontidae: Dioptinae): A hidden case of Müllerian mimicry. Zoological Journal of the Linnean Society 118: 1–45.

Miller, J. S., and J. W. Wenzel. 1995. Ecological characters and phylogeny. Annual Reviews of Entomology 40: 389–415.

Miller, L. D. 1968. The higher clasification, phylogeny and zoogeography of the Satyridae (Lepidoptera). Memoirs of the American Entomological Society (24), 174 pp.

Miller, R. B. 1978. The pollination ecology of *Aquilegia elegantula* and *A. caerulea* (Ranunculaceae) in Colorado. American Journal of Botany 65: 406–414.

———. 1981. Hawkmoths and the geographic patterns of floral variation in *Aquilegia caerulea*. Evolution 35: 763–774.

Miller, W. E. 1997. Diversity and evolution of tongue length in hawkmoths (Sphingidae). Journal of the Lepidopterists' Society 51: 9–31.

Miller, W. H., and G. D. Bernard. 1968. Butterfly glow. Journal of Ultrastructure Research 24: 286–294.

Minelli, A. 1993. *Biological systematics. The state of the art*. Chapman and Hall, London.

Mitchell, A., S. Cho, J. C. Regier, C. Mitter, R. W. Poole, and M. Matthews. 1997. Phylogenetic utility of elongation factor-α in Noctuoidea (Insecta: Lepidoptera): The limits of synonymous substitution. Molecular Biology and Evolution 14: 381–390.

Mitchell, J. F. B., T. C. Johns, J. M. Gregory, and S. Tett. 1995. Climate response to increasing levels of greenhouse gases and sulphate aerosols. Nature 376: 501–504.

Mitter, C., and D. R. Brooks. 1983. Phylogenetic aspects of coevolution. Pp. 65–98 in D. J. Futuyma and M. Slatkin, eds., *Coevolution*. Sinauer Associates, Sunderland, MA.

Mitter, C., B. Farrell, and D. J. Futuyma. 1991. Phylogenetic studies of insect-plant interactions: Insights into the genesis of diversity. Trends in Ecology and Evolution 6: 290–294.

Mitter, C., B. Farrell, and B. Weigmann. 1988. The phylogenetic study of adaptive zones: Has phytophagy promoted insect diversification? American Naturalist 132: 107–128.

Mitton, J. B. 1997. *Selection in natural populations*. Oxford University Press, New York.

Mitton, J. B., and R. K. Koehn. 1975. Genetic organization and adaptive response of allozymes to ecological variables in *Fundulus heteroclitus*. Genetics 79: 97–111.

Miyake, T., R. Yamaoka, and T. Yahara. 1998. Floral scents of hawkmoth-pollinated flowers in Japan. Journal of Plant Research 111: 199–205.

Miyako, Y., K. Arikawa, and E. Eguchi. 1993. Ultrastructure of the extraocular photoreceptor in the genitalia of a butterfly, *Papilio xuthus*. Journal of Comparative Neurology 327: 458–468.

Moilanen, A., and I. Hanski. 1998. Metapopulation dynamics: Effects of habitat quality and landscape structure. Ecology 79: 2503–2515.

Molyneux, R. J., and L. F. James. 1982. Loco intoxication: Indolizidine alkaloids of spotted locoweed (*Astragalus lentiginosus*). Science 216: 190–191.

Monserud, R. A., and R. Leemans. 1992. Comparing global vegetation maps with the Kappa statistic. Ecological Modelling 62: 275–293.

Monteiro, A., P. M. Brakefield, and V. French. 1994. The evolutionary genetics and developmental basis of wing pattern variation in the butterfly *Bicyclus anynana*. Evolution 48: 1147–1157.

———. 1997a. Butterfly eyespots: The genetics and development of the color rings. Evolution 51: 1207–1216.

———. 1997b. The genetics and development of an eyespot pattern in the butterfly *Bicyclus anynana:* Response to selection for eyespot shape. Genetics 146: 287–294.

———. 1997c. The relationship between eyespot shape and wing shape in the butterfly *Bicyclus anynana:* A genetic and morphological approach. Journal of Evolutionary Biology 10: 787–802.

Monteiro, A., V. French, G. Smit, P. M. Brakefield, and J. A. J. Metz. 2001. Butterfly eyespot patterns: Evidence for specification by a morphogen diffusion gradient. Acta Biotheoretica 49: 77–88.

Monteiro, A., and N. E. Pierce. 2001. Phylogeny of *Bicyclus* (Lepidoptera: Nymphalidae) inferred from COI, COII, and EF-1α gene sequences. Molecular Phylogenetics and Evolution 18: 264–281.

Moore, S. D. 1989. Patterns of juvenile mortality within an oligophagous insect population. Ecology 70: 1726–1737.

Moore, W. S. 1977. An evaluation of narrow hybrid zones in vertebrates. Quarterly Review of Biology 2: 263–277.

Mopper, S. 1998. Local adaptation and stochastic events in an oak leafminer population. Pp139–155 in S. Mopper and S. Y. Strauss, eds., *Genetic structure and local adaptation in natural insect populations*. Chapman and Hall, New York.

Morgan, A., and S. Lyon. 1928. Notes on amyl salicylate as an attractant to the tobacco hornworm moth. Journal of Economic Entomology 21: 189–191.

Morinaka, S., T. Maeyama, K. Maekawa, D. Erniwati, S. N. Prijono, I. K. Ginarsa, T. Nakazawa, and T. Hidaka. 1999. Molecular phylogeny of birdwing butterflies based on the representatives in most genera of the tribe Troidini (Lepidoptera: Papilionidae). Entomological Science 2: 347–358.

Morinaka, S., N. Minaka, M. Sekiguchi, D. Erniwati, S. N. Prijono, G. K. Ida, T. Miyata, and T. Hidaka. 2000. Molecular phylogeny of birdwing butterflies of the tribe Troidini (Lepidoptera: Papilionidae). Biogeography 2: 103–111.

Morisita, M. 1967. The seasonal distribution of butterflies in the suburbs of Kyoto. Pp. 95–132 in M. Morisita and T. Kira, eds., *Natural history—Ecological studies*. Chuo Koron, Tokyo.

Moritz, C. 1994a. Applications of mitochondrial DNA analysis in conservation: A critical review. Molecular Ecology 3: 401–411.

———. 1994b. Defining "evolutionary significant units" for conservation. Trends in Ecology and Evolution 9: 373–375.

———. 1995. Uses of molecular phylogenies for conservation. Philosophical Transactions of the Royal Society of London B 349: 113–118.

Moritz, C., S. Lavery, and R. Slade. 1995. Using allelic frequency and phylogeny to define units for conservation and management. American Fisheries Society Symposium 17: 249–262.

Morris, D. W. 1995. Earth's peeling veneer of life. Nature 373: 25.

Morris, R. F. 1963. Predictive population equations based on key factors. Memoirs Entomological Society Canada 32: 16–21.

Morris, W. F., D. Doak, M. Groom, P. Kareiva, J. Fieberg, L. Gerber, P. Murphy, and D. Thomson. 1999. *A practical handbook for population viability analysis.* The Nature Conservancy, Arlington, VA.

Motta, P. C. 1989. Análise filogenética de Ithomiinae (Lepidoptera, Nymphalidae) com base nos ovos: Relação com plantas hospedeiras. M.S. thesis, Universidade Estadual de Campinas, São Paulo.

Motten, A. F., and J. Antonovics. 1992. Determinants of outcrossing rate in a predominantiy self-fertilizing weed, *Datura stramonium* (Solanaceae). American Journal of Botany 79: 419–427.

Moya, S., and J. D. Ackerman. 1992. Variation in the floral fragrance of *Epidendrum ciliare* (Orchidaceae). Nordic Journal of Botany 13: 41–47.

Mueller, L. D., B. A. Wilcox, P. R. Ehrlich, D. G. Heckel, and D. D. Murphy. 1985. A direct assessment of the role of genetic drift in determining allele frequency variation in populations of *Euphydryas editha.* Genetics 110: 495–511.

Munroe, E. G. 1961. The classification of the Papilionidae. Canadian Entomologist Suppl. 17: 1–51.

Munroe, E. G. 1983. Wing patterns in the Lepidoptera. Canadian Entomologist 115: 103–112.

Munroe, E. G., and P. R. Ehrlich. 1960. Harmonization of concepts of higher classification of the Papilionidae. Journal of the Lepidopterists' Society 14: 169–175.

Murawski, D. A., and L. E. Gilbert. 1986. Pollen flow in *Psiguria warscewiczii:* A comparison of *Heliconius* butterflies and hummingbirds. Oecologia 68: 161–167.

Múrcia, C. 1991. Effect of flower morphology and temperature on pollen receipt and removal in *Ipomoea trichocarpa.* Ecology 71: 1098–1109.

Murdoch, W. W. 1994. Population regulation in theory and practice. Ecology 75: 271–287.

Murphy, D. D. 1984. Butterflies and their nectar plants: The role of the checkerspot butterfly *Euphydryas editha* as a pollen vector. Oikos 43: 113–116.

Murphy, D. D., A. E. Launer, and P. R. Ehrlich. 1983. The role of adult feeding in egg production and population dynamics of the checkerspot butterfly *Euphydryas editha.* Oecologia 56: 257–263.

Murphy, D. D., M. S. Menninger, and P. R. Ehrlich. 1984. Nectar source distribution as a determinant of oviposition host species in *Euphydryas chalcedona.* Oecologia 62: 269–277.

Murphy, D. D., and S. B. Weiss. 1988. Ecological studies and the conservation of the Bay checkerspot butterfly, *Euphydryas editha bayensis.* Biological Conservation 46: 183–200.

Murphy, D. D., and R. R. White. 1984. Rainfall, resources, and dispersal in southern populations of *Euphydryas editha* (Lepidoptera: Nymphalidae). Pan-Pacific Entomologist 60: 350–354.

Murray, K. G., P. Feinsinger, W. H. Busby, Y. B. Linhart, J. H. Beach, and S. Kinsman. 1987. Evaluation of character displacement among plants in two tropical pollination guilds. Ecology 68: 1283–1293.

Muyshondt, A., A Muyshondt Jr., and P. Muyshondt. 1976. Notas sobre la biologia de lepidopteros de El Salvador I. Revista Sociedad Mexicana de Lepidopterologia 2: 77–90.

Myers, J., and M. Walter. 1970. Olfaction in the Florida queen butterfly: Honey odor receptors. Journal of Insect Physiology 16: 573–578.

Nakanishi, A. 1988. Study of the first instar larvae of the subfamily Nymphalinae

(Lepidoptera, Nymphalidae). Special Bulletin of the Lepidopterological Society of Japan 6: 83–99.

Napolitano, M., and H. Descimon. 1994. Genetic structure of French populations of the mountain butterfly *Parnassius mnemosyne* L. (Lepidoptera: Papilionidae). Biological Journal of the Linnean Society 53: 325–341.

Naumann, C. M., P. Ockenfels, J. Schmitz, and W. Francke. 1991. Reactions of *Zygaena* moths to volatile compounds of *Knautia arvensis* (Lepidoptera: Zygaenidae). Entomologia Generales 15: 255–264.

Nee, S., and R. M. May. 1997. Extinction and the loss of evolutionary history. Science 278: 692–694.

Nei, M. 1972. Genetic distance between populations. American Naturalist 106: 283–292.

Nellen, D., R. Burke, G. Struhl, and K. Basler. 1996. Direct and long-range action of a dpp morphogen gradient. Cell 85: 357–368.

Nelson, G. 1971. "Cladism" as a philosophy of classification. Systematic Zoology 20: 373–376.

———. 1979. Cladistic analysis and synthesis: Principles and definitions, with a historical note on Adanson's Familles des Plantes (1763–1764). Systematic Zoology 28: 1–21.

———. 1984. Cladistics and Biogeography. Pp. 273–293 in T. Duncan and T. F. Stuessy, eds., *Cladistics: Perspectives on the reconstruction of evolutionary history.* Columbia University Press, New York.

Nelson, R., and N. Horning. 1993. AVHRR-LAC estimates of forest area in Madagascar, 1990. International Journal of Remote Sensing 14: 1463–1475.

Nève, G. L., B. Barascud, R. Hughes, J. Aubert, H. Descimon, P. Lebrun, and M. Baguette. 1996a. Dispersal, colonization power, and metapopulation structure in the vulnerable butterfly *Proclossiana eunomia* (Lepidoptera: Nymphalidae). Journal of Applied Ecology 33: 14–22.

Nève, G. L., L. Mousson, and M. Baguette. 1996b. Adult dispersal and genetic structure of butterfly populations in a fragmented landscape. Acta Oecologia 17: 621–626.

New, T. R., and N. M. Collins. 1991. *Swallowtail butterflies. An action plan for their conservation.* IUCN, Gland, Switzerland.

Newman, L. H. 1965. *Hawk-moths of Great Britain and Europe.* Cassell, Ltd, London.

Ng, D. 1988. A novel level of interactions in plant-insect systems. Nature 334: 611–612.

Nice, C. C., and A. M. Shapiro. 1999a. Molecular and morphological divergence in the butterfly genus *Lycaeides* (Lepidoptera: Lycaenidae) in North America: Evidence of recent speciation. Journal of Evolutionary Biology 12: 936–950.

———. 1999b. Population genetic evidence for host-race formation in the butterfly genus *Mitoura* (Lepidoptera: Lycaenidae). GenBank (http://www.ncbi.nlm.nih.gov).

———. 2001. Patterns of morphological, biochemical, and molecular evolution in the *Oeneis chryxus* complex (Lepidoptera: Satyridae): A test of historical biogeographical hypotheses. Molecular Phylogenetics and Evolution 20: 111–123.

Nicholson, A. J. 1933. The balance of animal populations. Journal of Animal Ecology 2: 132–178.

Nicholson, A. J., and V. A. Bailey. 1935. The balance of animal populations. Proceedings of the Zoological Society of London 3: 551–598.

Nielsen, E. S., and I. F. B. Common. 1991. Lepidoptera (moths and butterflies). The insects of Australia 2: 817–915. Melbourne University Press, Carlton, Victoria.

Nielsen, M. G., and W. B. Watt. 1998. Behavioural fitness component effects of the alba polymorphism of *Colias* (Lepidoptera, Pieridae): Resource and time budget analysis. Functional Ecology 12: 149–158.

Nijhout, H. F. 1980a. Ontogeny of the color pattern on the wings of *Precis coenia* (Lepidoptera: Nymphalidae). Developmental Biology 80: 275–288.

————. 1980b. Pattern formation on lepidopteran wings: Determination of an eyespot. Developmental Biology 80: 267–274.

————. 1984. Colour pattern modification by cold shock in Lepidoptera. Journal of Embryology and Experimental Morphology 81: 287–305.

————. 1985a. Cautery-induced colour patterns in *Precis coenia* (Lepidoptera: Nymphalidae). Journal of Embryology and Experimental Morphology 86: 191–203.

————. 1985b. The developmental physiology of colour patterns in Lepidoptera. Advances in Insect Physiology 18: 181–247.

————. 1991. *The development and evolution of butterfly wing patterns*. Smithsonian Institution Press, Washington, DC.

————. 1994a. Developmental perspectives on evolution of butterfly mimicry. BioScience 44: 148–157.

————. 1994b. Genes on the wing. Science 265: 44–45.

————. 2001. Elements of butterfly wing patterns. Journal of Experimental Zoology 291: 213–225.

Nijhout, H. F., and G. A. Wray. 1986. Homologies in the color patterns of the genus *Charaxes* (Lepidoptera: Nymphalidae). Biological Journal of the Linnean Society 28: 387–410.

Nijhout, H. F., G. A. Wray, and L. E. Gilbert. 1990. An analysis of the phenotypic effects of certain color pattern genes in *Heliconius* (Lepidoptera: Nymphalidae). Biological Journal of the Linnean Society 40: 357–372.

Nilsson, D.-E., M. F. Land, and J. Howard. 1984. A focal apposition optics in butterfly eyes. Nature 312: 561–563.

————. 1988. Optics of the butterfly eye. Journal of Comparative Physiology 162: 341–366.

Nilsson, L. A. 1978. Pollination ecology and adaptation in *Platanthera chlorantha* (Orchidaceae). Botaniska Notiser 131: 35–51.

————. 1988. The evolution of flowers with deep corolla tubes. Nature 334: 147–149.

Nilsson, L. A., L. Jonsson, L. Rason, and E. Randrianjohany. 1985. Monophily and pollination mechanisms in *Angraecum arachnites* Schltr. (Orchidaceae) in a guild of long-tongued hawkmoths (Sphingidae) in Madagascar. Biological Journal of the Linnean Society 26: 1–19.

————. 1987. Angraecoid orchids and hawkmoths in central Madagascar: Specialized pollination systems and generalist foragers. Biotropica 19: 310–318.

Nilsson, L. A., and E. Rabakonandrianina. 1988. Hawkmoth scale analysis and pollination specialization in the epilithic Malagasy endemic *Aerangis ellisii* (Reichenb. fil.) Schltr. (Orchidaceae). Botanical Journal of the Linnean Society 97: 49–61.

Nilsson, L. A., E. Rabokonandrianina, B. Pettersson, and J. Ranaivo. 1990. Ixoroid secondary pollen presentation and pollination by small moths in the Malagasy treelet *Ixora platythyrsa* (Rubiaceae). Plant Systematics and Evolution 170: 161–175.

Nilsson, L. A., E. Rabakonandrianina, R. Razananaivo, and J. Randriamanindry. 1992. Long pollinia on eyes: Hawkmoth pollination of *Cynorkis uniflora* Lindley (Orchidaceae) in Madagascar. Botanical Journal of the Linnean Society 109: 145–160.

Nitao, J. K., M. P. Ayres, R. C. Lederhouse, and J. M. Scriber. 1991. Larval adaptation to lauraceous hosts: Geographic divergence in the spicebush swallowtail butterfly. Ecology 72: 1428–1435.

NOAA. 1999. Weekly Weather and Crop Bull. NOAA/NWS/NCEP/CPC. Camp Springs, MD.

Norris, M. J. 1935. A feeding experiment on the adults of *Pieris rapae*. Entomologist 68: 125–127.

Noss, R. F. 1990. Indicators for monitoring biodiversity: A hierarchical approach. Conservation Biology 4: 355–364.

Noss, R. F., and A. Cooperrider. 1994. *Saving nature's legacy: Protecting and restoring biodiversity.* Island Press, Washington, DC.

Noss, R. F., E. T. LaRoe, and J. M. Scott. 1995. *Endangered ecosystems of the United States: A preliminary assessment of loss and degradation.* US Department of Interior Biological Report 28.

Nöthiger, R. 1981. Clonal analysis in imaginal discs. Pp. 109–114 in P. A. Lawrence, ed., *Insect development.* Symposium of the Royal Entomological Society of London VIII. Blackwell, Oxford.

Nothnagle, P. J., and J. C. Schultz. 1987. What is a forest pest? Pp. 59–80. in P. Barbosa and J. C. Shultz, eds., *Insect outbreaks.* Academic Press, San Diego.

Nylin, S. 1988. Host plant specialization and seasonality in a polyphagous butterfly, *Polygonia c-album* (Nymphalidae). Oikos 53: 381–386.

———. 1989. Effects of changing photoperiods in the life cycle regulation of the comma butterfly, *Polygonia c-album* (Nymphalidae). Ecological Entomology 14: 209–218.

Nylin, S., and K. Gotthard. 1998. Plasticity in life-history traits. Annual Review of Entomology 43: 63–83.

Nylin, S., K. Gotthard, and C. Wiklund. 1996a. Reaction norms for age and size at maturity in *Lasiommata* butterflies. Evolution 50: 1259–1264.

Nylin, S., and N. Janz. 1993. Oviposition preference and larval performance in *Polygonia c-album* (Lepidoptera: Nymphalidae): The choice between bad and worse. Ecological Entomology 18: 394–398.

———. 1999. Ecology and evolution of host plant range: Butterflies as a model group. Pp. 31–54 in H. Olff, V. K. Brown, and R. H. Drent, eds., *Herbivores: Between plants and predators.* Oxford: Blackwell.

Nylin, S., N. Janz, and N. Wedell. 1996b. Oviposition plant preference and offspring performance in the comma butterfly: Correlations and conflicts. Entomologica Experimentalis et Applicata 80: 141–144.

Nylin, S., K. Nyblom, F. Ronquist, N. Janz, J. Belicek, and M. Källersjö. 2001. Phylogeny of *Polygonia, Nymphalis* and related butterflies (Lepidoptera: Nymphalidae): A total-evidence analysis. Zoological Journal of the Linnean Society 132: 441–468.

Nylin, S., and N. Wedell. 1994. Sexual dimorphism and comparative methods. Pp. 253–280 in P. Eggleton and R. I. Vane-Wright, eds., *Phylogenetics and ecology.* Academic Press, London.

Nylin, S., P. O. Wickman, and C. Wiklund. 1989. Seasonal plasticity in growth and development of the speckled wood butterfly, *Pararge aegeria* (Satyrinae). Biological Journal of the Linnean Society 38: 155–171.

_____ . 1995. Life-cycle regulation and life history plasticity in the speckled wood butterfly: Are reaction norms predictable? Biological Journal of the Linnean Society 55: 143–157.

Nylin, S., C. Wiklund, P.-O. Wickman, and E. Garcia-Barros. 1993. Absence of trade-offs between sexual size dimorphism and early male emergence in a butterfly. Ecology 74: 1414–1427.

Obara, Y. 1964. Mating behaviour of the cabbage white, *Pieris rapae crucivora*. II. The "mate-refusal" posture. Zoological Magazine 73: 175–178.

_____ . 1970. Studies on the mating behavior of the white cabbage butterfly, *Pieris rapae crucivora* Boisduval. III. Near-ultraviolet reflection as the signal of intraspecific communication. Zeitschrift für Vergleichende Physiologie 69: 99–116.

Oberhauser, K. 1988. Male monarch butterfly spermatophore mass and mating strategies. Animal Behaviour 36: 1384–1388.

_____ . 1989. Effects of spermatophores on male and female monarch butterfly reproductive success. Behavioral Ecology and Sociobiology 25: 237–246.

_____ . 1992. Rate of ejaculate breakdown and intermating intervals in monarch butterflies. Behavioral Ecology and Sociobiology 31: 367–373.

O'Brien, D. M. 1998. Allocation of nectar nutrients to reproduction in *Amphion floridalis*, a novel quantitative method using stable carbon isotopes. Ph.D. dissertation, Princeton University, Princeton, NJ.

_____ . 1999. Fuel use in flight and its dependence on nectar feeding in the hawkmoth *Amphion floridalis*. Journal of Experimental Biology 202: 441–451.

O'Brien, D. M., M. Fogel, and C. L. Boggs. 2002. Renewable and non-renewable resources: The role of amino acid turnover in allocation to reproduction in Lepidoptera. Proceedings of the National Academy of Sciences USA 99: 4413–4418.

O'Brien, E. M. 1993. Climatic gradients in woody plant species richness: Towards an explanation based on an analysis of southern Africa's woody flora. Journal of Biogeography 20: 181–198.

_____ . 1998. Water-energy dynamics, climate, and prediction of woody plant species richness: An interim general model. Journal of Biogeography 25: 379–398.

O'Brochta, D. A., and P. J. Bryant. 1985. A zone of non-proliferating cells at a lineage restriction boundary in *Drosophila*. Nature 313: 138–141.

O'Carroll, D. J., N. J. Bidwell, S. B. Laughlin, and E. J. Warrant. 1996. Insect motion detectors matched to visual ecology. Nature 382: 63–66.

Odendaal, F. J., Y. Iwasa, and P. R. Ehrlich. 1985. Duration of female availability and its effect on butterfly mating systems. American Naturalist 125: 673–687.

Okubo, A. 1984. Critical patch size for plankton patchiness. Pp. 456–477 in S. A. Levin, T. G. Hallam, eds., *Mathematical ecology*. Lecture Notes in Biomathematics Number 54.

Oliveira, E., R. B. Srygley, and R. Dudley. 1998. Do Neotropical migrant butterflies navigate using a solar compass? Journal of Experimental Biology 201: 3317–3331.

Oliver, C. G. 1979a. Disturbance of eclosion sequence in hybrid Lepidoptera. Canadian Entomologist 115: 1445–1452.

_____ . 1979b. Genetic differentiation and hybrid viability within and between some Lepidoptera species. American Naturalist 114: 681–694.

Oliver, I. A., J. Beattie, and A. York. 1998. Spatial fidelity of plant, vertebrate, and invertebrate assemblages in multiple-use forest in eastern Australia. Conservation Biology 12: 822–835.

Olson, D. M., and E. Dinerstein. 1998. The global 200: A representation approach to conserving the earth's most biologically valuable ecoregions. Conservation Biology 12: 502–515.

Omura, H., K. Honda, and N. Hayashi. 1999a. Chemical and chromatic bases for preferential visiting by the cabbage butterfly *Pieris rapae* to rape flowers. Journal of Chemical Ecology 25: 1895–1906.

Omura, H., K. Honda, A. Nakagawa, and N. Hayashi. 1999b. The role of floral scent of the cherry tree, *Prunus yedoensis,* in the foraging behavior of *Leuhdorfia japonica* (Lepidoptera: Papilionidae). Applied Entomology and Zoology 34: 306–313.

Opler, P., H. G. Baker, and G. W. Frankie. 1975. Reproductive biology of some Costa Rican *Cordia* species (Boraginaceae). Biotropica 7: 234–247.

Opler, P., and R. L. Langston. 1968. A distributional analysis of the butterflies of Contra Costa, County, California. Journal of the Lepidopterists' Society 21: 89–107.

ORF-Finder. 1997. (http://www.ncbi.nlm.nih.gov/gorf/gorf.html).

Orr, H. A. 1987. Genetics of male and female sterility in hybrids of *Drosophila pseudoobscura* and *D. persimilis.* Genetics 116: 555–563.

———. 1989. Genetics of sterility in hybrids between two subspecies of *Drosophila.* Evolution 43: 180–189.

———. 1993. Haldane's rule has multiple genetic causes. Nature 361: 532–533.

———. 1995. The population genetics of speciation: The evolution of hybrid incompatibilities. Genetics 139: 1805–1813.

———. 1997. Haldane's Rule. Annual Review of Ecology and Systematics 28: 195–218.

Orr, H. A., and L. H. Orr. 1996. Waiting for speciation: The effect of population subdivision on the time to speciation. Evolution 50: 1742–1749.

Orr, M. R., and T. B. Smith. 1998. Ecology and speciation. Trends in Ecology and Evolution 13: 502–506.

Owen, D. F. 1969. Species diversity and seasonal abundance in tropical Sphingidae (Lepidoptera). Proceedings of the Royal Entomological Society of London (A) 44: 162–168.

———. 1971. *Tropical butterflies.* Clarendon, Ltd. Oxford.

Owen, D. F., and D. O. Chanter. 1972. Species diversity and seasonal abundance in *Charaxes* butterflies. Journal of Entomology A 46: 135–143.

Owen, D. F., T. G. Shreeve, and A. G. Smith. 1986. Colonization of Madeira by the speckled wood butterfly, *Pararge aegeria* (Lepidoptera: Satyridae), and its impact on the endemic *Pararge xiphia.* Ecological Entomology 11: 349–352.

Oyeyele, S. O., and M. P. Zalucki. 1990. Cardiac glycosides and oviposition by *Danaus plexippus* butterflies on *Asclepias fructicosa* in south-east Queensland (Australia) with notes on the effect of plant nitrogen content. Ecological Entomology 15: 177–185.

Packer, L. 1984. The ecological genetics of the speckled wood butterfly, *Pararge aegeria* L., a preliminary study. Heredity 52: 179–188.

Paetkau, D., and C. Strobeck. 1994. Microsatellite analysis of genetic variation in black bear populations. Molecular Ecology 3: 489–495.

———. 1995. The molecular basis and phylogenetic distribution of a microsatellite null allele in bears. Molecular Ecology 4: 519–520.

Paige, K. N., and T. G. Whitham. 1985. Individual and population shifts in flower color by scarlet gilia: A mechanism for pollinator tracking. Science 227: 315–317.

Panchen, A. L. 1992. *Classification, evolution, and the nature of biology.* Cambridge University Press, Cambridge.

Panganiban, G., A. Sebring, L. Nagy, and S. Carroll. 1995. The development of crustacean limbs and the evolution of arthropods. Science 270: 1363–1366.

Papaj, D. R. 1986a. Interpopulation differences in host preference and the evolution of learning in the butterfly *Battus philenor.* Ecology 40: 518–530.

_____. 1986b. Shifts in foraging behavior by a Battus philenor population: Field evidence for switching by individual butterflies. Behavioral Ecology and Sociobiology 19: 31–39.

Papaj, D. R., and M. D. Rausher. 1987. Components of conspecific host discrimination in the butterfly *Battus philenor.* Ecology 68: 245–253.

Papatsenko, D., G. Sheng, and C. Desplan. 1997. A new rhodopsin in R8 photoreceptors of *Drosophila:* Evidence for coordinate expression with Rh3 in R7 cells. Development 124: 1665–1673.

Parker, G. A. 1974. Assessment strategy and the evolution of fighting behaviour. Journal of Theoretical Biology 47: 223–243.

_____. 1982. Why are there so many tiny sperm? Sperm competition and the maintenance of two sexes. Journal of Theoretical Biology 96: 281–294.

_____. 1984. Sperm competition and the evolution of animal mating strategies. Pp. 1–60 in R. L. Smith, ed., *Sperm competition and the evolution of animal mating systems.* Academic Press, New York.

_____. 1990a. Sperm competition games: Raffles and roles. Proceedings of the Royal Society of London B 242: 120–126.

_____. 1990b. Sperm competition games: Sneaks and extra-pair copulations. Proceedings of the Royal Society of London B 242: 127–133.

_____. 1993. Sperm competition games: Sperm size and number under adult control. Proceedings of the Royal Society of London B 253: 245–254.

Parker, G. A., and S. P. Courtney. 1983. Seasonal incidence: Adaptive variation in the timing of life history stages. Journal of Theoretical Biology 105: 147–155.

Parker, G. A., and L. E. Simmons. 1996. Parental investment and the control of sexual selection: Predicting the direction of sexual competition. Proceedings of the Royal Society of London B 263: 315–321.

Parmesan, C. 1991. Evidence against plant 'apparency' as a constraint on evolution of insect search efficiency (Lepidoptera: Nymphalidae). Journal of Insect Behavior 4: 417–429.

_____. 1996. Climate and species' range. Nature 382: 765–766.

Parmesan, C., T. L. Root, M. R. Willig. 2000. Impacts of extreme weather and climate on terrestrial biota. Bulletin of the American Meteorological Society 81: 443–450.

Parmesan, C., N. Ryrholm, C. Stefanescu, J. K. Hill, C. D. Thomas, H. Descimon, B. Huntley, L. Kaila, J. Kullberg, T. Tammaru, J. Tennant, J. A. Thomas, and M. Warren. 1999. Polewards shifts in geographic ranges of butterfly species associated with regional warming. Nature 399: 579–583.

Parmesan, C., M. C. Singer, and I. Harris. 1995. Absence of adaptive learning from the oviposition foraging behaviour of a checkerspot butterfly. Animal Behaviour 50: 161–175.

Parsons, M. 1991. *Butterflies of the Bulolo-Wau Valley.* Bishop Museum Press, Honolulu.

———. 1996a. Gondwanan evolution of the troidine swallowtails (Lepidoptera: Papilionidae): Cladistic reappraisals using mainly immature stage characters, with focus on the birdwings *Ornithoptera* Boisduval. Bulletin Kitakyushu Museum Natural History 15: 43–118.

———. 1996b. A phylogenetic reappraisal of the birdwing genus *Ornithoptera* (Lepidoptera: Papilionidae: Troidini) and a new theory of its evolution in relation to Gondwanan vicariance biogeography. Journal of Natural History 30: 1707–1736.

———. 1999. *The butterflies of Papua New Guinea. Their systematics and biology.* Academic Press, London.

Pashley, D. P., and L. D. Ke. 1992. Sequence evolution in mitochondrial ribosomal and ND-1 genes in Lepidoptera: Implications for phylogenetic analyses. Molecular Biology and Evolution 9: 1061–1075.

Paterson, H. E. H. 1978. More evidence against speciation by reinforcement. South African Journal of Science 74: 369–371.

———. 1985. The recognition concept of species. Pp. 21–29 in E. S. Vrba, ed., *Species and speciation*. Transvaal Museum, Pretoria.

Patterson, C. 1980. Cladistics. Biologist 27: 234–240.

———. 1982. Morphological characters and homology. Pp. 21–74 in K. A. Joysey and A. E. Friday, eds., *Problems in phylogenetic reconstruction*. Academic Press, London.

Patterson, C., and D. Rosen. 1977. Review of the ichthyodectiform and other Mesozoic teleost fishes and the theory and practice of classifying fossils. Bulletin of the American Museum of Natural History 158: 81–172.

Patterson, C., D. M. Williams, and C. J. Humphries. 1993. Congruence between molecular and morphological phylogenies. Annual Review of Ecology and Systematics 24: 153–188.

Paulsen, S. M. 1994. Quantitative genetics of butterfly wing color patterns. Developmental Genetics 15: 79–91.

———. 1995. Quantitative genetics of the wing color pattern in the buckeye butterfly (*Precis coemia* and *Precis evarete*): Evidence against the constancy of G. Evolution 47: 593–618.

Paulsen, S. M., and H. F. Nijhout. 1993. Phenotypic correlation structure among elements of the color pattern in *Precis coenia* (Lepidoptera, Nymphalidae). Evolution 47: 593–618.

Pavlik, B. M., N. Ferguson, and M. Nelson. 1993. Assessing limitation on the growth of endangered plant populations II. Seed production and seed bank dynamics of *Erysimum capitatum* ssp. *angustatum* and *Oenothera deltoides* ssp. *howellii*. Biological Conservation 65: 267–278.

Pearson, D. L., and S. S. Carroll. 1998. Global patterns of species richness: Spatial models for conservation planning using bioindicator and precipitation data. Conservation Biology 12: 809–821.

Pellmyr, O. 1986. Three pollination morphs in *Cimicifuga simplex:* Incipient speciation due to inferiority in competition. Oecologia 78: 304–307.

Pemberton, J. M., J. Slate, D. R. Bancroft, and J. A. Barrett. 1995. Nonamplifying alleles at microsatellite loci: A caution for parentage and population studies. Molecular Ecology 4: 249–252.

Penz, C. M. 1999. Higher level phylogeny for the passion-vine butterflies (Nymphalidae: Heliconiinae) based on early stage and adult morphology. Zoological Journal of the Linnean Society 127: 277–344.

Penz, C. M., and P. J. DeVries. 1999. Preliminary assessment of the tribe Lemoniini (Lepidoptera: Riodinidae) based on adult morphology. American Museum Novitates (3284): 32pp.

Perez, S. M., O. R. Taylor, and R. Jander. 1997. A sun compass in monarch butterflies. Nature 387: 29.

Peterson, A. 1962. *Larvae of insects. I. Lepidoptera and plant infesting Hymenoptera.* Edwards Brothers, Columbus, Ohio.

Peterson, M. A. 1996. Long-distance gene flow in the sedentary butterfly, *Euphilotes enoptes* (Lepidoptera: Lycaenidae). Evolution 50: 1990–1999.

Pettersson, M. W. 1991. Pollination by a guild of fluctuating moth populations: Option for unspecialization in *Silene vulgaris.* Journal of Ecology 79: 591–604.

Phelan, P. L., and T. C. Baker. 1986. Male size-related courtship success and intersexual selection in the tobacco moth, *Ephestia eluthella.* Experimentia 42: 1291–1293.

Philippe, H. 1993. MUST: A computer package of management utilities for sequences and trees. Nucleic Acids Research 21: 5264–5272.

Pickett, S. T. A., and J. N. Thompson. 1978. Patch dynamics and the design of nature reserves. Biological Conservation 13: 27–37.

Pickett, S., V. Parker, and P. Fiedler. 1992. The new paradigm in ecology: Implication for conservation biology above the species level. Pp. 66–87 in P. Fiedler and S. Jain, eds., *Conservation biology: The theory and practice of nature conservation preservation and management.* Chapman and Hall, New York.

Pierce, N. E. 1983. The ecology and evolution of symbioses between lycaenid butterflies and ants. Ph.D. dissertation, Harvard University, Cambridge, MA.

_____. 1987. The evolution and biogeography of associations between lycaenid butterflies and ants. Pp. 89–116 in P. H. Harvey and L. Partridge, eds., *Ant-plant interactions. Oxford Surveys in Evolutionary Biology,* vol. 4. Oxford University Press, New York.

_____. 1989. Butterfly-ant mutualisms. Pp. 299–324 in P. J. Grubb and J. Whittaker, eds., *Towards a more exact ecology.* Blackwell, Oxford.

Pierce, N. E., M. F. Braby, A. Heath, D. J. Lohman, J. Mathew, D. B. Rand, and M. A. Travassos. 2002. The ecology and evolution of ant association in the Lycaenidae (Lepidoptera). Annual Review of Entomology 47: 733–771.

Pierce, N. E., and S. Easteal. 1986. The selective advantage of attendant ants for the larvae of a lycaenid butterfly *Glaucopsyche lygdamus.* Journal of Animal Ecology 55: 451–462.

Pivnick, K. A., and J. N. McNeil. 1986. Sexual differences in the thermoregulation of *Thymelicus lineola* adults (Lepidoptera: Hesperiidae). Ecology 67: 1024–1035.

_____. 1987. Puddling in butterflies: Sodium affects reproductive success in *Thymelicus lineola.* Physiological Entomology 12: 461–472.

Platnick, N. 1979. Philosophy and the transformation of cladistics. Systematic Zoology 28: 537–546.

_____. 1987. An empirical comparison of microcomputer parsimony programs. Cladistics 3: 121–144.

Platt, A. P. 1983. Evolution of North American Admiral Butterflies (*Limenitis:* Nymphalidae). Bulletin of the Entomological Society of America 29: 11–22.

Platt, A. P., and L. P. Brower. 1968. Mimetic versus disruptive coloration in intergrading populations of *Limenitis arthemis* and *astyanax* butterflies. Evolution 22: 699–718.

Platt, A. P., S. J. Harrison, and T. F. Williams. 1984. Absence of differential mate selection in the North American tiger swallowtail, *Papilio glaucus*. Pp. 245–249 in R. I. Vane-Wright and P. R. Ackery, eds., *The biology of butterflies*. Academic Press, London.

Pliske, T. E. 1973. Factors determining mating frequencies in some New World butterflies and skippers. Annals of the Entomological Society of America 66: 164–169.

Pliske, T. E. 1975. Attraction of Lepidoptera to plants containing pyrrolizidine alkaloids. Environmental Entomology 4: 455–473.

Pliske, T. E., J. A. Edgar, and C. C. J. Culvenor. 1976. The chemical basis of attraction of ithomiine butterflies to plants containing pyrrolizidine alkaloids. Journal of Chemical Ecology 2: 255–262.

Podolsky, A. S. 1984. *New phenology: Elements of mathematical forecasting in ecology*. John Wiley, New York.

Pogson, G. H. 1991. Expression of overdominance for specific activity at the phosphoglucomutase-2 locus in the Pacific oyster, *Crassostrea gigas*. Genetics 128: 133–141.

Polis, G. A., W. B. Anderson, and R. D. Holt. 1997. Toward an integration of landscape and food web ecology: The dynamics of spatially subsidized food webs. Annual Review of Ecology and Systematics 28: 289–316.

Pollard, E. 1979. Population ecology and change in range of the white admiral butterfly *Ladoga camilla* L. in England. Ecological Entomology 4: 61–74.

———. 1982. Monitoring butterfly abundance in relation to the management of a nature reserve. Biological Conservation 24: 317–328.

———. 1988. Temperature, rainfall and butterfly numbers. Journal of Applied Ecology 25: 819–828.

———. 1991a. Monitoring butterfly numbers. Pp. 87–111 in F. B. Goldsmith, ed., *Monitoring for conservation and ecology*. Chapman and Hall, London.

———. 1991b. Synchrony of population fluctuations: The dominant influence of widespread factors on local butterfly populations. Oikos 60: 7–10.

Pollard, E., and B. C. Eversham. 1995. Butterfly monitoring 2—interpreting the changes. Pp. 23–36 in A. S. Pullin, ed., *Ecology and conservation of butterflies*. Chapman and Hall, London.

Pollard, E., P. Rothery, and T. J. Yates. 1997. Annual growth rates in newly established populations of the butterfly *Pararge aegeria*. Ecological Entomology 21: 365–369.

Pollard, E., and T. J. Yates. 1992. The extinction and foundation of local butterfly populations in relation to population variability and other factors. Ecological Entomology 17: 249–254.

———. 1993. *Monitoring butterflies for ecology and conservation: The British butterfly monitoring scheme*. Chapman and Hall, London.

Pollock, D. D., W. B. Watt, V. K. Rashbrook, and E. V. Iyengar. 1998. Molecular phylogeny for *Colias* butterflies and their relatives (Lepidoptera: Pieridae). Annals of the Entomological Society of America 91: 524–531.

Pollock, J. A., and S. Benzer. 1988. Transcript localization of four opsin genes in the three visual organs of *Drosophila*: Rh2 is ocellus specific. Nature 333: 779–782.

Poole, R. W., and B. J. Rathcke. 1979. Regularity, randomness and aggregation in flowering phenologies. Science 203: 470–471.

Porter, A. H., and H. Geiger. 1995. Limitations to the inference of gene flow at regional geographic scales—an example from the *Pieris napi* group (Lepidoptera: Pieridae) in Europe. Biological Journal of the Linnean Society 54: 329–348.

Porter, A. H., and A. M. Shapiro. 1990. Lock-and-Key Hypothesis: Lack of mechanical isolation in a butterfly (Lepidoptera: Pieridae) hybrid zone. Annals of the Entomological Society of America 83: 107–114.

Porter, A. H., R. Wenger, H. Geiger, A. Scholl, and A. M. Shapiro. 1997. The *Pontia daplidice-edusa* hybrid zone in Northwestern Italy. Evolution 51: 1561–1573.

Porter, K., C. A. Steel, and J. A. Thomas. 1992. Butterflies and communities. Pp. 139–177 in R. H. Dennis, ed., *The ecology of butterflies in Britain.* Oxford University Press, Oxford.

Post, C. T. Jr., and T. H. Goldsmith. 1969. Physiological evidence for color receptors in the eye of a butterfly. Annals of the Entomological Society of America 62: 1497–1498.

Pounds, J. A., M. P. L. Fogden, and J. H. Campbell. 1999. Biological response to climate change in a highland tropical forest. Nature 398: 611–615.

Powell, J. A., and J. W. Brown. 1990. Concentrations of lowland sphingid and noctuid moths at high mountain passes in eastern Mexico. Biotropica 22: 316–319.

Powers, D. A. 1987. A multidisciplinary approach to the study of genetic variation within species. Pp. 102–134 in M. E. Feder, A. F. Bennett, W. W. Burggren, and R. B. Huey, eds., *New directions in ecological physiology.* Cambridge University Press, Cambridge.

Powers, D. A., T. Lauerman, D. Crawford, and L. DiMichele. 1991. Genetic mechanisms for adapting to a changing environment. Annual Review of Genetics 25: 629–659.

Powers, D. A., I. Ropson, D. C. Brown. R. Van Beneden, R. Cashon, L. I. Gonzalez-Villasenor, and J. A. DiMichele. 1986. Genetic variation in *Fundulus heroclitus:* Geographical distributions. American Zoologist 26: 131–144.

Prendergast, J. R., R. M. Quinn, J. H. Lawton, and B. C. Eversham. 1993. Rare species, the coincidence of diversity hotspots and conservation strategies. Nature 365: 335–337.

Presgraves, D. C., and H. A. Orr. 1998. Haldane's rule in taxa lacking a hemizygous X. Science 282: 952–954.

Primack, R. B. 1980. Variation in the phenology of natural populations of montane shrubs in New Zealand. Journal of Ecology 68: 849–862.

Prokopy, R. J., and E. D. Owens. 1983. Visual detection of plants by herbivorous insects. Annual Review of Entomology 28: 337–364.

Prowell, D. P. 1998. Sex linkage and speciation in Lepidoptera. Pp. 309–319 in D. J. Howard and S. H. Berlocher, eds., *Endless forms, species and speciation.* Oxford University Press, New York.

Pulliam, H. R. 1988. Sources, sinks, and population regulation. American Naturalist 132: 652–661.

———. 1996. Sources and sinks: Empirical evidence and population consequences. Pp. 45–69 in O. E. Rhodes Jr, R. K. Chester, and M. H. Smith, eds., *Population dynamics in ecological space and time.* University of Chicago Press, Chicago.

———. 2000. On the relationship between niche and distribution. Ecology Letters 3: 349–361.

Pullin, A. S., ed. 1995. *Ecology and conservation of butterflies.* Chapman and Hall, London.

Pyke, G. H., and N. M. Waser. 1981. The production of dilute nectars by hummingbird and honeyeater flowers. Biotropica 13: 260–270.

Questiau, S., M. C. Eybert, A. R. Gaginskaya, L. Gielly, and P. Taberlet. 1998. Recent divergence between two morphologically differentiated subspecies of bluethroat (Aves: Muscicapidae: *Luscinia svecica*) inferred from mitochondrial DNA sequence variation. Molecular Ecology 7: 239–245.

Rabinowitz, D., S. Cairns, and T. Dillon. 1986. Seven forms of rarity and their frequency in the flora of the British Isles. Pp. 182–204 in M. E. Soulé, ed., *Conservation biology: The science of scarcity and diversity.* Sinauer Associates, Sunderland, MA.

Radigue, F. 1994. Une invasion pacifique: La Carte géographique (*Araschnia levana* L.) dans l'Orne (1976–1992). *Alexanor* 18: 359–367.

Radtkey, R., and M. C. Singer. 1995. Repeated reversals of host preference evolution in a specialist insect herbivore. Evolution 49: 351–359.

Raguso, R. A. 2001. Floral scent, olfaction and scent-driven foraging behavior. In L. Chittka and J. D. Thomson, eds., *Pollinator behaviour and its implications for plant evolution.* Cambridge University Press, Cambridge.

Raguso, R. A., and D. M. Light. 1998. Electroantennogram responses of *Sphinx perelegans* (Lepidoptera: Sphingidae) to floral and vegetative compounds. Entomologica Experimentalis et Applicata 86: 287–293.

Raguso, R. A., D. M. Light, and E. Pickersky. 1996. Electroantennogram responses of *Hyles lineata* (Sphingidae: Lepidoptera) to floral volatile compounds from *Clarkia breweri* (Onagraceae) and other moth-pollinated flowers. Journal of Chemical Ecology 22: 1735–1766.

Raguso, R. A., and O. Pellmyr. 1998. Dynamic headspace analysis of floral volatiles: A comparison of methods. Oikos 81: 238–254.

Raguso, R. A., and M. A. Willis. 2002. The combination of visual and olfactory cues synergizes nectar feeding by naïve male *Manduca sexta* hawkmoths. Animal Behaviour.

Rainey, P. B., and M. Travisano. 1998. Adaptive radiation in a heterogeneous environment. Nature 394: 69–72.

Ralls, K., J. D. Ballou, and A. Templeton. 1988. Estimates of lethal equivalents and the cost of inbreeding in mammals. Conservation Biology 2: 185–193.

Ramaswamy, S. 1988. Host finding by moths: Sensory modalities and behaviours. Journal of Insect Physiology 34: 235–249.

Rand, D. B., A. Heath, T. Suderman, and N. E. Pierce. 2000. Phylogeny and life history evolution of the genus *Chrysoritis* within the Aphnaeini (Lepidoptera: Lycaenidae), inferred from mitochondrial cytochrome oxidase I sequences. Molecular Phylogenetics and Evolution 17: 85–96.

Rand, D. M., and R. G. Harrison. 1989. Ecological genetics of a mosaic hybrid zone: Mitochrondrial, nuclear, and reproductive differentiation of crickets by soil type. Evolution 43: 432–449.

Rapoport, E. H. 1982. *Areography: Geographical strategies of species.* Pergamon Press, Oxford.

Rathcke, B. 1984. Patterns of flowering phenologies: Testability and causal inference using a random model. Pp. 383–393 in D. R. Strong, J. H. Lawton, and R. Southwood, eds., *Insects on plants: Community patterns and mechanisms.* Harvard University Press, Cambridge, MA.

———. 1988. Flowering phenologies in a shrub community: Competition and restraints. Journal of Ecology 76: 975–994.

Rausher, M. D. 1978. Search image for leaf shape in a butterfly. Science 200: 1071–1073.

———. 1979a. Egg recognition: Its advantage to a butterfly. Animal Behaviour 27: 1034–1040.

————. 1979b. Larval habitat suitabiity and oviposition preference in three related butterflies. Ecology 60: 503–511.

————. 1984. The evolution of habitat preference in subdivided populations. Evolution 38: 596–608.

————. 1993. Behavioral ecology of oviposition in the pipevine swallowtail butterfly, *Battus philenor*. In M. R. Hunter, T. Ohgushi, P. W. Price, eds., *The effects of resource distribution on animal plant interactions*. Academic Press, New York.

Rausher, M. D., D. A. Mackay, and M. C. Singer. 1981. Pre- and post-alighting host discrimination by *Euphydryas editha* butterflies: The behavioral mechanisms causing clumped distributions of egg clusters. Animal Behaviour 29: 1220–1228.

Ravenscroft, N. 1994. Environmental influences on mate location in male chequered skipper butterflies, *Carterocephalus palaemon* (Lepidoptera: Hesperiidae). Animal Behaviour 47: 1179–1187.

Ray, T. A., and C. C. Andrews. 1980. Ant butterflies: Butterflies that follow army ants to feed on ant bird droppings. Science 210: 1147–1148.

Raymond, I. 1995. Approche phytoecologique sur l'évaluation qualitative et quantitative des utilisations villageoises des ressources naturelles en forèt dense humide sempervirente. Université d'Antananarivo, Antananarivo, Madagascar.

Raymond, M., and F. Rousset. 1995. Genepop 3.1: Population genetics software for exact tests and ecumenicism. Journal of Heredity 86: 248–249.

Razafimahatratra, V., and L. Andriamampianiana. 1995. Annexe V.4. Inventaire des deux groupes d'insectes Coleoptères: Scarabeidae et Cicindelidae de la Presqu'Ile Masoala et comparaisons biogéographiques. in C. Kremen, ed., *Proposition des limites du Parc National Masoala*. Care International Madagascar, Wildlife Conservation Society, and The Peregrine Fund, Antananarivo.

Razafindrakoto, Y. 1995. Contribution à l'étude des rongeurs et insectivores de la presqu'île de Masoala. Université d'Antananarivo, Antananarivo, Madagascar.

Read, A., and S. Nee. 1991. Is Haldane's rule significant? Evolution 45: 1707–1709.

Real, L. A. 1981. Uncertainty and pollinator-plant interactions: The foraging behavior of bees and wasps on artificial flowers. Ecology 62: 20–26.

Réal, P. 1962. Un phénomène écologique singulier, mais complexe, l'amphiphénotisme, observé chez les Piérides. Annales Scientifiques de l'Université de Besaçon Série II. 17: 87–95.

————. 1988. Lépidoptères nouveaux principalement jurassiens. Memoires du Comité de Liaison pour les Recherches Ecofaunistiques dans le Jura 4: 1–28.

Reavey, D., and J. H. Lawton. 1991. Larval contribution to fitness in leaf-eating insects. Pp. 293–329 in W. J. Bailey and J. Ridsdill-Smith, eds., *Reproductive behaviour of insects: Individuals and populations*. Chapman and Hall, London.

Reed, C. C. 1997. Responses of prairie insects and other arthropods to prescription burns. Natural Areas Journal 17: 380–385.

Reed, R. D., and F. A. H. Sperling. 1999. Interaction of process partitions in phylogenetic analysis: An example from the swallowtail butterfly genus *Papilio*. Molecular Biology and Evolution 16: 286–297.

Regier, J. C., Q. Q. Fang, C. Mitter, R. S. Peigler, T. P. Friedlander, and A. M. Solis. 1998. Evolution and phylogenetic utility of the period gene in Lepidoptera. Molecular Biology and Evolution 15: 1172–1182.

Reid, W. V. 1998. Biodiversity hotspots. Trends in Ecology and Evolution 13: 275–280.

Reig, O. 1968. Peuplement Vertébrés Tétrapodes de l'Amérique du Sud. In Delamarre-Deboutteville, C., and C. Rapoport eds. Biologie de l'Amérique Australe 4: 215–260.

Reinhold, K. 1998. Sex linkage among genes controlling sexually selected traits. Behavioral Ecology and Sociobiology 44: 1–7.

Reissinger, E. 1989. Checkliste Pieridae Duponchel, 1835, der Westpalaearctis (Europa, Nordwestafrika, Kaukasus, Kleinasien). Atalanta. 20: 149–185.

Remington, C. L. 1968a. A new sibling *Papilio* from the Rocky Mountains, with genetic and biological notes (Insecta, Lepidoptera). Postilla 119: 1–40.

———. 1968b. Suture-zones of hybrid interaction between recently joined biotas. Evolutionary Biology 2: 321–428.

Renwick, J. A. A., and F. S. Chew. 1994. Oviposition behavior in Lepidoptera. Annual Review of Entomology 39: 377–400.

Rhymer, J. M., and D. Simberloff. 1996. Extinction by hybridization and introgression. Annual Review of Ecology and Systematics 27: 83–109.

Ribi, W. A. 1979. Colored screening pigments cause red eye glow in pierid butterflies. Journal of Comparative Physiology 132: 2–9.

———. 1987. Anatomical identification of spectral receptor types in the retina and lamina of the Australian orchard butterfly, *Papilio aegeus aegeus*. Cell and Tissue Research 247: 393–407.

Rice, W. R. 1988. The effect of sex chromosomes on the rate of evolution. Trends in Ecology and Evolution 3: 2–3.

———. 1998. Intergenomic conflict, interlocus antagonistic coevolution, and the evolution of reproductive isolation. Pp. 261–270 in D. J. Howard and S. H. Berlocher, eds., *Endless forms, species and speciation.* Oxford University Press, New York.

Richardson, B., P. Baverstock, and M. Adams. 1986. *Allozyme electrophoresis.* Academic Press, San Diego.

Richerson, P., B. J. Dozier, and B. T. Maeda. 1976. The structure of phytoplankton associations in Lake Tahoe (California-Nevada). Verhandlungen—Internationale Vereinigung fur Theoretische und Angewandte Limnologie 19: 843–849.

Ricketts, T. H., G. C. Daily, P. R. Ehrlich, and J. P. Fay. 2001. Countryside biogeography of moths in native and human-dominated habitats. Conservation Biology 15: 378–388.

Ricklefs, R. 1966. The temporal component of diversity among species of birds. Evolution 20: 235–242.

Ridley, M. 1989. The timing and frequency of mating in insects. Animal Behaviour 37: 535–545.

Rieppel, O. 1988. *Fundamentals of comparative biology.* Birkhäuser, Basel.

Riesenberg, L. H., and J. F. Wendel. 1993. Introgression and its consequences. Pp. 70–109 in R. G. Harrison, ed., *Hybrid zones and the evolutionary process.* Oxford University Press, Oxford.

Rigamonti, M. M. 1993. Home range and diet in red ruffed lemurs (*Varecia variegata rubra*) on the Masoala Peninsula, Madagascar. Pp. 25–39 in P. M. Kappeler and J. U. Ganzhorn, eds., *Lemur social systems and their ecological basis.* Plenum Press, New York.

Ringo, J. 1996. Sexual receptivity in insects. Annual Review of Entomology 41: 473–494.

Ritchie, M. G., and G. M. Hewitt. 1995. Outcomes of negative heterosis. Pp. 157–174 in D. M. Lambert and H. G. Spencer, eds., *Speciation and the recognition concept: Theory and application.* John Hopkins University Press, Baltimore, MD.

Ritchie, M. G., and S. D. F. Phillips. 1998. The genetics of sexual isolation. Pp. 291–308 in D. J. Howard and S. H. Berlocher, eds., *Endless forms, species and speciation*. Oxford University Press, New York.

Ritland, D. B. 1986. The effect of temperature on the expression of the dark morph phenotype in female *Papilio glaucus* (Papilionidae). Journal of Research on Lepidoptera 25: 179–187.

Ritland, D. B., and J. M. Scriber. 1985. Larval developmental rates of three putative subspecies of tiger swallowtail butterflies, *Papilio glaucus,* and their hybrids in relation to temperature. Oecologia 65: 185–193.

Robbins, R. K. 1988a. Comparative morphology of the butterfly foreleg coxa and trochanter (Lepidoptera) and its systematic implications. Proceedings of the Entomological Society of Washington 90: 133–154.

_____ . 1988b. Male foretarsal variation in Lycaenidae and Riodinidae and the systematic placement of *Styx infernalis* (Lepidoptera). Proceedings of the Entomological Society of Washington 90: 356–368.

_____ . 1990. Systematic implications of butterfly leg structures that clean the antennae. Psyche 96: 209–222.

Robertson, P. A., S. A. Clarke, and M. S. Warren. 1995. Woodland management and butterfly diversity. Pp. 113–122 in A. S. Pullin, ed., *Ecology and conservation of butterflies*. Chapman and Hall, London.

Robinson, J. G., and K. H. Redford. 1991. *Neotropical wildlife use and conservation*. The University of Chicago Press, Chicago.

Robinson, R. 1971. *Lepidoptera genetics*. Pergamon Press, Oxford.

Rockey, S. J., J. H. Hainze, and J. M. Scriber. 1987a. Evidence of a sex-linked diapause response in *Papilio glaucus* subspecies and their hybrids. Physiological Entomology 12: 181–184.

_____ . 1987b. A latitudinal and obligatory response in three subspecies of the eastern tiger swallowtail, *Papilio glaucus* (Lepidoptera: Papilionidae) American Midland Naturalist 118: 162–168.

Roelofs, W., T. Glover, X. H. Tang, I. Streng, P. Robbins, C. Eckenrode, C. Lofstedt, B. S. Hansson, and B. O. Bengtsson. 1987. Sex pheromone production and perception in European corn borer moths is determined by both autosomal and sex-linked genes. Proceedings of the National Academy of Sciences USA 84: 7585–7589.

Roininen, H., and J. Tahvanainen. 1989. Host selection and larval performance of two willow-feeding sawflies. Ecology 70: 129–136.

Roland, J. 1982. Melanism and the diel activity of alpine *Colias* (Lepidoptera: Pieridae). Oecologia 53: 214–221.

Roland, J., N. Keyghobadi, and S. Fownes. 2000. Alpine *Parnassius* butterfly dispersal: Effects of landscape and population size. Ecology 81: 1642–1653.

Root, R. B., and P. M. Kareiva. 1984. The search for resources by cabbage butterflies (*Pieris rapae*): Ecological consequences and adaptive significance of Markovian movements in a patchy environment. Ecology 65: 147–165.

Rose, M. R., and T. J. Bradley. 1998. Evolutionary physiology of the cost of reproduction. Oikos 83: 443–451.

Rose, M. R., and G. V. Lauder, eds. 1996. *Adaptation*. Academic Press, New York.

Rosen, D. E. 1978. Vicariant patterns and historical explanation in biogeography. Systematic Zoology 27: 159–188.

Rosenberg, R. H. 1989. Genetic differentiation among populations of Weidemeyer's admiral butterfly. Canadian Journal of Zoology 67: 2294–2300.

Rosenberg, R. H., and M. Enqvist. 1991. Contest behavior in Weidemeyer's admiral butterfly *Limenitis weidemeyerii* (Nymphalidae): The effect of size and residency. Animal Behaviour 42: 805–811.

Rosenheim, J. A. 1996. An evolutionary argument for egg limitation. Evolution 50: 2089–2094.

———. 1999. The relative contributions of time and eggs to the cost of reproduction. Evolution 53: 376–385.

Ross, G. N. 1964. Life history studies on Mexican butterflies II. Early stages of *Anatole rossi* a new myrmecophilous metalmark. Journal of Research on Lepidoptera 3: 81–94.

———. 1966. Life-history studies on Mexican butterflies. IV. The ecology and ethology of *Anatole rossi,* a Myrmecophilous metalmark (Lepidoptera: Riodinidae). Annals of the Entomological Society of America 59: 985–1004.

Roth, V. L. 1991. Homology and hierarchies: Problems solved and unresolved. Journal of Evolutionary Biology 4: 167–194.

Rothman, E. D., and A. M. Templeton. 1980. A class of models of selectively neutral alleles. Theoretical Population Biology 18: 135–150.

Rothschild, M., and L. Schoonhoven. 1977. Assessment of egg load by *Pieris brassicae* (Lepidoptera: Pieridae). Nature 266: 352–355.

Rothschild, W., and K. Jordan. 1903. A revision of the lepidopterous family Sphingidae. Novitates Zoologicae, vol. 9. Hazell, Watson and Viney, Ltd., London. 813 pp.

———. 1906. A revision of the American *Papilios.* Novitates Zoologicae 13: 411–752.

Roubik, D. W. 1990. Mate location and male competition in males of stingless bees (Hymenoptera: Apidae: Meliponinae). Entomologia Generalis 15: 115–120.

Rountree, D. B., and H. F. Nijhout. 1995. Hormonal control of a seasonal polyphenism in *Precis coenia* (Lepidoptera: Nymphalidae). Journal of Insect Physiology 41: 987–992.

Roy, B. A., and R. A. Raguso. 1997. Olfactory vs. visual cues in a floral mimicry system. Oecologia 109: 414–426.

Roy, D. B., P. Rothery, D. Moss, E. Pollard, and J. A. Thomas. 2001. Butterfly numbers and weather: Predicting historical trends in abundance and the future effects of climate change. Journal of Animal Ecology 70: 201–217.

Roy, D. B., and T. H. Sparks. 2000. Phenology of British butterflies and climate change. Global Change Biology 6: 407–416.

Rutowski, R. L. 1977a. Chemical communication in the courtship of the small sulfur butterfly *Eurema lisa.* Journal of Comparative Physiology 115: 75–85.

———. 1977b. The use of visual cues in sexual and species discrimination by males of the small sulphur butterfly, *Eurema lisa* (Lepidoptera, Pieridae). Journal of Comparative Physiology 115: 61–74.

———. 1978a. The courtship behavior of the small sulfur butterfly *Eurema lisa.* Animal Behaviour 26: 892–903.

———. 1978b. The form and function of ascending flights in *Colias* butterflies. Behavioral Ecology and Sociobiology 3: 163–172.

———. 1979. The butterfly as an honest salesman. Animal Behaviour 27: 1269–1270.

———. 1980a. Courtship solicitation by females of the checkered white butterfly (*Pieris protodice*). Behavioral Ecology and Sociobiology 7: 113–117.

———. 1980b. Male scent-producing structures in *Colias* butterflies: Function, localization and adaptive features. Journal of Chemical Ecology 6: 13–26.

_____. 1981. Sexual discrimination using visual cues in the checkered white butterfly (*Pieris protodice*). Zeitschrift Tierpsychologie 55: 325–334.

_____. 1982. Epigamic selection by males as evidenced by courtship partner preferences in the checkered white butterfly (*Pieris protodice*). Animal Behaviour 30: 108–112.

_____. 1984. Sexual selection and the evolution of butterfly mating behaviour. Journal of Research on Lepidoptera 23: 125–142.

_____. 1991. The evolution of mate-locating behaviour in butterflies. American Naturalist 138: 1121–1139.

_____. 1997. Sexual dimorphism, mating systems and ecology in butterflies. Pp. 257–272 in J. C. Choe and B. J. Crespi, eds., *The evolution of mating systems in insects and arachnids.* Cambridge University Press, Cambridge.

_____. 1998. Mating strategies in butterflies. Scientific American July: 64–69.

_____. 2000. Eye size variation in butterflies: Inter- and intraspecfic patterns. Journal of Zoology 252: 187–195.

Rutowski, R. L., M. J. Demlong, and T. Leffingwell. 1994. Behavioral thermoregulation at mate encounter sites by male butterflies, *Asterocampa leilia* (Nymphalidae) at perching sites used in mate location. Journal of Research on Lepidoptera 30: 129–139.

Rutowski, R. L., and G. W. Gilchrist. 1986. Copulation in *Colias eurytheme* (Lepidoptera: Pieridae): Patterns and frequency. Journal of Zoology 209: 115–124.

Rutowski, R. L., G. W. Gilchrist, and B. Terkanian. 1987. Female butterflies mated with recently mated males show reduced reproductive output. Behavioral Ecology and Sociobiology 20: 319–322.

_____. 1991. Behavior of male desert hackberry butterflies, *Asterocampa leila* (Nymphalidae) at perching sites used in mate location. Journal of Research on Lepidoptera 30: 129–139.

Rutowski, R. L., C. E. Long, L. E. Marshall, and R. S. Vetter. 1981. Courtship solicitation by *Colias* females (Lepidoptera: Pieridae). American Midland Naturalist 105: 334–340.

Rutowski, R. L., and E. J. Warrant. 2002. Visual field structure in Empress Leilia, *Asterocampa leilia* (Lepidoptera: Nymphalidae): Dimensions and regional variation in acuity. Journal of Comparative Physiology 188: 1–12.

Ryan, M. J., J. H. Fox, W. Wilczynski, and S. A. Rand. 1990. Sexual selection for sensory exploitation in the frog, *Physalaemus pustulosis*. Nature 343: 66–67.

Ryan, M. J., and W. E. Wagner. 1987. Asymmetries in mating preferences between species: Female swordtails prefer heterospecific males. Science 236: 595–597.

Ryder, O. A. 1986. Species conservation and systematics: The dilemma of subspecies. Trends in Ecology and Evolution 1: 9–10.

Ryti, R. T. 1992. Effect of the focal taxon on the selection of nature reserves. Ecological Applications 2: 404–410.

Saccheri, I. J., P. M. Brakefield, and R. A. Nichols. 1996. Severe inbreeding depression and rapid fitness rebound in the butterfly *Bicyclus anynana* (Satyridae). Evolution 50: 200–213.

Saccheri, I. J., M. Kuussaari, M. Kankare, P. Vikman, W. Fortelius, and I. Hanski. 1998. Inbreeding and extinction in a butterfly metapopulation. Nature 392: 491–494.

Sachev-Gupta, K., C. D. Radke, and J. A. A. Renwick. 1992. Chemical recognition of diverse hosts by *Pieris rapae* butterflies. Pp. 136–138 in S. B. J. Menken, J. H. Visser, and P. Harrewijn, eds., *Proceedings of the 8th international symposium on insect-plant relationships.* Kluwer Academic, Dordrecht.

Sacktor, B. 1975. Biochemistry of insect flight. I. Utilization of fuels by muscle. Pp. 1–88 in D. J. Candy and B. A. Bilby, eds., *Insect biochemistry and function*. Chapman and Hall, London.

Saetersdal, M., J. M. Line, and H. J. B. Birks. 1993. How to maximize biological diversity in nature reserve selection: Vascular plants and breeding birds in deciduous woodlands, western Norway. Biological Conservation 66: 131–138.

Saetre, G. P., T. Moum, S. Bares, M. Kral, M. Adamjan, and J. Moreno. 1997. A sexually selected character displacement in flycatchers reinforces premating isolation. Nature 387: 589–592.

Sagarin, R. D., J. P. Barry, S. E. Gilman, and C. H. Baxter. 1999. Climate-related change in an intertidal community over short and long time scales. Ecological Monographs 69: 465–490.

Saitou, N., and M. Nei. 1987. The neighbor-joining method: A new method for reconstructing phylogenetic trees. Molecular Biology and Evolution 4: 406–425.

Sakamoto, K., O. Hisatomi, F. Tokunaga, and E. Eguchi. 1996. Two opsins from the compound eye of the crab *Hemigrapsus sanguineus*. Journal of Experimental Biology 199: 449–450.

Salcedo, E., A. Huber, S. Henrich, L. Chadwell, W.-H. Chou, R. Paulsen, and S. Britt. 1999. Blue- and green-absorbing visual pigments of *Drosophila*: Ectopic expression and physiological characterization of the R8 photoreceptor cell-specific Rh5 and Rh6 rhodopsins. Journal of Neuroscience 19: 10716–10726.

Sambrook, J., E. F. Fritsch, and T. Maniatis. 1989. *Molecular cloning: A laboratory manual*. Cold Spring Harbor Laboratory Press, Plainview, New York.

Samson, D. A., E. A. Rickart, and P. C. Gonzales. 1997. Ant diversity and abundance along an elevational gradient in the Philippines. Biotropica 29: 349–363.

Sanders, C. J., G. E. Daterman, and T. J. Ennis. 1977. Sex pheromone responses of *Choristoneura* spp., and their hybrids (Lepidoptera: Tortricidae). Canadian Entomologist 109: 1203–1220.

Sands, D. P. A., and P. F. Sawyer. 1977. An example of natural hybridization between *Troides oblongomaculatus papuensis* Wallace and *Ornithoptera priamus poseidon* Doubleday (Lepidoptera: Papilionidae). Journal of the Australian Entomological Society 16: 81–82.

Sasaki, T., K. Niino, H. Sakuma, and S. Sukawara. 1984a. Analysis of tobacco headspace volatiles using tenax GC or active carbon. Agricultural and Biological Chemistry 48: 3121–3128.

Sasaki, T., H. Sakuma, and S. Sugawara. 1984b. Analysis of the headspace volatiles of tobacco using an ether trap. Agricultural and Biological Chemistry 48: 2719–2724.

Savageau, M. A., and A. Sorribas. 1989. Constraints among molecular and systemic properties: Implications for physiological genetics. Journal of Theoretical Biology 141: 93–115.

Sbordoni, V., and S. Forestiero. 1984. *Butterflies of the world*. Crescent Books, New York.

Schaus, W. 1913. New species of Rhopalocera from Costa Rica. Proceedings of the Zoological Society of London 25: 339–367.

Schemscke, D. H. 1980. The evolution of floral display in the orchid *Brassavola nodosa*. Evolution 34: 489–493.

Schemscke, D. H., and C. C. Horvitz. 1984. Variation among floral visitors in pollination ability: A precondition for mutualism specialization. Science 225: 519–521.

Scherer, C., and G. Kolb. 1987a. Behavioral experiments on the visual processing of color stimuli in *Pieris brassicae* L. (Lepidoptera). Journal of Comparative Physiology A 160: 645–656.

———. 1987b. The influence of color stimuli on visually controlled behavior in *Aglais urticae* L., and *Pararge aegeria* L. (Lepidoptera). Journal of Comparative Physiology 161: 891–898.

Schlecht, P. 1979. Colour discrimination in dim light: An analysis of the photoreceptor arrangement in the moth *Deilephila*. Journal of Comparative Physiology A 129: 257–267.

Schluter, D. 2000. *Ecology and adaptive radiation.* Oxford University Press, New York.

Schmitt, J. B. 1938. The feeding mechanism of adult Lepidoptera. Smithsonian Miscellaneous Contributions 97 (4): 28.

Schmitz, H. 1994. Thermal characterization of butterfly wings: I. Absorption in relation to different color, surface structure and basking type. Journal of Thermal Biology 19: 403–412.

Schnelle, F. 1955. *Pflanzen-Phenologie.* Akademische Verlagsgesellschaft Geest und Portig, Leipzig.

Schoonhoven, L. M., E. A. M. Beerling, J. W. Klijnstra, and Y. van Vugt. 1990. Two related butterfly species avoid oviposition near each other's eggs. Experientia 46: 526–528.

Schreiber, H. 1978. Dispersal centres of Sphingidae (Lepidoptera) in the Neotropical region. Pp. 1–136 in J. Schmithüsen, ed., *Biogeographica,* vol. 10. Dr. W. Junk B. V., Publishers, The Hague.

Schultz, C. B. 1998a. Dispersal behavior and its implications for reserve design in a rare Oregon butterfly. Conservation Biology 12: 284–292.

———. 1998b. Ecology and conservation of the Fender's blue butterfly. Ph.D. dissertation, University of Washington, Seattle.

Schultz, C. B., and E. E. Crone. 1998. Burning prairie to restore butterfly habitat? A modeling approach to management tradeoffs for the Fender's blue. Restoration Ecology 6: 244–252.

———. 2001. Edge-mediated dispersal behavior in a prairie butterfly. Ecology 82: 1879–1892.

Schultz, C. B., and K. Dlugosch. 1999. Nectar and hostplant scarcity limits populations of an endangered butterfly. Oecologia 119: 231–238.

Schulz, S., M. Boppré, and R. I. Vane-Wright. 1993. Specific mixtures of secretions from male scent organs of Kenyan milkweed butterflies (Danainae). Philosophical Transactions of the Royal Society of London B 342: 161–181.

Schwagmeyer, P. L. 1995. Searching today for tomorrow's mates. Animal Behaviour 50: 759–767.

Schwartz, L. M., and J. W. Truman. 1983. Hormonal control of rates of metamorphic development in the tobacco hornworm *Manduca sexta*. Developmental Biology 99: 103–114.

Scoble, M. J. 1990a. A catalogue of the Hedylidae (Lepidoptera: Hedyloidea) with descriptions of two new species. Entomologica Scandinavica 21: 113–119.

———. 1990b. An identification guide to the Hedylidae (Lepidoptera: Hedyloidea). Entomologica Scandinavica 21: 121–158.

———. 1992. *The Lepidoptera: Form, function, and diversity.* Oxford University Press, Oxford.

Scott, J. A. 1970. Hilltopping as a mating mechanism to aid the survival of low density species. Journal of Research on Lepidoptera 7: 191–204.

———. 1973a. Mating of butterflies. Journal of Research on Lepidoptera 11: 99–127.

———. 1973b. Population biology and adult behavior of the circumpolar butterfly *Parnassius phoebus* F.(Papilionidae). Entomologica Scandinavica 4: 161–168.

———. 1974. Mate-locating behavior of butterflies. American Midland Naturalist 91: 103–117.

———. 1975. Flight patterns among eleven species of diurnal Lepidoptera. Ecology 56: 1367–1377.

———. 1983. Mate-locating behavior of western North American butterflies: II. New observations and morphological adaptations. Journal of Research on Lepidoptera 21: 177–187.

———. 1984. The phylogeny of butterflies (Papilionoidea and Hesperioidea). Journal of Research on Lepidoptera 23: 241–281.

———. 1986. *The butterflies of North America: A natural history and field guide.* Stanford University Press, California.

Scott, J. A., and M. Epstein. 1987. Factors affecting phenology in a temperate insect community. American Midland Naturalist 117: 103–118.

Scott, J. A., and D. M. Wright. 1990. Butterfly phylogeny and fossils. Pp. 152–208 in O. Kudrna, eds., *Butterflies of Europe*. Vol. 2. Aula-Verlag, Wiesbaden.

Scriber, J. M. 1973. Latitudinal gradients in larval feeding specialization of the world Papilionidae (Lepidoptera). Psyche 80: 355–373.

———. 1975. Comparative nutritional ecology of herbivorous insects: Generalized and specialized feeding strategies in the Papilionidae and Saturniidae (Lepidoptera). Ph.D. dissertation, Cornell University, Ithaca, NY.

———. 1982. Foodplants and speciation in the *Papilio glaucus* group. Pp. 307–314 in J. H. Visser and A. K. Minks, eds., *Proc. 5th Intern. Symp. Insect Plant Relationships*. PUDOC, Wageningen, Netherlands.

———. 1983. The evolution of feeding specialization, physiological efficiency, and host races. Pp. 373–412 in R. F. Denno and M. S. McClure, eds., *Variable plants and herbivores in natural and managed systems*. Academic Press, New York.

———. 1984a. Insect/Plant interactions—host suitability. Pp. 159–202 in W. Bell and R. Cardé, eds. *The chemical ecology of insects*. Chapman and Hall, London.

———. 1984b. Larval foodplant utilization by the world Papilionidae (Lepidoptera): Latitudinal gradients reappraised. Tokurana (Acta Rhopalocerologica) 2: 1–50.

———. 1986a. Origins of the regional feeding abilities in the tiger swallowtail butterfly: Ecological monophagy and the *Papilio glaucus australis* subspecies of Florida. Oecologia 71: 94–103.

———. 1986b. Allelochemicals and alimentary ecology: Heterosis in a hybrid zone? Pp. 43–71 in L. Brattsten and S. Ahmad, eds., *Molecular aspects of insect-plant associations*. Plenum, New York.

———. 1988. Tale of the tiger: Beringial biology, binomial classification, and breakfast choices in the *Papilio glaucus* complex of butterflies. Pp. 241–301 in K. C. Spencer, ed., *Chemical mediation of coevolution*. Academic Press, New York.

———. 1990. Interaction of introgression from *Papilio glaucus canadensis* and diapause in producing 'Spring form' Eastern tiger swallowtail butterflies, *P. glaucus*. Great Lakes Entomologist 23: 127–138.

———. 1992. Latitudinal trends in oviposition preferences: Ecological and genetic influences. Pp. 212–214 in S. B. J. Menken, J. H. Visser, and J. H. Harrewjin, eds., *Proc. of the 8th symposium on insect-plant relationships*. Kluwer Academic Publishers, Dordrecht, Netherlands.

———. 1993. Absence of behavioral induction in multi-choice oviposition preference studies with a generalist butterfly species, Papilio glaucus. Great Lakes Entomologist 28: 81–95.

———. 1994. Climatic legacies and sex chromosomes: Latitudinal patterns of voltinism, diapause, body size, and host-plant selection on two species of swallowtail butterflies at their hybrid zone. Pp. 133–171 in H. V. Danks, ed., *Insect life-cycle polymorphism: Theory, evolution and ecological consequences for seasonality and diapause control.* Kluwer Academic Publishers, Dordrecht, Netherlands.

———. 1995. An overview of swallowtail butterflies: Taxonomic and distributional latitude. Pp. 3–8 in J. M. Scriber, Y. Tsubaki, and R. C. Lederhouse, eds., *Swallowtail butterflies: Their ecology and evolutionary biology.* Scientific Publishers, Gainesville, FL.

———. 1996a. Tiger tales: Natural history of native North American swallowtails. American Entomologist 42: 19–32.

———. 1996b. A new "cold pocket" hypothesis to explain local host preference shifts in *Papilio canadensis.* Entomologica Experimentalis et Applicata 80: 315–319.

———. 1998. Inheritance of diagnostic larval traits for interspecific hybrids and *Papilio glaucus* and *P. canadensis.* Great Lakes Entomologist 31: 113–123.

———. 2002. The evolution of insect-plant relationships; Chemical constraints, coadaptation and concordance of insect/plant traits. Entomologica Experimentalis et Applicata. In press.

Scriber, J. M., M. D. Deering, L. Francke, W Wehling, and R. C. Lederhouse. 1998a. Notes on the population dynamics of three *Papilio* species in southcentral Florida. Holarctic Lepidoptera 5: 53–62.

Scriber, J. M., M. D. Deering, and A. Stump. 1998b. Evidence of long range transport of a swallowtail butterfly (*Papilio glaucus* L.) on a storm front into northern Michigan. Great Lakes Entomologist 31: 151–160.

Scriber, J. M., R. V. Dowell, R. C. Lederhouse, and R. H. Hagen. 1990b. Female color and sex ratio in hybrids between *Papilio glaucus glaucus* and *P. eurymedon, P. rutulus,* and *P. multicaudatus* (Papilionidae). Journal of the Lepidopterists' Society 44: 229–244.

Scriber, J. M., and M. H. Evans. 1986. An exceptional case of paternal transmission of the dark form female trait in the tiger swallowtail butterfly, *Papilio glaucus* (Lepidoptera: Papilionidae). Journal of Research on Lepidoptera 25: 110–120.

Scriber, J. M., M. H. Evans, and R. C. Lederhouse. 1990a. Hybridization of the Mexican tiger swallowtail, *Papilio alexiares garcia,* (Lepidoptera: Papilionidae) with other *Papilio glaucus* group species and survival of pure and hybrid larvae on potential host plants. Journal of Research on Lepidoptera 27: 222–232.

Scriber, J. M., M. H. Evans, and D. Ritland. 1987. Hybridization as a causal mechanism of mixed color broods and unusual color morphs of female offspring in the eastern tiger swallowtail butterflies, *Papilio glaucus.* Pp. 119–134 in M. Huettel, ed., *Evolutionary genetics of invertebrate behavior.* Plenum, New York.

Scriber, J. M., and P. P. Feeny. 1979. Growth of herbivorous caterpillars in relation to feeding specialization and to the growth form of their food plants. Ecology 60: 829–850.

Scriber, J. M., and S. Gage. 1995. Pollution and global climate change: Plant ecotones, butterfly hybrid zones, and biodiversity. Pp. 319–344 in J. M. Scriber,

Y. Tsubaki, and R. C. Lederhouse, eds., *Swallowtail butterflies: Their ecology and evolutionary biology.* Scientific Publishers, Gainesville, FL.

Scriber, J. M., B. L. Giebink, and D. Snider. 1991a. Reciprocal latitudinal clines in oviposition behaviour of *Papilio glaucus* and *P. canadensis* across the Great Lakes hybrid zone: Possible sex-linkage of oviposition preferences. Oecologia 87: 360–368.

Scriber, J. M., R. H. Hagen, and R. C. Lederhouse. 1996. Genetics of mimicry in the tiger swallowtail butterflies, *Papilio glaucus* and *P. canadensis* (Lepidoptera: Papilionidae). Evolution 50: 222–236.

Scriber, J. M., and J. H. Hainze. 1987. Geographic invasion and abundance as facilitated by different host plant utilization abilities. Pp. 433–468 in P. Barbosa and J. C. Schultz, eds., *Insect outbreaks: Ecological and evolutionary processes.* Academic Press, New York.

Scriber, J. M., M. K. Keefover, and S. Nelson. 2002. Hot summer temperatures may stop genetic introgression of *Papilio canadensis* south of the hybrid zone in the North American Great Lakes region? Ecography 25: 184–192.

Scriber, J. M., and R. C. Lederhouse. 1983. Temperature as a factor in the development and feeding ecology of tiger swallowtail caterpillars, *Papilio glaucus* (Lepidoptera). Oikos 40: 95–102.

——— . 1989. Hand-pairing of *Papilio glaucus glaucus* and *Papilio pilumnus* and hybrid survival on various host plants. Journal of Research on Lepidoptera 43: 93–101.

——— . 1992. The thermal environment as a resource dictating geographic patterns of feeding specialization of insect herbivores. Pp. 429–466 in M. R. Hunter, T. Ohgushi, and P. W. Price, eds., *Effects of resource distribution on animal-plant interactions.* Academic Press, New York.

Scriber, J. M., R. C. Lederhouse, and K. Brown. 1991b. Hybridization of Brazilian *Papilio* (*Pyrrhosticta*) (Section V) with North American Papilio (*Pterourus*) (Section III). Journal of Research on Lepidoptera 29: 21–32.

Scriber, J. M., R. C. Lederhouse, and R. V. Dowell. 1995a. Hybridization studies with North American swallowtails. Pp. 269–281 in J. M. Scriber, Y. Tsubaki, and R. C. Lederhouse, eds., *Swallowtail butterflies: Their ecology and evolutionary biology.* Scientific Publishers, Gainesville, FL.

Scriber, J. M., R. C. Lederhouse, and R. H. Hagen. 1991c. Foodplants and evolution within the *Papilio glaucus* and *Papilio troilus* species groups (Lepidoptera: Papilionidae) Pp. 341–373 in P. W. Price, T. M. Lewinsohn, G. W. Fernandez, and W. W. Benson, eds., *Plant-animal interactions: Evolutionary ecology in tropical and temperate regions.* Wiley, New York.

Scriber, J. M., R. L. Lindroth, and J. Nitao. 1989. Differential toxicity of a phenolic glycoside from quaking aspen leaves by *Papilio glaucus* subspecies, their hybrids, and backcrosses. Oecologia 81: 186–191.

Scriber, J. M., Y. Tsubaki, and R. C. Lederhouse, eds. 1995b. *Swallowtail butterflies: Their ecology and evolutionary biology.* Scientific Publishers, Gainsville, FL.

Scriber, J. M., K. Weir, D. Parry, and J. Deering. 1999. Using hybrid and backcross larvae of *Papilio canadensis* and *P. glaucus* to detect induced phytochemical resistance in hybrid poplars experimentally defoliated by gypsy moths. Entomologica Experimentalis et Applicata 91: 233–236.

Sculley, C. E., and C. L. Boggs. 1996. Mating systems and sexual division of foraging effort affect puddling behaviour by butterflies. Ecological Entomology 21: 193–197.

Sears, T. A. 1970. A possible explanation for seasonal emergence peaks of Macrolepidoptera in southern California. Pan-Pacific Entomologist 46: 82–83.

Seki, T., S. Fujishita, M. Ito, N. Matsuoka, and K. Tsukida. 1987. Retinoid composition in the compound eyes of insects. Experimental Biology 47: 95–103.

Sevenster, J. G., J. Ellers, and G. Driessen. 1998. An evolutionary argument for time limitation. Evolution 52: 1241–1244.

Shaffer, M. L. 1981. Minimum population size for species conservation. BioScience 31: 131–134.

Shapiro, A. M. 1974. Butterflies and skippers of New York State. Cornell University Agricultural Experiment Station Research 4: 1–60.

_____. 1975a. *Papilio "gothica"* and the phenotypic plasticity of *P. zelicaon* (Papilionidae). Journal of the Lepidopterists' Society 29: 79–84.

_____. 1975b. The temporal component of butterfly species diversity. Pp. 181–195 in M. L. Cody and J. M. Diamond, eds., *Ecology and evolution of communities.* Belknap Press, Harvard, Cambridge, MA.

_____. 1976. Seasonal polyphenism. Evolutionary Biology 9: 259–333.

_____. 1981. The pierid red-egg syndrome. American Naturalist 117: 276–294.

Shapiro, A. M., and K. K. Masuda. 1980. The opportunistic origin of a new citrus pest. California Agriculture 34: 4–5.

Shapiro, A. M., and A. R. Shapiro. 1973. The ecological associations of the butterflies of Staten Island (Richmond County, New York). Journal of Research on Lepidoptera 12: 65–126.

Sheck, A. L., and F. Gould. 1996. The genetic basis of differences in growth and behavior of specialist and generalist herbivore species: Selection on hybrids of *Heliothis virescens* and *Heliothis subflexa.* Evolution 50: 831–841.

Shelley, T. E., and D. Ludwig. 1985. Thermoregulatory behavior of the butterfly *Calisto nubila* (Satyridae) in a Puerto Rican forest. Oikos 44: 229–233.

Sheppard, P. M. 1962. Some aspects of the geography, genetics, and taxonomy of a butterfly. Publications Systematics Association 4: 135–152.

Sheppard, P. M., J. R. G. Turner, K. S. Brown, W. W. Benson, and M. C. Singer. 1985. Genetics and the evolution of Müllerian mimicry in *Heliconius* butterflies. Philosophical Transactions of the Royal Society of London B 308: 433–613.

Sherman, P. W., and W. B. Watt. 1973. The thermal physiological ecology of some *Colias* butterfly larvae. Journal of Comparative Physiology 83: 25–40.

Shields, O. 1968. Hilltopping. Journal of Research on Lepidoptera 6: 69–178.

_____. 1988. Butterflies of the foothill woodland (and chaparral) plant community in central California: Their ecology, affinities and ancestry. Utahensis 6: 18–39.

Shimada, T., Y. Kurimoto, and M. Kobayashi. 1995. Phylogenetic relationship of silkmoths inferred from sequence data of the arylphorin gene. Molecular Phylogenetics and Evolution 4: 223–234.

Shimohigashi, M., and Y. Tominaga. 1991. Identification of UV, green, and red receptors, and their projection to lamina in the cabbage butterfly, *Pieris rapae.* Cell Tissue Research 263: 49–59.

Shirôzu, T., and Yamamoto, H. 1957. Systematic position of the genus *Curetis* (Lepidoptera: Rhopalocera). Sieboldia 2: 43–51.

Showers, W. B. 1981. Geographic variation of the diapause response in the European corn borer. Pp. 97–11. in R. F. Denno and H. Dingle, eds., *Insect life history patterns: Habitat and geographic variation.* Springer-Verlag, New York.

Shreeve, T. G. 1984. Habitat selection, mate-location, and micro-climatic constraints on the activity of the speckled wood butterfly *Pararge aegeria.* Oikos 42: 371–377.

———. 1985. The population biology of the speckled wood butterfly *Pararge aegeria* (L.) (Lepidoptera: Satyridae). Ph.D. dissertation (CNAA), Oxford Polytechnic.

———. 1987. The mate-location behaviour of the male speckled wood butterfly *Pararge aegeria*, and the effect of phenotypic differences in hind-wing spotting. Animal Behaviour 35: 682–690.

———. 1990. The movements of butterflies. Pp. 512–532 in O. Kudrna, ed., *Butterflies of Europe, Vol. 2, Introduction to lepidopterology.* Aula-Verlag, Wiesbaden.

———. 1992a. Adult behaviour. Pp. 22–45 in R. L. H. Dennis, ed., *The ecology of butterflies in Britain.* Oxford University Press, Oxford.

———. 1992b. Monitoring butterfly movement. Pp. 120–138 in R. L. H. Dennis, ed., *The ecology of butterflies in Britain.* Oxford University Press, Oxford.

Shreeve, T. G., and A. G. Smith. 1992. The role of weather-related habitat use on the impact of European speckled wood butterfly *Pararge aegeria* on the endemic *Pararge xiphia* on the island of Madeira. Biological Journal of the Linnean Society 46: 59–75.

Shuey, J. A. 1986. Comments on Clench's temporal sequencing of Hesperiid communities. Journal of Research on Lepidoptera 25: 202–206.

Sibatani, A. 1980. Wing homeosis in Lepidoptera: A survey. Developmental Biology 79: a1–18.

Sibly, R. M., and P. Calow. 1984. Direct and absorption costing in the evolution of life cycles. Journal of Theoretical Biology 111: 463–473.

———. 1986. *Physiological ecology of animals.* Blackwell Scientific Publications, Oxford.

Silberbauer-Gottsberger, I., and G. Gottsberger. 1975. Über sphingophile angiospermen Brasiliens. Plant Systematics and Evolution 123: 157–184.

Silberglied, R. E. 1984. Visual communication and sexual selection among butterflies. Pp. 207–223 in R. I. Vane-Wright and P. R. Ackery, eds., *The biology of butterflies.* Academic Press, London.

Silberglied, R. E., and O. R. Taylor. 1978. Ultraviolet reflexion and its behavioral role in the courtship of the sulfur butterflies, *Colias eurytheme* and *C. philodice* (Lepidoptera: Pieridae). Behavioral Ecology and Sociobiology 3: 203–243.

Silberman, J. D., and P. J. Walsh. 1992. Species identification of spiny lobster phyllosome larvae via ribosomal DNA analysis. Molecular Marine Biology and Biotechnology 1: 195–205.

Sillén-Tullberg, B. 1988. Evolution of gregariousness in aposematic butterfly larvae: A phylogenetic analysis. Evolution 42: 293–305.

Simberloff, D. 1994. The ecology of extinction. Acta Palaeontologica Polonica 38: 159–174.

Simmons, L. W. 1995. Correlates of male quality in the field cricket, *Gryllus campestris* L.: Age, size, and symmetry determine pairing success in field populations. Behavioral Ecology 6: 376–381.

Simmons, L. W., and G. A. Parker. 1989. Nuptial feeding in insects: Mating effort versus paternal investment. Ethology 81: 332–343.

———. 1992. Individual variation in sperm competition success of yellow dungflies, *Scatophaga stercoraria.* Evolution 46: 366–375.

Simmons, R. E., M. Griffin, R. E. Griffin, E. Marais, and H. Kolberg. 1998. Endemism in Nambia: Patterns, processes and predictions. Biodiversity Conservation 7: 513–530.

Simon, C., F. Frati, A. Beckenbach, B. Crespi, H. Liu, and P. Flook. 1994. Evolution, weighting, and phylogenetic utility of mitochondrial gene sequences and a compilation of conserved polymerase chain reaction primers. Annals of the Entomological Society of America 87: 651–701.

Simpson, G. G. 1961. *Principles of animal taxonomy*. Columbia University Press, New York.

Simpson, S. J., and D. Raubenheimer. 1996. Feeding behaviour, sensory physiology and nutrient feedback: A unifying model. Entomologica Experimentalis et Applicata 80: 55–64.

Sinclair, A. R. E. 1989. Population regulation in animals. Pp. 197–242 in J. M. Cherrett, ed., *Ecological concepts*. Blackwell.

Singer, M. C. 1971a. Evolution of food-plant preference in the butterfly *Euphydrias editha*. Evolution 25: 383–389.

_____ . 1971b. Ecological studies on the butterfly *Euphydryas editha*. Ph.D. dissertation, Stanford University, Stanford, CA.

_____ . 1972. Complex components of habitat suitability within a butterfly colony. Science 173: 75–77.

_____ . 1982a. Quantification of host preference by manipulation of oviposition behavior in the butterfly *Euphydryas editha*. Oecologia 52: 224–229.

_____ . 1982b. Sexual selection for small size in male butterflies. American Naturalist 119: 440–443.

_____ . 1983. Determinants of multiple host use by a phytophagous insect population. Evolution 37: 389–403.

_____ . 1986. The definition and measurement of oviposition preference. Pp. 65–94 in J. Miller and T. A. Miller, eds., *Plant-insect interactions*. Springer-Verlag.

_____ . 1994. Behavioural constraints on the evolutionary expansion of insect diet: A case history from checkerspot butterflies. Pp. 279–296 in L. Real, ed., *Behavioural mechanisms in evolutionary ecology*. University of Chicago Press, Chicago.

_____ . 2000. Reducing ambiguity in describing plant-insect interactions: "preference," "acceptability" and "electivity." Ecology Letters 3: 159–162.

Singer, M. C., and P. R. Ehrlich. 1979. Population dynamics of the checkerspot butterfly *Euphydryas editha*. Fortschritte der Zoologie 25: 53–60.

Singer, M. C., and J. R. Lee. 2000. Discrimination within and between host species by a butterfly: Implications for design of preference experiments. Ecology Letters 3: 101–105.

Singer, M. C., D. Ng, and R. A. Moore. 1991. Genetic variation in oviposition preference between butterfly populations. Journal of Insect Behavior 4: 531–535.

Singer, M. C., D. Ng, and C. D. Thomas. 1988. Heritability of oviposition preference and its relationship to offspring performance within a single insect population. Evolution 42: 977–985.

Singer, M. C., D. Ng, D. Vasco, and C. D. Thomas. 1992a. Rapidly evolving associations among oviposition preferences fail to constrain evolution of insect diet. American Naturalist 139: 9–20.

Singer, M. C., and C. Parmesan. 1993. Sources of variation in patterns of plant-insect association. Nature 361: 251–253.

Singer, M. C., and C. D. Thomas. 1996. Evolutionary responses of a butterfly metapopulation to human- and climate-caused environmental variation. American Naturalist 148: S9-S39.

Singer, M. C., C. D. Thomas, H. L. Billington, and C. Parmesan. 1989. Variation among conspecific insect populations in the mechanistic basis of diet breadth. Animal Behaviour 37: 751–759.

———. 1994. Correlates of speed of evolution of host preference in a set of twelve populations of the butterfly *Euphydryas editha*. Ecoscience 1: 107–114.

Singer, M. C., C. D. Thomas, and C. Parmesan. 1993. Rapid human-induced evolution of insect diet. Nature 366: 681–683.

Singer, M. C., D. Vasco, C. Parmesan, C. D. Thomas, and D. Ng. 1992b. Distinguishing between 'preference' and 'motivation' in food choice: An example from insect oviposition. Animal Behaviour 44: 463–471.

Singer, R., and A. A. Cocucci. 1997. Eye attached hemipollinaria in the hawkmoth and settling moth pollination of *Habenaria* (Orchidaceae): A study on functional morphology in five species from subtropical South America. Botanica Acta 110: 328–337.

Skellam, J. G. 1951. Random dispersal in theoretical populations. Biometrika 38: 196–218.

Slatkin, M. 1985. Gene flow in natural populations. Annual Review of Ecology and Systematics 16: 393–430.

———. 1993. Isolation by distance in equilibrium and non-equilibrium populations. Evolution 47: 264–279.

Smedley, S. R., and T. Eisner. 1995. Sodium uptake by puddling in a moth. Science 270: 1816–1818.

Smiley, J. 1978. Plant chemistry and the evolution of host specificity: New evidence from *Heliconius* and *Passiflora*. Science 201: 745–747.

Smith, B. H. 1993. Merging mechanism and adaptation: An ethological approach to learning and generalization. Pp. 126–157 in D. R. Papaj and A. C. Lewis, eds., *Insect learning*. Chapman and Hall, New York.

Smith, B. H., and W. M. Getz. 1994. Nonpheromonal olfactory processing in insects. Annual Review of Entomology 39: 351–375.

Smith, D. A. 1984. Mate selection in butterflies: Competition, coyness, choice and chauvinism. Pp. 225–244 in R. I. Vane-Wright and P. R. Ackery, eds., *The biology of butterflies*. Academic Press, London.

Smith, J. M. 1983. The genetics of stasis and punctuation. Annual Review of Genetics 17: 11–25.

Smith, R. L. 1984. *Sperm competition and the evolution of animal mating systems*. Academic Press, New York.

Smouse, P. E., J. C. Long, and R. R. Sokal. 1986. Multiple regression and correlation extensions of the Mantel test of matrix correspondence. Systematic Zoology 35: 627–632.

Sokal, R. R. 1973. The species problem reconsidered. Systematic Zoology 22: 360–374.

Sokal, R. R., and F. Rohlf. 1995. *Biometry*. 3d ed. W. H. Freeman and Company, New York.

Sokal, R. R., and P. H. A. Sneath. 1963. *Principles of numerical taxonomy*. W. H. Freeman, San Francisco.

Solis, M. A., and M. G. Pogue. 1999. Lepidopteran biodiversity: Patterns and estimators. American Entomologist 45: 206–212.

Sota, T., and K. Kubota. 1998. Genital lock-and-key as a selective agent against hybridization. Evolution 52: 1507–1513.

Soto-Adames, F. N., H. M. Robertson, and S. H. Berlocher. 1994. Phylogenetic utility of partial DNA sequences of G6pdh at different taxonomic levels in Hexapoda with emphasis on Diptera. Annals of the Entomological Society of America 87: 723–736.

Soulé, M. E. 1986. *Conservation biology*. Sinauer Associates, Sunderland, MA.

Soulé, M. E., and B. A. Wilcox, eds. 1980. *Conservation biology: An evolutionary-ecological approach.* Sinauer Associates, Sunderland, MA.

Southwood, T. R. E. 1961. The number of species of insects associated with various trees. Journal of Animal Ecology 30: 1–8.

———. 1972. The insect-plant relationship-an evolutionary perspective. Symposium Royal Entomological Society 6: 3–30.

———. 1978. *Ecological methods.* Chapman and Hall, London.

Sparks, T. H., and P. D. Carey. 1995. The responses of species to climate over two centuries: An analysis of the Marsham phenological record, 1736–1947. Journal of Ecology 83: 321–329.

Sparks, T. H., and T. J. Yates. 1997. The effects of spring temperature on the appearance dates of British butterflies 1883–1993. Ecography 20: 368–374.

Spears, E. 1983. A direct measure of pollinator effectiveness. Oecologia 57: 196–199.

Speight, M. R., M. C. Hunter, and A. D. Watt. 1999. *Ecology of insects: Concepts and applications.* Blackwell Scientific, Oxford.

Sperling, F. A. H. 1987. Evolution of the *Papilio machaon* species group in western Canada (Lepidoptera: Papilionidae). Quaestiones Entomologicae 23: 198–315.

———. 1990. Natural hybrids of *Papilio* (Insecta: Lepidoptera): Poor taxonomy or interesting evolutionary problem? Canadian Journal of Zoology 68: 1790–1799.

———. 1991. Mitochondrial DNA phylogeny, speciation, and hostplant coevolution of *Papilio* butterflies. Ph.D. dissertation, Cornell University, Ithaca, NY.

———. 1993. Mitochondrial DNA variation and Haldane's rule in the *Papilio glaucus* and *P. troilus* species groups. Heredity 71: 227–233.

———. 1994. Sex-linked genes and species differences in Lepidoptera. Canadian Entomologist 126: 807–818.

Sperling, F. A. H., R. Byers, and D. Hickey. 1996. Mitochondrial DNA sequence variation among pheromotypes of the dingy cutworm, *Feltia jaculifera* (Gn.) (Lepidoptera: Noctuidae). Canadian Journal of Zoology 74: 2109–2117.

Sperling, F. A. H., and R. G. Harrison. 1994. Mitochondrial DNA variation within and between species of the *Papilio machaon* group of swallowtail butterflies. Evolution 48: 408–422.

Sperling, F. A. H., and N. G. Kondla. Alberta swallowtails and parnassians: Natural history, keys, and distribution. Blue Jay 49: 183–192.

Sperling, F. A. H., J.-F. Landry, and D. A. Hickey. 1995. DNA-based identification of introduced ermine moth species in North America (Lepidoptera: Yponomeutidae). Annals of the Entomological Society of America 88: 155–162.

Sperling, F. A. H., A. G. Raske, and I. S. Otvos. 1999. Mitochondrial DNA sequence variation among populations and host races of *Lambdina fiscellaria* (Gn.) (Lepidoptera: Geometridae). Insect Molecular Biology 8: 97–106.

Springer, P., and C. L. Boggs. 1986. Resource allocation to oocytes: Heritable variation with altitude in *Colias philodice eriphyle* (Lepidoptera). American Naturalist 127: 252–256.

Srgo, C. M., and L. Partridge. 1999. A delayed wave of death from reproduction in *Drosophila.* Science 286: 2521–2524.

Srygley, R. B. 1994. Locomotor mimimcry in butterflies? The associations of positions of centers of mass among groups of mimetic, unprofitable prey. Philosophical Transactions of the Royal Society of London B 343: 145–155.

———. 1999. Locomotor mimicry in *Heliconius* butterflies: Contrast analysis of flight morphology and kinematics. Philosophical Transactions of the Royal Society of London B 354: 203–214.

Srygley, R. B., and P. Chai. 1990a. Flight morphology of Neotropical butterflies: Palatability and distribution of mass to the thorax and abdomen. Oecologia 84: 491–499.

———. 1990b. Predation and the elevation of thoracic temperature in brightly colored Neotropical butterflies. American Naturalist 135: 766–787.

Srygley, R. B., E. Oliveira, and R. Dudley. 1996. Wind drift compensation, flyways, and conservation of diurnal migrant Neotropical Lepidoptera. Proceedings of the Royal Society of London B 263: 1351–1357.

Stacey, P. B., V. A. Johnson, and M. L. Taper. 1997. Migration with metapopulations: The impact upon local population dynamics. Pp. 267–292 in I. Hanski and M. E. Gilpin, eds., *Metapopulation biology.* Academic Press, San Diego.

Stair, R., and R. Johnston. 1953. Ultraviolet spectral radiant energy reflected from the moon. Journal of Research of the National Bureau of Standards 51: 81–84.

Stamp, N. E. 1980. Egg deposition patterns in butterflies: Why do some species cluster their eggs rather than deposit them singly? American Naturalist 115: 367–380.

———. 1982. Behavioural interactions of parasitoids and Baltimore checkerspot caterpillars (*Euphydryas phaeton*). Environmental Entomology 11: 100–104.

Stanton, M. L., and R. E. Cook. 1983. Sources of intraspecific variation in the hostplant seeking behavior of *Colias* butterflies. Oecologia 60: 365–370.

Stanton, M. L., A. A. Snow, and S. N. Handel. 1986. Floral evolution: Attractiveness to pollinators increases male fitness. Science 232: 1625–1627.

StatSoft France. 1997. STATISTICA pour Windows [Manuel du Programme]. StatSoft France, 72, quai des Carrières, 94220 Charenton-le-Pont.

Stavenga, D. G. 1975. Visual adaptation in butterflies. Nature 254: 435–437.

———. 1979. Pseudopupils of compound eyes. Pp. 357–439 in H. Autrum, ed., *Handbook of sensory physiology.* Vol. VII/6A. Springer Verlag, Berlin.

———. 1992. Eye regionalization and spectral tuning of retinal pigments in insects. Trends in Neuroscience 15: 213–218.

———. 1995. Insect retinal pigments: Spectral characteristics and physiological functions. Progress in Retinal Eye Research 15: 231–260.

Stavenga, D. G., M. Kinoshita, E.-C. Yang, and K. Arikawa. 2001. Retinal regionalization and heterogeneity of butterfly eyes. Naturwissenchaften 88: 477–481.

Stehr, F. W. 1987. Order Lepidoptera. Pp. 288–305 in F. W. Stehr, ed., *Immature insects.* Kendall/Hunt, Iowa.

Steiner, A. R. Paul, and R. Gemperlein. 1987. Retinal receptor types in *Aglais urticae* and *Pieris brassicae* (Lepidoptera), revealed by analysis of the electroretinogram obtained with Fourier interferometric stimulation (FIS). Journal of Comparative Physiology 160A: 247–258.

Sterling, E. J., and N. Rakotoarison. 1998. Rapid assessment of primate species richness and density on the Masoala Peninsula, eastern Madagascar. Folia Primatologica 69: 109–116.

Stern, D. L. 2000. Perspective: Evolutionary developmental biology and the problem of variation. Evolution 54: 1079–1091.

Stern, V. M., and R. F. Smith. 1960. Factors affecting egg production and oviposition in populations of *Colias philodice eurytheme* Boisduval (Lepidoptera: Pieridae). Hilgardia 29: 411–454.

Stevenson, R. D., K. Corbo, L. Baca, and Q. Le. 1995. Cage size and flight speed of the tobacco hawkmoth *Manduca sexta*. Journal of Experimental Biology 198: 1665–1672.

Stichel, H. 1928. *Nemeobiinae*. Walter de Gruyter, Berlin.

Stockhouse, R. E. II. 1976. A new method for studying pollen dispersal using micronized fluorescent dusts. American Midland Naturalist 96: 241–245.

Stone, G. N., and P. G. Willmer. 1989. Endothermy and temperature regulation in bees: A critique of 'grab and stab' measurement of body temperature. Journal of Experimental Biology 143: 211–223.

Straatman, R. 1962. Notes on certain Lepidoptera ovipositing on plants which are toxic to their larvae. Journal of the Lepidopterists' Society 16: 99–103.

Strauss, S. Y., and R. Karban. 1998. The strength of selection: Intraspecific variation in host-plant quality and the fitness of herbivores. Pp. 156–180 in S. Mopper and S. Y. Strauss, eds., *Genetic structure and local adaptation in natural insect populations*. Chapman and Hall, New York.

Strong, D. R. 1974. Rapid asymptotic species accumulation in phytophagous insect communities: The pests of cacao. Science 185: 1064–1066.

Struwe, G. 1972a. Spectral sensitivity of the compound eye in butterflies (*Heliconius*). Journal of Comparative Physiology A 79 191–196.

———. 1972b. Spectral sensitivity of single photoreceptors in the compound eye of a tropical butterfly. Journal of Comparative Physiology A 79: 197–201.

Stump, A. 2000. Lack of cryptic reproductive isolation between *Papilio canadensis* and *Papilio glaucus*; and population genetics near their hybrid zone. M.S. thesis, Michigan State University, East Lansing.

Stutt, A. D., and P. G. Willmer. 1998. Territorial defence in speckled wood butterflies: Do the hottest males always win? Animal Behaviour 55: 1341–1347.

Sugawara, T. 1979. Stretch reception in the bursa copulatrix of the butterfly *Pieris rapae crucivora* Boisduval (Lepidoptera: Pieridae), and its role in behaviour. Journal of Comparative Physiology 130: 191–199.

Sugden, E. 1986. Anthecology and pollinator efficacy of *Styrax officinale* subsp. *redivivum* (Styracaceae). American Journal of Botany 73: 919–930.

Sugden, E. A., P. S. Ward, A. M. Shapiro, and S. Teague. 1985. Invertebrates. Pp. 47–62 in W. W. Weathers and R. Cole, eds., *Flora and fauna of the Stebbins Cold Canyon Reserve*. Institute of Ecology, U.C. Davis, publ. 29.

Sutcliffe, O. L., C. D. Thomas, and D. Peggie. 1997a. Area-dependent migration by ringlet butterflies generates a mixture of patchy population and metapopulation attributes. Oecologia 109: 229–234.

Sutcliffe, O. L., C. D. Thomas, T. J. Yates, and J. N. Greatorex-Davis. 1997b. Correlated extinctions, colonisations and population fluctuations in a highly connected ringlet butterfly metapopulation. Oecologia 109: 235–241.

Sutherland, R. M., and J. M. Axton. 2000. PCR-RFLP and sequence identification of insect species in bird diet. GenBank (http://www.ncbi.nlm.nih.gov).

Sutton, S. L., and N. M. Collins. 1991. Insects and tropical forest conservation. Pp. 405–424 in N. M. Collins and J. A. Thomas, eds., *The conservation of insects and their habitats*. Academic Press, London.

Suzán, H., G. P. Nabhan, and D. T. Patten. 1994. Nurse plant and floral biology of a rare night-blooming Cereus, *Peniocereus striatus* (Brandegee) F. Buxbaum. Conservation Biology 8: 461–470.

Suzuki, N., and K. Matsumoto. 1992. Lifetime mating success of males in a natural population of the papilionid butterfly *Atrophaneura alcinous* (Lepidoptera: Papilionidae). Researches in Population Ecology (Kyoto) 34: 397–407.

Suzuki, Y. 1976. So-called territorial behavior of the small copper, *Lycaena phlaeas daimio* (Lepidoptera: Lycaenidae). Kontyu 44: 193–204.

Svärd, L., and C. Wiklund. 1986. Different ejaculate delivery strategies in first vs. subsequent matings in the swallowtail butterfly *Papilio machaon.* Behavioral Ecology and Sociobiology 18: 325–330.

———. 1988a. Prolonged mating in the monarch butterfly *Danaus plexippus,* and nightfall as a cue for sperm transfer. Oikos 52: 351–354.

———. 1988b. Fecundity, egg weight and longevity in relation to multiple mating in females of the monarch butterfly. Behavioral Ecology and Sociobiology 23: 39–43.

———. 1989. Mass and production rate of ejaculates in relation to monandry/polyandry in butterflies. Behavioral Ecology and Sociobiology 24: 395–402.

———. 1991. The effect of ejaculate mass on female reproductive output in the European swallowtail butterfly, *Papilio machaon.* Journal of Insect Behavior 4: 33–41.

Swihart, C. A. 1970. Colour selection and learned feeding preferences in the butterfly, *Heliconius charitonius* Linn. Animal Behaviour 18: 60–64.

———. 1971. Colour discrimination by the butterfly, *Heliconius charitonius* Linn. Animal Behaviour 19: 156–164.

Swihart, S. L. 1963. The electroretinogram of *Heliconius erato* (Lepidoptera) and its possible relation to established behavior patterns. Zoologica 48: 155–165.

———. 1967. Neural adaptations in the visual pathway of certain Heliconiine butterflies, and related forms, to variations in wing coloration. Zoologica 52: 1–14.

———. 1970. The neural basis of colour vision in the butterfly, *Papilio troilus.* Journal of Insect Physiology 16: 1623–1636.

Swofford, D. L. 1985. PAUP, Phylogenetic Analysis Using Parsimony. Vers. 2.4. Distributed by the Illinois Natural History Survey, Champaign, IL.

———. 1991. PAUP: Phylogenetic analysis using parsimony, version 3.0Q. Computer program distributed by the Illinois Natural History Survey, Champaign, IL.

———. 1998a. PAUP: Phylogenetic analysis using parsimony, version 4.0b1. Computer program distributed by Sinauer Associates, Sunderland, MA.

———. 1998b. PAUP*: Phylogenetic Analysis Using Parsimony and other methods. Test versions 4.0.0 d49–56. Laboratory of Molecular Systematics, Smithsonian Institution, Washington, D.C.

Swofford, D. L., and R. Selander. 1981. Biosys-1: A Fortran program for the comprehensive analysis of electrophoretic data in population genetics and systematics. Journal of Heredity 72: 281–283.

Symons, F. R., and G. W. Beccaloni. 1999. Phylogenetic indices for measuring the diet breadths of phytophagous insects. Oecologia 119: 427–434.

Szymura, J. M., and N. H. Barton. 1991. The genetic structure of the hybrid zone between the fire-bellied toads *Bombina bombina* and *B. variegata:* Comparisons between transects and between loci. Evolution 45: 237–261.

Tabashnik, B. E. 1983. Host range evolution: The shift from native legume hosts to alfalfa by the butterfly *Colias philodice eriphyle.* Evolution 37: 150–162.

Tabashnik, B. E., H. Wheelock, J. D. Rainbolt, and W. B. Watt. 1981. Individual variation in oviposition preference in the butterfly, *Colias eurytheme.* Oecologia 50: 225–230.

Tammaru, T., P. Kaitaniemi, and K. Ruohomaki. 1995. Oviposition choices of *Epirrita autumnata* (Lepidoptera: Geometridae) in relation to its eruptive population dynamics. Oikos 74: 296–304.

Tatar, M., and J. R. Carey. 1995. Nutrition mediates reproductive trade-offs with age-specific mortality in the beetle *Callosobruchus maculatus*. Ecology 76: 2066–2073.

Taylor, A. D. 1988. Large-scale spatial structure and population dynamics in arthropod predator-prey systems. Annales Zoologici Fennici 25: 63–74.

Taylor, A. H. 1995. Forest expansion and climate change in the mountain hemlock (*Tsuga mertensiana*) zone, Lassen Volcanic National Park, California, USA. Arctic Alpine Research 27: 207–216.

Taylor, M. F. J., S. W. McKechnie, N. Pierce, and M. Kreitman. 1993. The lepidopteran mitochondrial control region: Structure and evolution. Molecular Biology and Evolution 10: 1259–1272.

Templeton, A. R. 1989. The meaning of species and speciation: A genetic perspective. Pp. 3–27 in D. Otte and J. A. Endler, eds., *Speciation and its consequences*. Sinauer Associates, Sunderland, MA.

Templeton, A. R., and L. E. Gilbert. 1985. Population genetics and the coevolution of mutualism. Pp. 128–144 in D. H. Boucher, ed., *The biology of mutualisms*. Croom Helm, London, England.

Templeton, A. R., K. Shaw, E. Routman, and S. K. Davis. 1990. The genetic consequences of habitat fragmentation. Annals of the Missouri Botanical Garden 77: 13–27.

Tesar, D., and J. M. Scriber. 2002. Growth season constraints in climatic cold pockets: Intolerance of subfreezing temperatures by tiger swallowtail larvae. Holarctic Lepidoptera 7: 39–44.

Thomas, C. D. 1994. Extinction, colonization, and metapopulations: Environmental tracking by rare species. Conservation Biology 8: 373–378.

———. 1995. Ecology and conservation of butterfly metapopulations in the fragmented British landscape. Pp. 46–64 in A. S. Pullin, ed., *Ecology and conservation of butterflies*. Chapman and Hall, London.

Thomas, C. D., E. J. Bodsworth, R. J. Wilson, A. D. Simmons, Z. G. Davies, M. Musche, and L. Conradt. 2001. Ecological and evolutionary processes at expanding range margins. Nature 411: 577–581.

Thomas, C. D., and I. Hanski. 1997. Butterfly metapopulations. Pp. 359–386 in I. A. Hanski and M. E. Gilpin, eds., *Metapopulation dynamics: Ecology, genetics and evolution*. Academic Press, San Diego.

Thomas, C. D., and S. Harrison. 1992. Spatial dynamics of a patchily distributed butterfly species. Journal of Animal Ecology 61: 437–446.

Thomas, C. D., J. K. Hill, and O. T. Lewis. 1998. Evolutionary consequences of habitat fragmentation in a localized butterfly. Journal of Animal Ecology 67: 485–497.

Thomas, C. D., and T. M. Jones. 1993. Partial recovery of a skipper butterfly (*Hesperia comma*) from population refuges: Lessons for conservation in a fragmented landscape. Journal of Animal Ecology 62: 472–481.

Thomas, C. D., and J. J. Lennon. 1999. Birds extend their ranges northward. Nature 399: 213.

Thomas, C. D., D. Ng, M. C. Singer, J. L. B. Mallet, C. Parmesan, and H. L. Billington. 1987. Incorporation of a European weed into the diet of a North American herbivore. Evolution 41: 892–901.

Thomas, C. D., and M. C. Singer. 1987. Variation in host preference affects movement patterns in a butterfly population. Ecology 68: 1262–1267.

———. 1998. Scale-dependent evolution of specialization in a checkerspot butterfly. Pp. 343–374 in S. Mopper and S. Y. Strauss, eds., *Genetic structure and local adaptation in natural insect populations*. Chapman and Hall, New York.

Thomas, C. D., M. C. Singer, and D. A. Boughton. 1996. Catastrophic extinction of population sources in a butterfly metapopulation. American Naturalist 148: 957–975.

Thomas, C. D., J. A. Thomas, and M. S. Warren. 1992. Distributions of occupied and vacant butterfly habitats in fragmented landscapes. Oecologia 92: 563–567.

Thomas, C. D., D. A. Vasco, M. C. Singer, D. Ng, R. R. White, and D. Hinkley. 1990. Diet divergence in two sympatric congeneric butterflies: Community or species level phenomenon? Evolutionary Ecology 4: 62–74.

Thomas, J. A. 1980. Why did the large blue become extinct in Britain? Oryx 15: 243–247.

———. 1983a. The ecology and conservation of *Lysandra bellargus* (Lepidoptera: Lycaenidae) in Britain. Journal of Applied Ecology 20: 59–83.

———. 1983b. The ecology and status of *Thymelica acteon* (Lepidoptera: Hesperiidae) in Britain. Ecological Entomology 8: 427–435.

———. 1984. The conservation of butterflies in temperate countries: Past efforts and lessons for the future. Pp. 333–354 in R. I. Vane-Wright and P. R. Ackerly, eds., *The biology of butterflies*. Academic Press, London.

———. 1991. Rare species conservation: Case studies of European butterflies. Pp. 149–198 in I. F. Spellerberg, F. B. Goldsmith, and M. G. Morris, eds., *The scientific management of temperate communities for conservation*. Blackwell Scientific Publications, Oxford.

———. 1993. Holocene climate changes and warm man-made refugia may explain why a sixth of British butterflies possess unnatural early-successional habitats. Ecography 16: 278–284.

Thomas, J. A., and G. W. Elmes. 1992. The ecology and conservation of *Maculinea* butterflies and their ichneumon parasitoids. Pp. 116–123 in T. Pavlicek-vab Beek, A. H. Ovaa, and J. G. van der Made, eds., *Future of butterflies in Europe*. Department of Nature Conservation, Agricultural University, Wageningen.

Thomas, J. A., and R. Lewington. 1991. *The butterflies of Britain and Ireland*. Dorling Kindersley Lim., London.

Thompson, G. 1980. *The butterflies of Scotland*. Croom-Helm, London.

Thompson, J. N. 1988a. Evolutionary ecology of the relationship between oviposition preference and performance of offspring in phytophagous insects. Entomologica Experimentalis et Applicata 47: 3–14.

———. 1988b. Evolutionary genetics of oviposition preference in swallowtail butterflies. Evolution 42: 1223–1234.

———. 1993. Preference hierarchies and the origin of geographic specialization in host use in swallowtail butterflies. Evolution 47: 1585–1594.

———. 1994. *The coevolutionary process*. University of Chicago Press, Chicago.

———. 1995. The origins of host shifts in swallowtail butterflies versus other insects. Pp. 195–203 in J. M. Scriber, Y. Tsubaki, and R. C. Lederhouse, eds., *Swallowtail butterflies: Their ecology and evolutionary biology*. Scientific Publishers, Gainesville, FL.

———. 1997. Evaluating the dynamics of coevolution among geographically structured populations. Ecology 78: 1619–1623.

———. 1998. The evolution of diet breadth: Monophagy and polyphagy in swallowtail butterflies. Journal of Evolutionary Biology 11: 563–578.

Thompson, J. N., and O. Pellmyr. 1991. Evolution of oviposition behavior and host preference in Lepidoptera. Annual Review of Entomology 36: 65–89.

Thompson, J. N., W. Wehling, and R. Podolsky. 1990. Evolutionary genetics of host use in swallowtail butterflies. Nature 344: 148–150.

Thomson, G. 1977. The effect of a selected locus on linked neutral loci. Genetics 85: 753–788.

Thornhill, R. 1983. Cryptic female choice in the scorpionfly, *Harpobittacus nigriceps* and its implications. American Naturalist 122: 765–788.

———. 1992. Female preference from the pheromone of males with low fluctuating asymmetry in the Japanese scorpionfly (*Panorpa japonica:* Mecoptera), Behavioral Ecology 3: 277–283.

Thornhill, R., and J. Alcock. 1983. *The evolution of insect mating systems.* Harvard University Press, Cambridge, MA.

Thorpe, J. P. 1982. The molecular clock hypothesis: Biochemical evolution, genetic differentiation and systematics. Annual Review of Ecology and Systematics 13: 139–168.

Thorpe, R. S. 1984. Primary and secondary transition zones in speciation and population differentiation: A phylogenetic analysis of range expansion. Evolution 38: 233–243.

Thorstrom, R., J. Hart, and R. T. Watson. 1997. New record, ranging behaviour, vocalization and food habits of the Madagascar Red Owl. Ibis 139: 477–481.

Thorstrom, R., and R. T. Watson. 1997. Avian inventory and key species of the Masoala Peninsula, Madagascar. Bird Conservation International 7: 99–115.

Thorstrom, R., R. T. Watson, B. Damary, F. Toto, M. Baba, and V. Baba. 1995. Repeated sightings and first capture of a live Madagascar Serpent-eagle *Eutriorchis astur.* Bulletin of the British Ornithological Club 115: 40–45.

Thummel, C. S. 1995. From embryogeneisis to metamorphosis: The regulation and function of *Drosophila* nuclear receptor superfamily members. Cell 83: 871–877.

Tichenor, L. H., and D. S. Seigler. 1980. Electroantennogram and oviposition responses of *Manduca sexta* to volatile components of tobacco and tomato. Journal of Insect Physiology 26: 309–314.

Tilman, D., and P. Kareiva. 1997. *Spatial ecology: The role of space in population dynamics and interspecific interactions.* Princeton University Press, Princeton, NJ.

Tinbergen, N. 1958. *Curious naturalists.* Basic Books, New York.

Tinbergen, N., B. J. D. Meeuse, L. K. Boerema, and W. W. Varossieau. 1942. Die Balz des Samtfalters, *Eumenis (= Satyrus) semele.* Zeitschrift Tierpsychologie 5: 182–226.

Toh, Y., and M. Iwasaki. 1982. Ocellar system of the swallowtail butterfly larva. II. Projection of the retinular axons in the brain. Journal of Ultrastructure Research 78: 120–135.

Toh, Y., and H. Sagara. 1982. Ocellar system of the swallowtail butterfly larva. I. Structure of the lateral ocelli. Journal of Ultrastructure Research 78: 107–119.

Tolman, T. 1997. *Butterflies of Britain and Europe.* HarperCollins, London.

Tomlinson, A., and D. F. Ready. 1986. Sevenless: A cell-specific homeotic mutation of the *Drosophila* eye. Science 231: 400–403.

Tong, M. L., and A. M. Shapiro. 1989. Genetic differentiation among California populations of the anise swallowtail butterfly. Journal of the Lepidopterists' Society 43: 217–228.

Topazzini, A., M. Mazza, and P. Pelosi. 1990. Electroantennogram responses of five Lepidoptera species to 26 general odourants. Journal of Insect Physiology 36: 619–624.

Tosi, J. A. Jr. 1969. *Mapa ecológico, Republica de Costa Rica: Segun la classificacion de zonas de vida del mundo de L. H. Holdridge.* Centro Cientifico Tropical, San Jose.

Townson, S. M., B. S. W. Chang, E. Salcedo, L. V. Chadwell, N. E. Pierce, and S. G. Britt. 1998. Honeybee blue- and ultraviolet-sensitive opsins: Cloning, heterologous expression in *Drosophila,* and physiological characterization. Journal of Neuroscience 18: 2412–2422.

Traynier, R. M. M. 1984. Associative learning in the ovipositional behaviour of the cabbage butterfly, *Pieris rapae.* Physiological Entomology 9: 465–472.

Trigo, J. R., and P. C. Motta. 1990. Evolutionary implications of pyrrolizidine alkaloids assimilation by Ithomiinae larvae (Lepidoptera: Nymphalidae). Experientia 46: 332–334.

Trimen, R. 1869. On some remarkable mimetic analogies among African butterflies. Transactions of the Linnean Society 26: 497–522.

Tsuji, J. S., J. G. Kingsolver, and W. B. Watt. 1986. Thermal physiological ecology of *Colias* butterflies in flight. Oecologia 69: 161–170.

Turchin, P. 1986. Modelling the effect of patch host size on Mexican bean beetle emigration. Ecology 67: 124–132.

―――. 1995. Population regulation: Old arguments and a new synthesis. Pp. 19–40 in N. Cappuccino and P. Price, eds., *Population dynamics: New approaches and synthesis.* Academic Press, San Diego.

―――. 1998. *Quantitative analysis of movement: Measuring and modeling population redistribution in plants and animals.* Sinauer Associates, Sunderland, MA.

Turchin, P., F. J. Odendaal, and M. D. Rausher. 1991. Quantifying insect movement in the field. Environmental Entomology 20: 955–963.

Turelli, M. 1998. The causes of Haldane's rule. Science 282: 889–891.

Turelli, M., and H. A. Orr. 1995. The dominance theory of Haldane's rule. Genetics 140: 389–402.

Turner, J. R. G. 1963a. Geographical variation and evolution in the males of the butterfly *Papilio dardanus* Brown (Lepidoptera: Papilionidae). Transactions of the Royal Entomological Society of London 115: 239–259.

―――. 1963b. A quantitative study of a Welsh colony of the large heath butterfly *Coenonympha tullia.* Proceedings of the Royal Entomological Society of London A 38: 101–112.

―――. 1977. Butterfly mimicry: The genetical evolution of an adaptation. Evolutionary Biology 10: 163–206.

―――. 1981. Adaptation and evolution in *Heliconius:* A defense of neodarwinism. Annual Review of Ecology and Systematics 12: 99–121.

―――. 1983. Mimetic butterflies and punctuated equilibria: Some old light on a new paradigm. Biological Journal of the Linnean Society 20: 277–300.

―――. 1984. Mimicry: The palatability spectrum and its consequences. Pp. 141–161 in R. Vane-Wright and P. R. Ackery, eds., *The biology of butterflies.* Academic Press, London.

Turner, J. R. G., C. M. Gatehouse, and C. A. Corey. 1987. Does solar energy control organic diversity? Butterflies, moths and the British climate. Oikos 48: 195–205.

Turner, J. R. G., M. S. Johnson, and W. F. Eanes. 1979. Contrasted modes of evolution in the same genome: Allozymes and adaptive change in *Heliconius.* Proceedings of the National Academy of Sciences USA 76: 1924–1928.

Turner, J. R. G., and J. L. B. Mallet. 1996. Did forest islands drive the diversity of warningly coloured butterflies? Biotic drift and the shifting balance. Philosophical Transactions of the Royal Society of London B 351: 835–845.

Tyler, H. A. 1975. *The swallowtail butterflies of North America*. Naturegraph Publishers, Healdsburg, CA.

Tyler, H. A., K. S. Brown, and K. H. Wilson. 1994. *Swallowtail butterflies of the Americas. A study in biological dynamics, ecological diversity, biosystematics, and conservation*. Scientific Publishers, Gainesville, FL.

Umebachi, Y. 1985. Papiliochrome, a new pigment group of butterfly. Zoological Science 2: 163–174.

———. 1993. The third way of dopamine. Tr. Comparative Biochemistry and Physiology 1: 709–720.

Usher, R. R. 1986. *Wildlife conservation evaluation*. Chapman and Hall, London.

Väisänen, R., and P. Somerma. 1985. The status of *Parnassius mnemosyne* (Lepidoptera, Papilionidae) in Finland. Notulae Entomologicae 65: 109–118.

Valpine, P. de, and J. Harte. 2001. Plant response to experimental warming in a montane meadow. Ecology 82: 637–648.

Van den Bosch, F., J. A. J. Metz, and O. Diekmann. 1990. The velocity of spatial population expansion. Journal of Mathematical Biology 28: 529–565.

van der Pijl, L. 1961. Ecological aspects of floral evolution II. Zoophilous flower classes. Evolution 15: 44–59.

Van Dongen, S., T. Backeljau, E. Matthysen, and A. A. Dhondt. 1998. Genetic population structure of the winter moth (*Operophtera brumata* L.) (Lepidoptera, Geometridae) in a fragmented landscape. Heredity 80: 92–100.

van Doorn, G. S., A. J. Noest, and P. Hogeweg. 1998. Sympatric speciation and extinction driven by environment dependent sexual selection. Proceedings of the Royal Society of London B 265: 1915–1919.

Van Dyck, H., and E. Matthysen. 1998. Thermoregulatory differences between phenotypes of the speckled wood butterfly: Hot perchers and cold patrollers? Oecologia 114: 326–334.

———. 1999. Habitat fragmentation and insect flight: A changing 'design' in a changing landscape? Trends in Ecology and Evolution 14: 172–174.

Van Dyck, H., E. Matthysen, and A. A. Dhondt. 1997a. The effect of wing colour on male behavioural strategies in the speckled wood butterfly. Animal Behaviour 53: 39–51.

———. 1997b. Mate-locating strategies are related to relative body length and wing colour in the speckled wood butterfly *Pararge aegeria*. Ecological Entomology 22: 116–120.

Van Dyck, H., E. Matthysen, and C. Wiklund. 1998. Phenotypic variation in adult morphology and pupal colour within and among families of the speckled wood butterfly *Pararge aegeria* (L.). Ecological Entomology 23: 465–472.

Van Dyck, H., E. Matthysen, J. J. Windig, and A. A. Dhondt. 1997c. Seasonal phenotypic variation in the speckled wood butterfly (*Pararge aegeria* L.): Patterns in and relationships between wing characters. Belgian Journal Zoology 127: 167–178.

Van Dyck, H., and C. Wiklund. 2002. Seasonal butterfly design: Morphological plasticity among three developmental pathways relative to sex, flight and thermoregulation. Journal of Evolutionary Biology 15: 216–225.

Vane-Wright, R. I. 1978. Ecological and behavioural origins of diversity in butterflies. Symposium Royal Entomological Society London 9: 56–70.

_____ . 1996. Identifying priorities for the conservation of biodiversity: Systematic biological criteria within a socio-political framework. Pp. 309–344 in K. J. Gaston, ed., *Biodiversity: A biology of numbers and difference.* Blackwell Scientific, Oxford.

_____ . 2001. Taxonomy, methods of. Encyclopedia of Biodiversity 5: 589–606. Academic Press, San Diego.

Vane-Wright, R. I., and M. Boppré. 1993. Visual and chemical signalling in butterflies: Functional and phylogenetic perspectives. Philosophical Transactions of the Royal Society of London B 340: 197–205.

Vane-Wright, R. I., C. J. Humphries, and P. H. Williams. 1991. What to protect? Systematics and the agony of choice. Biological Conservation 55: 235–254.

Vane-Wright, R. I., D. C. Raheem, A. Cieslak, and A. P. Vogler. 1999. Evolution of the mimetic African swallowtail butterfly *Papilio dardanus:* Molecular data confirm relationships with *P. phorcas* and *P. constantinus*. Biological Journal of the Linnean Society 66: 215–229.

Vane-Wright, R. I., and C. R. Smith. 1991. Phylogenetic relationships of three African swallowtail butterflies, *Papilio dardanus, P. phorcas* and *P. constantinus:* A cladistic analysis (Lepidoptera: Papilionidae). Systematic Entomology 16: 275–291.

van Hateren, J. H., and D.-E. Nilsson. 1987. Butterfly optics exceed the theoretical limits of conventional apposition eyes. Biological Cybernetics 57: 159–168.

Vanjaarsveld, A. S., S. Freitag, C. S. L., C. Muller, S. Koch, H. Hull, C. Bellamy, M. Kruger, S. Endrodyyounga, M. W. Mansell, and C. H. Scholtz. 1998. Biodiversity assessment and conservation strategies. Science 279: 2106–2108.

van Loon, J. J. A., W. H. Frentz, and F. A. van Eeuwijk. 1992. Electroantennogram responses to plant volatiles in two species of *Pieris* butterflies. Entomologica Experimentalis et Applicata 62: 253–260.

Van Nouhuys, S., and I. Hanski. 2000. Apparent competition between parasitoids mediated by a shared hyperparasitoid. Ecology Letters 3: 82–84.

van Swaay, C. A. M. 1995. Measuring changes in butterfly abundance in The Netherlands. Pp. 230–247 in A. S. Pullin, ed., *Ecology and conservation of butterflies.* Chapman and Hall, London.

van Zandt Brower, J. 1958a. Experimental studies of mimicry in some North American butterflies. I. The Monarch, *Danaus plexippus,* and the Viceroy, *Limenitus archippus*. Evolution 12: 32–47.

_____ . 1958b. Experimental studies of mimicry in some North American butterflies. II. *Battus philenor* and *Papilio troilus, P. polyxenes,* and *P. glaucus*. Evolution 12: 123–136.

_____ . 1960. Experimental studies of mimicry in some North American butterflies. IV. The reaction of starlings to different proportions of models and mimics. American Naturalist 94: 271–282.

Varga, Z. 1970. Extension, Isolation, Micro evolution. Acta Biologica Debrecina 7–8: 193–209.

Vargas, F., I., J. Llorente B., and A. Luis M. 1991. Lepidópterofauna de Guerrero I: Distribución y fenología de los Papilionoidea de la Sierra de Atoyac. Publicaciones Especiales Museo Zoologica UNAM, 2: 1–127.

Vargas, J. M., R. Real, and L. J. Palomo. 1997. On identifying significant co-occurrence of species in space and time. Miscellanea Zoologica 20: 49–58.

Varley, G. C., and G. R. Gradwell. 1960. Key factors in population studies. Journal of Animal Ecology 29: 399–401.

Varvio, S., R. Chakraborty, and M. Nei. 1986. Genetic variation in subdivided populations and conservation genetics. Heredity 57: 189–198.

Vasey, N. 1996. Feeding and ranging behavior of red ruffed lemurs (*Vareica variegata rubra*) and white fronted lemurs (*Lemur fulvus albifrons*). American Journal of Physical Anthropology 22: 234–235.

———. 1997. How many red ruffed lemurs are left? International Journal of Primatology 18: 207–216.

Vasquez, L. G., and H. Perez. 1966. Nuevas observaciones sobre la biologia de *Baronia brevicornis* Salv. (Lepidoptera: Papilionidae-Baroniinae). Anales del Instituto de Biologia, Universidad de México 37: 195–204.

Veech, J. A., J. H. Bendix Jr., and D. J. Howard. 1996. Lack of calling song between two closely related ground crickets. Evolution 50: 1982–1989.

Venables, B. A. B. 1993. Phylogeny of the white and suphur butterflies (Pieridae). Ph.D. dissertation [draft]. University of Maryland, College Park.

Venables, B. A., and E. M. Barrows. 1985. Skippers: Pollinators or nectar thieves? Journal of the Lepidopterists' Society 39: 299–312.

Verity, R. 1919. The various modes of emergence and the number of annual broods of the Grypocera and of the Rhopalocera of southern Europe, illustrated by the Tuscan species. Entomologists' Record and Journal of Variation 31: 66–72, 104–110, 141–148.

———. 1920. On emergence of the Grypocera and Rhopalocera in relation to latitude and altitude. Entomologists' Record and Journal of Variation 32: 65–71, 107–110.

Via, S. 1986. Genetic covariance between oviposition preference and larval performance in an insect herbivore. Evolution 40: 778–785.

———. 1990. Ecological genetics and host adaptation in herbivorous insects: The experimental study of evolution in natural and agricultural systems. Annual Review of Entomology 35: 421–426.

Viader, J. 1993. Papallones de Catalunya: Araschnia levana (Linnaeus, 1758). Bull. Soc. Cat. Lep. 71: 49–62.

Viloria, P. A. L. 1998. Studies on the systematics and biogeography of some montane satyrid butterflies (Lepidoptera). Ph.D. dissertation, University of London.

Virdee, S. R. 1993. Unravelling Haldane's rule. Trends in Ecology and Evolution 11: 385–386.

Vogel, S. 1963. *The role of scent glands in pollination.* (English translation publ. 1990, Model Press, Ltd., New Delhi).

———. 1983. Ecophysiology of zoophilous pollination. Pp. 560–624 in O. L. Lange, P. S. Nobel, C. B. Osmond, H. Ziegler, eds., *Physiological plant ecology III: Effect of chemicals on plants.* Springer-Verlag, Berlin.

Vogler, A. P. 1998. Extinction and the evolutionary process in endangered species: What to conserve? Pp. 191–210 in R. DeSalle and B. Schierwater, eds., *Molecular approaches to ecology and evolution.* Birkhäuser, Basel.

Vogler, A. P., and R. DeSalle. 1994. Diagnosing units of conservation management. Conservation Biology 8: 354–363.

Voigt, C. C., and Y. Winter. 1999. Entergetic cost of hovering flight in nectar-feeding bats (Phyllostomidae: Glossophaginae) and its scaling in moths, birds and bats. Journal of Comparative Physiology B 169: 38–48.

Waage, J. K., J. T. Smiley, and L. E. Gilbert. 1981. The *Passiflora* problem in Hawaii: Prospects and problems of controlling the forest weed *P. mollissima* (Passifloraceae) with heliconiine butterflies. Entomophaga 26: 275–284.

Wagner, G. P. 1994. Homology and the mechanisms of development. Pp. 274–301 in B. K. Hall, ed., *Homology: The hierarchical basis of comparative biology.* Academic Press, New York.

_____. 1996. Homologues, natural kinds and the evolution of modularity. American Zoologist 36: 36–43.

Wagner, W. H. 1973. An orchid attractant for Monarch butterflies (Danaidae). Journal of the Lepidopterists' Society 27: 192–196.

_____. 1978. A possible natural hybrid of *Papilio eurymedon* and *P. rutulus* (Papilionidae) from Idaho. Journal of the Lepidopterists' Society 32: 226–228.

Wagner, W. H., M. K. Hansen, and M. R. Mayfield. 1981. True and false broods of *Callosamia promethea* (Lepidoptera: Saturniidae) in southern Michigan. Great Lakes Entomologist 14: 159–165.

Wahlberg, N., A. Moilanen, and I. Hanski. 1996. Predicting the occurrence of endangered species in fragmented landscapes. Science 273: 1536–1538.

Wahlberg, N., and M. Zimmermann. 2001. Pattern of phylogenetic relationships among members of the tribe Melitaeni (Lepidoptera: Nymphalidae) inferred from mtDNA sequences. Cladistics 16: 347–363.

Wainwright, P. C. 1994. Functional morphology as a tool in ecological research. Pp. 42–59 in P. C. Wainwright and S. M. Reilly, eds., *Ecological morphology, integrative organismal biology.* University of Chicago Press, Chicago.

Wald, G. 1968. Molecular basis of visual excitation. Science 162: 230–239.

Waldbauer, G. P., J. B. Sternburg, and A. W. Ghent. 1988. Lakes Michigan and Huron limit gene flow between the subspecies of the butterfly, *Limenitis arthemis.* Canadian Journal of Zoology 66: 1790–1795.

Wallace, A. R. 1865. On the phenomena of variation and geographical distribution as illustrated by the Papilionidae of the Malayan region. Transactions of the Linnean Society 25: 1–71.

Waller, D., and L. E. Gilbert. 1982. Roost recruitment and resource utilization: Observations on a *Heliconius charitonia* L. roost in Mexico (Nymphalidae). Journal of the Lepidoperists' Society 36: 178–184.

Walther, G.-R., E. Post, A. Menzel, P. Convey, C. Parmesan, F. Bairlen, T. Beebee, J. M. Fromont, and O. Hoegh-Guldberg. 2002. Ecological responses to recent climate change. Nature 416: 389–395.

Ward, P. I. 1998. A possible explanation for cryptic female choice in the Yellow Dung Fly, *Scathophaga stercoraria* (L.) Ethology 104: 97–110.

Warheit, K. I., J. D. Forman, J. B. Losos, and D. B. Miles. 1999. Morphological diversification and adaptive radiation: A comparison of two diverse lizard clades. Evolution 53: 1226–1234.

Warrant, E. J., and P. D. McIntyre. 1992. The tradeoff between resolution and sensitivity in compound eyes. Pp. 391–421 in R. B. Pinter and B. Nabet, eds., *Nonlinear vision.* CRC Press, Boca Raton, FL.

_____. 1993. Arthropod eye design and the physical limits to spatial resolving power. Progress in Neurobiology 40: 413–461.

Warren, M. S. 1987. The ecology and conservation of the heath fritillary butterfly, *Mellicta athalia.* III. Population dynamics and the effect of habitat management. Journal of Applied Ecology 24: 467–482.

_____. 1991. The successful conservation of an endangered species, the heath fritillary butterfly, *Mellicta athalia.* Britain. Biological Conservation 55: 37–56.

_____. 1992. The conservation of British butterflies. Pp. 246–274 in R. L. H. Dennis, ed., *The ecology of butterflies in Britain.* Oxford University Press, Oxford.

_____. 1995. Managing local microclimates for the high brown fritillary, *Argynnis adippe.* Pp. 198–210 in A. S. Pullin, ed., *Ecology and conservation of butterflies.* Chapman and Hall, London.

Warren, M. S., J. K. Hill, J. A. Thomas, J. Asher, R. Fox, B. Huntley, D. B. Roy, M. G. Telfer, S. Jeffcoate, P. Harding, G. Jeffcoate, S. G. Willis, J. N. Greatorex-Davies, D. Moss and C. D. Thomas. 2001. Climate versus habitat change: Opposing forces underly rapid changes to the distribution and abundances of British butterflies. Nature 414: 65–69.

Warren, M. S., E. Pollard, and T. J. Bibby. 1986. Annual and long-term changes in a population of the wood white butterfly, *Leptidea sinapis*. Journal of Animal Ecology 55: 707–719.

Warren, M. S., C. D. Thomas, and J. A. Thomas. 1984. The status of the heath fritillary butterfly, *Mellicta athalia* Rott. Britain. Biological Conservation 29: 287–305.

Warrington, S., and J. P. Brayford. 1995. Some aspects of the population ecology and dispersal of the small skipper butterfly *Thymelicus sylvestris* (Poda) in a series of linked grasslands. Entomologist 114: 201–209.

Warzecha, A.-K., and E. Egelhauf. 1995. Visual pattern discrimination in a butterfly. A behavioral study on the Australian Lurcher, *Yoma sabina*. Naturwissenschaften 82: 567–569.

Wasserthal, L. T. 1975. The role of butterfly wings in regulation of body temperature. Journal of Insect Physiology 21: 1921–1930.

––––––. 1993. Swing-hovering combined with long tongue in hawkmoths, an antipredator adaptation during flower visits. Pp. 77–87 in. W. Barthlott, C. Naumann, K. Schmidt-Loske, and K.-L. Schuchmann, eds., *Animal plant interactions in tropical environments*. Museum Koenig, Bonn.

––––––. 1997. The pollinators of the Malagasy Star Orchids, *Angraecum sesquipedale, A. sororium* and *A. compactum* and the evolution of extremely long spurs by pollinator shift. Botanica Acta 110: 343–359.

Watanabe, M. 1988. Multiple matings increase the fecundity of the yellow swallowtail butterfly, *Papilio xuthus,* in summer generations. Journal of Insect Behavior 1: 17–30.

Watanabe, M., C. Wiklund, and M. Bon'no. 1998. The effect of repeated matings on sperm numbers in successive ejaculates of the cabbage white butterfly *Pieris rapae*. Journal of Insect Behavior 11: 559–570.

Watson, R. T, M. C. Zinyowera, and R. H. Moss, eds. 1998. *The regional impacts of climate change, an assessment of vulnerability. A special report of the IPCC working group 2*. Cambridge University Press, Cambridge.

Watt, K. E. 1961. Mathematic models for use in insect pest control. Canadian Entomologist 93: 1–62.

Watt, W. B. 1968. Adaptive significance of pigment polymorphisms in *Colias* butterflies. I. Variation of melanin pigment in relation to thermoregulation. Evolution 22: 437–458.

––––––. 1977. Adaptation at specific loci. I. Natural selection on phosphoglucose isomerase of *Colias* butterflies: Biochemical and population aspects. Genetics 87: 177–194.

––––––. 1983. Adaptation at specific loci II. Demographic and biochemical elements in the maintenance of the *Colias* PGI polymorphism. Genetics 103: 691–724.

––––––. 1985a. Allelic isozymes and the mechanistic study of evolution. Isozymes: Current Topics in Biological and Medical Research 12: 89–132.

––––––. 1985b. Bioenergetics and evolutionary genetics—opportunities for new synthesis. American Naturalist 125: 118–143.

––––––. 1986. Power and efficiency as fitness indices in metabolic organization. American Naturalist 127: 629–653.

———. 1991. Biochemistry, physiological ecology and population genetics—the mechanistic tools of evolutionary biology. Functional Ecology 5: 145–154.

———. 1992. Eggs, enzymes, and evolution: Natural genetic variants change insect fecundity. Proceedings of the National Academy of Sciences USA 89: 10608–10612.

———. 1994. Allozymes in evolutionary genetics: Self-imposed burden or extraordinary tool? Genetics 136: 11–16.

———. 1995a. Allozymes in evolutionary genetics: Beyond the twin pitfalls of "neutralism" and "selectionism." Revue Suisse de Zoologie 102: 869–882.

———. 1995b. Descent with modification: Evolutionary study of *Colias* in the tradition of Charles Remington. Journal of the Lepidopterists' Society 49: 272–284.

———. 1997. Accuracy, anecdotes, and artifacts in the study of insect thermal ecology. Oikos 80: 399–400.

———. 2000. Avoiding paradigm-based limits to knowledge of evolution. Evolutionary Biology 32: 73–96.

Watt, W. B., and C. L. Boggs. 1987. Allelic isozymes as probes of the evolution of metabolic organization. Isozymes: Current Topics Biological Medical Research 15: 27–47.

Watt, W. B., P. A. Carter, and S. M. Blower. 1985. Adaptation at specific loci. IV. Differential mating success among glycolytic allozyme genotypes of *Colias* butterflies. Genetics 109: 157–175.

Watt, W. B., P. A. Carter, and K. Donohue. 1986. An insect mating system promotes the choice of "good genotypes" as mates. Science 233: 1187–1190.

Watt, W. B., K. Donohue, and P. A. Carter. 1996. Adaptation at specific loci. VI. Divergence vs. parallelism of polymorphic allozymes in molecular function and fitness-component effects among *Colias* species (Lepidoptera, Pieridae). Molecular Biology and Evolution 13: 699–709.

Watt, W. B., R. C. Cassin, and M. S. Swan. 1983. Adaptation at specific loci III. Field behavior and survivorship differences among *Colias* PGI genotypes are predictable from *in vitro* biochemistry. Genetics 103: 725–739.

Watt, W. B., F. S. Chew, L. R. G. Snyder, A. G. Watt, and D. E. Rothschild. 1977. Population structure of pierid butterflies I. Numbers and movements of some montane *Colias* species. Oecologia 27: 1–22.

Watt, W. B., and A. M. Dean. 2000. Molecular-functional studies of adaptive genetic variation in pro- and eukaryotes. Annual Reviews of Genetics 34: 593–622.

Watt, W. B., P. C. Hoch, and S. G. Mills. 1974. Nectar resource use by *Colias* butterflies: Chemical and visual aspects. Oecologia 14: 353–374.

Watt, W. B., C. W. Wheat, E. H. Meyer, and J.-F. Martin. 2002. Adaptation at specific loci. VII. Migration, selection, and the maintenance of genetic variation patterns in butterfly species complexes (*Colias:* Lepidoptera, Pieridae). Molecular Ecology. In press.

Weatherbee, S. D., and S. B. Carroll. 1999. Selector genes and limb identity in arthropods and vertebrates. Cell 97: 283–286.

Wedell, N. 1996. Mate quality affects reproductive effort in a paternally investing species. American Naturalist 148: 1075–1088.

Wedell, N., and P. A. Cook. 1998. Determinants of paternity in a butterfly. Proceedings of the Royal Society of London B 269: 625–630.

Weeks, P. J. D., I. D. Gauld, K. J. Gaston, and M. A. O'Neill. 1997. Automating the identification of insects: A new solution to an old problem. Bulletin of Entomological Research 87: 203–211.

Wehling, W. F., and J. N. Thompson. 1997. Evolutionary conservation of oviposition preference in a widespread polyphagous insect herbivore, *Papilio zelicaon*. Oecologia 111: 209–215.

Wehner, R. 1981. Spatial vision in arthropods. Pp. 287–615 in H. Autrum, ed., *Handbook of sensory physiology. VII/6C. Invertebrate visual centers.* Springer Verlag, Berlin.

Weir, B. S. 1979. Inferences about linkage disequilibrium. Biometrics 35: 235–254.

Weir, B. S., and C. C. Cockerham. 1978. Testing hypotheses about linkage disequilibrium with multiple alleles. Genetics 88: 633–642.

Weiss, M. R. 1995. Associative colour learning in a nymphalid butterfly. Ecological Entomology 20: 298–301.

———. 1997. Innate colour preferences and flexible colour learning in the pipevine swallowtail. Animal Behaviour 53: 1043–1052.

———. 2001. Vision and learning in some neglected pollinators: Beetles, flies, moths, and butterflies. In L. Chittka and J. D. Thompson, eds., *Pollinator behaviour and its implications for plant evolution.* Cambridge University Press, Cambridge.

Weiss, M. R., and B. B. Lamont. 1997. Floral color change and insect pollination: A dynamic relationship. Israel Journal of Plant Sciences 45: 185–199.

Weiss, S. B. 1999. Cars, cows, and checkerspot butterflies: Nitrogen deposition and management of nutrient-poor grasslands for a threatened species. Conservation Biology 13: 1476–1486.

Weiss, S. B., D. D. Murphy, P. R. Ehrlich, and C. F. Metzler. 1993. Adult emergence phenology in checkerspot butterflies: The effects of macroclimate, topography, and population history. Oecologia 96: 261–270.

Weiss, S. B., D. D. Murphy, and R. R. White. 1988. Sun, slope and butterflies: Topographic determinants of habitat quality in *Euphydryas editha*. Ecology 69: 1486–1496.

Weiss, S. B., R. R. White, D. D. Murphy, and P. R. Ehrlich. 1987. Growth and dispersal of larvae of the checkerspot butterfly *Euphydryas editha*. Oikos 50: 161–166.

Weller, S. J., and D. P. Pashley. 1995. In search of butterfly origins. Molecular Phylogenetics and Evolution 4: 235–246.

Weller, S. J., D. P. Pashley, and J. A. Martin. 1996. Reassessment of butterfly family relationships using independent genes and morphology. Annals of the Entomological Society of America 89: 184–192.

Weller, S. J., D. P. Pashley, J. A. Martin, and J. L. Constable. 1994. Phylogeny of noctuoid moths and the utility of combining independent nuclear and mitochondrial genes. Systematic Biology 43: 194–211.

Wen, Y. H. 1993. Sexual dimorphism and mate choice in *Hyalella azteca* (Amphipoda). American Midland Naturalist 129: 153–160.

Wenzel, J. W., and J. M. Carpenter. 1994. Comparing methods: Adaptive traits and tests of adaptation. Pp. 79–101 in P. Eggleton and R. I. Vane-Wright, eds., *Phylogenetics and ecology.* Academic Press, London.

White, R. H., R. S. Stevenson, R. R. Bennett, D. E. Cutler, and W. A. Haber. 1994. Wavelength discrimination and the role of ultraviolet vision in the feeding behavior of hawkmoths. Biotropica 26: 427–435.

White, R. R., and M. P. Levin. 1980. Temporal variation in vagility: Implications for evolutionary studies. American Midland Naturalist 105: 348–357.

Whitham, T. G., P. A. Morrow, and B. M. Potts. 1994. Plant hybrid zones as centers of biodiversity: The herbivore community of two endemic Tasmanian eucalypts. Oecologia 97: 481–490.

Whiting, M., J. C. Carpenter, Q. D. Wheeler, and W. C. Wheeler. 1997. The Strepsiptera problem: Phylogeny of the holometabolous insect orders inferred from 18s and 28s ribosomal DNA sequences and morphology. Systematic Biology 46: 1–68.

Whittaker, R. H. 1972. Evolution and the measurement of species diversity. Taxon 21: 213–251.

Wickman, P.-O. 1985a. The influence of temperature on the territorial and mate locating behaviour of the small heath butterfly, *Coenonympha pamphilus* (Lepidoptera: Satyridae). Behavioral Ecology and Sociobiology 16: 233–238.

———. 1985b. Territorial defence and mating success of the small heath butterfly, *Coenonympha pamphilus* (Lepidoptera: Satyridae). Animal Behaviour 33: 1162–1168.

———. 1986. Courtship solicitation by females of the small heath butterfly, *Coenonympha pamphilus* (L.) (Lepidoptera: Satyridae) and their behaviour in relation to male territories before and after copulation. Animal Behaviour 34: 153–157.

———. 1988. Dynamics of mate-searching behaviour in a hilltopping butterfly, *Lasiommata megera:* The effects of weather and male density. Zoological Journal of the Linnean Society 93: 357–377.

———. 1992a. Mating systems of *Coenonympha* butterflies in relation to longevity. Animal Behaviour 44: 141–148.

———. 1992b. Sexual selection and butterfly design—a comparative study. Evolution 46: 1525–1536.

Wickman, P.-O., E. Garcia-Barros, and C. Rappe-George. 1995. The location of leks in the small heath butterfly *Coenonympha pamphilus:* Support for the female preference model. Behavioral Ecology 6: 39–45.

Wickman, P.-O., and P. Jansson. 1997. An estimate of female mate searching costs in the lekking butterfly *Coenonympha pamphilus.* Behavioral Ecology and Sociobiology 40: 321–328.

Wickman, P.-O., and R. L. Rutowski. 1999. The evolution of mating dispersion in insects. Oikos 84: 463–472.

Wickman, P.-O., and C. Wiklund. 1983. Territorial defence and its seasonal decline in the speckled wood butterfly (*Pararge aegeria*). Animal Behaviour 31: 1206–1216.

Wiegmann, B. M. 1994. The earliest radiation of the Lepidoptera: Evidence from 18s rDNA. Ph.D. dissertation, University of Maryland, College Park.

Wiegmann, B. M., C. Mitter, J. C. Regier, T. P. Friedlander, D. M. Wagner, and E. S. Nielsen. 2000. Nuclear genes resolve Mesozoic-aged divergences in the insect order Lepidoptera. Molecular Phylogenetics and Evolution 15: 242–259.

Wiens, J. A., R. L. Schooley, and R. D. Weeks. 1997. Patchy landscapes and animal movements: Do beetles percolate? Oikos 78: 257–264.

Wiens, J. J. 1999. Polymorphism in systematics and comparative biology. Annual Review of Ecology and Systematics 30: 327–362.

Wiernasz, D. C. 1989. Female choice and sexual selection of male wing melanin pattern in *Pieris occidentalis* (Lepidoptera). Evolution 43: 1672–1682.

———. 1995. Male choice on the basis of female melanin pattern in *Pieris* butterflies. Animal Behaviour 49: 45–51.

Wiggins, D. 1980. *Sameness and substance.* Basil Blackwell, Oxford.

Wiklund, C. 1974. The concept of oligophagy and the natural habitats and host plants of *Papilio machaon* L. in Fennoscandia. Entomologica Scandinavica 5: 151–160.

————. 1975. The evolutionary relationship between adult oviposition preferences and larval host plant range in *Papilio machaon* L. Oecologia 18: 185–197.

————. 1977a. Courtship behaviour in relation to female monogamy in *Leptidea sinapis*. Oikos 29: 275–283.

————. 1977b. Oviposition, feeding and spatial separation of breeding and foraging habitats in a population of *Leptidea sinapis* (Lepidoptera). Oikos 28: 56–58.

————. 1981. Generalist vs., specialist oviposition behavior in *Papilio machaon* (Lepidoptera) and functional aspects on the hierarchy of oviposition preferences. Oikos 36: 163–170.

————. 1982. Behavioural shift from courtship solicitation to mate avoidance in female ringlet butterflies (*Aphantopus hyperantus*) after copulation. Animal Behaviour 30: 790–793.

————. 1984. Egg-laying patterns of butterflies in relation to their phenology and the visual apparency and abundance of their host plants. Oecologia 63: 23–29.

Wiklund, C., T. Eriksson, and H. Lundberg. 1979. The wood white butterfly *Leptidea sinapis* and its nectar plants: A case of mutualism or parasitism? Oikos 33: 358–362.

Wiklund, C., and T. Fagerström. 1977. Why do males emerge before females? A hypothesis to explain the incidence of protandry in butterflies. Oecologia 31: 153–158.

Wiklund, C., and J. Forsberg. 1985. Courtship and male discrimination between virgin and mated females in the orange tip butterfly, *Anthocharis cardamines*. Animal Behaviour 34: 328–332.

————. 1991. Sexual size dimorphism in relation to female polygamy and protandry in butterflies: A comparative study of Swedish Pieridae and Satyridae. Oikos 60: 373–381.

Wiklund, C., and A. Kaitala. 1995. Sexual selection for large male size in a polyandrous butterfly: The effect of body size on male versus female reproductive success in *Pieris napi*. Behavioral Ecology 6: 6–13.

Wiklund, C., A. Kaitala, V. Lindfors, and J. Abenius. 1993. Polyandry and its effect on female reproduction in the green-veined white butterfly (*Pieris napi* L.). Behavioral Ecology and Sociobiology 33: 25–33.

Wiklund, C., A. Kaitala, and N. Wedell. 1998. Decoupling of reproductive rates and parental expenditure in a polyandrous butterfly. Behavioral Ecology 9: 20–25.

Wiklund, C., B. Karlsson, and O. Leimar. 2001. Sexual conflict and cooperation in butterfly reproduction: A comparative study of polyandry and female fitness. Proceedings of the Royal Society of London B 268: 1661–1667.

Wiklund, C., V. Lindfors, and J. Forsberg. 1996. Early male emergence and reproductive phenology of the adult overwintering butterfly *Gonepteryx rhamni* in Sweden. Oikos 75: 227–240.

Wiklund, C., S. Nylin, and J. Forsberg. 1991. Sex-related variation in growth rate as a result of selection for large size in a bivoltine butterfly (*Pieris napi* L). Oikos 60: 241–250.

Wiklund, C., and A. Persson. 1983. Fecundity, egg weight variation and its relation to offspring fitness in the speckled wood butterfly, *Pararge aegeria*, or why don't butterfly females lay more eggs? Oikos 40: 53–63.

Wiklund, C., A. Persson, and P.-O. Wickman. 1983. Larval aestivation and direct development as alternative strategies in the speckled wood butterfly, *Pararge aegeria*, in Sweden. Ecological Entomology 8: 233–238.

Wiklund, C., and C. Solbreck. 1982. Adaptive versus incidental explanations for the occurrence of protandry in a butterfly *Leptidea sinapis*. Evolution 36: 56–62.

Wiley, E. O. 1978. The evolutionary species concept reconsidered. Systematic Zoology 27: 17–26.

———. 1981. *Phylogenetics: The theory and practice of phylogenetic systematics.* Wiley-Interscience, New York.

Williams, B. 2000. Conservation genetics, extinction and taxonomy: A case history of *Speyeria idalia* (Lepidoptera: Nymphalidae). GenBank (http://www.ncbi.nlm.nih.gov).

Williams, C. B. 1943. Area and the number of species. Nature 152: 264–267.

Williams, E. H. 1988. Habitat and range of *Euphydryas gillettii* (Nymphalidae). Journal of the Lepidopterists' Society 42: 37–45.

———. 1990. Dietary breadth in *Euphydryas gillettii* (Nymphalidae). Journal of the Lepidopterists' Society 44: 94–95.

Williams, J. A., S. W. Paddock, K. Vorwerk, and S. B. Carroll. 1994. Organization of wing formation and induction of a wing-patterning gene at the dorsal/ventral compartment boundary. Nature 368: 299–305.

Williams, K. S., and L. E. Gilbert. 1981. Insects as selective agents on plant vegetative morphology: Egg mimicry reduces egg laying in butterflies. Science 212: 467–469.

Williams, N. H. 1983. Floral fragrances as cues in animal behavior. Pp. 51–69 in C. E. Jones and R. J. Little, eds., *Handbook of experimental pollination biology.* Van Nostrand-Reinhold, New York.

Williams, P. H. 1998. WORLDMAP iv WINDOWS: Software and help document 4.1. Privately distributed by the author, London.

———. 2001. Complementarity. Encyclopedia of Biodiversity 1: 813–829. Academic Press, San Diego.

Williams, P. H., H. M. de Klerk, and T. M. Crowe. 1999. Interpreting biogeographical boundaries among Afrotropical birds: Spatial patterns in richness gradients and species replacement. Journal of Biogeography 26: 459–474.

Williams, P. H., and K. J. Gaston. 1994. Measuring more of biodiversity: Can higher taxon richness predict wholesale species richness? Biological Conservation 67: 211–217.

Williams, P. H., K. J. Gaston, and C. J. Humphries. 1994. Do conservationists and molecular biologists value differences between organisms in the same way? Biodiversity Letters 2: 67–78.

Williams, P. H., D. Gibbons, C. R. Margules, A. G. Rebelo, C. J. Humphries, and R. L. Pressey. 1996. A comparison of richness hotspots, rarity hotspots, and complementary areas for conserving diversity of British birds. Conservation Biology 10: 155–174.

Williams, P. H., and C. J. Humphries. 1996. Comparing character diversity among biotas. Pp. 54–76 in K. J. Gaston, ed., *Biodiversity: A biology of numbers and difference.* Blackwell, Oxford.

Williamson, M. 1981. *Island populations.* Oxford University Press, Oxford.

Willig, M. R., and S. K. Lyons. 1998. An analytical model of latitudinal gradients of species richness with an empirical test for marsupials and bats in the New World. Oikos 81: 93–98.

Willis, M. A., and E. Arbas. 1991. Odor-modulated upwind flight of the sphinx moth, *Manduca sexta.* Journal of Comparative Physiology A 169: 427–440.

Willmer, P. G. 1991. Thermal biology and mate acquisition in ectotherms. Trends in Ecology and Evolution 6: 369–399.

Willmott, A. P., and A. Búrquez. 1996. The pollination of *Merremia palmeri* (Convolvulaceae): Can hawkmoths be trusted? American Journal of Botany 83: 1050–1056.

Wilson, J. 1999. *Biological individuality: The identity and persistence of living entities.* Cambridge University Press, Cambridge.

Wiltshire, E. P. 1941. The phenological classification of Palearctic Lepidoptera. Entomologists' Record and Journal of Variation 53: 101–106.

Windig, J. J. 1991. Quantification of Lepidoptera wing patterns using an image analyzer. Journal of Research on Lepidoptera 30: 82–94.

Wink, M., L. Legal, and E. von Nickisch-Rosenegk. 1998. Response by Micheal Wink, Eva von Nickisch-Rosenegk, and Luc Legal. Journal of Chemical Ecology 24: 1285–1291.

Wink, M., and E. von Nickisch-Rosenegk. 1997. Sequence data of mitochondrial 16s rDNA of Arctiidae and Nymphalidae: Evidence for a convergent evolution of pyrrolizidine alkaloid and cardiac glycoside sequestration. Journal of Chemical Ecology 23: 1549–1568.

Wissel, C., and S. Stöcker. 1991. Extinction of populations by random influences. Theoretical Population Biology 39: 315–328.

Witkowski, Z., P. Adamski, A. Kosior, and P. Plonka. 1997. Extinction and reintroduction of *Parnassius Apollo* in the Pieniny National Park (Polish Carpathians). Biologia (Bratislava)52: 199–208.

Woiwod, I. P. 1997. Detecting the effects of climate change on Lepidoptera. Journal of Insect Conservation 1: 149–158.

Wolda, H. 1988. Insect seasonality: Why? Annual Review of Ecology and Systematics 19: 1–18.

Wolstenholme, D. R., and D. O. Clary. 1985. Sequence evolution of *Drosophila* mitochondrial DNA. Genetics 109: 725–744.

Woodward, A., E. G. Schreiner, and D. G. Silsbee. 1995. Climate, geography, and tree establishment in subalpine meadows of the Olympic Mountains, Washington, U.S.A. Arctic Alpine Research 27: 217–225.

Woodward, F. I. 1987. *Climate and plant distribution.* Cambridge University Press, Cambridge.

World Bank, United States Agency for International Development, Cooperation Suisse, UNESCO, United Nations Development Program, and Worldwide Fund for Nature. 1988. *Madagascar environmental action plan.* World Bank, Washington, D.C.

Wright, D. H. 1983. Species-energy theory: An extension of species-area theory. Oikos 41: 496–506.

Wright, S. 1931. Evolution in Mendelian populations. Genetics 16: 97–159.

――― . 1978. *Evolution and the genetics of populations.* Vol. 4. *Variability within and among natural populations.* University of Chicago Press, Chicago.

Wright, T. R. F. 1987. The genetics of biogenic amine metabolism, sclerotization, and melanization in *Drosophila melanogaster.* Advances in Genetics 24: 127–222.

Wu, C. I. 1992. A note on Haldane's rule: Hybrid inviability versus hybrid sterility. Evolution 46: 1584–1587.

Wu, C. I., and A. W. Davis. 1993. Evolution of post-mating reproductive isolation: The composite nature of Haldane's rule and its genetic bases. American Naturalist 142: 187–212.

Wu, C. I., and N. A. Johnson. 1996. Endless forms, several powers. Nature 382: 298–299.

Wynne, I., H. Loxdale, and C. Brookes. 1992. Use of a cellulose acetate system for allozyme electophoresis. Pp. 494–499 in R. J. Berry, T. J. Crawford, and G. M. Hewitt, eds., *Genes in Ecology*. Blackwell, Oxford.

Xu, P. X., X. Zhang, S. Heaney, A. Yoon, A. M. Michelson, and R. L. Maas. 1999. Regulation of Pax6 expression is conserved between mice and flies. Development 126: 383–395.

Yagi, N., and N. Koyama. 1963. *The compound eye of Lepidoptera: Approach from organic evolution*. Shinkyo Press, Tokyo.

Yagi, T., T. Katoh, A. Chichvarkhin, T. Shinkawa, K. Omoto. 2001. Molecular phylogeny of butterflies *Parnassius glacialis* and *P. stubbendorfii*. Genes and Genetic Systems 76: 229–234.

Yagi, T., G. Sasaki, and H. Takebe. 1999. Phylogeny of Japanese papilionid butterflies inferred from nucleotide sequences of mitochondrial *ND5* gene. Journal of Molecular Evolution 48: 42–48.

Yamamoto, M. 1973. A butterfly phenology at Jozankei (Sapporo), N. Japan. Journal Faculty of Science Hokkaido University 19: 465–473.

———. 1976. Further observations on butterfly phenology at Jozankei (Sapporo): Comparisons of the results in two successive years. Journal Faculty of Science Hokkaido University 20: 343–358.

———. 1977. A comparison of butterfly assemblages in and near Sapporo, northern Japan. Journal Faculty of Science Hokkaido University 20: 621–646.

Yamashita, K. 1995. Comparison of visual cues in mating behavior of four species of swallowtail butterflies. Pp. 133–144 in J. M. Scriber, Y. Tsubaki, and R. C. Lederhouse, eds., *Swallowtail butterflies: Their ecology and evolutionary biology*. Scientific Publishers, Gainesville, FL.

Yang, Z. 1998. On the best evolutionary rate for phylogenetic analysis. Systematic Biology 47: 125–133.

Yasuda, N., and M. Kimura. 1968. A gene-counting method of maximum likelihood for estimating gene frequencies in ABO and ABO-like systems. Annals of Human Genetics 31: 409–420.

Yokoyama, J., K. Odagiri, A. Yokoyama, and T. Fukuda. 1998. Phylogenetic relationship of genus *Japonica* subgenus *Yuhbae* (Lepidoptera: Lycaenidae) inferred from mitochondrial DNA sequences. GenBank (http://www.ncbi.nlm.nih.gov).

Yoshimoto, H. 2000. Wood whites (Pieridae), the most primitive pierids? Butterflies, Tokyo 26: 52–59.

Young, A. M. 1978. The biology of butterfly *Aeria eurimedea agna* (Nymphalidae: Ithomiinae: Oleriini) in Costa Rica. Journal of the Kansas Entomological Society 51: 1–10.

Zamudio, K. R., R. B. Huey, and W. D. Crill. 1995. Bigger isn't always better: Body size, developmental and parental temperature and male territorial success in *Drosophila melanogaster*. Animal Behaviour 49: 671–677.

Ziegler, R. 1991. Changes in lipid and carbohydrate metabolism during starvation in adult *Manduca sexta*. Journal of Comparative Physiology B 161: 125–131.

Ziemba, K. S., and R. L. Rutowski. 2000. Morphological correlates of sexual dimorphism in eye size in the desert hackberry butterfly, *Asterocampa leilia*. Psyche 103: 25–36.

Zimmermann, M., J. Aubert, and H. Descimon. 1999. Systématique moléculaire des Mélitées (Lepidoptera: Nymphalidae). Comptes Rendus de l'Academie des Sciences Serie III. Sciences de la Vie 322: 429–439.

Zimmermann, M., N. Wahlberg, and H. Descimon. 2000. Phylogeny of *Euphydryas* checkerspot butterflies (Lepidoptera: Nymphalidae) based on mitochondrial DNA sequence data. Annals of the Entomological Society of America 93: 347–355.

Zonneveld, C. 1996a. Being big or emerging early? Polyandry and the trade-off between size and emergence in male butterflies. American Naturalist 147: 946–965.

———. 1996b. Sperm competition cannot eliminate protandry. Journal of Theoretical Biology 178: 105–112.

Carol L. Boggs
Department of Biological Sciences
371 Serra Mall
Stanford University
Stanford, CA 94305-5020
cboggs@stanford.edu

Paul Brakefield
Institute of Ecological and
        Evolutionary Sciences
Leiden University
Kaiserstraat 63
2311 GP Leiden
The Netherlands
brakefield@rulsfb.leidenuniv.nl

Adriana Briscoe
Department of Ecology and
        Evolutionary Biology
321 Steinhaus Hall
University of California, Irvine
Irvine, CA 92697-2525
abriscoe@uci.edu

Dana L. Campbell
6516 41st Avenue
University Park, MD 20782
dana_campbell@harvard.post.edu

Elizabeth E. Crone
School of Forestry
The University of Montana

Missoula, MT 59812
ecrone@forestry.umt.edu

Mark Deering
Sophia Sachs Butterfly House
15193 Olive Blvd.
Chesterfield, MO 63017
entomology@butterflyhouse.org

Henri Descimon
Laboratoire de Systématique
        Evolutive
UPRES 2202 Biodiversité, Case 05
Université de Provence
3 Place Victor Hugo
13331 Marseille cedex
France
descimon@newsup.univ-mrs.fr

Erika I. Deinert
Organization for Tropical Studies
410 Swift Avenue
Duke University
Durham, NC 27701
deinert@cro.ots.ac.cr

Paul R. Ehrlich
Department of Biological Sciences
371 Serra Mall
Stanford University
Stanford, CA 94305-5020
pre@stanford.edu

John P. Fay
Center for Conservation Biology
Department of Biological Sciences
371 Serra Mall
Stanford University
Stanford, CA 94305-5020
jpfay@stanford.edu

Richard ffrench-Constant
Department of Biology and
        Biochemistry
University of Bath
Bath BA2 7AY
United Kingdom
bssrfc@bath.ac.uk

Sherri Fownes
Department of Biological Sciences
University of Alberta
Edmonton, Alberta T6G 2E9
Canada
sfownes@gpu.srv.ualberta.ca

Lawrence E. Gilbert
Department of Integrative Biology
University of Texas, Austin
Austin, TX 78712
lgilbert@mail.utexas.edu

André Gilles
Laboratoire D'Hydrobiologie, Case 36
3, Place Victor Hugo
13331 Marseille
France

Ilkka Hanski
Metapopulation Research Group
Division of Population Biology
Department of Ecology and Systematics
PO Box 65 (Viikinkaari 1)
FIN-00014 University of Helsinki
Finland
ilkka.hanski@helsinki.fi

Jane K. Hill
Department of Biology
PO Box 373
University of York
York YO10 5YW
United Kingdom

Brian Huntley
Department of Biological Sciences
University of Durham

South Road
Durham DH1 3LE
United Kingdom
brian.huntley@durham.ac.uk

Niklas Janz
Department of Zoology
Stockholm University
106 91 Stockholm
Sweden
niklas.janz@zoologi.su.se

Greg Kareofelas
1028 Cypress Lane
Davis, CA 95616

Nusha Keyghobadi
Academy of Natural Sciences
1900 Benjamin Franklin Parkway
Philadelphia, PA 19103
keyghobadi@acnatsci.org

P. Bernhard Koch
Abteilung Allgemeine Zoologie
Universität Ulm
Albert-Einstein-Allee 11
D-89069 Ulm
Germany
bernd.koch@biologie.uni-ulm.de

Claire Kremen
Department of Ecology and
        Evolutionary Biology
Princeton University
Guyot Hall, Washington Road
Princeton, NJ 08544
ckremen@princeton.edu

David Lees
Department of Paleontology
Natural History Museum
Cromwell Road
London SW7 5BD
United Kingdom
dcl@nhm.ac.uk

Jean-François Martin
CSIRO Division Entomology
Campus International de Baillarguet
34980 Montferrier-sur-Lez cedex
France
jef.martin@csuri-europe.org *or*
        jefmartin@hotmail.com

Antónia Monteiro
Department of Biological Sciences

107 Dorsheimer
State University of New York
    at Buffalo
Buffalo, NY 14260
monteiro@buffalo.edu

Paulo C. Motta
Depto. de Zoologia
Universidade de Brasilia
70910-900
Brasília, DF
Brazil
mottapc@unb.br

Camille Parmesan
Department of Integrative Biology
University of Texas, Austin
Austin, TX 78712
parmesan@mail.utexas.edu

William D. Patterson
2624 4th Avenue
Sacramento, CA 95818

Naomi E. Pierce
Department of Organismic and
    Evolutionary Biology
Harvard University
26 Oxford Street
Cambridge, MA 02138
npierce@oeb.harvard.edu

Robert A. Raguso
Department of Biology
University of South Carolina
Coker Life Sciences Building
Columbia, SC 29208
raguso@biol.sc.edu

Charles L. Remington
Department of Ecology/Evolutionary
    Biology
Yale University
New Haven, CT 06520

Jens Roland
Department of Biological Sciences
University of Alberta
Edmonton, Alberta T6G 2E9
Canada
jroland@ualberta.ca

Ronald L. Rutowski
Department of Zoology

Arizona State University
Tempe, AZ 85287-1501
r.rutowski@asu.edu

Cheryl B. Schultz
National Center for Ecological Analysis
    and Synthesis
735 State Street, Suite 300
Santa Barbara, CA 93101-3351
schultz@bren.ucsb.edu

J. Mark Scriber
Department of Entomology
Michigan State University
East Lansing, MI 48824
scriber@pilot.msu.edu

Arthur M. Shapiro
Center for Population Biology
University of California, Davis
Davis, CA 95616

Michael C. Singer
Department of Integrative Biology
University of Texas, Austin
Austin, TX 78712
sing@mail.utexas.edu

Felix Sperling
CW 405 Biological Sciences Centre
Department of Biological Sciences
University of Alberta
Edmonton, Alberta T6G 2E9
Canada
Felix.Sperling@ualberta.ca

Curt Strobeck
Department of Biological Sciences
University of Alberta
Edmonton, Alberta T6G 2E9
Canada
curtis.strobeck@ualberta.ca

Aram Stump
Biology Department
University of Notre Dame
Notre Dame, IN 46556
Aram.D.Stump.9@nd.edu

Chris D. Thomas
Centre for Biodiversity and
    Conservation
School of Biology
University of Leeds

Leeds, LS2 9JT
United Kingdom
c.d.thomas@leeds.ac.uk

Richard VanBuskirk
Department of Neurology, Physiology,
    and Behavior
University of California, Davis
Davis, CA 95616
rwvanbuskirk@ucdavis.edu

Hans Van Dyck
Department of Biology (U.I.A.)
University of Antwerp
Universiteitsplein 1
B-2610 Antwerp
Belgium
hvdyck@uia.ua.ac.be

Richard I. Vane-Wright
Keeper of Entomology
The Natural History Museum
Cromwell Road
London SW7 5BD

United Kingdom
rivw@nhm.ac.uk

Ward B. Watt
Department of Biological Sciences
371 Serra Mall
Stanford University
Stanford, CA 94305-5020
wbwatt@stanford.edu

Christer Wiklund
Department of Zoology
University of Stockholm
106 91 Stockholm
Sweden
christer.wiklund@zoologi.su.se

Mark A. Willis
Department of Biology
Case Western Reserve University
10900 Euclid Avenue
Cleveland, OH 44106-7080
maw27@po.cwru.edu

allozyme (cont.)
  See also esterase; phosphoglucose
    isomerase
amateur lepidopterists, xi, 2, 3, 322, 345,
    503, 515, 543, 560, 610
ant associations, 484
  evolution of, 395–408
  homology, assessing, 404–8
  independent evolution, 397, 403–8
  larval morphology, 403–8
  Lycaenidae/Riodinidae comparisons,
    403–8
  origins, 397, 403–4
Anthocharis cardamines, 76
Aphantopus hyperantus, 74, 150, 154,
    156–60, 165–67
apposition eye, 11. *See also* compound eye
Arizona, 43–64, 114, 441, 446
Asterocampa leilia, 12

basking, 71, 189, 322, 354, 358–59, 362
Battus philenor, 20, 40, 264, 267
Bicyclus anynana, 245–56
biochemical reaction kinetics, 324–25
bioenergetics, 4, 321–30, 341–43, 347–50
biogeography, 4, 320, 474, 496
  countryside, 5, 613
Britain, climate response surface, 151–67
British Butterfly Monitoring Scheme
    (BBMS), 114
butterfly higher classification
  cladistic primacy, 492–93
  cladograms as constructs, 491
  comparative biology, dependence on,
    490–97
  conservation priorities, 499–503
  dataset construction, 507–10
  doubt and certainty, 478–79
  Hedylidae, 489–90
  Hesperiidae, 479–80
  Lycaenidae, 395–403, 454, 478–79
  Nymphalidae, 488–89
  Papilionidae, 480–82
  Pieridae, 482–83
  Riodinidae, 485–86
  total evidence analysis, 479
  Troidini case example, difficulties,
    493–97
  See also classification; comparative
    biology; phylogenetic analysis
butterfly surveys, 117, 153, 297, 534, 557,
    561, 591

California, Vaca Hills, 116–47
Caligo sp., 11

candidate gene approach, 255, 407
checkerspot butterfly. *See Euphydryas*
chemical signals. *See* oviposition
cladistics, 3–4, 368, 395, 410, 462, 504–7
  comparative biology, dependence on,
    490–97
  phenetics, 477–78
  primacy, 492–93
  sampling, 507–10
  taxonomic identity, 504
  total evidence analysis, 507, 510, 512
  See also butterfly higher classification
classification, 5, 113, 477–78, 490–94
  conservation goals, 499–512
  continuous and discontinuous
    relationships, 506
  identity and, 503–6
  naturalness, 505–6
  relative relationships, 504–6
  species rank, 503–6
  taxonomic methods, 504–6
  See also butterfly higher classification
climate change, 109–12, 205, 584
  bioindicator attributes, butterfly,
    543–46
  environmental variation, 186, 200
  impact assessment, 541–43
  intergovernmental panel on, 149
  local extinctions, 553–59, 578, 581–82
  modeling species range changes,
    149–67
  multispecies poleward shift, 549–52
  phase relationship, 554–59
  phenological shifts, 543, 548
  species responses, 541–59
  See also range limit shifts due to climate
    change
climate response surface, 150–67
  current distribution simulations,
    156–59
  estimating dispersal rates, 161–63
  future distribution simulations,
    159–61, 165–67
  habitat availability, 157–59
  lag, habitat tracking, 156–57, 163–67,
    543
  model generation, 153–56, 159–60
  model species ecology, 151–53, 154
Coenonympha pamphilus, 21, 71–73,
    76–77
Coenonympha tullia, 73–74, 150, 154–67
coevolution, 341, 393
  between sexes, 85
  hotspots, 208

metabolism, 324
mimicry, 284, 313
nutrient transfer, 84
plant-insect, 3–8, 222, 343, 345, 351, 390, 409, 492
Colias, 76, 135, 200–201, 217, 223, 436
   adaptation test system, 320–51
   sex linkage, 436, 438, 458
color vision. *See* vision, color
comparative biology, 24, 62, 68, 244, 407, 442
   cladistics, dependence on , 490–97
   diet breadths, 497
   ecology and cladograms, 490–97
   gene expression, 256–57, 407
   mimicry, 284
   moths and butterflies, 45
   reproductive biology, 79, 82, 85, 203
   wing development, 256–57, 278
   See also butterfly higher classification
compound eye, 10, 11, 27, 484
   morphology, 28–31
   organization and function, 28
   screening pigments, 11
   selection pressure, 27–28
   See also vision; visual ecology
conservation biology, 2–6, 169
   biodiversity, 2, 5
   classification, 510–12
   countryside biogeography, 5, 613
   ecosystem services, 1, 2
   endemism, 518, 521–22
   gene flow barriers, 182–83
   global warming, 2, 5. *See also* climate change
   habitat patch size, minimum. *See* population persistence
   hybrids, 368
   indicator comparison, 2, 517–18, 529–31
   pattern and process, 510–12
   phenology, 111, 114
   phylogenetics and, 431–32, 438, 498–503, 506, 510–13
   planning and management convergence, 511–12
   plurality, need for, 510–12
   pollination, 44
   reintroduction population selection, 501–3
   species richness: cross taxonomic, 517–27; null model, 521
   umbrella species, 2

See also climate change; climate response surface; conservation biology, Madagascar; extinction; metapopulation; population persistence; species richness
conservation biology, Madagascar
   endemism patterns, 527–28
   indicator, evolutionary radiations as an, 529–31
   reserve: design, 532–38; selection, 531–32
   species richness patterns, 522–27
   species risk assessment, 532–38
   turnover patterns, 528–29
constraint, 3–4, 7, 320, 346–47
   allocation. *See* resource allocation
   host plant shifts, 221–26
   metabolic, 326–31, 334, 338–39, 350–51
   thermal, 323, 379, 390
   wing patterns, 246, 256, 308
   See also bioenergetics
cornea, 28, 32
Costa Rica, 95, 105, 281, 285, 293.
   See also Heliconius
crystalline cone, 10, 28, 505

Danus gilippus, 75, 80, 413
Danus plexippus, 19, 77, 89, 411, 413, 425–26, 496
Darwin, C. R., 46, 67–68, 74, 76, 81, 89, 112, 319, 491, 505
dispersal, 45, 110, 149, 218, 236, 309
   adaptation, 333–37
   behavior, 562–66, 571–75
   hybrid zones, 370, 385, 390
   landscape effects, 171–79, 182–83
   long-distance, 45
   morphology, 361–66
   rate, 161–66, 170
   See also climate change; climate response surface
Distal-less homeobox gene, 247–49, 255–56, 315, 407
Drosophila, 223, 226, 247, 274, 288–90, 348
   comparative genomics, 453, 455, 503, 505
   Haldane's rule, 435–37
   sex linkage, 385
   vision, 27, 34–35, 37–38, 41
   wing development, 247, 274, 288–90, 292, 296, 305, 311, 314–15
Dryas julia, 76

oviposition
  chemical signals, 19
  vision, role in, 19–20, 31, 33
oviposition preference, 207–27
  evolution, 223–25
  hierarchies, 223–26, 231–33, 236
  larval performance vs., 236–37
  ranking, 211, 229–35, 238–39
  See also sex linkage

palatability, 69–70, 302, 312, 316, 492
Papilio canadensis/P. glaucus hybrid zone,
    368–91
  markers, 368–71
  phylogenetic and ecological distances,
      372–73
  reproductive isolation, 373–76
  sex chromosomes and, 376–77, 442–44
Papilio demoleus, 40
Papilio glaucus species group, 439, 442–44
Papilio machaon species group, 439–42
Papilionidae, 372–73
  maintenance of genetic integrity,
      444–46
  phylogeny, 449
  vision, 16, 18
  See also butterfly higher classification
Papilionoidea
  phylogeny, 395–403
  See also ant associations
Papilio troilus, 40
Papilio xuthus
  color learning, 40
  vision, 17, 27–41
Pararge aegeria, 103, 150–67, 353–66
  climate and distribution, 150–66
  ejaculate, 81, 87
  mate location behavior, 71
Parnassius smintheus, 171–83
patrolling, perching. *See* mate location
    strategies
phenetics, 3–5, 463, 502, 504
  cladistics, 471, 477–78
  foundations, 477–78
phenofaunistics, 111–47
phenology, 111–47, 191, 227, 344, 550,
    595
  between- and within-site comparisons,
      127–46
  climate change and, 111, 543, 548,
      556–58
  emergence, 129–33
  first/last flight appearance, 133–46
  host shift barrier, 217–21

lepidopteran review, 113–15
  null models, 115–24
  pollination ecology methods, 115–16
  reasons to study, 111–12
  species boundaries, 436, 444, 459
  Vaca Hills example, 116–47
pheromone, 50, 94, 229, 509
  plumes, 51
  rejection, 75–76
  species boundaries, 437, 473, 509
phosphoglucose isomerase (PGI), 330–41,
    345–50, 469–70
photosensitive, photoreceptive cells, 10,
    14
  adult, 31
  genitalic, 31
  larval, 30–31
  microvilli, 18, 29–30
  physiology, 27, 32–33
  recovery rates, 17
  rhabdomeres, 29–30
  sensitivity, 16–17, 30
  spatial organization, 28
  See also acuity; ommatidia; vision;
      visual pigments
phylogenetic analysis, 27
  adaptation and, 338–39
  biological diversity, 498–503
  character numbers, 509
  cladistic primacy, 492–93
  cladograms as constructs, 491
  conservation biology, 498–503
  datasets: construction, 507–10;
      partitioning, 509–10
  distance, 372
  DNA marker relative utility, 455–57
  DNA sequence: compilation and
      assessment, 449–51; model
      organisms, 451
  gene phylogeny, modal, 448
  Ithomiinae, 409–28
  larval characters, using, 409–28
  mitochondrial DNA discussion, 451–53
  mitochondrial NADH dehydrogenase
      subunit 1 (ND1), 396, 402–3,
      452–55, 461–63
  molecular reliability, 447–49
  nuclear protein coding genes,
      discussion of, 454–55
  nuclear rRNA, discussion of, 453–54
  Papilionoidea, 397–403
  reliability, 447–49
  Riodinidae, 395–408
  sampling intensity, individual, 508–9

See also range limit shifts due to climate
    change
range limit shifts due to climate change
  directed search, 549–53
  early twentieth-century, 542–46
  emerging patterns, 546–48
  historical vs. modern, 542, 548–49
  individual level mechanisms, 553–57
  interpreting patterns, 545–46
  magnitude concordance, 553
  microclimate, 546
  mobility, 542–49
  nonclimatic factors, 545
  population-level mechanisms,
    557–59. *See also* climate response
    surface
refractory period, 60, 78, 85, 91
reproductive investment, 23, 79,
    81–86
  capital and income, 90
reproductive isolation, 367–70, 373–76,
    456
  lock and key hypothesis, 473
  measuring, 460
  postmating, 388
  premating, 385
  reinforcement, 385
  species concepts, 446, 472
resource allocation, 43, 114
  constraints, 185, 188, 197, 200–204,
    206, 208
  environmental variation effects, 110,
    185–206
  generalizations and, 201–6
  genetic variation, 348
  larval constraints, 86
  nuptial gift, 82–84
  phenology, 114
  population dynamics, effects, 199
  pupal mating, 94–95
  radiotracer studies, 83–84, 193–94, 197,
    203
  See also food availability; hawkmoth
    pollination
resource congruence, 188, 194, 196–97,
    201–3
resource foraging, 43
retina, 22, 28–40
rhabdomeres. *See* photosensitive,
    photoreceptive cells
Riodinidae
  phylogeny, 395–403
  See also ant associations; butterfly
    higher classification

scent. *See* floral scent; pheromone
sclerotization, 261–64, 268–74. *See also*
    wing color pattern
seasonality, 111–47
selection
  artificial, 248–58
  directional, 46
  intra- and intersexual, 67
  natural, stages of, 319–20, 331–34
  sexual, 8, 27, 67–90, 99, 312, 353,
    387–88, 435–37. *See also* mate
    choice; mate location strategies;
    mating behavior
senescence, 205
sex linkage, 394
  determining, 457
  faster evolution, 229
  genomic divergence, 438
  Haldane's rule and, 435–44
  host plant use, 229–39
  intra- and interspecific variation, 238
  ranking vs. specialization, 233–36
  speciation, 229, 373–77, 435–39
  species boundaries, 435–39
  See also melanism
sex ratio, 309, 566, 583
  operational, 75, 78, 87, 93, 353
  pupal mortality, 374
sexual dimorphism, 74, 361
Sonoran Desert, 44
speciation, 4, 351, 435, 471, 518
  conservation, 501, 518
  Haldane's rule, 374, 435. *See also main*
    entry
  host shifts, 215
  insights: from sibling species, 459–76;
    from species complexes, 284, 367,
    389, 439–47
  mechanisms, 376, 385, 389
  phylogenetics of, 500. *See also* wing
    color pattern
  sex-linked gene, 229, 239, 374, 385,
    436–39. *See also* sex linkage
  sympatric, 230
  theory, 459
species boundaries
  calibrating genetic divergence, 446–47
  difficulties, *Papilio* examples, 439–49
  markers, 439–44, 448, 455–56
  maternally inherited markers, 438–39
  See also Haldane's rule; sex linkage
species concepts, 336, 431, 439
  biological (BSC), 432–34, 471–73
  comparisons, 432–34, 471–73